Lecture Notes in Artificial Intelligence 4246

Edited by J. G. Carbonell and J. Siekmann

Subseries of Lecture Notes in Computer Science

T0142080

Miki Hermann   Andrei Voronkov (Eds.)

Logic for Programming, Artificial Intelligence, and Reasoning

13th International Conference, LPAR 2006
Phnom Penh, Cambodia, November 13-17, 2006
Proceedings

 Springer

Series Editors

Jaime G. Carbonell, Carnegie Mellon University, Pittsburgh, PA, USA
Jörg Siekmann, University of Saarland, Saarbrücken, Germany

Volume Editors

Miki Hermann
LIX , École Polytechnique
91128 Palaiseau, France
E-mail: hermann@lix.polytechnique.fr

Andrei Voronkov
University of Manchester, Department of Computer Science
Manchester M13 9PL, United Kingdom
E-mail: voronkov@cs.man.ac.uk

Library of Congress Control Number: 2006934988

CR Subject Classification (1998): I.2.3, I.2, F.4.1, F.3, D.2.4, D.1.6

LNCS Sublibrary: SL 7 – Artificial Intelligence

ISSN   0302-9743
ISBN-10   3-540-48281-4 Springer Berlin Heidelberg New York
ISBN-13   978-3-540-48281-9 Springer Berlin Heidelberg New York

Springer is a part of Springer Science+Business Media

springer.com

© Springer-Verlag Berlin Heidelberg 2006
Printed in Germany

Typesetting: Camera-ready by author, data conversion by Scientific Publishing Services, Chennai, India
Printed on acid-free paper   SPIN: 11916277   06/3142   5 4 3 2 1 0

Preface

This volume contains the papers presented at the 13th International Conference on Logic for Programming, Artificial Intelligence, and Reasoning (LPAR), held during November 13–17, 2006, in Phnom Penh, Cambodia, together with the 2nd International Workshop on Analytic Proof Systems (organized by Christian Fermüller and Matthias Baaz) and the 6th International Workshop on the Implementation or Logics (organized by Christoph Benzmüller, Bernd Fischer, and Geoff Sutcliffe).

The call for papers attracted 96 paper submissions, each of which was reviewed by at least three expert reviewers. The final decisions on the papers were taken during an electronic Program Committee meeting held on the Internet. The Internet-based submission, reviewing, and discussion software EasyChair, provided by the second PC Co-chair, supported each stage of the reviewing process. Nevertheless, the most important work was, of course, done by the 35 PC members and their external reviewers, who provided high-quality reviews. After intense discussions to resolve conflicts among the reviewers, the Program Committee decided to accept 38 papers.

The conference program also included an invited talk by Jean-Pierre Jouannaud, documented by an additional paper in these proceedings.

Apart from the authors, invited speaker, Program Committee members, and external reviewers, we would like to thank other people and organizations that made this LPAR conference a success: the Local Organization Chair, Sopheap Seng, and all the other people involved in the local organization; the Department of Information and Communication Technology Engineering at the Institut de Technologie du Cambodge in Phnom Penh, and the Kurt Gödel Society, which provided partial funding and support.

September 2006

Miki Hermann
Andrei Voronkov

Conference Organization

Program Chairs

Miki Hermann
Andrei Voronkov

Workshop Chair

Christelle Scharff

Program Committee

María Alpuente
Franz Baader
Matthias Baaz
Christoph Benzmüller
Koen Claessen
Javier Esparza
Bernd Fischer
Jürgen Giesl
Jean Goubault-Larrecq
Erich Grädel
Ziyad Hanna

Pascal van Hentenryck
Brahim Hnich
Ian Horrocks
Viktor Kuncak
Orna Kupferman
Christopher Lynch
Dale Miller
George Necula
Joachim Niehren
Luke Ong
Catuscia Palamidessi

Michel Parigot
Frank Pfenning
Reinhard Pichler
Michael Rusinowitch
Mooly Sagiv
Gernot Salzer
Christelle Scharff
Sopheap Seng
Geoff Sutcliffe
Sophie Tison
Margus Veanes

Local Organization

Uddam Chukmol
Seila Nuon

Sopheap Seng (Chair)

Touch Sereysethy
Kret Try

Supporting Institutions

Institut de Technologie du Cambodge, Phnom Penh, Cambodia

External Reviewers

Andreas Abel
Francis Alexandre
Torsten Altenkirch
Demis Ballis
Mike Barnett
Gregory Batt
Peter Baumgartner
Christoph Beierle
Sergey Berezin
Philippe Besnard
Nikolaj Bjørner
Bruno Blanchet
Frédéric Blanqui
Hendrik Blockeel
Bernard Boigelot
Charles Bouillaguet
Olivier Bournez
Gerhard Brewka
Chad Brown
Kai Brünnler
Maurice Bruynooghe
Elie Bursztein
Michael Butler
Diego Calvanese
Colin Campbell
Domenico Cantone
Felix Chang
Henning Christiansen
Agata Ciabattoni
Marco Comini
Álvaro Cortés
Jim Cunningham
Mehdi Dastani
Giorgio Delzanno
Stéphane Demri
Phan Minh Dung
Esra Erdem
Santiago Escobar
Wolfgang Faber
Ansgar Fehnker
Christian Fermüller
Michael Fink
Anders Franzén

Alexander Fuchs
Marco Gavanelli
Martin Giese
Bernhard Gramlich
Wolfgang Grieskamp
Yuri Gurevich
Volker Haarslev
Peter Habermehl
Matthew Hague
Dieter Hofbauer
Steffen Hölldobler
Rosalie Iemhoff
Radu Iosif
Florent Jacquemard
Gerda Janssens
Yevgeny Kazakov
Michael Kohlhase
Sebastien Konieczny
Adam Koprowski
Robert Kowalski
Ralf Kuesters
Temur Kutsia
Oliver Kutz
Barbara König
Gerardo Lafferriere
Ugo Dal Lago
Shuvendu Lahiri
Alexander Leitsch
Christopher Lepock
Tal Lev-Ami
Francesco Logozzo
Markus Lohrey
Salvador Lucas
Sebastian Maneth
Claude Marché
Joao Marques-Silva
Pierre Marquis
Viviana Mascardi
Ralph Matthes
Nancy Mazur
Stephen McCamant
Erik Meijer
George Metcalfe

Christian Michaux
Alexandre Miquel
Barbara Morawska
Ginés Moreno
Boris Motik
Huu Hai Nguyen
Robert Nieuwenhuis
Andreas Nonnengart
Dirk Nowotka
Nicola Olivetti
Bijan Parsia
Vicente Pelechano
Enrico Pontelli
Michael Poppleton
Florian Rabe
M. J. Ramírez-Quintana
Silvio Ranise
Christophe Ringeissen
Pritam Roy
Paul Rozière
Eric Rutten
Kostis Sagonas
Sam Sanjabi
Peter Schneider-Kamp
Danny De Schreye
Yann Secq
Lionel Seinturier
Jiří Srba
Colin Stirling
Lutz Straßburger
Sorin Stratulat
Niklas Sörensson
Jean-Marc Talbot
Sebastiaan Terwijn
Frank Theiss
René Thiemann
Nikolai Tillmann
Alwen Tiu
Salvatore La Torre
Josef Urban
Frank Valencia
Jean-Stéphane Varré
Bjorn Victor

Conferences Preceding LPAR-13

RCLP, 1990, Irkutsk, Soviet Union
RCLP 1991, Leningrad, Soviet Union, aboard the ship "Michail Lomonosov"
LPAR 1992, St. Petersburg, Russia, aboard the ship "Michail Lomonosov"
LPAR 1993, St. Petersburg, Russia
LPAR 1994, Kiev, Ukraine, aboard the ship "Marshal Koshevoi"
LPAR 1999, Tbilisi, Republic of Georgia
LPAR 2000, Réunion Island, France
LPAR 2001, Havana, Cuba
LPAR 2002, Tbilisi, Republic of Georgia
LPAR 2003, Almaty, Kazakhstan
LPAR 2004, Montevideo, Uruguay
LPAR 2005, Montego Bay, Jamaica

Table of Contents

Higher-Order Termination:
From Kruskal to Computability

Frédéric Blanqui[1], Jean-Pierre Jouannaud[2,*], and Albert Rubio[3]

[1] INRIA & LORIA, BP 101, 54602 Villiers-lés-Nancy CEDEX, France
[2] LIX, École Polytechnique, 91400 Palaiseau, France
[3] Technical University of Catalonia, Pau Gargallo 5, 08028 Barcelona, Spain

1 Introduction

Termination is a major question in both logic and computer science. In logic, termination is at the heart of proof theory where it is usually called strong normalization (of cut elimination). In computer science, termination has always been an important issue for showing programs correct. In the early days of logic, strong normalization was usually shown by assigning ordinals to expressions in such a way that eliminating a cut would yield an expression with a smaller ordinal. In the early days of verification, computer scientists used similar ideas, interpreting the arguments of a program call by a natural number, such as their size. Showing the size of the arguments to decrease for each recursive call gives a termination proof of the program, which is however rather weak since it can only yield quite small ordinals. In the sixties, Tait invented a new method for showing cut elimination of natural deduction, based on a *predicate* over the set of terms, such that the membership of an expression to the predicate implied the strong normalization property for that expression. The predicate being defined by induction on types, or even as a fixpoint, this method could yield much larger ordinals. Later generalized by Girard under the name of *reducibility* or *computability candidates*, it showed very effective in proving the strong normalization property of typed lambda-calculi with polymorphic types, dependent types, inductive types, and finally a cumulative hierarchy of universes. On the programming side, research on termination shifted from programming to executable specification languages based on rewriting, and concentrated on automatable methods based on the construction on well-founded orderings of the set of terms. The milestone here is Dershowitz's *recursive path ordering* (RPO), in the late seventies, whose well-foundedness proof is based on a powerful combinatorial argument, Kruskal's tree theorem, which also yields rather large ordinals. While the computability predicates must be defined for each particular case, and their properties proved by hand, the recursive path ordering can be effectively automated.

These two methods are completely different. Computability arguments show *termination*, that is, infinite decreasing sequences of expressions $e_0 \succ e_1 \succ \ldots e_n \succ e_{n+1} \ldots$ do not exist. Kruskal's based arguments show *well-orderedness*: for any infinite sequence of expressions $\{e_i\}_i$, there is a pair $j < k$ such that $e_j \preceq e_k$. It is easy to see that well-orderedness implies termination, but the converse is not true.

---

* Project LogiCal, Pôle Commun de Recherche en Informatique du Plateau de Saclay, CNRS, École Polytechnique, INRIA, Université Paris-Sud.

M. Hermann and A. Voronkov (Eds.): LPAR 2006, LNAI 4246, pp. 1–14, 2006.

In the late eighties, a new question arose: termination of a simply-typed lambda-calculus language in which beta-reduction would be supplemented with terminating first-order rewrite rules. Breazu-Tannen and Gallier on the one hand [12], and Okada [23] on the other hand, showed that termination was satisfied by the combination by using computability arguments. Indeed, when rewriting operates at basic types and is generated by first-order rewrite rules, beta-reduction and rewriting do not interfere. Their result, proved for a polymorphic λ-calculus, was later generalized to the calculus of constructions [1]. The situation becomes radically different with higher-order rewriting generated by rules operating on arrow-types, or involving lambda-bindings or higher-order variables. Such an example is provided by Gödel's system T, in which higher-order primitive recursion for natural numbers generated by Peano's constructors 0 and s is described by the following two higher-order rules:

$$rec(0, U, V) \rightarrow U$$
$$rec(s(X), U, V) \rightarrow @(V, X, rec(X, U, V))$$

where rec is a function symbol of type $\mathbb{N} \rightarrow T \rightarrow (\mathbb{N} \rightarrow T \rightarrow T) \rightarrow T$, U is a higher-order variable of type T and V a higher-order variable of type $\mathbb{N} \rightarrow T \rightarrow T$, for all type T. Jouannaud and Okada invented the so-called general-schema [17], a powerful generalization of Gödel's higher-order primitive recursion of higher types. Following the path initiated by Breazu-Tannen and Gallier on the one hand, and Okada on the other hand, termination of calculi based on the general schema was proved by using computability arguments as well [17,18,2]. The general schema was then reformulated by Blanqui, Jouannaud and Okada [3,4] in order to incorporate computability arguments directly in its definition, opening the way to new generalizations. Gödel's system T can be generalized in two ways, by introducing type constructors and dependent types, yielding the Calculus of Constructions, and by introducing strictly positive inductive types. Both together yield the Calculus of Inductive Constructions [24], the theory underlying the Coq system [14], in which rewrite rules like strong elimination operate on types, raising new difficulties. Blanqui gave a generalization of the general schema which includes the Calculus of Inductive Constructions as a particular case under the name of Calculus of Algebraic Constructions [6,7].

The general schema, however, is too simple to analyze complex calculi defined by higher-order rewrite rules such as encodings of logics. For that purpose, Jouannaud and Rubio generalized the recursive path ordering to the higher-order case, yielding the higher-order recursive path ordering (HORPO) [19]. The RPO well-foundedness proof follows from Kruskal's tree theorem, but no such theorem exists in presence of a binding construct, and it is not at all clear that such a theorem may exist. What is remarkable is that computability arguments fit with RPO's recursive structure. When applied to RPO, these arguments result in a new, simple, well-foundedness proof of RPO. One could even argue that this is the *first* well-foundedness proof of RPO, since Dershowitz showed *more*: well-orderedness.

Combining the general schema and the HORPO is indeed easy because their termination properties are both based on computability arguments. The resulting relation, HORPO with closure, combines an ordering relation with a membership predicate. In this paper, we reformulate and improve a recent idea of Blanqui [9] by defining a new version of the HORPO with closure which integrates smoothly the idea of the general schema into HORPO in the form of a new ordering definition.

So far, we have considered the kind of higher-order rewriting defined by using first-order pattern matching as in the calculus of constructions. These orderings need to contain β- and η-reductions. Showing termination of higher-order rewrite rules based on higher-order pattern matching, that is, rewriting modulo β and η now used as equalities, turns out to require simple modifications of HORPO [20]. We will therefore concentrate here on higher-order orderings containing β- and η-reductions.

We introduce higher-order algebras in Section 2. In Section 3, we recall the computability argument for this variation of the simply typed lambda calculus. Using a computability argument again, we show in Section 4 that RPO is well-founded. We introduce the general schema in section 5, and the HORPO in Section 6 before to combine both in Section 7. We end up with related work and open problems in the last two sections.

2   Higher-Order Algebras

The notion of a higher-order algebra given here is the monomorphic version of the notion of polymorphic higher-order algebra defined in [21]. Polymorphism has been ruled out for simplicity.

2.1   Types, Signatures and Terms

Given a set S of *sort symbols* of a fixed arity, denoted by $s : *^n \Rightarrow *$, the set $\mathcal{T}_S$ of *types* is generated from these sets by the arrow constructor:

$$\mathcal{T}_S := s(\mathcal{T}_S^n) \mid (\mathcal{T}_S \to \mathcal{T}_S)$$
$$\text{for } s : *^n \Rightarrow * \in S$$

Types headed by $\to$ are *arrow types* while the others are *basic types*. *Type declarations* are expressions of the form $\sigma_1 \times \cdots \times \sigma_n \to \sigma$, where n is the *arity* of the type declaration, and $\sigma_1, \ldots, \sigma_n, \sigma$ are types. A type declaration is *first-order* if it uses only sorts, otherwise *higher-order*.

We assume given a set of function symbols which are meant to be algebraic operators. Each function symbol f is equipped with a type declaration $f : \sigma_1 \times \cdots \times \sigma_n \to \sigma$. We use $\mathcal{F}_n$ for the set of function symbols of arity n. $\mathcal{F}$ is a *first-order signature* if all its type declarations are first-order, and a higher-order signature otherwise.

The set of *raw terms* is generated from the signature $\mathcal{F}$ and a denumerable set $\mathcal{X}$ of variables according to the grammar:

$$\mathcal{T} := \mathcal{X} \mid (\lambda \mathcal{X}.\mathcal{T}) \mid @(\mathcal{T}, \mathcal{T}) \mid \mathcal{F}(\mathcal{T}, \ldots, \mathcal{T}).$$

Terms generated by the first two grammar rules are called *algebraic*. Terms of the form $\lambda x.u$ are called *abstractions* while the terms of the form $@(u, v)$ are called *applications*. The term $@(u, \overline{v})$ is called a (partial) *left-flattening* of $@(\ldots @(@(u, v_1), v_2), \ldots, v_n)$, with u being possibly an application itself. Terms other than abstractions are said to be *neutral*. We denote by $\mathcal{V}ar(t)$ ($\mathcal{B}\mathcal{V}ar(t)$) the set of free (bound) variables of t. We may assume for convenience (and without further notice) that bound variables in a term are all different, and are different from the free ones.

Terms are identified with finite labeled trees by considering $\lambda x.$, for each variable x, as a unary function symbol. *Positions* are strings of positive integers, the empty string Λ denoting the root position. The *subterm* of t at position p is denoted by $t|_p$, and by $t[u]_p$ the result of replacing $t|_p$ at position p in t by u. We write $s \triangleright u$ if u is a strict subterm of s. We use $t[\ ]_p$ for a term with a hole, called a context. The notation $\bar{s}$ will be ambiguously used to denote a list, a multiset, or a set of terms $s_1, \ldots, s_n$.

2.2 Typing Rules

Typing rules restrict the set of terms by constraining them to follow a precise discipline. Environments are sets of pairs written $x : \sigma$, where x is a variable and σ is a type. Let $Dom(\Gamma) = \{x \mid x : \sigma \in \Gamma \text{ for some type } \sigma\}$. We assume there is a unique pair of the form $x : \sigma$ for every variable $x \in Dom(\Gamma)$. Our typing judgments are written as $\Gamma \vdash M : \sigma$ if the term M can be proved to have the type σ in the environment Γ. A term M has type σ in the environment Γ if $\Gamma \vdash M : \sigma$ is provable in the inference system of Figure 1. A term M is typable in the environment Γ if there exists a type σ such that M has type σ in the environment Γ. A term M is typable if it is typable in some environment Γ. Note that function symbols are uncurried, hence must come along with all their arguments.

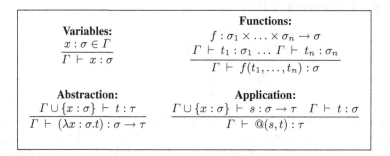

Fig. 1. Typing judgments in higher-order algebras

2.3 Higher-Order Rewrite Rules

Substitutions are written as in $\{x_1 : \sigma_1 \mapsto (\Gamma_1, t_1), \ldots, x_n : \sigma_n \mapsto (\Gamma_n, t_n)\}$ where, for every $i \in [1..n]$, t_i is assumed different from x_i and $\Gamma_i \vdash t_i : \sigma_i$. We also assume that $\bigcup_i \Gamma_i$ is an environment. We often write $x \mapsto t$ instead of $x : \sigma \mapsto (\Gamma, t)$, in particular when t is ground. We use the letter γ for substitutions and postfix notation for their application. Substitutions behave as endomorphisms defined on free variables. A (possibly higher-order) *term rewriting system* is a set of rewrite rules $R = \{\Gamma_i \vdash l_i \rightarrow r_i : \sigma_i\}_i$, where l_i and r_i are higher-order terms such that l_i and r_i have the same type σ_i in the environment Γ_i. Given a term rewriting system R, a term s rewrites to a term t at position p with the rule $l \rightarrow r$ and the substitution γ, written $s \xrightarrow[l \rightarrow r]{p} t$, or simply $s \rightarrow_R t$, if $s|_p = l\gamma$ and $t = s[r\gamma]_p$.

A term s such that $s \xrightarrow[R]{p} t$ is called *R-reducible*. The subterm $s|_p$ is a *redex* in s, and t is the *reduct* of s. Irreducible terms are said to be in *R-normal form*. A substitution γ is in *R*-normal form if $x\gamma$ is in *R*-normal form for all x. We denote by $\xrightarrow[R]{*}$ the reflexive, transitive closure of the rewrite relation $\xrightarrow[R]{}$.

Given a rewrite relation $\longrightarrow$, a term s is strongly normalizing if there is no infinite sequence of rewrites issuing from s. The rewrite relation itself is *strongly normalizing*, or *terminating*, if all terms are strongly normalizing, in which case it is called a *reduction*.

Three particular higher-order equation schemas originate from the λ-calculus, α-, β- and η-equality:

$$\lambda x.v \ =_\alpha \ \lambda y.v\{x \mapsto y\} \text{ if } y \notin \mathcal{B}\mathcal{V}ar(v) \cup (\mathcal{V}ar(v) \setminus \{x\})$$
$$@(\lambda x.v, u) \longrightarrow_\beta v\{x \mapsto u\}$$
$$\lambda x.@(u, x) \longrightarrow_\eta u \qquad \text{if } x \notin \mathcal{V}ar(u)$$

As usual, we do not distinguish α-convertible terms. β- and η-equalities are used as reductions, which is indicated by the long-arrow symbol instead of the equality symbol. The above rule-schemas define a rewrite system which is known to be terminating, a result proved in Section 3.

2.4 Higher-Order Reduction Orderings

We will make intensive use of well-founded orderings, using the vocabulary of rewrite systems for orderings, for proving strong normalization properties. For our purpose, an *ordering*, usually denoted by $\geq$, is a reflexive, symmetric, transitive relation compatible with α-conversion, that is, $s =_\alpha t \geq u =_\alpha v$ implies $s \geq v$, whose strict part $>$ is itself compatible. We will essentially use strict orderings, and hence, the word ordering for them too. We will also make use of order-preserving operations on relations, namely multiset and lexicographic extensions, see [15].

Rewrite orderings are *monotonic* and *stable* orderings, *reduction orderings* are in addition *well-founded*, while *higher-order reduction orderings* must also contain β- and η-reductions. Monotonicity of $>$ is defined as $u > v$ implies $s[u]_p > s[v]_p$ for all contexts $s[\ ]_p$. Stability of $>$ is defined as $u > v$ implies $s\gamma > t\gamma$ for all substitutions γ. Higher-order reduction orderings are used to prove termination of rewrite systems including β- and η-reductions by simply comparing the left hand and right hand sides of the remaining rules.

3   Computability

Simply minded arguments do not work for showing the strong normalization property of the simply typed lambda-calculus, for β-reduction increases the size of terms, which precludes an induction on their size, and preserves their types, which seems to preclude an induction on types.

Tait's idea is to generalize the strong normalization property in order to enable an induction on types. To each type σ, we associate a subset $[\![\sigma]\!]$ of the set of terms, called the *computability predicate* of type σ, or set of *computable terms* of type σ. Whether $[\![\sigma]\!]$ contains only typable terms of type σ is not really important, although it can help intuition. What is essential are the properties that the family of predicates should satisfy:

(i) computable terms are strongly normalizing;
(ii) reducts of computable terms are computable;
(iii) a neutral term u is computable iff all its reducts are computable;
(iv) $u : \sigma \to \tau$ is computable iff so is $@(u, v)$ for all computable v.

A (non-trivial) consequence of all these properties can be added to smooth the proof of the coming Main Lemma:

(v) $\lambda x.u$ is computable iff so is $u\{x \mapsto v\}$ for all computable v.

Apart from (v), the above properties refer to β-reduction via the notions of *reduct* and *strong normalization* only. Indeed, various computability predicates found in the literature use the same definition parametrized by the considered reduction relation.

There are several ways to define a computability predicate by taking as its definition some of the properties that it should satisfy. For example, a simple definition by induction on types is this:

$s : \sigma \in [\![\sigma]\!]$ for σ basic iff s is strongly normalizing;
$s : \theta \to \tau \in [\![\sigma \to \tau]\!]$ iff $@(s, u) : \tau \in [\![\tau]\!]$ for every $u : \theta \in [\![\theta]\!]$.

An alternative for the case of basic type is:

$$s : \sigma \in [\![\sigma]\!] \text{ iff } \forall t : \tau \,.\, s \longrightarrow t \text{ then } t \in [\![\tau]\!].$$

This formulation defines the predicate as a fixpoint of a monotonic functional. Once the predicate is defined, it becomes necessary to show the computability properties. This uses an induction on types in the first case or an induction on the definition of the predicate in the fixpoint case.

Tait's strong normalization proof is based on the following key lemma:

Lemma 1 (Main Lemma). *Let s be an arbitrary term and γ be an arbitrary computable substitution. Then $s\gamma$ is computable.*

Proof. By induction on the structure of terms.

1. s is a variable: $s\gamma$ is computable by assumption on γ.
2. $s = @(u, v)$. Since $u\gamma$ and $v\gamma$ are computable by induction hypothesis, $s\gamma = @(u\gamma, v\gamma)$ is computable by computability property (iv).
3. $s = \lambda x.u$. By computability property (v), $s\gamma = \lambda x.u\gamma$ is computable iff $u\gamma\{x \mapsto v\}$ is computable for an arbitrary computable v. Let now $\gamma' = \gamma \cup \{x \mapsto v\}$. By definition of substitutions for abstractions, $u\gamma\{x \mapsto v\} = u\gamma'$, which is usually ensured by α-conversion. By assumptions on γ and v, γ' is computable, and $u\gamma'$ is therefore computable by the main induction hypothesis. $\square$

Since an arbitrary term s can be seen as its own instance by the identity substitution, which is computable by computability property (iii), all terms are computable by the Main Lemma, hence strongly normalizing by computability property (i).

4   The Recursive Path Ordering and Computability

In this section, we restrict ourselves to first-order algebraic terms. Assuming that the set of function symbols is equipped with an ordering relation $\geq_{\mathcal{F}}$, called *precedence*, and a status function $stat$, writing $stat_f$ for $stat(f)$, we recall the definition of the recursive path ordering:

Definition 1. $s \succ_{rpo} t$ *iff*

1. $s = f(\overline{s})$ with $f \in \mathcal{F}$, and $u \underset{rpo}{\succeq} t$ for some $u \in \overline{s}$
2. $s = f(\overline{s})$ with $f \in \mathcal{F}$, and $t = g(\overline{t})$ with $f >_{\mathcal{F}} g$, and A
3. $s = f(\overline{s})$ and $t = g(\overline{t})$ with $f =_{\mathcal{F}} g \in Mul$, and $\overline{s}\,(\underset{rpo}{\succ})_{mul}\,\overline{t}$
4. $s = f(\overline{s})$ and $t = g(\overline{t})$ with $f =_{\mathcal{F}} g \in Lex$, and $\overline{s}\,(\underset{rpo}{\succ})_{lex}\,\overline{t}$ and A

$$\text{where } A = \forall v \in \overline{t}.\ s \underset{rpo}{\succ} v \quad \text{and} \quad s \underset{rpo}{\succeq} t \text{ iff } s \underset{rpo}{\succ} t \text{ or } s = t$$

We now show the well-foundedness of $\succ_{rpo}$ by using Tait's method. Computability is defined here as strong normalization, implying computability property (i). We prove the computability property:

(vii) Let $f \in \mathcal{F}_n$ and $\overline{s}$ be computable terms. Then $f(\overline{s})$ is computable.

Proof. The restriction of $\succ_{rpo}$ to terms smaller than or equal to the terms in $\overline{s}$ w.r.t. $\succ_{rpo}$ is a well-founded ordering which we use for building an outer induction on the pairs $(f, \overline{s})$ ordered by $(>_{\mathcal{F}}, (\succ_{rpo})_{stat_f})_{lex}$. This ordering is well-founded, since it is built from well-founded orderings by using mappings that preserve well-founded orderings.

We now show that $f(\overline{s})$ is computable by proving that t is computable for all t such that $f(\overline{s}) \succ_{rpo} t$. This property is itself proved by an (inner) induction on $|t|$, and by case analysis upon the proof that $f(\overline{s}) \succ_{rpo} t$.

1. subterm case: $\exists u \in \overline{s}$ such that $u \succ_{rpo} t$. By assumption, u is computable, hence so is its reduct t.
2. precedence case: $t = g(\overline{t})$, $f >_{\mathcal{F}} g$, and $\forall v \in \overline{t},\ s \succ_{rpo} v$. By inner induction, v is computable, hence so is $\overline{t}$. By outer induction, $g(\overline{t}) = t$ is computable.
3. multiset case: $t = f(\overline{t})$ with $f \in Mul$, and $\overline{s}(\succ_{rpo})_{mul}\overline{t}$. By definition of the multiset extension, $\forall v \in \overline{t}$, $\exists u \in \overline{s}$ such that $u \succeq_{rpo} v$. Since $\overline{s}$ is a vector of computable terms by assumption, so is $\overline{t}$. We conclude by outer induction that $f(\overline{t}) = t$ is computable.
4. lexicographic case: $t = f(\overline{t})$ with $f \in Lex$, $\overline{s}(\succ_{rpo})_{lex}\overline{t}$, and $\forall v \in \overline{t},\ s \succ_{rpo} v$. By inner induction, $\overline{t}$ is strongly normalizing, and by outer induction, so is $f(\overline{t}) = t$.

$\square$

The well-foundedness of $\succ_{rpo}$ follows from computability property (vii).

5   The General Schema and Computability

As in the previous section, we assume that the set of function symbols is equipped with a precedence relation $\geq_{\mathcal{F}}$ and a status function $stat$.

Definition 2. *The computability closure $CC(t = f(\bar{t}))$, with $f \in \mathcal{F}$, is the set $CC(t, \emptyset)$, s.t. $CC(t, \mathcal{V})$, with $\mathcal{V} \cap Var(t) = \emptyset$, is the smallest set of typable terms containing all variables in $\mathcal{V}$ and terms in $\bar{t}$, closed under:*

1. *subterm of basic type: let $s \in CC(t, \mathcal{V})$, and u be a subterm of s of basic type σ such that $Var(u) \subseteq Var(t)$; then $u \in CC(t, \mathcal{V})$;*
2. *precedence: let $f >_{\mathcal{F}} g$, and $\bar{s} \in CC(t, \mathcal{V})$; then $g(\bar{s}) \in CC(t, \mathcal{V})$;*
3. *recursive call: let $f(\bar{s})$ be a term such that terms in $\bar{s}$ belong to $CC(t, \mathcal{V})$ and $\bar{t}(\longrightarrow_{\beta} \cup \rhd)_{stat_f} \bar{s}$; then $g(\bar{s}) \in CC(t, \mathcal{V})$ for every $g =_{\mathcal{F}} f$;*
4. *application: let $s : \sigma_1 \to \ldots \to \sigma_n \to \sigma \in CC(t, \mathcal{V})$ and $u_i : \sigma_i \in CC(t, \mathcal{V})$ for every $i \in [1..n]$; then $@(s, u_1, \ldots, u_n) \in CC(t, \mathcal{V})$;*
5. *abstraction: let $s \in CC(t, \mathcal{V} \cup \{x\})$ for some $x \notin Var(t) \cup \mathcal{V}$; then $\lambda x.s \in CC(t, \mathcal{V})$;*
6. *reduction: let $u \in CC(t, \mathcal{V})$, and $u \longrightarrow_{\beta \cup \rhd} v$; then $v \in CC(t, \mathcal{V})$.*

We say that a rewrite system R satisfies the *general schema* iff

$$r \in CC(f(\bar{l})) \text{ for all } f(\bar{l}) \to r \in R$$

We now consider computability with respect to the rewrite relation $\longrightarrow_R \cup \longrightarrow_{\beta}$, and add the computability property (vii) whose proof can be easily adapted from the previous one. We can then add a new case in Tait's Main Lemma, for terms headed by an algebraic function symbol. As a consequence, the relation $\longrightarrow_{\beta} \cup \longrightarrow_R$ is strongly normalizing.

Example 1 (System T). We show the strong normalization of Gödel's system T by showing that its rules satisfy the general schema. This is clear for the first rule by the base Case of the definition. For the second rule, we have: $V \in CC(rec(s(X), U, V))$ by base Case; $s(X) \in CC(rec(s(X), U, V))$ by base Case again, and by Case 2 we have $X \in CC(rec(s(X), U, V))$, assuming $rec >_{\mathcal{F}} s$; $U \in CC(rec(s(X), U, V))$ by base Case, hence all arguments of the recursive call are in $CC(rec(s(X), U, V))$. Since $s(X) \rhd X$ holds, we have $rec(X, U, V) \in CC(rec(s(X), U, V))$. Therefore, we conclude with $@(V, X, rec(X, U, V)) \in CC(rec(s(X), U, V))$ by Case 4.

6   The Higher-Order Recursive Path Ordering

6.1   The Ingredients

– A quasi-ordering on types $\geq_{T_S}$ called *the type ordering* satisfying the following properties:
  1. *Well-foundedness:* $>_{T_S}$ is well-founded;
  2. *Arrow preservation:* $\tau \to \sigma =_{T_S} \alpha$ iff $\alpha = \tau' \to \sigma'$, $\tau' =_{T_S} \tau$ and $\sigma =_{T_S} \sigma'$;
  3. *Arrow decreasingness:* $\tau \to \sigma >_{T_S} \alpha$ implies $\sigma \geq_{T_S} \alpha$ or $\alpha = \tau' \to \sigma'$, $\tau' =_{T_S} \tau$ and $\sigma >_{T_S} \sigma'$;
  4. *Arrow monotonicity:* $\tau \geq_{T_S} \sigma$ implies $\alpha \to \tau \geq_{T_S} \alpha \to \sigma$ and $\tau \to \alpha \geq_{T_S} \sigma \to \alpha$;

  A convenient type ordering is obtained by restricting the subterm property for the arrow in the RPO definition.

- A quasi-ordering $\geq_{\mathcal{F}}$ on $\mathcal{F}$, called the *precedence*, such that $>_{\mathcal{F}}$ is well-founded.
- A *status* $stat_f \in \{Mul, Lex\}$ for every symbol $f \in \mathcal{F}$.

The higher-order recursive path ordering (HORPO) operates on typing judgments. To ease the reading, we will however forget the environment and type unless necessary. Let

$$A = \forall v \in \bar{t} \;\; s \underset{horpo}{\succ} v \text{ or } u \underset{horpo}{\succ} v \text{ for some } u \in \bar{s}$$

Definition 3. *Given two judgments* $\Gamma \vdash_{\Sigma} s : \sigma$ *and* $\Sigma \vdash_{\Sigma} t : \tau$,

$$s \underset{horpo}{\succ} t \text{ iff } \sigma \geq_{T_S} \tau \text{ and}$$

1. $s = f(\bar{s})$ with $f \in \mathcal{F}$, and $u \underset{horpo}{\succeq} t$ for some $u \in \bar{s}$
2. $s = f(\bar{s})$ with $f \in \mathcal{F}$, and $t = g(\bar{t})$ with $f >_{\mathcal{F}} g$, and A
3. $s = f(\bar{s})$ and $t = g(\bar{t})$ with $f =_{\mathcal{F}} g \in Mul$, and $\bar{s} \,(\underset{horpo}{\succ})_{mul} \bar{t}$
4. $s = f(\bar{s})$ and $t = g(\bar{t})$ with $f =_{\mathcal{F}} g \in Lex$, and $\bar{s} \,(\underset{horpo}{\succ})_{lex} \bar{t}$ and A
5. $s = @(s_1, s_2)$, and $s_1 \underset{horpo}{\succeq} t$ or $s_2 \underset{horpo}{\succeq} t$
6. $s = \lambda x : \alpha.u$ with $x \notin Var(t)$, and $u \underset{horpo}{\succeq} t$
7. $s = f(\bar{s})$ with $f \in \mathcal{F}$, $t = @(\bar{t})$ is a partial left-flattening of t, and A
8. $s = f(\bar{s})$ with $f \in \mathcal{F}$, $t = \lambda x : \alpha.v$ with $x \notin Var(v)$ and $s \underset{horpo}{\succ} v$
9. $s = @(s_1, s_2)$, $t = @(\bar{t})$, and $\{s_1, s_2\}(\underset{horpo}{\succ})_{mul} \bar{t}$
10. $s = \lambda x : \alpha.u$, $t = \lambda x : \beta.v$, $\alpha =_{T_S} \beta$, and $u \underset{horpo}{\succ} v$
11. $s = @(\lambda x : \alpha.u, v)$ and $u\{x \mapsto v\} \underset{horpo}{\succeq} t$
12. $s = \lambda x : \alpha.@(u, x)$, $x \notin Var(u)$ and $u \underset{horpo}{\succeq} t$

Example 2 (System T). The new proof of strong normalization of System T is even simpler. For the first rule, we apply Case 1. For the second, we apply Case 7, and show recursively that $rec(s(X), U, V) \succ_{horpo} V$ by Case 1, $rec(s(X), U, V) \succ_{horpo} X$ by Case 1 applied twice, and $rec(s(X), U, V) \succ_{horpo} rec(X, U, V)$ by Case 3, assuming a multiset status for rec, which follows from the comparison $s(X) \succ_{horpo} X$ by Case 1.

The strong normalization proof of HORPO is in the same style as the previous strong normalization proofs, although technically more complex [21]. This proof shows that HORPO and the general schema can be combined by replacing the membership $u \in \bar{s}$ used in case 1 by the more general membership $u \in \mathcal{CC}(f(\bar{s}))$. It follows that the HORPO mechanism is inherently more expressive than the closure mechanism.

Because of Cases 11 and 12, HORPO is not transitive. Indeed, there are examples for which the proof of $s \succ^+_{horpo} t$ requires guessing a middle term u such that $s \succ_{horpo} u$ and $u \succ_{horpo} t$. Guessing a middle term when necessary is automated in the implementations of HORPO and HORPO with closure available from the web page of the first two authors.

7   Unifying HORPO and the Computability Closure

A major advantage of HORPO over the general schema is its recursive structure. In contrast, the membership to the computability closure is undecidable due to its Case 3, but does not involve any type comparison. To combine the advantages of both, we now incorporate the closure construction into the HORPO as an ordering. Besides, we also incorporate the property that arguments of a type constructor are computable when the *positivity condition* is satisfied as it is the case for inductive types in the Calculus of Inductive Constructions [24,7].

$$s : \sigma \underset{horpo}{\succ} t : \tau \quad \text{iff}$$

$Var(t) \subseteq Var(s)$ and

1. $s = f(\bar{s})$ and $s \underset{comp}{\overset{\emptyset}{\succ}} t$

2. $s = f(\bar{s})$ and $\sigma \geq_{T_S} \tau$ and
   (a) $t = g(\bar{t})$, $f >_{\mathcal{F}} g$ and A
   (b) $t = g(\bar{t})$, $f =_{\mathcal{F}} g$,
       $\bar{s}(\underset{horpo}{\succ})_{stat_f}\bar{t}$ and A
   (c) $t = @(t_1, t_2)$ and A

3. $s = @(s_1, s_2), \sigma \geq_{T_S} \tau$ and
   (a) $t = @(t_1, t_2)$ and
       $\{s_1, s_2\}(\underset{horpo}{\succ})_{mul}\{t_1, t_2\}$
   (b) $s_1 \underset{horpo}{\succeq} t$ or $s_2 \underset{horpo}{\succeq} t$
   (c) $s_1 = \lambda x.u$ and
       $u\{x \mapsto s_2\} \underset{horpo}{\succeq} t$

4. $s = \lambda x : \alpha.u, \sigma \geq_{T_S} \tau$ and
   (a) $t = \lambda x : \beta.v, \alpha =_{T_S} \beta$
       and $u \underset{horpo}{\succ} v$
   (b) $x \notin Var(t)$ and $u \underset{horpo}{\succeq} t$
   (c) $u = @(v, x), x \notin Var(v)$
       and $v \underset{horpo}{\succeq} t$

where $A = \forall v \in \bar{t}$:
$s \underset{horpo}{\succ} v$ or $\exists u \in \bar{s} : u \underset{horpo}{\succ} v$

$$s = f(\bar{s}) \underset{comp}{\overset{\overline{X}}{\succ}} t \quad \text{iff}$$

1. $t \in \overline{X}$
2. $\exists s_i \in Acc(s) : s_i \underset{comp}{\overset{\overline{X}}{\succeq}} t$
3. $t = g(\bar{t})$, $f >_{T_S} g$ and
   $\forall v \in \bar{t} : s \underset{comp}{\overset{\overline{X}}{\succ}} v$
4. $t = g(\bar{t})$, $f =_{T_S} g$,
   $\forall v \in \bar{t} : s \underset{comp}{\overset{\overline{X}}{\succ}} v$ and
   $Acc(s)(\underset{horpo}{\succ})_{stat_f}\lambda\overline{X}.\bar{t}$
5. $t = @(u, v)$,
   $s \underset{comp}{\overset{\overline{X}}{\succ}} u$ and $s \underset{comp}{\overset{\overline{X}}{\succ}} v$
6. $t = \lambda x : \alpha.u$ and
   $s \underset{comp}{\overset{\overline{X}\cdot\{x:\alpha\}}{\succ}} u$

where $s_i \in Acc(f(\bar{s}))$
(s_i is accessible in s)
iff

1. s is the left hand side of
   an ancestor goal $s \succ_{horpo} u$
2. s is the left hand side of the
   current goal $s \succ_{comp} u$, and,
   either $f : \bar{\sigma} \to \sigma$ and
   σ occurs only positively in σ_i.

Example 3. We consider now the type of Brouwer's ordinals defined from the type $\mathbb{N}$ by the equation $Ord = 0 \uplus s(Ord) \uplus lim(\mathbb{N} \to Ord)$. Note that Ord occurs positively in the type $\mathbb{N} \to Ord$, and that $\mathbb{N}$ must be smaller or equal to Ord. The recursor for the type Ord is defined as:

$$rec(0, U, V, W) \rightarrow U$$
$$rec(s(X), U, V, W) \rightarrow @(V, X, rec(X, U, V, W))$$
$$rec(lim(F), U, V, W) \rightarrow @(W, F, \lambda n.rec(@(F, n), U, V, W))$$

We skip the first two rules and concentrate on the third:

1. $rec(lim(F), U, V, W) \succ_{horpo} @(W, F, \lambda n.rec(@(F, n), U, V, W))$
   which, by Case 1 of $\succ_{horpo}$ is replaced by the new goal:
2. $rec(lim(F), U, V, W) \succ^{\emptyset}_{comp} @(W, F, \lambda n.rec(@(F, n), U, V, W))$
   By Case 5 of $\succ_{comp}$, these three goals become:
3. $rec(lim(F), U, V, W) \succ^{\emptyset}_{comp} W$
4. $rec(lim(F), U, V, W) \succ^{\emptyset}_{comp} F$
5. $rec(lim(F), U, V, W) \succ^{\emptyset}_{comp} \lambda n.rec(@(F, n), U, V, W)$
   Since $rec(lim(F), U, V, W)$ originates from Goal 1,
   Goal 3 disappears by Case 2, while Goal 4 becomes:
6. $lim(F) \succ^{\emptyset}_{comp} F$
   which disappears by the same Case since F is accessible in $lim(F)$.
   thanks to the positivity condition. By Case 6, Goal 5 becomes:
7. $rec(lim(F), U, V, W) \succ^{\{n\}}_{comp} rec(@(F, n), U, V, W)$
   Case 4 applies with a lexicographic status for rec, yielding 5 goals:
8. $rec(lim(F), U, V, W) \succ^{\{n\}}_{comp} @(F, n)$
9. $rec(lim(F), U, V, W) \succ^{\{n\}}_{comp} U$
10. $rec(lim(F), U, V, W) \succ^{\{n\}}_{comp} V$
11. $rec(lim(F), U, V, W) \succ^{\{n\}}_{comp} W$
12. $\{lim(F), U, V, W\}(\succ_{horpo})_{lex}\{\lambda n.@(F, n), \lambda n.U, \lambda n.V, \lambda n.W\}$
    Goals 9, 10, 11 disappear by Case 2, while, by Case 5
    Goal 8 generates (a variation of) the solved Goal 4 and the new sub-goal:
13. $rec(lim(F), U, V, W) \succ^{\{n\}}_{comp} n$
    which disappears by Case 1. We are left with Goal 12, which reduces to:
14. $lim(F) \succ_{horpo} \lambda n.@(F, n)$
    which, by Case 1 of $\succ_{horpo}$, then 6 and 5 of $\succ_{comp}$ yields successively:
15. $lim(F) \succ^{\emptyset}_{comp} \lambda n.@(F, n)$
16. $lim(F) \succ^{\{n\}}_{comp} @(F, n)$
    which, by Case 5, generates (a variation of) the Goal 6 and the last goal:
17. $lim(F) \succ^{\{n\}}_{comp} n$
    which succeeds by Case 1, ending the computation.

To show the strong normalization property of this new definition of $\succ_{horpo}$, we need a more sophisticated predicate combining the predicates used for showing the strong normalization of HORPO [21] and CAC [6]. We have not done any proof yet, but we believe that it is well-founded.

It is worth noting that the ordering $\succ_{horpo}$ defined here is in one way less powerful than the one defined in Section 6 using the closure definition of Section 5 because it does not accumulate computable terms for later use anymore. Instead, it deconstructs its left hand side as usual with rpo, and remembers very few computable terms: the accessible ones only. On the other hand, it is more powerful since the recursive case 4 of the closure uses now the full power of $\succ_{horpo}$ for its last comparison instead of simply β-reduction (see [21]). Besides, there is no more type comparison in Case 1 of the definition of $\succ_{horpo}$, a key improvement which remains to be justified formally.

8   Related Work

Termination of higher-order calculi has recently attracted quite a lot of attention. The area is building up, and mostly, although not entirely, based on reducibility techniques.

The case of conditional rewriting has been recently investigated by Blanqui [8]. His results are presented in this conference.

Giesl's dependency pairs method has been generalized to higher-order calculi by using reducibility techniques as described here [25,10]. The potential of this line of work is probably important, but more work in this direction is needed to support this claim.

Giesl [22] has achieved impressive progress for the case of combinator based calculi, such as Haskell programs, by transforming all definitions into a first-order framework, and then proving termination by using first-order tools. Such transformations do not accept explicit binding constructs, and therefore, do not apply to rich λ-calculi such as those considered here. On the other hand, the relationship of these results with computability deserves investigation.

An original, interesting work is Jones's analysis of the flux of redexes in pure lambda-calculus [16], and its use for proving termination properties of functional programs. Whether this method can yield a direct proof of finite developments in pure λ-calculus should be investigated. We also believe that his method can be incorporated to the HORPO by using an interpretation on terms instead of a type comparison, as mentioned in Conclusion.

Byron Cook, Andreas Podelski and Andrey Ribalchenko [13] have developed a quite different and impressive method based on abstract interpretations to show termination of large imperative programs. Their claim is that large programs are more likely to be shown terminating by approximating them before to make an analysis. Note that the use of a well-founded ordering can be seen as a particular analysis. Although impressive, this work is indeed quite far from our objectives.

9   Conclusion

We give here a list of open problems which we consider important. We are ourselves working on some of these. The higher-order recursive path ordering should be seen as a firm step to undergo further developments in different directions, some of which are listed below.

- Two of them have been investigated in the first order framework: the case of associative commutative operators, and the use of interpretations as a sort of elaborated precedence operating on function symbols. The first extension has been carried out for the general schema [5], and the second for a weak form of HORPO [11]. Both should have an important impact for applications, hence deserve immediate attention.

- Enriching the type system with dependent types, a problem considered by Wału-kiewicz [26] for the original version of HORPO in which types were compared by a congruence. Replacing the congruence by HORPO recursively called on types as done in [21] for a simpler type discipline raises technical difficulties. The ultimate goal here is to generalize the most recent versions of the ordering including the present one, for applications to the Calculus of Inductive Constructions.
- HORPO does not contain and is not a well-order for the subterm relationship. However, its definition shows that it satisfies a weak subterm property, namely property A. It would be theoretically interesting to investigate whether some Kruskal-like theorem holds for higher-order terms with respect to the weak subterm property. This could yield an alternative, more abstract way of hiding away computability arguments.

References

1. F. Barbanera. Adding algebraic rewriting to the calculus of constructions: Strong normalization preserved. In *Proc. 2nd Int. Workshop on Conditional and Typed Rewriting Systems, Montreal, LNCS 516*, 1990.
2. F. Barbanera, M. Fernández, and H. Geuvers. Modularity of strong normalization and confluence in the λ-algebraic-cube. In *Proc. 9th IEEE Symp. Logic in Computer Science*, pages 406–415, 1994.
3. F. Blanqui, J.-P. Jouannaud, and M. Okada. The Calculus of Algebraic Constructions. In Paliath Narendran and Michael Rusinowitch, editors, *10th International Conference on Rewriting Techniques and Applications*, volume 1631 of *Lecture Notes in Computer Science*, Trento, Italy, July 1999. Springer Verlag.
4. F. Blanqui, J.-P. Jouannaud, and M. Okada. Inductive-Data-Type Systems. *Theoretical Computer Science*, 272(1-2):41–68, 2002.
5. F. Blanqui. Rewriting modulo in Deduction modulo. In *Proc. of the 14th International Conference on Rewriting Techniques and Applications*, volume 2706 of *LNCS*, 2003.
6. F. Blanqui. Definitions by rewriting in the Calculus of Constructions. *Mathematical Structures in Computer Science*, 15(1):37–92, 2005.
7. F. Blanqui. Inductive types in the Calculus of Algebraic Constructions. *Fundamenta Informaticae*, 65(1-2):61–86, 2005.
8. F. Blanqui and C. Riba. Combining typing and size constraints for checking termination of higher-order conditional rewriting systems. In *Proc. LPAR, to appear in LNAI*, LNCS, 2006.
9. F. Blanqui. (HO)RPO revisited, 2006. Manuscript.
10. F. Blanqui. Higher-order dependency pairs. In *Proceedings of the 8th International Workshop on Termination, 2006*.
11. Cristina Borralleras and Albert Rubio. A monotonic, higher-order semantic path ordering. In *Proceedings LPAR*, Lecture Notes in Computer Science. Springer Verlag, 2006.
12. Val Breazu-Tannen and Jean Gallier. Polymorphic rewriting conserves algebraic strong normalization. *Theoretical Computer Science*, 1990.
13. Andreas Podelski Byron Cook and Andrey Rybalchenko. Termination proofs for systems code, 2004. Manuscript.
14. Coq Development Team. *The Coq Proof Assistant Reference Manual, Version 8.0*. INRIA Rocquencourt, France, 2004. http://coq.inria.fr/.
15. Nachum Dershowitz and Jean-Pierre Jouannaud. Rewrite systems. In J. van Leeuwen, editor, *Handbook of Theoretical Computer Science*, volume B, pages 243–309. North Holland, 1990.

16. Neil Jones and Nina Bohr. Termination analysis of the untyped λ-calculus. In *Rewriting techniques and Applications*, pages 1–23. Springer Verlag, 2004. LNCS 3091.

17. Jean-Pierre Jouannaud and Mitsuhiro Okada. Executable higher-order algebraic specification languages. In *Proc. 6th IEEE Symp. Logic in Computer Science, Amsterdam*, pages 350–361, 1991.

18. Jean-Pierre Jouannaud and Mitsuhiro Okada. Abstract data type systems. *Theoretical Computer Science*, 173(2):349–391, February 1997.

19. Jean-Pierre Jouannaud and Albert Rubio. The higher-order recursive path ordering. In Giuseppe Longo, editor, *Fourteenth Annual IEEE Symposium on Logic in Computer Science*, Trento, Italy, July 1999.

20. Jean-Pierre Jouannaud and Albert Rubio. Higher-order orderings for normal rewriting. In *Proc. 17th International Conference on Rewriting Techniques and Applications, Seattle, Washington, USA*, 2006.

21. Jean-Pierre Jouannaud and Albert Rubio. Polymorphic higher-order recursive path orderings. *Journal of the ACM*, submitted.

22. Peter Scneider-Kamp Jürgen Giesl, Stephan Swiderski and René Thiemann. Automated termination analysis for haskell: Form term rewriting to programming languages. In *Rewriting techniques and Applications*, pages 297–312. Springer Verlag, 2006. LNCS 4098.

23. Mitsuhiro Okada. Strong normalizability for the combined system of the typed lambda calculus and an arbitrary convergent term rewrite system. In *Proc. of the 20th Int. Symp. on Symbolic and Algebraic Computation, Portland, Oregon, USA*, 1989.

24. Christine Paulin-Mohring. Inductive definitions in the system COQ. In *Typed Lambda Calculi and Applications*, pages 328–345. Springer Verlag, 1993. LNCS 664.

25. Masahiko Sakai and Keiichirou Kusakari. On dependency pairs method for proving termination of higher-order rewrite systems. *IEICE-Transactions on Information and Systems*, E88-D (3):583–593, 2005.

26. Daria Wałukiewicz-Chrzaszcz. Termination of rewriting in the Calculus of Constructions. In *Proceedings of the Workshop on Logical Frameworks and Meta-languages, Santa Barbara, California*, 2000. Satellite workshop of LICS'2000.

Deciding Satisfiability of Positive Second Order Joinability Formulae

Sébastien Limet and Pierre Pillot

LIFO, Université d'Orléans, France
{limet, pillot}@univ-orleans.fr

Abstract. This paper deals with a class of second order formulae where the only predicate is joinability modulo a conditional term rewrite system, first order variables range over ground terms and second order variables are interpreted as relations on ground terms (i.e. sets of tuples of ground terms). We define a generic algorithm that decides the satisfiability of positive second order joinability formulae when an algorithm is known to finitely represent solutions of first order formulae. When the answer is positive, the algorithm computes one particular instance for the second order variables. We apply this technique to the class of positive second order pseudo-regular formulae. The result is then a logic program that represents the instance of the second order variables. We define a transformation to translate this instance into a CTRS. This result can be used to automatically synthesize a program that defines a relation from its specification.

1 Introduction

Second order theories have been widely studied for a long time because of their practical applications in several fields of computer sciences. The most studied class is monadic second order logic. Many variants of this logic have been proved decidable using automata techniques (see [16] for a survey). The solutions of formulae in such a logic are represented by automata on strings or trees e.g. weak second order logic with k successors WSkS is solved using finite tree automata [15] that defines regular relations. Applications of monadic second order logic are numerous from circuit verification [5] which is the historical use, to program verification [7].

In this paper, we study a class of formulae based on the predicate $\downarrow_R^?$ (i.e. joinability modulo a term rewrite system). In the first order case, a solution of an equation $s \downarrow_R^? t$ is a substitution σ such that $s\sigma$ and $t\sigma$ rewrite into the same term. The term rewrite systems we consider are conditional term rewrite systems (CTRS for short). A CTRS defines a relation on terms by means of conditional rewrite rules of the form $l \to r \Leftarrow C$ (e.g. the CTRS of Example 1 below defines the relation $+$ on positive integers). In the second order formulae studied in the present paper, second order variables represent such a relation. For example, a solution of the formula $\forall x X(x) \downarrow_R^? x + x$ where x is a first order variable and X a second order one, is a relation (t_1, t_2) such that $t_2 = 2 \times t_1$. Our aim is to automatically build the rewrite rules that define this relation.

M. Hermann and A. Voronkov (Eds.): LPAR 2006, LNAI 4246, pp. 15–29, 2006.
© Springer-Verlag Berlin Heidelberg 2006

The first contribution of this paper is the definition of a general algorithm to decide the satisfiability of positive second order joinability formulae for classes where there exists an algorithm that produces a decidable finite representation of the solutions of first order joinability formulae. The output of the algorithm is the empty set when the second order formula is not satisfiable and a particular instance of the second order variables otherwise.

In a previous paper [9], we defined the class of first order pseudo-regular formulae and showed that the solutions of such a formula can be represented by a regular relation. Some restrictions are imposed on the rewrite system to ensure that the relations it defines are regular relations (those rewrite systems are called pseudo-regular TRS). The closure properties of regular relations are used to prove first that the solutions of a single equation are a regular relation, and then that the solutions of a formula are also regular. The technique used to represent and manipulate relations in that paper is based on logic programs and comes from [11]. The general algorithm is then used to show the decidability of the satisfiability of positive second order pseudo-regular formulae. When a formula is satisfiable, we obtain a logic program from which we compute a CTRS that defines one possible instance for the second order variables. This result can be used to automatically generate a CTRS (which can be considered as a program) from the specification of the intended results.

Example 1. The following CTRS is a pseudo-regular one. It represents the addition for positive integers represented by binary digit strings. In our encoding, the least significant bits are leftmost. For example the term $0(1(\bot))$ represents the binary number 10 i.e. the number 2. $+$ is addition and $\oplus$ addition with carry. The rules with n_1 or n_2 represent several rules where n_1 and n_2 can be replaced by 0 or 1.

$$\bot + n_1(y) \rightarrow n_1(y) \qquad\qquad n_1(y) + \bot \rightarrow n_1(y)$$
$$0(x) + 0(y) \rightarrow 0(x+y) \qquad\qquad 1(x) + 1(y) \rightarrow 0(x \oplus y)$$
$$n_1(x) + n_2(y) \rightarrow 1(x+y) \text{ if } n_1 \neq n_2 \qquad \bot + \bot \rightarrow \bot$$
$$s(\bot) \rightarrow 1(\bot) \qquad\qquad s(0(x)) \rightarrow 1(x)$$
$$s(1(x)) \rightarrow 0(s(x))$$
$$\bot \oplus 0(y) \rightarrow 1(y) \qquad\qquad \bot \oplus 1(y) \rightarrow 0(s(y))$$
$$0(y) \oplus \bot \rightarrow 1(y) \qquad\qquad 1(y) \oplus \bot \rightarrow 0(s(y))$$
$$0(x) \oplus 0(y) \rightarrow 1(x+y) \qquad\qquad 1(x) \oplus 1(y) \rightarrow 1(x \oplus y)$$
$$n_1(x) \oplus n_2(y) \rightarrow 0(x \oplus y) \text{ if } n_1 \neq n_2 \qquad \bot \oplus \bot \rightarrow 1(\bot)$$

This CTRS is not really conditional since there are no conditions in the rewrite rules. Let us consider the two following rules that define the elementwise substraction of two lists of integers.

$$sl(\bot, \bot) \rightarrow \bot$$
$$sl(c(x_1, y_1), c(x_2, y_2)) \rightarrow c(x_3, sl(y_1, y_2)) \Leftarrow x_2 + x_3 \downarrow_R x_1$$

In the context of TRS without condition, the function sl would need the explicit definition of subtraction between two integers.

$\forall x X(x) = x + x$ is a positive second order formula. Our procedure constructs automatically the following CTRS that defines the only possible instance for X.

$$f_X(\bot) \to \bot \qquad\qquad f'_X(\bot) \to 1(\bot)$$
$$f_X(0(x)) \to 0(f_X(x)) \qquad f'_X(0(x)) \to 1(f_X(x))$$
$$f_X(1(x)) \to 0(f'_X(x)) \qquad f'_X(1(x)) \to 1(f'_X(x))$$

Notice that f_X introduces a 0 in the units and shift the digits of the number which corresponds to doubling an integer represented by binary digits.

2 Preliminaries

We recall some basic notions and notation concerning terms, conditional term rewrite systems and logic programming; for details see [2,13].

First Order Terms and Relations. Let Σ be a finite set of symbols with arity, *Var* be an infinite set of variables, and $\mathcal{T}(\Sigma, \mathit{Var})$ be the first-order term algebra over $\Sigma \cup \mathit{Var}$. A term is *linear* if no variable occurs more than once in it and a term without variables is called a *ground term*. In this paper, Σ consists of three disjoint subsets: the set $\mathcal{F}$ of *defined function symbols*, the set $\mathcal{C}$ of *constructor symbols* and the set Pr of *predicate symbols*. The terms of $\mathcal{T}(\mathcal{C}, \mathit{Var})$ are called *data-terms* and those of the form $P(\vec{t})$ where P is a predicate symbol of arity n and $\vec{t}$ is a vector of $\mathcal{T}(\mathcal{F} \cup \mathcal{C}, \mathit{Var})^n$ are called *atoms*.

A *position* p is a string of integers whose length is denoted by $|p|$. For a term t, $Pos(t)$ denotes the set of *positions* in t, and $t|_u$ the *subterm* of t at position u. The term $t[u \leftarrow s]$ is obtained from t by replacing the subterm at position u by s. $Var(t)$ is the set of variables occurring in t. The set $\Sigma Pos(t) \subseteq Pos(t)$ denotes the set of non-variable positions, i.e., $t|_u \notin \mathit{Var}$ for $u \in \Sigma Pos(t)$ and $t|_u \in \mathit{Var}$ for $u \in Pos(t) \setminus \Sigma Pos(t)$. The *depth of a term* $t \in \mathcal{T}(\mathcal{F} \cup \mathcal{C}, \mathit{Var})$ denoted $Depth(t)$ is 0 if $t \in \mathit{Var}$ and $\max(\{\, |p| \mid p \in \Sigma Pos(t)\,\})$ otherwise. A term of depth 1 is said to be *flat*. The *depth of an atom* $P(\vec{t})$ denoted $Depth(P(\vec{t}))$ is $\max(\{\, Depth(s) \mid s \in \vec{t}\,\})$. An atom of depth 0 is said to be *flat*.

A substitution is a mapping from *Var* to $\mathcal{T}(\Sigma, \mathit{Var})$ where $x\sigma \neq x$ for a finite set of variables. The *domain* of a substitution σ, $Dom(\sigma)$, is the set $\{\, x \in \mathit{Var} \mid x\sigma \neq x \,\}$. For $V \subseteq \mathit{Var}$, $\sigma|_V$ denotes the *restriction of* σ to the variables in V, i.e., $x\sigma|_V = x\sigma$ for $x \in V$ and $x\sigma|_V = x$ otherwise. If for all $x \in Dom(\sigma)$, $x\sigma$ is a data-term then σ is called a *data substitution*. If a term t is an *instance* of a term s, i.e. $t = s\sigma$, we say that t *matches* s and s *subsumes* t.

Let $CVar = \{\, \Box_i \mid i \geq 1 \,\}$ be the set of *context variables* distinct from *Var*. An *n-context* is a term t in $T(\Sigma, \mathit{Var} \cup CVar)$ such that each $\Box_i$ $1 \leq i \leq n$ occurs once and only once in t and no other element of *CVar* occurs in t. $\Box_1$ (also denoted $\Box$) is called the *trivial context*; if C a term in $T(\mathcal{C}, \mathit{Var} \cup CVar)$ then C is a *constructor context*. For an n-context C, the expression $C[t_1, \ldots, t_n]$ denotes the term $C\{\, \Box_i \mapsto t_i \mid 1 \leq i \leq n \,\}$.

This paper mainly deals with relations on ground data-terms. A *data-relation* $\tilde{r}$ of *arity* n is a subset of $\mathcal{T}^{n+1}(\mathcal{C})$. Notice that what we call arity for a relation is its number of components minus 1 because in our context, a relation $\tilde{r}$ with n components models in fact a relation from $\mathcal{T}^{n-1}(\mathcal{C})$ to $\mathcal{T}(\mathcal{C})$. The notation $\tilde{r}(t_1, \ldots, t_{n-1})$ denotes the set $\{\, t_n \mid (t_1, \ldots, t_{n-1}, t_n) \in \tilde{r} \,\}$ of ground data-terms.

The set of all possible data-relations is recursively enumerable, so we associate to each data-relation of arity n a unique *relation symbol* of arity n different from $(\Sigma \cup Var)$ and call it the *name* of the relation. We denote the set of relation names $\mathcal{R}$.

Logic programs. If $H, A_1, \ldots, A_n$ are atoms then $H \Leftarrow A_1, \ldots, A_n$ is a *Horn clause*; H is said to be the *head* of the clause and $A_1, \ldots, A_n$ is said to be the body. The elements of $Var(A_1, \ldots, A_n) \setminus Var(H)$ are called *existential variables*. A *logic program* is a set of Horn clauses. The *Herbrand domain* is the set of all ground atoms. The body of the clause $H \Leftarrow \mathcal{B}$ is said to be linear iff every variable occurs at most once in $\mathcal{B}$. A clause is said to be *linear* if both the head and the body are linear. A set of ground atoms S is an *Herbrand model* of the clause $H \Leftarrow \mathcal{B}$ iff for all σ such that $H\sigma \Leftarrow \mathcal{B}\sigma$ is ground and $\mathcal{B}\sigma \subseteq S$, we have $H\sigma \in S$. S is a Herbrand model of the logic program $\mathcal{P}$ if it is a model of all clauses of $\mathcal{P}$. For a logic program $\mathcal{P}$ and a ground atom A we write $\mathcal{P} \models A$ if A belongs to the least Herbrand model of $\mathcal{P}$ (denoted $\mathcal{M}(\mathcal{P})$). The *language* described by an n-ary predicate symbol P w.r.t. a program $\mathcal{P}$ is the set $\{(t_1, \ldots, t_n) \mid \mathcal{P} \models P(t_1, \ldots, t_n)\}$ of n-tuples of ground terms.

Conditional Term Rewrite Systems. A *term rewrite system* (TRS) is a set of oriented equations built over $T(\mathcal{F} \cup \mathcal{C}, Var)$ and called *rewrite rules*. Lhs and rhs are shorthands for the left-hand and right-hand side of a rule, respectively. For a TRS R, the *rewrite relation* is denoted by $\rightarrow_R$ and is defined by $t \rightarrow_R s$ iff there exists a rule $l \rightarrow r$ in R, a non-variable position u in t, and a substitution σ, such that $t|_u = l\sigma$ and $s = t[u \leftarrow r\sigma]$. Such a step is written as $t \rightarrow_{[u,l\rightarrow r]} s$. If σ is a data-substitution then the step is called a *data-step*. If a term t cannot be reduced by any rewriting rule, it is said to be *irreducible*. The reflexive-transitive closure of $\rightarrow_R$ is denoted by $\rightarrow_R^*$. The *joinability relation* $\downarrow_R$ is defined by $t \downarrow_R s$ iff $t \rightarrow_R^* u$ and $s \rightarrow_R^* u$ for some term u. Notice that R-joinability is equivalent to R-unifiability for confluent rewrite systems.

A *conditional term rewrite system*, CTRS for short, is a finite set of rewrite rules of the form $l \rightarrow r \Leftarrow \mathcal{B}$ where $\mathcal{B}$ is a finite conjunction of conditions that must be checked before rewriting. There is a rewrite step, $t \rightarrow_R s$ iff there exists a conditional rule $l \rightarrow r \Leftarrow \mathcal{B}$ in R, a non-variable position u in t, and a substitution σ, such that $t|_u = l\sigma$ and $s = t[u \leftarrow r\sigma]$ and $\mathcal{B}\sigma$ is true. The notion of data-step extends trivially to the conditional case.

In this paper, we consider *join CTRS's* i.e. the conditions are pairs of terms $s \downarrow_R t$ which are verified for a substitution σ if $s\sigma$ and $t\sigma$ are R-joinable. Moreover, we focus on *constructor based CTRS*, i.e. CTRS where the lhs of rewrite rules are of the form $f(t_1, \ldots, t_n)$ where f is defined function symbol and each t_i $(1 \leq i \leq n)$ is a data-term.

In the context of constructor based CTRS, a *data-solution* of a joinability equation $s \downarrow_R^? t$ is a data-substitution σ such that $s\sigma \rightarrow_R^* u$ and $t\sigma \rightarrow_R^* u$ where u is a data term and all rewriting steps are data-steps. For a CTRS R and a defined function f, we denote by $\tilde{f}$ the data-relation $\tilde{f} = \{(t_1, \ldots, t_n, t) \in T^{n+1}(\mathcal{C}) \mid f(t_1, \ldots, t_n) \rightarrow_R^* t$ with data-steps only $\}$.

3 Positive Second Order Joinability Formulae

In this section, we present the kind of formulae we deal with and the way we solve them. We first define the second order algebra we consider.

3.1 Second Order Definitions

Let $\mathcal{X}$ be a set of second order variables with arity, different from $\Sigma \cup Var \cup \mathcal{R}$. The set of second order terms built over the signature $\mathcal{T}(\Sigma, Var, \mathcal{R}, \mathcal{X})$ is the smallest set such that

- Var is included in this set,
- if $t_1, \ldots, t_n$ are second order terms and f is either a symbol of arity n of Σ or a variable of arity n of $\mathcal{X}$ or a relation symbol of arity n of $\mathcal{R}$, then $f(t_1, \ldots, t_n)$ is a second order term.

For a second order term $Var(t)$ denotes the set of first order and second order variables of t. A second order term t is said to be *ground* if $Var(t)$ is empty. Let R be a CTRS, t be a ground second order term, then the *model* of t is denoted by $\mathcal{M}_R(t)$ and is the set of ground data terms inductively defined on the structure of the term [1]

- $\{ c(t_1, \ldots, t_n) \mid \forall 1 \le i \le n, t_i \in \mathcal{M}_R(s_i) \}$ if $t = c(s_1, \ldots, s_n)$ and $c \in \mathcal{C}$,
- $\{ \tilde{f}(t_1, \ldots, t_n) \mid \forall 1 \le i \le n, t_i \in \mathcal{M}_R(s_i) \}$ if $t = f(s_1, \ldots, s_n)$ and $f \in \mathcal{F}$,
- $\{ \tilde{r}(t_1, \ldots, t_n) \mid \forall 1 \le i \le n, t_i \in \mathcal{M}_R(s_i) \}$ if $t = \tilde{r}(s_1, \ldots, s_n)$ and $\tilde{r} \in \mathcal{R}$.

Notice that for a first order ground term t, $\mathcal{M}_R(t)$ is the set of ground data terms s such that $t \to_R^* s$ with a data-derivation. This is easily proved by induction on the height of the term t.

A *second order substitution* σ is a mapping from $Var \cup \mathcal{X}$ to $\mathcal{T}(\mathcal{F} \cup \mathcal{C}, Var) \cup \mathcal{R} \cup \mathcal{X}$ such that $x\sigma \ne x$ only for a finite subset of $Var \cup \mathcal{X}$ and

- if $x \in Var$, $x\sigma \in \mathcal{T}(\mathcal{F} \cup \mathcal{C}, Var)$
- if $x \in \mathcal{X}$ and x is of arity n, $x\sigma$ is either a symbol of $\mathcal{F} \cup \mathcal{R}$ of arity n or is x itself.

The domain of σ is the set of variables such that $x\sigma \ne x$. A second order substitution is called *data ground* if for all $x \in Dom(\sigma) \cap Var$, $x\sigma$ is a ground data term. We extend σ to $\mathcal{T}(\Sigma, Var, \mathcal{R}, \mathcal{X})$ homomorphically.

Example 2. Let us consider the CTRS of Example 1, the relation $\tilde{r} = \{(t_1, 0(t_1))\}$, t the second order term $X(x) + y$ and the substitution $\sigma = \{X \mapsto \tilde{r}, x \mapsto 1(\bot), y \mapsto 1(0(\bot))\}$. $Var(t) = Dom(\sigma) = \{X, x, y\}$. σ is data-ground. $t\sigma = \tilde{r}(1(\bot)) + 1(0(\bot))$ is a ground term and $\mathcal{M}_R(t\sigma) = \{0(0(1(\bot)))\}$ since $\mathcal{M}_R(x\sigma) = \{1(\bot)\}$ so $\mathcal{M}_R(\tilde{r}(x\sigma)) = \{0(1(\bot))\}$ and finally $\mathcal{M}_R(t\sigma)$ is the set $\{ \tilde{+}(t_1, t_2) \mid t_1 \in \mathcal{M}_R(\tilde{r}(x\sigma))$ and $t_2 \in \mathcal{M}_R(y\sigma) \}$ i.e. it is the set $\{\tilde{+}(0(1(\bot)), 1(0(\bot)))\} = \{1(1(\bot))\}$.

Notice that the model of the ground term $c(\bot, \bot) + 0(\bot)$ is empty since the first component of $\tilde{+}$ is never headed by the constructor symbol c.

---

[1] By convention, for a symbol s of arity 0 the notation $s(t_1, \ldots, t_n)$ (i.e. when n equals 0) denotes s itself.

3.2   Joinability Equations and Formulae

Definition 1. *Let R be a CTRS. A second order joinability equation $s \downarrow_R^? t$ is an equation such that s and t are second order terms. A first order joinability equation is an equation $s \downarrow_R^? t$ such that neither s nor t contains second order variables.*

Definition 2. *Let R be a CTRS, and $s \downarrow_R^? t$ be a second order joinability equation. A ground data substitution σ is a solution of $s \downarrow_R^? t$ iff $s\sigma$ and $t\sigma$ are ground terms and $\mathcal{M}_R(s\sigma) \cap \mathcal{M}_R(t\sigma) \neq \emptyset$.*

Let R be a CTRS, second order R-joinability formulae are defined by the following grammar:

$$e ::= s \downarrow_R^? t \mid \neg e \mid e \vee e \mid e \wedge e \mid \forall x e \mid \exists x e$$

where $s \downarrow_R^? t$ is a second order joinability equation and x is a first order variable.

Definition 3. *An R-joinability formula such that a second order variable does not occur within a negation is called a* positive second order R-joinability formula

The set of solutions of an R-joinability formula is defined as follows

- $SOL(s \downarrow_R^? t) = \{ \sigma \mid Dom(\sigma) = Var(s \downarrow_R^? t), \mathcal{M}_R(s\sigma) \cap \mathcal{M}_R(t\sigma) \neq \emptyset \}$
- $SOL(\neg e) = \{ \sigma \mid Dom(\sigma) = Var(e), \sigma \notin SOL(e) \}$
- $SOL(e_1 \wedge e_2) = \{ \sigma \mid Dom(\sigma) = Var(e_1 \wedge e_2), \sigma|_{Var(e_1)} \in SOL(e_1),$
  $\sigma|_{Var(e_2)} \in SOL(e_2) \}$
- $SOL(e_1 \vee e_2) = \{ \sigma \mid Dom(\sigma) = Var(e_1 \vee e_2), \sigma|_{Var(e_1)} \in SOL(e_1)$ or
  $\sigma|_{Var(e_2)} \in SOL(e_2) \}$
- $SOL(\exists x e) = \{ \sigma \mid Dom(\sigma) = Var(e) \setminus \{x\}, \exists \sigma' \in SOL(e), \sigma = \sigma'|_{Var(e) \setminus \{x\}} \}$
- $SOL(\forall x e) = \{ \sigma \mid Dom(\sigma) = Var(e) \setminus \{x\}, \forall t \in \mathcal{T}(\mathcal{C}), \sigma \cup \{x \mapsto t\} \in$
  $SOL(e), \sigma = \sigma'|_{Var(e) \setminus \{x\}} \}$

Example 3. Let us consider once more the CTRS of Example 1 and the following second order joinability formula $\forall x \exists y \, \neg(y + y \downarrow_R^? x) \vee X(x) \downarrow_R^? true$.

   This formula is a positive one. A solution of this formula instantiates the variable X to the relation $\tilde{e} = \{ (n, true) \mid n$ is an even number $\}$. Notice that any relation $\tilde{e}'$ such that $\tilde{e}' \supseteq \tilde{e}$ is also a solution of the formula since it is an implication and not an equivalence.

The set of solutions for the second order variables may be infinite, as in the previous example, and in the general case these solutions may be incomparable. This happens when the same second order variable occurs in both side of the connector $\vee$ like in the formula $\forall x \exists y \, \neg(y + y \downarrow_R^? x) \vee (X(x) \downarrow_R^? true \vee X(x) \downarrow_R^? 0)$. $\tilde{e}$ of Example 3 is a solution as well as $\tilde{e}'' = \{ (n, 0) \mid n$ is an even number $\}$ but $\tilde{e}$ and $\tilde{e}''$ cannot be compared. Therefore solving second order joinability in the general case would need to finitely represent infinite sets of relations in other words infinite sets of infinite sets. The cases where such a representation can be obtained are extremely rare and would need very strong restrictions on the CTRS. This is why we restrict ourselves to positive second order joinability formulae on the one hand, and on the other hand, we describe a decision algorithm that returns one solution if the formulae is satisfiable and the empty set otherwise.

3.3   Deciding Positive Second Order Formulae

The algorithm relies on the following idea: a positive second order formula is satisfiable iff its first order part is satisfiable. So the algorithm aims at separating the first order and second order equation, then solving the first order part of the formula and then computing an instance for the second order variables from the solutions of the first order part. The algorithm consists of two main steps. The first step flattens the equations of the formula. The second one transforms the result into its prenex disjunctive normal form.

The rules of Table 1 are used to transform any second order joinability equation to an equivalent formula whose equations are of the form $f(\vec{x}) \downarrow_R^? y$ where $f \in \mathcal{F} \cup \mathcal{C} \cup \mathcal{X}$ and $\vec{x}, y$ are first order variables. Such equations are called *flat equations*. A formula containing only flat equations is called a *flat formula*.

Table 1. Flattening second order equations

$$\frac{\top}{\delta(y) = \langle x, x \downarrow_R^? y \rangle} \quad \text{if } x, y \in Var \text{ and } x \neq y$$

$$\frac{\delta(t_1) = \langle x_1, e_1 \rangle \quad \cdots \quad \delta(t_n) = \langle x_n, e_n \rangle}{\delta(f(t_1, \ldots, t_n)) = \langle x, \exists x_1 \ldots x_n (f(x_1, \ldots, x_n) \downarrow_R^? x \wedge \bigwedge_{1 \leq i \leq n} e_i) \rangle}$$

if $f \in \mathcal{F} \cup \mathcal{X}$ and $x \notin \bigcup_{1 \leq i \leq n} Var(e_i)$ and the x_i's are pairwise different

$$\frac{\delta(s) = \langle x_s, e_s \rangle \quad \delta(t) = \langle x_t, e_t \rangle}{\delta(s \downarrow_R^? t) = \exists x_s, x_t \; x_s \downarrow_R^? x_t \wedge e_s \wedge e_t} \quad \text{if } x_s, x_t \in Var \text{ and } x_s \neq x_t$$

Notice that for a second order term t, $\delta(t)$ is unique up to a renaming of first order variables, therefore the side condition of the second rule on the x_i's is not a restriction. Moreover each e_i contains the corresponding x_i thus x is different from all the x_i's.

δ can be extended to flatten arbitrary second order formulae in the following way $\delta(\neg e) = \neg \delta(e)$, $\delta(e_1 \wedge e_2) = \delta(e_1) \wedge \delta(e_2)$, $\delta(e_1 \vee e_2) = \delta(e_1) \vee \delta(e_2)$, $\delta(\exists x \, e) = \exists x \, \delta(e)$ and $\delta(\forall x \, e) = \forall x \, \delta(e)$.

Lemma 1. *Let R be a CTRS and s a second order term such that $\delta(s) = \langle x, e \rangle$ and σ a ground data substitution $s\sigma$ is a ground term. If $t \in \mathcal{M}(s\sigma)$ then $\sigma \cup \{x \mapsto t\} \in SOL(e)$.*

The proof of this lemma is done by structural induction on the term s.

Lemma 2. *Let R be a CTRS and F a second order joinability formula. Then we have $SOL(F) = SOL(\delta(F))$.*

Proof. Let us consider a formula consisting of a single equation $s \downarrow_R^? t$. $\delta(s \downarrow_R^? t) = \langle \exists x_s, x_t, s \downarrow_R^? x_s \wedge t \downarrow_R^? x_t \wedge x_s \downarrow_R^? x_t \rangle$. If $\sigma \in SOL(s \downarrow_R^? t)$, there exists a term u such that $u \in \mathcal{M}(s\sigma) \cap \mathcal{M}(t\sigma)$. From Lemma 1 we know that $\sigma \cup \{x_s \mapsto s\} \in$

$SOL(e_s)$ and $\sigma \cup \{x_t \mapsto t\} \in SOL(e_t)$ thus $\sigma \cup \{x_s \mapsto s, x_t \mapsto t\} \in SOL(s \downarrow^?_R x_s \wedge t \downarrow^?_R x_t \wedge x_s \downarrow^?_R x_t)$ which implies that $\sigma \in SOL(\delta(e))$.

Now if $\sigma \in SOL(\delta(e))$ then there exists $\sigma' = \sigma \cup \{x_s \mapsto u_s, x_t \mapsto u_t\}$ which is a solution of $s \downarrow^?_R x_s \wedge t \downarrow^?_R x_t \wedge x_s \downarrow^?_R x_t$. We have $u_s \in \mathcal{M}(s\sigma')$ and $u_t \in \mathcal{M}(t\sigma')$. Since neither s nor t contain x_s and x_t, we have $s\sigma' = s\sigma$ and $t\sigma' = t\sigma$. Moreover $x_s\sigma' \downarrow^?_R x_t\sigma'$, so we have $u_s = u_t$, from which we can conclude that $u_s \in \mathcal{M}(s\sigma) \cap \mathcal{M}(t\sigma)$ so $\sigma \in SOL(s \downarrow^?_R t)$.

By an easy induction on the structure of the formula F we prove that $SOL(F) = SOL(\delta(F))$. $\square$

We study now the properties of unquantified conjunctive flat formulae since the algorithm works on prenex disjunctive normal form.

Let us consider a conjunctive formula F, of the form $fo(\vec{y}) \wedge X_1(\vec{x}_1) \downarrow^?_R x_1 \wedge \dots \wedge X_m(\vec{x}_m) \downarrow^?_R x_m$ where $fo(\vec{y})$ is a conjunction of first order equations and $\vec{y}$ the vector of the variables occurring in those equations.

In order to simplify the notations, we suppose that the set of solutions of the first order formula $fo(\vec{y})$ is represented by a logic program $\mathcal{P}_{fo(\vec{y})}$ which defines the predicate $P_{fo(\vec{y})}$ of arity $|\vec{y}|$ such that $\mathcal{P}_{fo(\vec{y})} \models P_{fo(\vec{y})}(\vec{t})$ iff the substitution $\{\vec{y}|_i \mapsto \vec{t}|_i \mid 1 \le i \le |\vec{y}|\} \in SOL(fo(\vec{y}))$. Let $SO(F)$ be the following set of clauses $\{P_{X_i}(\vec{x}_i, x_i) \Leftarrow P_{fo}(\vec{y}) \mid 1 \le i \le m\}$ and $\sigma_{SO(F)} = \{X_i \mapsto \tilde{r}^F_{X_i}\}$ where $\tilde{r}^F_{X_i} = \{(\vec{t}, t) \mid SO(F) \cup \mathcal{P}_{fo(\vec{y})} \models P_{X_i}(\vec{t}, t)\}$.

Lemma 3. *Let F be a positive second order flat conjunctive formula. F is satisfiable iff $F\sigma_{SO(F)}$ is satisfiable.*

Proof. It is obvious that if $F\sigma_{SO(F)}$ is satisfiable then F is satisfiable. Now suppose that F is satisfiable. This means that $fo(\vec{y})$ is satisfiable, therefore the model of $P_{fo}(\vec{y})$ is not empty. Hence $SO(F)$ instantiates each second order variable of F by a non-empty relation, thus $F\sigma_{SO(F)}$ is satisfiable since second order variables occur in trivial equations $X(\vec{x}) \downarrow^?_R x$. $\square$

The following lemma helps to characterize the instances of the second order variables we compute. It is used to prove that our algorithm gives a solution iff the whole formula is satisfiable. It is also important when one wants to synthesize a CTRS from a positive second order formula.

Lemma 4. *Let $F = fo(\vec{y}) \wedge X_1(\vec{x}_1) \downarrow^?_R x_1 \wedge \dots \wedge X_m(\vec{x}_m) \downarrow^?_R x_m$ be a conjunctive formula. Then $\sigma_{SO(F)}$ is the smallest solution of the following second order formula $\forall \vec{z} fo(\vec{y}) \Rightarrow X_1(\vec{x}_1) \downarrow^?_R x_1 \wedge \dots \wedge X_m(\vec{x}_m) \downarrow^?_R x_m$ where $\vec{z}$ is a vector composed of the union of the variables of $\vec{y}$, of $\vec{x}_i$ and x_i ($1 \le i \le m$).*

Proof. The proof of this lemma is obvious since $\sigma_{SO(F)}$ is computed from the set of clauses $P_{X_i}(\vec{x}_i, x_i) \Leftarrow P_{fo}(\vec{y})$ ($1 \le i \le n$). $\square$

We are now ready to describe the algorithm that decides the satisfiability of a positive second order formula and gives one instance of the second order variables and the set of corresponding solutions for the first order variables when the formula is satisfiable. This algorithm relies on the existence of an algorithm that solves first order joinability formulae and gives a finite representation of their solutions.

Algorithm 1. *Let $\mathcal{A}$ be an algorithm to solve first order joinability equations, R a CTRS and F a positive second-order formula.*

1. *Compute $\delta(F)$ the flattened form of F*
2. *Compute F' equivalent to $\delta(F)$ and in prenex disjunctive normal form. Let $C_1, \ldots, C_n$ be the conjunctive factors of F'.*
3. *For each C_i $(1 \leq i \leq n)$, use $\mathcal{A}$ to solve the first order part of C_i from which $\sigma_{SO(C_i)}$ is deduced.*
4. *Let $\sigma_{SO(F')} = \{ X_j \mapsto \tilde{r}'_{X_j} \mid X_j \in Var(F'), \tilde{r}'_{X_j} = \bigcup_{1 \leq i \leq n} \tilde{r}^{C_i}_{X_j} \}$. Use $\mathcal{A}$ to solve $F' \sigma_{SO(F')}$ considering second order variable symbols as defined function symbols [2].*
5. *If $SOL(F' \sigma_{SO(F')}) \neq \emptyset$ return $\sigma_{SO(F')}$ and the solutions of $F' \sigma_{SO(F')}$ else return $\emptyset$.*

Theorem 1. *Let $\mathcal{A}$ be an algorithm to solve first order joinability equations, R a CTRS and F a positive second-order formula. F is satisfiable iff the output of Algorithm 1 is not empty.*

Proof. From Lemma 2, we know that $SOL(F) = SOL(\delta(F))$ and therefore $SOL(F) = SOL(F')$.

Let $C_1, \ldots, C_n$ be the conjunctive factors of F'. Each C_i is of the form $fo_i(\vec{y}_i) \wedge so_i(\vec{x}_i, \vec{X}_i)$ where $fo_i(\vec{y}_i)$ is a conjunction of first order joinability equations whose variables are those of $\vec{y}_i$ and $so_i(\vec{x}_i, \vec{X}_i)$ is a conjunction of flat second order joinability equations of the form $X(\vec{x}) \downarrow^?_R x$ where $X \in X_i$ and the variables of $\vec{x}$ and x occur in $\vec{x}_i$.

The algorithm $\mathcal{A}$ can compute a finite representation of the solutions of $fo_i(\vec{y}_i)$ which gives the definition of $\sigma_{SO(C_i)}$. From Lemma 4, we know that $\sigma_{SO(C_i)}$ is the smallest model of the formula $\forall \vec{z}_i, fo_i(\vec{y}_i) \Rightarrow so_i(\vec{x}_i, \vec{X}_i)$. By definition of $\sigma_{SO(F')}$, we have $X \sigma_{SO(F')} \supseteq X \sigma_{SO(C_i)}$ for any second order variable of F' and any C_i $1 \leq i \leq n$. Hence, $\sigma_{SO(F')}$ is a model of the formulae $\forall \vec{z}_i, fo_i(\vec{y}_i) \Rightarrow so_i(\vec{x}_i, \vec{X}_i)$ which means that $\forall \vec{z}_i, fo_i(\vec{y}_i) \Rightarrow so_i(\vec{x}_i, \vec{X}_i) \sigma_{SO(F')}$ and of course $\forall \vec{z}_i, fo_i(\vec{y}_i) \Rightarrow fo_i(\vec{y}_i) \wedge so_i(\vec{x}_i, \vec{X}_i) \sigma_{SO(F')}$.

So we can deduce that any model of $fo_1(\vec{y}_1) \vee \ldots fo_n(\vec{y}_n)$ is a model of $(fo_1(\vec{y}_1) \wedge so_1(\vec{x}_1, \vec{X}_1) \sigma_{SO(F')}) \vee \ldots \vee (fo_n(\vec{y}_n) \wedge so_n(\vec{x}_n, \vec{X}_n) \sigma_{SO(F')})$. Let us suppose that $F' = Q\, C_1 \vee \ldots \vee C_n$ where Q represents the quantifications of the formula. If F is satisfiable, F' is also satisfiable as well as $Q\, fo_1(\vec{y}_1) \vee \ldots fo_n(\vec{y}_n)$. From the remark above we can deduce that $Q\, (fo_1(\vec{y}_1) \wedge so_1(\vec{x}_1, \vec{X}_1) \sigma_{SO(F')}) \vee \ldots \vee (fo_n(\vec{y}_n) \wedge so_n(\vec{x}_n, \vec{X}_n) \sigma_{SO(F')})$ is also satisfiable and therefore the algorithm $\mathcal{A}$ computes a non empty set of solutions.

---

[2] Formally, a CTRS R' that defines the functions f_{X_j} which model are the corresponding $\tilde{r}'$, should be synthesized from the result of algorithm $\mathcal{A}$, and the input of $\mathcal{A}$ should be $F'\{ X_j \mapsto f_{X_j} \mid X_j \in Var(F') \}$ and the CTRS $R \cup R'$.

On the other hand, if $\mathcal{A}$ computes a non empty set of solutions for $F'\sigma_{SO(F')}$, this means that $F'\sigma_{SO(F')}$ is satisfiable thus F' and F are also satisfiable.   □

Example 4. Let us consider again the formula of Example 3, i.e. $\forall x \exists y \neg (y + y \downarrow_R^? x) \vee X(x) \downarrow_R^?$ *true.* The flattened form of this formula is $\forall x \exists y \neg (y + y \downarrow_R^? x) \vee \exists z \, X(x) \downarrow_R^? z \wedge true \downarrow_R^? z$. Its prenex disjunctive normal form is $\forall x \exists y \exists z \neg (y + y \downarrow_R^? x) \vee X(x) \downarrow_R^? z \wedge true \downarrow_R^? z$ where $C_1 = \neg(y + y \downarrow_R^? x)$ and $C_2 = X(x) \downarrow_R^? z \wedge true \downarrow_R^? z$. The solutions of C_1 are the sets $\{ (y \mapsto n, x \mapsto m) \mid 2 \times n \neq m \}$ and the unique solution of $true \downarrow_R^? z$ is $\{z \mapsto true\}$ which can be represented by the logic program consisting of the clause $P(true) \Leftarrow$. Therefore $SO_X^{C_2} = \{P_X(x, z) \Leftarrow P(z)\}$ which means that $\tilde{r}_X^{C_2} = \{ t, true \mid t \in \mathcal{T}(\mathcal{C}) \}$. The output of the algorithm is then $X \mapsto \tilde{r}_X^{C_2}$ since all first order variables are quantified.

This solution is not the smallest one but the instance for X guarantees that each model of $true \downarrow_R^? z$ are models of $X(x) \downarrow_R^? z$ which is needed for the correctness of the algorithm.

To synthesize the even function, one can use the property stated by Lemma 4 and put the formula $\forall x \forall y \, y + y \downarrow_R^? x \wedge X(x) \downarrow_R^?$ *true* as input of the algorithm. Indeed this lemma states that the instance computed for X by the algorithm is the smallest solution of $\forall x, \forall y \, y + y \downarrow_R^? x \Rightarrow X(x) \downarrow_R^?$ *true.*

4   Pseudo-regular Formulae

In this section, we present a class of positive second order joinability equations which can be decided by Algorithm 1. The class of CTRS we consider is an extension to the conditional case of the class studied in [12]

Definition 4. *A conditional constructor based CTRS R is said to be pseudo-regular if all its rewrite rules are of the form*
$$f(t_1, \ldots, t_n) \to C[f_1(\vec{x}_1), \ldots, f_m(\vec{x}_m)] \Leftarrow f_1'(\vec{x}_1') \downarrow_R x_1' \ldots f_k'(\vec{x}_k') \downarrow_R x_k' \text{ where}$$

- C *is a constructor context, $f, f_1, \ldots, f_m, f_1', \ldots, f_k'$ are defined function symbols*
- $\bigcup_{1 \leq i \leq m}(\vec{x}_i) \cup \bigcup_{1 \leq i \leq k}(\vec{x}_i') \cup \bigcup_{1 \leq i \leq k}(x_k') \subseteq Var(f(t_1, \ldots, t_n)) \cup Var(C)$
- *there exists a mapping $\pi : Var \mapsto I\!N^+$, such that $\pi(x) = u$ implies that all occurrences of x in $t_1, \ldots, t_n$ and in C are at position u,*
- *all the variables of $\vec{x}_i'$ have the same image by π as x_i' ($1 \leq i \leq k$).*
- *the image by π of all the variables of $\vec{x}_i$ is u, the position of $f_i(\vec{x}_i)$ in $C[f_1(\vec{x}_1), \ldots, f_m(\vec{x}_m)]$ ($1 \leq i \leq m$).*

C *is said to be the* irreducible part *of $C[f_1(\vec{x}_1), \ldots, f_m(\vec{x}_m)]$, the terms $f_i(\vec{x}_i)$ are called* possible redexes *and the positions of the f_i in C the* possible redex positions *of $C[f_1(\vec{x}_1), \ldots, f_m(\vec{x}_m)]$*

Example 5. $R = \{f(s(c(x, y)), s(c(x, z))) \to s(c(g(x), f(y, y))) \Leftarrow g(z) \downarrow_R y, f(s(0), s(0)) \to 0, g(s(x)) \to s(x)\}$ is pseudo-regular. The irreducible part of the lhs of the first rule is $s(c(\square_1, \square_2))$ and it contains two possible redex positions namely 1.1 and 1.2 corresponding to the possible redexes $g(x)$ and $f(y, y)$. Notice that Definition 4 does not forbid duplicated variables in a single possible redex.

Definition 5. *Let R be a pseudo-regular CTRS, a pseudo-regular second order formula is a second order joinability formula that does not contain any constructor symbol.*

The formula of Example 3 is not a pseudo-regular second order formula since it contains the constructor symbol *true*. It can be easily transformed into a pseudo-regular one by introducing the new defined function symbol t and the pseudo regular rule $t \to true$ in the CTRS. Then the formula $\forall x \exists y \neg (y + y \downarrow_R^? x) \vee X(x) \downarrow_R^? t$ is pseudo-regular.

In [9], an algorithm for solving first order pseudo-regular formulae is given. This algorithm is defined in the non conditional case but relies on the fact that defined functions of a pseudo-regular TRS define regular relations (also called recognizable relations in [4]). For lack of space, we do not describe the algorithm, but we just show that defined function of pseudo-regular CTRS define also regular relations. For that we introduce the class of non-Greibach shared logic programs whose predicates define regular relations. The algorithms to decide membership and emptiness as well as the ones to compute set operations on regular relations represented by logic programs are described in [11] and [9].

Definition 6. *A Horn clause $H \Leftarrow \mathcal{B}$ is called non-Greibach shared pseudo-regular (NGSPR for short) iff it contains no existential variables, $\mathcal{B}$ contains no function symbols, none of the arguments of H is a variable and there exists a mapping $\pi \colon Var \mapsto \mathbb{N}^+$ such that $\pi(x) = u$ implies that all occurrences of x in the arguments of H are at position u and such that $\pi(x) = \pi(y)$ for all variables x and y occurring in the same body atom. A program is NGSPR if all its clauses are NGSPR.*

Example 6. The clause $P(d(y_1, x_1), c(x_1, y_2)) \Leftarrow P_1(x_1), P_2(y_1, y_2)$ is not NGSPR since x_1 is at position 2 in the first argument of the clause head and at position 1 in the second argument.

The clause $P(d(x_1, y_1), c(x_1, y_2)) \Leftarrow P_1(y_1), P_2(x_1, y_2)$ is also not NGSPR since x_1 and y_2 occur in the same body atom but they do not occur at the same position in the head of the clause.

The clause $P(c(s(x), y), s(s(z))) \Leftarrow P(x, z), Q(y)$ is NGSPR since x and z both occur at occurrence 1.1 in the arguments of the head.

We extend the technique presented in [12] that encodes the rewrite relation by a logic program in order to be able to deal with CTRS's. This translation intends to obtain logic programs that preserve as best as possible syntactic properties of the TRS. The obtained logic program encodes the rewrite relation with datasteps. The aim is to obtain an NGSPR program from a pseudo-regular CTRS.

Table 2 specifies the rules that transform terms and conditional rewrite rules to Horn clauses. P_{id} is a pseudo-regular predicate that defines the equality between data terms. Its set of clauses is denoted by $\mathcal{P}_{id}$ and is

$$\mathcal{P}_{id} = \{\, P_{id}(c(x_1, \ldots, x_n), c(y_1, \ldots, y_n)) \Leftarrow P_{id}(x_1, y_1), \ldots, P_{id}(x_n, y_n) \mid c \in \mathcal{C} \,\}$$

For a CTRS R, let $\mathcal{LP}(R)$ denote the logic program consisting of $\mathcal{P}_{id}$ and the set of clauses obtained by applying the fifth rule to all rewrite rules in R.

Table 2. Converting CTRS rules to Horn clauses

$$\frac{\top}{v \rightsquigarrow \langle v, \emptyset \rangle} \quad \text{if } v \in Var$$

$$\frac{s_1 \rightsquigarrow \langle t_1, \mathcal{G}_1 \rangle \ldots s_n \rightsquigarrow \langle t_n, \mathcal{G}_n \rangle}{f(s_1, \ldots, s_n) \rightsquigarrow \langle f(t_1, \ldots, t_n), \bigcup_i \mathcal{G}_i \rangle} \quad \text{if } f \in \mathcal{C}$$

$$\frac{s_1 \rightsquigarrow \langle t_1, \mathcal{G}_1 \rangle \ldots s_n \rightsquigarrow \langle t_n, \mathcal{G}_n \rangle}{f(s_1, \ldots, s_n) \rightsquigarrow \langle x, \bigcup_i \mathcal{G}_i \bigcup \{ P_f(t_1, \ldots, t_n, x) \} \rangle} \quad \text{if } f \in \mathcal{F}$$

$$\frac{s_1 \rightsquigarrow \langle t_1, \mathcal{G}_1 \rangle \qquad s_2 \rightsquigarrow \langle t_2, \mathcal{G}_2 \rangle}{s_1 \downarrow_R s_2 \rightsquigarrow \langle \varepsilon, \mathcal{G}_1 \cup \mathcal{G}_2 \cup P_{id}(t_1, t_2) \rangle}$$

$$\frac{s \rightsquigarrow \langle t, \mathcal{G} \rangle \quad c_1 \rightsquigarrow \langle \varepsilon, \mathcal{G}_1 \rangle \ldots c_k \rightsquigarrow \langle \varepsilon, \mathcal{G}_k \rangle}{f(s_1, \ldots, s_n) \rightarrow s \Leftarrow c_1 \ldots c_k \rightsquigarrow P_f(s_1, \ldots, s_n, t) \Leftarrow \mathcal{G} \cup \mathcal{G}_1 \cup \ldots \cup \mathcal{G}_k}$$

Note that the variables x introduced by the third rule are new fresh variables.

Remark 1. In the context of pseudo-regular CTRS, the conditions are of the form $f(x_1, \ldots, x_n) \downarrow_R y$. The transformation gives $P_f(x_1, \ldots, x_n, z), P_{id}(y, z)$ which we simplify by $P_f(x_1, \ldots, x_n, y)$.

For example, the first rewrite rule of Example 5 is transformed into
$$P_f(s(c(x, y)), s(c(x, z)), s(c(x_1, x_2))) \Leftarrow P_g(x, x_1), P_f(y, y, x_2), P_g(z, y).$$
The following theorem states the relation between a constructor based CTRS R and $\mathcal{LP}(R)$.

Theorem 2. *Let R be a CTRS, s a term such that $s \rightsquigarrow \langle s', \mathcal{G} \rangle$. $s \rightarrow^* t$ and t is a data-term holds iff $\mathcal{LP}(R) \models \mathcal{G}\mu$ and $t = s'\mu$ where μ is a data substitution.*

The proof of this theorem as well as the proof of the following lemma are essentially the same as the equivalent ones for pseudo-regular TRS. They can be found in [10].

Lemma 5. *If R is a pseudo-regular CTRS, $\mathcal{LP}(R)$ is a NGSPR logic program.*

Theorem 2 and Lemma 5 are sufficient to re-use the algorithm described in [9] to solve first order pseudo-regular formulae in the conditional case. This leads to the following result

Theorem 3. *Satisfiability of positive second order pseudo-regular formulae can be decided.*

Proof. Let us call $\mathcal{A}$ the algorithm to solve first order pseudo-regular formulae. From Theorem 1, we know that Algorithm 1 with $\mathcal{A}$, a pseudo-regular CTRS R and a positive second order pseudo-regular formula F as input, produces the empty set iff F is not satisfiable. □

The algorithm $\mathcal{A}$ produces an NGSPR logic program when the formula is satisfiable. It would be interesting to be able to give the corresponding CTRS so that the instance of second order variables are expressed in the same formalism as the relation defined by function symbols of the input CTRS. This transformation may be used to synthesize programs from second order pseudo-regular formulae.

For each flat atom A of the form $P(x_1, \ldots, x_{n-1}, x_n)$ we define $term(A) = f_P(x_1, \ldots, x_{n-1})$ and $equat(A) = f_P(x_1, \ldots, x_{n-1}) \downarrow_R x_n$. We extend $equat$ to a set of flat atoms $\mathcal{G}$ in the natural way i.e. $equat(\mathcal{G}) = \{ equat(A) \mid A \in \mathcal{G} \}$.

Definition 7. *Let* $\mathcal{C} = P(t_1, \ldots, t_{n-1}, C[x_1, \ldots, x_m]) \Leftarrow \mathcal{G}, \mathcal{G}'$ *be an NGSPR clause where* $\mathcal{G} = \{ P(\vec{x}, x) \mid x \in \{x_1, \ldots, x_m\}$ *and* x *occurs once in* $\mathcal{G}, \mathcal{G}' \}$

$\mathcal{RR}(\mathcal{C}) = f_P(t_1, \ldots, t_{n-1}) \to C[x_1, \ldots, x_m]\sigma \Leftarrow equat(\mathcal{G}')$ *where* $\sigma = \{ x \mapsto term(P(\vec{x}, x)) \mid P(\vec{x}, x) \in \mathcal{G} \}$.

For an NGSPR logic program $\mathcal{P}$, *let* $\mathcal{RR}(\mathcal{P})$ *denote the CTRS consisting of the rules* $\{ \mathcal{RR}(H \Leftarrow \mathcal{G}) \mid H \Leftarrow \mathcal{G} \in \mathcal{P} \}$.

For example, $P_f(s(x_1, y), s(x_2, y), s(z_1, z_2)) \Leftarrow P_f(x_2, x_1, z_1), P_f(x_1, x_1, x_2)$ is transformed into $f(s(x_1, y), s(x_2, y)) \to s(f(x_2, x_1), z_2) \Leftarrow f(x_1, x_1) \downarrow_R x_2$.

Lemma 6. *If* $\mathcal{P}$ *be an NGSPR logic program then* $\mathcal{RR}(\mathcal{P})$ *is a pseudo-regular CTRS.*

The proof of this lemma is mainly done by making a correspondence between body atoms of NGSPR clauses and function positions in the rhs of corresponding conditional rule.

Lemma 7. *If* $\mathcal{P}$ *be an NGSPR logic program then* $\mathcal{LP}(\mathcal{RR}(\mathcal{P})) = \mathcal{P}$ *modulo renaming of the introduced variables and the auxiliary predicate symbols.*

Proof. In this proof we consider that P_{f_P} is a notation for the predicate symbol P. Let $\mathcal{P}$ be an NGSPR logic program and $\mathcal{C}$ be a clause of $\mathcal{P}$. $\mathcal{C}$ is of the form $P(t_1, \ldots, t_{n-1}, C[x_1, \ldots, x_m]) \Leftarrow \mathcal{G}, \mathcal{G}'$.

$\mathcal{RR}(\mathcal{C}) = f_P(t_1, \ldots, t_{n-1}) \to C[x_1, \ldots, x_m]\sigma \Leftarrow equat(\mathcal{G}')$ where $\sigma = \{ x \mapsto term(P(\vec{x}, x)) \mid P(\vec{x}, x) \in \mathcal{G} \}$. For each atom $P(\vec{x}, x)$ of $\mathcal{G}'$, $equat(P(\vec{x}, x)) = f_P(\vec{x}) \downarrow_R x$. From Remark 1, each equation $f_P(\vec{x}) \downarrow_R x$ is transformed into $P_{f_P}(\vec{x}, x)$ (i.e $P(\vec{x}, x)$).

Each atom $P(\vec{x}, x)$ of $\mathcal{G}$ is transformed into the term $f_P(\vec{x})$. From Table 2 $f_P(\vec{x}) \rightsquigarrow \langle x, P_{f_P}(\vec{x}, x) \rangle$, therefore $C[x_1, \ldots, x_m]\sigma \rightsquigarrow \langle C[x_1, \ldots, x_m], \mathcal{G} \rangle$. Hence $f_P(t_1, \ldots, t_{n-1}) \to C[x_1, \ldots, x_m]\sigma \Leftarrow equat(\mathcal{G}') \rightsquigarrow \mathcal{C}$. □

Theorem 4. *Let* $\mathcal{P}$ *be an NGSPR logic program and* $P(\vec{t}, t)$ *be a ground atom.* $\mathcal{P} \models P(\vec{t}, t)$ *iff* $f_P(\vec{t}) \to^* t$.

Proof. From Lemma 7, we know that $\mathcal{LP}(\mathcal{RR}(\mathcal{P})) = \mathcal{P}$. The term $f_P(\vec{t})$ is transformed by $\rightsquigarrow$ to $\langle x, P(\vec{t}, x) \rangle$ because all the terms of $\vec{t}$ are ground data terms and we consider P_{f_P} as a notation for P. From Theorem 2 we know that $f_P(\vec{t}) \to^* t$ iff t is a ground data-term, $\mathcal{LP}(\mathcal{RR}(\mathcal{P})) \models P(\vec{t}, x)\mu$ and $t = x\mu$, in other words iff $\mathcal{P} \models P(\vec{t}, t)$. □

5   Conclusion

In this paper, we describe an algorithm to decide positive second order joinability formulae when an algorithm to compute a decidable representation of first order formulae exists. We have applied this algorithm to the class of pseudo-regular formulae by extending some of the results of [9] to conditional term rewrite systems. When the formula is satisfiable, the algorithm expresses the instances of second order variables by a CTRS. This result provides a mechanism for synthesizing CTRS which can be considered as functional logic programs.

Second order theories with second order variables occurring in the terms have been studied in the context of second order unification (see e.g. [8,14]). Our joinability equations are unifiability equations when the CTRS is confluent therefore solving pseudo-regular second order equations requires solving second order unification modulo a CTRS.

The synthesis of programs from a specification has been already investigated. In the context of functional programs for example [6,1] use term rewrite systems to provide a computational model for functional programming. The specification of the function to be synthesized is a set of equations that can be viewed as a positive conjunctive formula. Higher order logic has been used in [3] for specification in order to synthesize logic programs but some heuristics are used and the result is partially correct whereas our method is exact (i.e. we obtain a correct instance for second order variables). In most of the cases synthesis of programs (functional or not) uses induction with deductive methods to find partially correct results. As a consequence such methods generate more general programs than ours. In our framework, such partial solutions may be generated using some approximations during the computation of the operations on the regular relations.

Acknowledgements. We would like to thank the referees for their substantial comments and valuable suggestions.

References

1. M. Alpuente, D. Ballis, F. J. Correa, and M. Falaschi. Automated Correction of Functional Logic Programs. In P. Degano, editor, *Proc. of the European Symp. on Programming, ESOP 2003*, volume 2618 of *LNCS*, pages 54–68. Springer, 2003.
2. F. Baader and T. Nipkow. *Term Rewriting and All That.* Cambridge University Press, United Kingdom, 1998.
3. P. Bostrom, H. Idestam-Alquist. Induction of logic programs by example-guided unfolding. *Journal of Logic Programming*, 40:159–183, 1999.
4. H. Comon, M. Dauchet, R. Gilleron, D. Lugiez, S. Tison, and M. Tommasi. *Tree Automata Techniques and Applications (TATA).* http://www.grappa.univ-lille3.fr/tata, 1997.
5. D. A. Basin and N. Klarlund. Hardware verification using monadic second-order logic. In *Proceedings of the 7th International Conference On Computer Aided Verification*, volume 939, pages 31–41. Springer Verlag, 1995.

6. N. Dershowitz and E. Pinchover. Inductive synthesis of equationnal programs. In *Proc. of the Eighth National Conference on Artificial Intelligence*, pages 234–239. AAAI press, 1990.

7. J. L. Jensen, M. E. Jorgensen, N. Klarlund, and M. I. Schwartzbach. Automatic verification of pointer programs using monadic second-order logic. In *SIGPLAN Conference on Programming Language Design and Implementation*, pages 226–236, 1997.

8. L. Levy and M. Villaret. Linear second-order unification and context unification with tree-regular constraints. In *Proc. of the 11th Int. Conf. on Rewriting Techniques and Applications, RTA'00*, volume 1833 of *LNCS*, pages 156–171. Springer, 2000.

9. S. Limet and P. Pillot. Solving first order formulae of pseudo-regular theory. In *Proc. 2th Int. Conf. on Theorical Aspect of Computing (ICTAC'05)*, volume 3091 of *LNCS*, pages 110–124. Springer, 2005.

10. S. Limet and P. Pillot. On second order formulae of pseudo-regular theory. Technical report, LIFO, Université d'Orléans, 2006.

11. S. Limet and G. Salzer. Manipulating tree tuple languages by transforming logic programs. In Ingo Dahn and Laurent Vigneron, editors, *Electronic Notes in Theoretical Computer Science*, volume 86. Elsevier, 2003.

12. S. Limet and G. Salzer. Proving properties of term rewrite systems via logic programs. In V. van Oostrom, editor, *Proc. 15th Int. Conf. on Rewriting Techniques and Applications (RTA'04)*, volume 3091 of *LNCS*, pages 170–184. Springer, 2004.

13. J.W. Lloyd. *Foundations of Logic Programming*. Springer, 1984.

14. Joachim Niehren, Manfred Pinkal, and Peter Ruhrberg. On equality up-to constraints over finite trees, context unification and one-step rewriting. In *14th International Conference on Automated Deduction*, volume 1249 of *LNAI*, pages 34–48. Springer Verlag, 1997.

15. J. Thatcher and J. Wright. Generalized finite tree automata theory with an application to a descision problem of second-order logic. *Mathematical System Theory*, 2(1):57–81, 1968.

16. W. Thomas. *Handbook of Formal Language*, volume 3, chapter 7, pages 389–455. Springer Verlag, 1997.

SAT Solving for Argument Filterings[*]

Michael Codish[1], Peter Schneider–Kamp[2], Vitaly Lagoon[3],
René Thiemann[2], and Jürgen Giesl[2]

[1] Dept. of Computer Science, Ben-Gurion University, Israel
mcodish@cs.bgu.ac.il
[2] LuFG Informatik 2, RWTH Aachen, Germany
{psk, thiemann, giesl}@informatik.rwth-aachen.de
[3] Dept. of Computer Science and Software Engineering,
University of Melbourne, Australia
lagoon@cs.mu.oz.au

Abstract. This paper introduces a propositional encoding for lexicographic path orders in connection with dependency pairs. This facilitates the application of SAT solvers for termination analysis of term rewrite systems based on the dependency pair method. We address two main inter-related issues and encode them as satisfiability problems of propositional formulas that can be efficiently handled by SAT solving: (1) the combined search for a lexicographic path order together with an *argument filtering* to orient a set of inequalities; and (2) how the choice of the argument filtering influences the set of inequalities that have to be oriented. We have implemented our contributions in the termination prover APROVE. Extensive experiments show that by our encoding and the application of SAT solvers one obtains speedups in orders of magnitude as well as increased termination proving power.

1 Introduction

In recent work [5], Codish *et al.* introduce a propositional encoding of lexicographic path orders (LPO) and demonstrate that SAT solving can drastically speed up the solving of LPO termination problems. The key idea is that the encoding of a term rewrite system (TRS) $\mathcal{R}$ is satisfiable if and only if $\mathcal{R}$ is LPO-terminating and that each model of the encoding indicates a particular LPO which orients the rules in $\mathcal{R}$. However, lexicographic path orders on their own are too weak for many interesting termination problems and hence LPO is typically combined with more sophisticated termination proving techniques. One of the most popular and powerful such techniques is the *dependency pair* (DP) method [2]. Essentially, for any TRS the DP method generates a set of inequalities between terms. If one can find a well-founded order satisfying these inequalities, then termination is proved. A main advantage of the DP method is that it permits the use of orders which need not be monotonic. This allows the application of lexicographic path orders combined with *argument filterings*.

For every function symbol f, an argument filtering π specifies which parts of a term $f(\ldots)$ may be eliminated before comparing terms. As stated in [17],

---

[*] Supported by the Deutsche Forschungsgemeinschaft DFG under grant GI 274/5-1.

M. Hermann and A. Voronkov (Eds.): LPAR 2006, LNAI 4246, pp. 30–44, 2006.

"the dependency pairs method derives much of its power from the ability to use argument filterings to simplify constraints". However, argument filterings represent a severe bottleneck for the automation of dependency pairs, as the search space for argument filterings is enormous. In recent refinements of the DP method [11,23], the choice of π also influences the set of *usable rules* which contribute to the inequalities that have to be oriented.

This paper extends the approach of [5] by providing a propositional encoding which combines the search for an LPO with the search for an argument filtering. This extension is non-trivial as the choice of an argument filtering π influences the structure of the terms in the rules as well as the set of rules which contribute to the inequalities that need to be oriented. The key idea is to combine all of the constraints on π which influence the definition of the LPO and the definition of the usable rules and to encode these constraints in SAT. This encoding captures the synergy between precedences on function symbols and argument filterings. In our approach there exist an argument filtering π and an LPO which orient a set of inequalities if and only if the encoding of the inequalities is satisfiable. Moreover, each model of the encoding corresponds to a suitable argument filtering and a suitable LPO which orient the inequalities.

After the necessary preliminaries on LPO and on the DP method in Sect. 2, Sect. 3 extends the approach of [5] to consider argument filterings. Sect. 4 shows how to extend this encoding to account for the influence of an argument filtering on the set of usable rules. In Sect. 5 we describe the implementation of our results in the termination prover AProVE [14] and provide extensive experimental evidence indicating speedups in orders of magnitude. We conclude in Sect. 6.

2   Preliminaries

This section briefly describes the starting points for the rest of the paper: propositional encodings for lexicographic path orders [5,20] and the dependency pair framework [2,12,17]. We refer to [3] for further details on term rewriting.

We assume an algebra of terms constructed over given sets of symbols $\mathcal{F}$ and variables $\mathcal{V}$. Let $>_{\mathcal{F}}$ denote a (strict or non-strict) partial order on $\mathcal{F}$ (a so-called *precedence*) and let $\approx_{\mathcal{F}}$ denote the corresponding equivalence relation. We denote by $\sim$ the equality of terms up to equivalence of symbols. Observe that if $>_{\mathcal{F}}$ is strict then $\approx_{\mathcal{F}}$ and $\sim$ are the identity of symbols and terms respectively. Each precedence $>_{\mathcal{F}}$ on the symbols induces a lexicographic path order on terms.

Definition 1 (LPO [19]). *The lexicographic path order $\succ_{LPO}$ on terms induced by the partial order $>_{\mathcal{F}}$ is defined as $s = f(s_1, \ldots, s_n) \succ_{LPO} t$ if and only if one of the following holds:*

1. *$t = g(t_1, \ldots, t_m)$ and $s \succ_{LPO} t_j$ for all $1 \leq j \leq m$ and either*
   (i) $f >_{\mathcal{F}} g$ or   (ii) $f \approx_{\mathcal{F}} g$ and $\langle s_1, \ldots, s_n \rangle \succ_{LPO}^{lex} \langle t_1, \ldots, t_m \rangle$); or
2. *$s_i \succsim_{LPO} t$ for some $1 \leq i \leq n$.*

Here $\succ_{LPO}^{lex}$ is the lexicographic extension of $\succ_{LPO}$ to tuples of terms and $\succsim_{LPO}$ is the union of $\succ_{LPO}$ and $\sim$.

The classical approach to prove termination of a TRS $\mathcal{R}$ is to find a *reduction order* $\succ$ which orients all rules $\ell \to r$ in $\mathcal{R}$ (i.e., $\ell \succ_{LPO} r$). A reduction order is an order which is well founded, monotonic, and stable (closed under contexts and substitutions). In practice, most reduction orders amenable to automation are *simplification orders* [7], i.e., they contain the embedding relation $\succ_{emb}$.

The LPO is one of the most prominent simplification orders and raises the associated decision problem: For terms s and t, is there a precedence $>_{\mathcal{F}}$ such that $s \succ_{LPO} t$ holds? This decision problem comes in two flavors: "strict-LPO" and "quasi-LPO" depending on whether $>_{\mathcal{F}}$ is required to be strict or not. Finding $>_{\mathcal{F}}$ such that $s \succ_{LPO} t$ is tantamount to solving a constraint obtained by unfolding the definition of $s \succ_{LPO} t$, cf. [6,15].

As an example, let $\mathcal{F} = \{-, +, *\}$. Then there exists a strict precedence such that $-(x + y) \succ_{LPO} (-x) * (-y)$ if and only if the *partial order constraint* $(- >_{\mathcal{F}} *) \vee ((+ >_{\mathcal{F}} *) \wedge (+ >_{\mathcal{F}} -))$ has a solution. In [20] the authors show how such constraints can be encoded into propositional formulas. These formulas are satisfiable if and only if there exists a suitable partial order $>_{\mathcal{F}}$. A substantially improved encoding from such partial order constraints into propositional formulas is presented in [5].

It is well known that lexicographic path orders on their own are not very powerful for proving termination.

Example 2. Consider the following TRS $\mathcal{R}$ for division on natural numbers [2].

$$\mathsf{minus}(x, 0) \to x \qquad (1) \qquad \mathsf{quot}(0, \mathsf{s}(y)) \to 0 \qquad (3)$$
$$\mathsf{minus}(\mathsf{s}(x), \mathsf{s}(y)) \to \mathsf{minus}(x, y) \ (2) \quad \mathsf{quot}(\mathsf{s}(x), \mathsf{s}(y)) \to \mathsf{s}(\mathsf{quot}(\mathsf{minus}(x, y), \mathsf{s}(y))) \ (4)$$

Rules (1) - (3) can easily be oriented using an LPO, but rule (4) cannot. To see this, observe that if we instantiate y by $\mathsf{s}(x)$, we obtain $\mathsf{quot}(\mathsf{s}(x), \mathsf{s}(\mathsf{s}(x))) \prec_{emb}$ $\mathsf{s}(\mathsf{quot}(\mathsf{minus}(x, \mathsf{s}(x)), \mathsf{s}(\mathsf{s}(x))))$. Thus, no simplification order can show termination of $\mathcal{R}$. This drawback was the reason for developing more powerful approaches like the dependency pair method.

The dependency pair framework [12] is a modular reformulation and improvement of Arts and Giesl's dependency pair approach [2] which was also inspired by related work in [4,17]. To ease readability, the following presentation is slightly simplified yet sufficient to state the contributions of this paper. For further details on the dependency pair framework see [12].

For a term rewrite system $\mathcal{R}$ over the symbols $\mathcal{F}$, the set of *defined* symbols $\mathcal{D}_{\mathcal{R}} \subseteq \mathcal{F}$ is the set of all root symbols of left-hand sides of $\mathcal{R}$. With each defined symbol $f \in \mathcal{D}_{\mathcal{R}}$ we extend the signature $\mathcal{F}$ by a fresh *tuple symbol* F. For each rule $f(s_1, \ldots, s_n) \to r$ in a term rewrite system $\mathcal{R}$ and for each subterm $g(t_1, \ldots, t_m)$ of r with $g \in \mathcal{D}_{\mathcal{R}}$, $F(s_1, \ldots, s_n) \to G(t_1, \ldots, t_m)$ is a dependency pair, intuitively indicating that a function call to f may lead to a function call to g. The set of dependency pairs of $\mathcal{R}$ is denoted $DP(\mathcal{R})$.

Example 3. Recall the term rewrite system from Ex. 2. The defined symbols are minus and quot and there are three dependency pairs:

$$\text{MINUS}(s(x), s(y)) \rightarrow \text{MINUS}(x, y) \tag{5}$$
$$\text{QUOT}(s(x), s(y)) \rightarrow \text{MINUS}(x, y) \tag{6}$$
$$\text{QUOT}(s(x), s(y)) \rightarrow \text{QUOT}(\text{minus}(x, y), s(y)) \tag{7}$$

The main result underlying the dependency pair method states that a term rewrite system $\mathcal{R}$ is terminating if and only if there is no infinite (minimal) $\mathcal{R}$-*chain* of its dependency pairs $DP(\mathcal{R})$ [2]. In other words, there is no infinite sequence of dependency pairs $s_1 \rightarrow t_1, s_2 \rightarrow t_2, \ldots$ from $DP(\mathcal{R})$ such that for all i there is a substitution σ_i where $t_i\sigma_i$ is terminating with respect to $\mathcal{R}$ and $t_i\sigma_i \rightarrow_{\mathcal{R}}^* s_{i+1}\sigma_{i+1}$. To prove absence of such infinite chains automatically, we consider so-called *dependency pair problems*. A dependency pair problem $(\mathcal{P}, \mathcal{R})$ is a pair of term rewrite systems $\mathcal{P}$ and $\mathcal{R}$ and poses the question: "Is there an infinite $\mathcal{R}$-chain of dependency pairs from $\mathcal{P}$?" The goal is to solve the dependency pair problem $(DP(\mathcal{R}), \mathcal{R})$ in order to determine termination of $\mathcal{R}$.

Termination techniques now operate on dependency pair problems and are called *DP processors*. Formally, a DP processor *Proc* takes a dependency pair problem as input and returns a new dependency pair problem which then has to be solved instead. A processor *Proc* is *sound* if for all dependency pair problems $(\mathcal{P}, \mathcal{R})$ where $Proc(\mathcal{P}, \mathcal{R}) = (\mathcal{P}', \mathcal{R})$, there is an infinite $\mathcal{R}$-chain of pairs from $\mathcal{P}'$ whenever there is an infinite $\mathcal{R}$-chain of pairs from $\mathcal{P}$. Soundness of a DP processor is required to prove termination and in particular, to conclude that there is no infinite $\mathcal{R}$-chain if $Proc(\mathcal{P}, \mathcal{R}) = (\varnothing, \mathcal{R})$.

So termination proofs in the DP framework start with the initial DP problem $(DP(\mathcal{R}), \mathcal{R})$. Then the DP problem is simplified repeatedly by sound DP processors. If one reaches the DP problem $(\varnothing, \mathcal{R})$, then termination is proved. In the following, we present one of the most important processors of the framework, the so-called *reduction pair processor*. Additional processors are described in [12].

For a DP problem $(\mathcal{P}, \mathcal{R})$, the reduction pair processor generates inequality constraints which should be satisfied by a *reduction pair* $(\succsim, \succ)$ [21] where $\succsim$ is reflexive, transitive, monotonic, and stable and $\succ$ is a stable well-founded order compatible with $\succsim$ (i.e., $\succsim \circ \succ \subseteq \succ$ or $\succ \circ \succsim \subseteq \succ$). However, $\succ$ need not be monotonic. A typical choice for a reduction pair $(\succsim, \succ)$ is to use simplification orders in combination with *argument filterings* [2] (we adopt notation of [21]).

Definition 4 (Argument Filtering). *An argument filtering π maps every n-ary function symbol to an argument position $i \in \{1, \ldots, n\}$ or to a (possibly empty) list $[i_1, \ldots, i_p]$ with $1 \leq i_1 < \cdots < i_p \leq n$. An argument filtering π induces a mapping from terms to terms:*

$$\pi(t) = \begin{cases} t & \text{if } t \text{ is a variable} \\ \pi(t_i) & \text{if } t = f(t_1, \ldots, t_n) \text{ and } \pi(f) = i \\ f(\pi(t_{i_1}), \ldots, \pi(t_{i_p})) & \text{if } t = f(t_1, \ldots, t_n) \text{ and } \pi(f) = [i_1, \ldots, i_p] \end{cases}$$

For a relation $\succ$ on terms, let $\succ^\pi$ be the relation where $s \succ^\pi t$ holds if and only if $\pi(s) \succ \pi(t)$. An argument filtering with $\pi(f) = i$ is called collapsing *on f.*

Arts and Giesl show in [2] that if $(\succsim, \succ)$ is a reduction pair and π is an argument filtering then $(\succsim^\pi, \succ^\pi)$ is also a reduction pair. In particular, we focus on reduction pairs of the form $(\succsim^\pi_{LPO}, \succ^\pi_{LPO})$ to prove termination of examples like Ex. 2 where the direct application of simplification orders fails.

The constraints generated by the reduction pair processor require that (a) all dependency pairs in $\mathcal{P}$ are weakly or strictly decreasing and, (b) all *usable* rules $\mathcal{U}(\mathcal{P}, \mathcal{R})$ are weakly decreasing. Here, a rule $f(\ldots) \to r$ from $\mathcal{R}$ is *usable* if f occurs in the right-hand side of a dependency pair from $\mathcal{P}$ or of a usable rule. In Ex. 2, the symbols occurring in the right-hand sides of the dependency pairs (5) - (7) are MINUS, QUOT, s, and minus. Therefore the minus-rules (1) and (2) are usable. Since the right-hand sides of the minus-rules do not contain additional symbols, these are in fact all of the usable rules. Hence, the quot-rules (3) and (4) are not usable.

As shown in [16,23], under certain conditions on the reduction pair, Restriction (b) ensures that in chains $s_1 \to t_1, s_2 \to t_2, \ldots$ with $t_i \sigma_i \to^*_\mathcal{R} s_{i+1}\sigma_{i+1}$, we have $t_i \sigma_i \succsim s_{i+1}\sigma_{i+1}$. The required conditions hold in particular for any reduction pair constructed using simplification orders and argument filterings and specifically for $(\succsim^\pi_{LPO}, \succ^\pi_{LPO})$. Hence, the strictly decreasing pairs of $\mathcal{P}$ cannot occur infinitely often in chains. This enables the processor to delete such pairs from $\mathcal{P}$. In the following, for any term rewrite system $\mathcal{Q}$ and relation $\succ$, we denote $\mathcal{Q}_\succ = \{s \to t \in \mathcal{Q} \mid s \succ t\}$.

Theorem 5 (Reduction Pair Processor). *Let $(\succsim, \succ)$ be a reduction pair for a simplification order $\succ$ and let π be an argument filtering. Then the following DP processor Proc is sound.*

$$Proc(\mathcal{P}, \mathcal{R}) = \begin{cases} (\mathcal{P} \setminus \mathcal{P}_{\succ^\pi}, \mathcal{R}) & \text{if } \mathcal{P}_{\succ^\pi} \cup \mathcal{P}_{\succsim^\pi} = \mathcal{P} \text{ and } \mathcal{R}_{\succsim^\pi} \supseteq \mathcal{U}(\mathcal{P}, \mathcal{R}) \\ (\mathcal{P}, \mathcal{R}) & \text{otherwise} \end{cases}$$

Example 6. For the term rewrite system of Ex. 2, according to Thm. 5 we search for a reduction pair solving the following inequality constraints.

$$\text{MINUS}(\text{s}(x), \text{s}(y)) \overset{\succsim}{\underset{(\succsim)}{}} \text{MINUS}(x, y) \tag{8}$$
$$\text{minus}(x, 0) \succsim x \qquad \text{QUOT}(\text{s}(x), \text{s}(y)) \overset{\succsim}{\underset{(\succsim)}{}} \text{MINUS}(x, y) \tag{9}$$
$$\text{minus}(\text{s}(x), \text{s}(y)) \succsim \text{minus}(x, y) \qquad \text{QUOT}(\text{s}(x), \text{s}(y)) \overset{\succsim}{\underset{(\succsim)}{}} \text{QUOT}(\text{minus}(x, y), \text{s}(y)) \tag{10}$$

By Thm. 5, all dependency pairs corresponding to strictly decreasing inequalities (8) - (10) can be removed. To solve the inequalities we may take $(\succsim^\pi_{LPO}, \succ^\pi_{LPO})$ where $\pi(\text{minus})=1$, $\pi(\text{s})=\pi(\text{MINUS})=\pi(\text{QUOT})=[1]$, and where $\succsim_{LPO}$ and $\succ_{LPO}$ are induced by the partial order $\text{QUOT} >_\mathcal{F} \text{MINUS}$. For this choice, inequalities (8) - (10) are all strict and hence removed by the reduction pair processor. This results in the new DP problem $(\varnothing, \mathcal{R})$ which proves termination of Ex. 2.

We conclude this brief description of the dependency pair framework with a statement of the central *decision problem* associated with argument filterings, LPO, and dependency pairs:

For a given dependency pair problem $(\mathcal{P}, \mathcal{R})$, does there exist a reduction pair $(\succsim^\pi_{LPO}, \succ^\pi_{LPO})$ for some argument filtering π and lexicographic path order induced by some partial order $>_\mathcal{F}$ such that all rules in $\mathcal{P}$ and in $\mathcal{R}$ are weakly decreasing and at least one rule in $\mathcal{P}$ is strictly decreasing?

In the following section we show how to encode constraints like "$s \succ^{\pi}_{LPO} t$" and "$s \succsim^{\pi}_{LPO} t$" as propositional formulas. Such an encoding enables us to encode the decision problem stated above as a SAT problem. Based on the solution of the SAT problem one can then identify the dependency pairs which can be removed from $\mathcal{P}$.

3   Encoding LPO and Argument Filtering

In this section we consider lexicographic path orders with argument filterings and the corresponding decision problem. Consider first a naive brute force approach. For any given argument filtering π we generate the formula

$$\bigwedge_{\ell \to r \in \mathcal{U}(\mathcal{P}, \mathcal{R})} \pi(\ell) \succsim_{LPO} \pi(r) \;\; \wedge \;\; \bigwedge_{s \to t \in \mathcal{P}} \pi(s) \succsim_{LPO} \pi(t) \;\; \wedge \;\; \bigvee_{s \to t \in \mathcal{P}} \pi(s) \succ_{LPO} \pi(t) \quad (11)$$

The constraints "$\pi(s) \succsim_{LPO} \pi(t)$" and "$\pi(s) \succ_{LPO} \pi(t)$" can be encoded as described in Sect. 2. Then SAT solving can search for an LPO satisfying (11) for the given filtering π. However, this approach is hopelessly inefficient, potentially calling the SAT solver for each of the exponentially many argument filterings. Even if one considers the less naive enumeration algorithms implemented in [14] and [18], for many examples the SAT solver would be called exponentially often.

A contribution of this paper is to show instead how to encode the argument filterings into the propositional formula and delegate the search for an argument filtering to the SAT solver. In this way, the SAT solver is only called once with an encoding of Formula (11) and it can search for an argument filtering and for a precedence at the same time. This is clearly advantageous, since the filtering and the precedence highly influence each other.

So our goal is to encode constraints like "$s \succ^{\pi}_{LPO} t$" (or "$s \succsim^{\pi}_{LPO} t$") into propositional formulas such that every model of the encoding corresponds to a concrete filtering π and precedence $>_{\mathcal{F}}$ which satisfy "$s \succ^{\pi}_{LPO} t$" (or "$s \succsim^{\pi}_{LPO} t$"). We first provide an explicit definition which then provides the basis for specifying partial order and argument filtering constraints, satisfaction of which give "$s \succ^{\pi}_{LPO} t$" (or "$s \succsim^{\pi}_{LPO} t$"). The essential differences with Definition 1 are two: each of the two cases of Definition 1 is refined to consider the effect of π; and we define the weak version $\succsim^{\pi}_{LPO}$ of the order explicitly instead of just defining it via the equivalence on terms.

Definition 7 (LPO modulo π). Let $>_{\mathcal{F}}$ be a (strict or non-strict) precedence and let π be an argument filtering on $\mathcal{F}$. Let x denote a variable.

(I) The induced lexicographic path order $\succ^{\pi}_{LPO}$ on terms is defined as follows: $s = f(s_1, \ldots, s_n) \succ^{\pi}_{LPO} t$ if and only if one of the following holds:
1. $t = g(t_1, \ldots, t_m)$ and
    (a) $\pi(g) = j$ and $s \succ^{\pi}_{LPO} t_j$; or
    (b) $\pi(f) = [i_1, ..., i_p]$, $\pi(g) = [j_1, ..., j_q]$, $s \succ^{\pi}_{LPO} t_j$ for all $j \in [j_1, \ldots, j_q]$, and either (i) $f >_{\mathcal{F}} g$ or
        (ii) $f \approx_{\mathcal{F}} g$ and $\langle s_{i_1}, \ldots, s_{i_p} \rangle \succ^{\pi,lex}_{LPO} \langle t_{j_1}, \ldots, t_{j_q} \rangle$; or

2. (a) $\pi(f) = i$ and $s_i \succ^\pi_{LPO} t$; or

    (b) $\pi(f) = [i_1, \ldots, i_p]$ and for some $i \in [i_1, \ldots, i_p]$, $(s_i \succsim^\pi_{LPO} t)$.

(II) For tuples of terms we define $\langle s_1, \ldots, s_n \rangle \succ^{\pi,lex}_{LPO} \langle t_1, \ldots, t_m \rangle$ iff $n > 0$ and

    (a) $m = 0$ or

    (b) $m > 0$ and $((s_1 \succ^\pi_{LPO} t_1) \vee ((s_1 \succsim^\pi_{LPO} t_1) \wedge \langle s_2, \ldots, s_n \rangle \succ^{\pi,lex}_{LPO} \langle t_2, \ldots, t_m \rangle))$.

(III) $\succsim^\pi_{LPO}$ and $\succsim^{\pi,lex}_{LPO}$ are defined in an analogous way to $\succ^\pi_{LPO}$ and $\succ^{\pi,lex}_{LPO}$:

    (a) replacing $\succ^\pi_{LPO}$ by $\succsim^\pi_{LPO}$ in (I) 1(a) and 2(a); and

    (b) adding the case $x \succsim^\pi_{LPO} g(t_1, \ldots, t_m)$ iff $\pi(g) = j$ and $x \succsim^\pi_{LPO} t_j$, and the case $x \succsim^\pi_{LPO} x$ to (I); and

    (c) replacing $\succ^{\pi,lex}_{LPO}$ by $\succsim^{\pi,lex}_{LPO}$ in (I),(II) and adding $\langle \rangle \succsim^{\pi,lex}_{LPO} \langle \rangle$ to (II).

It follows directly from Definitions 1, 4, and 7 that for all terms s and t we have $s \succ^\pi_{LPO} t \Leftrightarrow \pi(s) \succ_{LPO} \pi(t)$ and $s \succsim^\pi_{LPO} t \Leftrightarrow \pi(s) \succsim_{LPO} \pi(t)$.

The decision problem associated with Def. 7 is stated as follows: For terms s and t, does there exist a partial order $>_{\mathcal{F}}$ and an argument filtering π such that $s \succ^\pi_{LPO} t$ resp. $s \succsim^\pi_{LPO} t$ holds. This problem again comes in two flavors: "strict-LPO" and "quasi-LPO" depending on whether $>_{\mathcal{F}}$ is required to be strict or not. Our aim is to encode these decision problems as constraints on $>_{\mathcal{F}}$ and π, similar to the encoding of $s \succ_{LPO} t$ as a partial order constraint in Sect. 2. The difference is that now we have two types of constraints: constraints on the partial order $>_{\mathcal{F}}$ and constraints on the argument filtering π. To express constraints on argument filterings we use atoms of the following forms: "$\pi(f) = i$" to constrain π to map f to the value i; "$\pi(f) \supseteq i$" to constrain π to map f either to a list containing i or to i itself; and "$list(\pi(f))$" to constrain π to map f to a list. So "$list(\pi(f))$" means that π is not collapsing on f.

Each of the definitions (I) - (III) in Def. 7 induces an encoding to constraints on partial orders and argument filterings. In the following definition, we illustrate the encoding of $s \succ^\pi_{LPO} t$ for the case of strict-LPO with argument filterings. The encoding for $s \succsim^\pi_{LPO} t$ and the encodings for quasi-LPO are defined in a similar way. In the following definition, τ_{1a}, τ_{1b} and τ_2 are the parts of the encoding corresponding to cases 1(a), 1(b) and 2(a-b) in Def. 7 (I).

Definition 8 (Encoding strict-LPO with Argument Filterings). *The strict-LPO encoding of $s \succ^\pi_{LPO} t$ is a mapping τ from pairs of terms s and t to constraints defined by the rules depicted in Fig. 1 (where x denotes a variable).*

Example 9. Consider the first arguments of QUOT in dependency pair (7). Using Def. 8, after simplification of conjunctions, disjunctions, and implications with *true* and *false* we obtain:

$$\tau(\mathsf{s}(x) \succ^\pi_{LPO} \mathsf{minus}(x, y)) = (\pi(\mathsf{minus}) = 1 \wedge list(\pi(\mathsf{s})) \wedge \pi(\mathsf{s}) \supseteq 1)$$
$$\vee (list(\pi(\mathsf{s})) \wedge list(\pi(\mathsf{minus})) \wedge (\mathsf{s} >_{\mathcal{F}} \mathsf{minus}) \wedge$$
$$(\pi(\mathsf{minus}) \supseteq 1 \rightarrow list(\pi(\mathsf{s})) \wedge \pi(\mathsf{s}) \supseteq 1) \wedge \neg(\pi(\mathsf{minus}) \supseteq 2))$$

Thus, $\mathsf{s}(x) \succ^\pi_{LPO} \mathsf{minus}(x, y)$ holds if and only if minus is collapsed to its first argument and s is not filtered or if s and minus are not collapsed, s is greater than minus in the precedence, the second argument of minus is filtered, and whenever minus keeps the first argument then s keeps the first argument, too.

Encoding I:

$$\tau(s \succ_{LPO}^{\pi} t) = \tau_{1a}(s \succ_{LPO}^{\pi} t) \;\vee\; \tau_{1b}(s \succ_{LPO}^{\pi} t) \;\vee\; \tau_2(s \succ_{LPO}^{\pi} t)$$

$$\tau_{1a}(x \succ_{LPO}^{\pi} t) = \tau_{1b}(x \succ_{LPO}^{\pi} t) = \tau_2(x \succ_{LPO}^{\pi} t) = \tau_{1a}(s \succ_{LPO}^{\pi} x) = \tau_{1b}(s \succ_{LPO}^{\pi} x) = \text{false}$$

$$\tau_{1a}(s \succ_{LPO}^{\pi} g(t_1, \ldots, t_m)) = \bigvee_{1 \le j \le m} \left((\pi(g) = j) \wedge \tau(s \succ_{LPO}^{\pi} t_j) \right) \text{ for non-variable } s$$

$$\tau_{1b}(f(s_1, \ldots, s_n) \succ_{LPO}^{\pi} g(t_1, \ldots, t_m)) = list(\pi(f)) \wedge list(\pi(g)) \wedge (f >_{\mathcal{F}} g) \wedge$$
$$\bigwedge_{1 \le j \le m} (\pi(g) \ni j) \to \tau(f(s_1, \ldots, s_n) \succ_{LPO}^{\pi} t_j) \text{ for } f \ne g$$

$$\tau_{1b}(f(s_1, \ldots, s_n) \succ_{LPO}^{\pi} f(t_1, \ldots, t_n)) = list(\pi(f)) \wedge$$
$$\tau(\langle s_1, \ldots, s_n \rangle \succ_{LPO,f}^{\pi,lex} \langle t_1, \ldots, t_n \rangle) \wedge$$
$$\bigwedge_{1 \le j \le n} (\pi(f) \ni j) \to \tau(f(s_1, \ldots, s_n) \succ_{LPO}^{\pi} t_j)$$

$$\tau_2(f(s_1, \ldots, s_n) \succ_{LPO}^{\pi} t) = \bigvee_{1 \le i \le n} \left((\pi(f) = i) \wedge \tau(s_i \succ_{LPO}^{\pi} t) \right) \quad \vee$$
$$\left(list(\pi(f)) \wedge \bigvee_{1 \le i \le n} (\pi(f) \ni i) \wedge \tau(s_i \succsim_{LPO}^{\pi} t) \right)$$

Encoding II:

$$\tau(\langle s_i, \ldots, s_n \rangle \succ_{LPO,f}^{\pi,lex} \langle t_i, \ldots, t_n \rangle) = \text{false if } n = 0 \text{ else}$$
$$((\pi(f) \ni i) \wedge \tau(s_i \succ_{LPO}^{\pi} t_i)) \vee$$
$$\left(((\pi(f) \ni i) \to \tau(s_i \succsim_{LPO}^{\pi} t_i)) \wedge \tau(\langle s_{i+1}, \ldots, s_n \rangle \succ_{LPO,f}^{\pi,lex} \langle t_{i+1}, \ldots, t_n \rangle) \right)$$

Fig. 1. Encoding LPO with Argument Filterings

We proceed to describe how partial order and argument filtering constraints are transformed into propositional logic. The propositional encoding of partial order constraints is presented in more detail in [5].

Let $|\mathcal{F}| = m$. The basic idea is to interpret the symbols in $\mathcal{F}$ as indices in a partial order taking finite domain values from the set $\{1, \ldots, m\}$. Each symbol $f \in \mathcal{F}$ is thus modeled as $\langle f_k, \ldots, f_1 \rangle$ with f_k the most significant bit and $k = \lceil \log_2 m \rceil$. The binary value of $\langle f_k, \ldots, f_1 \rangle$ represents the position of f in the partial order. Of course, $f_k, \ldots, f_1$ may be equal to $g_k, \ldots, g_1$ for $f \ne g$, if a (possibly strict) partial order imposes no order between f and g, or if a non-strict partial order imposes $f \approx_{\mathcal{F}} g$. Constraints of the form $(f >_{\mathcal{F}} g)$ or $(f \approx_{\mathcal{F}} g)$ on $\mathcal{F}$ are interpreted as constraints on indices and it is straightforward to encode them in k-bit arithmetic: A constraint of the form $(f \approx_{\mathcal{F}} g)$ is encoded in k bits by

$$\|(f \approx_{\mathcal{F}} g)\|_k = \bigwedge_{1 \le i \le k} (f_i \leftrightarrow g_i).$$

A constraint of the form $(f >_{\mathcal{F}} g)$ is encoded in k bits by

$$\|(f >_{\mathcal{F}} g)\|_k = \begin{cases} (f_1 \wedge \neg g_1) & \text{if } k = 1 \\ (f_k \wedge \neg g_k) \vee ((f_k \leftrightarrow g_k) \wedge \|(f > g)\|_{k-1}) & \text{if } k > 1 \end{cases}$$

To encode argument filtering constraints, we associate with each symbol $f \in \mathcal{F}$ of arity n the propositional variables $list_f$ (which is true if and only if π is not collapsing on f) and $arg_f^1, \ldots, arg_f^n$ (which indicate which arguments of f remain after filtering by π). We impose for each $f \in \mathcal{F}$ of arity n a constraint of the form $\neg list_f \rightarrow \bigoplus_{1 \leq i \leq n} arg_f^i$ where $\bigoplus_{1 \leq i \leq n} arg_f^i$ specifies that exactly one of the variables arg_f^i is *true* and the rest are *false*. The argument filtering constraints are then encoded as follows: $\|list(\pi(f))\| = list_f$; $\|\pi(f) \unrhd i\| = arg_f^i$; and $\|\pi(f) = i\| = \neg list_f \wedge arg_f^i$.

Example 10. Consider the encoding in Ex. 9 which contains partial order constraints and argument filtering constraints. Using the above encoding for these constraints, we obtain the following propositional formula. Since there are only $m = 2$ symbols s and minus, we choose $k = 1$ and encode the partial order constraint ($s >_{\mathcal{F}}$ minus) as ($s_1 \wedge \neg minus_1$).

$$\|\tau(\mathsf{s}(x) \succ^{\pi}_{LPO} \mathsf{minus}(x,y))\| = (\neg list_{\mathsf{minus}} \wedge arg_{\mathsf{minus}}^1 \wedge list_{\mathsf{s}} \wedge arg_{\mathsf{s}}^1)$$
$$\vee (list_{\mathsf{s}} \wedge list_{\mathsf{minus}} \wedge (\mathsf{s}_1 \wedge \neg minus_1) \wedge$$
$$(arg_{\mathsf{minus}}^1 \rightarrow list_{\mathsf{s}} \wedge arg_{\mathsf{s}}^1) \wedge \neg arg_{\mathsf{minus}}^2)$$

4   Argument Filterings and Usable Rules

Recent improvements of the DP method [11,23] significantly reduce the number of rules required to be weakly decreasing in the reduction pair processor of Thm. 5. We first recapitulate the improved reduction pair processor and then adapt our propositional encoding accordingly.

The idea is that one can restrict the set of usable rules by taking the argument filtering into account: in right-hand sides of dependency pairs or rules, an occurrence of f in the i-th argument of g will never be the cause to introduce a usable f-rule if the argument filtering eliminates g's i-th argument. For instance, when taking $\pi(\mathsf{QUOT}) = [2]$ in Ex. 2, the right-hand side of the *filtered* dependency pairs do not contain minus anymore. Thus, no rule is considered usable. In Def. 11, we define these restricted usable rules for a term t (initially corresponding to the right-hand side of a dependency pair). Here, we make the TRS $\mathcal{R}$ explicit to facilitate a straightforward encoding in Def. 14 afterwards.

Definition 11 (Usable Rules modulo π [11,23]). *Let $\mathcal{R}$ be a TRS and π an argument filtering. For any function symbol f, let $Rls_{\mathcal{R}}(f) = \{\ell \rightarrow r \in \mathcal{R} \mid root(\ell) = f\}$. For any term t, the usable rules $\mathcal{U}_{\pi}(t, \mathcal{R})$ modulo π are given by:*

$$\mathcal{U}_{\pi}(x, \mathcal{R}) = \varnothing \quad \text{for all variables } x$$
$$\mathcal{U}_{\pi}(f(t_1, \ldots, t_n), \mathcal{R}) = Rls_{\mathcal{R}}(f) \quad \cup$$
$$\bigcup_{\ell \rightarrow r \in Rls_{\mathcal{R}}(f)} \mathcal{U}_{\pi}(r, \mathcal{R} \setminus Rls_{\mathcal{R}}(f)) \quad \cup$$
$$\bigcup_{\pi(f) \unrhd i} \mathcal{U}_{\pi}(t_i, \mathcal{R} \setminus Rls_{\mathcal{R}}(f))$$

For a set of dependency pairs $\mathcal{P}$, let $\mathcal{U}_{\pi}(\mathcal{P}, \mathcal{R}) = \bigcup_{s \rightarrow t \in \mathcal{P}} \mathcal{U}_{\pi}(t, \mathcal{R})$.

We now refine the reduction pair processor of Thm. 5 to consider usable rules modulo π.

Theorem 12 (Reduction Pair Processor modulo π [23]). *Let $(\succsim, \succ)$ be a reduction pair for a simplification order $\succ$ and let π be an argument filtering. Then the following DP processor Proc is sound.*

$$Proc(\mathcal{P}, \mathcal{R}) = \begin{cases} (\mathcal{P} \setminus \mathcal{P}_{\succ^\pi}, \mathcal{R}) & \text{if } \mathcal{P}_{\succ^\pi} \cup \mathcal{P}_{\succsim^\pi} = \mathcal{P} \text{ and } \mathcal{R}_{\succsim^\pi} \supseteq \mathcal{U}_\pi(\mathcal{P}, \mathcal{R}) \\ (\mathcal{P}, \mathcal{R}) & \text{otherwise} \end{cases}$$

Example 13. Consider the following TRS (together with the minus-rules (1), (2))

$\mathsf{ge}(x, 0) \to \mathsf{true}$	(12)	$\mathsf{div}(x, y) \to \mathsf{if}(\mathsf{ge}(x, y), x, y)$	(15)
$\mathsf{ge}(0, \mathsf{s}(y)) \to \mathsf{false}$	(13)	$\mathsf{if}(\mathsf{true}, \mathsf{s}(x), \mathsf{s}(y)) \to \mathsf{s}(\mathsf{div}(\mathsf{minus}(x, y), \mathsf{s}(y)))$	(16)
$\mathsf{ge}(\mathsf{s}(x), \mathsf{s}(y)) \to \mathsf{ge}(x, y)$	(14)	$\mathsf{if}(\mathsf{false}, x, \mathsf{s}(y)) \to 0$	(17)

The usable rules are the minus- and ge-rules since minus occurs in the right-hand side of the dependency pair $\mathsf{IF}(\mathsf{true}, \mathsf{s}(x), \mathsf{s}(y)) \to \mathsf{DIV}(\mathsf{minus}(x, y), \mathsf{s}(y))$ resulting from rule (16) and ge occurs in the dependency pair $\mathsf{DIV}(x, y) \to \mathsf{IF}(\mathsf{ge}(x, y), x, y)$ resulting from rule (15). However, if one chooses an argument filtering with $\pi(\mathsf{DIV}) = [1]$ and $\pi(\mathsf{IF}) = [2]$, then the ge-rules are no longer usable since ge does not occur in the right-hand side of the filtered dependency pair $\mathsf{DIV}(x) \to \mathsf{IF}(x)$. Now Thm. 12 only requires the filtered minus-rules and the dependency pairs to be decreasing.

As demonstrated in [11,23] and confirmed by the experiments described in Sect. 5, introducing argument filterings to the specification of usable rules results in a significant gain of termination proving power. However, Thm. 12 is not straightforward to automate using SAT solvers. The technique of Sect. 3 assumes a given set of inequalities which is then encoded to a propositional formula. The problem with Thm. 12 is that that the set of inequalities to be oriented depends on the chosen argument filtering. Hence, the search for an argument filtering should be combined with the computation of the usable rules. As discussed before, an enumeration of argument filterings is hopelessly inefficient. Therefore, we modify the encoding of the inequalities in Formula (11) to consider for every rule $\ell \to r \in \mathcal{R}$, the condition under which $\ell \to r$ is usable. Only under this condition one has to require the inequality $\pi(\ell) \succsim_{LPO} \pi(r)$. To this end, instead of encoding formula (11) we encode the following formula.

$$\underbrace{\bigwedge_{\ell \to r \in \mathcal{U}_\pi(\mathcal{P}, \mathcal{R})} \ell \succsim_{LPO}^\pi r}_{(a)} \wedge \underbrace{\bigwedge_{s \to t \in \mathcal{P}} s \succsim_{LPO}^\pi t}_{(b)} \wedge \underbrace{\bigvee_{s \to t \in \mathcal{P}} s \succ_{LPO}^\pi t}_{(c)} \qquad (11')$$

The subformulas (b) and (c) are identical to those in Formula (11) and are encoded as a conjunction and disjunction of encodings of the forms $\tau(s \succsim_{LPO}^\pi t)$ and $\tau(s \succ_{LPO}^\pi t)$ using Def. 8. The definition of the usable rules in Def. 11 now induces the following encoding of subformula (a) as a propositional formula $\omega(\mathcal{P}, \mathcal{R})$.[1] As in Sect. 3, we use argument filtering constraints of the form "$\pi(f) \supseteq i$". Moreover, we introduce a new propositional variable u_f for every defined function symbol f of $\mathcal{U}(\mathcal{P}, \mathcal{R})$ which indicates whether f's rules are usable.

---

[1] The definition of ω can easily be adapted to more advanced definitions of usable rules as well, cf. e.g. [2,11,13].

Definition 14 (Encoding Usable Rules modulo Argument Filtering).
For a term t and a TRS $\mathcal{R}$ the formula $\omega(t, \mathcal{R})$ is defined as follows:

$$\omega(x, \mathcal{R}) = true \qquad\qquad\qquad\qquad\qquad\qquad for\ x \in \mathcal{V}$$
$$\omega(f(t_1, \ldots, t_n), \mathcal{R}) = \bigwedge_{1 \leq i \leq n} (\pi(f) \ni i \to \omega(t_i, \mathcal{R})) \qquad for\ f \notin \mathcal{D}_{\mathcal{R}}$$
$$\omega(f(t_1, \ldots, t_n), \mathcal{R}) = u_f\ \wedge \qquad\qquad\qquad\qquad\qquad for\ f \in \mathcal{D}_{\mathcal{R}}$$
$$\bigwedge_{\ell \to r \in Rls_{\mathcal{R}}(f)} \omega(r, \mathcal{R} \setminus Rls_{\mathcal{R}}(f))\ \wedge$$
$$\bigwedge_{1 \leq i \leq n} (\pi(f) \ni i \to \omega(t_i, \mathcal{R} \setminus Rls_{\mathcal{R}}(f)))$$

For a set of dependency pairs $\mathcal{P}$, let

$$\omega(\mathcal{P}, \mathcal{R}) = \left(\bigwedge_{s \to t \in \mathcal{P}} \omega(t, \mathcal{R}) \right) \wedge \left(\bigwedge_{f \in \mathcal{D}_{\mathcal{U}(\mathcal{P}, \mathcal{R})}} u_f \to \left(\bigwedge_{\ell \to r \in Rls_{\mathcal{R}}(f)} \tau(\ell \succsim_{LPO}^{\pi} r) \right) \right).$$

For a DP problem $(\mathcal{P}, \mathcal{R})$ we encode the formula (11'). Every model of this encoding corresponds to a precedence $>_{\mathcal{F}}$ and an argument filtering π satisfying the constraints of the improved reduction pair processor from Thm. 12. Thus, we can now use SAT solving to automate Thm. 12 as well.

Example 15. Consider the TRS $\mathcal{R}$ from Ex. 13. Using the encoding of Def. 14, for $\mathcal{P} = DP(\mathcal{R})$ we obtain:

$$\omega(\mathcal{P}, \mathcal{R}) = (\pi(\mathsf{DIV}) \ni 1 \to u_{\mathsf{minus}}) \wedge (\pi(\mathsf{IF}) \ni 1 \to u_{\mathsf{ge}}) \wedge$$
$$(u_{\mathsf{minus}} \to (\tau(\mathsf{minus}(x, 0) \succsim_{LPO}^{\pi} x) \wedge \tau(\mathsf{minus}(\mathsf{s}(x), \mathsf{s}(y)) \succsim_{LPO}^{\pi} \mathsf{minus}(x, y)))) \wedge$$
$$(u_{\mathsf{ge}} \to (\tau(\mathsf{ge}(x, 0) \succsim_{LPO}^{\pi} \mathsf{true}) \wedge \tau(\mathsf{ge}(0, \mathsf{s}(y)) \succsim_{LPO}^{\pi} \mathsf{false}) \wedge$$
$$\tau(\mathsf{ge}(\mathsf{s}(x), \mathsf{s}(y)) \succsim_{LPO}^{\pi} \mathsf{ge}(x, y))))$$

5 Implementation and Experiments

The propositional encodings for LPO with argument filterings and for the reduction pair processors described in Sect. 3 and 4 are implemented and integrated in the termination prover AProVE available from [9]. This Java implementation consists of the following main components: **(a)** An encoder from DP problems to formulas with partial order and argument filtering constraints (approx. 1700 lines). **(b)** A propositional encoder for partial order constraints following [5] and for argument filtering constraints (approx. 300 lines). **(c)** Interfaces to several SAT solvers (approx. 300 lines). In our experiments to evaluate the contributions of this paper, we applied the MiniSAT solver [8]. For the translation to conjunctive normal form (CNF) we used the implementation of Tseitin's algorithm [24] offered by SAT4J [22] - a freely available Java implementation of MiniSAT. Our implementation uses several optimizations to minimize encoding size:

1. We apply basic simplification axioms for *true* and *false* as well as standard Boolean simplifications to flatten nested conjunctions and disjunctions.
2. When building the formulas top-down, at each point we maintain the sets of atomic constraints (partial order and argument filtering) that must be *true*

and *false* from this point on. This information is then applied to simplify all constraints generated below (in the top-down process) and to prune the encoding process.

3. We memo and identify identical subformulas in the propositional encodings and represent formulas as directed acyclic graphs (or Boolean circuits) instead of trees. This decreases the size of the representation considerably. (The usefulness of sharing when solving LPO constraints was already discussed in [10].) For instance, consider the constraint from Ex. 9. Already in this tiny example, the subformula $list(\pi(\mathsf{s})) \wedge \pi(\mathsf{s}) \supseteq 1$ occurs twice, since it results from the encoding of both $\mathsf{s}(x) \succ^\pi_{LPO} x$ and $\mathsf{s}(x) \succ^\pi_{LPO} y$.

Optimization (2) typically reduces the number of propositional variables in the resulting CNF by a factor of at least 2. Optimizations (1) and (3) together further reduce the number of propositional variables by a typical factor of 10.

To evaluate our new SAT-based implementation, we performed extensive experiments to compare it with the corresponding methods in the current non-SAT-based implementations of AProVE [14] and of the Tyrolean Termination Tool (TTT) [18]. In the annual *International Competition of Termination Tools* 2004 and 2005 [1], AProVE and TTT were the two most powerful tools for termination analysis of term rewriting. For our experiments, both AProVE and TTT were configured to consider all argument filterings.[2]

We ran the three tools on all 773 TRSs from the *Termination Problem Data Base 2005*. This is the collection of examples from the annual competition of termination tools. It contains 99 TRSs that are known to be non-terminating and which serve as an error-checking mechanism. As expected, all three implementations fail to show termination of these TRSs. For the experiments, the TTT analyzer was applied via its web interface and ran on a Xeon 2.24GHz dual-CPU platform. The AProVE analyzer and our new SAT-based analyzer were run on an AMD Athlon 64 at 2.2 GHz.

Apart from the reduction pair processor, we also used the *dependency graph processor* [2,12,17], which is the other main processor of the dependency pair framework. This processor is used to split up dependency pair problems into smaller ones. As AProVE and TTT use slightly different techniques for estimating dependency graphs in the dependency graph processor and as they run on different machines, their performance is not directly comparable.

For a fair comparison of the three different implementations, we did not use any of the many other termination analysis techniques available in AProVE and TTT. In particular we did not use any techniques to preprocess the TRSs and we did not apply any other DP processors.

Tables 1 and 2 summarize the results using the DP processors based on Thm. 5 and 12 respectively. The tools are indicated as: TTT, APR (AProVE) and SAT (AProVE with our SAT-based encoding). For each of the experiments we considered reduction pairs based on *strict-* and *quasi*-LPO. Each of the experiments was performed with a time-out of 60 seconds (corresponding to the

---

[2] TTT offers two algorithms to search for argument filterings. We used the "divide-and-conquer"-algorithm, since it is usually the more efficient one.

way tools are evaluated in the annual competition) and with a time-out of 10 minutes. We indicate by "*Yes*", "*Fail*", and "*RL*" the number of TRSs for which proving termination with the given technique succeeds, fails, or encounters a resource limit (time-out or exhausts memory). Finally, we give the total time in seconds for analyzing all 773 examples. Individual runtimes and proof details are available from our empirical evaluation web site [9].

Table 1. Strict–LPO (left) and Quasi-LPO (right) with the DP processor of Thm. 5

	LPO - 60sec t/o				LPO - 10min t/o				QLPO - 60sec t/o				QLPO - 10min t/o			
Tool	Yes	Fail	RL	Time	Yes	Fail	RL	Time	Yes	Fail	RL	Time	Yes	Fail	RL	Time
TTT	268	448	57	4202	269	465	39	28030	297	395	81	6241	297	408	68	43540
APR	310	358	105	6936	310	365	98	60402	320	331	122	7913	326	341	106	67764
SAT	327	446	0	82	327	446	0	82	359	414	0	183	359	414	0	183

Table 2. Strict-LPO (left) and Quasi-LPO (right) with the DP processor of Thm. 12

	LPO - 60sec t/o				LPO - 10min t/o				QLPO - 60sec t/o				QLPO - 10min t/o			
Tool	Yes	Fail	RL	Time	Yes	Fail	RL	Time	Yes	Fail	RL	Time	Yes	Fail	RL	Time
APR	338	368	67	4777	341	383	49	33329	357	323	93	6100	359	336	78	49934
SAT	348	425	0	82	348	425	0	82	380	393	0	193	380	393	0	193

The comparison of the corresponding SAT-based and non-SAT-based configurations in Table 1 shows that the analyzers based on SAT solving with our proposed encoding are faster by orders of magnitude. Moreover, the power (i.e., the number of examples where termination can be proved) also increases substantially in the SAT-based configurations. It is also interesting to note that there are no time-outs in the SAT-based configurations, whereas the non-SAT-based configurations have many time-outs.[3]

Table 2 provides results using the improved reduction pair processor of Thm. 12. Again, the SAT-based configuration is much faster than the corresponding non-SAT-based one. The comparison with Table 1 shows that replacing the processor of Thm. 5 by the one of Thm. 12 increases power significantly and has no negative influence on runtimes.

In both tables, the comparison between strict- and quasi-LPO (of corresponding configurations) shows that quasi-LPO is more powerful but also slower than strict-LPO. However, for the SAT-based analyses, the overall runtimes are still extremely fast in comparison to the non-SAT-based configurations.

Table 3 highlights 5 examples which could not be solved by any tool in the termination competition 2005, whereas the SAT-based configuration proves termination for all 5 in a total of 4.3 seconds. In fact, except for the second example, neither TTT nor AProVE are able to prove termination within 10 minutes in their fully

---

[3] To evaluate the optimizations on p. 40, we also tested the SAT-based configuration with strict-LPO and the 10-minute time-out in a version where optimizations (2) and (3) are switched off. Here, the total runtime increases from 82 to 1968 seconds. Thus, optimizations (2) and (3) decrease total runtime by a factor of more than 20.

automatic mode (which uses many other termination techniques in addition to LPO and argument filtering). This demonstrates that our encoding advances the state of the art of automated termination analysis. The third example could be proven terminating by TTT or AProVE if they employed a strategy which applies LPO earlier. But due to efficiency considerations, both tools did not do this yet in their fully automatic mode. However, with the speed of our new SAT-based approach one can now develop strategies which try LPO and argument filtering as one of the first termination techniques. Since failure of LPO is now detected very quickly, one can still use other termination techniques afterwards.

The columns TTT, APR, and SAT indicate for the 3 tools the analysis times in seconds (including parsing, producing proofs, computing dependency graphs, etc.) and "t/o" indicates a 10 minute timeout. For each of the examples and tools, the time indicated is for the fastest configuration from those described in Tables 1 and 2. For the second and third example, TTT's "divide-and-conquer"-algorithm times out, but its "enumeration"-algorithm (which is usually less efficient) finds a solution within 10 minutes. Therefore, here the runtimes are given in brackets. The last four columns give details for the largest CNF which occurred during the termination proof with SAT (ranging over all dependency pair problems encountered). Columns 4 and 5 indicate the number of clauses and the number of literals of this CNF while Columns 6 and 7 indicate the time (in milliseconds) for encoding to propositional logic and for SAT solving.

Table 3. Five hard examples: SAT solving increases termination proving power

Example	TTT	APR	SAT	# clauses	# literals	encod. time	SAT time
Ex26_Luc03b_Z	t/o	t/o	1.15	12462	32027	90	48
Ex2_Luc02a_C	(476.8)	t/o	0.69	8478	21200	137	20
Ex49_GM04_C	(25.8)	44.4	0.81	7040	17638	212	16
ExSec11_1_Luc02a_C	t/o	t/o	0.78	10968	28265	145	12
ExSec11_1_Luc02a_GM	t/o	t/o	0.87	19782	50608	155	72

6   Conclusion

In [5] the authors demonstrate the power of propositional encoding and application of SAT solving to LPO termination analysis. This paper extends the SAT-based approach to consider the more realistic setting of dependency pair problems with LPO and argument filtering. The main challenge derives from the strong dependencies between the notions of LPO, argument filterings, and the set of rules which need to be oriented. The key to a solution is to introduce and encode in SAT all of the constraints originating from these notions into a single search process. We introduce such an encoding and through implementation and experimentation prove that it meets the challenge yielding speedups in orders of magnitude over existing termination tools as well as increasing termination proving power. To experiment with our SAT-based implementation and for further details on our experiments please visit our web page at http://aprove.informatik.rwth-aachen.de/eval/SATLPO [9].

References

1. Annual International Competition of Termination Tools. `http://www.lri.fr/marche/termination-competition`.
2. T. Arts and J. Giesl. Termination of term rewriting using dependency pairs. *Theoretical Computer Science*, 236:133–178, 2000.
3. F. Baader and T. Nipkow. *Term Rewriting and All That*. Cambridge, 1998.
4. C. Borralleras. *Ordering-based methods for proving termination automatically*. PhD thesis, Universitat Politècnica de Catalunya, Spain, 2003.
5. M. Codish, V. Lagoon, and P. J. Stuckey. Solving partial order constraints for LPO termination. In *Proc. RTA '06*, LNCS 4098, pages 4–18, 2006.
6. H. Comon, P. Narendran, R. Nieuwenhuis, and M. Rusinowitch. Decision problems in ordered rewriting. In *Proc. LICS '98*, pages 276–286, 1998.
7. N. Dershowitz. Termination of rewriting. *J. Symb. Comput.*, 3(1,2):69–116, 1987.
8. N. Eén and N. Sörensson. An extensible SAT-solver. In *Proc. SAT '03*, LNCS 2919, pages 502–518, 2004.
9. Empirical evaluation of "SAT Solving for Argument Filterings". `http://aprove.informatik.rwth-aachen.de/eval/SATLPO`.
10. T. Genet and I. Gnaedig. Termination proofs using GPO ordering constraints with shared term data structure. In *Proc. TAPSOFT '97*, LNCS 1214, pp. 249-260, 1997.
11. J. Giesl, R. Thiemann, P. Schneider-Kamp, and S. Falke. Improving dependency pairs. In *Proc. LPAR '03*, LNAI 2850, pages 165–179, 2003.
12. J. Giesl, R. Thiemann, and P. Schneider-Kamp. The dependency pair framework: Combining techniques for automated termination proofs. In *Proc. LPAR '04*, LNAI 3452, pages 301–331, 2005.
13. J. Giesl, R. Thiemann, and P. Schneider-Kamp. Proving and disproving termination of higher-order functions. In *Proc. FroCoS '05*, LNAI 3717, pp. 216-231, 2005.
14. J. Giesl, P. Schneider-Kamp, and R. Thiemann. AProVE 1.2: Automatic termination proofs in the DP framework. *Proc. IJCAR '06*, LNAI 4130, pp. 281-286, 2006.
15. N. Hirokawa and A. Middeldorp. Tsukuba Termination Tool. In *Proc. RTA '03*, LNCS 2706, pages 311–320, 2003.
16. N. Hirokawa and A. Middeldorp. Dependency pairs revisited. In *Proc. RTA '04*, LNCS 3091, pages 249–268, 2004.
17. N. Hirokawa and A. Middeldorp. Automating the dependency pair method. *Information and Computation*, 199(1,2):172–199, 2005.
18. N. Hirokawa and A. Middeldorp. Tyrolean Termination Tool. In *Proc. RTA '05*, LNCS 3467, pages 175–184, 2005.
19. S. Kamin and J. J. Lévy. Two generalizations of the recursive path ordering. Unpublished Manuscript, University of Illinois, IL, USA, 1980.
20. M. Kurihara and H. Kondo. Efficient BDD encodings for partial order constraints with application to expert systems in software verification. In *Proc. IEA/AIE '04*, LNCS 3029, pages 827–837, 2004.
21. K. Kusakari, M. Nakamura, and Y. Toyama. Argument filtering transformation. In *Proc. PPDP '99*, LNCS 1702, pages 47–61, 1999.
22. SAT4J satisfiability library for Java. `http://www.sat4j.org`.
23. R. Thiemann, J. Giesl, and P. Schneider-Kamp. Improved modular termination proofs using dependency pairs. In *Proc. IJCAR '04*, LNAI 3097, pages 75–90, 2004.
24. G. Tseitin. On the complexity of derivation in propositional calculus. In *Studies in Constructive Mathematics and Mathematical Logic*, pages 115–125. 1968. Reprinted in J. Siekmann and G. Wrightson (editors), *Automation of Reasoning*, vol. 2, pages 466-483, Springer, 1983.

Inductive Decidability Using Implicit Induction[*]

Stephan Falke and Deepak Kapur

Computer Science Department, University of New Mexico, Albuquerque, NM, USA
{spf, kapur}@cs.unm.edu

Abstract. Decision procedures are widely used in automated reasoning tools in order to reason about data structures. In applications, many conjectures fall outside the theory handled by a decision procedure. Often, reasoning about user-defined functions on those data structures is needed. For this, inductive reasoning has to be employed. In this work, classes of function definitions and conjectures are identified for which inductive validity can be automatically decided using implicit induction methods and decision procedures for an underlying theory. The class of equational conjectures considered in this paper significantly extends the results of Kapur & Subramaniam (CADE, 2000) [15], which were obtained using explicit induction schemes. Firstly, nonlinear conjectures can be decided automatically. Secondly, function definitions can use other defined functions in their definitions, thus allowing mutually recursive functions and decidable conjectures about them. Thirdly, conjectures can have general terms from the decidable theory on inductive positions. These contributions are crucial for successfully integrating inductive reasoning into decision procedures, thus enabling their use in push-button mode in applications including verification and program analysis.

1 Introduction

Inductive reasoning about recursively defined data structures and recursive functions defined on such data structures is often needed for verifying properties of computational descriptions, both in hardware and software. Decision procedures about commonly used data structures including numbers and data structures generated using free constructors (such as lists and trees) are being widely used in software and hardware verification. Push-button tools for program analysis and verification based on decision procedures have been explored. However, most tools based on decision procedures, including BLAST [9] and SLAM [3], are limited in their capabilities because of their inability to reason about recursively defined functions.

One of the major challenges is to integrate inductive reasoning with decision procedures and, in particular, to identify a subclass of inductive conjectures about recursively defined functions whose validity can be decided automatically. This line of research was initiated by Kapur, Giesl, and Subramaniam [15,7,8,12]. The aim of identifying inductive conjectures whose validity is decidable is achieved by imposing restrictions on the structure of function definitions,

---

[*] Partially supported by NSF grants ITR CCR-0113611 and CCR-0203051.

M. Hermann and A. Voronkov (Eds.): LPAR 2006, LNAI 4246, pp. 45–59, 2006.

as well as on the conjectures about these functions. Kapur *et al.* use the framework of explicit inductive reasoning based on the cover set method proposed in [20].

This paper uses the framework of implicit induction for automating inductive reasoning in order to extend the results given in [15]. Implicit induction methods, while less widely applicable, are considered to be more amenable to automation. A benefit of the implicit induction methods is that conjectures requiring mutual induction can be handled more easily than in the explicit induction framework.

In [15], the concept of theory-based functions is introduced. In the definition of a theory-based function, the only recursive calls permitted are to the same function again. The conjectures whose validity is shown decidable in [15] are equational conjectures $r_1 \approx r_2$, where r_2 is a term in the decidable theory and r_1 contains theory-based functions. The arguments to those theory-based functions are required to be distinct variables. In [7], Boolean combinations of those conjectures are considered. In [8], the class of conjectures is extended to linear equational conjectures containing theory-based functions on both sides.

In this paper, we substantially extend the results from [15] in three ways that are orthogonal to the extensions of [7,8]. Firstly, the permitted conjectures are generalized to include nonlinear conjectures and conjectures with general terms from the decidable theory on inductive positions, such as $\mathsf{gcd}(x, x) \approx x$ and $x \leq \mathsf{s}(x) \approx \mathsf{true}$, whose validity can be decided automatically. For handling such nonlinear conjectures, conditions on function definitions are identified which can easily be checked a priori using a decision procedure (Section 4). The second generalization is to allow the definition of a theory-based function to use theory-based functions other than the function being defined. A group of theory-based function symbols can thus be viewed as being defined jointly together. This extension allows for mutually recursive theory-based definitions (Section 5). As in [15], conjectures about these groups of function symbols can have nested function calls (Section 6). For each of these classes, a decision procedure based on implicit induction methods is given. The considered classes of conjectures are highly relevant in practice and can readily be handled using implicit induction methods. They are quite challenging for explicit inductive reasoning techniques.

Due to lack of space, almost all proofs are omitted. They may be found in the extended version of this paper [5], together with more details on the examples.

2   Background

We generally assume familiarity with the concepts of term rewriting [1]. We use many-sorted first-order logic where "$\approx$" is the only predicate symbol and "$\approx$" is reflexive, symmetric, transitive, and congruent. For a signature $\mathcal{F}$ and an infinite set of variables $\mathcal{V}$, we denote the set of (well-typed) *terms over $\mathcal{F}$ and $\mathcal{V}$* by $\mathit{Terms}(\mathcal{F}, \mathcal{V})$ and the set of ground terms by $\mathit{Terms}(\mathcal{F})$. We often write x^* to denote a tuple of (not necessarily pairwise distinct) variables, and denote by x_i the ith element of this tuple. Analogously, s^* denotes a tuple of terms s_i.

A theory $\mathcal{T}$ is given by a finite signature $\mathcal{F}_{\mathcal{T}}$ and a set of axioms (i.e., closed formulas) $AX_{\mathcal{T}}$ over the signature $\mathcal{F}_{\mathcal{T}}$. The (quantifier-free) theory $\mathcal{T}$ is defined to be the set of all quantifier-free formulas φ over $\mathcal{F}_{\mathcal{T}}$ such that $AX_{\mathcal{T}} \models \forall^*. \varphi$, where $\forall^*. \varphi$ is the universal closure of φ. In this case we also say that φ is *valid*. We often write $s \approx_{\mathcal{T}} t$ as a shorthand for $AX_{\mathcal{T}} \models \forall^*. s \approx t$ and $s \not\approx_{\mathcal{T}} t$ as a shorthand for $AX_{\mathcal{T}} \not\models \forall^*. s \approx t$.

For the theory $\mathcal{T}_C$ of *free constructors*, $AX_{\mathcal{T}_C}$ consists of the universal closures of the following formulas:

$$\neg(c(x_1, \ldots, x_n) \approx c'(y_1, \ldots y_m)) \text{ for all } c, c' \in \mathcal{F}_{\mathcal{T}_C} \text{ where } c \neq c'$$
$$c(x_1, \ldots, x_n) \approx c(y_1, \ldots, y_n) \Longrightarrow x_1 \approx y_1 \wedge \ldots \wedge x_n \approx y_n \text{ for all } c \in \mathcal{F}_{\mathcal{T}_C}$$
$$\bigvee_{c \in \mathcal{F}_{\mathcal{T}_C}} \exists y_1, \ldots, y_n. \, x \approx c(y_1, \ldots, y_n)$$
$$\neg(c_1(\ldots c_2(\ldots c_n(\ldots x \ldots) \ldots) \ldots) \approx x) \text{ for all sequences } c_1 \ldots c_n \in \mathcal{F}_{\mathcal{T}_C}^*, n > 0$$

Note that the last type of axioms usually results in infinitely many formulas. Here, "$\ldots$" in the arguments of c_i stands for pairwise distinct variables.

We use the following definition for the equational sub-theory $\mathcal{T}_{PA}$ of *Presburger arithmetic* on natural numbers: $\mathcal{F}_{\mathcal{T}_{PA}} = \{0, 1, +\}$ and $AX_{\mathcal{T}_{PA}}$ consists of the universal closures of the following formulas:

$$
\begin{array}{ll}
(x + y) + z \approx x + (y + z) & \neg(1 + x \approx 0) \\
x + y \approx y + x & x + y \approx x + z \Longrightarrow y \approx z \\
0 + y \approx y & x \approx 0 \vee \exists y. \, x \approx y + 1
\end{array}
$$

We often write *flattened* terms since "$+$" is associative and commutative. For $t \in \mathit{Terms}(\mathcal{F}_{\mathcal{T}_{PA}}, \mathcal{V})$ with $\mathcal{V}(t) = \{x_1, \ldots, x_n\}$, there exist $a_i \in \mathbb{N}$ such that $t \approx_{\mathcal{T}_{PA}} a_0 + a_1 \cdot x_1 + \ldots + a_n \cdot x_n$. Here, "$a \cdot x$" denotes the term $x + \ldots + x$ (a times) and "a_0" denotes $1 + \ldots + 1$ (a_0 times).

Instead of *validity*, we are usually interested in *inductive validity*. The formula φ is *inductively valid in a theory* $\mathcal{T}$ (denoted $AX_{\mathcal{T}} \models_{ind} \varphi$) iff $AX_{\mathcal{T}} \models \varphi\sigma$ for all ground substitutions σ, i.e., σ substitutes all variables of φ by ground terms from $\mathit{Terms}(\mathcal{F}_{\mathcal{T}})$. In general, validity implies inductive validity, but not vice versa. We restrict ourselves to theories like $\mathcal{T}_C$ and $\mathcal{T}_{PA}$ which are decidable and inductively complete, i.e., inductive validity of an equation $r_1 \approx r_2$ over $\mathcal{F}_{\mathcal{T}}$ also implies its validity.

We assume that for all sets $U = \{s_1 \approx_{\mathcal{T}}^? t_1, \ldots, s_n \approx_{\mathcal{T}}^? t_n\}$ with $s_i, t_i \in \mathit{Terms}(\mathcal{F}_{\mathcal{T}}, \mathcal{V})$ for all $1 \leq i \leq n$, a finite minimal complete set $\mathcal{CU}_{\mathcal{T}}(U)$ of $\mathcal{T}$-unifiers is computable. If $U = \{s \approx_{\mathcal{T}}^? t\}$ we also write $\mathcal{CU}_{\mathcal{T}}(s, t)$.

We use *term rewrite systems* (TRSs) over a signature $\mathcal{F} \supseteq \mathcal{F}_{\mathcal{T}}$ as our specification language and require that all left sides of rules have the form $f(s^*)$ for a tuple s^* of terms from $\mathit{Terms}(\mathcal{F}_{\mathcal{T}}, \mathcal{V})$ and $f \notin \mathcal{F}_{\mathcal{T}}$. Let $\mathcal{F}_d = \mathcal{F} \setminus \mathcal{F}_{\mathcal{T}}$ denote the set of *defined symbols*. We use the concept of rewriting modulo a theory ($\to_{\mathcal{R}/\mathcal{T}}$), where $\to_{\mathcal{R}/\mathcal{T}}$ must be decidable. We restrict ourselves to terminating, confluent, and sufficiently complete TRSs $\mathcal{R}$, where $\mathcal{R}$ is *terminating* if $\to_{\mathcal{R}/\mathcal{T}}$ is well-founded, it is *confluent* if $\to_{\mathcal{R}/\mathcal{T}}$ is confluent, and it is *sufficiently complete* if for all (well-typed) ground terms $t \in \mathit{Terms}(\mathcal{F})$ there exists a ground term $q \in \mathit{Terms}(\mathcal{F}_{\mathcal{T}})$ such that $t \to_{\mathcal{R}/\mathcal{T}}^* q$. When regarding $\to_{\mathcal{R}/\mathcal{T}}^*$, we usually do not distinguish between terms that are equal w.r.t. $\approx_{\mathcal{T}}$.

A *reduction order* is a strict, well-founded order $\succ$ on $Terms(\mathcal{F}, \mathcal{V})$ that is closed under contexts ($C[s] \succ C[t]$ whenever $s \succ t$) and substitutions ($s\sigma \succ t\sigma$ whenever $s \succ t$). We say that $\succ$ is *compatible* with $\mathcal{T}$ if $\approx_{\mathcal{T}} \circ \succ \circ \approx_{\mathcal{T}} \subseteq \succ$, i.e., $\succ$ does not distinguish between terms that are equal w.r.t. $\approx_{\mathcal{T}}$.

The rules in $\mathcal{R}$ are considered as equational axioms extending the underlying theory $\mathcal{T}$. This results in a new theory with the signature $\mathcal{F}$ and the axioms $AX_{\mathcal{T}} \cup \{l \approx r \mid l \to r \in \mathcal{R}\}$. To ease readability, we write $AX_{\mathcal{T}} \cup \mathcal{R}$ instead of $AX_{\mathcal{T}} \cup \{l \approx r \mid l \to r \in \mathcal{R}\}$. This extension is *conservative*, i.e., it does not change inductive validity of equations over $\mathcal{F}_{\mathcal{T}}$ [8]. If $AX_{\mathcal{T}} \cup \mathcal{R} \models_{ind} r_1 \approx r_2$ we say that the equation $r_1 \approx r_2$ is an *inductive consequence* of $AX_{\mathcal{T}} \cup \mathcal{R}$.

3   Implicit Induction Methods and $\mathcal{T}$-Based Functions

Implicit induction is a proof method that was derived in [18] from the Knuth-Bendix completion procedure. Since its initial formulation, various improvements have been made to the basic method, see, e.g., [10,13,11,6,14,17,2,19,4].

In this paper, we follow the presentation in [19]. The results, however, are largely independent of this presentation and extend to other proposed methods like the ones in [14,2,4].

Here, as in [19], the implicit induction method is given by an inference system. The system $\mathcal{I}_{\mathcal{T}}$ shown in Figure 1 is parameterized by a TRS $\mathcal{R}$ and a reduction order $\succ$ which is compatible with $\mathcal{T}$ and orients $\mathcal{R}$. It operates on two sets of equations:

1. $\mathcal{E}$, containing the set of equations to be proven, and
2. $\mathcal{H}$, containing the equations (oriented as rewrite rules by $\succ$) which can be used as inductive hypotheses.

Here, $\mathcal{CP}(\mathcal{R}, l \to r)$ is the set of *critical pairs* of $\mathcal{R}$ on $l \to r$, i.e, $\mathcal{CP}(\mathcal{R}, l \to r) = \bigcup_{p \in \mathcal{FPos}(l)} \mathcal{CP}'(\mathcal{R}, l \to r, p)$, where $\mathcal{FPos}(l)$ denotes the non-variable positions in l and $\mathcal{CP}'(\mathcal{R}, l \to r, p) = \{r\sigma \approx l\sigma[r'\sigma]_p \mid l' \to r' \in \mathcal{R}, \sigma \in \mathcal{CU}_{\mathcal{T}}(l|_p, l')\}$. For this, the variables in $l' \to r'$ are suitably renamed to be disjoint from the variables in l. Notice that we use $\mathcal{T}$-unification in order to compute the critical pairs. We use $r_1 \mathrel{\dot{\approx}} r_2$ to stand for either $r_1 \approx r_2$ or $r_2 \approx r_1$. The inference rules Theory$_1$ and Theory$_2$ are replaced by a decision procedure for $\mathcal{T}$ in practice.

The following theorem is obtained by extending [19, Proposition 18].

Theorem 1. *If there is a successful $\mathcal{I}_{\mathcal{T}}$-derivation $(\mathcal{E}_0, \emptyset) \vdash_{\mathcal{I}_{\mathcal{T}}} (\mathcal{E}_1, \mathcal{H}_1) \vdash_{\mathcal{I}_{\mathcal{T}}} \ldots \vdash_{\mathcal{I}_{\mathcal{T}}} (\emptyset, \mathcal{H}_n)$, then all equations in $\mathcal{E}_0$ are inductive consequences of $AX_{\mathcal{T}} \cup \mathcal{R}$. If there is a refuting $\mathcal{I}_{\mathcal{T}}$-derivation $(\mathcal{E}_0, \emptyset) \vdash_{\mathcal{I}_{\mathcal{T}}} (\mathcal{E}_1, \mathcal{H}_1) \vdash_{\mathcal{I}_{\mathcal{T}}} \ldots \vdash_{\mathcal{I}_{\mathcal{T}}} \bot$, then some equation in $\mathcal{E}_0$ is not an inductive consequence of $AX_{\mathcal{T}} \cup R$.*

In [15], the concept of a $\mathcal{T}$-based function is introduced: in the rewrite rules defining a function f, all arguments to f are terms from $Terms(\mathcal{F}_{\mathcal{T}}, \mathcal{V})$, and the right side becomes a term in $Terms(\mathcal{F}_{\mathcal{T}}, \mathcal{V})$ after subterms of the form $f(t^*)$, if any, are abstracted using new variables.

$$
\begin{array}{ll}
\text{Expand} & \dfrac{\mathcal{E} \cup \{r_1 \stackrel{\approx}{\approx} r_2\}, \mathcal{H}}{\mathcal{E} \cup \mathcal{E}', \mathcal{H} \cup \{r_1 \to r_2\}} \quad \text{if } r_1 \succ r_2 \text{ and } \mathcal{E}' = \mathcal{CP}(\mathcal{R}, r_1 \to r_2) \\[3ex]
\text{Simplify} & \dfrac{\mathcal{E} \cup \{r_1 \stackrel{\approx}{\approx} r_2\}, \mathcal{H}}{\mathcal{E} \cup \{r_1' \approx r_2\}, \mathcal{H}} \quad \text{if } r_1 \to_{\mathcal{R} \cup \mathcal{H}/\mathcal{T}} r_1'
\end{array}
$$

$$
\begin{array}{llll}
\text{Theory}_1 & \dfrac{\mathcal{E} \cup \{r_1 \approx r_2\}, \mathcal{H}}{\mathcal{E}, \mathcal{H}} & \text{Theory}_2 & \dfrac{\mathcal{E} \cup \{r_1 \approx r_2\}, \mathcal{H}}{\bot} \\[2ex]
& \text{if } r_1 \approx_{\mathcal{T}} r_2 & & \text{if } r_1 \not\approx_{\mathcal{T}} r_2
\end{array}
$$

Fig. 1. The inference system $\mathcal{I}_{\mathcal{T}}$

Definition 2 ($\mathcal{T}$-based Functions [15]). *A function* $f \in \mathcal{F}_d$ *is* $\mathcal{T}$-*based if all rules* $l \to r \in \mathcal{R}$ *with* $l(\Lambda) = f$ *have the form* $f(s^*) \to C[f(t_1^*), \ldots, f(t_n^*)]$, *where* $s^*, t_1^*, \ldots, t_n^* \in \mathit{Terms}(\mathcal{F}_{\mathcal{T}}, \mathcal{V})$, *and* C *is a context over* $\mathcal{F}_{\mathcal{T}}$.

The *inductive positions* of a function f are those positions such that subterms on those positions change by applying the rules defining f.

Definition 3 (Inductive Positions). *For a* $\mathcal{T}$-*based* f, *position* i *with* $1 \leq i \leq \mathsf{arity}(f)$ *is non-inductive if for all rules* $f(s_1, \ldots, s_m) \to C[f(t_{1,1}, \ldots, t_{1,m}), \ldots, f(t_{n,1}, \ldots, t_{n,m})]$ *where* C *is a context over* $\mathcal{F}_{\mathcal{T}}$, *we have* $s_i \in \mathcal{V}$, $t_{k,i} = s_i$, *and* $s_i \notin \mathcal{V}(s_j) \cup \mathcal{V}(t_{k,j})$ *for all* $j \neq i$ *and all* $1 \leq k \leq n$. *Otherwise, the position is inductive.*

We generally assume that the first n positions of any function f are inductive, while the remaining positions are non-inductive, for some $0 \leq n \leq \mathsf{arity}(f)$.

Example 4. Let $\mathcal{R}$ be the TRS defining "$-$" on natural numbers over $\mathcal{T}_C$.

$$
1 : x - 0 \to x \qquad 2 : 0 - s(y) \to 0 \qquad 3 : s(x) - s(y) \to x - y
$$

Then both position 1 and position 2 of "$-$" are inductive positions. $\Diamond$

4 Nonlinear Simple Conjectures

In [15], a class of conjectures about theory-based functions of the form $f(x^*, s^*) \approx r$, where all variables in x^* are pairwise distinct and do not occur in s^*, is defined. This rules out nonlinear conjectures like $x' - x' \approx 0$. The restrictions were imposed to ensure that the inductive hypothesis is applicable. Below, we show how the restriction on linearity in the left side can be relaxed, thus substantially expanding the class of conjectures which can be decided automatically.

Example 5. Continuing Example 4, we want to prove $x' - x' \approx 0$. Indeed,

$$
\begin{aligned}
(\{x' - x' \approx 0\}, \emptyset) &\vdash_{\mathsf{Expand}} (\{0 \approx 0, 0 \approx x - x\}, \{x' - x' \to 0\}) \\
&\vdash_{\mathsf{Simplify}} (\{0 \approx 0\}, \{x' - x' \to 0\}) \\
&\vdash_{\mathsf{Theory}_1} (\emptyset, \{x' - x' \to 0\})
\end{aligned}
$$

is a successful derivation. $\Diamond$

The reason this derivation is successful is that whenever the terms on the inductive positions in the left side of a rule have a relationship (in this case, equality), the terms on those positions of the recursive calls in the right side have the same relationship, which is needed to apply the inductive hypothesis. This observation is formalized using the set $\mathcal{ImpEq}(\mathsf{f})$.

Definition 6 ($\mathcal{ImpEq}(\mathsf{f})$). *Let f be $\mathcal{T}$-based and defined by the rules $\mathsf{f}(s_i^*) \rightarrow C_i[\mathsf{f}(t_{i,1}^*), \ldots, \mathsf{f}(t_{i,n_i}^*)]$ for $1 \leq i \leq n$. Then we define $\langle l_1, l_2, \mathcal{C} \rangle \in \mathcal{ImpEq}(\mathsf{f})$ iff $\mathcal{C} = \{ \langle k_{j,1}, k_{j,2} \rangle \mid 1 \leq j \leq m \}$ for some m such that $1 \leq l_1 < l_2 \leq \mathsf{arity}(\mathsf{f})$, $1 \leq k_{j,1} < k_{j,2} \leq \mathsf{arity}(\mathsf{f})$ for all $1 \leq j \leq m$,*

$$\bigwedge_{j=1}^{m} s_{i,k_{j,1}} \approx s_{i,k_{j,2}} \implies \bigwedge_{j=1}^{n_i} t_{i,j,l_1} \approx t_{i,j,l_2}$$

is $\mathcal{T}$-valid for all $1 \leq i \leq n$, and there is no $\mathcal{C}' \subsetneq \mathcal{C}$ with this property.

Hence, if a term of the form $\mathsf{f}(s_i^*)\sigma$ is simplified using the rule $\mathsf{f}(s_i^*) \rightarrow C_i[\mathsf{f}(t_{i,1}^*), \ldots, \mathsf{f}(t_{i,n_i}^*)]$, then $t_{i,k,l_1}\sigma \approx_{\mathcal{T}} t_{i,k,l_2}\sigma$ for all $1 \leq k \leq n_i$ if $s_{i,k_{j,1}}\sigma \approx_{\mathcal{T}} s_{i,k_{j,2}}\sigma$ for all $1 \leq j \leq m$.

Example 7. Continuing Example 5, we get $\mathcal{ImpEq}(-) = \{ \langle 1, 2, \{\langle 1, 2 \rangle\} \rangle \}$. For rule 1, $x \approx 0 \implies \mathtt{true}$ is obviously $\mathcal{T}_C$-valid. Also, $0 \approx \mathsf{s}(y) \implies \mathtt{true}$ obtained from rule 2 is $\mathcal{T}_C$-valid. For rule 3, $\mathsf{s}(x) \approx \mathsf{s}(y) \implies x \approx y$ is $\mathcal{T}_C$-valid as well. ◊

Clearly, the set $\mathcal{ImpEq}(\mathsf{f})$ can be computed at compile-time from the rules defining f with the help of a decision procedure for $\mathcal{T}$.

Below, we extend the definition of simple conjectures in [15] to consider nonlinear conjectures by relaxing the requirement that variables on inductive positions need to be pairwise distinct.

Definition 8 (Simple Conjectures). *A simple conjecture is a conjecture of the form $\mathsf{f}(x^*, s^*) \approx r$ such that[1] $\mathsf{f}(x^*, s^*) \succ r$, the function f is $\mathcal{T}$-based, $s^*, r \in \mathcal{Terms}(\mathcal{F}_\mathcal{T}, \mathcal{V})$, the x_i are on f's inductive positions and do not appear in the s_j, and if $x_{l_1} = x_{l_2}$ then there exists $\langle l_1, l_2, \mathcal{C} \rangle \in \mathcal{ImpEq}(\mathsf{f})$ such that $x_{k_1} = x_{k_2}$ for all $\langle k_1, k_2 \rangle \in \mathcal{C}$.*

The following theorem gives a decision procedure based on the implicit induction framework for the class of simple conjectures which includes nonlinear as well as linear conjectures.

Theorem 9. *The inductive validity of a simple conjecture is decidable using the strategy[2] $\mathsf{Expand} \cdot \mathsf{Simplify}^* \cdot (\mathsf{Theory}_1 \cup \mathsf{Theory}_2)^*$.*

Proof. Let $\mathsf{f}(x^*, s^*) \approx r$ be a simple conjecture, and let

---

[1] Here, $\succ$ is the same reduction order used to orient $\mathcal{R}$. In practice this means that $\mathcal{R} \cup \{\mathsf{f}(x^*, s^*) \rightarrow r\}$ is terminating.

[2] Here, $\cdot^*$ means that the inference rule is applied exhaustively.

$$\mathcal{R}' = \{\, f(s_1^*, y^*) \to C_1[f(t_{1,1}^*, y^*), \ldots, f(t_{1,n_1}^*, y^*)],$$

$$\ldots,$$

$$f(s_m^*, y^*) \to C_m[f(t_{m,1}^*, y^*), \ldots, f(t_{m,n_m}^*, y^*)]\,\}$$

be the definition of the $\mathcal{T}$-based function f.

Applying Expand to $(\{f(x^*, s^*) \approx r\}, \emptyset)$, we obtain the state

$$\mathcal{E} = \{\, C_{i_1}[f(t_{i_1,1}^*, y^*), \ldots, f(t_{i_1,n_{i_1}}^*, y^*)]\sigma_{i_1} \approx r\sigma_{i_1},$$

$$\ldots,$$

$$C_{i_l}[f(t_{i_l,1}^*, y^*), \ldots, f(t_{i_l,n_{i_l}}^*, y^*)]\sigma_{i_l} \approx r\sigma_{i_l} \quad \},$$

$$\mathcal{H} = \{\, f(x^*, s^*) \to r \qquad\qquad\qquad\qquad\qquad\qquad \}$$

for some $i_1, \ldots, i_l \in \{1, \ldots, m\}$, where $\sigma_{i_j} \in \mathcal{CU}_\mathcal{T}(\{x^* \approx_\mathcal{T}^? s_{i_j}^*, y^* \approx_\mathcal{T}^? s^*\})$. The i_j are such that the arguments of $f(x^*, s^*)$ and $f(s_{i_j}^*, y^*)$ are $\mathcal{T}$-unifiable. To ease readability, we assume that every complete set of unifiers has cardinality 1.

If $n_{i_j} = 0$, then $C_{i_j}[f(t_{i_j,1}^*, y^*), \ldots, f(t_{i_j,n_{i_j}}^*, y^*)]\sigma_{i_j} = C_{i_j}\sigma_{i_j} \in \mathit{Terms}(\mathcal{F}_\mathcal{T}, \mathcal{V})$. Hence, either Theory$_1$ or Theory$_2$ applies to $C_{i_j}\sigma_{i_j} \approx r\sigma_{i_j}$.

If $n_{i_j} > 0$, then

$$C_{i_j}[f(t_{i_j,1}^*, y^*), \ldots, f(t_{i_j,n_{i_j}}^*, y^*)]\sigma_{i_j}$$
$$= C_{i_j}\sigma_{i_j}[f(t_{i_j,1}^*\sigma_{i_j}, s^*), \ldots, f(t_{i_j,n_{i_j}}^*\sigma_{i_j}, s^*)].$$

Now, if $x_{l_1} = x_{l_2}$, then there exists $\langle l_1, l_2, \mathcal{C} \rangle \in \mathcal{ImpEq}(f)$ such that $x_{k_1} = x_{k_2}$ for all $\langle k_1, k_2 \rangle \in \mathcal{C}$. But since the arguments of $f(x^*, s^*)$ and $f(s_{i_j}^*, y^*)$ are $\mathcal{T}$-unifiable by σ_{i_j}, this means $s_{i_j,k_1}\sigma_{i_j} \approx_\mathcal{T} s_{i_j,k_2}\sigma_{i_j}$ for all $\langle k_1, k_2 \rangle \in \mathcal{C}$. Now, the definition of $\mathcal{ImpEq}(f)$ implies $t_{i_j,k,l_1}\sigma_{i_j} \approx_\mathcal{T} t_{i_j,k,l_2}\sigma_{i_j}$ for all $1 \leq k \leq n_{i_j}$.

Hence, Simplify applies n_{i_j} times to $C_{i_j}\sigma_{i_j}[f(t_{i_j,1}^*\sigma_{i_j}, s^*), \ldots, f(t_{i_j,n_{i_j}}^*\sigma_{i_j}, s^*)]$ using the rule $f(x^*, s^*) \to r \in \mathcal{H}$, to get $C_{i_j}\sigma_{i_j}[r\tau_{i_j,1}, \ldots, r\tau_{i_j,n_{i_j}}] \approx r\sigma_{i_j}$, where $\tau_{i_j,k} = \{x^* \mapsto t_{i_j,k}^*\sigma_{i_j}\}$. Since both sides are in $\mathit{Terms}(\mathcal{F}_\mathcal{T}, \mathcal{V})$, either Theory$_1$ or Theory$_2$ applies. $\qquad\square$

With this theorem many conjectures can be handled which did not fall in the class of simple conjectures in [15].

Example 10. Consider this TRS over $\mathcal{T}_C$.

$\max(0, y) \to y$	$\max(s(x), 0) \to s(x)$	$\max(s(x), s(y)) \to s(\max(x, y))$
$\min(0, y) \to 0$	$\min(s(x), 0) \to 0$	$\min(s(x), s(y)) \to s(\min(x, y))$
$x < 0 \to \mathsf{false}$	$0 < s(y) \to \mathsf{true}$	$s(x) < s(y) \to x < y$
$0 \leq y \to \mathsf{true}$	$s(x) \leq 0 \to \mathsf{false}$	$s(x) \leq s(y) \to x \leq y$

Then, the following conjectures can be decided using Theorem 9:

$$\min(x, x) \approx x \qquad\qquad \max(x, x) \approx x$$
$$x < x \approx \mathsf{false} \qquad\qquad x \leq x \approx \mathsf{true}$$
$$x < x \approx \mathsf{true} \qquad\qquad x \leq x \approx \mathsf{false}$$

For this, we notice that $\mathcal{ImpEq}(f) = \{\langle 1, 2, \{\langle 1, 2 \rangle\}\rangle\}$ for $f \in \{\min, \max, <, \leq\}$. $\lozenge$

4.1   Relaxing $\mathcal{ImpEq}$

In some cases, the conditions of Definition 8 can be relaxed. Firstly, there can be conjectures for which the inductive hypotheses need not be applied if the recursive calls already rewrite to terms in the decidable theory using $\mathcal{R}$.

Example 11. Consider the TRS defining gcd over $\mathcal{T}_{PA}$.

$$
\begin{array}{ll}
1: \quad \gcd(x, 0) \to x & 3: \gcd(x + y + 1, y + 1) \to \gcd(x, y + 1) \\
2: \gcd(0, y + 1) \to y + 1 & 4: \gcd(x + 1, x + y + 1) \to \gcd(x + 1, y)
\end{array}
$$

Assume the conjecture $\gcd(x', x') \approx x'$ is to be proven. Theorem 9 cannot be used, since $\langle 1, 2, \{1, 2\}\rangle \notin \mathcal{ImpEq}(\gcd)$ because $x + y + 1 \approx y + 1 \Longrightarrow x \approx y + 1$, which is obtained from rule 3, is not $\mathcal{T}_{PA}$-valid.

However, there is a successful derivation.

$$
\begin{array}{ll}
& (\{\gcd(x', x') \approx x'\}, \emptyset) \\
\vdash_{\mathsf{Expand}} & (\{0 \approx 0, y + 1 \approx \gcd(0, y + 1), x + 1 \approx \gcd(x + 1, 0)\}, \{\gcd(x', x') \to x'\}) \\
\vdash_{\mathsf{Simplify}} & (\{0 \approx 0, y + 1 \approx y + 1, x + 1 \approx \gcd(x + 1, 0)\}, \{\gcd(x', x') \to x'\}) \\
\vdash_{\mathsf{Simplify}} & (\{0 \approx 0, y + 1 \approx y + 1, x + 1 \approx x + 1\}, \{\gcd(x', x') \to x\}) \\
\vdash^3_{\mathsf{Theory}_1} & (\emptyset, \{\gcd(x', x') \to x'\})
\end{array}
$$

The key observation is that the recursive calls that are generated by Expand simplify to terms in $\mathit{Terms}(\mathcal{F}_{\mathcal{T}_{PA}}, \mathcal{V})$ using just rewrite rules in $\mathcal{R}$, without using the inductive hypothesis.   ◇

Secondly, general terms from a decidable theory can be allowed on inductive positions in a conjecture if it can be ensured that the hypotheses will be applicable if they are needed. Notice that applicability of a hypothesis means that it $\mathcal{T}$-matches the recursive call generated by Expand.

Example 12. Continuing Example 10, we attempt to prove the conjecture $x' < \mathsf{s}(x') \approx \mathsf{true}$, which is nonlinear and has the term $\mathsf{s}(x')$ on an inductive position. The proof attempt is as follows:

$$
\begin{array}{l}
(\{x' < \mathsf{s}(x') \approx \mathsf{true}\}, \emptyset) \vdash_{\mathsf{Expand}} (\{\mathsf{true} \approx \mathsf{true}, \mathsf{true} \approx x < \mathsf{s}(x)\}, \{x' < \mathsf{s}(x') \to \mathsf{true}\}) \\
\qquad\qquad \vdash_{\mathsf{Simplify}} (\{\mathsf{true} \approx \mathsf{true}\}, \{x' < \mathsf{s}(x') \to \mathsf{true}\}) \\
\qquad\qquad \vdash_{\mathsf{Theory}_1} (\emptyset, \{x' < \mathsf{s}(x') \to \mathsf{true}\}).
\end{array}
$$

The key observation is that the recursive call generated by Expand has the "right" form for the inductive hypothesis to apply, i.e., $(x < y)\sigma$ has the form $z < \mathsf{s}(z)$ where σ is the substitution generated by Expand from the third rule defining "$<$", i.e, $\sigma = \{y \mapsto \mathsf{s}(x), x' \mapsto \mathsf{s}(x)\}$.   ◇

For formalizing these observations, we define the set $\mathcal{TPat}(\mathsf{f})$. In the following, we identify two tuples p^*, q^* of the same length containing terms from $\mathit{Terms}(\mathcal{F}_{\mathcal{T}}, \mathcal{V})$ if q^* can be obtained from p^* by means of a variable renaming.

Definition 13 ($\mathcal{TPat}(\mathsf{f})$). *Let* f *be* $\mathcal{T}$*-based and defined by the rules* $\mathsf{f}(s_i^*) \rightarrow C_i[\mathsf{f}(t_{i,1}^*), \ldots, \mathsf{f}(t_{i,n_i}^*)]$ *for* $1 \leq i \leq n$. *Then we define* $p^* \in \mathcal{TPat}(\mathsf{f})$ *for* $p^* \in Terms(\mathcal{F}_{\mathcal{T}}, \mathcal{V})$ *iff for all* $1 \leq i \leq n$, *all* $\sigma \in \mathcal{CU}_{\mathcal{T}}(s_i^* \approx_{\mathcal{T}}^? p^*)$[3] *and all* $1 \leq k \leq n_i$ *either*

1. p^* $\mathcal{T}$*-matches* $t_{i,k}^*\sigma$, *or*
2. $\mathsf{f}(t_{i,k}^*)\sigma \rightarrow_{\mathcal{R}/\mathcal{T}}^* q$ *for some* $q \in Terms(\mathcal{F}_{\mathcal{T}}, \mathcal{V})$.

Condition (1.) ensures that the inductive hypothesis is applicable, as demonstrated in Example 12. Condition (2.) is for cases like Example 11 where the inductive hypothesis is not needed. Also, notice that condition (1.) subsumes $\mathcal{ImpEq}(\mathsf{f})$.

The set $\mathcal{TPat}(\mathsf{f})$ is in general infinite. However, it does not have to be computed at compile-time. Instead, it can be generated *lazily* as needed and cached for later reuse.

Definition 14 (Generalized Simple Conjectures). *A generalized simple conjecture is a conjecture of the form* $\mathsf{f}(p^*) \approx r$ *such that* $\mathsf{f}(p^*) \succ r$, *the function* f *is* $\mathcal{T}$*-based,* $r \in Terms(\mathcal{F}_{\mathcal{T}}, \mathcal{V})$, *and* $p^* \in \mathcal{TPat}(\mathsf{f})$.

Example 15. Continuing Example 11, the conjecture $\gcd(x', x') \approx x'$ is generalized simple since $(x', x') \in \mathcal{TPat}(\gcd)$. Indeed, for rule 3, $\mathcal{CU}_{T_{PA}}(\{x' \approx_{T_{PA}}^? x + y + 1, x' \approx_{T_{PA}}^? y + 1\}) = \{\sigma\}$ where $\sigma = \{x \mapsto 0, x' \mapsto y + 1\}$, and for this σ we have $\gcd(x, y + 1)\sigma = \gcd(0, y + 1) \rightarrow_{\mathcal{R}/T_{PA}} y + 1 \in Terms(\mathcal{F}_{T_{PA}}, \mathcal{V})$, i.e., (2.) in Definition 13 applies. For rule 4, we get $\sigma = \{y \mapsto 0, x' \mapsto x + 1\}$ and $\gcd(x + 1, y)\sigma = \gcd(x + 1, 0) \rightarrow_{\mathcal{R}/\mathcal{T}} x + 1 \in Terms(\mathcal{F}_{T_{PA}}, \mathcal{V})$. ◊

The following theorem gives a decision procedure for generalized simple conjectures, a substantially expanded class compared to the class of simple conjectures in [15], which allows nonlinear conjectures as well as conjectures in which general terms from a decidable theory can appear on inductive positions.

Theorem 16. *The inductive validity of a generalized simple conjecture is decidable using the strategy* $\mathsf{Expand} \cdot \mathsf{Simplify}^* \cdot (\mathsf{Theory}_1 \cup \mathsf{Theory}_2)^*$.

Example 17. Continuing Example 12, the conjecture $x' < \mathsf{s}(x') \approx \mathsf{true}$ is generalized simple since $(x', \mathsf{s}(x')) \in \mathcal{TPat}(<)$. Indeed, for $\mathsf{s}(x) < \mathsf{s}(y) \rightarrow x < y$, we get $\mathcal{CU}_{T_C}(\{\mathsf{s}(x) \approx_{T_C}^? x', \mathsf{s}(y) \approx_{T_C}^? \mathsf{s}(x')\}) = \{\sigma\}$ where $\sigma = \{x' \mapsto \mathsf{s}(x), y \mapsto \mathsf{s}(x)\}$, and $(x < y)\sigma = x < \mathsf{s}(x)$, where $(x, \mathsf{s}(x))$ is $\mathcal{T}_C$-matched by $(x', \mathsf{s}(x'))$. ◊

Example 18. Continuing Example 11, we consider the conjecture $\gcd(2 \cdot x', 2) \approx 2$ about gcd. We show that $(2 \cdot x', 2) \in \mathcal{TPat}(\gcd)$. For rules 1 and 2, there are no recursive calls on the right sides. For rule 3, $\mathcal{CU}_{T_{PA}}(\{2 \cdot x' \approx_{T_{PA}}^? x + y + 1, 2 \approx_{T_{PA}}^? y + 1\}) = \{\sigma\}$, where $\sigma = \{x' \mapsto z + 1, y \mapsto 1, x \mapsto 2 \cdot z\}$ for a fresh variable z. Now, $\gcd(x, y + 1)\sigma = \gcd(2 \cdot z, 2)$, where $(2 \cdot z, 2)$ is $\mathcal{T}_{PA}$-matched by $(2 \cdot x', 2)$. Rule 4 yields $\mathcal{CU}_{T_{PA}}(\{2 \cdot x' \approx_{T_{PA}}^? x + 1, 2 \approx_{T_{PA}}^? x + y + 1\}) = \{\sigma\}$, with $\sigma = \{x' \mapsto 1, x \mapsto 1, y \mapsto 0\}$. Now, $\gcd(x + 1, y)\sigma = \gcd(2, 0) \rightarrow_{\mathcal{R}/\mathcal{T}} 2 \in Terms(\mathcal{F}_{T_{PA}}, \mathcal{V})$. Thus, the conjecture $\gcd(2 \cdot x', 2) \approx 2$ is generalized simple. ◊

---

[3] The variables in p^* are suitably renamed to be disjoint from the variables in s_i^*.

5   Jointly $\mathcal{T}$-Based Functions

The class of $\mathcal{T}$-based functions is quite restrictive in the sense that a $\mathcal{T}$-based function f can only make recursive calls to f, but not to any other function g. This restriction is imposed to ensure that the strategy Expand · Simplify* leads to conjectures in $\mathcal{T}$. Below, we generalize the definition of a $\mathcal{T}$-based function by allowing a finite number of $\mathcal{T}$-based functions to be defined together as a group, where a function in the group may call other functions in the group in its definition. This generalization allows for mutually recursive functions and classes of conjectures about them that can be decided automatically.

Example 19. We define maxlist using the function max from Example 10.

$$\text{maxlist}(x, \text{nil}) \rightarrow \text{nil} \qquad\qquad \text{maxlist}(\text{nil}, \text{cons}(x', y')) \rightarrow \text{nil}$$
$$\text{maxlist}(\text{cons}(x, y), \text{cons}(x', y')) \rightarrow \text{cons}(\text{max}(x, x'), \text{maxlist}(y, y'))$$

While max is $\mathcal{T}_C$-based, maxlist is not $\mathcal{T}_C$-based since it calls max. Hence, the conjecture $\text{maxlist}(x'', x'') \approx x''$ is not simple. Indeed, an attempt to prove this conjecture gets stuck since one ends up with $\text{cons}(x, y) \approx \text{cons}(\text{max}(x, x), y)$, which cannot be simplified without knowing $\text{max}(x, x) \approx x$ in conjunction with the original conjecture.   ◊

Below, we relax the restriction on $\mathcal{T}$-based functions by introducing the notion of a *jointly $\mathcal{T}$-based* set of functions. A set F of functions is jointly $\mathcal{T}$-based if the rules defining F make recursive calls only to functions in F again. It is now possible for a recursive definition to use other functions in the group as well.

Definition 20 (Jointly $\mathcal{T}$-based Functions). *The set* $\mathsf{F} = \{\mathsf{f}_1, \ldots, \mathsf{f}_n\}$ *of functions* $\mathsf{f}_i \in \mathcal{F}_d$ *is jointly $\mathcal{T}$-based if all rules* $l \rightarrow r \in \mathcal{R}$ *with* $l(\Lambda) \in \mathsf{F}$ *have the form* $\mathsf{f}_i(s^*) \rightarrow C[\mathsf{f}_{i_1}(t_1^*), \ldots, \mathsf{f}_{i_n}(t_n^*)]$, *where* $s^*, t_j^* \in \textit{Terms}(\mathcal{F}_{\mathcal{T}}, \mathcal{V})$, $\mathsf{f}_{i_j} \in \mathsf{F}$ *for all* $1 \leq j \leq n$, *and C is a context over* $\mathcal{F}_{\mathcal{T}}$.

In particular, this definition allows for, but is not limited to, mutually recursive functions. Clearly, f is $\mathcal{T}$-based iff $\{\mathsf{f}\}$ is jointly $\mathcal{T}$-based, hence Definition 20 subsumes Definition 2.

To handle nonlinear conjectures for jointly $\mathcal{T}$-based functions, $\mathcal{I}mp\mathcal{E}q(\mathsf{f})$ does not suffice in order to guarantee that the inductive hypotheses are applicable. Instead, the whole set F of jointly $\mathcal{T}$-based functions has to be taken into consideration. The set $\mathcal{I}mp\mathcal{E}q(\mathsf{F})$ generalizes the set $\mathcal{I}mp\mathcal{E}q(\mathsf{f})$ by carrying the function symbols along with the positions $l_1, l_2, k_{j,1}, k_{j,2}$ from Definition 6. A formal definition of the set $\mathcal{I}mp\mathcal{E}q(\mathsf{F})$ can be found in [5, Definition 17]. If $\mathsf{F} = \{\mathsf{f}\}$, we identify $\mathcal{I}mp\mathcal{E}q(\mathsf{F})$ and $\mathcal{I}mp\mathcal{E}q(\mathsf{f})$. The set $\mathcal{I}mp\mathcal{E}q(\mathsf{F})$ can be computed from $\mathcal{R}$ with the help of a decision procedure for $\mathcal{T}$. See [5, Appendix A] for details. $\mathcal{T}Pat(\mathsf{f})$ can similarly be extended to $\mathcal{T}Pat(\mathsf{F})$.

Example 21. Considering the jointly $\mathcal{T}$-based set $\mathsf{F} = \{\text{max}, \text{maxlist}\}$ from Example 19, we get $\mathcal{I}mp\mathcal{E}q(\mathsf{F}) = \{\langle \text{max}, 1, 2, \{\langle \text{max}, 1, 2\rangle, \langle \text{maxlist}, 1, 2\rangle\}\rangle, \langle \text{maxlist}, 1, 2, \{\langle \text{maxlist}, 1, 2\rangle\}\rangle\}$ since all of $\mathsf{s}(x) \approx \mathsf{s}(y) \Longrightarrow x \approx y$, $\text{cons}(x, y) \approx \text{cons}(x', y') \Longrightarrow x \approx x'$ (for max), and $\text{cons}(x, y) \approx \text{cons}(x', y') \Longrightarrow y \approx y'$ (for maxlist) are $\mathcal{T}_C$-valid.   ◊

Now, a *conjunctive simple conjecture* has to make a conjecture about each function in a set F of jointly $\mathcal{T}$-based functions.

Definition 22 (Conjunctive Simple Conjectures). *A conjunctive simple conjecture is a conjecture of the form* $f_1(x_1^*) \approx r_1 \wedge \ldots \wedge f_n(x_n^*) \approx r_n$ *such that* $f_i(x_i^*) \succ r_i$ *for all* $1 \leq i \leq n$, *the set* $F = \{f_1, \ldots, f_n\}$ *is jointly* $\mathcal{T}$-based, $r_i \in \mathit{Terms}(\mathcal{F}_\mathcal{T}, \mathcal{V})$ *for all* $1 \leq i \leq n$, *and if* $x_{i,l_1} = x_{i,l_2}$ *then exists* $\langle f_i, l_1, l_2, \mathcal{C} \rangle \in \mathcal{ImpEq}(F)$ *such that* $x_{j,k_1} = x_{j,k_2}$ *for all* $\langle f_j, k_1, k_2 \rangle \in \mathcal{C}$.

Example 23. Continuing Example 21, $\mathsf{maxlist}(x'', x'') \approx x'' \wedge \mathsf{max}(y'', y'') \approx y''$ is a conjunctive simple conjectures. $\diamondsuit$

The following theorem generalizes Theorem 9 and gives a decision procedure for conjunctive simple conjectures. An analogous theorem can be obtained for *conjunctive generalized simple conjectures* which use $\mathcal{TPat}$ instead of $\mathcal{ImpEq}$ [5].

Theorem 24. *The inductive validity of a conjunctive simple conjecture is decidable using the strategy* $\mathsf{Expand}^* \cdot \mathsf{Simplify}^* \cdot (\mathsf{Theory}_1 \cup \mathsf{Theory}_2)^*$, *where* Expand *is applied once to each equation of the conjecture.*

Example 25. Consider the following TRS over $\mathcal{T}_C$, where mix takes two lists l_1, l_2 and constructs a new list by taking elements on odd numbered positions from l_1 and elements on even numbered positions from l_2.

$$\mathsf{mix}(x, \mathsf{nil}) \to \mathsf{nil} \qquad\qquad \mathsf{mix}(\mathsf{nil}, \mathsf{cons}(x', y')) \to \mathsf{nil}$$
$$\mathsf{mix}(\mathsf{cons}(x, y), \mathsf{cons}(x', y')) \to \mathsf{cons}(x, \mathsf{mix}'(y, y'))$$
$$\mathsf{mix}'(x, \mathsf{nil}) \to \mathsf{nil} \qquad\qquad \mathsf{mix}'(\mathsf{nil}, \mathsf{cons}(x', y')) \to \mathsf{nil}$$
$$\mathsf{mix}'(\mathsf{cons}(x, y), \mathsf{cons}(x', y')) \to \mathsf{cons}(x', \mathsf{mix}(y, y'))$$

$\langle \mathsf{mix}, 1, 2, \{\langle \mathsf{mix}', 1, 2 \rangle\} \rangle$ and $\langle \mathsf{mix}', 1, 2, \{\langle \mathsf{mix}, 1, 2 \rangle\} \rangle$ are in $\mathcal{ImpEq}(\{\mathsf{mix}, \mathsf{mix}'\})$. Thus, $\mathsf{mix}(x'', x'') \approx x'' \wedge \mathsf{mix}'(y'', y'') \approx y''$ is a conjunctive simple conjecture. $\diamondsuit$

6 Nonlinear Complex Conjectures

So far, we have considered conjectures in which only a single defined function symbol appears in the left side of each equation within a conjecture. Similar to [15,8], conjectures in which the left side has nested $\mathcal{T}$-based functions can also be decided automatically provided their definitions are *compatible*. Furthermore, the results from the previous two sections extend to such complex conjectures under the same conditions as in [15]. Below, we show this with a particular emphasis on illustrating our ideas with examples. More technical details and proofs can be found in [5].

Since a complex conjecture with nested function symbols can have many nonvariable subterm positions where Expand is applicable we make use of *inductively complete positions*, which are a special case of the general definition in [6]. This enables us to select a position in a nested term to which the computation of critical pairs can be restricted. This notion is not needed for simple conjectures since for them there is only one position on which critical pairs can be computed.

Definition 26 (Inductively Complete Positions). *A position p in a term t is* inductively complete *if $t|_p = f(q^*)$, where $f \in \mathcal{F}_d$ and $q^* \in \mathit{Terms}(\mathcal{F}_\mathcal{T}, \mathcal{V})$.*

From now on, the inference rule Expand is replaced by the inference rule Expand' given in Figure 2.

$$\text{Expand'}\quad \frac{\mathcal{E} \cup \{r_1 \mathrel{\dot{\approx}} r_2\}, \mathcal{H}}{\mathcal{E} \cup \mathcal{E}', \mathcal{H} \cup \{r_1 \to r_2\}} \quad \begin{array}{l} \text{if } r_1 \succ r_2 \text{ and } \mathcal{E}' = \mathcal{CP}'(\mathcal{R}, r_1 \to r_2, p) \\ \text{for an inductively complete position } p \text{ in } r_1 \end{array}$$

Fig. 2. The inference rule Expand'

A function g is *jointly compatible* with a set of functions F on argument j if in any term $g(\ldots, f(\ldots), \ldots)$, where $f(\ldots)$ is on the jth argument of g and $f \in F$, every context created by rewriting f will move outside the term by rewriting g.

Definition 27 (Jointly Compatible Functions). *Let $F = \{f_1, \ldots, f_n\}$ be jointly $\mathcal{T}$-based, let g be $\mathcal{T}$-based, let $1 \leq j \leq m = \text{arity}(g)$. Then g is jointly compatible with F on argument j if all rules $f_i(s^*) \to C[f_{i_1}(t_1^*), \ldots, f_{i_n}(t_n^*)]$ satisfy*

$$g(x_1, \ldots, x_{j-1}, C[z_1, \ldots, z_n], x_{j+1}, \ldots, x_m) \;\to^*_{\mathcal{R}/\mathcal{T}}$$
$$D[g(x_1, \ldots, x_{j-1}, z_{i_1}, x_{j+1}, \ldots, x_m), \ldots, g(x_1, \ldots, x_{j-1}, z_{i_k}, x_{j+1}, \ldots, x_m)]$$

for a context D over $\mathcal{F}_\mathcal{T}$, $i_1, \ldots, i_k \in \{1, \ldots, n\}$, and $z_i \notin \mathcal{V}(D)$ for all $1 \leq i \leq n$.

The notion of compatibility in [8] is a special case of this definition. If $F = \{f\}$ we also say that g is compatible with f.

Example 28. Consider this TRS over $\mathcal{T}_C$.

$$
\begin{array}{ll}
1 : \text{zip}(x, \text{nil}) \to \text{pnil} & 2 : \text{zip}(\text{nil}, \text{cons}(x', y')) \to \text{pnil} \\
3 : \text{zip}(\text{cons}(x, y), \text{cons}(x', y')) \to \text{pcons}(\text{pair}(x, x'), \text{zip}(y, y')) \\
4 : \text{fst}(\text{pnil}) \to \text{nil} & 5 : \text{fst}(\text{pcons}(\text{pair}(x, x'), y)) \to \text{cons}(x, \text{fst}(y))
\end{array}
$$

Then, fst is compatible with zip on argument 1. For rules 1 and 2, C is pnil (a context without holes), and fst(pnil) rewrites to nil using rule 4, i.e., $D = \text{nil}$. For rule 3, C is pcons(pair(x, x'), $\square$) and fst(pcons(pair(x, x'), z_1)) rewrites to cons(x, fst(z_1)) by rule 5, i.e., $D = \text{cons}(x, \square)$. $\diamondsuit$

As in [15,8], the concept of compatibility can be extended to arbitrarily deep nestings. To this end, we define the notion of a *compatibility sequence*.

Definition 29 (Joint Compatibility Sequences). *Let $L = \{l_1, \ldots, l_n\}$ be a set of terms in $\mathit{Terms}(\mathcal{F}, \mathcal{V})$, let $g_1, \ldots, g_d$ be $\mathcal{T}$-based for some $d \geq 0$, and let the set of function symbols $F = \{f_1, \ldots, f_n\}$ be jointly $\mathcal{T}$-based. The sequence $\langle g_1, \ldots, g_d, F \rangle$ is a* joint compatibility sequence *on arguments $\langle j_1, \ldots, j_d \rangle$ and the set $L = \{l_1, \ldots, l_n\}$ of terms has* this joint compatibility sequence *if*

1. g_i is compatible with g_{i+1} on argument j_i for all $1 \leq i \leq d - 1$, and g_d is jointly compatible with F, and

2. $l_k = g_1(p_1^*, g_2(p_2^*, \ldots g_d(p_d^*, f_k(x_k^*), q_d^*) \ldots, q_2^*), q_1^*)$, where the $x_{k,i}$ do not occur elsewhere in l_k, all $p_i^*, q_i^* \in Terms(\mathcal{F}_{\mathcal{T}}, \mathcal{V})$, and $g_i(p_i^*, g_{i+1}(\ldots), q_i^*)|_{j_i} = g_{i+1}(\ldots)$ for all $1 \le i \le d-1$, as well as $g_d(p_d^*, f_k(x_k^*), q_d^*)|_{j_d} = f_k(x_k^*)$.

Informally, this definition ensures that the l_i are constructed using (jointly) compatible functions in the appropriate positions.

Again, the compatibility sequences of [8] are a special case of this definition. If $L = \{l\}$ (and thus $F = \{f\}$) we also say that l has a compatibility sequence where we write f instead of F in the last component.

If l_i is as in the definition, then the position $p = j_1.j_2.\cdots.j_d$ is an inductively complete position in l_i.

Definition 30 (Conjunctive Complex Conjectures). A conjunctive complex conjecture is a conjecture of the form $l_1 \approx r_1 \wedge \ldots \wedge l_n \approx r_n$ such that $l_i \succ r_i$ for all $1 \le i \le n$, where the r_i are in $Terms(\mathcal{F}_{\mathcal{T}}, \mathcal{V})$, the $l_i = D[f_i(x_i^*)]$ have a joint compatibility sequence, the set $F = \{f_1, \ldots, f_n\}$ is jointly $\mathcal{T}$-based, and if $x_{i,l_1} = x_{i,l_2}$ then exists $\langle f_i, l_1, l_2, \mathcal{C} \rangle \in Imp\mathcal{E}q(F)$ such that $x_{j,k_1} = x_{j,k_2}$ for all $\langle f_j, k_1, k_2 \rangle \in \mathcal{C}$.

If the group of joint $\mathcal{T}$-based functions consists of a single function, then we call a conjecture as defined above complex, but in contrast to the complex conjectures of [15] we allow for nonlinear complex conjectures.

The following theorem extends the results from the previous two sections to conjunctive complex conjectures and gives a decision procedure for this class.

Theorem 31. The inductive validity of a conjunctive complex conjecture is decidable using the strategy Expand'*·Simplify*·(Theory$_1$∪Theory$_2$)*, where Expand' is applied once to each equation of the conjecture at the innermost position, i.e., at the f_i for all $1 \le i \le n$.

Example 32. Continuing Example 28, the term $fst(zip(x'', x''))$ has the compatibility sequence $\langle fst, zip \rangle$ on arguments $\langle 1 \rangle$. Furthermore we have $\langle 1, 2, \{\langle 1, 2 \rangle\} \rangle \in Imp\mathcal{E}q(zip)$. Thus, $fst(zip(x'', x'')) \approx x''$ is a complex conjecture. Due to the nonlinearity, it is not permitted in [15]. $\Diamond$

Example 33. We consider mutually recursive functions in this example. Take the function fst defined in Example 28, and add the following rules defining stitch, where pair is a new constructor.

$$stitch(x, nil) \rightarrow pnil \qquad\qquad stitch(nil, cons(x', y')) \rightarrow pnil$$
$$stitch(cons(x, y), cons(x', y')) \rightarrow pcons(pair(x, x'), stitch'(y, y'))$$
$$stitch'(x, nil) \rightarrow pnil \qquad\qquad stitch'(nil, cons(x', y')) \rightarrow pnil$$
$$stitch'(cons(x, y), cons(x', y')) \rightarrow pcons(pair(x', x), stitch(y, y'))$$

Then $F = \{stitch, stitch'\}$ is jointly $\mathcal{T}$-based and fst is jointly compatible with F, since for the third stitch-rule, the term $fst(pcons(pair(x, x'), z_1))$ rewrites to $cons(x, fst(z_1))$, and similarly for the third stitch'-rule. Furthermore, the set $L = \{fst(stitch(x'', x'')), fst(stitch'(y'', y''))\}$ has the joint compatibility sequence

$\langle \mathsf{fst}, \{\mathsf{stitch}, \mathsf{stitch}'\} \rangle$ on arguments $\langle 1 \rangle$. Thus, the conjecture $\mathsf{fst}(\mathsf{stitch}(x'', x'')) \approx x'' \wedge \mathsf{fst}(\mathsf{stitch}'(y'', y'')) \approx y''$ is a conjunctive complex conjecture since also both $\langle \mathsf{stitch}, 1, 2, \{\langle \mathsf{stitch}', 1, 2 \rangle\} \rangle$ and $\langle \mathsf{stitch}', 1, 2, \{\langle \mathsf{stitch}, 1, 2 \rangle\} \rangle$ are in $\mathcal{I}mp\mathcal{E}q(\mathsf{F})$. $\Diamond$

For a conjunctive complex conjectures, $\mathcal{T}\mathcal{P}at(\mathsf{F})$ can only be used if condition (2.) in Definition 13 is not needed. The class of *conjunctive generalized complex conjectures* is obtained from Definition 30 by replacing $\mathcal{I}mp\mathcal{E}q$ with $\mathcal{T}\mathcal{P}at$ using this restriction.

Example 34. Consider the TRS defining zip and fst from Example 28 and the conjecture $\mathsf{fst}(\mathsf{zip}(y'', \mathsf{cons}(x'', y''))) \approx y''$. Firstly, $(y'', \mathsf{cons}(x'', y'')) \in \mathcal{T}\mathcal{P}at(\mathsf{zip})$. For rule 3, we get $\mathcal{CU}_{\mathcal{T}_C}(\{y'' \approx^?_{\mathcal{T}_C} \mathsf{cons}(x, y), \mathsf{cons}(x'', y') \approx^?_{\mathcal{T}_C} \mathsf{cons}(x', y')\}) = \{\sigma\}$, where $\sigma = \{x' \mapsto x'', y' \mapsto \mathsf{cons}(x, y), y'' \mapsto \mathsf{cons}(x, y)\}$. Now, $\mathsf{zip}(y, y')\sigma = \mathsf{zip}(y, \mathsf{cons}(x, y))$, and $(y, \mathsf{cons}(x, y))$ is $\mathcal{T}_C$-matched by $(y'', \mathsf{cons}(x'', y''))$. Thus, the conjecture is generalized complex. $\Diamond$

7   Conclusion and Further Work

This paper shows how implicit induction methods can be used to integrate inductive reasoning into decision procedures without losing automation. We have given decision procedures based on implicit induction methods for the inductive validity of large classes of simple and complex conjectures about recursively defined theory-based functions, satisfying certain conditions that are checkable syntactically or using the decision procedure for the underlying theory.

We have broadened the class of decidable inductive conjectures permitted in [15] significantly by allowing nonlinear conjectures as well as general terms from the decidable theory on inductive positions. We have extended the notion of theory-based functions to allow for recursive calls to other function symbols as long as all the functions are being defined together. This extension allows us to decide inductive properties of mutually recursive functions automatically.

In [8], the class of conjectures whose inductive validity can be decided is expanded to linear conjectures having defined function symbols on both sides. We believe that this class can be decided using implicit induction methods as well (if the conjecture can be oriented). However, this possibility needs to be investigated further. Then it should also be possible to extend the class in [8] to non-linear conjectures and jointly theory-based functions.

It is shown in this paper that a conjunction of conjectures about all jointly theory-based definitions has to be considered simultaneously. We are confident that it is possible to decide a conjecture about a single function in a set of jointly defined functions by automatically generating conjectures about other functions in the set which are needed in a proof attempt. This might require techniques similar to the ones in [16]. We are planning to examine this idea further.

A preliminary implementation and evaluation of the results given in this paper for $\mathcal{T}_C$ is available at http://www.cs.unm.edu/~spf/sail/. On average, checking whether a conjecture satisfies the conditions that make it decidable takes half the time of the actual proof attempt.

Acknowledgments. We thank Mahadevan Subramaniam and the anonymous referees for useful comments.

References

1. F. Baader and T. Nipkow. *Term Rewriting and All That.* Cambridge University Press, 1998.
2. L. Bachmair. Proof by consistency in equational theories. In *Proc. LICS '88*, pages 228–233, 1988.
3. T. Ball and S. K. Rajamani. The SLAM toolkit. In *Proc. CAV '01*, LNCS 2102, pages 260–264, 2001.
4. A. Bouhoula. Automated theorem proving by test set induction. *Journal of Symbolic Computation*, 23(1):47–77, 1997.
5. S. Falke and D. Kapur. Implicit induction methods and decision procedures. Technical Report TR-CS-2006-04, Department of Computer Science, University of New Mexico, available at http://www.cs.unm.edu/research/, 2006.
6. L. Fribourg. A strong restriction of the inductive completion procedure. *Journal of Symbolic Computation*, 8(3):253–276, 1989.
7. J. Giesl and D. Kapur. Decidable classes of inductive theorems. In *Proc. IJCAR '01*, LNCS 2083, pages 469–484, 2001.
8. J. Giesl and D. Kapur. Deciding inductive validity of equations. In *Proc. CADE '03*, LNAI 2741, pages 17–31, 2003.
9. T. A. Henzinger, R. Jhala, R. Majumdar, and G. Sutre. Software verification with BLAST. In *Proc. SPIN '03*, LNCS 2648, pages 235–239, 2003.
10. G. P. Huet and J.-M. Hullot. Proofs by induction in equational theories with constructors. *Journal of Computer and Systems Sciences*, 25(2):239–266, 1982.
11. J.-P. Jouannaud and E. Kounalis. Automatic proofs by induction in theories without constructors. *Information and Computation*, 82(1):1–33, 1989.
12. D. Kapur, J. Giesl, and M. Subramaniam. Induction and decision procedures. *Revista de la Real Academia de Ciencias, Serie A*, 98(1):153–180, 2004.
13. D. Kapur and D. R. Musser. Proof by consistency. *Artificial Intelligence*, 31(2):125–157, 1987.
14. D. Kapur, P. Narendran, and H. Zhang. Automating inductionless induction using test sets. *Journal of Symbolic Computation*, 11(1–2):81–111, 1991.
15. D. Kapur and M. Subramaniam. Extending decision procedures with induction schemes. In *Proc. CADE '00*, LNCS 1831, pages 324–345, 2000.
16. D. Kapur and M. Subramaniam. Automatic generation of simple lemmas from recursive definitions using decision procedures—preliminary report. In *Proc. ASIAN '03*, LNCS 2896, pages 125–145, 2003.
17. W. Küchlin. Inductive completion by ground proof transformation. In *Resolution of Equations in Algebraic Structures Vol. 2*, pages 211–244. Academic Press, 1989.
18. D. R. Musser. On proving inductive properties of abstract data types. In *Proc. POPL '80*, pages 154–162, 1980.
19. U. S. Reddy. Term rewriting induction. In *Proc. CADE '90*, LNCS 449, pages 162–177, 1990.
20. H. Zhang, D. Kapur, and M. S. Krishnamoorthy. A mechanizable induction principle for equational specifications. In *Proc. CADE '88*, LNCS 310, pages 162–181, 1988.

Matching Modulo Superdevelopments
Application to Second-Order Matching

Germain Faure

Université Henri Poincaré & LORIA
BP 239, F-54506 Vandoeuvre-lès-Nancy France
faure@loria.fr

Abstract. To perform higher-order matching, we need to decide the $\beta\eta$-equivalence on λ-terms. The first way to do it is to use simply typed λ-calculus and this is the usual framework where higher-order matching is performed. Another approach consists in deciding a restricted equivalence based on finite superdevelopments. We consider higher-order matching modulo this equivalence over untyped λ-terms for which we propose a terminating, sound and complete matching algorithm.

This is in particular of interest since all second-order β-matches are matches modulo superdevelopments. We further propose a restriction to second-order matching that gives exactly all second-order matches.

Introduction

Higher-order matching and unification are two operations fundamental in various fields such as higher-order logic programming [Mil90] and logical frameworks [Pfe01], computational linguistics [DSP91], program transformation [HL78, Shi94, Vis05], higher-order rewriting [vOvR93, MN98, NP98], proof theory etc.

Higher-order matching is usually defined as the following problem: given a set of equations $s_i = t_i$ between *typed* λ-terms where the t_i do not contain free variables, is there a substitution σ such that for all i $s_i\sigma$ is equal to t_i modulo the usual $\beta(\eta)$ relation.

In [dMS01] O. De Moor and G. Sittampalam introduced a new approach to higher-order matching for automatic program transformation in an untyped setting. Matching equations are solved modulo a one-step reduction for an appropriate parallel β-reduction notion that does not coincide with the standard one of Tait and Martin-Löf. As the authors suggest in the paper, this operation, that always terminates even in an untyped context, represents in a certain sense an approximation of the β-normalization process.

The standard approximation of β-normal forms is given by complete developments [Bar84]. But the parallel β-normal forms used in [dMS01] provide a more precise approximation than the complete developments. Actually, the latter parallel β-reduction was introduced first by P. Aczel in [Acz78] and the corresponding approximation was introduced by F. van Raamsdonk [vR93] under the name of superdevelopments. They are an extended notion of finite developments

M. Hermann and A. Voronkov (Eds.): LPAR 2006, LNAI 4246, pp. 60–74, 2006.

that were introduced to prove the confluence of a general class of reduction systems containing λ-calculus and term rewrite systems. A superdevelopment is a reduction sequence that may reduce the redexes of the term, its residuals and some created redexes but not those created by the substitution of a variable in functional position by a λ-abstraction. The approximation given by superdevelopments coincides with β-normal forms when considering second-order terms.

In this paper, we consider matching equations built over untyped λ-terms and solve them modulo superdevelopments. The matching problems are of interest particularly because the set of matches modulo superdevelopments contains, but is not restricted to, second-order β-matches.

The one-step reduction modulo which one considers matching equations in [dMS01] "may be a little difficult to understand" as the authors of the original paper said. In this paper, we shed light on this reduction by giving a clear relationship with superdevelopments (and quoting the original definition of P. Aczel). The original algorithm is presented using transformation rules as suggested in [GS89]. This method provides an abstract and elegant way to give a clear separation between the operational and logical issues.

The main goal of this paper is convince that superdevelopments constitute a right tool for tackling the matching problems. We also claim that the background theory of superdevelopments provides nice intuitions and simplifications of the different proofs (w.r.t. [dMS01, Sit01]) especially *w.r.t.* the application to second-order matching.

In fact, the general approach of solving equations modulo a restricted notion of reduction can be useful to deal with higher-order matching in calculi for which a simple type system that ensures termination is difficult to find. This is for example the case of simply typed ρ-calculus [CLW03] which is not terminating. Higher-order matching in the ρ-calculus or in pure pattern calculus [JK06] are useful in the transformation of pattern-matching programs or in proof theory that handles rich proof-terms in the generalized deduction modulo [Wac06].

Road-map. The paper is organized as follows. The first section introduces the syntax and the superdevelopments. The second section is devoted to the presentation of matching modulo superdevelopments and its link with usual higher-order matching (second-order matching, third-order matching and matching of patterns à la Miller). Section 3 presents and studies[1] an algorithm to perform matching modulo superdevelopements in the λ-calculus. Section 4 explicitly analyzes the optional role of the η rule in the matching process. Throughout the paper, many examples are taken.

1   Preliminaries

In this section, we first recall some basic definitions and set some notations related to the λ-calculus. Then we define in two different ways superdevelopments as a restriction of the β-reduction. We refer the reader to [Bar84] or [Dow01] for the fundamental definitions and results on the λ-calculus.

---

[1] The proofs not given in the paper will be available in a journal paper.

1.1   Typed λ-Calculus and β-Reduction

Given a set of base types $\mathfrak{T}_0$, we define the set of types $\mathfrak{T}$ inductively as the smallest set containing $\mathfrak{T}_0$ and such that if $\alpha, \beta \in \mathfrak{T}$ then $(\alpha \to \beta) \in \mathfrak{T}$. The order of a type α denoted $\mathfrak{o}(\alpha)$ is equal to 1, if $\alpha \in \mathfrak{T}_0$. The order of a type $\alpha \to \beta$ is equal to $max(\mathfrak{o}(\alpha) + 1, \mathfrak{o}(\beta))$.

Definition 1 (Typed λ-terms). *Let $\mathcal{K}$ be a set of constants, having a unique type. For each type $\alpha \in \mathfrak{T}$, we assume given two countably infinite and disjoint sets of that type, denoted $\mathcal{X}_\alpha$ and $\mathcal{V}_\alpha$. Let $\mathcal{X} = \cup_{\alpha \in \mathfrak{T}} \mathcal{X}_\alpha$ be the set of variables and let $\mathcal{V} = \cup_{\alpha \in \mathfrak{T}} \mathcal{V}_\alpha$ be the set of matching variables. The set $\mathcal{T}_t$ of typed λ-terms is inductively defined as the smallest set containing all variables, all matching variables and all constants, and closed under the following rules:*
— If $A, B \in \mathcal{T}_t$ with type resp. $\alpha \to \beta$ and α then $(A \, B) \in \mathcal{T}_t$ with type β.
— If $A \in \mathcal{T}_t$ with type β, and $x \in \mathcal{X}_\alpha$ then $\lambda x \,.\, A \in \mathcal{T}_t$ with type $\alpha \to \beta$.

There are two different sets of "variables": the variables belonging to $\mathcal{X}$ on which we abstract and the matching variables belonging to $\mathcal{V}$ sometimes called unknowns. We justify the use of the two sets in Section 3.

The symbols $A, B, C, \ldots$ range over the set $\mathcal{T}_t$ of terms, the symbols $x, y, z, \ldots$ range over the set $\mathcal{X}$ of variables ($\mathcal{X} \subseteq \mathcal{T}_t$), the symbols $a, b, c, \ldots, f, g, h$ range over a set $\mathcal{K}$ of term constants ($\mathcal{K} \subseteq \mathcal{T}_t$). The symbols $X, Y, \ldots$ range over the set $\mathcal{V}$ of matching variables. Finally, the symbol ε ranges over the set of atoms, which consists of variables, matching variables and constants. All symbols can be indexed. Positions in λ-terms are denoted by $p_1, \ldots, p_n$. We denote by $\preceq$ the canonical order on positions. The subterm of A at position p_1 is denoted by $A_{|p_1}$.

The order of a constant or a matching variable is defined as the order of its type. The order of a redex $(\lambda x \,.\, A) \, B$ is defined as the order of the abstraction $\lambda x \,.\, A$. We consider the usual notion of free and bound variables that concerns the variables (matching variables cannot be bound). A term is said to be closed if it contains no matching variables and no free variables. We denote by $\mathcal{FV}(A)$ the set of the free variables of A.

The substitution of variables is defined as usual and avoids variable capture using α-conversion when needed. The substitution of the variable x by A in B is denoted by $B\{A/x\}$.

As in any calculus involving binders, we work modulo the α-*conversion* of Church, and modulo the *hygiene-convention* of Barendregt [Bar84], *i.e.*, free and bound variables have different names.

We denote a β-reduction step by $\to_\beta$, by $\twoheadrightarrow_\beta$ its reflexive and transitive closure and by $=_\beta$ its reflexive, symmetric and transitive closure. A λ-term is said to be β-*normal* or simply *normal* if it is in normal form for $\to_\beta$.

1.2   Untyped Labelled λ-Calculus and β_l-Reduction

When no ambiguity is possible, we use the same notation for both typed and untyped (labelled) terms. Labels are simply elements of $\mathbb{N}$.

Definition 2 (Labelled λ-terms). *Let $\mathcal{K}$ be a set of constants. Let $\mathcal{X}$ and $\mathcal{V}$ be two countably infinite and disjoint sets respectively for variables and matching variables. The set $\mathcal{T}_l$ of labelled λ-terms is defined as the smallest set containing all variables, matching variables, constants and closed under the following rules:*

— *If $A \in \mathcal{T}_l$ and $p \in \mathbb{N}$, then $\lambda_p x.A \in \mathcal{T}_l$.*
— *If $M, N \in \mathcal{T}_l$ and $p \in \mathbb{N}$, then $(MN)^p \in \mathcal{T}_l$.*

We define β_l-reduction on the set of labelled λ-terms as follows:

$$((\lambda_p x.A)B)^p \rightarrow_{\beta_l} A\{B/x\}$$

In order to define superdevelopements we will restrict attention to terms that are labelled such that the label of an application cannot be equal to the label of a λ-abstraction that is not in its scope.

Definition 3 (Well-labelled and initially labelled terms). *A labelled term $A \in \mathcal{T}_l$ is said to be* well-labelled *if for all positions such that $A_{|p_1} = (B_0 B_1)^p$ and $A_{|p_2} = \lambda_p x.C$ then $p_1 \preceq p_2$. It is is* initially labelled *if moreover for all positions such that $A_{|p_1} = \lambda_p x.C$ and $A_{|p_2} = \lambda_p x'.C'$ then $p_1 = p_2$.*

In the following, we will suppose that all labelled terms are well-labelled. We can remark that the set of well-labelled terms is closed by β_l-reduction.

1.3 Untyped λ-Calculus and Superdevelopments

The untyped λ-calculus is defined as the labelled λ-calculus by simply erasing all labels (both in terms and reduction). The set of untyped λ-terms is denoted by $\mathcal{T}$. We introduce a generalization of (finite) developments [Bar84] called superdevelopments. This notion, initially introduced in [vR93], is related to the three ways to create redexes in the λ-calculus [Lév78]:

1. $((\lambda x . \lambda y . A) B) C \quad \rightarrow_\beta \quad (\lambda y . A\{B/x\}) C$
2. $((\lambda x . x) (\lambda y . A)) B \quad \rightarrow_\beta \quad (\lambda y . A) B$
3. $(\lambda x . A)(\lambda y . B) \quad\quad \rightarrow_\beta \quad A\{\lambda y . B/x\}$
    if there is a position p_1 such that $A_{|p_1} = x A_0$

For the first two ways of creating a β-redex, one can say that the creation is "upwards", whereas in the last case it can be said to be "downwards". By restricting to well-labelled terms we exactly restrict to upwards creations.

A superdevelopment is a β-rewrite sequence that may reduce both the redexes that are residuals of redex occurrences in the initial term (like in developments) and the redex occurrences that are created in the first or second way.

In the λ-calculus, superdevelopments are, as developments, finite.

Definition 4 (Superdevelopments). *A β-rewrite sequence ς of the λ-calculus is a β-superdevelopment if it exists a β_l-rewrite sequence σ in the labelled λ-calculus that starts with an initially labelled term and stops on a term in β_l-normal form and such that $\Upsilon(\sigma) = \varsigma$, where Υ is the canonical mapping from labelled λ-terms to λ-terms and from β_l-reduction to β-reduction that simply erases labels.*

For example, the β-rewrite sequence $(\lambda x \,.\, \lambda y \,.\, xy)zz' \to_\beta (\lambda y \,.\, zy)z' \to_\beta zz'$ is a superdevelopment since it corresponds to the β_l-rewrite sequence $(((\lambda_1 x.\lambda_2 y.xy)z)^1)z')^2 \to_{\beta_l} ((\lambda_2 y.zy)z')^2 \to_{\beta_l} zz'$.

However, the rewrite sequence $(\lambda x \,.\, xx)(\lambda x \,.\, xx) \to_\beta (\lambda x \,.\, xx)(\lambda x \,.\, xx) \to_\beta \ldots$ is not a superdevelopment.

Given a λ-term, we can "label" this term (and thus obtaining a labelled λ-term) in order to β_l-reduce redexes created in the first or in the second way but not in the third way. This is exactly why we restrict ourselves to well-labelled terms.

The corresponding β_l-rewrite sequence associated to a superdevelopment is no more given in the following (this a good exercise left to the reader). We now give four examples of β-reductions that are superdeveloppements.

[**Finite development**] Residuals of redexes present in the initial term can be contracted:
$$(\lambda x \,.\, f(x,x))\,((\lambda y \,.\, y)\,a)$$
$$\to_\beta f((\lambda y \,.\, y)\,a, (\lambda y \,.\, y)\,a)$$
$$\to_\beta f(a, (\lambda y \,.\, y)\,a)$$
$$\to_\beta f(a,a)$$

[**Redex creation of type 1**] In the following superdevelopment, the new redex obtained after one β-rewrite step is reduced:
$$((\lambda x \,.\, \lambda y \,.\, f(x,y))a)b$$
$$\to_\beta (\lambda y \,.\, f(a,y))b$$
$$\to_\beta f(a,b)$$

[**Redex creation of type 2**] As in the previous example, a redex is created and reduced during reduction, but in a different way: $((\lambda x \,.\, x)(\lambda y \,.\, y))a$
$$\to_\beta (\lambda y \,.\, y)a$$
$$\to_\beta a$$

[**Redex creation of type 3**] There is no superdevelopment from the term $(\lambda x \,.\, xa)(\lambda y \,.\, y)$ to the term a:
$$(\lambda x \,.\, xa)(\lambda y \,.\, y)$$
$$\to_\beta (\lambda y \,.\, y)a$$

1.4   Another Characterization of Superdevelopments

As finite developments coincide with the classical parallel reduction of Tait and Martin-Löf, finite superdevelopments coincide with Aczel's parallel reduction [Acz78] called in the following strong parallel β-reduction. It is denoted by $\Longrightarrow_{\beta_{sd}}$ and we say that a term A β_{sd}-reduces to a term B if $A \Longrightarrow_{\beta_{sd}} B$. It is defined inductively in Figure 1.

The only difference with the parallel reduction of Tait and Martin-Löf is the rule $(Red - \beta_s)$ that replaces the rule $(Red - \beta)$ of the parallel reduction given by

$$\frac{\lambda x \,.\, A_1 \Longrightarrow_\beta \lambda x \,.\, A_2 \quad B_1 \Longrightarrow_\beta B_2}{(\lambda x \,.\, A_1)B_1 \Longrightarrow_\beta A_2\{B_2/x\}} \ (Red - \beta)$$

The following result states that superdevelopments coincide with strong parallel β-reduction. This characterization is the essence of the matching algorithm.

Theorem 1. *There exists a superdevelopment from A to B iff $A \Longrightarrow_{\beta_{sd}} B$.*

$$\frac{}{\varepsilon \Longrightarrow_{\beta_{sd}} \varepsilon} \ (Red-\varepsilon) \qquad \frac{A_1 \Longrightarrow_{\beta_{sd}} A_2}{\lambda x . A_1 \Longrightarrow_{\beta_{sd}} \lambda x . A_2} \ (Red-\lambda)$$

$$\frac{A_1 \Longrightarrow_{\beta_{sd}} A_2 \quad B_1 \Longrightarrow_{\beta_{sd}} B_2}{A_1 B_1 \Longrightarrow_{\beta_{sd}} A_2 B_2} \ (Red-@)$$

$$\frac{A_1 \Longrightarrow_{\beta_{sd}} \lambda x . A_2 \quad B_1 \Longrightarrow_{\beta_{sd}} B_2}{A_1 B_1 \Longrightarrow_{\beta_{sd}} A_2 \{B_2/x\}} \ (Red-\beta_s)$$

Fig. 1. Strong parallel β-reduction

2   Matching Modulo Superdevelopments

In this section, we first define matching modulo superdevelopments, also called β_{sd}-matching. We then relate it with second and third order matching.

2.1   Definition of β_{sd}-Matching

Definition 5 (Substitution). *A matching substitution or simply a substitution $\varphi : V \to T$ is a function from matching variables to terms. If $\varphi = \{A_1/X_1, \ldots, A_n/X_n\}$ then the domain of φ is the set $\{X_i\}_{i=1}^n$. We overload the notation used for substitutions of variables and we denote by $B\{A/X\}$ the substitution of A for the matching variable X in B. In this work, we only consider closed and normal substitutions that are substitutions of closed normal terms.*

Since we consider classes of terms modulo α-conversion, when applying a substitution the appropriate representatives are always chosen in order to avoid potential variable captures.

Definition 6 (Union). *Two substitutions coincide if their images coincide on the intersection of their domains. We then straightforwardly define the union of two substitutions σ and φ that coincide and denote it by $\sigma \cup \varphi$.*

Definition 7 (Matching equation–System). *A β_{sd}-matching equation or simply a matching equation is a pair of terms denoted $A \leqslant_{\beta_{sd}} B$ such that B is normal and does not contain matching variables. A matching system is a multiset of matching equations.*

For example, $XY \leqslant_{\beta_{sd}} \lambda x . x$ and $(\lambda x . x)X \leqslant_{\beta_{sd}} a$ are β_{sd}-matching equations whereas $XY \leqslant_{\beta_{sd}} (\lambda x . x)a$ is not.

Every solution of a matching equation is supposed to be a *closed* substitution. We say that a matching variable belongs to a system S and we note $X \in S$ if X occurs in one equation of S.

Definition 8 (β_{sd}-match). *A substitution φ on matching variables is a β_{sd}-match or simply a match for the matching equation $A \leqslant_{\beta_{sd}} B$ if and only if $A\varphi \Longrightarrow_{\beta_{sd}} B$. A substitution is a match of a system if it matches each equation. The set of all matches of a system S is denoted $M(S)$.*

For example, $\{\lambda xy\,.\,y/X\}$ and $\{\lambda y\,.\,y/X, \lambda x\,.\,x/Y\}$ are β_{sd}-matches for the equation $XY \leqslant_{\beta_{sd}} \lambda x\,.\,x$. The substitution $\{\lambda z\,.\,z(\lambda x\,.\,x)/X, \lambda y\,.\,y/Y\}$ is not a β_{sd}-match because $(\lambda z\,.\,z(\lambda x\,.\,x))(\lambda y\,.\,y)$ does not β_{sd}-reduce to $\lambda x\,.\,x$. (although it β-reduces).

The application of a substitution to a matching equation $B \leqslant_{\beta_{sd}} C$ is the equation $B\varphi \leqslant_{\beta_{sd}} C$. The application of a substitution φ to a system, denoted $\mathbb{S}\varphi$ consists in the application of the substitution φ to each matching equation of $\mathbb{S}$.

Definition 9 (Solved form). *A matching equation $X \leqslant_{\beta_{sd}} A$ is in* solved form *if A contain no free variables. The corresponding substitution is defined by $\{\;\}AX$. A system is in* solved form *if all its equations are in solved form and if the left-hand sides are pairwise disjoint. The corresponding susbtitutution of such a system is the union of the corresponding substitutions of each equation (of the system). It is denoted by $\sigma_{\mathbb{S}}$.*

Definition 10 (Complete match set). *Let $\mathbb{S}$ be a matching system. A complete match set of $\mathbb{S}$ is a set of substitutions $\mathbb{M}$ such that:*

1. **Soundness** *For all $\varphi \in \mathbb{M}$, φ is a β_{sd}-match of $\mathbb{S}$.*
2. **Completeness** *For all φ such that φ is a β_{sd}-match of $\mathbb{S}$ there exists $\psi \in \mathbb{M}$ such that $\psi \leq \varphi$, i.e., there exists a substitution ξ such that $\varphi = \xi \circ \psi$ where $\circ$ denotes substitution composition.*

The following lemma gives the relevance of solved forms:

Lemma 1. *If $\mathbb{S}$ is a system in solved form then $\{\sigma_{\mathbb{S}}\}$ is a complete match set of $\mathbb{S}$.*

2.2 Comparison with Usual Higher-Order Matching

Comparison with Second-Order Matching. First, we relate β_{sd}-matching with second-order matching (*i.e.*, typed higher-order β-matching where all matching variables are second-order and where constants are third-order). We show that all solutions of a given second-order system are β_{sd}-matches. In this section, all terms are supposed to be typable, *i.e.*, belong to $\mathcal{T}_t$.

We simply recall the definition of β-matching and we refer to [GS89] for a more complete and self-contained presentation.

Definition 11 (β-matching equation and β-match). *A β-matching equation is a pair of β-normal typed λ-terms of the same type denoted $A \leqslant_\beta B$ such that B does not contain matching variables. A substitution φ, that preserves types, is a β-match for the matching equation $A \leqslant_\beta B$ if and only if $A\varphi =_\beta B$. We generalize the definition to matching systems as in Def. 8.*

If we erase the types, then all β-matching equations are β_{sd}-matching equations. We will switch from the former to the latter without explicit mentions.

The following results were already proved in [dMS01]. Nevertheless, the formalization using superdevelopments (and not only strong β-parallel reduction) introduced in this paper gives quite simple and clear proofs.

First, a technical result on the creation of redexes.

Lemma 2. *For all terms $A_1, \ldots, A_n$ such that there exists a superdevelopment $A_1 \to_\beta \ldots \to_\beta A_n$ and A_n contains a redex of third order order (or more), then A_1 contains also a redex of third order (or more).*

Proof. We prove the result by induction on n. We look at the induction case. By induction hypothesis, we know that A_2 contains a redex of a least third order that we call in the following $R = (\lambda x . C)\, D$. First, if R is a residual of a redex of A_1 then the result is obvious. Secondly, if not, and if R is created during the reduction from A_1 to A_2 in the first way mentioned before then A_1 must contain a subterm of the form $(((\lambda z . \lambda x . C')\, E)\, D$ with $C = C'\{E/z\}$. Then the order of the redex $(\lambda z . \lambda x . C')\, E$ is greater or equal to the of order R. This concludes the case. Finally, if not, and if R is created during the reduction from A_1 to A_2 in the second way mentioned before then A_1 must contain a subterm of the form $(\lambda y . y)\, (\lambda x . C)\, D$. The order of the redex $(\lambda y . y)\, (\lambda x . C)$ is strictly greater than the one of R. This concludes the case. $\qquad\square$

Proposition 1. *Consider a second-order β-matching equation. If a substitution φ is a β-match then it is a β_{sd}-match.*

Proof. The proof is by contradiction. Let φ be a β-match of the β-matching equation $A \leqslant_\beta B$ that is not a β_{sd}-match. Then we have $A\varphi =_\beta B$, that A does not contain any β-redex, that φ does not contain any term of order greater than 2. Finally, $A\varphi \not\twoheadrightarrow_{\beta_{sd}} B$ and $A\varphi =_\beta B$. Thus there exist $(A_i)_i$ such that $A\varphi \to_\beta A_1 \to_\beta \cdots \to_{\beta_{sd}} A_n$ is a superdevelopments and A_n contains a β-redex $(\lambda x . C)D$ which is not reduced by superdevelopments. This means that this redex is a residual of a redex created when reducing A_{i_0}. Since the redex is not reduced by superdevelopments then this creation is of type 3 and thus induces a redex of order at least 3. Lemma 2 implies that $A\varphi$ contains a redex of order at least three. Since both A and φ range in the set of β-normal forms, then there exists a position p_l and a term E such that $A_{|p_l} = XE$ where X is mapped by φ to a λ-abstraction of at least third order. This contradicts the hypothesis on the order of the initial matching problem. $\qquad\square$

This proposition for second-order β-equations can be easily generalised to second-order β-systems.

Creations of redexes in the third way induce intrinsically redexes of at least third order. This intuitively explains why second-order matches modulo β are β_{sd}-matches. The reader familiar with the second-order matching algorithm of G. Huet and B. Lang may notice that during this matching process, we can restrict β-normalization to β_{sd}-normalization.

Comparison with Third-Order Matching. As soon as we consider third-order matching problems, the set of minimal solutions may be infinite. Since matching modulo superdevelopments generates finitely many minimal solutions, we remark that matching modulo superdevelopments cannot be complete *w.r.t.* third-order matching.

Example 1. The substitution $\{\lambda x \,.\, \lambda f \,.\, fx/X\}$ is a β-match for the matching equation $\lambda z \,.\, (X \quad z \quad (\lambda y \,.\, y)) \leqslant \lambda z \,.\, z$ whereas it is not a β_{sd}-match. In fact, $\lambda z \,.\, ((\lambda x \,.\, \lambda f \,.\, fx) \, z \, (\lambda y \,.\, y)) \, \beta_{sd}$-reduces to $\lambda z \,.\, (\lambda y \,.\, y)z$ but not to $\lambda z \,.\, z$.

The last example is classical and taken from [Dow01]. The third-order matching equation has an infinite number of (minimal) solutions of type $\iota \to (\iota \to \iota) \to \iota$ that are given by the Church numbers $\lambda x \,.\, \lambda f \,.\, (f \ldots (f \, x) \ldots)$.

Comparison with Patterns à la Miller. In the case of matching of patterns à la Miller [Mil91, Qia96], the restriction of the β-reduction given by superdevelopments is powerful enough:

Proposition 2. *Let φ be a match of an equation $P \leqslant_\beta A$ where P is a pattern à la Miller. Then there exists a superdevelopment $P\varphi \Vdash\!\!\twoheadrightarrow_\beta A$.*

3   An Algorithm for Matching Modulo Superdevelopments

In this section, we first present an algorithm for matching modulo superdevelopments. We illustrate it on several examples and finally state its main properties.

3.1   Presentation of the Algorithm

We propose in Figure 2 an algorithmic description of matching modulo superdevelopments using transformation rules [GS89]:

— A system is transformed by successively applying the rules until we get to a normal form (it always exists since the rules terminate) that gives a solution (the algorithm is sound).
— By exploring all possible reductions (the rule are non-deterministic in the sense that at each step there are possibly several rules that can applied) and collecting all solved forms we get a complete match set (since the algorithm is sound and complete).

   We write $\mathbb{S} \to \mathbb{S}'$ if there exists a transformation rule that can be applied to transform $\mathbb{S}$ into $\mathbb{S}'$ and $\mathbb{S} \Vdash\!\!\twoheadrightarrow \mathbb{S}'$ if there exist $n \geq 0$ systems $\mathbb{S}_1, \ldots, \mathbb{S}_n$ such that $\mathbb{S} \to \mathbb{S}_1 \to \ldots \mathbb{S}_n \to \mathbb{S}'$. The matching algorithm follows the definition of strong β-parallel reduction:

The ε rules: deal with atoms. The rules (ε_c) and (ε_v) are trivial rules dealing with variables and constants. The rule (ε_X) substitutes a matching variable by its corresponding value. Remark first that we do not substitute by terms containing free variables and then that we do not normalize when applying a substitution (otherwise the rule (ε_X) would not be sound ; see the long version for further

$(x \leqslant_{\beta_{sd}} x)$, $\mathbb{S}$	$\to_{\varepsilon_v}$	$\mathbb{S}$
$(a \leqslant_{\beta_{sd}} a)$, $\mathbb{S}$	$\to_{\varepsilon_c}$	$\mathbb{S}$
$(X \leqslant_{\beta_{sd}} A)$, $\mathbb{S}$	$\to_{\varepsilon_X}$	$X \leqslant_{\beta_{sd}} A$, $\mathbb{S}\{A/X\}$
		if $\mathcal{FV}(A) = \emptyset$ **and** $X \in \mathbb{S}$
$(\lambda x . A \leqslant_{\beta_{sd}} \lambda x . B)$, $\mathbb{S}$	$\to_{\lambda_\lambda}$	$(A \leqslant_{\beta_{sd}} B)$, $\mathbb{S}$
$(A_1 B_1 \leqslant_{\beta_{sd}} A_2 B_2)$, $\mathbb{S}$	$\to_{@_@}$	$(A_1 \leqslant_{\beta_{sd}} A_2)$, $(B_1 \leqslant_{\beta_{sd}} B_2)$, $\mathbb{S}$
$(A_1 B_1 \leqslant_{\beta_{sd}} C)$, $\mathbb{S}$	$\to_{@_\pi}$	$(A_1 \leqslant_{\beta_{sd}} \lambda x . C)$, $\mathbb{S}$
		where x **fresh**
$(A_1 B_1 \leqslant_{\beta_{sd}} C)$, $\mathbb{S}$	$\to_{@_\beta}$	$(A_1 \leqslant_{\beta_{sd}} \lambda x . A_2)$, $(B_1 \leqslant_{\beta_{sd}} B_2)$, $\mathbb{S}$
		where $A_2\{B_2/x\} = C$
		and x fresh, $x \in \mathcal{FV}(A_2)$
		and A_2, B_2 normal forms

Fig. 2. Matching algorithm for higher-order matching modulo superdevelopments

details). In the rule (ε_X), we compel that the substituted term contains no free variables. This is not a stricly needed condition but if the condition is not verified there is no interest to apply the rule since the system will never lead to a solved form (precisely because of the condition is not verified).

The λ rule: deals with abstraction by mimicking the $(Red - \lambda)$ rule (thanks to the implicit α-renaming, we can suppose that the two bound variables are the same). This rule illustrates the use of two different sets of "variables": we can "unbind" a variable safely without possible confusion with a matching variable (recall that we only consider *closed* substitutions). Many algorithms use a single set of variables. In this case, since matching variables are the free variables of the left-hand side of the equation, we have to remember the variables that were bound in the initial equation. The two choices are relevant.

A similar rule is used in the works on unification in the λ-calculus with explicit substitutions and de Bruijn indices [DHK00].

The @ rules: deal with application. The $(@_@)$ rule is in one-to-one correspondance with the rule $(Red - @)$ and thus does not need further comments. The rules $(@_\pi)$ and $(@_\beta)$ are both related to the rule $(Red - \beta_s)$. We try to express the right-hand side C of the equation as the result of a β-reduction let us say $A_2\{B_2/x\}$. Depending on the presence of x in A_2, we obtain the rule $(@_\pi)$ or $(@_\beta)$. If x does not belong to A_2, then we obtain the rule $(@_\pi)$: the left-hand side of the application is mapped to an abstraction that ignores its argument and returns the right-hand side of the matching equation. Otherwise (if x belongs to A_2), we obtain the rule $(@_\beta)$ by mimicking the $(Red - \beta_s)$ for all terms such that $A_2\{B_2/x\} = C$ where x belongs to A_2 and A_2, B_2 are normal. To find the terms

A_2 and B_2 we first remark that B_2 must be a subterm of C (since x belongs to A_2). We can thus choose one of them. Then, choose a subset of the set of positions on which B_2 appears in C. Then A_2 is obtained from C by putting x at every position of the chosen set. Notice that there are finitely many pairs (A_2, B_2) satisfying the conditions.

Notice that the matching algorithm does not introduce new matching variables (this is not the case in [HL78]). This is for example pertinent in [Ali05].

Example 2. We consider the matching equation $XY \leqslant_{\beta_{sd}} ab$. Since the left and right-hand sides of the matching equation are applications, we can apply the rules $(@_\pi)$, $(@_@)$ or $(@_\beta)$.

1. Rule $(@_\pi)$: $XY \leqslant_{\beta_{sd}} ab \rightarrow X \leqslant_{\beta_{sd}} \lambda x . ab$.
2. Rule $(@_@)$: $XY \leqslant_{\beta_{sd}} ab \rightarrow X \leqslant_{\beta_{sd}} a$, $Y \leqslant_{\beta_{sd}} b$.
3. Rule $(@_\beta)$: to find A_1 and A_2 such that $A_1\{A_2/x\} = ab$ first we choose A_2 as one of the subterm of "ab": a, b and ab. There is only one subset of the set of positions on which A_2 appears in ab (since each subterm of ab appears once). Then we can apply the rule $(@_\beta)$ in different ways corresponding to the three subterms of the right-hand side of the equation:
   (a) $XY \leqslant_{\beta_{sd}} ab \rightarrow X \leqslant_{\beta_{sd}} \lambda x . xb$, $Y \leqslant_{\beta_{sd}} a$.
   (b) $XY \leqslant_{\beta_{sd}} ab \rightarrow X \leqslant_{\beta_{sd}} \lambda x . ax$, $Y \leqslant_{\beta_{sd}} b$.
   (c) $XY \leqslant_{\beta_{sd}} ab \rightarrow X \leqslant_{\beta_{sd}} \lambda x . x$, $Y \leqslant_{\beta_{sd}} ab$.

Example 3. We consider the equation $X(YX) \leqslant_{\beta_{sd}} a$. We can apply either the rule $(@_\pi)$ or $(@_\beta)$.

1. Rule $(@_\pi)$: $X(YX) \leqslant_{\beta_{sd}} a \rightarrow X \leqslant_{\beta_{sd}} \lambda x . a$.
2. Rule $(@_\beta)$: $X(YX) \leqslant_{\beta_{sd}} a \rightarrow X \leqslant_{\beta_{sd}} \lambda x . x$, $YX \leqslant_{\beta_{sd}} a$.
   To simplify $YX \leqslant_{\beta_{sd}} a$ we can apply either the rule $(@_\pi)$ or the rule $(@_\beta)$.
   (a) Rule $(@_\pi)$: $X \leqslant_{\beta_{sd}} \lambda x . x$, $YX \leqslant_{\beta_{sd}} a \rightarrow X \leqslant_{\beta_{sd}} \lambda x . x, Y \leqslant_{\beta_{sd}} \lambda x . a$.
   (b) Rule $(@_\beta)$
   $$X \leqslant_{\beta_{sd}} \lambda x . x, \; YX \leqslant_{\beta_{sd}} a \rightarrow X \leqslant_{\beta_{sd}} \lambda x . x, Y \leqslant_{\beta_{sd}} \lambda x . x, X \leqslant_{\beta_{sd}} a$$
   $$\rightarrow X \leqslant_{\beta_{sd}} \lambda x . x, Y \leqslant_{\beta_{sd}} \lambda x . x,$$
   $$\lambda x . x \leqslant_{\beta_{sd}} a.$$

In the last case, the system is not in solved form (although no transformation rules can be applied) and thus it gives no solutions. The initial matching equation has only two solutions.

3.2   Properties

Proposition 3 (Termination).   *The set of transformation rules of Figure 2 is terminating.*

Proposition 4 (Correctness). *For all systems S and S' such that $S \mapsto\!\!\!\twoheadrightarrow S'$ and S' is in solved form, we have $\sigma_{S'} \in M(S)$.*

Proposition 5 (Completeness). *For any system* S, *if* $\varphi \in \mathsf{M}(\mathsf{S})$ *then there exists a sequence of transformations starting from* S *and ending on a system* S_n *such that* S_n *is in solved form and* $\sigma_{\mathsf{S}_n} \leq \varphi$.

Proof. By induction on the appropriate extension of the $\Longrightarrow_{\beta_{sd}}$ on multisets.

Theorem 2 (Finite complete match set). *Let* $A \leqslant_{\beta_{sd}} B$ *be a matching equation and* $\mathsf{M} = \{\sigma_{\mathsf{S}} \mid A \leqslant_{\beta_{sd}} B \longmapsto \mathsf{S}$ *and* S *is in solved form* $\}$. *Then the set* M *is a complete match set for the equation* $A \leqslant_{\beta_{sd}} B$. *It is always finite.*

We can remark that there are some second-order β-match equations that have no solutions but that the corresponding β_{sd}-equation has a solution[2]:

Example 4. Let $g(XY, XZ) \leqslant_\beta g(fa, fb)$ be a β-match equation with types $a : \iota_2$, $b : \iota_2$, $f : \iota_2 \to \iota_1$, $g : \iota_1 \to \iota_1 \to \iota_1$, $X : \iota_3 \to \iota_1$, $Y : \iota_3$ and $Z : \iota_3$.

We consider the solutions of the β_{sd}-equations $XY \leqslant_{\beta_{sd}} fa$ and $XZ \leqslant_{\beta_{sd}} fb$.

$XY \leqslant_{\beta_{sd}} fa$		$XZ \leqslant_{\beta_{sd}} fb$	
$X \leqslant_{\beta_{sd}} f,$	$Y \leqslant_{\beta_{sd}} a$	$X \leqslant_{\beta_{sd}} f,$	$Z \leqslant_{\beta_{sd}} b$
$X \leqslant_{\beta_{sd}} \lambda x . fa$		$X \leqslant_{\beta_{sd}} \lambda x . fb$	
$X \leqslant_{\beta_{sd}} \lambda x . fx, Y \leqslant_{\beta_{sd}} a$		$X \leqslant_{\beta_{sd}} \lambda x . fx, Z \leqslant_{\beta_{sd}} b$	
$X \leqslant_{\beta_{sd}} \lambda x . xa, Y \leqslant_{\beta_{sd}} f$		$X \leqslant_{\beta_{sd}} \lambda x . xb, Z \leqslant_{\beta_{sd}} f$	
$X \leqslant_{\beta_{sd}} \lambda x . x, \quad Y \leqslant_{\beta_{sd}} fa$		$X \leqslant_{\beta_{sd}} \lambda x . x, \quad Z \leqslant_{\beta_{sd}} fb$	

The only two well-typed solutions (that is, solutions such that the term associated to a matching variable has the same type than this matching variable) are respectively $X \leqslant_{\beta_{sd}} \lambda x . fa$ and $X \leqslant_{\beta_{sd}} \lambda x . fb$. Of course, they do not lead to a substitution for $g(XY, XZ) \leqslant_{\beta_{sd}} g(fa, fb)$. Thus, we have found a second-order β-match equation that has no solution[3] even if the β_{sd}-equation has.

We now work in the framework of the typed λ-calculus *to solve second-order matching equations.* As in any higher-order matching algorithm for typed λ-calculi, we only consider well-typed equations that are pairs of typed terms of the *same* type. In particular, transformation rules are applied only if the resulting systems is well typed (that is, each equation is well-typed). In this context, we have the following result.

Theorem 3 (Second-order matching algorithm). *The rules given in Fig. 2 applied in the context of the typed λ-calculus gives a sound and complete matching algorithm for second-order matching.*

---

[2] Thus we cannot deduce from the NP-completeness of the second-order matching, the NP-completeness of the matching modulo superdeveloppements.

[3] Since there is no well-typed substitutions modulo superdevelopments, there are no second-order substitution for $g(XY, XZ) \leqslant_\beta g(fa, fb)$ (applying prop. 1).

4 Matching Modulo Superdevelopments and η

The gap between higher-order matching modulo β and higher-order matching modulo $\beta\eta$ is mainly explained by the fundamental use of η-long normal forms when matching is performed modulo $\beta\eta$. In the context of higher-order matching modulo superdevelopments, the use of η-equivalence does not strongly influence our algorithm, as explained below.

A $\beta_{sd}\eta$-matching equation is a pair (A, B) of terms such that B is $\beta\eta$-normal and contains no matching variable. It is denoted by $A \leqslant^{\eta}_{\beta_{sd}} B$. A substitution φ is a $\beta_{sd}\eta$-match if there exists a term C such that $A\varphi \Longrightarrow_{\beta_{sd}} C \to^{*}_{\eta} B$. The algorithm described in Section 3 has to be adapted $w.r.t.$ two aspects:

First, η-expansion is performed on demand by adding a rule to the matching algorithm:

$$(\lambda x . A \leqslant^{\eta}_{\beta_{sd}} B), \, \mathbb{S} \to_{\lambda_-} (A \leqslant^{\eta}_{\beta_{sd}} Bx), \mathbb{S}$$
$$\text{if } B \text{ is not a } \lambda\text{-abstraction and } x \text{ is fresh}$$

In one step, this rule first replaces the right hand side B by $\lambda y . (By)$ and then performs λ-abstraction elimination as in the rule (λ_{λ}).

Secondly, we must add a side condition in the rule $(@_{\beta})$ so that $\lambda x . A_2$ and A_1 are in $\beta\eta$-normal form (and not only in β-normal form).

The algorithm enjoys the same properties (termination, soundness and completeness) as before. Moreover, if we apply this algorithm to an equation whose first term is a pattern à la Miller then we obtain a complete match set consisting exactly of the more general match.

Example 5. If we consider the match-equation of Ex. 2 we can remark that solving the equation modulo $\beta_{sd}\eta$ we get only 4 solutions. In fact, the rule $(@_{\beta})$ applies now only twice. The following two solutions found in Ex. 2 are η-equivalent: $X \leqslant_{\beta_{sd}} a$, $Y \leqslant_{\beta_{sd}} b$ and $X \leqslant_{\beta_{sd}} \lambda x . ax$, $Y \leqslant_{\beta_{sd}} b$.

Example 6. Consider the equation $(\lambda x . X(Yx), a)$. It has no β_{sd}-solution whereas it has two $\beta_{sd}\eta$-matches given by $\{a/X, \lambda z . z/Y\}$ and $\{\lambda z . z/X, a/Y\}$.

$$
\begin{array}{lll}
\lambda x . X(Yx) \leqslant^{\eta}_{\beta_{sd}} a & \to & X(Yx) \leqslant^{\eta}_{\beta_{sd}} ax \\
& \to & X \leqslant^{\eta}_{\beta_{sd}} a, \, Yx \leqslant^{\eta}_{\beta_{sd}} x \\
& \to & X \leqslant^{\eta}_{\beta_{sd}} a, \, Y \leqslant^{\eta}_{\beta_{sd}} \lambda z . z \\
\\
\lambda x . X(Yx) \leqslant^{\eta}_{\beta_{sd}} a & \to & X(Yx) \leqslant^{\eta}_{\beta_{sd}} ax \\
& \to & X \leqslant^{\eta}_{\beta_{sd}} \lambda z . z, \, Yx \leqslant^{\eta}_{\beta_{sd}} ax \\
& \to & X \leqslant^{\eta}_{\beta_{sd}} \lambda z . z, \, Y \leqslant^{\eta}_{\beta_{sd}} a
\end{array}
$$

5 Conclusion

We proposed a new approach to study higher-order matching following [dMS01]: instead of working in the typed λ-calculus modulo full β-reduction we propose to work in the untyped λ-calculus modulo a restriction of β-equivalence, namely superdevelopments. The essence of the restriction induces that all second-order β-matches are matches modulo superdevelopments. The algorithms are described in a mathematically elegant way that allow us to write intuitive proofs (termination, soundness and completeness). Since we consider untyped frameworks the use of the η-equivalence does not influence the behavior and design of our algorithms.

An implementation of the algorithm of matching modulo superdevelopments was done in the TOM language [MRV03].

Higher-order formalisms and especially higher-order rewriting generally choose the typed λ-calculus modulo β (or $\beta\eta$) as a meta-language. In the case of CRS [KvOvR93], the meta-language is the untyped λ-calculus with developments. The next step is thus to study higher-order rewriting with the untyped λ-calculus modulo superdevelopments as a meta-language (in other words to consider higher-order rewriting with the untyped λ-calculus with superdevelopments as a substitution calculus in the sense of [Oos94]).

As far as it concerns the transformations of pattern-matching programs, the work of [dMS01] motivates by several examples higher-order matching in pattern-calculi such as the ρ-calculus [CLW03] or pure pattern calculi [JK06]. Since a simple type system that ensures termination is difficult to find in this context, this paper should give useful guidelines.

Acknowledgments. We would like to thank E. Bonelli for some comments that motivated this work. It benefited of the discussions we had with H. Cirstea, C. Kirchner and G. Nadathur. Finally, we sincerely thank the referees for their deep remarks on the paper.

References

[Acz78]   P. Aczel. A general church rosser theorem. Technical report, University of Mancherster, July 1978.

[Ali05]   C. Alias. *Program Optimization by Template Recognition and Replacement*. PhD thesis, University of Versailles, Versailles, France, December 2005.

[Bar84]   H. Barendregt. *The Lambda-Calculus, its syntax and semantics*. Elsevier Science Publishers B. V. (North-Holland), 1984.

[CLW03]   H. Cirstea, L. Liquori, and B. Wack. Rewriting calculus with fixpoints: Untyped and first-order systems. volume 3085. Springer, 2003.

[DHK00]   G. Dowek, T. Hardin, and C. Kirchner. Higher-order unification via explicit substitutions. *Information and Computation*, 157(1/2):183–235, 2000.

[dMS01]   O. de Moor and G. Sittampalam. Higher-order matching for program transformation. *Theoretical Computer Science*, 269, 2001.

[Dow01]   G. Dowek. Higher-order unification and matching. In *Handbook of Automated Reasoning*. Elsevier, 2001.

[DSP91]   M. Dalrymple, S. M. Shieber, and F. Pereira. Ellipsis and higher-order unification. *Linguistics and Philosophy*, 14:399–452, 1991.

[GS89]   J. Gallier and W. Snyder. Higher-order unification revisited: Complete
            sets of transformations. *JSCOMP: Journal of Symbolic Computation*, 8,
            1989.

[HL78]   G. Huet and B. Lang. Proving and applying program transformations
            expressed with second-order patterns. *Acta Informatica*, 11, 1978.

[JK06]   C. B. Jay and D. Kesner. Pure pattern calculus. In *Proceedings of the
            European Symposium on Programming (ESOP) LNCS 3924*, 2006.

[KvOvR93]   Klop, van Oostrom, and van Raamsdonk. Combinatory reduction sys-
            tems: Introduction and survey. *TCS: Theoretical Computer Science*, 121,
            1993.

[Lév78]   J.-J. Lévy. *Reductions Correctes et Optimales dans le Lambda-Calcul*.
            Ph.D. thesis, Université de Paris, 1978.

[Mil90]   D. Miller. Higher-order logic programming. In *Int. Conf. on Logic Pro-
            gramming*, page 784, 1990.

[Mil91]   D. Miller. A logic programming language wiith lambda-abstraction, func-
            tion variables, and simple unification. *Jour. of Log. and Comp.*, 1991.

[MN98]   R. Mayr and T. Nipkow. Higher-order rewrite systems and their conflu-
            ence. *Theoretical Computer Science*, 192, 1998.

[MRV03]   P.-E. Moreau, C. Ringeissen, and M. Vittek. A pattern matching compiler
            for multiple target languages. In *Compiler Construction*, 2003.

[NP98]   T. Nipkow and C. Prehofer. Higher-order rewriting and equational rea-
            soning. In *Automated Deduction: A Basis for Applications*. Kluwer, 1998.

[Oos94]   V. V. Oostrom. *Confluence for abstract and higher-order rewriting*. PhD
            thesis, Vrije Universiteit, 1994.

[Pfe01]   F. Pfenning. Logical frameworks. In *Handbook of Automated Reasoning*,
            volume II, chapter 17, pages 1063–1147. Elsevier Science, 2001.

[Qia96]   Z. Qian. Unification of higher-order patterns in linear time and space. *J.
            Log. Comput*, 1996.

[Shi94]   H. Shi. *Extended matching with applications to program transformation*.
            PhD thesis, Universität Bremen, 1994.

[Sit01]   G. Sittampalam. *Higher-order Matching for Program Transformation*.
            PhD thesis, Magdalen College, 2001.

[Vis05]   E. Visser. A survey of strategies in rule-based program transformation
            systems. *Journal of Symbolic Computation*, 40(1), 2005.

[vOvR93]   V. van Oostrom and F. van Raamsdonk. Comparing combinatory re-
            duction systems and higher-order rewrite systems. volume 816 of *LNCS*,
            1993.

[vR93]   F. van Raamsdonk. Confluence and superdevelopments. *Rewriting Tech-
            niques and Applications*, 1993.

[Wac06]   B. Wack. A Curry-Howard-De Bruijn Isomorphism Modulo. *Under sub-
            mission*, 2006.

Derivational Complexity of Knuth-Bendix Orders Revisited

Georg Moser

Institute of Computer Science
University of Innsbruck
6020 Innsbruck, Austria
georg.moser@uibk.ac.at

Abstract. We study the derivational complexity of rewrite systems $\mathcal{R}$ compatible with KBO, if the signature of $\mathcal{R}$ is infinite. We show that the known bounds on the derivation height are preserved, if $\mathcal{R}$ fulfils some mild conditions. This allows us to obtain bounds on the derivational height of non simply terminating TRSs. Furthermore, we re-establish the 2-recursive upper-bound on the derivational complexity of finite rewrite systems $\mathcal{R}$ compatible with KBO.

1 Introduction

One of the main themes in rewriting is *termination*. Over the years powerful methods have been introduced to establish termination of a given term rewriting system (TRS) $\mathcal{R}$. Earlier research mainly concentrated on inventing suitable reduction orders—for example simplification orders, see Chapter 6, authored by Zantema in [1]—capable of proving termination directly. In recent years the emphasis shifted towards transformation techniques like the *dependency pair method* or *semantic labelling*, see [1]. The dependency pair method is easily automatable and lies at the heart of many successful termination provers like T$_T$T [2] or AProVE [3]. Semantic labelling with infinitely labels was conceived to be unsuitable for automation. Hence, only the variant with finitely many elements was incorporated (for example in AProVE [3] or TORPA [4]). Very recently this belief was proven wrong. TPA [5] implements semantic labelling with natural numbers, in combination with recursive path orders (RPOs) efficiently. As remarked in [6] a sensible extension of this implementation is the combination of semantic labelling with Knuth–Bendix orders (KBOs).

In order to assess the power and weaknesses of different termination techniques it is natural to look at the length of derivation sequences, induced by different techniques. This program has been suggested in [7]. The best known result is that for finite rewrite systems, RPOs induce primitive recursive derivational complexity. This bound is essentially optimal, see [8,9]. Similar optimal results have been obtained for lexicographic path orders (LPOs) and KBOs. Weiermann [10] showed that LPOs induce multiply recursive derivational complexity. In [11] Lepper showed that for term rewriting systems (TRSs) compatible with KBOs, the derivational complexity is bounded by the Ackermann function.

M. Hermann and A. Voronkov (Eds.): LPAR 2006, LNAI 4246, pp. 75–89, 2006.
© Springer-Verlag Berlin Heidelberg 2006

These results not only assess different proof techniques for termination, but constitute an a priori complexity analysis for term rewriting systems provably terminating by RPOs, LPOs, or KBOs. The application of termination provers as basis for the termination analysis of logic or functional programs is currently a very hot topic. Applicability of an a priori complexity analysis for TRSs in this direction seems likely.

While the aforementioned program has spawned a number of impressive results, not much is known about the derivational complexity induced by the dependency pair method or semantic labelling (for fixed base orders, obviously). We indicate the situation with an example.

Example 1. Consider the TRS $(\mathcal{F}, \mathcal{R})$ [12] consisting of the following rewrite rules:

$$f(h(x)) \rightarrow f(i(x)) \qquad\qquad h(a) \rightarrow b$$
$$g(i(x)) \rightarrow g(h(x)) \qquad\qquad i(a) \rightarrow b \,.$$

It is not difficult to see that termination of $\mathcal{R}$ cannot be established directly with path orders or KBOs. On the other hand, termination is easily shown via the dependency pair method or via semantic labelling. For the sake of the argument we show termination via semantic labelling with KBOs.

We use natural numbers as semantics and as labels. As interpretation for the function symbols we use $a_\mathbb{N} = b_\mathbb{N} = g_\mathbb{N}(n) = f_\mathbb{N}(n) = 1$, $i_\mathbb{N}(n) = n$, and $h_\mathbb{N}(n) = n + 1$. The resulting algebra $(\mathbb{N}, >)$ is a quasi-model for $\mathcal{R}$. It suffices to label the symbol f. We define the labelling function $\ell_f \colon \mathbb{N} \rightarrow \mathbb{N}$ as $\ell_f(n) = n$. Replacing

$$f(h(x)) \rightarrow f(i(x)) \,,$$

by the infinitely many rules

$$f_{n+1}(h(x)) \rightarrow f_n(i(x)) \,,$$

we obtain the labelled TRS, $(\mathcal{F}_{\mathrm{lab}}, \mathcal{R}_{\mathrm{lab}})$. Further the TRS $(\mathcal{F}_{\mathrm{lab}}, \mathcal{D}ec)$ consists of all rules

$$f_{n+1}(x) \rightarrow f_n(x) \,.$$

Now we can show termination of $\mathcal{R}' := \mathcal{R}_{\mathrm{lab}} \cup \mathcal{D}ec$ by an instance $\succ_{\mathsf{kbo}}$ of Knuth-Bendix order (KBO). We set the weight for all occurring function symbols to 1. Further, the precedence is defined as

$$f_{n+1} \succ f_n \succ \cdots \succ f_0 \succ i \succ h \succ g \succ a \succ b \,.$$

It is easy to see that $\mathcal{R}' \subseteq \succ_{\mathsf{kbo}}$. Thus termination of $\mathcal{R}$ is guaranteed.

As the rewrite system $\mathcal{R}'$ is infinite we cannot directly apply the aforementioned result on the derivational complexity induced by Knuth-Bendix order. A careful study of [11] reveals that the crucial problem is not that $\mathcal{R}'$ is infinite, but that the signature $\mathcal{F}_{\mathrm{lab}}$ is infinite, as Lepper's proof makes explicit use of the finiteness of the signature: To establish an upper-bound on the derivational complexity of a

TRS $\mathcal{R}$, compatible with KBO, an interpretation function $\mathcal{I}$ is defined, where the cardinality of the underlying signature is hard-coded into $\mathcal{I}$, cf. [11].

We study the situation by giving an alternative proof of Lepper's result compare [11]. The outcome of this study is that the assumption of finiteness of the rewrite system can be weakened. By enforcing conditions that are still weak enough to treat interesting rewrite systems, we show that for (possibly infinite) TRSs $\mathcal{R}$ over infinite signatures, compatible with KBO, the derivation height of $\mathcal{R}$ can be bounded by the Ackermann function. Using an example that stems from [8] we show that this upper-bound is essentially optimal.

Specialised to Example 1, our results provide an upper bound on the derivation height function with respect to $\mathcal{R}$: For every $t \in \mathcal{T}(\mathcal{F})$ there exists a constant c (depending only on t, $\mathcal{R}'$, and $\succ_{\mathsf{kbo}}$) such that the derivation height $\mathsf{dh}_{\mathcal{R}}(t)$ with respect to $\mathcal{R}$ is $\leq \mathsf{Ack}(c^n, 0)$. As the constant c can be made precise, the method is capable of automation.

This paper is organised as follows: In Section 2 and 3 some basic facts on rewriting, set theory and KBOs are recalled. In Section 4 we define an embedding from $\succ_{\mathsf{kbo}}$ into $>^{\mathsf{lex}}$, the lexicographic comparison of sequences of natural numbers. This embedding renders an alternative description of the derivation height of a term, based on the partial order $>^{\mathsf{lex}}$. This description is discussed in Section 5 and linked to the Ackermann function in Section 6. The above mentioned central result is contained in Section 7. Moreover in Section 7 we apply our result to a non simply terminating TRS, whose derivational complexity cannot be primitive recursively bounded.

2   Preliminaries

We assume familiarity with term rewriting. For further details see [1]. Let $\mathcal{V}$ denote a countably infinite set of variables and $\mathcal{F}$ a signature. We assume that $\mathcal{F}$ contains at least one constant. The set of terms over $\mathcal{F}$ and $\mathcal{V}$ is denoted as $\mathcal{T}(\mathcal{F}, \mathcal{V})$, while the set of ground terms is written as $\mathcal{T}(\mathcal{F})$. The set of variables occurring in a term t is denoted as $\mathsf{Var}(t)$. The set of function symbols occurring in t is denoted as $\mathsf{FS}(t)$. The *size* of a term t, written as $\mathsf{Size}(t)$, is the number of variables and functions symbols in it. The number of occurrences of a symbol $a \in \mathcal{F} \cup \mathcal{V}$ in t is denoted as $|t|_a$. A *TRS* $(\mathcal{F}, \mathcal{R})$ over $\mathcal{T}(\mathcal{F}, \mathcal{V})$ is a set of rewrite rules. The smallest rewrite relation that contains $\mathcal{R}$ is denoted as $\to_{\mathcal{R}}$. The transitive closure of $\to_{\mathcal{R}}$ is denoted by $\to_{\mathcal{R}}^{+}$, and its transitive and reflexive closure by $\to_{\mathcal{R}}^{*}$. A TRS $(\mathcal{F}, \mathcal{R})$ is called *terminating* if there is no infinite rewrite sequence. As usual, we frequently drop the reference to the signature $\mathcal{F}$.

A *partial order* $\succ$ is an irreflexive and transitive relation. The converse of $\succ$ is written as $\prec$. A partial order $\succ$ on a set A is *well-founded* if there exists no infinite descending sequence $a_1 \succ a_2 \succ \cdots$ of elements of A. A rewrite relation that is also a partial order is called *rewrite order*. A well-founded rewrite order is called *reduction order*. A TRS $\mathcal{R}$ and a partial order $\succ$ are *compatible* if $\mathcal{R} \subseteq \succ$. We also say that $\mathcal{R}$ is compatible with $\succ$ or vice versa. A TRS $\mathcal{R}$ is terminating iff it is compatible with a reduction order $\succ$.

Let $(\mathcal{A}, >)$ denote a well-founded weakly monotone $\mathcal{F}$-algebra. $(\mathcal{A}, >)$ consists of a carrier A, interpretations $f_{\mathcal{A}}$ for each function symbol in $\mathcal{F}$, and a well-founded partial order $>$ on A such that every $f_{\mathcal{A}}$ is weakly monotone in all arguments. We define a quasi-order $\geqslant_{\mathcal{A}}$: $s \geqslant_{\mathcal{A}} t$ if for all assignments $\alpha\colon \mathcal{V} \to A$ $[\alpha]_{\mathcal{A}}(s) \geqslant [\alpha]_{\mathcal{A}}(t)$. Here $\geqslant$ denotes the reflexive closure of $>$. The algebra $(\mathcal{A}, >)$ is a *quasi-model* of a TRS $\mathcal{R}$, if $\mathcal{R} \subseteq \geqslant_{\mathcal{A}}$.

A *labelling* ℓ for $\mathcal{A}$ consists of a set of labels L_f together with mappings $\ell_f\colon A^n \to L_f$ for every $f \in \mathcal{F}$, f n-ary. A labelling is called *weakly monotone* if all labelling functions ℓ_f are weakly monotone in all arguments. The labelled signature $\mathcal{F}_{\mathrm{lab}}$ consists of n-ary functions symbols f_a for every $f \in \mathcal{F}$, $a \in L_f$, together with all $f \in \mathcal{F}$, such that $L_f = \emptyset$. The TRS $\mathcal{Dec}$ consists of all rules

$$f_{a+1}(x_1, \ldots, x_n) \to f_a(x_1, \ldots, x_n) \,,$$

for all $f \in \mathcal{F}$. The x_i denote pairwise different variables. Our definition of $\mathcal{Dec}$ is motivated by a similar definition in [6]. Note that the rewrite relation $\to^*_{\mathcal{Dec}}$ is not changed by this modification of $\mathcal{Dec}$. For every assignment α, we inductively define a mapping $\mathsf{lab}_\alpha\colon \mathcal{T}(\mathcal{F}, \mathcal{V}) \to \mathcal{T}(\mathcal{F}_{\mathrm{lab}}, \mathcal{V})$:

$$\mathsf{lab}_\alpha(t) := \begin{cases} t & \text{if } t \in \mathcal{V}\,, \\ f(\mathsf{lab}_\alpha(t_1), \ldots, \mathsf{lab}_\alpha(t_n)) & \text{if } t = f(t_1, \ldots, t_n) \text{ and } L_f = \emptyset\,, \\ f_a(\mathsf{lab}_\alpha(t_1), \ldots, \mathsf{lab}_\alpha(t_n)) & \text{otherwise}\,. \end{cases}$$

The label a in the last case is defined as $l_f([\alpha]_{\mathcal{A}}(t_1), \ldots, [\alpha]_{\mathcal{A}}(t_n))$. The *labelled* TRS $\mathcal{R}_{\mathrm{lab}}$ over $\mathcal{F}_{\mathrm{lab}}$ is defined as

$$\{\mathsf{lab}_\alpha(l) \to \mathsf{lab}_\alpha(r) \mid l \to r \in \mathcal{R} \text{ and } \alpha \text{ an assignment}\}\,.$$

Theorem 1 (Zantema [13]). *Let $\mathcal{R}$ be a TRS, $(\mathcal{A}, >)$ a well-founded weakly monotone quasi-model for $\mathcal{R}$, and ℓ a weakly monotone labelling for $(\mathcal{A}, >)$. Then $\mathcal{R}$ is terminating iff $\mathcal{R}_{\mathrm{lab}} \cup \mathcal{Dec}$ is terminating.*

The proof of the theorem uses the following lemma.

Lemma 1. *Let $\mathcal{R}$ be a TRS, $(\mathcal{A}, >)$ a quasi-model of $\mathcal{R}$, and ℓ a weakly monotone labelling for $(\mathcal{A}, >)$. If $s \to_{\mathcal{R}} t$, then $\mathsf{lab}_\alpha(s) \to^*_{\mathcal{Dec}} \cdot \to_{\mathcal{R}_{\mathrm{lab}}} \mathsf{lab}_\alpha(t)$ for all assignments α.*

We briefly review a few basic concepts from set-theory in particular ordinals, see [14]. We write $>$ to denote the well-ordering of ordinals. Any ordinal $\alpha \neq 0$, smaller than ϵ_0, can uniquely be represented by its *Cantor Normal Form (CNF)*:

$$\omega^{\alpha_1} n_1 + \ldots \omega^{\alpha_k} n_k \qquad \text{with } \alpha_1 > \cdots > \alpha_k\,.$$

To each well-founded partial order $\succ$ on a set A we can associate a (set-theoretic) ordinal, its *order type*. First we associate an ordinal to each element a of A by setting $\mathrm{otype}_{\succ}(a) := \sup\{\mathrm{otype}_{\succ}(b) + 1\colon b \in A \text{ and } b \succ a\}$. The *order type* of $\succ$, denoted by $\mathrm{otype}(\succ)$, is the supremum of $\mathrm{otype}_{\succ}(a) + 1$ with $a \in A$. For two partial orders $\succ$ and $\succ'$ on A and A', respectively, a mapping $o\colon A \to A'$ *embeds* $\succ$ into $\succ'$ if for all $p, q \in A$, $p \succ q$ implies $o(p) \succ' o(q)$. Such a mapping is an *order-isomorphism* if it is bijective and the partial orders $\succ$ and $\succ'$ are linear .

3   The Knuth Bendix Orders

A *weight function* for $\mathcal{F}$ is a pair (w, w_0) consisting of a function $w \colon \mathcal{F} \to \mathbb{N}$ and a minimal weight $w_0 \in \mathbb{N}$, $w_0 > 0$ such that $w(c) \geq w_0$ if c is a constant. A weight function (w, w_0) is called *admissible* for a precedence $\succ$ if $f \succ g$ for all $g \in \mathcal{F}$ different from f, when f is unary with $w(f) = 0$. The function symbol f (if present) is called *special*. The *weight* of a term t, denoted as $w(t)$ is defined inductively. Assume t is a variable, then set $w(t) := w_0$, otherwise if $t = g(t_1, \ldots, t_n)$, we define $w(t) := w(g) + w(t_1) + \cdots + w(t_n)$.

The following definition of KBO is tailored to our purposes. It is taken from [11]. We write $s = f^a s'$ if $s = f^a(s')$ and the root symbol of s' is distinct from the special symbol f. Let $\succ$ be a precedence. The *rank* of a function symbol is defined as: $\mathrm{rk}(f) := \max\{\mathrm{rk}(g) + 1 \mid f \succ g\}$. (To assert well-definedness we stipulate $\max(\emptyset) = 0$.)

Definition 1. *Let* (w, w_0) *denote an admissible weight function for* $\mathcal{F}$ *and let* $\succ$ *denote a precedence on* $\mathcal{F}$. *We write f for the special symbol. The* Knuth Bendix *order $\succ_{\mathrm{KBO2}}$ on $\mathcal{T}(\mathcal{F}, \mathcal{V})$ is inductively defined as follows: $s \succ_{\mathrm{KBO2}} t$ if $|s|_x \geq |t|_x$ for all $x \in \mathcal{V}$ and*

1. $w(s) > w(t)$, *or*
2. $w(s) = w(t)$, $s = f^a s'$, $t = f^b t'$, *where* $s' = g(s_1, \ldots, s_n)$, $t' = h(t_1, \ldots, t_m)$, *and one of the following cases holds.*
   (a) $a > b$, *or*
   (b) $a = b$ *and* $g \succ h$, *or*
   (c) $a = b$, $g = h$, *and* $(s_1, \ldots, s_n) \succ^{\mathrm{lex}}_{\mathrm{KBO2}} (t_1, \ldots, t_n)$.

Let $\succ_{\mathsf{kbo}}$ denote the KBO on terms in its usual definition, see [1]. The following lemma, taken from [11], states that both orders are interchangeable.

Lemma 2 (Lepper [11]). *The orders $\succ_{\mathsf{kbo}}$ and $\succ_{\mathrm{KBO2}}$ coincide.*

In the literature *real-valued* KBOs and other generalisations of KBOs are studied as well, cf. [15,16]. However, as established in [17] any TRS shown to be terminating by a real-valued KBO can be shown to be terminating by a integer-valued KBO.

4   Exploiting the Order-Type of KBOs

We write $\mathbb{N}^*$ to denote the set of finite sequences of natural numbers. Let $p \in \mathbb{N}^*$, we write $|p|$ for the *length* of p, i.e. the number of positions in the sequence p. The ith element of the sequence a is denoted as $(p)_{i-1}$. We write $p \frown q$ to denote the concatenation of the sequences p and q. The next definition is standard but included here, for sake of completeness.

Definition 2. *We define the* lexicographic order *on* $\mathbb{N}^*$. *If $p, q \in \mathbb{N}^*$, then $p >^{\mathrm{lex}} q$ if,*

- $|p| > |q|$, *or*
- $|p| = |q| = n$ *and there exists* $i \in [0, n-1]$, *such that for all* $j \in [0, i-1]$
  $(p)_j = (q)_j$ *and* $(p)_i > (q)_i$.

It is not difficult to see that $\mathrm{otype}(>^{\mathrm{lex}}) = \omega^\omega$, moreover in [11] it is shown that $\mathrm{otype}(\succ_{\mathsf{kbo}}) = \omega^\omega$. Hence $\mathrm{otype}(>^{\mathrm{lex}}) = \mathrm{otype}(\succ_{\mathsf{kbo}})$, a fact we exploit below. However, to make this work, we have to restrict our attention to signatures $\mathcal{F}$ with bounded arities. The maximal arity of $\mathcal{F}$ is denoted as $\mathsf{Ar}(\mathcal{F})$.

Definition 3. *Let the signature $\mathcal{F}$ and a weight function (w, w_0) for $\mathcal{F}$ be fixed. We define an embedding* $\mathsf{tw}\colon \mathcal{T}(\mathcal{F}, \mathcal{V}) \to \mathbb{N}^*$. *Set* $b := \max\{\mathsf{Ar}(\mathcal{F}), 3\} + 1$.

$$
\mathsf{tw}(t) := \begin{cases} (w_0, a, 0) \frown 0^m & \text{if } t = f^a x, \; x \in \mathcal{V}, \\ (\mathrm{w}(t), a, \mathsf{rk}(g)) \frown \mathsf{tw}(t_1) \frown \cdots \frown \mathsf{tw}(t_n) \frown 0^m & \text{if } t = f^a g(t_1, \ldots, t_n). \end{cases}
$$

The number m is set suitably, so that $|\mathsf{tw}(t)| = b^{\mathrm{w}(t)+1}$.

The mapping tw flattens a term t by transforming it into a concatenation of triples. Each triple holds the weight of the considered subterm r, the number of leading special symbols and the rank of the first non-special function symbol of r. In this way all the information necessary to compare two terms via $\succ_{\mathsf{kbo}}$ is expressed as a very simple data structure: a list of natural numbers.

Lemma 3. tw *embeds* $\succ_{\mathsf{kbo}}$ *into* $>^{\mathrm{lex}}$: *If* $s \succ_{\mathsf{kbo}} t$, *then* $\mathsf{tw}(s) >^{\mathrm{lex}} \mathsf{tw}(t)$.

Proof. The proof follows the pattern of the proof of Lemma 9 in [11].

Firstly, we make sure that the mapping tw is *well-defined*, i.e., we show that the length restriction can be met. We proceed by induction on t; let $t = f^a t'$. We consider two cases (i) $t' \in \mathcal{V}$ or (ii) $t' = g(t_1, \ldots, t_n)$. Suppose the former:

$$
|(w_0, a, 0)| = 3 \le b^{\mathrm{w}(t)+1} .
$$

Now suppose case (ii): Let $j = \mathsf{rk}(g)$, we obtain

$$
|(\mathrm{w}(t), a, j) \frown \mathsf{tw}(t_1) \frown \cdots \frown \mathsf{tw}(t_n)| = 3 + b^{\mathrm{w}(t_1)+1} + \cdots + b^{\mathrm{w}(t_n)+1}
$$
$$
\le 3 + n \cdot b^{\mathrm{w}(t)} \le b^{\mathrm{w}(t)+1} .
$$

Secondly, we show the following, slight generalisation of the lemma:

$$
s \succ_{\mathsf{kbo}} t \wedge |\mathsf{tw}(s) \frown r| = |\mathsf{tw}(t) \frown r'| \implies \mathsf{tw}(s) \frown r >^{\mathrm{lex}} \mathsf{tw}(t) \frown r' . \tag{1}
$$

To prove (1) we proceed by induction on $s \succ_{\mathsf{kbo}} t$. Set $p = \mathsf{tw}(s) \frown r$, $q = \mathsf{tw}(t) \frown r'$.

CASE $\mathrm{w}(s) > \mathrm{w}(t)$: By definition of the mapping tw, we have: If $\mathrm{w}(s) > \mathrm{w}(t)$, then $(\mathsf{tw}(s))_0 > (\mathsf{tw}(t))_0$. Thus $p >^{\mathrm{lex}} q$ follows.

CASE $\mathrm{w}(s) = \mathrm{w}(t)$: We only consider the sub-case where $s = f^a g(s_1, \ldots, s_n)$ and $t = f^a g(t_1, \ldots, t_n)$ and there exists $i \in [1, n]$ such that $s_1 = t_1, \ldots, s_{i-1} = t_{i-1}$, and $s_i \succ_{\mathsf{kbo}} t_i$. (The other cases are treated as in the case above.) The induction hypotheses (IH) expresses that if $|\mathsf{tw}(s_i) \frown v| = |\mathsf{tw}(t_i) \frown v'|$, then $\mathsf{tw}(s_i) \frown v >^{\mathrm{lex}} \mathsf{tw}(t_i) \frown v'$. For $j = \mathsf{rk}(g)$, we obtain

$$p = \overbrace{(\mathsf{w}(s), a, j) \frown \mathsf{tw}(s_1) \frown \cdots \frown \mathsf{tw}(s_{i-1})}^{w} \frown \mathsf{tw}(s_i) \frown \cdots \frown \mathsf{tw}(s_n) \frown r \,,$$

$$q = \underbrace{(\mathsf{w}(s), a, j) \frown \mathsf{tw}(s_1) \frown \cdots \frown \mathsf{tw}(s_{i-1})}_{w} \frown \mathsf{tw}(t_i) \frown \cdots \frown \mathsf{tw}(t_n) \frown r' \,.$$

Due to $|p| = |q|$, we conclude

$$|\mathsf{tw}(s_i) \frown \cdots \frown \mathsf{tw}(s_n) \frown r| = |\mathsf{tw}(t_i) \frown \cdots \frown \mathsf{tw}(t_n) \frown r'| \,.$$

Hence IH is applicable and we obtain

$$\mathsf{tw}(s_i) \frown \cdots \frown \mathsf{tw}(s_n) \frown r >^{\mathrm{lex}} \mathsf{tw}(t_i) \frown \cdots \frown \mathsf{tw}(t_n) \frown r' \,,$$

which yields $p >^{\mathrm{lex}} q$. This completes the proof of (1).

Finally, to establish the lemma, we assume $s \succ_{\mathsf{kbo}} t$. By definition either $\mathsf{w}(s) > \mathsf{w}(t)$ or $\mathsf{w}(s) = \mathsf{w}(t)$. In the latter case $\mathsf{tw}(s) >^{\mathrm{lex}} \mathsf{tw}(t)$ follows by (1). While in the former $\mathsf{tw}(s) >^{\mathrm{lex}} \mathsf{tw}(t)$ follows as $\mathsf{w}(s) > \mathsf{w}(t)$ implies $|\mathsf{tw}(s)| > |\mathsf{tw}(t)|$. $\qquad\square$

5   Derivation Height of Knuth-Bendix Orders

Let $\mathcal{R}$ be a TRS and $\succ_{\mathsf{kbo}}$ a KBO such that $\succ_{\mathsf{kbo}}$ is compatible with $\mathcal{R}$. The TRS $\mathcal{R}$ and the KBO $\succ_{\mathsf{kbo}}$ are fixed for the remainder of the paper. We want to extract an upper-bound on the length of derivations in $\mathcal{R}$. We recall the central definitions. Note that we can restrict the definition to the set ground terms. The *derivation height* function $\mathsf{dh}_{\mathcal{R}}$ (with respect to $\mathcal{R}$ on $\mathcal{T}(\mathcal{F})$) is defined as follows.

$$\mathsf{dh}_{\mathcal{R}}(t) := \max(\{n \mid \exists (t_0, \ldots, t_n)\; t = t_0 \to_{\mathcal{R}} t_1 \to_{\mathcal{R}} \ldots \to_{\mathcal{R}} t_n\}) \,.$$

We introduce a couple of *measure functions* for term and sequence complexities, respectively. The first measure $\mathsf{sp} \colon \mathcal{T}(\mathcal{F}, \mathcal{V}) \to \mathbb{N}$ bounds the maximal nesting of special symbols in the term:

$$\mathsf{sp}(t) := \begin{cases} a & \text{if } t = f^a x, \; x \in \mathcal{V} \,, \\ \max(\{a\} \cup \{\mathsf{sp}(t_j) \mid j \in [1, n]\}) & \text{if } t = f^a g(t_1, \ldots, t_n) \,. \end{cases}$$

The second and third measure $\mathsf{rk} \colon \mathcal{T}(\mathcal{F}, \mathcal{V}) \to \mathbb{N}$ and $\mathsf{mrk} \colon \mathcal{T}(\mathcal{F}, \mathcal{V}) \to \mathbb{N}$ collect information on the ranks of non special function symbols occurring:

$$\mathsf{rk}(t) := \begin{cases} 0 & \text{if } t = f^a x, \; x \in \mathcal{V} \,, \\ j & \text{if } t = f^a g(t_1, \ldots, t_n) \text{ and } \mathsf{rk}(g) = j \,, \end{cases}$$

$$\mathsf{mrk}(t) := \begin{cases} 0 & \text{if } t = f^a x, \; x \in \mathcal{V} \,, \\ \max(\{j\} \cup \{\mathsf{mrk}(t_i) \mid i \in [1, n]\}) & \text{if } t = f^a g(t_1, \ldots, t_n), \; \mathsf{rk}(g) = j \,. \end{cases}$$

The fourth measure $\mathbf{max}\colon \mathbb{N}^* \to \mathbb{N}$ considers sequences p and bounds the maximal number occurring in p:

$$\mathbf{max}(p) := \max(\{(p)_i \mid i \in [0, |p| - 1]\}) \ .$$

It is immediate from the definitions that for any term t: $\mathsf{sp}(t), \mathsf{rk}(t), \mathsf{mrk}(t) \leq \mathbf{max}(\mathsf{tw}(t))$. We write $r \trianglelefteq t$ to denote the fact that r is a subterm of t.

Lemma 4. *If $r \trianglelefteq t$, then $\mathbf{max}(\mathsf{tw}(t)) \geq \mathbf{max}(\mathsf{tw}(r))$.*

We informally argue for the correctness of the lemma. Suppose r is a subterm of t. Then clearly $\mathsf{w}(r) \leq \mathsf{w}(t)$. The maximal occurring nesting of special symbols in r is smaller (or equal) than in t. And the maximal rank of a symbol in r is smaller (or equal) than in t. The mapping tw transforms r to a sequence p whose coefficients are less than $\mathsf{w}(t)$, less than the maximal nesting of special symbols and less than the maximal rank of non-special function symbol in r . Hence $\mathbf{max}(\mathsf{tw}(t)) \geq \mathbf{max}(\mathsf{tw}(r))$ holds.

Lemma 5. *If $p = \mathsf{tw}(t)$ and $q = \mathsf{tw}(f^a t)$, then $\mathbf{max}(p) + a \geq \mathbf{max}(q)$.*

Proof. The proof of the lemma proceeds by a case distinction on t.   □

Lemma 6. *We write $m \,\dot{-}\, n$ to denote $\max(\{m - n, 0\})$. Assume $s \succ_{\mathsf{kbo}} t$ with $\mathsf{sp}(t) \leq K$ and $(\mathsf{mrk}(t) \,\dot{-}\, \mathsf{rk}(s)) \leq K$. Let σ be a substitution and set $p = \mathsf{tw}(s\sigma)$, $q = \mathsf{tw}(t\sigma)$. Then $p >^{\mathrm{lex}} q$ and $\mathbf{max}(p) + K \geq \mathbf{max}(q)$.*

Proof. It suffices to show $\mathbf{max}(p) + K \geq \mathbf{max}(q)$ as $p >^{\mathrm{lex}} q$ follows from Lemma 3. We proceed by induction on t; let $t = f^a t'$.

CASE $t' \in \mathcal{V}$: Set $t' = x$. We consider two sub-cases: Either (i) $x\sigma = f^b y$, $y \in \mathcal{V}$ or (ii) $x\sigma = f^b g(u_1, \ldots, u_m)$. It suffices to consider sub-case (ii), as sub-case (i) is treated in a similar way. From $s \succ_{\mathsf{kbo}} t$, we know that for all $y \in \mathcal{V}$, $|s|_y \geq |t|_y$, hence $x \in \mathsf{Var}(s)$ and $x\sigma \trianglelefteq s\sigma$. Let $l := \mathsf{rk}(g)$; by Lemma 4 we conclude $\mathbf{max}(\mathsf{tw}(x\sigma)) \leq \mathbf{max}(p)$. I.e. $b, l, \mathbf{max}(\mathsf{tw}(u_1)), \ldots, \mathbf{max}(\mathsf{tw}(u_m)) \leq \mathbf{max}(p)$. We obtain

$$
\begin{aligned}
\mathbf{max}(q) &= \max(\{w_0, a + b, l\} \cup \{\mathbf{max}(\mathsf{tw}(u_j)) \mid i \in [1, m]\}) \\
&\leq \max(\{\mathsf{w}(s\sigma), \mathsf{sp}(t) + \mathbf{max}(p), \mathbf{max}(p)\} \cup \{\mathbf{max}(p)\}) \\
&\leq \max(\{\mathsf{w}(s\sigma), \mathbf{max}(p) + K\} \cup \{\mathbf{max}(p)\}) = \mathbf{max}(p) + K \ .
\end{aligned}
$$

CASE $t' = g(t_1, \ldots, t_n)$: Let $j = \mathsf{rk}(g)$. By Definition 1 we obtain $s \succ_{\mathsf{kbo}} t_i$. Moreover $\mathsf{sp}(t_i) \leq \mathsf{sp}(t) \leq K$ and $\mathsf{mrk}(t_i) \leq \mathsf{mrk}(t)$. Hence for all i: $\mathsf{sp}(t_i) \leq K$ and $(\mathsf{mrk}(t_i) \,\dot{-}\, \mathsf{rk}(s)) \leq K$ holds. Thus IH is applicable: For all i: $\mathbf{max}(\mathsf{tw}(t_i\sigma)) \leq \mathbf{max}(p) + K$. By using the assumption $(\mathsf{mrk}(t) \,\dot{-}\, \mathsf{rk}(s)) \leq K$ we obtain:

$$
\begin{aligned}
\mathbf{max}(q) &= \max(\{\mathsf{w}(t\sigma), a, j\} \cup \{\mathbf{max}(\mathsf{tw}(t_i\sigma)) \mid i \in [1, n]\}) \\
&\leq \max(\{\mathsf{w}(t\sigma), \mathsf{sp}(t), \mathsf{rk}(s) + K\} \cup \{\mathbf{max}(p) + K\}) \\
&\leq \max(\{\mathsf{w}(s\sigma), \mathsf{sp}(t), \mathsf{rk}(s\sigma) + K\} \cup \{\mathbf{max}(p) + K\}) \\
&\leq \max(\{\mathsf{w}(s\sigma), K, \mathbf{max}(p) + K\} \cup \{\mathbf{max}(p) + K\}) = \mathbf{max}(p) + K \ .
\end{aligned}
$$

□

In the following, we assume that the set

$$M := \{\mathsf{sp}(r) \mid l \to r \in \mathcal{R}\} \cup \{(\mathsf{mrk}(r) \doteq \mathsf{rk}(l)) \mid l \to r \in \mathcal{R}\} \tag{2}$$

is finite. We set $K := \max(M)$ and let K be fixed for the remainder.

Example 2. With respect to the TRS $\mathcal{R}' := \mathcal{R}_{\text{lab}} \cup \mathcal{D}ec$ from Example 1, we have $M = \{(\mathsf{mrk}(r) \doteq \mathsf{rk}(l)) \mid l \to r \in \mathcal{R}'\}$. Note that the signature of $\mathcal{R}'$ doesn't contain a special symbol.

Clearly M is finite and it is easy to see that $\max(M) = 1$. Exemplary, we consider the rule schemata $f_{n+1}(h(x)) \to f_n(i(x))$. Note that the rank of i equals 4, the rank of h is 3, and the rank of f_n is given by $n+5$. Hence $\mathsf{mrk}(f_n(i(x))) = n+5$ and $\mathsf{rk}(f_{n+1}(h(x))) = n+6$. Clearly $(n+5 \doteq n+6) \leq 1$.

Lemma 7. *If* $s \to_{\mathcal{R}} t$, $p = \mathsf{tw}(s)$, $q = \mathsf{tw}(t)$, *then* $p >^{\text{lex}} q$ *and* $u(\mathbf{max}(p), K) \geq \mathbf{max}(q)$, *where* u *denotes a monotone polynomial such that* $u(n, m) \geq 2n + m$.

Proof. By definition of the rewrite relation there exists a context C, a substitution σ and a rule $l \to r \in R$ such that $s = C[l\sigma]$ and $t = C[r\sigma]$. We prove $\mathbf{max}(q) \leq u(\mathbf{max}(p), K)$ by induction on C. Note that C can only have the form (i) $C = f^a[\square]$ or (ii) $C = f^a g(u_1, \ldots, C'[\square], \ldots, u_n)$.

CASE $C = f^a[\square]$: By Lemma 6 we see $\mathbf{max}(\mathsf{tw}(r\sigma)) \leq \mathbf{max}(\mathsf{tw}(l\sigma)) + K$. Employing in addition Lemma 5 and Lemma 4, we obtain:

$$\begin{aligned}
\mathbf{max}(q) = \mathbf{max}(\mathsf{tw}(f^a r\sigma)) &\leq \mathbf{max}(\mathsf{tw}(r\sigma)) + a \\
&\leq \mathbf{max}(\mathsf{tw}(l\sigma)) + K + a \\
&\leq \mathbf{max}(p) + K + \mathbf{max}(p) \leq u(\mathbf{max}(p), K) .
\end{aligned}$$

CASE $C = f^a g(u_1, \ldots, C'[\square], \ldots, u_n)$: As $C'[l\sigma] \to_{\mathcal{R}} C'[r\sigma]$, IH is applicable: Let $p' = \mathsf{tw}(C'[l\sigma])$, $q' = \mathsf{tw}(C'[r\sigma])$. Then $\mathbf{max}(q') \leq u(\mathbf{max}(p'), K)$. For $\mathsf{rk}(g) = l$, we obtain by application of IH and Lemma 4:

$$\begin{aligned}
\mathbf{max}(q) = \mathbf{max}(\{\mathsf{w}(t), a, l\} &\cup \{\mathbf{max}(\mathsf{tw}(u_1)), \ldots, \mathbf{max}(q'), \ldots, \mathbf{max}(\mathsf{tw}(u_n))\}) \\
&\leq \mathbf{max}(\{\mathsf{w}(s), a, l\} \cup \\
&\quad \cup \{\mathbf{max}(\mathsf{tw}(u_1)), \ldots, u(\mathbf{max}(p'), K), \ldots, \mathbf{max}(\mathsf{tw}(u_n))\}) \\
&\leq \mathbf{max}(\{\mathsf{w}(s), a, l\} \cup \{\mathbf{max}(p), u(\mathbf{max}(p), K)\}) = u(\mathbf{max}(p), K) . \qquad \square
\end{aligned}$$

We define *approximations* of the partial order $>^{\text{lex}}$.

$$p >^{\text{lex}}_n q \quad \text{iff} \quad p >^{\text{lex}} q \text{ and } u(\mathbf{max}(p), n) \geq \mathbf{max}(q) ,$$

where u is defined as in Lemma 7. Now Lemma 6 can be concisely expressed as follows, for K as above.

Proposition 1. *If* $s \to_{\mathcal{R}} t$, *then* $\mathsf{tw}(s) >^{\text{lex}}_K \mathsf{tw}(t)$.

In the spirit of the definition of derivation height, we define a family of functions $\mathsf{Ah}_n \colon \mathbb{N} \to \mathbb{N}$:

$$\mathsf{Ah}_n(p) := \max(\{m \mid \exists(p_0, \ldots, p_m) \ p = p_0 >_n^{\text{lex}} p_1 >_n^{\text{lex}} \cdots >_n^{\text{lex}} p_m\}) \ .$$

The following proposition is an easy consequence of the definitions and Proposition 1.

Theorem 2. *Let $(\mathcal{F}, \mathcal{R})$ be a TRS, compatible with KBO. Assume the set $M :=$ $\{\mathsf{sp}(r) \mid l \to r \in \mathcal{R}\} \cup \{(\mathsf{mrk}(r) \doteq \mathsf{rk}(l)) \mid l \to r \in \mathcal{R}\}$ is finite and the arities in of the symbols in $\mathcal{F}$ are bounded; set $K := \max(M)$. Then $\mathsf{dh}_{\mathcal{R}}(t) \leq \mathsf{Ah}_K(\mathsf{tw}(t))$.*

In the next section we show that Ah_n is bounded by the Ackermann function Ack. Thus providing the sought upper-bound on the derivation height of $\mathcal{R}$.

6   Bounding the Growth of Ah_n

Instead of directly relating the functions Ah_n to the Ackermann function, we make use of the fast-growing *Hardy* functions, cf. [18]. The Hardy functions form a hierarchy of unary functions $\mathsf{H}_\alpha \colon \mathbb{N} \to \mathbb{N}$ indexed by ordinals. We will only be interested in a small part of this hierarchy, namely in the set of functions $\{\mathsf{H}_\alpha \mid \alpha < \omega^\omega\}$.

Definition 4. *We define the embedding $o \colon \mathbb{N}^* \to \omega^\omega$ as follows:*

$$o(p) := \omega^{\ell-1}(p)_0 + \ldots \omega(p)_{\ell-2} + (p)_{\ell-1} \ ,$$

where $\ell = |p|$.

The next lemma follows directly from the definitions.

Lemma 8. *If $p >^{\text{lex}} q$, then $o(p) > o(q)$.*

We associate with every $\alpha < \omega^\omega$ in *CNF* an ordinal α_n, where $n \in \mathbb{N}$. The sequence $(\alpha_n)_n$ is called *fundamental sequence* of α. (For the connection between rewriting and fundamental sequences see e.g. [19].)

$$\alpha_n := \begin{cases} 0 & \text{if } \alpha = 0 \, , \\ \beta & \text{if } \alpha = \beta + 1 \, , \\ \beta + \omega^{\gamma+1} \cdot (k-1) + \omega^\gamma \cdot (n+1) & \text{if } \alpha = \beta + \omega^{\gamma+1} \cdot k \, . \end{cases}$$

Based on the definition of α_n, we define $\mathsf{H}_\alpha \colon \mathbb{N} \to \mathbb{N}$, for $\alpha < \omega^\omega$ by transfinite induction on α:

$$\mathsf{H}_0(n) := n \qquad \mathsf{H}_\alpha(n) := \mathsf{H}_{\alpha_n}(n+1) \ .$$

Let $>_{(n)}$ denote the transitive closure of $(.)_n$, i.e. $\alpha >_{(n)} \beta$ iff $\alpha_n >_{(n)} \beta$ or $\alpha_n = \beta$. Suppose $\alpha, \beta < \omega^\omega$. Let $\alpha = \omega^{\alpha_1} n_1 + \ldots \omega^{\alpha_k} n_k$ and $\beta = \omega^{\beta_1} m_1 + \ldots \omega^{\beta_l} m_l$. Recall that any ordinal $\alpha \neq 0$ can be uniquely written in CNF, hence we can assume that $\alpha_1 > \cdots > \alpha_k$ and $\beta_1 > \cdots > \beta_l$. Furthermore by our assumption that $\alpha, \beta < \omega^\omega$, we have $\alpha_i, \beta_j \in \mathbb{N}$. We write $\mathsf{NF}(\alpha, \beta)$ if $\alpha_k \geq \beta_1$.

Before we proceed in our estimation of the functions Ah_n, we state some simple facts that help us to calculate with the function H_α.

Lemma 9.   *1. If $\alpha >_{(n)} \beta$, then $\alpha >_{(n+1)} \beta + 1$ or $\alpha = \beta + 1$.*
2. If $\alpha >_{(n)} \beta$ and $n \geq m$, then $\mathsf{H}_\alpha(n) > \mathsf{H}_\beta(m)$.
3. If $n > m$, then $\mathsf{H}_\alpha(n) > \mathsf{H}_\alpha(m)$.
4. If $\mathsf{NF}(\alpha, \beta)$, then $\mathsf{H}_{\alpha+\beta}(n) = \mathsf{H}_\alpha \circ \mathsf{H}_\beta(n)$; $\circ$ denotes function composition.

We relate the Hardy functions with the Ackermann function. The stated upper-bound is a gross one, but a more careful estimation is not necessary here.

Lemma 10. *For $n \geq 1$: $\mathsf{H}_{\omega^n}(m) \leq \mathsf{Ack}(2n, m)$.*

Proof. We recall the definition of the Ackermann function:

$$\mathsf{Ack}(0, m) = m + 1$$
$$\mathsf{Ack}(n + 1, 0) = \mathsf{Ack}(n, 1)$$
$$\mathsf{Ack}(n + 1, m + 1) = \mathsf{Ack}(n, \mathsf{Ack}(n + 1, m))$$

In the following we sometimes denote the Ackermann function as a unary function, indexed by its first argument: $\mathsf{Ack}(n, m) = \mathsf{Ack}_n(m)$. To prove the lemma, we proceed by induction on the lexicographic comparison of n and m. We only present the case, where n and m are greater than 0. As preparation note that $m + 1 \leq \mathsf{H}_{\omega^n}(m)$ holds for any n and $\mathsf{Ack}_n^2(m + 1) \leq \mathsf{Ack}_{n+1}(m + 1)$ holds for any n, m.

$$\begin{aligned}
\mathsf{H}_{\omega^{n+1}}(m + 1) &= \mathsf{H}_{\omega^n(m+2)}(m + 2) \\
&\leq \mathsf{H}_{\omega^n(m+2)+\omega^n}(m + 1) &&\text{Lemma 9(3,4)} \\
&= \mathsf{H}_{\omega^n}^2 \mathsf{H}_{\omega^n(m+1)}(m + 1) &&\text{Lemma 9(4)} \\
&= \mathsf{H}_{\omega^n}^2 \mathsf{H}_{\omega^{n+1}}(m) \\
&\leq \mathsf{Ack}_{2n}^2 \mathsf{Ack}_{2(n+1)}(m) &&\text{IH} \\
&\leq \mathsf{Ack}_{2n+1} \mathsf{Ack}_{2(n+1)}(m) \\
&= \mathsf{Ack}(2(n + 1), m + 1) \, . &&\square
\end{aligned}$$

Lemma 11. *Assume $u(m, n) \leq 2m + n$ and set $\ell = |p|$. For all $n \in \mathbb{N}$:*

$$\mathsf{Ah}_n(p) \leq \mathsf{H}_{\omega^2 \cdot o(p)}(u(\max(p), n) + 1) < \mathsf{H}_{\omega^{4+\ell}}(\max(p) + n) \, . \qquad (3)$$

Proof. To prove the first half of (3) , we make use of the following fact:

$$p >^{\mathrm{lex}} q \wedge n \geq \max(q) \implies o(p) >_{(n)} o(q) \, . \qquad (4)$$

To prove (4), one proceeds by induction on $>^{\mathrm{lex}}$ and uses that the embedding $o \colon \mathbb{N}^* \to \omega^\omega$ is essentially an order-isomorphism. We omit the details.
By definition, we have $\mathsf{Ah}_n(p) = \max(\{\mathsf{Ah}_n(q) + 1 \mid p >_n^{\mathrm{lex}} q\})$. Hence it suffices to prove

$$p >^{\mathrm{lex}} q \wedge u(\max(p), n) \geq \max(q) \implies \mathsf{Ah}_n(q) < \mathsf{H}_{\omega^2 \cdot o(p)}(u(\max(p), n)+1) \quad (5)$$

We fix p fulfilling the assumptions in (5); let $\alpha = o(p), \beta = o(q), v = u(\max(q), n)$. We use (4) to obtain $\alpha >_{(v)} \beta$. We proceed by induction on p.

Consider the case $\alpha_v = \beta$. As $p >^{\text{lex}} q$, we can employ IH to conclude $\mathsf{Ah}_n(q) \leq H_{\omega^2 \cdot o(q)}(u(\mathbf{max}(q), n)+1)$. It is not difficult to see that for any $p \in \mathbb{N}^*$ and $n \in \mathbb{N}$, $4\,\mathbf{max}(p) + 2n + 1 \leq H_{\omega^2}(u(\mathbf{max}(p), n))$. In sum, we obtain:

$$
\begin{aligned}
\mathsf{Ah}_n(q) &\leq H_{\omega^2 \cdot o(q)}(u(\mathbf{max}(q), n) + 1) \\
&\leq H_{\omega^2 \cdot \alpha_v}(u(u(\mathbf{max}(p), n), n) + 1) && \mathbf{max}(q) \leq u(\mathbf{max}(p), n) \\
&\leq H_{\omega^2 \cdot \alpha_v}(4\,\mathbf{max}(p) + 2n + 1) && \text{Definition of } u \\
&\leq H_{\omega^2 \cdot \alpha_v} H_{\omega^2}(u(\mathbf{max}(p), n)) \\
&= H_{\omega^2 \cdot (\alpha_v + 1)}(u(\mathbf{max}(p), n)) && \text{Lemma 9(4)} \\
&< H_{\omega^2 \cdot (\alpha_v + 1)}(u(\mathbf{max}(p), n) + 1) && \text{Lemma 9(3)} \\
&\leq H_{\omega^2 \cdot \alpha}(u(\mathbf{max}(p), n) + 1) && \text{Lemma 9(2)}
\end{aligned}
$$

The application of Lemma 9(2) in the last step is feasible as by definition $\alpha >_{(v)} \alpha_v$. An application of Lemma 9(1) yields $\alpha_v + 1 \leq_{(v+1)} \alpha$. From which we deduce $\omega^2 \cdot (\alpha_v + 1) \leq_{(v+1)} \omega^2 \cdot \alpha$.

Secondly, consider the case $\alpha_v >_{(v)} \beta$. In this case the proof follows the pattern of the above proof, but an additional application of Lemma 9(4) is required. This completes the proof of (5).

To prove the second part of (3), we proceed as follows: The fact that $\omega^\ell > o(p)$ is immediate from the definitions. Induction on p reveals that even $\omega^\ell >_{(\mathbf{max}(p))} o(p)$ holds. Thus in conjunction with the first part of (3), we obtain:

$$
\begin{aligned}
\mathsf{Ah}_n(p) &\leq H_{\omega^2 \cdot o(p)}(u(\mathbf{max}(p), n) + 1) \leq H_{\omega^{2+\ell}}(u(\mathbf{max}(p), n) + 1) \\
&\leq H_{\omega^{4+\ell}}(\mathbf{max}(p) + n) \,.
\end{aligned}
$$

The last step follows as $2\,\mathbf{max}(p) + n + 1 \leq H_{\omega^2}(\mathbf{max}(p) + n)$. $\qquad\square$

As a consequence of Lemma 10 and 11, we obtain the following proposition.

Theorem 3. *For all $n \geq 1$: If $\ell = |p|$, then $\mathsf{Ah}_n(p) \leq \mathsf{Ack}(2\ell + 8, \mathbf{max}(p) + n)$.*

7   Derivation Height of TRSs over Infinite Signatures Compatible with KBOs

Based on Theorem 2 and 3 we obtain that the derivation height of $t \in \mathcal{T}(\mathcal{F})$ is bounded in the Ackermann function.

Theorem 4. *Let $(\mathcal{F}, \mathcal{R})$ be a TRS, compatible with KBO. Assume the set $M := \{\mathsf{sp}(r) \mid l \to r \in \mathcal{R}\} \cup \{(\mathsf{mrk}(r) \dot{-} \mathsf{rk}(l)) \mid l \to r \in \mathcal{R}\}$ is finite and the arities of the symbols in $\mathcal{F}$ are bounded; set $K := \max(M)$. Then $\mathsf{dh}_\mathcal{R}(t) \leq \mathsf{Ack}(\mathcal{O}(|\mathsf{tw}(t)|) + \mathbf{max}(\mathsf{tw}(t)) + K, 0)$.*

Proof. We set $u(n, m) = 2n + m$ and keep the polynomial u fixed for the remainder. Let $p = \mathsf{tw}(t)$ and $\ell = |p|$. Due to Theorem 2 we conclude that $\mathsf{dh}_\mathcal{R}(t) \leq \mathsf{Ah}_K(p)$. It is easy to see that $\mathsf{Ack}(n, m) \leq \mathsf{Ack}(n + m, 0)$. Using this fact and Theorem 3 we obtain: $\mathsf{Ah}_K(p) \leq \mathsf{Ack}(\mathcal{O}(\ell), \mathbf{max}(p) + K) \leq \mathsf{Ack}(\mathcal{O}(\ell) + \mathbf{max}(p) + K, 0)$. Thus the theorem follows. $\qquad\square$

For fixed $t \in \mathcal{T}(\mathcal{F})$ we can bound the argument of the Ackermann function in the above theorem in terms of the size of t. We define

$$r_{\max} := \mathsf{mrk}(t) \qquad\qquad w_{\max} := \max(\{\mathsf{w}(u) \mid u \in \mathsf{FS}(t) \cup \mathsf{Var}(t)\}) \,.$$

Lemma 12. *For* $t \in \mathcal{T}(\mathcal{F})$, *let* $r_{\max}$, $w_{\max}$ *be as above. Let* $b := \max\{\mathsf{Ar}(\mathcal{F}), 3\} + 1$, *and set* $n := \mathsf{Size}(t)$. *Then* $\mathsf{w}(t) \leq w_{\max} \cdot n$, $\mathsf{sp}(t) \leq n$, $\mathsf{mrk}(t) \leq r_{\max}$. *Hence* $|\mathsf{tw}(t)| \leq b^{w_{\max}(n) \cdot n + 1}$ *and* $\max(\mathsf{tw}(t)) \leq w_{\max}(n) \cdot n + r_{\max}$.

Proof. The proof proceeds by induction on t. □

Corollary 1. *Let* $(\mathcal{F}, \mathcal{R})$ *be a TRS, compatible with a KBO* $\succ_{\mathsf{kbo}}$. *Assume the set* $\{\mathsf{sp}(r) \mid l \rightarrow r \in \mathcal{R}\} \cup \{(\mathsf{mrk}(r) \doteq \mathsf{rk}(l)) \mid l \rightarrow r \in \mathcal{R}\}$ *is finite and the arites of the symbols in* $\mathcal{F}$ *are bounded. Then for* $t \in \mathcal{T}(\mathcal{F})$, *there exists a constant* c—*depending on* t, $(\mathcal{F}, \mathcal{R})$, *and* $\succ_{\mathsf{kbo}}$—*such that* $\mathsf{dh}_{\mathcal{R}}(t) \leq \mathsf{Ack}(c^n, 0)$.

Proof. The corollary is a direct consequence of Theorem 4 and Lemma 12. □

Remark 1. Note that it is not straight-forward to apply Theorem 4 to classify the derivational complexity of $\mathcal{R}$, over infinite signature, compatible with KBO. This is only possible in the (unlikely) case that for every term t the maximal rank $\mathsf{mrk}(t)$ and the weight $\mathsf{w}(t)$ of t can be bounded uniformly, i.e. independent of the size of t.

We apply Corollary 1 to the motivating example introduced in Section 1.

Example 3. Recall the definition of $\mathcal{R}$ and $\mathcal{R}' := \mathcal{R}_{\mathrm{lab}} \cup \mathcal{Dec}$ from Example 1 and 2 respectively. Let $s \in \mathcal{T}(\mathcal{F}_{\mathrm{lab}})$ be fixed and set $n := \mathsf{Size}(s)$.

Clearly the arities of the symbols in $\mathcal{F}_{\mathrm{lab}}$ are bounded. In Example 2 we indicated that the set $M = \{(\mathsf{mrk}(r) \doteq \mathsf{rk}(l)) \mid l \rightarrow r \in \mathcal{R}'\}$ is finite. Hence, Corollary 1 is applicable to conclude the existence of $c \in \mathbb{N}$ with $\mathsf{dh}_{\mathcal{R}'}(s) \leq \mathsf{Ack}(c^n, 0)$. In order to bound the derivation height of $\mathcal{R}$, we employ Lemma 1 to observe that for all $t \in \mathcal{T}(\mathcal{F})$: $\mathsf{dh}_{\mathcal{R}}(t) \leq \mathsf{dh}_{\mathcal{R}'}(\mathsf{lab}_\alpha(t))$, for arbitrary α. As $\mathsf{Size}(t) = \mathsf{Size}(\mathsf{lab}_\alpha(t))$ the above calculation yields

$$\mathsf{dh}_{\mathcal{R}}(t) \leq \mathsf{dh}_{\mathcal{R}'}(\mathsf{lab}_\alpha(t)) \leq \mathsf{Ack}(c^n, 0) \,.$$

Note that c depends only on t, $\mathcal{R}'$ and the KBO $\succ_{\mathsf{kbo}}$ employed.

The main motivation of this work was to provide an alternative proof of Lepper's result that the derivational complexity of any *finite* TRS, compatible with KBO, is bounded by the Ackermann function, see [11]. We recall the definition of the *derivational complexity*:

$$\mathsf{dc}_{\mathcal{R}}(n) := \max(\{\mathsf{dh}_{\mathcal{R}}(t) \mid \mathsf{Size}(t) \leq n\}) \,.$$

Corollary 2. *Let* $(\mathcal{F}, \mathcal{R})$ *be a TRS, compatible with KBO, such that* $\mathcal{F}$ *is finite. Then* $\mathsf{dh}_{\mathcal{R}}(n) \leq \mathsf{Ack}(2^{\mathcal{O}(n)}, 0)$.

Proof. As $\mathcal{F}$ is finite, the $K = \max(\{(\text{mrk}(r) \dot{-} \text{rk}(l)) \mid l \rightarrow r \in \mathcal{R}'\})$ and $\text{Ar}(\mathcal{F})$ are obviously well-defined. Theorem 4 yields that $\text{dh}_{\mathcal{R}}(t) \leq \text{Ack}(\mathcal{O}(|\text{tw}(t)|) + \textbf{max}(\text{tw}(t)) + K, 0)$. Again due to the finiteness of $\mathcal{F}$, for any $t \in \mathcal{T}(\mathcal{F})$, $\text{mrk}(t)$ and $\text{w}(t)$ can be estimated independent of t. A similar argument calculation as in Lemma 12 thus yields $\text{dh}_{\mathcal{R}}(t) \leq \text{Ack}(2^{\mathcal{O}(\text{Size}(t))}, 0)$. Hence the result follows.   □

Remark 2. Note that if we compare the above corollary to Corollary 19 in [11], we see that Lepper could even show that $\text{dc}_{\mathcal{R}}(n) \leq \text{Ack}(\mathcal{O}(n), 0)$. On the other hand, as already remarked above, Lepper's result is not admissible if the signature is infinite.

In concluding, we want to stress that the method is also applicable to obtain bounds on the derivational height of non simply terminating TRSs, a feature only shared by Hofbauer's approach to utilise context-dependent interpretations, cf. [20].

Example 4. Consider the TRS consisting of the following rules:

$$f(x) \circ (y \circ z) \rightarrow x \circ (f^2(y) \circ z) \qquad\qquad a(a(x)) \rightarrow a(b(a(x)))$$
$$f(x) \circ (y \circ (z \circ w)) \rightarrow x \circ (z \circ (y \circ w))$$
$$f(x) \rightarrow x$$

Let us call this TRS $\mathcal{R}$ in the following. Due to the rule $a(a(x)) \rightarrow a(b(a(x)))$, $\mathcal{R}$ is not simply terminating. And due to the three rules, presented on the left, the derivational complexity of $\mathcal{R}$ cannot be bounded by a primitive recursive function, compare [8].

Termination can be shown by semantic labelling, where the natural numbers are used as semantics and as labels. The interpretations $a_{\mathbb{N}}(n) = n+1$, $b_{\mathbb{N}}(n) = \max(\{0, n-1\})$, $f_{\mathbb{N}}(n) = n$, and $m \circ_{\mathbb{N}} n = m+n$ give rise to a quasi-model. Using the labelling function $\ell_a(n) = n$, termination of $\mathcal{R}' := \mathcal{R}_{\text{lab}} \cup \mathcal{D}ec$ can be shown by an instance $\succ_{\text{kbo}}$ of KBO with weight function $(\text{w}, 1)$: $\text{w}(\circ) = \text{w}(f) = 0$, $\text{w}(b) = 1$, and $\text{w}(a_n) = n$ and precedence: $f \succ \circ \succ \dots a_{n+1} \succ a_n \succ \dots \succ a_0 \succ b$. The symbol f is special. Clearly the arities of the symbols in $\mathcal{F}_{\text{lab}}$ are bounded. Further, it is not difficult to see that the set $M = \{\text{sp}(r) \mid l \rightarrow r \in \mathcal{R}'\} \cup \{(\text{mrk}(r) \dot{-} \text{rk}(l)) \mid l \rightarrow r \in \mathcal{R}'\}$ is finite and $K := \max(M) = 2$.

Proceeding as in Example 3, we see that for each $t \in \mathcal{T}(\mathcal{F})$, there exists a constant c (depending on t, $\mathcal{R}'$ and $\succ_{\text{kbo}}$) such that $\text{dh}_{\mathcal{R}}(t) \leq \text{Ack}(c^n, 0)$.

References

1. Terese: Term Rewriting Systems. Volume 55 of Cambridge Tracks in Theoretical Computer Science. Cambridge University Press (2003)
2. Hirokawa, N., Middeldorp, A.: Tyrolean termination tool. In: RTA 2005. Number 3467 in LNCS, Springer Verlag (2005) 175–184
3. Giesl, J., Thiemann, R., Schneider-Kamp, P., Falke, S.: Automated termination proofs with Aprove. In: RTA 2004. Number 3091 in LNCS, Springer Verlag (2004) 210–220

4. Zantema, H.: Termination of string rewriting proved automatically. J. Automated Reasoning **34** (2005) 105–109

5. Koprowski, A.: TPA: Termination Proved Automatically (System Description). In: RTA 2006. Number 4098 in LNCS, Springer Verlag (2006) 257–266

6. Koprowski, A., Zantema, H.: Recursive Path Ordering for Infinite Labelled Rewrite Systems. In: IJCAR 2006. (2006) To appear.

7. Hofbauer, D., Lautemann, C.: Termination proofs and the length of derivations. In: RTA 1989. Number 355 in LNCS, Springer Verlag (1989) 167–177

8. Hofbauer, D.: Termination Proofs and Derivation Lengths in Term Rewriting Systems. PhD thesis, Technische Universität Berlin (1991)

9. Hofbauer, D.: Termination proofs by multiset path orderings imply primitive recursive derivation lengths. Theor. Comput. Sci. **105** (1992) 129–140

10. Weiermann, A.: Termination proofs for term rewriting systems with lexicographic path ordering imply multiply recursive derivation lengths. Theor. Comput. Sci. **139** (1995) 355–362

11. Lepper, I.: Derivation lengths and order types of Knuth-Bendix order. Theor. Comput. Sci. **269** (2001) 433–450

12. Bachmair, L.: Proof methods for equational theories. PhD thesis, University of Illionois (1987)

13. Zantema, H.: Termination of term rewriting by semantic labelling. Fundamenta Informaticae **24** (1995) 89–105

14. Jech, T.: Set Theory. Springer Verlag (2002)

15. Martin, U.: How to chose weights in the Knuth-Bendix ordering. In: RTA 1987. Number 256 in LNCS, Springer Verlag (1987) 42–53

16. Dershowitz, N.: Termination of Rewriting. J. Symbolic Computation (1987)

17. Korovin, K., Voronkov, A.: Orienting rewrite rules with the Knuth-Bendix order. Information and Compuation **183** (2003) 165–186

18. Rose, H.: Subrecursion: Functions and Hierarchies. Oxford University Press (1984)

19. Moser, G., Weiermann, A.: Relating derivation lengths with the slow-growing hierarchy directly. In: RTA 2003. Number 2706 in LNCS, Springer Verlag (2003) 296–310

20. Hofbauer, D.: Termination proofs by context-dependent interpretations. In: RTA 2001. Number 2051 in LNCS, Springer Verlag (2001) 108–121

A Characterization of Alternating Log Time by First Order Functional Programs

Guillaume Bonfante, Jean-Yves Marion, and Romain Péchoux

Loria-INPL, École Nationale Supérieure des Mines de Nancy, B.P. 239, 54506
Vandoeuvre-lès-Nancy Cedex, France
Guillaume.Bonfante@loria.fr, Jean-Yves.Marion@loria.fr,
Romain.Pechoux@loria.fr

Abstract. We a give an intrinsic characterization of the class of functions which are computable in NC^1 that is by a uniform, logarithmic depth and polynomial size family circuit. Recall that the class of functions in $ALogTime$, that is in logarithmic time on an Alternating Turing Machine, is NC^1. Our characterization is in terms of first order functional programming languages. We define measure-tools called Sup-interpretations, which allow to give space and time bounds and allow also to capture a lot of program schemas. This study is part of a research on static analysis in order to predict program resources. It is related to the notion of Quasi-interpretations and belongs to the implicit computational complexity line of research.

1 Introduction

This study concerns interpretation methods for proving complexity bounds of first order functional programs. Such methods provide machine independent characterization of functional complexity classes, that Cobham [15] initiated. They also provide static analysis of the computational resources, which are necessary to run a program. Such an analysis should guarantee the amount of memory, time or processors which are necessary to execute a program on all inputs.

Implicit computational complexity (ICC) proposes syntactic characterizations of complexity classes, which lean on a data ramification principle like safe recursion [7], lambda-calculus [26] or data tiering [24]. We mention this line of works because they are inherently fundamentals, in the sense that one has to introduce such characterizations before one can proceed with the development of further studies and applications. Here, the term ICC is use as a name for characterizations of complexity classes which are syntactic and do not explicitly refer to computational resources.

It bears stressing to discuss on the two main difficulties that we have to face in order to provide a compelling resource static analysis. The first is that the method should capture a broad class of programs in order to be useful. From a theoretical perspective, this means that we are trying to characterize a large class of programs, which represents functions in some complexity classes. Traditional results focus on capturing all functions of a complexity class and we should

M. Hermann and A. Voronkov (Eds.): LPAR 2006, LNAI 4246, pp. 90–104, 2006.

call this approach extensional whereas our approach is rather intentional. This change of point of view is difficult because we have to keep in mind that the set of polynomial time programs is Σ_2-complete. The second difficulty is related to the complexity of the static analysis suggested. The resource analysis procedure should be decidable and easily checkable. But inversely, a too "easy" resource analysis procedure won't, certainly, delineate a meaningful class of programs.

There are at least four directions inspired by ICC approaches which are related with our topic and that we briefly review. The first direction deals with linear type disciplines in order to restrict computational time and began with the seminal work of Girard [20] which defined Light Linear Logic. The second direction is due to Hofmann [21], which introduced a resource atomic type, the diamond type, into the linear type system for higher order functional programming. Unlike the two former approaches and the next one, the third one considers imperative programming language and is developed by Kristiansen-Jones [22], Niggl-Wunderlich [31], and Marion-Moyen [30].

Lastly, the fourth approach is the one on which we focus in this paper. It concerns term rewriting systems and interpretation methods for proving complexity bounds. This method consists in giving an interpretation to computed functions, which provides an upper bound on function output sizes. The method analyses the program data flow in order to measure the program complexity. We have developed two kinds of interpretation methods for proving complexity. The first method concerns Quasi-interpretations, which is surveyed in [10]. The second method, which concerns this paper, is the *sup-interpretation method*, that we introduced in [29]. The main features of interpretation methods for proving complexity bounds are the following.

1. The analysis include broad classes of algorithms, like greedy algorithms, dynamic programming [28] and deal with non-terminating programs [29].
2. Resource verification of bytecode programs is obtained by compiling first order functional and reactive programs. See for example [3,2,18].
3. There are heuristics to determine program complexity. See [1,11]

1.1   Backgrounds on *ALogTime* and *NC^1*

We write $\log(n)$ to mean $\lceil \log_2(n+1) \rceil$. Recall that the floor function $\lfloor x \rfloor$ is the greatest integer $\leq x$, and the ceiling function $\lceil x \rceil$ is least integer $\geq x$.

We refer to *Random Access Alternating Turing Machine* of [13], called ATM. An ATM has random access read only input tapes as well as work tapes. The states of the ATM are classified as either conjunctive, disjunctive or reading. The computation of an ATM proceeds in two stages. The first stage consists in spawning two successor configurations from a root configuration. The second stage consists in evaluating backward the configuration tree generated in the first stage. An ATM outputs a single bit. A function $F : \{0,1\}^* \to \{0,1\}^*$ is bitwise computable in *ALogTime* if the function $F_{bit} : \{0,1\}^* \times \{0,1\}^* \to \{0,1\}$ is computable by an ATM in time $O(\log(n))$. The function F_{bit} is defined by $F_{bit}(x,u)$ is equal to the i'th bit of $F(x)$, where i is the integer that u represents in binary. Following Cook [17], we say that a function $F : \{0,1\}^* \to \{0,1\}^*$ is computed in *ALogTime* if ϕ is bitwise computable in *ALogTime* and ϕ is polynomially bounded.

A circuit C_n is a directed acyclic graph built up from Boolean gates *And*, *Or* and *Not*. Each gate has an in-degree less or equal to two. A circuit has n input nodes and $g(n)$ output nodes, where $g(n) = O(n^c)$ for some constant $c \geq 1$. Thus, a circuit C_n computes a function $f_n : \{0,1\}^n \to \{0,1\}^{g(n)}$. A circuit family is a sequence of Boolean circuits $C = (C_n)_n$, which computes a family of finite functions (f_n) over $\{0,1\}^*$. Inversely a function f is computed by a circuit family $(C_n)_n$ if the restriction of f to inputs of size n is computed by C_n. The complexity of a circuit depends on its height (that is the longest path from an input to an output gate) and its size (that is the number of gates).

The class of NC^1 functions is the set of functions which are computed by U_{E^*}-uniform circuit families of polynomial size (i.e. bounded $O(n^d)$ for some degree d) and of depth $O(\log(n))$ where n is the circuit input length.

NC^1 contains functions associated with binary addition, subtraction, and more generally prefix sum of associative operators. Buss [12] showed that the evaluation of Boolean formulae is a complete problem for NC^1. The class NC^1 contains functions which are computed by very fast parallel algorithms.

Uniformity condition ensures that there is a procedure which, given n, produces a description of the circuit C_n. All along, we shall consider U_{E^*}-uniform family of circuits, which is sufficient one to establish the equivalent Theorem 1. Barrington, Immerman and Straubing [6] studied other equivalent uniform conditions. The U_{E^*}-uniformity condition is the following. The extended connection language L_{EC} of $C = (C_n)_n$ is a set of quadruplets (n, g, p, y) where the gate indicated by the path p from the gate numbered g is of type y in C_n. For NC^1, knowing whether an element is in the extended connection language L_{EC} for C is decidable in time $O(\log(n))$ by an ATM.

In [32], Ruzzo demonstrated the following equivalence.

Theorem 1. *A function* $\phi : \{0,1\}^* \to \{0,1\}^*$ *is in* NC^1 *if and only if* ϕ *is computed in ALogTime.*

The class NC^1 is included in the class Logspace, and so in the Ptime. Furst, Saxe and Spiser [19] and Atjai [5] established that AC^0 is strictly included in NC^1. Following [6] opinion, NC^1 is at the frontier where we begin to have some separation results, which is a motivation to study NC^1.

1.2   Results and Related Works

We consider a first order functional programming language over constructor term algebra. We define a class of programs that we call *explicitly additive arboreal* programs. We demonstrate that functions, which are computable by these programs, are exactly the functions computed in *ALogTime*. That is, they are computable in NC^1. To our knowledge, this is the first result, which connects a small class of parallel functions and term rewriting systems.

There are various characterizations of *ALogTime*, which are surveyed in [14] based on bounded recursion schema. Compton and Laflamme [16] give a characterization of *ALogTime* based on finite global functions. These results are clearly a guideline for us. However, there are only a few characterizations of *ALogTime* from which a resource static analysis is conceivable. Bloch [8] gives a characterization of *ALogTime* using a divide and conquer ramified recursion schema. Leivant and Marion [27] propose another characterization based on linear ramified recursion with substitutions. It is also worth mentioning [25,9] which capture *NC*. These purely syntactic characterizations capture a few algorithmic patterns. On the contrary, this work tries to delineate a broad class of algorithms. Parallel algorithms are difficult to design. Employing the sup-interpretation method leads to delineate efficient parallel programs amenable to circuit computing. Designing parallel implementations of first order functional programs with interpretation methods for proving complexity bounds, might be thus viable in the near future.

2 First Order Functional Programming

2.1 Syntax of Programs

We define a generic first order functional programming language. The vocabulary $\Sigma = \langle Cns, Op, Fct \rangle$ is composed of three disjoint domains of symbols. The arity of a symbol is the number n of arguments that it takes. The program grammar is the following.

$$
\begin{array}{llll}
\text{(Constructor terms)} & \mathcal{T}(Cns) \ni v & ::= & \mathbf{c} \mid \mathbf{c}(v_1, \cdots, v_n) \\
\text{(terms/Expressions)} & \mathcal{T}(Cns, Fct, Var) \ni t & ::= & \mathbf{c} \mid x \mid \mathbf{c}(t_1, \cdots, t_n) \\
& & & \mid \mathbf{op}(t_1, \cdots, t_n) \mid \mathbf{f}(t_1, \cdots, t_n) \\
\text{(patterns)} & Patterns \ni p & ::= & \mathbf{c} \mid x \mid \mathbf{c}(p_1, \cdots, p_n) \\
\text{(rules)} & \mathcal{R} \ni r & ::= & \mathbf{f}(p_1, \cdots, p_n) \rightarrow e^{\mathbf{f}}
\end{array}
$$

where $\mathbf{c} \in Cns$ is a constructor, $\mathbf{op} \in Op$ is an operator, $\mathbf{f} \in Fct$ is a function symbol. The set of variables Var is disjoint from Σ and $x \in Var$. In a rule, a variable of $e^{\mathbf{f}}$ occurs in the patterns $p_1, \cdots, p_n$ of the definition of $\mathbf{f}$. A program $\mathbf{p}$ is a list of rules. The program's main function symbol is the first function symbol in the program's list of rules. Throughout, we consider only orthogonal programs, that is, rule patterns are disjoint and linear. So each program is confluent.

Throughout, we write $\bar{e}$ to mean a sequence of expressions, that is $\bar{e} = e_1, \ldots, e_n$, for some n clearly determined by the context.

2.2 Semantics

The domain of computation of a program $\mathbf{p}$ is the constructor algebra $\texttt{Values} = \mathcal{T}(Cns)$. Put $\texttt{Values}^* = \texttt{Values} \cup \{\mathbf{Err}\}$ where $\mathbf{Err}$ is the value associated when an error occurs. An operator $\mathbf{op}$ of arity n is interpreted by a function $[\![\mathbf{op}]\!]$ from $\texttt{Values}^n$ to $\texttt{Values}^*$. Operators are essentially basic partial functions like destructors or characteristic functions of predicates like $=$.

The language has a usual closure-based call-by-value semantics which is displayed in Figure 1. The computational domain is $\mathtt{Values}^{\#} = \mathtt{Values} \cup \{\mathbf{Err}, \bot\}$ where $\bot$ means that a program is non-terminating. A program $\mathbf{p}$ computes a partial function $[\![\mathbf{p}]\!] : \mathtt{Values}^n \rightarrow \mathtt{Values}^{\#}$ defined as follows. For all $v_i \in \mathtt{Values}$, $[\![\mathbf{p}]\!](v_1, \cdots, v_n) = w$ iff $\mathbf{p}(v_1, \cdots, v_n) \downarrow w$. Otherwise $[\![\mathbf{p}]\!](v_1, \cdots, v_n) = \bot$. The meaning of $e \downarrow w$ is that e evaluates to the value w of $\mathtt{Values}$. By definition, if no rule is applicable, then an error occurs and $e \downarrow \mathbf{Err}$.

A substitution σ is a finite function from variables to $\mathtt{Values}$. The application of a substitution σ to a term e is noted $e\sigma$.

$$\frac{t_1 \downarrow w_1 \ldots t_n \downarrow w_n}{\mathbf{c}(t_1, \cdots, t_n) \downarrow \mathbf{c}(w_1, \cdots, w_n)} \quad \mathbf{c} \in Cns \text{ and } \forall i, w_i \neq \mathbf{Err}$$

$$\frac{t_1 \downarrow w_1 \ldots t_n \downarrow w_n}{\mathbf{op}(t_1, \cdots, t_n) \downarrow [\![\mathbf{op}]\!](w_1, \cdots, w_n)} \quad \mathbf{op} \in Op$$

$$\frac{t_1 \downarrow w_1 \ldots t_n \downarrow w_n \quad \mathbf{f}(p_1, \cdots, p_n) \rightarrow e \quad e\sigma \downarrow w}{\mathbf{f}(t_1, \cdots, t_n) \downarrow w} \quad \text{where } \sigma(x_i) = w_i \ \forall i = 1, \ldots, n$$

Fig. 1. Call by value semantics of ground terms wrt a program $\mathbf{p}$

3   Sup-interpretations

Let us now turn our attention to the sup-interpretation method which is the main tool to analyze a program complexity. For this purpose, we define a special kind of program interpretation called *sup-interpretation*, which is associated to a *lightweight*, to provide a complexity measure.

3.1   Partial Assignments

A partial assignment $\mathcal{I}$ is a partial mapping from a vocabulary Σ such that for each symbol $\mathbf{f}$ of arity n, in the domain of $\mathcal{I}$, it yields a partial function $\mathcal{I}(f) : (\mathbb{R}_+)^n \longmapsto \mathbb{R}_+$, where $\mathbb{R}_+$ is the set of non-negative real numbers. The domain of a partial assignment $\mathcal{I}$ is noted $\mathrm{dom}(\mathcal{I})$. Because it is convenient, we shall always assume that partial assignments that we consider, are defined on constructors and operators. That is $Cns \cup Op \subseteq \mathrm{dom}(\mathcal{I})$.

An expression e is defined over $\mathrm{dom}(\mathcal{I})$ if each symbol belongs to $\mathrm{dom}(\mathcal{I})$ or is a variable of Var. Assume that an expression e is defined over $\mathrm{dom}(\mathcal{I})$ and has n variables. Take a denumerable sequence $X_1, \ldots, X_n, \ldots$. The partial assignment of e wrt $\mathcal{I}$ is the homomorphic extension that we write $\mathcal{I}^*(e)$. It denotes a function from $\mathbb{R}_+^n$ to $\mathbb{R}_+$ and is defined as follows:

1. If x_i is a variable of Var, let $\mathcal{I}^*(x_i) = X_i$
2. If b is a 0-ary symbol of Σ, then $\mathcal{I}^*(b) = \mathcal{I}(b)$.
3. If f is a symbol of arity $n > 0$ and $e_1, \cdots, e_n$ are expressions, then

$$\mathcal{I}^*(f(e_1, \cdots, e_n)) = \mathcal{I}(f)(\mathcal{I}^*(e_1), \ldots, \mathcal{I}^*(e_n))$$

3.2 Sup-interpretations and Lightweights

Definition 1 (Sup-interpretation). *A sup-interpretation is a partial assignment θ which verifies the three conditions below :*

1. *The assignment θ is weakly monotonic. That is, for each symbol $f \in dom(\theta)$, the function $\theta(f)$ satisfies for every $i = 1, \ldots, n$*

$$X_i \geq Y_i \Rightarrow \theta(f)(X_1, \cdots, X_n) \geq \theta(f)(Y_1, \cdots, Y_n)$$

2. *For each $v \in$ Values,*

$$\theta^*(v) \geq |v|$$

   The size of an expression e is noted $|e|$ and is defined by $|\mathbf{c}| = 0$ where $\mathbf{c}$ is a 0-ary symbol and $|\mathbf{b}(e_1, \ldots, e_n)| = 1 + \sum_i |e_i|$ where $\mathbf{b}$ is a n-ary symbol.
3. *For each symbol $f \in dom(\theta)$ of arity n and for each value $v_1, \ldots, v_n$ of Values, if $[\![f]\!](v_1, \ldots, v_n)$ is defined, that is $[\![f]\!](v_1, \ldots, v_n) \in$ Values, then*

$$\theta^*(f(v_1, \ldots, v_n)) \geq \theta^*([\![f]\!](v_1, \ldots, v_n))$$

An expression e admits a sup-interpretation $\theta^*(e)$, wrt θ, if e is defined over $dom(\theta)$. Intuitively, the sup-interpretation is a special program interpretation. Instead of yielding the program denotation, a sup-interpretation provides an approximation from above of the size of the outputs of the function denoted by the program.

Lemma 1. *Let e be an expression with no variable and which admits a sup-interpretation θ. Assume that $[\![e]\!]$ is defined, that is $[\![e]\!] \in$ Values. We then have (i) $\theta^*([\![e]\!]) \leq \theta^*(e)$ and (ii) $|[\![e]\!]| \leq \theta^*(e)$.*

Example 1. We illustrate the notion of sup-interpretation by a function, which divides by two a number. For this, we define the set of tally numbers thus,

$$\mathtt{Uint} = \mathbf{0} \mid \mathbf{S}(\mathtt{Uint})$$

We note $\overline{n} = \mathbf{S}^n(\mathbf{0})$. Next, we define the function $[\![\mathtt{half}]\!]$ such that $[\![\mathtt{half}]\!] = \lfloor \frac{\overline{n}}{2} \rfloor$ by the program below.

$$\mathtt{half}(\mathbf{0}) \to \mathbf{0} \qquad \mathtt{half}(\mathbf{S}(\mathbf{0})) \to \mathbf{0} \qquad \mathtt{half}(\mathbf{S}(\mathbf{S}(y))) \to \mathbf{S}(\mathtt{half}(y))$$

Now, a sup-interpretation of $\mathbf{0}$ is $\theta(\mathbf{0}) = 0$ and a sup-interpretation of $\mathbf{S}$ is $\theta(\mathbf{S})(X) = X + 1$. Clearly, for any n, $\theta^*(\overline{n}) \geq |\overline{n}| = n$. Then, we set $\theta(\mathtt{half})(X) = \lfloor \frac{X}{2} \rfloor$, which is a monotonic function. We check that condition (3) of Definition 1 is satisfied because $\theta^*(\mathtt{half}(\overline{n})) = \lfloor \frac{\overline{n}}{2} \rfloor$. Notice that such a sup-interpretation is not a quasi-interpretation (a fortiori not an interpretation for proof termination) since it violates the subterm property.

We end by defining lightweights which are used to control the depth of recursive data-flows.

Definition 2 (Lightweight). *A lightweight ω is a partial assignment which ranges over Fct. To a given function symbol f of arity n it assigns a total function ω_f from $\mathbb{R}^n_+$ to $\mathbb{R}_+$ which is weakly monotonic.*

3.3   Additive Assignments

Definition 3. *A partial assignment $\mathcal{I}$ is additive if*

1. *For each symbol f of arity n in $dom(\mathcal{I})$, $\mathcal{I}(f)$ is bounded by a polynomial of $\mathbb{R}_+[X_1, \cdots , X_n]$.*
2. *For each constructor $\mathbf{c} \in dom(\theta)$ of arity > 0,*

$$\theta(\mathbf{c})(X_1, \cdots , X_n) = \sum_{i=1}^{n} X_i + \alpha_{\mathbf{c}} \qquad\qquad \alpha_{\mathbf{c}} \geq 1$$

Lemma 2. *Assume that $\mathcal{I}$ is an additive assignment. There is a constant α such that for each value $\mathbf{u}$ of $\mathtt{Values}$, the following inequality is satisfied : $|\mathbf{u}| \leq \theta^*(\mathbf{u}) \leq \alpha \times |\mathbf{u}|$*

Throughout the following paper we consider sup-interpretations and lightweights, which are additive assignments.

4   Arboreal Programs

4.1   Fraternities

Given a program $\mathbf{p}$, we define *precedence* $\geq_{Fct}$ on function symbols. Set $f \geq_{Fct} g$ if there is a $\mathbf{p}$-rule $f(p_1, \cdots , p_n) \rightarrow e$ and g is in e. Then, take the reflexive and transitive closure of $\geq_{Fct}$, also noted $\geq_{Fct}$. Next, we define $f \approx_{Fct} g$ and $f >_{Fct} g$ as usual. We define a rank function rk as a morphism from $(Fct, \geq_{Fct})$ into $(\mathbb{N}, \geq)$, so satisfying : rk(g) < rk(f), if $f \geq_{Fct} g$, and rk(f) = rk(g), if $f \approx_{Fct} g$.

A *context* is an expression $\mathsf{C}[\diamond_1, \cdots , \diamond_r]$ containing one occurrence of each $\diamond_i$. Here, we suppose that the $\diamond_i$'s are new symbols which are neither in Σ nor in *Var*. The substitution of each $\diamond_i$ by an expression d_i is noted $\mathsf{C}[d_1, \cdots , d_r]$.

Definition 4. *Given a program $\mathbf{p}$, a term $\mathsf{C}[g_1(\overline{t_1}), \ldots , g_r(\overline{t_r})]$ is a fraternity activated by $f(p_1, \cdots , p_n)$ iff*

1. *There is a rule $f(p_1, \cdots , p_n) \rightarrow \mathsf{C}[g_1(\overline{t_1}), \ldots , g_r(\overline{t_r})]$.*
2. *For each $i \in \{1, r\}$, $g_i \approx_{Fct} f$.*
3. *For every function symbol h in the context $\mathsf{C}[\diamond_1, \cdots , \diamond_r]$, $f >_{Fct} h$.*

4.2 Arboreal Programs

Definition 5 (Arboreal). *A program p admits an* arboreal *sup-interpretation iff there is a sup-interpretation θ, a lightweight ω and a constant $K > 1$ such that for every fraternity $C[g_1(\overline{t_1}), \ldots, g_r(\overline{t_r})]$ activated by $f(p_1, \cdots, p_n)$, and any substitutions σ, both conditions are satisfied:*

$$\omega_f(\theta^*(p_1\sigma), \ldots, \theta^*(p_n\sigma)) > 1 \tag{1}$$
$$\omega_f(\theta^*(p_1\sigma), \ldots, \theta^*(p_n\sigma)) \geq K \times \omega_{g_i}(\theta^*(t_{i,1}\sigma), \ldots, \theta^*(t_{i,m}\sigma)) \quad \forall 1 \leq i \leq r \tag{2}$$

The constant K is called the arboreal coefficient *of p.*

Example 2. We show how to compute prefix sum, which is one of the canonical examples of an efficient parallel circuit computation. Suppose that $\odot$ is a binary associative operation over A. The prefix sum of a list $[x_1, \ldots, x_n]$ of elements of A, is $x_1 \odot \ldots \odot x_n$. Lists over A are defined as usual

$$\mathtt{List}(A) = [\,] \mid [A, \mathtt{List}(A)]$$

We take two operators **Left** and **Right**, which cut a list in two half.

$$\mathbf{Left}([\,]) = [\,] \qquad \mathbf{Left}([x_1, \ldots, x_n]) = [x_1, \ldots, x_{\lfloor \frac{n}{2} \rfloor}]$$
$$\mathbf{Right}([\,]) = [\,] \qquad \mathbf{Right}([x_1, \ldots, x_n]) = [x_{\lfloor \frac{n}{2} \rfloor + 1}, \ldots, x_n]$$

We write $[x_1, \ldots, x_n]$ instead of $[x_1, [x_2, \ldots, x_n]]$. Now, the prefix sum of a list is computed as follows.

$$\mathtt{sum}([x]) = x$$
$$\mathtt{sum}([x, y, L]) = \mathtt{sum}(\mathbf{Left}([x, y, L])) \odot \mathtt{sum}(\mathbf{Right}([x, y, L]))$$

Here, we consider $\odot$ as an infix operator using familiar conventions. Actually, the pattern $[x, y, L]$ captures a list of length at least 2.

The constructors and the operators admit the following sup-interpretations.

$$\theta([\,]) = 0 \qquad \theta([X, L]) = X + L + 1$$
$$\theta(\mathbf{Left})(N) = \lfloor \frac{N}{2} \rfloor \qquad \theta(\mathbf{Right})(N) = \lceil \frac{N}{2} \rceil$$

Indeed, since the size of a list is the number of its elements, we see that for any list L, we have $|L| = \theta(L)$. We might also check that $|[\![\mathbf{Left}(L)]\!]| \leq \theta(\mathbf{Left}(L))$ and $|[\![\mathbf{Right}(L)]\!]| \leq \theta(\mathbf{Right}(L))$. Next, $\mathtt{sum}$ satisfies the arboreal condition by taking $\omega_{\mathtt{sum}}(L) = L$ and $K = \frac{3}{2}$ (Hint : $L \geq 2$). Lastly, we shall see in a short while that $\mathtt{sum}$ is an example of an explicitly additive arboreal program.

We shall now show that a program admitting an arboreal sup-interpretation is terminating. Actually, the termination of an arboreal program may be established by the dependency pair method of Arts and Giesl [4], or by the size change principle for program termination of Lee, Jones and Ben-Amram [23]. However, it is worth to have a direct demonstration in order to establish an upper bound on derivation lengths.

4.3   Weighted Call-Trees

We now describe the notion of call-trees which is a representation of a program state transition sequences. Next, we show that, when we consider arboreal programs, we can assign weights to state transitions in such way that a state transition sequence is associated to a sequence of strictly decreasing weights. Lastly, weights provide a measure which gives us an upper bound on derivation lengths.

Call-Trees. Suppose that we have a program $\mathbf{p}$. A *state* $\langle \mathbf{f}, \mathbf{u}_1, \cdots, \mathbf{u}_n \rangle$ of $\mathbf{p}$ is a tuple where $\mathbf{f}$ is a function symbol of arity n and $\mathbf{u}_1, \cdots, \mathbf{u}_n$ are values of Values*.

A *state transition* of $\mathbf{p}$ is a triplet $\eta_1 \rightsquigarrow \eta_2$ between two states $\eta_1 = \langle \mathbf{f}, \mathbf{u}_1, \ldots, \mathbf{u}_n \rangle$ and $\eta_2 = \langle \mathbf{g}, \mathbf{v}_1, \cdots, \mathbf{v}_m \rangle$ where

1. $\mathbf{f}(p_1, \cdots, p_n) \to e$ is a rule of $\mathbf{p}$
2. there is a substitution σ such that $p_i \sigma \downarrow \mathbf{u}_i$ for any $1 \leq i \leq n$,
3. $e = \mathsf{C}[\mathbf{g}(d_1, \cdots, d_m)]$ and for any $1 \leq i \leq m$, $d_i \sigma \downarrow \mathbf{v}_i$

We write $\overset{*}{\rightsquigarrow}$ to mean the transitive closure of $\rightsquigarrow$. We define the $\langle \mathbf{f}, \mathbf{u}_1, \cdots, \mathbf{u}_n \rangle$ call-tree as a tree where (i) the set of nodes are labeled by states of $\{\eta \mid \langle \mathbf{f}, \mathbf{u}_1, \cdots, \mathbf{u}_n \rangle \overset{*}{\rightsquigarrow} \eta\}$, (ii) there is an edge between two nodes if there is a transition between both states, which labels the nodes. (iii) the root is a node labeled by the state $\langle \mathbf{f}, \mathbf{u}_1, \cdots, \mathbf{u}_n \rangle$.

A $\langle \mathbf{f}, \mathbf{u}_1, \cdots, \mathbf{u}_n \rangle$ call-tree may be an infinite tree. In this case, König's Lemma implies that there is a reduction strategy which leads to a infinite sequence of reductions.

Weighted Call-Trees. Throughout, it is convenient to use $\theta^*(\overline{v_j})$ to abbreviate $\theta^*(v_{j,1}), \ldots, \theta^*(v_{j,n})$. Given a sup-interpretation θ and a lightweight ω of a program, we assign to each state transition a weight, which is a pair (p, q) in $\mathbb{N} \cup \{\bot\} \times \mathbb{N} \cup \{\bot\}$ as follows. We have $\eta_1 = \langle \mathbf{f}, \mathbf{u}_1, \cdots, \mathbf{u}_n \rangle \overset{(p, q)}{\rightsquigarrow} \eta_2 = \langle \mathbf{g}, \mathbf{v}_1, \cdots, \mathbf{v}_m \rangle$ iff

- If $\mathbf{f} >_{Fct} \mathbf{g}$, then $(p, q) = (\mathrm{rk}(\mathbf{f}), 0)$.
- If $\mathbf{f} \approx_{Fct} \mathbf{g}$ and $\omega_{\mathbf{f}}(\theta^*(\overline{\mathbf{u}})) \geq 1$, then $(p, q) = (\mathrm{rk}(\mathbf{f}), \lceil \log_K (\omega_{\mathbf{f}}(\theta^*(\overline{\mathbf{u}}))) \rceil)$
- Otherwise, $(p, q) = (\bot, \bot)$.

In the two first cases above, the weight is said to be defined,

Lemma 3. *Assume that $\mathbf{p}$ admits an arboreal sup-interpretation. The weight which is assigned to each state transition of $\mathbf{p}$ is defined.*

Proof. It suffices to prove that when $\mathbf{f} \approx_{Fct} \mathbf{g}$, we have $\omega_{\mathbf{f}}(\theta^*(\mathbf{u}_1), \ldots, \theta^*(\mathbf{u}_n)) \geq 1$. Since $\mathbf{p}$ admits an arboreal sup-interpretation, the situation is the following. $\mathbf{f}(\mathbf{u}_1, \cdots, \mathbf{u}_n)$ matches a unique rule $\mathbf{f}(p_1, \cdots, p_n) \to e$ because $\mathbf{p}$ is orthogonal. By definition of a state transition, $\mathbf{g}$ is in e. Since $\mathbf{f} \approx_{Fct} \mathbf{g}$, e is a fraternity activated by $\mathbf{f}(p_1, \cdots, p_n)$ such that $e = \mathsf{C}[\ldots, \mathbf{g}(\ldots), \ldots]$. Therefore, the condition (1) of Definition 5 holds, which completes the proof.

Intuitively, the weight associated to a transition indicates what is decreasing. In fact, there is two possibilities. In the first one, the function rank is strictly decreasing. In the second one, it is the lightweight which is strictly decreasing.

Theorem 2. *Assume that the program $\mathbf{p}$ admits an arboreal sup-interpretation. Then $\mathbf{p}$ is terminating. That is, for every function symbol f and for any values $\mathbf{u}_1, \cdots, \mathbf{u}_n$ in* Values, $[\![f]\!](\mathbf{u}_1, \cdots, \mathbf{u}_n)$ *is in* Values*.

Proof. Let $\langle \mathbf{f}, \mathbf{u}_1, \cdots, \mathbf{u}_n \rangle$ be a state of $\mathbf{p}$. Take a branch of the $\langle \mathbf{f}, \mathbf{u}_1, \cdots, \mathbf{u}_n \rangle$ call-tree $\eta_0 \overset{(p_0, q_0)}{\rightsquigarrow} \eta_1 \overset{(p_1, q_1)}{\rightsquigarrow} \eta_2 \overset{(p_2, q_2)}{\rightsquigarrow} \ldots$ where $\eta_j = \langle \mathbf{f}_j, \overline{v_j} \rangle$.

We define an ordering on $\mathbb{N} \times \mathbb{N}$ by $(n, m) < (p, q)$ if $n < p$ or $n = p$ and $m < q$. We show that for any i such that $\eta_i \overset{(p_i, q_i)}{\rightsquigarrow} \eta_{i+1} \overset{(p_{i+1}, q_{i+1})}{\rightsquigarrow} \eta_{i+2}$, we have $(p_i, q_i) > (p_{i+1}, q_{i+1})$. There are three cases to examine.

1. Suppose that $\mathbf{f}_i >_{Fct} \mathbf{f}_{i+1}$. Then, we have $p_i = \mathrm{rk}(\mathbf{f}_i) > p_{i+1} = \mathrm{rk}(\mathbf{f}_{i+1})$.
2. Suppose that $\mathbf{f}_i \approx_{Fct} \mathbf{f}_{i+1}$ and $\mathbf{f}_{i+1} >_{Fct} \mathbf{f}_{i+2}$. We have $p_i = \mathrm{rk}(\mathbf{f}_i) = p_{i+1} = \mathrm{rk}(\mathbf{f}_{i+1})$ and $q_i = \lceil \log_K(\omega_{\mathbf{f}_i}(\theta^*(\overline{v_i}))) \rceil > q_{i+1} = 0$, since $\omega_{\mathbf{f}_i}(\theta^*(\overline{v_i})) > 1$
3. Suppose that $\mathbf{f}_i \approx_{Fct} \mathbf{f}_{i+1}$ and $\mathbf{f}_{i+1} \approx_{Fct} \mathbf{f}_{i+2}$. As in the previous case, we have $p_i = p_{i+1}$. Now, we also have $q_i = \lceil \log_K(\omega_{\mathbf{f}_i}(\theta^*(\overline{v_i}))) \rceil > q_{i+1} = \lceil \log_K(\omega_{\mathbf{f}_{i+1}}(\theta^*(\overline{v_{i+1}}))) \rceil$. Indeed intuitively, each recursive state corresponds to the division of its lightweight by the arboreal constant $K > 1$. Formally, Condition (2) of Definition 5 claims that

$$\omega_{\mathbf{f}_i}(\theta^*(\overline{v_i})) \geq K \times \omega_{\mathbf{f}_{i+1}}(\theta^*(\overline{v_{i+1}}))$$
$$\lceil \log_K(\omega_{\mathbf{f}_i}(\theta^*(\overline{v_i}))) \rceil \geq \lceil \log_K(\omega_{\mathbf{f}_{i+1}}(\theta^*(\overline{v_{i+1}}))) \rceil + 1$$

In the three cases above, we have established that $(p_i, q_i) > (p_{i+1}, q_{i+1})$. Since the ordering $<$ is well-founded, the weight sequence is finite, which completes the proof.

5 Main Result

5.1 Explicitly Defined Functions

Given a program $\mathbf{p}$, a function symbol $\mathbf{f}$ is *explicitly defined* iff for each rule like $\mathbf{f}(p_1, \cdots, p_n) \to e$, the expression e is built from variables, constructors, operators and explicitly defined function symbols whose precedence is strictly less than $\mathbf{f}$. An expression e is *explicit* in $\mathbf{p}$ iff each function symbol occurring in e is explicitly defined in $\mathbf{p}$.

An explicit function is a function which is defined by a program in which any function symbols are explicitly defined.

Definition 6. *A program $\mathbf{p}$ is* explicitly fraternal *if and only if for each fraternity $C[g_1(\overline{t_1}), \ldots, g_r(\overline{t_r})]$ of $\mathbf{p}$, the context $C[\diamond_1, \cdots, \diamond_r]$ and each $\overline{t_i}$ are explicitly defined in $\mathbf{p}$.*

5.2   Characterization of Alogtime

We encode the elements of $\mathtt{Values}^*$ by binary words of $\{0,1\}^*$ using a mapping $code : \mathtt{Values}^* \rightarrow \{0,1\}^*$ such that (i) $code$ is computed in $ALogTime$, and (ii) each constructor of Cns is computed by an U_{E^*}-uniform, polynomial size, and constant depth circuit family wrt the encoding $code$.

A program $\mathbf{p}$ has flat operators if every operator of Op is computed by an U_{E^*}-uniform, polynomial size, and constant depth circuit family using the same encoding $code$.

A program $\mathbf{p}$ admits an *additive arboreal* sup-interpretation if it admits an arboreal sup-interpretation for which the sup-interpretation θ and the lightweight ω are additive assignments.

Definition 7. *A program $\mathbf{p}$ is* explicitly additive arboreal *if $\mathbf{p}$ admits an additive arboreal sup-interpretation, which is explicitly fraternal and all operators are flat.*

Given a function $\phi : \mathtt{Values}^k \rightarrow \mathtt{Values}$, we associate a function $\tilde{\phi} : \{0,1\}^* \rightarrow \{0,1\}$, which is defined by $\phi(\mathbf{u}) = \tilde{\phi}(code(\mathbf{u}))$, for any $\mathbf{u} \in \mathtt{Values}$. A function ϕ over $\mathtt{Values}$ is computed in $ALogTime$ if the function $\tilde{\phi}$ is also computed in $ALogTime$.

Theorem 3. *A function ϕ over $\mathtt{Values}$ is computed by a explicitly additive arboreal program if and only if ϕ is computed in $ALogTime$.*

Proof. It is a consequence of Lemma 7 and Lemma 9.

6   Circuit Evaluation of Exp. Add. Arboreal Programs

We now move toward an implementation of programs by uniform family of circuits. It will be appropriate to do this in several steps that we shall describe in more or less intuitive fashion. Indeed implementation details are not difficult but tedious, and will be written in the full forthcoming paper. Actually, the demonstration of Theorem 3 leans essentially on Lemmas 5 and 6.

6.1   Explicit Functions Are Constant Depth Computable

In the first step, we show that an explicit functions are computed in constant parallel time.

Lemma 4. *Assume that $\phi : \mathtt{Values}^k \rightarrow \mathtt{Values}^*$ is an explicit function from flat operators. Then, ϕ is computed by an U_{E^*}-uniform, polynomial size, and constant depth circuit family.*

Proof. An explicit function ϕ is defined by composition from constructors and operators. So, we complete the construction by a straightforward induction on the definition length, and by using a circuit implementation of constructors and destructors. The program which defines ϕ provides the U_{E^*}-uniformity.

6.2   Upper Bounds on Height and Size

In the second step, we establish a logarithmic upper bound on derivation lengths. Then, we show that computed values are polynomially bounded.

The height of a weighted call tree is the length of the longest branch.

Lemma 5. *Let p be an explicitly additive arboreal program. Let $\langle f, u_1, \cdots, u_n \rangle$ be a state of p. The height of the $\langle f, u_1, \cdots, u_n \rangle$ call tree is bounded by $d \times \log(\max(|u_1|, \ldots, |u_n|))$ for some constant d.*

Proof. Put $n = \max_i(|u_i|)$. We refine the demonstration of Theorem 2 by looking more carefully to a finite strictly decreasing sequence $(p_0, q_0) > \ldots > (p_\ell, q_\ell)$ of a branch of the $\langle f, u_1, \cdots, u_n \rangle$ call-tree.

By definition of the partial ordering $<$ on $\mathbb{N} \times \mathbb{N}$, we have $\ell \leq (p_0 + 1) \times (q_0 + 1)$. Since, $p_0 \leq \max_f(\mathrm{rk}(f))$ and $q_0 \leq \lceil \log_K(\max_f(\omega_f(\theta^*(\overline{u})))) \rceil$, we see that $\ell \leq \max_f(\mathrm{rk}(f)) \times \lceil \log_K(\max_f(\omega_f(\theta^*(\overline{u})))) \rceil$.

The fact that p admits an additive assignment implies that there is a polynomial P such that $\max_f(\omega_f(\theta^*(\overline{u})) \leq P(\alpha \times n)$, where the constant α is given by Lemma 2. Putting altogether, there is a constant d such that $\ell \leq d \times \log_2(n)$.

Lemma 6. *Assume that p is an explicitly additive arboreal program. Then, there is a polynomial P such that for any values $u_1, \cdots, u_n$ and function symbol f, we have*

$$|[\![f]\!](u_1, \cdots, u_n)| \leq P(\max_i(|u_i|))$$

Proof (Sketch of proof). Suppose that f is recursively defined, and so its computation implies fraternities. Each fraternity is explicitly defined, which means that the output size is linearly bounded by $a \times m + b$ where a and b are some constants, m is the input size, because of Lemma 4. The computation of $\langle f, u_1, \cdots, u_n \rangle$ is made by iterating ℓ times the computation of explicit fraternity. So the output size is bounded by $a^\ell m + b \times \ell$. The length ℓ is bounded by the height of the $\langle f, u_1, \cdots, u_n \rangle$ call-tree. By lemma 5, $\ell \leq d \times \log(\max(|u_1|, \ldots, |u_n|))$, for some constant d. Therefore, there is a polynomial P whose degree depends on the arboreal coefficient K and a such that $|[\![f]\!](u_1, \cdots, u_n)| \leq P(\max_i(|u_i|))$.

6.3   Programs Are in NC^1

In the third step, we construct an U_{E^*}-uniform, polynomial size, and constant depth circuit family which computes an explicitly additive arboreal program.

Lemma 7. *Suppose that a function $\phi : \texttt{Values}^k \to \texttt{Values}$ is defined by an explicitly additive arboreal program p. Then, an U_{E^*}-uniform, polynomial size, and logarithmic depth circuit family computes $\tilde{\phi}$.*

Proof. Given an upper bound m on the input size, we construct a circuit C_m by induction on function symbol rank of p. Actually, the depth of a circuit is bounded by $d \times \log(n)$ for some constant d because of Lemma 5. Lemma 6 states that the size of the inputs and the outputs of each circuit layer is bounded by a polynomial. We see that circuits have a logarithmic depth and polynomial size. The U_{E^*}-uniformity condition is not too difficult to check, because the extended connection language is based on $\mathbf{p}$, which is given and on the upper-bounds obtained in the previous section.

7   Simulation of *ALogTime* Computable Functions

In this section, we prove that a function in *ALogTime* is computed by an explicitly additive arboreal program.

For this purpose, we consider the characterization [27] of *ALogTime* instead of dealing directly with ATM. There are at least two reasons to proceed in this way. The first is that it simplifies proofs which otherwise would require a lot of encodings. The second is that, as we say in the introduction, there is closed connection between ramified recursion used in implicit computational complexity and our approach.

In [27], the characterization is based on linear ramified recursion with substitution, called *LRRS*, using well-balanced trees as internal data structures.

LRRS functions compute over binary tree algebra T. Initial functions consist of constructors, conditionals and destructors over T. *LRRS* functions use one ramified recursion over 2 tiers, and is defined as follows.

$$\mathbf{f}(\mathbf{c}, \overline{u}; \overline{x}) = \mathbf{g_c}(\overline{u}; \overline{x}) \qquad\qquad \mathbf{c} = 0, 1, \bot$$
$$\mathbf{f}(t * t', \overline{u}; \overline{x}) = \mathbf{g}(; \mathbf{f}(t, \overline{u}; \mathbf{h}_1(; \overline{x})), \ldots, \mathbf{f}(t', \overline{u}; \mathbf{h}_k(; \overline{x})), \overline{x})$$

where $\mathbf{g}, \mathbf{g}_c$ and the substitution functions $\mathbf{h}_1, \ldots, \mathbf{h}_k$ are previously defined functions. We separate tiers by a semicolon. A flat function is a function whose domain and range are at the same tier. A crucial point is that $\mathbf{g}$ and the substitution functions $\mathbf{h}_1, \ldots, \mathbf{h}_k$ are flat functions. Indeed, it was proved that flat functions are definable by composition of initial functions.

A function ϕ over the algebra of words $\mathbb{W} = \{0, 1\}^*$ is said to be representable in *LRRS* if it is representable by some function f definable in *LRRS* and whose inputs represent the shortest (in the height) encoding of words by full binary trees.

Theorem 4 (Marion and Leivant). *A function f over $\{0, 1\}^*$ is representable in LRRS if and only if it is bitwise in ALogTime and its growth is bounded by a polynomial in the size of the inputs.*

Now we are going to use this result in order to establish the completeness of our characterization:

Lemma 8. *A function ϕ which is representable in LRRS, is computed by an explicitly additive arboreal program $\mathbf{p}$.*

Proof (Sketch of proof). The simulation of *LRRS* functions is based on three points. The first point concerns the encoding of well balanced trees. In the simulation, we reduce *LRRS* trees into a list like in Example 2. The operator **Left** and **Right** allow to simulate well-balanced tree.

The second point is to see that a flat function of $LRRS$ is explicitly defined.

The third point is to replace the linear ramified recursion scheme with parameter substitutions over binary trees by the following scheme:

$$\mathtt{f}([\mathbf{c}], \overline{u}, \overline{x}) \to \mathbf{g_c}(\overline{u}, \overline{x}) \quad \mathbf{c} = \mathbf{0}, \mathbf{1}, \bot$$
$$\mathtt{f}([\mathbf{c}, \mathbf{b}, l], \overline{u}, \overline{x}) \to \mathtt{g}(\mathtt{f}(\mathbf{Left}([\mathbf{c}, \mathbf{b}, l]), \overline{u}, \mathtt{h}_1(\overline{x})), .., \mathtt{f}(\mathbf{Right}([\mathbf{c}, \mathbf{b}, l]), \overline{u}, \mathtt{h}_k(\overline{x})), \overline{x})$$

The program defined by the previous rules is explicitly fraternal, because $\mathtt{g}$, $\mathbf{g_c}$, and $(\mathtt{h}_i)_i$ are flat functions.

The above Lemma entails the following one:

Lemma 9. *Every function ϕ in ALogTime is computable by an explicitly additive arboreal program $\mathbf{p}$.*

References

1. R. Amadio. Synthesis of max-plus quasi-interpretations. *Fundamenta Informaticae*, *65(1–2)*, 2005.
2. R. Amadio, S. Coupet-Grimal, S. Dal-Zilio, and L. Jakubiec. A functional scenario for bytecode verification of resource bounds. In *CSL*, volume 3210 of *LNCS*, pages 265–279, 2004.
3. R. Amadio and S. Dal-Zilio. Resource control for synchronous cooperative threads. In *CONCUR*, volume 3170 of *LNCS*, pages 68–82, 2004.
4. T. Arts and J. Giesl. Termination of term rewriting using dependency pairs. *TCS*, 236:133–178, 2000.
5. M. Atjai. Σ_1^1-formulae on finite strutures. *Annals of Pure and Applied Logic*, 24:1–48, 1983.
6. D. Barrington, N. Immerman, and H. Straubing. On uniformity within nc. *J. of Computer System Science*, 41(3):274–306, 1990.
7. S. Bellantoni and S. Cook. A new recursion-theoretic characterization of the polytime functions. *Computational Complexity*, 2:97–110, 1992.
8. S. Bloch. Function-algebraic characterizations of log and polylog parallel time. *Computational complexity*, 4(2):175–205, 1994.
9. G. Bonfante, R. Kahle, J.-Y. Marion, and I. Oitavem. Towards an implicit characterization of NCk. In *CSL'06*, LNCS, 2006.
10. G. Bonfante, J.-Y. Marion, and J.-Y. Moyen. Quasi-interpretation: a way to control ressources. *survey submitted, revision.* http://www.loria/~marionjy.
11. G. Bonfante, J.-Y. Marion, J.-Y. Moyen, and R. Péchoux. Synthesis of quasi-interpretations. *Workshop on Logic and Complexity in Computer Science, LCC2005, Chicago,* 2005. http://www.loria/~pechoux.
12. S. Buss. The boolean formula value problem is in ALOGTIME. In *STOC*, pages 123–131, 1987.
13. A. Chandra, D. Kozen, and L. Stockmeyer. Alternation. *Journal of the ACM*, 28:114–133, 1981.
14. P. Clote. Computational models and function algebras. In D. Leivant, editor, *LCC'94*, volume 960 of *LNCS*, pages 98–130, 1995.
15. A. Cobham. The intrinsic computational difficulty of functions. In *Conf. on Logic, Methodology, and Philosophy of Science*, pages 24–30. North-Holland, 1962.

16. K.J. Compton and C. Laflamme. An algebra and a logic for nc. *Inf. Comput.*, 87(1/2):240–262, 1990.
17. S.A. Cook. A taxonomy of problems with fast parallel algorithms. *Information and Control*, 64(1-3):2–21, 1985.
18. S. Dal-Zilio and R. Gascon. Resource bound certification for a tail-recursive virtual machine. In *APLAS 2005*, volume 3780 of *LNCS*, pages 247–263, 2005.
19. M. Furst, J. Saxe, and M. Spiser. Parity, circuits, and the polynomial time hierarchy. *Math. Systems Theory*, 17:13–27, 1984.
20. J.-Y. Girard. Light linear logic. In D. Leivant, editor, *LCC'94*, number 960 in LNCS, 1995.
21. M. Hofmann. Programming languages capturing complexity classes. *SIGACT News Logic Column 9*, 2000.
22. L. Kristiansen and N.D. Jones. The flow of data and the complexity of algorithms. In *New Computational Paradigms*, number 3526 in LNCS, pages 263–274, 2005.
23. C. S. Lee, N. D. Jones, and A. M. Ben-Amram. The size-change principle for program termination. In *POPL*, volume 28, pages 81–92, 2001.
24. D. Leivant. Predicative recurrence and computational complexity I: Word recurrence and poly-time. In *Feasible Mathematics II*, pages 320–343. Birkhäuser, 1994.
25. D. Leivant. A characterization of NC by tree recurrence. In *39th Annual Symposium on Foundations of Computer Science, FOCS'98*, pages 716–724, 1998.
26. D. Leivant and J.-Y. Marion. Lambda Calculus Characterizations of Poly-Time. *Fundamenta Informaticae*, 19(1,2):167–184, September 1993.
27. D. Leivant and J.-Y. Marion. A characterization of alternating log time by ramified recurrence. *TCS*, 236(1-2):192–208, Apr 2000.
28. J.-Y. Marion and J.-Y. Moyen. Efficient first order functional program interpreter with time bound certifications. In *LPAR*, volume 1955 of *LNCS*, pages 25–42, 2000.
29. J.-Y. Marion and R. Péchoux. Resource analysis by sup-interpretation. In *FLOPS 2006*, volume 3945 of *LNCS*, pages 163–176, 2006.
30. J.-Y. Moyen. *Analyse de la complexité et transformation de programmes*. Thèse d'université, Nancy 2, Dec 2003.
31. K.-H. Niggl and H. Wunderlich. Certifying polynomial time and linear/polynomial space for imperative programs. *SIAM J. on Computing*. to appear.
32. W. Ruzzo. On uniform circuit complexity. *J. of Computer System Science*, 22(3):365–383, 1981.

Combining Typing and Size Constraints for Checking the Termination of Higher-Order Conditional Rewrite Systems

Frédéric Blanqui (INRIA) and Colin Riba (INPL)

LORIA*, Campus Scientifique, BP 239
54506 Vandoeuvre-lès-Nancy Cedex, France

Abstract. In a previous work, the first author extended to higher-order rewriting and dependent types the use of size annotations in types, a termination proof technique called type or size based termination and initially developed for ML-like programs. Here, we go one step further by considering conditional rewriting and explicit quantifications and constraints on size annotations. This allows to describe more precisely how the size of the output of a function depends on the size of its inputs. Hence, we can check the termination of more functions. We first give a general type-checking algorithm based on constraint solving. Then, we give a termination criterion with constraints in Presburger arithmetic. To our knowledge, this is the first termination criterion for higher-order conditional rewriting taking into account the conditions in termination.

1 Introduction

We are interested in automatically checking the termination of the combination of β-reduction and higher-order conditional rewrite rules. There are two important approaches to higher-order rewriting: rewriting on $\beta\bar{\eta}$-normal forms [17], and the combination of β-reduction and term rewriting [16]. The relation between both has been studied in [20]. The second approach is more atomic since a rewrite step in the first approach can be directly encoded by a rewrite step together with β-steps in the second approach. In this paper, we consider the second approach, restricted to first-order pattern-matching (we do not allow abstractions in rule left-hand side). Following [7], our results could perhaps be extended to higher-order pattern-matching.

The combination of β-reduction and rewriting is naturally used in proof assistants implementing the proposition-as-type and proof-as-object paradigm. In these systems, two propositions equivalent modulo β-reduction and rewriting are identified (*e.g.* $P(2 + 2)$ and $P(4)$). This is essential for enabling users to formalize large proofs with many computations, as recently shown by Gonthier and Werner's proof of the Four Color Theorem in the Coq proof assistant. However, for the system to be able to check the correctness of user proofs, it must

---

* UMR 7503 CNRS-INPL-INRIA-Nancy2-UHP.

M. Hermann and A. Voronkov (Eds.): LPAR 2006, LNAI 4246, pp. 105–119, 2006.

at least be able to check the equivalence of two terms. Hence, the necessity to have termination criteria for the combination of β-reduction and rewriting.

In Coq, rewriting is restricted to the reductions associated to inductive types like in functional programming languages with pattern-matching. Such reductions correspond to constructor-based rewriting. This is the kind of rewrite systems we are going to consider in this paper. A more general form of rewriting is studied in [9,6] (matching on defined symbols and matching modulo).

Currently, Coq accepts only functions in the definition of which recursive calls are made on arguments that are structurally smaller. For first-order functions, this corresponds to restrict rewrite systems to simply terminating ones, that is, to the ones that can be proved terminating by an ordering containing the subterm relation. However, many interesting systems are not simply terminating. Consider for instance the following definition of division on natural numbers:

$$
\begin{array}{rcl}
\mathsf{minus}\,0\,x & \to & 0 \\
\mathsf{minus}\,x\,0 & \to & x \\
\mathsf{minus}\,(\mathsf{s}\,x)\,(\mathsf{s}\,y) & \to & \mathsf{minus}\,x\,y \\
\mathsf{div}\,0\,y & \to & 0 \\
\mathsf{div}\,(\mathsf{s}\,x)\,y & \to & \mathsf{s}\,(\mathsf{div}\,(\mathsf{minus}\,x\,y)\,y)
\end{array}
$$

Considering that minus is applied to strongly normalizing arguments and that the *size* of a term is the height of its normal form, one can easily prove, by induction on the size of t, that the size of $v = (\mathsf{minus}\,t\,u)$ is less than or equal to the size of t, hence that this definition of minus terminates:

- If v matches the first rule, then $t = 0$ and the normal form of v, which is 0, has the same size as t.
- If v matches the second rule, then v has the same normal form as t.
- If v matches the third rule, then $t = \mathsf{s}t'$, $u = \mathsf{s}u'$ and, by induction hypothesis, the normal form of v has a size smaller than t', hence smaller than t.

The idea of size or type based termination, initiated in [15] and developed by various authors for ML-like definitions [11,22,1,2,3,4] and rewriting and dependent types [8,5], consists in extending the underlying type system by replacing a base type B by an infinite family of base types $(\mathsf{B}^{\mathfrak{a}})_{\mathfrak{a}\in\mathbb{N}}$, a term of type $\mathsf{B}^{\mathfrak{a}}$ being by construction of size smaller than or equal to $\mathfrak{a}$ (except in [22], see later). Then, for ensuring termination, one can restrict in function definitions recursive calls to arguments whose size, by typing, is smaller.

For instance, in all these systems, one can easily (type-)check that minus has for type something similar to $\forall\alpha\beta\mathsf{N}^{\alpha} \Rightarrow \mathsf{N}^{\beta} \Rightarrow \mathsf{N}^{\alpha}$. Hence, assuming that $x : \mathsf{N}^{\alpha}$ and $y : \mathsf{N}^{\beta}$, one can easily (type-)check that $\mathsf{minus}\,x\,y : \mathsf{N}^{\alpha}$ while $\mathsf{s}x : \mathsf{N}^{\alpha+1}$. Thus, the recursive call to div in the last rule can be allowed.

Note that higher-order inductive types, *i.e.* types having constructors with recursive arguments of higher-order type, require families indexed by ordinals. In the present paper, we restrict our attention to first-order inductive types since higher-order inductive types have already been studied in previous works. Note also that interpreting $\mathsf{B}^{\mathfrak{a}}$ by the set of terms of size smaller than or equal to $\mathfrak{a}$ requires subtyping since $t : \mathsf{B}^{\mathfrak{b}}$ whenever $t : \mathsf{B}^{\mathfrak{a}}$ and $\mathfrak{a} \leq \mathfrak{b}$.

However, without explicit existential quantifications and constraints over size annotations, one cannot (type-)check that the following function has type $N \Rightarrow \forall \alpha L^\alpha \Rightarrow \exists \beta \gamma (\alpha = \beta + \gamma) L^\beta \times L^\gamma$:

$$
\begin{aligned}
\text{pivot}\, x\, \text{nil} &\rightarrow (\text{nil}, \text{nil}) \\
\text{pivot}\, x\, (\text{cons}\, y\, l) &\rightarrow \text{let}\, z = \text{pivot}\, x\, l\, \text{in} \\
& \quad \text{if}\, (\text{le}\, y\, x)\, \text{then}\, (\text{cons}\, y\, (\text{fst}\, z), \text{snd}\, z) \\
& \quad \text{else}\, (\text{fst}\, z, \text{cons}\, y\, (\text{snd}\, z))
\end{aligned}
$$

Such a type is necessary for proving that some sorting functions are size preserving, *i.e.* have type $\forall \alpha L^\alpha \Rightarrow L^\alpha$. To the best of our knowledge, only Xi considers such explicit quantifications and constraints [22]. In this work, B^α is interpreted as the set of terms of size α. Note that, with this interpretation, the type of terms of size smaller than α can be represented by $\exists \alpha(\alpha \leq \alpha)B^\alpha$. However, we cannot apply Xi's results on the problem we are interested in for the following reasons:

- Xi considers ML-like function definitions based on `letrec`/`match` constructions while we are interested in definitions based on rewrite rules.
- Xi is interested in the termination of closed terms with call-by-value evaluation strategy while we are interested in the strong normalization of open terms.
- Xi has a two-level approach. He considers an intermediate system where not only types but also terms are annotated by size informations, and proves that terms typable in this system are terminating. Then, for proving the termination of an unannotated term, he must infer the necessary size annotations, which may not be possible. This elaboration process is described in [21].

In the present paper, we extend the simply typed part of [8] with conditional rewriting and explicit quantifications and constraints over size annotations, without using an intermediate system. As Xi and in contrast with [8], we do not consider higher-order inductive types and interpret B^α as the set of terms of size α. The integration of both works should not create too much difficulties. Hence, we get a powerful termination criterion for the combination of β-reduction and higher-order conditional rewriting, based on type-checking and constraint solving. To our knowledge, this is the first termination criterion for higher-order conditional rewriting taking into account the conditions in termination.

In Section 2, we define a system with constrained types. In Section 3, we give a general type-checking algorithm based on constraint solving. In Section 4, we present a general termination proof technique based on Tait's method for proving the termination of β-reduction. In Section 5, we give a termination criterion based on type-checking with constraints in Presburger arithmetic.

2 A System with Constrained Types

Terms. The set $\mathcal{T}$ of *terms* is inductively defined as follows:

$$t \in \mathcal{T} ::= x \mid c \mid f \mid \lambda x t \mid tt \mid (t, t) \mid \text{fst}\, t \mid \text{snd}\, t \mid \text{let}\, x = t\, \text{in}\, t \mid \text{if}\, t\, \text{then}\, t\, \text{else}\, t$$

where $x \in \mathcal{X}$ is a term variable, $c \in \mathcal{C}$ is a *constructor* symbol and $f \in \mathcal{F}$ is a *function symbol*. We assume that $\mathcal{C}$ contains true and false. As usual, terms are considered up to renaming of bound variables. By t, we denote a sequence of terms $t_1, \ldots, t_n$ of length $|t| = n \geq 0$. Term substitutions are denoted by $\sigma, \theta, \ldots$ or their explicit mappings $(\frac{t}{x})$. By $\sigma + \theta$, we denote the substitution equal to θ on $\mathrm{dom}(\theta)$ and to σ on $\mathrm{dom}(\sigma) \setminus \mathrm{dom}(\theta)$. The set $\mathcal{P}$ of (constructor) *patterns* is inductively defined by $p \in \mathcal{P} ::= x \mid c\,p$.

Size annotations. Let $\mathcal{S} = \{nat, bool\}$ be the set of *size sorts*. We assume given a $\mathcal{S}$-sorted first-order term algebra $\mathcal{A}$ for *size expressions* $a, b, \ldots$ whose variables are denoted by $\alpha, \beta, \ldots$ We assume that $\mathcal{A}$ at least contains the symbols $0 : nat$, $1 : nat$, $+ : nat \times nat \Rightarrow nat$, $max : nat \times nat \Rightarrow nat$, $t : bool$ and $f : bool$. For each sort s, we assume given a well-founded interpretation domain $(\mathcal{D}_s, >_{\mathcal{D}_s})$. For $bool$, we take $\mathcal{D}_{bool} = \{t, f\}$. In the following, let $\mathsf{true}^* = t$ and $\mathsf{false}^* = f$; $t^* = t$ and $f^* = f$; $t^* = \mathsf{true}$ and $f^* = \mathsf{false}$. Elements of $\mathcal{D}_s$ are denoted by $\mathfrak{a}, \mathfrak{b}, \ldots$ Valuations are denoted by $\mu, \nu, \ldots$ Size substitutions are denoted by $\varphi, \psi, \ldots$

Constraints. Let a *constraint* be a first-order formula over $\mathcal{A}$, $\mathbb{C}$ be a class of constraints containing $\top$ and $\mathrm{FV}(C)$ be the variables free in C. We denote by $\mu \models C$ the fact that a valuation μ satisfies C; by $\vdash C$ the fact that, for all valuation μ such that $\mathrm{FV}(C) \subseteq \mathrm{dom}(\mu)$, $\mu \models C$, and by $C \equiv D$ the fact that $\vdash C \Leftrightarrow D$. We consider constraints up to the logical equivalence $\equiv$.

Types. We assume given a set $\mathcal{B}$ of type names containing bool. Let $\kappa_{\mathsf{bool}} = bool$ and, for all $\mathsf{B} \neq bool$, $\kappa_{\mathsf{B}} = nat$ (except bool that is annotated by booleans, types are annotated by natural numbers). Types are defined as follows:

$$\begin{aligned}
\text{types } T \in \mathbb{T} &::= \mathsf{B}^a \mid T \Rightarrow T \mid T \times T \mid \forall \alpha P T \mid \exists \alpha P T \\
\text{simple types } S \in \mathbb{S} &::= \exists \alpha \mathsf{B}^\alpha \mid S \Rightarrow S \mid S \times S \\
\text{basic types } B \in \mathbb{B} &::= \mathsf{B}^a \mid B \times B \\
\exists\text{-basic types } E \in \mathbb{E} &::= B \mid \exists \alpha P E \quad \text{with } \vdash \exists \alpha P
\end{aligned}$$

where $\mathsf{B} \in \mathcal{B}$ is a type name, $a \in \mathcal{A}$ is a size expression of sort κ_{B} and $P \in \mathbb{C}$ is a constraint. In the following, we use the following abbreviations: $\forall \alpha T = \forall \alpha \top T$ and $\mathsf{B} = \exists \alpha \mathsf{B}^\alpha$. There is a natural transformation from $\mathbb{T}$ to $\mathbb{S}$: let $\overline{\mathsf{B}^a} = \exists \alpha \mathsf{B}^\alpha$, $\overline{\exists \alpha P T} = \overline{\forall \alpha P T} = \overline{T}$, $\overline{T \Rightarrow U} = \overline{T} \Rightarrow \overline{U}$ and $\overline{T \times U} = \overline{T} \times \overline{U}$.

Subtyping. We define a constraint-based subtyping relation. Let $C \vdash T \leq U$ iff $\vdash C \supset (\!|T \leq U|\!)$ where $(\!|T \leq U|\!)$ is inductively defined as follows:

- $(\!|\mathsf{B}^a \leq \mathsf{B}^b|\!) = (a = b)$
- $(\!|T \Rightarrow U \leq T' \Rightarrow U'|\!) = (\!|T' \leq T|\!) \wedge (\!|U \leq U'|\!)$
- $(\!|T \times U \leq T' \times U'|\!) = (\!|T \leq T'|\!) \wedge (\!|U \leq U'|\!)$
- $(\!|T \leq \exists \alpha P U|\!) = \exists \alpha (P \wedge (\!|T \leq U|\!)) \ (\alpha \notin T, T \neq \exists \beta Q V)$
- $(\!|\exists \alpha P U \leq T|\!) = \forall \alpha (P \supset (\!|U \leq T|\!)) \ (\alpha \notin T)$
- $(\!|T \leq \forall \alpha P U|\!) = \forall \alpha (P \supset (\!|T \leq U|\!)) \ (\alpha \notin T)$
- $(\!|\forall \alpha P U \leq T|\!) = \exists \alpha (P \wedge (\!|U \leq T|\!)) \ (\alpha \notin T, T \neq \forall \beta Q V)$

Typing. An *environment* is a finite mapping Γ from $\mathcal{X}$ to $\mathbb{T}$. Let $\Gamma, x : T$ be the environment Δ such that $x\Delta = T$ and $y\Delta = y\Gamma$ if $y \neq x$. Two environments Γ_1 and Γ_2 are *compatible* if, for all x, $x\Gamma_1 = x\Gamma_2$.

$$(\text{var}) \quad \frac{x \in \text{dom}(\Gamma)}{C; \Gamma \vdash_\tau x : x\Gamma} \qquad (\text{symb}) \quad \frac{\mathsf{s} \in \mathcal{C} \cup \mathcal{F}}{C; \Gamma \vdash_\tau \mathsf{s} : \tau_\mathsf{s}}$$

$$(\text{abs}) \quad \frac{C; \Gamma, x : T \vdash_\tau u : U \quad x \notin \Gamma}{C; \Gamma \vdash_\tau \lambda x u : T \Rightarrow U} \qquad (\text{app}) \quad \frac{C; \Gamma \vdash_\tau t : U \Rightarrow V \quad C; \Gamma \vdash_\tau u : U}{C; \Gamma \vdash_\tau tu : V}$$

$$(\text{pair}) \quad \frac{C; \Gamma \vdash_\tau u : U \quad C; \Gamma \vdash_\tau v : V}{C; \Gamma \vdash_\tau (u, v) : U \times V}$$

$$(\text{fst}) \quad \frac{C; \Gamma \vdash_\tau t : U \times V}{C; \Gamma \vdash_\tau \mathsf{fst}\, t : U} \qquad (\text{snd}) \quad \frac{C; \Gamma \vdash_\tau t : U \times V}{C; \Gamma \vdash_\tau \mathsf{snd}\, t : V}$$

$$(\text{if}) \quad \frac{C; \Gamma \vdash_\tau t : \mathsf{bool} \quad C; \Gamma \vdash_\tau u : T \quad C; \Gamma \vdash_\tau v : T \quad T \;\exists\text{-basic}}{C; \Gamma \vdash_\tau \mathsf{if}\, t \,\mathsf{then}\, u \,\mathsf{else}\, v : T}$$

$$(\text{let}) \quad \frac{C; \Gamma \vdash_\tau t : T \quad C; \Gamma, x : T \vdash_\tau u : U \quad x \notin \Gamma}{C; \Gamma \vdash_\tau \mathsf{let}\, x = t \,\mathsf{in}\, u : U}$$

$$(\forall\text{intro}) \quad \frac{C \wedge P; \Gamma \vdash_\tau t : T \quad \vdash C \supset \exists \alpha P \quad \alpha \notin C, \Gamma}{C; \Gamma \vdash_\tau t : \forall \alpha P T}$$

$$(\forall\text{elim}) \quad \frac{C; \Gamma \vdash_\tau t : \forall \alpha P T \quad \vdash C \supset P^a_\alpha}{C; \Gamma \vdash_\tau t : T^a_\alpha}$$

$$(\exists\text{intro}) \quad \frac{C; \Gamma \vdash_\tau t : T^a_\alpha \quad \vdash C \supset P^a_\alpha}{C; \Gamma \vdash_\tau t : \exists \alpha P T}$$

$$(\exists\text{elim}) \quad \frac{C; \Gamma \vdash_\tau t : \exists \alpha P T \quad C \wedge P; \Gamma, x : T \vdash_\tau u : U \quad \vdash C \supset \exists \alpha P \quad \alpha, x \notin C, \Gamma, U}{C; \Gamma \vdash_\tau \mathsf{let}\, x = t \,\mathsf{in}\, u : U}$$

$$(\text{sub}) \quad \frac{C; \Gamma \vdash_\tau t : T \quad C \vdash T \leq T'}{C; \Gamma \vdash_\tau t : T'}$$

Fig. 1. Typing rules

A type assignment is a function $\tau : \mathcal{C} \cup \mathcal{F} \to \mathbb{T}$ such that $\tau_\mathsf{true} = \mathsf{bool}^\mathsf{t}$, $\tau_\mathsf{false} = \mathsf{bool}^\mathsf{f}$ and, for all $\mathsf{s} \in \mathcal{C} \cup \mathcal{F}$, τ_s is closed. To every type assignment τ, we associate a typing relation $\vdash_\tau$ defined in Figure 1. Note that, in contrast with [22], the typing of u and v in (if) does not depend on t. This is because we consider strong normalization instead of weak normalization. This does not reduce the expressive power of the system since we consider conditional rewriting.

A term t is typable wrt τ if there are C, Γ, T such that $\vdash C$ and $C; \Gamma \vdash_\tau t : T$. Let $\Lambda(\tau)$ be the set of terms typable wrt τ. A term t is *simply typable* if there are Γ, T simple such that $\top; \Gamma \vdash_{\overline{\tau}} t : T$ without ($\exists$intro), ($\forall$intro), ($\exists$elim), ($\forall$elim), (sub). Let $\overline{\Lambda}(\overline{\tau})$ be the set of terms simply typable wrt $\overline{\tau}$.

Example 1. Consider the symbols append : $\forall \beta \gamma \mathsf{L}^\beta \Rightarrow \mathsf{L}^\gamma \Rightarrow \mathsf{L}^{\beta+\gamma}$ and pivot : $\mathsf{N} \Rightarrow \forall \alpha \mathsf{L}^\alpha \Rightarrow \exists \beta \gamma (\alpha = \beta + \gamma) \mathsf{L}^\beta \times \mathsf{L}^\gamma$. Let $\Gamma = x : \mathsf{N}$, $l : \mathsf{L}^\alpha$, $u = (\mathsf{let}\, z = t \,\mathsf{in}\, v)$, $t = \mathsf{pivot}\, x\, l$ and $v = \mathsf{append}\,(\mathsf{fst}\, z)(\mathsf{snd}\, z)$. Then, $\top; \Gamma \vdash t : \exists \beta \gamma (\alpha = \beta + \gamma) \mathsf{L}^\beta \times \mathsf{L}^\gamma$ and $\alpha = \beta + \gamma$; $\Gamma, z : \mathsf{L}^\beta \times \mathsf{L}^\gamma \vdash v : \mathsf{L}^\alpha$. Thus, by ($\exists$elim), $\Gamma \vdash u : \mathsf{L}^\alpha$.

Rewriting. Let $\to_\beta$ be the smallest relation stable by context containing the *head-β-reduction relation* $\to_{\beta h}$ defined as follows:

$$(\lambda x u)t \ \to_{\beta h} \ u_x^t \qquad \mathsf{fst}\,(u,v) \ \to_{\beta h} \ u \qquad \text{if true then } u \text{ else } v \ \to_{\beta h} \ u$$
$$\mathsf{let}\, x = t \,\mathsf{in}\, u \ \to_{\beta h} \ u_x^t \qquad \mathsf{snd}\,(u,v) \ \to_{\beta h} \ v \qquad \text{if false then } u \text{ else } v \ \to_{\beta h} \ v$$

A *conditional rewrite rule* is an expression of the form $\boldsymbol{t} = \mathbf{c} \supset l \to r$ such that l is of the form $\mathbf{f} l$, $\boldsymbol{l}$ are patterns, $\mathbf{c} \in \{\mathsf{true}, \mathsf{false}\}$ and $\mathrm{FV}(r, t) \subseteq \mathrm{FV}(l)$. A rule $\boldsymbol{t} = \mathbf{c} \supset l \to r$ *defines* $\mathsf{f} \in \mathcal{F}$ if l is of the form $\mathsf{f} l$. In the following, we assume given a set $\mathcal{R}$ of rules. The associated rewrite relation is the smallest relation $\to_\mathcal{R}$ stable by context and substitution such that, for all $\boldsymbol{t} = \mathbf{c} \supset l \to r \in \mathcal{R}$, $l\sigma \to_\mathcal{R} r\sigma$ whenever $t\sigma \to^* \mathbf{c}$, where $\to^*$ is the reflexive and transitive closure of $\to = \to_\beta \cup \to_\mathcal{R}$.

Our goal is to prove the strong normalization of $\to = \to_\beta \cup \to_\mathcal{R}$ on the set of simply typable terms $\overline{\Lambda}(\overline{\tau})$.

Assumption: We assume that $\to$ is locally confluent.

Hence, any strongly normalizing term t has a unique normal form $t{\downarrow}$. Note that $\to$ is locally confluent whenever $\to_\mathcal{R}$ so is. See [10] for general conditions on the confluence of β-reduction and higher-order conditional rewriting.

It should be noted that ($\exists$elim) makes subject reduction fail. For instance, with $\Gamma = x : \exists \alpha \mathsf{N}^\alpha, y : \forall \alpha \mathsf{N}^\alpha \Rightarrow \exists \beta \mathsf{N}^\beta$, we have $\top; \Gamma \vdash \mathsf{let}\, z = x \,\mathsf{in}\, yz : \exists \beta \mathsf{N}^\beta$ while yx is not typable in $\top; \Gamma$. It could be fixed by replacing in ($\exists$elim) $\mathsf{let}\, x = t \,\mathsf{in}\, u$ by u_x^t. It does not matter since our termination proof technique does not need subject reduction. Note however that subject reduction holds on simply typed terms.

An example of higher-order conditional rule is given by the following definition of $\mathsf{filter} : (\mathsf{N} \Rightarrow \mathsf{N}) \Rightarrow \forall \alpha \mathsf{L}^\alpha \Rightarrow \exists \beta (\beta \leq \alpha) \mathsf{L}^\beta$:

$$
\begin{aligned}
\mathsf{filter}\, f \,\mathsf{nil} \quad &\to \quad \mathsf{nil} \\
f\, x = \mathsf{true} \supset \mathsf{filter}\, f\,(\mathsf{cons}\, x\, l) \quad &\to \quad \mathsf{cons}\,(f\, x)\,(\mathsf{filter}\, f\, l) \\
f\, x = \mathsf{false} \supset \mathsf{filter}\, f\,(\mathsf{cons}\, x\, l) \quad &\to \quad \mathsf{filter}\, f\, l
\end{aligned}
$$

3   Type-Checking Algorithm

Type-checking is the following problem: given τ, C, Γ, t and T, do we have C satisfiable and $C; \Gamma \vdash_\tau t : T$?

Because of the rules ($\exists$elim) and (conv), type-checking does not seem to be decidable. Similarly, in [22], the elaboration process is not complete. It is however possible to give an algorithm that either succeed or fails, a failure meaning that we don't know. To this end, we inductively define in Figure 2 two relations in the style of bi-directional type inference [12,2]. In the type inference relation $C; \Gamma \vdash t \uparrow T$, C and T are produced according to Γ and t. In the type checking relation $C; \Gamma \vdash t \downarrow T$, C is produced according to Γ, t and T. An actual algorithm is a strategy for applying the rules defining these relations.

$$\text{(type-check)} \quad \frac{D; \Gamma \vdash t \downarrow T \quad \vdash C \supset D \quad C \text{ satisfiable}}{C; \Gamma \vdash^? t : T}$$

$$\text{($\uparrow$var)} \quad \frac{x \in \text{dom}(\Gamma)}{\top; \Gamma \vdash x \uparrow x\Gamma} \qquad \text{($\uparrow$symb)} \quad \top; \Gamma \vdash s \uparrow \tau_s$$

$$\text{($\uparrow$app)} \quad \frac{C; \Gamma \vdash t \uparrow U \Rightarrow V \quad D; \Gamma \vdash u \downarrow U}{C \wedge D; \Gamma \vdash tu \uparrow V}$$

$$\text{($\uparrow$pair)} \quad \frac{C; \Gamma \vdash u \uparrow U \quad D; \Gamma \vdash v \uparrow V}{C \wedge D; \Gamma \vdash (u,v) \uparrow U \times V}$$

$$\text{($\uparrow$fst)} \quad \frac{C; \Gamma \vdash t \uparrow U \times V}{C; \Gamma \vdash \text{fst}\, t \uparrow U} \qquad \text{($\uparrow$snd)} \quad \frac{C; \Gamma \vdash t \uparrow U \times V}{C; \Gamma \vdash \text{snd}\, t \uparrow V}$$

$$\text{($\uparrow$let)} \quad \frac{C; \Gamma \vdash t \uparrow T \quad D; \Gamma, x : T \vdash u \uparrow U}{C \wedge D; \Gamma \vdash \text{let}\, x = t \,\text{in}\, u \uparrow U}$$

$$\text{($\uparrow\forall$elim)} \quad \frac{C; \Gamma \vdash t \uparrow \forall\alpha PT \quad \alpha \notin C, \Gamma}{C \wedge P; \Gamma \vdash t \uparrow T}$$

$$\text{($\uparrow\exists$elim)} \quad \frac{C; \Gamma \vdash t \uparrow \exists\alpha PT \quad D; \Gamma, x : T \vdash u \uparrow U \quad x \notin \Gamma \quad \alpha \notin C, \Gamma}{C \wedge \exists\alpha P \wedge \forall\alpha(P \supset D); \Gamma \vdash \text{let}\, x = t \,\text{in}\, u \uparrow \exists\alpha PU}$$

$$\text{($\downarrow$abs)} \quad \frac{C; \Gamma, x : T \vdash u \downarrow U \quad x \notin \Gamma}{C; \Gamma \vdash \lambda xu \downarrow T \Rightarrow U}$$

$$\text{($\downarrow$if)} \quad \frac{C; \Gamma \vdash t \downarrow \exists\alpha \text{bool}^\alpha \quad D; \Gamma \vdash u \downarrow T \quad E; \Gamma \vdash v \downarrow T \quad T \,\exists\text{-basic}}{C \wedge D \wedge E; \Gamma \vdash \text{if}\, t \,\text{then}\, u \,\text{else}\, v \downarrow T}$$

$$\text{($\downarrow\forall$intro)} \quad \frac{C; \Gamma \vdash t \downarrow T \quad \alpha \notin \Gamma}{\exists\alpha P \wedge \forall\alpha(P \supset C); \Gamma \vdash t \downarrow \forall\alpha PT}$$

$$\text{($\downarrow\forall$elim)} \quad \frac{C; \Gamma \vdash t \uparrow \forall\alpha PT}{C \wedge P_\alpha^a; \Gamma \vdash t \downarrow T_\alpha^a}$$

$$\text{($\downarrow\exists$intro)} \quad \frac{C; \Gamma \vdash t \downarrow T \quad \alpha \notin \Gamma}{\exists\alpha(C \wedge P); \Gamma \vdash t \downarrow \exists\alpha PT}$$

$$\text{($\downarrow\exists$elim)} \quad \frac{C; \Gamma \vdash t \uparrow \exists\alpha PT \quad D; \Gamma, x : T \vdash u \downarrow U \quad \alpha \notin C, \Gamma, U}{C \wedge \exists\alpha P \wedge \forall\alpha(P \supset D); \Gamma \vdash \text{let}\, x = t \,\text{in}\, u \downarrow U}$$

$$\text{($\downarrow$sub)} \quad \frac{C; \Gamma \vdash t \uparrow T'}{C \wedge (\!| T' \leq T |\!); \Gamma \vdash t \downarrow T}$$

Fig. 2. Rules for deciding type-checking

Let $\overline{\mathbb{C}}$ be the closure of $\mathbb{C}$ by conjunction, implication, existential and universal quantification. If one starts with $C \in \mathbb{C}$, then the constraints generated by such an algorithm are in $\mathbb{C}$ too. Hence, if $\mathbb{C}$ only contains linear inequalities, then $\overline{\mathbb{C}}$

are formulas of Presburger arithmetic which is known to be decidable [18] and whose complexity is doubly exponential in the size of the formula [13]. This high complexity is not so important in our case since the terms we intend to consider are small (rule right-hand sides). It would be however interesting to study in more details the complexity of type-checking wrt $\mathbb{C}$.

For proving the correctness of the rule ($\downarrow\exists$intro), we need to assume that the size expression language $\mathcal{A}$ is complete wrt the interpretation domains $\mathcal{D}_s$, that is, to every $\mathfrak{a} \in \mathcal{D}_s$ corresponds a closed term $a \in \mathcal{A}$ whose denotation in $\mathcal{D}_s$ is $\mathfrak{a}$. Note that this is indeed the case when $\mathcal{D}_s = \mathbb{N}$ and $\mathcal{A}$ contains 0, 1 and +.

See Example 3 at the end of the paper for an example of derivation.

Theorem 1. *Consider the rules of Figure 2. If $C; \Gamma \vdash^? t : T$, then C is satisfiable and $C; \Gamma \vdash t : T$.*

Proof. First, one can easily check that, for every rule, if the constraint in the conclusion is satisfiable, then the constraints in the premises are satisfiable too. Then, we prove that, if C is satisfiable and $C; \Gamma \vdash t \uparrow T$ or $C; \Gamma \vdash t \downarrow T$, then $C; \Gamma \vdash t : T$. We only detail some cases.

($\uparrow\exists$**elim**) Let $E = C \wedge \exists \alpha P \wedge \forall \alpha (P \supset D)$. Since $E \supset C$ and $(E \wedge P) \supset D$, by induction hypothesis and weakening, $E; \Gamma \vdash t : \exists \alpha PT$ and $E \wedge P; \Gamma \vdash u : U$. Since $(E \wedge P) \supset P$, by ($\exists$intro), $E \wedge P; \Gamma \vdash u : \exists \alpha PU$. Since $E \supset \exists \alpha P$ and $\alpha \notin \exists \alpha PU$, by ($\exists$elim), $E; \Gamma \vdash \text{let } x = t \text{ in } u : \exists \alpha PU$.

($\downarrow\forall$**intro**) Let $E = \exists \alpha P \wedge \forall \alpha (P \supset C)$. Since $(E \wedge P) \supset C$, by induction hypothesis and weakening, $E \wedge P; \Gamma \vdash t : T$. Since $E \supset \exists \alpha P$, we can conclude by ($\forall$intro).

($\downarrow\forall$**elim**) Let $E = C \wedge P_\alpha^a$. By induction hypothesis and weakening, $E; \Gamma \vdash t : \forall \alpha PT$. Since $E \supset P_\alpha^a$, we can conclude by ($\forall$elim).

($\downarrow\exists$**intro**) Let $E = \exists \alpha (C \wedge P)$. Since E is satisfiable, C is satisfiable too. By completeness, there is a such that $F = C_\alpha^a \wedge P_\alpha^a$ is satisfiable. By induction hypothesis, $C; \Gamma \vdash t : T$. By substitution and weakening, $F; \Gamma \vdash t : T_\alpha^a$. Since $F \supset P_\alpha^a$, by ($\exists$intro), $F; \Gamma \vdash t : \exists \alpha PT$. Since $E \supset F$, we can conclude by weakening.

($\downarrow\exists$**elim**) Let $E = C \wedge \exists \alpha P \wedge \forall \alpha (P \supset D)$. Since $E \supset C$ and $(E \wedge P) \supset D$, by induction hypothesis and weakening, $E; \Gamma \vdash t : \exists \alpha PT$ and $E \wedge P; \Gamma \vdash u : U$. Since $E \supset \exists \alpha P$ and $\alpha \notin U$, by ($\exists$elim), $E; \Gamma \vdash \text{let } x = t \text{ in } u : U$. $\square$

4   Termination Proof Technique

In this section, we present a general method for proving the strong normalization of β-reduction and rewriting on well-typed terms. It is based on Tait's method for proving the strong normalization of β-reduction [19]. The idea is to interpret types by particular sets of strongly normalizing terms, called saturated, and prove that every well-typed term belongs to the interpretation of its type.

Following [2], we define the *weak-head-β-reduction relation* $\to_{\beta wh}$ as the relation such that $E[t] \to_{\beta wh} E[u]$ iff $t \to_{\beta h} u$ and $E \in \mathcal{E}$, where the set of *elimination contexts* $\mathcal{E}$ is inductively defined as follows:

$$E \in \mathcal{E} ::= [] \mid E\,t \mid \mathsf{fst}\,E \mid \mathsf{snd}\,E$$

Definition 1 (Saturated sets). *The set* SAT *of saturated sets is the set of all the sets of terms S such that:*

(1) If $t \in S$, then $t \in$ SN.
(2) If $t \in S$ and $t \to t'$, then $t' \in S$.
(3) If $E[x] \in$ SN, then $E[x] \in S$.
(4) If $t \in$ SN, $t \to_{\beta h} t'$ and $E[t'] \in S$, then $E[t] \in S$.

We also define the following operations on sets of terms:

- $S_1 \Rightarrow S_2 = \{t \in \mathcal{T} \mid \forall u \in S_1, tu \in S_2\}$
- $S_1 \times S_2 = \{t \in \mathcal{T} \mid \mathsf{fst}\,t \in S_1 \wedge \mathsf{snd}\,t \in S_2\}$

Let $\mathcal{N}$ be the set of terms of the form $\mathsf{f}t$, $\mathsf{if}\,t\,\mathsf{then}\,u\,\mathsf{else}\,v$, $\mathsf{fst}\,t$ or $\mathsf{snd}\,t$. A saturated set S has the neutral term property *if $s \in S$ whenever $s \in \mathcal{N}$ and $\to(s) \subseteq S$.*

Lemma 1. SAT *is a complete lattice for inclusion with $\bigcup$ as lub, $\bigcap$ as glb and* SN *as greatest element. It is also stable by $\Rightarrow$ and $\times$.*

All this is more or less well known. See for instance [2]. The key difference with the first author work [8] is that we use saturated sets instead of reducibility candidates. See [14] for a comparison between the two kinds of sets. With reducibility candidates, (4) is replaced by the neutral term property.

Reducibility candidates are saturated but the converse does not hold since candidates are not stable by union. Hence, with candidates, $\exists \alpha PT$ cannot be interpreted as an union, which is essential if one wants to interpret B^a as the set of terms of size a in order to give precise types to function symbols.

However, reducibility candidates extend well to rewriting and polymorphism since, for proving that $\mathsf{f}t \in S$, it suffices to prove that $\to(\mathsf{f}t) \subseteq S$. In Lemma 2, we prove that this property still holds with saturated sets when S is the interpretation of an existentially quantified basic type.

Definition 2 (Interpretation of types). *A base type interpretation is a function I which, to every pair (B, a) with $\mathsf{B} \neq$ bool, associates a set $I_{\mathsf{B}}^a \in$ SAT. We extend I to bool by taking $I_{\mathsf{bool}}^a = \{t \in$ SN $\mid t\!\downarrow \neq a^*\}$. Given such an interpretation, types are interpreted by saturated sets as follows:*

- $[\![\mathsf{B}^a]\!]_\mu^I = I_{\mathsf{B}}^{a\mu}$
- $[\![U \times V]\!]_\mu^I = [\![U]\!]_\mu^I \times [\![V]\!]_\mu^I$
- $[\![U \Rightarrow V]\!]_\mu^I = [\![U]\!]_\mu^I \Rightarrow [\![V]\!]_\mu^I$
- $[\![\forall \alpha PT]\!]_\mu^I = \bigcap_{\mu + \frac{a}{\alpha} \models P} [\![T]\!]_{\mu + \frac{a}{\alpha}}^I$ if $\vdash \exists \alpha P$, $[\![\forall \alpha PT]\!]_\mu^I =$ SN *otherwise*
- $[\![\exists \alpha PT]\!]_\mu^I = \bigcup_{\mu + \frac{a}{\alpha} \models P} [\![T]\!]_{\mu + \frac{a}{\alpha}}^I$ if $\vdash \exists \alpha P$, $[\![\exists \alpha PT]\!]_\mu^I = \bigcap$ SAT *otherwise*

Let $I_{\mathsf{B}}^\omega = [\exists \alpha \mathsf{B}^\alpha]$. A symbol $\mathsf{s} \in \mathcal{C} \cup \mathcal{F}$ is computable if $\mathsf{s} \in [\![\tau_{\mathsf{s}}]\!]^I$. A pair (μ, σ) is valid for $C; \Gamma$, written $(\mu, \sigma) \models C; \Gamma$, if $\mu \models C$ and, for all $x \in \mathrm{dom}(\Gamma)$, $x\sigma \in [\![x\Gamma]\!]_\mu^I$. A base type interpretation I is valid if every constructor is computable and, for every $\exists$-basic type T, $[\![T]\!]_\mu^I$ has the neutral term property.

Note that $I_{\mathsf{bool}}^{\mathsf{a}} \in \mathrm{SAT}$ has the neutral term property and $[\![T\varphi]\!]_\mu^I = [\![T]\!]_{\varphi\mu}^I$.

Theorem 2. *Assume that I is a valid base type interpretation and every $\mathsf{f} \in \mathcal{F}$ is computable. If $C; \Gamma \vdash t : T$ and $(\mu, \sigma) \models C; \Gamma$, then $t\sigma \in [\![T]\!]_\mu^I$.*

Proof. By induction on $C; \Gamma \vdash t : T$. We only detail some cases.

(abs) We must prove that $s = (\lambda xu)\sigma \in [\![T \Rightarrow U]\!]_\mu^I$. Wlog, we can assume that $x \notin \sigma$. Then, $s = \lambda x(u\sigma)$. Let $t \in [\![T]\!]_\mu^I$. We must prove that $st \in [\![U]\!]_\mu^I$. By induction hypothesis, $u\sigma \in [\![U]\!]_\mu^I$. Let now $\sigma' = \sigma +_x^t$. Since $(\mu, \sigma') \models C; \Gamma, x : T$, by induction hypothesis, $u\sigma' \in [\![U]\!]_\mu^I$. Hence, $st \in \mathrm{SN}$ since, by induction on $(u\sigma, t)$ with $\to_{\mathrm{lex}}$ as well-founded ordering, $\to(st) \subseteq \mathrm{SN}$. Therefore, $st \in [\![U]\!]_\mu^I$ since $st \to_{\beta h} u\sigma' \in [\![U]\!]_\mu^I$ and $st \in \mathrm{SN}$.

(if) Let $s = (\mathrm{if}\ t\ \mathrm{then}\ u\ \mathrm{else}\ v)\sigma$. By induction hypothesis, $t\sigma \in I_{\mathsf{bool}}^\omega$ and $t_i\sigma \in [\![T]\!]_\mu^I$. Since $s \in \mathcal{N}$ and T is an $\exists$-basic type, by the neutral term property, it suffices to prove that $\to(s) \subseteq [\![T]\!]_\mu^I$. This follows by induction on $(t\sigma, u\sigma, v\sigma)$ with $\to_{\mathrm{lex}}$ as well-founded ordering.

($\exists$elim) We must prove that $s = (\mathrm{let}\ x = t\ \mathrm{in}\ u)\sigma \in [\![U]\!]_\mu^I$. Wlog, we can assume that $x \notin \sigma$. Then, $s = \mathrm{let}\ x = t\sigma\ \mathrm{in}\ u\sigma$. Let $\sigma' = \sigma_x^{t\sigma}$. By induction hypothesis, $t\sigma \in [\![\exists\alpha PT]\!]_\mu^I$. Since $\vdash C \supset \exists\alpha P$, there is $\mathbf{a}$ such that $\mu +_\alpha^{\mathbf{a}} \models P$ and $t\sigma \in [\![T]\!]_{\mu+_\alpha^{\mathbf{a}}}^I$. Therefore, by induction hypothesis, $u\sigma' \in [\![U]\!]_{\mu+_\alpha^{\mathbf{a}}}^I = [\![U]\!]_\mu^I$.

(sub) By induction on T and T', one can easily prove that $[\![T]\!]_\mu^I \subseteq [\![U]\!]_\mu^I$ whenever $\mu \models (T \leq U)$. $\qquad\square$

Corollary 1. *Assume that I is a valid base type interpretation and every $\mathsf{f} \in \mathcal{F}$ is computable. Then, $\to$ is strongly normalizing on $\Lambda(\tau)$.*

Corollary 2. *Assume that, for all $\mathsf{s} \in \mathcal{C} \cup \mathcal{F}$, τ_{s} is of the form $\boldsymbol{T} \Rightarrow \forall \alpha \mathsf{B}^\alpha \Rightarrow T$ with $\boldsymbol{T}$ simple, B basic and T an $\exists$-basic type. If every symbol is computable, then $\to$ is strongly normalizing on $\overline{\Lambda}(\overline{\tau})$.*

Proof. It suffices to prove that, for all s, $\mathsf{s} \in [\![\overline{\tau_{\mathsf{s}}}]\!]^I$. We have $\overline{\tau_{\mathsf{s}}} = \boldsymbol{T} \Rightarrow \mathsf{B} \Rightarrow \overline{B}$. Let $\boldsymbol{t} \in [\![\boldsymbol{T}]\!]^I$ and $u \in I_{\mathsf{B}}^\omega$. We must prove that $\mathsf{f}\boldsymbol{t}u \in [\![B]\!]^I$. There is $\alpha\mu$ such that $u \in I_{\mathsf{B}}^{\alpha\mu}$. Assume that $T = \forall \delta PB$. Since $\mathsf{f} : \boldsymbol{T} \Rightarrow \forall \alpha \mathsf{B}^\alpha \Rightarrow T$ is computable, $\mathsf{f}\boldsymbol{t}u \in [\![T]\!]_\mu^I = \bigcup_{\mu+_\delta^{\mathsf{o}} \models P} [\![B]\!]_{\mu+_\delta^{\mathsf{o}}}^I$. Let $\nu = \mu +_\delta^{\mathsf{o}} \models P$. We are left to prove that $[\![B]\!]_\nu^I \subseteq [\![\overline{B}]\!]^I$. We proceed by induction on B. $\qquad\square$

5   Termination Criterion

We now provide conditions to obtain the computability of defined symbols.

A *precedence* is a quasi-ordering $\geq$ whose strict part $> = \geq \setminus \leq$ is well-founded. Let $\simeq = \geq \cap \leq$ be its associated equivalence relation. We assume given a precedence $\geq_\mathcal{B}$ on $\mathcal{B}$ and a precedence $\geq_\mathcal{F}$ on $\mathcal{F}$. We are going to define some base type interpretation and prove that every function symbol is computable by induction on these precedences.

Assumption: For all $c \in \mathcal{C}$, we assume that τ_c is of the form[1] $\mathbf{C} \Rightarrow \forall \alpha \mathbf{B}^\alpha \Rightarrow \mathbf{B}^a$ with $\mathbf{C} <_\mathcal{B} \mathbf{B}$, $\mathbf{B} \simeq_\mathcal{B} \mathbf{B}$, $a = 0$ if $|\alpha| = 0$, and $a = 1 + max(\alpha)$ if $|\alpha| > 0$.

Example 2. The type N of natural numbers has constructors $0 : \mathsf{N}^0$ and $\mathsf{s} : \forall \alpha \mathsf{N}^\alpha \Rightarrow \mathsf{N}^{\alpha+1}$. The type L of lists has constructors $\mathsf{nil} : \mathsf{L}^0$ and $\mathsf{cons} : \mathsf{N} \Rightarrow \forall \alpha \mathsf{L}^\alpha \Rightarrow \mathsf{L}^{\alpha+1}$. The type T of binary trees has constructors $\mathsf{leaf} : \mathsf{N} \Rightarrow \mathsf{T}^0$ and $\mathsf{node} : \forall \alpha \beta \mathsf{T}^\alpha \Rightarrow \mathsf{T}^\beta \Rightarrow \mathsf{T}^{1+max(\alpha,\beta)}$.

We define the base type interpretation as follows:

- $I_\mathsf{B}^0 = \{t \in \mathrm{SN} \mid \forall c : \mathbf{C} \Rightarrow \forall \alpha \mathbf{B}^\alpha \Rightarrow \mathbf{B}^a, \forall tu, |t| = |\mathbf{C}| \wedge |u| = |\alpha| \wedge t \rightarrow^* ctu \Rightarrow t \in I_\mathsf{\underline{C}}^\omega \wedge |\alpha| = a = 0\}$
- $I_\mathsf{B}^{a+1} = \{t \in \mathrm{SN} \mid \forall c : \mathbf{C} \Rightarrow \forall \alpha \mathbf{B}^\alpha \Rightarrow \mathbf{B}^a, \forall tu, |t| = |\mathbf{C}| \wedge |u| = |\alpha| \wedge t \rightarrow^* ctu \Rightarrow t \in I_\mathsf{\underline{C}}^\omega \wedge a = 1 + max(\alpha) \wedge (\exists b)\, a = max(b) \wedge u \in I_\mathsf{B}^b\}$

Lemma 2. *I is a valid base type interpretation.*

Proof. One can easily check that I_b^a is saturated and that every constructor is computable. We now prove that $[\![T]\!]_\mu^I$ has the neutral term property whenever T is $\exists$-basic.

We first remark that, if $t \in \mathrm{SN}$ and $t \rightarrow^* t' \in I_\mathsf{B}^a$, then $t \in I_\mathsf{B}^a$. We prove it by induction on (B, a) with $(>_\mathcal{B}, >_{\mathcal{D}_{\kappa_\mathcal{B}}})_{\mathrm{lex}}$ as well-founded ordering. Let $c : \mathbf{C} \Rightarrow \forall \alpha \mathbf{B}^\alpha \Rightarrow \mathbf{B}^a$, t and u such that $|t| = |\mathbf{C}|$, $|u| = |\alpha|$ and $t \rightarrow^* ctu$. By confluence, $t' \rightarrow^* ct'u'$ with $tu \rightarrow^* t'u'$. We proceed by case on a.

- $a = \mathsf{t}$. Then, $t' \not\rightarrow^* \mathsf{false}$. Hence, $t \not\rightarrow^* \mathsf{false}$ and $t \in I_\mathsf{B}^a$.
- $a = \mathsf{f}$. Idem.
- $a = 0$. Since $t' \in I_\mathsf{B}^a$, $t' \in I_\mathsf{\underline{C}}^\omega$ and $|\alpha| = a = 0$. Since $\mathbf{C} <_\mathcal{B} \mathbf{B}$, by induction hypothesis, $t \in I_\mathsf{\underline{C}}^\omega$. Thus, $t \in I_\mathsf{B}^a$.
- $a > 0$. Since $t' \in I_\mathsf{B}^a$, $t' \in I_\mathsf{\underline{C}}^\omega$, $a = 1 + max(\alpha)$ and there are b such that $a = 1 + max(b)$ and $u' \in I_\mathsf{B}^b$. Since $\mathbf{C} <_\mathcal{B} \mathbf{B}$ and $b < a$, by induction hypothesis, $t \in I_\mathsf{\underline{C}}^\omega$ and $u \in I_\mathsf{B}^b$. Thus, $t \in I_\mathsf{B}^a$.

Let now $T = \exists \alpha P B$ be an $\exists$-basic type. We have $S = \bigcup_{\mu+_\alpha^a \models P}[\![B]\!]_{\mu+_\alpha^a}^I$. We first prove that there are a such that $\nu = \mu+_\alpha^a \models P$ and $\rightarrow(s) \subseteq S' = [\![B]\!]_\nu^I$. If $\rightarrow(s) = \emptyset$, this is immediate. So, assume that there is $t \in \rightarrow(s)$. Since $t \in S$, there are a such that $\nu = \mu+_\alpha^a \models P$ and $t \in S' = [\![B]\!]_\nu^I$. Let now $u \in \rightarrow(s)$. By confluence, there is v such that $t, u \rightarrow^* v$. Since $t \in S'$, we have $v \in S'$. Thus, $u \in S'$ too. Hence, $\rightarrow(s) \subseteq S'$.

We now prove that $s \in S'$ whenever $\rightarrow(s) \subseteq S'$ by induction on B. $\square$

Lemma 3. *We assume given an injection ε from term variables to size variables. Consider the rules of Figure 3. If $\alpha = a; \Gamma \rightsquigarrow t : \mathsf{B}^\alpha$ and $t\sigma \in I_\mathsf{B}^{\alpha\mu}$, then there is ν such that $(\mu + \nu, \sigma) \models \alpha = a; \Gamma$.*

---

[1] The order of types is not relevant. We take this order for the sake of simplicity.

$$(1) \quad \alpha = \varepsilon_x; x : \mathsf{B}^{\varepsilon_x} \rightsquigarrow x : \mathsf{B}^\alpha$$

$$(2) \quad \frac{c : T \Rightarrow \mathsf{B}^0 \quad \mathsf{B} \neq \mathsf{bool}}{\alpha = 0; x : T \rightsquigarrow cx : \mathsf{B}^\alpha} \qquad (2') \quad \frac{c : \mathsf{bool}^{c^*}}{\alpha = c^*; \emptyset \rightsquigarrow c : \mathsf{bool}^\alpha}$$

$$(3) \quad \frac{c : T \Rightarrow \forall \alpha \mathsf{B}^\alpha \Rightarrow \mathsf{B}^{1+max(\alpha)} \quad \alpha = a; \Gamma \rightsquigarrow u : \mathsf{B}^\alpha \quad \alpha \notin a}{x : T, \Gamma \text{ are compatible}}$$
$$\frac{}{\alpha = 1 + max(a); x : T, \Gamma \rightsquigarrow cxu : \mathsf{B}^\alpha}$$

Fig. 3. Matching constraints

Proof. We say that $\mathfrak{a}$ is minimal for $t \in [\![\mathsf{B}]\!]^\omega$ if $t \in [\![\mathsf{B}]\!]^{\mathfrak{a}}$ and, for all $\mathfrak{b} < \mathfrak{a}$, $t \notin [\![\mathsf{B}]\!]^{\mathfrak{b}}$. We prove the lemma by induction on $\alpha = a; \Gamma \rightsquigarrow t : \mathsf{B}^\alpha$ with the additional requirement that ν is minimal whenever μ so is.

(1) It suffices to take $\varepsilon_x \nu = \alpha \mu$.

(2) and (2') It suffices to take $\nu = \emptyset$.

(3) We have $t\sigma = cx\sigma u\sigma$. Thus, μ is minimal, $x\sigma \in [\![T]\!]$ and there is μ' minimal such that $u\sigma \in I_\mathsf{B}^{\alpha\mu'}$ and $\alpha\mu = 1 + max(\alpha\mu')$. Now, by induction hypothesis, there are ν minimal such that $(\mu' + \nu, \sigma) \models \alpha = a; \Gamma$. Since ν are minimal, if $x\sigma \in I_{\mathsf{B}_i}^{\varepsilon_x \nu_i} \cap I_{\mathsf{B}_j}^{\varepsilon_x \nu_j}$, then $\varepsilon_x \nu_i = \varepsilon_x \nu_j$. Thus, we can define $\nu = \Sigma \nu$. Since ν is minimal, we are left to prove that $(\mu + \nu, \sigma) \models \alpha = 1 + max(a); \Gamma$. First, we have $\mu + \nu \models \alpha = 1 + max(a)$ since $\alpha\mu = 1 + max(\alpha\mu') = 1 + max(a\nu)$. Second, let $x \in u_i$. Then, $x\sigma \in [\![x\Gamma]\!]_{\nu_i}^I = [\![x\Gamma]\!]_{x\nu}^I$. $\qquad \square$

Theorem 3 (Termination criterion). *Assume that, for every* $\mathsf{f} \in \mathcal{F}$:

(1) τ_f *is of the form* $T \Rightarrow \forall \alpha \mathsf{B}^\alpha \Rightarrow T$ *with* T *an* $\exists$-*basic type;*

(2) *there is a constraint* $(\beta <_\mathsf{f} \alpha)$ *such that the ordering* $\succ_\mathsf{f}$ *defined by* $\alpha\mu \succ_\mathsf{f} \beta\mu$ *iff* $\mu \models \beta <_\mathsf{f} \alpha$ *is well-founded;*

(3) *for every* $\mathsf{g} \simeq_\mathcal{F} \mathsf{f}$, τ_g *is of the form* $U \Rightarrow \forall \alpha \mathsf{B}^\alpha \Rightarrow U$ *and* $<_\mathsf{f} = <_\mathsf{g}$;

and, for every rule $t = \mathsf{c} \supset l \rightarrow r$ *defining* f:

(4) l *is of the form* $\mathsf{f}xl$ *with* $|x| = |T|$ *and* $|l| = |\alpha|$;

(5) *there are* Γ *compatible and* a *such that* $\alpha = a; \Gamma \rightsquigarrow l : \mathsf{B}^\alpha$;

(6) *every symbol occurring in* r *is* $\leq_\mathcal{F} \mathsf{f}$;

(7) $\alpha = a; x : T, \Gamma \vdash_{\tau_<} t : \mathsf{bool}^b$;

(8) $b = \mathsf{c}^*; \alpha = a; x : T, \Gamma \vdash_{\tau_<} r : T$.

where:

(9) *for every* $\mathsf{g} <_\mathcal{F} \mathsf{f}$, $\tau_\mathsf{g}^< = \tau_\mathsf{g}$;

(10) *for every* $\mathsf{g} \simeq_\mathcal{F} \mathsf{f}$, $\tau_\mathsf{g}^< = U \Rightarrow \forall \alpha'(\alpha' <_\mathsf{f} \alpha)\mathsf{B}^{\alpha'} \Rightarrow U$ *with* $\alpha' \notin \alpha$ *whenever* $\tau_\mathsf{g} = U \Rightarrow \forall \alpha' \mathsf{B}^{\alpha'} \Rightarrow U$.

Then, $\rightarrow$ *is strongly normalizing on* $\Lambda(\tau)$ *and* $\overline{\Lambda}(\overline{\tau})$.

Proof. We must prove that, for all $\mathsf{f} : T \Rightarrow \forall \alpha \mathsf{B}^\alpha \Rightarrow T$, $t \in [\![T]\!]$, μ and $u \in I_\mathsf{B}^{\alpha\mu}$, $\mathsf{f}tu \in [\![T]\!]_\mu^I$. We proceed by induction on $(\mathsf{f}, \alpha\mu, tu)$ with $(>_\mathcal{F}, \succ_\mathsf{f}, \rightarrow_{\mathsf{lex}})_{\mathsf{lex}}$ as well-founded ordering. By Lemma 2, it suffices to prove that $\rightarrow(s) \subseteq S$. If the reduction takes place in tu, we conclude by induction hypothesis. Assume now that there are $f x l \to r \in \mathcal{R}$ and σ such that $x\sigma = t$ and $l\sigma = u$. We must prove that $r\sigma \in [\![T]\!]_\mu^I$. After Lemma 3, since Γ are compatible, there is ν such that $(\mu + \nu, \sigma) \models \alpha = a; \Gamma$. By induction hypothesis, for all $g \leq_\mathcal{F} f$, $g \in [\![\tau_g^<]\!]$ (considering α as constants interpreted by $\alpha\mu$). Thus, letting $\eta = \mu + \nu$, by Theorem 2, we have $t\sigma \in I_{\text{bool}}^{b\eta}$. Since $t\sigma \to^* \mathbf{c} \in I_{\text{bool}}^{\mathbf{c}^{**}}$, we have $b\eta = \mathbf{c}^{**}$. Thus, $\eta \models b = \mathbf{c}^*$ and, by Theorem 2 again, $r\sigma \in [\![T]\!]_\eta^I = [\![T]\!]_\mu^I$.   □

The size variables α in the type of f (1) represents the sizes of the recursive arguments of f. The user-defined predicate $<_f$ in (2) expresses the measure that must decrease in recursive calls. One can for instance take lexicographic or multiset comparisons together with linear combinations of the arguments. The condition (5) provides the constraints on α when a term matches the rule left hand-side $l = f x l$. The condition (7) implies that the terms t are terminating whenever the arguments of the left hand-side so are. The condition (8) implies that the right-hand-side is terminating whenever the arguments of the left hand-side so are and $t \to^* \mathbf{c}$. The fact that $t \to^* \mathbf{c}$ is expressed by the additional constraint $b = \mathbf{c}^*$. Termination is ensured by doing type-checking in the system $\vdash_{\mathcal{T}<}$ where, by condition (10), function symbols equivalent to f can only be applied to arguments smaller than α in $<_f$. This is in contrast with [8] where a new type system (called the computability closure) restricting the use of (app) must be introduced.

Example 3. We detail the criterion with the second rule of pivot given in the introduction. Let r be the right-hand side of the rule and u (resp. v) be the first (resp. second) branch of if in r.

We take pivot $: \mathsf{N} \Rightarrow \forall \alpha \mathsf{L}^\alpha \Rightarrow T(\alpha)$ with $T(\alpha) = \exists \beta \gamma (\alpha = \beta + \gamma) \mathsf{L}^\beta \times \mathsf{L}^\gamma$, $<_f = <$, $\succ_f = >_\mathbb{N}$ and le $: \mathsf{N} \Rightarrow \mathsf{N} \Rightarrow$ bool. Let $\Gamma = y : \mathsf{N}, l : \mathsf{L}^\delta$ and $\Delta = x : \mathsf{N}, \Gamma$.

Matching constraint: $\alpha = \delta + 1; \Gamma \rightsquigarrow \mathsf{cons}\, y\, l : \mathsf{L}^\alpha$ (we take $\varepsilon_l = \delta$).

We must check that $\alpha = \delta + 1; \Delta \vdash r : T(\alpha)$ with pivot $: \mathsf{N} \Rightarrow \forall \alpha'(\alpha' < \alpha)\mathsf{L}^{\alpha'} \Rightarrow T(\alpha')$. Let $\Delta = \Gamma, z : \mathsf{L}^\beta \times \mathsf{L}^\gamma$.

One can easily check that $\delta < \alpha; \Gamma \vdash$ pivot $x\, l \uparrow T(\delta)$, $\top; \Delta \vdash$ le $y\, x \uparrow$ bool, $\top; \Delta \vdash u \uparrow \mathsf{L}^{\beta+1} \times \mathsf{L}^\gamma$, $\top; \Delta \vdash v \uparrow \mathsf{L}^\beta \times \mathsf{L}^{\gamma+1}$.

Thus, by ($\downarrow$sub), $\beta + 1 = \beta' \wedge \gamma = \gamma'; \Delta \vdash u \downarrow \mathsf{L}^{\beta'} \times \mathsf{L}^{\gamma'}$ and $\beta = \beta' \wedge \gamma + 1 = \gamma'; \Delta \vdash u \downarrow \mathsf{L}^{\beta'} \times \mathsf{L}^{\gamma'}$.

By ($\downarrow\exists$intro), $D; \Delta \vdash u \downarrow T(\alpha)$ where $D = \exists \beta' \gamma'(\beta + 1 = \beta' \wedge \gamma = \gamma' \wedge \alpha = \beta' + \gamma')$, and $E; \Delta \vdash v \downarrow T(\alpha)$ where $E = \exists \beta' \gamma'(\beta = \beta' \wedge \gamma + 1 = \gamma' \wedge \alpha = \beta' + \gamma')$. Note that $D \equiv E \equiv (\alpha = \beta + \gamma + 1)$.

By ($\downarrow$if), $\alpha = \beta + \gamma + 1; \Delta \vdash$ if (le $y\, x$) then u else $v : T(\alpha)$.

By ($\downarrow\exists$elim), $F; \Gamma \vdash r \downarrow T(\alpha)$ where $F = \delta < \alpha \wedge (\exists \beta \gamma (\alpha = \beta + \gamma)) \wedge (\forall \beta \gamma (\delta = \beta + \gamma \supset \alpha = \beta + \gamma + 1))$.

Therefore, $\alpha = \delta + 1; \Delta \vdash r : T(\alpha)$ if $\vdash \alpha = \delta + 1 \supset F$, which is true.

Example 4. Consider the following definition of Mc Carthy's 91 function:

$$\text{le}\, x\, 100 = \text{true} \supset f\, x \to f\,(f\,(\text{plus}\, x\, 11))$$
$$\text{le}\, x\, 100 = \text{false} \supset f\, x \to \text{minus}\, x\, 10$$

We assume that $\mathcal{A}$ contains le $: nat \times nat \Rightarrow bool$ interpreted as expected.

We assume that $\text{le} : \forall\alpha\beta N^\alpha \Rightarrow N^\beta \Rightarrow \text{bool}^{le(\alpha,\beta)}$, plus $: \forall\alpha\beta N^\alpha \Rightarrow N^\beta \Rightarrow N^{\alpha+\beta}$, minus $: \forall\alpha\beta N^\alpha \Rightarrow N^\beta \Rightarrow \exists\gamma PN^\gamma$ with $P = (\alpha \le \beta \wedge \gamma = 0) \vee (\alpha > \beta \wedge \alpha = \beta + \gamma)$, and $\text{f} : \forall\alpha N^\alpha \Rightarrow \exists\beta QN^\beta$ with $Q = (\alpha \le 100 \wedge \beta = 91) \vee (\alpha > 100 \wedge \alpha = \beta + 10)$. Taking $\Gamma = x : N^\alpha$, we get that $\top; \Gamma \vdash \text{le}\, x\, 100 : \text{bool}^{le(\alpha,100)}$. The condition $le(\alpha, 100) = \text{t}$ is equivalent to $\alpha \le 100$, hence the termination.

6   Conclusion and Future Work

We extended the simply typed part of [8] with conditional rewriting and explicit quantifications and constraints over size annotations. This allows to precisely describe the relation between the size of the output of a function and the size of its inputs. This also provides a powerful termination criterion for the combination of β-reduction and higher-order conditional rewriting, based on type-checking and constraint solving. To our knowledge, this is the first termination criterion for higher-order conditional rewriting taking into account conditions in termination. We plan to extend this work in various directions:

- As in [22], we did not consider constructors with recursive arguments of higher-order type since this is already studied in [8]. The integration of both works should not create too much difficulties. We already have preliminary results in this direction.
- The complexity of Presburger arithmetic is high. Although it is not so important in our case since the constraints we consider are small (rule right-hand sides are generally not very big terms), it would be interesting to study the complexity in more details, depending on the allowed size annotations.
- Our long term goal is to extend the present work to polymorphic and dependent type systems that serve as basis for proof assistants like Coq, *e.g.* the Calculus of Algebraic Constructions [9].
- We assume that constrained types of function symbols are given and check that they imply termination. It would be very interesting to infer these constraints automatically.

References

1. A. Abel. Termination and productivity checking with continuous types. In *Proc. of TLCA'03*, LNCS 2701.
2. A. Abel. Termination checking with types. *Theoretical Informatics and Applications*, 38(4):277–319, 2004.
3. G. Barthe, M. J. Frade, E. Giménez, L. Pinto, and T. Uustalu. Type-based termination of recursive definitions. *Mathematical Structures in Computer Science*, 14(1):97–141, 2004.
4. G. Barthe, B. Grégoire, and F. Pastawski. Practical inference for type-based termination in a polymorphic setting. In *Proc. of TLCA'05*, LNCS 3461.
5. F. Blanqui. Decidability of type-checking in the Calculus of Algebraic Constructions with size annotations. In *Proc. of CSL'05*, LNCS 3634.
6. F. Blanqui. Rewriting modulo in Deduction modulo. *Proc. of RTA'03*, LNCS 2706.

7. F. Blanqui. Termination and confluence of higher-order rewrite systems. In *Proc. of RTA'00*, LNCS 1833.

8. F. Blanqui. A type-based termination criterion for dependently-typed higher-order rewrite systems. In *Proc. of RTA'04*, LNCS 3091.

9. F. Blanqui. Definitions by rewriting in the Calculus of Constructions. *Mathematical Structures in Computer Science*, 15(1):37–92, 2005.

10. F. Blanqui, C. Kirchner, and C. Riba. On the confluence of λ-calculus with conditional rewriting. In *Proc. of FoSSaCS'06*, LNCS 3921.

11. W. N. Chin and S. C. Khoo. Calculating sized types. *Journal of Higher-Order and Symbolic Computation*, 14(2-3):261–300, 2001.

12. R. Davies and F. Pfenning. Intersection types and computational effects. In *Proc. of ICFP'00*, SIGPLAN Notices35(9).

13. M. Fischer and M. Rabin. Super-exponential complexity of presburger arithmetic. In *Proceedings of the SIAM-AMS Symposium in Applied Mathematics*, 1974.

14. J. Gallier. On Girard's "Candidats de Réductibilité". In P.-G. Odifreddi, editor, *Logic and Computer Science*. North-Holland, 1990.

15. J. Hughes, L. Pareto, and A. Sabry. Proving the correctness of reactive systems using sized types. In *Proc. of POPL'96*.

16. J. W. Klop, V. van Oostrom, and F. van Raamsdonk. Combinatory reduction systems. *Theoretical Computer Science*, 121:279–308, 1993.

17. R. Mayr and T. Nipkow. Higher-order rewrite systems and their confluence. *Theoretical Computer Science*, 192(2):3–29, 1998.

18. M. Presburger. ber die vollst ndigkeit eines gewissen systems der arithmetik ganzer zahlen, in welchem die addition als einzige operation hervortritt. In *Sprawozdanie z I Kongresu Matematykow Krajow Slowcanskich, Warszawa, Poland*, 1929.

19. W. W. Tait. A realizability interpretation of the theory of species. In R. Parikh, editor, *Proceedings of the 1972 Logic Colloquium*, volume 453 of *Lecture Notes in Mathematics*, 1975.

20. V. van Oostrom and F. van Raamsdonk. Comparing Combinatory Reduction Systems and Higher-order Rewrite Systems. In *Proc. of HOA'93*, LNCS 816.

21. H. Xi. *Dependent types in practical programming*. PhD thesis, Carnegie-Mellon, Pittsburgh, United States, 1998.

22. H. Xi. Dependent types for program termination verification. *Journal of Higher-Order and Symbolic Computation*, 15(1):91–131, 2002.

On a Local-Step Cut-Elimination Procedure for the Intuitionistic Sequent Calculus

Kentaro Kikuchi

RIEC, Tohoku University
Katahira 2-1-1, Aoba-ku, Sendai 980-8577, Japan
kentaro@nue.riec.tohoku.ac.jp

Abstract. In this paper we investigate, for intuitionistic implicational logic, the relationship between normalization in natural deduction and cut-elimination in a standard sequent calculus. First we identify a subset of proofs in the sequent calculus that correspond to proofs in natural deduction. Then we define a reduction relation on those proofs that exactly corresponds to normalization in natural deduction. The reduction relation is simulated soundly and completely by a cut-elimination procedure which consists of local proof transformations. It follows that the sequent calculus with our cut-elimination procedure is a proper extension that is conservative over natural deduction with normalization.

1 Introduction

In his seminal paper [6], Gentzen introduced natural deduction systems and sequent calculi for intuitionistic and classical logics, and proved the logical equivalence of the systems for each logic as well as the cut-elimination theorems for sequent calculi. In [10], Prawitz systematically studied normalization processes in natural deduction, and gave a construction of a cut-free proof from a normal proof for the purpose of proving the cut-elimination theorems through normalization results in natural deduction (Appendix A.3 of [10]). The construction by Prawitz differs from Gentzen's in that it assigns a *cut-free* proof to each normal proof in natural deduction. Under the Curry-Howard correspondence [8], the computational meaning of the cut-free proofs can be considered as the simply typed λ-terms corresponding to the normal proofs in natural deduction.

To obtain a meaningful Curry-Howard correspondence for sequent calculus, we therefore need to define a mapping from non-normal proofs in natural deduction to some proofs in sequent calculus, and investigate the relationship between normalization and cut-elimination processes. In particular, it is crucial to identify the cut-elimination procedure that corresponds to β-reduction in the simply typed λ-calculus. This would also open the way for understanding the computational or constructive meaning of various logics, including those logics which allow natural cut-elimination procedures in their sequent calculi but do not have an appropriate natural deduction system and normalization in it (e.g. modal logics and substructural logics).

M. Hermann and A. Voronkov (Eds.): LPAR 2006, LNAI 4246, pp. 120–134, 2006.

In this paper, we define a mapping from proofs in natural deduction to a subset of proofs in a standard sequent calculus for intuitionistic logic. We syntactically characterize the image of the mapping, and show that it is a bijection between proofs in natural deduction and the subset of proofs in the sequent calculus. We also define a reduction relation on the subset of proofs, and show that it coincides with the β-reduction relation under the bijection. Thus the identification of β-reduction in the sequent calculus is achieved. The problem then reduces to investigating the relationship between the image of β-reduction and cut-elimination in the sequent calculus. In this paper we introduce a fairly standard cut-elimination procedure, except that in some circumstances it allows a cut to pass over another cut. Then the image of β-reduction is shown to be simulated by the cut-elimination procedure. It is also shown that the cut-elimination procedure is sound in regard to β-reduction, i.e., it does not break β-reducibility in the isomorphic image of natural deduction.

Allowing cuts to pass over other cuts is one of the criteria stated in [12,13]. (It was also noted in [7,2] for Herbelin's sequent calculus). Using the strong normalization result of a cut-elimination procedure that satisfies the criteria, Urban [12] proved strong normalization of the simply typed λ-calculus. Note however that inferring strong normalization of β-reduction and identifying β-reduction in a sequent calculus are different, and the latter is more appropriate to obtain a relevant Curry-Howard correspondence for sequent calculus. In [12], Urban also defined another cut-elimination procedure which consists of local proof transformations. For the cut-elimination procedure to satisfy the criteria, he introduced labelled cut-rules whose instances are allowed to pass over usual cuts. The cut-elimination procedure we introduce in this paper also consists of local proof transformations, but uses only one cut-rule. Instead of introducing labelled cut-rules and allowing any labelled cuts to pass over usual cuts, we derive minimal requirements on permutation of cuts for the simulation of β-reduction from a thorough analysis of our proof of the simulation.

For Herbelin-style sequent calculi (i.e., sequent calculi with stoup), it is known that there is an isomorphism between natural deduction and a fragment of those sequent calculi [4,3,5]. In such a system, one can distinguish cuts according to information on the stoups of sequents, and know in which case a cut should be allowed to pass over another cut. This is analogous to the situation using the labelled cuts mentioned above. Also, the proof terms for Herbelin-style sequent calculi are constructed involving an additional syntactic category called applicative context. In contrast, we establish an isomorphism using only proof terms for the standard sequent calculus, as found in [9].

The organization of the paper is as follows. In Section 2 we introduce sequent calculus and our cut-elimination procedure. In Section 3 we establish an isomorphism between a fragment of the sequent calculus and natural deduction. In Section 4 we discuss simulation of β-reduction by our cut-elimination procedure. In Section 5 we conclude and give suggestions for further work.

To save space we omit some of the details, but a full version with all the details is available at http://www.nue.riec.tohoku.ac.jp/user/kentaro/ .

2 Sequent Calculus

In this section we introduce a term notation for proofs in a standard sequent calculus for intuitionistic implicational logic. Our cut-elimination procedure is represented as reduction rules for those terms. For proof terms and normalization in natural deduction, we use the ordinary simply typed λ-calculus.

First, the set of raw terms for sequent proofs is defined by the grammar: $t ::= x \mid \lambda x.t \mid \langle xt/x \rangle t \mid [t/x]t$ where x ranges over a denumerable set of variables. $\langle \_\_/\_\rangle\_$ and $[\_/\_]\_$ are 4-ary and 3-ary function symbols, respectively, and may be regarded as two kinds of explicit substitutions. We use letters x, y, z, w for variables and t, s, r, u for terms. The notions of free and bound variables are defined as usual, with an additional clause that the variable x in $\langle ys/x \rangle t$ or $[s/x]t$ binds the free occurrences of x in t. The set of free variables of a term t is denoted by $FV(t)$. We often use the notation $\langle \underline{x}s/y \rangle t$ to denote $\langle xs/y \rangle t$ if $x \notin FV(s) \cup FV(t)$. For such terms and variables, we define the notion of *fresh head variable* as follows: $FHV(x) = x$ and $FHV(\langle \underline{x}s/y \rangle t) = x$. The symbol $\equiv$ denotes syntactic equality modulo α-conversion.

Table 1. Sequent calculus

$$
Ax \; \frac{}{\Gamma, x : A \vdash x : A}
\qquad
L \supset \; \frac{\Gamma \vdash s : A \quad \Gamma, y : B \vdash t : C}{\Gamma, x : A \supset B \vdash \langle xs/y \rangle t : C} \; y \notin \Gamma
$$

$$
R \supset \; \frac{\Gamma, x : A \vdash t : B}{\Gamma \vdash \lambda x.t : A \supset B} \; x \notin \Gamma
\qquad
Cut \; \frac{\Gamma \vdash s : A \quad \Gamma, x : A \vdash t : B}{\Gamma \vdash [s/x]t : B} \; x \notin \Gamma
$$

$\langle \underline{x}s/y \rangle t$ is used for $\langle xs/y \rangle t$ when $x \notin FV(s) \cup FV(t)$. In that case we assume $x \notin \Gamma$ in the rule $L \supset$.

(1)	$[t/x]y \to y \quad (y \not\equiv x)$
(2)	$[t/x]x \to t$
(3)	$[s/x](\lambda y.t) \to \lambda y.[s/x]t$
(4)	$[r/z]\langle xs/y \rangle t \to \langle x([r/z]s)/y \rangle [r/z]t \quad (x \not\equiv z)$
(5)	$[r/x]\langle xs/y \rangle t \to [r/x]\langle \underline{x}([r/x]s)/y \rangle [r/x]t \quad$ if $x \in FV(s) \cup FV(t)$
(6)	$[z/x]\langle \underline{x}s/y \rangle t \to \langle zs/y \rangle t$
(7)	$[\langle xs/y \rangle t/z]r \to \langle xs/y \rangle [t/z]r$
(Beta)	$[\lambda z.r/x]\langle \underline{x}s/y \rangle t \to [[s/z]r/y]t$
(Perm₁)	$[[r/x]\langle \underline{x}s/y \rangle t/z]\langle \underline{z}s'/w \rangle t' \to [r/x][\langle \underline{x}s/y \rangle t/z]\langle \underline{z}s'/w \rangle t'$
(Perm₂)	$[u/w][\lambda z.r/x]\langle \underline{x}s/y \rangle t \to [[u/w](\lambda z.r)/x][u/w]\langle \underline{x}s/y \rangle t$

The term assignment for sequent proofs of intuitionistic implicational logic is given in Table 1. We define a context, ranged over by Γ, as a finite set of pairs $\{x_1 : A_1, \ldots, x_n : A_n\}$ where the variables are pairwise distinct. The context $\Gamma, x : A$ denotes the union $\Gamma \cup \{x : A\}$, and $x \notin \Gamma$ means that x does not appear in Γ. For precise representation of proofs by terms, we should specify formulas on binders, but we will omit them for brevity. If $x \notin FV(s) \cup FV(t)$ in the term $\langle xs/y\rangle t$, we assume $x \notin \Gamma$ in the rule $L \supset$, which means the formula $A \supset B$ is introduced without implicit contraction.

The reduction rules in Table 1 define a cut-elimination procedure for sequent proofs. The notion of cut-reduction is defined by the contextual closures of these reduction rules. We use $\rightarrow_{\mathrm{cut}}$ for one-step reduction, $\overset{+}{\rightarrow}_{\mathrm{cut}}$ for its transitive closure, and $\overset{*}{\rightarrow}_{\mathrm{cut}}$ for its reflexive transitive closure. These kinds of notations are also used for the notions of other reductions in this paper.

The reduction rules (1) through (5) correspond to cut-elimination steps that permute a cut upwards through its right subproof. Similarly, the rules (6) and (7) correspond to steps permuting a cut upwards through its left subproof. The rule (Beta) corresponds to the key-case which breaks a cut on an implication into two cuts on its subformulas. The rules $(Perm_1)$ and $(Perm_2)$ are the new rules introduced in this paper. They permute two cuts with some restrictions. In $(Perm_1)$, the left rule over the lower cut is another cut, and the right rules over both cuts must be $L \supset$ that introduces the cut-formula without implicit contraction. In $(Perm_2)$, the right rule over the lower cut is another cut, which must construct a proof corresponding to a redex of the rule (Beta).

3   Pure Terms

Table 2 presents the syntax of *pure terms*, which are the subset of proof terms for sequent calculus that correspond to simply typed λ-terms, i.e., proof terms for natural deduction. We use letters $l, l', \ldots$ for variables or pure terms of the form $\langle y_1 s_1/y_2\rangle \ldots \langle y_{n-1} s_{n-1}/y_n\rangle y_n$. The intuitive idea behind the syntax is that we translate a λ-term $xM_1M_2 \ldots M_n$ to $\langle xs_1/y_1\rangle\langle y_1 s_2/y_2\rangle \ldots \langle y_{n-1} s_n/y_n\rangle y_n$, and $(\lambda z.N)M_1M_2 \ldots M_n$ to $[\lambda z.r/x]\langle \underline{x} s_1/y_1\rangle\langle y_1 s_2/y_2\rangle \ldots \langle y_{n-1} s_n/y_n\rangle y_n$, where $N, M_1, M_2, \ldots, M_n$ are translated to $r, s_1, s_2, \ldots, s_n$ $(n \geqslant 1)$. So a non-normal proof corresponding to $(\lambda z.N)M_1M_2 \ldots M_n$ is translated to a cut of the form:

$$\dfrac{\dfrac{\Gamma, z : A \vdash r : B}{\Gamma \vdash \lambda z.r : A \supset B} \ R\supset \quad \dfrac{\Gamma \vdash s_1 : A \quad \Gamma, y_1 : B \vdash l : C}{\Gamma, x : A \supset B \vdash \langle \underline{x} s_1/y_1\rangle l : C} \ L\supset}{\Gamma \vdash [\lambda z.r/x]\langle \underline{x} s_1/y_1\rangle l : C} \ Cut$$

where $l \equiv \langle y_1 s_2/y_2\rangle \ldots \langle y_{n-1} s_n/y_n\rangle y_n$. We refer to this kind of cut as a β-cut.

For the definition of β-reduction on pure terms, we need a meta-substitution $\{\_/\_\}\_$. Since we cannot in general replace the free variable w in $\langle ws/y\rangle l$ by a pure term, we need a further meta-operation $\langle\{\_\}\_/\_\rangle\_$. The term $\langle\{u\}s/y\rangle l$ may be seen as an abbreviation for $\{u/w\}\langle \underline{w}s/y\rangle l$, and defined by induction on the structure of the pure term u. Note that if $FHV(l) = y$ then $FHV(\{u/w\}l) =$

Table 2. Pure terms

$t, s, r ::= x \mid \lambda x.t \mid \langle xs/y\rangle l \mid [\lambda z.r/x]\langle \underline{x}s/y\rangle l$
$l ::= x \mid \langle \underline{x}s/y\rangle l$
where $FHV(l) = y$ in the right hand sides.

$(\beta) \qquad\qquad [\lambda z.r/x]\langle \underline{x}s/y\rangle l \;\rightarrow\; \{\{s/z\}r/y\}l$

where

$$\{u/w\}x =_{def} x \qquad (x \not\equiv w)$$
$$\{u/w\}w =_{def} u$$
$$\{u/w\}(\lambda x.t) =_{def} \lambda x.\{u/w\}t$$
$$\{u/w\}\langle xs/y\rangle l =_{def} \langle x(\{u/w\}s)/y\rangle\{u/w\}l \qquad (x \not\equiv w)$$
$$\{u/w\}\langle ws/y\rangle l =_{def} \langle \{u\}(\{u/w\}s)/y\rangle\{u/w\}l$$
$$\{u/w\}[\lambda z.r/x]\langle \underline{x}s/y\rangle l =_{def} [\lambda z.\{u/w\}r/x]\langle \underline{x}(\{u/w\}s)/y\rangle\{u/w\}l$$

$$\langle \{x\}s'/y\rangle l' =_{def} \langle xs'/y\rangle l'$$
$$\langle \{\lambda x.t\}s'/y\rangle l' =_{def} [\lambda x.t/w]\langle \underline{w}s'/y\rangle l'$$
$$\langle \{\langle xs/w\rangle l\}s'/y\rangle l' =_{def} \langle xs/w\rangle\langle \{l\}s'/y\rangle l'$$
$$\langle \{[\lambda z.r/x]\langle \underline{x}s/w\rangle l\}s'/y\rangle l' =_{def} [\lambda z.r/x]\langle \underline{x}s/w\rangle\langle \{l\}s'/y\rangle l'$$

---

y ($w \not\equiv y$) and $FHV(\langle \{l\}s'/w\rangle l') = y$, so the meta-operations are well-defined on pure terms. The operation $\langle \{\_\}\_/\_\rangle\_$ corresponds to the cut-elimination process where the right rule over the cut is $L \supset$ introducing the cut-formula without implicit contraction, and the cut is permuted upwards through its left subproof. (Meta-operations based on similar ideas are found in [12,13,4,3], but not for the pure terms we defined above.)

In the rest of this section we establish an isomorphism between pure terms and λ-terms. For this we define the translations ρ and φ as shown in Table 3. (It can be shown that these translations preserve the types of terms.) For normal proofs, the translation ρ agrees with Prawitz's translation [10]. While Prawitz defined his translation by induction on the structure of normal proofs, we define the translation ρ by induction on the usual syntax of λ-terms, since we need to show that the same translation also preserves β-reduction which is based on the meta-substitution defined along with the usual syntax of λ-terms.

Now we consider bijection and preservation of β-reduction in order.

3.1 ρ and φ Are Bijective

Lemma 1. *Let t, u be pure terms. If $x \notin FV(t)$, then $\{u/x\}t \equiv t$.*

Proof. By induction on the structure of t.   □

Table 3. Translations ρ and φ

$$\rho(x) =_{def} x$$
$$\rho(MN) =_{def} \langle\{\rho(M)\}\rho(N)/x\rangle x$$
$$\rho(\lambda x.M) =_{def} \lambda x.\rho(M)$$

$$\varphi(x) =_{def} x$$
$$\varphi(\lambda x.t) =_{def} \lambda x.\varphi(t)$$
$$\varphi(\langle xs/y\rangle l) =_{def} \{x\varphi(s)/y\}\varphi(l)$$
$$\varphi([\lambda z.r/x]\langle \underline{x}s/y\rangle l) =_{def} \{(\lambda z.\varphi(r))\varphi(s)/y\}\varphi(l)$$

Lemma 2. *Let u, s, l, s', l' be pure terms with $FHV(l) = w$ and $FHV(l') = y$. Then $\langle\{\langle\{u\}s/w\rangle l\}s'/y\rangle l' \equiv \langle\{u\}s/w\rangle\langle\{l\}s'/y\rangle l'$.*

Proof. By induction on the structure of u. We treat some cases.

(a) $u \equiv \langle xr/z\rangle l''$. Then

$$
\begin{aligned}
\langle\{\langle\{\langle xr/z\rangle l''\}s/w\rangle l\}s'/y\rangle l' &\equiv \langle\{\langle xr/z\rangle\langle\{l''\}s/w\rangle l\}s'/y\rangle l' \\
&\equiv \langle xr/z\rangle\langle\{\langle\{l''\}s/w\rangle l\}s'/y\rangle l' \\
&\equiv \langle xr/z\rangle\langle\{l''\}s/w\rangle\langle\{l\}s'/y\rangle l' \quad \text{(by IH)} \\
&\equiv \langle\{\langle xr/z\rangle l''\}s/w\rangle\langle\{l\}s'/y\rangle l'
\end{aligned}
$$

(b) $u \equiv [\lambda z.r/x]\langle \underline{x}t/y'\rangle l''$. Then

$$
\begin{aligned}
\langle\{\langle\{[\lambda z.r/x]\langle \underline{x}t/y'\rangle l''\}s/w\rangle l\}s'/y\rangle l' & \\
\equiv \langle\{[\lambda z.r/x]\langle \underline{x}t/y'\rangle\langle\{l''\}s/w\rangle l\}s'/y\rangle l' & \\
\equiv [\lambda z.r/x]\langle \underline{x}t/y'\rangle\langle\{\langle\{l''\}s/w\rangle l\}s'/y\rangle l' & \\
\equiv [\lambda z.r/x]\langle \underline{x}t/y'\rangle\langle\{l''\}s/w\rangle\langle\{l\}s'/y\rangle l' & \quad \text{(by IH)} \\
\equiv \langle\{[\lambda z.r/x]\langle \underline{x}t/y'\rangle l''\}s/w\rangle\langle\{l\}s'/y\rangle l' &
\end{aligned}
$$

$\square$

Lemma 3. *Let u, t, s', l' be pure terms with $FHV(l') = y$ and $x \not\equiv y$. Then $\{u/x\}\langle\{t\}s'/y\rangle l' \equiv \langle\{\{u/x\}t\}\{u/x\}s'/y\rangle\{u/x\}l'$.*

Proof. By induction on the structure of t. We treat some cases.

(a) $t \equiv \langle x's/w\rangle l$ ($x' \not\equiv x$). Then

$$
\begin{aligned}
\{u/x\}\langle\{\langle x's/w\rangle l\}s'/y\rangle l' & \\
\equiv \{u/x\}\langle x's/w\rangle\langle\{l\}s'/y\rangle l' & \\
\equiv \langle x'\{u/x\}s/w\rangle\{u/x\}\langle\{l\}s'/y\rangle l' & \\
\equiv \langle x'\{u/x\}s/w\rangle\langle\{\{u/x\}l\}\{u/x\}s'/y\rangle\{u/x\}l' & \quad \text{(by IH)} \\
\equiv \langle\{\langle x'\{u/x\}s/w\rangle\{u/x\}l\}\{u/x\}s'/y\rangle\{u/x\}l' & \\
\equiv \langle\{\{u/x\}\langle x's/w\rangle l\}\{u/x\}s'/y\rangle\{u/x\}l' &
\end{aligned}
$$

(b) $t \equiv \langle xs/w \rangle l$. Then

$$\{u/x\}\langle\{\{\langle xs/w\rangle l\}s'/y\rangle l'$$
$$\equiv \{u/x\}\langle xs/w\rangle\langle\{l\}s'/y\rangle l'$$
$$\equiv \langle\{u\}\{u/x\}s/w\rangle\{u/x\}\langle\{l\}s'/y\rangle l'$$
$$\equiv \langle\{u\}\{u/x\}s/w\rangle\langle\{\{u/x\}l\}\{u/x\}s'/y\rangle\{u/x\}l' \qquad \text{(by IH)}$$
$$\equiv \langle\{\langle\{u\}\{u/x\}s/w\rangle\{u/x\}l\}\{u/x\}s'/y\rangle\{u/x\}l' \qquad \text{(by Lemma 2)}$$
$$\equiv \langle\{\{u/x\}\langle xs/w\rangle l\}\{u/x\}s'/y\rangle\{u/x\}l'$$

(c) $t \equiv [\lambda z.r/y']\langle y's/w\rangle l$. Then

$$\{u/x\}\langle\{\{[\lambda z.r/y']\langle y's/w\rangle l\}s'/y\rangle l'$$
$$\equiv \{u/x\}[\lambda z.r/y']\langle y's/w\rangle\langle\{l\}s'/y\rangle l'$$
$$\equiv [\lambda z.\{u/x\}r/y']\langle y'\{u/x\}s/w\rangle\{u/x\}\langle\{l\}s'/y\rangle l'$$
$$\equiv [\lambda z.\{u/x\}r/y']\langle y'\{u/x\}s/w\rangle\langle\{\{u/x\}l\}\{u/x\}s'/y\rangle\{u/x\}l' \qquad \text{(by IH)}$$
$$\equiv \langle\{[\lambda z.\{u/x\}r/y']\langle y'\{u/x\}s/w\rangle\{u/x\}l\}\{u/x\}s'/y\rangle\{u/x\}l'$$
$$\equiv \langle\{\{u/x\}[\lambda z.r/y']\langle y's/w\rangle l\}\{u/x\}s'/y\rangle\{u/x\}l'$$

$$\square$$

Lemma 4. *Let N, M be λ-terms. Then $\rho(\{N/x\}M) \equiv \{\rho(N)/x\}\rho(M)$.*

Proof. By induction on the structure of M. We treat the case $M \equiv M_0M_1$. Then

$$\rho(\{N/x\}(M_0M_1)) \equiv \rho(\{N/x\}M_0\{N/x\}M_1)$$
$$\equiv \langle\{\rho(\{N/x\}M_0)\}\rho(\{N/x\}M_1)/y\rangle y$$
$$\equiv \langle\{\{\rho(N)/x\}\rho(M_0)\}\{\rho(N)/x\}\rho(M_1)/y\rangle y \qquad \text{(by IH)}$$
$$\equiv \langle\{\{\rho(N)/x\}\rho(M_0)\}\{\rho(N)/x\}\rho(M_1)/y\rangle\{\rho(N)/x\}y$$
$$\equiv \{\rho(N)/x\}\langle\{\rho(M_0)\}\rho(M_1)/y\rangle y \qquad \text{(by Lemma 3)}$$
$$\equiv \{\rho(N)/x\}\rho(M_0M_1)$$

$$\square$$

Lemma 5. *Let u, s', l' be pure terms with $FHV(l') = y$. Then $\varphi(\langle\{u\}s'/y\rangle l') \equiv \{\varphi(u)\varphi(s')/y\}\varphi(l')$.*

Proof. By induction on the structure of u. We treat some cases.

(a) $u \equiv \langle xs/w\rangle l$. Then

$$\varphi(\langle\{\langle xs/w\rangle l\}s'/y\rangle l') \equiv \varphi(\langle xs/w\rangle\langle\{l\}s'/y\rangle l')$$
$$\equiv \{x\varphi(s)/w\}\varphi(\langle\{l\}s'/y\rangle l')$$
$$\equiv \{x\varphi(s)/w\}\{\varphi(l)\varphi(s')/y\}\varphi(l') \qquad \text{(by IH)}$$
$$\equiv \{\{x\varphi(s)/w\}\varphi(l)\varphi(s')/y\}\varphi(l') \qquad (*)$$
$$\equiv \{\varphi(\langle xs/w\rangle l)\varphi(s')/y\}\varphi(l')$$

where the step $(*)$ is established since we can assume $w \notin FV(s') \cup FV(l')$ and so $w \notin FV(\varphi(s')) \cup FV(\varphi(l'))$.

(b) $u \equiv [\lambda z.r/x]\langle \underline{x}s/w\rangle l$. Then

$$
\begin{aligned}
\varphi(\langle\{[\lambda z.r/x]\langle \underline{x}s/w\rangle l\}s'/y\rangle l') \\
\equiv\ & \varphi([\lambda z.r/x]\langle \underline{x}s/w\rangle\langle\{l\}s'/y\rangle l') \\
\equiv\ & \{\lambda z.\varphi(r)\varphi(s)/w\}\varphi(\langle\{l\}s'/y\rangle l') \\
\equiv\ & \{\lambda z.\varphi(r)\varphi(s)/w\}\{\varphi(l)\varphi(s')/y\}\varphi(l') && \text{(by IH)} \\
\equiv\ & \{\{\lambda z.\varphi(r)\varphi(s)/w\}\varphi(l)\varphi(s')/y\}\varphi(l') && (*) \\
\equiv\ & \{\varphi([\lambda z.r/x]\langle \underline{x}s/w\rangle l)\varphi(s')/y\}\varphi(l')
\end{aligned}
$$

where the step $(*)$ is established since we can assume $w \notin FV(s') \cup FV(l')$ and so $w \notin FV(\varphi(s')) \cup FV(\varphi(l'))$.   □

Lemma 6. *Let s, r, l be pure terms with $FHV(l) = y$. Then*

1. $\{\langle xs/w\rangle w/y\}l \equiv \langle xs/y\rangle l$,
2. $\{[\lambda z.r/x]\langle \underline{x}s/w\rangle w/y\}l \equiv [\lambda z.r/x]\langle \underline{x}s/y\rangle l$.

Proof. By cases on l.   □

Proposition 1. $\varphi \circ \rho = id$ *and* $\rho \circ \varphi = id$.

Proof. The first part is by induction on the structure of λ-terms. We treat the case $M \equiv M_0 M_1$. Then

$$
\begin{aligned}
(\varphi \circ \rho)(M_0 M_1) \equiv\ & \varphi(\langle\{\rho(M_0)\}\rho(M_1)/x\rangle x) \\
\equiv\ & \{\varphi(\rho(M_0))\varphi(\rho(M_1))/x\}\varphi(x) && \text{(by Lemma 5)} \\
\equiv\ & \{M_0 M_1/x\}x && \text{(by IH)} \\
\equiv\ & M_0 M_1
\end{aligned}
$$

The second part is by induction on the structure of pure terms. We treat some cases.

(a) $t \equiv \langle xs/y\rangle l$. Then

$$
\begin{aligned}
(\rho \circ \varphi)(\langle xs/y\rangle l) \equiv\ & \rho(\{x\varphi(s)/y\}\varphi(l)) \\
\equiv\ & \{\rho(x\varphi(s))/y\}\rho(\varphi(l)) && \text{(by Lemma 4)} \\
\equiv\ & \{\rho(x\varphi(s))/y\}l && \text{(by IH)} \\
\equiv\ & \{\langle\{\rho(x)\}\rho(\varphi(s))/w\rangle w/y\}l \\
\equiv\ & \{\langle\{\rho(x)\}s/w\rangle w/y\}l && \text{(by IH)} \\
\equiv\ & \{\langle\{x\}s)/w\rangle w/y\}l \\
\equiv\ & \{\langle xs/w\rangle w/y\}l \\
\equiv\ & \langle xs/y\rangle l && \text{(by Lemma 6 (1))}
\end{aligned}
$$

(b) $t \equiv [\lambda z.r/x]\langle \underline{x}s/y\rangle l$. Then

$$
\begin{aligned}
(\rho \circ \varphi)([\lambda z.r/x]\langle \underline{x}s/y\rangle l) &\equiv \rho(\{(\lambda z.\varphi(r))\varphi(s)/y\}\varphi(l)) \\
&\equiv \{\rho((\lambda z.\varphi(r))\varphi(s))/y\}\rho(\varphi(l)) \quad \text{(by Lemma 4)} \\
&\equiv \{\rho((\lambda z.\varphi(r))\varphi(s))/y\}l \quad\quad\quad \text{(by IH)} \\
&\equiv \{\langle\{\rho(\lambda z.\varphi(r))\}\rho(\varphi(s))/w\rangle w/y\}l \\
&\equiv \{\langle\{\rho(\lambda z.\varphi(r))\}s/w\rangle w/y\}l \quad\quad \text{(by IH)} \\
&\equiv \{\langle\{\lambda z.\rho(\varphi(r))\}s/w\rangle w/y\}l \\
&\equiv \{\langle\{\lambda z.r\}s/w\rangle w/y\}l \quad\quad\quad\quad \text{(by IH)} \\
&\equiv \{[\lambda z.r/x]\langle \underline{x}s/w\rangle w/y\}l \\
&\equiv [\lambda z.r/x]\langle \underline{x}s/y\rangle l \quad\quad\quad \text{(by Lemma 6 (2))}
\end{aligned}
$$

□

3.2 ρ and φ Preserve β-Reduction

Lemma 7. *Let u,t be pure terms. Then $\varphi(\{u/x\}t) \equiv \{\varphi(u)/x\}\varphi(t)$.*

Proof.

$$
\begin{aligned}
\varphi(\{u/x\}t) &\equiv \varphi(\{\rho(\varphi(u))/x\}\rho(\varphi(t))) \quad \text{(by Proposition 1)} \\
&\equiv \varphi(\rho(\{\varphi(u)/x\}\varphi(t))) \quad\quad \text{(by Lemma 4)} \\
&\equiv \{\varphi(u)/x\}\varphi(t) \quad\quad\quad\quad \text{(by Proposition 1)}
\end{aligned}
$$

□

Lemma 8. *Let u,u',s,s',l be pure terms with $FHV(l) = y$.*

1. *If $u \rightarrow_\beta u'$ then $\langle\{u\}s/y\rangle l \rightarrow_\beta \langle\{u'\}s/y\rangle l$.*
2. *If $s \rightarrow_\beta s'$ then $\langle\{u\}s/y\rangle l \rightarrow_\beta \langle\{u\}s'/y\rangle l$.*

Proof. 1. By induction on the structure of u. We treat some cases where $u \equiv [\lambda z.r/x]\langle \underline{x}s_0/w\rangle l_0$.

(a) The β-reduction is at the root, i.e., $u' \equiv \{\{s_0/z\}r/w\}l_0$. Then

$$
\begin{aligned}
&\langle\{[\lambda z.r/x]\langle \underline{x}s_0/w\rangle l_0\}s/y\rangle l \\
&\equiv [\lambda z.r/x]\langle \underline{x}s_0/w\rangle\langle\{l_0\}s/y\rangle l \\
&\rightarrow_\beta \{\{s_0/z\}r/w\}\langle\{l_0\}s/y\rangle l \\
&\equiv \langle\{\{\{s_0/z\}r/w\}l_0\}\{\{s_0/z\}r/w\}s/y\rangle\{\{s_0/z\}r/w\}l \quad \text{(by Lemma 3)} \\
&\equiv \langle\{\{\{s_0/z\}r/w\}l_0\}s/y\rangle l \quad\quad\quad\quad\quad\quad \text{(by Lemma 1)}
\end{aligned}
$$

(b) The β-reduction is internal, e.g., $l_0 \rightarrow_\beta l_0'$. Then

$$
\begin{aligned}
&\langle\{[\lambda z.r/x]\langle \underline{x}s_0/w\rangle l_0\}s/y\rangle l \\
&\equiv [\lambda z.r/x]\langle \underline{x}s_0/w\rangle\langle\{l_0\}s/y\rangle l \\
&\rightarrow_\beta [\lambda z.r/x]\langle \underline{x}s_0/w\rangle\langle\{l_0'\}s/y\rangle l \quad \text{(by IH)} \\
&\equiv \langle\{[\lambda z.r/x]\langle \underline{x}s_0/w\rangle l_0'\}s/y\rangle l
\end{aligned}
$$

2. By induction on the structure of u, similarly to 1.   □

Lemma 9. *Let l be a pure term with $FHV(l) = y$. Then y occurs exactly once in $\varphi(l)$.*

Proof. By induction on the structure of l.   □

Theorem 1.

1. *For any λ-terms M, M', if $M \to_\beta M'$ then $\rho(M) \to_\beta \rho(M')$.*
2. *For any pure terms t, t', if $t \to_\beta t'$ then $\varphi(t) \to_\beta \varphi(t')$.*

Proof.   1. By induction on the structure of M.

(a) $M \equiv (\lambda x.M_0)M_1 \to_\beta \{M_1/x\}M_0 \equiv M'$. Then

$$
\begin{aligned}
\rho((\lambda x.M_0)M_1) &\equiv \langle\{\rho(\lambda x.M_0)\}\rho(M_1)/y\rangle y \\
&\equiv \langle\{\lambda x.\rho(M_0)\}\rho(M_1)/y\rangle y \\
&\equiv [\lambda x.\rho(M_0)/w]\langle\underline{w}\rho(M_1)/y\rangle y \\
&\to_\beta \{\{\rho(M_1)/x\}\rho(M_0)/y\}y \\
&\equiv \{\rho(M_1)/x\}\rho(M_0) \\
&\equiv \rho(\{M_1/x\}M_0) \qquad \text{(by Lemma 4)}
\end{aligned}
$$

(b) $M \equiv M_0M_1$ and $M_0 \to_\beta M_0'$. By the induction hypothesis, $\rho(M_0) \to_\beta \rho(M_0')$. Hence

$$
\begin{aligned}
\rho(M_0M_1) &\equiv \langle\{\rho(M_0)\}\rho(M_1)/y\rangle y \\
&\to_\beta \langle\{\rho(M_0')\}\rho(M_1)/y\rangle y \qquad \text{(by Lemma 8 (1))} \\
&\equiv \rho(M_0'M_1)
\end{aligned}
$$

(c) $M \equiv M_0M_1$ and $M_1 \to_\beta M_1'$. Similar, using Lemma 8 (2).

(d) $M \equiv \lambda x.M_0$ and $M_0 \to_\beta M_0'$. By the induction hypothesis, $\rho(M_0) \to_\beta \rho(M_0')$. Hence $\rho(\lambda x.M_0) \equiv \lambda x.\rho(M_0) \to_\beta \lambda x.\rho(M_0') \equiv \rho(\lambda x.M_0')$.

2. By induction on the structure of t.

(a) $t \equiv \lambda x.t_0$ and $t_0 \to_\beta t_0'$. By the induction hypothesis, $\varphi(t_0) \to_\beta \varphi(t_0')$. Hence $\varphi(\lambda x.t_0) \equiv \lambda x.\varphi(t_0) \to_\beta \lambda x.\varphi(t_0') \equiv \varphi(\lambda x.t_0')$.

(b) $t \equiv \langle xs/y\rangle l$ and $s \to_\beta s'$. By the induction hypothesis, $\varphi(s) \to_\beta \varphi(s')$. By Lemma 9, y has exactly one occurrence in $\varphi(l)$. Hence $\varphi(\langle xs/y\rangle l) \equiv \{x\varphi(s)/y\}\varphi(l) \to_\beta \{x\varphi(s')/y\}\varphi(l) \equiv \varphi(\langle xs'/y\rangle l)$.

(c) $t \equiv \langle xs/y\rangle l$ and $l \to_\beta l'$. Similar, using the induction hypothesis.

(d) $t \equiv [\lambda z.r/x]\langle xs/y\rangle l$.

    i. The β-reduction is at the root, i.e., $t' \equiv \{\{s/z\}r/y\}l$. Then

$$
\begin{aligned}
\varphi([\lambda z.r/x]\langle xs/y\rangle l) &\equiv \{(\lambda z.\varphi(r))\varphi(s)/y\}\varphi(l) \\
&\to_\beta \{\{\varphi(s)/z\}\varphi(r)/y\}\varphi(l) \\
&\equiv \{\varphi(\{s/z\}r)/y\}\varphi(l) \qquad \text{(by Lemma 7)} \\
&\equiv \varphi(\{\{s/z\}r/y\}l) \qquad \text{(by Lemma 7)}
\end{aligned}
$$

ii. The β-reduction is internal, e.g., $r \to_\beta r'$. By the induction hypothesis, $\varphi(r) \to_\beta \varphi(r')$. Hence

$$\varphi([\lambda z.r/x]\langle \underline{x}s/y \rangle l) \equiv \{(\lambda z.\varphi(r))\varphi(s)/y\}\varphi(l)$$
$$\to_\beta \{(\lambda z.\varphi(r'))\varphi(s)/y\}\varphi(l)$$
$$\equiv \varphi([\lambda z.r'/x]\langle \underline{x}s/y \rangle l)$$

The other cases are similar, using the induction hypothesis.   □

4   Simulation of β-Reduction

In this section we investigate the relation between $\to_{\mathrm{cut}}$ and $\to_\beta$ on pure terms. This relates normalization in natural deduction and our cut-elimination procedure in the sequent calculus, since pure terms are the isomorphic image of proof terms for natural deduction, as shown in the previous section. It is important that on the one hand, the cut-reduction simulates β-reduction, and on the other hand, the cut-reduction is sound in regard to β-reduction (i.e., a pure term t reaches another pure term t' by the cut-reduction only if t is β-reducible to t').

The following lemmas show that the cut-reduction correctly simulates the meta-operations on pure terms.

Lemma 10. *Let* u, s, l *be pure terms with* $FHV(l) = w$. *Then* $[u/y]\langle \underline{y}s/w \rangle l \xrightarrow{*}_{\mathrm{cut}} \langle \{u\}s/w \rangle l$.

Proof. By induction on the structure of u.

(a) $u \equiv x$. Then $[x/y]\langle \underline{y}s/w \rangle l \to_{\mathrm{cut}} \langle \underline{x}s/w \rangle l \equiv \langle \{x\}s/w \rangle l$.
(b) $u \equiv \lambda x.t$. Then $[\lambda x.t/y]\langle \underline{y}s/w \rangle l \equiv \langle \{\lambda x.t\}s/w \rangle l$.
(c) $u \equiv \langle \underline{x}s'/w' \rangle l'$. Then

$$[\langle \underline{x}s'/w' \rangle l'/y]\langle \underline{y}s/w \rangle l \to_{\mathrm{cut}} \langle \underline{x}s'/w' \rangle[l'/y]\langle \underline{y}s/w \rangle l$$
$$\xrightarrow{*}_{\mathrm{cut}} \langle \underline{x}s'/w' \rangle\langle \{l'\}s/w \rangle l \qquad \text{(by IH)}$$
$$\equiv \langle \{\langle \underline{x}s'/w' \rangle l'\}s/w \rangle l$$

(d) $u \equiv [\lambda z.r/x]\langle \underline{x}s'/w' \rangle l'$. Then

$$[[\lambda z.r/x]\langle \underline{x}s'/w' \rangle l'/y]\langle \underline{y}s/w \rangle l \to_{\mathrm{cut}} [\lambda z.r/x][\langle \underline{x}s'/w' \rangle l'/y]\langle \underline{y}s/w \rangle l$$
$$\to_{\mathrm{cut}} [\lambda z.r/x]\langle \underline{x}s'/w' \rangle[l'/y]\langle \underline{y}s/w \rangle l$$
$$\xrightarrow{*}_{\mathrm{cut}} [\lambda z.r/x]\langle \underline{x}s'/w' \rangle\langle \{l'\}s/w \rangle l \qquad \text{(by IH)}$$
$$\equiv \langle \{[\lambda z.r/x]\langle \underline{x}s'/w' \rangle l'\}s/w \rangle l$$

□

Lemma 11. *Let* u, t *be pure terms. Then* $[u/y]t \xrightarrow{*}_{\mathrm{cut}} \{u/y\}t$.

Proof. By induction on the structure of t.

(a) $t \equiv x$ $(x \not\equiv y)$. Then $[u/y]x \rightarrow_{\text{cut}} x \equiv \{u/y\}x$.

(b) $t \equiv y$. Then $[u/y]y \rightarrow_{\text{cut}} u \equiv \{u/y\}y$.

(c) $t \equiv \lambda z.r$. Then $[u/y](\lambda z.r) \rightarrow_{\text{cut}} \lambda z.[u/y]r \overset{\text{IH*}}{\rightarrow}_{\text{cut}} \lambda z.\{u/y\}r \equiv \{u/y\}(\lambda z.r)$.

(d) $t \equiv \langle xs/w \rangle l$ $(x \not\equiv y)$. Then

$$
\begin{aligned}
[u/y]\langle xs/w \rangle l \ \ &\rightarrow_{\text{cut}} \ \langle x([u/y]s)/w \rangle [u/y]l \\
&\overset{*}{\rightarrow}_{\text{cut}} \ \langle x(\{u/y\}s)/w \rangle \{u/y\}l && \text{(by IH)} \\
&\equiv \ \{u/y\}\langle xs/w \rangle l
\end{aligned}
$$

(e) $t \equiv \langle ys/w \rangle l$ $(y \in FV(s) \cup FV(l))$. Then

$$
\begin{aligned}
[u/y]\langle ys/w \rangle l \ \ &\rightarrow_{\text{cut}} \ [u/y]\langle \underline{y}([u/y]s)/w \rangle [u/y]l \\
&\overset{*}{\rightarrow}_{\text{cut}} \ [u/y]\langle \underline{y}(\{u/y\}s)/w \rangle \{u/y\}l && \text{(by IH)} \\
&\overset{*}{\rightarrow}_{\text{cut}} \ \langle \{u\}(\{u/y\}s)/w \rangle \{u/y\}l && \text{(by Lemma 10)} \\
&\equiv \ \{u/y\}\langle ys/w \rangle l
\end{aligned}
$$

(f) $t \equiv \langle \underline{y}s/w \rangle l$. Then

$$
\begin{aligned}
[u/y]\langle \underline{y}s/w \rangle l \ \ &\overset{*}{\rightarrow}_{\text{cut}} \ \langle \{u\}s/w \rangle l && \text{(by Lemma 10)} \\
&\equiv \ \langle \{u\}(\{u/y\}s)/w \rangle \{u/y\}l && \text{(by Lemma 1)} \\
&\equiv \ \{u/y\}\langle \underline{y}s/w \rangle l
\end{aligned}
$$

(g) $t \equiv [\lambda z.r/x]\langle \underline{x}s/w \rangle l$. Then

$$
\begin{aligned}
[u/y][\lambda z.r/x]\langle \underline{x}s/w \rangle l \ \ &\rightarrow_{\text{cut}} \ [[u/y](\lambda z.r)/x][u/y]\langle \underline{x}s/w \rangle l \\
&\rightarrow_{\text{cut}} \ [\lambda z.[u/y]r/x][u/y]\langle \underline{x}s/w \rangle l \\
&\rightarrow_{\text{cut}} \ [\lambda z.[u/y]r/x]\langle \underline{x}([u/y]s)/w \rangle [u/y]l \\
&\overset{*}{\rightarrow}_{\text{cut}} \ [\lambda z.\{u/y\}r/x]\langle \underline{x}(\{u/y\}s)/w \rangle \{u/y\}l && \text{(by IH)} \\
&\equiv \ \{u/y\}[\lambda z.r/x]\langle \underline{x}s/w \rangle l
\end{aligned}
$$

$\square$

Now we are ready to show that the cut-reduction simulates β-reduction.

Theorem 2. *For any pure terms t, t', if $t \rightarrow_\beta t'$ then $t \overset{+}{\rightarrow}_{\text{cut}} t'$.*

Proof. By induction on the structure of t. We treat the case $t \equiv [\lambda z.r/x]\langle \underline{x}s/y \rangle l$, $t' \equiv \{\{s/z\}r/y\}l$. Then use $\rightarrow_{Beta}$ to create $[[s/z]r/y]l$, and use Lemma 11 to reach $\{\{s/z\}r/y\}l$. $\square$

The proof of Theorem 2 indicates how to simulate normalization in natural deduction by our cut-elimination procedure in the sequent calculus. Specifically, a redex in natural deduction is translated into a β-cut corresponding to a *Beta*-redex $[\lambda z.r/x]\langle \underline{x}s/y \rangle l$. Then the transformation corresponding to the rule (*Beta*)

Table 4. Translation $\widehat{\varphi}$

$$
\begin{aligned}
\widehat{\varphi}(x) &=_{def} x \\
\widehat{\varphi}(\lambda x.t) &=_{def} \lambda x.\widehat{\varphi}(t) \\
\widehat{\varphi}(\langle xs/y\rangle t) &=_{def} \{x\widehat{\varphi}(s)/y\}\widehat{\varphi}(t) \\
\widehat{\varphi}([s/x]t) &=_{def} \{\widehat{\varphi}(s)/x\}\widehat{\varphi}(t)
\end{aligned}
$$

is performed to create the proof corresponding to $[[s/z]r/y]l$, followed by cut-elimination steps to reach the proof corresponding to $\{\{s/z\}r/y\}l$.

From the above proofs of Lemmas 10 and 11, we see that for simulation of β-reduction, the reduction rules (7) and $(Perm_1)$ can be restricted to the following forms:

$$(7') \qquad [\langle xs/y\rangle t/z]\langle \underline{z}s'/w\rangle t' \to \langle xs/y\rangle[t/z]\langle \underline{z}s'/w\rangle t'$$

$$(Perm_1') \quad [[\lambda z.r/x]\langle \underline{x}s/y\rangle t/z]\langle \underline{z}s'/w\rangle t' \to [\lambda z.r/x][\langle \underline{x}s/y\rangle t/z]\langle \underline{z}s'/w\rangle t'$$

These reduction rules specify some strategies for cut-elimination. The rule $(7')$ makes the cut-elimination procedure first permute a cut upwards through its right subproof and then through its left subproof. The rule $(Perm_1')$ restricts the cut-elimination procedure so that permutation of two cuts is allowed only when the upper cut corresponds to a *Beta*-redex.

Next we show that the cut-reduction is sound in regard to β-reduction. For this we define a translation $\widehat{\varphi}$ of all terms for sequent proofs into λ-terms, as shown in Table 4.

Proposition 2. *For any pure term t, $\widehat{\varphi}(t) \equiv \varphi(t)$.*

Proof. By induction on the structure of t. We treat the case $t \equiv [\lambda z.r/x]\langle \underline{x}s/y\rangle l$. Then

$$
\begin{aligned}
\widehat{\varphi}([\lambda z.r/x]\langle \underline{x}s/y\rangle l) &\equiv \{\widehat{\varphi}(\lambda z.r)/x\}\widehat{\varphi}(\langle \underline{x}s/y\rangle l) \\
&\equiv \{\lambda z.\widehat{\varphi}(r)/x\}\{x\widehat{\varphi}(s)/y\}\widehat{\varphi}(l) \\
&\equiv \{(\lambda z.\widehat{\varphi}(r))\widehat{\varphi}(s)/y\}\widehat{\varphi}(l) & (*) \\
&\equiv \{(\lambda z.\varphi(r))\varphi(s)/y\}\varphi(l) & \text{(by IH)} \\
&\equiv \varphi([\lambda z.r/x]\langle \underline{x}s/y\rangle l)
\end{aligned}
$$

where the step $(*)$ is established since $x \notin FV(s) \cup FV(l)$ and so $x \notin FV(\widehat{\varphi}(s)) \cup FV(\widehat{\varphi}(l))$. □

Now we show that the cut-reduction projects onto β-reduction.

Lemma 12 (Projection). *If $u \to_{cut} u'$, then $\widehat{\varphi}(u) \overset{*}{\to}_\beta \widehat{\varphi}(u')$.*

Proof. By induction on the structure of u. If the cut-reduction is not at the root then the lemma easily follows from the induction hypothesis. If the cut-reduction is at the root, for example, if $u \equiv [[r/x]\langle \underline{x}s/y\rangle t/z]\langle \underline{z}s'/w\rangle t' \to_{cut} [r/x][\langle \underline{x}s/y\rangle t/z]\langle \underline{z}s'/w\rangle t' \equiv u'$ then

$$\widehat{\varphi}([[r/x]\langle \underline{x}s/y\rangle t/z]\langle \underline{z}s'/w\rangle t') \equiv \widehat{\varphi}([[r/x]\langle \underline{x}s/y\rangle t/z]\langle \underline{z}s'/w\rangle t')$$
$$\equiv \{\widehat{\varphi}([r/x]\langle \underline{x}s/y\rangle t)/z\}\widehat{\varphi}(\langle \underline{z}s'/w\rangle t')$$
$$\equiv \{\{\widehat{\varphi}(r)/x\}\widehat{\varphi}(\langle \underline{x}s/y\rangle t)/z\}\widehat{\varphi}(\langle \underline{z}s'/w\rangle t')$$
$$\equiv \{\widehat{\varphi}(r)/x\}\{\widehat{\varphi}(\langle \underline{x}s/y\rangle t)/z\}\widehat{\varphi}(\langle \underline{z}s'/w\rangle t') \qquad (*)$$
$$\equiv \{\widehat{\varphi}(r)/x\}\widehat{\varphi}([\langle \underline{x}s/y\rangle t/z]\langle \underline{z}s'/w\rangle t')$$
$$\equiv \widehat{\varphi}([r/x][\langle \underline{x}s/y\rangle t/z]\langle \underline{z}s'/w\rangle t')$$

where the step $(*)$ is established since we can assume $x \notin FV(\langle \underline{z}s'/w\rangle t')$ and so $x \notin FV(\widehat{\varphi}(\langle \underline{z}s'/w\rangle t'))$.   □

As a result, we have that $\to_{\mathrm{cut}}$ is a sound refinement of $\to_\beta$.

Corollary 1. *For any pure terms t, t', if $t \xrightarrow{*}_{\mathrm{cut}} t'$ then $t \xrightarrow{*}_\beta t'$.*

Proof. Suppose that $t \xrightarrow{*}_{\mathrm{cut}} t'$. Then by Lemma 12, $\widehat{\varphi}(t) \xrightarrow{*}_\beta \widehat{\varphi}(t')$, so by Proposition 2, $\varphi(t) \xrightarrow{*}_\beta \varphi(t')$. Now by Theorem 1 (1), $\rho(\varphi(t)) \xrightarrow{*}_\beta \rho(\varphi(t'))$, and so by Proposition 1, we have $t \xrightarrow{*}_\beta t'$.   □

5   Conclusion and Further Work

We have investigated the relationship between normalization in natural deduction and cut-elimination in a standard sequent calculus, using term notations for both systems. We have identified a subset of sequent proofs that correspond to simply typed λ-terms, and showed that the isomorphic image of β-reduction is simulated by our cut-elimination procedure. Since the cut-elimination procedure is also sound in regard to β-reduction, the sequent calculus can be considered as a conservative extension of natural deduction in both proofs and reduction relation. Moreover, we have derived minimal requirements for simulation of β-reduction by a local-step cut-elimination procedure, analyzing our proof of the simulation.

It is expected that our cut-elimination procedure satisfies the strong normalization property. However, unlike in the case using labelled cuts [12], a standard method for inferring strong normalization of explicit substitution calculus [1] is not directly applied to our case. One of the reasons is that the subcalculus (i.e., the reduction system without the rule (*Beta*)) is not confluent (e.g., the critical pair $w \leftarrow [\langle \underline{x}s/y\rangle t/z]w \to \langle \underline{x}s/y\rangle[t/z]w$ is not joinable). So we might need more powerful methods for proving strong normalization, which will be investigated in future work.

Acknowledgements. I would like to thank Takafumi Sakurai and Stéphane Lengrand for useful discussions concerning the subject of this paper. I also thank the anonymous referees for valuable comments. This research was partially supported by the Japanese Ministry of Education, Culture, Sports, Science and Technology, Grant-in-Aid for Young Scientists (B) 17700003.

References

1. R. Bloo and H. Geuvers. Explicit substitution: On the edge of strong normalization. *Theoretical Computer Science*, 211:375–395, 1999.
2. R. Dyckhoff and L. Pinto. Cut-elimination and a permutation-free sequent calculus for intuitionistic logic. *Studia Logica*, 60:107–118, 1998.
3. R. Dyckhoff and C. Urban. Strong normalization of Herbelin's explicit substitution calculus with substitution propagation. *Journal of Logic and Computation*, 13:689–706, 2003.
4. J. Espírito Santo. Revisiting the correspondence between cut elimination and normalisation. In *Proceedings of ICALP'00*, Lecture Notes in Computer Science 1853, pages 600–611. Springer-Verlag, 2000.
5. J. Espírito Santo. An isomorphism between a fragment of sequent calculus and an extension of natural deduction. In *Proceedings of LPAR'02*, Lecture Notes in Computer Science 2514, pages 352–366. Springer-Verlag, 2002.
6. G. Gentzen. Untersuchungen über das logische Schliessen. *Mathematische Zeitschrift*, 39:176–210, 405–431, 1935. English translation in [11], pages 68–131.
7. H. Herbelin. A λ-calculus structure isomorphic to Gentzen-style sequent calculus structure. In *Proceedings of CSL'94*, Lecture Notes in Computer Science 933, pages 61–75. Springer-Verlag, 1995.
8. W. A. Howard. The formulae-as-types notion of construction. In J. P. Seldin and J. R. Hindley, editors, *To H. B. Curry: Essays on Combinatory Logic, Lambda-Calculus and Formalism*, pages 479–490. Academic Press, 1980.
9. F. Pfenning. Structural cut elimination: I. intuitionistic and classical logic. *Information and Computation*, 157:84–141, 2000.
10. D. Prawitz. *Natural Deduction, A Proof-Theoretical Study*. Almquist and Wiksell, 1965.
11. M. E. Szabo, editor. *The Collected Papers of Gerhard Gentzen*. North-Holland, 1969.
12. C. Urban. *Classical Logic and Computation*. PhD thesis, University of Cambridge, 2000.
13. C. Urban and G. M. Bierman. Strong normalisation of cut-elimination in classical logic. *Fundamenta Informaticae*, 45:123–155, 2001.

Modular Cut-Elimination: Finding Proofs or Counterexamples

Agata Ciabattoni[1,*] and Kazushige Terui[2,**]

[1] Institute für Diskrete Mathematik und Geometrie, TU Wien
agata@logic.at
[2] National Institute of Informatics, Tokyo, Japan
terui@nii.ac.jp

Abstract. Modular cut-elimination is a particular notion of "cut-elimination in the presence of non-logical axioms" that is preserved under the addition of suitable rules. We introduce syntactic necessary and sufficient conditions for modular cut-elimination for standard calculi, a wide class of (possibly) multiple-conclusion sequent calculi with generalized quantifiers. We provide a "universal" modular cut-elimination procedure that works uniformly for any standard calculus satisfying our conditions. The failure of these conditions generates counterexamples for modular cut-elimination and, in certain cases, for cut-elimination.

1 Introduction

Cut-elimination is one of the most important techniques in proof theory. The removal of cuts corresponds to the elimination of intermediate statements (lemmas) from proofs, resulting in calculi in which proofs are *analytic* in the sense that all statements in the proofs are subformulae of the result.

A great many different cut-elimination proofs for various sequent calculi have been published since Gentzen's proofs for **LK** and **LJ** (sequent calculi for classical and intuitionistic first-order logic, respectively), most using heavy syntactic arguments and based on case distinctions, usually written without filling in the details[1]. However since it is often the case that "the devil is in the details" (this also explains why so many wrong cut-elimination proofs appear in the literature, e.g. [5]), it is natural to investigate *general criteria* that a sequent calculus should satisfy in order to admit cut-elimination. Such criteria should support a *modular view* of cut-elimination in sequent calculi (i.e. decomposability of the whole calculus into local components when proving cut-elimination), and also provide useful information in the negative case, where a particular cut-elimination method cannot be applied or a cut-elimination proof cannot be found at all.

Necessary and sufficient conditions for cut-elimination were defined in [14] for *canonical calculi*, which are sequent calculi containing identity axioms, the usual structural rules (weakening, exchange and contraction) and possibly "standard" rules for connectives and quantifiers. Canonical calculi extended with (k, n)-ary connectives

---

* Research supported by FWF Project P18731.
** Partially supported by Grant-in-Aid for Scientific Research, MEXT, Japan.

[1] Notable exceptions are the cut-elimination proofs for classical and intuitionistic logic of [7].

M. Hermann and A. Voronkov (Eds.): LPAR 2006, LNAI 4246, pp. 135–149, 2006.

which bind k variables and connect n formulas were investigated in [15] where sufficient conditions for cut-elimination have been introduced in the case $k = 0, 1$. In the context of substructural logics, syntactic and semantic criteria for (additive) structural rules to preserve cut-elimination when added to full Lambek calculus were introduced in [12]. Terui's work was generalized in [3] to provide necessary and sufficient conditions for a large class of propositional single-conclusion sequent calculi to admit reductive cut-elimination, a naturally strengthened version of Buss' free-cut elimination [1] which additionally aims to shift non-eliminable cuts upwards as much as possible. The proposed criteria have two equivalent forms: syntactic (*reductivity* and *weak substitutivity*) and semantic (coherence and propagation). The former arises by weakening the sufficient conditions in [2] while the latter generalize the results in [12].

In this paper we focus on the syntactic aspects of cut-elimination. We refine and extend the (syntactic) results of [3] to *standard calculi*, i.e. commutative (not necessarily single-conclusion) sequent calculi possibly containing (fancy) structural rules and rules for (k, n)-ary connectives, for all k and n. Examples of standard calculi are Maehara's calculus **LJ'** for intuitionistic predicate logic, the calculus **GD** for the logic of constant domains [5], the multiplicative additive fragment of linear logic extended with any structural rule, or the calculi investigated in [15]. We investigate *modular cut-elimination* in standard calculi, a particular notion of "cut-elimination in the presence of non-logical axioms," that is preserved under the addition of suitable rules. *Weak substitutivity* and *reductivity*, the syntactic conditions of [3], are adapted to standard sequent calculi (Section 4), and shown to be necessary and sufficient for modular cut-elimination (the former holds when logical rules satisfy some additional properties, see Section 5). The necessity result is used for *counterexamples generation*: given a standard sequent calculus for which our criteria fail, counterexamples for modular cut-elimination are automatically generated and, in certain cases, lead to counterexamples for cut-elimination. The sufficient result is shown by providing a constructive proof of modular cut-elimination, from which a concrete cut-elimination procedure can be read off (Section 6). Remarkably enough this procedure is "universal" in the sense that when a standard sequent calculus admits modular cut-elimination, then our procedure always transforms derivations with cuts into cut-free derivations (Corollary 3).

Our results also support a modular view of cut-elimination. Indeed when adding a new connective and/or a new structural rule to a standard calculus for which modular cut-elimination has been already established, it is enough to show that the newly added rules are reductive and weakly substitutive. Moreover the task of proving modular cut-elimination for a standard calculus can be decomposed into the sub-tasks of proving cut-elimination for appropriate sub-calculi. In particular, in analogy with *Toyama's Lemma*[2] in term rewriting theory, modular cut-elimination is preserved by taking the disjoint union of two (sets of rules of) standard sequent calculi (Corollary 2).

2   Standard Calculi

We start by formalizing the notion of a standard sequent calculus. In the following we consider formulas built over a *vocabulary* $\mathcal{V}$ consisting of (countably many): (term)

---

[2] It states that the disjoint union of two confluent term rewriting systems is also confluent.

variables $x, y, z, \ldots$, for each $n \geq 0$, n-ary function and predicate symbols, as well as (m, n)-ary connectives $\star_1, \star_2, \ldots$ for each $m, n \geq 0$. As usual, *terms* $t, u, v, \ldots$ (in the vocabulary $\mathcal{V}$) are built up from variables using function symbols while atomic formulae are built up from terms using predicate symbols. A *formula* (in the vocabulary $\mathcal{V}$) is either an atomic formula or a compound formula of the form $\star_i \boldsymbol{x}(\boldsymbol{A})$ with $\star_i$ an (m, n)-ary connective, which binds $\boldsymbol{x} \equiv x_1, \ldots, x_m$ distinct variables, and connect formulas $\boldsymbol{A} \equiv A_1, \ldots, A_n$. Given a formula, its free and bound variables are defined in the standard way. As usual, we identify formulas only differing in the names of bound variables (i.e. formulas are considered up to α-equivalence).

Example 1.

1. The standard quantifiers $\forall$ and $\exists$ can be seen as $(1, 1)$-ary connectives, while propositional connectives as $(0, n)$-ary connectives, for some $n \geq 1$.
2. The Henkin quantifier Q_H (see e.g. [15]) can be seen as a $(4, 1)$-ary connective.
3. Bounded quantified formulae $\forall x \leq t.A$, $\exists x \leq t.A$ can be built with $(1, 2)$-ary connectives $\forall^b x(X, Y)$, $\exists^b x(X, Y)$ with the proviso that the meta-variable X is always instantiated by an inequation of the form $x \leq t$.

We indicate with $\Gamma, \Delta, \Pi, \Sigma, \ldots$ multisets of formulae. When $\lambda \geq 0$, Γ^λ denotes $\Gamma, \ldots, \Gamma$ (λ times). A *sequent* $\Gamma \Rightarrow \Delta$ (Γ said to be *antecedent* and Δ *consequent*) is *atomic* if all formulae in Γ and Δ are atomic. $\Gamma \Rightarrow \Delta$ is *single-conclusion* if Δ contains at most one formula, otherwise it is *multiple-conclusion*.

To specify inference rules we use *meta-variables* $X, Y, Z, X[^t/_{\boldsymbol{x}}] \ldots (t \equiv t_1, \ldots, t_m$ and $\boldsymbol{x} \equiv x_1, \ldots, x_m)$ standing for arbitrary formulae and $\Theta, \Xi, \Phi, \Psi, \Upsilon, \ldots$ for (possibly empty) multisets of meta-variables.

Definition 1. *A standard* sequent calculus $\mathcal{L}$ *consists of:*

- identity axiom *of the form* $X \Rightarrow X$
- *the multiplicative version of the* cut rule, *i.e.*

$$\frac{\Theta \Rightarrow \Xi, X \quad X, \Theta' \Rightarrow \Xi'}{\Theta, \Theta' \Rightarrow \Xi', \Xi} \ (CUT)$$

- structural inference rules *of the form* ($n > 0$):

$$\frac{\Theta_1 \Rightarrow \Xi_1 \quad \cdots \quad \Theta_n \Rightarrow \Xi_n}{\Theta \Rightarrow \Xi} \ (R_i)$$

satisfying the conditions

(str0) Θ *and* Ξ *are disjoint.*

(str1) *any meta-variable occurring in* $\Theta_1, \ldots, \Theta_n$ *occurs in* Θ *and any meta-variable occurring in* $\Xi_1, \ldots, \Xi_n$ *occurs in* Ξ.

(Note that since $\Theta, \Xi, \ldots$ *are multisets, we implicitly assume that permutation rule(s) always belong to* $\mathcal{L}$)

– left logical rules $\{(\star, l, \boldsymbol{y})_i\}_{i \in \Lambda}$ and right logical rules $\{(\star, r, \boldsymbol{z})_j\}_{j \in \Lambda'}$ (Λ and Λ' could be empty) for each (k, l)-ary connective $\star$, with $k, l, m, n \geq 0$:

$$\frac{\Upsilon_1 \Rightarrow \Psi_1 \quad \cdots \quad \Upsilon_n \Rightarrow \Psi_n}{\star \boldsymbol{x}(\boldsymbol{X}), \Theta \Rightarrow \Xi} (\star, l, \boldsymbol{y})_i \qquad \frac{\Upsilon_1' \Rightarrow \Psi_1' \quad \cdots \quad \Upsilon_m' \Rightarrow \Psi_m'}{\Theta \Rightarrow \Xi, \star \boldsymbol{x}(\boldsymbol{X})} (\star, r, \boldsymbol{z})_j$$

where $\boldsymbol{x} \equiv x_1, \ldots x_k$, $\boldsymbol{X} \equiv X_1, \ldots, X_l$ and for each $i = 1, \ldots l$, $X_i[^t/_{\boldsymbol{x}}]$ ($\boldsymbol{t} \equiv t_1, \ldots, t_k$, where each t_i is a term) may appear in $\Upsilon_j \Rightarrow \Psi_j, \Upsilon_{j'}' \Rightarrow \Psi_{j'}$ with $j = 1, \ldots, n$ and $j' = 1, \ldots, m$. $\boldsymbol{y}$ and $\boldsymbol{z}$ are the eigenvariables of the rules.
$(\star, l, \boldsymbol{y})_i$ must satisfy the following conditions
(log0) Θ, Ξ and $\{\boldsymbol{X}\}$ are mutually disjoint.
(log1) Any meta-variable occurring in $\Upsilon_1, \ldots, \Upsilon_n$ occurs in Θ or it is of the form $X_i[^t/_{\boldsymbol{x}}]$ where $X_i \in \boldsymbol{X}$. Any meta-variable occurring in $\Psi_1, \ldots, \Psi_n$ occurs in Ξ or it is of the form $X_i[^t/_{\boldsymbol{x}}]$ where $X_i \in \boldsymbol{X}$.
The corresponding conditions hold for $(\star, r, \boldsymbol{z})_j$.

Remark 1. Conditions **(str1)** and **(log1)** ensure that rules satisfy the subformula property and do not allow meta-variables in Θ and Ξ to move from antecedent to consequent of sequents and vice versa.

We identify rules up to the renaming of meta-variables and logical rules up to the renaming of (term) variables.

Definition 2. Instances *(resp.* atomic instances*) of identity axiom, (CUT), and structural rules are obtained by substituting arbitrary formulae (resp. atomic formulae) for meta-variables. An* instance *(resp.* atomic instance*) of a logical rule $(\star, l, \boldsymbol{y})_i$ or $(\star, r, \boldsymbol{y})_j$ is obtained*

1. *by replacing each meta-variable Y with a formula (resp. atomic formula) that does not contain $\boldsymbol{y}$ as free variables.*
2. *when a meta-variable X_i ($\in \boldsymbol{X}$) in its conclusion is replaced by a formula (resp. atomic formula) A (that does not contain $\boldsymbol{y}$ as free variables), then each meta-variable $X_i[^t/_{\boldsymbol{x}}]$ in its premises is replaced with the formula (resp. atomic formula) A in which all free occurrences of the variable x_j (if any) are replaced by the term t_j, for $j = 1, \ldots, k$.*

A derivation *in $\mathcal{L}$ is obtained by composing instances of axioms and rules of $\mathcal{L}$.*

Condition 1. above ensures that the eigenvariable condition is satisfied.

Definition 3. *In logical and structural rules (or their instances) the meta-variables (formulae) in Θ are called* left context meta-variables *(left context formulae), those in Ξ* right context meta-variables *(right context formulae), and (in the former rules) the meta-variables (formulae) of the form $X_i, X_i[^t/_{\boldsymbol{x}}]$* active meta-variables *(active formulae).*

In a logical rule (or its instance) the introduced $\star \boldsymbol{x}(\boldsymbol{X})$ (or the formula of the form $\star \boldsymbol{x}(A_1, \ldots, A_l)$) is called principal formula. *Moreover, the two occurrences of the formula instantiating the meta-variable X in (CUT) are called* left *and* right *cut formulae (and the corresponding premises of (CUT) are called* left *and* right premises).

Example 2.

1. Simple sequent calculi with permutation (see [3]) are particular standard calculi in which each sequent is single-conclusion and whose connectives are of type $(0, n)$.
2. The ordinary rules for quantifiers fit into our framework. For instance, the left and right rules for $\forall$ are represented by the following rules:

$$\frac{X[^t/_x], \Theta \Rightarrow \Xi}{\forall x(X), \Theta \Rightarrow \Xi} \; (\forall, l, \emptyset) \qquad \frac{\Theta \Rightarrow \Xi, X[^y/_x]}{\Theta \Rightarrow \Xi, \forall x(X)} \; (\forall, r, y)$$

   where t is an arbitrary term and Θ, Ξ are arbitrary multisets of meta-variables.
3. Canonical calculi with (n, k)-ary connectives (see [15]) are particular standard calculi that contain all the structural rules (weakening, contraction and exchange).

3   Modular Cut-Elimination

Generalizations of cut-elimination with extra (non-logical) axioms have been considered e.g. in [13,1,11]. They play an important role in the proof theory of formalized mathematical theories such as fragments of arithmetic. Given a deduction in **LK** of a sequent S_0 from a set S of non-logical axioms closed under substitutions, *free-cut elimination* described in [1] aims at finding a deduction of S_0 containing only *anchored-cuts*, i.e. cuts whose premises (at least one, for cuts with compound cut-formulas) derive from sequents in S. If S consist of atomic sequents closed under mix (and substitutions) then Gentzen's cut-elimination method generates a cut-free **LK**-derivation of S_0, see e.g. [13]. To characterize the "stepwise process of local transformations to eliminate cuts" in a large class of propositional single-conclusion sequent calculi we introduced in [3] reductive cut-elimination, a naturally strengthened version of free-cut elimination which in addition aims to shift upward anchored-cuts in these calculi *as much as possible*.

Here below we rework the above notions of cut-elimination in the presence of axioms to define a "modular" cut-elimination for standard calculi, namely if such calculi enjoy it, they also do when extended by any rule satisfying suitable conditions (weak substitutivity and reductivity, see Section 4).

Definition 4. *A set S of sequents* (non-logical axioms) *is called* elementary *if*

1. *all formulae in S are atomic.*
2. *S is closed under substitutions: whenever $S(x) \in S$ and t is any term, the sequent $S(t)$, obtained by substituting in S the term t for all free occurrences of x, is in S.*
3. *S is closed under cuts: whenever $\Gamma_1 \Rightarrow \Delta_1, A$ and $A, \Gamma_2 \Rightarrow \Delta_2$ belong to S, so does $\Gamma_1, \Gamma_2 \Rightarrow \Delta_1, \Delta_2$.*
4. *it is not the case that sequents of the forms $\Gamma \Rightarrow \Delta, A, A$ and $A, A, \Sigma \Rightarrow \Pi$, both belong to S.*

Definition 5. *A standard sequent calculus $\mathcal{L}$ admits* modular cut-elimination *if whenever a sequent S_0 is derivable in $\mathcal{L}$ from an elementary set S of sequents in $\mathcal{L}$, S_0 has a cut-free derivation in $\mathcal{L}$ from S.*

Remark 2. Modular cut-elimination implies the ordinary cut-elimination (set $\mathcal{S} = \emptyset$).

Notice that if we remove condition 4 from Def. 4, the resulting notion of cut-elimination is not admitted e.g. by **LK**: indeed $\mathcal{S} \equiv \{A, A \Rightarrow ; \Rightarrow A, A ; A \Rightarrow A\}$ with A atomic satisfies the conditions 1-3 of Def. 4. It is easy to check that the empty sequent $\Rightarrow$ is derivable from $\mathcal{S}$ in **LK** only using (CUT).

4   Syntactic Criteria

In this section we introduce the notions of reductive logical rules and weakly substitutive rules for standard calculi. Intuitively, a logical rule is reductive if it allows the replacement of cuts by "smaller" cuts, and a rule is weakly substitutive when any cut can be permuted upward. Reductivity and weak substitutivity are obtained by suitably modifying the homonymous conditions of [3] defined for simple calculi (see Ex. 2.1).

Let S be a sequent, A a formula, $T_1 \equiv A, \Sigma \Rightarrow \Pi$ and $T_2 \equiv \Sigma \Rightarrow \Pi, A$. We define

$$[S \hookleftarrow^r_A T_1] = \{\Gamma, \Sigma^\lambda \Rightarrow \Delta, \Pi^\lambda \mid S \equiv \Gamma \Rightarrow \Delta, A^\lambda \text{ with } \lambda \geq 0\}$$
$$[S \hookleftarrow^l_A T_2] = \{\Gamma, \Sigma^\lambda \Rightarrow \Delta, \Pi^\lambda \mid S \equiv A^\lambda, \Gamma \Rightarrow \Delta \text{ with } \lambda \geq 0\}$$

Namely, each $U \in [S \hookleftarrow^r_A T_1]$ is obtained by applying (CUT) possibly several times between S and (several copies of) T_1 with cut formula A. $[S \hookleftarrow^l_A T_2]$ is dually defined. In case T does not contain any occurrence of A in the antecedent (resp. consequent), we define $[S \hookleftarrow^r_A T] = \{S\}$ (resp. $[S \hookleftarrow^l_A T] = \{S\}$).

Definition 6. *Let $\mathcal{L}$ be a standard sequent calculus. A rule (R) is said to be* weakly substitutive *in $\mathcal{L}$ if for each instance of (R) with premises $S_1, \ldots, S_n$ and conclusion S_0 the following condition holds:*

(*) for any $c \in \{r, l\}$, context formula A and any sequent T of $\mathcal{L}$ (which does not contain any eigenvariable of (R)), every $U \in [S_0 \hookleftarrow^c_A T]$ has a derivation from $\bigcup_{i=1}^n [S_i \hookleftarrow^c_A T]$ only using structural rules and, when (R) is a left (resp. right) logical rule with principal formula B, left (resp. right) logical rules with principal formula B.

Remark 3. The above condition was defined (in fact, using rule *schemas* instead of rule *instances*) in [3] only for structural rules. Indeed, the logical rules considered there satisfy a condition stronger than (*), namely: for any $c \in \{r, l\}$, context formula A (right or left context formula, depending on c) and single-conclusion sequent T, every $U \in [S_0 \hookleftarrow^c_A T]$ is derivable from $\bigcup_{i=1}^n [S_i \hookleftarrow^c_A T]$ with an application of (R).

Example 3. The rules of **LJ** (resp. **LK**) are weakly substitutive in **LJ** (resp. **LK**). Consider now:

1. Maehara's calculus **LJ'** for intuitionistic logic, that is an equivalent version of Gentzen's **LJ** where the intuitionistic restriction (i.e. consequent of sequents contain at most one formula) applies not generally but only in the case of the right rules for $\rightarrow$, $\neg$ and $\forall$, see e.g. [11].

2. The calculus **GD** for the logic of constant domains[3]. **GD** was defined in [5] by modifying **LK** as follows: (1) the sequents of **GD** have at most two formulas in their consequents and (2) the rules $(\rightarrow, r, \emptyset)$ and $(\neg, r, \emptyset)$ obey the intuitionistic restriction.

It is easy to see that e.g. the rule $(\rightarrow, r, \emptyset)$ is weakly substitutive neither in **LJ'** nor in **GD**. Indeed, take any instance of $(\rightarrow, r, \emptyset)$, say

$$\frac{S_1}{S_0} \equiv \frac{\Gamma, C, A \Rightarrow B}{\Gamma, C \Rightarrow A \rightarrow B} \ (\rightarrow, r, \emptyset)$$

and $T \equiv \Sigma \Rightarrow \Pi, C$, where Π contains at least one formula. Then $\Gamma, \Sigma \Rightarrow A \rightarrow B, \Pi \in [S_0 \hookleftarrow^l_C T]$ is in general not cut-free derivable from $[S_1 \hookleftarrow^l_C T]$ in **LJ'** or **GD**.

Although Definition 6 refers to *all* instances of any rule, in practice to check that a particular rule is weakly substitutive it is enough to consider *certain atomic* instances.

Definition 7. *Let (R_0) be any instance of a structural rule. The associated atomic instance $\langle R_0 \rangle$ is defined by replacing each context formula occurrence A with a new atomic formula $\langle A, c \rangle$ with no free variables (c is either l or r according to whether the formula occurrence appears in the antecedent or consequent of sequents in (R_0)).*

When (R_0) is an instance of a logical rule with the principal formula $\star x(A)$ with $x \equiv x_1, \ldots, x_k$ and $A \equiv A_1, \ldots, A_l$, the associated atomic instance $\langle R_0 \rangle$ is defined by replacing

- *each context formula A with $\langle A, c \rangle$ as above,*
- *its principal formula $\star x(A)$ with $\star x(\langle A_1, 1 \rangle(x), \ldots \langle A_l, l \rangle(x))$, where for each $i = 1, \ldots, l$ $\langle A_i, i \rangle$ is a new k-ary predicate symbol*
- *each $A_i[t/x]$ with $\langle A_i, i \rangle(t)$.*

Note that $\langle R_0 \rangle$ strictly distinguishes active, left and right context formulae.

Lemma 1. *(1) If (R_0) is an instance of a rule (R), so is $\langle R_0 \rangle$. (2) If condition (*) of Def. 6 holds for $\langle R_0 \rangle$ then the same condition holds for (R_0).*

Proof. (1) Follows by conditions (**str0**), (**str1**), (**log0**) and (**log1**). (2) Easy.

To introduce reductivity we need some additional notation and terminology. Given a set $\mathcal{S}$ of sequents (resp. a set $\mathcal{A}$ of formulae), we denote by $\mathcal{S}^s$ (resp. $\mathcal{A}^s$) the least set containing $\mathcal{S}$ (resp. $\mathcal{A}$) and closed under substitutions. We call any instance of (CUT) with cut-formula in $\mathcal{A}$ an $\mathcal{A}$-cut.

Definition 8. *Let $\mathcal{L}$ be a standard sequent calculus. We call its logical rules $\{(\star, r, y)_j\}_{j \in \Lambda}$ and $\{(\star, l, z)_k\}_{k \in \Lambda'}$ for introducing a (k, l)-ary connective $\star$ reductive in $\mathcal{L}$ if*

1. *either Λ or Λ' is empty or*
2. *for any pair of instances of left and right logical rules with principal formula $\star x(A)$:*

---

[3] A Hilbert calculus for this logic is obtained by adding to that of intuitionistic logic the shifting law of universal quantifiers w.r.t. $\vee$, i.e. $\forall x(A(x) \vee B) \rightarrow \forall x A(x) \vee B$, where x does not appear free in B.

$$\frac{S_1 \quad \cdots \quad S_n}{\Gamma \Rightarrow \Delta, \star x(A)} \qquad \frac{T_1 \quad \cdots \quad T_m}{\star x(A), \Sigma \Rightarrow \Pi}$$

($\star$) $\Gamma, \Sigma \Rightarrow \Delta, \Pi$ *is derivable from* $\{S_1, \ldots, S_n, T_1, \ldots, T_m\}^s$ *only using* $\{A\}^s$-*cuts and structural rules.*

Remark 4. The above definition generalizes the reductivity condition of [3] and the principal formula condition of [8], both defined for propositional calculi (single-conclusion, in case of the former). Reductivity is also related to the coherence criterion of [6].

Lemma 2. *If condition* ($\star$) *of Def. 8 holds for* $\langle R_0 \rangle$ *then it holds for* (R_0).

Example 4. Consider the $(1, 1)$-ary logical connectives $\flat, \natural$ defined by the following rules:

$$\frac{X[^t/_x], \Theta \Rightarrow \Xi}{\flat x(X), \Theta \Rightarrow \Xi} \; (\flat, l, \emptyset) \qquad \frac{\Theta \Rightarrow \Xi, X[^t/_x]}{\Theta \Rightarrow \Xi, \flat x(X)} \; (\flat, r, \emptyset)$$

$$\frac{X[^y/_x], \Theta \Rightarrow \Xi}{\natural x(X), \Theta \Rightarrow \Xi} \; (\natural, l, y) \qquad \frac{\Theta \Rightarrow \Xi, X[^y/_x]}{\Theta \Rightarrow \Xi, \natural x(X)} \; (\natural, r, y)$$

The rules for $\natural$ are reductive in **LK** while those for $\flat$ are not.

Example 5. Let $\mathcal{L}_1$ be the standard calculus that consists of the following rules introducing the $(0, 2)$-ary connective $\sqcap$ (together with permutation rules and identity axioms)

$$\frac{\Theta \Rightarrow X, \Xi \quad \Theta \Rightarrow Y, \Xi}{\Theta \Rightarrow X \sqcap Y, \Xi} \; (\sqcap, r, \emptyset) \qquad \frac{\Theta, X, Y \Rightarrow \Xi}{\Theta, X \sqcap Y \Rightarrow \Xi} \; (\sqcap, l, \emptyset)$$

$(\sqcap, r, \emptyset)$ and $(\sqcap, l, \emptyset)$ are not reductive in $\mathcal{L}_1$.

5   Necessary Conditions

We show that reductivity and weak substitutivity are necessary conditions for modular cut-elimination in standard sequent calculi whose logical rules satisfy certain additional conditions. Specifically, for each logical rule $(\star, l, \boldsymbol{y})_i$ and $(\star, r, \boldsymbol{z})_j$ we define the following conditions:

$$\frac{\Upsilon_1 \Rightarrow \Psi_1 \quad \cdots \quad \Upsilon_n \Rightarrow \Psi_n}{\star x(X), \Theta \Rightarrow \Xi} \; (\star, l, \boldsymbol{y})_i \qquad \frac{\Upsilon_1 \Rightarrow \Psi_1 \quad \cdots \quad \Upsilon_n \Rightarrow \Psi_n}{\Theta \Rightarrow \Xi, \star x(X)} \; (\star, r, \boldsymbol{z})_j$$

(log2) if any active meta-variable $X[^t/_x]$ occurs in $\Upsilon_1, \ldots, \Upsilon_n$, then no $X[^{t'}/_{x'}]$ (for any t', x') occurs in $\Psi_1, \ldots, \Psi_n$, and *vice versa*.

(log3) each active meta-variable X_i $(1 \le i \le l)$ occurs at most once in each premise $\Upsilon_j \Rightarrow \Psi_j$ $(1 \le j \le n)$.

Theorem 1. *Let* $\mathcal{L}$ *be a standard sequent calculus. If* $\mathcal{L}$ *admits modular cut-elimination, (i) its structural rules are weakly substitutive and (if in addition each logical rule of* $\mathcal{L}$ *satisfies* **(log2)**) *(ii) its logical rules are weakly substitutive.*

Proof. We prove (ii) since (i) is similar. Let (R_0) be any instance of a logical rule with principal formula B. By Lemma 1 it is enough to prove condition (*) of Definition 6 for the associated atomic instance $\langle R_0 \rangle$ with premises $S_1, \ldots S_n$ and conclusion S_0. Let $c \in \{l, r\}$, T an atomic sequent without free variables and A any atomic formula. W.l.o.g. we may assume that T does not share any atomic formula other than A with S_0. Let S be the least set that contains $\{S_1, \ldots, S_n, T\}$ and is closed under substitutions and cuts. By condition **(log2)** and the definition of $\langle R_0 \rangle$ and T, S is elementary and is equivalent to $\bigcup_{i=1,\ldots,n} [S_i \hookleftarrow_A^c T]$.

Then, any $U \in [S_0 \hookleftarrow_A^c T]$ is derivable from S using $\langle R_0 \rangle$ and (CUT). Hence by modular cut-elimination, U has a cut-free derivation d from $\bigcup_{i=1,\ldots,n} [S_i \hookleftarrow_A^c T]$. Since B is the only compound formula in U, d uses only structural rules and logical rules introducing B. $\qquad \square$

Theorem 2. *Let $\mathcal{L}$ be any standard sequent calculus whose logical rules satisfy **(log2)** and **(log3)**. If $\mathcal{L}$ admits modular cut-elimination, then its logical rules are reductive.*

Proof. Let $(\star, r, \boldsymbol{y})_k$ and $(\star, l, \boldsymbol{z})_j$ be a pair of instances of right and left logical rules for $\star$ in $\mathcal{L}$ and $\langle \star, r, \boldsymbol{y} \rangle_k$ and $\langle \star, l, \boldsymbol{z} \rangle_j$ be the associated atomic instances (see Def. 7):

$$\frac{S_1 \quad \cdots \quad S_n}{\Gamma \Rightarrow \Delta, \star[\boldsymbol{x}](A)} \; \langle \star, r, \boldsymbol{y} \rangle_k \qquad \frac{T_1 \quad \cdots \quad T_m}{\star[\boldsymbol{x}](A), \Sigma \Rightarrow \Pi} \; \langle \star, l, \boldsymbol{z} \rangle_j$$

Without loss of generality, we may assume that (†) the context formulae of $\langle \star, r, \boldsymbol{y} \rangle_k$ are distinct from those of $\langle \star, l, \boldsymbol{z} \rangle_j$. Thus the active formulae (in $\{A\}^s$) are the only formulae that occur both in the antecedent of a premise and in the consequent of another. Let S be the least set that contains $\{S_1, \ldots, S_n, T_1, \ldots, T_m\}$ and is closed under substitutions and cuts. S is elementary due to conditions **(log2)** and **(log3)** and the definition of $\langle \star, r, \boldsymbol{y} \rangle_k$ and $\langle \star, l, \boldsymbol{z} \rangle_j$. By modular cut-elimination $\Gamma, \Sigma \Rightarrow \Delta, \Pi$ is cut-free derivable from S. Hence it is derivable from $\{S_1, \ldots, S_n, T_1, \ldots, T_m\}^s$ only using $\{A\}^s$-cuts and structural rules. The claim follows by Lemma 2. $\qquad \square$

6   Sufficient Conditions

Weak substitutivity and reductivity are sufficient conditions for a standard sequent calculus to admit *modular cut-elimination* (and hence cut-elimination). Here below we give a constructive proof of this result.

In the sequel, $\mathcal{L}$ denotes a standard calculus whose rules are weakly substitutive and whose logical rules are reductive while S_0 any elementary set of non-logical axioms.

Definition 9. *The length $|d|$ of a derivation d is the maximal number of inference rules + 1 occurring on any branch of d. The complexity $|A|$ of a formula A is defined as the number of occurrences of its (n, k)-ary connectives. The cut rank $\rho(d)$ of d is (the maximal complexity of the cut-formulae in d) + 1 ($\rho(d) = 0$ if d has no cuts). Given a compound formula B and $c \in \{l, r\}$, $\sharp_B^c(d)$ is the maximal number of c-side (left or right) logical rules with principal formula B on any branch of d.*

To prove modular cut-elimination for $\mathcal{L}$, we proceed by removing cuts which are topmost among all cuts with cut rank equal to the rank of the whole deduction. Let, e.g.

$$
\frac{\begin{array}{ccc} S_0 & & S_0 \\ \vdots\, d_1 & & \vdots\, d_2 \\ \Gamma \Rightarrow \Delta, A & & A, \Sigma \Rightarrow \Pi \end{array}}{\Gamma, \Sigma \Rightarrow \Delta, \Pi} \text{(CUT)}
$$

be a subderivation ending in such a cut. Roughly speaking our strategy is as follows: If the cut-formula A is a compound formula, using the fact that rules are weakly substitutive, we shift up this cut over d_2 *as much as possible* until we meet (a) an identity axiom or (b) a logical rule introducing the cut formula A (Lemma 5). In the first case the cut is easily eliminated while in case (b) is replaced by cuts with smaller complexity. The latter can be done being logical rules reductive (Lemma 4 and Lemma 5). If A is atomic, the cut is shifted upward over d_2 or d_1 (according to whether the elementary set S_0 contains a sequent of the form $\Phi \Rightarrow \Psi, A, A$ or $\Phi, A, A \Rightarrow \Psi$, respectively) until we meet (a) an identity axiom or (b) a non-logical axiom in S_0 (Lemma 6.(ii)). In both cases the cut can be easily eliminated (for case (b) see Lemma 6.(i)).

Henceforth we write $d, S \vdash_{\mathcal{L}} S$ if d is a derivation in $\mathcal{L}$ of S from a set S of sequents.

Lemma 3 (Substitution). *Let S be any set of sequents closed under substitutions and $d, S \vdash_{\mathcal{L}} S(x)$. Then for any term t there is a derivation d' with $|d'| = |d|$ and $\rho(d') = \rho(d)$ such that $d', S \vdash_{\mathcal{L}} S(t)$. Moreover, for any compound formula A which contains neither x nor an eigenvariable of a rule in d and for any $c \in \{l, r\}$, $\sharp_A^c(d') = \sharp_A^c(d)$.*

Proof. By induction on $|d|$. The crucial case is when the last inference (R) in d is a logical rule with eigenvariables $\boldsymbol{y}$ and with premises $S_1(x, \boldsymbol{y}), \ldots, S_n(x, \boldsymbol{y})$. The term t might contain eigenvariables $\boldsymbol{y}$. So, take fresh variables $\boldsymbol{z}$. Then each $S_i(t, \boldsymbol{z})$ ($i = 1, \ldots, n$) has derivations with the required properties. We can now apply (R) and obtain $S(t)$. Since A contains neither x nor $\boldsymbol{y}$, $\sharp_A^c(d)$ remains unchanged. $\qquad\square$

The following lemma shows how to *reduce* a cut on a compound formula B (i.e. replace it by cuts with cut-formula smaller than B) in case one of its premises is the conclusion of a logical rule introducing B on the left hand side and with atomic context formulae. This lemma is needed when proving the general case: reducing any cut on a compound formula (Lemma 5).

Lemma 4. *Let*

$$
\frac{T_1 \quad \cdots \quad T_m}{T} \equiv B, \Sigma \Rightarrow \Pi
$$

be an instance of a left logical rule with principal formula B and in which all context formulae are atomic. If $d_1, S_0 \cup \{T_1, \ldots, T_m\}^s \vdash_{\mathcal{L}} S$ with $\rho(d_1) < |B|$ then each $U \in [S \hookleftarrow_B^r T]$ has a derivation $d, S_0 \cup \{T_1, \ldots, T_m\}^s \vdash_{\mathcal{L}} U$ with $\rho(d) < |B|$ and $\sharp_B^r(d) \le \sharp_B^r(d_1)$.

Of course, one could derive U by applying (CUT), but the resulting derivation would have cut rank $|B| + 1$.

Proof. Proceeds by a double induction on $(\#_B^r(d_1), |d_1|)$. Let $\mathcal{T} = \{T_1, \ldots, T_m\}^s$.

Base case: $|d_1| = 1$. Then S is either an identity axiom or belongs to $\mathcal{S}_0 \cup \mathcal{T}$. In the former case $U \in [S \hookleftarrow_B^r T]$ is S or T, while in the latter case U is S (since S does not contain B). Hence the claim is trivial.

Inductive case: $|d_1| > 1$. If $U \equiv S$ the claim is trivial. Otherwise, suppose that d_1 ends in a rule (R) with premises $S_1, \ldots, S_n$ and conclusion S. Two cases can arise:

(Case 1) (R) is not a right logical rule with principal formula B. Since (R) is weakly substitutive, (previously applying Lemma 3, if needed) $U \in [S \hookleftarrow_B^r T]$ has a derivation d' from $U_1, \ldots, U_k \in \bigcup_{i=1}^n [S_i \hookleftarrow_B^r T]$, in which neither (CUT) nor a rule introducing B in the consequent is used. By the inductive hypothesis, we can find derivations $d'_i, \mathcal{S}_0 \cup \mathcal{T} \vdash_{\mathcal{L}} U_i$ with $\rho(d'_i) < |B|$ and $\#_B^r(d'_i) \leq \#_B^r(d_1)$ for $1 \leq i \leq k$. Therefore the required derivation for U can be obtained by plugging $d'_1, \ldots, d'_k$ into d'.

(Case 2) Otherwise, S can be written as $\Gamma \Rightarrow \Delta, B$. Let U_0 be $\Gamma, \Sigma \Rightarrow \Delta, \Pi$. Then,
   (1) $U \in [U_0 \hookleftarrow_B^r T]$,
   (2) U_0 has a derivation d'_0 from $U_1, \ldots, U_k \in \{S_1, \ldots, S_n, T_1, \ldots, T_m\}^s$ only using structural rules and $\{A\}^s$-cuts, being (R) reductive. In particular, no rule introducing B in the consequent is used in d'_0.
   By hypothesis, each S_i ($i = 1, \ldots, n$) has a derivation δ_i from $\mathcal{S}_0 \cup \mathcal{T}$ with cut-rank $< |B|$ and and $\#_B^r(\delta_i) < \#_B^r(d_1)$. By Lemma 3, each U_i has a derivation $d'_i, \mathcal{S}_0 \cup \mathcal{T} \vdash_{\mathcal{L}} U_i$ with $\rho(d'_i) < |B|$ and $\#_B^r(d'_i) < \#_B^r(d_1)$ for $1 \leq i \leq k$. Therefore by plugging $d'_1, \ldots, d'_k$ into d'_0, we obtain a derivation $d', \mathcal{S}_0 \cup \mathcal{T} \vdash_{\mathcal{L}} U_0$ with $\rho(d') < |B|$ and $\#_B^r(d') < \#_B^r(d_1)$. The required derivation for U can be obtained by (1) and the inductive hypothesis.   □

To reduce any cut on a compound formula we use a similar argument as in the previous lemma. Here we need more care of the parameter on which the induction proceeds. To this aim we consider the *marking* (or *decoration*, see [2]) of some formulae occurring in a derivation. Let us fix a formula $B \equiv \star x(A)$. A *marked sequent* is a sequent with some (possibly zero) underlined occurrences of B in the antecedent. A *marked derivation* d consists of marked sequents, with the following proviso:

(!) for any instance of a rule (R) used in d and any occurrence of B in the conclusion of (R) which instantiates a meta-variable X, if that occurrence is marked, so are all occurrences of B in the premises which instantiate X.

Given a not marked sequent $S \equiv \Gamma \Rightarrow \Delta, B$ and a marked sequent T, $[T \hookleftarrow_{\underline{B}}^l S]$ stands for $\{\Gamma^\lambda, \Sigma \Rightarrow \Delta^\lambda, \Pi \mid T \equiv \underline{B}^\lambda, \Sigma \Rightarrow \Pi$ with $\lambda \geq 0\}$. (Notice that Σ may contain other occurrences of $\underline{B}$.) Finally, let $\#_{\underline{B}}^l(d)$ be the maximal number of logical rules introducing *marked* occurrences of B on the left side on any branch of d.

Lemma 5 (Compound formulae). *Let B be any compound formula, T be a marked sequent in which some occurrences of B in the antecedent are marked and $d_2, \mathcal{S}_0 \vdash_{\mathcal{L}} T$ be a marked derivation. Assume $d_1, \mathcal{S}_0 \vdash_{\mathcal{L}} S$ (d_1 and S are not marked) where $\rho(d_1), \rho(d_2) < |B|$. Then, each $U \in [T \hookleftarrow_{\underline{B}}^l S]$ has a marked derivation $d, \mathcal{S}_0 \vdash_{\mathcal{L}} U$ with $\rho(d) < |B|$ and $\#_{\underline{B}}^l(d) \leq \#_{\underline{B}}^l(d_2)$.*

Proof. Proceed by a double induction on $(\sharp_{\underline{B}}^l(d_2), |d_2|)$.

Base case: $|d_2| = 1$. T is either an identity axiom or $(B \notin T$ and$)$ $T \in \mathcal{S}_0$. Then U is either S or T, and the required derivation d is either d_1 or just consists of T. In both cases, we have $\rho(d) < |B|$ and $\sharp_{\underline{B}}^l(d_1) = 0$. Hence our claim holds.

Inductive case: $|d_2| > 1$. If $U \equiv T$, the claim is trivial. Otherwise, assume that d_2 ends with an instance of a rule (R) with premises $T_1, \ldots, T_m$ and conclusion T. Two cases can arise:

(Case 1) (R) is not a left logical rule introducing a marked occurrence of B. This case is similar to (Case 1) in the proof of Lemma 4.

(Case 2) Otherwise, we may assume that T is of the form $\underline{B}, \Sigma \Rightarrow \Pi$ and S of the form $\Gamma \Rightarrow \Delta, B$. Let U_0 be $\Gamma, \Sigma \Rightarrow \Delta, \Pi$. Then any $U \in [T \hookleftarrow_{\underline{B}}^l S]$ other than T also belongs to $[U_0 \hookleftarrow_{\underline{B}}^l S]$. Hence it is enough to find a derivation $d, \mathcal{S}_0 \vdash_{\mathcal{L}} U_0$ with $\rho(d) < |B|$ and $\sharp_{\underline{B}}^l(d) < \sharp_{\underline{B}}^l(d_2)$. The claim will then be established by the inductive hypothesis.

Let us replace the principal formula $\underline{B}$ by B and each context formula $C(\boldsymbol{y})$ (resp. marked context formula $\underline{C}(\boldsymbol{y})$) in $T, T_1, \ldots, T_m$ with free variables $\boldsymbol{y}$ by a fresh atomic formula $\langle C \rangle(\boldsymbol{y})$ (resp. $\langle \underline{C} \rangle(\boldsymbol{y})$) to obtain sequents $\langle T \rangle, \langle T_1 \rangle, \ldots, \langle T_m \rangle$. In particular, $\langle T \rangle$ is of the form $B, \langle \Sigma \rangle \Rightarrow \langle \Pi \rangle$ and $\langle T_1 \rangle, \ldots, \langle T_m \rangle / \langle T \rangle$ is an instance of (R) in which context formulas are atomic. Since $\langle U_0 \rangle \equiv \Gamma, \langle \Sigma \rangle \Rightarrow \Delta, \langle \Pi \rangle \in [S \hookleftarrow_B^r \langle T \rangle]$, Lemma 4 implies that there is a derivation $d_0, \mathcal{S}_0 \cup \{\langle T_1 \rangle, \ldots, \langle T_m \rangle\}^s \vdash \langle U_0 \rangle$ with $\rho(d_0) < |B|$ and $\sharp_{\underline{B}}^l(d_0) = 0$ (since d_0 does not contain any $\underline{B}$). From this, we can easily obtain a derivation $d_0', \mathcal{S}_0 \cup \{T_1, \ldots, T_m\}^s \vdash_{\mathcal{L}} U_0$ with the same property. On the other hand, by hypothesis and Lemma 3 any $U' \in \{T_1, \ldots, T_m\}^s$ has a derivation $d', \mathcal{S}_0 \vdash_{\mathcal{L}} U'$ with $\rho(d') < |B|$ and $\sharp_{\underline{B}}^l(d') < \sharp_{\underline{B}}^l(d_2)$. Hence by plugging them into d_0', we obtain the required derivation d for U_0.   □

Lemma 6 (Atomic formulae). *(i) Suppose that a sequent S has a cut-free derivation d_1 from $\mathcal{S}_0$ and $T \in \mathcal{S}_0$. Then, for any atomic formula A and any $c \in \{l, r\}$, each $U \in [S \hookleftarrow_A^c T]$ has a cut-free derivation from $\mathcal{S}_0$.*

(ii) Let d_1 and d_2 be cut-free derivations of $d_1, \mathcal{S}_0 \vdash_{\mathcal{L}} S$ and $d_2, \mathcal{S}_0 \vdash_{\mathcal{L}} T$ and A be an atomic formula. Then, each $U \in [T \hookleftarrow_A^l S]$ (resp. each $U \in [S \hookleftarrow_A^r T]$) has a cut-free derivation $d, \mathcal{S}_0 \vdash_{\mathcal{L}} U$ provided that no sequent of the form $A, A, \Sigma \Rightarrow \Pi$ (resp. $\Gamma \Rightarrow \Delta, A, A$) belongs to $\mathcal{S}_0$.

Proof. (i) Proceeds by induction on $|d_1|$, similarly as (Case 1) in the proof of Lemma 4. (ii) Proceeds by induction on $|d_2|$ (resp. $|d_1|$). When $|d_2| = 1$, then T is an identity axiom or $T \in \mathcal{S}_0$. If $U \equiv T$ or $U \equiv S$ the claim is trivial. Otherwise, since T does not contain more than one occurrence of A in the antecedent, $U \in [T \hookleftarrow_A^l S]$ also belongs to $[S \hookleftarrow_A^r T]$. Hence the claim follows by (i). The case $|d_2| > 1$ is as before.   □

Theorem 3 (Modular Cut-Elimination). *Any standard sequent calculus $\mathcal{L}$ whose rules are weakly substitutive and whose logical rules are reductive admits modular cut-elimination.*

Proof. Let $\mathcal{S}_0$ be an elementary set of non-logical axioms in $\mathcal{L}$, d a derivation in $\mathcal{L}$ from $\mathcal{S}_0$ with $\rho(d) > 0$. The proof proceeds by a double induction on $(\rho(d), n\rho(d))$, where

$n\rho(d)$ is the number of cuts in d with cut rank $\rho(d)$. Let us take in d an uppermost cut with cut rank $\rho(d)$. Let $d_1, S_0 \vdash_{\mathcal{L}} \Gamma \Rightarrow \Delta, A$ and $d_2, S_0 \vdash_{\mathcal{L}} A, \Sigma \Rightarrow \Pi$ its premises.

When A is not atomic, let d_2' be a marking of d_2 in which the indicated A is marked, and apply Lemma 5 to d_1 and d_2'. When A is atomic, apply Lemma 6 (ii) to d_1 and d_2 (by Definition 4, multiple copies of A cannot occur both in the antecedent and consequent positions of any sequent in S_0). In any case, either $\rho(d)$ or $n\rho(d)$ decreases.   □

When a standard sequent calculus satisfies some additional properties, weak substitutivity and reductivity *characterize* modular cut-elimination:

Corollary 1. *Let $\mathcal{L}$ be a standard sequent calculus satisfying* **(log2)** *and* **(log3)**. *Then $\mathcal{L}$ admits modular cut-elimination if and only if all rules are weakly substitutive and all logical rules are reductive.*

Theorem 3 allows us to prove cut-elimination for a given standard sequent calculus in an "incremental" way:

Corollary 2 (Modularity). *Let $\mathcal{L}$ and $\mathcal{L}'$ be standard calculi with disjoint sets of logical connectives (and the same cut rule). Suppose that their logical rules satisfy* **(log2)** *and* **(log3)**. *If both $\mathcal{L}$ and $\mathcal{L}'$ admit modular cut elimination, so does $\mathcal{L} \cup \mathcal{L}'$, obtained by taking the union of logical connectives and rules in $\mathcal{L}$ and $\mathcal{L}'$.*

Remark 5. The same result does not hold for cut-elimination. E.g. let $\mathcal{L}_1'$ be the calculus containing exchange and the rules for implication in linear logic. $\mathcal{L}_1'$ admits cut-elimination and so does (trivially) the calculus $\mathcal{L}_1$ of Example 5 (the only sequents provable in $\mathcal{L}_1$ are instances of identity axioms) while $\mathcal{L}_1 \cup \mathcal{L}_1'$ does not anymore.

Our modular cut-elimination procedure is 'universal' for standard sequent calculi with additional conditions in the following sense:

Corollary 3. *Let $\mathcal{L}$ be a standard sequent calculus satisfying* **(log2)** *and* **(log3)**. *If $\mathcal{L}$ admits modular cut-elimination and $\vdash_{\mathcal{L}} S$, the procedure described in this section always provides a cut-free derivation in $\mathcal{L}$ for S.*

Remark 6. The same does not hold for cut-elimination and e.g. the procedures of Gentzen [4] and Schütte-Tait [10,9]. Indeed, Gentzen's cut-elimination method can be applied only when suitable "ad hoc" (derivable) generalizations of the cut rule (e.g. Gentzen's mix) are found. These generalizations, needed to cope with rules duplicating formulas (e.g. contraction), are not needed for the Schütte-Tait method whose applicability relies on the inversion of (at least) one of the premises of the cut. This cannot always be done in calculi that admit cut-elimination. For example let $\mathcal{L}_2$ be the calculus consisting of weakening, exchange and the following rules:

$$\frac{\Theta \Rightarrow X_1 \quad \Theta' \Rightarrow X_2}{\Theta, \Theta' \Rightarrow X_1 \wedge X_2} \; (\wedge, r) \qquad \frac{\Theta, X_i \Rightarrow Y}{\Theta, X_1 \wedge X_2 \Rightarrow Y} \; (\wedge, l)_{i=1,2}$$

$\mathcal{L}_2$ admits cut-elimination (e.g. using our method: it is easy to check that these rules are reductive and weakly substitutive) although neither of the premises of a cut with cut formula $A \wedge B$ can be inverted in the usual way and hence the Schütte-Tait procedure does not apply.

7   Counterexamples to (Modular) Cut-Elimination

We have introduced syntactic criteria (weak substitutivity and reductivity) that when met by a standard sequent calculus $\mathcal{L}$, $\mathcal{L}$ admits modular cut-elimination. If the logical rules of $\mathcal{L}$ satisfy (**log2**) and (**log3**) our conditions are also necessary and hence a *counterexample for modular cut-elimination* (i.e. a derivation in $\mathcal{L}$ from an elementary set of sequents in which cuts cannot be eliminated) can be extracted from their failure.

Now, what can we say about plain cut-elimination? The failure of weak substitutivity or reductivity for a standard calculus $\mathcal{L}$ is not enough to conclude that $\mathcal{L}$ does not admit cut-elimination, being modular cut-elimination a notion strictly stronger than cut-elimination (e.g. both **LJ'** and $\mathcal{L}_1$ admit cut-elimination although they do not admit modular cut-elimination, see Examples 3, 5 and Remark 5).

Our conditions are however useful for pinning down the difficulty of (dis)proving cut-elimination and reduce the search space when finding counterexamples for cut-elimination (or cut-admissibility). Indeed

Definition 10. *Let $\mathcal{L}$ be a standard sequent calculus. The following derivations d in $\mathcal{L}$ are called* candidates of counterexamples *for $\mathcal{L}$.*

– *Let (R) be an instance of a rule in $\mathcal{L}$ which is not weakly substitutive. Let S_0 be its conclusion and $S_1, \ldots, S_n$ its premises. Take a sequent T, a formula A, $c \in \{l, r\}$ and $U \in [S_0 \leftrightarrow^c_A T]$ which violates condition (*) of Def. 6. Then let d be the following:*

$$\frac{T \quad \dfrac{S_1 \quad \cdots \quad S_n}{S_0}}{U} \ (CUT)$$

– *Let $\star$ be a connective in $\mathcal{L}$ whose rules are not reductive. Take a pair of instances of left and right logical rules with conclusions $\Gamma \Rightarrow \Delta, \star x(A)$ and $\star x(A), \Sigma \Rightarrow \Pi$ which violates the condition $(\star)$ of Def. 8. Then let d be the following:*

$$\frac{\dfrac{S_1 \quad \cdots \quad S_n}{\Gamma \Rightarrow \Delta, \star x(A)} \quad \dfrac{T_1 \quad \cdots \quad T_m}{\star x(A), \Sigma \Rightarrow \Pi}}{\Gamma, \Sigma \Rightarrow \Delta, \Pi} \ (CUT)$$

A candidate of counterexamples $d, U_1, \ldots, U_n \vdash_{\mathcal{L}} U_0$ is resolvable *if whenever $U_1, \ldots, U_n$ are provable in $\mathcal{L}$, U_0 is cut-free provable in $\mathcal{L}$.*

Example 6. The rule $(\rightarrow, r, \emptyset)$ is weakly substitutive neither in Maehara's **LJ'** nor in **GD** (see Example 3). A candidate of counterexamples for **LJ'** and **GD**, that is also a counterexample for modular cut-elimination is then provided by any cut-free derivable sequent with one implicative formula on its right end side, e.g. $D \Rightarrow C \rightarrow D$ and any set of non-logical axioms containing the sequent $\Gamma \Rightarrow D, \Delta$, for any Δ that contains at least one formula. This counterexample for modular cut-elimination can be easily turned into a *counterexample for cut-elimination* in **GD** by suitably choosing Γ, Δ and D such that $\vdash_{\mathbf{GD}} \Gamma \Rightarrow D, \Delta$ while $\vdash_{\mathbf{GD}} \Gamma \Rightarrow C \rightarrow D, \Delta$ only using (CUT). E.g. take $\Gamma \equiv \forall x(P(x) \vee B)$, $D \equiv \forall x P(x)$ and $\Delta \equiv B$, it is easy to see that the sequent $\forall x(P(x) \vee B) \Rightarrow C \rightarrow \forall x P(x), B$ is not cut-free derivable in **GD** while a derivation with (CUT) is as follows:

$$\dfrac{\dfrac{\dfrac{\dfrac{P(a) \Rightarrow P(a) \quad B \Rightarrow B}{P(a) \vee B \Rightarrow P(a), B}\ (\vee,\text{l})}{\forall x(P(x) \vee B) \Rightarrow P(a), B}\ (\forall,\text{l})}{\forall x(P(x) \vee B) \Rightarrow \forall x P(x), B}\ (\forall,\text{r}) \qquad \dfrac{\dfrac{\forall x P(x) \Rightarrow \forall x P(x)}{\forall x P(x), C \Rightarrow \forall x P(x)}\ (\text{w},\text{l})}{\forall x P(x) \Rightarrow C \rightarrow \forall x P(x)}\ (\rightarrow,\text{r})}{\forall x(P(x) \vee B) \Rightarrow C \rightarrow \forall x P(x), B}\ (\text{CUT})$$

This proves that **GD** does not admit cut-elimination (in contrast with the claim in [5]).

Notice that all candidates of counterexamples are resolvable in **LJ'**. Indeed, a careful inspection of the modular cut-elimination proof shows:

Theorem 4. *Let $\mathcal{L}$ be a standard sequent calculus for which either weak substitutivity or reductivity fails. Then $\mathcal{L}$ admits cut-elimination if and only if all candidates of counterexamples for $\mathcal{L}$ are resolvable.*

To conclude, although our conditions do not directly yield a counterexample for cut-elimination, they do provide the class of candidates among which, if a standard calculus does not admit cut-elimination, such a counterexample can be found.

References

1. S. Buss. An Introduction to Proof Theory. *Handbook of Proof Theory*, Elsevier Science, pp. 1–78, 1998.
2. A. Ciabattoni. Automated Generation of Analytic Calculi for Logics with Linearity. *Proceedings of CSL'04*, vol. 3210 LNCS, pp. 503–517, 2004.
3. A. Ciabattoni and K. Terui. Towards a semantic characterization of cut-elimination. *Studia Logica*. Vol. 82(1). pp. 95 - 119. 2006.
4. G. Gentzen. Untersuchungen über das logische Schliessen I, II. *Mathematische Zeitschrift*, 39: 176–210, 405–431. 1934.
5. E. G. K. Lopez-Escobar. On the Interpolation Theorem for the Logic of Constant Domains. *J. Symb. Log.*. 46(1). pp. 87-88. 1981.
6. D. Miller and E. Pimentel, Tableaux'02, LNAI, Using Linear Logic to reason about sequent systems, 2-23, 2002.
7. F. Pfenning. Structural Cut Elimination: I. Intuitionistic and Classical Logic. *Inf. Comput.* 157. pp. 84-141. 2000.
8. G. Restall. *An Introduction to Substructural Logics*. Routledge, London, 1999.
9. K. Schütte. *Beweistheorie*. Springer Verlag. 1960.
10. W.W. Tait. Normal derivability in classical logic. In *The Sintax and Semantics of infinitary Languages*, LNM 72, 204–236. 1968.
11. G. Takeuti. *Proof Theory*, 2nd edition, North-Holland, 1987.
12. K. Terui. Which Structural Rules Admit Cut Elimination? — An Algebraic Criterion. To appear in *Journal of Symbolic Logic*.
13. A. S. Troelstra and H. Schwichtenberg. *Basic Proof Theory (2nd Edition)*. Cambridge Tracts in Theoretical Computer Science, Cambridge University Press, 2000.
14. A. Zamanski and A. Avron. Cut-Elimination and Quantification in Canonical Systems. *Studia Logica*, Vol. 82(1), pp. 157–176. 2006.
15. A. Zamanski and A. Avron. Canonical Gentzen-type calculi with (n,k)-ary quantifiers. *Proceedings of IJCAR'06*. To appear.

An Executable Formalization
of the HOL/Nuprl Connection
in the Metalogical Framework Twelf[*]

Carsten Schürmann[1] and Mark-Oliver Stehr[2]

[1] Yale University, Department of Computer Science
51 Prospect St., New Haven, CT 06520, USA
carsten@cs.yale.edu
[2] University of Illinois at Urbana Champaign, Siebel Center for Computer Science
201 N. Goodwin, Urbana, IL 61801, USA
stehr@cs.uiuc.edu

Abstract. Howe's HOL/Nuprl connection is an interesting example of a translation between two fundamentally different logics, namely a typed higher-order logic and a polymorphic extensional type theory. In earlier work we have established a proof-theoretic correctness result of the translation in a way that complements Howe's semantics-based justification and furthermore goes beyond the original HOL/Nuprl connection by providing the foundation for a proof translator. Using the Twelf logical framework, the present paper goes one step further. It presents the first rigorous formalization of this treatment in a logical framework, and hence provides a safe alternative to the translation of proofs.

1 Introduction

Doug Howe's HOL/Nuprl connnection [7,10] establishes a link between two very different logics, namely the classical logic of the HOL system [5] and a classical variant of the Nuprl type theory [4], so that formal developments in Nuprl can integrate theorems or entire libraries developed in HOL.

Based on a proof-theoretic understanding of the HOL/Nuprl connection obtained in earlier work [20], we present a rigorous formalization of the relevant parts of HOL and Nuprl as deductive systems, and a foundational transformation between the two in the logical framework Twelf [16]. Both encodings of the deductive systems are adequate, the transformation is executable and machine-verified, using Twelf's termination [17], coverage [18], and uniquness checker [2].

According to [20], the HOL/Nuprl connection as it was originally implemented in [11] proceeds in two stages:

1. The first stage is a *translation* of an *axiomatic HOL theory* into an *axiomatic Nuprl theory*. The use of the term "axiomatic" emphasizes the fact that the

---

[*] This research has been funded in part by the NSF grants CCR-0325808 and CCR-0133502 and the ONR Grant N00014-02-1-0715.

M. Hermann and A. Voronkov (Eds.): LPAR 2006, LNAI 4246, pp. 150–166, 2006.

theories are not necessarily only definitional extensions of the base logic. The translation is, by its very nature, metalogical, in the sense that, by relating two different logics, it is semantically beyond the scope of each of them.[1] It is a critical stage whose correctness has not been reduced to that of the two theorem provers involved and requires careful analysis.

2. The second stage is the *interpretation* of an axiomatic Nuprl theory inside Nuprl. In this way we can often obtain a *computationally meaningful* theory, which is closer to the spirit of Nuprl, that favors definitional extensions. As in Howe's extension of Nuprl, this interpretation stage can take place inside the Nuprl system in a formally rigorous way.

The key correctness property established in [20] is the soundness of the translation. If $\mathcal{L}$ and $\mathcal{L}'$ are the source and target logics, respectively, and α is the mapping of $\mathcal{L}$ into $\mathcal{L}'$ then *soundness* is the property that $\Gamma \vdash_{\mathcal{L}} P$ implies $\alpha(\Gamma) \vdash_{\mathcal{L}'} \alpha(P)$ for any set Γ of axioms and any formula P. Hence, a proof of soundness would demonstrate that for each proof of P from Γ in $\mathcal{L}$ there is a corresponding proof of $\alpha(P)$ from $\alpha(\Gamma)$ in $\mathcal{L}'$. Although soundness is a necessary requirement for the correctness of the translator, it is noteworthy that soundness can always be achieved by extending the target system by additional axioms and inference rules. Of course, such an extension could make the target system inconsistent, which is why the soundness proof is meaningful only in the presence of a consistency proof for the target system extension, which for the classical variant of Nuprl has been achieved by Howe's hybrid computational/set-theoretic semantics [8,9].

It has been recognized in [20] that, since the soundness proof is conducted in a constructive way, it implicitly contains an algorithm for proof translation. In fact, a proof translator based on our earlier study has been developed by Pavel Naumov as an extension of the Nuprl system [13]. In spite of the high degree of safety achieved by translating proofs, we have found that, computationally, proof translation can be very expensive if the proofs are large and unstructured.

An unexplored alternative, which guarantees absolute assurance, is formal verification. This paper can be seen as a first step in that direction by giving a fully formal account of the translation and its correctness proof in the logical framework of Twelf. The translation is completely independent of tactics; one translates concrete and efficient encodings of HOL derivations into Nuprl derivations instead of heuristic recipes or methods. The resulting Twelf specification is executable, and hence constitutes a uniform certified translator that can translate theories as well as proofs.

In summary we present in this paper a lightweight formalization of [20] with a few simplifications: (1) We do not make explicit the categorical structure, e.g. the fact that the translation constitutes a natural transformation. (2) We use higher-order abstract syntax to represent terms in the object logics HOL and Nuprl. (3) We use signatures of the metalogical framework Twelf to uniformly represent

---

[1] Syntactially, however, the formal systems and the translation can be represented using a metalogic, which could be a metalogical framework like Twelf in this paper or even one of the object logics, Nuprl or HOL. In the latter case one would speak of a reflective approach (see e.g. [3] for some recent advances on reflection in Nuprl).

signatures and theories of the object logics. (4) Without loss of generality we work with a simplified notion of sentences that are obtained from sequents by a universal closure. (5) We confine ourselves to a fixed HOL theory (namely the logical theory of HOL) and represent the composition of theory translation and the subsequent theory interpretation by a single function.

The paper is organized as follows. After a brief introduction to Twelf we give representations of the objects logics HOL and Nuprl in Sections 3 and 4, respectively. Then, in Section 5, we present the translation as formalized in Twelf, followed by Section 6, which establishes its correctness. Details about the formalization of Nuprl and selected Twelf proofs can be found in [19].

2   The Twelf Logical Framework

The Twelf logical framework is an implementation of LF [6] designed as a meta-language for the representation of deductive systems and used in this work for representing the relevant rules of HOL and Nuprl. Judgments are represented as types, and derivations as objects leading to the three standard syntactical categories of the Twelf system.

$$\begin{array}{lll} \text{Kinds:} & K & ::= \; \texttt{type} \; | \; \Pi x{:}A. \; K \; | \; A \to K \\ \text{Types:} & A, B & ::= \; a \; | \; A \, M \; | \; \Pi x{:}A. \; B \; | \; A \to B \\ \text{Objects:} & M & ::= \; c \; | \; \texttt{x} \; | \; \lambda x{:}A. \; M \; | \; M_1 \, M_2 \end{array}$$

We write a for type level constants (also called type families), and c for object level constants. Type-level constants and object-level constants declarations form signatures in Twelf, and thus, the entire formal development of the HOL-Nuprl connection can be thought of as one signature that we explain piece by piece. Type constants are declared in form of declarations "$a \; : \; K$.", and object level constant are either declared "$c \; : \; A$.", or defined "$c \; : \; A = M$." Constants c may be be used infix.

Among the many algorithms that Twelf offers, we comment only on the most important that are directly relevant to the formalization of the HOL-Nuprl connection. The type inference algorithm [15] permits inferable arguments to remain implicitly Π-quantified indicated by logic variables that start with an uppercase letter. The logic programming engine Elf [15] as part of Twelf defines an operational interpration of the Twelf signature. For example, a type $\texttt{a} \; M_1 \; \texttt{X}$ defines a query, whose execution results in an object M and an instantiation M_2 of $\texttt{X}$, such that $M \; : \; \texttt{a} \; M_1 \; M_2$ holds. Twelf's mode system [17] assigns input/output roles to arguments of type families. For example a declaration $\%\texttt{mode} \; a \; \texttt{+X} \; \texttt{-Y}$ indicates that the first argument to a plays the role of an input, and the second the role of an output. Furthermore, once modes are declared, the logic program can be checked for termination, coverage and totality properties [17,18].

3   The Logic of HOL

HOL [5] is a proof development system based on higher-order logic. It uses a Hindley-Milner-style polymorphic λ-calculus together with an axiomatization of the logic using polymorphic equality, implication, and Hilbert's choice operator as basic ingredients. As most higher-order logics it is a logic of total functions. The HOL system favors conservative theory extensions (to introduce new constants and/or new data types) but axiomatic extensions are also supported. The following higher-order abstract syntax representation of HOL in Twelf is close to the informal presentation of [5].

3.1 Syntax

We introduce a Twelf type tp to represent the set of *HOL types* σ with o representing the type of *HOL formulas* and infix operator `-->` the *HOL function type* constructor.

```
tp : type.    --> : tp → tp → tp.    o : tp.
```

A dependent Twelf type tm σ is used to represent the set of *HOL terms* (including *HOL formulas*) over a given HOL type σ with => representing *logical implication*, == representing *polymorphic equality*, @ representing *polymorhic function application*, and \ representing *polymorphic λ-abstraction*. Since => and == represent HOL constants, we also introduce convenience functions ==> and === that can be directly applied as infix operators to HOL formulas/terms.

```
tm  : tp → type.
=>  : tm (o --> o --> o).
==  : tm (A --> A --> o).
@   : tm (A --> B) → tm A → tm B.
\   : (tm A → tm B) → tm (A --> B).
==> : tm o → tm o → tm o
    = λH:tm o. λG:tm o. => @ H @ G.
=== : tm A → tm A → tm o
    = λH:tm A. λG:tm A. == @ H @ G.
```

HOL theories, more precisely their signatures, provide a way to extend the syntax of HOL by additional constants. We define an *HOL type constant declaration* as a Twelf declaration of the form $c :$ tp $\rightarrow$ tp $\rightarrow \ldots \rightarrow$ tp. An *HOL constant declaration* is a Twelf declaration of the form $c : \varPi\alpha_1 :$ tp. $\ldots \varPi\alpha_n :$ tp. σ, where σ is an HOL type over $\alpha_1 \ldots \alpha_n$ and where each type variable α_i occurs in σ. An *HOL signature* Σ is a Twelf signature consisting of *HOL type constant declarations* and *HOL constant declarations*. The categoy of HOL signatures equipped with the standard notion of signature morphism (see [20]) will be denoted by **HolSign**.

An *HOL sentence* over Σ has the form $\varPi\alpha_1 :$ tp. $\ldots \varPi\alpha_n :$ tp. A with an HOL formula A over $\alpha_1 \ldots \alpha_n$. The set of sentences over a given HOL signature Σ is denoted by $HolSen(\Sigma)$. This notion of an HOL sentence is less general than that of an HOL sequent used in [5], but it is sufficient for our purposes, because each HOL sequent can be converted into an equivalent HOL sentence of the form above by means of a universal closure.

3.2 Deduction in HOL

In this section we inductively define the *HOL derivability predicate* that characterizes all derivable HOL sentences. Using the propositions-as-types interpretation (sometimes called judgements-as-types interpretation in this setting) this predicate is formalized in Twelf as follows.

```
|- : tm o → type.
```

Each HOL deduction rule is then represented as a function in Twelf that operates on proofs of derivability. The function allows us to construct a proof of the conclusion if we provide a proof for each premise.

```
mp    : |- H → |- H ==> G → |- G.
disch : (|- H → |- G) → |- H ==> G.
refl  : |- H === H.
beta  : |- \ (λx:tm A₂. H x) @ G === H G.
sub   : ΠG:tm A → tm o. |- H₁ === H₂ → |- G H₁ → |- G H₂.
abs   : (Πx:tm A₁. |- H x === G x)
            → |- \ (λx:tm A₁. H x) === \ (λx:tm A₁. G x).
```

We do not need an explicit representation of HOL's assumption and type instantiation rules, because they are inherited from the logical framework. The latter is a special case of Twelf's substitution rule.

Given a signature Σ, the *HOL entailment relation* $(\vdash_{\Sigma}^{Hol}) \subseteq \mathcal{P}_{\text{fin}}(HolSen(\Sigma)) \times HolSen(\Sigma)$ is defined as follows: $\{\phi_1, ..., \phi_n\} \vdash_{\Sigma}^{Hol} \phi$ holds iff a proof of $|-\phi$ can be constructed from proofs of $|-\phi_1 ... |-\phi_n$ in Twelf. Using the terminology of [12], the structure (**HolSign**, $HolSen, \vdash^{Hol}$) constitutes an entailment system. We call it the *entailment system of HOL*.

3.3 Theories

An *(axiomatic) HOL theory* (Σ, Γ) consists of a signature Σ together with a set Γ of sentences over Σ called *axioms*. A signature morphism $H : \Sigma \to \Sigma'$ is said to be a *theory morphism* $H : (\Sigma, \Gamma) \to (\Sigma', \Gamma')$ iff $\Gamma' \vdash_{\Sigma'}^{Hol} HolSen(H)(\phi)$ for all $\phi \in \Gamma$. This gives a category of theories that will be denoted by **HolTh**.

All mathematical developments in HOL take place in *standard theories* extending the *logical theory* bool. Therefore, for the remainder of this paper we define bool as o, and we use bool to emphasize that we are working with classical extensional logic. The logical theory bool has a signature Σ which contains the standard type constant bool (i.e. o) and the standard constants == and =>. The remaining constants of Σ together with their definitional axioms in Γ are:

```
true  : tm bool = \ (λx:tm bool. x) === \ (λx:tm bool. x).
all|   : tm ((A --> bool) --> bool)
         = \ (λP:tm (A --> bool). P === \ (λx:tm A. true)).
all   = λP:tm (A --> bool). all| @ P.
false : tm bool = all (\ (λP:tm bool. P)).
```

```
neg   : tm (bool --> bool) = \ (λP:tm bool. P ==> false).
/|\   : tm (bool --> bool --> bool)
      = \ (λP. \ (λQ. all (\ (λR. (P ==> Q ==> R) ==> R)))).
/\    = λP:tm bool. λQ:tm bool. /|\ @ P @ Q.
\|/   : tm (bool --> bool --> bool)
      = \ (λP. \ (λQ. all (\ (λR. (P ==> R) ==> (Q ==> R) ==> R)))).
\/    = λP:tm bool. λQ:tm bool. \|/ @ P @ Q.
the|  : tm ((A --> bool) --> A).
the   = λP:tm (A --> bool). the| @ P.
ex|   : tm ((A --> bool) --> bool)
      = \ (λP:tm (A --> bool). P @ the (\ (λx:tm A. P @ x))).
ex    = λP:tm (A --> bool). ex| @ P.
```

We use the symbols /|\ and \|/ to represent the HOL constants for conjuction and disjunction, respectively, and we introduce corresponding convenience infix operators /\ and \/ in Twelf. Similarly, we have HOL constants all|, ex|, and the| for universal and existential quantification, and Hilbert's ϵ-operator, again with their corresponding convenience functions all, ex, and the.

Moreover, there are some nondefinitional axioms in Γ, namely

```
bool-cases-ax  : |- all (\ (λx:tm bool. x === true \/ x === false)).
imp-antisym-ax : |- all (\ (λx:tm bool. all (\ (λy:tm bool.
                     (x ==> y) ==> (y ==> x) ==> x === y)))).
eta-ax         : |- \ (λx:tm A. F @ x) === F.
select-ax      : |- all (\ (λP:tm (A --> o). all (\ (λx:tm A.
                     P @ x ==> P @ the P)))).
```

Some HOL contants and axioms have been omitted, because they are unnecessary for the core fragment of the translation. These are: (1) an atomic type constant ind together with an axiom stating that ind has an infinite number of elements; and (2) some additional constants with definitional axioms facilitating the introduction of new data types in a conservative way.

Our encoding of HOL in Twelf is adequate. This means that every derivation of a sentence ϕ in HOL corresponds bijectively to an object in β-normal η-long form of type $|-\ulcorner\phi\urcorner$, where $\ulcorner\phi\urcorner$ stands for the representation of the sentence ϕ in Twelf. The reverse direction also holds. Furthermore, the encoding is compositional, in the sense, that the substitution property of HOL is captured by Twelf's built-in β-rule.

4 The Type Theory of Nuprl

Nuprl's type theory [4] is a variant of Martin-Löf's 1982 polymorphic, extensional type theory (the version contained in [14] with extensional equality). Although Nuprl has very advanced features (e.g. subset types, subtyping, quotient types, recursive types, intersection types, partial functions, and direct computation, which make these type theories rather different), semantically Nuprl can be viewed as an extension of Martin-Löf's type theory, in the sense that it has a richer variety of types and more flexible rules which give rise to a richer collection of well-typed terms.[2]

In contrast to HOL, terms in Nuprl are neither explicitly nor implicitly equipped with types. Instead types are ordinary terms, and the judgement that a type can be *assigned* to a term is a sentence in the logical language which is not decidable in general. Indeed, since Nuprl is polymorphic, a term may be associated with different types.

Even though the advanced features of Nuprl provide an important motivation for the HOL/Nuprl connection, the connection itself does not rely on features that go beyond Martin-Löf's type theory as presented in [14]. Hence, we have selected a set of rules as the basis of our formalization that can be derived in both Martin-Löf's type theory as well as in Nuprl. We do not attempt to give a complete presentation of these type theories, but we rather show that the given rules are sufficient to establish the connection to HOL. In the following we give a simplified presentation of Nuprl based on [4]. As for HOL we use a Twelf representaton based on higher-order abstract syntax.

4.1 Syntax

We introduce a Twelf type `n-tm` to represent the set of *Nuprl terms* which as discussed above also includes all potential *Nuprl types*. The subsets of well-typed Nuprl terms and types are determined by the deduction rules of Nuprl given in the next subsection.

Nuprl has the following term or type constructors. We begin with the term `uni` K representing the predicative Nuprl universe at level K. Levels are encoded by Twelf's `integer` constraint domain, which provides the usual arithmetical operations.

```
n-tm : type.    uni : integer → n-tm.
```

We use `eq` M N T to represent Nuprl's typed equality, that is M and N are equal at type T. Membership, written $N \# T$, is a derived notion in Nuprl and stands for `eq` N N T. The constant `axiom` is an element that denotes an anonymous proof in Nuprl, e.g. a proof by means of a computation or decision procedure.

```
eq     : n-tm → n-tm → n-tm → n-tm.
#      : n-tm → n-tm → n-tm = λN:n-tm. λT:n-tm. eq N N T
axiom : n-tm.
```

In the following, `pi` represents the Nuprl dependent function type constructor with the infix operator `->>` representing the special case of ordinary function types. The constants `app` and `lam` represent function application and the untyped λ-abstraction of Nuprl. For instance, we represent Nuprl's dependent function type $x : S \to T$ as $\ulcorner x : S \to T \urcorner =$ `pi` $\ulcorner S \urcorner$ $(\lambda x : \text{n-tm}.\ulcorner T \urcorner)$, where $\ulcorner x \urcorner = x$, where $\ulcorner \cdot \urcorner$ denotes the representation function into Twelf.

---

[2] For some subtle differences between Martin-Löf's type theory and Nuprl see [1].

```
pi  : n-tm → (n-tm → n-tm) → n-tm.
->> : n-tm → n-tm → n-tm = λS:n-tm. λT:n-tm. pi S (λx:n-tm. T).
app : n-tm → n-tm → n-tm.
lam : (n-tm → n-tm) → n-tm.
```

Nuprl has strong existential types (also called strong Σ-types) represented by the function **sigma** with an element constructor **pair** and projections **fst** and **snd**.

```
sigma : n-tm → (n-tm → n-tm) → n-tm.        fst : n-tm → n-tm.
pair  : n-tm → n-tm → n-tm.                 snd : n-tm → n-tm.
```

The function **+** represents the disjoint sum type constructor. It comes with left and right injections **inl** and **inr**, and a function **decide** to perform case analysis.

```
+ : n-tm → n-tm → n-tm.     inl : n-tm → n-tm.     inr : n-tm → n-tm.
decide : n-tm → (n-tm → n-tm) → (n-tm → n-tm) → n-tm.
```

Finally, we have Nuprl's singleton type **unit** with **bullet** as its only element, and the empty type **void** with a function **any** for the elimination principle.

```
void : n-tm.     any : n-tm → n-tm.     unit : n-tm.     bullet : n-tm.
```

Finally, the HOL/Nuprl connection makes use of Nuprl's subset types, here represented by the type constructor —set—. A set $\{x : T \mid P\}$ in Nuprl is then represented as $\ulcorner\{x : T \mid P\}\urcorner = $ **set** $\ulcorner T \urcorner (\lambda x : \text{n-tm}.\ulcorner P \urcorner)$ where $\ulcorner x \urcorner = x$.

```
set : n-tm → (n-tm → n-tm) → n-tm.
```

Similar to HOL, the Nuprl syntax can be extended by additional (untyped) constants. A *Nuprl signature* Σ is a Twelf signature consisting of *Nuprl constant declaration* of the form $c : \text{n} - \text{tm}$. The category of Nuprl signatures equipped with the standard notion of signature morphism (see [20]) will be denoted by **NuprlSign**. Given a signature Σ, we define *Nuprl sentences* simply as Nuprl terms over Σ (in practice these will be Nuprl types interpreted as propositions). Although this is more restrictive that the Nuprl sequents of [4], there is no loss of generality, because by universal closure each sequent can be converted to a Nuprl sentence of this form. The set of sentences over Σ is denoted by $NuprlSen(\Sigma)$.

It is worthwhile mentioning that there is another reason why the notion of Nuprl sentence is a proper specialization of the judgements admitted in [4], which (disregarding the left-hand side) take the form $\vdash T [\text{ext } P]$, the pragmatic intention being that the extraction term P is usually hidden from the user, but it can be extracted from a completed proof. In this paper we are not interested in the extraction term P. Therefore we will only use *abstract judgements* of the form $\vdash T$. We define such an abstract judgement to be derivable iff $\vdash T [\text{ext } P]$ is derivable for some P.

4.2   Deduction in Nuprl

In this section we inductively define the *Nuprl derivability predicate*. We consider derivability in the fragment of Classical Nuprl given by the inference rules below, which are either basic inference rules or trivially derivable in Nuprl. Similar to derivability in HOL we formalize the derivability predicate of Nuprl as follows:

```
!- : n-tm → type.
```

There is no need to formalize the basic Nuprl assumption, weakening, and cut rules, because they are inherited from Twelf. We begin with the representation of the rules for Nuprl's hierarchy of universes. There is a formation rule for each universe and a rule stating that the hierarchy is cummulative.

```
uni-form : J - 1 >= I → !- uni I # uni J.
uni-culm : !- T # uni I → J - 1 >= I → !- T # uni J.
```

For Nuprl's equality we have a formation rule, and rules for symmetry, transitivity and substitution. Reflexivity is a trivial consequence of the fact that membership $N \# T$ is defined as a special case of equality eq, namely as eq $N\ N\ T$.

```
equality-form  : !- N # T → !- M # T → !- T # uni K
                    → !- eq M N T # uni K.
equality-symm  : !- eq M N T → !- eq N M T.
equality-trans : !- eq M M' T → !- eq M' M" T → !- eq M M" T.
subst          : (Πx:n-tm. !- x # T → !- P x # uni K) → !- eq N N' T
                    → !- eq M M' (P N') → !- eq M M' (P N).
```

The following rule `ax-intro` implies that `axiom` serves as an anonymous proof of every membership. The next rule `ax-elim` allows us to abstract from a proof.

```
ax-intro : !- M # T → !- axiom # (M # T).
ax-elim  : !- M # T → !- T.
```

Dependent function types are at the core of Nuprl's type theory. We follow the standard scheme to first give a formation rule, which introduces the type, and then introduction and elimination rules for the elements of this type, followed by equational/computation rules.[3]

```
fun-form  : !- S # uni K → (Πx:n-tm. !- x # S → !- T x # uni K)
                 → !- pi S (λx:n-tm. T x) # uni K.
fun-intro : !- S # uni K → (Πx:n-tm. !- x # S → !- M x # T x)
                 → !- lam (λx:n-tm. M x) # pi S (λx:n-tm. T x).
fun-elim  : !- M # pi S (λx:n-tm. T x) → !- N # S
                 → !- app M N # T N.
fun-xi    : (Πx:n-tm. !- x # S → !- eq (M x) (N x) (T x))
                 → !- S # uni K
                 → !- eq (lam (λx:n-tm. M x)) (lam (λx:n-tm. N x))
                      (pi S (λx:n-tm. T x)).
```

---

[3] Instead of Nuprl's untyped computation rules, we use the weaker typed computation rules to cover Martin-Löf's type theory as well.

```
fun-beta  : (Πx:n-tm. !- x # S → !- M x # T x) → !- N # S
              → !- eq (app (lam (λx:n-tm. M x)) N) (M N) (T N).
fun-ext   : (Πx:n-tm. !- x # S → !- eq (app M x) (app N x) (T x))
              → !- N # pi S (λx:n-tm. T x)
              → !- M # pi S (λx:n-tm. T x)
              → !- eq M N (pi S (λx:n-tm. T x)).
```

For sake of brevity we have omitted the rules concerned with Σ-types and subset types, but the interested reader can find them in [19].

Nuprl has a singleton type unit with one element bullet.

```
unit-form : !- unit # uni 1.      unit-intro : !- bullet # unit.
unit-eq   : !- N # unit → !- M # unit → !- eq M N unit.
```

Finally, we have the rules for the empty type void that does not have any introduction rules, but an elimination rule that allows us to prove anything from the existence of an element in void.

```
void-form : !- void # uni 1.
void-elim : !- T # uni K → !- N # void → !- any N # T.
```

The heavily used Nuprl type boolean is defined as a disjoint union in Nuprl:

```
boolean : n-tm = unit + unit.    tt = inl bullet.    ff = inr bullet.
if = λM:n-tm.λM₁:n-tm.λM₂:n-tm. decide M (λz:n-tm. M₁) (λz:n-tm. M₂).
```

The propositions-as-types interpretation is made explicit using the following logical abbreviations. We also introduce the abbreviation nP K for uni K to emphasize that we are interpreting types in this universe in a logical way. n/\, n\/, =n=>, and n<=> are used in infix notation.

```
nP     = λk:integer. uni k.     ntrue  = unit.     nfalse = void.
n/\    = λT:n-tm. λS:n-tm. sigma T (λx:n-tm. S).
n\/    = λT:n-tm. λS:n-tm. T + S.
nall   = λT:n-tm. λS:n-tm → n-tm. pi T (λx:n-tm. S x).
nex    = λT:n-tm. λS:n-tm → n-tm. sigma T (λx:n-tm. S x).
=n=>   = λT:n-tm. λS:n-tm. pi T (λx:n-tm. S).
n~     = λT:n-tm. T =n=> nfalse.
n<=>   = λT:n-tm. λS:n-tm. (T =n=> S) n/\ (T =n=> S).
```

4.3 Classical Extension

The translation described in the next section makes use of Nuprl's operator

```
^       = λM:n-tm. if M ntrue nfalse.
^-form : ΠM:n-tm. !- M # boolean → !- ^ M # uni 1
```

which converts an element of boolean into a (propositional) type. The following properties have been proved using Twelf:

```
fact₅ : !- N # nall boolean (λx:n-tm. ^ x # nP 1).
fact₄ : !- N # nall boolean (λx:n-tm. eq x tt boolean =n=> ^ x).
fact₆ : !- N # nall boolean (λx:n-tm. ^ x =n=> eq x tt boolean).
```

For the translation of HOL's equality we wish to define a boolean polymorphic equality using Nuprl's propositional equality, but so far we do not have any means for converting a proposition into a boolean, which amounts to deciding whether a propositional type is inhabited. So we add a standard constant `inhabited` and we assume the following family of axioms stating that `inhabited` T decides if its argument, a type T in `uni` K, is inhabited, and that it returns an element of T if this is the case. Under the logical reading this assumption is known as the *axiom of the excluded middle*.

```
inhabited : n-tm.
inh-intro : !- inhabited # pi (uni K) (λx:n-tm. x + (x ->> void)).
```

Equipped with this axiom we can easily define an operator `v` casting a propositional type into a boolean value deciding the proposition:

```
v = λP:n-tm. decide (app inhabited P) (λx:n-tm. tt) (λy:n-tm. ff).
```

Recall that `decide` performs case analysis for elements of a disjoint union type. The following *casting lemmas* have been verified using Twelf:

```
v-form :  !- N # uni K → !- v N # boolean.
law₄   :  !- N # nall (nP K) (λp:n-tm. v p # boolean).
law₅   :  !- N # nall (nP K) (λp:n-tm. ^ v p =n=> p).
law₆   :  !- N # nall (nP K) (λp:n-tm. p =n=> ^ v p).
```

In complete analogy to the entailment relation of HOL we now define the *Nuprl entailment relation* $(\vdash_{\Sigma}^{Nuprl}) \subseteq \mathcal{P}_{\text{fin}}(NuprlSen(\Sigma)) \times NuprlSen(\Sigma)$ where $\{\phi_1, ..., \phi_n\} \vdash_{\Sigma}^{Nuprl} \phi$ holds iff a proof of !-ϕ can be constructed from proofs of !-ϕ_1 ... !-ϕ_n in Twelf. The structure (**NuprlSign**, $NuprlSen$, $\vdash^{Nuprl}$) constitutes an entailment system. We call it the *entailment system of Nuprl*.

4.4   Theories

An *(axiomatic) Nuprl theory* (Σ, Γ) consists of a signature Σ together with a set Γ of sentences over Σ called *axioms*. A signature morphism $H : \Sigma \to \Sigma'$ is said to be a *theory morphism* $H : (\Sigma, \Gamma) \to (\Sigma', \Gamma')$ iff $\Gamma' \vdash_{\Sigma'}^{Nuprl} NuprlSen(H)(\phi)$ for all $\phi \in \Gamma$. This gives a category of theories that will be denoted by **NuprlTh**.

Our encoding of Nuprl and its classical extension in Twelf are adequate. As in the case of HOL, this means that every derivation of a sentence ϕ in Nuprl corresponds bijectively to an object in β-normal η-long form of type !- ϕ, where ϕ stands for the representation of the sentence ϕ in Twelf. The reverse direction also holds. Again, the encoding is compositional, in the sense, that the substitution property of Nurpl is captured by Twelf's built-in β-rule.

5   Theory Translation

In [13] the translation from HOL theories to Nuprl theories is given by a functor $\Phi : \textbf{HolSign} \to \textbf{NuprlTh}$ which translates HOL signatures into Nuprl theories together with a natural transformation $\alpha : HolSen \to NuprlSen \circ \Phi$ which translates HOL sentences into Nuprl sentences.

Since signatures of the object logics do not have a formal status in our Twelf formalization beyond being represented as Twelf signatures, we cannot express a function like Φ in our current formalization. Instead, we will show in Section 5.1 how to translate a concrete signature using the logical theory of HOL as an example. In the following, we focus on the formalization of the core translation function α, which has three main components. In the logic-programming-style of Twelf functions are represented as predicates, and uniqueness and totality are established independently.

The first component is the translation of HOL types into Nuprl types. Notice that the above HOL type o of propositions is translated classically as the Nuprl data type `boolean`. The `%mode` assigns + position the role of input arguments, and - positions the role of output arguments.

```
transtp    : tp → n-tm → type.              %mode transtp +A -N.
transtp--> : transtp A T → transtp B S
                → transtp (A --> B) (pi T (λx:n-tm. S)).
transtpo   : transtp o boolean.
```

The second component of the translation function α is the translation of HOL terms into Nuprl terms:

```
transtm  : tm A → n-tm → type.              %mode transtm +H -N.
trans=>  : transtm => =p=>.
trans==  : transtp A N → transtm == (=p= N).
trans@   : transtm H T → transtm G S → transtm (H @ G) (app T S).
trans\   : transtp A N₁
             → (Πx:tm A. Πy:n-tm. transtm x y → transtm (H x) (M y))
             → transtm (\ (λx:tm A. H x)) (lam (λx:n-tm. M x)).
```

where we have employed the abbreviations (where =b=> is an infix operator)

```
=p=> = lam (λx:n-tm. lam (λy:n-tm. if x y tt)).
=b=> = λM:n-tm. λN:n-tm. app (app =p=> M) N.
=p=  = λT:n-tm. lam (λx:n-tm. lam (λy:n-tm. v (eq x y T))).
=b=  = λT:n-tm. λM:n-tm. λN:n-tm. app (app (=p= T) M) N.
```

The final component of α is the translation of HOL sentences into Nuprl sentences. Here, a Nuprl term is obtained from the translation of an HOL formula, and hence we only need to cast it into a propositional type to obtain a meaningful Nuprl sentence.

```
transsen : tm o → n-tm → type.
t-base   : transtm H M → transsen H (^ M).
```

5.1 Interpreting the Logical Theory

It might be surprising that the logical HOL theory `bool` is a theory like every other HOL theory, but that is simply the way it is implemented in the HOL system and presented in [5]. In practice, all HOL theories are extensions of `bool`, because together with the HOL inference rules this makes HOL a higher-order classical logic. In contrast to most other theories used in practice, it is noteworthy that bool is not a purely definitional theory in HOL. We follow [11] where the proof obligations have been verified inside Nuprl using the interpretation given below, but first we recall the general concept of a theory interpretation.

Given Nuprl theories (Σ, Γ) and (Σ', Γ'), we say that (Σ, Γ) is *interpreted* in (Σ', Γ') by I iff $I : (\Sigma, \Gamma) \to (\Sigma', \Gamma')$ is a theory morphism in the category **NuprlTh**. Notice that these morphisms are not necessarily axiom-preserving, since it is typically the point of such an interpretation to get rid of axioms. Instead, we have to verify $\Gamma' \vdash_{\Sigma'}^{Nuprl} NuprlSen(I)(\phi)$ for all $\phi \in \Gamma$, the sentences $NuprlSen(I)(\phi)$ are called *proof obligations*. As explained in the introduction of this paper, the activity of setting up a theory morphism and verifying the proof obligations characterizes the second stage of the HOL/Nuprl connection which requires user interaction in general.

In [20] each HOL constant is translated into a Nuprl constant with the same name. If the HOL constant is polymorphic the resulting Nuprl constant is a function representing a family of constants indexed by types. In the interpretation stage this Nuprl constant is then interpreted. In most cases the interpretation is the same constant but with an associated definitional axiom which equates the constant to a Nuprl term.

To accomplish this in Twelf for the concrete logical HOL theory bool we simply extend transtm by the composition of: (1) the translation of HOL constants into Nuprl contants and (2) the interpretation of Nuprl constants by their associated Nuprl terms. As a result, transtm represents the composition of the translation and the interpretation function in our formalization.

```
tc-true   : transtm true tt.      tc-false : transtm false ff.
tc-neg    : transtm neg (lam (λx:n-tm. if x ff tt)).
tc-/|\    : transtm /|\ (lam (λx:n-tm. lam (λy:n-tm. if x y ff))).
tc-\|/    : transtm \|/ (lam (λx:n-tm. lam (λy:n-tm. if x tt y))).
tc-all|   : transtp A T
          → transtm all| (lam (λp:n-tm. v (pi T (λx:n-tm. ^ app p x)))).
tc-ex|    : transtp A T
          → transtm ex| (lam (λp:n-tm. v (sigma T (λx:n-tm. ^ app p x)))).
```

As abbreviations we introduce inh T to express that a type T is nonempty and arb T, which picks an arbitrary element inhabiting a nonempty type T.

```
inh = λT:n-tm. nex T (λy:n-tm. ntrue).
arb = λT:n-tm. decide (app inhabited T) (λx:n-tm. x) (λx:n-tm. bullet).
arb-intro : ΠM:n-tm. !- M # (S # uni 1) n/\ inh S → !- arb S # S
```

Hilbert's choice operator the P, where P is a boolean predicate on some type A, picks an element of the subset of A specified by P if this subset is nonempty, or yields an arbitrary element of A otherwise.

```
tc-the|  : transtp A T
         → transtm the| (lam (λp:n-tm. decide (app inhabited
           (set T (λx:n-tm. ^ app p x))) (λx:n-tm. x) (λx:n-tm. arb T))).
```

Using this interpretation, all the proof obligations, i.e. the translated axioms of the HOL theory bool, can be derived in Classial Nuprl. The fact that HOL types are nonempty is critical to verify the proof obligation corresponding to the declaration of Hilbert's ϵ-operator.

6   Correctness of the Translation

The key property of a map of entailment systems [12] is soundness, i.e. the preservation of entailment. In our lightweight formalization in Twelf this boils down to `lemma5`, which is given at the end of this section. Its proof closely follows the informal proof given in [20], but instead of using the Nuprl system to prove some intermediate lemmas, all parts of the proof have been uniformly conducted in Twelf. We begin with a number of simple Nuprl lemmas:

```
refl_lemma : !- N # nall (uni 1) (λt:n-tm. nall t (λx:n-tm.
    ^ app (app (=p= t) x) x))
disch_lemma: !- N # nall boolean (λp:n-tm. nall boolean (λq:n-tm.
    (^ p =n=> ^ q) =n=> ^ (p =b=> q)))
mp_lemma   : !- N # nall boolean (λp:n-tm. nall boolean (λq:n-tm.
    ^ (p =b=> q) =n=> ^ p =n=> ^ q))
beta_lemma : !- N # nall (uni 1) (λt:n-tm.
    nall t (λx:n-tm. nall t (λy:n-tm. eq x y t =n=> ^ =b= t x y)))
beta_inv   : !- N # nall (uni 1) (λt:n-tm.
    nall t (λx:n-tm. nall t (λy:n-tm. ^ =b= t x y =n=> eq x y t)))
```

To prove soundness as expressed by `lemma5`, it remains to show that the translation of each HOL rule can be derived in Nuprl. Most of the translated inference rules have surprisingly short proofs (see [19]) in Nuprl if we use the lemmas above together with the following well-formedness lemmas for translated HOL types and HOL terms, which have been proved in Twelf by induction over HOL types and HOL terms, respectively.

```
lemma₁  :  ΠA:tp. transtp A T → type.
lemma₂  :  ΠH:tm A. ΠM:n-tm. transtm H M → type.
lemma₃  :  transtp A T → !- N # (T # uni 1) n/\ inh T → type.
lemma₄  :  transtm H N → transtp A T → !- N # T → type.

theorem₅ :  |- H → transsen H T → !- N # T → type.
```

Informally, `theorem₅` states that the translation T of each derivable HOL sentence H is inhabited in Nuprl by some term N. The proof goes by induction on the structure of the HOL derivation. In the case that the derivation ends in `|- G ==> H` by the `disch` rule, the premiss D_1 (of type `|- G → |- H`) is given as well. Two appeals to `lemma₂` yields translations TTM_1 for H to Nuprl term T_1 and TTM_2 for G to Nuprl term T_2. Since H and G are both HOL formulas, they are of type o, and consequently, `transtpo` provides the evidence that o translates to `boolean` necessary to justify two applications to `lemma₄`, which yields in turn two Nuprl proofs ND_1, ND_2 of `!- N₁ # T₁` and `!- N₂ # T₂`, respectively, for some Nuprl terms N_1 and N_2. Next, we introduce an HOL assumption u: `|- H` and the corresponding Nuprl assumption v:!- y # ^ T_1 for a fresh Nuprl term y, and appeal to the induction hypothesis on D_1 u and the proof that sentence G translates to T_2. The result is a hypothetical Nuprl derivation ND y v, which proves !- N' y # T_2 in Nuprl. By cleverly combining the derivations TTM_1 and TTM_2, and ND_1, ND_2, and ND we provide evidence for the translation of G ==> H and a proof of its derivability in Nuprl.

```
case₅₂ :
  theorem₅ (disch (λu:|- H. D₁ u))
    (t-base (trans@ (trans@ trans=> TTM₁) TTM₂))
    (=n=>-elim (nall-elim (nall-elim disch_lemma ND₁) ND₂)
      (=n=>-intro
        (boolean-if (uni-form (+>= 1 0>=0)) ND₁ ntrue-form nfalse-form)
        (λx:n-tm. λu:!- x # if T₁ unit void. ND x u)))
    ← lemma₂ H T₁ TTM₁ ← lemma₂ G T₂ TTM₂
    ← lemma₄ TTM₁ transtpo ND₁ ← lemma₄ TTM₂ transtpo ND₂
    ← (Πu:|- H. Πy:n-tm. Πv:!- y # ^ T₁.
        theorem₅ u (t-base TTM₁) v
          → theorem₅ (D₁ u) (t-base TTM₂) (ND y v)).
```

All lemmas and theorem₅ have been mechanically checked for termination, coverage, and totality. In two cases we were forced to manually verify the totality due to an incompleteness in Twelf's totality checker. The Twelf implementation is constructive, executable and by a realizability interpretation illustrates the soundness of the HOL/Nuprl connection.

7 Final Remarks

We have presented a lightweight formalization of earlier work [20] complementing Howe's semantics-based justification of the HOL/Nuprl connection with a proof-theoretic counterpart. Our correctness result does not only provide a formal proof-theoretic justification for *translating theories*, but it simultaneously provides a formalization of *proof translation* that was beyond the scope of the original HOL/Nuprl connection. A noteworthy point is that the translation does not rely on the more advanced features of Nuprl that go beyond Martin-Löf's extensional polymorphic type theory as presented in [14]. Therefore, the translation can also be regarded as a translation between HOL and a classical variant of Martin-Löf's type theory. This paper makes use of a few simplifications, but on the other hand it goes beyond [20] in the sense that is precisely spells out the rules that are sufficient to establish the logical connection. Furthermore, the entire development including some verifications that were delegated to Nuprl in [20] has been uniformly verified in Twelf. In addition to the translation, there is the logical theory interpretation stage, which seems less critical, because the associated proof obligations have been verified by Howe inside the Nuprl system. We still plan to extend our formalization to include a detailed verification of the interpretation stage in Twelf.

The feasibility of proof translation has been demonstrated by the proof translator presented in [13], but a remaining practical problem is that proof translation can be computationally very expensive, especially in view of the large size of HOL proofs generated by some HOL tactics. The approach taken in this paper is a rigorously formal certification of the translator by formalizing not only the translation function but also the deductive system of the logics involved and the soundness proof in a metalogical framework like Twelf. So instead of verifying the correctness of each single translated HOL proof in Nuprl, so to say at runtime, we have formalized our general soundness result, which enhances our confidence in the correctness of our earlier informal mathematical treatment, and hence can be regarded as a resonable safe alternative to proof translation.

One the other hand, if the high assurance of proof translation is needed, the Twelf specification can serve as a certified proof translator. However, the practical feasibility of translating actual HOL proofs in this way has not been investigated yet and is left as a possible direction for future work. Other items for future work include the explicit representation of theories as objects in Twelf as well as a more modular development that separates the two stages of theory translation and theory interpretation.

The complete formal development of the HOL/Nuprl connection in Twelf can be found at www.logosphere.org.

References

1. S. Allen. *A Non-Type-Theoretic Semantics for Type-Theoretic Language*. PhD thesis, Cornell University, September 1987.
2. Penny Anderson and Frank Pfenning. Verifying uniqueness in a logical framework. In *Proceedings of the 17th International Conference on Theorem Proving in Higher Order Logics (TPHOLs'04)*, Park City, Utah, September 2004. Springer Verlag.
3. E. Barzilay, S.F. Allen, and R. L. Constable. Practical reflection in nuprl. In P. Kolaitis, editor, *Proceedings of 18th IEEE Symposium on Logic in Computer Science, June 22 - 25, 2003, Ottawa, Canada*, 2003.
4. R. L. Constable, S. Allen, H. Bromely, W. Cleveland, et al. *Implementing Mathematics with the Nuprl Development System*. Prentice-Hall, 1986.
5. M. J. C. Gordon and Thomas F. Melham. *Introduction to HOL: A theorem proving environment for higher order logic*. Cambridge University Press, 1993.
6. Robert Harper, Furio Honsell, and Gordon Plotkin. A framework for defining logics. *Journal of the Association for Computing Machinery*, 40(1):143–184, January 1993.
7. D. J. Howe. Importing mathematics from HOL into Nuprl. In J. Von Wright, J. Grundy, and J. Harrison, editors, *Theorem Proving in Higher Order Logics, 9th International Conference, TPHOLs'96, Turku, Finland, August 26-30, 1996, Proceedings*, volume 1125 of *Lecture Notes in Computer Science*, pages 267–282. Springer Verlag, 1996.
8. D. J. Howe. Semantical foundations for embedding HOL in Nuprl. In M. Wirsing and M. Nivat, editors, *Algebraic Methodology and Software Technology*, volume 1101 of *Lecture Notes in Computer Science*, pages 85–101, Berlin, 1996. Springer-Verlag.
9. D. J. Howe. A classical set-theoretic model of polymorphic extensional type theory. Manuscript, 1997.

10. D. J. Howe. Toward sharing libraries of mathematics between theorem provers. In *Frontiers of Combining Systems, FroCoS'98, ILLC, University of Amsterdam, October 2–4, 1998, Proceedings.* Kluwer Academic Publishers, 1998.

11. D. J. Howe. Source Code of the HOL-Nuprl Translator (including Extensions to Nuprl), January 1999.

12. J. Meseguer. General logics. In H.-D. Ebbinghaus et al., editors, *Logic Colloquium'87, Granada, Spain, July 1987, Proceedings*, pages 275–329. North-Holland, 1989.

13. P. Naumov, M.-O. Stehr, and J. Meseguer. The HOL/NuPRL proof translator — A practical approach to formal interoperability. In *Theorem Proving in Higher Order Logics, 14th International Conference, TPHOLs'2001, Edinburgh, Scotland, UK, September 3–6, 2001, Proceedings*, volume 2152 of *Lecture Notes in Computer Science*, pages 329 – 345. Springer-Verlag, 2001.

14. K. Petersson, J. Smith, and B. Nordstroem. *Programming in Martin-Löf's Type Theory. An Introduction.* International Series of Monographs on Computer Science. Oxford: Clarendon Press, 1990.

15. F. Pfenning. Elf: A language for logic definition and verified meta-programming. In *Fourth Annual Symposium on Logic in Computer Science*, pages 313–322, Pacific Grove, California, June 1989. IEEE Computer Society Press.

16. F. Pfenning and C. Schürmann. System description: Twelf — a meta-logical framework for deductive systems. In H. Ganzinger, editor, *Proceedings of the 16th International Conference on Automated Deduction (CADE-16)*, pages 202–206, Trento, Italy, July 1999. Springer-Verlag LNAI 1632.

17. E. Rohwedder and F. Pfenning. Mode and termination checking for higher-order logic programs. In Hanne Riis Nielson, editor, *Proceedings of the European Symposium on Programming*, volume 1058 of *Lecture Notes in Computer Science*, pages 296–310, Linköping, Sweden, April 1996. Springer-Verlag.

18. C. Schürmann and F. Pfenning. A coverage checking algorithm for LF. In David Basin and Burkhart Wolff, editors, *Proccedings of Theorem Proving in Higher Order Logics (TPHOLs'03)*, volume 2758 of *Lecture Notes in Computer Science*, Rome, Italy, 2003. Springer-Verlag.

19. C. Schürmann and M.-O. Stehr. An executable formalization of the HOL/Nuprl connection in the metalogical framework Twelf. Technical report, Yale University, Computer Science Department, 2005. YALEU/DCS/TR-1312.

20. M.-O. Stehr, P. Naumov, and J. Meseguer. A proof-theoretic approach to HOL-Nuprl connection with applications to proof translation (extended abstract). In *WADT/CoFI'01, 15th International Workshop on Algebraic Development Techniques and General Workshop of the CoFI WG, Genova, Italy, April 1-3, 2001*, 2001. Full version available at `http://formal.cs.uiuc.edu/stehr/biblio_stehr.html` .

A Semantic Completeness Proof for TaMeD

Richard Bonichon and Olivier Hermant

Université Paris 6 - LIP6
8 rue du Capitaine Scott, 75015 Paris, France
{richard.bonichon, olivier.hermant}@lip6.fr

Abstract. Deduction modulo is a theoretical framework designed to introduce computational steps in deductive systems. This approach is well suited to automated theorem proving and a tableau method for first-order classical deduction modulo has been developed. We reformulate this method and give an (almost constructive) semantic completeness proof. This new proof allows us to extend the completeness theorem to several classes of rewrite systems used for computations in deduction modulo. We are then able to build a counter-model when a proof fails for these systems.

1 Introduction

Efficient treatment of equality and equational theories is still a challenging problem to tackle in the domain of automated theorem proving. The proof of as simple a statement as $(a + b) + ((c + d) + e) = a + ((b + c) + (d + e))$ might take a long time within a theory with the usual associativity and identity axioms if one uses an ineffective strategy. The resolving process should eventually be a deterministic and terminating method where we only have to check if the two terms are indeed the same modulo our theory. We would like to use computation (blind execution) instead of deduction (non-deterministic search), thus expressing the associativity axiom as a *rewrite rule on terms*.

Orienting equational theories through rewriting is not unusual, but *rewrite rules on propositions* are almost never considered. However it can be useful to allow them. One framework to handle such rewrite rules is deduction modulo [9]. The axiom $\forall x\, \forall y\, (x * y = 0 \iff (x = 0 \vee y = 0))$ yields by orientation the rewrite rule $x * y = 0 \rightarrow x = 0 \vee y = 0$, which is useful to prove $\exists z(a * a = z \Rightarrow a = z)$ by adapted automated deduction methods (see [2, 9]) which handle propositional rewriting by extended narrowing.

The use of both propositional and term rewrite rules in deduction modulo instead of unoriented axioms should result in a speed up in the proof search. However, deduction modulo has other interesting consequences: propositional rewrite rules like $P(a) \rightarrow \forall x P(x)$ can be used to restart the deductive process. The deduction modulo is powerful enough to express axiomatic theories such as arithmetic [11] or HOL [10] as sets of rewrite rules. Deduction modulo also produces shorter (regarding the size of the proof tree), more readable, proofs containing only purely deductive steps (the "important" ones to humans) and no computational details anymore.

M. Hermann and A. Voronkov (Eds.): LPAR 2006, LNAI 4246, pp. 167–181, 2006.

In [2], a syntactic completeness proof of a tableau method for deduction modulo (TaMeD) is given. Our semantic completeness proof sheds.

- We first recall in Sec. 2 the sequent calculus modulo as the setting of our proof-search procedure.
- Then we define in Sec. 3 a new free-variable tableau calculus with constraints as a basis for a systematic tableau construction algorithm upon which we build a completeness proof. The need for a model construction forced us to give this proof-search algorithm. This is an improvement over [2].
- Section 4 eventually presents this new semantic completeness proof. The use of general semantic methods allows us to precisely give some categories of rewrite systems for which the completeness theorem holds. It is an improvement over both [2, 9] and [19]. The completeness proofs of the first two papers assume that certain properties such as cut elimination in the sequent calculus modulo are enjoyed by the considered rewrite systems, without describing any possible candidate. More precise conditions than just cut elimination are given in this paper. The classes of rewrite systems described in Sec. 4 also subsumes those generated by the order condition of the completeness proof of [19].
- We finally illustrate our systematic tableau procedure on an example in Sec. 5 and discuss further (mainly practical) improvements.

2   Deduction Modulo for First-Order Classical Logic

We present the sequent calculus modulo we use as a basis for the tableau method. We consider first-order classical logic without equality where formulas are built using atoms, connectors $(\wedge, \vee, \neg, \Rightarrow)$ and quantifiers $(\forall, \exists)$. In the rest of the paper, formulas are denoted by capital letters such as $A, B, P, Q, ...$, (multi)sets of formulas by Γ, Δ, constants by $a, b, c, ...$, function symbols by $f, g, h, ...$, terms by $t, u, v, ...$, variables by $x, y, z, ..$, free variables by $X, Y, Z, ...$; the usual substitution avoiding capture of x by t in P is denoted $P[x := t]$. A constraint is an equation $t \approx u$ where t and u are terms to unify. An immediate subformula is defined as usual : $P(t)$ is an immediate subformula of $\forall x P(x)$ for any t. Similarly, A is an immediate subformula of $A \wedge B$, and so on. We consider *confluent* rewrite systems $(\mathcal{R})$ formed by term rewrite rules and propositional rewrite rules where left members are atomic propositions. We use the single arrow for rewriting: $\longrightarrow_{\mathcal{R}}$ is a single step, $\longrightarrow_{\mathcal{R}}^{n}$ n steps, $\longrightarrow_{\mathcal{R}}^{*}$ is the reflexive and transitive closure of $\longrightarrow_{\mathcal{R}}$. $A{\downarrow}_{\mathcal{R}}$ represents the normal form of A by a rewrite system $\mathcal{R}$. $P \equiv_{\mathcal{R}} Q$ if they have a common reduct.

A similar sequent calculus is presented in [9]. Therefore we will only exhibit a representative fragment of the rules (see Fig. 1). Extending the transformations (i.e. adding side conditions) to the whole set of rules of LK is not more difficult than what we have in Fig. 1. Notice that the side condition is not a constraint: it liberalizes the corresponding rule of LK.

$$\frac{}{P \vdash_\mathcal{R} Q} \text{ axiom if } P \equiv_\mathcal{R} Q \qquad \frac{\Gamma, P \vdash_\mathcal{R} \Delta \qquad \Gamma \vdash_\mathcal{R} Q, \Delta}{\Gamma \vdash_\mathcal{R} \Delta} \text{ cut if } P \equiv_\mathcal{R} Q$$

$$\frac{\Gamma, Q[t/x] \vdash_\mathcal{R} \Delta}{\Gamma, P \vdash_\mathcal{R} \Delta} \forall\text{-l if } P \equiv_\mathcal{R} \forall x\, Q \qquad \frac{\Gamma, P \vdash_\mathcal{R} \Delta \qquad \Gamma, Q \vdash_\mathcal{R} \Delta}{\Gamma, R \vdash_\mathcal{R} \Delta} \lor\text{-l if } R \equiv_\mathcal{R} P \lor Q$$

Fig. 1. Some inference rules of sequent calculus modulo

3 Tableaux Modulo Revisited

We introduce in this section a new version of the tableaux modulo of [2]. We use constrained a form of constrained tableaux which borrows ideas from those of [5, 6, 7, 13]. We represent tableaux as multisets of branches. A *branch* is thus a multiset of formulas written $\Gamma, \Delta....$ Γ, P denotes the multiset $\Gamma \cup \{P\}$; $\mathcal{T}|\Gamma$ stands for $\mathcal{T} \cup \{\Gamma\}$. A constrained tableau is a pair $\mathcal{T} \cdot \mathcal{C}$ of a tableau $\mathcal{T}$ and a set of unification constraints $\mathcal{C}$. A branch can be *closed* when two opposite unifiable formulas can be found on it (the base case consists in having P and $\neg P$). A tableau is closed when all its branches can be (simultaneously) closed, i.e. there is a unifier closing all branches simultaneously.

Tableaux for Deduction Modulo. We present tableaux for deduction modulo as an extension of first-order classical tableaux. We define an alternate *nondestructive* version which combines the usual tableau expansion rules (see [12, 18] for details) on formulas — called α (conjunction), β (disjunction), γ (universal) and δ (existential) — with a rule handling explicitly rewriting on terms and propositions.. Our tableau calculus works more precisely on *constrained labelled formulas*: every formula has an added label storing variables used in δ-rule for skolemization and a local constraint store which keeps track of unification constraints produced by rewriting steps. Hence formulas are written P_c^l where c is the constraint and l is the label. Note that there are two type of constraints: local constraints (attached to formulas) and global ones (attached to a tableau) which interfere only in the case of the closure rule. We also assume that variables of input formulas are renamed in order to avoid unification problems between syntactically equal but semantically independent variables.

In a γ-rule, a *globally fresh* free variable is substituted for the universally quantified variable x. This free variable is also added to the label of the formula.

In a δ-rule, the skolemization is done as follows: `sko` is a fresh Skolem function symbol whose arguments are the variables in the label of the formula. This δ-rule guarantees for example if we have the rewrite rule $x*0 \longrightarrow_\mathcal{R} 0$, the two equivalent (with respect to the rewrite rules) formulas $\forall x \exists y P(0, y)$ and $\forall x \exists y P(x*0, y)$ are skolemized in the same way.

In the `rw` rule, we add a constraint to formulas resulting of rewriting steps. It keeps track of the needed unification between the originating occurrence ω of a rewritable formula in P ($P_{|\omega}$) and the left part of the applied rewrite rule (l) if we are to use the rewritten formula ($P[r]_{|\omega}$) later in our tableau. There is still

$$\frac{\Gamma_1, \beta(P,Q)_c^l \mid ... \mid \Gamma_n}{\Gamma_1, \beta(P,Q)_c^l, P_c^l \mid \Gamma_1, \beta(P,Q)_c^l, Q_c^l \mid ... \mid \Gamma_n} \, \beta \qquad \frac{\Gamma_1, \alpha(P,Q)_c^l \mid ... \mid \Gamma_n}{\Gamma_1, \alpha(P,Q)_c^l, P_c^l, Q_c^l \mid ... \mid \Gamma_n} \, \alpha$$

$$\frac{\Gamma_1, \gamma(x,P)_c^l \mid ... \mid \Gamma_n}{\Gamma_1, P(x:=X)_c^{l\cup\{X\}}, \gamma(x,P)_c^l \mid ... \mid \Gamma_n} \, \gamma \qquad \frac{\Gamma_1, \delta(x,P)_c^l \mid ... \mid \Gamma_n}{\Gamma_1, P_c^l[\text{x}:=\text{sko}(l)], \delta(x,P)_c^l \mid ... \mid \Gamma_n} \, \delta$$

$$\frac{\Gamma_1, P_c^l \mid ... \mid \Gamma_n \cdot \mathcal{C}}{\Gamma_1, P_c^l, P_{\mathcal{K}}^l[r]_\omega \mid ... \mid \Gamma_n \cdot \mathcal{C}} \, \text{rw if } l \longrightarrow_{\mathcal{R}} r, \text{ and } \mathcal{K} = (c \cup \{P_{|\omega} \approx l\}$$

$$\frac{\Gamma_1, P_{c_1}^{l_1}, \neg P_{c_2}^{l_2} \mid ... \mid \Gamma_n \cdot \mathcal{C}}{(\Gamma_2 \mid ... \mid \Gamma_n) \cdot \mathcal{C} \cup c_1 \cup c_2 \cup \{P^{l_1} \approx P^{l_2}\}} \, \text{closure } (\odot)$$

Fig. 2. Tableau modulo expansion and closure rules

no need to put the constraints globally as we are unable to guess if the formula will be used in a closure rule. Note that no new variables are created during rewriting in deduction modulo, so there is no risk of capture.

The `closure` rule erases the closable branch provided its constraints are unifiable. It is the usual binary closure rule. Note that the labels of P and $\neg P$ need not be same (this would be the case of $P(X)$ and $\neg P(a)$), therefore we must unify some subterms of the two formulas (this is denoted by $P^{l_1} \approx P^{l_2}$) and apply the substitution to the whole tableau. The local formula constraints are transferred to the global store in `closure`. In the global constraint store, syntactically equal variables are semantically the same: what looked like possible separate branch closure might be non unifiable globally due to rigid free-variables introduced in the calculus.

There are some differences between TaMeD in [2] and these tableaux: TaMeD combines in effect a normalization procedure (yielding a kind of disjunctive normal form) of the formula which occurs *before* any application of extended narrowing and branch closure rules. Our tableau calculus here mixes formula decomposition (α, β, γ and δ rules) with closure and rewriting steps — and this allows non-atomic closure. The extended closure rule with $\mathcal{RE}$-unification of[2] constraints is now a binary closure with first-order unification constraints as $\mathcal{R}$-unification is encoded in the application of `rw`. The `rw` rule rewriting propositions do not necessitate an immediate post-decomposition of the branch it is applied on : for example, if we use $P \longrightarrow_{\mathcal{R}} Q \wedge R$ on the branch Γ, P, we keep the rewritten form $\Gamma, Q \wedge R$ instead of requiring to immediately have Γ, Q, R .

The soundness theorem holds for the following notion of model, that is a natural extension of the usual boolean model definition to deduction modulo:

Definition 1. *A boolean model is said to be a model of a rewrite system $\mathcal{R}$ if and only if for any propositions $P \equiv_{\mathcal{R}} Q$, $|P| = |Q|$. $|.|$ is then noted $|.|_{\mathcal{R}}$.*

As usual, a boolean model is mainly a total interpretation function from propositions into $\{0,1\}$ satisfying the conditions of Def. 2. In the later, the term *model* will always mean a boolean model of the considered rewrite system $\mathcal{R}$ (clear from context).

Theorem 1 (Soundness). *If Γ has a model, then we can not derive the closed tableau $\odot$ from Γ using the rules of Fig. 2.*

Proof. The proof is standard: we check by induction on the tableau derivation that any tableau rooted at Γ, at least one branch remains true in the model.   □

Systematic Tableau Generation. We now define a systematic tableau procedure which resembles the incremental closure of [13] as the first step towards our semantic completeness proof. We must ensure that our strategy is fair, which is now more complicated due to the addition of rewriting steps. We construct step by step an approximation of a complete tableau (if Γ is not provable).

First, attach a boolean (of value **true**) to the input branch. Its value will be used to alternatively use γ-rules or **rw**: ensuring completeness forces us to use them infinitely many times while remaining fair. Two orderings are used to select the formula to expand: on branches, $\mathcal{B}_1 \preceq_{\mathcal{B}} \mathcal{B}_2$ if $\text{size}(\mathcal{B}_1) \leq \text{size}(\mathcal{B}_2)$ where $\text{size}(\mathcal{B})$ returns the number of formulas on $\mathcal{B}$ and on formulas on a given branch $\mathcal{B}$, $\preceq_f$ is defined as $\alpha \prec_f \delta \prec_f \beta \prec_f \textbf{rw} \prec_f \gamma$ if $\text{boolean}(\mathcal{B}) =$**true**, and $\alpha \prec_f \delta \prec_f \beta \prec_f \gamma \prec_f \textbf{rw}$ otherwise. Now proceed as follows:

1. Tag every formula of the input branch as *unused*. If we apply α, β, δ: the considered formula becomes *used* — to forbid the same expansion again as in a destructive method — and the branch boolean is inherited by the produced branch(es). In the case of **rw** for a given rewrite rule $r \in \mathcal{R}$ used on formula P on branch $\mathcal{B}$, P is tagged as *used(r)* to forbid applying twice the same rewrite rule to it. Name b the boolean of the expanded branch, then $b \leftarrow \neg\text{boolean}(\mathcal{B})$. In any case, produced formulas are *unused*.

2. (a) On each branch, generate from unifiable formulas on it the set of constraints which can close it. Take the intersection of these local sets to get the global set of constraints which could simultaneously close the tableau. If a unifier exist for the global store then *return 'unsatisfiable'*. Otherwise if a branch can be closed *without* unification, remove it from the tableau as in the **closure** rule (and its set of constraints is also removed from the global set).

   (b) Then select the smallest expandable branch (according to $\prec_{\mathcal{B}}$) and its set S of smallest formulas according to $\prec_f$. Apply the related expansion rule on every *unused* (or unused(r) if we apply **rw** with r) formulas of S. If we could not apply any expansion *return 'satisfiable'*, else **go to 2a**.

We do not rewrite formulas when we know (we check it) that we cannot unify them with the left part of the rewrite rule. More generally we do not add in the constraint stores provably non-unifiable terms.

4   Semantic Completeness

In this section, we prove that the systematic tableau procedure of Sec. 3 is complete with respect to the models of Def. 1.

We will need to define a model interpretation for all propositions, even those that do not appear in the tableau. We also will need some conditions on $\mathcal{R}$, since the method cannot be complete for all confluent terminating rewrite systems, as shown in [10, 16]. Two of them are presented in Sec. 4.6.

4.1 Preliminaries

Semi-valuations have first been defined by Schütte, and correspond to Hintikka sets. The idea is that they correspond to open branches of the systematic tableau, and this is the first step toward a model. Partial valuations are a bottom-up extension of them. They differ from model interpretations by the fact that both are *partial* functions.

Definition 2 (Semi-valuation(Partial valuation)). *An interpretation is a partial function $V : \mathcal{P} \mapsto \{0,1\}$. It is called* semi- *(resp.* partial*) valuation iff:*

- *if $V(\neg P) = 0$ then (resp. iff) $V(P) = 1$*
- *if $V(\neg P) = 1$ then (resp. iff) $V(P) = 0$*
- *if $V(P \vee Q) = 0$ then (resp. iff) $V(P) = V(Q) = 0$*
- *if $V(P \vee Q) = 1$ then (resp. iff) $V(P) = 1$ or $V(Q) = 1$*
- *if $V(P \wedge Q) = 0$ then (resp. iff) $V(P) = 0$ or $V(Q) = 0$*
- *if $V(P \wedge Q) = 1$ then (resp. iff) $V(P) = V(Q) = 1$*
- *if $V(P \Rightarrow Q) = 0$ then (resp. iff) $V(P) = 1$ and $V(Q) = 0$*
- *if $V(P \Rightarrow Q) = 1$ then (resp. iff) $V(P) = 0$ or $V(Q) = 1$*
- *if $V(\forall x P) = 0$ then (resp. iff) for some ground term t, $V(P[x := t]) = 0$*
- *if $V(\forall x P) = 1$ then (resp. iff) for any ground term t, $V(P[x := t]) = 1$*
- *if $V(\exists x P) = 0$ then (resp. iff) for any ground term t, $V(P[x := t]) = 0$*
- *if $V(\exists x P) = 1$ then (resp. iff) for some ground term t, $V(P[x := t]) = 1$*

Definition 3 (Semi-valuation in deduction modulo). *A semi-valuation (resp. partial valuation) V is said to be compatible with a rewrite system $\mathcal{R}$ iff when $P \equiv_{\mathcal{R}} Q$ and $V(P)$ is defined, we have $V(Q) = V(P)$.*

This definition is a natural extension to deduction modulo of the previous one. The next four sections deal with the construction of a partial valuation in the sense of Def. 3.

4.2 Defining a Semi-valuation from a Complete Branch of a Tableau

Because of the free variables, the construction of a semi-valuation from an open complete branch is not so easy: their meaning is not determined once and for all, and an open branch might be closed by some unifier θ. A tableau is non closable when at any step n of our tableau construction no (finite) unifier θ can be found such that all branches can be closed at the same time.

We have to generate a σ, that enumerates all γ-terms. Remark that if a γ-formula P appears in a non closed branch of a complete tableau, then for infinitely many fresh variables X_n, $P[x := X_n]$ appears (the γ rule is infinitely repeated). Since in the open branch γ-formulas are countable, and *free variables are new when introduced*, we define an enumeration of $\langle \gamma_i, X_j^i \rangle$, the couples of a γ-formula (indexed by i) and its corresponding free variables (indexed by j). We fix also an enumeration of the terms of the full language (including the Skolem symbols introduced). Then, we define successive approximations of the needed substitution σ:

- σ_0 is the empty substitution.
- $\sigma_{n+1} = \sigma_n + \langle X_{j_n}^{i_n} := t_{j_n} \rangle$

Section 3 describes a process to construct $T_0, ..., T_n, ...$ that represent successive approximations to a complete tableau, that is a tableau where all possible rules have been applied. We supposed it non closable: hence for any n, there exists some open branch $\mathcal{B}$ of T_n under σ_n. Moreover, we can choose this branch such that for any further step of the systematic tableau procedure, it is never closed by any σ_p.

Given a formula γ, a term t, for some step n of the systematic tableau generation, $\gamma(t)$ appears on this branch, since it is also open under σ_n with n such that $t = t_{j_n}$ and $\gamma = \gamma_{i_n}$ (from the enumeration).

We obtain a complete open branch under σ that possesses all the needed properties, and we define our semi-valuation V:

- if a proposition P_c with free variables and constraints c appears on the branch, and if σ satisfies c, set $V(P\sigma) = 1$.
- if $\neg P_c$ appear with constraints c, and if σ satisfies c, set $V(P\sigma) = 0$.
- if the constraints are not satisfiable, drop the proposition.

It is easy to prove that all properties of Def. 2 for a semi-valuation hold: the constraints are not modified by the application of any of the α-, β-, γ-, δ-rules so if, say, an α-formula is interpreted by V, so are its two immediate subformulas. The semi-valuation hereby defined is well defined. Forcing a proposition to have two different interpretations, means that σ closes the branch: we cannot have $V(P\sigma) \neq V(P'\sigma)$ for $P\sigma = P'\sigma$.

4.3   Basic Results on V

We must have that V is a semi-valuation for the rewrite system $\mathcal{R}$. This is not yet the case (think about $A \to B$, $V(B)$ defined although $V(A)$ is not defined), so it has to be extended. We first need to prove some technical properties of V.

Our starting point is: the systematic tableau generation of Sec. 3 ensures that for any atomic proposition, if $P = R\sigma$ appears, then each of its one-step reduct $Q = R'\sigma$ appear, since we exhaustively try to apply rewrite rules to any atomic proposition, and if $P \to Q$, σ unifies the constraints of R'.

Lemma 1. *Let P_0, P_n atomic formulas such that $V(P_0)$ is defined and $P_0 \to^1 P_1 \to^1 \ldots \to^1 P_n \to^1 P_{n+1}$ (P_{n+1} atomic or not), with $\to^1$ the one-step reduct relation. For any $i \leq n+1$, $V(P_i)$ is defined.*

Proof. By induction on n. We first show that the one-step reduct P_1 is interpreted under V. The process of Sec. 3 tries to one-step rewrite any literal with all possible rewrite rules. So if $P_0 = R\sigma \to^1 P_1$, with R_c appearing on the tableau, there exists by construction a $R'_{c'}$ such that $P' = R'\sigma$ and the associated constraints c' are satisfied by σ (since σ satisfies c and $P \to P'$).

Hence $V(P_1)$ is defined. If $n = 0$ we are done, else we apply the induction hypothesis on $P_1 \to^1 ... \to^1 P_n \to^1 P_{n+1}$.   □

Lemma 2. *Let P, Q be two propositions such that $P \equiv_{\mathcal{R}} Q$. $V(P) = V(Q)$ if they are defined.*

Proof. By confluence there exists a proposition R such that $P \to^n R {}^m \leftarrow Q$. We prove Lemma 2 by induction on the pair $\langle n + m, \min(\#P, \#Q)\rangle$, where $\#P$ stands for P's number of logical connectors.

If $n = m = 0$, $Q = P = R$ and the result is trivial.

If P or Q is an atomic proposition (suppose it is P, without loss of generality), then $P \to^p P' \to^1 R' \to^q R$ with P' atomic. By Lemma 1, $V(R')$ is defined. We use induction hypothesis on R' and Q, since $p_2 < n$.

If both P and Q are compound propositions, remember that V is a semi-valuation and apply induction hypothesis.

For instance, if $P = \forall x S$, confluence implies $Q = \forall x S'$, and $R = \forall x S''$. Suppose that $V(P) = 1$ and $V(Q) = 0$. Then there exists a t such that $V(S'[x := t]) = 0$. But $V(S[x := t]) = 1$ by definition 2. We find a contradiction by applying induction hypothesis on $S[x := t] \to^n S''[x := t]^m \leftarrow S'[x := t]$ □

4.4   Extending V into a Semi-valuation for $\mathcal{R}$

Lemma 2 is not sufficient: to fit with Def. 3 we need to ensure that $V(Q)$ is defined whenever $V(P)$ is. So we extend the semi-valuation V into a semi-valuation $\mathcal{V}$ for $\mathcal{R}$. Fix an enumeration P_n of the propositions of the language, such that a proposition Q is seen infinitely many times (it boils down to an enumeration of $\langle Q, n\rangle$ where Q describes the propositions and n describes $\mathbb{N}$).

Set $V_0 = V$. Set $V_{n+1} = V_n$ and extend it with P_n if $V_n(P_n)$ is not defined:

1. set $V_{n+1}(P_n) = V_n(Q)$ if for some Q, $Q \equiv_{\mathcal{R}} P_n$ and $V_n(Q)$ is defined.
2. if P_n is a compound proposition, look at the interpretation under V_n of its immediate subformulas. If we have enough information, then set $V_{n+1}(P_n)$ accordingly. For instance, if $P_n = \forall x R$ and for any t, $V_n(R[x := t]) = 1$, set $V_{n+1}(P_n) = 1$. Conversely if there is at least one t such that $V_n(R[x := t]) = 0$, set $V_{n+1}(P_n) = 0$. Even if for some $t', V_n(R[x := t'])$ is not defined.

We set $\mathcal{V}$ as the limit of the V_n. $\mathcal{V}(P) = V_n(P)$, if it is defined for some n. We do not know anything yet about $\mathcal{V}$ (a compound proposition can be defined by the first rule). That's why we need the following technical lemmas, where we adopt the convention $n - 1 = n$ if $n = 0$.

Lemma 3. *Let n an integer, P an atomic formula, suppose $V_n(P)$ defined. Then there exist Q such that $P \equiv_{\mathcal{R}} Q$ and either $V(Q)$ is defined, or Q is compound and $V_{n-1}(Q)$ is defined. In any case all interpretations are equal.*

Proof. By induction on n. If $n = 0$, $V_0 = V$ and we are done. If $V_{n-1}(P)$ is defined, apply induction hypothesis. Else, since P is atomic, $V_n(P)$ is equal to $V_{n-1}(P')$ for some $P' \equiv_{\mathcal{R}} P$. If P' is a compound proposition, take $Q = P'$. If it is an atomic formula, then apply the induction hypothesis on $V_{n-1}(P')$, we find a fitting $Q \equiv_{\mathcal{R}} P' \equiv_{\mathcal{R}} P$.   □

Corollary 1. *Let P an atomic formula, such that $V_n(P)$ is defined, and that there exists a compound formula Q such that $P \equiv_{\mathcal{R}} Q$.*

Then there exists a compound formula R such that $P \equiv_{\mathcal{R}} R$ and $V_{n-1}(R)$ is defined and equal to $V_n(P)$.

Proof. Apply Lemma 3. If we obtain an atomic $S \equiv_{\mathcal{R}} P$ such that $V(S)$ is defined, we use confluence and apply Lemma 1 on the following reduction chain, obtained by confluence:

$$S \to^* S_q \to^1 R \to^* Q{\downarrow}$$

such that R is the first non-atomic proposition ($Q \downarrow$ is not atomic). From Lemma 3, Lemma 2, and since every V_{p+1} is a conservative extension of V_p, we get:

$$V_n(P) = V(S) = V(R) = V_{n-1}(R)$$

Else, S is already compound and all interpretations are equal.   □

Lemma 4. *Let $P \equiv_{\mathcal{R}} Q$ be two propositions. Suppose that $\mathcal{V}(P)$ is defined. Then $\mathcal{V}(Q) = \mathcal{V}(P)$.*

Proof. Let m the least integer for which $V_m(P)$ or $V_m(Q)$ is defined, and suppose without loss of generality that $V_m(Q)$ is defined.

If $m = 0$ and $V_0(P)$ is also defined, the result comes from Lemma 2.

Else, since the enumeration has infinite repetition, P is considered at some later step n. And $V_n(P)$ is defined by the first extension rule, since the conditions for its application hold. Therefore, $\mathcal{V}(P) = V_n(P) = V_m(Q) = \mathcal{V}(Q)$.   □

Lemma 5. *$\mathcal{V}$ is a semi-valuation.*

Proof. We prove by induction that if a (compound) proposition P is defined at step n, then enough of its immediate subformulas are interpreted in $\mathcal{V}$ so as to ensure that $\mathcal{V}$ is a semi-valuation.

If $n = 0$, then this is because V is a semi-valuation.

If P is defined at step n by the second extension rule: it is immediate.

If P is defined at step n by the first rule, let Q be the proposition such that $P \equiv_{\mathcal{R}} Q$ and $V_n(P)$ is defined equal to $V_{n-1}(Q)$. Corollary 1 allows us to choose Q non-atomic. By confluence they have the same main connector. By induction hypothesis, enough immediate subformulas of Q receive an interpretation under $\mathcal{V}$. Let R_i those subformulas and R_i' their counterparts in P. We have $R_i \equiv_{\mathcal{R}} R_i'$. Applying Lemma 4, we get $\mathcal{V}(R_i) = \mathcal{V}(R_i')$, and therefore enough subformulas of P are interpreted in $\mathcal{V}$.   □

Lemma 6. *$\mathcal{V}$ is a semi-valuation for the rewrite system $\mathcal{R}$.*

Proof. This is the combination of Lemmas 4 and 5.   □

4.5   Extending a Semi-valuation into a Partial Valuation

$\mathcal{V}$ is not a partial valuation for $\mathcal{R}$. Indeed, suppose $V(\forall x \ (A(x) \wedge B(x)))$ is not defined and that for any t, $V(A(t)) = V(B(t)) = 1$. We would like to have $\mathcal{V}(\forall x \ Q) = 1$, since $\mathcal{V}(A(t) \wedge B(t)) = 1$ for any t. But we can find no n such that $V_n(A(t) \wedge B(t)) = 1$ for any t, therefore we can never have $V_{n+1}(\forall x \ (A(x) \wedge B(x))) = 1$. So we need to extend $\mathcal{V}$ as in section 4.4. But no finite step of this process is sufficient.

We define $\tilde{V}$ as the least fixpoint of this semi-valuation extension operation: this is possible, since we can define a partial order on the semi-valuations: $V \prec V'$ if V interprets less formulas than V', and if V' is conservative over V.

It is then immediate to prove the following lemma:

Lemma 7. $\tilde{V}$ *is a partial valuation for $\mathcal{R}$ and agrees with V.*

Proof. $\tilde{V}$ is a semi-valuation for $\mathcal{R}$ by construction (the extension operation respects those properties). It is also a partial valuation: if we know enough information about the subformulas of Q, then the extension operation sets the interpretation of Q. Since $\tilde{V}$ is its own extension, $\tilde{V}(Q)$ is defined.   □

4.6   Transforming a Partial Valuation into a Model for $\mathcal{R}$

We prove the following theorem:

Theorem 2 (Completeness). *Let $\mathcal{R}$ a terminating confluent rewrite system, and Γ a set of propositions. If the systematic tableau procedure of Sec. 3 rooted at Γ does not terminate, then Γ has a model, under both conditions below.*

In usual first-order logic, once one has a semi-valuation, one ends the completeness proof very easily: we extend the semi-valuation into a model by defining randomly the truth value of uninterpreted atoms by V. This is no more the case in deduction modulo, since we have to ensure that the model we construct is a model of $\mathcal{R}$. At this point, we must introduce some more conditions on $\mathcal{R}$, since model construction differ with respect to those conditions.

An Order Condition. has been introduced by Stuber in [19] and used in [15, 16] for proving semantic completeness theorems (of the resolution ENAR and the cut-free sequent calculus). We consider a confluent rewrite system and a well-founded order $\prec$ such that:

- if $P \to Q$ then $Q \prec P$.
- if A is a subformula of B then $A \prec B$.

The domain of the model is the set of the ground terms appearing in the partial valuation $\tilde{V}$ constructed in the previous section. And we construct the interpretation by induction on the order:

- if A is a normal atom, set $|A|_{\mathcal{R}} = \tilde{V}(A)$, if defined. Else set $|A|_{\mathcal{R}}$ arbitrarily.
- if A is not a normal atom, set $|A|_{\mathcal{R}} = |A\!\downarrow|_{\mathcal{R}}$.
- if P is a compound proposition, set $|P|_{\mathcal{R}}$ from the interpretation of its immediate subformulas.

This definition is well-founded. We prove as in [15] the following results (in this order):

- $P \mapsto |P|_{\mathcal{R}}$ defines a model interpretation.
- $|P|_{\mathcal{R}} = |P{\downarrow}|_{\mathcal{R}}$.
- $P \mapsto |P|_{\mathcal{R}}$ defines a model of $\mathcal{R}$.
- $P \mapsto |P|_{\mathcal{R}}$ is a conservative extension of $\tilde{V}$.

Turning back to the proof of Theorem 2, in the model defined, $|P|_{\mathcal{R}} = 1$, for any $P \in \Gamma$. The tableau method is thus proved complete for all rewrite systems $\mathcal{R}$ that verifies this order condition.

A Positivity Condition. We now suppose that the rewrite system $\mathcal{R}$, besides confluence and termination, verifies a **positivity** condition: all propositional rewrite rules $l \rightarrow r \in \mathcal{R}$ are such that all atoms occurring in r occur positively: they occur under an even times of negations and as left member of an implication. r will be called a positive formula. For instance, the following rewrite rule respects the positivity condition: $P(0) \rightarrow \forall x P(x)$

The domain of the model is the ground terms. We define the interpretation rather differently:

- if A is an atom, and if $\tilde{V}(A)$ is defined, set $|A|_{\mathcal{R}} = \tilde{V}(A)$.
- if A is an atom, and if $\tilde{V}(A)$ is not defined, set $|A|_{\mathcal{R}} = 1$.
- if P is a compound proposition, set $|P|_{\mathcal{R}}$ accordingly to Def. 2.

Notice that we defined the interpretation of even non-normal atoms, disregarding rewrite rules (for now).

Lemma 8. $P \mapsto |P|_{\mathcal{R}}$ *defines a model interpretation. Let P be a proposition. If $\tilde{V}(P)$, is defined, then $|P|_{\mathcal{R}} = \tilde{V}(P)$.*

Proof. The first part of the lemma is by construction of the interpretation. The second part is proved by induction on the structure of P, using the fact that $\tilde{V}$ is a partial valuation (Def. 2). $\qquad\square$

So if any tableau rooted at Γ cannot be closed, Γ has a boolean model. But we have not yet spoken about a needed property of the interpretation $|\ |_{\mathcal{R}}$: it has to be a model of $\mathcal{R}$.

If $P \equiv_{\mathcal{R}} Q$, and $\tilde{V}(P)$ is defined, $\tilde{V}$ being a partial valuation, and by Lemma 8:

$$|P|_{\mathcal{R}} = \tilde{V}(P) = \tilde{V}(Q) = |Q|_{\mathcal{R}}$$

The problem arises from the propositions that are *not* defined by the partial valuation $\tilde{V}$. We do not know anything, *a priori*.

We can restrain ourselves to a simpler subcase: consider only $P \rightarrow Q$ instead of its full reflexive-transitive-symmetric closure $\equiv_{\mathcal{R}}$. Also, considering P atomic is not harmful since the rewriting steps proceed always on atoms.

Now, remember that $\mathcal{R}$ is a positive rewrite system. Hence Q is a positive proposition (noted Q^+). The crucial point *was* to define the interpretation $|A|_{\mathcal{R}}$

of an non-valued atom under $\tilde{V}$ to be *the same for all atoms* (whatever: we could have set 0 or 1). Since Q^+ is positive, the intuition is that since its atoms will also be interpreted by 1, Q^+ itself will be interpreted by 1.

We however have to be very careful: first, it could have been that $\tilde{V}(Q^+)$ is defined, and set to 0. Fortunately, $\tilde{V}$ is a partial valuation, hence if $\tilde{V}(Q)$ is defined, so should be $\tilde{V}(P)$. But it still might be that some subformulas of Q are interpreted under $\tilde{V}$. We have to generalize a bit the result, in order to be able to prove it:

Lemma 9. *Let P^+ a positive and Q^- a negative ($\neg Q^-$ is positive) proposition that does not receive an interpretation under $\tilde{V}$. Then $|P^+|_{\mathcal{R}} = 1$ and $|Q^-|_{\mathcal{R}} = 0$.*

Proof. By induction over the proposition structure. The base case (P atomic) is immediate from the definition of $P \mapsto |P|_{\mathcal{R}}$. There is no base case for Q^- since an atom is positive.

We detail the case of an universally quantified proposition. If $P^+ = \forall x R^+$. Let t be a term. Since $\tilde{V}$ is a partial valuation, it can not be that $\tilde{V}(R^+[x := t]) = 0$, else $\tilde{V}(P)$ would have been defined. Hence, $|R^+[x := t]|_{\mathcal{R}} = 1$ either by Lemma 8 (if $\tilde{V}(R^+[x := t]) = 1$), or by induction hypothesis (if $\tilde{V}(R^+[x := t])$ is not defined). Since it is true for any term t, we conclude that $|P|_{\mathcal{R}} = 1$.

If $Q^- = \forall x R^-$. Since $\tilde{V}$ is a partial valuation, it can not be that $\tilde{V}(R^-[x := t]) = 1$ for any ground term t. By hypothesis we can find no t such that $\tilde{V}(R^-[x := t]) = 0$. Hence, there is a t_0 such that $\tilde{V}(R^-[x := t_0])$ is not defined, and we conclude by induction hypothesis that $|R^-[x := t_0]|_{\mathcal{R}} = 0$. Hence $|Q^-|_{\mathcal{R}} = 0$. □

We then can easily prove the lemma:

Lemma 10. *The interpretation $P \mapsto |P|_{\mathcal{R}}$ defines a model for $\mathcal{R}$.*

Proof. Let $A \rightarrow^1 P$. Either $\tilde{V}(A)$ is defined, and we conclude by Lemma 8, or it is not, and by the preceding lemma we have that $|A|_{\mathcal{R}} = |P|_{\mathcal{R}} = 1$. We then extend it to compound propositions by structural induction. At last, we extend it by induction on the number of rewrite steps to the relation $\equiv_{\mathcal{R}}$. □

The tableau method is then proved complete for the positive rewrite systems.

5   Example

We prove $2 = 2 \Rightarrow \exists x \, (x + x = 2)$ where $=$ has no special property. Insignificant formulas are omitted but we list every applied inference. Let $\mathcal{R}$ be the following fragment of Peano's arithmetic (see [11] for arithmetic as a theory modulo):

$$x + 0 \longrightarrow_{\mathcal{R}} 0 \tag{1}$$
$$x + s(y) \longrightarrow_{\mathcal{R}} s(x + y) \tag{2}$$

Notice that in the first rewrite step, rule 1 is not applied, since 0 trivially does not unify with $2 = s(s(0))$. Notice also that after that rewrite step, we could have replaced X_1 by $s(Y_1)$ yielding a faster solution. As a side comment, the two formulas under the fourth horizontal bar are produced from the formula over it using respectively $\mathtt{rw}(1)$ and $\mathtt{rw}(2)$.

$$
\cfrac{
  \cfrac{
    \cfrac{
      \cfrac{2 = 2, \forall x(x + x \neq 2)}{X + X \neq 2} \; \gamma
    }{s(X_1 + Y_1) \neq 2 \cdot \mathcal{C} := \{X \approx X_1, X \approx s(Y_1)\}} \; \mathtt{rw}(2)
  }{
    \cfrac{X' + X' \neq 2}{s(X_2) \neq 2 \cdot \mathcal{C}' := \mathcal{C} \cup \{X_1 \approx X_2, \mathbf{Y_1 \approx 0}\}} \; \gamma
  } \; \mathtt{rw}(1), \mathtt{rw}(2)
}{
  \cfrac{s(s(X_3 + Y_3)) \neq 2 \cdot \mathcal{C}'' := \mathcal{C} \cup \{X_1 \approx X_3, Y_1 \approx s(Y_3)\}}{\odot \cdot \{X \approx 1\}} \; \mathtt{closure}(\mathcal{C}')
}
$$

6   Conclusion and Further Work

We have given a new (more liberal) formulation of tableaux for deduction modulo which is better suited to automated theorem proving. For example, it does not force atomic closure anymore, which was done in [2] where branches were fully expanded before eventually applying closure. Moreover, rewriting is not a separated process anymore and can now occur after any tableau expansion (and not after all expansions have been done). We have shown its semantic completeness through a systematic generation and detailed the model construction for specific classes of rewrite systems.

Our systematic tableau construction can be seen as the first step towards an effective (but not efficient) implementation of the method. Many improvements are to be made for it to be effective.

For example, labels are an explicit way to store arguments for Skolem functions, but they may contain variables which are not present in the formula we skolemize. Moreover, if an existential quantifier is inside a universal one (as in the formula $\forall x \, \exists y \, P(x, y)$), we generate a new Skolem symbol each time we use δ after a new γ although we could simply use the same one over and over. This inefficiency could be solved either by removing the rule and preskolemizing the input formula or by using one of the improved δ-rules: δ^+ ([14]) (or better δ^{++} ([1]) or one of the other ones surveyed in [4]. Our completeness proof should not be changed by the use of one the two δ^+ rules.

Then, the δ-rule in a calculus with free-variables complicates any syntactic soundness proofs with respect to sequent calculus modulo, especially cut-free. Indeed, we can no more ensure the freshness condition. So, we are not able to translate δ-rules into deduction steps in cut-free sequent calculus modulo. The workaround should be a Skolem theorem for cut-free sequent calculus modulo, that is yet to be investigated. The link between ground tableaux and a constructive cut elimination theorem is well-known in classical logic, and studied in the intuitionistic frame in [3].

The completeness proof is not constructive at only one point: we need König's lemma to identify an infinite branch. Such a branch is useful only because we consider *boolean* models, where truth and falsity are split by construction. The workaround is well-known ([17]): we should consider models base only on truth: $\neg P$ is true means that if P is true, then every proposition is true in the model. So, reconsidering the semi-valuation definition from this point of view, we believe that this work could be shifted in a perfectly constructive framework.

Adding rewrite rules to the tableau already complicates the completeness proof even with such conditions as confluence or termination of the rewrite system. We proved this for an order condition and a positivity condition. In [3, 15] some more conditions are studied from the point of view of semantic completeness (of cut-free sequent calculus and intuitionistic tableaux) such as a mix of the two previous conditions or the formulation of HOL in first-order logic modulo given in [10]. Those results should be easily extendable to the study of tableau completeness, since we already have a partial valuation.

Concerning deduction modulo, the restriction to atomicity of the left-hand side of propositional rewrite rules can sometimes be relaxed as shown in [8] where the (first-order) sequent calculus is presented as (non-atomic) propositional rewrite rules: the system obtained is similar to a tableau calculus (no surprise here) and it exhibits the fact that the real deductive process lies within the quantifiers. Sadly, no criterion exists regarding the safe introduction of non-atomic propositional rewrite rules: this remains yet another area to be explored, which could be interesting regarding the implementation of proof-search procedures modulo.

References

[1] B. Beckert, R. Hähnle, and P. Schmitt. *The even more liberalized δ-rule in free variable Semantic Tableaux*, volume 713. June 1993.

[2] R. Bonichon. Tamed: A tableau method for deduction modulo. In *IJCAR*, pages 445–459, 2004.

[3] R. Bonichon and O. Hermant. On constructive cut admissibility in deduction modulo (submitted). http://www-spi.lip6.fr/~bonichon/papers/occad-fl.ps .

[4] D. Cantone and M. Nicolosi Asmundo. A sound framework for delta-rule variants in free variable semantic tableaux. In *FTP*, 2005.

[5] A. Degtyarev and A. Voronkov. The undecidability of simultaneous rigid e-unification. *Theoretical Computer Science*, 166(1-2):291–300, 1996.

[6] A. Degtyarev and A. Voronkov. What you always wanted to know about rigid e-unification. *J. Autom. Reason.*, 20(1-2):47–80, 1998.

[7] A. Degtyarev and A. Voronkov. *Equality Reasoning in Sequent-based Calculi*, chapter 10. Elsevier Science Publishers B.V., 2001.

[8] E. Deplagne. Sequent calculus viewed modulo. In Catherine Pilière, editor, *Proceedings of the ESSLLI-2000 Student Session*, pages 66–76, Birmingham, england, August 2000. University of Birmingham.

[9] G. Dowek, T. Hardin, and C. Kirchner. Theorem proving modulo. *Journal of Automated Reasoning*, (31):33–72, 2003.

[10] G. Dowek and B. Werner. Proof normalization modulo. *The Journal of Symbolic Logic*, 68(4):1289–1316, December 2003.

[11] G. Dowek and B. Werner. Arithmetic as a theory modulo. In J. Giesel, editor, *Term rewriting and applications*, Lecture Notes in Computer Science. Springer-Verlag, 2005.

[12] M. Fitting. *First Order Logic and Automated Theorem Proving*. Springer-Verlag, 2nd edition, 1996.

[13] M. Giese. Incremental Closure of Free Variable Tableaux. In *Proc. Intl. Joint Conf. on Automated Reasoning, Siena, Italy*, number 2083 in LNCS, pages 545–560. Springer-Verlag, 2001.

[14] R. Hähnle and P. Schmitt. The liberalized δ-rule in free variable semantic tableaux. *Journal of Automated Reasoning*, 13(2):211–221, 1994.

[15] O. Hermant. *Méthodes Sémantiques en Déduction Modulo*. PhD thesis, Université Paris 7 - Denis Diderot, 2005.

[16] O. Hermant. Semantic cut elimination in the intuitionistic sequent calculus. *Typed Lambda-Calculi and Applications*, pages 221–233, 2005.

[17] J.-L. Krivine. Une preuve formelle et intuitionniste du théorème de complétude de la logique classique. *The Bulletin of Symbolic Logic*, 2:405–421, 1996.

[18] R. Smullyan. *First Order Logic*. Springer, 1968.

[19] J. Stuber. A model-based completeness proof of extended narrowing and resolution. *Lecture Notes in Computer Science*, 2083:195+, 2001.

Saturation Up to Redundancy
for Tableau and Sequent Calculi

Martin Giese

Johann Radon Institute for Computational and Applied Mathematics
Altenbergerstr. 69, A-4040 Linz, Austria
martin.giese@oeaw.ac.at

Abstract. We discuss an adaptation of the technique of saturation up to redundancy, as introduced by Bachmair and Ganzinger [1], to tableau and sequent calculi for classical first-order logic. This technique can be used to easily show the completeness of optimized calculi that contain destructive rules e.g. for simplification, rewriting with equalities, etc., which is not easily done with a standard Hintikka-style completeness proof. The notions are first introduced for Smullyan-style ground tableaux, and then extended to constrained formula free-variable tableaux.

1 Introduction

The usual Hintikka-style completeness proof for tableau or sequent calculi requires branches to be *saturated*. This means that for any formula appearing on a branch and any inference possible on that formula, all formulae introduced by that inference on at least one of the created branches also appear on the branch.

While this condition poses no problem in the standard calculi for classical logic, more complicated calculi might allow several different inferences on the same formula. In that case, none of these inferences may in general delete the original formula, since it has to remain available for the other inferences to achieve saturation.

In many cases, destructive rules would make a calculus more efficient. Examples are rewriting with equalities [5], type reasoning [7], as well as various domain specific calculi, see e.g. [3], which all use non-destructive rules. The completeness of destructive variants of these calculi cannot be shown using a Hintikka-style proof. Sometimes, proof transformation techniques can be used to cope with destructiveness, see e.g. [6], but these require plenty of creativity and are very specific to the calculus at hand.

In the context of resolution theorem proving, Bachmair and Ganzinger have established the admirable framework of *saturation up to redundancy*, see e.g. [1]. The idea is that a clause can be deleted from a clause set if it is *redundant* with respect to the other clauses. Precise definitions are given for what constitutes a valid redundancy criterion, and then completeness is shown for all inference systems that obey certain restrictions.

In this paper, the results of Bachmair and Ganzinger are transferred to the setting of tableau and sequent calculi for classical first-order logic. After intro-

M. Hermann and A. Voronkov (Eds.): LPAR 2006, LNAI 4246, pp. 182–196, 2006.

ducing in Sect. 2 some basic notions about the type of calculi we are going to consider, Sect. 3 presents notions of redundancy and a generic completeness theorem for tableaux. In the next two sections, the technique is demonstrated on two simple calculi. We then extend our notions to free variable calculi in Sect. 6. This is again followed by a case study, before we conclude the paper in Sect. 8.

2   Semi-sequent Calculi

We simplify our presentation by considering only *semi-sequent* calculi. A semi-sequent calculus is like a sequent calculus in which the right hand side, the succedent, of every sequent is empty. Such calculi are also known as *block tableau* [8] calculi.

Definition 1. *A semi-sequent is a set of formulae written $\phi_1, \ldots, \phi_n \vdash$. With the notation $\phi_1, \ldots, \phi_n, \Gamma \vdash$, we mean a semi-sequent that consists of the set of formulae $\{\phi_1, \ldots, \phi_n\} \cup \Gamma$.*

Definition 2. *A tableau for a semi-sequent calculus is a tree where each node is labeled with a semi-sequent.*

A derivation consists of a sequence of tableaux, each of which is constructed from the previous one through the application of an inference on one of the leaves. The first tableau consists of only the root node, which is labeled with the initial semi-sequent. A derivation for a formula ϕ is a derivation with initial semi-sequent $\phi \vdash$.

A semi-sequent is called closed *if it contains $\bot$, the false formula, otherwise it is called* open. *A tableau is called closed, if the semi-sequents in all leaves are closed.*

The general form of an inference in a semi-sequent calculus is

$$\frac{\phi_{11}, \ldots, \phi_{1m_1}, \Gamma \vdash \quad \cdots \quad \phi_{n1}, \ldots, \phi_{nm_n}, \Gamma \vdash}{\phi_{01}, \ldots, \phi_{0m_0}, \Gamma \vdash}$$

We refer to the upper semi-sequents as *premises* and the lower one as *conclusion* of the inference. One of the formulae in the conclusion of every inference is identified and called the *main formula* of the conclusion, the others are the *side formulae*.

Application of such an inference requires all formulae $\phi_{01}, \ldots, \phi_{0m_0}$ of the conclusion to be present in a leaf semi-sequent. The tree is then expanded by appending n children to the leaf containing the modified sequents given by the premises.[1]

Given a finite or infinite derivation $(\mathcal{T}_i)_{i \in \mathbb{N}}$, we can easily define its limit $\mathcal{T}^\infty$, which may in general be an infinite tree. This possibly infinite tree consists of

---

[1] It may be a bit confusing that proof construction starts from the conclusion and adds more premises, but this is the common terminology in sequent calculi. A possible reading is "to conclude that Γ_0 is unsatisfiable, we have to show that Γ_1 to Γ_n are unsatisfiable."

possibly infinitely many possibly infinite branches, which again are sequences $(\Gamma_i)_{i \in \mathbb{N}}$ of semi-sequents. While each tableau in the derivation is contained in each of its successors, this is not necessarily the case for the semi-sequents on a tableau branch: inferences might remove formulae from semi-sequents. Still, one can form a limit semi-sequent,

$$\Gamma^\infty := \bigcup_{i \in \mathbb{N}} \bigcap_{j \geq i} \Gamma_j$$

consisting of all *persistent* formulae on the branch.

3   Redundancy

The definitions, lemmas and proofs in this section follow those of [1] very closely. The main difference is that tableaux and sequent proofs can split into several branches, which adds a quantifier to most of the notions and requires deciding whether something should hold for all formulae in one of the new goals or for one formula in each of the goals, etc. The other difference is that the presentation is adapted to better fit the style in which tableau/sequent calculi are usually presented.

We start with a very general notion of redundancy criterion:

Definition 3. *A* redundancy criterion *is a pair* $(\mathcal{R}_\mathcal{F}, \mathcal{R}_\mathcal{I})$ *of mappings from sets of formulae to sets of formulae, resp. sets of inferences, such that for all sets of formulae Γ and Γ':*

(R1) *if $\Gamma \subseteq \Gamma'$ then $\mathcal{R}_\mathcal{F}(\Gamma) \subseteq \mathcal{R}_\mathcal{F}(\Gamma')$, and $\mathcal{R}_\mathcal{I}(\Gamma) \subseteq \mathcal{R}_\mathcal{I}(\Gamma')$.*
(R2) *if $\Gamma' \subseteq \mathcal{R}_\mathcal{F}(\Gamma)$ then $\mathcal{R}_\mathcal{F}(\Gamma) \subseteq \mathcal{R}_\mathcal{F}(\Gamma \setminus \Gamma')$, and $\mathcal{R}_\mathcal{I}(\Gamma) \subseteq \mathcal{R}_\mathcal{I}(\Gamma \setminus \Gamma')$.*
(R3) *if Γ is unsatisfiable, then so is $\Gamma \setminus \mathcal{R}_\mathcal{F}(\Gamma)$.*

The criterion is called effective *if, in addition,*

(R4) *an inference is in $\mathcal{R}_\mathcal{I}(\Gamma)$, whenever it has at least one premise introducing only formulae $P = \{\phi_{k1}, \dots \phi_{km_k}\}$ with $P \subseteq \Gamma \cup \mathcal{R}_\mathcal{F}(\Gamma)$.*

The formulae, resp. inferences in $\mathcal{R}_\mathcal{F}(\Gamma)$ resp. $\mathcal{R}_\mathcal{I}(\Gamma)$ are called redundant *with respect to Γ.*

For an effective redundancy criterion, any inference is redundant that has at least one premise where no new formula is introduced. This means that inferences that destroy regularity are redundant.

In contrast to resolution calculi, sequent calculi are usually written in such a way that an inference can simultaneously add new formulae and remove old ones that have become redundant. We therefore introduce the following notion:

Definition 4. *A* calculus *conforms to a redundancy criterion, if its inferences remove formulae from a branch only if they are redundant with respect to the formulae in the resulting semi-sequent.*

The following two Lemmas are taken almost verbatim from [1], where their proofs can be found.

Lemma 1. *Let $(\Gamma_i)_{i\in\mathbb{N}}$ be a branch of some limit derivation in a conforming calculus. Then $\mathcal{R}_{\mathcal{F}}(\bigcup_i \Gamma_i) \subseteq \mathcal{R}_{\mathcal{F}}(\Gamma^\infty)$, and $\mathcal{R}_{\mathcal{I}}(\bigcup_i \Gamma_i) \subseteq \mathcal{R}_{\mathcal{I}}(\Gamma^\infty)$.*

The next lemma is slightly different from the resolution setting, in that the implication holds in only one direction, due to the splitting into several branches.

Lemma 2. *Let $(\Gamma_i)_{i\in\mathbb{N}}$ be a branch of some limit derivation in a conforming calculus. If Γ^∞ is satisfiable, then also Γ_0 is satisfiable.*

We now define saturation up to redundancy which is what a derivation should approach on each branch.

Definition 5. *A set of formulae Γ is* saturated up to redundancy *with respect to a given calculus and redundancy criterion, if all inferences from formulae in $\Gamma \setminus \mathcal{R}_{\mathcal{F}}(\Gamma)$ are in $\mathcal{R}_{\mathcal{I}}(\Gamma)$.*

A tableau $\mathcal{T}$ is saturated up to redundancy *with respect to a given calculus and redundancy criterion if all its limit branches Γ^∞ are saturated.*

While saturation is desired for limit tableaux, the following notion gives a better idea of how a theorem prover might achieve it.

Definition 6. *A derivation $(\mathcal{T}_i)_{i\in\mathbb{N}}$ in a calculus that conforms to an effective redundancy criterion is called* fair *if for every limit branch $(\Gamma_i)_{i\in\mathbb{N}}$ of $\mathcal{T}^\infty$, and any non-redundant inference possible on non-redundant formulae in Γ^∞, all formulae of at least one of the premises of the inference are either in $\bigcup_i \Gamma_i$ or redundant in $\bigcup_i \Gamma_i$.*

Theorem 1. *If a derivation in a calculus that conforms to an effective redundancy criterion is fair, then the limit tableau it produces is saturated.*

Proof. Let γ be an inference from non-redundant formulae of some limit-branch Γ^∞ of a fair derivation. Due to fairness, for at least one premise produced by γ, $P \subseteq \bigcup_i \Gamma_i \cup \mathcal{R}_{\mathcal{F}}(\bigcup_i \Gamma_i)$, where P are the formulae γ introduces on that premise. According to (R4), γ is redundant in $\bigcup_i \Gamma_i$, and due to Lemma 1 also in Γ^∞. $\square$

We will now make our discussion more concrete by defining a *standard redundancy criterion* which is sufficient to prove completeness of most calculi. We will prove in Theorems 2 and 3 that this standard redundancy criterion is indeed an effective redundancy criterion according to Def. 3 under certain conditions. To define the criterion, we require a fixed Noetherian order $\succ$ on formulae. We place the restriction on this ordering that $\bot$ must be smaller than all other formulae.

Definition 7. *The* standard redundancy criterion *is defined as follows: A formula ϕ is* redundant *with respect to a set of formulae Γ, iff there are formulae $\phi_1,\ldots,\phi_n \in \Gamma$, such that $\phi_1,\ldots,\phi_n \models \phi$ and $\phi \succ \phi_i$ for $i = 1,\ldots,n$.*

An inference with main formula ϕ and side formulae $\phi_1,\ldots\phi_n$ is redundant *w.r.t. a set of formulae Γ, iff it has one premise such that for all formulae ξ introduced in that premise, there are formulae $\psi_1,\ldots,\psi_m \in \Gamma$, such that $\psi_1,\ldots,\psi_m,\phi_1,\ldots,\phi_n \models \xi$ and $\phi \succ \psi_i$ for $i = 1,\ldots,m$.*

Theorem 2. *The standard redundancy criterion of Def. 7 is indeed a redundancy criterion according to Def. 3.*

Proof. Property (R1) follows directly from Def. 7. For property (R2), if $\phi \in \mathcal{R}_{\mathcal{F}}(\Gamma)$, consider all finite sets $\Gamma_0 \subseteq \Gamma$ of formulae smaller than ϕ which imply ϕ. Every finite set can be considered a multiset, so they can be ordered according to the multiset extension of $\succ$. Take a minimal such set. No element of Γ_0 can be redundant in Γ, since otherwise it could be replaced by some even smaller elements of Γ, contradicting the minimality of Γ_0. Therefore $\Gamma_0 \subseteq \Gamma \setminus \mathcal{R}_{\mathcal{F}}(\Gamma)$, which means that $\phi \in \mathcal{R}_{\mathcal{F}}(\Gamma \setminus \mathcal{R}_{\mathcal{F}}(\Gamma))$, and since this holds for arbitrary redundant ϕ,

$$\mathcal{R}_{\mathcal{F}}(\Gamma) \subseteq \mathcal{R}_{\mathcal{F}}(\Gamma \setminus \mathcal{R}_{\mathcal{F}}(\Gamma)) \tag{$*$}$$

To show the $\mathcal{R}_{\mathcal{F}}$ part of (R2), let $\Gamma' \subseteq \mathcal{R}_{\mathcal{F}}(\Gamma)$. This implies that $\Gamma \setminus \mathcal{R}_{\mathcal{F}}(\Gamma) \subseteq \Gamma \setminus \Gamma'$. From (R1) we get $\mathcal{R}_{\mathcal{F}}(\Gamma \setminus \mathcal{R}_{\mathcal{F}}(\Gamma)) \subseteq \mathcal{R}_{\mathcal{F}}(\Gamma \setminus \Gamma')$, and together with $(*)$, $\mathcal{R}_{\mathcal{F}}(\Gamma) \subseteq \mathcal{R}_{\mathcal{F}}(\Gamma \setminus \Gamma')$. For the $\mathcal{R}_{\mathcal{I}}$ part of (R2), we consider a premise where every new formula ξ is implied by the side formulae and some formulae smaller than ϕ. The same argument as for $\mathcal{R}_{\mathcal{F}}$ can be applied to each of these ξ.

For (R3), we just showed that every redundant formula $\phi \in \mathcal{R}_{\mathcal{F}}(\Gamma)$ is implied by some non-redundant ones. Therefore $\Gamma \setminus \mathcal{R}_{\mathcal{F}}(\Gamma) \models \mathcal{R}_{\mathcal{F}}(\Gamma)$, from which (R3) follows.   □

No inference in a calculus conforming to this redundancy criterion can remove $\bot$ from a semi-sequent, since $\bot$, as the smallest formula, is not redundant with respect to any set of formulae. In other words, the literal $\bot$ is always persistent. Under the following restriction, the standard redundancy criterion is *effective:*

Definition 8. *A calculus is called* reductive *if all new formulae introduced by an inference are smaller than the main formula of the inference.*

Theorem 3. *The standard redundancy criterion is an effective redundancy criterion for any reductive calculus.*

Proof. Let an inference with main formula ϕ introduce a formula $\xi \in \Gamma \cup \mathcal{R}_{\mathcal{F}}(\Gamma)$ on some premise. In a reductive calculus, $\phi \succ \xi$. If $\xi \in \Gamma$, then ξ is itself a formula smaller than ϕ which implies ξ. If $\xi \in \mathcal{R}_{\mathcal{F}}(\Gamma)$, then ξ is implied by formulae in Γ which are smaller than ξ and therefore also smaller than ϕ. If this is the case for all formulae introduced in one premise of the inference, that inference is redundant according to Def. 7.   □

For the following concept, we assume a fixed *model functor* I, which maps any saturated[2] set of formulae Γ that does not contain $\bot$ to a model $I(\Gamma)$, as well as a fixed Noetherian order $\succ$ on formulae.

Definition 9. *Let Γ be saturated up to redundancy with respect to some redundancy criterion. A* counterexample *for $I(\Gamma)$ in Γ is a formula $\phi \in \Gamma$ with $I(\Gamma) \not\models \phi$. Since $\succ$ is Noetherian, if there is a counterexample for $I(\Gamma)$ in Γ, then there is also a minimal one.*

---

[2] This is a slight enhancement to the presentation of Bachmair and Ganzinger, who require the model functor to be defined on any (multi-)set. Knowing that the set is saturated can make it easier to define a suitable model in some cases.

A calculus has the counterexample reduction property, *if for any saturated Γ not containing $\bot$ and minimal counterexample ϕ, the calculus permits an inference*

$$\frac{\phi_{11},\ldots,\phi_{1m_1},\Gamma_0 \vdash \quad \cdots \quad \phi_{n1},\ldots,\phi_{nm_n},\Gamma_0 \vdash}{\phi,\phi_{01},\ldots,\phi_{0m_0},\Gamma_0 \vdash}$$

with main formula ϕ where $\Gamma = \{\phi,\phi_{01},\ldots,\phi_{0m_0}\} \cup \Gamma_0$ such that $I(\Gamma)$ satisfies all side formulae, i.e. $I(\Gamma) \models \phi_{01},\ldots,\phi_{0m_0}$, and each of the premises contains an even smaller counterexample ϕ_{ik_i}, i.e. $I(\Gamma) \not\models \phi_{ik_i}$ and $\phi \succ \phi_{ik_i}$.

The following lemma is similar in purpose to the usual 'model lemma' in a Hintikka-style completeness proof.

Lemma 3. *Given a calculus that*

- *conforms to the standard redundancy criterion, and*
- *is reductive, and*
- *has the counterexample reduction property,*

any set of formulae Γ that is saturated up to redundancy w.r.t. that calculus and the standard redundancy criterion, and that does not contain $\bot$, is satisfiable, specifically, $I(\Gamma) \models \Gamma$.

Proof. If the model $I(\Gamma)$ is not a model for Γ, then Γ contains a minimal counterexample ϕ. This ϕ cannot be redundant w.r.t. Γ since it would otherwise have to be a logical consequence of formulae smaller than ϕ in Γ, and all such formulae are satisfied by $I(\Gamma)$. Since the calculus has the counterexample reduction property, there is an inference with main formula ϕ, and $I(\Gamma)$ satisfying all side formulae $\phi_1,\ldots,\phi_n$, which produces a smaller counterexample ϕ' on each new premise. Since Γ is saturated, this inference must be redundant. This means that the inference has one premise, such that for the smaller counterexample ϕ' in that premise (like for all other introduced formulae), there are formulae $\psi_1,\ldots,\psi_m \in \Gamma$, all smaller than ϕ, with $\psi_1,\ldots,\psi_m,\phi_1,\ldots,\phi_n \models \phi'$. Since the ψ_i are smaller than ϕ, they too are valid in $I(\Gamma)$, and so $I(\Gamma) \models \phi'$, so ϕ' cannot be a counterexample after all. We conclude that $I(\Gamma)$ *is* a model for Γ. $\square$

Theorem 4. *If a calculus*

- *conforms to the standard redundancy criterion, and*
- *is reductive, and*
- *has the counterexample reduction property, then*

any fair derivation for an unsatisfiable formula ϕ contains a closed tableau.

Proof. Assume that there is a fair derivation $\mathcal{T}_0, \mathcal{T}_1, \mathcal{T}_2, \ldots$ with a limit $\mathcal{T}^\infty$, where none of the $\mathcal{T}_i$ is closed. $\mathcal{T}^\infty$ has at least one branch $(\Gamma_i)_{i\in\mathbb{N}}$ that does not contain $\bot$. For assume that all limit branches contain $\bot$. These persistent formulae were introduced by some inferences in the sequence $(\mathcal{T}_i)$. Make a new tableau $\mathcal{T}'$ by cutting off every branch below the introduction of a $\bot$ literal. Then $\mathcal{T}'$ has only branches of finite length and is finitely branching. Thus, by

König's Lemma, T' must be a finite closed tableau for ϕ. One of the tableaux T_i must contain T' as initial sub-tableau, and thus T_i is closed, contradicting the assumption that there is no closed tableau in the derivation.

Now consider such an open limit branch $(\Gamma_i)_{i \in \mathbb{N}}$ with persistent formulae $\Gamma^\infty \not\ni \bot$. Due to fairness, Γ^∞ is saturated. Lemma 3 tells us that Γ^∞ is satisfiable, and due to Lemma 2, also the initial sequent Γ_0 and with it ϕ is satisfiable, contradicting our assumptions. $\square$

4   Case Study: Smullyan Style NNF Tableaux

We will start by studying a familiar calculus, namely a semi-sequent calculus for first-order formulae in negation normal form (NNF). Completeness of this calculus can easily be shown with a Hintikka-style proof, but it is also a good introductory example for our new technique.

$$\alpha \; \frac{\phi, \psi, \Gamma \vdash}{\phi \wedge \psi, \Gamma \vdash} \qquad \beta \; \frac{\phi, \Gamma \vdash \quad \psi, \Gamma \vdash}{\phi \vee \psi, \Gamma \vdash}$$

$$\gamma \; \frac{[x/t]\phi, \forall x.\phi, \Gamma \vdash}{\forall x.\phi, \Gamma \vdash} \qquad \delta \; \frac{[x/c]\phi, \Gamma \vdash}{\exists x.\phi, \Gamma \vdash}$$

$$\text{for any ground term } t \qquad\quad \text{for some new constant } c$$

$$\text{CLOSE} \; \frac{\bot \vdash}{L, \neg L, \Gamma \vdash}$$

In the CLOSE rule, we consider $\neg L$ to be the main formula, and L a side formula, since $\neg L$ is always larger than $\bot$. For the model functor, we take the set of all ground terms as domain, and we define that $I(\Gamma) \models L$ exactly for positive literals $L \in \Gamma$. We let $\succ$ order formulae by the number of boolean connectives and quantifiers appearing.

The calculus conforms to the standard redundancy criterion, since for each of the rules, the formulae deleted from the semi-sequent are clearly implied by the remaining ones. In particular for the CLOSE rule, the false formula $\bot$ implies any other formula. For the γ rule, the new formula $[x/t]\phi$ does *not* imply the original $\forall x.\phi$, but this is not required, since the original formula is kept.

The calculus is also reductive, since all rules introduce only formulae smaller than the respective main formula. Moreover, the calculus has the counterexample reduction property. For assume that $I(\Gamma) \not\models \phi$ for some $\phi \in \Gamma$. If $\phi = \phi_1 \wedge \phi_2$ is a conjunction, this means that $I(\Gamma)$ does not satisfy one of the conjuncts, w.l.o.g. ϕ_1. An α inference on ϕ is possible which produces ϕ_1, which is smaller than ϕ.

If $\phi = \phi_1 \vee \phi_2$ is a disjunction, then $I(\Gamma)$ fails to satisfy both disjuncts, and therefore each of the premises produced by the β rule contains a smaller counterexample.

In the case of a universally quantified formula, $\phi = \forall x.\phi_1$, there has to be some term t such that $I(\Gamma) \not\models [x/t]\phi_1$. The γ rule can be used to introduce $[x/t]\phi_1$, and clearly $\forall x.\phi_1 \succ [x/t]\phi_1$, so we have reduced the counterexample. For an existentially quantified formula, $I(\Gamma) \not\models \exists x.\phi_1$, in particular $I(\Gamma) \not\models [x/c]\phi_1$, so $[x/c]\phi_1$ is a smaller counterexample.

ϕ cannot be a positive literal, since $I(\Gamma)$ is defined to satisfy all positive literals. Finally, if $\phi = \neg L$ is a negative literal, then $I(\Gamma) \models L$, and therefore $L \in \Gamma$. This allows an application of the CLOSE rule, which produces the smaller counterexample $\bot$. Note that $I(\Gamma)$ does indeed satisfy the side formula L.

Thus, Theorem 4 allows us to conclude that this calculus is complete for first order formulae in negation normal form.

5   Case Study: NNF Hyper-tableaux

We now consider a negation normal form (NNF) version of the hyper-tableaux calculus. See [6] for an explanation of how this calculus relates to the clausal hyper-tableau calculus.

We will use the concept of *disjunctive paths* (d-paths) through formulae. The set of d-paths of a formula ϕ, denoted $dp(\phi)$, is defined by induction over the structure of ϕ as follows.

- If ϕ is a literal or a quantified formula $\forall x.\phi_1$ or $\exists x.\phi_1$, then $dp(\phi) := \{\langle \phi \rangle\}$.
- If $\phi = \phi_1 \wedge \phi_2$ is a conjunction, then $dp(\phi) := dp(\phi_1) \cup dp(\phi_2)$.
- If $\phi = \phi_1 \vee \phi_2$ is a disjunction, then $dp(\phi) := \{uv \mid u \in dp(\phi_1), v \in dp(\phi_2)\}$, where uv is the concatenation of two paths u and v.

For instance, for the formula $\phi = (p \wedge \neg p) \vee (q \wedge \neg q)$, this definition gives:

$$dp(p \wedge \neg p) = \{\langle p \rangle, \langle \neg p \rangle\}$$
$$dp(q \wedge \neg q) = \{\langle q \rangle, \langle \neg q \rangle\}$$
$$dp(\phi) = \{\langle p, q \rangle, \langle p, \neg q \rangle, \langle \neg p, q \rangle, \langle \neg p, \neg q \rangle\}$$

Note that we do not consider paths below quantifiers, in order to keep our discussion as simple as possible. A *positive d-path* is a d-path that contains no negated literal. In the example, $\langle p, q \rangle$ is the only positive d-path. Any d-path that is not positive must contain at least one negated literal, and in particular a left-most one. Let $lmn(\phi)$ be the set of left-most negated literals of the d-paths of ϕ. In the example, $lmn(\phi) = \{\neg q, \neg p\}$.

Consider the following semi-sequent calculus for NNF formulae:

$$\alpha \;\frac{\phi, \psi, \Gamma \vdash}{\phi \wedge \psi, \Gamma \vdash} \qquad \text{CLOSE} \;\frac{\bot \vdash}{L, \neg L, \Gamma \vdash}$$

$$\gamma \;\frac{[x/t]\phi, \forall x.\phi, \Gamma \vdash}{\forall x.\phi, \Gamma \vdash} \qquad\qquad \delta \;\frac{[x/c]\phi, \Gamma \vdash}{\exists x.\phi, \Gamma \vdash}$$
$$\text{for any ground term } t \qquad\qquad \text{for some new constant } c$$

$$\beta \;\frac{\phi, \Gamma \vdash \quad \psi, \Gamma \vdash}{\phi \vee \psi, \Gamma \vdash}$$
$$\text{where } \phi \vee \psi \text{ has at least one positive d-path.}$$

$$\text{SIMP } \frac{L, \phi[L], \Gamma \vdash}{L, \phi, \Gamma \vdash}$$

$$\text{where } \neg L \in lmn(\phi).$$

In the CLOSE rule and the SIMP rule, L is a side formula. By $\phi[L]$ we denote the result of replacing the negative literal $\neg L$ by the falsum $\perp$, and then simplifying the formula by repeated application of the transformations $\phi \wedge \perp \Rightarrow \perp$ and $\phi \vee \perp \Rightarrow \phi$. For instance, $((\neg p \wedge q) \vee r)[p] \Rightarrow (\perp \wedge q) \vee r \Rightarrow \perp \vee r \Rightarrow r$.

We again define the model functor, such that the domain of $I(\Gamma)$ consists of all ground terms, and $I(\Gamma) \models L$ for a positive literal L, exactly if $L \in \Gamma$. We will also use the same ordering as in the previous section.

The α, β, γ, δ, and CLOSE rules conform to the standard redundancy criterion as before. In the SIMP rule, the formula ϕ is dropped. Since $\neg L \in lmn(\phi)$, the simplification to $\phi[L]$ is indeed going to reduce the size of the formula, and an induction over the transformation steps leading to $\phi[L]$ easily convinces us that indeed $L, \phi[L] \models \phi$, so ϕ is redundant in the new sequent.

Also, the calculus is clearly still reductive, since if $\neg L \in lmn(\phi)$, then $\phi \succ \phi[L]$. As for the counterexample reduction property, the arguments are the same as in the previous section for literals, conjunctions, and quantified formulae. For disjunctions, there are two cases. If $\phi = \phi_1 \vee \phi_2$ has at least one positive d-path, a β inference will reduce the counterexample as before. Otherwise, every d-path of ϕ contains some negative literal. Then, there are again two cases: In the first case, Γ contains some L with $\neg L \in lmn(\phi)$. In particular, L is then smaller than ϕ, and therefore $I(\Gamma) \models L$. Similarly as before, we can convince ourselves that then $I(\Gamma) \not\models \phi[L]$, so the SIMP rule produces a smaller counterexample. In the second case, there is no $L \in \Gamma$ with $\neg L \in lmn(\phi)$. Due to our definition of I this means that every left-most negative literal is satisfied by $I(\Gamma)$, and therefore every d-path of ϕ contains at least one satisfied literal. Now a simple induction on the structure of ϕ, taking into account the definition of d-paths, tells us that also $I(\Gamma) \models \phi$ contradicting the assumption that ϕ is a counterexample.

Theorem 4 now tells us that also this calculus is complete.

6   Free Variable Tableaux

In this section, we shall lift the presented technique to a certain type of free variable tableaux, namely *constrained formula* free variable tableaux. They differ from the tableaux we have considered until now in two ways:

First, the formulae in the semi-sequents may contain free variables, although the formulae in the initial Γ_0 shouldn't. Free variables are used as placeholders for instantiations that a theorem prover would otherwise have to guess.

Second, semi-sequents actually contain *constrained formulae* $\phi \ll C$ consisting of a formula ϕ and a *constraint* C. For our purposes, the constraint is a formula of a subset of first order logic that will be interpreted over the domain of ground terms, using fixed interpretations for any predicate symbols. For instance in some calculi, the constraint language might be restricted to conjunctions of equations, written $s \equiv t$ denoting the syntactic equality of terms, in other cases, disjunction and negation or even quantifiers may be allowed in the constraint language, or ordering constraints $s > t$ may be available to compare terms with respect to some term ordering. For us, it is only important that there is a function Sat which for any constraint produces the set of ground substitutions that satisfy the constraint. For instance, one will usually have[3]

$$\text{Sat}(s \equiv t) = \{\sigma \in \mathcal{G} \mid \sigma s = \sigma t\}$$
$$\text{Sat}(C \,\&\, D) = \text{Sat}(C) \cap \text{Sat}(D) \tag{†}$$
$$\text{Sat}(!\,C) = \mathcal{G} \setminus \text{Sat}(C)$$

etc., so & denotes conjunction of constraints, ! negation of constraints, where $\mathcal{G}$ is the set of all ground substitutions.

A constrained formula $\phi \ll C$ in a semi-sequent means that the formula has resulted from some sequence of inferences that are only sound (or more generally desired) in cases where the free variables get instantiated as described by C. Ultimately, the constraints will get propagated until they reach $\bot \ll C$, of which a suitable combination has to be found to close all branches of the proof.

Definition 10. *A tableau of a constrained formula tableau calculus is closed under σ, where σ is a ground substitution for the occurring free variables, iff every leaf sequent of the tableau contains a constrained formula $\phi \ll C$ with $\sigma \in \text{Sat}(C)$. A tableau is* closable *if there exists a σ under which it is closed.*

The following definition describes how to apply a substitution to a semi-sequent or to a whole tableau, while discarding any formulae which carry a constraint that is not satisfied by that substitution.

Definition 11. *Let Γ be a set of constrained formulae. We define*

$$\sigma\Gamma := \{\sigma\phi \mid \phi \ll C \in \Gamma \text{ with } \sigma \in \text{Sat}(C)\} \quad.$$

Let $\mathcal{T}$ be a tableau. We construct $\sigma\mathcal{T}$ by replacing the semi-sequent Γ in each node of $\mathcal{T}$ by $\sigma\Gamma$.

The next definition uses these notions of substitution to establish a tight correspondence between constrained variable calculi and the non-free-variable, non-constrained calculi described in the previous sections. The correspondence is actually the same as that between Smullyan-style first order tableaux and Fitting-style [4] free variable tableaux.

Definition 12. *Let*

$$\frac{\Gamma_1 \vdash \quad \cdots \quad \Gamma_n \vdash}{\Gamma_0}$$

be an inference of a constrained formula tableau calculus. The corresponding ground inference under σ for some ground substitution σ is

$$\frac{\sigma\Gamma_1 \vdash \quad \cdots \quad \sigma\Gamma_n \vdash}{\sigma\Gamma_0} \quad.$$

---

[3] We use the prenex notation "σt", etc., for the application of substitutions.

The corresponding ground calculus *is the calculus consisting of all corresponding ground inferences under any σ of any inferences in the constrained formula calculus.*

We use the word 'ground' for notions without free variables. There might well be quantifiers in the formulae involved. Any given inference of the constrained formula calculus can in general have infinitely many different corresponding ground inferences for different σ, but each of them is an ordinary, finite ground inference.

Using the correspondence to a ground calculus, we can define the same properties as before for constrained formula tableaux:

Definition 13. *A constrained formula calculus* conforms *to a given redundancy criterion, has the* counterexample reduction property, *or is* reductive *iff the corresponding ground calculus has that property.*

Note that a constrained formula calculus can always discard a formula with an unsatisfiable constraint, since it disappears under any substitution. Therefore, a ground inference corresponding to the deletion of a formula with unsatisfiable constraint does not change the semi-sequent, so it trivially conforms to any redundancy criterion.

Finally, a notion of fairness is needed. Again this definition is heavily based on the 'ground' notion. We will discuss its implications after Theorem 5.

Definition 14. *A constrained formula tableau derivation* $(\mathcal{T}_i)_{i\in\mathbb{N}}$ *in a calculus that conforms to an effective redundancy criterion is called* fair *if there is a ground substitution σ for the free variables, such that $(\sigma\mathcal{T}_i)_{i\in\mathbb{N}}$ is a fair derivation of the corresponding ground calculus. We call such a σ a* fair instantiation *for the constrained formula tableau derivation.*

It is now easy to show completeness for well-behaved calculi:

Theorem 5. *If a constrained formula calculus*

- *conforms to the standard redundancy criterion and*
- *is reductive*
- *has the counterexample reduction property, then*

a fair derivation for an unsatisfiable formula ϕ contains a closable tableau.

Proof. Let σ be a fair instantiation for $(\mathcal{T}_i)_{i\in\mathbb{N}}$. Then $(\sigma\mathcal{T}_i)_{i\in\mathbb{N}}$ is a fair derivation of the corresponding ground calculus and $\sigma\mathcal{T}_0 = \mathcal{T}_0$, since the initial formula ϕ does not contain free variables. Theorem 4 ensures that some $\sigma\mathcal{T}_i$ is closed. Therefore, $\mathcal{T}_i$ is closed under σ. □

The big question is of course whether a constrained formula calculus actually admits fair derivations, and how these can be constructed algorithmically. There are two issues to be discussed here.

The first is that a series of inferences on a branch might 'change' the constraint of a formula ϕ, successively deriving $\phi \ll C_0$, $\phi \ll C_1, \ldots$. None of these formulae is persistent in the usual sense of the word. Still, there can be a substitution $\sigma \in \text{Sat}(C_0) \cap \text{Sat}(C_1) \cap \cdots$. The *instantiation* $\sigma\phi$ is therefore persistent, and a fair derivation must eventually perform inferences that correspond to ground inferences on $\sigma\phi$.

Consider for instance a calculus with the following hypothetical rules:

$$\text{STEP} \; \frac{p(t) \ll A, p(f(t)) \ll A, \Gamma \vdash}{p(t) \ll A, \Gamma \vdash} \qquad \text{CLOSE} \; \frac{\bot \ll A \vdash}{r(t) \ll A, \Gamma \vdash}$$
$$\text{for any term } t \qquad\qquad \text{for any term } t$$

$$\text{REDUCE} \; \frac{q(s) \ll A \,\&\, B \,\&\, s \equiv t, r(s) \ll A \,\&\, !(B \,\&\, s \equiv t), p(t) \ll B, \Gamma \vdash}{r(s) \ll A, p(t) \ll B, \Gamma \vdash}$$
$$\text{for any terms } s, t$$

where & is conjunction and ! is negation of constraints, and $\equiv$ denotes syntactic equality, as described by the equations (†). From a sequent

$$r(X),\, p(a) \vdash$$

we can derive, using REDUCE

$$q(X) \ll X \equiv a,\, r(X) \ll !\, X \equiv a,\, p(a) \vdash$$

and then, with STEP,

$$q(X) \ll X \equiv a,\, r(X) \ll !\, X \equiv a,\, p(a),\, p(f(a)) \vdash \quad .$$

Now we apply REDUCE again:

$$q(X) \ll X \equiv f(a),\, q(X) \ll X \equiv a,\, r(X) \ll !\, X \equiv a\,\&!\, X \equiv f(a),\, p(a),\, p(f(a) \vdash$$

and so on. The constraint on $r(X)$ gets more and more complicated, and none of the constrained formulae is persistent. But for fairness, we must eventually apply CLOSE, since this will not become redundant whatever the instantiation for X (unless there are other rules which eventually close the branch).

For some calculi, like standard free variable tableaux without constraints, such situations simply cannot occur. If they can however, a possible solution is to use a theorem proving procedure that achieves fairness not by managing a queue of formulae that remain to be processed, but a queue of rule applications: Any new constrained formula introduced to a branch should be checked for possible inferences in combination with other present formulae. All possible inferences should eventually be considered in a fair manner, *even if the original constrained formula gets deleted or changed.* When an inference's turn has come, it should be checked whether there are *now* formulae in the semi-sequent on which it can be applied.

The second issue is that of the fair instantiation of free variables. In many calculi, free variables are only introduced by a γ rule like[4]

$$\gamma \; \frac{[x/X]\phi, \forall x.\phi, \Gamma \vdash}{\forall x.\phi, \Gamma \vdash}$$

with a new free variable X.

The corresponding ground inferences are

$$\frac{[x/t]\phi, \forall x.\phi, \Gamma \vdash}{\forall x.\phi, \Gamma \vdash}$$

for any term t. In general, if a formula $\forall x.\phi$ is persistent on some branch of a fair ground derivation, this rule needs to be applied for *all* ground terms t, with the possible exception of terms for which $[x/t]\phi$ happens to be redundant. Therefore, in the calculus with free variables, a fair instantiation can in general only exist if infinitely many copies of $[x/X_i]\phi$ with different free variables are introduced on the branch. Therefore, the theorem proving procedure has to apply the γ rule again and again. The fair instantiation can then be defined by taking for instance an enumeration $(t_i)_{i\in\mathbb{N}}$ of all ground terms and requiring that $\sigma X_i = t_i$.

This is not necessarily the case for every rule that introduces a free variable. For instance, in Sect. 6 of [5], a constrained formula tableau version of the basic ordered paramodulation rule [2] is given, in which the new free variable is constrained to only one possible instantiation. Therefore, this rule needs to be applied only once.

Although these observations about fairness should cover the most common cases, in the framework given so far, the question ultimately has to be considered for each calculus. It will be an interesting topic for future research to find sensible restrictions of the given framework that permit general statements about fairness.

Another general remark is in order concerning our 'lifting', i.e. the relation between our free variable calculi to ground calculi. In particular for equality handling by rewriting, it is important to restrict the application of equalities to non-variable positions. This means that an inference that acts only on the instantiation of some free variables should not be needed. The framework presented so far does not help in excluding such inferences. A corresponding refinement is a further topic for future research.

7   Case Study: Free Variable NNF Hyper-tableaux

We will now study a constrained formula version of the NNF hyper-tableaux calculus of Sect. 5. Completeness of such a calculus has previously been shown using proof transformation arguments [6], but the proof using saturation up to

---

[4] When we don't write constraints, we mean the trivial constraint that is satisfied by all instantiations of the free variables.

redundancy will be a lot simpler. We will start from pre-skolemized formulae that contain no existential quantifiers, to avoid discussing the soundness issues that arise in connection with free variables in δ rules.

The rules of our calculus are as follows:

$$\alpha \; \frac{\phi \ll A, \psi \ll A, \Gamma \vdash}{\phi \wedge \psi \ll A, \Gamma \vdash} \qquad\qquad \beta \; \frac{\phi \ll A, \Gamma \vdash \quad \psi \ll A, \Gamma \vdash}{\phi \vee \psi \ll A, \Gamma \vdash}$$

where $\phi \vee \psi$ has at least one positive d-path.

$$\gamma \; \frac{[x/X]\phi \ll A, \forall x.\phi \ll A, \Gamma \vdash}{\forall x.\phi \ll A, \Gamma \vdash} \qquad \text{CLOSE} \; \frac{\bot \ll L \equiv M \,\&\, A \,\&\, B \vdash}{L \ll A, \neg M \ll B, \Gamma \vdash}$$

for a new free variable X

$$\text{SIMP} \; \frac{\mu\phi[\mu L] \ll L \equiv M \,\&\, A \,\&\, B, \phi \ll A \,\&\, !(L \equiv M \,\&\, B), L \ll B, \Gamma \vdash}{\phi \ll A, L \ll B, \Gamma \vdash}$$

where $\neg M \in lmn(\phi)$ and μ is a most general unifier of L and M.

It is not hard to see that the ground instances corresponding to the α, β, γ, and CLOSE rules are exactly the inferences of the respective rules in Sect. 4. For the SIMP rule, the corresponding ground inference under some instantiation $\sigma \in \text{Sat}(L \equiv M \,\&\, A \,\&\, B)$ is

$$\frac{\sigma\phi[\sigma L], \sigma L, \Gamma \vdash}{\sigma\phi, \sigma L, \Gamma \vdash}$$

which is just the SIMP rule of Sect. 5. For all $\sigma \notin \text{Sat}(L \equiv M \,\&\, A \,\&\, B)$, the constraints ensure that the corresponding ground inference under σ does not change the sequent. It follows that apart from the missing δ rule, the corresponding ground calculus is exactly the one from Sect. 5.

We conclude that any proof procedure that produces fair derivations in this calculus is complete. Let us analyze what is needed for fairness: free variables can only be introduced by the γ rule, so as discussed before, it needs to be applied infinitely often on each branch for any persistent occurrence of a constrained formula $\forall x.\phi \ll C$, producing formulae $[x/X_i]\phi$ with distinct variables. Since there are no rules that could delete such an occurrence, *all* occurrences of universally quantified formulae are persistent. The corresponding fair instantiation σ needs to make sure that if $\sigma \in \text{Sat}(C)$, then there is an X_i with $\sigma X_i = t$ for every ground term t. This is of course a well-known ingredient in many tableau completeness proofs.

Do we have the fairness problem of persistent ground instances $\sigma\phi$ of non-persistent formulae $\phi \ll C$ described in the previous section? Yes, we do! The SIMP rule can lead to similar chains of inferences as the REDUCE rule. Consider a formula $\phi = (\neg p(X) \wedge \neg p(b)) \vee q(X)$ in the place of the $r(X)$ in the REDUCE example. From a series of literals $p(a), p(f(a)), \ldots$, the SIMP rule allows to derive $q(a), q(f(a)), \ldots$, constantly changing the constraint on ϕ, although a SIMP on the other left-most negative literal $\neg p(b)$ might be possible all the time and necessary for completeness.

In this calculus, there is an easier way of coping with this problem than the one we hinted at in Sect. 6: Theorem 3 of [6] establishes the interesting fact that under certain sensible restrictions, our calculus always permits only a finite number of inferences without intervening γ inferences. This means that we can obtain fairness simply by requiring derivations to be built in such a way that γ inferences may only be applied when there are no more possible SIMP inferences.

This illustrates that the fairness question can be quite subtle, depending on the particular calculus at hand.

8   Conclusion

We have introduced a notion of saturation up to redundancy for tableau and sequent calculi, closely following the work of Bachmair and Ganzinger [1] for resolution calculi. We have shown a generic completeness theorem that makes it easy to show completeness of calculi with destructive rules. Notions and proofs were lifted to the case of free variable tableaux with constrained formulae. Some examples were given to illustrate the method.

Future work includes finding a generic way of achieving fairness for free variable calculi. A method of lifting that does not require inferences below variable positions would be needed to apply our technique to equality reasoning. One might also consider defining when whole branches are redundant with respect to the rest of a tableau, to allow redundancy elimination on the branch level. It might also be interesting to adapt the idea of 'histories' used in [5] instead of constraints with negations to our framework.

References

1. L. Bachmair and H. Ganzinger. Resolution theorem proving. In A. Robinson and A. Voronkov, editors, *Handbook of Automated Reasoning*, volume I, chapter 2, pages 19–99. Elsevier Science B.V., 2001.
2. L. Bachmair, H. Ganzinger, C. Lynch, and W. Snyder. Basic paramodulation. *Information and Computation*, 121(2):172–192, 1995.
3. D. Cantone and C. G. Zarba. A tableau calculus for integrating first-order reasoning with elementary set theory reasoning. In R. Dyckhoff, editor, *Proc. TABLEAUX 2000*, volume 1847 of *LNCS*, pages 143–159. Springer, 2000.
4. M. C. Fitting. *First-Order Logic and Automated Theorem Proving*. Springer, second edition, 1996.
5. M. Giese. A model generation style completeness proof for constraint tableaux with superposition. In U. Egly and C. G. Fermüller, editors, *Proc. TABLEAUX 2002*, volume 2381 of *LNCS*, pages 130–144. Springer, 2002.
6. M. Giese. Simplification rules for constrained formula tableaux. In M. Cialdea Mayer and F. Pirri, editors, *Proc. TABLEAUX 2003*, volume 2796 of *LNCS*, pages 65–80. Springer, 2003.
7. M. Giese. A calculus for type predicates and type coercion. In B. Beckert, editor, *Proc. TABLEAUX 2005*, volume 3702 of *LNAI*, pages 123–137. Springer, 2005.
8. R. M. Smullyan. *First-Order Logic*, volume 43 of *Ergebnisse der Mathematik und ihrer Grenzgebiete*. Springer, 1968.

Branching-Time Temporal Logic Extended with Qualitative Presburger Constraints

Laura Bozzelli and Régis Gascon

LSV, CNRS & ENS Cachan, France
{bozzelli, gascon}@lsv.ens-cachan.fr

Abstract. Recently, *LTL* extended with atomic formulas built over a constraint language interpreting variables in $\mathbb{Z}$ has been shown to have a decidable satisfiability and model-checking problem. This language allows to compare the variables at different states of the model and include periodicity constraints, comparison constraints, and a restricted form of quantification. On the other hand, the *CTL* counterpart of this logic (and hence also its *CTL** counterpart which subsumes both *LTL* and *CTL*) has an undecidable model-checking problem. In this paper, we substantially extend the decidability border, by considering a meaningful fragment of *CTL** extended with such constraints (which subsumes both the universal and existential fragments, as well as the *EF*-like fragment) and show that satisfiability and model-checking over relational automata that are abstraction of counter machines are decidable. The correctness and the termination of our algorithm rely on a suitable well quasi-ordering defined over the set of variable valuations.

1 Introduction

Model-checking of infinite-state counter systems. The formal verification of infinite-state systems has benefited from numerous decidable model-checking problems. This is the case for instance of timed automata [AD94], or subclasses of counter systems, see e.g. [CJ98]. Counter systems are finite state machines operating on a finite set of variables (counters or registers) interpreted as integers. Though simple problems like reachability are already undecidable for 2-counter Minsky machines [Min67], many interesting restrictions of counter systems have been studied, for which reachability and richer temporal properties have been shown to be decidable. For instance, Petri nets represent the subclass of counter systems obtained by removing the ability to test a counter for zero. Other examples include reversal-bounded counter machines [Iba78], flat counter systems [Boi98,BFLP03,LS04] and constraint automata with qualitative constraints on $\mathbb{Z}$ between the states of variables at different steps of the execution [DG05]. "Qualitative" means that the relationship between the constrained variables is not sharp, like $x < y$. This last class of systems can be seen as an abstraction of counter systems where increments and decrements are abstracted by comparisons and congruence relations modulo some integer. For example, $x = y + 1$ can be abstracted by $x > y \wedge x \equiv_{2^k} y + 1$. This is very common in various programming languages performing arithmetic operations modulo some integer, typically modulo 2^{32} or 2^{64} (see [MOS05]). Periodicity constraints have also found applications in formalisms dealing with calendars [LM01] and temporal reasoning in database access control [BBFS98].

M. Hermann and A. Voronkov (Eds.): LPAR 2006, LNAI 4246, pp. 197–211, 2006.
© Springer-Verlag Berlin Heidelberg 2006

Temporal logics extended with Presburger constraints. Classical problems studied on counter systems often reduce to the reachability of some control state. Recently, richer temporal properties have been investigated and formalized by introducing fragments of Presburger constraints in temporal logics. In this setting, atomic formulas are Presburger arithmetic constraints over variables (counters) taking values in $\mathbb{Z}$. Furthermore, these formalisms involve an hybrid of temporal logic and constraints, with varying degrees of interaction. For instance, one may be allowed to refer to the value of a variable x on the next time instant, leading to constraints of the form $x > Ox$. More generously, one may be permitted to refer to a future value of a variable x a certain number n of steps further. We denote this value by $O \ldots Ox$ where x is prefixed by n times the symbol O (in the following such an expression is abbreviated by $O^n x$). For linear-time temporal logics, such extensions can be found in numerous works, see for instance [BEH95,CC00,DD03]. However, full Presburger *LTL* is undecidable, and to regain decidability, one can either restrict the underlying constraint language, see e.g. [DD03,DG05], or restrict the logical language, see e.g. [BEH95,CC00]. In [DG05], full *LTL* extended with a wide set of qualitative constraints, including comparison and periodicity constraints, has been shown to have PSPACE-complete satisfiability and model-checking problems (over constraint automata mentioned above). Similar extensions have also been considered for description logics where models are Kripke structures, see for instance [Lut04]. On the other hand, to the best of our knowledge, very few works deal with decidable fragments of branching-time temporal logics enhanced with Presburger constraints. Actually, we can only refer to the work [Čer93], in which *CTL** extended with only comparison constraints is shown to have an undecidable model checking problem for *Integral Relational Automata* (undecidability already holds for the *CTL*-like fragment). However, model-checking for the existential and universal fragments are shown to be decidable. Note that the logic proposed in [Čer93] does not exhibit any form of interaction between the temporal operators and the comparison constraints (in particular, atomic formulas of the form $x < Oy$ are not considered).

Our contribution. In this paper, we introduce the logic *CCTL** as an extension of the branching–time temporal logic *CTL** with a wide set of qualitative constraints including periodicity constraints of the form $x \equiv_k y + c$, comparison constraints of the form $x < y$ and a restricted form of quantification. This logic is the branching–time counterpart of the constraint *LTL* defined in [DG05] and extends the logic from [Čer93] by introducing richer constraints and the possibility to compare counters at different states of the model. The operational models on which we check temporal properties expressed in this logic are extensions of Integral Relational Automata (*IRA*, for short) [BBK77,Čer93,ACJT96] introduced in [BBK77] as a model for studying possibilities of automated complete test set generation for data processing programs. Our extension is obtained by adding periodicity constraints and makes the new formalism an equivalent variant of the constraint automata with qualitative constrains mentioned above. However, *IRA* provide a representation that is more intuitive and closer to the operational semantics of programs manipulating integers.

Model-checking this extension of *IRA* against full *CCTL** is undecidable (also for the *CTL*-like fragment) as a consequence of [Čer93]. Thus, in this paper we investigate a meaningful fragment, which subsume both the existential and universal fragments as well as the *EF*-like fragment. For instance, the formula $A\Box E\Box(x = Ox)$ is in this fragment and states that for any reachable state, there is a computation starting from it in which the value of counter x remains constant. For this fragment, we show that both satisfiability and model checking of the proposed extension of *IRA* are decidable. The existential and universal fragments of *CCTL** are strictly more expressive than the constraint *LTL* defined in [DG05]. Moreover, the symbolic algorithm we describe builds a finite representation of the set of states satisfying a given formula, a very substantial information compared to the symbolic representation used in [DG05].

IRA belong to the class of well–structured transition systems which have been intensively studied, see e.g. [ACJT96,FS01]. Hence, one can define a decidable well-quasi ordering on the set of states, which is also a simulation. This property is sufficient to guarantee decidability of simple problems such as coverability, but not to decide richer properties like liveness properties[1] which can be expressed in our logical framework. Thus, we need to use a more sophisticated approach, which is a technical non-trivial generalization and refinement of the one used in [Čer93] combining automata-based techniques, theory of well quasi-ordering, and the theory of a specific class of linear inequality systems (used to represent upward closed sets of states). The correctness and the termination of the algorithm rely on a suitable well quasi-ordering defined over these inequality systems. Another major contribution consists in extending to a larger framework the original and difficult proof from [Čer93] and in clarifying all the technical lemmas needed in the last part of the algorithm, which are omitted in [Čer93].

Due to lack of space, many proofs are omitted and can be found in [BG06].

2   Preliminaries

2.1   Language of Constraints

Let VAR be a countable set of variables. For $D \subseteq$ VAR, a *valuation* over D is a map $v : D \to \mathbb{Z}$. For all $x \in D$, we denote by $v.x$ the value assigned to x in v.

The *language of constraints p*, denoted by *IPC** [DG05], is defined as follows: [2]

$$p ::= t \mid x \sim y \mid p \wedge p \mid \neg p$$
$$t ::= x \equiv_k [c_1, c_2] \mid x \equiv_k y + [c_1, c_2] \mid x = y \mid x \sim c \mid t \wedge t \mid \neg t \mid \exists x\, t$$

where $\sim \in \{<, \leq, >, \geq, =\}$, $x, y \in$ VAR, $k \in \mathbb{N} \setminus \{0\}$, and $c_1, c_2, c \in \mathbb{Z}$. For a constraint p and a valuation v over VAR, the satisfaction relation $v \models p$ is defined as follows (we omit the standard clauses for negation, conjunction, and inequalities):

$$- v \models x \equiv_k [c_1, c_2] \stackrel{\text{def}}{\Leftrightarrow} \exists\, c_1 \leq c \leq c_2 \text{ and } m \in \mathbb{Z}.\ v.x = c + m \cdot k;$$
$$- v \models x \equiv_k y + [c_1, c_2] \stackrel{\text{def}}{\Leftrightarrow} \exists\, c_1 \leq c \leq c_2 \text{ and } m \in \mathbb{Z}.\ v.x = v.y + c + m \cdot k;$$
$$- v \models \exists x\, t \stackrel{\text{def}}{\Leftrightarrow} \exists\, c \in \mathbb{Z}.\ v[x \leftarrow c] \models t$$

---

[1] For instance, liveness properties in lossy channel systems are undecidable [AJ94].

[2] Note that constraints of the form $\exists x$, $x < y$ are not allowed since they leads to the undecidability already for the corresponding LTL extension (see [DG05]).

where $v[x \leftarrow c].x' = v.x'$ if $x \neq x'$ and $v[x \leftarrow c].x = c$. A constraint p is *atomic* if it has one of the following forms: $x \equiv_k c \mid x \sim y \mid x \sim c$, where $\sim \in \{<, \leq, >, \geq, =\}$ and $x \equiv_k c$ is an abbreviation for $x \equiv_k [c, c]$. Evidently, for a constraint p, whether a valuation v satisfies p depends only on the values of v over the finite set $Vars(p)$ of free variables occurring in p. Thus, in the following as interpretations of a constraint p we consider the set of valuations over finite supersets of $Vars(p)$.

Lemma 1 ([DG05]). *Any IPC* constraint can be effectively converted into an equivalent positive boolean combination of atomic IPC* constraints.*

The translation implies an exponential blowup of the size of the formula w.r.t the constants used. However, the results in the following do not refer to complexity issues.

2.2 The Constrained Branching-Time Temporal Logic (*CCTL**)

We introduce the *constrained branching-time temporal logic (CCTL*)* as an extension of the standard propositional logic *CTL** [EH86] where atomic propositions are replaced by *IPC** constraints between terms representing the value of variables at different sates of the model. We denote these atomic formulae by $p[x_1 \leftarrow O^{i_1} x_{j_1}, \ldots, x_r \leftarrow O^{i_r} x_{j_r}]$, where p is an *IPC** constraint with free variables $x_1, \ldots, x_r$ and we substitute each occurrence of variable x_l with $O^{i_l} x_{j_l}$ (corresponding to variable x_{j_l} preceded by i_l "next" symbols). The expression $O^i x$ represents the value of the variable x at the ith next state. For example, $Oy \equiv_2 x + 1$ and $x < Oy$ are atomic formulae of *CCTL**.

As for standard *CTL**, there are two types of formulas in *CCTL**: *state formulas* ξ whose satisfaction is related to a specific state, and *path formulas* ψ, whose satisfaction is related to a specific path. Their syntax is inductively defined as follows:

$$\xi := \top \mid \xi \vee \xi \mid \xi \wedge \xi \mid A \psi \mid E \psi$$
$$\psi := \xi \mid p[x_1 \leftarrow O^{i_1} x_{j_1}, \ldots, x_r \leftarrow O^{i_r} x_{j_r}] \mid \psi \vee \psi \mid \psi \wedge \psi \mid O\psi \mid \Box\psi \mid \psi U \psi$$

where $\top$ denotes "true", E ("for some path") and A ("for all paths") are path quantifiers, and O ("next"), U ("until"), and $\Box$ ("always") are the usual linear temporal operators.[3] The set of state formulas ξ forms the language *CCTL**. For a set X of state formulas, the set of path formulas ψ defined only from state formulas in X is denoted by $PLF(X)$.

For a *CCTL** formula ξ, let $Val(\xi)$ be the set of valuations over finite sets $D \subseteq \text{VAR}$ such that D contains the variables occurring in ξ. The interpretations for the formula ξ are labelled graphs $\mathcal{G} = \langle S, \rightarrow, \mu \rangle$, where S is a (possible infinite) set of vertices (here, called states), $\rightarrow \subseteq S \times S$ is the edge relation, which is total (i.e., for every $s \in S$, $s \rightarrow s'$ for some $s' \in S$), and $\mu : S \rightarrow Val(\xi)$ maps each state $s \in S$ to a valuation in $Val(\xi)$. A path is a sequence of states $\pi = s_0, s_1, \ldots$ such that $s_{i-1} \rightarrow s_i$ for any $1 \leq i < |\pi|$. We denote the suffix $s_i, s_{i+1}, \ldots$ of π by π^i, and the i-th state of π by $\pi(i)$. Let $s \in S$ and π be a infinite path of $\mathcal{G}$. For a state (resp., path) formula ξ (resp., ψ), the satisfaction relation $(\mathcal{G}, s) \models \xi$ (resp., $(\mathcal{G}, \pi) \models \psi$), meaning that ξ (resp., ψ) holds at state s (resp., holds along π) in $\mathcal{G}$, is defined by induction. The clauses for conjunction and disjunction are standard. For the other clauses we have:

---

[3] We have defined a positive normal form of the logic *CCTL**, i.e. negation is used only in atomic formulae. Moreover, the given syntax is complete since the dual $\tilde{U}$ of the until operator can be expressed in terms of the until and always operator: $\psi_1 \tilde{U} \psi_2 \equiv \Box\psi_2 \vee (\psi_2 U(\psi_1 \wedge \psi_2))$.

- $(\mathcal{G}, s) \models A\,\psi \overset{\text{def}}{\Leftrightarrow}$ for each infinite path π from s, $(\mathcal{G}, \pi) \models \psi$;
- $(\mathcal{G}, s) \models E\,\psi \overset{\text{def}}{\Leftrightarrow}$ there exists an infinite path π from s such that $(\mathcal{G}, \pi) \models \psi$;
- $(\mathcal{G}, \pi) \models \xi \overset{\text{def}}{\Leftrightarrow} (\mathcal{G}, \pi(0)) \models \xi$;
- $(\mathcal{G}, \pi) \models p[x_1 \leftarrow \mathsf{O}^{i_1} x_{j_1}, \ldots, x_r \leftarrow \mathsf{O}^{i_r} x_{j_r}] \overset{\text{def}}{\Leftrightarrow}$
  $\mu(\pi(0))[x_1 \leftarrow \mu(\pi(i_1)).x_{j_1}, \ldots, x_r \leftarrow \mu(\pi(i_r)).x_{j_r}] \models p$;
- $(\mathcal{G}, \pi) \models \mathsf{O}\psi \overset{\text{def}}{\Leftrightarrow} (\mathcal{G}, \pi^1) \models \psi$;
- $(\mathcal{G}, \pi) \models \Box\psi \overset{\text{def}}{\Leftrightarrow}$ for all $i \geq 0$, $(\mathcal{G}, \pi^i) \models \psi$;
- $(\mathcal{G}, \pi) \models \psi_1 \mathsf{U} \psi_2 \overset{\text{def}}{\Leftrightarrow} \exists i \geq 0.\ (\mathcal{G}, \pi^i) \models \psi_2$ and $\forall j < i.\ (\mathcal{G}, \pi^j) \models \psi_1$.

$\mathcal{G}$ is a *model* of ξ, written $\mathcal{G} \models \xi$ iff $(\mathcal{G}, s) \models \xi$ for some state s. We denote by $[\![\xi]\!]_{SAT}$ the set of valuations v over $Vars(\xi)$ such that $(\mathcal{G}, s) \models \xi$ for some model $\mathcal{G}$ and state s of $\mathcal{G}$ with $\mu(s) = v$. A $CCTL^*$ formula ξ is *satisfiable* iff there exists a model of ξ.

Assumption: By Lemma 1, we can assume w.l.o.g. that the IPC^* constraints p associated with atomic formulas $p[x_1 \leftarrow \mathsf{O}^{i_1} x_{j_1}, \ldots, x_r \leftarrow \mathsf{O}^{i_r} x_{j_r}]$ are atomic.

The existential fragment $E\text{--}CCTL^*$ and the dual universal fragment $A\text{--}CCTL^*$ of $CCTL^*$ are obtained by disallowing respectively the universal and the existential path quantifier. In order to consider a fragment as large as possible, we also introduce CEF^+ which subsumes $E\text{--}CCTL^*$, $A\text{--}CCTL^*$ and the IPC^*-constrained counterpart of EF logic, a well-know fragment of standard CTL closed under boolean connectives (see e.g., [May01]). CEF^+ is defined as follows (where ξ_E is an $E\text{--}CCTL^*$ formula):

$$\xi := \xi_E \mid \neg\xi \mid \xi \vee \xi \mid E(\xi_E \mathsf{U} \xi) \mid E\mathsf{O}\xi$$

2.3   Integral Relational Automata

In this section we recall the framework of *Integral Relational Automata* (IRA) introduced in [BBK77]. An *IRA* consists of a finite-state machine enhanced with a finite number of counters. The operation repertoire of *IRA* includes assignment, input/output operations and guards of the form $x \sim y$ or $x \sim c$ with $\sim \in \{<, \leq, >, \geq, =\}$. We extend this operational model by allowing periodicity constraints as guards. Note that if we also allow guards of the form $x \leq y + c$, then the resulting formalism is Turing-complete (since we can easily simulate unrestricted counter machines). Let OP be the set of operations defined as follows:

$$p \mid ?x \mid !x \mid !c \mid x \leftarrow y \mid x \leftarrow c \mid \text{NOP}$$

where p is an *atomic IPC** constraint, $x, y \in \text{VAR}$ and $c \in \mathbb{Z}$. Informally, $?x$ assigns a new integral value to the variable x, $!x$ (resp $!c$) outputs the value of variable x (resp., constant c), $x \leftarrow y$ (resp. $x \leftarrow c$) assigns the value of variable y (resp., constant c) to x, and NOP is the dummy operation. The atomic IPC^* constraints are used as guards.

An *Integral Relational Automaton* (IRA) is a tuple $P = \langle V(P), E(P), \ell_V, \ell_E \rangle$, where $V(P)$ is the finite set of *vertices*, $E(P) \subseteq V(P) \times V(P)$ is the set of *edges*, $\ell_V : V(P) \to OP$ associates an operation to every vertex, and $\ell_E : E(P) \to \{+, -\}$ is a labelling of the edges (used for tests).

Let $Vars(P)$ be the set of all P variables (used in the operations of P) and $Cons(P)$ $\subseteq \mathbb{Z}$ be the least set containing all the P constants and such that $0 \in Cons(P)$ and for all $c_1, c_2 \in Cons(P)$, $c_1 \leq c \leq c_2$ implies $c \in Cons(P)$. Moreover, let $Mod(P)$ be the set of the *modulo constants* k used in the periodicity constrains $x \equiv_k c$ of P.

Notation: For convenience, we define $v.c = c$ for any valuation v and constant $c \in \mathbb{Z}$.

The semantics of an *IRA* P is described by a labelled graph $\mathcal{G}(P) = \langle \mathcal{S}(P), \rightarrow, \mu \rangle$, where the set of states $\mathcal{S}(P)$ is the set of pairs $\langle n, v \rangle$ such that $n \in V(P)$ is a vertex and v is a valuation over $Vars(P)$, $\mu(\langle n, v \rangle) = v$ for all $\langle n, v \rangle \in \mathcal{S}(P)$, and $\langle n, v \rangle \rightarrow \langle n', v' \rangle$ if and only if $e = (n, n') \in E(P)$ and one of the following conditions holds:

- $\ell_V(n) = ?x$ and $v'.y = v.y$ for every $y \in Vars(P) \setminus \{x\}$,
- $\ell_V(n) = !x$ or $\ell_V(n) = !c$ or $\ell_V(n) = \text{NOP}$ and $v' = v$,
- $\ell_V(n) = x \leftarrow a$, $v'.x = v.a$, and $v'.y = v.y$ for every $y \in Vars(P) \setminus \{x\}$,
- $\ell_V(n) = p$, $v' = v$, and *either* $\ell_E(e) = +$ and $v \models p$, or $\ell_E(e) = -$ and $v \not\models p$.

Note that $\mathcal{G}(P)$ is infinitely-branching because of input operations. An *history* of P is a path of $\mathcal{G}(P)$. An infinite history is also called a *computation*. A path $\overline{n}$ of P is a path in the finite–state graph $\langle V(P), E(P) \rangle$. For a finite path $\overline{n}$ of P, two tuples $\mathcal{N} = \langle n_1, \ldots, n_k \rangle$ and $\mathcal{N}' = \langle n'_1, \ldots, n'_h \rangle$ of P-vertices, we say that $\overline{n}$ is a path from $\mathcal{N}$ to $\mathcal{N}'$ iff $|\overline{n}| \geq h + k$ and $n_1, \ldots, n_h$ (resp., $n'_1, \ldots, n'_h$) is a prefix (resp., suffix) of P. The notion of path $\overline{n}$ from a tuple of vertices is similar. These notions can be extended to histories of P in a natural way. Let $\overline{n}_1$ be a P path from $\mathcal{N}_1$ to $\mathcal{N}$ and $\overline{n}_2$ be a P path from $\mathcal{N}$. We denote by $[\overline{n}_1 + \overline{n}_2]_\mathcal{N}$ the P path obtained by concatenating $\overline{n}_1$ with the path obtained from $\overline{n}_2$ by eliminating the prefix corresponding to $\mathcal{N}$. This notion of concatenation can be extended to histories in a natural way. In the following, a k-tuple $\langle \langle n_1, v_1 \rangle, \ldots, \langle n_k, v_k \rangle \rangle$ of P states is also denoted by $\langle \langle n_1, \ldots, n_k \rangle, \langle v_1, \ldots, v_k \rangle \rangle$.

We say that an *IRA* P is *complete* if the edge relation $E(P)$ is total and for each vertex n labelled by an *IPC** constraint and each flag $f \in \{+, -\}$, there is an edge labelled by f and having n as source. W.l.o.g. we assume that the *IRA* under our consideration are complete (this implies that the edge relation in $\mathcal{G}(P)$ is total).

Extended Integral Relational Automata: for technical reasons, we introduce *Extended IRA (EIRA)*. An *EIRA* is a pair $\langle P, \ell_{EXT} \rangle$ where P is an *IRA* and ℓ_{EXT} is an additional P-vertex-labelling, mapping each vertex $n \in V(P)$ to a finite set (interpreted as conjunction) of *CCTL** atomic formulas $p[x_1 \leftarrow O^{i_1} x_{j_1}, \ldots, x_r \leftarrow O^{i_r} x_{j_r}]$ (where p is an atomic *IPC** constraint). This labelling induces constraints between the variables of the current state and the variables of succeeding states (along a computation).

For a (finite or infinite) P-history $\pi = \langle n_1, v_1 \rangle, \langle n_2, v_2 \rangle, \ldots$, we say that π is *fair* if π is consistent with the ℓ_{EXT}–labelling. Formally, we require that for all $1 \leq k \leq |\pi|$ and $p[x_1 \leftarrow O^{i_1} x_{j_1}, \ldots, x_r \leftarrow O^{i_r} x_{j_r}] \in \ell_{EXT}(n_k)$, the following holds: if $k + i_p \leq |\pi|$ for all $1 \leq p \leq r$, then $v_k[x_1 \leftarrow v_{k+i_1}.x_{j_1}, \ldots, x_r \leftarrow v_{k+i_r}.x_{j_r}] \models p$.

In this paper we are interested in the following problem:

Model Checking Problem of IRA Against CCTL* : given an *IRA* P, a state s_0 of P, and a *CCTL** formula ξ with $Vars(\xi) \subseteq Vars(P)$, does $(\mathcal{G}(P), s_0) \models \xi$ hold?

In the following, we denote by $[\![\xi]\!]_P$ the set of P states s such that $(\mathcal{G}(P), s) \models \xi$. Model checking *IRA* against full *CCTL** is undecidable (also for the *CTL*-like fragment) as a consequence of [Čer93]. Thus, in the following, we analyze the fragment CEF^+. consider the satisfiability problem for CEF^+. We start by giving a symbolic model checking algorithm for IRA against E–$CCTL^*$.

3   Symbolic Model Checking of IRA Against E–$CCTL^*$

In this section we show that given an IRA P and an E–$CCTL^*$ formula ξ with $Vars(\xi) \subseteq Vars(P)$, we can compute a finite representation of $[\![\xi]\!]_P$. In the following, we can assume w.l.o.g. that $Cons(\xi) \subseteq Cons(P)$ and $Mod(\xi) \subseteq Mod(P)$, where $Cons(\xi)$ (resp., $Mod(\xi)$) denote the set of constants (resp., modulo constants) occurring in ξ.

First, we recall some basic notions. For a set S, a *quasi-ordering* (*qo*, for short) $\preceq$ over S is a reflexive and transitive (binary) relation on S. Given such a *qo*, we say that $U \subseteq S$ is an *upward closed set* if for all $x \in S$ and $y \in U$, $y \preceq x$ implies $x \in U$. We say that $\preceq$ is a *partial-order* (*po*, for short) iff $x \preceq y$ and $y \preceq x$ imply $x = y$. Finally, we say that the *qo* $\preceq$ is a *well quasi-ordering* (*wqo*, for short) if for every infinite sequence $x_0, x_1, x_2, \ldots$ of elements of S there exist indices $i < j$ such that $x_i \preceq x_j$.

Following [Čer93], we define a *wqo* on the set $\mathcal{S}(P)$ of P states (that is also a *po*). Then, in order to solve the model-checking problem, we will show that: (1) $[\![\xi]\!]_P$ is an upward closed set; (2) we can compute a finite representation $R([\![\xi]\!]_P)$ of this set; (3) we can check whether a given a state s belongs to $R([\![\xi]\!]_P)$.

We start by defining such a *wqo*. Let κ be the least common multiple of the constants in $Mod(P) \cup \{1\}$. We define a *po* $\preceq$ over tuples of valuations over $Vars(P)$ as follows: $\langle v_1, \ldots, v_h \rangle \preceq \langle v'_1, \ldots, v'_k \rangle$ iff $h = k$ and for all $1 \leq i, j \leq h$ and $a, b \in Cons(P) \cup Vars(P)$, the following holds: (1) $v_i.a \geq v_j.b$ iff $v'_i.a \geq v'_j.b$, (2) $v_i.a \equiv_\kappa v'_i.a$, and (3) if $v_i.a \geq v_j.b$, then $v'_i.a - v'_j.b \geq v_i.a - v_j.b$.[4] We write simply $v_1 \preceq v'_1$ if $h = 1$. Note that $v_i \preceq v'_i$ for all $1 \leq i \leq h$ does not imply that $\langle v_1, \ldots, v_h \rangle \preceq \langle v'_1, \ldots, v'_h \rangle$. Finally, for two h-tuples of states $\langle \mathcal{N}, \mathcal{V} \rangle, \langle \mathcal{N}', \mathcal{V}' \rangle$, we write $\langle \mathcal{N}, \mathcal{V} \rangle \preceq \langle \mathcal{N}', \mathcal{V}' \rangle$ to mean that $\mathcal{N} = \mathcal{N}'$ and $\mathcal{V} \preceq \mathcal{V}'$. The proofs of the following two results are given in [BG06].

Proposition 1. *For every $h \geq 1$, the partial order $\preceq$ is a* wqo *over the set of h-tuples of valuations over $Vars(P)$.*

Lemma 2 (Simulation Lemma)

1. *Let $\pi = \langle n_1, v_1 \rangle, \ldots, \langle n_h, v_h \rangle$ be an history and $v'_1 \succeq v_1$. Then, there is an history $\pi' = \langle n_1, v'_1 \rangle, \ldots, \langle n_h, v'_h \rangle$ such that $\langle v'_1, \ldots, v'_h \rangle \succeq \langle v_1, \ldots, v_h \rangle$;*
2. *Let $\pi = \langle n_1, v_1 \rangle, \langle n_2, v_2 \rangle, \ldots$ be a computation and $v'_1 \succeq v_1$. Then, there is a computation $\pi' = \langle n_1, v'_1 \rangle, \langle n_2, v'_2 \rangle, \ldots$ s.t. for all $h \geq 1$, $\langle v'_1, \ldots, v'_h \rangle \succeq \langle v_1, \ldots, v_h \rangle$.*

Thanks to the Simulation Lemma, we can prove the first important result.

Proposition 2. $[\![\xi]\!]_P$ *is an upward closed set with respect to $\preceq$.*

Proof. The proof is by structural induction on ξ. The cases $\xi = \top$, $\xi = \xi_1 \vee \xi_2$, and $\xi = \xi_1 \wedge \xi_2$ are obvious since $[\![\top]\!]_P = \mathcal{S}(P)$, $[\![\xi_1 \vee \xi_2]\!]_P = [\![\xi_1]\!]_P \cup [\![\xi_2]\!]_P$, $[\![\xi_1 \wedge \xi_2]\!]_P = [\![\xi_1]\!]_P \cap [\![\xi_2]\!]_P$, and upward closed sets are closed under union and intersection.

---

[4] So, the relation $\preceq$ depends on parameters $Vars(P), Cons(P)$, and κ.

Now, assume that $\xi = E\psi$ for some path formula ψ. Then, there is a set X of state sub-formulas of ξ such that $\psi \in PLF(X)$. Let $s_1 \in [\![E\psi]\!]_P$ and $\bar{s}_1 \succeq s_1$. We claim that $\bar{s}_1 \in [\![E\psi]\!]_P$. Since $s_1 \in [\![E\psi]\!]_P$, there is a computation $\pi = s_1, s_2, \ldots$ such that $(\mathcal{G}(P), \pi) \models \psi$. Since $\bar{s}_1 \succeq s_1$, by Property 2 of Simulation Lemma and definition of $\preceq$, it easily follows that there is a computation $\bar{\pi} = \bar{s}_1, \bar{s}_2, \ldots$ such that for all $i \geq 1$ and atomic formula $\psi_{at} = p[x_1 \leftarrow O^{i_1} x_{j_1}, \ldots, x_r \leftarrow O^{i_r} x_{j_r}]$ with constants in $Cons(P)$ and modulo constants in $Mod(P)$: $\bar{s}_i \succeq s_i$ and $(\mathcal{G}(P), \pi^i) \models \psi_{at}$ if and only if $(\mathcal{G}(P), \bar{\pi}^i) \models \psi_{at}$. Moreover, for all $i \geq 1$ and $\xi' \in X$, by the induction hypothesis and the fact that $\bar{s}_i \succeq s_i$, we have that $s_i \in [\![\xi']\!]_P$ implies $\bar{s}_i \in [\![\xi']\!]_P$. These properties evidently imply $(\mathcal{G}(P), \bar{\pi}) \models \psi$, i.e. $\bar{s}_1 \in [\![E\psi]\!]_P$. Therefore, the claim holds.   □

In the following subsection, we introduce the framework of *modulo–κ Graphose in-equality Systems* (κ–*GS*, for short) as a finite representation of upward closed sets of P states (w.r.t. $\preceq$). In Subsection 3.2, we show some technical results on extended *IRA* and finally, in Subsection 3.3, we describe an algorithm to compute a κ-*GS* representation of the upward closed set $[\![\xi]\!]_P$.

3.1   Modulo–κ Graphose Inequality Systems

κ-*GS* extend *Graphose inequality Systems* introduced in [Čer93] by allowing to specify periodicity constraints on the set of solutions. Formally, for $\kappa \geq 1$, a κ–*GS* is a tuple $G = \langle D, C, w, mod \rangle$, where $D \subseteq$ VAR is a finite set of variables, $C \subseteq \mathbb{Z}$ is a finite set of integral constants, $w : A \times A \to \mathbb{Z}^-$ for $A = D \cup C$ and $\mathbb{Z}^- = \mathbb{Z} \cup \{-\infty\}$ is a *weight function*, and *mod* is a map $mod : A \to \{0, \ldots, \kappa - 1\}$.

The semantics of a κ–*GS* G is given by specifying the set $Sol(G)$ of its *solutions*. A valuation v over D is said to be a solution of G iff for all $a, b \in A$,

$$v.a - v.b \geq w(a, b) \quad \text{and} \quad v.a \equiv_\kappa mod(a)$$

where by definition for $c \in C$, $mod(c) \equiv_\kappa c$. The κ–*GS* G can be interpreted as a graph with set of vertices A and such that there is an edge from $a \in A$ to $b \in A$ with the *weight* $w(a, b)$ whenever $w(a, b) \neq -\infty$. Finding a solution of G means assigning integral values to the variable vertices so that the constraints imposed by *mod* are satisfied and for every edge in G, the difference between its source and target vertex values is at least the weight associated with the edge.

A κ-*GS* $G = \langle D, C, w, mod \rangle$ is called *consistent* if it has a solution. Furthermore, we say that G is *positive* if for all $a, b \in D \cup C$, either $w(a, b) = -\infty$ or $w(a, b) \geq 0$. A positive κ-*GS* is also denoted by κ-*PGS*. A κ-*GS* $G = \langle D, C, w, mod \rangle$ is *normalized* iff for all $a, b, c \in D \cup C$, (1) $w(a, b) \geq w(a, c) + w(c, b)$ and (2) $w(a, b) \neq -\infty$ implies $w(a, b) \equiv_\kappa mod(a) - mod(b)$.

Proposition 3 (Effectiveness of the κ-*GS* representation). *We can decide whether a κ-GS $G = \langle D, C, w, mod \rangle$ is consistent. In this case we can build effectively an equivalent normalized κ-GS $|G| = \langle D, C, |w|, mod \rangle$, called normal form of G, such that: (1) $Sol(|G|) = Sol(G)$, (2) $|G|$ is positive if G is positive, (3) every solution of the restriction of $|G|$ to a subset of D can be extended to a complete solution of $|G|$.*

Given an *IRA* P, let κ be the least common multiple of the integers in $Mod(P) \cup \{1\}$. A κ-*GS* $H = \langle D, C, w, mod \rangle$ is called *local* for P iff $D = Vars(P)$ and $C = Cons(P)$. A set of states $Y \subseteq \mathcal{S}(P)$ is said to be κ-*GS-represented* by a family of finite sets $(\mathcal{H}_n)_{n \in V(P)}$ of local κ-*GS* if for every state $\langle n, v \rangle \in Y$ we have $v \in Sol(H)$ for some $H \in \mathcal{H}_n$. By definition of *wqo* $\preceq$, it easily follows that local *positive* κ-*GS* constitute an effective representation of upward closed sets of states in $\mathcal{S}(P)$ (see details in [BG06]).

Proposition 4. κ-GS *representations are effectively closed under complementation.*

Proposition 5. *For every set of states* $U \subseteq \mathcal{S}(P)$, U *is* κ-PGS-*representable iff* U *is an upward closed set.*

Definition 1 (Intersection of κ-GS). *Given two* κ-GS $G_1 = \langle D_1, C_1, w_1, mod_1 \rangle$ *and* $G_2 = \langle D_2, C_2, w_2, mod_2 \rangle$, *their intersection* $G_1 \bigotimes G_2 = \langle D_1 \cup D_2, C_1 \cup C_2, w, mod \rangle$ *is defined by:*

- $G_1 \bigotimes G_2 = \text{nil}^5$ *if there is* $a \in D_1 \cap D_2$ *such that* $mod_1(a) \neq mod_2(a)$;
- *otherwise for all* $a, b \in D_1 \cup D_2 \cup C_1 \cup C_2$, $mod(a) = max\{mod_1'(a), mod_2'(a)\}$ *and* $w(a, b) = max\{w_1'(a, b), w_2'(a, b)\}$ *where (for* $i = 1, 2$)
  - *if* $a \in D_i \cup C_i$ *then* $mod_i'(a) = mod_i(a)$, *else* $mod_i'(a) = -\infty$
  - *if* $a, b \in D_i \cup C_i$ *then* $w_i'(a, b) = w_i(a, b)$, *else* $w_i'(a, b) = -\infty$.

Note that intersection of κ-*GS* preserves positiveness. Moreover, the following holds.

Proposition 6. *Let* $G = \langle D, C, w, mod \rangle$ *and* $G' = \langle D', C', w', mod' \rangle$ *be two* κ-GS. *Then, for* $v : D \cup D' \to \mathbb{Z}$, $v \in Sol(G \bigotimes G')$ *iff* $v|_D \in Sol(G)$ *and* $v|_{D'} \in Sol(G')$. *In particular, for* $D = D'$, $Sol(G \bigotimes G') = Sol(G) \cap Sol(G')$.

3.2 Symbolic Characterization of Fair Computations in *EIRA*

In this section, we essentially show that given an *EIRA*, we can compute a *PGS*-representation of the set of states s such that there is a *fair* computation starting from s. This technical result non-trivially generalizes [Čer93, Lemma 5.11] and is used in the following to solve model-checking of *IRA* against *E–CCTL**.

Let $\langle P, \ell_{EXT} \rangle$ be an *EIRA* and $\mathcal{K}$ the maximal natural number i such that a term of the form $O^i x$ occurs in $\langle P, \ell_{EXT} \rangle$ for some variable x. W.l.o.g., we can assume that $\mathcal{K} \geq 1$ and all the constants (resp., modulo constants) occurring in the atomic formulas of $\langle P, \ell_{EXT} \rangle$ are in $Cons(P)$ (resp. $Mod(P)$). We denote by κ the least common multiple of the integers in $Mod(P) \cup \{1\}$ and $\mathcal{S}(P)^\dagger$ be the set of tuples of P states. In the following we consider only κ-*PGS* or κ-*GS* but we write simply *PGS* or *GS*.

Assume that $U \subseteq \mathcal{S}(P)$ is an *upward closed set* given by a *PGS*-representation. For a set $F \subseteq V(P)$ of P vertices, we denote by $[\![E \square^F U]\!]_P$ the set of P states s such that there is a *fair* computation from s that only visits states of U and contains infinite occurrences of states $\langle n, v \rangle$ with $n \in F$. The main result of this subsection is the following:

---

^{5} nil denotes some inconsistent κ-*PGS* over $D_1 \cup D_2$ and $C_1 \cup C_2$.

Theorem 1. *Given a set $F \subseteq V(P)$ of P vertices, one can build a PGS representation of the set $[\![E \square^F U]\!]_P$.*

To prove this result, we show two important preliminary results (Theorems 2 and 3).

For two tuples $\langle \mathcal{N}, \mathcal{V} \rangle$ and $\langle \mathcal{N}', \mathcal{V}' \rangle$ of P states, a P path $\overline{n}$ from $\mathcal{N}$ to $\mathcal{N}'$, we write:

- $\langle \mathcal{N}, \mathcal{V} \rangle \overset{\mathcal{K}}{\rightsquigarrow}{}^U \langle \mathcal{N}', \mathcal{V}' \rangle$ to mean that there is a *fair* history π from $\langle \mathcal{N}, \mathcal{V} \rangle$ to $\langle \mathcal{N}', \mathcal{V}' \rangle$ visiting only states in U, where $|\pi| = m \cdot \mathcal{K}$ with $m \geq 2$ (*fair reachability relation*);
- $\langle \mathcal{N}, \mathcal{V} \rangle \rightsquigarrow{}^U_{\overline{n}} \langle \mathcal{N}', \mathcal{V}' \rangle$ to mean that $\langle \mathcal{N}, \mathcal{V} \rangle \overset{\mathcal{K}}{\rightsquigarrow}{}^U \langle \mathcal{N}', \mathcal{V}' \rangle$ by a fair history π whose projection on $V(P)$ is the path $\overline{n}$.

For all $i \geq 1$, let $Vars_i$ be a fresh copy of $Vars(P)$ (we need this notation to formalize access to several copies of P variables), $\mathcal{K}Vars = \bigcup_{i=1}^{i=\mathcal{K}} Vars_i = \{y_1 \ldots, y_p\}$ and $\mathcal{K}Vars' = \{y'_1, \ldots, y'_p\}$. Given a $\mathcal{K}$-tuple $\mathcal{V} = \langle v_1, \ldots, v_{\mathcal{K}} \rangle$ of valuations over $Vars(P)$, for all $x \in \mathcal{K}Vars$ such that $x \in Vars_i$ (for some $1 \leq i \leq \mathcal{K}$) is a copy of variable $y \in Vars(P)$, $\mathcal{V}.x$ denotes the value of the component y of v_i.

A GS $G = \langle D, C, w, mod \rangle$ is called $\mathcal{K}$–*local* for P iff $D = \mathcal{K}Vars$ and $C = Cons(P)$. We denote by $Sat(G)$ the set of $\mathcal{K}$-tuples $\mathcal{V}$ of valuations over $Vars(P)$ that *satisfy* G, where $\mathcal{V}$ satisfies G iff the mapping $v : D \to \mathbb{Z}$ defined as $v.x = \mathcal{V}.x$ is a solution of G. We use $\mathcal{K}$–*local GS* to represent sets of $\mathcal{K}$-tuples of P states. Intuitively, a $\mathcal{K}$–*local GS* contains all the informations needed to evaluate an atomic constraint where all the terms of the form $O^i x$ are such that $i \leq \mathcal{K}$. A set $X \subseteq \mathcal{S}(P)^{\mathcal{K}}$ of $\mathcal{K}$-tuples of P states is *GS-represented* by a family of finite sets $(\mathcal{G}_{\mathcal{N}})_{\mathcal{N} \in V(P)^{\mathcal{K}}}$ of $\mathcal{K}$–local GS if $\langle \mathcal{N}, \mathcal{V} \rangle \in X$ iff $\mathcal{V} \in Sat(G)$ for some GS $G \in \mathcal{G}_{\mathcal{N}}$.

A PGS $G = \langle D, C, w, mod \rangle$ is called $\mathcal{K}$–*transitional* for P iff $D = \mathcal{K}Vars \cup \mathcal{K}Vars'$ and $C = Cons(P)$. A pair $\langle \mathcal{V}, \mathcal{V}' \rangle$ of $\mathcal{K}$-tuples of valuations over $Vars(P)$ *satisfies* G iff the mapping $v : D \to \mathbb{Z}$ defined as $v.x = \mathcal{V}.x$ and $v.x' = \mathcal{V}'.x$, for each $x \in \mathcal{K}Vars$, is a solution of G. We denote by $Sat(G)$ the set of pairs of $\mathcal{K}$-tuples of valuations over $Vars(P)$ that satisfy G. We also extend the operator Sat to sets of $\mathcal{K}$–transitional PGS as follows: for a set $\mathcal{G}$ of $\mathcal{K}$–transitional PGS, $Sat(\mathcal{G}) = \bigcup_{G \in \mathcal{G}} Sat(G)$. Given a relation $\rightsquigarrow_0 \subseteq \mathcal{S}(P)^{\dagger} \times \mathcal{S}(P)^{\dagger}$, a pair $\langle \mathcal{N}, \mathcal{N}' \rangle$ of $\mathcal{K}$-tuples of P vertices and a finite set $\mathcal{G}$ of $\mathcal{K}$–transitional PGS, we say that $\mathcal{G}$ *characterizes* $\rightsquigarrow_0$ with respect to the pair $\langle \mathcal{N}, \mathcal{N}' \rangle$ iff $Sat(\mathcal{G}) = \{\langle \mathcal{V}, \mathcal{V}' \rangle \mid \langle \mathcal{N}, \mathcal{V} \rangle \rightsquigarrow_0 \langle \mathcal{N}', \mathcal{V}' \rangle\}$.

Remark 1. Let π_1 be a *fair* history from $\langle \mathcal{N}_1, \mathcal{V}_1 \rangle$ to $\langle \mathcal{N}, \mathcal{V} \rangle$ and π_2 be a *fair* history from $\langle \mathcal{N}, \mathcal{V} \rangle$ with $\langle \mathcal{N}, \mathcal{V} \rangle \in \mathcal{S}(P)^{\mathcal{K}}$. Then, $[\pi_1 + \pi_2]_{\langle \mathcal{N}, \mathcal{V} \rangle}$ is a *fair* history.

As first result, we show that the fair reachability relation $\overset{\mathcal{K}}{\rightsquigarrow}{}^U$ can be *PGS*-characterized.

Theorem 2. *For each pair $\langle \mathcal{N}, \mathcal{N}' \rangle$ of $\mathcal{K}$–tuples of P vertices, one can build effectively a finite set $\mathcal{G}^U(\mathcal{N}, \mathcal{N}')$ of $\mathcal{K}$–transitional PGS that characterizes the fair reachability relation $\overset{\mathcal{K}}{\rightsquigarrow}{}^U$ w.r.t. the pair $\langle \mathcal{N}, \mathcal{N}' \rangle$. Moreover, for each $G \in \mathcal{G}^U(\mathcal{N}, \mathcal{N}')$, $\{G\}$ characterizes the fair reachability relation $\rightsquigarrow{}^U_{\overline{n}}$ for some path $\overline{n}$ from $\mathcal{N}$ to $\mathcal{N}'$.*

The algorithm we propose relies on Remark 1, properties of normalized PGS (see Proposition 3), and its termination is guaranteed by a suitable decidable *wqo*, which is defined over the set of *PGS* [6] (for a fixed set of variables and constants). More details are given in [BG06].

For a set $X \subseteq \mathcal{S}(P)^{\mathcal{K}}$, let us define $re^U(X) = \{\langle n, v \rangle \in \mathcal{S}(P) \mid \exists \langle \mathcal{N}, \mathcal{V} \rangle \in X.$ $\langle n, v \rangle \overset{\mathcal{K}}{\leadsto}^U \langle \mathcal{N}, \mathcal{V} \rangle\}$. By Proposition 3 and Theorem 2, we easily obtain the following important corollary.

Corollary 1. *Given a family of $\mathcal{K}$–local GS (resp., PGS) representing a set $X \subseteq \mathcal{S}(P)^{\mathcal{K}}$, we can construct a GS (resp., PGS) representation of $re^U(X)$.*

The second preliminary result for the proof of Theorem 1 essentially relies on properties of *PGS*. Its proof is highly technical (full details are given in [BG06]). For a $\mathcal{K}$-tuple $\mathcal{N}$ of vertices and a P path h from $\mathcal{N}$ to $\mathcal{N}$, we define the following sets of $\mathcal{K}$-tuples of valuations over $Vars(P)$:

- $Sp(h) := \{\mathcal{V} \mid \exists \mathcal{V}'. \langle \mathcal{N}, \mathcal{V} \rangle \leadsto_h^U \langle \mathcal{N}, \mathcal{V}' \rangle$ and $\mathcal{V}' \succeq \mathcal{V}\}$;
- $Rea^\infty(h) := \{\mathcal{V} \mid \langle \mathcal{N}, \mathcal{V} \rangle \leadsto_{h^\infty}^U\}$.

where $\langle \mathcal{N}, \mathcal{V} \rangle \leadsto_{h^\infty}^U$ means that there is a fair U-computation π starting from $\langle \mathcal{N}, \mathcal{V} \rangle$ whose projection on $V(P)$ is the path h^∞ (h^∞ is the infinite path $h, h_1, h_1, \ldots$, where h_1 is obtained from h by eliminating the prefix corresponding to $\mathcal{N}$). By Simulation Lemma $Sp(h) \subseteq Rea^\infty(h)$.

Theorem 3. *Let $\mathcal{N}$ be a $\mathcal{K}$-tuple of vertices, h be a path from $\mathcal{N}$ to $\mathcal{N}$, and $G(h)$ be a $\mathcal{K}$–transitional PGS such that $\{G(h)\}$ characterizes the fair reachability relation $\leadsto_h^U$. Then, we can construct a $\mathcal{K}$–local PGS H^h such that $Sp(h) \subseteq Sat(H^h) \subseteq Rea^\infty(h)$.*

The idea behind this result is that we can build a *PGS*-representation H^h having the properties needed to prove Theorem 1 instead of considering $Sp(h)$ and $Rea^\infty(h)$ (see the following proof). Now, we can prove the main result of this subsection.

Proof of Theorem 1. Let $F_{\mathcal{K}}$ be the set of $\mathcal{K}$–tuples $\mathcal{N}$ of vertices such that some component of $\mathcal{N}$ is in F. By Theorem 2, for each $\mathcal{N} \in F_{\mathcal{K}}$, we can construct a finite set $\mathcal{G}^U(\mathcal{N}, \mathcal{N})$ of $\mathcal{K}$-transitional *PGS* characterizing $\overset{\mathcal{K}}{\leadsto}^U$ w.r.t. the pair $(\mathcal{N}, \mathcal{N})$. Moreover, there is *finite* set of *representative* paths h from $\mathcal{N}$ to $\mathcal{N}$, denoted by $Repr(\mathcal{N})$, such that $\mathcal{G}^U(\mathcal{N}, \mathcal{N}) = \bigcup_{h \in Repr(\mathcal{N})} \{G(h)\}$, where $\{G(h)\}$ characterizes $\leadsto_h^U$. By Theorem 3, for every $\mathcal{N} \in F_{\mathcal{K}}$, we can compute a family $\{H_{\mathcal{N}}^h\}_{h \in Repr(\mathcal{N})}$ of $\mathcal{K}$–local *PGS* such that $Sp(h) \subseteq Sat(H_{\mathcal{N}}^h) \subseteq Rea^\infty(h)$ for every $h \in Repr(\mathcal{N})$. Let us consider the set X of $\mathcal{K}$-tuples of P states defined as follows:

$$X = \{\langle \mathcal{N}, \mathcal{V} \rangle \mid \mathcal{N} \in F_{\mathcal{K}}, \exists h \in Repr(\mathcal{N}) : \mathcal{V} \in Sat(H_{\mathcal{N}}^h)\}$$

Note that X is *PGS*-represented by the family $\{\mathcal{H}_{\mathcal{N}}\}_{\mathcal{N} \in F_{\mathcal{K}}}$ of $\mathcal{K}$-local *PGS*, where $\mathcal{H}_{\mathcal{N}} = \bigcup_{h \in Repr(\mathcal{N})} \{H_{\mathcal{N}}^h\}$. Therefore, by Corollary 1, Theorem 1 directly follows from the following claim: $re^U(X) = [\![E\Box^F U]\!]_P$. It remains to prove this claim.

$re^U(X) \subseteq [\![E\Box^F U]\!]_P$: let $\langle n, v \rangle \in re^U(X)$. Then, there is $\mathcal{N} \in F_{\mathcal{K}}$, $h \in Repr(\mathcal{N})$, and $\mathcal{V} \in Sat(H_{\mathcal{N}}^h)$ such that $\langle n, v \rangle \overset{\mathcal{K}}{\leadsto}^U \langle \mathcal{N}, \mathcal{V} \rangle$. Since $Sat(H_{\mathcal{N}}^h) \subseteq Rea^\infty(h)$, it

---

[6] The hypothesis of positiveness is crucial.

holds that $\langle \mathcal{N}, \mathcal{V} \rangle \rightsquigarrow_{h^\infty}^U$. Since h^∞ contains infinite occurrences of accepting vertices, by Remark 1 we deduce that $\langle n, v \rangle \in [\![E\square^F U]\!]_P$. $[\![E\square^F U]\!]_P \subseteq re^U(X)$: let $\langle n, v \rangle \in [\![E\square^F U]\!]_P$. Then, there is a fair U-computation π starting from $\langle n, v \rangle$ that visits some vertex in F infinitely many times. Hence, we deduce the existence of an infinite sequence

$$\langle n, v \rangle \overset{\mathcal{K}}{\rightsquigarrow}^U \langle \mathcal{N}_0, \mathcal{V}_0 \rangle \overset{\mathcal{K}}{\rightsquigarrow}^U \langle \mathcal{N}_1, \mathcal{V}_1 \rangle \overset{\mathcal{K}}{\rightsquigarrow}^U \langle \mathcal{N}_2, \mathcal{V}_2 \rangle \dots$$

with $\mathcal{N}_i \in F_{\mathcal{K}}$ for each $i \geq 0$. Due to well quasi-ordering of $\preceq$, there are $i < j$ such that $\mathcal{N}_i = \mathcal{N}_j$ and $\mathcal{V}_i \preceq \mathcal{V}_j$. Since $\langle \mathcal{N}_i, \mathcal{V}_i \rangle \overset{\mathcal{K}}{\rightsquigarrow}^U \langle \mathcal{N}_i, \mathcal{V}_j \rangle$, by Properties of $\mathcal{G}^U(\mathcal{N}_i, \mathcal{N}_i)$, there is $h \in Repr(\mathcal{N}_i)$ such that $\langle \mathcal{N}_i, \mathcal{V}_i \rangle \rightsquigarrow_h^U \langle \mathcal{N}_i, \mathcal{V}_j \rangle$. Since $\mathcal{V}_i \preceq \mathcal{V}_j$, it follows that $\mathcal{V}_i \in Sp(h) \subseteq Sat(H_{\mathcal{N}}^h)$. As $\langle n, v \rangle \overset{\mathcal{K}}{\rightsquigarrow}^U \langle \mathcal{N}_i, \mathcal{V}_i \rangle$, it holds that $\langle n, v \rangle \in re^U(X)$. □

3.3 Symbolic Model-Checking Algorithm

We fix an *IRA* P and an *E–CCTL** formula ξ such that $Vars(\xi) \subseteq Vars(P)$, $Cons(\xi) \subseteq Cons(P)$, and $Mod(\xi) \subseteq Mod(P)$. Let κ be the least common multiple of the constants in $Mod(P) \cup \{1\}$. In the following, by using Theorem 1 and a generalization of the standard tableau-based construction for *LTL* model-checking, we show that we can construct a κ-*PGS* representation of the set of states $[\![\xi]\!]_P$. Hence, model-checking *IRA* against *E–CCTL** is decidable (note that the membership problem for κ-*PGS* representations is trivially decidable).

Let $\psi \in PLF(X)$ be a path *E–CCTL** formula with $X = \{\xi_1, \dots, \xi_k\}$. The *closure* of ψ, denoted by $cl(\psi)$, is the smallest set containing $\xi_1, \dots, \xi_k$, each *subformula* of ψ (considering $\xi_1, \dots, \xi_k$ as atomic propositions), and satisfying: (1) if $\psi_1 U \psi_2 \in cl(\psi)$, then $O(\psi_1 U \psi_2) \in cl(\psi)$, (2) if $\square \psi_1 \in cl(\psi)$, then $O\square \psi_1 \in cl(\psi)$. An *LTL-atom* of ψ is a set $A \subseteq cl(\psi)$ satisfying the following properties:

- for $\psi_1 \vee \psi_2 \in cl(\psi)$, $\psi_1 \vee \psi_2 \in A$ iff either $\psi_1 \in A$ or $\psi_2 \in A$;
- for $\psi_1 \wedge \psi_2 \in cl(\psi)$, $\psi_1 \wedge \psi_2 \in A$ iff $\psi_1 \in A$ and $\psi_2 \in A$;
- for $\psi_1 U \psi_2 \in cl(\psi)$, $\psi_1 U \psi_2 \in A$ iff either $\psi_2 \in A$ or $\{\psi_1, O(\psi_1 U \psi_2)\} \subseteq A$;
- for $\square \psi_1 \in cl(\psi)$, $\square \psi_1 \in A$ iff $\{\psi_1, O\square \psi_1\} \subseteq A$.

Let $Atoms(\psi)$ be the set of *LTL*-atoms of ψ. When an until-formula $\psi_1 U \psi_2$ is asserted at a state along a computation, we must make sure that the liveness requirement ψ_2 is eventually satisfied. This is done (as for *LTL*) using a generalized Büchi condition, one for each until formula. Formally, we denote by $\mathcal{F}(\psi)$ the family of subsets of $Atoms(\psi)$ defined as: for any until formula $\psi_1 U \psi_2 \in cl(\psi)$, there is a component $F \in \mathcal{F}(\psi)$ that contains all and only the *LTL*-atoms A such that either $\psi_2 \in A$ or $\psi_1 U \psi_2 \notin A$.

The main step of the proposed algorithm is represented by the following result.

Lemma 3. *Let $\psi \in PLF(X)$ be a path sub-formula of ξ such that $X = \{\xi_1, \dots, \xi_k\}$ and for each $1 \leq i \leq k$, $[\![\xi_i]\!]_P$ is given by a family $(\mathcal{H}_n^{\xi_i})_{n \in V(P)}$ of local κ-PGS. Then, we can construct a κ-PGS representation of $[\![E\psi]\!]_P$.*

Proof (Sketch). We build an *EIRA* $\langle P', \ell_{EXT} \rangle$, a set $F \subseteq V(P')$, and a family $\mathcal{H} = (\mathcal{H}_{n'})_{n' \in V(P')}$ of sets of local κ-PGS (w.r.t. P') such that $Vars(P') = Vars(P)$, $Cons(P') = Cons(P)$, $Mod(P') = Mod(P)$, $V(P') = V(P) \times Atoms(\psi) \times \{0, \dots, |\mathcal{F}(\psi)|\}$, and

Claim 1. for all $\langle n, v \rangle \in \mathcal{S}(P)$, $\langle n, v \rangle \in [\![E\psi]\!]_P$ if and only if $\langle \langle n, A, 0 \rangle, v \rangle \in [\![E\square^F \ulcorner \mathcal{H} \urcorner]\!]_{P'}$ for some *LTL*-atom $A \in Atoms(\psi)$ such that $\psi \in A$ (where $\ulcorner \mathcal{H} \urcorner$ denotes the upward closed subset of $\mathcal{S}(P')$ that is κ–*PGS* represented by $\mathcal{H}$).

Evidently, the current Lemma directly follows from the claim above and Theorem 1. The *EIRA* $\langle P', \ell_{EXT} \rangle$ and $F \subseteq V(P')$ are defined as (where $\mathcal{F}(\psi) = \{F_1, \ldots, F_m\}$):

- $V(P') = V(P) \times Atoms(\psi) \times \{0, \ldots, m\}$. A P' vertex is a triple $\langle n, A, i \rangle$, where n is a P vertex, A is an atom that intuitively represents the set of formulas that hold at n (along the current computation), and i is a finite counter used to check the fulfillment of the generalized Büchi condition $\mathcal{F}(\psi)$;
- $\langle \langle n, A, i \rangle, \langle n', A', j \rangle \rangle \in E(P')$ if and only if (1) $\langle n, n' \rangle \in E(P)$, (2) for all $O\psi' \in cl(\psi)$, $O\psi' \in A$ iff $\psi' \in A'$ (i.e., the next-requirements in A are met in A'), and (3) $j = i$ if $i < m$ and $A' \notin F_{i+1}$, and $j = (i + 1) \; mod \; (m + 1)$ otherwise;
- the labelling ℓ'_V and ℓ'_E of P' are consistent with those of P, i.e. $\ell'_V(\langle n, A, i \rangle) = \ell_V(n)$ and $\ell'_E(\langle \langle n, A, i \rangle, \langle n', A', i' \rangle \rangle) = \ell_E(\langle n, n' \rangle)$; $\ell_{EXT}(\langle n, A, i \rangle)$ is the set of atomic formulas $p[x_1 \leftarrow O^{i_1} x_{j_1}, \ldots, x_r \leftarrow O^{i_q} x_{j_q}]$ in A;
- $F = \{\langle n, A, m \rangle \in V(P')\}$.

It remains to define the family $\mathcal{H} = (\mathcal{H}_{n'})_{n' \in V(P')}$ of sets of local κ-*PGS*. Let $n' = \langle n, A, i \rangle$ with $A \cap X = \{\xi_{j_1}, \ldots, \xi_{j_r}\}$. Intuitively, $A \cap X$ represents the set of "atomic" state formulas asserted at n along the current computation. Thus, we have to require that $Sat(\mathcal{H}_{n'}) = \{v \mid \langle n, v \rangle \in \bigcap_{i=1}^{i=r} [\![\xi_{j_i}]\!]_P\}$. Formally, $\mathcal{H}_{n'} = \{H \mid H = H^1 \otimes \ldots \otimes H^r$ with $H^h \in \mathcal{H}_n^{\xi_{j_h}}$ for all $1 \le h \le r\}$. A full proof of Claim 1 is given in [BG06]. $\square$

Now, we can prove the desired result.

Theorem 4. *We can construct a κ-PGS representation $(\mathcal{H}_n^\xi)_{n \in V(P)}$ of $[\![\xi]\!]_P$.*

Proof. By structural induction on ξ. The case $\xi = \top$ is obvious. If $\xi = \xi_1 \vee \xi_2$ (resp., $\xi = \xi_1 \wedge \xi_2$), then for all $n \in V(P)$, $\mathcal{H}_n^\xi = \mathcal{H}_n^{\xi_1} \cup \mathcal{H}_n^{\xi_2}$ (resp., $\mathcal{H}_n^\xi = \{H_1 \otimes H_2 \mid H_i \in \mathcal{H}_n^{\xi_i}, \; i = 1, 2\}$), where $(\mathcal{H}_n^{\xi_i})_{n \in V(P)}$ is the κ-*PGS* representation of ξ_i with $i = 1, 2$. Finally, the case $\xi = E\psi$ follows from the induction hypothesis and Lemma 3. $\square$

4 Satisfiability and Model-Checking for *CEF*$^+$

In this section we show the main result of this paper, i.e. satisfiability and model-checking for *CEF*$^+$ are decidable. We need the following preliminary result.

Lemma 4. *For an E–CCTL* formula ξ, we can construct in polynomial time an IRA P with a distinguished vertex n_0 and a new E–CCTL* formula ξ' such that $[\![\xi]\!]_{SAT} = \{v \mid \langle n_0, v' \rangle \in [\![\xi']\!]_P$ where $v'.x = v.x$ for every $x \in Vars(\xi)\}$.*

Proof. Let $Var(\xi) = \{x_1, \ldots, x_k\}$. The *IRA* P is defined as follows:

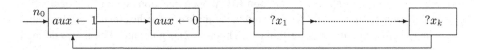

This *IRA* essentially consists of a sequence of inputs operations and we use an auxiliary variable aux to distinguish the state where all the values of the variables have been updated, which correspond to a new valuation.

Now consider the map f over *E–CCTL** formulas defined as: $f(O^i x \sim O^j y) = O^{i(k+2)} x \sim O^{j(k+2)} y$, $f(O^i x \equiv_k c) = f(O^{i(k+2)} x) \equiv_k c$, f is homomorphic w.r.t. the positive boolean operators, $f(O\psi) = O^{(k+2)} f(\psi)$, $f(\psi U \psi') = ((aux = 1) \Rightarrow f(\psi)) U ((aux = 1) \wedge f(\psi'))$, $f(\Box \psi) = \Box ((aux = 1) \Rightarrow f(\psi))$, $f(E\psi) = Ef(\psi)$. We can check that $v \in [\![\xi]\!]_{SAT}$ iff there is a valuation v' over $Vars(\xi) \cup \{aux\}$ such that $v'.x = v.x$ for every $x \in Vars(\xi)$ and $\langle n_0, v' \rangle \in [\![f(\xi)]\!]_P$.   □

Theorem 5

(1) The model checking problem of IRA *against* CEF+ *is decidable.*
(2) Satisfiability of CEF+ *is decidable.*

Proof (1) For given *IRA* P and *CEF+* formula ξ, we prove by structural induction on ξ that we can build a κ-GS representation of $[\![\xi]\!]_P$ (where κ is defined as in Section 3). The cases in which ξ is a *E–CCTL** formula or a disjunction of formulas directly follow from Theorem 4, while the case $\xi = \neg \xi'$ follows from Proposition 4. For the case $\xi = E(\xi_1 U \xi_2)$ where ξ_1 is an *E–CCTL** formula, we observe that $[\![\xi]\!]_P = re^{[\![\xi_1]\!]_P}([\![\xi_2]\!]_P)$, and the result follows from Theorem 4 and Corollary 1 (setting $\mathcal{K} = 1$). Finally, the case $\xi = EO\xi'$ follows from a simple variant of Corollary 1.

(2) For a *CEF+* formula ξ, we construct a κ-GS representation of $[\![\xi]\!]_{SAT}$ (where κ and κ-GS representation have an obvious meaning). For the boolean connectives we proceed as above. The case in which ξ is an *E–CCTL** formula easily follows from Proposition 3, Lemma 4, and Theorem 4. Finally, we observe that (1) $[\![E(\xi_1 U \xi_2)]\!]_{SAT} = \emptyset$ if $[\![\xi_2]\!]_{SAT} = \emptyset$, and $[\![E(\xi_1 U \xi_2)]\!]_{SAT} = [\![\xi_1]\!]_{SAT} \cup [\![\xi_2]\!]_{SAT}$ otherwise, (2) $[\![EO\xi]\!]_{SAT}$ contains all valuations over $Vars(\xi)$ if $[\![\xi]\!]_{SAT} \neq \emptyset$, and $[\![EO\xi]\!]_{SAT} = \emptyset$ otherwise.   □

5   Conclusion

We have considered an extension of standard *CTL**, called *CCTL**, whose atomic formulas are constraints from *IPC** with comparison of variables at different states. For this logic, we have addressed two problems: satisfiability and model checking of Integral Relational Automata [BBK77,Čer93] extended with periodicity constraints. Since model checking *IRA* against full *CCTL** is undecidable (also for the *CTL*-like fragment), we have considered a meaningful fragment of *CCTL**, namely *CEF+* (which subsumes both the existential and universal fragment of *CCTL** and the *EF*-like fragment) showing that for this fragment both satisfiability and model checking of *IRA* are decidable. Furthermore, using a symbolic approach based on theory of κ-GS, the theory of well quasi-ordering, and automata-theoretic techniques, we have shown that it is possible to compute a finite representation of the set of states of the given *IRA* that satisfy a given formula. There are still interesting and non-trivial open questions such as the decidability status of satisfiability of full *CCTL** and the complexity for the considered decidable fragment (termination of our algorithm (see Theorem 2) is guaranteed by a *wqo* defined over the set of κ-PGS for a fixed set of variables and constants).

References

[ACJT96] P. A. Abdulla, K. Cerans, B. Jonsson, and Yih-Kuen Tsay. General decidability theorems for infinite-state systems. In *LICS'96*, pages 313–321. IEEE Computer Society Press, 1996.

[AD94] R. Alur and D. Dill. A theory of timed automata. *Theoretical Computer Science*, 126:183–235, 1994.

[AJ94] P.A. Abdulla and B. Jonsson. Undecidable verification problems for programs with unreliable channels. In *ICALP'04*, volume 820 of *LNCS*. Springer, 1994.

[BBFS98] E. Bertino, C. Bettini, E. Ferrari, and P. Samarati. An access control model supporting periodicity constraints and temporal reasoning. *ACM TODS*, 23(3):231–285, 1998.

[BBK77] J. Bardzin, J. Bicevskis, and A. Kalninsh. Automatic construction of complete sample systems for program testing. In *IFIP Congress*, pages 57–62, 1977.

[BEH95] A. Bouajjani, R. Echahed, and P. Habermehl. On the verification problem of nonregular properties for nonregular processes. In *LICS'95*, pages 123–133. IEEE Computer Society Press, 1995.

[BFLP03] S. Bardin, A. Finkel, J. Leroux, and L. Petrucci. FAST: Fast Acceleration of Symbolic Transition systems. In *CAV'03*, volume 2725 of *LNCS*, pages 118–121. Springer, 2003.

[BG06] L. Bozzelli and R. Gascon. Branching-time temporal logic extended with Presburger constraints. Technical Report LSV-06-10, LSV, May 2006.

[Boi98] B. Boigelot. *Symbolic methods for exploring infinite state spaces*. PhD thesis, Université de Liège, 1998.

[CC00] H. Comon and V. Cortier. Flatness is not a weakness. In *CSL'00*, volume 1862 of *LNCS*, pages 262–276. Springer, 2000.

[Čer93] K. Čerāns. Deciding properties of integral relational automata. Technical Report No. 73, Dept. of Computer Sciences, Chalmers University of Technology, Göteborg, Sweden, 1993. An extended abstract appeared in Proc. of ICALP'04, LNCS 820.

[CJ98] H. Comon and Y. Jurski. Multiple counters automata, safety analysis and Presburger arithmetic. In *CAV'98*, volume 1427 of *LNCS*, pages 268–279. Springer, 1998.

[DD03] S. Demri and D. D'Souza. An automata-theoretic approach to constraint LTL. Technical Report LSV-03-11, 2003. An extended abstract appeared in Proc. of FSTTCS'02.

[DG05] S. Demri and R. Gascon. Verification of qualitative $\mathbb{Z}$-constraints. In *CONCUR'05*, volume 3653 of *LNCS*, pages 518–532. Springer, 2005.

[EH86] E.A. Emerson and J.Y. Halpern. Sometimes and not never revisited: On branching versus linear time. *Journal of ACM*, 33(1):151–178, 1986.

[FS01] A. Finkel and Ph. Schnoebelen. Well-structured transition systems everywhere! *Theoretical Computer Science*, 256(1-2):63–92, 2001.

[Iba78] O. Ibarra. Reversal-bounded multicounter machines and their decision problems. *Journal of ACM*, 25(1):116–133, 1978.

[LM01] U. Dal Lago and A. Montanari. Calendars, time granularities, and automata. In *SSTD'01*, volume 2121 of *LNCS*, pages 279–298. Springer, 2001.

[LS04] J. Leroux and G. Sutre. On flatness for 2-dimensional vector addition systems with states. In *CONCUR'04*, volume 3170 of *LNCS*, pages 402–416. Springer, 2004.

[Lut04] C. Lutz. NEXPTIME-complete description logics with concrete domains. *ACM Transactions on Computational Logic*, 5(4):669–705, 2004.

[May01] Richard Mayr. Decidability of model checking with the temporal logic EF. *Theoretical Computer Science*, 256:31–62, 2001.

[Min67] M. Minsky. *Computation: Finite and Infinite Machines*. Prentice Hall, 1967.

[MOS05] M. Müller-Olm and H. Seidl. Analysis of modular arithmetic. In *ESOP'05*, volume 3444 of *LNCS*, pages 46–60. Springer, 2005.

Combining Supervaluation and Degree Based Reasoning Under Vagueness

Christian G. Fermüller and Robert Kosik

Technische Universität Wien, Austria

Abstract. Two popular approaches to formalize adequate reasoning with vague propositions are usually deemed incompatible: On the one hand, there is supervaluation with respect to precisification spaces, which consist in collections of classical interpretations that represent admissible ways of making vague atomic statements precise. On the other hand, t-norm based fuzzy logics model truth functional reasoning, where reals in the unit interval $[0, 1]$ are interpreted as degrees of truth. We show that both types of reasoning can be combined within a single logic $\mathbf{SŁ}$, that extends both: Łukasiewicz logic $Ł$ and (classical) $\mathbf{S5}$, where the modality corresponds to '... is true in all complete precisifications'. Our main result consists in a game theoretic interpretation of $\mathbf{SŁ}$, building on ideas already introduced by Robin Giles in the 1970s to obtain a characterization of $Ł$ in terms of a Lorenzen style dialogue game combined with bets on the results of binary experiments that may show dispersion. In our case the experiments are replaced by random evaluations with respect to a given probability distribution over permissible precisifications.

1 Introduction

Providing adequate logical calculi for systematic reasoning about vague information is a major challenge in the intersection of logic, AI, and computer science. Many different models of reasoning with vague notions are on the market. In fact, the literature on so-called theories of vagueness is almost unsurmountable large and still fast growing. (We refer to the book [20], the reader [21], and the more recent collection [1] for further references.) Still, one can single out two quite different approaches as particularly popular—albeit popular in different communities. On the one hand, there is *fuzzy logic* 'in Zadeh's narrow sense' (see, e.g., [15,17]) focusing on the study of truth functional logics, based on a (potential) continuum of degrees of truth, usually identified with the real closed unit interval $[0, 1]$. On the other hand, there is the concept of *supervaluation* (see, e.g., [11,20,27]), which maintains that vague statements have to be evaluated with respect to all their admissible precisifications. The slogan 'truth is supertruth' in the latter context entails the thesis that a logical formula built up from vague atomic propositions is true if and only if it is true in each of its (classical) precisifications. Whereas this is often understood as a vindication of classical logic (even) in contexts of vague information[1], all degree based fuzzy logics agree upon the rejection of the logical validity

---

[1] One should mention that the extent to which supervaluation leads to classical validity and consequence relations is hotly debated. See, in particular [22] for proofs that compactness, upwards and downwards Löwenheim-Skolem, and recursive axiomatizability fail for 'natural' supervaluation based consequence relations.

M. Hermann and A. Voronkov (Eds.): LPAR 2006, LNAI 4246, pp. 212–226, 2006.
© Springer-Verlag Berlin Heidelberg 2006

of *tertium non datur* $(A \lor \neg A)$. Consequently it is not surprising that supervaluation and degree based reasoning, respectively, are deemed fundamentally incompatible.

We think that a formal assessment, relating the scope and limits of both types of logical reasoning with each other, is essential for judging their adequateness for applications in information processing (as argued in [9]). As a first step towards such an evaluation we seek to identify a common formal framework for degree based logics and supervaluation. The main purpose of this paper is to show that supervaluation as well as t-norm based fuzzy logics can be interpreted as referring to classical precisifications at different levels of formula evaluation. The resulting semantic framework allows to *combine* both forms of reasoning within a single logic. The main tool for achieving an appropriate mathematical analysis of corresponding analytic reasoning is borrowed from the dialogue based characterization of infinite-valued Łukasiewicz logic developed by Robin Giles in the 1970s [13,14]. In particular, our extension of Giles's game for **Ł** will lead us to a tableau style calculus for the evaluation of formulas over precisification spaces.

We like to emphasize that it is *not* the purpose of this work to (just) introduce yet another modal extension of a particular fuzzy logic. Rather we seek to derive an adequate logic for the combination of supervaluation and degree based reasoning from first principles about the formalization of vague notions and propositions. Still, a short comparison with similar extensions of fuzzy logics will be presented in Section 5.

We also point out that throughout the paper we only deal with propositional logics.

2 Supervaluation, Sorites, and t-Norm Based Fuzzy Logics

The use of supervaluation to obtain a semantics for languages that accommodate (also) *vague* propositions was introduced by Kit Fine in [11] and has remained an important point of reference for investigations into logic and vagueness ever since (see, e.g., [20,27,28,9]. The main idea is to evaluate propositions not simply with respect to classical interpretations—i.e., assignments of the truth values 0 ('false') and 1 ('true') to atomic statements—but rather with respect to a whole *space* Π of (possibly) partial interpretations. For every partial interpretation I in Π, Π is required to contain also a classical interpretation I' that extends I. I' is called an *admissible (complete) precisification* of I. A proposition is called *supertrue* in Π if it evaluates to 1 in all admissible precisifications, i.e., in all classical (i.e., complete) interpretations contained in Π.

Example 1. To illustrate supervaluation let us briefly describe how the famous *Sorites paradox* (see, e.g, [20,28,3]) is solved in this context. Suppose that h_i stands for the proposition "i (properly arranged) sand-corns make a heap of sand". Let us further agree that h_1 is false (i.e., a single sand-corn is not a heap of sand) but that h_{10000} is true. The paradox consists in the fact that also the proposition $h_i \supset h_{i-1}$—read: "If i sand-corns make a heap then also $i - 1$ sand-corns make a heap"—seems to be true for each $i > 1$. However, from these implicative propositions and h_{10000} we can derive h_1 using modus ponens only. In other words, classical logic is at variance with the above mentioned, seemingly innocent intuitions. Using supervaluation we can easily accommodate the intuition that h_1 is definitely false while h_{10000} is definitely true by assigning 0 to h_1 and 1 to h_{10000} in each admissible precisification in a corresponding space Π. On the other hand, at least one statement h_i, where $1 < i < 10000$ is taken to be *vague*, i.e., neither definitely false nor definitely true. This means that for some i the space Π contains admissible precisifications I and I' such that h_i evaluates to 0 in I, but to 1 in I'. Assuming further that h_j is true in an admissible precisification, whenever already h_i is true there for some $i < j$, we obtain that there is an i such that $h_i \supset h_{i-1}$ is not true in all interpretations contained in Π. In other words: while h_{10000} is supertrue and h_1 is superfalse, at least one statement of the form $h_i \supset h_{i-1}$ is neither supertrue nor superfalse.

Note that the inference from h_{10000} to h_1 is blocked since the conclusion of modus ponens is guaranteed to be supertrue only if both premises are supertrue. In fact, supervaluationists like to identify truth with supertruth and thus feel justified in claiming to have 'saved' classical logic also in context of vague propositions. (See, e.g., [20].)

Note, that no reference to (strictly) partial interpretations is needed to determine which propositions are supertrue. The partial interpretations represent additional information that is used to model the semantics of modal operators like 'definitely' or 'indefinitely'. However, we will not investigate such operators here and thus may simplify the notion of a space Π by assuming that Π contains admissible complete precisifications, i.e., classical interpretations only. We will use the term 'precisification space' henceforth for such structures.

One complaint about the above analysis of the Sorites paradox focuses on the fact that we seem to have good reasons to insist that 'taking away one sand-corn from a heap does not result in a non-heap' formalized as $h_i \supset h_{i-1}$ is, if not simply true, at least *almost true* for all $i > 1$. Supervaluation itself does not accommodate this intuition. In contrast, *fuzzy logics* 'in Zadeh's narrow sense' are often claimed to solve the Sorites paradox while respecting all mentioned intuitions. Indeed, in fuzzy logics one may assign an intermediary truth value, close to 1 to all instances of $h_i \supset h_{i-1}$. Using a properly generalized (from $\{0,1\}$ to $[0,1]$) truth function for implication and generalized modus ponens, respectively, one may still block the inference from h_{10000} to h_1, even if h_{10000} is interpreted as definitely true (1) and h_0 as as definitely false 0. (For a detailed analysis of Sorites in the context of t-norm based fuzzy logics we refer to [18].)

Supervaluation and fuzzy logics can be viewed as capturing contrasting, but individually coherent intuitions about the role of logical connectives in vague statements. Consider a sentence like

(*) "The sky is blue and is not blue".

When formalized as $b \& \neg b$, (*) is superfalse in all precisification spaces, since either b or $\neg b$ is evaluated to 0 in each precisification. This fits Kit Fine's motivation in [11] to capture 'penumbral connections' that prevent any mono-colored object from having two colors at the same time. According to Fine's intuition the statement "The sky is blue" absolutely contradicts the statement "The sky is not blue", even if neither statement is definitely true or definitely false. Consequently (*) is judged as definitely false, although admittedly composed of vague sub-statements. On the other hand, by asserting (*) one may intend to convey the information that both component statements are true *only to some degree*, different from 1 but also from 0. Under this reading and certain 'natural' choices of truth functions for & and $\neg$ the statement $b \& \neg b$ is *not* definitely false, but receives some intermediary truth value.

We are motivated by the fact that, although supervaluation is usually deemed incompatible with fuzzy logics, one may (and should) uncover a substantial amount of common ground between both approaches to reasoning under vagueness. This common ground becomes visible if one relates the (in general intermediary) truth value of an atomic proposition p as stipulated in fuzzy logics to the 'density' of those interpretations in a precisification space Π that assign 1 to p.

Example 2. Let $h_1,\ldots,h_{10000}$ be as in Example 1 and let these h_i be the only atomic propositions taken into consideration. We define a corresponding precisification space Π as follows: Π consists in the set of all classical interpretations I, that fulfill the following conditions, which model 'penumbral connections' in the sense of [11]. (We write $I(p)$ for the value $\in \{0,1\}$ that is assigned to proposition p in I).

1. $I(h_1) = 0$ and $I(h_{10000}) = 1$
2. $i \leq j$ implies $I(h_i) \leq I(h_j)$ for all $i, j \in \{1,\ldots,10000\}$

The first condition makes h_1 superfalse and h_{10000} supertrue in Π. The second condition captures the assumption that, if some precisification declares i sand-corns to form a heap, then, for all $j \geq i$, j sand-corns also form a heap under the same precisification. Note that supervaluation leaves the semantic status of all statements $h_i \supset h_{i-1}$, where $1 < i \leq 10000$, undecided. However, we can observe that $I(h_i \supset h_{i-1}) = 1$ in *all but one* of the, in total, 99999 interpretations I in Π, whenever $1 < i \leq 10000$. It is thus tempting to say that Π itself (but not supervaluation!) respects the intuition that $h_i \supset h_{i-1}$—informally read as "taking away one sand-corn from a heap still leaves a heap"—is (at least) 'almost true'. Once one accepts the idea that truth may come in degrees, it seems natural to identify what could be called the 'global truth value of h_i with respect to Π' with the fraction of admissible precisifications $I \in S$ where $I(h_i) = 1$. We thus obtain $\frac{i-1}{99999}$ as global truth value of h_i, here.

Following this example we will use *global truth values* $\in [0,1]$ to make information explicit that is implicit in precisification spaces, but is not used in supervaluation. A simple way to extract a global truth value for an atomic proposition p from a given precisification space Π is suggested by Example 2: just divide the number of interpretations I in Π that assign 1 to p by the total number of interpretations in Π. This is feasible if Π is represented by a finite set or multiset of interpretations. (For related ideas underlying the so-called 'voting semantics' of fuzzy logics, we refer to [26,12].) More generally, since we view the interpretations in Π as corresponding to different ways of making all atomic propositions precise, it seems natural not just to count those precisifications, but to endow Π with a probability measure μ on the σ-algebra formed by all subsets of precisifications in Π, where μ is intended to represent the relative plausibility (or 'frequency in non-deterministic evaluations') of different precisifications. Suppose, e.g., that in refining Example 2 we want to model the intuition that a 'cut-off' point n between heaps and non-heaps—i.e., an n where $I(h_n) \neq I(h_{n+1})$—is more plausibly assumed to be near $n = 100$ than near $n = 9500$. Then we may take $\mu(\mathscr{J}_{\sim 100})$ to be higher than $\mu(\mathscr{J}_{\sim 9500})$, where $\mathscr{J}_{\sim n}$ denotes the set of all interpretations I where the 'cut-off' point is near n, in the sense that $I(h_{n-c}) = 0$ but $I(h_{n+c}) = 1$ for some fixed smallish c, say $c = 10$.

Note that if we insist on *truth functional* semantics, then we cannot simply extend the above method for extracting truth values from Π from atomic propositions to logically complex propositions. E.g., in general, the fraction of interpretations I in a finite precisification space Π for which $I(p\&q) = 1$ is not uniquely determined by the fractions of interpretations that assign 1 to p and q, respectively.

Obviously, the question arises which truth functions should be used for the basic logical connectives. For this we follow Hájek (and many others) in making the following 'design choices' (see, e.g., [15,17]):

1. The truth function for conjunction is a continuous, commutative, associative, and monotonically non-decreasing function $* : [0,1]^2 \mapsto [0,1]$, where $0*x = 0$ as well as $1*x = x$. In other words: $*$ is a continuous t-norm.
2. The residuum $\Rightarrow_*$ of the t-norm $*$—i.e., the unique function $\Rightarrow_*: [0,1]^2 \mapsto [0,1]$ satisfying $x \Rightarrow_* y = \sup\{z \mid x*z \leq y\}$—serves as the truth function for implication.
3. The truth function for negation is defined as $\lambda x[x \Rightarrow_* 0]$.

Given a continuous t-norm $*$ with residuum $\Rightarrow_*$, one obtains a fuzzy logic $\mathbf{L}(*)$ based on a language with binary connectives $\supset$ (implication), $\&$ (strong conjunction), constant $\bot$ (falsum), and defined connectives $\neg A =_{def} A \supset \bot$, $A \wedge B =_{def} A\&(A \supset B)$, $A \vee B =_{def} ((A \supset B) \supset B) \wedge ((B \supset A) \supset A)$ (negation, weak conjunction and disjunction, respectively) as follows. A *valuation* for $\mathbf{L}(*)$ is a function v assigning to each propositional variable a truth value from the real unit interval $[0,1]$, uniquely extended to v^* for formulas by:

$$v^*(A\&B) = v^*(A) * v^*(B), \quad v^*(A \supset B) = v^*(A) \Rightarrow_* v^*(B), \quad v^*(\bot) = 0$$

Formula F is valid in $\mathbf{L}(*)$ iff $v^*(F) = 1$ for all valuations v^* pertaining to the t-norm $*$.

Three fundamental continuous t-norms and their residua are:

	t-norm	associated residuum
Łukasiewicz	$x *_{\mathbf{L}} y = \sup\{0, x+y-1\}$	$x \Rightarrow_{\mathbf{L}} y = \inf\{1, 1-x+y\}$
Gödel	$x *_{\mathbf{G}} y = \inf\{x,y\}$	$x \Rightarrow_{\mathbf{G}} y = \begin{cases} 1 \text{ if } x \leq y \\ y \text{ otherwise} \end{cases}$
Product	$x *_{\mathbf{P}} y = x \cdot y$	$x \Rightarrow_{\mathbf{P}} y = \begin{cases} 1 \quad \text{ if } x \leq y \\ y/x \text{ otherwise} \end{cases}$

Any continuous t-norm is obtained by an ordinal sum construction based on these three (see, [25,15]). The logics $\mathbf{L}(*_{\mathbf{L}})$, $\mathbf{L}(*_{\mathbf{G}})$, and $\mathbf{L}(*_{\mathbf{P}})$, are called Łukasiewicz logic $\mathbf{Ł}$, Gödel logic $\mathbf{G}$, and Product logic $\mathbf{P}$, respectively.

The mentioned logics have different features that render them adequate for different forms of applications. E.g., Gödel logic $\mathbf{G}$, is the only t-norm based logic, where the truth value of every formula A only depends on the relative order of truth values of atomic subformulas of A, but not on the absolute values of these subformulas. However, Example 2 suggests another *desideratum*, that we formulate as an additional design choice:

4. Small changes in $v^*(A)$ or $v^*(B)$ result in, at most, small changes in $v^*(A \supset B)$. More precisely: the truth function $\Rightarrow_*$ for implication is continuous.

Design choices 1-4 jointly determine a unique logic:

Proposition 1. Ł *is the only logic of type* **L**(∗), *where* $\Rightarrow_*$ *is continuous.*

Proof. Let $x, y, u \in [0, 1]$. For any continuous t-norm $*$ we have (see [16]):

- If $x < u \leq y$ and $u = u * u$ is idempotent then $(y \Rightarrow_* x) = x$.
- If $y \leq x$ then $(y \Rightarrow_* x) = 1$.

Putting $y = u$ in these inequalities we get for idempotent u:

- $(u \Rightarrow_* x) = x$ for $x < u$
- $(u \Rightarrow_* x) = 1$ for $x \geq u$

It follows that $\Rightarrow_*$ is not continuous at (u, u) if u is idempotent and $0 < u < 1$. By the ordinal sum representation of [25] each continuous t-norm is the generalized sum of order isomorphic copies of the Łukasiewicz and product t-norms. In this construction boundaries of an interval are mapped to idempotent elements. It follows that the only continuous t-norms with no idempotent elements except 0 and 1 are given by a single interval whose boundaries are mapped to 0 and 1. The corresponding t-norms are order isomorphic to Łukasiewicz or product t-norm respectively.

The residuum $x \Rightarrow_* y$ of product t-norm is not continuous at $(0, 0)$. Hence the only continuous t-norms with continuous implication are order isomorphic to the Lukasiewicz t-norm. The unique corresponding logic is Łukasiewicz logic Ł.   ◇

Note that we have used the same symbols for classical conjunction, negation, and implication as for their respective counterparts in t-norm based fuzzy logics. In principle, one might keep the classical logical vocabulary apart from the logical vocabulary for fuzzy logics in defining a logic that combines supervaluation with t-norm based valuations. However, the results in Section 3, below, can be seen as a justification of our choice of a unified logical syntax for the logic **SŁ** that extends Łukasiewicz logic, but incorporates also classical logic. The crucial link between classical and $*_Ł$- based valuation over precisification spaces is obtained by making the concept of supertruth explicit also in our language. For this we introduce the (unary) connective **S**—read: "It is supertrue that ..."—which will play the role of an **S5**-like modal operator. Modal extensions of fuzzy logics have already been studied in other contexts; see, e.g., chapter 8 of [15] and [8]. However **SŁ** is different from the modal extensions of Ł studied by Hájek, Godo, Esteva, Montagna, and others, since it combines classical reasoning with many-valued reasoning in a different way, as will get clear below. (See also Section 5.)

Formulas of **SŁ** are built up from the propositional variables $p \in V = \{p_1, p_2, \ldots\}$ and the constant $\bot$ using the connectives & and $\supset$. The additional connectives $\neg$, $\wedge$, and $\vee$ are defined as explained above. In accordance with our earlier (informal) semantic considerations, a precisification space is formalized as a triple $\langle W, e, \mu \rangle$, where $W = \{\pi_1, \pi_2, \ldots\}$ is a non-empty (countable) set, whose elements π_i are called *precisification points*, e is a mapping $W \times V \mapsto \{0, 1\}$, and μ is a probability measure on the σ-algebra formed by all subsets of W. Given a precisification space $\Pi = \langle W, e, \mu \rangle$ a *local truth value* $\|A\|_\pi$ is defined for every formula A and every precisification point $\pi \in W$ inductively by

$$\|p\|_\pi = e(\pi, p), \text{ for } p \in V \tag{1}$$

$$\|\bot\|_\pi = 0 \tag{2}$$

$$\|A\&B\|_\pi = \begin{cases} 1 \text{ if } \|A\|_\pi = 1 \text{ and } \|B\|_\pi = 1 \\ 0 \text{ otherwise} \end{cases} \tag{3}$$

$$\|A \supset B\|_\pi = \begin{cases} 1 \text{ if } \|A\|_\pi = 1 \text{ and } \|B\|_\pi = 0 \\ 0 \text{ otherwise} \end{cases} \tag{4}$$

$$\|SA\|_\pi = \begin{cases} 1 \text{ if } \forall \sigma \in W : \|A\|_\sigma = 1 \\ 0 \text{ otherwise} \end{cases} \tag{5}$$

Local truth values are classical and do not depend on the underlying t-norm $*_{\text{Ł}}$. In contrast, the *global truth value* $\|A\|_\Pi$ of a formula A is defined by

$$\|p\|_\Pi = \mu(\{\pi \in W | e(\pi, p) = 1\}), \text{ for } p \in V \tag{6}$$

$$\|\bot\|_\Pi = 0 \tag{7}$$

$$\|A\&B\|_\Pi = \|A\|_\Pi *_{\text{Ł}} \|B\|_\Pi \tag{8}$$

$$\|A \supset B\|_\Pi = \|A\|_\Pi \Rightarrow_{\text{Ł}} \|B\|_\Pi \tag{9}$$

$$\|SA\|_\Pi = \|SA\|_\pi \text{ for any } \pi \in W \tag{10}$$

Note that $\|SA\|_\pi$ is the same value (either 0 or 1) for all $\pi \in W$. In other words: 'local' supertruth is in fact already global; which justifies the above clause for $\|SA\|_\Pi$. Also observe that we could have used clauses 8 and 9 also to define $\|A\&B\|_\pi$ and $\|A \supset B\|_\pi$ since the (global) t-norm based truth functions coincide with the (local) classical ones, when restricted to $\{0, 1\}$. (However that might have obscured their intended meaning.)

A formula A is called *valid* in **SŁ** if $\|A\|_\Pi = 1$ for all precisification spaces Π. In stating the following proposition we identify not only **SŁ**, but also Łukasiewicz logic **Ł** and the (classical) modal logic **S5** with their respective sets of valid formulas.

Proposition 2. **SŁ** *restricted to formulas without occurrences of* S *coincides with* **Ł**. *On the other hand,* $\{A \mid SA \in \textbf{SŁ}\}$ *coincides with* **S5**.

Proof. The first part of the claim follows immediately from clauses 7, 8 and 9, above; and the fact that all values $v(p_i) \in [0, 1]$ for some propositional variable $p_i \in \{p_1, \ldots p_n\}$ can be obtained as $\mu(\{\pi \in W | e(\pi, p) = 1\})$ for a suitable precisification space $\langle W, e, \mu \rangle$ where W and e correspond to all 2^n assignments of 0 or 1 to the p_i.

The second part follows from clauses 1-5 and 10 using the well known fact that in any Kripke model $\langle W, R, e \rangle$ for **S5**—where W is the set of possible worlds, R is the accessibility relation, and e the mapping that assigns 0 or 1 to each propositional variable in each world—R can be assumed to be the total relation $W \times W$. $\diamond$

We have the following finite model property.

Proposition 3. *A formula* F *is valid in* **SŁ** *if and only if* F *is valid in all those precisification spaces* $\langle W, e, \mu \rangle$ *where* W *is finite.*

Proof. Let $\Pi = \langle W, e, \mu \rangle$ and let $V_F = \{p_1, \ldots, p_n\}$ be the propositional variables occurring in F. Moreover, let $\mathscr{B}_F$ be the set of all classical truth value assignments $I : V_F \mapsto \{0, 1\}$. We write $I = e(\pi)$ if $\forall p \in V_F : I(p) = e(\pi, p)$ and define a new precisification space $\Pi^f = \langle W^f, e', \mu' \rangle$ as follows:

- $W_f = \{I \in \mathscr{B}_F \mid \exists \pi \in W : I = e(\pi)\}$
- $e'(I, p) = e(\pi, p)$, where $I = e(\pi)$
- $\mu'(\{I\}) = \mu(\{\pi \mid I = e(\pi)\})$, which uniquely extends to all subsets of W_f.

It is straightforward to check that $\|F\|_\Pi = \|F\|_{\Pi^f}$. Thus we have shown that in evaluating F it suffices to consider precisification spaces with at most $2^{p(F)}$ precisification points, where $p(F)$ is the number of different propositional variables occurring in F. $\diamond$

3   Reasoning Via Dialogue Games

We have defined the logic $S\!\math8L$ in an attempt to relate supervaluation and 'fuzzy valuation' in a common framework based on precisification spaces. But we have not yet said anything about proof systems or—more generally—about formal *reasoning* in this context. We claim that a Hilbert-style calculus for $S\math8L$ can be obtained by extending any system for $\math8L$ with the following axioms

$A1$: $S(A \vee \neg A)$ $A2$: $SA \vee \neg SA$

$A3$: $S(A \supset B) \supset (SA \supset SB)$ $A4$: $SA \supset A$

$A5$: $SA \supset SSA$ $A6$: $\neg SA \supset S \neg SA$

and the Necessitation Rule $\dfrac{A}{SA}$ for supertruth. However, mainly due to space constraints, we defer a corresponding soundness and completeness proof to an extended version of this paper and concentrate on an analysis of $S\math8L$ that seems more revealing with respect to its intended semantics and also more important from a computational point of view. Building on an extension of (a variant of) Robin Giles's dialogue and betting game for $\math8L$ (see [13,14,10]) we provide a game based characterization of $S\math8L$. Our game will be seen to correspond to a tableau style system for analytic reasoning over given precisification spaces. It consists of two largely independent building blocks:

(1) Betting for Random Verifications. Assume that two players—let's say me and you—agree to pay $1\,\text{\euro}$ to the opponent player for each assertion of an atomic statement, which is false according to a randomly chosen admissible precisification. More formally, given a precisification space $\Pi = \langle W, e, \mu \rangle$ the *risk value* $\langle p \rangle_\Pi$ associated with a propositional variable p is defined as $\langle p \rangle_\Pi = \mu(\{\pi \in W \mid e(\pi, p) = 0\})$; moreover we define $\langle \bot \rangle_\Pi = 1$. Note that $\langle p \rangle_\Pi$ corresponds to the probability (as determined by μ) of having to pay $1\,\text{\euro}$, when asserting p.

Let $p_1, p_2, \ldots, q_1, q_2, \ldots$ denote atomic statements, i.e., propositional variables or $\bot$. By $[p_1, \ldots, p_m \| q_1, \ldots, q_n]$ we denote an *elementary state* in the game, where I assert each of the q_i in the multiset $\{q_1, \ldots, q_n\}$ of atomic statements and you, likewise, assert each atomic statement $p_i \in \{p_1, \ldots, p_m\}$. To illustrate this notions consider the elementary state $[p \| q, q]$. According to the outlined arrangement, we have to evaluate p once, and q twice in randomly chosen precisifications. If, e.g., all three evaluations result in 0 then I owe you 2€ and you owe me 1€, implying a total loss of 1€ for me.

The *risk* associated with a multiset $P = \{p_1, \ldots, p_m\}$ of atomic formulas is defined as $\langle p_1, \ldots, p_m \rangle_\Pi = \sum_{i=1}^m \langle p_i \rangle_\Pi$. The risk $\langle \rangle_\Pi$ associated with the empty multiset is 0. Note that $\langle P \rangle_\Pi$ thus denotes the average amount of money that I expect to have to pay to you according to the above arrangements if I have asserted the atomic formulas in P. The risk associated with an elementary state $[p_1, \ldots, p_m \| q_1, \ldots, q_n]$ is calculated from my point of view. Therefore the condition $\langle p_1, \ldots, p_m \rangle_\Pi \geq \langle q_1, \ldots, q_n \rangle_\Pi$, which we will call *success condition*, expresses that I do not expect any loss (but possibly some gain) when betting on the truth of atomic statements as explained above. Returning to our example of the elementary state $[p \| q, q]$, I expect an average loss of 0.5€ with respect to $\Pi = \langle W, e, \mu \rangle$, where μ is the uniform contribution over a finite set of precisification points W with $|\{\pi \in W \mid e(\pi, r) = 1\}| = |\{\pi \in W \mid e(\pi, r) = 0\}|$ for $r = p$ and $r = q$, implying $\langle p \rangle_\Pi = \langle q \rangle_\Pi = 0.5$. If for some alternative precisification space Π' we have $\langle p \rangle_{\Pi'} = 0.8$ and $\langle q \rangle_{\Pi'} = 0.3$ then my average loss is negative; more precisely, I can expect a gain of 0.2€ in average.

(2) A Dialogue Game for the Analysis of Complex Formulas. We follow Giles and Paul Lorenzen (see, e.g., [23]) in constraining the meaning of connectives by reference to rules of a dialogue game that proceeds by systematically reducing arguments about compound formulas to arguments about their subformulas.

For the sake of clarity, we first assume that formulas are built up from propositional variables and $\bot$ using the connectives $\supset$ and S only. (Note that in Ł, and therefore also in SŁ, one can define strong conjunction and consequently also all other connectives using $A \& B =_{def} (A \supset (B \supset \bot)) \supset \bot)$. However, we will present a more direct analysis of conjunction and disjunction, below.)

The dialogue rule for implication can be stated as follows (cf. [13,14]):

$(R_\supset)$ If I assert $A \supset B$ then, whenever you choose to attack this statement by asserting A, I have to assert also B. (And *vice versa*, i.e., for the roles of me and you switched.)

Note that a player may also choose not to attack the opponent's assertions of $A \supset B$. This rule reflects the idea that the *meaning of implication* entails the principle that an assertion of "If A then B." obliges one to assert also B if the opponent in a dialogue grants (i.e., asserts) A.

The dialogue rule for the supertruth modality involves a relativization to specific precisification points:

(R_S) If I assert SA then I also have to assert that A holds at any precisification point π that you may choose. (And *vice versa*, i.e., for the roles of me and you switched.)

Let us henceforth use A^π as shorthand for 'A holds at the precisification point π' and speak of A as a *formula indexed* by π, accordingly. Note that using rule (R_S) entails that we have to deal with indexed formulas also in rule $(R_\supset)$. However, we don't have to change the rule itself, which will turn out to be adequate independently of the kind of evaluation—degree based or supervaluation based—that we aim at in a particular context. Rather, we only need to stipulate that in applying $(R_\supset)$ the precisification point index of $A \supset B$ (if there is any) is inherited by the subformulas A and B. If, on the other hand, we apply rule (R_S) to an already indexed formula $(SA)^\rho$ then the index ρ is overwritten by whatever index π is chosen by the opponent player; i.e., we have to continue with the assertion A^π. Of course, we also have to account for indices of formulas in elementary states. This is achieved in the obvious way: we simply augment the definition of *risk* (with respect to $\Pi = \langle W, e, \mu \rangle$) by $\langle p^\pi \rangle_\Pi = 1 - e(\pi, p)$. In other words, the probability of having to pay 1€ for claiming that p holds at the precisification point π is 0 if p is true at π and 1 if p is false at π.

To simplify notations we will use the special *global index* ε ($\notin W$) to indicate that a formula is *not* referring to a particular precisification point. Thus *every* formula is indexed now, but A^ε means that A is asserted 'globally', i.e., without reference to a particular precisification.

We use $[A_1^{\pi_1}, \ldots, A_m^{\pi_m} \| B_1^{\rho_1}, \ldots, B_n^{\rho_n}]$ to denote an arbitrary (not necessarily elementary) *state* of the game, where $\{A_1^{\pi_1}, \ldots, A_m^{\pi_m}\}$ is the multiset of formulas that are currently asserted by you, and $\{B_1^{\rho_1}, \ldots, B_n^{\rho_n}\}$ is the multiset of formulas that are currently asserted by me. (Note that this implies, that we don't care about the order in which formulas are asserted.)

A *move initiated by me* (m-move) in state $[\Gamma \| \Delta]$ consists in my picking of some non-atomic formula A^π from the multiset Γ and proceeding as follows:

- If $A^\pi = (A_1 \supset A_2)^\pi$ then I may either *attack* by asserting A_1^π in order to force you to assert A_2^π in accordance with $(R_\supset)$, or *admit* A^π. In the first case the successor state is $[\Gamma', A_2^\pi \| \Delta, A_1^\pi]$, in the second case it is $[\Gamma' \| \Delta]$, where $\Gamma' = \Gamma - \{A^\pi\}$.
- If $A^\pi = SB^\pi$ then I choose an arbitrary $\sigma \in W$ thus forcing you to assert B^σ. The successor state is $[\Gamma', B^\sigma \| \Delta]$, where $\Gamma' = \Gamma - \{A^\pi\}$.

A *move intiated by you* (y-move) is symmetric, i.e., with the roles of me and you interchanged. A run of the game consists in a sequence of states, each resulting from a move in the immediately preceding state, and ending in an elementary state $[p_1^{\pi_1}, \ldots, p_m^{\pi_m} \| q_1^{\rho_1}, \ldots, q_n^{\rho_n}]$. I *succeed* in this run if this final state fulfills the success condition, i.e., if

$$\sum_{j=1}^{n} \langle q_j^{\rho_j} \rangle_\Pi - \sum_{i=1}^{m} \langle p_i^{\pi_i} \rangle_\Pi \leq 0. \tag{11}$$

The term at the left hand side of inequality 11 is my *expected loss* at this state. In other words, I succeed if my expected loss is 0 or even negative, i.e., in fact a gain.

As mentioned above, other connectives can be reduced to implication and *falsum*. However, using the corresponding definitions directly hardly results in dialogue rules that are as natural as $(R_\supset)$. In the following we will formulate dialogue rules only from my point of view, with the implicit understanding that the corresponding rule for you is completely symmetric. For conjunction *two* candidate rules seem natural:

$(R_\wedge)$ If I assert $A_1 \wedge A_2$ then I have to assert also A_i for any $i \in \{1, 2\}$ that you may choose.

$(R_{\wedge'})$ If I assert $A_1 \wedge' A_2$ then I have to assert also A_1 as well as A_2.

Rule $(R_\wedge)$ is dual to the following natural candidate for a disjunction rule:

$(R_\vee)$ If I assert $A_1 \vee A_2$ then I have to assert also A_i for some $i \in \{1,2\}$ that I myself may choose.

Moreover it is clear how $(R_\wedge)$ generalizes to a rule for universal quantification. Note that the modality S can be seen as a kind of universal quantifier over corresponding classical propositions at all precisification points; which is reflected in the form of the rules $(R_\wedge)$ and (R_S), respectively.

It follows already from results in [13,14] that rules $(R_\wedge)$ and $(R_\vee)$ are adequate for weak conjunction and disjunction in **Ł**, respectively. $\wedge$ and $\vee$ are also called 'lattice connectives' in the context of fuzzy logics, since their truth functions are given by

$$v^*(A \wedge B) = \inf\{v^*(A), v^*(B)\} \quad \text{and} \quad v^*(A \vee B) = \sup\{v^*(A), v^*(B)\}.$$

The question arises, whether we can use the remaining rule $(R_{\wedge'})$ to characterize strong disjunction $(\&)$. However, rule $(R_{\wedge'})$ is inadequate in the context of our betting scheme for random evaluation in a precisification space. The reason for this is that we have to make sure that for any (not necessarily atomic) assertion we make, we risk a *maximal* loss of 1€. It is easy to see that rules $(R_\supset)$, $(R_\wedge)$, $(R_\vee)$, and (R_S) comply with this constraint; however if I assert $p \wedge' q$ and we play according to $(R_{\wedge'})$, then I end up with an expected loss of 2€, in case both p and q are superfalse. There is a simply way to redress this situation to obtain a rule that is adequate for $(\&)$: Allow any player who asserts $A_1 \& A_2$ to hedge her possible loss by asserting $\bot$ instead; which of course corresponds to the obligation to pay 1€ (but not more) in the resulting final state. We thus obtain:

$(R_\&)$ If I assert $A_1 \& A_2$ then I either have to assert also A_1 as well as A_2, or else I have to assert $\bot$.

All discussed rules induce definitions of corresponding *moves* in the game, analogously to the case of $(R_\supset)$ and (R_S), illustrated above.

4   Adequacy of the Game

To prove that the game presented in Section 3 indeed characterizes logic **SŁ**, we have to analyse all possible runs of the game starting with some arbitrarily complex assertion by myself. A *strategy* for me will be a tree-like structure, where a branch represents a possible run resulting from particular choices made by myself, taking into account all of your possible choices in (y- or m-moves) that are compatible with the rules. We will only have to look at strategies for *me* and thus call a strategy *winning* if I succeed in all corresponding runs (according to condition 11).

Remember that by Proposition 3 we can assume that the set W of the underlying precisification space $\Pi = \langle W, e, \mu \rangle$ is finite. The construction of strategies can be viewed as systematic proof search in an analytic tableau calculus with the following rules:

$$\frac{[\Gamma\|\Delta,(A_1 \supset A_2)^\pi]}{[\Gamma,A_1^\pi\|\Delta,A_2^\pi]\mid[\Gamma\|\Delta]}(\supset_y) \qquad \frac{[\Gamma,(A_1 \supset A_2)^\pi\|\Delta]}{[\Gamma,A_2^\pi\|\Delta,A_1^\pi]}(\supset_m^1) \qquad \frac{[\Gamma,(A_1 \supset A_2)^\pi\|\Delta]}{[\Gamma\|\Delta]}(\supset_m^2)$$

$$\frac{[\Gamma\|\Delta,(A_1 \& A_2)^\pi]}{[\Gamma\|\Delta,A_1^\pi,A_2^\pi]}(\&_y^1) \qquad \frac{[\Gamma\|\Delta,(A_1 \& A_2)^\pi]}{[\Gamma\|\Delta,\bot^\pi]}(\&_y^2) \qquad \frac{[\Gamma,(A_1 \& A_2)^\pi\|\Delta]}{[\Gamma,A_1^\pi,A_2^\pi\|\Delta]\mid[\Gamma,\bot^\pi\|\Delta]}(\&_m)$$

$$\frac{[\Gamma\|\Delta,(A_1 \wedge A_2)^\pi]}{[\Gamma\|\Delta,A_1^\pi]\mid[\Gamma\|\Delta,A_2^\pi]}(\wedge_y) \qquad \frac{[\Gamma,(A_1 \wedge A_2)^\pi\|\Delta]}{[\Gamma,A_1^\pi\|\Delta]}(\wedge_m^1) \qquad \frac{[\Gamma,(A_1 \wedge A_2)^\pi\|\Delta]}{[\Gamma,A_2^\pi\|\Delta]}(\wedge_m^2)$$

$$\frac{[\Gamma\|\Delta,(A_1 \vee A_2)^\pi]}{[\Gamma\|\Delta,A_1^\pi]}(\vee_y^1) \qquad \frac{[\Gamma\|\Delta,(A_1 \vee A_2)^\pi]}{[\Gamma\|\Delta,A_2^\pi]}(\vee_y^2) \qquad \frac{[\Gamma,(A_1 \vee A_2)^\pi\|\Delta]}{[\Gamma,A_1^\pi\|\Delta]\mid[\Gamma,A_2^\pi\|\Delta]}(\vee_m)$$

$$\frac{[\Gamma\|\Delta,(SA)^\pi]}{[\Gamma\|\Delta,A^{\pi_1}]\mid\ \ldots\ \mid[\Gamma\|\Delta,A^{\pi_n}]}(S_y) \qquad \frac{[\Gamma,(SA)^\pi\|\Delta]}{[\Gamma,A^\rho\|\Delta]}(S_m)$$

In all rules π can denote any index, including the global index ε. In rule (S_y) we assume that $W=\{\pi_1,\ldots,\pi_m\}$ and in rule (S_m) the index ρ can be any element of W. Note that, in accordance with the definition of a strategy for *me*, your choices in the moves induce branching, whereas for my choices a single successor state that is compatible with the dialogue rules is chosen.

The finiteness assumption for W is not needed in proving the following theorem.

Theorem 1. *A formula F is valid in $S\!\L$ if and only if for every precisification space Π I have a winning strategy for the game starting in state $[\|F]$.*

Proof. Note that every run of the game is finite. For every final elementary state $[p_1^{\pi_1},\ldots,p_m^{\pi_m}\|q_1^{\rho_1},\ldots,q_n^{\rho_n}]$ the success condition says that we have to compute the risk $\sum_{j=1}^n\langle q_j^{\rho_j}\rangle_\Pi - \sum_{i=1}^m\langle p_i^{\pi_i}\rangle_\Pi$, where $\langle r^\pi\rangle_\Pi = \mu(\{\rho \in W | e(\rho,r)=0\})$ if $\pi=\varepsilon$ and $\langle r^\pi\rangle_\Pi = 1 - e(\pi,r)$ otherwise, and check whether the resulting value (in the following denoted by $\langle p_1^{\pi_1},\ldots,p_m^{\pi_m}\|q_1^{\rho_1},\ldots,q_n^{\rho_n}\rangle_\Pi$) is ≤ 0 to determine whether I 'win' the game. To obtain my minimal final risk (i.e., my minimal expected loss) that I can enforce in any given state S by playing according to an optimal strategy, we have to take into account the supremum over all risks associated with the successor states to S that you can enforce by a choice that you may have in a (y- or m-)move S. On the other hand, for any of my choices I can enforce the infimum of risks of corresponding successor states. In other words, we prove that we can extend the definition of *my expected loss* from elementary states to arbitrary states such that the following conditions are satisfied:

$$\langle\Gamma,(A \supset B)^\pi\|\Delta\rangle_\Pi = \inf\{\langle\Gamma\|\Delta\rangle_\Pi,\langle\Gamma,B^\pi\|A^\pi,\Delta\rangle_\Pi\} \tag{12}$$

$$\langle\Gamma,(A \& B)^\pi\|\Delta\rangle_\Pi = \sup\{\langle\Gamma,A^\pi,B^\pi\|\Delta\rangle_\Pi,\langle\Gamma,\bot^\pi\|\Delta\rangle_\Pi\} \tag{13}$$

$$\langle\Gamma,(A \wedge B)^\pi\|\Delta\rangle_\Pi = \inf\{\langle\Gamma,A^\pi\|\Delta\rangle_\Pi,\langle\Gamma,B^\pi\|\Delta\rangle_\Pi\} \tag{14}$$

$$\langle\Gamma,(A \vee B)^\pi\|\Delta\rangle_\Pi = \sup\{\langle\Gamma,A^\pi\|\Delta\rangle_\Pi,\langle\Gamma,B^\pi\|\Delta\rangle_\Pi\} \tag{15}$$

for assertions by you and, for my own assertions:

$$\langle\Gamma\|(A \supset B)^\pi,\Delta\rangle_\Pi = \sup\{\langle\Gamma,A^\pi\|B^\pi,\Delta\rangle_\Pi,\langle\Gamma\|\Delta\rangle_\Pi\} \tag{16}$$

$$\langle\Gamma\|(A \& B)^\pi,\Delta\rangle_\Pi = \inf\{\langle\Gamma\|A^\pi,B^\pi,\Delta\rangle_\Pi,\langle\Gamma\|\bot,\Delta\rangle_\Pi\} \tag{17}$$

$$\langle\Gamma\|(A \wedge B)^\pi,\Delta\rangle_\Pi = \sup\{\langle\Gamma\|A^\pi,\Delta\rangle_\Pi,\langle\Gamma\|B^\pi,\Delta\rangle_\Pi\} \tag{18}$$

$$\langle\Gamma\|(A \vee B)^\pi,\Delta\rangle_\Pi = \inf\{\langle\Gamma\|A^\pi,\Delta\rangle_\Pi,\langle\Gamma\|B^\pi,\Delta\rangle_\Pi\} \tag{19}$$

Furthermore we have

$$\langle \Gamma \| (SA)^\pi, \Delta \rangle_\Pi = \sup_{\rho \in W} \{ \langle \Gamma \| A^\rho, \Delta \rangle_\Pi \} \tag{20}$$

$$\langle \Gamma, (SA)^\pi \| \Delta \rangle_\Pi = \inf_{\rho \in W} \{ \langle \Gamma, A^\rho \| \Delta \rangle_\Pi \} \tag{21}$$

We have to check that $\langle \cdot \| \cdot \rangle_\Pi$ is well-defined; i.e., that conditions 12-21 together with the definition of my expected loss (risk) for elementary states indeed can be simultaneously fulfilled and guarantee uniqueness. To this aim consider the following generalisation of the truth function for S$Ł$ to multisets Γ of indexed formulas:

$$\|\Gamma\|_\Pi =_{def} \sum_{A^\pi \in \Gamma, \pi \neq \varepsilon} \|A\|_\pi + \sum_{A^\varepsilon \in \Gamma} \|A\|_\Pi.$$

Note that

$$\|A\|_\Pi = \|\{A^\varepsilon\}\|_\Pi = 1 \ \text{iff} \ \langle \|A^\varepsilon \rangle_\Pi \leq 0.$$

In words: A is valid in S$Ł$ iff my risk in the game starting with my assertion of A is non-positive. Moreover, for elementary states we have

$$\langle p_1^{\pi_1}, \dots, p_m^{\pi_m} \| q_1^{\rho_1}, \dots, q_n^{\rho_n} \rangle_\Pi = n - m + \|p_1^{\pi_1}, \dots, p_m^{\pi_m}\|_\Pi - \|q_1^{\rho_1}, \dots, q_n^{\rho_n}\|_\Pi.$$

We generalize the risk function to arbitrary states by

$$\langle \Gamma \| \Delta \rangle_\Pi^* =_{def} |\Delta| - |\Gamma| + \|\Gamma\|_\Pi - \|\Delta\|_\Pi$$

and check that it satisfies conditions 12-21. We only spell out two cases. To avoid case distinctions let $\|A\|_\varepsilon =_{def} \|A\|_\Pi$. For condition 12 we have

$$\langle \Gamma, (A \supset B)^\pi \| \Delta \rangle_\Pi^* = |\Delta| - |\Gamma| - 1 + \|\Gamma\|_\Pi + \|(A \supset B)\|_\pi - \|\Delta\|_\Pi$$
$$= \langle \Gamma \| \Delta \rangle_\Pi^* - 1 + \|(A \supset B)\|_\pi = \langle \Gamma \| \Delta \rangle_\Pi^* - 1 + (\|A\|_\pi \Rightarrow_Ł \|B\|_\pi)$$
$$= \langle \Gamma \| \Delta \rangle_\Pi^* - 1 + \inf\{1, 1 - \|A\|_\pi + \|B\|_\pi\} = \langle \Gamma \| \Delta \rangle_\Pi^* - 1 + \inf\{1, 1 + \langle B^\pi \| A^\pi \rangle_\Pi^*\}$$
$$= \langle \Gamma \| \Delta \rangle_\Pi^* + \inf\{0, \langle B^\pi \| A^\pi \rangle_\Pi^*\} = \inf\{\langle \Gamma \| \Delta \rangle_\Pi^*, \langle \Gamma, B^\pi \| A^\pi, \Delta \rangle_\Pi^*\}$$

For condition 20 we have

$$\langle \Gamma \| (SA)^\pi, \Delta \rangle_\Pi^* = |\Delta| + 1 - |\Gamma| + \|\Gamma\|_\Pi - \|\Delta\|_\Pi - \|SA\|_\pi$$
$$= \langle \Gamma \| \Delta \rangle_\Pi^* + 1 - \|SA\|_\pi = \langle \Gamma \| \Delta \rangle_\Pi^* + 1 - \inf_{\rho \in W}\{\|A\|_\rho\}$$
$$= \langle \Gamma \| \Delta \rangle_\Pi^* + \sup_{\rho \in W}\{\|A\|_\rho\} = \sup_{\rho \in W}\{\langle \Gamma, A^\rho \| \Delta \rangle_\Pi^*\} \qquad \diamond$$

Remark 1. It already follows from a well known general theorem ('saddle point theorem') about finite games with perfect information that conditions 12-21 uniquely extend any given risk assignment from final states to arbitrary states. However, our proof above yields more information, namely that the extended risk function indeed matches the semantics of logic S$Ł$, as defined in Section 2.

By a *regulation* we mean an assignment of game states to labels '*you move next*' and '*I move next*' that constrain the possible runs of the game in the obvious way. A regulation is *consistent* if the label '*you (I) move next*' is only assigned to states where such a move is possible, i.e., where I (you) have asserted a non-atomic formula. As a simple but nice corollary to our proof of Theorem 1, we obtain:

Corollary 1. *The total expected loss* $\langle \Gamma \| \Delta \rangle_{\Pi}^{*}$ *that I can enforce in a game over* Π *starting in state* $[\Gamma \| \Delta]$ *only depends on* Γ, Δ, *and* Π. *In particular, it is the same for every consistent regulation that may be imposed on the game.*

5   Remarks on Related Work

Various kinds of modal extensions of fuzzy logics have been considered in the literature. E.g., chapter 8 of the central monograph [15] presents the family **S5**(L) for t-norm based fuzzy logics L by letting the truth value $e(w, p)$ assigned to a proposition p at a world $w \in W$ of a Kripke model range over $[0, 1]$ instead of $\{0, 1\}$. The truth function for the modality $\square$ is given by $\|\square A\|_w = \inf_{v \in W} \|A\|_v$. Of course, $\square$, thus defined, behaves quite differently from supertruth S. In particular $\square A \vee \neg \square A$ is not valid. On the other hand, $\triangle A \vee \neg \triangle A$ is valid for the widely used 'definiteness' operator $\triangle$ as axiomatized in [2]. However also $\triangle$ over Ł is quite different from S in SŁ, as can be seen by considering the distribution axiom $\triangle (A \vee B) \supset (\triangle A \vee \triangle B)$ of [2]: Replacing $\triangle$ by S yields a formula that is not valid in **SŁ**. For the same reason the modal extensions of logic **MTL** considered in [5] are not able to express 'supertruth'.

Yet another type of natural extension of fuzzy logics arises when one considers the propositional operator Pr for 'It is probable that …'. In [15,19,8] model structures that are essentially like our precisification spaces are used to specify the semantics of Pr. More exactly, one defines $\|Pr(A)\|_w = \mu(\{w \in W \mid e(w, A) = 1\})$, which implies that, for atomic propositions p, $Pr(p)$ is treated like p itself in **SŁ**. However, supertruth S cannot be expressed using Pr, already for the simple reason that the syntax of the mentioned 'fuzzy probability logics' does not allow for nesting of Pr. Moreover, classical and degree based connectives are separated at the syntactic level; whereas our dialogue game based analysis justifies the syntactic identification of both types of connectives in the context of precisification spaces.

Our way to define evaluation over a precisification space is also related to ideas of Dorothy Egdington [7]. However, while Edgington also refers to 'truth on proportions of precisifications', she insists on evaluations that are not truth functional.

Finally we mention that some of the ideas underlying our presentation of SŁ are already—at least implicitly—present in [10]. However no corresponding formal definitions or results have been presented there.

6   Conclusion and Future Work

We have presented an analysis of logical reasoning with vague propositions that incorporates two seemingly different approaches to semantics: supervaluation and degree based valuation. The resulting logic SŁ has been characterized as the set of those formulas which a player can assert in a natural dialogue+betting game over precisification spaces, without having to expect a loss of money.

The agenda for related future work includes the 'lifting' of our tableau style evaluation system to a hypersequent calculus, that abstracts away from particular underlying precisification spaces. This will lead to a proof system related to the calculi in [24] and in [4], and should be a good basis for exploring also other t-norm based evaluations over precisification spaces. Moreover we want to investigate the extension of S**Ł** by further modal operators that seem relevant in modelling propositional attitudes arising in contexts of vagueness.

References

1. J.C. Beall (ed.): *Liars and Heaps*. Oxford University Press 2003.
2. Matthias Baaz: Infinite-valued Gödel logics with 0-1-projections and relativizations. In: *Gödel 96. Kurt Gödel's Legacy*, Springer LNL 6 (1996), 23-33.
3. Linda C. Burns: *Vagueness: an Investigation Into Natural Language and the Sorites Paradox*, Dordrecht, Kluwer Academic Publishers, 1991.
4. A. Ciabattoni, C.G. Fermüller, G. Metcalfe: Uniform Rules and Dialogue Games for Fuzzy Logics. In: *LPAR 2004*, F. Baader, A. Voronkov (eds.), Springer LNAI 3452 (2005), 496-510.
5. A. Ciabattoni, F. Montagna, G. Metcalfe: Adding Modalities to MTL and its Extensions. *Linz Symposium 2005*, to appear.
6. R. Cignoli, I.M.L. D'Ottaviano, D. Mundici: Algebraic Foundations of Many-valued Reasoning. Trends in Logic, Volume 7. Kluwer Academic Publishers, Dordrecht, 1999.
7. D. Edgington: Validity, Uncertainty and Vagueness. *Analsis* 52/4 (1992), 193-204.
8. T. Flaminio, F. Montagna: A logical and algebraic treatment of conditional probability. Arch. Math. Logic 44, 245-262 (2005).
9. Christian G. Fermüller: Theories of Vagueness Versus Fuzzy Logic: Can Logicians Learn from Philosophers? *Neural Network World Journal* 13(5) (2003), 455-466.
10. Christian G. Fermüller: Revisiting Giles's Game. *Logic, Games and Philosophy: Foundational Perspectives*, Prague Colloquium October 2004, to appear.
11. Kit Fine: Vagueness, Truth and Logic, *Synthése* 30, 265-300, 1975.
12. B.R. Gaines. Foundations of fuzzy reasoning. *International Journal of Man-Machine Studies*, 8:623–668, 1976.
13. Robin Giles: A non-classical logic for physics. *Studia Logica* 33, vol. 4, (1974), 399-417.
14. Robin Giles: A non-classical logic for physics. In: R. Wojcicki, G. Malinkowski (Eds.) *Selected Papers on Łukasiewicz Sentential Calculi*. Polish Academy of Sciences, 1977, 13-51.
15. Petr Hájek: *Metamathematics of Fuzzy Logic*. Kluwer, 1998.
16. Petr Hájek: Basic fuzzy logic and BL-algebras. *Soft Computing* 2 (1998), 124-128
17. Petr Hájek: Why fuzzy logic?. In *A Companion to Philosophical Logic* (D. Jackquette, ed.), Blackwell, 2002, 595-606.
18. Petr Hájek, Vilém Novák: The sorites paradox and fuzzy logic. *Intl. J. of General Systems* 32/4 (2003) 373-383
19. Petr Hájek, Lluis Godo, Francesc Esteva: Fuzzy logic and probability. *11th Conference on Uncertainty in Artificial Intelligence (UAI-95*, Morgan Kaufmann 1995, 237-244.
20. Keefe, Rosanna: *Theories of Vagueness*, Cambridge University Press, 2000.
21. Rosanna Keefe, Peter Smith (eds.): *Vagueness: A Reader*, Massachusetts, MIT Press, 1987.
22. Philip Kremer and Michael Kremer: Some Supervaluation-based Consequence Relations. *Journal of Philosophical Logic* 32(3), June 2003, 225-244.
23. P. Lorenzen: Logik und Agon. In *Atti Congr. Internaz. di Filosofia*, Sansoni, 1960, 187-194.
24. G. Metcalfe, N. Olivetti, D. Gabbay: Sequent and hypersequent calculi for abelian and Łukasiewicz logics. *ACM Transactions on Computational Logic* 6(3), 578-613, 2005.
25. P.S. Mostert, A.L. Shields: On the structure of semigroups on a compact manifold with boundary. *Annals of Mathematics* 65 (1957), 117-143.
26. Jeff Paris: Semantics for Fuzzy Logic Supporting Truth Functionality. In: *Discovering the World with Fuzzy Logic*. Physica-Verlag, Heidelberg, 2000, 82-104.
27. Achille Varzi: Vagueness, Logic, and Ontology, *The Dialogue 1*, 135-154.
28. Timothy Williamson: *Vagueness*, London, Routledge, 1994.

A Comparison of Reasoning Techniques for Querying Large Description Logic ABoxes

Boris Motik and Ulrike Sattler

University of Manchester
Manchester, UK

Abstract. Many modern applications of description logics (DLs) require answering queries over large data quantities, structured according to relatively simple ontologies. For such applications, we conjectured that reusing ideas of deductive databases might improve scalability of DL systems. Hence, in our previous work, we developed an algorithm for reducing a DL knowledge base to a disjunctive datalog program. To test our conjecture, we implemented our algorithm in a new DL reasoner KAON2, which we describe in this paper. Furthermore, we created a comprehensive test suite and used it to conduct a performance evaluation. Our results show that, on knowledge bases with large ABoxes but with simple TBoxes, our technique indeed shows good performance; in contrast, on knowledge bases with large and complex TBoxes, existing techniques still perform better. This allowed us to gain important insights into strengths and weaknesses of both approaches.

1 Introduction

Description logics (DLs) are a family of knowledge representation formalisms with applications in numerous areas of computer science. They have long been used in information integration [1, Chapter 16], and they provide a logical foundation for OWL—a standardized language for ontology modeling in the Semantic Web [10]. A DL knowledge base is typically partitioned into a terminological (or schema) part, called a *TBox*, and an assertional (or data) part, called an *ABox*. Whereas some applications rely on reasoning over large TBoxes, many DL applications involve answering queries over knowledge bases with small and simple TBoxes, but with large ABoxes. For example, the documents in the Semantic Web are likely to be annotated using simple ontologies; however, the number of annotations is likely to be large. Similarly, the data sources in an information integration system can often be described using simple schemata; however, the data contained in the sources is usually very large.

Reasoning with large data sets was extensively studied in the field of deductive databases, resulting in several techniques that have proven themselves in practice. Motivated by the prospect of applying these techniques to query answering in description logics, in our previous work we described a novel reasoning algorithm [12] that reduces a $\mathcal{SHIQ}$ knowledge base KB to a disjunctive datalog program $\mathsf{DD}(KB)$ while preserving the set of relevant consequences. This

M. Hermann and A. Voronkov (Eds.): LPAR 2006, LNAI 4246, pp. 227–241, 2006.
© Springer-Verlag Berlin Heidelberg 2006

algorithm is quite different from tableau algorithms [1, Chapter 2] and their optimizations [9], used in state-of-the-art DL reasoners such as RACER [8], FaCT++
[22], or Pellet [17].

We conjectured that our algorithm will scale well to knowledge bases with
large ABoxes and simple TBoxes. In particular, we expected great benefits from
techniques such as magic sets [4] or join-order optimizations. Furthermore, we
identified a Horn fragment of $\mathcal{SHIQ}$ [13], for which our algorithm exhibits polynomial data complexity (that is, the complexity measured in the size of the
ABox, assuming the TBox is fixed in size).

To test our conjecture, we implemented the reduction algorithm in a new DL
reasoner KAON2.[1] To obtain an efficient system, we developed several optimizations of the initial algorithm and of known implementation techniques. In this
paper we outline the design of the system and overview the employed techniques.
Due to lack of space, we are unable to present all optimizations in full detail; for
more information, please refer to [15].

Providing an objective account of the performance of our approach proved
to be difficult because there are no widely recognized benchmarks for query
answering. To fill this gap, we created a benchmark suite consisting of several
ontologies with TBoxes of varying size and complexity, and with large ABoxes.
In this paper, we discuss the guidelines we followed in selecting the test data.
Our benchmarks are freely available on the Web,[2] and we hope that they can
provide a starting point for a standard DL test suite.

Finally, we conducted extensive performance tests with KAON2, RACER, and
Pellet. To obtain a complete picture of the performance of our algorithms, apart
from ABox reasoning tests, we also performed several TBox reasoning tests. The
results were twofold, and were roughly in line with our expectations. Namely, on
ontologies with a small TBox but a large ABox, our algorithm outperformed its
tableau counterparts; however, on ontologies with a complex TBox but a small
ABox, existing algorithms exhibited superior performance. We discuss these results, and provide insight into strengths and weaknesses of either algorithm. This
may provide useful guidance to developers of future DL systems.

Summing up, our reasoning algorithm provides good performance for knowledge bases which do not rely too heavily on modal reasoning, but are more akin
to logic programs. However, the boundary between the two extreme use-cases
is not clear-cut. As a consequence, we now have a more comprehensive set of
reasoning techniques for expressive DLs, allowing the users to choose the one
that best suits the needs of their application.

2   Preliminaries

We now present the syntax and the semantics of the DL $\mathcal{SHIQ}$ [11]—the formalism underlying KAON2. Given a set of role names N_R, a $\mathcal{SHIQ}$ *role* is either
some $R \in N_R$ or an *inverse role* R^- for $R \in N_R$. A $\mathcal{SHIQ}$ *RBox* $KB_\mathcal{R}$ is a

---

[1] http://kaon2.semanticweb.org/

[2] http://kaon2.semanticweb.org/download/test_ontologies.zip

Table 1. Semantics of $\mathcal{SHIQ}$ by Mapping to FOL

Translating Concepts to FOL	
$\pi_y(A, X) = A(X)$	$\pi_y(C \sqcap D, X) = \pi_y(C, X) \wedge \pi_y(D, X)$
$\pi_y(\neg C, X) = \neg \pi_y(C, X)$	$\pi_y(\forall R.C, X) = \forall y : R(X, y) \rightarrow \pi_x(C, y)$
$\pi_y(\geq n\, S.C, X) = \exists y_1, \ldots, y_n : \bigwedge S(X, y_i) \wedge \bigwedge \pi_x(C, y_i) \wedge \bigwedge y_i \not\approx y_j$	
Translating Axioms to FOL	
$\pi(C \sqsubseteq D) = \forall x : \pi_y(C, x) \rightarrow \pi_y(D, x)$	$\pi(C(a)) = \pi_y(C, a)$
$\pi(R \sqsubseteq S) = \forall x, y : R(x, y) \rightarrow S(x, y)$	$\pi(R(a, b)) = R(a, b)$
	$\pi(a \circ b) = a \circ b$ for $\circ \in \{\approx, \not\approx\}$
$\pi(\mathsf{Trans}(R)) = \forall x, y, z : R(x, y) \wedge R(y, z) \rightarrow R(x, z)$	
Translating KB to FOL	
$\pi(R) = \forall x, y : R(x, y) \leftrightarrow R^-(y, x)$	
$\pi(KB) = \bigwedge_{R \in N_R} \pi(R) \wedge \bigwedge_{\alpha \in KB_{\mathcal{T}} \cup KB_{\mathcal{R}} \cup KB_{\mathcal{A}}} \pi(\alpha)$	

X is a meta variable and is substituted by the actual variable. π_x is obtained from π_y by simultaneously substituting $x_{(i)}$ for all $y_{(i)}$, respectively, and π_y for π_x.

finite set of role inclusion axioms $R \sqsubseteq S$ and transitivity axioms $\mathsf{Trans}(R)$, for R and S $\mathcal{SHIQ}$ roles. For $R \in N_R$, we set $\mathsf{Inv}(R) = R^-$ and $\mathsf{Inv}(R^-) = R$, and assume that $R \sqsubseteq S \in KB_{\mathcal{R}}$ ($\mathsf{Trans}(R) \in KB_{\mathcal{R}}$) implies $\mathsf{Inv}(R) \sqsubseteq \mathsf{Inv}(S) \in KB_{\mathcal{R}}$ ($\mathsf{Trans}(\mathsf{Inv}(R)) \in KB_{\mathcal{R}}$). A role R is said to be *simple* if $\mathsf{Trans}(S) \notin KB_{\mathcal{R}}$ for each $S \sqsubseteq^* R$, where $\sqsubseteq^*$ is the reflexive-transitive closure of $\sqsubseteq$.

Given a set of *concept names* N_C, the set of $\mathcal{SHIQ}$ concepts is the minimal set such that each $A \in N_C$ is a $\mathcal{SHIQ}$ concept and, for C and D $\mathcal{SHIQ}$ concepts, R a role, S a simple role, and n a positive integer, $\neg C$, $C \sqcap D$, $\forall R.C$, and $\geq n\, S.C$ are also $\mathcal{SHIQ}$ concepts. We use $\top$, $\bot$, $C_1 \sqcup C_2$, $\exists R.C$, and $\leq n\, S.C$ as abbreviations for $A \sqcup \neg A$, $A \sqcap \neg A$, $\neg(\neg C_1 \sqcap \neg C_2)$, $\neg \forall R. \neg C$, and $\neg(\geq (n+1)\, S.C)$, respectively. A TBox $KB_{\mathcal{T}}$ is a finite set of concept inclusion axioms of the form $C \sqsubseteq D$. An ABox $KB_{\mathcal{A}}$ is a finite set of axioms $C(a)$, $R(a, b)$, and (in)equalities $a \approx b$ and $a \not\approx b$. A knowledge base KB is a triple $(KB_{\mathcal{R}}, KB_{\mathcal{T}}, KB_{\mathcal{A}})$. The semantics of KB is given by translating it into first-order logic by the operator π from Table 1.

A *query* Q over KB is a conjunction of literals $A(s)$ and $R(s, t)$, where s and t are variables or constants, R is a role, and A is an atomic concept. In our work, we assume that all variables in a query should be mapped to individuals explicitly introduced in the ABox. Then, a mapping θ of the free variables of Q to constants is an *answer* of Q over KB if $\pi(KB) \models Q\theta$.

3 KAON2 Architecture

KAON2 is a DL reasoner developed at the University of Manchester and the University of Karlsruhe. The system can handle $\mathcal{SHIQ}$ knowledge bases extended with *DL-safe* rules—first-order clauses syntactically restricted in a way that makes the clauses applicable only to individuals mentioned in the ABox, thus ensuring decidability. KAON2 implements the following reasoning tasks: deciding knowledge base and concept satisfiability, computing the subsumption hierarchy, and answering conjunctive queries withoutdistinguished variables (i.e.,

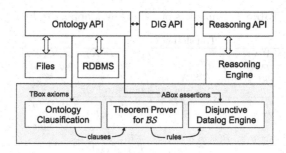

Fig. 1. KAON2 Architecture

all variables of a query can be bound only to explicit ABox individuals, and not to individuals introduced by existential quantification). It has been implemented in Java 1.5.

Figure 1 describes the technical architecture of KAON2. The *Ontology API* provides ontology manipulation services, such as adding and retrieving axioms. The API fully supports OWL and the Semantic Web Rule Language (SWRL) at the syntactic level. Several similar APIs already exist, such as the OWL API [3] or Jena.[3] However, to obtain an efficient system, we needed complete control over the internals of the API, and could thus not reuse an existing implementation. Ontologies can be saved in files, using either OWL RDF[4] or OWL XML[5] syntax. Alternatively, ABox assertions can be stored in a relational database (RDBMS): by mapping ontology entities to database tables, KAON2 will query the database on the fly during reasoning.

The *Reasoning API* allows one to invoke various reasoning tasks, and to retrieve their results.

All APIs can be be invoked either locally, using KAON2 as a dynamic library, or remotely, for example, through the DL Implementors Group (DIG) interface.

The central component of KAON2 is the *Reasoning Engine*, which is based on the algorithm for reducing a $\mathcal{SHIQ}$ knowledge base KB to a disjunctive datalog program $\mathsf{DD}(KB)$ [12]. To understand the intuition behind this algorithm, considering the knowledge base $KB = \{C \sqsubseteq \exists R.E_1, E_1 \sqsubseteq E_2, \exists R.E_2 \sqsubseteq D\}$. For an individual x in C, the first axiom implies existence of an R-successor y in E_1. By the second axiom, y is also in E_2. Hence, x has an R-successor y in E_2, so, by the third axiom, x is in D. The program $\mathsf{DD}(KB)$ contains the rules $E_2(x) \leftarrow E_1(x)$ and $D(x) \leftarrow R(x,y), E_2(x)$, corresponding to the second and the third axiom, respectively. However, the first axiom of KB is not represented in $\mathsf{DD}(KB)$; instead, $\mathsf{DD}(KB)$ contains the rule $D(x) \leftarrow C(x)$. The latter rule can be seen as a "macro": it combines into one step the effects of all mentioned inference steps, without expanding the R-successors explicitly.

---

[3] http://jena.sourceforge.net/

[4] http://www.w3.org/TR/owl-semantics/

[5] http://www.w3.org/TR/owl-xmlsyntax/

Computing all relevant "macro" rules is performed by saturating the TBox of KB using *basic superposition* $(\mathcal{BS})$ [2,16] (a clausal refutation calculus), which is implemented in the *Theorem Prover* subcomponent of the Reasoning Engine. Although there are several efficient theorem provers for first-order logic (e.g., Vampire [19], E [20], or Otter [14]), we decided to implement our own theorem prover, due to the following reasons. First, we are unaware of an existing implementation of basic superposition. Second, existing systems usually do not come with a comprehensive API, which makes their integration into other systems difficult. Third, our theorem prover is not used primarily to check TBox inconsistency (an inconsistent TBox is usually a modeling error); rather, it is used to compute all "macro" rules that logically follow from a TBox. Hence, whereas most theorem provers are geared towards unsatisfiable problems, ours is geared towards satisfiable problems. This allows us to make several simplifying assumptions. For example, unlike most existing theorem provers, ours spends very little time in deciding which clause to work on next (in most cases, all clauses must be considered anyway). Fourth, we were not interested in building a general theorem prover; rather, we wanted a prover that implements our algorithm efficiently. This allowed the implementation to be further simplified. In particular, our algorithm must handle only unary and binary literals containing shallow terms, for which unification can be implemented in constant time. Furthermore, clauses can be efficiently indexed using a variant of feature vector indexing [21].

The *Ontology Clausification* subcomponent of the Reasoning Engine is responsible for translating the TBox of a $\mathcal{SHIQ}$ knowledge base KB into a set of first-order clauses. As our experiments confirm, it is very important to reduce the number of clauses produced in the translation. To this purpose, we use several simple optimizations of the clausification algorithm. In particular, if several axioms contain the same nested subconcept, we replace all their occurrences with a new atomic concept. For example, in axioms $C \sqsubseteq \exists R.\exists S.D$ and $E \sqsubseteq \forall T.\exists S.D$ the concept $\exists S.D$ occurs twice, so we replace all its occurrences with a new concept Q. We thus obtain the set of equisatisfiable axioms $C \sqsubseteq \exists R.Q$, $E \sqsubseteq \forall T.Q$, and $Q \sqsubseteq \exists S.D$, which produces fewer clauses than the original one. Another optimization involves functional roles: if R is functional, the existential quantifier in each occurrence of a formula $\exists y : [R(x,y) \wedge C(y)]$ (stemming from a concept $\exists R.C$) can be skolemized using the same function symbol.

The *Disjunctive Datalog Engine* subcomponent of the Reasoning Engine is used for answering queries in the disjunctive datalog program obtained by the reduction. Although several disjunctive datalog engines exist (e.g., DLV [5]), we decided to implement our own engine, due to the following reasons. First, existing engines do not come with a comprehensive API, which makes their integration into other systems difficult. Second, our reduction produces only positive datalog programs—that is, programs without negation-as-failure. We also do not rely on the minimal model semantics of disjunctive datalog. Thus, we can eliminate the minimality test from our implementation and avoid unnecessary overhead. Third, model building is an important aspect of reasoning in disjunctive datalog. To compute the models, disjunctive datalog engines usually ground the disjunctive program. Although this process has been optimized using *intelligent grounding* [6], grounding can be very expensive on large data sets. In contrast, the models of our programs are of no interest. To avoid grounding, we answer queries using hyperresolution with answer literals. Fourth, disjunctive datalog engines typically do not provide for the first-order equality predicate, which we use to correctly support number restrictions.

Due to space constraints, we cannot present the implementation techniques used in KAON2 in more detail; for more information, please see [15].

4   Benchmarks for ABox and TBox Reasoning

Comparing the performance of DL reasoning systems objectively is difficult because there are no widely accepted benchmarks. Certain ontologies have established themselves as standards for testing TBox reasoning; however, to the best of our knowledge, there are no such standard tests for ABox reasoning. Hence, we constructed our own data set, which we present in this section. The data set is freely available from the KAON2 Web site,[6] and we hope it can be used as a foundation for an extensive DL benchmark suite.

4.1   Selecting Test Data

We wanted to base our tests as much as possible on ontologies created and used in real projects; our intuition was that such ontologies reflect the relevant use cases more accurately than the synthetically generated ones. However, most ontologies currently used in practice seem to fall into two categories: they either have a complex TBox, but no ABox, or they have a large ABox, but a very simple TBox. To obtain tests with interesting TBoxes, we used synthetic ontologies as well. Furthermore, to obtain ABoxes of sufficient size, we applied *replication*—copying an ABox several times with appropriate renaming of individuals in axioms.

One of our goals was to study the impact of various DL constructors on the reasoning performance. In particular, we expected that the presence of equality (stemming from number restrictions), existential quantifiers, and disjunctions will have adverse effects on the performance of reasoning. Therefore, we selected test ontologies that specifically use (a combination of) these constructors.

For some ontologies, the authors also supplied us with the queries used in their projects, which we then reused in our tests. Namely, these queries were usually sent to us because they caused performance problems in practice, so there is reason to believe that they are "hard." Moreover, we expect these queries to better reflect the practical use cases of their respective ontologies.

4.2   Test Ontologies and Queries

VICODI[7] is an ontology about European history, manually created in the EU-funded project VICODI. The TBox is relatively small and simple: it consists of

---

[6] http://kaon2.semanticweb.org/download/test_ontologies.zip

[7] http://www.vicodi.org/

role and concept inclusion axioms, and of domain and range specifications; furthermore, it does not contain disjunctions, existential quantification, or number restrictions. However, the ABox is relatively large and it contains many interconnected individuals. Because the TBox does not contain existential quantifiers, equality, or disjunctions, it can be converted into a nondisjunctive equality-free datalog program directly, without invoking the reduction algorithm. Hence, query answering for VICODI can be realized using a deductive database only; furthermore, it is possible to deterministically compute the canonical model of the ontology.

With vicodi_0 we denote the ontology from the project, and with vicodi_n the one obtained by replicating n times the ABox of vicodi_0.

From the ontology author we received the following two queries, which are characteristic of the queries used in the project. The first one is a simple concept retrieval, and the second one is a more complex conjunctive query.

$$Q_{V_1}(x) \equiv Individual(x)$$
$$Q_{V_2}(x, y, z) \equiv Military\text{-}Person(x), hasRole(y, x), related(x, z)$$

$SEMINTEC$ is an ontology about financial services, created in the SEMINTEC project[8] at the University of Poznan. Like VICODI, this ontology is relatively simple: it does not use existential quantifiers or disjunctions; it does, however, contain functionality assertions and disjointness constraints. Therefore, it requires equality reasoning, which is known to be hard for deductive databases.

With semintec_0 we denote the ontology from the project, and with semintec_n the one obtained by replicating n times the ABox of semintec_0.

From the ontology author, we obtained the following two queries, which are characteristic of the queries used in the project.

$$Q_{S_1}(x) \equiv Person(x)$$
$$Q_{S_2}(x, y, z) \equiv Man(x), isCreditCardOf(y, x), Gold(y), livesIn(x, z), Region(z)$$

$LUBM$[9] is a benchmark developed at the Lehigh University for testing performance of ontology management and reasoning systems [7]. The ontology describes organizational structure of universities and it is relatively simple: it does not use disjunctions or number restrictions, but it does use existential quantifiers, so our reduction algorithm must be used to eliminate function symbols. Due to the absence of disjunctions and equality, the reduction algorithm produces an equality-free Horn program. In other words, query answering on LUBM can be performed deterministically.

LUBM comes with a generator, which we used instead of ABox replication to obtain the test data. With lubm_n de note the ontology obtained from the generator by setting the number of universities to n. The test generator creates many small files; to make these ontologies easier to handle, we merged them into a single file.

---

[8] http://www.cs.put.poznan.pl/alawrynowicz/semintec.htm
[9] http://swat.cse.lehigh.edu/projects/lubm/index.htm

The LUBM Web site provides 14 queries for use with the ontology, from which we selected the following three. With Q_{L_1} we test the performance of concept retrieval, with Q_{L_2} we test how the performance changes if Q_{L_1} is extended with additional atoms, and with Q_{L_3} we make sure that our results are not skewed by the particular choice of concepts.

$$Q_{L_1}(x) \equiv Chair(x)$$
$$Q_{L_2}(x, y) \equiv Chair(x), worksFor(x, y), Department(y),$$
$$subOrganizationOf(y, \text{``http://www.University0.edu''})$$
$$Q_{L_3}(x, y, z) \equiv Student(x), Faculty(y), Course(z), advisor(x, y),$$
$$takesCourse(x, z), teacherOf(y, z)$$

$Wine^{10}$ is an ontology containing a classification of wines. It uses nominals, which our algorithms cannot handle, so we apply a sound but an incomplete approximation: we replace each enumerated concept $\{i_1, \ldots, i_n\}$ with a new concept O and add assertions $O(i_k)$. This approximation of nominals is incomplete for query answering: for completeness one should further add a clause $\neg O(x) \vee x \approx i_1 \vee \ldots \vee x \approx i_n$; however, doing this would destroy the termination property of our algorithms. The resulting ontology is relatively complex: it contains functional roles, disjunctions, and existential quantifiers.

With wine_0, we denote the original ontology, and with wine_n the one obtained by replicating 2^n times the ABox of wine_0.

Elimination of nominals changes the semantics of most concepts in the knowledge base. Hence, we ran only the following query, which involved computing several nontrivial answers:

$$Q_{W_1}(x) \equiv AmericanWine(x)$$

It is justified to question whether the Wine ontology is suitable for our tests. However, as we already mentioned, we were unable to find an ontology with a complex TBox and an interesting ABox. The approximated Wine ontology was the only one that, at least partially, fulfilled our criteria.

$DOLCE^{11}$ is a foundational ontology developed at the Laboratory for Applied Ontology of the Italian National Research Council. It is very complex, and no reasoner currently available can handle it. Therefore, the ontology has been factored into several modules. We used the DOLCE OWL version 397, up to the Common module (this includes the DOLCE-Lite, ExtDnS, Modal and Common modules). Because the ontology does not have an ABox, we used it only for TBox testing.

We have observed that the performance of KAON2 on DOLCE significantly depends on the presence of transitivity axioms. Hence, we included in our benchmarks a version of DOLCE obtained by removing all transitivity axioms.

---

[10] http://www.schemaweb.info/schema/SchemaDetails.aspx?id=62
[11] http://www.loa-cnr.it/DOLCE.html

Table 2. Statistics of Test Ontologies

KB	$C \sqsubseteq D$	$C \equiv D$	$C \sqcap D \sqsubseteq \bot$	functional	domain	range	$R \sqsubseteq S$	$C(a)$	$R(a,b)$
vicodi_0								16942	36711
vicodi_1								33884	73422
vicodi_2	193	0	0	0	10	10	10	50826	110133
vicodi_3								67768	146844
vicodi_4								84710	183555
semintec_0								17941	47248
semintec_1								35882	94496
semintec_2	55	0	113	16	16	16	6	53823	141744
semintec_3								71764	188992
semintec_4								89705	236240
lubm_1								18128	49336
lubm_2	36	6	0	0	25	18	9	40508	113463
lubm_3								58897	166682
lubm_4								83200	236514
wine_0								247	246
wine_1								741	738
wine_2								1235	1230
wine_3								1729	1722
wine_4								2223	2214
wine_5	126	61	1	6	6	9	9	2717	2706
wine_6								5187	5166
wine_7								10127	10086
wine_8								20007	19926
wine_9								39767	39606
wine_10								79287	78966
dolce	203	27	42	2	253	253	522	0	0
galen	3237	699	0	133	0	0	287	0	0

GALEN[12] is a medical terminology developed in the GALEN project [18]. It has a very large and complex TBox and no ABox, and has traditionally been used as a benchmark for terminological reasoning.

Table 2 shows the number of axioms for each ontology.

5   Performance Evaluation

The main goal of our performance evaluation was to test the scalability of our algorithm—that is, to see how performance of query answering depends on the amount of data and on the complexity of different ontologies. This should give us an idea about the kinds of ontologies that can be efficiently handled using our algorithm. Additionally, we wanted to compare our reasoning algorithm with its tableau counterparts. This goal turned out to be somewhat difficult to achieve. Namely, we are only able to compare *implementations*, and not the algorithms themselves. DL algorithms are complex, and overheads in maintaining data structures or memory management can easily dominate the run time; furthermore, the implementation language itself can introduce limitations that

---

[12] We obtained GALEN through private communication with Ian Horrocks.

become evident when dealing with large data sets. Therefore, the results we present in this section should be taken qualitatively, rather than quantitatively.

5.1 Test Setting

We compared the performance of KAON2 with RACER and Pellet. To the best of our knowledge, these are the only reasoners that provide sound and complete algorithms for $\mathcal{SHIQ}$ with ABoxes.

RACER[13] [8] was developed at the Concordia University and the Hamburg University of Technology, and is written in Common Lisp. We used the version 1.8.2, to which we connected using the JRacer library. RACER provides an optimized reasoning mode (so-called nRQL mode 1), which provides significant performance improvements, but which is complete only for certain types of knowledge bases. When we conducted the evaluation, RACER did not automatically recognize whether the optimized mode is applicable to a particular knowledge base, so we used RACER in the mode which guarantees completeness (so-called nRQL mode 3). Namely, determining whether optimizations are applicable is a form of reasoning which, we believe, should be taken into account in a fair comparison.

Pellet[14] [17] was developed at the University of Maryland, and was the first system to fully support OWL-DL, taking into account all the nuances of the specification. It is implemented in Java, and is freely available with the source code. We used the version 1.3 beta.

We asked the authors of each tool for an appropriate sequence of API calls for running tests. For each reasoning task, we started a fresh instance of the reasoner and loaded the test knowledge base. Then, we measured the time required to execute the task. We made sure that all systems return the same answers.

Many optimizations of tableau algorithms involve caching computation results, so the performance of query answering should increase with each subsequent query. Furthermore, both RACER and Pellet check ABox consistency before answering the first query, which typically takes much longer than computing query results. Hence, starting a new instance of the reasoner for each query might seem unfair. However, we did not yet consider caching for KAON2; furthermore, materialized views were extensively studied in deductive databases, and were successfully applied to ontology reasoning [23]. Also, KAON2 does not perform a separate ABox consistency test because ABox inconsistency is discovered automatically during query evaluation; we consider this to be an advantage of our approach.

Due to these reasons, we decided to measure only the performance of the actual reasoning algorithm, and to leave a study of possible materialization and caching strategies for future work. Since ABox consistency checking is a significant source of overhead for tableau systems, we measured the time required to execute it separately. Hence, in our tables, we distinguish the one-time *setup*

---

[13] http://www.racer-systems.com/
[14] http://www.mindswap.org/2003/pellet/index.shtml

time (S) from the query processing time (Q) for Pellet and RACER. This some-what compensates for the lack of caching: most caches are computed during setup time, so one can expect that subsequent queries will be answered in time similar to the one required for the first query after setup.

The time for computing the datalog program in KAON2 was comparatively small to the time required to evaluate the program. Therefore, in our test results, we simply included the reduction time into the total query time.

All tests were performed on a laptop computer with a 2 GHz Intel processor, 1 GB of RAM, running Windows XP Service Pack 2. For Java-based tools, we used Sun's Java 1.5.0 Update 5. The virtual memory of the Java virtual machine was limited to 800 MB, and each test was allowed to run for at most 5 minutes.

The results of all tests are shown in Figure 2. Tests which ran either out of memory or out of time are denoted with a value of 10000.

5.2   Querying Large ABoxes

VICODI. The results show that Pellet and RACER spend the bulk of their time in checking ABox consistency by computing a completion of the ABox. Because the ontology is simple, no branch splits are performed, so the process yields a single completion representing a model. Query answering is then very fast in Pellet, as it just requires model lookup. Note that, other than for vicodi_0, the time KAON2 takes to answer queries depends very little on the data size.

It may seem odd that KAON2 takes longer to answer Q_{V_1} on vicodi_0 than on vicodi_1. Repeated tests produced results consistent with the ones reported here. After further analysis, we discovered that this is caused by choosing a suboptimal sideways information passing strategy in the magic sets transformation. We shall try to address this problem in our future research.

SEMINTEC. The SEMINTEC ontology is roughly of the same size as the VI-CODI ontology; however, the time that KAON2 takes to answer a query on SEMINTEC is one order of magnitude larger than for the VICODI ontology. This is mainly due to equality, which is difficult for deductive databases. Namely, since any part of the knowledge base can imply two individuals to be equal, techniques such as magic sets that localize reasoning to a portion of the ABox are less effective. Also, notice that all three tools exhibit roughly the same dependency on the size of the data set.

LUBM. As our results show, LUBM does not pose significant problems for KAON2; namely, the translation produces an equality-free Horn program, which KAON2 evaluates in polynomial time. Hence, the time required to answer a query for KAON2 grows moderately with the size of the data set.

Although LUBM is roughly of the same size as VICODI, both Pellet and RACER performed better on the latter; namely, Pellet was not able to answer any of the LUBM queries within the given resource constraints, and RACER performed significantly better on VICODI than on LUBM. We were surprised by this result: the ontology is still Horn, so an ABox completion can be computed

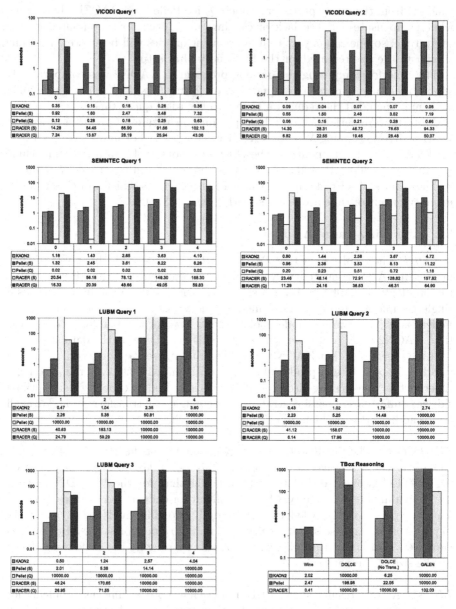

Note: (S) — one-time setup time (including ABox consistency check)

(Q) — time required to process the query

Fig. 2. Test Results

in advance and used as a cache for query answering. By analyzing a run of Pellet
on lubm_1 in a debugger, we observed that the system performs disjunctive

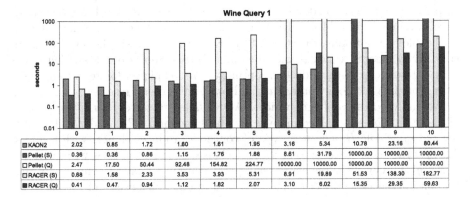

	0	1	2	3	4	5	6	7	8	9	10
KAON2	2.02	0.85	1.72	1.80	1.61	1.95	3.16	5.34	10.78	23.16	80.44
Pellet (S)	0.36	0.36	0.86	1.15	1.76	1.88	8.61	31.79	10000.00	10000.00	10000.00
Pellet (Q)	2.47	17.50	50.44	92.48	154.82	224.77	10000.00	10000.00	10000.00	10000.00	10000.00
RACER (S)	0.68	1.58	2.33	3.53	3.93	5.31	8.91	19.89	51.53	138.30	182.77
RACER (Q)	0.41	0.47	0.94	1.12	1.82	2.07	3.10	6.02	15.35	29.35	59.63

Fig. 2. Test Results (*continued*)

reasoning (i.e., it performs branch splits). Further investigation showed that this is due to *absorption* [9]—a well-known optimization technique used by all tableau reasoners. Namely, an axiom of the form $C \sqsubseteq D$, where C is a complex concept, increases the amount of don't-know nondeterminism in a tableau because it yields a disjunction $\neg C \sqcup D$ in the label of each node. If possible, such an axiom is transformed into an equivalent *definition* axiom $A \sqsubseteq C'$ (where A is an atomic concept), which can be handled in a deterministic way. The LUBM ontology contains several axioms that are equivalent to $A \sqsubseteq B \sqcap \exists R.C$ and $B \sqcap \exists R.C \sqsubseteq A$. Now the latter axiom contains a complex concept on the left-hand side of $\sqsubseteq$, so it is absorbed into an equivalent axiom $B \sqsubseteq A \sqcup \forall R.\neg C$. Whereas this is a definition axiom, it contains a disjunction on the right-hand side, and thus causes branch splits. This could perhaps be improved by extending the tableau calculus with an inference rule similar to hyperresolution. Namely, an axiom $B \sqcap \exists R.C \sqsubseteq A$ is equivalent to the clause $B(x) \wedge R(x,y) \wedge C(y) \rightarrow A(x)$. In resolution, one can select the literals on the left-hand side of the implication, which allows the clause to "fire" only if all three literals can be resolved simultaneously. It remains to see whether this is possible in a tableau setting without affecting the correctness and the termination of the calculus.

Wine. The results show that the ontology complexity affects the performance: the ontology wine_0 is significantly smaller than, say, lubm_1, but the times for KAON2 are roughly the same in the two cases. In fact, KAON2 exhibits roughly the same performance as RACER on this test. The degradation of performance in KAON2 is mainly due to disjunctions. On the theoretical side, disjunctions increase the data complexity of our algorithm from P to NP [13]. On the practical side, the technique for answering queries in disjunctive programs used in KAON2 should be further optimized.

5.3   TBox Reasoning

Our TBox reasoning tests clearly show that the performance of KAON2 lags behind the performance of the tableau reasoners. This should not come as a surprise: in the past decade, many optimization techniques for TBox reasoning were developed for tableau algorithms, and these techniques are not directly applicable to the resolution setting. Still, KAON2 can classify DOLCE without transitivity axioms, which is known to be a fairly complex ontology. Hence, we believe that developing additional optimization techniques for resolution algorithms might yield some interesting and practically useful results.

We analyzed the problems which KAON2 failed to solve. Roughly speaking, all these problems contained many concepts of the form $\exists R.C$ and $\forall R.D$ involving the same role R. The first type of concepts produces clauses with a literal $R(x, f(x))$, whereas the second type of clauses produces clauses with a literal $\neg R(x, y)$. Obviously, these clauses can participate in a quadratic number of resolution inferences in the beginning of a saturation, which eventually leads to an exponential blowup. This explains why KAON2 is not able to classify the original DOLCE ontology, but why it works well if the transitivity axioms are removed: the approach for dealing with transitivity in KAON2 introduces axioms that, when clausified, produce many clauses with such literals.

6   Conclusion

In this paper, we described KAON2—a DL reasoner based on a novel reasoning algorithm that allows for the application of optimization techniques from deductive databases to DL reasoning. To verify our conjecture that such algorithms will scale well in practice, we created a set of benchmarks and conducted a thorough performance evaluation. The results were roughly in line with our expectations: for ontologies with rather simple TBoxes, but large ABoxes, our algorithm indeed provides good performance; however, for ontologies with large and complex TBoxes, existing algorithms still provide superior performance.

For our future work, the main challenge is to extend the reduction algorithm to handle nominals. Furthermore, we believe that optimizations based on ABox statistics will provide further significant improvements. Finally, we shall investigate further optimizations of TBox reasoning.

References

1. F. Baader, D. Calvanese, D. McGuinness, D. Nardi, and P. F. Patel-Schneider, editors. *The Description Logic Handbook: Theory, Implementation and Applications.* Cambridge University Press, January 2003.
2. L. Bachmair, H. Ganzinger, C. Lynch, and W. Snyder. Basic Paramodulation. *Information and Computation*, 121(2):172–192, 1995.
3. S. Bechhofer, R. Volz, and P. W. Lord. Cooking the Semantic Web with the OWL API. In *Proc. ISWC 2003*, volume 2870 of *LNCS*, pages 659–675, Sanibel Island, FL, USA, October 20–23 2003. Springer.
4. C. Cumbo, W. Faber, G. Greco, and N. Leone. Enhancing the Magic-Set Method for Disjunctive Datalog Programs. In *Proc. ICLP 2004*, volume 3132 of *LNCS*, pages 371–385, Saint-Malo, France, September 6–10 2004. Springer.

5. T. Eiter, W. Faber, N. Leone, and G. Pfeifer. Declarative problem-solving using the DLV system. *Logic-Based Artificial Intelligence*, pages 79–103, 2000.
6. T. Eiter, N. Leone, C. Mateis, G. Pfeifer, and F. Scarcello. A Deductive System for Non-Monotonic Reasoning. In *Proc. LPNMR '97*, volume 1265 of *LNAI*, pages 364–375, Dagstuhl, Germany, July 28–31 1997. Springer.
7. Y. Guo, Z. Pan, and J. Heflin. An Evaluation of Knowledge Base Systems for Large OWL Datasets. In *Proc. ISWC 2004*, volume 3298 of *LNCS*, pages 274–288, Hiroshima, Japan, November 7–11 2004. Springer.
8. V. Haarslev and R. Möller. RACER System Description. In *Proc. IJCAR 2001*, volume 2083 of *LNAI*, pages 701–706, Siena, Italy, June 18–23 2001. Springer.
9. I. Horrocks. *Optimising Tableaux Decision Procedures for Description Logics*. PhD thesis, University of Manchester, UK, 1997.
10. I. Horrocks and P. F. Patel-Schneider. Reducing OWL entailment to description logic satisfiability. *Journal of Web Semantics*, 1(4):345–357, 2004.
11. I. Horrocks, U. Sattler, and S. Tobies. Practical Reasoning for Very Expressive Description Logics. *Logic Journal of the IGPL*, 8(3):239–263, 2000.
12. U. Hustadt, B. Motik, and U. Sattler. Reducing $\mathcal{SHIQ}^-$ Description Logic to Disjunctive Datalog Programs. In *Proc. KR 2004*, pages 152–162, Whistler, Canada, June 2–5, 2004 2004. AAAI Press.
13. U. Hustadt, B. Motik, and U. Sattler. Data Complexity of Reasoning in Very Expressive Description Logics. In *Proc. IJCAI 2005*, pages 466–471, Edinburgh, UK, July 30–August 5 2005. Morgan Kaufmann Publishers.
14. W. W. McCune. OTTER 3.0 Reference Manual and Guide. Technical Report ANL-94/6, Argonne National Laboratory, January 1994.
15. B. Motik. *Reasoning in Description Logics using Resolution and Deductive Databases*. PhD thesis, Univesität Karlsruhe, Germany, 2006.
16. R. Nieuwenhuis and A. Rubio. Theorem Proving with Ordering and Equality Constrained Clauses. *Journal of Symbolic Computation*, 19(4):312–351, 1995.
17. B. Parsia and E. Sirin. Pellet: An OWL-DL Reasoner. Poster, In Proc. ISWC 2004, Hiroshima, Japan, November 7–11, 2004.
18. A. L. Rector, W. A. Nowlan, and A. Glowinski. Goals for concept representation in the galen project. In *Proc. SCAMC '93*, pages 414–418, Washington DC, USA, November 1–3 1993. McGraw-Hill.
19. A. Riazanov and A. Voronkov. The design and implementation of VAMPIRE. *AI Communications*, 15(2–3):91–110, 2002.
20. S. Schulz. E—A Brainiac Theorem Prover. *AI Communications*, 15(2–3):111–126, 2002.
21. S. Schulz. Simple and Efficient Clause Subsumption with Feature Vector Indexing. In *Proc. ESFOR, IJCAR 2004 Workshop*, Cork, Ireland, July 4–8 2004.
22. D. Tsarkov and I. Horrocks. Ordering Heuristics for Description Logic Reasoning. In *Proc. IJCAI 2005*, pages 609–614, Edinburgh, UK, July 30 – August 5 2005. Morgan Kaufmann Publishers.
23. R. Volz. *Web Ontology Reasoning With Logic Databases*. PhD thesis, Universität Fridericiana zu Karlsruhe (TH), Germany, 2004.

A Local System for Intuitionistic Logic

Alwen Tiu

Australian National University and National ICT Australia

Abstract. This paper presents systems for first-order intuitionistic logic and several of its extensions in which all the propositional rules are *local*, in the sense that, in applying the rules of the system, one needs only a fixed amount of information about the logical expressions involved. The main source of non-locality is the contraction rules. We show that the contraction rules can be restricted to the atomic ones, provided we employ *deep-inference*, i.e., to allow rules to apply anywhere inside logical expressions. We further show that the use of deep inference allows for modular extensions of intuitionistic logic to Dummett's intermediate logic LC, Gödel logic and classical logic. We present the systems in the calculus of structures, a proof theoretic formalism which supports deep-inference. Cut elimination for these systems are proved indirectly by simulating the cut-free sequent systems, or the hypersequent systems in the cases of Dummett's LC and Gödel logic, in the cut free systems in the calculus of structures.

Keywords: proof theory, intuitionistic logic, intermediate logics, deep inference, calculus of structures, locality.

1   Introduction

This paper presents systems for intuitionistic logic and its extensions, which are properly included in classical logic, in which all the propositional rules are *local*, in the sense of [4]. That is, in applying the rules of the system, one needs only a fixed amount of information about the logical expressions involved. For example, the usual contraction rule in sequent calculus, i.e.,

$$cL \frac{B, B, \Gamma \vdash C}{B, \Gamma \vdash C}$$

is non-local, since in order to apply the rule one has to check that two formulae are syntactically equal, and since B can be arbitrary formula, the "cost" of this checking varies with the size of B. Other examples include the (non-atomic) identity and cut rules, and the promotion rule in linear logic [11]. In [7], it is shown that it is possible to give a system for classical logic in which all the rules are local. This means in particular that the contraction, weakening, the cut and the identity rules are restricted to atomic forms. As it is shown in [5], this is difficult to achieve without some form of *deep inference*, i.e., to allow rules to apply anywhere inside logical expressions. The classical system in [7], called

M. Hermann and A. Voronkov (Eds.): LPAR 2006, LNAI 4246, pp. 242–256, 2006.

SKS, is presented in *the calculus of structures* [13], a formalism which allows deep inference in a way which preserves interesting proof theoretical notions and properties. We shall use the same formalism to present the intuitionistic systems to follow.

Deep inference and locality have been shown to allow for finer analyses on proofs, in particular, proofs in the deep-inference presentation of classical logic, i.e., the system SKS, have been shown to admit non-trivial categorical [18] and geometric interpretations [14]. Classical logic is among a number of logical systems that have been presented in the calculus of structures, e.g., non-commutative extension of linear logic [13], linear logic [21] and modal logics [20]. In these systems, the above notion of locality has been consistently exhibited. However, the logical systems in the calculus of structures studied so far have been those which are symmetric, in the sense that they have involutive negations and can be presented in one-sided sequent systems. The work presented in this paper is an attempt to find "good" presentations of asymmetric (two-sided) sequent systems in the calculus of structures, where locality is one important criteria. This will hopefully lead to further categorical or geometric models for two-sided sequent proofs for intuitionistic and intermediate logics. Another advantage of adopting deep inference is that it allows for modular presentations of several extensions of intuitionistic logic, e.g., intermediate logics and classical logic: different logical systems can be obtained by adding rules which are derived straightforwardly from the axiomatic definitions of the extended systems. Our work can hopefully serve as a basis to give a uniform presentation for various intermediate logics.

We adopt the presentation of intuitionistic logic in the calculus of structures using positive and negative contexts, due to Kai Bruennler [6] and Phillipe de Groote[1]. Negative context corresponds to the left-hand side of a sequent and positive context corresponds to the right-hand side. In this presentation, rules are divided into negative rules, which apply under negative context, naturally, and positive rules which apply under positive context. Note that however since applying a rule would require checking for negative/positive context, the rules formalized this way are no longer local in the sense of [4]. But we can still achieve a weaker form of locality, that is, all rules that duplicate structures can be restricted to atomic forms. This system is then refined to a fully local one by exploiting the fact that all rule schemes in the system preserve polarities (see Section 6).

In Brünnler's intuitionistic system [6], it seems difficult, if not impossible, to reduce contraction to its atomic form. This is partly due to the fact that the contraction rule in this system (as it is the case with most sequent systems for intuitionistic logic) is *asymmetric*, i.e., contraction is allowed on the left (or negative context) but not on the right (positive context), while reducing contraction to its atomic form seems to require a symmetric contraction. The solution proposed here for reducing contraction to atomic is inspired by the multiple-conclusion intuitionistic system in sequent calculus [9,23]. In this

---

[1] The author thanks Lutz Strassburger for pointing out the contribution of de Groote.

system, contraction and weakening are allowed on both sides of the sequent. The asymmetry of intuitionistic logic is captured by the implication rule:

$$\supset R \, \frac{\Gamma, A \vdash B}{\Gamma \vdash A \supset B, \Delta}$$

One can see for instance that the classical theorem of excluded middle, i.e., $A \vee (A \supset \bot)$, is not provable. In the calculus of structures, this is reflected by the absence of certain "logical rules" under disjunctive context (see Section 2).

There exist numerous systems for intuitionistic and intermediate logics in the literature. These systems can be roughly divided into two categories: systems which are designed with decidability and proof search in mind, e.g., contraction-free sequent systems [16,10], and those which are mainly concerned with generality of the formalisms, such as *labelled deduction* systems [3], hypersequents [1] and display calculi [12]. Our work is more in the latter category. In terms of expressivity, the calculus of structures is certainly at least as expressive as the non-standard sequent systems (display, hypersequents, and labelled systems), as one can simulate these systems inside cut-free systems in the calculus of structures. A common feature to these extended sequent systems is that they all employ some sort of structural extensions to sequents in order to capture various extensions of intuitionistic logic. In contrast, in the calculus of structures, there is no additional structural elements added to the proof system: one simply introduces more rules to get the extended logics. Moreover, these extended rules are derived straightforwardly from their axiomatic formulations (i.e., in Hilbert's systems). However, one of the drawbacks of the formulation of deep inference systems in our work is that we currently have no "internal" proof of cut-elimination. Our cut-elimination proof is indirect via translations to other systems, notably, sequent and hypersequent systems. Methodology for proof search in deep inference systems is not yet fully developed, although there is some work in this direction [17].

The rest of the paper is organized as follows. In Section 2, we present an intuitionistic system with the general (non-local) contraction rules, called SISgq. This is then followed by the soundness and completeness proof of SISgq with respect to a multiple-conclusion sequent system for intuitionistic logic and the cut elimination proof in Section 3. Section 4 shows how to extend SISg to cover Dummett's LC, Gödel logic and classical logic. Cut elimination for LC and Gödel logic are proved indirectly by simulating the corresponding hypersequent systems for these logics [1,2]. In Section 5, the system SISg and its extensions are refined to systems in which the contraction rules are restricted to their atomic forms, but with additional *medial rules*. In Section 6 we show how to remove the context dependency in the propositional rules in all of the above logical systems, resulting in purely local systems for the propositional fragments, by introducing polarities into logical expressions. Section 7 discusses future work. Detailed proofs of the lemmas and the theorems in this paper can be found in an extended version of the paper.

2   An Intuitionistic System in the Calculus of Structures

Inference rules in the calculus of structures can be seen as rewrite rules on formulae, i.e., the rules are of the form

$$\rho \, \frac{F\{B\}}{F\{C\}}$$

where ρ is the name of the rule, $F\{\}$ is a formula-context and B and C are formulae. Basically, any sound implication $B \supset C$ can be turned into a rule. The question is of course whether doing so would result in a good proof theory. The design philosophy of the calculus of structures has been centered around the concept of *interaction* and *symmetry* in inference rules. Just as the left and right rules in sequent calculus and introduction and elimination rules in natural deduction, a rule in the calculus of structures always has its dual, called its *co-rule*, which is obtained from the rule by taking the contrapositive of the implication defining the rule. The concept of interaction replaces the notion of identity and cut in sequent calculus. In classical logic [4], the interaction rules are (using the standard notation for classical formulae)

$$\mathsf{i}{\downarrow} \, \frac{S\{\top\}}{S\{A \vee \neg A\}} \qquad \mathsf{i}{\uparrow} \, \frac{S\{A \wedge \neg A\}}{S\{\bot\}}$$

In intuitionistic logic, we shall have a slightly different notation for the interaction rules, but the idea is essentially the same: the $\mathsf{i}{\downarrow}$-rule creates a dual pair of formulas (reading the rule top-down) while the $\mathsf{i}{\uparrow}$ rule destructs them.

In formulating the rules in the calculus of structures, one encounters certain rules which correspond to some logical equivalences in the logic being formalized. Some of the trivial equivalences, e.g., commutativity and associativity of conjunction, are more appropriately represented as equations rather than rules. We thus consider formulae modulo these equivalences. In the terms of the calculus of structures, these equivalent classes of formulae are referred to as *structures*. We shall be concerned with the following language of structures

$$S := p(t) \mid \mathsf{t} \mid \mathsf{f} \mid \langle S; S \rangle \mid [S, S] \mid (S, S) \mid \forall x R \mid \exists x R$$

where p is a predicate symbol, t is a term and the rest correspond to true, false, implication, disjunction, conjunction, universal and existential quantifications. For simplicity of presentation, we consider only unary predicates, but generalization to predicates of arbitrary arities is straightforward.

Note that we opt to use the above bracketing notations instead of the more traditional ones of connectives to simplify the presentation of the inference rules and derivations. Structures are ranged over by R, T, U, V, W and atomic structures are ranged over by a, b, c, d. A *structure context*, or context for short, is a structure with a hole, denoted by $S\{\ \}$. Given a structure R and a context $S\{\ \}$, we write $S\{R\}$ to denote the structure that results from replacing the hole $\{\ \}$ in $S\{\ \}$ with R. In presenting a structure R in a context $S\{\ \}$, we often omit

Units:
$$[\mathsf{t},\mathsf{t}] = \mathsf{t} \quad (\mathsf{f},\mathsf{f}) = \mathsf{f} \quad \langle\mathsf{f};\mathsf{t}\rangle = \mathsf{t} \quad \langle\mathsf{f};\mathsf{f}\rangle = \mathsf{t}$$
$$[\mathsf{f}, R] = R \quad (\mathsf{t}, R) = R \quad \langle\mathsf{t}; R\rangle = R$$

Associativity:
$$[R, [T, U]] = [[R, T], U] \quad (R, (T, U)) = ((R, T), U)$$

Commutativity:
$$[R, T] = [T, R] \quad (R, T) = (T, R)$$

Currying:
$$\langle(R, T); U\rangle = \langle R; \langle T; U\rangle\rangle$$

Quantifiers:
$$\forall x.R = \exists x.R = R, \text{ if } x \text{ is not free in } R.$$
$$\forall x.R = \forall y.R[y/x], \exists x.R = \exists y.R[y/x], \ y \text{ is not free in } \forall x.R.$$

Congruence:
$$S\{R\} = S\{T\}, \text{ if } R = T.$$

Fig. 1. Syntactic equality of structures

$$\mathsf{i}{\downarrow}\, \frac{S^+\{\mathsf{t}\}}{S^+\langle R; R\rangle} \qquad \mathsf{cr}{\downarrow}\, \frac{S^+[R, R]}{S^+\{R\}} \qquad \mathsf{cl}{\downarrow}\, \frac{S^-(R, R)}{S^-\{R\}} \qquad \mathsf{wr}{\downarrow}\, \frac{S^+\{\mathsf{f}\}}{S^+\{R\}} \qquad \mathsf{wl}{\downarrow}\, \frac{S^-\{\mathsf{t}\}}{S^-\{R\}}$$

$$\mathsf{s}{\downarrow}\, \frac{S^+([R, T], U)}{S^+[R, (T, U)]} \qquad \mathsf{sc}{\downarrow}\, \frac{S^+(\langle R; T\rangle, U)}{S^+\langle R; (T, U)\rangle} \qquad \mathsf{sd}{\downarrow}\, \frac{S^+(\langle R; T\rangle, \langle U; V\rangle)}{S^+\langle [R, U]; [T, V]\rangle}$$

$$\mathsf{sid}{\downarrow}\, \frac{S^+[\langle R; T\rangle, U]}{S^+\langle R; [T, U]\rangle} \qquad \mathsf{sic}{\downarrow}\, \frac{S^+(R, \langle T; U\rangle)}{S^+\langle\langle R; T\rangle; U\rangle} \qquad \mathsf{sac}{\downarrow}\, \frac{S^+(\forall x R, \forall x T)}{S^+\{\forall x(R, T)\}}$$

$$\mathsf{sa}{\downarrow}\, \frac{S^+\{\forall x\langle R; T\rangle\}}{S^+\langle R; \forall x T\rangle} \qquad \mathsf{se}{\downarrow}\, \frac{S^+\{\forall x\langle R; T\rangle\}}{S^+\langle\exists x R; T\rangle} \qquad \mathsf{nr}{\downarrow}\, \frac{S^+\{R[t/x]\}}{S^+\{\exists x R\}} \qquad \mathsf{nl}{\downarrow}\, \frac{S^-\{R[t/x]\}}{S^-\{\forall x R\}}$$

Fig. 2. System ISgq: an intuitionistic system in the calculus of structures. The rules sa↓ and se↓ have the provisos that x is not free in R and T, respectively.

the curly braces surrounding the R, if R is composed with a binary relation, e.g., we shall write $S[U, V]$ instead of $S\{[U, V]\}$. Structures are considered modulo the syntactic equivalence given in Figure 1. Note that we assume the domain of the quantification is non-empty. This is reflected in the equations concerning quantifiers.

We distinguish between *positive contexts* and *negative contexts*. Positive and negative contexts are defined inductively as follows:

1. { } is a positive context,
2. if $S\{\ \}$ is a positive context then $(S\{\ \}, R)$, $(R, S\{\ \})$, $[S\{\ \}, R]$, $[R, S\{\ \}]$, $\forall x\{\ \}$, $\exists x\{\ \}$ and $\langle R; S\{\ \}\rangle$ are positive contexts, otherwise they are negative contexts,
3. if $S\{\ \}$ is a positive context then $\langle S\{\ \}; R\rangle$ is a negative context, otherwise it is a positive context.

Given a positive context $S\{\ \}$, we often write it as $S^+\{\ \}$ to emphasize that it is a positive context. Similarly we write $S^-\{\ \}$ to emphasize that $S\{\ \}$ is a negative context.

The inference rules for the general system (non-local) for intuitionistic logic is given in Figure 2. We refer to this system as ISgq. As we have noted previously,

$$\mathsf{i}{\uparrow}\,\frac{S^-\langle R;R\rangle}{S^-\{t\}} \qquad \mathsf{cr}{\uparrow}\,\frac{S^-\{R\}}{S^-[R,R]} \qquad \mathsf{cl}{\uparrow}\,\frac{S^+\{R\}}{S^+(R,R)} \qquad \mathsf{wr}{\uparrow}\,\frac{S^-\{R\}}{S^-\{f\}} \qquad \mathsf{wl}{\uparrow}\,\frac{S^+\{R\}}{S^+\{t\}}$$

$$\mathsf{s}{\uparrow}\,\frac{S^-[R,(T,U)]}{S^-([R,T],U)} \qquad \mathsf{sc}{\uparrow}\,\frac{S^-\langle R;(T,U)\rangle}{S^-(\langle R;T\rangle,U)} \qquad \mathsf{sd}{\uparrow}\,\frac{S^-\langle[R,U];[T,V]\rangle}{S^-(\langle R;T\rangle,\langle U;V\rangle)}$$

$$\mathsf{sid}{\uparrow}\,\frac{S^-\langle R;[T,U]\rangle}{S^-[\langle R;T\rangle,U]} \qquad \mathsf{sic}{\uparrow}\,\frac{S^-\langle\langle R;T\rangle;U\rangle}{S^-(R,\langle T;U\rangle)} \qquad \mathsf{sac}{\uparrow}\,\frac{S^-\{\forall x(R,T)\}}{S^-(\forall xR,\forall xT)}$$

$$\mathsf{sa}{\uparrow}\,\frac{S^-\langle R;\forall xT\rangle}{S^-\{\forall x\langle R;T\rangle\}} \qquad \mathsf{se}{\uparrow}\,\frac{S^-\langle\exists xR;T\rangle}{S^-\{\forall x\langle R;T\rangle\}} \qquad \mathsf{nr}{\uparrow}\,\frac{S^-\{\exists xR\}}{S^-\{R[t/x]\}} \qquad \mathsf{nl}{\uparrow}\,\frac{S^+\{\forall xR\}}{S^+\{R[t/x]\}}$$

Fig. 3. System clSgq: the dual of lSgq

each rule in the calculus of structures has its co-rule. In the case of lSgq, the co-rule of a rule ρ is obtained from ρ by exchanging the premise with the conclusion and reversing the condition on the context of the rule (i.e., positive to negative and vice versa). The name of a rule is usually suffixed with an up or a down arrow, and its co-rule has the same name but with the arrow reversed. We use the term *up-rules* to denote rules with up-arrow in their names and *down-rules* if their names contain down-arrow. The rule $\mathsf{i}{\downarrow}$ corresponds to the identity rule in sequent calculus. Its co-rule, $\mathsf{i}{\uparrow}$ (see Figure 3), corresponds to cut. Together they are referred to as the *interaction rules*. The rules $\mathsf{cl}{\downarrow}$ and $\mathsf{cr}{\downarrow}$ are the contraction left and right rules, and $\mathsf{wl}{\downarrow}$ and $\mathsf{wr}{\downarrow}$ are the weakening left and right rules. The rules prefixed with the letter s are the *switch* rules, using the terminology of [13]. The notation $[t/x]$ in the $\mathsf{nr}{\downarrow}$ and $\mathsf{nl}{\downarrow}$ rules denotes capture-avoiding substitutions.

Notice that if we take the dual of the rules of lSgq, we obtain another, "dual" system of intuitionistic logic. This system, called clSgq, is shown in Figure 3. Each of the systems lSgq and clSgq is incomplete in its own, since either cut or identity is missing. The fully symmetric system for intuitionistic logic is thus obtained by combining the two, and is referred to as SlSgq. SlSgq naturally corresponds to first-order LJ and either one of lSgq or clSgq corresponds to the cut-free fragment of first-order LJ. Note that either system can be chosen to represent the cut-free LJ; it is just a matter of convention that we fix our choice to lSgq. We refer to the propositional fragment of SlSgq (lSgq) as SlSg (respectively, lSg).

Definition 1. *A* derivation *Δ in a system in the calculus of structures is a finite chain of instances of inference rules in the system. A derivation can consist of just one structure. The topmost structure in a derivation is called the* premise *of the derivation, and the structure at the bottom is called its* conclusion. *A* proof *Π in the calculus of structures is a derivation whose premise is* t. *A rule ρ is* derivable *in a system $\mathscr{S}$ if $\rho \notin \mathscr{S}$ and for every instance of $\rho\,\dfrac{T}{R}$ there is a* *derivation with premise R and conclusion T in $\mathscr{S}$. Two systems are equivalent if they have the same set of provable structures.*

3   Soundness, Completeness and Cut Elimination

We shall now prove that the system SISgq is sound and complete with respect to intuitionistic logic and that it has cut-elimination. The notion of cut-elimination in the calculus of structures is more general than that of sequent calculus, that is, not only the cut rule (the $\mathsf{i\uparrow}$) is admissible, but the entire up-rules are also admissible. We prove the soundness and completeness of SISgq with respect to a multiple-conclusion sequent system for intuitionistic logic [9]. We refer to this system as LJm. Its rules are those of Gentzen's LK, except for the right introduction rules for universal quantifier and implication:

$$\supset R \, \frac{\Gamma, A \vdash B}{\Gamma \vdash A \supset B, \Psi} \qquad \forall R \, \frac{\Gamma \vdash A[y/x]}{\Gamma \vdash \forall x A, \Psi}$$

where y in the $\forall R$ rule is not free in the lower sequent. Cut-elimination for SISgq is obtained indirectly via the cut-elimination theorem in sequent calculus, by observing that all the rules in LJm, except the cut, are derivable in ISgq, i.e., the fragment of SISgq without the up-rules.

The formulae of LJm are given by the following grammar:

$$F ::= p(t) \mid \top \mid \bot \mid F \supset F \mid F \vee F \mid F \wedge F \mid \forall x F \mid \exists x F.$$

As in structures, p here denotes a unary predicate, and the rest of the constants correspond to true, false, implication, disjunction, conjunction, universal and existential quantifiers.

Definition 2. *The functions* $\underline{}_s$ *and* $\underline{}_\lrcorner$ *given below transform formulae in LJm into structures and vice versa:*

$$
\begin{array}{llll}
\underline{\top}_s = \mathsf{t} & \underline{\bot}_s = \mathsf{f} & \underline{\mathsf{t}}_\lrcorner = \top & \underline{\mathsf{f}}_\lrcorner = \bot \\
\underline{p(t)}_s = p(t) & \underline{A \wedge B}_s = (\underline{A}_s, \underline{B}_s) & \underline{p(t)}_\lrcorner = p(t) & \underline{(R,T)}_\lrcorner = \underline{R}_\lrcorner \wedge \underline{R}_\lrcorner \\
\underline{A \vee B}_s = [\underline{A}_s, \underline{B}_s] & \underline{A \supset B}_s = \langle \underline{A}_s ; \underline{B}_s \rangle & \underline{[R,T]}_\lrcorner = \underline{R}_\lrcorner \vee \underline{T}_\lrcorner & \underline{\langle R; T \rangle}_\lrcorner = \underline{R}_\lrcorner \supset \underline{T}_\lrcorner \\
\underline{\forall x A}_s = \forall x \underline{A}_s & \underline{\exists x A}_s = \exists x \underline{A}_s & \underline{\forall x R}_\lrcorner = \forall x \underline{R}_\lrcorner & \underline{\exists x R}_\lrcorner = \exists x \underline{R}_\lrcorner
\end{array}
$$

The function $\underline{}_s$ *is generalized to sequents as follows:*

$$\underline{A_1, \ldots, A_n \vdash B}_s = \forall x_1 \ldots \forall x_n \langle (\underline{A_1}_s, \ldots, \underline{A_n}_s); \underline{B}_s \rangle$$

where $x_1, \ldots, x_n$ are the eigenvariables of the sequent, and empty conjunction is interpreted as the constant t.

The key to proving soundness is to show that each instance of a rule in SISgq corresponds to an implication in LJm and that equivalent structures map to logically equivalent formulas. For instance, the soundness of the $\mathsf{sc\downarrow}$ rule is demonstrated by the left derivation in Figure 4.

$$\mathsf{sc}{\downarrow}\ \frac{(\langle \Gamma_1; [A, \Psi_2]\rangle, \langle (B, \Gamma_2); \Psi_1\rangle)}{\langle \Gamma_1; ([A, \Psi_2], \langle (B, \Gamma_2); \Psi_1\rangle)\rangle}$$
$$=\ \frac{}{\langle \Gamma_1; (\langle \Gamma_2; \langle B; \Psi_1\rangle\rangle, [A, \Psi_2])\rangle}$$
$$\mathsf{sc}{\downarrow}\ \frac{}{\langle \Gamma_1; \langle \Gamma_2; (\langle B; \Psi_1\rangle, [A, \Psi_2])\rangle\rangle}$$
$$=\ \frac{}{\langle (\Gamma_1, \Gamma_2); ([A, \Psi_2], \langle B; \Psi_1\rangle)\rangle}$$
$$\mathsf{s}{\downarrow}\ \frac{}{\langle (\Gamma_1, \Gamma_2); [(A, \langle B; \Psi_1\rangle), \Psi_2]\rangle}$$
$$\mathsf{sic}{\downarrow}\ \frac{}{\langle (\Gamma_1, \Gamma_2); [\langle\langle A; B\rangle; \Psi_1\rangle, \Psi_2]\rangle}$$
$$\mathsf{sid}{\downarrow}\ \frac{}{\langle (\Gamma_1, \Gamma_2); \langle\langle A; B\rangle; [\Psi_1, \Psi_2]\rangle\rangle}$$
$$=\ \frac{}{\langle (\Gamma_1, \Gamma_2, \langle A; B\rangle); [\Psi_1, \Psi_2]\rangle}$$

$$id\ \frac{}{R \vdash R} \qquad id\ \frac{}{T \vdash T}$$
$$\supset L\ \frac{}{R \supset T, R \vdash T} \qquad id\ \frac{}{U \vdash U}$$
$$\wedge R\ \frac{R \supset T, U, R \vdash T \wedge U}{}$$
$$\wedge L\ \frac{(R \supset T) \wedge U, R \vdash T \wedge U}{}$$
$$\supset R\ \frac{(R \supset T) \wedge U \vdash R \supset (T \wedge U)}{}$$

Fig. 4. A correspondence between ISgq and LJm

Theorem 3. *For every structure R, R is provable in* SISgq *if and only if $\underline{R}_{\lrcorner}$ is provable in LJm.*

To prove completeness, and cut-elimination, we show that ISgq can simulate all the sequent rules of LJm. For instance, we show in the right derivation in Figure 4 a simulation of the left introduction rule for implication:

$$\supset L\ \frac{\Gamma_1 \vdash A, \Psi_1 \quad B, \Gamma_2 \vdash \Psi_2}{\Gamma_1, \Gamma_2, A \supset B \vdash \Psi_1, \Psi_2}$$

Notice that the branching in the rule is mapped to the conjunctive structural relation in ISgq.

Theorem 4. *For every structure R, R is provable in* SISgq *if and only if it is provable in* ISgq.

4 Intermediate and Classical Logics

We now consider three extensions of intuitionistic logic: Dummett's LC [8], Gödel logic [22] and classical logic. Dummett's LC is obtained by adding the following axiom $A \supset B \vee B \supset A$ to the propositional fragment of intuitionistic logic. Gödel logic is obtained by adding to LC the axiom $\forall x(A \vee B) \supset \forall x A \vee B$, where x is not free in B. Classical logic is obtained, obviously, by dropping the restriction on the contexts in the introduction rules for implication and universal quantifiers. We discuss each of these extension in the following.

4.1 Dummett's LC

Dummett's LC can be formalized in the calculus of structures by adding the following rules to SISg (i.e., the propositional fragment of SISgq).

$$\mathsf{com}{\downarrow}\ \frac{S^+(\langle R; T\rangle, \langle U; V\rangle)}{S^+[\langle R; V\rangle, \langle U; T\rangle]} \qquad \mathsf{com}{\uparrow}\ \frac{S^-[\langle R; V\rangle, \langle U; T\rangle]}{S^-(\langle R; T\rangle, \langle U; V\rangle)}$$

These rules are called the *communication* rules, and are inspired by the corresponding rules in the hypersequent formulation of LC [1,2]. With the com$\downarrow$ rule, we can derive the axiom $A \supset B \vee B \supset A$ as follows:

$$
\mathsf{com}\downarrow \frac{\mathsf{i}\downarrow \frac{\mathsf{i}\downarrow \frac{= \dfrac{\mathsf{t}}{(\mathsf{t},\mathsf{t})}}{(\mathsf{t}, \langle B; B \rangle)}}{(\langle A; A \rangle, \langle B; B \rangle)}}{[\langle A; B \rangle, \langle B; A \rangle]}
$$

We refer to the system SISg extended with both rules as SCSg. We call the down fragment of SCSg, i.e., ISg plus the com$\downarrow$ rule, the system CSg. As we will see, it is enough to consider CSg since it is equivalent to SCSg.

Both com$\downarrow$ and com$\uparrow$ rules correspond to the formula

$$(R \supset T) \wedge (U \supset V) \supset (R \supset V) \vee (U \supset T).$$

This formula can be easily shown to be provable from the following three formulas:

1. $(T \supset V) \vee (V \supset T)$,
2. $(R \supset T) \wedge (T \supset V) \supset (R \supset V)$,
3. $(U \supset V) \wedge (V \supset T) \supset (U \supset T)$.

The first formula is an axiom of LC, the second and the third are intuitionistic theorems. Therefore the com$\downarrow$ and com$\uparrow$ rules are sound with respect to LC. The completeness proof of CSg (and SCSg) is more involved; it uses a translation from a hypersequent system for LC to CSg. We state the result here and refer the interested reader to the extended version of the paper for the detailed proofs.

Theorem 5. *For every structure R, R is provable in* CSg *if and only if $\underline{R}$ is provable in* LC.

4.2   Gödel Logic

Gödel logic is obtained by adding com$\downarrow$, com$\uparrow$ and the following rules to SISgq:

$$
\mathsf{g}\downarrow \frac{S^+\{\forall x[R,T]\}}{S^+[\forall x R, T]} \qquad \mathsf{g}\uparrow \frac{S^-[\forall x R, T]}{S^-\{\forall x[R,T]\}}
$$

We refer to the formulation of this logic as SGSg. The down fragment, i.e., CSg plus the g$\downarrow$ rule, is referred to as GSg.

The rules g$\downarrow$ and g$\uparrow$ are obviously sound since they correspond directly to the axiom $\forall x(R \vee T) \supset \forall x R \vee T$. To prove completeness and cut-elimination, we encode a hypersequent system for Gödel logic, i.e., the system HIF [2] (also known as first-order intuitionistic fuzzy logic) in GSg. The details of the encoding can be found in the appendix.

Theorem 6. *For every structure R, R is provable in* GSg *if and only if $\underline{R}$ is provable in* HIF.

4.3   Classical Logic

Classical logic is obtained by adding $g{\downarrow}$, $g{\uparrow}$ and the following rules

$$\mathsf{ci}{\downarrow}\,\frac{S^{+}\langle R;[T,U]\rangle}{S^{+}[\langle R;T\rangle,U]} \qquad \mathsf{ci}{\uparrow}\,\frac{S^{-}[\langle R;T\rangle,U]}{S^{-}\langle R;[T,U]\rangle}$$

to SISgq. These rules allow one to simulate the right-introduction rules for implication and universal quantifier in LK:

$$\supset R\,\frac{\Gamma,A\vdash B,\Psi}{\Gamma\vdash A\supset B,\Psi} \qquad \forall R\,\frac{\Gamma\vdash A[y/x],\Psi}{\Gamma\vdash\forall xA,\Psi}$$

More precisely, these rules are derived as follows:

$$\mathsf{ci}{\downarrow}\,\frac{=\dfrac{\langle(\Gamma,A);[B,\Psi]\rangle}{\langle\Gamma;\langle A;[B,\Psi]\rangle\rangle}}{\langle\Gamma;[\langle A;B\rangle,\Psi]\rangle} \qquad \mathsf{g}{\downarrow}\,\frac{\mathsf{sa}{\downarrow}\,\dfrac{\forall y\langle\Gamma;[A[y/x],\Psi]\rangle}{\langle\Gamma;\forall y[A[y/x],\Psi]\rangle}}{=\dfrac{\langle\Gamma;[\forall y.A[y/x],\Psi]\rangle}{\langle\Gamma;[\forall xA,\Psi]\rangle}}$$

We refer to the system SISgq extended with $\mathsf{ci}{\downarrow}$, $\mathsf{ci}{\uparrow}$, $g{\downarrow}$ and $g{\uparrow}$ as SKS_{2g}. The down fragment, i.e., ISgq extended with $\mathsf{ci}{\downarrow}$ and $g{\downarrow}$, is referred to as KS_{2g}.

Theorem 7. *For every structure R, R is provable in KS_{2g} if and only if $\underline{R}$ is provable in LK.*

5   Atomic Contraction

We shall now refine the system SISgq and its extensions to systems in which the interaction rules (i.e., the $\mathsf{i}{\downarrow}$ and $\mathsf{i}{\uparrow}$ rules), contraction and weakening are restricted to atomic propositions. The transformations required to reduce the interaction, weakening and contraction rules to their atomic forms are independent of the particular extensions to SISgq, so without loss of generality we shall work only with the system SISgq in this section. The main challenge in reducing contraction to its atomic form is in finding the right *medial rules*, just like those in SKS [4]. They are basically some form of distributivity among the connectives. In order to reduce contraction in negative context to atomic ones, it is crucial that we allow contraction on positive context as well. This is due to the reversal of polarity introduced by the implication connective.

The atomic versions of the interaction, contraction and weakening rules are as follows:

$$\mathsf{ai}{\downarrow}\,\frac{S^{+}\{\mathsf{t}\}}{S^{+}\langle a;a\rangle} \quad \mathsf{acr}{\downarrow}\,\frac{S^{+}[a,a]}{S^{+}\{a\}} \quad \mathsf{acl}{\downarrow}\,\frac{S^{-}(a,a)}{S^{-}\{a\}} \quad \mathsf{awr}{\downarrow}\,\frac{S^{+}\{\mathsf{f}\}}{S^{+}\{a\}} \quad \mathsf{awl}{\downarrow}\,\frac{S^{-}\{\mathsf{t}\}}{S^{-}\{a\}}$$

and their respective duals, obtained by exchanging the premise and the conclusion, with the polarity of the context reversed. Here we denote with a an atomic formula.

$$\mathsf{ml}\,\frac{S^-([R,T],[U,V])}{S^-[(R,U),(T,V)]} \qquad \mathsf{mr}\,\frac{S^+[(R,U),(T,V)]}{S^+([R,T],[U,V])}$$

$$\mathsf{mil}{\downarrow}\,\frac{S^-(\langle R;U\rangle,\langle T;V\rangle)}{S^-\langle[R,T];(U,V)\rangle} \qquad \mathsf{mir}{\downarrow}\,\frac{S^+[\langle R;U\rangle,\langle T;V\rangle]}{S^+\langle(R,T);[U,V]\rangle}$$

$$\mathsf{mal}{\downarrow}\,\frac{S^-(\forall x R,\forall x T)}{S^-\{\forall x(R,T)\}} \qquad \mathsf{mar}{\downarrow}\,\frac{S^+[\forall x R,\forall x T]}{S^+\{\forall x[R,T]\}}$$

$$\mathsf{mel}{\downarrow}\,\frac{S^-(\exists x R,\exists x T)}{S^-\{\exists x(R,T)\}} \qquad \mathsf{mer}{\downarrow}\,\frac{S^+[\exists x R,\exists x T]}{S^+\{\exists x[R,T]\}}$$

Fig. 5. The medial rules for reducing contraction to atomic

The medial rules for intuitionistic logic are given in Figure 5. The classical medial rule m of SKS [7] splits into two rules: the (right) medial rule mr and the (left) medial rule ml. This is because we have contraction on both the positive and negative contexts. Notice that mr and ml are dual to each other, that is, mr is the up-version of ml and vice versa. There are extra medial rules that deal with implication and quantifiers. All those rules are derivable from the contraction and weakening rules in lSgq, and hence their soundness follows from the soundness of lSgq. By taking the duals of the medial rules in Figure 5, we obtain the *co-medial* rules, which by symmetry, are needed to reduce the *co-contraction* (i.e., the up-version of the contraction rules) to atomic. The co-medial rules are denoted by the same name but with the arrows reversed.

The general interaction rules i↓ and the weakening rule wr↓ can be shown reducible to their atomic versions, and the contraction rule cr↓ can be reduced to the atomic one with the medial rules. We illustrate here a step in the reduction of the contraction rule; more details can be found in the appendix. Consider for instance, contractions on an implication structure, on both the positive and negative context:

$$\mathsf{cr}{\downarrow}\,\frac{S^+[\langle R;T\rangle,\langle R;T\rangle]}{S^+\langle R;T\rangle} \qquad \mathsf{cl}{\downarrow}\,\frac{S^-(\langle R;T\rangle,\langle R;T\rangle)}{S^-\langle R;T\rangle}$$

These instances of contractions can be replaced by the following derivations:

$$\mathsf{cl}{\downarrow}\,\frac{\mathsf{cr}{\downarrow}\,\frac{\mathsf{mir}{\downarrow}\,\frac{S^+[\langle R;T\rangle,\langle R;T\rangle]}{S^+\langle(R,R);[T,T]\rangle}}{S^+\langle(R,R);T\rangle}}{S^+\langle R;T\rangle} \qquad \mathsf{cr}{\downarrow}\,\frac{\mathsf{cl}{\downarrow}\,\frac{\mathsf{mil}{\downarrow}\,\frac{S^-[\langle R;T\rangle,\langle R;T\rangle]}{S^-\langle[R,R];(T,T)\rangle}}{S^-\langle[R,R];T\rangle}}{S^-\langle R;T\rangle}$$

Notice that in the above derivations, contractions are applied to a subformula of the original formula. Repeating this process, we eventually end up with contractions on atomic formulas only.

Definition 8. *System* lSaq *is obtained from* lSgq *by replacing the interaction rule* i↓ *with* ai↓*, the weakening rules* wr↓ *and* wl↓ *with* awr↓ *and* awl↓*, the*

Units: $\quad [t^+, t^+]^+ = t^+ \quad (f^+, f^+)^+ = f^+ \quad \langle f^-; t^+ \rangle^+ = t^+ \quad \langle f^-; f^+ \rangle^+ = t^+$
$\qquad\qquad\qquad [f^+, R^+]^+ = R^+ \quad (t^+, R^+)^+ = R^+ \quad \langle t^-; R^+ \rangle^+ = R^+$

Associativity: $\quad [R, [T, U]^+]^+ = [[R, T]^+, U]^+ \qquad (R, (T, U)^+)^+ = ((R, T)^+, U)^+$

Commutativity: $\qquad\qquad [R, T]^+ = [T, R]^+ \qquad (R, T)^+ = (T, R)^+$

Currying: $\qquad\qquad\qquad \langle (R, T)^-; U \rangle^+ = \langle R; \langle T; U \rangle^+ \rangle^+$

Orthogonality: $\qquad\qquad\qquad \overline{R} = \overline{T}, \text{ if } R = T.$

Congruence: $\qquad\qquad\qquad S\{R\} = S\{T\}, \text{ if } R = T.$

Fig. 6. Syntactic equality for polarized structures

contraction rules cr↓ *and* cl↓ *with* acr↓, acl↓ *and the medial rules in Figure 5. System* SISaq *is obtained by adding to* ISaq *its own dual rules. The propositional fragment of* SISaq *and* ISaq *are referred to as* SISa *and* ISa, *respectively.*

Theorem 9. *The systems* SISgq, SISaq, SISaq *and* ISaq *are equivalent.*

6 A Local System for Propositional Intuitionistic Logic

The rules in both SISgq and SISaq are non-local since in order to apply the rules, one has to check whether the redex is in a positive or negative context. However, if one carefully observes the rules, one notices a certain conservation of *polarities* in the rules. That is to say there is never the case where a structure in a positive context is moved to a negative context and vice versa. For example, in the rule sc↓ in Figure 2, the substructures R, T, U and V have the same polarities in both the premise and the conclusion of the rule. That is R is in negative context in both premise and conclusion, T is in positive context, and so on. This observation leads to the following idea: When proving a structure, we first label each substructure with either a '+' or a '−' depending on whether the substructure is in a positive or a negative context respectively. Each time a structure is modified by a rule, the premise of the rule is relabelled consistently, that is, substructures are labelled depending on which context they reside in. The polarity-preserving property of the rules guarantees that there is no need of relabelling of substructures which are not affected by the rule. For the sc↓ rule, the labelled version would be:

$$\text{sc↓} \; \frac{S(\langle R; T \rangle^+, U)^+}{S\langle R; (T, U)^+ \rangle^+}$$

This modified rule of sc↓ is local since we need only to check for polarity of three substructures in the rule, instead of checking the entire context. We shall give a fully local system for the propositional fragment of ISaq by introducing polarities into structures.

$$\text{ai}\downarrow \frac{S\{t^+\}}{S\langle a^-;a^+\rangle^+} \qquad \text{acr}\downarrow \frac{S[a^+,a^+]^+}{S\{a^+\}} \qquad \text{acl}\downarrow \frac{S(a^-,a^-)^-}{S\{a^-\}} \qquad \text{awr}\downarrow \frac{S\{f^+\}}{S\{a^+\}} \qquad \text{wl}\downarrow \frac{S\{t^-\}}{S\{a^-\}}$$

$$\text{s}\downarrow \frac{S([R,T]^+,U)^+}{S[R,(T,U)^+]^+} \qquad \text{sc}\downarrow \frac{S(\langle R;T\rangle^+,U)^+}{S\langle R;(T,U)^+\rangle^+} \qquad \text{sd}\downarrow \frac{S(\langle R;T\rangle^+,\langle U;V\rangle^+)^+}{S\langle [R,U]^-;[T,V]^+\rangle^+}$$

$$\text{sid}\downarrow \frac{S[\langle R;T\rangle^+,U]^+}{S\langle R;[T,U]^+\rangle^+} \qquad \text{sic}\downarrow \frac{S(R,\langle T;U\rangle^+)^+}{S\langle\langle R;T\rangle^+;U\rangle^+}$$

$$\text{ml}\frac{S([R,T]^-,[U,V]^-)^-}{S[(R,U)^-,(T,V)^-]^-} \qquad \text{mr}\frac{S[(R,U)^+,(T,V)^+]^+}{S([R,T]^+,[U,V]^+)^+}$$

$$\text{mil}\downarrow \frac{S(\langle R;U\rangle^-,\langle T;V\rangle^-)^-}{S\langle[R,T]^+;(U,V)^-\rangle^-} \qquad \text{mir}\downarrow \frac{S[\langle R;U\rangle^+,\langle T;V\rangle^+]^+}{S\langle(R,T)^-;[U,V]^+\rangle^+}$$

Fig. 7. System ISp

Definition 10. Polarized structures *are expressions generated from the following grammar:*

$$S ::= P \mid N$$
$$P ::= a^+ \mid t^+ \mid f^+ \mid (P,P)^+ \mid [P,P]^+ \mid \langle N;P\rangle^+$$
$$N ::= a^- \mid t^- \mid f^- \mid (N,N)^- \mid [N,N]^- \mid \langle P;N\rangle^-$$

A positive polarized structure, or positive structure for short, is a polarized structure labelled with '+', and a negative polarized structure, *or* negative structure, *is a polarized structure labelled with '−'. Positive structures are often denoted by R^+ and negative structures by R^-. The* orthogonal *of a structure R, denoted by $\overline{R}$, is the structure obtained from R by exchanging the labels '+' with '−' and vice versa. A* polarized context *is a polarized structure with a hole { }. Given a polarized context S{ } and a polarized structure R, the placement of R in S{ }, i.e., S{R}, is allowed only if doing so results in a well-formed polarized structure. Polarized structures are considered modulo the equality in Figure 6.*

The propositional intuitionistic system with polarized structures is given in Figure 7. We refer to this system as ISp. Each polarized rule has a dual version which is obtained by exchanging the premise and the conclusion and exchanging the polarities. The system obtained by adding ISp to its own duals is is referred to as SISp. Both the inference rules and the structural equality are derived straightforwardly from the inference rules and structural equality of SISa, that is, by giving appropriate labels to the structures. Care has to be taken to ensure that the rules and the equality between polarized structures preserve polarity. We shall now proceed to prove formally that SISp, SISa, ISp and ISa are all equivalent in terms of provability.

The notion of derivations in SISp is the same as that in SISa. The notion of proof is slightly different.

Definition 11. *A proof of a polarized structure* R *in* $\mathscr{S}$ *is a derivation in* $\mathscr{S}$ *with premise* t^+ *and conclusion* R.

By this definition, it is obvious that all provable polarized structures are positive structures since all rules in SISp preserve polarities.

The key idea to proving the correspondence between SISp and the propositional fragment of SISaq is the following: the polarity of any substructure R in $S\{R\}$ should determine the polarity of the context. In particular, positive structures R and $S\{R\}$ are translated to some structures T and $S'\{T\}$ such that $S'\{\ \}$ corresponds to $S\{\ \}$ and T corresponds to R, and most importantly, $S'\{\ \}$ is a positive context. In this way, rules that apply to positive substructures in SISp translate to the same rules that apply under positive context in SISa, and a simple observation on the inference rules of SISp and SISa shows that they co-incide. The same observation holds for negative structures and negative contexts. In the following theorems, we denote with $\underline{R}_{\mathsf{s}}$, where R is a polarized structure, the structure obtained from R by dropping all the polarity signs.

Theorem 12. *For every polarized structure* R, R *is provable in* ISp *if and only if* $\underline{R}_{\mathsf{s}}$ *is provable in* ISa.

7 Future Work

Properties of proofs and derivations in the systems SISgq and its extensions remain to be studied. An immediate future works would be to find direct proofs (i.e., without the detour through sequent calculus or hypersequent) of cut-elimination. It would also be interesting to investigate various substructural logics that arise from either restricting or extending the base system SISgq. For instance, it would be interesting to see what sort of logic we get from dropping the atomic contraction rules but keeping the medial rules. Another open problem is to come up with a fully local first-order intuitionistic system. The rules which instantiate quantifiers, i.e., $\mathsf{nr}{\downarrow}$ and $\mathsf{nl}{\downarrow}$, involve substitutions which are non-local. This can probably be made local by giving rules which effectively "implement" explicit substitutions. On the more general problem of formalizing asymmetric systems, it would be intereting to see if the methodology presented here can be generalized to formalize non-standard asymmetric systems such as Bunched Logic [19]. Some preliminary result in this direction can be found in [15]. The current work focusses mainly on the proof theoretic aspects. It would be interesting to see if the analyses on the deep inference systems, in particular the notions of locality and atomicity, will be useful for implementing proof search for these logics.

Acknowledgement. The author would like to thank Alessio Guglielmi for his useful comments and suggestions, in particular the one concerning the use of polarities. The author would also like to thank Kai Brünnler, Lutz Strassburger and the anonymous referees for their useful comments and suggestions on earlier drafts of the paper. The author is grateful for the support he received from INRIA Lorraine/LORIA during the start of this work in 2005.

References

1. A. Avron. Hypersequents, logical consequence and intermediate logics for concurrency. *Ann. Math. Artif. Intell.*, 4:225–248, 1991.
2. M. Baaz and A. Ciabattoni. A Schütte-Tait style cut-elimination proof for first-order Gödel logic. In U. Egly and C. G. Fermüller, editors, *TABLEAUX*, volume 2381 of *Lecture Notes in Computer Science*, pages 24–37. Springer, 2002.
3. V. Balat and D. Galmiche. Labelled proof systems for intuitionistic provability. pages 1–32, 2000.
4. K. Brünnler. *Deep Inference and Symmetry in Classical Proofs*. PhD thesis, TU Dresden, September 2003.
5. K. Brünnler. Two restrictions on contraction. *Logic Journal of the IGPL*, 11(5):525–529, 2003.
6. K. Brünnler. Intuitionistic logic in the calculus of structures. Unpublished notes, 2004.
7. K. Brünnler and A. F. Tiu. A local system for classical logic. In R. Nieuwenhuis and A. Voronkov, editors, *LPAR 2001*, volume 2250 of *LNCS*, pages 347–361. Springer-Verlag, 2001.
8. M. Dummett. A propositional calculus with denumerable matrix. *J. Symbolic Logic*, 24(2):97–106, 1959.
9. M. Dummett. *Element of Intuitionism*. Oxford University Press, 1977.
10. R. Dyckhoff. Contraction-free sequent calculi for intuitionistic logic. *Journal of Symbolic Logic*, 57(3):795–807, 1992.
11. J.-Y. Girard. Linear logic. *Theoretical Computer Science*, 50:1–102, 1987.
12. R. Goré. Substructural logics on display. *Logic Journal of the IGPL*, 6(3):451–504, 1998.
13. A. Guglielmi. A system of interaction and structure. Technical Report WV-02-10, TU Dresden, 2002. Accepted by ACM Transactions on Computational Logic.
14. Y. Guiraud. The three dimensions of proofs. To appear in Annals of Pure and Applied Logic, 2006.
15. B. Horsfall. Towards BI in the calculus of structures. Accepted at ESSLLI 2006.
16. J. Hudelmaier. Bounds on cut-elimination in intuitionistic propositional logic. *Archive for Mathematical Logic*, 31:331–354, 1992.
17. O. Kahramanoğulları. Reducing nondeterminism in the calculus of structures. Accepted at LPAR 2006.
18. R. McKinley. *Classical Categories and Deep Inference*. PhD thesis, University of Bath, 2006.
19. P. O'Hearn and D. Pym. The logic of bunched implications. *Bulletin of Symbolic Logic*, 5(2):215–243, June 1999.
20. C. Stewart and P. Stouppa. A systematic proof theory for several modal logics. In R. Schmidt, I. Pratt-Hartmann, M. Reynolds, and H. Wansing, editors, *Advances in Modal Logic*, volume 5 of *King's College Publications*, pages 309–333, 2005.
21. L. Straßburger. *Linear Logic and Noncommutativity in the Calculus of Structures*. PhD thesis, Technische Universität Dresden, 2003.
22. G. Takeuti and S. Titani. Intuitionistic fuzzy logic and intuitionistic fuzzy set theory. *J. Symbolic Logic*, 49(3):851–866, 1984.
23. A. Troelstra and H. Schwichtenberg. *Basic Proof Theory*. Cambridge University Press, 1996.

CIC^: Type-Based Termination of Recursive Definitions in the Calculus of Inductive Constructions[*]

Gilles Barthe[1], Benjamin Grégoire[1], and Fernando Pastawski[1,2]

[1] INRIA Sophia-Antipolis, France
{Gilles.Barthe, Benjamin.Gregoire,
Fernando.Pastawski}@sophia.inria.fr
[2] FaMAF, Univ. Nacional de Córdoba, Argentina

Abstract. Sized types provides a type-based mechanism to enforce termination of recursive definitions in typed λ-calculi. Previous work has provided strong indications that type-based termination provides an appropriate foundation for proof assistants based on type theory; however, most work to date has been confined to non-dependent type systems. In this article, we introduce a variant of the Calculus of Inductive Constructions with sized types and study its meta theoretical properties: subject reduction, normalization, and thus consistency and decidability of type-checking and of size-inference. A prototype implementation has been developed alongside case studies.

1 Introduction

Proof assistants based on dependent type theory rely on termination of typable programs to guarantee decidability of convertibility and hence decidability of typing. In order to enforce termination of programs, proof assistants typically require that recursive calls in a function definition are always performed on structurally smaller arguments; in the Coq proof assistant, which forms the focus of this article, the requirement is captured by a guard predicate $\mathcal{G}$ on expressions, that is applied to the body of recursive definitions for deciding whether or not the function should be accepted. Providing a liberal yet intuitive and correct syntactic guard criterion to guarantee termination is problematic.

Type-based termination is an alternative approach to enforce termination of recursive definitions through an extended type system that manipulates *sized types*, i.e. types that convey information about the size of their inhabitants. In a nutshell, the key ingredients of type-based termination are the explicit representation of the successive approximations of datatypes in the type system, a subtyping relation to reflect inclusion of the successive approximations and the adoption of appropriate rules for constructors, case expressions, and fixpoints.

Previous work by the authors [6,7] and by others (see Section 2) has shown that type-based termination is an intuitive and robust mechanism, and a good candidate for enforcing termination in proof assistants based on dependent type theories. However, these works were concerned with non-dependent type systems. The contribution of the

---

[*] More details on difficulties with Coq, case studies, remaining issues and proofs and an implementation are available from the second author's web page.

M. Hermann and A. Voronkov (Eds.): LPAR 2006, LNAI 4246, pp. 257–271, 2006.

paper is an extension of these results to dependent type theories, and more precisely to the Calculus of Inductive Constructions; concretely, we introduce CIC‸, a variant of the Calculus of Inductive Constructions that enforces termination of recursive definitions through sized types. Besides, we show that the system CIC‸ enjoys essential properties required for proof assistants, in particular logical consistency and decidability of type-checking, and decidability of size-inference. We have developed a prototype implementation of CIC‸ and used it to prove the correctness of quicksort.

2   Related Work

The idea of ensuring termination and productivity of fixpoint definitions by typing can be traced back to early work by Mendler [21] on recursion schemes, and to work by Hughes, Pareto and Sabry [18] on the use of sized types to ensure productivity of programs manipulating infinite objects. We refer the reader to [2,6] for a review of related work, and focus on work that deals with dependent types or with size inference.

Inference. Chin and Khoo [14] were among the first to study size inference in a non-dependent setting; they provided an algorithm that generates formulae of Presburger arithmetic to witness termination for a class of strongly normalizing terms typable in a (standard) simply typed λ-calculus with recursive definitions.

   Type-checking algorithms for systems that enforce type-based termination were developed by Xi [25] for a system with restricted dependent types and by Abel [1,2] for a higher order polymorphic λ-calculus. More recently, Blanqui and Riba [12] have shown (termination and) decidability of type checking for a simply typed λ-calculus extended with higher-order rewriting and based on constraint-based termination, a generalization of type-based termination inspired from [14].

Dependent types. Giménez [17] was the first to consider a dependent type theory that uses type-based termination: concretely, he defined a variant of the Calculus of Inductive Constructions with type-based termination, and stated strong normalization for his system. The paper does not contain proofs and does not deal with size inference; besides, Giménez does not use an explicit representation of stages, which makes the system impractical for mutually recursive definitions. This work was pursued by Barras [4], who considered a variant of Giménez system with an explicit representation of stages, and proved in Coq decidability of type-checking assuming strong normalization.

   Blanqui [10,11] has defined a type-based variant of the Calculus of Algebraic Constructions (CAC) [9], an extension of the Calculus of Constructions with higher-order rewriting à la Jouannaud-Okada [19], and showed termination and decidability of type-checking. It is likely that strong normalization for CIC‸ (which we conjecture) can be derived from [10], in the same way that strong normalization of CIC can be derived from strong normalization of CAC [9]. On the other hand, our inference result is more powerful than [11]. Indeed, our system only requires terms to carry a minimal amount of size annotations, and uses a size inference algorithm to compute these annotations, whereas size annotations are pervasive in Blanqui's system, and merely checked. We believe that size inference has a significant impact on the usability of the system, and is a requirement for a practical use of type-based termination in a proof-assistant.

3   A Primer on Type-Based Termination

The object of this section is to provide a (necessarily) brief introduction to type-based termination. For more information (including a justification of some choices for the syntax of non-dependent systems and inherited here), we refer the reader to [6,7].

Consider for example the datatype of lists; in our system, the user declares the datatype with a declaration

$$\text{List } [A : \mathbf{Set}] : \mathbf{Set} := \text{nil} : \text{List} \mid \text{cons} : A \to \text{List} \to \text{List}$$

Lists are then represented by an infinite set of approximations $\text{List}^s \, A$, where s is a size (or stage) expression taken from the following grammar:

$$s ::= \imath \mid \widehat{s} \mid \infty$$

where $\widehat{}$ denotes the successor function on stage expressions, and where we adopt the convention that $\widehat{\infty} = \infty$. Intuitively, $\text{List}^s \, A$ denotes the type of A-lists of size at most s, and in particular, $\text{List}^\infty \, A$ denotes the usual type of A-lists. In order to reflect inclusion between successive approximations of lists, we introduce a subtyping relation with the rules

$$\text{List}^s \, A \leq \text{List}^{\widehat{s}} \, A \qquad \text{List}^s \, A \leq \text{List}^\infty \, A$$

together with the usual rules for reflexivity, transitivity, and function space.

The typing rules for constructors confirm the intuitive meaning that the size of a constructor term is one plus the maximum size of its subterms:

$$\frac{\Gamma \vdash A : \omega}{\Gamma \vdash \text{nil} \, |A| : \text{List}^{\widehat{\imath}} \, A} \qquad \frac{\Gamma \vdash A : \omega \qquad \Gamma \vdash a : A \qquad \Gamma \vdash l : \text{List}^s \, A}{\Gamma \vdash \text{cons} \, |A| \, a \, l : \text{List}^{\widehat{s}} \, A}$$

Note that the empty list cannot be of type $\text{List}^\imath$ because it would break normalization. Furthermore, note that parameters in constructors do not carry any size annotations (they are removed by the erasure function $|.|$), both to ensure subject reduction and to guarantee that we do not have multiple canonical inhabitants for parametrized types: e.g. in this way we guarantee that nil Nat is the only empty list in List Nat^∞; otherwise we would have for each stage s an empty list nil Nat^s of type List Nat^∞.

Then, the typing rule for fixpoints ensures that recursive function calls are always performed on arguments smaller than the input:

$$\frac{\Gamma, f : \text{List}^\imath \, A \to B \vdash e : \text{List}^{\widehat{\imath}} \, A \to B[\imath := \widehat{\imath}]}{\Gamma \vdash (\text{fix } f : |\text{List}^\imath \, A \to B|^\imath := e) : \text{List}^s \, A \to B[\imath := s]}$$

where $\imath$ occurs positively in B and does not occur in Γ, A. Note that the tag of f in the recursive definition does not carry size annotations (we use the erasure function $|.|^\imath 2$); instead, it simply carries position annotations in some places, to indicate which recursive arguments have a size related to the decreasing argument. The purpose of position annotations is to guarantee the existence of compact most general typings (without position annotations we would need union types), see [7].

In the conclusion, the stage s is arbitrary, so the system features some *implicit stage polymorphism*. Further, the substitution in the conclusion is useful to compute so-called *precise typings*. For example, CIC^ allows the precise typings for map and filter:

$$\text{map} : \Pi A : \textbf{Set}. \ \Pi B : \textbf{Set}. \ (A \to B) \to (\text{list}^s \ A) \to (\text{list}^s \ B)$$
$$\text{filter} : \Pi A : \textbf{Set}. \ (A \to \text{bool}) \to (\text{list}^s \ A) \to (\text{list}^s \ A)$$

to reflect that the map and filter function outputs a list whose length is smaller or equal to the length of the list that they take as arguments. In turn, the precise typing of filter is used to type functions that are rejected by many syntactic criteria of termination, such as the quicksort function. Wahlstedt[23] presents a size-change principle that accepts many recursion schemes that escape our type system but is unable to gain expressiveness from size preserving functions.

4   System CIC^

The system CIC^ is a type-based termination version of the Calculus of Inductive Constructions (CIC) [24]. The latter is an extension of the Calculus of Constructions with (co-)inductive types, and the foundation of the Coq proof assistant. In this paper, we omit co-inductive types. On the other hand, we present CIC^ as an instance of a Sized Inductive Type System, which is an extension of Pure Type Systems [3] with inductive types using size-based termination.

Specifications. The type system is implicitly parametrized by a specification that is a quadruple of sorts $\mathcal{S}$, axioms Axioms, product rules Rules, and elimination rules Elim. Sorts are the universes of the type system; typically, there is one sort **Prop** of propositions and a sort **Set** of types. Axioms establish typing relations between sorts, product rules determine which dependent products may be formed and in which sort they live, and elimination rules determine which case analysis may be performed. The specification for CIC^ is that of CIC [22].

Terms. Following $F^{\wedge}$ [7], CIC^ features three families of expressions to ensure subject reduction and efficient type inference. The first family is made of bare expressions that do not carry any size information: bare expressions are used in the tags of λ-abstractions and case expressions and as parameters in inductive definitions/constructors. The second family is made of positions expressions that are used in the tags of recursive definitions and rely on a mark $\star$ to denote (in a recursive definition) which positions have a size related to that of the recursive argument. Finally, the third family is made of sized expressions that carry annotations (except in their tags).

Definition 1 (Stages and expressions)

1. The set $\mathcal{S}$ of stage expressions *is given by the abstract syntax: $s, r ::= \imath \mid \infty \mid \widehat{s}$. Stage substitution is defined in the obvious way, and we write $s[\imath := s']$ to denote the stage obtained by replacing $\imath$ by s' in s. Furthermore, the base stage of a stage expression is defined by the clauses $\lfloor \imath \rfloor = \imath$ and $\lfloor \widehat{s} \rfloor = \lfloor s \rfloor$ (the function is not defined on stages that contain ∞).*

$$\frac{}{\mathsf{WF}([\,])}\ \text{empty}\qquad \frac{\mathsf{WF}(\Gamma)\quad \Gamma\vdash T:\omega}{\mathsf{WF}(\Gamma(x:T))}\ \text{cons}\qquad \frac{\mathsf{WF}(\Gamma)\quad (\omega,\omega')\in\mathsf{Axioms}}{\Gamma\vdash\omega:\omega'}\ \text{sort}$$

$$\frac{\mathsf{WF}(\Gamma)\quad \Gamma(x)=T}{\Gamma\vdash x:T}\ \text{var}\qquad \frac{\Gamma\vdash T:\omega_1\quad \Gamma(x:T)\vdash U:\omega_2\quad (\omega_1,\omega_2,\omega_3)\in\mathsf{Rules}}{\Gamma\vdash \Pi x:T.\,U:\omega_3}\ \text{prod}$$

$$\frac{\Gamma\vdash \Pi x:T.\,U:\omega\quad \Gamma(x:T)\vdash u:U}{\Gamma\vdash \lambda x:|T|.\,u:\Pi x:T.\,U}\ \text{abs}\qquad \frac{\Gamma\vdash u:\Pi x:T.\,U\quad \Gamma\vdash t:T}{\Gamma\vdash u\,t:U[x:=t]}\ \text{app}$$

$$\frac{\Gamma\vdash t:T\quad \Gamma\vdash U:\omega\quad T\preceq U}{\Gamma\vdash t:U}\ \text{conv}\qquad \frac{\mathsf{WF}(\Gamma)\quad I\in\Sigma}{\Gamma\vdash I^s:\mathsf{TypeInd}(I)}\ \text{ind}$$

$$\frac{I\in\Sigma\quad \Gamma(x:\mathsf{TypeConstr}(c,s))\vdash x\,\boldsymbol{p}\,\boldsymbol{a}:U}{\mathsf{params}(c)=\#\boldsymbol{p}\quad \mathsf{args}(c)=\#\boldsymbol{a}\quad x\ \text{fresh in}\ \Gamma,\boldsymbol{p},\boldsymbol{a}}{\Gamma\vdash c(|\boldsymbol{p}|,\boldsymbol{a}):U}\ \text{constr}$$

$$\frac{\Gamma\vdash t:I^{\hat{s}}\,\boldsymbol{p}\,\boldsymbol{a}\quad I\in\Sigma\quad \Gamma\vdash P:\mathsf{TypePred}(I,s,\boldsymbol{p},\omega')}{(I.\omega,\omega')\in\mathsf{Elim}\quad \mathsf{params}(I)=\#\boldsymbol{p}\quad \Gamma\vdash b_i:\mathsf{TypeBranch}(c_i,s,P,\boldsymbol{p})}{\Gamma\vdash \mathsf{case}_{|P|}\,t\ \text{of}\ \{c_i\Rightarrow b_i\}:P\,\boldsymbol{a}\,t}\ \text{case}$$

$$\frac{T=\Pi\Delta.\,\Pi x:I^\imath\,\boldsymbol{u}.\,U\quad \imath\ \mathsf{pos}\ U\quad \#\Delta=n-1}{\imath\ \text{does not occur in}\ \Delta,\boldsymbol{u},\Gamma,t\quad \Gamma\vdash T:\omega\quad \Gamma(f:T)\vdash t:T[\imath:=\hat{\imath}]}{\Gamma\vdash(\mathsf{fix}_n\,f:|T|^\imath:=t):T[\imath:=s]}\ \text{fix}$$

Fig. 1. Typing rules

2. *The set of* $\mathcal{P}$ *size positions is defined as* $\{\star,\epsilon\}$.
3. *The generic set of terms over the set* a *is defined by the abstract syntax:*

$$\mathcal{T}[a]::=\Omega\mid \mathcal{X}\mid \lambda\mathcal{X}:\mathcal{T}°.\,\mathcal{T}[a]\mid \mathcal{T}[a]\,\mathcal{T}[a]\mid \Pi\mathcal{X}:\mathcal{T}[a].\,\mathcal{T}[a]\mid \mathcal{C}(\mathcal{T}°,\mathcal{T}[a])\mid \mathcal{I}^a$$
$$\mid\ \mathsf{case}_{\mathcal{T}°}\,\mathcal{T}[a]\ \text{of}\ \{\mathcal{C}\Rightarrow\mathcal{T}[a]\}\mid \mathsf{fix}_n\,\mathcal{X}:\mathcal{T}^\star:=\mathcal{T}[a]$$

where Ω, $\mathcal{X}$, $\mathcal{I}$ *and* $\mathcal{C}$ *range over sorts, variables, datatypes and constructors.*
4. *The set of bare expressions, position expressions, and sized expressions are defined by the clauses* $\mathcal{T}°::=\mathcal{T}[\epsilon]$ *and* $\mathcal{T}^\star::=\mathcal{T}[\mathcal{P}]$ *and* $\mathcal{T}::=\mathcal{T}[\mathcal{S}]$.

Note that we require that constructors are fully applied; as mentioned above, we also separate arguments of constructors into parameters that do not carry any size information and arguments that may carry size information. Besides, the fixpoint definition carries an index n that determines the recursive argument of the function. Finally, observe that case expressions are tagged with a function that gives the type of each branch, as required in a dependently typed setting.

Reduction and Conversion. The computational behavior of expressions is given by the usual rules for β-reduction (function application), ι-reduction (pattern matching) and μ-reduction (unfolding of recursive definitions). The definition of these rules relies on substitution, whose formalization must be adapted to deal with the different categories of expressions.

Definition 2 (Erasure and substitution)

1. *The function* $|.| : \mathcal{T}^\star \cup \mathcal{T} \to \mathcal{T}^\circ$ *is defined as the obvious erasure function from sized terms (resp. position terms) to bare terms.*
2. *The function* $|.|^\imath : \mathcal{T} \to \mathcal{T}^\star$ *is defined as the function that replaces stage annotations* s *with* $\star$ *if the base stage of* s *is* $\imath$ ($\lfloor s \rfloor = \imath$) *and by* ϵ *otherwise.*
3. *The substitution of* x *by* N *into* M *is written as* $M[x := N]$. *(In fact we need three substitution operators, one for each category of terms; all are defined in the obvious way, and use the erasure functions when required.)*
4. *The substitution of stage variable* $\imath$ *by stage expression* s *is defined as* $M[\imath := s]$.

We are now in position to define the reduction rules.

Definition 3 (Reduction rules and conversion)

- *The reduction relation* $\to$ *is defined as the compatible closure of the rules:*

$$(\lambda x : T^\circ. M)\, N \;\to\; M[x := N] \qquad\qquad (\beta)$$
$$\mathsf{case}_{T^\circ}\, c_j(\boldsymbol{p}^\circ, \boldsymbol{a})\ \mathsf{of}\ \{c_i \Rightarrow t_i\} \;\to\; t_j\, \boldsymbol{a} \qquad\qquad (\imath)$$
$$(\mathsf{fix}_n\, f : T^\star := M)\, \boldsymbol{b}\, c(\boldsymbol{p}^\circ, \boldsymbol{a}) \;\to\; M[f := (\mathsf{fix}_n\, f : T^\star := M)]\, \boldsymbol{b}\, c(\boldsymbol{p}^\circ, \boldsymbol{a})\ (\mu)$$

  where $\boldsymbol{b}$ *is of length* $n - 1$.
- *We write* $\xrightarrow{*}$ *and* $\approx$ *respectively for the reflexive-transitive and reflexive-symmetric-transitive closure of* $\to$.

Both reduction and conversion are closed under substitution. Moreover, reduction is Church-Rosser.

Lemma 1 (Church-Rosser). *For every expressions* u *and* v *such that* $u \approx v$ *there exists* t *such that* $u \xrightarrow{*} t$ *and* $v \xrightarrow{*} t$.

In particular normal forms are unique, hence we write $\mathrm{NF}(A)$ for the normal form of A (if it exists) w.r.t. $\to$.

Subtyping. In order to increase its expressiveness, the type system features a subtyping relation that is derived from a partial order on stages. The partial order reflects two intuitions: first, that an approximation $\mathcal{J}^s$ is contained in its successor approximation $\mathcal{J}^{\hat{s}}$; second, that $\mathcal{J}^\infty$ is closed under constructors, and the fixpoint of the monotonic operator attached to inductive types.

Definition 4 (Substage). *The relation* s *is a substage of* s', *written* $s \sqsubseteq s'$, *is defined by the rules:*

$$\frac{}{s \sqsubseteq s} \qquad \frac{s \sqsubseteq r \quad r \sqsubseteq p}{s \sqsubseteq p} \qquad \frac{}{s \sqsubseteq \hat{s}} \qquad \frac{}{s \sqsubseteq \infty}$$

The substage relation defines a subtyping relation between types, using for each inductive type a declaration that indicate the polarity of its parameters.

Definition 5 (Polarity declaration). *We assume that each inductive type I comes with a vector $I.\nu$ of polarity declarations, where each element of a polarity declaration can be positive, negative or invariant:*

$$\nu ::= + \mid - \mid \circ$$

Subtyping is then defined in the expected way, using an auxiliary relation that defines subtyping between vectors of expressions relative to a vector of positivity declarations.

Definition 6 (Subtyping)

- *Let R be an equivalence relation stable under substitution of terms and stages. The subtyping relations $\preceq_R$ and $\preceq_R^\nu$ are simultaneously defined by the rules:*

$$\frac{t_1 \, R \, t_2}{t_1 \preceq_R t_2} \qquad \frac{T_2 \preceq_R T_1 \quad U_1 \preceq_R U_2}{\Pi x{:}T_1.\, U_1 \preceq_R \Pi x{:}T_2.\, U_2} \qquad \frac{s \sqsubseteq s' \quad t_1 \preceq_R^{I.\nu} t_2}{I^s \, t_1 \preceq_R I^{s'} \, t_2}$$

$$\frac{t_1 \, R \, u_1 \quad t \preceq_R^\nu u}{t_1.t \preceq_R^{\circ.\nu} u_1.u} \qquad \frac{t_1 \preceq_R u_1 \quad t \preceq_R^\nu u}{t_1.t \preceq_R^{+.\nu} u_1.u} \qquad \frac{u_1 \preceq_R t_1 \quad t \preceq_R^\nu u}{t_1.t \preceq_R^{-.\nu} u_1.u} \qquad \frac{t \, R \, u}{t \preceq_R^\emptyset u}$$

- *We define $\preceq$ as the transitive closure of $\preceq_\approx$. (Note that $\preceq$ is reflexive and allows redex elimination through $\approx$.)*
- *We define $\leq$ as $\preceq_=$. (Note that $\leq$ is reflexive and transitive.)*

The subtyping relation $\preceq$ shall be used to define the type system of CIC⁻, whereas the subtyping relation $\leq$ shall be used by the inference algorithm. The two subtyping relations are related by the following lemma.

Lemma 2. *If A and A' are normalizing, then $A \preceq A'$ iff $\mathsf{NF}(A) \leq \mathsf{NF}(A')$.*

Positivity. In order to formulate the type system and to specify which inductive definitions are correct and supported by CIC⁻, we need several notions of positivity and strict positivity. Strict positivity is used to guarantee termination of recursive functions, whereas positivity is used to verify that polarity declarations are correct and in the rule for fixpoints. We begin by defining positivity of stage variables. In contrast to simple type systems, positivity cannot be defined syntactically, and we are forced to use a semantic definition.

Definition 7 (Positivity of stage variables). *$\imath$ is positive in T, written $\imath$ pos T, iff $T[\imath := s_1] \preceq T[\imath := s_2]$ for all s_1, s_2 such that $s_1 \sqsubseteq s_2$.*

The above definition involves a universal quantification and thus is not practical for algorithmic purposes. We provide an equivalent definition that can be used for type checking.

Lemma 3 (Redefinition of positivity). *If T is normalizing then*

$$\imath \text{ pos } T \Leftrightarrow T \preceq T[\imath := \hat{\imath}] \Leftrightarrow \mathsf{NF}(T) \leq \mathsf{NF}(T[\imath := \hat{\imath}])$$

We can generalize the notion of positivity to term variables.

Definition 8 (Positivity of term variables)

- x *is positive in* T, *written* x pos T, *iff* $T[x := t_1] \preceq T[x := t_2]$ *for all* t_1, t_2 *such that* $t_1 \preceq t_2$.
- x *is negative in* T, *written* x neg T, *iff* $T[x := t_2] \preceq T[x := t_1]$ *for all* t_1, t_2 *such that* $t_1 \preceq t_2$.

We conclude this section with a definition of strict positivity. Indeed, contrary to earlier work with non-dependent type systems, we cannot allow positive inductive types in our system, because it would lead to an inconsistency [15].

Definition 9 (Strictly positive). *A variable* x *is strictly positive in* T, *written* x POS T, *if* x *does not appear in* T *or if* $T \approx \Pi\Delta$. $x\,t$ *and* x *does not appear in* Δ *and* t.

Inductive Types. Inductive definitions are declared in a signature Σ; each inductive definition is introduced with a declaration of the form

$$\mathrm{Ind}(I[\Delta_p]^\nu : \Pi\Delta_a.\,\omega := \overrightarrow{c_i : \Pi\Delta_i.\,\delta\,t_i})$$

where I is the name of the inductive type, Δ_p is a context defining its parameters and their type, Δ_a is a context defining its arguments and their type, ω is a sort and ν is its polarity declaration. To the right of the := symbol, we find a list of constructors with their types: c_i represents the name of the i-th constructor, and Δ_i is the context for its arguments, and $\delta\,t_i$ represents the type of the resulting constructor term—for technical reasons, we use a special variable δ representing the current inductive type. In the sequel, we shall use some notations to deal with inductive definitions. First, we write $I \in \Sigma$ for $\mathrm{Ind}(I[\Delta_p]^\nu : \Pi\Delta_a.\,\omega := \overrightarrow{c_i : \Pi\Delta_i.\,\delta\,t_i}) \in \Sigma$. Figure 2 introduces further notations referring to inductive definitions : $I.\omega$ and $\mathsf{TypeInd}(I)$ are respectively the sort and the type of I; $\mathsf{params}(I) = \mathsf{params}(c)$ indicates the number of parameters of the inductive type and of its constructors. Then, we define the type of a constructor ($\mathsf{TypeConstr}(c, s)$), of the case predicate ($\mathsf{TypePred}(I, s, p, \omega')$) and the type of case branches $\mathsf{TypeBranch}(c_i, s, P, p)$.

As usual, we separate between parameters and arguments of inductive types—they are handled differently in the syntax and shall be handled differently in the conversion rule—and assume that inductive types do not share constructors. Furthermore, contexts of inductive definitions are subject to well-formedness constraints; some constraints rely on the type system defined in the next paragraph. A context of inductive definitions is well-formed if it is empty [] or if it is of the form $\Sigma; \mathrm{Ind}(...)$ where Σ is well formed and all of the following hold:

1. the inductive definition is well-typed, i.e. $\vdash \Pi\Delta_p.\ \Pi\Delta_a.\ \omega : \omega'$ for some ω' is a valid typing judgment with signature Σ;
2. the constructors are well-typed, i.e. $\Delta_p\,(\delta : \Pi\Delta_a.\,\omega) \vdash \Pi\Delta_i.\,\delta\,t_i : \omega_i$ for some ω_i is a valid typing judgment with signature Σ;
3. variable δ is strictly positive in the type of every constructor argument (δ pos Δ_i).
4. each occurrence of inductive types in $\Delta_p, \Delta_a, \Delta_i$ is annotated with ∞;
5. each variable in Δ_p satisfies the polarity condition in the type of each constructor. This means $\mathrm{dom}(\Delta_p)$ pos $^{I.\nu}\Delta_p$ and for every constructor c_i, $\mathrm{dom}(\Delta_p)$ pos $^{I.\nu}\Delta_i$.

$$
\begin{array}{ll}
I.\omega & := \omega \\
\mathsf{TypeInd}(I) & := \Pi\Delta_p.\ \Pi\Delta_a.\ \omega \\
\mathsf{params}(I) & := \#\Delta_p \\
\mathsf{params}(c) & := \#\Delta_p \\
\mathsf{args}(c) & := \#\Delta_i \\
\mathsf{TypeConstr}(c_i, s) & := \Pi\Delta_p.\ \Pi(\Delta_i[\delta := I^s\ \mathsf{dom}(\Delta_p)]).\ I^{\hat{s}}\ \mathsf{dom}(\Delta_p)\ t_i \\
\mathsf{TypePred}(I, s, p, \omega') & := \Pi\Delta_a[\mathsf{dom}(\Delta_p) := p].\ \Pi x : I^{\hat{s}}\ p\ \mathsf{dom}(\Delta_a).\ \omega' \\
\mathsf{TypeBranch}(c_i, s, P, p) & := (\Pi\Delta_i.\ P\ t_i\ c_i(|p|, \mathsf{dom}(\Delta_i)))\,[\mathsf{dom}(\Delta_p) := p][\delta := I^s\ p]
\end{array}
$$

Fig. 2. Definitions over inductive constructions

6. positive and negative variables in Δ_p do not appear in arguments t_i that appear in the types of constructors.
7. from subtyping rules, we have that $p_1 \preceq^{I \cdot \nu} p_2$ implies $I\ p_1 a \preceq I\ p_2 a$. We require $\mathsf{dom}(\Delta_p)$ pos $^{I \cdot \nu} \Delta_a$ to guarantee that if $I\ p_1 a$ and all the components of p_2 are well typed, then $I\ p_2 a$ will be well typed.

Clause 3 ensures termination, whereas Clause 4 ensures that constructors use previously defined datatypes, but not approximations of previously defined datatypes—it is not clear whether lifting such a restriction would make the system more useful and how much the theory would be impacted. Clauses 5 and 6 reflect the subtyping rules for inductive types, and are used in the proof of subject reduction. Lastly, clause 7 is required to guarantee the completeness of type inference.

Typing. Typing judgments are defined in the usual way. They are implicitly parameterized by a signature of inductive declarations, and by a specification that consists of a set of axioms, product rules, and elimination rules. Axioms establish typing relations between sorts, product rules determine which dependent products may be formed and in which sort they live, and elimination rules determine which case analysis may be performed. For example, Coq does not allow $\mathsf{Elim}(\mathbf{Prop}, \mathbf{Set})$.

Definition 10 (Contexts and judgments)

– *A context is a finite list of declarations* $\Gamma := (x_1 : T_1) \ldots (x_n : T_n)$ *where* $x_1, \ldots, x_n$ *are pairwise disjoint variables and* $T_1, \ldots, T_n$ *are expressions.*
– *A typing judgment is a tuple of the form* $\Gamma \vdash t : T$, *where* Γ *is a context, t and T are expressions.*
– *A judgment is derivable iff it can be obtained using the rules of Figure 1.*

5 Meta-theory

This section states the main properties that CIC⁻ inherits from its non-dependent ancestors, and that justifies it as a foundation for proof assistants. Once the distinction between terms and types is reestablished for CIC⁻, the algorithm and most proofs may be adapted with only minor modifications inherent to the complexity of CIC. All properties are proved for arbitrary specifications, and rely on the assumption of normalization.

$$\mathsf{Check}(V, \Gamma, e^\circ, T) \quad = \quad V_e, C_e \cup T_e \preceq T, e$$
$$\text{where } (V_e, C_e, e, T_e) := \mathsf{Infer}(V, \Gamma, e^\circ)$$

$$\mathsf{Infer}(V, \Gamma, \omega) \quad = \quad V, \emptyset, \omega, \mathsf{axioms}(\omega)$$

$$\mathsf{Infer}(V, \Gamma, x) \quad = \quad V, \emptyset, x, \Gamma(x)$$

$$\mathsf{Infer}(V, \Gamma, \lambda x{:}T_1^\circ. e^\circ) \quad = \quad V_e, C_1 \cup C_e, \lambda x{:}T_1^\circ. e, \Pi x{:}T_1. T_2$$
$$\text{where } (V_1, C_1, T_1, W_1) := \mathsf{Infer}(V, \Gamma, T_1^\circ) \text{ and } \mathsf{whnf}(W_1) = \omega_1$$
$$(V_e, C_e, e, T_2) := \mathsf{Infer}(V_1, \Gamma; x{:}T_1, e^\circ)$$

$$\mathsf{Infer}(V, \Gamma, \Pi x{:}T_1^\circ. T_2^\circ) \quad =$$
$$V_2, C_1 \cup C_2, \Pi x{:}T_1. T_2, \mathsf{rules}(\omega_1, \omega_2)$$
$$\text{where } (V_1, C_1, T_1, W_1) := \mathsf{Infer}(V, \Gamma, T_1^\circ) \text{ and } \mathsf{whnf}(W_1) = \omega_1$$
$$(V_2, C_2, T_2, W_2) := \mathsf{Infer}(V_1, \Gamma; x{:}T_1, T_2^\circ)$$
$$\text{and } \mathsf{whnf}(W_2) = \omega_2$$

$$\mathsf{Infer}(V, \Gamma, e_1^\circ \, e_2^\circ) \quad = \quad V_2, C_1 \cup C_2, e_1 \, e_2, T[x := e_2]$$
$$\text{where } (V_1, C_1, e_1, T_1) := \mathsf{Infer}(V, \Gamma, e_1^\circ)$$
$$\mathsf{whnf}(T_1) = \Pi x{:}T_2. T$$
$$(V_2, C_2, e_2) := \mathsf{Check}(V_1, \Gamma, e_2^\circ, T_2)$$

$$\mathsf{Infer}(V, \Gamma, I) \quad = \quad V \cup \{\alpha\}, \emptyset, I^\alpha, \mathsf{TypeInd}(I) \quad \text{with } \alpha \notin V$$

$$\mathsf{Infer}(V, \Gamma, c(\boldsymbol{p}^\circ, \boldsymbol{a}^\circ)) \quad = \quad V_c, C, c(\boldsymbol{p}^\circ, \boldsymbol{a}), T$$
$$\text{where } T_c := \mathsf{TypeConstr}(c, \alpha) \quad \text{with } \alpha \notin V$$
$$\mathsf{params}(c) = \#\boldsymbol{p}^\circ \text{ and } \mathsf{args}(c) = \#\boldsymbol{a}^\circ \text{ and } x \text{ free in } \Gamma, \boldsymbol{p}, \boldsymbol{a}$$
$$(V_c, C, x \, \boldsymbol{p} \, \boldsymbol{a}, T) = \mathsf{Infer}(V \cup \{\alpha\}, \Gamma(x : T_c), x \, \boldsymbol{p}^\circ \, \boldsymbol{a}^\circ)$$

$$\mathsf{Infer}(V, \Gamma, \mathsf{case}_{P^\circ} \, e_c^\circ \text{ of } \{c_i \Rightarrow e_i^\circ\}) \quad =$$
$$V_n, C_c \cup C_p \cup \bigcup_{i=0}^n C_i, \mathsf{case}_{P^\circ} \, e_c \text{ of } \{c_i \Rightarrow e_i\}, P \, \boldsymbol{a} \, e_c$$
$$\text{where } (V_c, C_c, e_c, T_c) := \mathsf{Infer}(V, \Gamma, e_c^\circ)$$
$$\mathsf{whnf}(T_c) = I^r \, \boldsymbol{p} \, \boldsymbol{a} \text{ and } \mathsf{params}(I) = \#\boldsymbol{p} \text{ and } \alpha \notin V_c$$
$$(V_P, C_P, P, T_P) := \mathsf{Infer}(V_c \cup \{\alpha\}, \Gamma, P^\circ) \text{ and } T_{P_0} := T_P$$
$$\forall i = 1 \dots \mathsf{args}(I) + 1, \Pi x_i{:}T_i. T_{P_i} := \mathsf{whnf}(T_{P_{i-1}})$$
$$\omega' := \mathsf{whnf}(T_{P_{\mathsf{args}(I)+1}}) \text{ and } \mathsf{elim}(I.\omega, \omega')$$
$$C_0 := r \sqsubseteq \widehat{\alpha} \cup T_P \preceq \mathsf{TypePred}(I, \alpha, \boldsymbol{p}, \omega')) \text{ and } V_0 := V_P$$
$$\forall i = 1 \dots n, (V_i, C_i, e_i) :=$$
$$\mathsf{Check}(V_{i-1}, \Gamma, e_i^\circ, \mathsf{TypeBranch}(c_i, \alpha, P, \boldsymbol{p}))$$

$$\text{given } T^\star \equiv \Pi\Delta^\circ. \Pi x{:}I^\star \, \boldsymbol{u}^\circ. U^\star \quad \text{with } \#\Delta^\circ = n - 1$$
$$\mathsf{Infer}(V, \Gamma, \mathsf{fix}_n \, f{:}T^\star := e_B^\circ) \quad =$$
$$V_B, C_f, \mathsf{fix}_n \, f{:}T^\star := e_B, \Pi\Delta. \Pi x{:}I^\alpha \, \boldsymbol{u}. U$$
$$\text{where } (V_T, C_T, \Pi\Delta. \Pi x{:}I^\alpha \, \boldsymbol{u}. U, W) := \mathsf{Infer}(V, \Gamma, |T^\star|)$$
$$\text{and } \mathsf{whnf}(W) = \omega$$
$$(V^\star, \widehat{U}) := \mathsf{shift}(U, U^\star) \text{ and } T' := \Pi\Delta. \Pi x{:}I^\alpha \, \boldsymbol{u}. U$$
$$(V_B, C_B, e_B) :=$$
$$\mathsf{Check}(V_T, \Gamma(f : T'), e_B^\circ, \Pi\Delta. \Pi x{:}I^\alpha \, \boldsymbol{u}. \widehat{U})$$
$$C_f := \mathsf{RecCheck}(\alpha, V^\star, V_B \backslash V^\star, C_T \cup C_B \cup U \preceq \widehat{U})$$

Fig. 3. Inference Algorithm

Subject Reduction and Consistency. In order to prove subject reduction, we must first establish substitution lemmas, generation lemmas, correctness of types and inversion of products.

Lemma 4

- *Correctness of types: If $\Gamma \vdash t : T$ then there exists $\omega \in \mathcal{S}$ such that $T = \omega$ or $\Gamma \vdash T : \omega$*
- *Inversion of product If $\Pi x : A.\ B \preceq \Pi x : C.\ D$ then $C \preceq A$ and also $B \preceq D$*
- *Subject reduction If $\Gamma \vdash M : T$ and $M \to M'$ then $\Gamma \vdash M' : T$*

The proof of subject reduction is in most parts analogous to the one for CIC. The difficulty posed by fixpoint reduction is dealt with thanks to a lemma stating preservation of typing under stage substitution[6].

As usual, subject reduction and confluence allow to deduce consistency from normalization.

Size Inference. Proof assistants based on dependent type theory rely on the Curry-Howard isomorphism to reduce proof-checking to type-checking. In this context, it is important to be able to decide whether a term is typable or not. Furthermore, it is important for usability that size annotations should not be provided by users, for whom sized types should be as transparent as possible. Thus, we want to device a procedure that takes as input a context and a bare expression and returns a decoration of the bare expression and a most general typing if it exists, or an error if no decoration of the expression is typable.

There are two fundamental steps in designing a type-checking algorithm for dependent types—without subtyping and inductive types. The first step is to give a syntax-directed formulation of the typing rules, with conversion used only in specific places; the second step is to give a procedure to decide the convertibility of two terms. The syntax-directed algorithm always calls convertibility checking on typable terms, which are thus known to be normalizing, and convertibility is decidable in this case— thanks to confluence and normalization, one can compute both normal forms and check the equality.

In our setting, convertibility is replaced by subtyping $T \preceq U$, but we can adopt the strategy for testing convertibility for well typed terms (that are strongly normalizing): compute both normal forms and check whether they are related by subtyping $\leq$, see Lemma 2. However, termination is enforced with size information, which must be inferred during type-checking. Although it would be tempting to perform type-checking using erased types and perform termination checking afterwards, this is not possible with dependent types because it would entail not knowing termination at type-checking, which itself results in undecidability. Thus, we must check termination during type-checking, and more concretely when checking recursive definitions. Informally, we achieve the desired effect by creating and propagating constraints between stages while checking expressions, and resolving the constraints while checking a recursive definition.

Formally, our algorithm returns for every context Γ and unannotated expression e° either an error if no annotation e of e° is typable in Γ or else a most general annotation e

of e° and typing of the form $C \Rightarrow T$ where C is a set of constraints (stage inequalities), and T is an annotated type subject to the following properties:

Soundness: for every stage substitution ρ satisfying C, we have $\rho\Gamma \vdash \rho e : \rho T$.

Completeness: for every stage substitution ρ' and annotation e' of e° such that $\rho'\Gamma \vdash e' : T'$, there exists ρ, a stage substitution such that ρ satisfies C and $\rho\Gamma = \rho'\Gamma$ and $\rho e = e'$ and $\rho T \preceq T'$.

The notion of constraint system and satisfaction are defined formally as follows.

Definition 11 (Constraint and constraint systems)

1. A stage constraint *is a pair of stages, written* $s_1 \sqsubseteq s_2$.
2. A constraint system *is a finite set of stage constraints.*
3. *A stage substitution* ρ *satisfies a constraint system* C, *written* $\rho \models C$, *if for every constraint* $s_1 \sqsubseteq s_2$ *in* C, *we have* $\rho(s_1) \sqsubseteq \rho(s_2)$.

Note that the stage substitution that maps all stage variables to ∞ is a solution of all constraint systems.

We now turn to the formal description of the algorithm, which is adapted from [7]. The inference algorithm $\mathsf{Infer}(V, \Gamma, e^\circ)$ takes as input a context Γ, an unannotated expression e° and an auxiliary parameter V that represents the stage variables that have been previously used during inference (we need the latter to guarantee that we only introduce fresh variables). It returns a tuple (V', C, e, T) where e is an annotated version of e°, T is a sized type, C is a constraint system, and V' is an extended set of stage variables that has been used by the algorithm. The invariants are $\mathsf{FV}(\Gamma) \subseteq V$ and $V \subseteq V'$ and $\mathsf{FV}(C, e, T) \subseteq V'$. For practical reasons, we also use a second algorithm $\mathsf{Check}(V, \Gamma, e^\circ, T)$ which returns a tuple (V', C, e), where e is an annotated version of e° such that e has type T in environment Γ (and fails if no such e exists). The invariants are $\mathsf{FV}(\Gamma, T) \subseteq V$ and $V \subseteq V'$ and $\mathsf{FV}(C, e) \subseteq V'$.

Definition 12. *The algorithms* Infer *and* Check *are defined in Figure 3.*

The algorithms rely on several auxiliary functions. First, there are functions axioms , rules , elim that verify compatibility with the specification—here we assume Axioms and Rules to be functional. Then, there is an auxiliary function whnf that computes the weak head normal form of an expression—here we assume that the type system is normalizing, and use the fact that the function will only be called on typable expressions. As mentioned above, we also need an auxiliary function that generates constraints from subtyping judgments—the function is used in Check and the rule for fixpoints. Besides, there are auxiliary functions for fixpoints.

The algorithm is close to the usual type checking algorithm of CIC. The most difficult part is the case of fixpoints. First, the algorithm type checks the type annotation $T^\star = \Pi\Delta^\circ.\ \Pi x : I^\star\ u^\circ.\ U^\star$ and gets, as part of the result, an annotated term T that corresponds to the final type of the recursive definition, as well as it's sort, W. Here, we identify the stage variable α annotating the decreasing inductive argument. Next, we compute from U and $U^\star$, the expected return type, $\widehat{U}$, for the body of the recursive definition using the shift function, which replaces all stage annotations s in recursive positions by $\widehat{s}$; in addition, shift returns the set $V^\star$ of replaced variables. Once done, we check that the body e° can be decorated into an expression e of type $\widehat{T} = \Pi\Delta.\ \Pi x : I^{\widehat{\alpha}}\ \boldsymbol{u}.\ \widehat{U}$. Finally, we call the auxiliary function RecCheck to guarantee termination. The function RecCheck takes as input:

- the stage variable α which corresponds to the recursive argument, and which must be mapped to a fresh base stage $\imath$;
- a set of stage variables $V^\star$ that must be mapped to a stage expression with the same base stage as α. The set $V^\star$ is determined by the position types in the tag of the recursive definition. In particular, we have $\alpha \in V^\star$;
- a set of stage variables $V^{\neq}$ that must be mapped to a stage expression with a base stage different from $\imath$;
- a set of constraints C';

and returns an error or a set of constraints subject to some conditions. In [7], we provide an implementation of RecCheck and a proof of some soundness and completeness conditions. We use these results in the proof of the proposition below.

Proposition 1. *Assume that typable terms and normalizing and that the specification is functional.*

- Check *and* Infer *are sound:*

$$\mathsf{Check}(V, \Gamma, e^\circ, T) = (V', C, e) \quad \Rightarrow \quad \forall \rho \models C.\ \rho\Gamma \vdash \rho e : \rho T$$
$$\mathsf{Infer}(V, \Gamma, e^\circ) = (V', C, e, T) \quad \Rightarrow \quad \forall \rho \models C.\ \rho\Gamma \vdash \rho e : \rho T$$

- Check *and* Infer *terminate and are complete:*
  1. *If* $\rho\Gamma \vdash e : \rho T$ *and* $\mathsf{FV}(\Gamma, T) \subseteq V$ *then there exist* V', C, e', ρ' *such that* $\rho' \models C$ *and* $\rho =_V \rho'$ *and* $\rho'e' = e$ *and* $\mathsf{Check}(V, \Gamma, |e|, T) = (V', C, e')$.
  2. *If* $\rho\Gamma \vdash e : T$ *and* $\mathsf{FV}(\Gamma) \subseteq V$ *there exist* V', C, e', T', ρ' *such that* $\rho' \models C$ *and* $\rho'T' \preceq T$ *and* $\rho' =_V \rho$ *and* $\rho'e' = e$ *and* $\mathsf{Infer}(V, \Gamma, |e|) = (V', C, e', T')$.

Proof. By simultaneous induction on the structure of e° for soundness and on the typing derivation for completeness.

Normalization. Both consistency and decidability of type checking and size inference rely on normalization.

Conjecture 1. *If* $\Gamma \vdash M : A$ *taking as specification that of CIC [22] then* M *is strongly normalizing.*

Our earlier work on non-dependent systems demonstrates that it is rather direct to adapt existing model constructions to type-based termination, and that the resulting model is in fact easier to justify than for systems that use a syntactic guard predicate to enforce termination. Thus we strongly believe—but have not checked details—that existing model constructions for CIC, e.g. [16,24], can be adapted immediately to CIC^, using the construction of [6] for inductive definitions. As discussed in Section 2, it is likely that the conjecture can also be deduced from [10].

6 Implementation and Case Studies

We have developed a prototype implementation of the type checker and size inference algorithm for a fragment of CIC⁻, and used it to program quicksort and prove its
correctness.

We have also used CIC⁻ to define general recursive functions, following the approach developed by Bove and Capretta [13] for Martin-Löf's type theory—we have
not carried this work with the prototype because it currently does not support inductive families. In a nutshell, the approach consists in defining an inductive predicate
that characterizes the domain of the function to be defined, and to define the function
by induction on the proof that the argument is in the domain. One difficulty with this
approach is that it requires to prove some inversion lemmas in a very contrived way,
not using Coq standard tactics for inversion [5,8]. In a type-based setting, the problem
disappears, i.e. there is no restriction on the way the lemmas are proved, because the
statements make it clear that the recursive call will be performed on a smaller proof.
The example illustrates that type-based termination makes it easier to define general
recursive definitions, and suggests that CIC⁻ is a more appropriate setting than CIC to
pursue the program of [5] to support general recursive definitions via tools that generate
termination proofs for functions that are shown terminating with e.g. the size-change
principle [20].

7 Concluding Remarks

We have defined CIC⁻, a variant of the Calculus of Inductive Constructions that enforces termination of recursive definitions via sized types, and shown that it enjoys the
required meta-theoretical properties to serve as a basis for proof assistants. A prototype
implementation has been developed and applied on medium size case studies.

The immediate objective for further work is to resolve outstanding issues that CIC⁻
inherited from F⁻, and that must be solved prior to integrating type-based termination
in Coq, namely mutually recursive types and global definitions. Our longer term goal
is to integrate type-based termination in Coq. We believe that it shall result in a more
robust and flexible system that is easier for users to understand and for developers to
evolve.

References

1. A. Abel. Termination checking with types. *RAIRO– Theoretical Informatics and Applications*, 38:277–320, October 2004.
2. A. Abel. *A Polymorphic Lambda-Calculus with Sized Higher-Order Types*. PhD thesis,
   Ludwig-Maximilians-Universität München, 2006.
3. H. Barendregt. Lambda calculi with types. In S. Abramsky, D. Gabbay, and T. Maibaum, editors, *Handbook of Logic in Computer Science*, pages 117–309. Oxford Science Publications,
   1992. Volume 2.
4. B. Barras. *Auto-validation d'un système de preuves avec familles inductives*. PhD thesis,
   Université Paris 7, 1999.

5. G. Barthe, J. Forest, D. Pichardie, and V. Rusu. Defining and reasoning about recursive functions: a practical tool for the Coq proof assistant. In M. Hagiya and P. Wadler, editors, *Proceedings of FLOPS'06*, volume 3945 of *Lecture Notes in Computer Science*, pages 114–129. Springer-Verlag, 2006.
6. G. Barthe, M. J. Frade, E. Giménez, L. Pinto, and T. Uustalu. Type-based termination of recursive definitions. *Mathematical Structures in Computer Science*, 14:97–141, February 2004.
7. G. Barthe, B. Grégoire, and F. Pastawski. Practical inference for typed-based termination in a polymorphic setting. In P. Urzyczyn, editor, *Proceedings of TLCA'05*, volume 3641 of *Lecture Notes in Computer Science*, pages 71–85. Springer-Verlag, 2005.
8. Y. Bertot and P. Castéran. *Interactive Theorem Proving and Program Development— Coq'Art: The Calculus of Inductive Constructions*. Texts in Theoretical Computer Science. Springer-Verlag, 2004.
9. F. Blanqui. *Théorie des Types et Récriture*. PhD thesis, Université Paris XI, Orsay, France, 2001. Available in english as "Type theory and Rewriting".
10. F. Blanqui. A type-based termination criterion for dependently-typed higher-order rewrite systems. In V. van Oostrom, editor, *Proceedings of RTA'04*, volume 3091 of *Lecture Notes in Computer Science*, pages 24–39, 2004.
11. F. Blanqui. Decidability of type-checking in the calculus of algebraic constructions with size annotations. In C.-H.L. Ong, editor, *Proceedings of CSL'05*, volume 3634 of *Lecture Notes in Computer Science*, pages 135–150. Springer-Verlag, 2005.
12. F. Blanqui and C. Riba. Constraint based termination. Manuscript, 2006.
13. A. Bove and V. Capretta. Modelling general recursion in type theory. *Mathematical Structures in Computer Science*, 15:671–708, February 2005.
14. W.-N. Chin and S.-C. Khoo. Calculating sized types. *Higher-Order and Symbolic Computation*, 14(2–3):261–300, September 2001.
15. T. Coquand and C. Paulin. Inductively defined types. In P. Martin-Löf and G. Mints, editors, *Proceedings of COLOG'88*, volume 417 of *Lecture Notes in Computer Science*, pages 50–66. Springer-Verlag, 1988.
16. H. Geuvers. A short and flexible proof of strong normalisation for the Calculus of Constructions. In P. Dybjer, B. Nordström, and J. Smith, editors, *Proceedings of TYPES'94*, volume 996 of *Lecture Notes in Computer Science*, pages 14–38. Springer-Verlag, 1995.
17. E. Giménez. Structural recursive definitions in Type Theory. In K.G. Larsen, S. Skyum, and G. Winskel, editors, *Proceedings of ICALP'98*, volume 1443 of *Lecture Notes in Computer Science*, pages 397–408. Springer-Verlag, 1998.
18. J. Hughes, L. Pareto, and A. Sabry. Proving the correctness of reactive systems using sized types. In *Proceedings of POPL'96*, pages 410–423. ACM Press, 1996.
19. J.-P. Jouannaud and M. Okada. Executable higher-order algebraic specification languages. In *Proceedings of LICS'91*, pages 350–361. IEEE Computer Society Press, 1991.
20. C.-S. Lee, N. D. Jones, and A. M. Ben-Amram. The size-change principle for program termination. In *Proceedings of POPL'01*, pages 81–92. ACM Press, 2001.
21. N. P. Mendler. Inductive types and type constraints in the second-order lambda calculus. *Annals of Pure and Applied Logic*, 51(1-2):159–172, March 1991.
22. C. Paulin-Mohring. *Définitions Inductives en Theorie des Types d'Ordre Superieur*. Habilitation à diriger les recherches, Université Claude Bernard Lyon I, 1996.
23. David Wahlstedt. Type theory with first-order data types and size-change termination. Technical report, Chalmers University of Technology, 2004. Licentiate thesis 2004, No. 36L.
24. B. Werner. *Méta-théorie du Calcul des Constructions Inductives*. PhD thesis, Université Paris 7, 1994.
25. H. Xi. Dependent Types for Program Termination Verification. In *Proceedings of LICS'01*, pages 231–242. IEEE Computer Society Press, 2001.

Reducing Nondeterminism in
the Calculus of Structures

Ozan Kahramanoğulları

Department of Computing, Imperial College London, UK
ozank@doc.ic.ac.uk

Abstract. The calculus of structures is a proof theoretical formalism
which generalizes the sequent calculus with the feature of deep inference: In contrast to the sequent calculus, inference rules can be applied
at any depth inside a formula, bringing shorter proofs than any other
formalisms supporting analytical proofs. However, deep applicability of
the inference rules causes greater nondeterminism than in the sequent
calculus regarding proof search. In this paper, we introduce a new technique which reduces nondeterminism without breaking proof theoretical
properties and provides a more immediate access to shorter proofs. We
present this technique on system BV, the smallest technically non-trivial
system in the calculus of structures, extending multiplicative linear logic
with the rules mix, nullary mix, and a self-dual non-commutative logical operator. Because our technique exploits a scheme common to all
the systems in the calculus of structures, we argue that it generalizes to
these systems for classical logic, linear logic, and modal logics.

1 Introduction

Developing new representations of logics, which address properties that are central to computer science applications, has been one of the challenging goals of
proof theory. In this regard, a proof theoretical formalism must be able to provide a rich combinatorial analysis of proofs while being able to address properties
such as modularity and locality that are important for applications.

The calculus of structures [6,8] is a proof theoretical formalism, like natural
deduction, the sequent calculus and proof nets, for specifying logical systems
while keeping the above mentioned computational aspects in focus (see, e.g.,
[3,19]). The calculus of structures is a generalization of the sequent calculus.
Structures are expressions intermediate between formulae and sequents which
unify these two latter entities. This way, they provide a greater control over the
mutual dependencies of logical relations. The main feature that distinguishes
this formalism is *deep inference*: In contrast to the sequent calculus, the calculus
of structures does not rely on the notion of main connective and permits the
application of the inference rules at any depth inside a structure. Derivations
are not trees like in the sequent calculus, but chains of inferences.

The calculus of structures was originally conceived to introduce the logical
system BV which admits a self-dual non-commutative logical operator resem-
bling sequential composition in process algebras: System BV is an extension of

M. Hermann and A. Voronkov (Eds.): LPAR 2006, LNAI 4246, pp. 272–286, 2006.

multiplicative linear logic with the rules mix, nullary mix, and a self-dual non-commutative logical operator. Bruscoli showed in [4] that this operator captures precisely the sequential composition of the process algebra CCS. System BV cannot be designed in any standard sequent calculus, as it was shown by Tiu in [23], because deep inference is crucial for deriving the provable structures of system BV. System BV is NP-complete [13].

The calculus of structures also provides systems which bring new insights to proof theory of other logics: In [2], Brünnler presents systems in the calculus of structures for classical logic; in [20], Straßburger presents systems for different fragments of linear logic. In [18], Stewart and Stouppa give systems for a class of modal logics. Tiu presents, in [22], a local system for intuitionistic logic. All these systems follow a scheme in which two of the three rules of system BV, namely atomic interaction and switch rule (i.e., rules ai↓ and s in Figure 2), are common to all these systems. For instance, these two rules give the multiplicative linear logic, whereas a system for classical logic is obtained by adding the contraction and weakening rules to these two rules (see Definition 9). Furthermore, the third rule in system BV (i.e., rule q↓ in Figure 2), which is responsible for the non-commutative context management, is also common to the Turing-complete [21] extension of system BV, presented in [9].

Availability of deep inference does not only provide a richer combinatorial analysis of the logic being studied, but also provides shorter proofs than in the sequent calculus [7]: Applicability of the inference rules at any depth inside a structure makes it possible to start the construction of a proof by manipulating and annihilating substructures. This provides many more different proofs of a structure, some of which are shorter than in the sequent calculus. However, deep inference causes a greater nondeterminism: Because the inference rules can be applied at many more positions than in the sequent calculus, the breadth of the search space increases rather quickly.

Reducing nondeterminism in proof search without losing the completeness of the subject system requires combinatorial techniques which work in harmony with the proof theoretical formalism. Because the rules of the sequent calculus act on the main connective and the notion of main connective resolves in the systems with deep inference, it is not possible to use the techniques of the sequent calculus, e.g., focusing [1] (see Section 7), in the systems with deep inference.

In this paper, we introduce a new technique in the calculus of structures that reduces nondeterminism in proof search and makes the shorter proofs more immediately accessible. For this purpose, we employ system BV that exposes the core of our problem, and argue that these ideas generalize to other systems in the calculus of structures. By exploiting an interaction schema on the structures, we redesign the inference rules by means of restrictions such that the inference rules act on the structures only in those ways which promote the interactions between dual atoms and reduce the interaction between atoms which are not duals of each other. These restrictions on the inference rules reduce the breadth of the search space drastically while preserving the shorter proofs, that are available due to deep inference.

Although this technique is quite intuitive, the completeness argument turned out to be difficult. In order to prove the completeness of these systems, we exploit the strong relation between cut elimination and completeness: We resort to a technique, called *splitting*, introduced in [6] for proving cut elimination for system BV. This technique was used also in [20] and [2] for proving cut elimination for linear logic and classical logic, respectively. Because splitting is closely related with cut elimination, it also justifies the cleanness of our technique. Because our technique exploits a scheme which is common to all the systems in the calculus of structures, we argue that it generalizes to other systems for other logics such as classical logic and linear logic. As evidence, we demonstrate this technique on system KSg, a system for classical logic in the calculus of structures.

The present paper extends our previous work in [13], where we have shown that system BV is NP-complete, and in [10,14], where we have have presented implementations of system BV. We applied the technique presented in this paper to these implementations, and observed a performance improvement in various amounts depending on the structure being proved.

The rest of the paper is organized as follows: In Section 2, we re-collect the notions and notations of the calculus of structures and system BV. Then in the sections 3, 4, and 5 we introduce our technique for reducing nondeterminism at different levels and provide experimental results. In Section 6, we show this technique on a calculus of structures system for classical logic, i.e., system KSg. Section 7 concludes the paper. Space restrictions did not allow us to give the complete proofs of the results. We refer to technical report [12].

2   The Calculus of Structures and System BV

In this section, we collect some notions and definitions of the calculus of structures and system BV, following [6].

In the language of BV atoms are denoted by $a, b, c, \ldots$ Structures are denoted by $R, S, T, \ldots$ and generated by

$$S ::= \circ \mid a \mid \langle \underbrace{S; \ldots; S}_{>0} \rangle \mid [\underbrace{S, \ldots, S}_{>0}] \mid (\underbrace{S, \ldots, S}_{>0}) \mid \bar{S} \ ,$$

where $\circ$, the *unit*, is not an atom. $\langle S; \ldots; S \rangle$ is called a *seq structure*, $[S, \ldots, S]$ is called a *par structure*, and $(S, \ldots, S)$ is called a *copar structure*, $\bar{S}$ is the *negation* of the structure S. A structure R is called a *proper par structure* if $R = [R_1, R_2]$ where $R_1 \neq \circ$ and $R_2 \neq \circ$. Structures are considered equivalent modulo the relation $\approx$, which is the smallest congruence relation induced by the equations shown in Figure 1. A *structure context*, denoted as in $S\{\ \}$, is a structure with a hole that does not appear in the scope of negation. The structure R is a *substructure* of $S\{R\}$ and $S\{\ \}$ is its *context*. Context braces are omitted if no ambiguity is possible: For instance $S[R, T]$ stands for $S\{[R, T]\}$. A structure, or a structure context, is in *normal form* when the only negated structures appearing in it are atoms and no unit $\circ$ appears in it. The BV structures whose normal forms do not contain seq structures are called *flat*.

Associativity	Commutativity	Negation
$\langle\langle R;T\rangle;U\rangle \approx \langle R;\langle T;U\rangle\rangle$	$[R,T] \approx [T,R]$	$\bar{\circ} \approx \circ$
$[[R,T],U] \approx [R,[T,U]]$	$(R,T) \approx (T,R)$	$\overline{\langle R;T\rangle} \approx \langle \bar{R};\bar{T}\rangle$
$((R,T),U) \approx (R,(T,U))$	**Units**	$\overline{[R,T]} \approx (\bar{R},\bar{T})$
Context Closure	$\langle \circ;R\rangle \approx \langle R;\circ\rangle \approx \langle R\rangle$	$\overline{(R,T)} \approx [\bar{R},\bar{T}]$
if $R \approx T$ then $S\{R\} \approx S\{T\}$	$[\circ,R] \approx [R]$	$\bar{\bar{R}} \approx R$
and $\bar{R} \approx \bar{T}$	$(\circ,R) \approx (R)$	

Fig. 1. Equivalence relations underlying BV

In the calculus of structures, an *inference rule* is a scheme of the kind $\rho\,\dfrac{S\{T\}}{S\{R\}}$ where ρ is the *name* of the rule, $S\{T\}$ is its *premise* and $S\{R\}$ is its *conclusion*. Such an inference rules specifies the implication $T \Rightarrow R$ inside a generic context $S\{\ \}$, which is the implication being modeled in the system. An inference rule is called an *axiom* if its premise is empty. Rules with empty contexts correspond to the case of the sequent calculus.

A (formal) *system* $\mathscr{S}$ is a set of inference rules. A derivation Δ in a certain formal system is a finite chain of instances of inference rules in the system. A derivation can consist of just one structure. The topmost structure in a derivation, if present, is called the *premise* of the derivation, and the bottommost structure is called its *conclusion*. A derivation Δ whose premise is T, conclusion is R, and inference rules are in $\mathscr{S}$ will be written as $\begin{smallmatrix}T\\ \Delta\|\mathscr{S}\\ R\end{smallmatrix}$. Similarly, $\begin{smallmatrix}\Pi\|\mathscr{S}\\ R\end{smallmatrix}$ will denote a *proof* Π which is a finite derivation whose topmost inference rule is an axiom. The *length* of a derivation (proof) is the number of instances of inference rules appearing in it.

We say that two systems $\mathscr{S}$ and $\mathscr{S}'$ are *strongly equivalent* if for every derivation $\begin{smallmatrix}T\\ \Delta\|\mathscr{S}\\ R\end{smallmatrix}$ there exists a derivation $\begin{smallmatrix}T\\ \Delta\|\mathscr{S}'\\ R\end{smallmatrix}$ and vice versa. Two systems $\mathscr{S}$ and $\mathscr{S}'$ are *(weakly) equivalent* if for every proof of a structure T in system $\mathscr{S}$, there exists a proof of T in system $\mathscr{S}'$ and vice versa.

The system $\{\circ\downarrow, \mathsf{ai}\downarrow, \mathsf{s}, \mathsf{q}\downarrow\}$, shown in Figure 2, is denoted by BV, and called *basic system* V. The rules of the system are called *unit* ($\circ\downarrow$), *atomic interaction* ($\mathsf{ai}\downarrow$), *switch* (s), and *seq* ($\mathsf{q}\downarrow$). The system $\{\circ\downarrow, \mathsf{ai}\downarrow, \mathsf{s}\}$ is called *flat system* BV, and denoted by FBV.

Guglielmi proves the following result in [6].

Proposition 1. *System* BV *is a conservative extension of system* FBV, *that is, if a flat structure R is provable in* BV, *then it is also provable in* FBV.

$$\circ\downarrow \frac{}{\circ} \qquad \text{ai}\downarrow \frac{S\{\circ\}}{S[a,\bar{a}]} \qquad \text{s} \frac{S([R,T],U)}{S[(R,U),T]} \qquad \text{q}\downarrow \frac{S\langle[R,U];[T,V]\rangle}{S[\langle R;T\rangle,\langle U;V\rangle]}$$

Fig. 2. System BV

There is a straightforward correspondence between flat BV structures and formulae of multiplicative linear logic (MLL) which do not contain the units 1 and ⊥. For example $[(a,b),\bar{c},\bar{d}]$ corresponds to $((a \otimes b) \,\mathscr{V}\, c^{\perp} \,\mathscr{V}\, d^{\perp})$, and vice versa. Units 1 and ⊥ are mapped into ∘, since $1 \equiv \perp$, when the rules mix and mix0 are added to MLL (see, e.g., [6]). In fact, system FBV proves those structures, which are syntactic variations of the formulae that are provable in MLL + mix + mix0. However, as Tiu showed in [23], system BV cannot be designed in a standard sequent calculus, because a notion of deep rewriting is necessary in order to derive all the provable structures of system BV. For a more detailed discussion on the proof theory of BV and the precise relation between BV and MLL, the reader is referred to [6].

3 The Switch Rule

In this section, we redesign the switch rule such that this rule can be applied only in those ways which promote a specific mutual relation between dual atoms in the structure to which it is applied.[1] Below definition puts this mutual relation between atoms formally.

Definition 1. *Given a structure S, the notation* at *S indicates the set of all the atoms appearing in S. We talk about* atom occurrences *when considering all the atoms appearing in S as distinct (for example, by indexing them so that two atoms which are equal get different indices). The notation* occ *S indicates the set of all the atom occurrences appearing in S. The* size *of S is the cardinality of the set* occ *S. Given a structure S in normal form, we define the* structural relation $\downarrow \subseteq$ (occ $S)^2$ *as follows: for every* $S'\{\ \}$, *U, and V and for every a in U and b in V, if* $S = S'[U,V]$ *then* $a \downarrow_S b$. *To a structure that is not in normal form we associate the structural relation obtained from any of its normal forms, since they yield the same relation* $\downarrow_S$.

In order to see the above definition at work, consider the following structure: $S = [a,b,(\bar{b},[\langle\bar{a};c\rangle,\bar{c}])]$. We have at $S = $ occ $S = \{a,\bar{a},b,\bar{b},c,\bar{c}\}$. Then, we have $a \downarrow b$, $a \downarrow \bar{b}$, $a \downarrow \bar{a}$, $a \downarrow c$, $a \downarrow \bar{c}$, $b \downarrow \bar{b}$, $b \downarrow \bar{a}$, $b \downarrow c$, $b \downarrow \bar{c}$, $\bar{a} \downarrow \bar{c}$, $c \downarrow \bar{c}$ (we omit the symmetric relations, e.g., $b \downarrow a$).

---

[1] These relations emerge from a graphic representation of structures, called *relation webs*, justified by the equivalence relations in Figure 1. However, in this paper we give a partial exposure to relation webs, referring the reader to [6].

Intuitively, one can consider the relation $\downarrow_S$ as a notion of interaction: The atoms which are related by $\downarrow_S$ are interacting atoms, whereas others are non-interacting. Proofs are constructed by isolating the atoms, by breaking the interaction between some atoms, and this way promoting the interaction between dual atoms, till dual atoms establish a closer interaction in which they can annihilate each other at an application of the atomic interaction rule. During a bottom-up proof search episode, while acting on structures, inference rules perform such an isolation of atoms: In an instance of an inference rule with the conclusion S, a subset of $\downarrow_S$ holds in the premise. For example, consider the following three instances of the switch rule with the same structure at the conclusion:

$$(i.) \quad \mathsf{s}\,\frac{([\bar{a},a,b],\bar{b})}{[(\bar{a},\bar{b}),a,b]} \qquad (ii.) \quad \mathsf{s}\,\frac{[([\bar{a},b],\bar{b}),a]}{[(\bar{a},\bar{b}),a,b]} \qquad (iii.) \quad \mathsf{s}\,\frac{[(\bar{a},\bar{b},a),b]}{[(\bar{a},\bar{b}),a,b]}$$

While going up, from conclusion to premise, in $(i.)$ $a \downarrow b$ and $b \downarrow \bar{b}$; in $(ii.)$ $b \downarrow \bar{b}$; in $(iii.)$ $a \downarrow \bar{a}$ and $a \downarrow \bar{b}$ cease to hold. However, none of these derivations can lead to a proof. Following proposition expresses the intuition behind this.

Proposition 2. *If a structure R has a proof in* BV *then, for all the atoms a that appear in R, there is an atom $\bar{a}$ in R such that $a \downarrow_R \bar{a}$.*

Often, inference rules can be applied to a structure in many different ways, however only few of these applications can lead to a proof. For example, to the structure $[(\bar{a},\bar{b}),a,b]$ switch rule can be applied bottom-up in twelve different ways, three of them which are given above, but only two of these twelve instances can lead to a proof. With the below definition, we will redesign the switch rule such that only these applications will be possible.

Definition 2. *Let* interaction switch *be the rule*

$$\mathsf{is}\,\frac{S([R,W],T)}{S[(R,T),W]} \quad,$$

where $\mathrm{at}\,\overline{W} \cap \mathrm{at}\,R \neq \emptyset$.

Definition 3. *Let* system BV with interaction switch, *or system* BVs *be the system* $\{\circ\downarrow, \mathsf{ai}\downarrow, \mathsf{is}, \mathsf{q}\downarrow\}$. *Let* system BV with lazy interaction switch, *or system* BVsl *be the system resulting from replacing the rule* is *in* BVs *with its instance, called* lazy interaction switch, *or* lis, *where the structure W is not a proper par structure.*

The switch rule can be safely replaced with the lazy interaction switch rule in system BV without losing completeness. In the following, we will collect some definitions and lemmas which are necessary to prove this result.

Definition 4. *Let R,T be* BV *structures such that $R \neq \circ \neq T$. R and T are* independent *iff, for $\mathscr{S} \in \{$BV, BVs, BVsl$\}$,*

$$\frac{\ \|^{\mathscr{S}}}{[R,T]} \quad implies \quad \|^{\mathscr{S}}_R \quad and \quad \|^{\mathscr{S}}_T \quad.$$

Otherwise, they are dependent.

Proposition 3. *For any* BV *structures* R *and* T, *if* at $\bar{R}$ $\cap$ at $T = \emptyset$ *then* R *and* T *are independent.*

Lemma 1. *For any* BV *structures* R, P, *and* U,

$$
\text{if} \quad \begin{array}{c} \Pi \,\big\|\,\text{BVsl} \\[2pt] [P,U] \end{array} \quad \text{then there is a derivation} \quad \begin{array}{c} R \\ \big\|\,\text{BVsl} \\[2pt] [(R,P),U] \end{array} \ .
$$

Sketch of Proof: If U is not a proper par structure Lemma is proved. Otherwise, by consequent application of the rule Iis bring the partition of the structure U which is dependent with P into the same par context as P.   □

Proposition 4. *In* BV *(*BVs, BVsl*)*, $\langle R; T \rangle$ *is provable if and only if* R *and* T *are provable and* (R, T) *is provable if and only if* R *and* T *are provable.*

The following theorem is a specialization of the shallow splitting theorem which was introduced in [6] for proving cut elimination for system BV. Exploiting the fact that systems in the calculus of structures follow a scheme, in which the rules atomic interaction and switch are common to all these systems, this technique was used also to prove cut elimination for classical logic [2], linear logic [20], and system NEL [9,21] (Turing-complete extension of BV with the exponentials of linear logic). As the name suggests, this theorem splits the context of a structure so that the proof of the structure can be partitioned into smaller pieces in a systematic way. Below we show that splitting theorem can be specialized to system BVsl where the switch rule in system BV is replaced with the lazy interaction switch rule.

Theorem 1. *(Shallow Splitting for* BVsl*) For all structures* R, T *and* P:

1. *if* $[\langle R; T \rangle, P]$ *is provable in* BVsl *then there exists* P_1, P_2 *and* $\begin{array}{c} \langle P_1; P_2 \rangle \\ \Delta \,\|\,\text{BVsl} \\ P \end{array}$ *such*

    that $[R, P_1]$ *and* $[T, P_2]$ *are provable in* BVsl.

2. *if* $[(R, T), P]$ *is provable in* BVsl *then there exists* P_1, P_2 *and* $\begin{array}{c} [P_1, P_2] \\ \Delta \,\|\,\text{BVsl} \\ P \end{array}$ *such*

    that $[R, P_1]$ *and* $[T, P_2]$ *are provable in* BVsl.

Sketch of Proof: Proof by induction, with Lemma 1, similar to the proof of shallow splitting for system BV in [6]: Single out the bottom-most rule instance ρ in the given proof, and do case analysis on ρ.   □

Because inference rules can be applied at any depth inside a structure, we need the following theorem for accessing the deeper structures.

Theorem 2. (Context Reduction for BVsl) *For all structures* R *and for all contexts* $S\{\ \}$ *such that* $S\{R\}$ *is provable in* BVsl, *there exists a structure* U *such that for all structures* X *there exist derivations:*

$$\begin{array}{ccc} [X,U] & & \Vert_{\mathsf{BVsl}} \\ \Vert_{\mathsf{BVsl}} & \quad and \quad & \\ S\{X\} & & [R,U] \end{array} \quad .$$

Sketch of Proof: Proof by induction, with Proposition 4 and Lemma 1, similar to the proof of context reduction for system BV in [6]: Do case analysis on the context $S\{\ \}$. □

We can now prove the following two results:

Theorem 3. *Systems* BV, BVsl, *and* BVs *are equivalent.*

Sketch of Proof: Observe that every proof in BVsl is also a proof in BVs and every proof in BVs is a proof in BV. For the other direction, single out the upper-most instance of the switch rule in the BV proof which is not an instance of the lazy interaction switch rule. Apply Theorem 2 to reduce the context of the premise. Construct a proof in BVsl with Lemma 1 by partitioning the resulting proof by Theorem 1. Repeat the above procedure inductively until all the instances of the switch rule that are not instances of lazy interaction switch rule are removed. □

Let us now consider the rule lis on some examples: In the proof search space of $[(\bar{a},\bar{b}),a,b]$ there are 12 instances of the switch rule. In system FBV, these instances result in 358 different derivations. However, only 6 of these derivations are proofs. Let FBVi denote the system obtained from system FBV by replacing the switch rule with the rule lis. In system FBVi, we observe that we have only the following instances, which lead to 6 proofs mentioned above.

$$\mathsf{lis}\,\frac{[([\bar{a},a],\bar{b}),b]}{[(\bar{a},\bar{b}),a,b]} \qquad\qquad \mathsf{lis}\,\frac{[([\bar{b},b],\bar{a}),a]}{[(\bar{a},\bar{b}),a,b]}$$

When we consider deeply nested structures, we observe that the switch rule can be applied in many more ways due to the deep inference feature. For instance, consider the structure $[([\bar{a}_1,(\bar{a}_2,\bar{b}_2),a_2,b_2],\bar{b}_1),a_1,b_1]$ which is obtained by nesting the structure $[(\bar{a},\bar{b}),a,b]$ in itself. To this structure switch rule can be applied in 51 different ways, but only 4 of these instances provide a proof. These 4 instances are the only possible instances of the rule lis. In particular, the deeper instances of the rule lis (marked above) provide shorter proofs which are not possible in the sequent calculus.

We have implemented the systems above in Maude [5] as described in [10,11]. In these implementations, inference rules are expressed as (conditional) term rewriting rules. For proof search, we use the built-in breadth-first search function. Some representative examples of our experiments for comparing the performance of systems FBV and FBVi are as follows: (All the experiments below are performed on an Intel Core Duo 1.83 GHz processor.)

1. $[a,b,(\bar{a},\bar{c}),(\bar{b},c)]$ 2. $[a,b,(\bar{a},\bar{b},[a,b,(\bar{a},\bar{b})])]$

3. $[a,b,(\bar{a},\bar{b},[c,d,(\bar{c},\bar{d})])]$ 4. $[a,b,(\bar{a},\bar{b},[c,d,(\bar{c},\bar{d},[e,f,(\bar{e},\bar{f})])])]$

Query	System	# states explored	finds a proof in # ms (cpu)	Query	System	# states explored	finds a proof in # ms (cpu)
1.	FBV	342	60	2.	FBV	1041	100
	FBVi	34	10		FBVi	264	0
3.	FBV	1671	310	4.	FBV	(*)	
	FBVi	140	0		FBVi	6595	1370

(∗) On this query, search halted by running out of memory after having spent approximately 3GB memory and 80 minutes (cpu).

4   The Seq Rule

At a first glance, the rules switch and seq appear to be different in nature due to the different logical operators they work on. However, at a closer inspection of these rules, one can observe that both of these rules manage the context of the structures they are applied at: While the switch rule reduces the interaction in the structures involving a copar structure in a bottom-up application, the seq rule does the same with the structures involving seq structures. In this section, exploiting this observation, we will carry the ideas from the previous section to the seq rule.

Definition 5. *Let the system consisting of the rules*

$$q_1\downarrow \frac{S\langle [R,T];[U,V]\rangle}{S[\langle R;U\rangle,\langle T;V\rangle]} \quad q_2\downarrow \frac{S\langle R;T\rangle}{S[R,T]} \quad lq_3\downarrow \frac{S\langle [R,W];T\rangle}{S[W,\langle R;T\rangle]} \quad lq_4\downarrow \frac{S\langle R;[T,W]\rangle}{S[W,\langle R;T\rangle]}$$

where W is not a proper par structure, and none of the structures R, T, U, V, W is the unit $\circ$, be the lazy seq system V, *or* QVl.

In the above definition, we partition the seq rule, making its instances with respect to the unit specific. This way, one can also observe the similarity between the switch rule and seq rule, in particular the rules $lq_3\downarrow$ and $lq_4\downarrow$. In fact, Retoré gives similar rules for Pomset Logic in [17], which is conjectured to be equivalent to BV in [6]. However he does not provide a cut-elimination proof. The following proposition, that we proved in [11], shows that in any system the seq rule can be safely replaced with the system QVl.

Proposition 5. *System QVl and system $\{q\downarrow\}$ are strongly equivalent.*

Proposition 6. *Let $\mathscr{S} \in \{$BV, BVs, BVsl$\}$. The system resulting from replacing the rule $q\downarrow$ in $\mathscr{S}$ with system QVl and system BV are equivalent.*

Below, we will carry the ideas of the previous section to the seq rule.

Definition 6. *The following rules are called* interaction seq rule 1, lazy interaction seq rule 3, *and* lazy interaction seq rule 4, *respectively,*

$$\mathsf{iq_1}{\downarrow}\ \frac{S\langle[R,T];[U,V]\rangle}{S[\langle R;U\rangle,\langle T;V\rangle]} \qquad \mathsf{liq_3}{\downarrow}\ \frac{S\langle[R,W];T\rangle}{S[W,\langle R;T\rangle]} \qquad \mathsf{liq_4}{\downarrow}\ \frac{S\langle T;[R,W]\rangle}{S[W,\langle T;R\rangle]}$$

where in $\mathsf{iq_1}{\downarrow}$ *we have* at $\overline{R}\cap$ at $T\neq\emptyset$ *and* at $\overline{U}\cap$ at $V\neq\emptyset$; *in* $\mathsf{liq_3}{\downarrow}$ *and in*
$\mathsf{liq_4}{\downarrow}$ *we have* at $\overline{R}\cap$ at $W\neq\emptyset$ *and* W *is not a proper par structure. The system
resulting from replacing the seq rule in system* BVsl *with the rules* $\mathsf{iq_1}{\downarrow}$, $\mathsf{q_2}{\downarrow}$,
$\mathsf{liq_3}{\downarrow}$, *and* $\mathsf{liq_4}{\downarrow}$ *is called* interaction system BV, *or* BVi.

Definition 7. *The following rules are called* non-interaction seq rule 1, non-
interaction seq rule 3 *and* non-interaction seq rule 4, *respectively,*

$$\mathsf{niq_1}{\downarrow}\ \frac{S\langle[R,T];[U,V]\rangle}{S[\langle R;U\rangle,\langle T;V\rangle]} \qquad \mathsf{niq_3}{\downarrow}\ \frac{S\langle[R,W];T\rangle}{S[W,\langle R;T\rangle]} \qquad \mathsf{niq_4}{\downarrow}\ \frac{S\langle T;[R,W]\rangle}{S[W,\langle T;R\rangle]}$$

where in $\underline{\mathsf{niq_1}}{\downarrow}$ *we have* at $\overline{R}\cap$ at $T=\emptyset$ *or* at $\overline{U}\cap$ at $V=\emptyset$; *in* $\mathsf{niq_3}{\downarrow}$ *and in* $\mathsf{niq_4}{\downarrow}$
we have at $\overline{R}\cap$ at $W=\emptyset$.

Remark 1. Every instance of the rule $\mathsf{q}{\downarrow}$ is an instance of one of the rules $\mathsf{iq_1}{\downarrow}$,
$\mathsf{niq_1}{\downarrow}$, $\mathsf{q_2}{\downarrow}$, $\mathsf{liq_3}{\downarrow}$, $\mathsf{niq_3}{\downarrow}$, $\mathsf{liq_4}{\downarrow}$, $\mathsf{niq_4}{\downarrow}$.

Below, we will see that system BV and BVi are equivalent. However, using the
splitting technique, in the form it was used in the previous section, will not be
possible for proving this argument. In order to see the reason for this consider
the structure $[\langle[a,b,c];[d,e]\rangle,\bar{a},\langle\bar{b};\bar{d}\rangle,\langle\bar{c};\bar{e}\rangle]$ which is provable in BVsl (and also
in system BVi). By applying Theorem 1, we can obtain the derivation

$$\mathsf{q_3}{\downarrow}\ \frac{\langle[\bar{a},\bar{b},\bar{c}];[\bar{d},\bar{e}]\rangle}{\mathsf{q_1}{\downarrow}\ \dfrac{[\bar{a},\langle[\bar{b},\bar{c}];[\bar{d},\bar{e}]\rangle]}{[\bar{a},\langle\bar{b};\bar{d}\rangle,\langle\bar{c};\bar{e}\rangle]}} \qquad \text{such that} \qquad \begin{array}{c}\varPi\big\|\mathsf{BVsl}\\ [\bar{a},\bar{b},\bar{c},a,b,c]\end{array} \quad \text{and} \quad \begin{array}{c}\varPi\big\|\mathsf{BVsl}\\ [\bar{d},\bar{e},d,e]\end{array}\ .$$

However, the derivation on the left-hand side above is not possible in system
BVi. For this reason, in the following, we will introduce a generalization of the
splitting Theorem for system BVi.

Theorem 4. *(Shallow Splitting for* BVi*) For all structures* R, T, *and* P: *if
the structure* $[\langle L;R\rangle,U]$ *or the structure* $[(L,R),U]$ *has a proof* $\varPi$ *in* BVsl,
then there are structures $L_1,\ldots,L_m$, $P_{1,1},\ldots,P_{s,2}$, $R_1,\ldots,R_n$ *and there exist
a derivation*

$$[L_1,\ldots,L_m,\langle P_{1,1};P_{1,2}\rangle,\ldots,\langle P_{s,1};P_{s,2}\rangle,R_1,\ldots,R_n]$$
$$\big\|\mathsf{BVi}$$
$$U$$

and proofs

$$\begin{array}{c}\big\|\mathsf{BVi}\\ [L,L_1,\ldots,L_m,P_{1,1},\ldots,P_{s,1}]\end{array} \qquad \text{and} \qquad \begin{array}{c}\big\|\mathsf{BVi}\\ [R,P_{1,2},\ldots,P_{s,2},R_1,\ldots,R_n]\end{array}\ .$$

Sketch of Proof: Proof by induction: Apply Theorem 1 to the proof Π. This delivers a derivation Δ and two proofs Π_1 and Π_2 in BVsl. Take the derivation Δ and permute down all the instances of $\mathsf{niq}_1\!\downarrow$, $\mathsf{niq}_3\!\downarrow$, and $\mathsf{niq}_4\!\downarrow$ in Δ and apply the induction hypothesis to the proofs Π_1 and Π_2.   □

Corollary 1. *Systems* BV *and* BVi *are equivalent.*

Sketch of Proof: Observe that every proof in BVi is also a proof in BV. For the other direction, first construct proof in BVsl by Theorem 3, and then construct a proof in BVi by Theorem 4.   □

Let us now consider system BV and BVi with respect to our Maude implementations. Some representative examples for comparing the performance of systems BV and BVi are as follows:

1. $[\langle a; [b, c]\rangle, \langle [\bar{a}, \bar{b}]; \bar{c}\rangle]$
2. $[\langle\langle([d, \bar{d}], \langle a; b\rangle); c\rangle, \langle \bar{a}; (\langle \bar{b}; \bar{c}\rangle, [e, \bar{e}])\rangle\rangle]$
3. $[\langle\langle(b, c); [d, e]\rangle, \langle [\bar{b}, \bar{c}]; (\bar{d}, \bar{e})\rangle\rangle]$
4. $[\bar{a}, (a, \langle d; \bar{b}\rangle), (b, c), \langle \bar{d}; \bar{c}\rangle]$

Query	System	# states explored	finds a proof in # millisec.	Query	System	# states explored	finds a proof in # millisec.
1.	BV	1263	630	2.	BV	8069	890
	BVi	995	480		BVi	2138	620
3.	BV	11191	1740	4.	BV	123154	5010
	BVi	3696	560		BVi	20371	1050

The restrictions that are imposed on the inference rules of system BVi succeed in eliminating unsuccessful branches in the proof search space of BV structures. However, the rule $\mathsf{q}_2\!\downarrow$ causes still a huge amount of redundant nondeterminism in proof search: For instance, consider the BV structure $[a, \bar{a}, b, \bar{b}]$ which can be trivially proved by applying the rule $\mathsf{ai}\!\downarrow$ twice. To this structure, the rule $\mathsf{q}_2\!\downarrow$ can be applied in 50 different ways, but removing this rule from system BVi results in an incomplete system, because some provable BV structures, e.g., $[\langle a; [b, c]\rangle, \langle [\bar{a}, \bar{b}]; \bar{c}\rangle]$, are not provable without this rule.

5   Cautious Rules

In a bottom-up application of the rules switch and seq in proof construction, besides promoting interactions between some atoms, the interaction between some atoms are broken (for instance, consider the example derivations (*i.*), (*ii.*), and (*iii.*) in Section 3.). However, if the structure being proved consists of pairwise distinct atoms, breaking the interaction between dual atoms, in a bottom-up inference step delivers a structure which cannot be proved. The following definition introduces a further restriction on these inference rules, which exploits this observation and allows only cautious instances of the inference rules which do not break the interaction between dual atoms.

Definition 8. *Let* pruned switch *be the rule* ps *below where* at $\overline{T}$ ∩ at $W = \emptyset$, *and let* pruned seq *be the rule* pq↓ *below where* at $\overline{T}$ ∩ at $U = \emptyset$ *and* at $\overline{R}$ ∩ at $V = \emptyset$:

$$\text{ps } \frac{S([R,W],T)}{S[(R,T),W]} \qquad \text{pq↓ } \frac{S\langle [R,T]; [U,V]\rangle}{S[\langle R;U\rangle, \langle T;V\rangle]} \quad,$$

Let pruned system BV, *or system* BVp *be the system* {o↓, ai↓, ps, pq↓}.

Proposition 7. *Let* P *be a* BV *structure that consists of pairwise distinct atoms and* Π *be a proof of* P *in* BV *(*BVs*,* BVsl*, respectively). In* Π*, all the instances of the rule* s *(*is*,* lis*, respectively) are instances of the rule* ps*; and all the instances of the rule* q↓ *are instances of the rule* pq↓.

Sketch of Proof: It suffices to show that, by Proposition 2, a bottom-up application of the inference rules without respecting the above restrictions result in a structure which is not provable in BV. □

Proposition 8. *Let* P *be a* BV *structure that consists of pairwise distinct atoms and* Π *be a proof of* P *in* BVi*. In* Π*, all the instances of the rule* s *are instances of the rule* ps*; and all the instances of the rule* $\text{iq}_1\downarrow$*,*$\text{q}_2\downarrow$*,* $\text{liq}_3\downarrow$*, and* $\text{liq}_4\downarrow$ *are instances of the rule* pq↓.

Sketch of Proof: Follows immediately from Remark 1 and Proposition 7. □

6 Nondeterminism in Classical Logic

Systems in the calculus of structures follow a common scheme where the context management of the commutative operators is performed by the switch rule. System KSg for classical logic [2] is no exception to this. In this section, we will see that, similar to system BV, the switch rule of system KSg can be safely replaced with the lazy interaction switch rule in order to reduce nondeterminism in proof search.

Definition 9. *The system* KSg *is the system consisting of the rules*

$$\text{tt↓ } \frac{}{\text{tt}} \,, \quad \text{ai↓ } \frac{S\{\text{tt}\}}{S[a,\bar{a}]} \,, \quad \text{s } \frac{S([R,U],T)}{S[(R,T),U]} \,, \quad \text{w↓ } \frac{S\{\text{ff}\}}{S\{R\}} \,, and \quad \text{c↓ } \frac{S[R,R]}{S\{R\}} \,.$$

The rules of the system KSg *are called* axiom, atomic interaction, switch, weakening, *and* contratction, *respectively.* KSg *structures are defined as* FBV *structures with the difference that* ff *is the unit for the* disjunction $[\_,\_]$ *and* tt *is the unit for the* conjunction $(\_,\_)$ *and we also impose the equalities* $[\text{tt},\text{tt}] \approx \text{tt}$ *and* $(\text{ff},\text{ff}) \approx \text{ff}$. *The system* KSgi *is the system obtained from system* KSg *by replacing the rule* s *with the rule* lis.

Theorem 5. *A structure* R *has a proof in* KSg *if and only if there is a structure* R' *and there is a proof of the form*

$$\begin{array}{c} \Big\Vert {\scriptstyle \{s,ai\downarrow\}} \\ R' \\ \Vert {\scriptstyle \{w\downarrow,c\downarrow\}} \\ R \end{array} \quad.$$

Sketch of Proof: If R is provable in KSg, then we can construct the conjunctive normal form of R while going up in the derivation by first applying only the rule c↓ and then only the rule s. Then a proof of conjunctive normal form of R can be constructed by applying first only the rule w↓ and then the rule ai↓. By permuting all the instances of w↓ under the instances of s, we get the desired proof.   □

The reader might realize that there is a significant similarity between the systems {ai↓, lis} and the system FBVi (FBV) (the system for multiplicative linear logic extended by the rules mix and nullary mix). Indeed, these two systems are the same up to the inference rules. However, the treatment of the units in these systems is quite different: In system FBV there is a single unit, which is shared by all the connectives. On the other hand, in system {ai↓, lis}, there are two different units, tt and ff, which are units for different operators. We can now state the main result of this section:

Theorem 6. *System* KSg *and* KSgi *are equivalent.*

Sketch of Proof: Observe that every proof in KSgi is a proof in system KSg. For the other direction, replace the proof Π in {s, ai↓}, delivered from Theorem 5 with a proof Π' in {lis, ai↓} similar to the proof of Theorem 3.   □

7   Discussion

We presented a novel technique for reducing nondeterminism in proof search by restricting the application of the inference rules. This resulted in a class of equivalent systems to system BV where nondeterminism is reduced at different levels. We have also seen that this technique generalizes to system KSg for classical logic. In these systems, inference rules can be applied only in certain ways that promote the interaction, in the sense of a specific mutual relation, between dual atoms. Because of the splitting argument that we use in our completeness proof, which is strongly related to cut elimination, our rules remain clean from a proof theoretic point of view. Because proofs are constructed by annihilating dual atoms, these restrictions reduce the breadth of the search space drastically and preserve the shorter proofs that are available due to deep inference.

We have implemented the proof search for the systems BV and BVi in the lines of [10]. These implementations makes use of the simple high level language, the term rewriting features, and the built-in breadth-first function of the language Maude [5]. In [14], we have presented another implementation of system BV in Java, where different search strategies can be easily employed. This implementation uses the pattern matching preprocessor TOM [16] that makes it possible to integrate term rewriting features into Java. The Maude modules[2] together with representative proof search queries, the source code of the Java implementation[3], and a proof search applet[4] are available online.

---

[2] http://www.iccl.tu-dresden.de/~ozan/maude_cos.html

[3] http://tom.loria.fr

[4] http://tom.loria.fr/examples/structures/BV.html

In our approach, in order to prove the completeness of the restricted systems, we use the *splitting* technique which was introduced and used by Guglielmi in [6] for proving cut elimination in system BV. In [20], Straßburger used the splitting technique to prove cut elimination in the calculus of structures systems for different fragments of linear logic. All the systems in the calculus of structures follow a scheme where the context management is performed by the *switch* rule. Because splitting technique is common to these other systems, our technique should generalize to other systems for linear logic. In Section 6, we have seen that for the case of classical logic, switch rule can be replaced with the lazy interaction switch rule in system KSg. In the light of this result, we conjecture that this technique generalizes to the calculus of structures systems for a class of modal logics [18] that extend system KSg with the modal rules.

Although our technique attacks the same problem as Miller's Forum [15] where Andreoli's focusing technique [1] is used for reducing nondeterminism in linear logic proofs, our approach is different, in essence, than uniform proofs: Focusing technique is based on permuting different phases of a proof by distinguishing between asynchronous (deterministic) and synchronous (nondeterministic) parts of a proof. This approach depends on the fact that in the sequent calculus asynchronous connectives, e.g., par, and synchronous connectives, e.g., copar, can be treated in isolation. However, in the calculus of structures connectives are never in isolation: Asynchronous connectives are always matched to a synchronous connective at each inference step. Furthermore, asynchronous parts of a proof normally spread the object level, given by the logical operators, onto the meta-level. For instance, par operators are mapped to commas. In the systems with deep inference, because what is meta-level in the sequent calculus is brought to the object level, thus there is no meta-level, this is a superfluous operation.

Acknowledgements. The author would like to thank Alessio Guglielmi, Lutz Straßburger, Kai Brünnler, Alwen Tiu, and the anonymous referees for valuable remarks and improvements. This work has been supported by the DFG Graduiertenkolleg 446 at the University of Leipzig, and accomplished during author's stay at the ICCL–TU Dresden as a visiting researcher.

References

1. J.-M. Andreoli. Logic programming with focussing proofs in linear logic. *Journal of Logic and Compututation*, 2(3):297–347, 1992.
2. K. Brünnler. *Deep Inference and Symmetry in Classical Proofs*. PhD thesis, TU Dresden, 2003.
3. K. Brünnler and A. F. Tiu. A local system for classical logic. In R. Nieuwenhuis and A. Voronkov, editors, *LPAR 2001*, volume 2250 of *LNAI*, pages 347–361. Springer, 2001.
4. P. Bruscoli. A purely logical account of sequentiality in proof search. In P. J. Stuckey, editor, *Logic Prog., 18th Int. Conf.*, volume 2401 of *LNCS*, pages 302–316. Springer, 2002.

5. M. Clavel, F. Durán, S. Eker, P. Lincoln, N. Martí-Oliet, J. Meseguer, and C. Talcott. The Maude 2.0 system. In Robert Nieuwenhuis, editor, *Rewriting Techniques and Applications, Proc. of the 14th Int. Conf.*, volume 2706. Springer, 2003.

6. A. Guglielmi. A system of interaction and structure. Technical Report WV-02-10, TU Dresden, 2002. Accepted by ACM Transactions on Computational Logic.

7. A. Guglielmi. Polynomial size deep-inference proofs instead of exponential size shallow-inference proofs. Available on the web at http://cs.bath.ac.uk/ag/p/AG12.pdf, 2004.

8. A. Guglielmi and L. Straßburger. Non-commutativity and MELL in the calculus of structures. In L. Fribourg, editor, *CSL 2001*, volume 2142 of *LNCS*, pages 54–68. Springer, 2001.

9. A. Guglielmi and L. Straßburger. A non-commutative extension of MELL. In M. Baaz and A. Voronkov, editors, *LPAR 2002*, volume 2514 of *LNAI*, pages 231–246. Springer, 2002.

10. O. Kahramanoğulları. Implementing system BV of the calculus of structures in Maude. In L. Alonso i Alemany and P. Égré, editors, *Proc. of the ESSLLI-2004 Student Session*, pages 117–127, Université Henri Poincaré, Nancy, France, 2004.

11. O. Kahramanoğulları. System BV without the equalities for unit. In C. Aykanat, T. Dayar, and I. Körpeoğlu, editors, *Proc. of the 19th Int. Symp. on Comp. and Inform. Sciences, ISCIS'04*, volume 3280 of *LNCS*. Springer, 2004.

12. O. Kahramanoğulları. Reducing nondeterminism in the calculus of structures. Technical Report WV-06-01, TU Dresden, 2006. Available at http://www.ki.inf.tu-dresden.de/~ozan/redNondet.pdf.

13. O. Kahramanoğulları. System BV is NP-complete. In R. de Queiroz, A. Macintyre, and G. Bittencourt, editors, *WoLLIC 2005*, volume 143 of *ENTCS*, pages 87–99, Florianapolis, Brazil, 2006. Elsevier.

14. O. Kahramanoğulları, P.-E. Moreau, and A. Reilles. Implementing deep inference in TOM. In P. Bruscoli, F. Lamarche, and C. Stewart, editors, *Structures and Deduction'05 (ICALP'05 Workshop)*, pages 158–172, Lisbon, Portugal, 2005.

15. D. Miller. Forum: A multiple-conclusion specification logic. *Theoretical Computer Science*, 165:201–232, 1996.

16. P.-E. Moreau, C. Ringeissen, and M. Vittek. A pattern matching compiler for multiple target languages. In G. Hedin, editor, *12th Conference on Compiler Construction, Warsaw*, volume 2622 of *LNCS*, pages 61–76. Springer, 2003.

17. C. Retoré. Pomset logic: A non-commutative extension of classical linear logic. In Ph. de Groote and J. R. Hindley, editors, *Typed Lambda Calculus and Applications, TLCA'97*, volume 1210 of *LNCS*, pages 300–318. Springer, 1997.

18. C. Stewart and P. Stouppa. A systematic proof theory for several modal logics. In R. Schmidt, I. Pratt-Hartmann, M. Reynolds, and H. Wansing, editors, *Advances in Modal Logic*, volume 5 of *King's College Publications*, pages 309 – 333, 2005.

19. L. Straßburger. A local system for linear logic. In M. Baaz and A. Voronkov, editors, *LPAR 2002*, volume 2514 of *LNAI*, pages 388–402. Springer, 2002.

20. L. Straßburger. *Linear Logic and Noncommutativity in the Calculus of Structures.* PhD thesis, TU Dresden, 2003.

21. L. Straßburger. System NEL is undecidable. In R. de Queiroz, E. Pimentel, and L. Figueiredo, editors, *WoLLIC 2003*, volume 84 of *ENTCS*. Elsevier, 2003.

22. A. F. Tiu. A local system for intuitionistic logic. Accepted at LPAR 2006.

23. A. F. Tiu. A system of interaction and structure II: The need for deep inference. to appear on Logical Methods in Computer Science, 2005.

A Relaxed Approach to Integrity and Inconsistency in Databases

Hendrik Decker[1] and Davide Martinenghi[2]

[1] Instituto Tecnológico de Informática
Ciudad Politécnica de la Innovación
Campus de Vera, edificio 8G
E-46071 Valencia, Spain
hendrik@iti.es

[2] Free University of Bozen/Bolzano
Computer Science Department
Piazza Domenicani, 3
I-39100 Bolzano, Italy
martinenghi@inf.unibz.it

Abstract. We demonstrate that many, though not all integrity checking methods are able to tolerate inconsistency, without having been aware of it. We show that it is possible to use them to beneficial effect and without further ado, not only for preserving integrity in consistent databases, but also in databases that violate their constraints. This apparently relaxed attitude toward integrity and inconsistency stands in contrast to approaches that are much more cautious wrt the prevention, identification, removal, repair and tolerance of inconsistent data that violate integrity. We assess several well-known methods in terms of inconsistency tolerance and give examples and counter-examples thereof.

1 Introduction

Integrity constraints are conditions meant to always be satisfied during the lifetime of a database. They are imposed for ensuring that no data may be entered or deleted that would render the information semantically inconsistent. For instance, in a civil registry database containing information about citizens including their marital status, entering the tuple *married(john, mary)* will violate a constraint forbidding bigamy if the tuple *married(john, susan)* is already stored. Also, in the presence of this tuple, a constraint requiring an entry for each spouse of each married couple in the *person* table of the database will signal violation upon an attempt to delete the entry about *susan*.

Semantic inconsistency in databases is supposed to be prevented by methods for checking integrity constraints for satisfaction or violation. Some prominent methods in the literature are [22,20,25,14,7]. Despite the precautions taken by running integrity checking methods, data that violate integrity may sneak into the database in various ways, and usually do so in practice. For instance, the tuples *married(john, mary)* and *married(john, emily)* may both be present in

M. Hermann and A. Voronkov (Eds.): LPAR 2006, LNAI 4246, pp. 287–301, 2006.

the database because the second couple divorced in a foreign country which was therefore not acknowledged at home and the more recent marriage has been entered when the integrity checking module was switched off due to a migration of the database to a new machine, or the second tuple was deleted but reappeared after a faulty backup reload.

Several cautionary ways of dealing with inconsistent data have been discussed in the literature, e.g., [4,9]. These may involve actions of identifying, undoing or repairing inconsistency. However, experience shows that, in general, there is hardly a feasible way to guarantee completely consistency all the time, and even less so in very large databases. Thus, cautious approaches to live with violated integrity constraints have been developed for database query answering. These approaches are able to compute answers to queries in inconsistent databases that are correct in all possible repaired and consistent states that would differ from the given one in some minimal way (in [2] and several works to follow).

As opposed to the cautious measures taken by various approaches to prevent, rectify or tolerate integrity violation, as mentioned above, we propose a much more relaxed manner to tolerate manifest database inconsistencies while preserving consistent cases of integrity. Surprisingly, it turns out that conventional integrity checking methods can be used for that without further ado.

An unquestioned assumption made by all methods for integrity checking in the literature so far has been that constraints are satisfied before each update. This has been deemed necessary for improving the efficiency of determining integrity satisfaction or violation after the update. For several methods, we are going to show what happens, when this assumption is abandoned. Intuitively speaking, we define an integrity checking method to be inconsistency-tolerant if it can guarantee that each instance of any satisfied constraint will remain satisfied after each update attempt, including the rejection of updates that would cause new integrity violations. Importantly, it also includes that (possibly unnoticed) instances of violated constraints may remain so after updates. We demonstrate the usefulness of our definitions by showing that several well-known approaches to database integrity can indeed afford to abandon the consistency assumption without losing their efficiency, while their applicability is vastly increased.

The main contributions of this paper are as follows. (i) We capture with a very general definition the essence of integrity checking methods and soundness and completeness thereof. (ii) We introduce the notion of inconsistency tolerance with respect to integrity checking. (iii) We prove inconsistency (in)tolerance of several well-known integrity checking methods.

After some preliminaries including an abstract definition of the soundness and completeness of integrity checking in section 2, we define and discuss inconsistency tolerance in section 3, where we also specify, independently of any method, a general sufficient condition for inconsistency tolerance. We then verify this property for several methods in section 4. More related work and concluding remarks are addressed in section 5, with an outlook on a broader notion of inconsistency tolerance. Longer proofs have been omitted due to space constraints.

2   A General View of Integrity Checking

Throughout we assume the usual terminological and notational conventions for relational and deductive databases, as known from the standard literature (e.g., [1]). In particular, we refer to the notion of *clause*, i.e., a formula $A \leftarrow L_1 \wedge \cdots \wedge L_n$ where A is an atom and $L_1, \ldots, L_n$ are literals, with the usual understanding of variables being implicitly universally quantified; A is called the *head* and $L_1 \wedge \cdots \wedge L_n$ the *body* of the clause. If the head is missing (understood as *false*) the clause is called a *denial*. A *rule* is a clause whose head is intensional, and a *fact* is a clause whose head is extensional and ground and whose body is empty (understood as *true*). A *database* is a finite set of facts and rules.

With regard to approaches to database integrity, we refer to [22,8,20,25,7] and others as surveyed in [21]. However, the definitions we provide in the following do not rely on any concrete approach. We only point out that integrity constraints are usually conceived as closed well-formed formulae of first-order predicate calculus in the underlying language of the database. Two standard representations of integrity constraints are used in this paper: prenex normal form (where all quantifiers are outermost and all negation symbols are innermost) and denial form. An *integrity theory* is a finite set of integrity constraints. We write $D(IC) = sat$ to indicate that an integrity theory IC is satisfied in a database D, and $D(IC) = vio$ when it is violated.

Different methods employ different notions (commonly the *stable models* [1] or other semantic notions) to define integrity satisfaction and violation, and use different criteria to determine these properties. In fact, each method $\mathcal{M}$ can be identified with its criteria, which in turn can be formalized as a function that takes as input a database (i.e., a set of database facts and rules), a finite set of integrity constraints, and an update (i.e., a bipartite finite set of database clauses to be deleted and inserted, resp.), and outputs upon termination one of the values $\{sat, vio\}$. For a database D and an update U, let D^U denote the updated database (D and D^U are also usually referred to as the old and the new state, respectively). Thus, soundness and completeness of an integrity checking method $\mathcal{M}$ can be stated as follows.

Definition 1 (Integrity checking)
An integrity checking method $\mathcal{M}$ is sound *iff, for any database D, any integrity theory IC such that $D(IC) = sat$ and any update U, the following holds.*

$$\text{If } \mathcal{M}(D, IC, U) = sat \text{ then } D^U(IC) = sat. \tag{1}$$

An integrity checking method $\mathcal{M}$ is complete *iff, for any database D, any integrity theory IC such that $D(IC) = sat$ and any update U, the following holds.*

$$\text{If } D^U(IC) = sat \text{ then } \mathcal{M}(D, IC, U) = sat. \tag{2}$$

It is easy to see that this general definition can be applied to virtually any given concrete method of integrity checking known in the literature, as will also be discussed in the next section.

For several significant classes of logic databases including relational ones, completeness has been shown to hold for the methods in [22,20,25,7] and others in the respective original papers. In particular, the methods discussed here also assume each integrity constraint to be range-restricted, i.e., any variable in an integrity constraint must occur at least in a positive literal in the body. Other methods (e.g., [18,15]) are only shown to be sound and thus provide sufficient conditions that guarantee integrity of the updated database.

We note here that some methods conform to a so-called *compiled* approach, i.e., they do not take into account the input database D, but rather provide an integrity checking condition parametric wrt the database, that is calculated on the integrity theory and the update only. Such condition, referred to as *simplification* (in [22]), is then checked against a specific database.

Example 1. Let $b(\text{ISBN}, \text{TITLE})$ be a relation storing information about books and W the integrity constraint $\leftarrow b(X,Y) \wedge b(X,Z) \wedge Y \neq Z$ stating that no two books with the same ISBN may have different titles. Suppose U is the addition of tuple $b(i,t)$. The method of [22] (and virtually all methods to follow based on a compiled approach) provides the simplified formula $W' = \leftarrow b(i,Y) \wedge Y \neq t$ to be tested on the database whose integrity is to be checked. For any database D, the updated database D^U is guaranteed to have integrity iff $D^U(W') = sat$.

The advantages of such simplifications have amply been appraised in the literature and mainly consist in major gains in efficiency (compare the complexity of W with that of W' in example 1) and in the fact that they can be generated so to speak statically (without knowing the actual database, but only its integrity theory and the update), thus without burdening run time database performance with potentially heavy optimizations. One may object that the update is known only at run time, but, as recognized in later approaches (e.g., [15,12,7]), simplifications can be generated for parameterized patterns of updates conceived by the database designer; when an actual update is executed, the parameters in the simplification are replaced by the actual values and tested against the database. For example, i and t in example 1 may well be considered as placeholders for actual ISBNs and titles, so when book 4 with ISBN 5 is inserted, these values should replace t and i, respectively, in W' and the resulting formula be checked against the database.

Among the methods based on a compiled approach, it is worthwhile to distinguish between simplifications to be checked in the new state (henceforth called *post-tests* and considered, e.g., in [22,20,12,23,19]) and simplifications to be checked in the old state (studied, e.g., in [24,7] and henceforth called *pre-tests*). The advantage of pre-tests is that updates are executed only if known to lead to a consistent database, whereas with a post-test, one needs to execute the update anyway, and then roll it back if the reached database is inconsistent.

Definition 2. *Let IC, IC' be integrity theories and U an update. Consider:*

$$D(IC') = sat \text{ iff } D^U(IC) = sat \tag{3}$$

$$D^U(IC') = sat \text{ iff } D^U(IC) = sat \tag{4}$$

IC' is a pre-test of IC for U if (3) holds for every database D s.t. $D(IC) = sat$.
IC' is a post-test of IC for U if (4) holds for every database D s.t. $D(IC) = sat$.
IC' is a plain pre-test (resp., plain post-test) if (3) (resp. (4)) holds for every database D.

The notion of plain test intuitively indicates a simplification that does not exploit satisfaction of IC in the old state. Indeed, the assumption of integrity in the old state, common to virtually all integrity checking methods, is a key factor for the generation of simplifications that are indeed easier than the original integrity constraints. Simplifications returned by actual methods are therefore expected to be at least as "good" as plain tests, which can thus be used for benchmarking purposes. Next, we show how the integrity assumption may be relaxed.

3   Inconsistency Tolerance of Integrity Checking

In this section we formally define the notion of inconsistency tolerance. As indicated above, the intuition of inconsistency tolerance of an approach $\mathcal{M}$ to integrity checking is that we want to tolerate (or, rather, be able to live with) cases of violated constraints as long as we can ensure that no new cases of integrity violation are introduced. In this way, the cases of integrity that are satisfied before the update will remain satisfied afterwards. To clarify what we mean by "case", we employ the notion of *substitution*, i.e., a mapping from variables to terms (for compactness, vector notation is used to indicate sequences of terms). A substitution σ may also be written as $\{\vec{X}/\vec{t}\}$ to indicate that the variables in $\vec{X}$ are orderly mapped to the terms in $\vec{t}$; the notation $Rng(\sigma)$ refers to the set of variables in $\vec{X}$, $Img(\sigma)$ to the set of variables in $\vec{t}$. Whenever E is a term (resp. formula) and σ is a substitution $\{\vec{X}/\vec{t}\}$, the notation $E\sigma$ denotes the term (resp. formula) that arises from E when each free occurrence of a variable in $\vec{X}$ is simultaneously replaced by the corresponding term in $\vec{t}$; $E\sigma$ is called an *instance* of E. A formula or term which contains no variables is called *ground*. A substitution $\{\vec{X}/\vec{Y}\}$ is called a *renaming* iff $\vec{Y}$ is a permutation of $\vec{X}$. Formulas F, G are *variants* of one another if $F = G\rho$ for some renaming ρ.

Furthermore, a variable x occurring in an integrity constraint W is a *global variable* in W if it is $\forall$-quantified but not dominated by any $\exists$ quantifier (i.e., $\exists$ does not occur left of the quantifier of x in W) in the prenex normal form of W; $Glb(W)$ denotes the set of global variables in W.

Definition 3 (Case). *Let W be an integrity constraint. Then $W\sigma$ is called a case of W if σ is a substitution s. t. $Rng(\sigma) \subseteq Glb(W)$ and $Img(\sigma) \cap Glb(W) = \emptyset$.*

Clearly, each variable in a constraint W represented in denial form is a global variable of W. Note that cases of an integrity constraint need not be ground, and that each constraint W as well as each variant of W is a case of W. Inconsistency tolerance of an integrity checking method $\mathcal{M}$ can be defined as follows.

Definition 4 (Inconsistency tolerance). *An integrity checking method $\mathcal{M}$ is inconsistency-tolerant if, for any database D, any update U, any integrity theory*

IC, any finite set IC' of cases of constraints in IC such that $D(IC') = sat$, the following holds.

$$\text{If } \mathcal{M}(D, IC, U) = sat \text{ then } D^U(IC') = sat. \tag{5}$$

Note that, even though there may well be an infinity of cases of constraints in IC, the finiteness requirement for IC' entails no loss of generality: (5) guarantees satisfaction of any number of cases, if $\mathcal{M}$ returns sat. Note that (5) is a "soundness" condition wrt. inconsistency tolerance. Its dual would define a notion of completeness wrt. inconsistency tolerance, which, however, is hopelessly complied with by any method, since a method returning sat for an empty integrity theory (which it should, as an empty theory is always satisfied), should then also return sat for *any* integrity theory, the empty theory being just an empty set of cases. We therefore only concentrate on soundness wrt. inconsistency tolerance.

Clearly, for checking integrity with an inconsistency-tolerant method $\mathcal{M}$, (5) suggests to compute the very same function as in the traditional case, where satisfaction of all of IC in D is required. Hence, with this relaxation, no efficiency is lost, whereas the gains are immense: with an inconsistency-tolerant method, it is possible to continue database operations even in the presence of (obvious or hidden, known or unknown) violations of integrity (which is rather the rule than the exception in practice), while maintaining the integrity of all cases which comply with the constraints. Whenever $\mathcal{M}$ is employed, no new cases of integrity violation will be introduced, while existing "bad" cases may disappear (by intention or even accidentally) by executing given updates which have passed the integrity test of $\mathcal{M}$. With the strict requirement of integrity satisfaction in the old state, not the least bit of integrity violation was tolerable; hence, the results of virtually all approaches to database integrity would remain nearly useless in practice, unless they can be shown to be inconsistency-tolerant. Fortunately, most known approaches to database integrity are indeed inconsistency-tolerant.

Example 2. [1 continued] Suppose the facts $b(1, 2)$ and $b(1, 3)$ are in D. Clearly, $D(W) = vio$. However, if the fact $b(4, 5)$ is added to D, this is not going to introduce new violations as long as the test $\leftarrow b(4, Y) \wedge Y \neq 5$ obtained in example 1 succeeds. In other words, the method that returned the test tolerates inconsistency in D and can be used to guarantee that all the cases of W that were satisfied in D will still be satisfied in the new state.

It is easily verified that a method based on a compiled approach always returning a plain test is inconsistency-tolerant. To this end, we overload our terminology by applying the notion of inconsistency tolerance to (pre- or post-) tests.

Definition 5. *A pre-test (resp., post-test) IC' of an integrity theory IC for an update U is inconsistency-tolerant whenever, for any case W of a constraint in IC, $D^U(W) = sat$ if $D(IC') = sat$ (resp., $D^U(IC') = sat$) for every database D s.t. $D(W) = sat$.*

Theorem 1. *Let IC be an integrity theory and U an update. Then, any plain (pre- or post-) test of IC for U is inconsistency-tolerant.*

Proof. Assume that IC' is a plain pre-test of IC for U. By definition of plain pre-test, we have $D^U(IC) = sat$ iff $D(IC') = sat$ for every D. Since W is a case of a constraint in IC and, hence, entailed by IC, then $D^U(W) = sat$ if $D^U(IC) = sat$. By transitivity, we have $D^U(W) = sat$ if $D(IC') = sat$ for every D and, hence, a fortiori, for every D consistent with W. The proof is analogous if IC' is a plain post-test of IC for U.   □

Clearly, a method $\mathcal{M}$ that, for any input D, IC, and U, always calculates a plain test of IC for U and then evaluates it in D is inconsistency-tolerant.

3.1 A Sufficient Condition for Proving Inconsistency Tolerance

For any given method $\mathcal{M}$, it is easy to see that its inconsistency tolerance as expressed by (5) directly follows from soundness of integrity checking if condition (6) below is satisfied for each database D, each integrity theory IC, each finite set IC' of cases of constraints in IC s. t. $D(IC') = sat$, and each update U:

$$\text{If } \mathcal{M}(D, IC, U) = sat \text{ then } \mathcal{M}(D, IC', U) = sat \qquad (6)$$

i.e., if satisfaction of $\mathcal{M}$ for an integrity theory entails satisfaction of $\mathcal{M}$ for any set of cases thereof. Hence, we immediately have the following result.

Theorem 2. *Let $\mathcal{M}$ be a sound method for integrity checking. Then, $\mathcal{M}$ is inconsistency-tolerant if (6) holds.*

Proof. For a database D, an update U and a finite set IC' of cases of constraints in IC such that IC' is satisfied in D, a special case of (1) obviously is

$$\text{If } \mathcal{M}(D, IC', U) = sat \text{ then } D^U(IC') = sat \qquad (7)$$

By transitivity between (6), which is assumed to hold, and (7) we obtain (5).   □

Condition (6) is verified for the approaches in [22,20] in section 4. Such methods generate simplified forms of constraints, such that, roughly speaking, the truth value of the simplified form of any case of a constraint W is implied by the truth value of the simplified form of W itself, from which (6) follows. The condition is also verified for methods that are not based on a compiled approach, e.g., [25]. However, it would be wrong to think that inconsistency tolerance came for free with any sound approach to integrity whatsoever, and section 4 also shows examples of methods that are *not* inconsistency-tolerant.

4 Inconsistency Tolerance of Known Methods

4.1 The Method of Nicolas

We show here that the well-known simplification method for integrity checking in [22], henceforth denoted $\mathcal{M}_N$, is inconsistency-tolerant. We do so by a direct generalization of the "if" half of the equivalence statement of its central

Theorem 1. All preparatory results in [22] straightfordwardly hold also in our framework, once we assume that each integrity constraint is range-restricted and a sufficiently large underlying language which remains fixed across updates is used.

For a database D, an integrity constraint W in prenex conjunctive normal form and a tuple r to be inserted into some relational table R, Nicolas' simplification method automatically generates a simplification $\Gamma_{r,W}^+ = W\gamma_1 \wedge \ldots \wedge W\gamma_m$, $m \geq 0$, where the γ_i are unifiers of r and m different occurrences of negated atoms in W that unify with r. The simplification is denoted by Γ_R^+ in [22]; for convenience, we make the updated tuple r and the constraint W explicit. (Symmetrically, for a tuple s to be deleted, a simplification consisting of conjuncts obtained by instantiating W with unifiers of s and non-negated occurrences of matches of s is generated; for simplicity, we only deal with the insertion theorem here; the result about deletions and its proof are completely symmetrical.)

The simplification theorem in [22] states that, if W is known to hold in D, then W holds in the updated state D^U iff $\Gamma_{r,W}^+$ holds in D^U. We now state formally that checking the simplification of W obtained from the update is sufficient for verifying that those cases of W that were satisfied in the old state remain satisfied in the new, updated state, independently of any violations of other cases of W and other constraints.

Theorem 3. *Let D be a database, W an integrity constraint in prenex normal form, W' its matrix, r a tuple to be inserted, and $\Gamma_{r,W}^+$ the simplification of W for r as generated by $\mathcal{M}_N$. For a substitution ζ of some of variables in $Glb(W)$, let $W^* = \forall(W'\zeta)$ be a case of W such that $D(W^*) = sat$. Then, $D^U(W^*) = sat$ if $D^U(\Gamma_{r,W}^+) = sat$.*

Proof. According to condition (6), it suffices to show, under the premise that $D^U(W^*) = sat$, the following.

If $D^U(\Gamma_{r,W}^+) = sat$ then $D^U(\Gamma_{r,W^*}^+) = sat$

where Γ_{r,W^*}^+ is the simplification of W^* for the insertion of r as generated by $\mathcal{M}_N$.

For each negated literal $\sim r_i\zeta$ in W^* such that $r_i\zeta$ unifies with r, we have *a fortiori* that also r_i unifies with r, since $r_i\zeta$ is more specific than r_i. In particular, we have $r_i\zeta\beta_i = r_i\gamma_i = r$, where β_i and γ_i are the substitutions used to compute Γ_{r,W^*}^+ and $\Gamma_{r,W}^+$, respectively. So, we have that, for each conjunct $W^*\beta_i$ in Γ_{r,W^*}^+, there is an identical conjunct $W\gamma_i$ in $\Gamma_{r,W}^+$. Since there may be some r_i that unifies with r whereas the corresponding $r_i\zeta$ does not, $\Gamma_{r,W}^+$ may have some extra conjuncts that have no counterpart in $\Gamma_{r,W\zeta}^+$. Hence $\Gamma_{r,W}^+$ entails Γ_{r,W^*}^+. $\qquad\square$

4.2   The Method of Lloyd, Sonenberg and Topor

Let $W = \forall W'$ be an integrity constraint in prenex normal form and $W^* = \forall(W'\zeta)$ a case of W. In this section, we show that the integrity checking method by

Lloyd, Sonenberg and Topor [20], here denoted $\mathcal{M}_{LST}$, is inconsistency-tolerant. We do so by following the structure of corresponding statements of results and proofs in [20], which actually generalize the basic result in [22] and its proof step by step. In particular, we assume that sets $pos_{D,D'}$ and $neg_{D,D'}$ for capturing the difference between two databases D and D' such that $D \subseteq D'$ be defined precisely as in [20]. The two sets consist of atoms that either are the head of some clause in $U = D' \setminus D$ or the head of a database clause in D that is possibly affected by reasoning forward from clauses in U. It is easy to see by their original definition that these sets capture a superset of facts that are actually inserted ($pos(D, D')$), i.e., provable after the update but not before, or deleted ($neg(D, D')$), i.e., provable before but not after the update. Note that, due to negative literals in the body of clauses that are affeced by an update U, explicit insertions in U may lead to implicit but provable deletions, and explicit deletions in U may lead to implicit but provable insertions.

Let D be a stratified database and U an update which preserves stratification and is partitioned into a set of deletions U_1 and a set of insertions U_2 such that executing the deletions first leads to an intermediate state $D" = D^{U_1}$. Applying U_2 to $D"$ then leads to the updated state $D^U = (D")^{U_2}$. For D^U, we also write D' as in [20]. It is shown in [20] that the sets $pos(D", D')$, $neg(D", D')$, $pos(D", D)$, $neg(D", D)$ capture a superset of facts that are actually inserted ($pos(D", D')$ and $neg(D", D)$) or deleted ($neg(D", D')$ and $pos(D", D)$) by U. Recall that the pos and neg sets are defined only for pairs (D_1, D_2) of databases such that $D_1 \subseteq D_2$, but U may contain any finite amount of clauses to be inserted in or deleted from D. This is why facts actually inserted by the deletions leading from D to $D"$ are captured in $neg(D", D)$ as if they were actually deleted by an inverse update leading from $D"$ to D; and conversely, facts actually deleted by the deletions from D to $D"$ are captured in $pos(D", D)$ as it they were actually inserted by an inverse update from $D"$ to D.

Thus, the following rules for identifying relevant constraints that are potentially violated by an update, as established in [22] for relational databases and generalized to deductive databases in [8], apply as follows. Only those atoms in $pos(D", D') \cup neg(D", D)$ that unify with the atom of a negative literal in W by some mgu ϕ capture a possibly inserted fact that may violate integrity, which is then checked by evaluating $W\phi$. And only those atoms in $neg(D", D') \cup pos(D", D)$ that unify with the atom of a positive literal in W by some mgu ϕ' capture a possibly deleted fact that may violate integrity, which is then checked by evaluating $W\phi'$. Let $\Phi(W)$ be the set of all such substitutions ϕ and ϕ'. In [20], $\Phi(W)$ is obtained as the union of two sets Θ and Ψ of substitutions, which both depend on W. However, this and other details in the proof of 4 in [20], are not relevant in the proof of theorem 5 below.

We now can re-state the simplification theorem in [20] as follows. Part (a) expresses the soundness of the method $\mathcal{M}_{LST}$. Part (b) says that it can be computed with SLDNF. Thereafter, we state that $\mathcal{M}_{LST}$ is inconsistency-tolerant.

Theorem 4 ([20] Lloyd et al.'s simplification theorem)
Suppose $D(W) = sat$. Then we have the following:

(a) $D^U(W) = sat$ if $D^U(\forall(W'\phi)) = sat$ for all ϕ in $\Phi(W)$.
(b) If $D^U \cup \{\leftarrow \forall(W'\phi)\}$ has an SLDNF refutation for all ϕ in $\Phi(W)$, then $D^U(W) = sat$.

Theorem 5 (Inconsistency tolerance of Lloyd et al.'s simplification)
Suppose $D(W^*) = sat$. Then the following holds.
(a) $D^U(W^*) = sat$ if $D^U(\forall(W'\phi)) = sat$ for all ϕ in $\Phi(W, D, U)$.
(b) If $D^U \cup \{\leftarrow \forall(W'\phi)\}$ has an SLDNF refutation for all ϕ in $\Phi(W)$, then $D^U(W^*) = sat$.

We finally remark that inconsistency-tolerant versions of the two corollaries of Theorem 4 in [20] for single clause insertions or deletions can be obtained as straightforwardly as the original results.

4.3   The Method of Sadri and Kowalski

In this subsection, we are going to verify condition (6) for the integrity checking method in [25], henceforth referred to as $\mathcal{M}_{SK}$.

We first note that none of the proofs of the theorems and corollaries in [25] effectively makes use of the assumption that integrity is satisfied in the old state, except the completeness results following from theorems numbered 4 and 5 in [25]. This already provides a certain form of tolerance of $\mathcal{M}_{SK}$ with regard to integrity violation, in the following sense: whenever $\mathcal{M}_{SK}(D, IC, U) = vio$, then the correctly indicated violation of integrity is independent of the integrity status before the update. However, rather than integrity violation, we are after inconsistency tolerance wrt. integrity satisfaction, as expressed in (5). The independence of detecting integrity violation via $\mathcal{M}_{SK}$ from the integrity status before the update is trivial, and was addressed above only to be precise about what we are dealing with. The main result of this subsection is the following.

Theorem 6. *The integrity checking method $\mathcal{M}_{SK}$ is inconsistency-tolerant.*

The function $\mathcal{M}_{SK}(D, IC, U)$ determines integrity violation and satisfaction by the existence or, respectively, absence of a refutation in the search space of the theorem-prover defined in [25] with an element from U as top clause. We illustrate its inconsistency tolerance by an example adapted from [17].

Example 3. Consider a database D consisting of clauses C_1–C_5 shown in figure 1 for unary relations r (regular residence), c (citizen), d (deported) and binary relation w (works for) and the integrity constraint W, expressing that it is impossible to both have a regular residence status and be registered as a deported person at the same time. The given update U inserts a new rule asserting that people working for a registered citizen also have regular residence status.

Clearly, W is not satisfied in D, since $r(jo)$ is derivable via C_1 and C_3, and $d(jo)$ is a fact (C_4). However, $W' = \leftarrow r(tom) \wedge d(tom)$ is a case of W that is satisfied in D since $d(tom)$ does not hold in D.

If W were satisfied in D, the approach of [25] would traverse the search space given by the tree shown in figure 1 (selected literals are underlined), with U

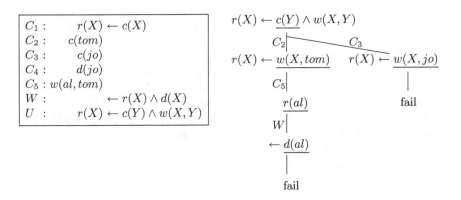

$C_1:$	$r(X) \leftarrow c(X)$
$C_2:$	$c(tom)$
$C_3:$	$c(jo)$
$C_4:$	$d(jo)$
$C_5: w(al, tom)$	
$W:$	$\leftarrow r(X) \wedge d(X)$
$U:$	$r(X) \leftarrow c(Y) \wedge w(X, Y)$

Fig. 1. Clauses and derivation tree of example 3

as top clause. Since this tree is finitely failed, we can conclude that U will not introduce new cases of inconsistency: all cases of integrity constraints that were satisfied in D remain satisfied in D^U. In particular, W' is also satisfied in D^U.

4.4 The Method of Gupta et al.

As we anticipated, not all methods comply with the requirements of definition 5. The well-known method by Gupta et al. [14], henceforth referred to as $\mathcal{M}_{GSUW}$, is indeed *not* inconsistency-tolerant. The integrity constraints considered by their method are of the form

$$\leftarrow L \wedge R_1 \wedge \ldots \wedge R_n \wedge C_1 \wedge \ldots \wedge C_k \qquad (8)$$

in which L is a literal referring to a *local* (and thus accessible) predicate, the R_i's are literals referring to *remote* predicates that cannot be accessed to check the integrity status of the database, while the C_j's are arithmetic comparisons such that the variables occurring in them also occur in L or one of the R_i's[1]; an update, for $\mathcal{M}_{GSUW}$, is an insertion of a tuple in L's relation.

Their main result (theorem 5.2 in [14]) is based on the notion of *reduction* of a constraint W of the form (8): the reduction of W by tuple t inserted in L's local predicate, written $RED(t, L, W)$, is obtained by substituting the components of t for the corresponding variables in L, and then eliminating L. Then to check whether W is satisfied after the insertion of t, and assuming W was satisfied before the insertion, it suffices to check whether $RED(t, L, W) \subseteq \cup_{s \text{ in } L} RED(s, L, W)$, where $\subseteq$ denotes query containment.

For example, $W = \leftarrow l(X, Y) \wedge r(Z) \wedge X \le Z \le Y$ indicates that no Z in r may occur in an interval whose ends are specified by l. Suppose $D = \{l(3, 6), l(5, 10)\}$ and U is the insertion of $l(4, 8)$; then one concludes that $D^U(W) = sat$, since

---

[1] We omit other restrictions, not relevant for the present discussion, included in [14] for technical reasons.

$$r(Z) \wedge 4 \leq Z \leq 8 \subseteq (r(Z) \wedge 3 \leq Z \leq 6) \cup (r(Z) \wedge 5 \leq Z \leq 10),$$

which holds basically because $[4,8] \subseteq [3,10]$.

To show that here we do not have inconsistency tolerance, consider a case $W' = \leftarrow l(4,8) \wedge r(Z) \wedge 4 \leq Z \leq 8$ of W, a database $D = \{l(3,6), l(5,10), r(7)\}$ and the same update U as before. Clearly, W is violated in D whereas W' is satisfied. Again, the method guarantees that U cannot violate integrity provided that D has integrity (for the same containment as before), i.e., $\mathcal{M}_{GSUW}(D,W,U) = sat$. However, satisfaction of W' is not preserved in D^U, therefore $\mathcal{M}_{GSUW}$ is not inconsistency-tolerant.

4.5   The Method of Christiansen and Martinenghi

The method of [6,7] is based on the generation of pre-tests. Given an integrity theory IC and an update U, it consists of the following two steps:

- first, a specific plain pre-test of IC for U is obtained, denoted $\mathsf{After}^U(IC)$, as described in definition 6 below;
- second, $\mathsf{After}^U(IC)$ is reduced in size ("optimized") by removing from it all denials and literals that can be proved to be redundant in it by assuming that IC holds. The result is denoted $\mathsf{Optimize}^{IC}(\mathsf{After}^U(IC))$ and the $\mathsf{Optimize}$ transformation is described in definition 7.

The After operator takes as input an integrity theory and an update and is proved in [7] to return a plain pre-test thereof.

Definition 6. *Let IC be an integrity theory[2] and U an update. The notation $\mathsf{After}^U(IC)$ refers to a copy of IC in which all atoms of the form $p(\vec{t})$ have been simultaneously replaced by $(p(\vec{t}) \wedge \vec{t} \neq \vec{b}_1 \wedge \cdots \wedge \vec{t} \neq \vec{b}_m) \vee \vec{t} \doteq \vec{a}_1 \vee \cdots \vee \vec{t} \doteq \vec{a}_n$, where $p(\vec{a}_1), \ldots, p(\vec{a}_n)$ are all facts that U adds to p and $p(\vec{b}_1), \ldots, p(\vec{b}_m)$ are all facts that U deletes from p.*

It is assumed that $\mathsf{After}^U(IC)$ is represented as a set of denials, which can be obtained by straightforward application of De Morgan's laws. This is then optimized via a terminating proof procedure ($\vdash$) based on resolution and subsumption. We do not delve into the details here and just assume $\vdash$ to be sound.

Definition 7. *Let Σ, Δ be integrity theories; $\mathsf{Optimize}^\Delta(\Sigma)$ is the result of applying on Σ the following rewrite rules as long as possible*

1. $\{\leftarrow C \wedge L\} \cup \Sigma' \Rightarrow \{\leftarrow C\} \cup \Sigma'$ *if* $\Delta \cup \Sigma' \cup \{\leftarrow C\} \vdash \leftarrow C \wedge L$
2. $\{\sigma\} \sqcup \Sigma' \Rightarrow \Sigma'$ *if* $\Delta \cup \Sigma' \vdash \sigma$

where Σ' is an integrity theory, C a conjunction of literals, L a literal, σ an integrity constraint, and $\vdash$ a sound and terminating implementation of provability.

---

[2] Assumed here, for simplicity, to refer to extensional predicates only. The full definition is found in [7,6].

An application of the method, denoted here $\mathcal{M}_{CM}(D, IC, U)$, consists then of evaluating in D the expression $\mathsf{Optimize}^{IC}(\mathsf{After}^{U}(IC))$, which is proved in [7] to be a pre-test of IC for U. Although one can easily derive from theorem 1 that $\mathsf{After}^{U}(IC)$ is an inconsistency-tolerant pre-test of IC for U, step 2 of $\mathsf{Optimize}$ may destroy inconsistency tolerance. In fact, examples can be found where the method does not behave tolerantly with respect to inconsistency.

Example 4. Consider $IC = \{\leftarrow t \wedge p, \leftarrow t \wedge \sim p, \leftarrow t \wedge q(X) \wedge r(X)\}$. Let U be the addition of $q(a)$. The pre-test IC' of IC for U returned by $\mathcal{M}_{CM}$ is $\emptyset$ (the update cannot violate integrity if the database before the update has integrity), since $\leftarrow t$ can be derived from IC, which subsumes all denials belonging to $\mathsf{After}^{U}(IC) = \{\leftarrow t \wedge p, \leftarrow t \wedge \sim p, \leftarrow t \wedge q(X) \wedge r(X), \leftarrow t \wedge r(a)\}$.

Now, let $D = \{t, r(a)\}$ and consider a case $W = \leftarrow t \wedge q(a) \wedge r(a)$ of a constraint in IC. We have: $D(IC) = vio$, $D(W) = sat$ and $D(IC') = sat$. However, $D^{U}(W) = vio$, which shows that $\mathcal{M}_{CM}$ is not inconsistency-tolerant.

One may object that IC above had redundancies, since it is equivalent to $\leftarrow t$ and, if it had been expressed like that, there will be no discussion about satisfaction of a case $\leftarrow t \wedge q(a) \wedge r(a)$ simply because $\leftarrow t \wedge q(a) \wedge r(a)$ would not have been a case. This indicates that inconsistency tolerance by case was lost because the method optimized "too much". It can be shown with a similar example that $\mathcal{M}_{CM}$ is not unsatisfiability-tolerant either (indeed, IC in example 4 is unsatisfiable if t is in D). However, excessive optimizations coming from the interplay between different constraints are avoided if IC contains a single constraint (or constraints that, pairwise, have no predicate in common, which is a likely circumstance).

Theorem 7. *Let $IC = \{W\}$ be an integrity theory, W a denial, U an update. Then the pre-test IC' of IC for U obtained by $\mathcal{M}_{CM}$ is inconsistency-tolerant.*

5   Discussion

Efficient integrity checking has been recognized by a large body of research as a fundamental database topic for more than two decades. As mentioned, methods exist in which the checking phase proper is preceded by a compilation phase that generates either a pre-test [16,24,7] or a post-test [22,19] for integrity. Other methods regard integrity checking as an instance of query answering and modify the behavior of the query engine for this purpose [8,25]. Indeed, integrity checking can be regarded as a special case of materialized view maintenance: integrity constraints are defined as views that must always remain empty for the database to be consistent [13,10].

Intuitively, it seems unrealistic to assume that integrity in databases is always completely satisfied. This, however, is exactly the premise for virtually all known approaches to integrity checking. The unease about this intuitive conflict has motivated our relaxation of the consistency requirement on the basis of the notion of satisfaction by "cases" of an integrity constraint.

One of the main purposes of integrity checking and enforcement is to make data comply with their semantic requirements and thus to have trustable query answers. The results shown in this paper provide us with tools that pave the way towards better data semantics: in this sense, one may "measure" the amount of inconsistency in a database, in a sense that can be defined, e.g., as in [11], and show that such measure cannot increase as long as an inconsistency-tolerant approach is used. In turn, this guarantees, at least in a probabilistic sense, that query answers will tend to be more trustable. For example, in a relational database, the percentage of the data that participate in inconsistencies will necessarily decrease in the new state if the update consists only of insertions.

Methods based on logic programming such as [25] do not take into account irrelevant clauses for refuting denial constraints, and thus, in a procedural sense, do not show the explosive behavior predicted by first-order logic in the presence of inconsistency. However, to the best of our knowledge, the declarative inconsistency tolerance of integrity checking has never been studied nor even defined before. Yet, we reckon that all the mentioned approaches can be reconsidered in terms of this declarative understanding of inconsistency tolerance and most of them can actually be characterized as inconsistency-tolerant. We also observe that all of the performance gains obtained by such integrity checking methods are inherited by their inconsistency-tolerant counterparts, while their applicability is greatly extended. Indeed, in some contexts, certain violations of integrity constraints may be considered acceptable or even unavoidable, e.g., in distributed or federated systems or when data come from unverified sources.

We remark that the inconsistency intolerance of the methods analyzed in this paper may be understood as an indication that approaches to integrity which implement special treatment for certain cases (as $\mathcal{M}_{GSUW}$) or that optimize beyond the scope of a single constraint (as $\mathcal{M}_{CM}$) tend to be less inconsistency-tolerant than other methods. To this end, it should be interesting to study other definitions of inconsistency tolerance that are not based on the notion of case.

The related problems of restoring integrity once inconsistencies are detected (tackled since [2] with the notion of *repair*) and of using active rules for much the same purpose [4], certainly give way to inconsistency tolerance, but cannot be directly used to detect inconsistencies for integrity checking purposes.

Future work will investigate in which sense also other integrity checking methods are inconsistency-tolerant (the literature in this field is indeed immense, as witnessed by, e.g., [21]). To this end, it will be interesting to study how the notion of inconsistency tolerance can be extended to query evaluation and how this relates to consistent query answering in inconsistent databases (e.g., [3]). We also intend to investigate the feasibility of implementing inconsistency-tolerant integrity checking in replicated databases.

References

1. S. Abiteboul, R. Hull, and V. Vianu. *Foundations of Databases.* 1995.
2. M. Arenas, L. E. Bertossi, and J. Chomicki. Consistent query answers in inconsistent databases. In *Proceedings of PODS*, pages 68–79. ACM Press, 1999.

3. L. E. Bertossi and J. Chomicki. Query answering in inconsistent databases. In *Logics for Emerging Applications of Databases*, pages 43–83, 2003.
4. S. Ceri and J. Widom. Deriving production rules for constraint maintainance. In *Proceedings of VLDB 90*, pages 566–577. Morgan Kaufmann, 1990.
5. C. L. Chang and R. C. Lee. *Symbolic Logic and Mechanical Theorem Proving*. Academic Press, 1973.
6. H. Christiansen and D. Martinenghi. Incremental integrity checking: Limitations and possibilities. In *Proceedings of LPAR 2005*, volume 3835 of *LNCS*, pages 712–727. Springer, 2005.
7. H. Christiansen and D. Martinenghi. On simplification of database integrity constraints. *Fundamenta Informaticae*, 71(4):371–417, 2006.
8. H. Decker. Integrity enforcement on deductive databases. In *Proceedings of EDS'86*, pages 381–395. Benjamin/Cummings, 1987.
9. H. Decker. Translating advanced integrity checking technology to SQL. In *Database integrity: challenges and solutions*, pages 203–249. Idea Group, 2002.
10. G. Dong and J. Su. Incremental Maintenance of Recursive Views Using Relational Calculus/SQL. *SIGMOD Record*, 29(1):44–51, 2000.
11. J. Grant and A. Hunter. Measuring inconsistency in knowledgebases. *Journal of Intelligent Information Systems*, in press.
12. J. Grant and J. Minker. Integrity constraints in knowledge based systems. In *Knowledge Engineering Vol II, Applications*, pages 1–25. McGraw-Hill, 1990.
13. A. Gupta and I. S. Mumick, editors. *Materialized views: techniques, implementations, and applications*. MIT Press, 1999.
14. A. Gupta, Y. Sagiv, J. D. Ullman, and J. Widom. Constraint checking with partial information. In *Proceedings of PODS 1994*, pages 45–55. ACM Press, 1994.
15. L. Henschen, W. McCune, and S. Naqvi. Compiling constraint-checking programs from first-order formulas. In *Advances In Database Theory*, volume 2, pages 145–169. Plenum Press, New York, 1984.
16. A. Hsu and T. Imielinski. Integrity checking for multiple updates. In S. B. Navathe, editor, *Proceedings of SIGMOD 1985*, pages 152–168. ACM Press, 1985.
17. R. A. Kowalski, F. Sadri, and P. Soper. Integrity checking in deductive databases. In *Proceedings of VLDB'87*, pages 61–69. Morgan Kaufmann, 1987.
18. S. Y. Lee and T. W. Ling. Further improvements on integrity constraint checking for stratifiable deductive databases. In *VLDB'96*, pages 495–505. Kaufmann, 1996.
19. M. Leuschel and D. de Schreye. Creating specialised integrity checks through partial evaluation of meta-interpreters. *JLP*, 36(2):149–193, 1998.
20. J. W. Lloyd, L. Sonenberg, and R. W. Topor. Integrity constraint checking in stratified databases. *JLP*, 4(4):331–343, 1987.
21. D. Martinenghi, H. Christiansen, and H. Decker. Integrity checking and maintenance in relational and deductive databases, and beyond. In Z. Ma, editor, *Intelligent Databases: Technologies and Applications*, chapter X, page to appear. Idea Group Publishing, 2006.
22. J.-M. Nicolas. Logic for improving integrity checking in relational data bases. *Acta Informatica*, 18:227–253, 1982.
23. A. Olivé. Integrity constraints checking in deductive databases. In *Proceedings of VLDB 1991*, pages 513–523. Morgan Kaufmann, 1991.
24. X. Qian. An effective method for integrity constraint simplification. In *ICDE 88*, pages 338–345. IEEE Computer Society, 1988.
25. F. Sadri and R. Kowalski. A theorem-proving approach to database integrity. In *Foundations of Deductive Databases and Logic Programming*, pages 313–362. Kaufmann, Los Altos, CA, 1988.

On Locally Checkable Properties

Orna Kupferman[1,*], Yoad Lustig[1], and Moshe Y. Vardi[2,3,**]

[1] Hebrew University, School of Eng. and Computer Science,
Jerusalem 91904, Israel
{orna, yoadl}@cs.huji.ac.il
http://www.cs.huji.ac.il/~{orna, yoadl}
[2] Rice University, Department of Computer Science,
Houston, TX 77251, U.S.A.
[3] Microsoft Research
vardi@cs.rice.edu
http://www.cs.rice.edu/~vardi

Abstract. The large computational price of formal verification of general ω-regular properties has led to the study of restricted classes of properties, and to the development of verification methodologies for them. Examples that have been widely accepted by the industry include the verification of safety properties, and bounded model checking. We introduce and study another restricted class of properties – the class of *locally checkable* properties. For an integer $k \geq 1$, a language $L \subseteq \Sigma^\omega$ is *k-checkable* if there is a language $R \subseteq \Sigma^k$ (of "allowed subwords") such that a word w belongs to L iff all the subwords of w of length k belong to R. A property is locally checkable if its language is k-checkable for some k. Locally checkable properties, which are a special case of safety properties, are common in the specification of systems. In particular, one can often bound an eventuality constraint in a property by a fixed time frame.

The practical importance of locally checkable properties lies in the low memory demand for their run-time verification. A monitor for a k-checkable property needs only a record of the last k computation cycles. Furthermore, even if a large number of k-checkable properties are monitored, the monitors can share their memory, resulting in memory demand that do not depend on the number of properties monitored. This advantage of locally checkable properties makes them particularly suitable for run-time verification. In the paper, we define locally checkable languages, study their relation to other restricted classes of properties, study the question of deciding whether a property is locally checkable, and study the relation between the size of the property (specified by an LTL formula or an automaton) and the smallest k for which the property is k-checkable.

* Supported in part by BSF grant 9800096, and by a grant from Minerva.
** Supported in part by NSF grants CCR-9988322, CCR-0124077, CCR-0311326, and ANI-0216467, by BSF grant 9800096, and by Texas ATP grant 003604-0058-2003. Part of this work was done while the author was visiting the Isaac Newton Institute for Mathematical Science, as part of a Special Programme on Logic and Algorithms, supported by a Guggenheim Fellowship.

M. Hermann and A. Voronkov (Eds.): LPAR 2006, LNAI 4246, pp. 302–316, 2006.
© Springer-Verlag Berlin Heidelberg 2006

1   Introduction

It is generally acknowledged that one of the main obstacles to the development of complex computerized systems lies in the process of system verification. In system verification we try to ensure that a model of the system satisfies some specification. Common specification formalisms are based on temporal logic [14] and automata on infinite words [12,19]. Such formalisms are very expressive, for example automata over infinite objects can specify all ω-regular properties. Expressiveness, however, comes at a cost, as verifying a general ω-regular property is sometimes very costly in terms of the resources needed for the verification. As a result, an effort is being made to identify and study less expressive formalisms that allow for an easier verification process. An example of a class of properties that gain a lot of attention is the class of *safety properties* [2,16]. Safety properties require the system to always stay within some allowed region, and their verification can be reduced to invariant checking [10]. A large portion of the properties actually checked in the industry are safety properties. As a result, specialized algorithms for safety properties were developed and are successfully used in practice [5].

Even a larger effect on industrial verification was made by the introduction of *bounded model-checking* (BMC) [6]. In BMC, only a bounded interval of time at the beginning of the computation is checked. While BMC techniques can be applied to general temporal logic properties, they correspond the class of *bounded properties* – properties that regard only an interval of length k, for some $k \geq 0$, in the beginning of the computation [11]. In practice, it is possible to apply BMC to significantly large systems. Thus, focusing on a bounded interval of interest at the beginning of the computation is extremely fruitful in practice.

While BMC techniques check bounded properties, and thus computations are evaluated from their initial state, it is possible to check bounded properties also from an arbitrary state of the computation. This is done in symbolic trajectory evaluation (GTE) [15,1]. In this work we study properties that are similar to properties checked by STE: while still focusing our interest on intervals of a bounded length $k \geq 0$, we would like to regard every k-long time interval throughout the computation.

Let us start with an example: a classical no-starvation specification has the form "throughout the computation, whenever a *req* signal is raised, it is followed by an *ack* signal raised sometime in the future". Such a specification can be seen as characterizing "events" of an unbounded length. The event begins when a *req* signal is raised, and ends when an *ack* signal is raised. In real systems, one can often bound the time frame within which the event should occur. The user may expect, for example, that the following bounded version of the no-starvation specification holds: "throughout the computation, whenever a *req* signal is raised, it is followed by an *ack* signal raised within seven computation cycles".

We introduce in this paper the novel concept of checkability. A language $L \subseteq \Sigma^\omega$ is *k-checkable* if there exists a finite language $R \subseteq \Sigma^k$ such that for every word $w \in \Sigma^\omega$ it holds that $w \in L$ iff all the k-long subwords of w are elements of R. In such a case, we say that L is induced by R. A language is *locally checkable* (or simply checkable) if it is k-checkable for some k. Note that our bounded version of "no starvation" can be characterized by an 8-checkable language. For example, a language in which all 8-long subwords are permissible except those in which a *req* was raised in the first cycle but no *ack* was raised later.

Intuitively, checkable languages are languages that can be verified by a verifier with a bounded memory – one that has access only to the last k-computation cycles. The practical importance of this distinction lies the context of runtime verification [8,4,7]. Run-time verification of a property amounts to executing a monitor together with the system allowing the detection of errors in run time. Run-time monitors for checkable specifications have low memory demand. Furthermore, in the case of general ω-regular properties, when several properties are checked, we need a monitor for each property, and since the properties are independent of each other, so are the state spaces of the monitors. Thus, the memory demand (as well as the resources needed to maintain the memory) grow linearly with the number of properties monitored. Such a memory demand is a real problem in practice. In contrast, we show that a monitor for a k-checkable property needs only a record of the last k computation cycles. Furthermore, even if a large number of k-checkable properties are monitored, the monitors can share their memory, resulting in memory demand that do not depend on the number of properties monitored. This advantage of checkable languages make them particularly suited to be used as specification formalism for run-time verification.

An extensively studied family of languages related to checkable languages is that of *locally testable* languages [13,20]. A language L is locally testable if the answer to the question "is the word w in L?" is determined by a bounded prefix of w and by the set of subwords of w of some bounded length k. Thus, checkable languages are a special case of testable languages: in the case of checkable languages, the only question one might ask of the set of subwords of length k is about their containment in a set R. Note that the bounded-memory advantage that holds for checkable languages does not hold for general testable languages. Indeed, in the case of testable languages, one must maintain the set of all subswords of length k seen so far in order to establish membership, and this involves remembering which subwords were seen at the beginning of the computation. In fact, we prove that locally testable languages constitute a much more expressive formalism. In particular, there are locally testable properties that are not locally checkable at all, and for an arbitrarily large k, there are 2-testable properties that are k-checkable but not $(k-1)$-checkable.

In this paper we define k-checkable and locally checkable languages and study their properties. We provide some basic constructions and observations, and study the relation between locally checkable languages and other fragments of ω-regular properties such as safety properties, bounded properties, uninitialized properties, and testable properties. In addition, we study the problem of deciding whether a specification is locally checkable, or k-checkable, and the relation between the size of the smallest Büchi automaton or LTL formula for a checkable specification and the smallest k for which the specification is k-checkable.

Due to space limitations, some of the proofs appear only in the full version of this paper, available at the authors' web sites.

2   Preliminaries

Consider an alphabet Σ. For a word $w = w_1 w_2 w_3 \ldots$ over Σ, we denote the length of w by $|w|$. Note that $|w|$ is either a natural number (in case $w \in \Sigma^*$), or the first infinite ordinal ω (in case $w \in \Sigma^\omega$). For $i, j \in \mathbb{N}$ such that $i \le j \le |w|$, we denote by $w^i = w_i w_{i+1} \ldots$ the suffix of w starting at the ith letter and denote by $w[i..j] = w_i w_{i+1} \ldots w_j$ the subword between the ith and jth letters. For $w \in \Sigma^\omega$, we denote by $\mathit{suff}(w)$ the set of suffixes of w, i.e. $\mathit{suff}(w) = \{w^i \mid i \ge 0\}$. For a word $w \in \Sigma^\omega$, we denote by $\mathit{sub}(w)$ the set of finite subwords of w, formally, $\mathit{sub}(w) = \{y \in \Sigma^* \mid \exists x \in \Sigma^*, z \in \Sigma^\omega \text{ such that } w = xyz\}$. For $k \ge 0$, we denote by $\mathit{sub}(w, k)$ the set of subwords of w of length k, i.e., $\mathit{sub}(w, k) = \mathit{sub}(w) \cap \Sigma^k$.

A language $L \subseteq \Sigma^\omega$ is k-*checkable* if there exists a finite language $R \subseteq \Sigma^k$ such that $w \in L$ iff all the k-long subwords of w are elements of R. That is, $L = \{w \in \Sigma^\omega \mid \mathit{sub}(w, k) \subseteq R\}$. In such a case, we say that L is induced by R. A language is *locally checkable* (or simply *checkable*) if it is k-checkable for some k. A language $L \subseteq \Sigma^\omega$ is k-*co-checkable* if there exists a finite language $R \subseteq \Sigma^k$ such that $w \in L$ iff there exists a k-long subword of w that is a an element of R. That is, $L = \{w \in \Sigma^\omega \mid \mathit{sub}(w, k) \cap R \ne \emptyset\}$. A language is *locally co-checkable* (or simply *co-checkable*) if it is k-co-checkable for some k.

We assume the reader is familiar with nondeterministic Büchi word automata (NBWs) [17]. We describe an NBW by a tuple $\mathcal{A} = \langle \Sigma, Q, Q_0, \delta, F \rangle$, where Σ is the alphabet, Q is the set of states, $Q_0 \subseteq Q$ is the set of initial states, $\delta : Q \times \Sigma \to 2^Q$ is the transition function, and $F \subseteq Q$ is the set of accepting states. When $|Q_0| = 1$ and $|\delta(q, \sigma)| = 1$ for all $q \in Q$ and $\sigma \in \Sigma$, we say that $\mathcal{A}$ is a deterministic Büchi automaton (DBW). For $S \subseteq Q$, we denote by $\mathcal{A}^S$ the NBW obtained from $\mathcal{A}$ by changing the set of initial states to S; i.e. $\mathcal{A}^S = \langle \Sigma, Q, S, \delta, F \rangle$. For $s \in Q$ we use A^s to denote $A^{\{s\}}$. We denote the language of $\mathcal{A}$ by $L(\mathcal{A})$. For a fragment of the ω-regular languages (e.g., k-checkable) and an NBW $\mathcal{A}$, we say that $\mathcal{A}$ is in the fragment (e.g., $\mathcal{A}$ is a k-checkable NBW) iff $L(\mathcal{A})$ is in the fragment.

Example 1. Let $\Sigma = \{0, 1, 2\}$. The DBW $\mathcal{A}$ below recognizes the language L of all the words that contain 10, 120 or 220 as subwords. Note that L is the 3-co-checkable language L co-induced by $R = \{010, 110, 210, 100, 101, 102, 120, 220\}$. Indeed, a word w is in L iff $\mathit{sub}(w, 3) \cap R \ne \emptyset$.

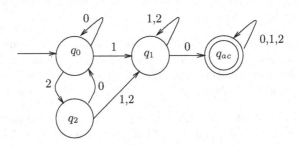

The DFA in Example 1 exhibits some of the subtlety to be found in co-checkable languages. At first glance, one would assume that the traversal through a minimal sub-word of the inducing set should not contain a cycle. This impression, however, is misleading, as demonstrated in the DBW above, where a traversal through the subword 120 contains a cycle.

Consider a language $R \subseteq \Sigma^k$ of words of length k. We denote by $check(R)$ the checkable language induced by R. Formally, $check(R) = \{w \in \Sigma^\omega | sub(w,k) \subseteq R\}$. Similarly, we denote by $co\text{-}check(R)$ the language $\{w \in \Sigma^\omega | sub(w,k) \cap R \neq \emptyset\}$. For a checkable (co-checkable) language L, we denote by $width(L)$ the smallest natural number k for which there exists a set $R \subseteq \Sigma^k$ such that $L = check(R)$ (resp. $L = co\text{-}check(R)$).

Note that a checkable language L may be induced by more than one language of words of length $width(L)$. For example, let $\Sigma = \{a,b,c\}$ and $L = a^\omega + a^*c^\omega + c^\omega$. Both $R_1 = \{aa, ac, cc\}$ and $R_2 = \{aa, ac, cc, ab\}$ induce L. In this case, however, R_2 clearly contains a redundant word.

Proposition 2

1. *For each checkable language L there exists a unique minimal inducing set, denoted $induce(L)$.*
2. *For each co-checkable language L there exists a unique maximal inducing set, denoted $co\text{-}induce(L)$.*
3. *For every checkable language L, it holds that $check(induce(L)) = L$. For every co-checkable language L, it holds that $co\text{-}check(co\text{-}induce(L)) = L$.*

3 Basic Observations

In this section we study some basic properties of checkable (and co-checkable) languages. We begin with the closure of checkable languages with respect to set operations. For a language $R \subseteq \Sigma^*$, the complement of R is the language $\Sigma^* \setminus R$. For a language $L \subseteq \Sigma^\omega$ the complement of L is the language $\Sigma^\omega \setminus L$. In either case, we denote the complement of L by $comp(L)$. It is easy to see that checkable languages are not closed under complementation. For example, the language $\{a^\omega\}$ over the alphabet $\{a,b\}$ is 1-checkable whereas its complement $\{a,b\}^\omega \setminus \{a^\omega\}$ is not checkable. As we now show, however, checkable and co-checkable languages complement each other.

Proposition 3. *Checkable and co-checkable languages complement each other in the following ways:*

1. *The complement of a k-checkable language is k-co-checkable and vice-versa.*
2. *A finite language $R \subseteq \Sigma^k$ induces the k-checkable language L iff $\Sigma^k \setminus R$ co-induces the k-co-checkable language $comp(L)$.*
3. *For a co-checkable language L, $co\text{-}induce(L) = \Sigma^{width(L)} \setminus induce(comp(L))$.*

Note that in the context of verification, we expect specifications of the type "whenever a *req* signal is raised, it is followed by an *ack* signal raised within seven computation cycles", rather then specifications of the type "there exists time window in which a *req* signal is raised, and it is followed by an *ack* signal raised within seven computation cycles". Thus, checkable specifications are more suitable for verification then co-checkable specifications[1].

Proposition 4. *Let L_1 and L_2 be k-checkable languages. Then, $L_1 \cap L_2$ is k-checkable, but $L_1 \cup L_2$ need not be checkable.*

As we discuss further in the sequel, the closure of checkable properties under intersection is crucial for efficient run-time verification.

We now proceed with generic constructions of automata for checkable and co-checkable languages.

Theorem 5

1. *For every $R \subseteq \Sigma^k$ there exists a DBW $\mathcal{A}$, with at most $O(|\Sigma|^k)$ states, such that $L(\mathcal{A}) = check(R)$. Similarly, there exists a DBW $\mathcal{A}'$, with the same parameters, for which $L(\mathcal{A}') = co\text{-}check(R)$. Furthermore, both $\mathcal{A}$ and $\mathcal{A}'$ can be constructed using polynomial space.*
2. *For every $R \subseteq \Sigma^k$, there exists an NBW $\mathcal{A}$, with at most $O(k|R|)$ states, such that $L(\mathcal{A}) = co\text{-}check(R)$. Furthermore, $\mathcal{A}$ can be constructed in polynomial time.*

Intuitively, the DBW construction is based on maintaining the last $k-1$ letters read. The NBW construction is based on guessing where a subword from *co-check(R)* appears, and verifying the guess. In addition, there exists $R \subseteq \Sigma^k$ for which the smallest NBW for *check(R)* has at least $|\Sigma|^{k-1}$ states. Thus, applying nondeterminism in order to get an improved construction is possible only for co-checkable languages.

The basic observations made so far suggest that locally checkable specifications have properties that are desirable in the context of verification. The closure of checkable properties under intersection is crucial for the fact, discussed in Section 1, that run-time verification of several checkable properties requires bounded memory, which does not depend on the number of properties checked. Indeed, combining the monitors of several k-checkable properties, one gets a new single monitor, with the same state space as each of the single monitors. Indeed, if the languages $L_1, L_2, \ldots, L_n$, for n different k-checkable properties, are induced by $R_1, R_2, \ldots, R_n$, respectively, then the intersection $R = R_1 \cap R_2 \cap \cdots \cap R_n$ induces $L_1 \cap L_2 \cap \cdots \cap L_n$. A DBW for *check(R)*, described in Theorem 5, can then serve as a monitor for all the properties: the DBW is run in parallel to the verified system, and once it moves to the rejecting sink (note that all other states are accepting) an error is reported. Note also that while the number of states of the single monitor is exponential in k, the memory demand is linear in k.

---

[1] This is the case since checkable specifications are safety while co-checkable specifications are co-safety (see Proposition 6).

Finally, in the context of model checking we enjoy both the fact that we do not need our monitors to be deterministic, and the fact that we work with complemented specifications, which are co-checkable. Therefore, in the context of model checking, the smaller nondeterministic monitors for co-checkable specifications can be used.

4   Deciding Checkability

In this section we study decision problems related to checkability. We start by investigating the relations between checkable and co-checkable languages and other restricted fragments of ω-regular languages. We then use these observations in order to decide checkability of languages.

4.1   Relation to Other Families of Languages

We first consider safety, co-safety, and bounded languages. Let L be a language of infinite words over Σ. A finite word $x \in \Sigma^*$ is a *bad prefix* for L if for all infinite words $y \in \Sigma^\omega$, the concatenation $x \cdot y$ of x and y is not in L. Thus, a bad prefix for L is a finite word that cannot be extended into an infinite word in L. In a similar fashion, a finite word $x \in \Sigma^*$ is a *good prefix* for L, if for all infinite words $y \in \Sigma^\omega$, the concatenation $x \cdot y$ of x and y is in L. A language L is a *safety language* if every word not in L has a finite bad prefix. A language L is a *co-safety language* if every word in L has a finite good prefix [2]. For a co-safety language L we denote by $good(L)$ the set of good prefixes for L. For $k \geq 0$, a language L is *bounded with bound k* if every k-long word $x \in \Sigma^k$ is either a good prefix, or a bad prefix for L. A language L is *bounded* if there exists $k \geq 0$ for which the language is bounded with bound k. A language is bounded iff it is both safety and co-safety [11].

Two other related families of languages we study are *uninitialized* [9] (also called suffix closed) and *liveness* [2] languages. A language is uninitialized if for every word w in L, every suffix of w is also in L. Thus, a language L is uninitialized iff $suff(L) \subseteq L$. A language L is *liveness* if for every word w in L and every word $v \in \Sigma^\omega$, if w is a suffix of v, then $v \in L$. Thus, L is liveness iff $\Sigma^* \cdot L \subseteq L$. Note that a language L is uninitialized iff $comp(L)$ is liveness

Proposition 6

1. *Checkable languages are both safety and uninitialized. Co-checkable languages are both co-safety and liveness.*
2. *There exists a safety uninitialized language that is not checkable. There exists a co-safety liveness language that is not co-checkable.*
3. *No language, other then $\emptyset$ and Σ^ω, is both bounded and checkable (or co-checkable).*

As discussed in Section 1, checkable languages are a special case of testable languages. A language L is *k-testable* [13,20] if for every two words $w_1, w_2 \in \Sigma^\omega$, if $w_1[0..k-1] = w_2[0..k-1]$ and $sub(w_1, k) = sub(w_2, k)$ then $w_1 \in L$ iff $w_2 \in L$. A language is *locally testable* (or simply *testable*) if it is k-testable for some $k \geq 0$. Every checkable (or co-checkable) language is trivially testable. The other direction, however, does not hold. As discussed in Section 1, the expressive power of testable languages has a computational price, as the memory demand for a general k-testable property is exponential in k. Indeed, while a monitor for a k-checkable language only has to remember the last k letters, a monitor for a k-testable language has to remember all the subwords of length k seen so far.

Proposition 7

1. *There are testable languages that are neither checkable nor co-checkable.*
2. *For every $k \geq 0$, there exists a 2-testable language that is k-checkable but not $(k-1)$-checkable.*
3. *For every k-testable property there is an NBW with at most $2^{|\Sigma|^{O(k)}}$ states.*
4. *There are k-testable properties for which every NBW has at least $2^{|\Sigma|^{\Omega(k)}}$ states.*

4.2   Decision Problems

We now turn to the problem of deciding whether a property is checkable or co-checkable. We consider properties given as NBWs. We first need to study some more properties of checkable languages.

Consider a language L. A word $x \in \Sigma^*$ is a *minimal good prefix* for L if it is a good prefix, and no strict prefix or strict suffix of x are good prefixes. Consider for example the language $L = a\Sigma^\omega \cup bc^*a\Sigma^\omega$. It is easy to see that L is a co-safety language and that the good prefixes of L are the words in $a\Sigma^*$ and $bc^*a\Sigma^*$. Note that a is a good prefix, and since ϵ is not a good prefix, clearly a is a minimal good prefix. On the other hand, a appears as a subword in any good prefix, and therefore a is the only minimal good prefix. The set of minimal good prefixes of L is denoted $min(L)$. For an automaton $\mathcal{A}$, we denote by $min(\mathcal{A})$ the set $min(L(\mathcal{A}))$.

The decision criteria is based on the intuition that a co-checkable language has a finite set of minimal good prefixes. We would have liked to argue that this is a sufficient condition for a language to be co-checkable. This, however, is not true as can be seen by the previous example. Indeed $L = a\Sigma^\omega \cup bc^*a\Sigma^\omega$ has a finite set of minimal good prefixes (namely $\{a\}$), but is not co-checkable.

Theorem 8. *A language L is co-k-checkable iff L is co-safety, liveness, and $min(L)$ is contained in Σ^k. Dually, a language L is k-checkable iff L is safety, uninitialized, and $min(comp(L))$ is contained in Σ^k.*

Proof. We prove the characterization for co-k-checkable languages. The one for k-checkable languages is dual. Assume first that L is co-k-checkable. Then, by Theorem 6, L is co-safety and liveness. We prove that $min(L)$ is is contained in Σ^k. Let $R = co\text{-}induce(L)$, and let $sub(R)$ denote all the subwords of words in R. In the full version, we prove that $min(L) \subseteq sub(R)$. Since $R \subseteq \Sigma^k$, so is $sub(R)$, implying that $min(L) \subseteq \Sigma^k$.

For the other direction, let L be a co-safety and liveness language with $min(L) \subseteq \Sigma^k$. Let R be the set of k-long words that contain minimal good prefixes as subwords. In the full version, we prove that $L = co\text{-}check(R)$.   □

Corollary 9. *A language L is co-checkable iff L is co-safety, liveness, and $min(L)$ is finite. Dually, a language L is checkable iff L is safety, uninitialized, and $min(comp(L))$ is finite.*

We can now use the criteria from Corollary 9 in order to decide whether a given NBW $\mathcal{A}$ is checkable or co-checkable. The most challenging part is the test for the finiteness of the set of minimal good prefixes. For the proof of the next claim we need the following definition: an NBW $\mathcal{A}$ is *co-looping* if it has a single accepting state that is a sink.

Theorem 10

1. *For a co-safety DBW $\mathcal{A}$, deciding whether $min(\mathcal{A})$ is finite is in* NLOGSPACE.
2. *For a co-safety NBW $\mathcal{A}$, deciding whether $min(\mathcal{A})$ is finite is in* PSPACE.

Proof. The NBW case reduces to the DBW case by using the determinization of safety and co-safety NBWs [10]. As the test described below for DBW uses only nondeterministic logarithmic space, we get a polyspace test for NBW.

Given a DBW $\mathcal{A}$, our strategy is to construct a DFW $\mathcal{A}'$ whose language is $min(\mathcal{A})$, and decide whether $L(\mathcal{A}')$ is finite. We now show how to construct $\mathcal{A}'$.

Let $\mathcal{A}$ be an n-states co-safety DBW with language $L \subseteq \Sigma^\omega$. As a first step we construct a co-looping DFW $\mathcal{A}_g$ with $O(n)$ states such that $L(\mathcal{A}_g) = good(L(\mathcal{A}))$.

Let $nonmin(L) = good(L) \setminus min(L)$ be the set of non-minimal good prefixes of L. Given a word $w = w_1 \cdots w_l \in good(L)$, the word w is in $nonmin(L)$ iff either of the following holds.

1. $w[2..l] \in good(L)$ (we classify such words as words of type 1), or
2. $w[1..l-1] \in good(L)$ (we classify such words as words of type 2).

We can construct a DFW $\mathcal{A}_1$, for words of type 1, by adding to $\mathcal{A}_g$ a new state q_{in}^1, making it the initial state, and adding to the transition function of $\mathcal{A}_g$ a transition from q_{in}^1 to the original initial state of $\mathcal{A}_g$, labeled by all the letters in Σ. We denote the set of states of $\mathcal{A}_1$ by Q_1, and its accepting sink by q_{ac}^1.

We can also construct a DFW $\mathcal{A}_2$, for words of type 2, by adding a new accepting sink state q_{ac2}^2 to $\mathcal{A}_g$, making the former accepting state q_{ac}^2 non-accepting, and adding to the transition function of $\mathcal{A}_2$ a transition from q_{ac}^2 to q_{ac2}^2 labeled by all the letters in Σ. Note that a word w is in $good(L)$ iff a run of $\mathcal{A}_2$ on w ends in either q_{ac}^2 or q_{ac2}^2.

We denote by $\mathcal{A}_{min}$ the cross product of $\mathcal{A}_1$ and $\mathcal{A}_2$, where the accepting states set is $(Q_1 \setminus \{q_{ac}^1\}) \times \{q_{ac}^2\}$. The words accepted by $\mathcal{A}_{min}$ are exactly $good(L) \setminus nonmin(L)$ as needed. The number of state of $\mathcal{A}_{min}$ is quadratic in the number of states of the DBW $\mathcal{A}$. Since deciding DFW finiteness amounts to deciding if there exists a cycle on a path between the initial state and an accepting state, deciding finiteness of DFW is in NLOGSPACE and the complexity result follows.   □

We can now combine the tests as suggested in Corollary 9.

Theorem 11. *The problem of deciding checkability is* NLOGSPACE-*complete for DBWs and* PSPACE-*complete for NBWs.*

Proof. For the upper bounds, we follow the characterization in Corollary 9 and check whether $L(\mathcal{A})$ is safety [3], uninitialized [9], and $min(comp(L))$ is finite. In order to check the latter, we construct a deterministic DBW $\tilde{\mathcal{A}}_g$ for $good(comp(L(\mathcal{A})))$. In case $\mathcal{A}$ is an NBW, we construct a DBW $\tilde{\mathcal{A}}$ for $comp(\mathcal{A})$ in polynomial space [10], and can proceed as in Theorem 10.

In case $\mathcal{A}$ is DBW, we proceed as follows: We say that a state q of $\mathcal{A}$ is *useless* if $L(\mathcal{A}^q) = \emptyset$. Since $\mathcal{A}$ is deterministic, after reading a bad prefix $\mathcal{A}$ must be in a useless state. Thus, replacing all the useless states by a single sink, marking the new sink accepting, and the rest of the states non-accepting, results in a DFW $\mathcal{A}_g$ for the bad prefixes of $L(\mathcal{A})$ which are the good prefixes of $comp(\mathcal{A})$.

Note that deciding whether a state is not useless amounts to searching for a cycle with an accepting state reachable from it. Therefore, deciding uselessness in can be done in nondeterministic logarithmic space.

Once we constructed $\mathcal{A}_g$, we proceed by checking the finiteness of $min(\mathcal{A}_g)$ as in Theorem 10.

The lower bound for NBWs is proven by a standard reduction from NBW universality. The same argument applied to DBW implies NLOGSPACE-hardness.
                                                                       □

For the dual case, where we want to test an automaton for being co-checkable, we again use the characterization in Corollary 9:

Theorem 12. *Deciding co-checkability is* NLOGSPACE-*complete for DBWs and* PSPACE-*complete for NBWs.*

Proof. For the upper bounds, we apply the criteria of Corollary 9. We have to check co-safety, liveness and finiteness of $min(L)$. We start with the NBW case. To check whether $L(\mathcal{A})$ is co-safety we apply the procedure of [16][2]. Checking for liveness can be done as in [3]; note that the procedure suggested in [3] can be done in polynomial space. Checking the finiteness of $min(L)$ can be done as in Theorem 10.

As for DBWs, checking for both properties liveness and co-safety can be done in NLOGSPACE. Checking for finiteness of $min(L(\mathcal{A}))$ can be done as in Theorem 10.

---

[2] [16] suggests a procedure for deciding and automaton is safety. We can check for co-safety by complementing $\mathcal{A}$ and checking $comp(\mathcal{A})$ for safety. While complementing $\mathcal{A}$ has an exponential blow-up, this blow-up does not increase the complexity of the decision procedure, since the decision procedure in [16] already involves complementation.

The lower bound for deciding NBWs co-checkability is proven by a reduction from NBW universality, using the same argument as in Theorem 13. For DBW, NLOGSPACE hardness can be proven by a reduction from graph non reachability.   □

We now turn to study the problem of deciding whether L is k-checkable or k-co-checkable for a given k. We describe the reasoning for the case of co-checkability. The considerations in the case of k-checkability are dual.

From Theorem 8 we know that finding the width of a co-checkable language L can be reduced to finding the length of its longest minimal good prefix, and deciding whether L is k-co-checkable can be reduced to checking that L is checkable yet no minimal good prefix of it is of length $k' > k$. In Theorem 10, we constructed a DFW $\mathcal{A}_{min}$ that accepts exactly all the minimal good prefixes of L. Recall that when L is co-checkable, the language of $\mathcal{A}_{min}$ is finite, so $\mathcal{A}_{min}$ contains no cycles. Hence, checking a bound on the length of accepting paths in $\mathcal{A}_{min}$ can be done nondeterministically in space that is logarithmic in the size of $\mathcal{A}_{min}$ (a longer path can be guessed). Accordingly, we have the following.

Theorem 13

1. *Given a DBW $\mathcal{A}$ and an integer k, deciding whether $\mathcal{A}$ is k-checkable (or co-k-checkable) is* NLOGSPACE-*complete.*
2. *Given an DBW $\mathcal{A}$ and an integer k, deciding whether $\mathcal{A}$ is k-checkable (or co-k-checkable) is* PSPACE-*complete.*

By translating LTL formulas to NBWs, the results above imply an EXPSPACE upper bound to the problem of deciding whether an LTL formula is checkable or k-checkable, for a given k. We leave open the question of the tightness of this bound. As we shall see in Section 5, the fact LTL formulas can be easily complemented leads, in the case of width bound, to an upper bound that is tighter than the one obtained by going through NBWs.

5   Bounding the Width

In this section we study the relations between the width of a checkable (or co-checkable) language, and the size of automata or LTL formulas for the language.

5.1   Width vs. Automata Size

We start with Büchi automata. At first sight, it seems that the width of a language of a checkable language can be bounded by the diameter of the smallest DBW recognizing the language. Indeed, it appears that in an accepting run, the traversal through the minimal good prefix should not contain a cycle. This impression, however, is misleading, as demonstrated in the DBW $\mathcal{A}$ from Example 1, where a traversal through the subword 120 contains a cycle. The diameter of the DBW $\mathcal{A}$ is 3, so a bound by the diameter is still possible, but remains open. As detailed below, our bound depends on the size of $\mathcal{A}$ and not only in its diameter. We start with an upper bound:

Theorem 14

1. *For a checkable (or co-checkable) DBW $\mathcal{A}$ with n states, the width of $L(\mathcal{A})$ is bounded by $O(n^2)$.*
2. *For a checkable (or co-checkable) NBW $\mathcal{A}$ with n states, the width of $L(\mathcal{A})$ is bounded by $2^{O(n)}$.*

The proof is based on an analysis of $\mathcal{A}_{min}$ from Theorem 10.

We now prove an exponential lower bounds on the gap between width and size of automata by presenting small NBWs that accept checkable and co-checkable languages of large width. The crucial observation is that an NBW with n states can "characterize" a word w of length exponential in n, in the sense it accepts all strings but w.

For natural numbers $i, n \geq 0$, we denote by $m_n(i) \in \{0,1\}^n$ the n-bit binary string encoding of $i \bmod 2^n$ (e.g. $m_4(5) = 0101$). We denote by $counter(n)$ the string $m_n(0) \cdot \# \cdot m_n(1) \cdots \# \cdot m_n(2^n - 1) \cdot \#$. For example, $counter(3) = 000\#001\#010\#011\#100\#101\#110\#111\#$. Note that the length of $counter(n)$ is $(n+1)2^n$. The word $counter(n)$ is characterized by its first $n+1$ letters (i.e. $00\cdots0\#$), and by the fact that when a letter σ is read, the letter σ' at distance $n+1$ from σ is fixed by simple rules: if σ is $\#$, then so is σ'. If σ is 0, then σ' is 1 if all the letters between σ and the next $\#$ are 1 and is 0 otherwise. Similar rules hold if σ is 1. We refer to these rules as the $(n+1)$-distance rules.

Each of the $(n+1)$-distance rules, as well as the contents of the first $(n+1)$ letters, can be easily checked. Therefore, we can construct an NBW that accepts words that violate one of those rules (simply by guessing which rule is violated and where).

Theorem 15. *There exists an NBW $\mathcal{A}$ with $O(n)$ states such that $L(\mathcal{A})$ is k-checkable but not $(k-1)$-checkable, for $k = (n+1)2^n + 2$.*

Proof. Let Σ be $\{0, 1, \#, b, e\}$. For $n \geq 0$, let x_n be the word $b \cdot counter(n) \cdot e$, and let L be the language of all words that do not contain x_n as a subword. Thus, $L = check(\Sigma^{|x_n|} \setminus \{x_n\})$ and therefore L is $(|x_n|)$-checkable. On the other hand, every word of length $|x_n| - 1$ can be extended to a word in L, so L is not $|x_n| - 1$ checkable. (Details as to see why L can be accepted by an NBW $\mathcal{A}$ of size $O(n)$ can be found in the full version). □

Theorem 16. *There exists an NBW $\mathcal{A}$ with $O(n^2)$ states such that $L(\mathcal{A})$ is k-co-checkable but not $(k-1)$-co-checkable, for $k = 2(n+1)2^n$.*

Proof. We prove the theorem in two steps. First, we describe a language (based on the word $counter(n)$) that is $(n+1)$-co-checkable and has an NBW of size $O(n)$. Next, we examine a small variation of the language, one that still has a small NBW accepting it, but is only k-co-checkable for k exponential in n.

For $n \geq 0$, we denote by L the language $suff(counter(n)^\omega)$ of all the suffixes of the word $counter(n)^\omega$. Like $counter(n)$, all the words in L follow the $(n+1)$-distance rules. Furthermore, every word that begins with an $(n+1)$-long subword of $counter(n)$ and follows the $(n + 1)$-distance rules, is in L. Since the $(n + 1)$-distance rules specify a letter by its preceding $(n + 1)$ letters, these rules can be seen as a set of permissible subwords of length $(n + 2)$. Therefore, L is $(n + 2)$-checkable, and $comp(L)$ is $(n + 2)$-co-checkable. It is also not hard to see that $comp(L)$ is accepted by an NBW of size $O(n)$ that looks for a violation of the $(n + 1)$-distance rules, or a flaw in the first $n + 1$ letters

We now look at a variation of $counter(n)$. Let $\$$ be a new letter. For $n \geq 0$, we denote by $counter^\$(n)$ the word $m_n(0)\cdot\#\cdot m_n(1)\cdots\#\cdot m_n(2^n-1)\cdot\$$ which differs from $counter(n)$ only in the last letter. The word $counter^\$(n)$ is characterized by rules slightly different from the $(n + 1)$-distance rules: the rules now allow $\$$ to appear at distance $n + 1$ from $\#$, but require that $\$$ is preceded by a block of n 1's. We refer to these rules as the $(n + 1)$-$\$$-distance rules. As in the case of $counter(n)$, there exists an NFW of size $O(n)$ that detects $(n + 1)$-$\$$-distance rules violations.

Consider now the language $L' = suff(counter(n)^\omega)) \cup suff(counter^\$(n)^\omega)$, i.e., the language of all words that are either a suffix of $counter(n)^\omega$ or a suffix of $counter^\$(n)^\omega$. The crucial point is that the word is of one of these types, and therefore the letter after a block of n 1's is either always $\#$, or always $\$$. In the full version, we show that while L' is $2|counter(n)|$-checkable and $comp(L')$ is $2|counter(n)|$-co-checkable, L' is not $(2|counter(n)| - 1)$-checkable. Also, an NBW $\mathcal{A}$ for $comp(L')$ has $O(n^2)$ states. Thus, $\mathcal{A}$ is a checkable NBW with $O(n^2)$ states whose language is of width $2(n + 1)2^n$. □

5.2   Width vs. Formula Size

We now turn to consider bounds on the width of a language in terms of an LTL formula defining the language. The main technical tool used in the proof of Theorem 16 is the fact that there is a small NBW detecting violations of the $(d+1)$-distance rules. Since these rules can be easily specified by an LTL formula of size $O(d)$, a lower bound on the width of languages of LTL formulas follows:

Theorem 17

(1) There is an LTL formula φ such that $L(\varphi)$ is checkable of width $2^{\Omega(|\varphi|)}$.
(2) There is an LTL formula φ such that $L(\varphi)$ is co-checkable of width $2^{\Omega(|\varphi|)}$.

Note that since LTL has a negation operand, Claim (2) above follows trivially from Claim (1).

It follows that the gap between the size of an LTL formula defining a checkable language and its width might be exponential. In fact, since LTL formulas are exponentially more succinct than NBWs, Theorems 15 and 16 hint that the gap may be even doubly exponential. Nevertheless, we now show that the gap cannot be larger then an exponential.

Theorem 18. *For a checkable (or co-checkable) LTL formula φ, the width of $L(\varphi)$ is bounded by $2^{|\varphi|^3+2}$.*

Proof. Let φ be a checkable LTL formula, and let L be its language. We denote the of width of L by k. Let $\mathcal{A}$ be an n states NBW for L, and let $\tilde{\mathcal{A}}$ be an $\tilde{n}$ states NBW for $comp(L)$. The crux of the proof is the observation that while k may depend exponentially on n, it depends polynomially on $\max(n, \tilde{n})$. Since complementation in LTL is trivial, the exponential construction of an NBW for the language of an LTL formula bounds both n and $\tilde{n}$ [18]. We prove, by a pumping-lemma type argument, that k is bounded by $n^2\tilde{n} + 3$.

By Theorem 3, we have that $comp(L)$ is co-induced by $\Sigma^k \setminus induce(L)$. We first claim that there is a word $w \in \Sigma^{k-2}$ such that there are $\sigma, \tau \in \Sigma$, for which the following hold. **(1)** $\sigma \cdot w \cdot \tau \in \Sigma^k \setminus induce(L)$, **(2)** there is $\sigma' \in \Sigma$ such that $\sigma' \cdot w \cdot \tau \in induce(L)$, and **(3)** there is $\tau' \in \Sigma$ such that $\sigma \cdot w \cdot \tau' \in induce(L)$.

The existence of w that satisfies Conditions 1-3 follows from the minimality of k. Since $induce(L)$ contains no redundancies, we also know that **(4)** there is $t' \in \Sigma^\omega$ such that $\sigma' \cdot w \cdot \tau \cdot t' \in L$ and **(5)** there is $t \in \Sigma^\omega$ such that $\sigma \cdot w \cdot \tau' \cdot t \in L$.

Assume by way of contradiction that $k \geq n^2\tilde{n} + 3$. Consider the infinite words $u = \sigma \cdot w \cdot \tau \cdot t'$, $v = \sigma' \cdot w \cdot \tau \cdot t'$, and $p = \sigma \cdot w \cdot \tau' \cdot t$. The word u contains the subword $\sigma \cdot w \cdot \tau$, which is (Condition 1) in $\Sigma^k \setminus induce(L)$. Therefore, $u \notin L$. By Conditions 4 and 5, the words v and p are in L.

Let r_u be an accepting run of $\tilde{\mathcal{A}}$ on u, and let r_v and r_p be accepting runs of $\mathcal{A}$ on v and p, respectively. Since $k \geq n^2\tilde{n} + 3$, we also have $k - 2 \geq n^2\tilde{n} + 1$, thus there is a triple of states s_u, s_v, and s_p, of $\tilde{\mathcal{A}}, \mathcal{A}$, and $\mathcal{A}$ respectively, and there is a partition of w to $x \cdot y \cdot z$, with $y \neq \epsilon$, such that the run r_u visits s_u after reading $\sigma' \cdot x$ and after reading $\sigma' \cdot x \cdot y$, the run r_v visits s_v after reading $\sigma \cdot x$ and after reading $\sigma \cdot x \cdot y$, and the run r_p visits s_p after reading $\sigma \cdot x$ and after reading $\sigma \cdot x \cdot y$,

It follows that for all $i \geq 0$, we have the following: $\sigma \cdot x \cdot y^i \cdot z \cdot \tau \cdot t' \notin L$, $\sigma' \cdot x \cdot y^i \cdot z \cdot \tau \cdot t' \in L$, and $\sigma \cdot x \cdot y^i \cdot z \cdot \tau' \cdot t \in L$. From the last two facts, all subwords of length k of $\sigma' \cdot x \cdot y^2 \cdot z \cdot \tau \cdot t'$ and of $\sigma \cdot x \cdot y^2 \cdot z \cdot \tau' \cdot t$ are in $induce(L)$. Hence, so are all the subwords of length k of $\sigma \cdot x \cdot y^2 \cdot z \cdot \tau \cdot t'$, contradicting the fact it is not in L. □

6   Conclusions

We defined k-checkable and locally checkable languages and studied their properties. We showed that memory demand for monitoring k-checkable properties is independent of the number of properties checked. This advantage of checkable languages make them particularly suited to be used as specification formalism for run-time verification.

We studied the relation between locally checkable languages and other fragments of ω-regular properties and showed that safety properties, uninitialized properties, and testable properties, all strictly contain checkable properties. We considered the problem of deciding whether a specification is locally checkable, or k-checkable for a given k, and showed that both problems are PSPACE-complete. Finally, we studied the relation between the width of a checkable language and the size of an NBW or LTL formula for the language, and showed that NBWs and LTL formulas can define checkable languages with an exponentially larger width. An interesting problem that remains open is the relation between the width of a co-checkable language and the size of a DBW for it.

References

1. M. Aagaard, R.B. Jones, and C.-J.H Seger. Combining theorem proving and trajectory evaluation in an industrial environment. In *35th DAC*, pp. 538–541, 1998.
2. B. Alpern and F.B. Schneider. Defining liveness. *IPL*, 21:181–185, 1985.
3. B. Alpern and F.B. Schneider. Recognizing safety and liveness. *Distributed computing*, 2:117–126, 1987.
4. H. Barringer, A. Goldberg, K. Havelund, and K. Sen. Rule-based runtime verification. In *Proc. 5th VMCAI*, LNCS 2937, pages 44–57, 2004.
5. I. Beer, S. Ben-David, and A. Landver. On-the-fly model checking of RCTL formulas. In *Proc. 10th CAV*, LNCS 1427, pages 184–194, 1998.
6. E. M. Clarke, A. Bierea, R. Raimi, and Y. Zhu. Bounded model checking using satisfiability solving. *FMSD*, 19(1):7–34, 2001.
7. M. d'Amorim and G. Rosu. Efficient monitoring of omega-languages. In *Proc. 17th CAV*, LNCS 3576 , 2005.
8. K. Havelund and G. Rosu. Synthesizing monitors for safety properties. In *Proc. 8th TACAS*, LNCS 2280, pages 342–356, 2002.
9. T.A. Henzinger, S.C. Krishnan, O. Kupferman, and F.Y.C. Mang. Synthesis of uninitialized systems. In *Proc. 29th ICALP*, LNCS 2380, pages 644–656, 2002.
10. O. Kupferman and M.Y. Vardi. Model checking of safety properties. *Formal methods in System Design*, 19(3):291–314, November 2001.
11. O. Kupferman and M.Y. Vardi. On bounded specifications. In *Proc. 8th LPAR*, LNCS 2250, pages 24–38. 2001.
12. R.P. Kurshan. *Computer Aided Verification of Coordinating Processes*. Princeton Univ. Press, 1994.
13. R. McNaughton and S. Papert. *counter-free automata*. MIT Pres, 1971.
14. A. Pnueli. The temporal semantics of concurrent programs. *TCS*, 13:45–60, 1981.
15. C.J.H. Seger and R.E. Bryant. Formal verification by symbolic evaluation of partially-ordered trajectories. *FMSD*, 6:147–189, 1995.
16. A.P. Sistla. Safety, liveness and fairness in temporal logic. *Formal Aspects of Computing*, 6:495–511, 1994.
17. W. Thomas. Automata on infinite objects. *Handbook of Theoretical Computer Science*, pages 133–191, 1990.
18. M.Y. Vardi and P. Wolper. An automata-theoretic approach to automatic program verification. In *Proc. 1st LICS*, pages 332–344, 1986.
19. M.Y. Vardi and P. Wolper. Reasoning about infinite computations. *Information and Computation*, 115(1):1–37, November 1994.
20. T. Wilke. Locally threshold testable languages of infinite words. In *10th STACS*, LNCS 665, pages 607–616. 1993.

Deciding Key Cycles for Security Protocols[*]

Véronique Cortier and Eugen Zălinescu

Loria UMR 7503 & INRIA Lorraine projet Cassis & CNRS, France

Abstract. Many recent results are concerned with interpreting proofs of security done in symbolic models in the more detailed models of computational cryptography. In the case of symmetric encryption, these results stringently demand that no key cycle (e.g. $\{k\}_k$) can be produced during the execution of protocols. While security properties like secrecy or authentication have been proved decidable for many interesting classes of protocols, the automatic detection of key cycles has not been studied so far.

In this paper, we prove that deciding the existence of key-cycles is NP-complete for a bounded number of sessions. Next, we observe that the techniques that we use are of more general interest and apply them to reprove the decidability of a significant existing fragment of protocols with timestamps.

1 Introduction

Security protocols are small programs that aim at securing communications over a public network like Internet. The design of such protocols is difficult and error-prone; many attacks are discovered even several years after the publication of a protocol. Two distinct approaches for the rigorous design and analysis of cryptographic protocols have been pursued in the literature: the so-called Dolev-Yao, symbolic, or formal approach on the one hand and the cryptographic, computational, or concrete approach on the other hand. In the symbolic approach, messages are modeled as formal terms that the adversary can manipulate using a fixed set of operations. The main advantage of this approach is its relative simplicity which makes it amenable to automated analysis tools (see, e.g., [7,3,22]). In the cryptographic approach, messages are bit strings and the adversary is an arbitrary probabilistic polynomial-time Turing machine. While results in this model yield strong security guarantees, the proofs are often quite involved and only rarely suitable for automation (see, e.g., [16,6]).

Starting with the seminal work of Abadi and Rogaway [1], recent results investigate the possibility of bridging the gap between the two approaches. The goal is to obtain the best of both worlds: simple, automated security proofs that entail strong security guarantees. The approach usually consists in proving that the abstraction of cryptographic primitives made in the Dolev-Yao model is correct as soon as strong enough primitives are used in the implementation. For example, in the case of asymmetric encryption, it has been shown [21] that the *perfect encryption assumption* is a sound abstraction for IND-CCA2, which corresponds to a well-established security level. The perfect encryption assumption intuitively states that encryption is a black-box that can be opened only when one has the inverse key. Otherwise, no information can be learned from a ciphertext about the underlying plaintext.

---

[*] This work has been partially supported by the ACI-SI Satin and the ARA SSIA Formacrypt.

M. Hermann and A. Voronkov (Eds.): LPAR 2006, LNAI 4246, pp. 317–331, 2006.

However, it is not always sufficient to find the right cryptographic hypotheses. Formal models may need to be amended in order to be correct abstractions of the cryptographic models. This is in particular the case for symmetric encryption. For example, in [4], the authors consider extra-rules for the formal intruder in order to reflect the ability of a real intruder to choose its own keys in a particular manner.

A more widely used requirement is to control how keys can encrypt other keys. In a passive setting, soundness results [1,18] require that no key cycles can be generated during the execution of a protocol. Key cycles are messages like $enc(k, k)$ or $enc(k_1, k_2), enc(k_2, k_1)$ where a key encrypts itself or more generally when the encryption relation between keys contains a cycle. Such key cycles have to be disallowed simply because usual security definitions for encryption schemes do not provide any guarantees when such key cycles occur. In the active setting, the typical hypotheses are even stronger. For instance, in [4,17] the authors require that a key k_1 never encrypts a key k_2 generated before k_1.

Some authors circumvent the problem of key cycles by providing new security definitions for encryption that allow key cycles [2,5]. However, the standard security notions do not imply these new definitions and ad-hoc encryption schemes have to be constructed in order to satisfy the definitions. These constructions use the random oracle model which is provably non implementable. As a consequence, it is not known how to implement encryption schemes that satisfy the new definitions. In particular, none of the usual, implemented encryption schemes have been proved to satisfy the requirements.

Our main contribution is an NP-complete decision procedure for detecting the generation of key cycles during the execution of a protocol, in the presence of an intruder, for a bounded number of sessions. To the best of our knowledge, this problem has not been addressed before. We therefore provide a necessary component for automated tools used in proving strong, cryptographical security properties, using existing soundness results. Our result has been obtained following the classical approach of Rusinowitch-Turuani [25], revisited by Comon-Lundh [11,13], where protocols are represented by constraint systems. Since this initial procedure is already implemented in Avispa [3] for deciding secrecy and authentication properties, we believe that our algorithm can be easily implemented since it can be adapted from the existing procedure.

Our second contribution is to provide a generic approach derived from [11,13] to decide general security properties. Comon-Lundh showed that any constraint system can be transformed in (possibly several) much simpler constraint systems that are called *solved forms*. We show using (almost) the same transformation rules that, in order to verify a property on a constraint system, it is always sufficient to verify the property on the solved forms obtained after transformation. Compared to [11,13], the framework is slightly extended since we consider sorted terms, symmetric and asymmetric encryption, pairing and signatures. We use this approach to first prove NP-completeness of the key-cycle problem but also to show co-NP-completeness of secrecy for protocols with timestamps. We actually retrieve a significant fragment of the decidable class identified by Bozga *et al* [9]. We believe our result can lead more easily to an implementation since, again, we only need to adapt the procedure implemented in Avispa [3] while Bozga *et al* have designed a completely new decision procedure, which *de facto* has not been implemented.

The messages and the intruder capabilities are modeled in Section 2. In Section 3.1, we define constraint systems and show how they can be used to express protocol executions. In Section 3.2, we define security properties and the notion of satisfiability of constraint systems. In 3.3, we explain how the satisfiability problem of any security property can be reduced to the satisfiability of the same problem but on simpler constraint systems. We show in Section 4.1 how this approach can be used to obtain our main result of NP-completeness of the generation of key cycles and in Section 4.2 how it can be used to derive NP-completeness for protocols with timestamps. Some concluding remarks about further work can be found in Section 5.

2   Messages and Intruder Capabilities

2.1   Syntax

Cryptographic primitives are represented by function symbols. More specifically, we consider the *signature* $(\mathcal{S}, \mathcal{F})$ made of a set of *sorts* $\mathcal{S} = \{s, s_1 \ldots\}$ and a set of *symbols* $\mathcal{F} = \{\mathrm{enc}, \mathrm{enca}, \mathrm{sign}, \langle \rangle, \mathrm{pub}, \mathrm{priv}\}$ together with arities of the form $\mathrm{ar}(f) = s_1 \times s_2 \rightarrow s$ for the four first symbols and $\mathrm{ar}(f) = s \rightarrow s'$ for the two last ones. The symbol $\langle \rangle$ represents the pairing function. The terms $\mathrm{enc}(m, k)$ and $\mathrm{enca}(m, k)$ represent respectively the message m encrypted with the symmetric (resp. asymmetric) key k. The term $\mathrm{sign}(m, k)$ represents the message m signed by the key k. The terms $\mathrm{pub}(a)$ and $\mathrm{priv}(a)$ represent respectively the public and private keys of an agent a.

We fix an infinite set of *names* $\mathcal{N} = \{a, b \ldots\}$ and an infinite set of *variables* $\mathcal{X} = \{x, y \ldots\}$. We assume that names and variables are given with sorts. The set of *terms of sort s* is defined inductively by

$$
\begin{array}{ll}
t ::= & \text{term of sort } s \\
\quad | \quad x & \text{variable } x \text{ of sort } s \\
\quad | \quad a & \text{name } a \text{ of sort } s \\
\quad | \quad f(t_1, \ldots, t_k) & \text{application of symbol } f \in \mathcal{F}
\end{array}
$$

where for the last case, we further require that t_i is a term of some sort s_i and $\mathrm{ar}(f) = s_1 \times \ldots \times s_k \rightarrow s$. We assume a special sort Msg that subsumes all the other sorts and such that any term is of sort Msg.

As usual, we write $\mathcal{V}(t)$ for the set of variables occurring in t. A term is *ground* or *closed* if and only if it has no variables. The *size* of a term t, denoted $|t|$, is defined inductively as usual: $|t| = 1$ if t is a variable or a name and $t = 1 + \sum_{i=1}^{n} |t_i|$ if $t = f(t_1, \ldots, t_n)$ for $f \in \mathcal{F}$. If T is a set of terms then $|T|$ denotes the sum of the sizes of its elements. We denote by $St(t)$ the set of subterms of t.

Substitutions are written $\sigma = \{x_1 = t_1, \ldots, x_n = t_n\}$ with $\mathrm{dom}(\sigma) = \{x_1, \ldots, x_n\}$. We only consider *well-sorted* substitutions, that is substitutions for which x_i and t_i have the same sort. σ is *closed* if and only if all of the t_i are closed. The application of a substitution σ to a term t is written $\sigma(t) = t\sigma$.

Sorts are mostly left unspecified in this paper. They can be used in applications to express that certain operators can be applied only to some restricted terms. For example, sorts can be used to require that messages are encrypted only by atomic keys.

$$\frac{S \vdash x \quad S \vdash y}{S \vdash \langle x, y \rangle} \qquad \frac{S \vdash x \quad S \vdash y}{S \vdash \mathrm{enc}(x, y)} \qquad \frac{S \vdash x \quad S \vdash y}{S \vdash \mathrm{enca}(x, y)} \qquad \frac{S \vdash x \quad S \vdash y}{S \vdash \mathrm{sign}(x, y)}$$

$$\frac{S \vdash \langle x, y \rangle}{S \vdash x} \qquad \frac{S \vdash \langle x, y \rangle}{S \vdash y} \qquad \frac{S \vdash \mathrm{enc}(x, y) \quad S \vdash y}{S \vdash x}$$

$$\frac{S \vdash \mathrm{enca}(x, \mathrm{pub}(y)) \quad S \vdash \mathrm{priv}(y)}{S \vdash x} \qquad \frac{S \vdash \mathrm{sign}(x, \mathrm{priv}(y))}{S \vdash x} \; (optional) \qquad \frac{}{S \vdash x} \, x \in S$$

Fig. 1. Intruder deduction system

2.2 Intruder Capabilities

The ability of the intruder is modeled by a deduction system described in Figure 1 and corresponds to the usual Dolev-Yao rules. The first line describes the *composition* rules, the two last lines describe the *decomposition* rules and the axiom. Intuitively, these deduction rules say that an intruder can compose messages by pairing, encrypting and signing messages provided he has the corresponding keys and conversely, it can decompose messages by projecting or decrypting provided it has the decryption keys. For signatures, the intruder is also able to *verify* whether a signature $\mathrm{sign}(m, k)$ and a message m match (provided she has the verification key), but this does not give her any new message. That is why this capability is not represented in the deduction system. We also consider an optional rule $\frac{S \vdash \mathrm{sign}(x, \mathrm{priv}(y))}{S \vdash x}$ that expresses that an intruder can retrieve the whole message from its signature. This property may or may not hold depending on the signature scheme, and that is why this rule is optional. Note that this rule is necessary for obtaining soundness properties w.r.t. cryptographic digital signatures. Our results hold in both cases (that is, when the deduction relation $\vdash$ is defined with or without this rule).

A term u is *deducible* from a set of terms S, denoted by $S \vdash u$ if there exists a *proof i.e.* a tree such that the root is $S \vdash u$, the leaves are of the form $S \vdash v$ with $v \in S$ (*axiom* rule) and every intermediate node is an instance of one of the rules of the deduction system.

Example 1. The term $\langle k_1, k_2 \rangle$ is deducible from the set $S_1 = \{\mathrm{enc}(k_1, k_2), k_2\}$. A proof of $S_1 \vdash \langle k_1, k_2 \rangle$ is:

$$\frac{\dfrac{S_1 \vdash \mathrm{enc}(k_1, k_2) \quad S_1 \vdash k_2}{S_1 \vdash k_1} \quad S_1 \vdash k_2}{S_1 \vdash \langle k_1, k_2 \rangle}$$

3 Constraint Systems and Security Properties

Constraint systems are quite common (see e.g. [13,25]) in modeling security protocols. We recall here their formalism and show how they can be used to specify general security properties. Then we prove that any constraint system can be transformed into a simpler constraint system.

3.1   Constraint Systems

Definition 1. *A constraint system C is a finite set of expressions $T_i \Vdash tt$ or $T_i \Vdash u_i$, where T_i is a non empty set of terms, tt is a special symbol that represents an always deducible term, and u_i is a term, $1 \leq i \leq n$, such that:*

- *$T_i \subseteq T_{i+1}$, for all $1 \leq i \leq n-1$;*
- *if $x \in \mathcal{V}(T_i)$ then $\exists j < i$ such that $T_j = \min\{T \mid (T \Vdash u) \in C, x \in \mathcal{V}(u)\}$ (for the inclusion relation) and $T_j \subsetneq T_i$.*

The *left-hand side* (*right-hand side*) of a constraint $T \Vdash u$ is T (respectively u). The *left-hand side* of a constraint system C, denoted by $lhs(C)$, is the maximal set of messages T_n. The *right-hand side* of a constraint system C, denoted by $rhs(C)$, is the set of right-hand sides of its constraints. $\mathcal{V}(C)$ denotes the set of variables occurring in C. $\bot$ denotes the unsatisfiable system. The *size* of a constraint system is defined as $|C| \overset{\text{def}}{=} |lhs(C)| + |rhs(C)|$.

A constraint system is denoted as a conjunction of expressions. The left-hand side of a constraint system C usually represents the messages sent on the network.

Example 2. Consider the famous Needham-Schroeder asymmetric key authentication protocol [23] designed for mutual authentication.

$$A \rightarrow B : \quad \text{enca}(\langle N_A, A \rangle, \text{pub}(B))$$
$$B \rightarrow A : \quad \text{enca}(\langle N_A, N_B \rangle, \text{pub}(A))$$
$$A \rightarrow B : \quad \text{enca}(N_B, \text{pub}(B))$$

The agent A sends to B his name and a fresh nonce (a randomly generated value) encrypted with the public key of B. The agent B answers by copying A's nonce and adds a fresh nonce N_B, encrypted by A's public key. The agent A acknowledges by forwarding B's nonce encrypted by B's public key. We assume that a potential intruder has a complete control of the network: he may intercept, block and send new messages to arbitrary agents.

Let $T_0 = \{a, b, i, \text{pub}(a), \text{pub}(b), \text{pub}(i), \text{priv}(i)\}$ be the initial knowledge of the intruder. The following constraint system C_1 models a scenario where A starts a session with a corrupted agent I (whose private key is known to the intruder) and B is willing to answer to A. We consider this scenario for simplicity, but of course we could also consider for example A talking to B and B responding to I.

$$T_1 \overset{\text{def}}{=} T_0 \cup \{\text{enca}(\langle n_a, a \rangle, \text{pub}(i))\} \Vdash \text{enca}(\langle x, a \rangle, \text{pub}(b)) \tag{1}$$

$$T_2 \overset{\text{def}}{=} T_1 \cup \{\text{enca}(\langle x, n_b \rangle, \text{pub}(a))\} \Vdash \text{enca}(\langle n_a, y \rangle, \text{pub}(a)) \tag{2}$$

$$T_3 \overset{\text{def}}{=} T_2 \cup \{\text{enca}(y, \text{pub}(i))\} \Vdash \text{enca}(n_b, \text{pub}(b)) \tag{3}$$

where n_a and n_b are names of sort Msg and x and y are variables of sort Msg. The set T_1 represents the messages known to the intruder once A has contacted the corrupted agent I. Then the equations 1 and 2 can be read as follows: if a message of the form $\text{enca}(\langle x, a \rangle, \text{pub}(b))$ can be sent on the network, then B would answer to this message by $\text{enca}(\langle x, n_b \rangle, \text{pub}(a))$, which is added to T_1. Subsequently, if a message of the form $\mathsf{enca}(\langle n_a, y \rangle, \mathsf{pub}(a))$ can be sent on the network, then A would answer by $\mathsf{enca}(y, \mathsf{pub}(i))$ since A believes she is talking to I. The run is successful if B can finish his session by receiving the message $\mathsf{enca}(n_b, \mathsf{pub}(b))$. Then B believes he has talked to A while A actually talked to I. If the protocol was secure, such a constraint system should not have a solution. The variables represent those parts of messages that are *a priori* unknown to the agents.

3.2 Security Properties

A security property is modeled by a predicate on (lists of) terms. The terms represent some information about the execution of the protocol, for example the messages that are sent on the network.

Definition 2. *A security property is a predicate on lists of messages. For a list L we denote by L_s the set of messages of the list L.*

Let C be a constraint system, L a list of terms such that $\mathcal{V}(L_s) \subseteq \mathcal{V}(C)$ and P a security property. A solution of C for P w.r.t. L is a closed substitution θ such that $\forall (T \Vdash u) \in C, T\theta \vdash u\theta$ and $P(L\theta)$ holds. Every substitution satisfies $T \Vdash \mathsf{tt}$ and none satisfies $\perp$.

Example 3. If the predicate P is simply the **true** predicate (which holds for any list of terms) and the only sort is Msg then we simply retrieve the usual constraint system deduction problem, which is known to be NP-complete [11,25].

Example 4. Secrecy can be easily expressed by requiring that the secret data is not deducible from the messages sent on the network. We consider again the constraint system C_1 defined in Example 2. Let L_1 be a list of the messages in $lhs(C_1)$. We define the predicate P_1 to hold on a list of messages if and only if n_b is deducible from it. That is, $P_1(L) = \mathbf{true}$ iff $L_s \vdash n_b$. Then the substitution $\sigma_1 = \{x = n_a, y = n_b\}$ is a solution of C_1 for the property P_1 w.r.t. L_1 and corresponds to the attack found by G. Lowe [19]. Note that such a deduction-based property can be directly encoded in the constraint system by adding a constraint $T \Vdash n_b$ where $T = lhs(C_1)$.

Example 5. Authentication can also be defined using a predicate P_2 on lists of messages. For this purpose we use corresponding assertions and we introduce, following the syntax of Avispa [3], two new function symbols witness and request of arity 4 with the following intuition: $\mathsf{request}(a, b, id, m)$ says that the agent a (*id* being simply a constant identifying the request since there might be several requests in one execution of a protocol) *now believes* that it is really agent b who sent the message m (that is, a authenticates b on m), and $\mathsf{witness}(b, a, id, m)$ says that b has just sent the message m to a. The predicate P_2 holds on a list L of messages if whenever $\mathsf{request}(a, b, id, m)$ appears in the list there is a corresponding occurrence $\mathsf{witness}(b, a, id, m)$ (defining an injection) appearing before it in the list (that is, at a smaller position), for any agents a, b different from the intruder. Choosing L_2 to be a list of the messages in $lhs(C)$ following the order induced by the constraints (that is m appears before m' in L_2 whenever $m \in T_i$, $m \notin T_j$, $m' \in T_j$, $T_i \subseteq T_j$) we obtain Lowe's definition of injective agreement [20]. Formally, a protocol has an attack on the authentication property iff the constraint system C has a solution for $\overline{P_2}$ w.r.t. L_2, where $\overline{P_2}$ is the negation of P_2.

R_1	$C \wedge T \Vdash u \leadsto C \wedge T \Vdash \ttt$	if $T \cup \{x \mid (T' \Vdash x) \in C, T' \subsetneq T\} \vdash u$
R_2	$C \wedge T \Vdash u \leadsto_\sigma C\sigma \wedge T\sigma \Vdash u\sigma$	if $\sigma = \mathrm{mgu}(t, u)$, $t \in St(T)$, $t \neq u$, t, u not variables
R_3	$C \wedge T \Vdash u \leadsto_\sigma C\sigma \wedge T\sigma \Vdash u\sigma$	if $\sigma = \mathrm{mgu}(t_1, t_2)$, $t_1, t_2 \in St(T)$, $t_1 \neq t_2$, t_1, t_2 not variables
R_4	$C \wedge T \Vdash u \leadsto \perp$	if $\mathcal{V}(T, u) = \emptyset$ and $T \not\vdash u$
R_f	$C \wedge T \Vdash f(u, v) \leadsto C \wedge T \Vdash u \wedge T \Vdash v$	for $f \in \{\langle \rangle, \mathrm{enc}, \mathrm{enca}, \mathrm{sign}\}$

Fig. 2. Simplification rules

Consider again the constraint system C_1 defined in Example 2 where T_0 is replaced by $T'_0 = T_0 \cup \{\mathrm{enca}(\langle n'_a, a\rangle, \mathrm{pub}(b))\}$: the agent A also initiates a session with B, and $T'_1 = T'_0 \cup T_1 \cup \{\mathrm{witness}(b, a, 1, x), \mathrm{request}(b, a, 2, n_b)\}$: B asserts that A should rely on the value of x for his authentication to A, and now B believes he talked with A. The substitution σ_1 defined in Example 4 is a solution of C_1 for the property $\overline{P_2}$ w.r.t. L_2, since there is no corresponding witness assertion for $\mathrm{request}(b, a, 2, n_b)$ in L_2.

In Section 4, we provide other examples of predicates which encode time constraints or express that no key cycles are allowed.

3.3 General Approach

Using some simplification rules, solving general constraint systems can be reduced to solving simpler constraint systems that we called solved. We say that a constraint system is *solved* if it is different from $\perp$ and each of its constraints are of the form $T \Vdash \ttt$ or $T \Vdash x$, where x is a variable. This corresponds to the notion of solved form in [13].

Solved constraint systems with the single sort Msg are particularly simple in the case of the **true** predicate since they always have a solution, as noticed in [11]. Indeed, let T_1 be the smallest (w.r.t. inclusion) left hand side of a constraint. From the definition of a constraint system we have that T_1 is non empty and has no variables. Let $t \in T_1$. Then the substitution θ defined by $x\theta = t$ for every variable x is a solution since $T \vdash x\theta = t$ for any constraint $T \Vdash x$ of the solved system.

The *simplification rules* we consider are defined in Figure 2. All the rules are in fact indexed by a substitution: when there is no index then the identity substitution is implicitly considered. We write $C \leadsto_\sigma^n C'$ if there are $C_1, \ldots, C_n$ with $n \geq 1$, $C' = C_n$, $C \leadsto_{\sigma_1} C_1 \leadsto_{\sigma_2} \cdots \leadsto_{\sigma_n} C_n$ and $\sigma = \sigma_1 \sigma_2 \ldots \sigma_n$. We write $C \leadsto_\sigma^* C'$ if $C \leadsto_\sigma^n C'$ for some $n \geq 1$, or if $C' = C$ and σ is the empty substitution.

The simplification rules are correct, complete and terminating in polynomial time.

Theorem 1. *Let C be a constraint system, θ a substitution, P a security property and L a list of messages such that $\mathcal{V}(L_s) \subseteq \mathcal{V}(C)$.*

1. *(Correctness) If $C \leadsto_\sigma^* C'$ for some constraint system C' and some substitution σ and if θ is a solution of C' for the property P w.r.t. $L\sigma$ then $\sigma\theta$ is a solution of C for the property P w.r.t. L.*

2. *(Completeness) If θ is a solution of C for the property P w.r.t. L, then there exist a constraint system C' and substitutions σ, θ' such that $\theta = \sigma\theta'$, $C \leadsto_\sigma^* C'$ and θ' is a solution of C' for the property P w.r.t. $L\sigma$.*

3. *(Termination) If $C \leadsto_\sigma^n C'$ for some constraint system C' and some substitution σ then n is polynomially bounded in the size of C.*

Theorem 1 extends the result of [11] to sorted messages and general security properties. This last point simply relies on the fact that whenever $C \leadsto_\sigma^* C'$ then $L(\sigma\theta) = (L\sigma)\theta$ for any substitution θ. We introduced explicit sorts since soundness results are usually obtained for models with atomic sorts for keys and nonces for example. The proof is actually a simple extension of [11] and all the details can be found in [14].

The following corollary is easily obtained from the previous theorem by observing that we can guess the simplification rules which lead to a solved form.

Corollary 1. *Any property P that can be decided in polynomial time on solved constraint systems can be decided in non-deterministic polynomial time on arbitrary constraint systems.*

4   Decidability of Some Specialized Security Properties

Using the general approach presented in the previous section, verifying particular properties like the existence of key cycles or the conformation to an *a priori* given order relation on keys can be reduced to deciding these properties on solved constraint systems. We deduce a new decidability result, useful in models designed for proving cryptographic properties. This approach also allows us to retrieve a significant fragment of [9] for protocols with timestamps.

4.1   Encryption Cycles

To show that formal models (like the one presented in this article) are sound with respect to cryptographical ones, the authors usually assume that no key cycle can be produced during the execution of a protocol or, even stronger, assume that the "encrypts" relation on keys follows an *a priori* given order.

In this section we restrict our attention to key cycles and key order on symmetric keys since there are very few papers constraining the key relations in an asymmetric setting. We consider atomic keys for symmetric encryption since soundness results are only obtained in this setting. In particular, there exists no general definition (with a cryptographic interpretation) of key cycles in the case of arbitrary composed keys. More precisely, we assume a sort Key $\subset$ Msg and we assume that the sort of enc is Msg $\times$ Key $\to$ Msg. All the other symbols are of sort Msg $\times \cdots \times$ Msg $\to$ Msg. Hence only names and variables can be of sort Key.

Key Cycles. Many definitions of key cycles are available in the literature. They are defined by considering cycles in the *encrypts* relation between keys. But this relation differs from one article to another. For example, the early definition proposed by Abadi and Rogaway [1] says that k encrypts k' as soon as there exists a term enc(m, k) such that k' is a subterm of m. For example, both $enc(k, k)$ and $enc(enc(a, k), k)$ contain key cycles. However, in the definition proposed by Laud [18], $enc(enc(a, k), k)$ does not contain a key cycle since the relation "k encrypts k'" is restricted to keys k' that occur in plaintext. We consider the two variants for the notion of key cycles.

We write $s <_{st} t$ if and only if s is a subterm of t. We define recursively the least reflexive and transitive relation $\sqsubseteq$ satisfying: $s_1 \sqsubseteq (s_1, s_2)$, $s_2 \sqsubseteq (s_1, s_2)$, and if $s \sqsubseteq t$ then $s \sqsubseteq enc(t, t')$. Intuitively, $s \sqsubseteq t$ if s is a subterm of t that occurs (at least once) in a plaintext position.

Definition 3. *Let ρ_1 be a relation chosen in $\{<_{st}, \sqsubseteq\}$. Let S be a set of messages and k, k' two terms of sort Key. We say that k encrypts k' in S (denoted $k \rho_e^S k'$) if there exist $m \in S$ and a term m' such that*

$$k' \rho_1 m' \text{ and } enc(m', k) \sqsubseteq m.$$

With $\rho_1 = <_{st}$, we retrieve the definition of Abadi and Rogaway. With $\rho_1 = \sqsubseteq$ we retrieve the definition of Laud. For simplicity, we may write ρ_e instead of ρ_e^S if S is clear from the context.

We say that a set of messages S *contains a key cycle* if there is a cycle in the relation ρ_e^S. If m is a message we denote by ρ_e^m the relation $\rho_e^{\{m\}}$ and say that m contains a cycle if $\{m\}$ contains a cycle.

Definition 4. *Let K be a set of names of sort Key. We define the predicate P_{kc}^K as follows: P_{kc}^K holds on a list of messages L if and only if $S = L_s \cup \{m \mid L_s \vdash m\}$ contains a key cycle $(k_1, \ldots, k_n)$, with $n \geq 1$ and $k_i \in K$ for all $1 \leq i \leq n$.*

Definition of Key Order. In order to establish soundness of formal models in a symmetric encryption setting, the requirements on the encrypts relation can be even stronger, in particular in the case of an active intruder. In [4] and [17], the authors require that a key never encrypts a younger key. More precisely, the encrypts relation has to be compatible with the order in which the keys are generated. Hence we also want to check whether there exist executions of the protocol for which the encrypts relation is incompatible with an *a priori* given order on keys.

Definition 5. *Let $\leq$ be a partial order on a set of names K of sort Key. We define the predicate $P_{\leq}^K$ as follows: $P_{\leq}^K$ holds on a list of messages L if and only if the encrypts relation ρ_e^S (restricted to $K \times K$), where $S = L_s \cup \{m \mid L_s \vdash m\}$, is compatible with $\leq$, that is*

$$k \rho_e^m k' \Rightarrow k' \not\leq k, \text{ for all } k, k' \in K.$$

For example, in [4,17] the authors choose $\leq$ to be the order in which the keys are generated: $k \leq k'$ if k has been generated before k'. We denote by $\overline{P}_{\leq}^K$ the negation of $P_{\leq}^K$. Indeed, an attack in this context is an execution such that the encrypts relation is incompatible with $\leq$, that is the predicate $\overline{P}_{\leq}^K$ holds.

The following proposition states that in the passive case a key cycle can be deduced from a set S only if it already appears in S.

Proposition 1. *Let L be a list of messages, K a set of names of sort* Key *and $\leq$ a partial order on K. The predicate P_{kc}^K (resp. $\overline{P}_{\leq}^K$) holds on L if and only if*

- *there is $k \in K$ such that k is deducible from L_s, that is $L_s \vdash k$, or*
- *L_s contains a key cycle (resp. the encrypts relation on L_s is not compatible with $\leq$).*

Indeed if k is deducible from L_s then $enc(k,k)$ is deducible from L_s. Hence there is a deducible message containing a key cycle and for which the encrypts relation is not compatible with the order $\leq$. If there are no deducible keys then it can be easily shown that the encrypts relation on any deducible message is included in the encrypts relation on L_s, hence the equivalences in the proposition.

Decidability. In what follows, a solution of C for the **true** predicate w.r.t. an arbitrary list is said to be a *partial* solution to C. A *key* is a term of sort Key.

We show how to decide the existence of key cycles or the conformation to an order in polynomial time for solved constraint systems without variables of sort Key. Indeed, the instantiation of key variables can be guessed in advance (see the next section). Note that the set of messages on which our two predicates are applied usually contains all messages sent on the network and possibly some additional intruder knowledge.

Proposition 2. *Let C be a solved constraint system without variables of sort* Key *and L be a list of messages such that $\mathcal{V}(L_s) \subseteq \mathcal{V}(C)$ and $lhs(C) \subseteq L_s$. Let K be a set of names of sort* Key *such that $L_s\theta \not\vdash k$ for any θ partial solution of C and for any $k \in K$. Let $\leq$ be a partial order on K.*

- *Deciding whether C has a solution for P_{kc}^K w.r.t. L can be done in $\mathcal{O}(|L|+|K|^2)$.*
- *Deciding whether C has a solution for $\overline{P}_{\leq}^K$ w.r.t. L can be done in $\mathcal{O}(|L|+|K|^2)$.*

Since the keys of K are not deducible from $L_s\theta$, for any θ partial solution of C, we know by Proposition 1 that it is sufficient to look at the encrypts relation only on $L_s\theta$ (and not on every deducible term).

Since C is solved, any constraint of C is of the form $T \Vdash x$ or $T \Vdash tt$. For each variable x of C we denote $T_x = \min\{T \mid T \Vdash x \in C\}$. Let t_x be the term obtained by pairing all terms of T_x (in some arbitrary order). We construct the following substitution $\tau = \tau_1 \ldots \tau_q$, where q is the number of variables in C, and τ_j is defined inductively as follows:

- $dom(\tau_1) = \{x_1\}$ and $x_1\tau_1 = t_{x_1}$
- $\tau_{j+1} = \tau_j \cup \{{}^{t_{x_i}\tau_j}/_{x_i}\}$, where $i = \min\{i' \mid x_{i'} \notin dom(\tau_j)\}$.

The construction is correct by the definition of a constraint system. It is clear that τ is a partial solution of C.

We construct the following directed graph $G = (K, A)$ as follows: if k encrypts k' in L_s then $(k, k') \in A$; and, if k encrypts x in L_s (where $x \in \mathcal{V}(L_s)$) then $(k, k') \in A$ for all $k' \rho_1 x\tau$. The graph captures exactly the encrypts relation induced by τ on C and any possible encrypts relation is contained in the graph.

Lemma 1. *Let θ be a partial solution of C and $k, k' \in K$ be two non deducible keys, that is $L_s\theta \not\vdash k, k'$. If $k \rho_e^{L_s\theta} k'$, that is k encrypts k' in $L_s\theta$ then $(k, k') \in A$. Conversely, if $(k, k') \in A$ then $k \rho_e^{L_s\tau} k'$, that is k encrypts k' in $L_s\tau$.*

We deduce that deciding whether C has a solution for P_{kc}^K w.r.t. L can be done simply by deciding whether the graph G has cycles. Indeed, if there is a solution θ such that there is a cycle $(k_1, \ldots, k_n)$ in $L_s\theta$, that is, for each i we have $k_i \rho_e^{L_s\theta} k_{i+1}$, then (by Lemma 1) $(k_i, k_{i+1}) \in A$ for each i, that is $(k_1, \ldots, k_n)$ is a cycle in the graph G. Conversely, if $(k_1, \ldots, k_n)$ is a cycle in G then, again by Lemma 1, τ is a solution of C for P_{kc}^K w.r.t. L.

Deciding whether C has a solution for $\overline{P}_{\leq}^K$ w.r.t. L can be done by deciding whether the graph G has the following property P_G: there is $(k, k') \in A$ such that $k \leq k'$. And indeed, if there is a solution θ such that $\overline{P}_{\leq}^K$ holds on $L\theta$, that is $P_{\leq}^K$ does not hold on $L\theta$, then there are $k, k' \in K$ such that $k\rho_e^{L_s\theta}k'$ and $k \leq k'$. Hence $(k, k') \in A$ and $k \leq k'$. That is the property P_G on the graph G holds. Conversely, if the property P_G holds then there are $k, k' \in K$ such that k encrypts k' in $L\tau$ and $k \leq k'$, that is τ is a solution of C for $\overline{P}_{\leq}^K$ w.r.t. L.

The graph can be constructed in $\mathcal{O}(|L_s| + |K|^2)$. Testing for cycles and verifying property P_G can be simply done by traversing the graph in $\mathcal{O}(|K|^2)$.

NP-Completeness. Consider a constraint system C, a set K of names of sort Key and a list of messages L such that $\mathcal{V}(L_s) \subseteq \mathcal{V}(C)$ and $lhs(C) \subseteq L_s$. We want to decide the existence of a solution of C for P_{kc}^K (resp. $P_{\leq}^K$) w.r.t. L. By Proposition 1, there is a solution if and only if

1. either there exists $k \in K$ such that there exists a partial solution to $C_k \overset{\text{def}}{=} C \wedge L_s \Vdash k$,
2. or no key from $k \in K$ is deducible (that is $L_s\theta \nvdash k$, for all θ partial solution of C) and C has a solution for P_{kc}^K (resp. $P_{\leq}^K$) w.r.t. L.

We guess whether we are in case 1 or 2 and in case 1 we also guess which key is deducible. In the first case, we check whether C_k has a partial solution in non-deterministic polynomial time using Corollary 1. In the second case, we guess an instantiation θ of variables of sort Key and of codomain the set of keys appearing in L (a finite set). Then we check whether $C\theta$ has a solution for P_{kc}^K (resp. $P_{\leq}^K$) w.r.t. $L\theta$ using Theorem 1 and Proposition 2.

NP-hardness is obtained by adapting the construction for NP-hardness provided in [25]. More precisely, we consider the reduction of the 3SAT problem to our problem. For any 3SAT boolean formula we construct a protocol such that the intruder can deduce a key cycle if and only if the formula is satisfiable. The construction is the same as in [25] (pages 15 and 16) except that, in the last rule, the participant responds with the term $enc(k, k)$, for some fresh key k (initially secret), instead of $Secret$. Then it is easy to see that the only way to produce a key cycle on a secret key is to play this last rule which is equivalent, using [25], to the satisfiability of the corresponding 3SAT formula.

4.2 Timestamps

For modeling timestamps, we introduce a new sort Time $\subseteq$ Msg for time and we assume an infinite number of names of sort Time, represented by rational numbers or integers. We assume that the only two sorts are Time and Msg. Any value of time should be known to an intruder, that is why we add to the deduction system the rule $\dfrac{}{S \vdash a}$ for any name a of sort Time. All the previous results can be easily extended to such a deduction system since ground deducibility remains decidable in polynomial time.

To express relations between timestamps, we use timed constraints. An *integer timed constraint* or a *rational timed constraint* T is a conjunction of formulas of the form

$$\Sigma_{i=1}^{k}\alpha_i x_i \ltimes \beta,$$

where the α_i and β are rational numbers, $\ltimes \in \{<, \leq\}$, and the x_i are variables of sort Time. A *solution* of a rational (resp. integer) timed constraint T is a closed substitution $\sigma = \{x_1 = c_1, \ldots, x_k = c_k\}$, where the c_i are rationals (resp. integers), that satisfies the constraint.

Timed constraints between the variables of sort Time are expressed through satisfiability of security properties.

Definition 6. *A predicate P is a* timed property *if P is generated by some (rational or integer) timed constraint T, that is if T has variables $x_1, \ldots, x_k$ then for any list L of messages $P(L)$ holds if and only if*

- *L contains exactly k messages $t_1, \ldots, t_k$ of sort Time that appear in this order in the list, and*
- *$T(t_1, \ldots, t_k)$ is true.*

Such timed properties can be used for example to say that a timestamp x_1 must be fresher than a timestamp x_2 ($x_1 \geq x_2$) or that x_1 must be at least 30 seconds fresher than x_2 ($x_1 \geq x_2 + 30$).

Example 6. We consider the Wide Mouthed Frog Protocol [10].

$$A \rightarrow S : A, \mathrm{enc}(\langle T_a, B, K_{ab} \rangle, K_{as})$$
$$S \rightarrow B : \mathrm{enc}(\langle T_s, A, K_{ab} \rangle, K_{bs})$$

A sends to a server S a fresh key K_{ab} intended for B. If the timestamp T_a is fresh enough, the server answers by forwarding the key to B, adding its own timestamps. B simply checks whether this timestamp is older than any other message he has received from S. As explained in [10], this protocol is flawed because an attacker can use the server to keep a session alive as long as he wants by replaying the answers of the server. This protocol can be modeled by the following constraint system:

$$S_1 \stackrel{\text{def}}{=} \{a, b, \langle a, \mathrm{enc}(\langle 0, b, k_{ab} \rangle, k_{as}) \rangle\} \Vdash \langle a, \mathrm{enc}(\langle x_{t_1}, b, y_1 \rangle, k_{as}) \rangle, x_{t_2} \qquad (4)$$

$$S_2 \stackrel{\text{def}}{=} S_1 \cup \{\mathrm{enc}(\langle x_{t_2}, a, y_1 \rangle, k_{bs})\} \Vdash \langle b, \mathrm{enc}(\langle x_{t_3}, a, y_2 \rangle, k_{bs}) \rangle, x_{t_4} \qquad (5)$$

$$S_3 \stackrel{\text{def}}{=} S_2 \cup \{\mathrm{enc}(\langle x_{t_4}, b, y_2 \rangle, k_{as})\} \Vdash \langle a, \mathrm{enc}(\langle x_{t_5}, b, y_3 \rangle, k_{as}) \rangle, x_{t_6} \qquad (6)$$

$$S_4 \stackrel{\text{def}}{=} S_3 \cup \{\mathrm{enc}(\langle x_{t_6}, a, y_3 \rangle, k_{bs})\} \Vdash \mathrm{enc}(\langle x_{t_7}, a, k_{ab} \rangle, k_{bs}) \qquad (7)$$

where y_1, y_2, y_3 are variables of sort Msg and $x_{t_1}, \ldots, x_{t_7}$ are variables of sort Time. We add explicitly the timestamps emitted by the agents on the right hand side of the constraints (that is in the messages expected by the participants) since the intruder can schedule the message transmission whenever he wants.

Initially, the intruder simply knows the names of the agents and A's message at time 0. Then S answers alternatively to requests from A and B. Since the intruder controls the network, the messages can be scheduled as slow (or fast) as the intruder needs it. The server S should not answer if A's timestamp is too old (let's say older than 30 seconds) thus S's timestamp cannot be too much delayed (no more than 30 seconds). This means that we should have $x_{t_2} \leq x_{t_1} + 30$. Similarly, we should have $x_{t_4} \leq x_{t_3} + 30$ and $x_{t_6} \leq x_{t_5} + 30$. The last rule corresponds to B's reception. In this scenario, B does not perform any check on the timestamp since it is the first message he receives.

We say that there is an attack if there is a solution to the constraint system that satisfies the previously mentioned time constraints and such that the timestamp received by B is too fresh to come from A: $x_{t_7} \geq 30$. Formally, we consider the timed property generated by the following timed constraint: $x_{t_2} \leq x_{t_1} + 30 \wedge x_{t_4} \leq x_{t_3} + 30 \wedge x_{t_6} \leq x_{t_5} + 30 \wedge x_{t_7} \geq 30$. Then the substitution corresponding to the attack is $\sigma = \{y_1 = y_2 = y_3 = y_4 = k_{ab}, x_{t_1} = 0, x_{t_2} = x_{t_3} = 30, x_{t_4} = x_{t_5} = 60, x_{t_6} = x_{t_7} = 90\}$.

Proposition 3. *Any timed property can be decided in non-deterministic polynomial time on solved constraints.*

Proof (sketch). Let C be a solved constraint, P a timed property and T a timed constraint generating P. Let $y_1, \ldots, y_n$ be the variables of sort Msg in C and $x_1, \ldots, x_k$ the variables of sort Time in C. Clearly, any substitution σ of the form $\sigma(y_i) = u_i$ where $u_i \in S_i$ for some $S_i \Vdash y_i \in C$ and $\sigma(x_i) = t_i$ for t_i any constant of sort Time is a solution of C for the **true** property. Let σ' be a the restriction of σ to the timed variables $x_1, \ldots, x_k$.

Clearly, σ is a solution of C for P if and only if σ' is a solution to T. Thus there exists a solution of C for P if and only if T is satisfiable. The satisfiability of T is solved by usual linear programming [26]. It is polynomial in the case of rational timed constraints and it is NP-complete in the case of integer timed constraints, thus the result.

NP-Completeness. We deduce by combining Theorem 1 and Proposition 2 that the problem of deciding timed properties on arbitrary constraint systems is in NP.

NP-hardness directly follows from the NP-hardness of constraint system solving by considering a predicate corresponding to an empty timed constraint.

5   Further Work

We have shown how the generic approach we have derived from [11,13,25] can be used to retrieve two NP-completeness results. The first one enables us to detect key cycles while the second one enables us to solve constraint systems with timed constraints. In both cases, we had to provide a decision procedure only for a simple class of constraint systems. Since the constraint-based approach [11,13,25] has already been implemented in Avispa [3], we plan, using our results, to adapt this implementation to the case of key cycles and timestamps.

More generally, taking advantage of our generic approach, we would like to explore how decision procedures of distinct security properties can be combined on solved constraint systems. In addition, in our two cases, decidability on solved constraints systems was quite simple. It would be interesting to understand which classes of properties can be decided in the same manner.

Regarding key cycles, our approach is valid for a bounded number of sessions only. Secrecy is undecidable in general [15] for an unbounded number of sessions. Such an undecidability result could be easily adapted to the problem of detecting key cycles. Several decidable fragments have been designed [24,12,8,27] for secrecy and an unbounded number of sessions. We plan to investigate how such fragments could be used to decide key cycles.

Acknowledgment. We are particularly grateful to Michaël Rusinowitch and Bogdan Warinschi for their very helpful suggestions.

References

1. M. Abadi and Ph. Rogaway. Reconciling two views of cryptography (the computational soundness of formal encryption). *Journal of Cryptology*, 2:103–127, 2002.
2. P. Adão, G. Bana, J. Herzog, and A. Scedrov. Soundness of formal encryption in the presence of key-cycles. In *Proc. 10th European Symposium on Research in Computer Security (ESORICS'05)*, volume 3679 of *LNCS*, pages 374–396, 2005.
3. A. Armando, D. Basin, Y. Boichut, Y. Chevalier, L. Compagna, J. Cuellar, P. Hankes Drielsma, P.C. Héam, O. Kouchnarenko, J. Mantovani, S. Mödersheim, D. von Oheimb, M. Rusinowitch, J. Santiago, M. Turuani, L. Viganò, and L. Vigneron. The Avispa tool for the automated validation of internet security protocols and applications. In *Proc. of Computer Aided Verification (CAV'05)*, volume 3576 of *LNCS*, 2005.
4. M. Backes and B. Pfitzmann. Symmetric encryption in a simulatable Dolev-Yao style cryptographic library. In *Proc. 17th IEEE Computer Science Foundations Workshop (CSFW'04)*, pages 204–218, 2004.
5. M. Backes, B. Pfitzmann, and A. Scedrov. Key-dependent message security under active attacks. Cryptology ePrint Archive, Report 2005/421, 2005.
6. M. Bellare and P. Rogaway. Entity authentication and key distribution. In *Advances in Cryptology – Crypto '93, 13th Annual International Cryptology Conference*, volume 773 of *LNCS*, pages 232–249, 1993.
7. B. Blanchet. An efficient cryptographic protocol verifier based on Prolog rules. In *Proc. 14th IEEE Computer Security Foundations Workshop (CSFW'01)*, pages 82–96, 2001.
8. B. Blanchet and A. Podelski. Verification of cryptographic protocols: Tagging enforces termination. In Andrew Gordon, editor, *Foundations of Software Science and Computation Structures (FoSSaCS'03)*, volume 2620 of *LNCS*, April 2003.
9. L. Bozga, C. Ene, and Y. Lakhnech. A symbolic decision procedure for cryptographic protocols with time stamps. In *Proc. 15th International Conference on Concurrency Theory (CONCUR'04)*, LNCS, pages 177–192, London, England, 2004. Springer-Verlag.
10. J. Clark and J. Jacob. A survey of authentication protocol literature. Available at http://www.cs.york.ac.uk/~jac/papers/drareviewps.ps, 1997.
11. H. Comon-Lundh. Résolution de contraintes et recherche d'attaques pour un nombre borné de sessions. Available at http://www.lsv.ens-cachan.fr/~comon/CRYPTO/bounded.ps.

12. H. Comon-Lundh and V. Cortier. New decidability results for fragments of first-order logic and application to cryptographic protocols. In *Proc. of the 14th Int. Conf. on Rewriting Techniques and Applications (RTA'2003)*, volume 2706 of *LNCS*, pages 148–164. Springer-Verlag, June 2003.

13. H. Comon-Lundh and V. Shmatikov. Intruder deductions, constraint solving and insecurity decision in presence of exclusive or. In *Proc. of 18th Annual IEEE Symposium on Logic in Computer Science (LICS '03)*, pages 271–280, 2003.

14. V. Cortier and E. Zălinescu. Deciding key cycles for security protocols, extended version. Available at http://www.loria.fr/~zalinesc/papers/cz_keycycles.ps.

15. N. Durgin, P. Lincoln, J. Mitchell, and A. Scedrov. Undecidability of bounded security protocols. In *Proc. of the Workshop on Formal Methods and Security Protocols*, 1999.

16. S. Goldwasser and S. Micali. Probabilistic encryption. *Journal of Computer and System Sciences*, 28:270–299, 1984.

17. R. Janvier, Y. Lakhnech, and L. Mazare. (De)Compositions of Cryptographic Schemes and their Applications to Protocols. Cryptology ePrint Archive, Report 2005/020, 2005.

18. P. Laud. Encryption cycles and two views of cryptography. In *Nordic Workshop on Secure IT Systems (NORDSEC'02)*, 2002.

19. G. Lowe. Breaking and fixing the Needham-Schroeder public-key protocol using FDR. In *Tools and Algorithms for the Construction and Analysis of Systems (TACAS'96)*, volume 1055 of *LNCS*, pages 147–166. Springer-Verlag, March 1996.

20. G. Lowe. A hierarchy of authentication specification. In *10th Computer Security Foundations Workshop (CSFW '97)*, pages 31–44, 1997.

21. D. Micciancio and B. Warinschi. Soundness of formal encryption in the presence of active adversaries. In *Proc. 1st Theory of Cryptography Conference (TCC'04)*, volume 2951 of *LNCS*, pages 133–151, 2004.

22. J. K. Millen and V. Shmatikov. Constraint solving for bounded-process cryptographic protocol analysis. In *Proc. 8th ACM Conference on Computer and Communications Security (CCS'01)*, pages 166–175, 2001.

23. R. M. Needham and M. D. Schroeder. Using encryption for authentication in large networks of computers. *Commun. ACM*, 21(12):993–999, 1978.

24. R. Ramanujam and S. P. Suresh. Tagging makes secrecy decidable for unbounded nonces as well. In *Proc. of the 23rd Conference on Foundations of Software Technology and Theoretical Computer Science (FSTTCS'03)*, Mumbai, 2003.

25. M. Rusinowitch and M. Turuani. Protocol insecurity with finite number of sessions and composed keys is NP-complete. *Theoretical Computer Science*, 299:451–475, 2003.

26. A. Schrijver. *Theory of Linear and Integer Programming*. Wiley, 1998.

27. K. N. Verma, H. Seidl, and T. Schwentick. On the complexity of equational Horn clauses. In *Proc. of the 22th International Conference on Automated Deduction (CADE 2005)*, Lecture Notes in Computer Science, pages 337–352. Springer-Verlag, 2005.

Automating Verification of Loops by Parallelization*

Tobias Gedell and Reiner Hähnle

Department of Computing Science, Chalmers University of Technology
S-412 96 Göteborg, Sweden
{gedell, reiner}@chalmers.se

Abstract. Loops are a major bottleneck in formal software verification, because
they generally require user interaction: typically, induction hypotheses or invariants must be found or modified by hand. This involves expert knowledge of the
underlying calculus and proof engine. We show that one can replace interactive
proof techniques, such as induction, with automated first-order reasoning in order to deal with parallelizable loops, where a loop can be parallelized whenever
it avoids dependence of the loop iterations from each other. We develop a dependence analysis that ensures parallelizability. It guarantees soundness of a proof
rule that transforms a loop into a universally quantified update of the state change
information represented by the loop body. This makes it possible to use automatic first order reasoning techniques to deal with loops. The method has been
implemented in the KeY verification tool. We evaluated it with representative case
studies from the JAVA CARD domain.

1 Introduction

It is generally agreed that loops and recursive calls are the main bottleneck in formal
software verification. The source of the problem is that loops and recursion are proof
theoretically handled either with invariant rules or with induction. In both cases, it is
necessary in general to strengthen invariants and induction hypotheses in order to make
proofs go through. There are also many technicalities with those rules that make their
application difficult. A number of heuristic techniques have been developed to guide
induction proofs and to find appropriate induction hypotheses (for example, [6,8]).

The context of the present work is formal verification of functional properties of sequential JAVA programs [1]. Here the situation is aggravated by the fact that the above
mentioned techniques have been developed for relatively simple functional programming languages and are not readily applicable to a complex, imperative, object-based
language such as JAVA (similar comments apply to C, C++, or C#). Hence, not only is
there a lack of heuristic techniques that help to automate proofs about loops in JAVA, but
due to the complexity of loop rules in imperative languages [5] user interaction involves
a high amount of technical knowledge and is extremely expensive.

A recent divide-and-conquer technique for decomposition of induction proofs [15]
works for imperative programs, but it is targeted at simplifying user interaction rather

---

* This work was funded in part by a STINT institutional grant and by the IST programme of the
EC, Future and Emerging Technologies under the IST-2005-015905 MOBIUS project. This
article reflects only the author's views and the Community is not liable for any use that may
be made of the information contained therein.

M. Hermann and A. Voronkov (Eds.): LPAR 2006, LNCS 4246, pp. 332–346, 2006.

than eliminating it. In order to deal *automatically* with loops in verification of JAVA-like languages there are not too many options at present: abstraction [13] and approximation [10] are incomplete and in some scenarios even unsound. They also impose limits on what can be expressed in specifications. If the number of loop iterations is known and small then it is possible to use symbolic execution with finite unwinding [11]. The state of the art in JAVA verification is, however, that complex user interaction is unavoidable for almost all loops [7].

In this paper we present an *automatic* deductive verification technique that is applicable to many loops occurring in practically relevant JAVA programs. Like any automatic method it cannot handle all loops, but it is seamlessly integrated with a complete interactive verification system. In addition, it computes useful information even when it fails. To make things concrete, we look at an example (where e(i) is an expression with an occurrence of i):   **for** (**int** i = 0; i < a.length; i++)a[i] = e(i);

The effect of this piece of code is simply to initialize all elements of the array a with the expression $e(i)$ at index i. Since the length of a is in general unknown, it is not possible to deal with this loop by finite unwinding. An abstraction of this program has difficulties to record that the value a.length depends on a. On the other hand, in most cases it is overkill to use induction on such a simple problem. In order to describe the effect of such loops it is usually sufficient to be able to quantify universally over state update expressions that are performed in parallel. From a proof theoretic point of view, quantified state modifiers can be handled by skolemization and simplification [17], hence, they are amenable to automated proof search.

In general, the initialization, guard and step expressions, as well as the loop body could be more complicated than in the example above. We are looking for a technique that does not rely on the target program being in a particular syntactic form. Of course, we need to make certain assumptions to ensure that the effect of a loop is expressible as a quantified update. This problem is closely related to loop vectorization and parallelization and it is possible to use notions developed in these fields. The main issue is to exclude certain data dependencies. For example, in the case of $e(i) \equiv$ a[i - 1] the code above cannot be transformed into a quantified state update, because there exist dependencies between the updates.

The contribution of this paper is a deductive verification method for treating loops[1] based on the ideas just sketched. Its main properties are:

Robustness. The target program needs not to be in a particular syntactic form. This is achieved by computing the accumulated effect of the expressions and statements occurring in the loop by symbolic execution *before* checking the dependencies in the loop body (Section 4 and Section 5).

Soundness. There is an automatic dependence analysis that guarantees sound applicability (Section 6).

Automation. Proof theoretic treatment of the effect of loops is not by induction but by universally quantified state modification and is automatic (Section 7).

---

[1] The technique is applicable both to for- and while-loops. In this presentation we concentrate on the former to make the presentation more concise, and because for-loops are much more common in our application domain JAVA CARD.

Relevance. The method applies not only to a few academic examples, but to a substantial number of loops in realistic programs. An experimental evaluation of a number of realistic JAVA CARD programs confirms this (Section 9).

2 Basic Definitions

The platform for our experiments is the KeY tool [1], which features an interactive theorem prover for formal verification of sequential JAVA programs.

2.1 Dynamic Logic for JAVA CARD

In KeY the target program to be verified and its specification are both modeled in an instance of a dynamic logic (DL) [12] calculus called JAVA DL [3]. JAVA DL extends other variants of DL used for theoretical investigations or verification purposes, because it handles such phenomena as side effects, aliasing, object types, exceptions, and finite integer types. JAVA DL axiomatizes full JAVA minus multi-threading, floating point types, and dynamic class loading.

Deduction in the JAVA DL calculus is based on symbolic program execution and simple program transformations and so is close to a programmer's understanding of JAVA. It can be seen as a modal logic with a modality $\langle p \rangle$ for every program p, where $\langle p \rangle$ refers to the final state (if p terminates normally) that is reached after executing p.

The *program formula* $\langle p \rangle \phi$ expresses that the program p terminates in a state in which ϕ holds without throwing an exception. A formula $\phi \rightarrow \langle p \rangle \psi$ is valid if for every state S satisfying precondition ϕ a run of the program p starting in S terminates normally, and in the terminating state the postcondition ψ holds.

The programs in JAVA DL formulas are basically JAVA code. Each rule of the JAVA DL calculus specifies how to execute symbolically one particular statement, possibly with additional restrictions. When a loop or a recursive method call is encountered, it is in general necessary to perform induction over a suitable data structure. In this paper we show how induction can be avoided in the case of parallelizable loops.

2.2 State Updates

In JAVA (as in other object-oriented programming languages), different object type variables may refer to the same object. This phenomenon, called aliasing, causes difficulties for the handling of assignments in a calculus for JAVA DL. For example, whether or not the formula $o1.f \doteq 1$, where $\doteq$ denotes equality, holds after (symbolic) execution of the assignment $o2.f = 2;$, depends on whether $o1$ and $o2$ refer to the same object. Therefore, JAVA assignments cannot be symbolically executed by syntactic substitution. In the JAVA DL calculus a different solution is used, based on the notion of (state) *updates*.

Definition 1. Atomic updates *are of the form* $loc := val$, *where* val *is a logical term without side effects and* loc *is either (i) a program variable v, or (ii) a field access o.f, or (iii) an array access a[i]. Updates may appear in front of any formula, where they are surrounded by curly brackets for easy parsing. The semantics of* $\{loc := val\}\phi$ *is the same as that of* $\langle loc=val; \rangle \phi$.

Definition 2. *General* updates *are defined inductively based on atomic updates. If $\mathcal{U}$ and $\mathcal{U}'$ are updates then so are: (i) $\mathcal{U}$, $\mathcal{U}'$* (parallel composition), *(ii) $\mathcal{U}$; $\mathcal{U}'$* (sequential composition), *(iii) $\mathcal{U}\mathcal{U}'$* (applied on update), *(iv)* \if (b) $\{\mathcal{U}\}$, *where b is a quantifier-free formula* (conditional execution), *(v)* \for T s; $\mathcal{U}(s)$, *where s is a variable over a well-ordered type T and $\mathcal{U}(s)$ is an update with occurrences of s* (quantification).

The semantics of sequential updates, conditional updates and updates applied on updates is obvious; the meaning of a parallel update is the simultaneous application of all its constituent updates except when two left hand sides refer to the same location: in this case the syntactically later update wins. This models natural program execution flow. The semantics of \for T s; $\mathcal{U}(s)$ *is the parallel execution of all updates in $\bigcup_{x \in T} \{s := x; \mathcal{U}(s)\}$. As for parallel updates, a last-win clash-semantics is in place: the maximal update with respect to the well-order on T and the syntactic order within each $\mathcal{U}(s)$ wins.*

The restriction that right-hand sides of updates must be side effect-free is not limiting: by introducing fresh local variables and symbolic execution of complex expressions the JAVA DL calculus rules normalize arbitrary assignments so that they meet the restrictions of updates. A full formal treatment of updates is in [17].

3   Outline of the Approach

Let us look at the following example:

```
for (int i = 1; i < a.length; i++)
    if (c != 0) a[i] = b[i+1];
    else a[i] = b[i-1];
```

In a first step the loop initialization expression is transformed out of the loop and symbolically executed. The reason is that the initialization expression might be complex and have side effects. This results in a state $S = \{i := 1\}$. The remaining loop now has the form: **for** (; i < a.length; i++)...

We proceed to symbolically execute the loop body, the step expression and the guard for a generic value of i. In order to do this correctly, we must eliminate from the current state all locations that can potentially be modified in the body, step, or guard. In Section 4 we describe an algorithm that approximates such a set of locations rather precisely. Applied to the present example we obtain i and a[i] as modifiable locations. Consequently, generic execution of the loop body, step, and guard starts in the empty state. Note that the set of modifiable locations does not include, for example, c. This is important, because if S contains, say, c := 1, we would start the execution in the state $\{c := 1\}$ and the resulting state would be much simplified.

In our example, symbolic execution of one loop iteration starting in the empty state gives $S' = \{i := i + 1, \text{\if } (c \not\doteq 0) \{a[i] := b[i+1]\}, \text{\if } (c \doteq 0) \{a[i] := b[i-1]\}\}$, where the step and guard expressions were executed as well.

The next step is to check whether the state update S' resulting from the execution of the generic iteration contains dependencies that make it impossible to represent the effect of the loop as a quantified update. For S' this is the case if and only if c is 0 and a and b are the same array. In this case, the body amounts to the statement a[i] = a[i-1] which contains a data dependence that cannot be parallelized. All other dependencies can be captured by parallel execution of updates with last-win clash-semantics. The details of the dependence analysis are explained in Section 6. In the example it results in a logical constraint C that, among other things, contains the disjunction of $c \neq 0$ and $a \neq b$. A further logical constraint $\mathcal{D}$ strengthening C is computed which, in addition, ensures that the loop terminates normally. In the example, normal termination is ensured by a and b not being **null** and b having enough elements, that is, $b.length > a.length$.

At this point the proof is split into two cases using cut formula $\mathcal{D}$. Under the assumption $\mathcal{D}$ the loop can be transformed into a quantified update. If $\mathcal{D}$ is not provable, then the loop must be also tackled with a conventional induction rule, but one may use the additional assumption $\neg\mathcal{D}$, which may well simplify the proof.

For the sake of illustration assume now S and S' both contain $\{c:=1\}$ and the termination constraint in $\mathcal{D}$ holds. In this case, we can additionally simplify S' to $\{c:=1, i:=i+1, a[i]:=b[i+1]\}$.

In the final step we synthesize from (i) the initial state S, (ii) the effect of a generic execution of an iteration S' and (iii) the guard, a state update, where the loop variable i is universally quantified. The details are explained in Section 7. The result for the example is:

$$\text{\textbackslash for int } l;\ \{i:=l\}\{\text{\textbackslash if } (i \geq 1 \wedge i < a.length)\ \{c:=1,\ i:=i+1,\ a[i]:=b[i+1]\}\}$$

The for-expression is a universal first order quantifier whose scope is an update that contains occurrences of the variable i (see Def. 2 and [17]). Subexpressions are first order terms that are simplified eagerly while symbolic execution proceeds. First order quantifier elimination rules based on skolemization and instantiation are applicable, for example, for any positive value j such that $j < a.length$ we obtain immediately the update $a[j]:=b[j+1]$ by instantiation. Proof search is performed by the usual first order strategies without user interaction.

4   Computing State Modifications

In this section we describe how we compute the state modifications performed by a generic loop iteration. As a preliminary step we move the initialization out of the loop and execute it symbolically, because the initialization expression may contain side-effects. We are left with a loop consisting of a guard, a step expression and a body:

$$\textbf{for } (;\ guard;\ step)\ body \tag{1}$$

We want to compute the state modifications performed by a generic iteration of the loop. A single loop iteration consists of executing the body, evaluating the step expression, and testing the guard expression. This behavior is captured in the following compound statement where dummy is needed, because JAVA expressions are not statements.

$$body;\ step;\ \textbf{boolean } dummy = guard; \tag{2}$$

We proceed to symbolically execute the compound statement (2) for a generic value of the loop variable. This is quite similar to computing the strongest post condition of a given program. Platzer [16] has worked out the details of how to compute the strongest post condition in the specific JAVA program logic that we use and our methods are based on the same principles. Our method handles the fragment of JAVA that the symbolic execution machinery of KeY handles, which is JAVA CARD.

Let p be the code in (2). The main idea is to try to prove validity of the program formula $S\langle p \rangle\, F$, where F is an arbitrary but unspecified non-rigid predicate that signifies when to stop symbolic execution. Symbolic execution of p starting in state S eventually yields a proof tree whose open leaves are of the form $\Gamma \rightarrow \mathcal{U} F$ for some update expression $\mathcal{U}$. The predicate F cannot be shown to be true or false in the program logic. Therefore, after all instructions in p have been executed, symbolic execution is stuck. At this stage we extract two vectors $\vec{\Gamma}$ and $\vec{\mathcal{U}}$ consisting of corresponding Γ and $\mathcal{U}$ from all open leaf nodes. Different leaves correspond to different computation branches in the loop body.

Example 1. Consider the following statement p:

```
if (i > 2) a[i] = 0 else a[i] = 1; i = i + 1;
```

After the attempt to prove $\langle p \rangle\, F$ becomes stuck, i.e. all instructions have been symbolically executed, there are two open leaves:

$$V \wedge i > 2 \rightarrow \{\texttt{a[i]} := 0, \texttt{i} := \texttt{i}+1\} F$$
$$V \wedge i \not> 2 \rightarrow \{\texttt{a[i]} := 1, \texttt{i} := \texttt{i}+1\} F$$

where V stands for $\neg(\texttt{a} = \textbf{null}) \wedge i \geq 0 \wedge \texttt{i} < \texttt{a.length}$. From these we extract the following vectors:

$$\vec{\Gamma} \equiv \langle V \wedge i > 2, V \wedge i \not> 2 \rangle$$
$$\vec{\mathcal{U}} \equiv \langle \{\texttt{a[i]} := 0, \texttt{i} := \texttt{i}+1\}, \{\texttt{a[i]} := 1, \texttt{i} := \texttt{i}+1\} \rangle$$

$\square$

If the loop iteration throws an exception, abruptly terminates the loop, or when the automatic strategies are not strong enough to execute all instructions in p to completion, some open leaf will contain unhandled instructions and be of a form different from $\Gamma \rightarrow \mathcal{U} F$. We call these *failed leaves* in contrast to leaves of the form $\Gamma \rightarrow \mathcal{U} F$ that are called *successful*.

If a failed leaf can be reached from the initial state, our method cannot handle the loop. We must, therefore, make sure that our method is only applied to loops for which we have proven that no failed leaf can be reached. In order to do this we create a vector $\vec{\mathcal{F}}$ consisting of the Γ extracted from all failed leaves and let the negation of $\vec{\mathcal{F}}$ become a condition that needs to be proven when applying our method.

Example 2. In Example 1 only the successful leaves are shown. When all instructions have been symbolically executed, there are in addition failed leaves of following form:

$$\texttt{a} \doteq \textbf{null} \qquad\qquad\qquad \rightarrow \ldots F$$
$$\texttt{a} \not\doteq \textbf{null} \wedge \texttt{i} < 0 \qquad\qquad \rightarrow \ldots F$$
$$\texttt{a} \not\doteq \textbf{null} \wedge \texttt{i} \not< \texttt{a.length} \rightarrow \ldots F$$

From these we extract the following vector:

$$\vec{\mathcal{F}} \equiv \langle \texttt{a} \doteq \textbf{null}, \texttt{a} \neq \textbf{null} \wedge \texttt{i} < 0, \texttt{a} \neq \textbf{null} \wedge \texttt{i} \not< \texttt{a.length} \rangle \qquad \square$$

Note that symbolic execution discards any code that cannot be reached. As a consequence, an exception that occurs at a code location that cannot be reached from the initial state will not occur in the leaves of the proof tree. This means that our method is not restricted to code that cannot throw any exception, which would be very restrictive.

So far we said nothing about the state in which we start a generic loop iteration. Choosing a suitable state requires some care, as the following example shows.

Example 3. Consider the following code:

```
c = 1;
i = 0;
for (; i < a.length; i++) {
    if (c != 0) a[i] = 0;
    b[i] = 0; }
```

At the beginning of the loop we are in state $S = \{\texttt{c}:=1, \texttt{i}:=0\}$. It is tempting, but wrong, to start the generic loop iteration in this state. The reason is that i has a specific value, so one iteration would yield $\{\texttt{a[0]}:=0, \texttt{b[0]}:=0, \texttt{i}:=1\}$, which is the result after the *first* iteration, not a generic one. The problem is that S contains information that is not invariant during the loop. Starting the loop iteration in the empty state is sound, but suboptimal. In the example, we get $\{\backslash\texttt{if} \ (\texttt{c} \neq 0) \ \{\texttt{a[i]}:=0\}, \texttt{b[i]}:=0, \texttt{i}:=\texttt{i}+1\}$, which is unnecessarily imprecise, since we know that c is equal to 1 during the entire execution of the loop. $\qquad \square$

We want to use as much information as possible from the state S_{init} at the beginning of the loop and only remove those parts that are not invariant during all iterations of the loop. Executing the loop in the largest possible state corresponds to performing dead code elimination. When we reach a loop of the form (1) in state S_{init} we proceed as follows:

1. Execute **boolean** dummy = guard; in state S_{init} and obtain S. We need to evaluate the guard since it may have side effects. Evaluation of the guard might cause the proof to branch, in which case we apply the following steps to *each* branch. If our method cannot be applied to at least one of the branches we backtrack to state S_{init} and use the standard rules to prove the loop.
2. Compute the vectors $\vec{\Gamma}$, $\vec{\mathcal{U}}$ and $\vec{\mathcal{F}}$ from (2) starting in state S.
3. Obtain S' by removing from S all those locations that are modified in a successful leaf, more formally: $S' = \{(\ell:=e) \in S \mid \ell \notin mod(\vec{\mathcal{U}})\}$, where $mod(\vec{\mathcal{U}})$ is the set of locations whose value in $\vec{\mathcal{U}}$ differs from its value in S.
4. If $S = S'$ then stop; otherwise let S become S' and goto step 2.

The algorithm terminates since the number of locations that can be removed from the initial state is bound both by the textual size of the loop and all methods called by the loop. and, in case the state does not contain any quantified update, the size of the state itself. The final state of this algorithm is a greatest fixpoint containing as much information as possible from the initial state S. Let us call this final state S_{iter}.

Example 4. Example 3 yields the following sequence of states:

Round	Start state	State modifications	New state	Remark
1	$\{c:=1, i:=0\}$	$\{a[0]:=0, b[0]:=0, i:=1\}$	$\{c:=1\}$	
2	$\{c:=1\}$	$\{a[i]:=0, b[i]:=0, i:=i+1\}$	$\{c:=1\}$	Fixpoint

Computing the set $mod(\vec{\mathcal{U}})$ can be difficult. Assume S contains $a[c]:=0$ and $\vec{\mathcal{U}}$ contains $a[i]:=1$. If i and c can have the same value then $a[c]$ should be removed from S, otherwise it is safe to keep it. In general it is undecidable whether two variables can assume the same value. One can use a simplified version of the dependence analysis described in Section 6 (modified to yield always a boolean answer) to obtain an approximation of location collision. The dependence analysis always terminates so this does not change the overall termination behavior.

A similar situation occurs when S contains $a.f:=0$ and $\vec{\mathcal{U}}$ contains $b.f:=1$. If a and b are references to the same object then $a.f$ must be removed from the new state. Here we make a safe approximation and remove $a.f$ unless we can show that a and b refer to different objects.

5 Loop Variable and Loop Range

For the dependence analysis and for creating the quantified state update later we need to identify the loop variable and the loop range. In addition, we need to know the value that the loop variable has in each iteration of the loop, that is, the function from the iteration number to the value of the loop variable in that iteration. This is a hard problem in general, but whenever the loop variable is incremented or decremented with a constant value in each iteration, it is easy to construct this function. At present we impose this as a restriction: the update of the loop variable must have the form $l := l$ op e, where l is the loop variable and e is invariant during loop execution. It would be possible to let the user provide this function at the price of making the method less automatic.

To identify the loop variable we compute a set of candidate pairs (l, e) where l is a location that is assigned the expression e, satisfying the above restriction, in all successful leaf nodes of the generic iteration. Formally, this set is defined as $\{(l, e) \mid \bigwedge_{u \in \vec{\mathcal{U}}} \{l:=e\} \in \mathcal{U}\}$. The loop variable is supposed to have an effect on the loop range; therefore, we remove all those locations from the candidate set that do not occur in the guard. If the resulting set consists of more than one location, we arbitrarily choose one.

The remaining candidates should be eliminated, because they will all cause data flow-dependence. A candidate is eliminated by transforming its expression into one which is not dependent on the candidate location. For example, the candidate l, introduced by the assignment $l = l + c;$, can be eliminated by transforming the assignment into $l = init + I * c;$, where $init$ is the initial value of l and I the iteration number.

Example 5. Consider the code in Example 1 which gives the following vector $\vec{\mathcal{U}}$ of updates occurring in successful leaves:

$$\vec{\mathcal{U}} \equiv \langle \{a[i]:=0, i:=i+1\}, \{a[i]:=1, i:=i+1\}\rangle$$

We identify the location i as the loop variable, assuming that i occurs in the guard. □

To determine the loop range we begin by computing the specification of the guard in a similar way as we computed the state modifications of a generic iteration in the previous section. We attempt to prove $\langle$**boolean** dummy = guard;$\rangle$ F. From the open leaves of the form $\Gamma \rightarrow \{$dummy:= e, ...$\}$ F, we create the formula GS which characterizes when the guard is true. Formally, GS is defined as $\bigvee_{\Gamma \in \bar{\Gamma}}(\Gamma \wedge e \doteq$ **true**$)$. The formula GF characterizes when the guard is not successfully evaluated. We let GF be the disjunction of all Γ from the open leaves that are not of the form above.

Example 6. Consider the following guard g $\equiv$ i < a.length. When all instructions in the formula $\langle$**boolean** dummy = g;$\rangle$ F have been symbolically executed, there are two successful leaves:

$$a \neq \textbf{null} \wedge \texttt{i} < \texttt{a.length} \rightarrow \{\texttt{dummy}:= \textbf{true}\} F$$
$$a \neq \textbf{null} \wedge \texttt{i} \not< \texttt{a.length} \rightarrow \{\texttt{dummy}:= \textbf{false}\} F$$

From these we extract the following formula GS (before simplification):

$$(a \neq \textbf{null} \wedge \texttt{i} < \texttt{a.length} \wedge \textbf{true} \doteq \textbf{true}) \vee$$
$$(a \neq \textbf{null} \wedge \texttt{i} \not< \texttt{a.length} \wedge \textbf{false} \doteq \textbf{true})$$

When the instructions have been executed, there is also the failed leaf $a \doteq \textbf{null} \rightarrow ... F$. From it we extract the following formula $GF \equiv a \doteq \textbf{null}$. □

After having computed the specification of the guard and identified the loop variable we determine the initial value *start* of the loop variable from the initial state S_{init}. If an initial value cannot be found we let it be unknown. We try to determine the final value *end* of the loop variable from the successful leaves of the guard specification. Currently, we restrict this to guards of the form 1 op e. If we cannot determine the final value, we let it be unknown. We had already computed the *step* value during loop variable identification.

The formula LR characterizes when the value of i is within the loop range. It is defined as follows, which expresses that there exists an iteration with the particular value of the loop variable and that the iteration can be reached:

$$LR \equiv GS \wedge \exists n. \left(\begin{array}{c} n \geq 0 \wedge \texttt{i} \doteq start + n * step \wedge \\ \forall m. \ 0 \leq m < n \rightarrow \{\texttt{i}:= start + m * step\} GS \end{array} \right)$$

It is important that the loop terminates, otherwise, our method is unsound. We, therefore, create a termination constraint LT that needs to be proven when applying our method. The termination constraint says that there exists a number of iterations, n, after which the guard formula evaluates to false. The constraint LT is defined as:

$$LT \equiv \exists n. \ n \geq 0 \wedge \{\texttt{i}:= start + n * step\} \neg GS$$

6   Dependence Analysis

Transforming a loop into a quantified state update is only possible when the iterations of the loop are independent of each other. Two loop iterations are independent of each other if the execution of one iteration does not affect the execution of the other. According to this definition, the loop variable clearly causes dependence, because each iteration both reads its current value and updates it. We will, however, handle the loop variable by quantification. Therefore, it is removed from the update before the dependence analysis is begun. The problem of loop dependencies was intensely studied in loop vectorization and parallelization for program optimization on parallel architectures. Some of our concepts are based on results in this field [2,18].

6.1 Classification of Dependencies

In our setting we encounter three different kinds of dependence; *data flow-dependence*, *data anti-dependence*, and *data output-dependence*.

Example 7. It is tempting to assume that it is sufficient for independence of loop iterations that the final state after executing a loop is independent of the order of execution, but the following example shows this to be wrong:

```
for (int i = 0, sum = 0; i < a.length; i++) sum += a[i];
```

The loop computes the sum of all elements in the array a which is independent of the order of execution, however, running all iterations in parallel gives the wrong result, because reading and writing of sum collide.   □

Definition 3. *Let S_J be the final state after executing a generic loop iteration over variable i during which it has value J and let $<$ be the order on the type of i.*
There is a data input-dependence *between iterations $K \neq L$ iff S_K writes to a location (i.e., appears on the left-hand side of an update) that is read (appears on the right hand side or in a guard of an update) in S_L. We speak of* data flow-dependence *when $K < L$ and of* data anti-dependence, *when $K > L$. There is* data output-dependence *between iterations $K \neq L$ iff S_K writes to a location that is overwritten in S_L.*

Example 8. When executing the second iteration of the following loop, the location a[1], modified by the first iteration, is read, indicating data flow-dependence:

```
for (int i = 1; i < a.length; i++) a[i] = a[i - 1];
```

The following loop exhibits data output-dependence:

```
for (int i = 1; i < a.length; i++) last = a[i];
```

Each iteration assigns a new value to last. When the loop terminates, last has the value assigned to it by the last iteration.   □

Loops with data flow-dependencies cannot be parallelized, because each iteration must wait for a preceding one to finish before it can perform its computation.

In the presence of data anti-dependence swapping two iterations is unsound, but parallel execution is possible provided that the generic iteration acts on the original state before loop execution begins. In our translation of loops into quantified state updates in Section 7 below, this is ensured by simultaneous execution of all updates. Thus, we can handle loops that exhibit data anti-dependence. The final state of such loops depends on the order of execution, so independence of the order of executions is not only insufficient (Example 7) but even unnecessary for parallelization.

Even loops with data output-dependence can be parallelized by assigning an ordinal to each iteration. An iteration that wants to write to a location first ensures that no iteration with higher ordinal has already written to it. This requires a total order on the iterations. As we know the step expression of the loop variable, this order can easily be constructed. The order is used in the quantified state update together with a last-win clash-semantics to obtain the desired behavior.

6.2 Comparison to Traditional Dependence Analysis

Our dependence analysis is different from most existing analyses for loop parallelization in compilers [2,18]. The major difference is that these analyses must not be expensive in terms of computation time, because the user waits for the compiler to finish. Traditionally, precision is traded off for cost. Here we use dependence information to avoid using induction which comes with an extremely high cost, because it typically requires user interaction. In consequence, we strive to make the dependence analysis as precise as possible as long as it is still fully automatic. In particular, our analysis can afford to try several algorithms that work well for different classes of loops.

A second difference to traditional dependence analysis is that we do not require a definite answer. When used during compilation to a parallel architecture, a dependence analysis must give a Boolean answer as to whether a given loop is parallelizable or not. In our setting it is useful to know that a loop is parallelizable relative to satisfaction of a symbolic constraint. Then we can let a theorem prover validate or refute this constraint, which typically is a much easier problem than proving the original loop.

6.3 Implementation

Our dependence analysis consists of two parts. The first part analyzes the loop and symbolically computes a *constraint* that characterizes when the loop is free of dependencies. The advantage of the constraint-based approach is that we can avoid to deal with a number of very hard problems such as aliasing: for example, locations $a[i]$ and $b[i]$ are the same iff a and b are references to the same array, which can be difficult to determine. Our analysis side-steps the aliasing problem simply by generating a constraint saying that *if* a is not the same array as b *then* there is no dependence. The second part of the dependence analysis is a tailor-made theorem prover that simplifies the integer equations occurring in the resulting constraints as much as possible.

The computation of the dependence constraints uses the vectors $\vec{\Gamma}$ and $\vec{\mathcal{U}}$ that represent successful leaves in the symbolic execution of the loop body and were obtained as the result of a generic loop iteration in Section 4. Let Γ_k and $\mathcal{U}_k$ be the precondition, respectively, the resulting update in the k-th leaf. If the preconditions of two leaves are true for different values in the loop range we need to ensure that the updates of the leaves are independent of each other (Def. 3). Formally, if there exist two distinct values K and L in the loop range and (possibly identical) leaves r and s, for which $\{i:=K\}\Gamma_r$ and $\{i:=L\}\Gamma_s$ are true, then we need to ensure independence of $\mathcal{U}_r$ and $\mathcal{U}_s$. We run our dependence analysis on $\mathcal{U}_r$ and $\mathcal{U}_s$ to compute the dependence constraint $C_{r,s}$.

We do this for all pairs of leaves and define the dependence constraint for the entire loop as follows where *LR* is the loop range predicate:

$$C \equiv \bigwedge_{r,s}(((\exists K,L.\ (K \neq L \wedge \{\mathtt{i}:=K\}(LR \wedge \Gamma_r) \wedge \{\mathtt{i}:=L\}(LR \wedge \Gamma_s))) \rightarrow C_{r,s})$$

Example 9. Consider the following loop that reverses the elements of the array a:

```
int half = a.length / 2 - 1;
for (int i = 0; i <= half; i++) {
  int tmp = a[i];
  a[i] = a[a.length - 1 - i];
  a[a.length - 1 - i] = tmp; }
```

When running the dependence analysis we get the following constraint:

$$C_{0,0} \equiv \mathtt{a.length} < 2 \vee \mathtt{half} * 2 < \mathtt{a.length}$$

For this loop, the state S_{iter} contains half:=a.length / 2 - 1 and the constraint is, therefore, simplified to a.length $< 2 \vee$ (a.length/2) $* 2 <$ a.length $+ 2$. This is simplified to **true** which makes C true and means that the loop does not contain any dependencies that cannot be handled by our method.   □

7 Constructing the State Update

If we can show that the iterations of a loop are independent of each other (i.e., the constraint C defined in the previous section holds), we can capture all state modifications of the loop in one update (Def. 2). Concretely, we use the following quantified update (T is the type of the loop variable i; LR, Γ_r, $\mathcal{U}_r$ were defined in Sections 4 and 5):

$$\mathcal{U}_{loop} \equiv \backslash\mathtt{for}\ T\ I;\ \{\mathtt{i}:=I\}\{\backslash\mathtt{if}\ (LR)\ \{\bigcup_r \backslash\mathtt{if}\ (\Gamma_r)\ \{\mathcal{U}_r\}\}\} \qquad (3)$$

The conditional update inside (3) corresponds to one loop iteration, where i has the value I. In each state only one Γ can be true so we do not need to ensure any particular order of the updates $\vec{\mathcal{U}}$.

The guard LR ensures that i is within the loop range. We must take care when using last-win clash-semantics to handle data output-dependence. When the step is positive, the iteration with the highest value of the loop variable should have priority over all other iterations. This is ensured by the standard well-order on the JAVA integer types.

A complication arises when the step is negative. Then we need to reverse the order so that the iteration with the lowest value of the loop variable has priority. Since each type has a fixed order we need to change the state update instead: it is sufficient to replace in (3) the update i:=I with i:=$-I$.

8 Using the Analysis in a Correctness Proof

When we encounter a loop during symbolic execution we analyze it for parallelizability as described above and compute the dependence constraint. We replace the loop by (3) if no failed leaves for the iteration statement or the guard expression can be reached (see Section 4), the loop terminates (formula LT, see Section 5), and the dependence constraint C in Section 6.3 is valid. Taken together, this yields:

$$\mathcal{D} \equiv \neg (\exists I. \{i := I\}(LR \wedge \bigvee_i \mathcal{F}_i)) \wedge \neg GF \wedge LT \wedge C$$

If $\mathcal{D}$ does not hold, we fall back to the standard rules to verify the loop (usually induction). In many cases it is not trivial to immediately validate or refute $\mathcal{D}$. Then we perform a cut on $\mathcal{D}$ in the proof and replace the loop by the quantified state update $\mathcal{U}_{loop}$ (3) in the proof branch where $\mathcal{D}$ is assumed to hold. The general outline of a proof using a cut on $\mathcal{D}$ is as follows:

$$\frac{\begin{array}{cc} \text{If not } \Gamma \Rightarrow \mathcal{D}, & \\ \text{use standard induction} & \Gamma, \mathcal{D} \Rightarrow \mathcal{U}\mathcal{U}_{loop}\langle \ldots \rangle \phi \\ \hline \Gamma \Rightarrow \mathcal{U}\langle \text{for } \ldots ; \ldots \rangle \phi, \mathcal{D} \quad \Gamma, \mathcal{D} \Rightarrow \mathcal{U}\langle \text{for } \ldots ; \ldots \rangle \phi \end{array}}{\Gamma \Rightarrow \mathcal{U}\langle \text{for } \ldots ; \ldots \rangle \phi} \; cut$$

$$\vdots$$

If we can validate or refute $\mathcal{D}$ we can close one of the two branches. Typically, this involves to show that there is no aliasing between the variables occurring in the dependence constraint. Even when it is not possible to prove or to refute $\mathcal{D}$ our analysis is useful, because $\mathcal{D}$ in succedent of the left branch can make it easier to close.

9   Evaluation

We evaluated our method with three representative JAVA CARD programs [14]: De-Money, SafeApplet and IButtonAPI that together consist of ca. 2200 lines of code (not counting comments). In these programs there exist 17 loops. Out of these, our method can be applied to five (sometimes, a simple code transformation like v += e to v = v0 + i * e is required). Additionally, four loops can be handled if we allow object creation in the quantified updates (which is currently not realized). The remaining eight loops cannot be handled because they contain abrupt termination and irregular step functions. The results are summarized in the following table:

	DeMoney	SafeApplet	IButtonAPI	Total
LoC	1633	514	102	2249
Size (kB)	182	22	3	207
# loops	10	6	1	17
handled	4	0	1	5
with ext.	3	1	0	4
remaining	3	5	0	8

All loops in the row "handled" are detected automatically as parallelizable and are transformed into quantified updates. The evaluation shows that a considerable number of loops in realistic legacy programs can be formally verified without resorting to interactive and, therefore, expensive techniques such as induction. Interestingly, the percentage of loops that can be handled differs drastically among the three programs. A closer inspection reveals that the reason is not that, for example, all the loops in SafeApplet are inherently not parallelizable. Some of them could be rewritten so that they become parallelizable. This suggests to develop programming guidelines (just as they exist for compilation on parallel architectures) that ensure parallelizability of loops.

10 Conclusion

We presented a method for formal verification of loops that works by transforming loops into automizable first order constructs (quantified updates) instead of interactive methods such as invariants or induction. The approach is restricted to loops that can be parallelized, but an analysis of representative programs from the JAVA CARD domain shows that such loops occur frequently. The method can be applied to most initialization and array copy loops but also to more complex loops as shown by Example 9.

The method relies on the capability to represent state change information effecting from symbolic execution of imperative programs explicitly in the form of syntactic updates [3,17]. With the help of updates the effect of a generic loop iteration is represented so that it can be analyzed for the presence of data dependencies. Ideas for the dependency analysis are taken from compiler optimization for parallel architectures, but the analysis is not merely static. Loops that are found to be parallelizable are transformed into first order quantified updates to be passed on to an automated theorem prover.

A main advantage of our method is its robustness in the presence of syntactic variability in the target programs. This is achieved by performing symbolic execution before doing the dependence analysis. The method is also fully automatic whenever it is applicable and gives useful results in the form of symbolic constraints even if it fails.

Future Work. The analysis can be improved in various ways. One example is the function from iteration number to value of the loop variable (see Section 5). In addition, straightforward automatic program transformations that reduce the amount of dependencies (for example, v += e; into v = vInit + i * e;) could be derived by looking at the updates from a generic loop iteration. We also intend to develop general programming guidelines that ensure parallelizability of loops. Recent work on automatic termination analysis [9] could be adapted to the present setting for proving the termination constraint in Section 5.

Critical dependencies exhibited during the analysis are likely to cause problems as well in a proof attempt based on invariants or induction, so one could try to use the obtained information on dependencies to guide the generalization of loop invariants.

At the moment we observe JAVA integer semantics only by checking for overflow. The integer model could be made more precise by computing all integer operators modulo the the size of the underlying integer type. This would require changes in the dependence analysis; the JAVA DL calculus covers full JAVA integer semantic already [4].

Finally, the discussion in this paper stops after a loop has been transformed into a quantified update. So far, our theorem prover has limited capabilities for automatic reasoning over first order quantified updates. Since quantified updates occur in many other scenarios it is worth to spend more effort on that front.

Acknowledgments. Many thanks to Richard Bubel whose help with the implementation was invaluable! Thanks are also due to Philipp Rümmer for many inspiring discussions.

References

1. W. Ahrendt, T. Baar, B. Beckert, R. Bubel, M. Giese, R. Hähnle, W. Menzel, W. Mostowski, A. Roth, S. Schlager, and P. H. Schmitt. The KeY tool: integrating object oriented design and formal verification. *Software and System Modeling*, 4(1):32–54, 2005.
2. U. Banerjee, S.-C. Chen, D. J. Kuck, and R. A. Towle. Time and parallel processor bounds for Fortran-like loops. *IEEE Trans. Computers*, 28(9):660–670, 1979.
3. B. Beckert. A dynamic logic for the formal verification of Java Card programs. In I. Attali and T. Jensen, editors, *Java on Smart Cards: Programming and Security. Revised Papers, Java Card 2000, Cannes, France*, LNCS 2041, pages 6–24. Springer, 2001.
4. B. Beckert and S. Schlager. Software verification with integrated data type refinement for integer arithmetic. In E. A. Boiten, J. Derrick, and G. Smith, editors, *Proc. , Intl. Conf. on Integrated Formal Methods*, volume 2999 of *LNCS*, pages 207–226. Springer, 2004.
5. B. Beckert, S. Schlager, and P. H. Schmitt. An improved rule for while loops in deductive program verification. In K.-K. Lau, editor, *Proc. , Seventh Intl. Conf. on Formal Engineering Methods (ICFEM), Manchester, UK*, LNCS. Springer-Verlag, 2005.
6. R. S. Boyer and J. S. Moore. *A Computational Logic Handbook*. Academic Press, 1988.
7. C.-B. Breunesse. *On JML: Topics in Tool-assisted Verification of Java Programs*. PhD thesis, Radboud University of Nijmegen, 2006.
8. A. Bundy, D. Basin, D. Hutter, and A. Ireland. *Rippling: Meta-Level Guidance for Mathematical Reasoning*, volume 56 of *Cambridge Tracts in Theoretical Computer Science*. Cambridge University Press, June 2005.
9. B. Cook, A. Podelski, and A. Rybalchenko. Termination proofs for systems code. In *Proc. ACM SIGPLAN Conf. on Programming Language Design and Implementation*. ACM Press, to appear, 2006.
10. C. Flanagan, K. R. M. Leino, M. Lillibridge, G. Nelson, J. B. Saxe, and R. Stata. Extended static checking for Java. In *Proc. ACM SIGPLAN 2002 Conf. on Programming Language Design and Implementation, Berlin*, pages 234–245. ACM Press, 2002.
11. R. Hähnle and W. Mostowski. Verification of safety properties in the presence of transactions. In G. Barthe, L. Burdy, M. Huisman, J.-L. Lanet, and T. Muntean, editors, *Post Conf. Proc. of CASSIS: Construction and Analysis of Safe, Secure and Interoperable Smart devices, Marseille*, volume 3362 of *LNCS*, pages 151–171. Springer, 2005.
12. D. Harel, D. Kozen, and J. Tiuryn. *Dynamic Logic*. MIT Press, 2000.
13. G. J. Holzmann. Software analysis and model checking. In E. Brinksma and K. G. Larsen, editors, *Proc. Intl. Conf. on Computer-Aided Verification CAV, Copenhagen*. Springer, 2002.
14. W. Mostowski. Formalisation and verification of Java Card security properties in dynamic logic. In M. Cerioli, editor, *Proc. Fundamental Approaches to Software Engineering (FASE), Edinburgh*, volume 3442 of *LNCS*, pages 357–371. Springer, Apr. 2005.
15. O. Olsson and A. Wallenburg. Customised induction rules for proving correctness of imperative programs. In B. Beckert and B. Aichernig, editors, *Proc. , Software Engineering and Formal Methods (SEFM), Koblenz, Germany*, pages 180–189. IEEE Press, 2005.
16. A. Platzer. Using a program verification calculus for constructing specifications from implementations. Master's thesis, Univ. Karlsruhe, Dept. of Computer Science, 2004.
17. P. Rümmer. Sequential, parallel, and quantified updates of first-order structures. In *Proceedings, 13th International Conference on Logic for Programming, Artificial Intelligence and Reasoning*, LNCS. Springer, 2006. To appear.
18. M. J. Wolfe. *Optimizing Supercompilers for Supercomputers*. The MIT Press, 1989.

On Computing Fixpoints in Well-Structured Regular Model Checking, with Applications to Lossy Channel Systems*

Christel Baier[1], Nathalie Bertrand[2], and Philippe Schnoebelen[2]

[1] Universität Bonn, Institut für Informatik I, Germany
[2] LSV, ENS de Cachan & CNRS, France

Abstract. We prove a general finite convergence theorem for "upward-guarded" fixpoint expressions over a well-quasi-ordered set. This has immediate applications in regular model checking of well-structured systems, where a main issue is the eventual convergence of fixpoint computations. In particular, we are able to directly obtain several new decidability results on lossy channel systems.

1 Introduction

Regular model checking [19,11] is a popular paradigm for the symbolic verification of models with infinite state space. It has been applied to varied families of systems ranging from distributed algorithms and channel systems to hybrid systems and programs handling dynamic data structures.

In regular model checking, one works with regular sets of states and handles them via finite descriptions, e.g., finite-state automata or regular expressions. Models amenable to regular model checking are such that, when $S \subseteq \mathit{Conf}$ is regular, then $Post(S)$ (or $Pre(S)$), the set of 1-step successors (resp., predecessors), is again a regular set that can be computed effectively from S. Since regular sets are closed under Boolean operations, one can[1] try to compute the reachability set $Post^*(Init)$, as the limit of the sequence

$$S_0 := Init; \quad S_1 := S_0 \cup Post(S_0); \quad \ldots \quad S_{n+1} := S_n \cup Post(S_n); \quad \ldots \qquad (*)$$

Since equality of regular sets is decidable, the computation of (*) can contain a test that detects if the limit is reached in finite time, i.e., if $S_{n+1} = S_n$ for some $n \in \mathbb{N}$,

With infinite-state models, the main difficulty is *convergence*. It is very rare that a fixpoint computation like (*) converges in finite time [10].

Well-structured transition systems (WSTS) are a generic family of models for which the co-reachability set $Pre^*(Final)$ can be computed symbolically with a backward-chaining version of (*) [3,16]. For WSTS's, convergence of the fixpoint computation is ensured by WQO theory: one handles upward-closed sets, and increasing sequences

---

* The first author is supported by the DFG-NWO project VOSS II and the DFG-project PROB-POR. The last two authors were supported by the ACI Sécurité & Informatique project Persée.
[1] Actually, such symbolic computations are possible with any class of representation closed under, and providing algorithms for, *Pre* or *Post*, Boolean operations, vacuity [19,18].

M. Hermann and A. Voronkov (Eds.): LPAR 2006, LNAI 4246, pp. 347–361, 2006.
© Springer-Verlag Berlin Heidelberg 2006

of upward-closed sets always converge in finite time when the underlying ordering is a well-quasi-ordering (a WQO), as is the case with WSTS's.

Computing $Pre^*(Final)$ for reachability analysis is just a special case of fixpoint computation. When dealing with richer temporal properties, one is interested in more complex fixpoints. E.g., the set of states satisfying the CTL formula $\exists[Cond U Goal]$ is definable via a least-fixpoint expression: $\mu X.Goal \cup (Cond \cap Pre(X))$. For game-theoretic properties, similar fixpoints are involved. E.g., the states from which one can enforce reaching a goal in a turn-based game is given by $\mu X.Goal \cup Pre(\overline{Pre(\overline{X})})$.

Our Contribution. In this paper, we define a notion of μ-expressions where recursion is guarded by upward-closure operators, and give a general finite convergence theorem for all such expressions. The consequence is that these fixpoint expressions can be evaluated symbolically by an iterative procedure. The guarded fragment we isolate is very relevant for the verification of well-structured transition systems as we demonstrate by providing several new decidability results on channel systems.

Related Work. Henzinger *et al.* give general conditions for the convergence of fix-points computations for temporal [18] or game-theoretic [14] properties, but the underlying framework (finite quotients) is different and has different applications (timed and hybrid systems). Our applications to well-structured transition systems generalize results from [2,27,28,21] that rely on more ad-hoc finite convergence lemmas.

2   A Guarded Mu-Calculus

We assume basic understanding of μ-calculi techniques (otherwise see [7]) and of well-quasi-ordering (WQO) theory (otherwise see [24,20], or simply [16, sect. 2.1]).

Let $(W, \sqsubseteq)$ be a well-quasi-ordered set. A subset V of W is *upward-closed* if $w \in V$ whenever $v \sqsubseteq w$ for some $v \in V$. From WQO theory, we mostly need the following:

Fact 2.1 (Finite convergence). *If $V_0 \subseteq V_1 \subseteq V_2 \subseteq \cdots$ is an infinite increasing sequence of upward-closed subsets of W, then for some index $k \in \mathbb{N}$, $\bigcup_{i \in \mathbb{N}} V_i = V_k$.*

The *upward-closure* of $V \subseteq W$, denoted $C_\uparrow(V)$, is the smallest upward-closed set that contains V. The *upward-kernel* of V, denoted $K_\uparrow(V)$, is the largest upward-closed set included in V. There are symmetric notions of *downward-closed* subset of W, of *downward-closure*, $C_\downarrow(V)$, and of *downward-kernel*, $K_\downarrow(V)$, of V. The complement of an upward-closed subset is downward-closed. Observe that $C_\uparrow(V) = V = K_\uparrow(V)$ iff V is upward-closed, and that $C_\uparrow$ and $K_\downarrow$ (resp., $C_\downarrow$ and $K_\uparrow$) are dual:

$$W \smallsetminus K_\uparrow(V) = C_\downarrow(W \smallsetminus V), \qquad W \smallsetminus K_\downarrow(V) = C_\uparrow(W \smallsetminus V). \qquad (1)$$

Monotonic Region Algebra. In symbolic model-checking, a *region algebra* is a family of sets of states (subsets of W) that is closed under Boolean and other relevant operators like Pre and $Post$ [18].

Here we consider regions generated by a family $O = \{o_1, o_2, \ldots\}$ of (monotonic) operators. By a k-ary *operator*, we mean a monotonic mapping $o : (2^W)^k \to 2^W$ that associates a subset $o(V_1, \ldots, V_k) \subseteq W$ with any k subsets $V_1, \ldots, V_k$. Monotonicity means that $o(V_1,\ldots,V_k) \subseteq o(V_1',\ldots,V_k')$ when $V_i \subseteq V_i'$ for $i = 1,\ldots,k$. We allow nullary operators, i.e., fixed subsets of W. Finally, we require that O contains at least four special unary operators: $C_\uparrow$, $C_\downarrow$, $K_\uparrow$, $K_\downarrow$, and two special nullary operators: $\emptyset$ and W.

The *region algebra generated by* O, denoted with $\mathcal{R}_O$, or simply $\mathcal{R}$, is the set of all the subsets of W, called *regions*, that can be obtained by applying operators from O on already constructed regions, starting with nullary operators. Equivalently, $\mathcal{R}$ is the least subset of 2^W that is closed under O.

We say the region algebra generated by O is *effective* if there are algorithms implementing the operators in O and an effective membership algorithm saying whether $w \in R$ for some $w \in W$ and some region $R \in \mathcal{R}_O$. Such effectiveness assumptions presuppose a finitary encoding of regions and elements of W: if there are several possible encodings for a same region, we assume an effective equality test.

Extending the Region Algebra with Fixpoints. Let $\chi = \{X_1, X_2, \cdots\}$ be a countable set of variables. $L_\mu(W, \sqsubseteq, O)$, or shortly L_μ when $(W, \sqsubseteq)$ and O are understood, is the set of *O-terms with least and greatest fixpoints* given by the following abstract syntax:

$$L_\mu \ni \varphi, \psi ::= o(\varphi_1,\ldots,\varphi_k) \mid X \mid \mu X.\varphi \mid \nu X.\varphi \mid C_\uparrow(\varphi) \mid C_\downarrow(\varphi) \mid K_\uparrow(\varphi) \mid K_\downarrow(\varphi)$$

where X runs over variables from χ, and o over operators from O. $\mu X.\varphi$ and $\nu X.\varphi$ are fixpoint expressions. Free and bound occurrences of variables are defined as usual. We assume that no variable has both bound and free occurrences in some φ, and that no two fixpoint subterms bind the same variable: this can always be ensured by renaming bound variables. (The abstract syntax for L_μ could be shorter but we wanted to stress that $C_\uparrow$, $C_\downarrow$, $K_\uparrow$, and $K_\downarrow$ are required to be present in O.)

The meaning of L_μ terms is as expected: an *environment* is a mapping $env : \chi \to 2^W$ that interprets each variable $X \in \chi$ as a subset of W. Given env, a term $\varphi \in L_\mu$ denotes a subset of W, written $[\![\varphi]\!]_{env}$ and defined by induction on the structure of φ:

$$[\![X]\!]_{env} \stackrel{\text{def}}{=} env(X) \qquad\qquad [\![o(\varphi_1,\ldots,\varphi_k)]\!]_{env} \stackrel{\text{def}}{=} o([\![\varphi_1]\!]_{env},\ldots,[\![\varphi_k]\!]_{env})$$

$$[\![C_\uparrow(\varphi)]\!]_{env} \stackrel{\text{def}}{=} C_\uparrow([\![\varphi]\!]_{env}) \qquad\qquad [\![C_\downarrow(\varphi)]\!]_{env} \stackrel{\text{def}}{=} C_\downarrow([\![\varphi]\!]_{env})$$

$$[\![K_\uparrow(\varphi)]\!]_{env} \stackrel{\text{def}}{=} K_\uparrow([\![\varphi]\!]_{env}) \qquad\qquad [\![K_\downarrow(\varphi)]\!]_{env} \stackrel{\text{def}}{=} K_\downarrow([\![\varphi]\!]_{env})$$

$$[\![\mu X.\varphi]\!]_{env} \stackrel{\text{def}}{=} \mathrm{lfp}(\Omega[\varphi,X,env]) \qquad\qquad [\![\nu X.\varphi]\!]_{env} \stackrel{\text{def}}{=} \mathrm{gfp}(\Omega[\varphi,X,env])$$

where, for all φ, X, and env, $\Omega[\varphi, X, env] : 2^W \to 2^W$ is a unary operator defined by $\Omega[\varphi, X, env](V) \stackrel{\text{def}}{=} [\![\varphi]\!]_{env[X:=V]}$, using the standard variant notation "$env[X := V]$" for the environment that agrees with env everywhere except on X where it returns V. As usual, $[\![\varphi]\!]_{env}$ does not depend on $env(X)$ if X is not free in φ, so that we may shortly write $[\![\varphi]\!]$ when φ is a closed term, i.e., a term with no free variables.

We recall that the semantics of the fixpoint terms is well-defined since, for every φ, X and env, $\Omega[\varphi, X, env]$ is monotonic (and since $(2^W, \subseteq)$ is a complete lattice). Moreover, if env and env' are such that $env(X) \subseteq env'(X)$ for all $X \in \chi$, shortly written $env \subseteq env'$, then $\mathrm{lfp}(\Omega[\varphi, X, env]) \subseteq \mathrm{lfp}(\Omega[\varphi, X, env'])$ and $\mathrm{gfp}(\Omega[\varphi, X, env]) \subseteq \mathrm{gfp}(\Omega[\varphi, X, env'])$.

Definition 2.2 (Upward- and downward-guardedness)

1. *A variable X is* upward-guarded *in φ if all free occurrences of X in φ are in the scope of either a $C_\uparrow$ or a $K_\uparrow$ operator, i.e., appear in a subterm of the form $C_\uparrow(\psi)$ or $K_\uparrow(\psi)$.*
2. *Dually, X is* downward-guarded *in φ if all its free occurrences are in the scope of a $C_\downarrow$ or a $K_\downarrow$ operator.*
3. *A term φ is* guarded *if all its least-fixpoint subterms $\mu X.\psi$ have X upward-guarded in ψ, and all its greatest-fixpoint subterms $\nu X.\psi$ have X downward-guarded in ψ.*

Given some φ, X and env, the approximants of $\mathrm{lfp}(\Omega[\varphi,X,env])$ are given by the sequence $(M_i)_{i\in\mathbb{N}}$ of subsets of W defined inductively by $M_0 = \emptyset$ and $M_{i+1} = [\![\varphi]\!]_{env[X:=M_i]}$. Monotonicity yields

$$M_0 \subseteq M_1 \subseteq M_2 \subseteq \cdots \subseteq \mathrm{lfp}(\Omega[\varphi,X,env]). \tag{2}$$

Similarly we define $(N_i)_{i\in\mathbb{N}}$ by $N_0 = W$ and $N_{i+1} = [\![\varphi]\!]_{env[X:=N_i]}$, so that

$$N_0 \supseteq N_1 \supseteq N_2 \supseteq \cdots \supseteq \mathrm{gfp}(\Omega[\varphi,X,env]). \tag{3}$$

Lemma 2.3 (Finite convergence of approximants). *If X is upward-guarded in φ, then there exists an index $k \in \mathbb{N}$ such that*

$$[\![\mu X.\varphi]\!]_{env} = M_k = M_{k+1} = M_{k+2} = \ldots \tag{4}$$

Dually, if X is downward-guarded in φ, then there exists a $k' \in \mathbb{N}$ such that

$$[\![\nu X.\varphi]\!]_{env} = N_{k'} = N_{k'+1} = N_{k'+2} = \ldots \tag{5}$$

Proof. We only prove the first half since the other half is dual. Let $\psi_1,\ldots,\psi_m$ be the maximal subterms of φ that are immediately under the scope of a $C_\uparrow$ or a $K_\uparrow$ operator. Then φ can be decomposed under the form

$$\varphi \equiv \Phi(\Uparrow \psi_1, \ldots, \Uparrow \psi_m)$$

where the context $\Phi(Y_1,\ldots,Y_m)$ uses fresh variables $Y_1,\ldots,Y_m$ to be substituted in, and where $\Uparrow \psi_i$ is either $C_\uparrow(\psi_i)$ or $K_\uparrow(\psi_i)$, depending on how ψ_i appears in φ. In either case, and for any environment env', the set $[\![\Uparrow \psi_i]\!]_{env'}$ is upward-closed.

For $V_1,\ldots,V_m \subseteq W$ we shortly write $[\![\Phi]\!](V_1,\ldots,V_m)$ for $[\![\Phi]\!]_{env[Y_1:=V_1,\ldots,Y_m:=V_m]}$. Since X is upward-guarded in φ, it has no occurrence in Φ, only in the ψ_i's, so that

$$M_{i+1} = [\![\varphi]\!]_{env[X:=M_i]} = [\![\Phi]\!]([\![\Uparrow \psi_1]\!]_{env[X:=M_i]}, \ldots, [\![\Uparrow \psi_m]\!]_{env[X:=M_i]})$$
$$= [\![\Phi]\!](L_{i,1},\ldots,L_{i,m})$$

writing $L_{i,j}$ for $[\![\Uparrow \psi_j]\!]_{env[X:=M_i]}$. From $M_0 \subseteq M_1 \subseteq M_2 \subseteq \cdots$, we deduce $L_{0,j} \subseteq L_{1,j} \subseteq L_{2,j} \subseteq \cdots$ Since $K_\uparrow$ and $C_\uparrow$ return upward-closed sets, the $L_{i,j}$'s are upward-closed subsets of W. For all $j = 1,\ldots,m$, Fact 2.1 implies that there is an index k_j such that $L_{i,j} = L_{k_j,j}$ for all $i \geq k_j$. Picking $K = \max(k_1,\ldots,k_j)$ gives for any $i \geq K$

$$M_{i+1} = [\![\Phi]\!](L_{i,1},\ldots,L_{i,m}) = [\![\Phi]\!](L_{k_1,1},\ldots,L_{k_m,m}) = [\![\Phi]\!](L_{K,1},\ldots,L_{K,m}) = M_{K+1}.$$

Thus, $\bigcup_{i\in\mathbb{N}} M_i = M_{K+1} = M_{K+2}$ and M_{K+1} is a fixpoint of $\Omega[\varphi,X,env]$, hence the least one thanks to (2). Picking $k = K + 1$ satisfies (4). $\qquad\square$

Regions with Guarded Fixpoints. We can now prove our main result: subsets defined by L_μ terms are regions (and can be computed effectively if the underlying region algebra is effective).

By a *region-environment* we mean an environment $env : \chi \to \mathcal{R}$ that associates regions with variables. If env is a region-environment, and φ has only free variables, i.e., has no fixpoint subterms, then $[\![\varphi]\!]_{env}$ is a region.

Theorem 2.4. *If $\varphi \in L_\mu$ is guarded and env is a region-environment then $[\![\varphi]\!]_{env}$ is a region. Furthermore, if the region algebra is effective, then $[\![\varphi]\!]_{env}$ can be computed effectively from φ and env.*

Proof. By structural induction on the structure of φ. If $\varphi = o()$ is a nullary operator, the result holds by definition of the region algebra. If $\varphi = o(\varphi_1, \cdots, \varphi_k)$, the $[\![\varphi_i]\!]_{env}$'s are (effectively) regions by induction hypothesis, so that $[\![\varphi]\!]_{env}$ is an (effective) region too by definition. In particular, this argument applies when o is a nullary operator, or is one of the unary operators we singled out: $C_\uparrow$, $C_\downarrow$, $K_\uparrow$, and $K_\downarrow$.

If $\varphi = \mu X.\psi$, we can apply Lemma 2.3 after we have proved that each one of the approximants $M_0, M_1, M_2, \ldots,$ of $[\![\varphi]\!]_{env}$ are regions. In particular, $M_0 = \emptyset$ is a region, and if M_i is a region, then $M_{i+1} = [\![\psi]\!]_{env[X:=M_i]}$ is one too, since $env' = env[X := M_i]$ is a region-environment, and since by induction hypothesis $[\![\psi]\!]_{env'}$ is a region when env' is a region-environment. When $\mathcal{R}_O$ is effective, the M_i can be computed effectively, and one can detect when $M_k = M_{k+1}$ since region equality is decidable by definition. Then $[\![\varphi]\!]_{env} = M_k$ can be computed effectively. Finally, the case where $\varphi = \nu X.\psi$ is dual.   □

Corollary 2.5 (Decidability for guarded $\mathcal{L}_\mu$ properties). *The following problems are decidable for effective monotonic region algebras:*

Model-checking: *"Does $w \in [\![\varphi]\!]$?" for a $w \in W$ and a closed and guarded $\varphi \in L_\mu$.*
Satisfiability: *"Is $[\![\varphi]\!]$ non-empty?" for a closed and guarded $\varphi \in L_\mu$.*
Universality: *"Does $[\![\varphi]\!] = W$?" for a closed and guarded $\varphi \in L_\mu$.*

A Region Algebra of Regular Languages. Consider $W = \Sigma^*$, the set of finite words over some finite alphabet Σ. The *subword ordering*, defined by "$u \sqsubseteq v$ iff u can be obtained by erasing some letters from v", is a WQO (Higman's Lemma). Regular languages over Σ are a natural choice for regions: observe that the closure operators $C_\uparrow$ and $C_\downarrow$ preserve regularity and have effective implementations.[2] Natural operators to be considered in O are $\cup$ (union) and $\cap$ (intersection). However, any operation on languages that is monotonic, preserve regularity, and has an effective implementation on regular languages can be added. This includes concatenation (denoted $R.R'$), star-closure (denote R^*), left- and right-residuals ($R^{-1}R' \stackrel{\text{def}}{=} \{v \mid \exists u \in R, uv \in R'\}$), shuffle product (denoted $R \parallel R'$), reverse (denoted $\overleftarrow{R}$), conjugacy ($\widetilde{R} \stackrel{\text{def}}{=} \{vu \mid uv \in R\}$), homomorphic and inverse-homomorphic images, and many more [26]. Complementation is not allowed in O (it is not monotonic) but the duals of all above-mentioned operators can be

---

[2] From a FSA for R, one obtains a FSA for $C_\uparrow(R)$ simply by adding loops $q \stackrel{a}{\to} q$ on all states q of the FSA and for all letters $a \in \Sigma$. A FSA for $C_\downarrow(R)$ is obtained by adding ε-transitions $q \stackrel{\varepsilon}{\to} q'$ whenever there is a $q \stackrel{a}{\to} q'$. From this, $K_\uparrow$ and $K_\downarrow$ can be implemented using (1).

included in O (without compromising effectiveness) so that, for all practical purposes, complement can be used with the restriction that bound variables in L_μ terms are under an even number of complementations.

An application of Theorem 2.4 is that, if R_1 and R_2 are regular languages, then the language defined as $\mu X . \nu Y . \left(K_\uparrow \left[R_1 \parallel (X^* \cap C_\downarrow (Y^{-1} \overleftarrow{X} \cap X^{-1} R_2)) \right] \right)$ is regular and a finite representation for it (e.g., a regular expression or a minimal DFA) can be constructed from R_1 and R_2.

3 Verification of Lossy Channel Systems

Theorem 2.4 has several applications for regular model checking of lossy channel systems [5] (LCS) and other families of well-structured systems [3,16]. In the rest of this paper we concentrate on LCS's.

3.1 Channel Systems, Perfect and Lossy

A channel system is a tuple $\mathcal{L} = (Q, \mathsf{C}, \mathsf{M}, \Delta)$ consisting of a finite set $Q = \{p, q, \ldots\}$ of *locations*, a finite set $\mathsf{C} = \{c, \ldots\}$ of *channels*, a finite *message alphabet* $\mathsf{M} = \{m, \ldots\}$ and a finite set $\Delta = \{\delta, \ldots\}$ of *transition rules*. Each transition rule has the form $q \xrightarrow{op} p$ where op is an *operation*: $c!m$ (sending message $m \in \mathsf{M}$ along channel $c \in \mathsf{C}$), $c?m$ (receiving message m from channel c), or $\sqrt{}$ (an internal action to some process, no I/O-operation).

Operational Semantics. Let $\mathcal{L} = (Q, \mathsf{C}, \mathsf{M}, \Delta)$ be a channel system. A *configuration* (also, a *state*) is a pair $\sigma = (q, w)$ where $q \in Q$ is a location and $w : \mathsf{C} \to \mathsf{M}^*$ is a channel valuation that associates with any channel its content (a sequence of messages). The set $Q \times \mathsf{M}^{*\mathsf{C}}$ of all configurations is denoted by $\mathit{Conf} = \{\sigma, \rho, \ldots\}$. For a subset V of Conf, we let $\overline{V} \stackrel{\text{def}}{=} \mathit{Conf} \smallsetminus V$.

Steps between configurations are as expected. Formally, $\sigma = (q, w)$ leads to $\sigma' = (q', w')$ by firing $\delta = p \xrightarrow{op} r$, denoted $\sigma \xrightarrow{\delta}_{\mathrm{perf}} \sigma'$, if and only if $q = p$, $q' = r$ and w' is obtained from w by the effect of op (the "perf" subscripts emphasizes that the step is perfect: without losses). Precisely

$$w'(c) = \begin{cases} w(c)m & \text{if } op = c!m, \\ m^{-1}w(c) & \text{if } op = c?m, \end{cases}$$

where the notation "$w(c)m$" (for concatenation) and "$m^{-1}w(c)$" (for left-residuals) are as in section 2. Furthermore, $w'(c) = w(c)$ for all channels c that are not touched upon by op.

Thus, when $op = c?m$, w' is only defined if $w(c)$ starts with m and indeed this is the intended condition for firing δ. Whenever $\sigma \xrightarrow{\delta} \rho$ for some ρ, we say that δ is *enabled* in σ, written $\delta \in \Delta(\sigma)$.

Below we restrict our attention to LCS's where from each $q \in Q$ there is at least one rule $q \xrightarrow{op} p$ in Δ where op is not a receiving action: this ensures that the LCS has no deadlock states and simplifies many technical details without losing any generality.

Lossy Systems. In *lossy* channel systems, losing messages is formalized via the sub-word ordering, extended from M^* to *Conf*: $(q, w) \sqsubseteq (q', w')$ if $q = q'$ and $w(c) \sqsubseteq w'(c)$ for all channels $c \in C$.

A (possibly lossy) step in the LCS is made of a perfect step followed by arbitrary losses:[3] formally, we write $\sigma \xrightarrow{\delta} \rho$ whenever there is a perfect step $\sigma \xrightarrow{\delta}_{\text{perf}} \sigma'$ such that $\rho \sqsubseteq \sigma'$. This gives rise to a labeled transition system $LTS_L \overset{\text{def}}{=} (Conf, \Delta, \rightarrow)$.

Remark 3.1. Our choice of operational semantics has the consequence that LTS_L is *not* turned into a WSTS by $\sqsubseteq$ because message losses only occur after a step. However, the WSTS structure is recovered with the following relation: $\sigma \preceq \rho \overset{\text{def}}{\Leftrightarrow} \sigma \sqsubseteq \rho \wedge \Delta(\sigma) = \Delta(\rho)$. Both $\sqsubseteq$ and $\preceq$ turns *Conf* into a WQO. From now on we assume, for the sake of simplicity, that $(Conf, \sqsubseteq)$ is the WQO on which L_μ is defined.   □

Following standard notations for transition systems $(Conf, \Delta, \rightarrow)$ labeled over some Δ, we write $Pre[\delta](\sigma) \overset{\text{def}}{=} \{\rho \in Conf \mid \rho \xrightarrow{\delta} \sigma\}$ for the set of predecessors via δ of σ in L. Then $Pre(\sigma) \overset{\text{def}}{=} \bigcup_{\delta \in \Delta} Pre[\delta](\sigma)$ has all 1-step predecessors of σ, and $Pre(V) = \bigcup_{\sigma \in V} Pre(\sigma)$ has all 1-step predecessors of states in V. The dual $\widetilde{Pre}$ of Pre is defined by $\widetilde{Pre}(V) = \overline{Pre(\overline{V})}$. Thus $\sigma \in \widetilde{Pre}(V)$ iff all 1-step successors of σ are in V (this includes the case where σ is a deadlock state).

Seen as unary operators on 2^{Conf}, both Pre and $\widetilde{Pre}$ are monotonic and even continuous for all transition systems [30]. For LCS's, the following lemma states that Pre is compatible with the WQO on states, which will play a crucial role later when we want to show that some L_μ term is guarded.

Lemma 3.2. *Let $V \subseteq Conf$ in the transition system LTS_L associated with a LCS L. Then $Pre(V) = Pre(C_\uparrow(V))$ and $\widetilde{Pre}(V) = \widetilde{Pre}(K_\downarrow(V))$.*

Proof. $V \subseteq C_\uparrow(V)$ implies $Pre(V) \subseteq Pre(C_\uparrow(V))$. Now $\sigma \in Pre(C_\uparrow(V))$ implies that $\sigma \rightarrow \rho \sqsupseteq \rho'$ for some $\rho' \in V$. But then $\sigma \rightarrow \rho'$ by definition of lossy steps and $\sigma \in Pre(V)$. The second equality is dual.   □

An Effective Region Algebra for LCS's. We are now ready to apply the framework of section 2 to regular model checking of lossy channel systems. Assume $L = (Q, C, M, \Delta)$ is a given LCS. A region $R \in \mathcal{R}$ is any "regular" subset of *Conf*. More formally, it is any set $R \subseteq Conf$ that can be written under the form

$$R = \sum_{i \in I} (q_i, R_i^1, \ldots, R_i^{|C|})$$

---

[3] Note that, with this definition, message losses only occur *after* steps (thus, not in the initial configuration). The usual definition allows arbitrary losses before and after a step [5]. There is no essential semantic difference between these two ways of grouping atomic events into single "steps", except for the first step. The definition from [5] is technically smoother when LCS's are viewed as nondeterministic systems, but becomes unnatural in situations where several adversarial processes compete, e.g., in probabilistic LCS's [9] or the game-theoretical settings we explore in sections 4 and 5.

where I is a *finite* index set, the q_i's are locations from Q, and each R_i^j is a regular language on alphabet M. The notation has obvious interpretation, with summation denoting set union (the empty sum is denoted $\emptyset$). We are not more precise on how such regions could be effectively represented (see [6]), but they could be handled as, e.g., regular expressions or FSAs over the extended alphabet $M \cup Q \cup \{'(',')',',',\}$.

The set O of operators includes union, intersection, $C_\uparrow$, $C_\downarrow$, $K_\uparrow$, $K_\downarrow$: these are monotonic, regularity-preserving, and effective operators as explained in our example at the end of section 2. Operators specific to regular model-checking are Pre and $\widetilde{Pre}$. That they are regularity-preserving and effective is better seen by first looking at the special case of perfect steps. We use

$$Pre_{\text{perf}}[p \xrightarrow{c_i?m} q](q, R_p^1, \cdots, R_p^{|C|}) = (p, R_p^1, \ldots, R_p^{i-1}, mR_p^i, R_p^{i+1}, \ldots, R_p^{|C|}),$$

$$Pre_{\text{perf}}[p \xrightarrow{c_i!m} q](q, R_p^1, \cdots, R_p^{|C|}) = (p, R_p^1, \ldots, R_p^{i-1}, R_p^i m^{-1}, R_p^{i+1}, \ldots, R_p^{|C|})$$

completed with the obvious

$$Pre_{\text{perf}}[p \xrightarrow{op} q](r, R_p^1, \cdots, R_p^{|C|}) = \emptyset \text{ when } r \neq q,$$

$$Pre_{\text{perf}}\left(\sum_{i \in I}(q_i, R_i^1, \ldots, R_i^{|C|})\right) = \sum_{i \in I}\sum_{\delta \in \Delta} Pre_{\text{perf}}[\delta](q_i, R_i^1, \ldots, R_i^{|C|}).$$

Then lossy steps are handled with $Pre(R) = Pre_{\text{perf}}(C_\uparrow(R))$.

Clearly, both Pre_{perf} and Pre are effective operators on regions.

3.2   Regular Model-Checking for Lossy Channel Systems

Surprising decidability results for lossy channel systems is what launched the study of this model [15,5,12]. We reformulate several of these results as a direct consequence of Theorem 2.4, before moving to new problems and new decidability results in the next sections. Note that our technique is applied here to a slightly different operational semantics (cf. footnote 3) but it would clearly apply as directly to the simpler semantics.

Reachability Analysis. Thanks to Lemma 3.2, the co-reachability set can be expressed as a guarded L_μ term:

$$Pre^*(V) = \mu X.V \cup Pre(X) = \mu X.V \cup Pre(C_\uparrow(X)). \tag{6}$$

Corollary 3.3. *For regular* $V \subseteq Conf$, *$Pre^*(V)$ is regular and effectively computable.*

Safety Properties. More generally, safety properties can be handled. In CTL, they can be written $\forall(V_1 R V_2)$. Recall that R, the Release modality, is dual to Until: a state σ satisfies $\forall(V_1 R V_2)$ if and only if along all paths issuing from σ, V_2 always holds until maybe V_1 is visited. Using Lemma 3.2, $[\![\forall(V_1 R V_2)]\!]$, the set of states where the safety property holds, can be defined as a guarded L_μ term:

$$[\![\forall(V_1 R V_2)]\!] = \nu X.\left(V_2 \cap (\widetilde{Pre}(X) \cup V_1)\right) = \nu X.\left(V_2 \cap (\widetilde{Pre}(K_\downarrow(X)) \cup V_1)\right). \tag{7}$$

Corollary 3.4. *For regular $V_1, V_2 \subseteq Conf$, $[\![\forall(V_1 R V_2)]\!]$ is regular and effectively computable.*

Another formulation is based on the duality between the "$\forall R$" and the "$\exists U$" modalities.

Theorem 3.5. *[21, sect. 5] If f is a temporal formula in the $\mathsf{TL}(\exists U, \exists X, \wedge, \neg)$ fragment of CTL (using regions for atomic propositions), then $[\![f]\!]$ is regular and effectively computable.*

Proof. By induction on the structure of f, using $[\![\exists X f]\!] \overset{\text{def}}{=} Pre([\![f]\!])$, and the fact that regions are (effectively) closed under complementation. $\square$

Beyond Safety. Inevitability properties, and recurrent reachability can be stated in L_μ. With temporal logic notation, this yields

$$[\![\forall \Diamond V]\!] = \mu X.\big(V \cup (Pre(Conf) \cap \widetilde{Pre}(X))\big),$$
$$[\![\exists \Box \Diamond V]\!] = \nu X.\big(\mu Y.((V \cup Pre(Y)) \cap Pre(X))\big).$$

These two terms are not guarded and Lemma 3.2 is of no help here. However this is not surprising: firstly, $\sigma \models \exists \Box \Diamond V$ is undecidable [4]; secondly, and while $\sigma \models [\![\forall \Diamond V]\!]$ is decidable, the set $[\![\forall \Diamond V]\!]$ cannot be computed effectively [23].

3.3   Generalized Lossy Channel Systems

Transition rules in LCS's do not carry guards, aka preconditions, beyond the implicit condition that a reading action $c?m$ is only enabled when $w(c)$ starts with m. This barebone definition is for simplification purpose, but actual protocols sometimes use guards that probe the contents of the channel before taking this or that transition. The simplest such guards are emptiness tests, like "$p \xrightarrow{c=\varepsilon?} q$" that only allows a transition from p to q if $w(c)$ is empty.

We now introduce *LCS's with regular guards* (GLCS's), an extension of the barebone model where any regular set of channel contents can be used to guard a transition rule. This generalizes emptiness tests, occurrence tests (as in [25]), etc., and allows expressing priority between rules since whether given rules are enabled is a regular condition.

Formally, we assume rules in Δ now have the form $p \xrightarrow{G:op} q$ with p, q, op as before, and where G, the guard, can be any regular region. The operational semantics is a expected: when $\delta = p \xrightarrow{G:op} q$, there is a perfect step $\sigma \xrightarrow{\delta}_{\text{perf}} \theta$ iff $\sigma \in G$ and θ is obtained from σ by the rule $p \xrightarrow{G:op} q$ (without any guard). Then, general steps $\sigma \xrightarrow{\delta} \rho$ are obtained from perfect steps $\sigma \xrightarrow{\delta}_{\text{perf}} \sigma'$ by message losses $\rho \sqsubseteq \sigma'$.

Verification of GLCS's. For GLCS's, *Pre* and *Post* are effective monotonic regularity-preserving operators as in the LCS case since

$$Pre[p \xrightarrow{G:op} q](R) = G \cap Pre[p \xrightarrow{op} q](R),$$
$$Post[p \xrightarrow{G:op} q](R) = Post[p \xrightarrow{op} q](G \cap R).$$

Observe that Lemma 3.2 holds for GLCS's as well, so that Equations (6) and (7) entail a generalized version of Theorem 3.5:

Theorem 3.6. *For all GLCS's L and formulae f in the* $\mathsf{TL}(\exists\mathsf{U},\exists\mathsf{X},\wedge,\neg)$ *fragment,* $[\![f]\!]$
is regular and effectively computable.

4 Solving Games on Lossy Channel Systems

In this section, we consider turn-based games on GLCS's where two players, A and
B, alternate their moves. Games play a growing role in verification where they address
situations in which different agents have different, competing goals. We assume a basic
understanding of the associated concepts: arena, play, strategy, etc. (otherwise see [17]).

Games on well-structured systems have already been investigated in [2,27,28]. The
positive results in these three papers rely on ad-hoc finite convergence lemmas that are
special cases of our Theorem 2.4.

4.1   Symmetric LCS-Games with Controllable Message Losses

We start with the simplest kind of games on a GLCS: A and B play in turn, choosing the
next configuration, i.e., picking what rule $\delta \in \Delta$ is fired, and what messages are lost.

Formally, a *symmetric LCS-game* is a GLCS $L = (Q_A, Q_B, C, M, \Delta)$ where the set
of locations $Q = Q_A \cup Q_B$ is partitioned into two sets, one for each player, and where
the rules ensure strict alternation: for all $p \xrightarrow{G:op} q \in \Delta$, $p \in Q_A$ iff $q \in Q_B$. Below, we
shortly write $Conf_A$ for $Q_A \times M^{*|C|}$, the regular region where it is A's turn to play. $Conf_B$
is defined similarly. Strict alternation means that the arena, LTS_L, is a bipartite graph
partitioned in $Conf_A$ and $Conf_B$.

Reachability Games. Reachability and invariance are among the simplest objectives
for games. In a reachability game, A tries to reach a state in some set V, no matter how
B behaves. This goal is denoted $\Diamond V$. It is known that such games are determined and
that memoryless strategies are sufficient [17]. The set of winning configurations for A
is denoted with $\langle\!\langle A \rangle\!\rangle \Diamond V$, and can be defined in L_μ:

$$\langle\!\langle A \rangle\!\rangle \Diamond V = \mu X . \Big[V \cup [Conf_A \cap Pre(X)] \cup [Conf_B \cap \widetilde{Pre}(X)] \Big]. \tag{8}$$

The first occurrence of X can be made upward-guarded by replacing $Pre(X)$ with
$Pre(C_\uparrow(X))$ (Lemma 3.2). For the second occurrence, we can unfold the term, relying
on the fixpoint equation $[\![\mu X . \varphi(X)]\!] = [\![\mu X . \varphi(\varphi(X))]\!]$. This will replace $Conf_B \cap \widetilde{Pre}(X)$
in (8) with

$$Conf_B \cap \widetilde{Pre}\Big(V \cup [Conf_A \cap Pre(X)] \cup [Conf_B \cap \widetilde{Pre}(X)] \Big). \tag{+}$$

Now, the strict alternation between $Conf_A$ and $Conf_B$ lets us simplify (+) into

$$Conf_B \cap \widetilde{Pre}\Big(V \cup Pre(X) \Big). \tag{9}$$

Hence (8) can be rewritten into

$$\langle\!\langle A \rangle\!\rangle \Diamond V = \mu X . \Big[V \cup [Conf_A \cap Pre(C_\uparrow(X))] \cup [Conf_B \cap \widetilde{Pre}(V \cup Pre(C_\uparrow(X)))] \Big]. \tag{8'}$$

Invariance Games. In invariance games, A's goal is to never leave some set $V \subseteq Conf$, no matter how B behaves. Invariance games are dual to reachability games, and the set of winning configurations $\langle\!\langle A \rangle\!\rangle \Box V$ is exactly $\overline{\langle\!\langle B \rangle\!\rangle \Diamond \overline{V}}$.

Repeated Reachability Games. Here A's goal is to visit V infinitely many times, no matter how B behaves. The set of winning configurations is given by the following L_μ term:

$$\langle\!\langle A \rangle\!\rangle \Box \Diamond V = \nu Y.\langle\!\langle A \rangle\!\rangle \Diamond \left[V \cap (\varphi_A(Y) \cup \varphi_B(Y)) \right], \qquad (10)$$

where

$$\varphi_A(Y) \overset{\text{def}}{=} Conf_A \cap Pre\big(C_\uparrow(\widetilde{Pre}(K_\downarrow(Y)))\big),$$
$$\varphi_B(Y) \overset{\text{def}}{=} Conf_B \cap \widetilde{Pre}(K_\downarrow(Y)).$$

and where we reuse (8') for $\langle\!\langle A \rangle\!\rangle \Diamond [\ldots]$.

Persistence Games. In a persistence game, A aims at remaining inside V from some moment on, no matter how B behaves. Dually, this can be seen as a repeated reachability game for B. Note that $\langle\!\langle A \rangle\!\rangle \Diamond \Box V \neq \langle\!\langle A \rangle\!\rangle \Diamond (\langle\!\langle A \rangle\!\rangle \Box V)$.

Theorem 4.1 (Decidability of symmetric LCS-games). *For symmetric LCS-games $\mathcal{L}$ and regular regions V, the four sets $\langle\!\langle A \rangle\!\rangle \Diamond V$, $\langle\!\langle A \rangle\!\rangle \Box V$, $\langle\!\langle A \rangle\!\rangle \Diamond \Box V$, and $\langle\!\langle A \rangle\!\rangle \Box \Diamond V$, are (effective) regions. Hence reachability, invariance, repeated reachability, and persistence symmetric games are decidable on GLCS's.*

Proof (Sketch). The winning sets can be defined by guarded L_μ terms.

Remark 4.2. There is no contradiction between the undecidability of $\exists \Box \Diamond V$ and the decidability of $\langle\!\langle A \rangle\!\rangle \Box \Diamond V$. In the latter case, B does not cooperate with A, making the goal harder to reach for A (and the property easier to decide for us).   □

4.2   Asymmetric LCS-Games with 1-Sided Controlled Loss of Messages

Here we adopt the setting considered in [2]. It varies from the symmetric setting of section 4.1 in that only player B can lose messages (and can control what is lost), while player A can only make perfect steps. Note that this generalizes games where A plays moves in the channel system, and B is an adversarial environment responsible for message losses. We use the same syntax as for symmetric LCS-games.

Reachability and Invariance Games. Let us first consider games where one player tries to reach a regular region V (goal $\Diamond V$), no matter how the other player behaves.

The configurations where B can win a reachability game are given by:

$$\langle\!\langle B \rangle\!\rangle \Diamond V = \mu X.V \cup \left(Conf_B \cap Pre(X) \right) \cup \left(Conf_A \cap \widetilde{Pre}_{\text{perf}}(X) \right)$$
$$= \mu X.V \cup \left(Conf_B \cap Pre(C_\uparrow(X)) \right) \cup \left(Conf_A \cap \widetilde{Pre}_{\text{perf}}(V \cup Pre(C_\uparrow(X))) \right)$$

where guardedness is obtained via Lemma 3.2 and unfolding.

When we consider a reachability game for A, the situation is not so clear:

$$\langle\!\langle A \rangle\!\rangle \Diamond V = \mu X.V \cup \left(Conf_A \cap Pre_{\text{perf}}(X)\right) \cup \left(Conf_B \cap \widetilde{Pre}(X)\right).$$

Neither Lemma 3.2 nor unfolding techniques can turn this into a guarded term. This should be expected since the set $\langle\!\langle A \rangle\!\rangle \Diamond V$ cannot be computed effectively [2].

Theorem 4.3 (Decidability of asymmetric LCS-games [2]). *For asymmetric LCS-games L and regular regions V, the sets $\langle\!\langle B \rangle\!\rangle \Diamond V$ and $\langle\!\langle A \rangle\!\rangle \Box V$ are (effective) regions. Hence reachability games for B, and invariance games for A are decidable on GLCS's.*

Proof (Sketch). Invariance games are dual to reachability games, and the winning set $\langle\!\langle B \rangle\!\rangle \Diamond V$ is defined by a guarded L_μ term.

5   Channel Systems with Probabilistic Losses

LCS's where messages losses follow probabilistic rules have been investigated as a less pessimistic model of protocols with unreliable channels (see [29,1,9] and the references therein).

In [9], we present decidability results for LCS's seen as combining *nondeterministic* choice of transition rules with *probabilistic* message losses. The semantics is in term of Markovian decision processes, or $1\frac{1}{2}$-player games, whose solutions can be defined in L_μ. Indeed, we found the inspiration for L_μ and our Theorem 2.4 while extending our results in the MDP approach to richer sets of regions.

In this section, rather than rephrasing our results on $1\frac{1}{2}$-player games on LCS's, we show how to deal with $2\frac{1}{2}$-player games [13] on LCS's, i.e., games opposing players A and B (as in section 4) but where message losses are probabilistic. This relies on new characterizations, like equations (11) or (12) below, for which the proof will be found in the full version of this paper.

Formally, a *symmetric probabilistic LCS-game* $L = (Q_A, Q_B, C, M, \Delta)$ is exactly like a symmetric LCS-game but with an altered semantics: in state $\sigma \in Conf_A$, player A selects a fireable rule $\delta \in \Delta$ (B picks the rule if $\sigma \in Conf_B$) and the system moves to a successor state ρ where $\sigma \xrightarrow{\delta}_{\text{perf}} \sigma' \sqsupseteq \rho$ and ρ is chosen probabilistically in $C_\downarrow(\{\sigma'\})$. The definition of the probability distribution $\mathbf{P}(\sigma, \delta, \rho)$ can be found in [29,9] where it is called *the local-fault model*. It satisfies $\mathbf{P}(\sigma, \delta, \rho) > 0$ iff $\rho \sqsubseteq \sigma'$ (assuming $\sigma \xrightarrow{\delta}_{\text{perf}} \sigma'$). Additionally it guarantees a *finite-attractor property*: the set of states where all channels are empty will be visited infinitely many times almost surely [1,8].

Reachability Games. Assume A tries to reach region V (goal $\Diamond V$) *with probability 1* no matter how B behaves. The set $\langle\!\langle A \rangle\!\rangle [\Diamond V]_{=1}$ of states in which A has an almost-sure winning strategy is given by

$$\langle\!\langle A \rangle\!\rangle [\Diamond V]_{=1} = \nu Y.\mu X.\left(\begin{array}{l} V \cup \left[Conf_A \cap Pre_{\text{perf}}(C_\uparrow(X) \cap K_\downarrow(Y))\right] \\ \cup \left[Conf_B \cap \widetilde{Pre}_{\text{perf}}(C_\uparrow(X) \cap K_\downarrow(Y))\right] \end{array}\right). \tag{11}$$

Remark 5.1. Justifying (11) is outside the scope of this paper, but we can try to give an intuition of why it works: the inner fixpoint "$\mu X.V \cup \cdots$" define the largest set from which A has a strategy to reach V no matter what B does *if the message losses are favorable*. However, whatever messages are lost, A's strategy also guarantees that the system will remain in Y, from which it will be possible to retry the strategy for $\Diamond V$ as many times as necessary. This will eventually succeed almost surely thanks to the finite-attractor property.   □

Invariance Games. Assume now A tries to stay in V almost surely (goal $[\Box V]_{=1}$), no matter how B behaves. Then A must ensure $\Box V$ surely and we are considering a 2-player game where message losses are adversarial and could as well be controlled by B. This leads to

$$
\begin{aligned}
\langle\!\langle A \rangle\!\rangle [\Box V]_{=1} &= \nu X.V \cap \Big(\big[Conf_A \cap Pre_{\text{perf}}(K_\downarrow(X)) \big] \cup \big[Conf_B \cap \widetilde{Pre}(X) \big] \Big) \\
&= \nu X.V \cap \Big(\big[Conf_A \cap Pre_{\text{perf}}(K_\downarrow(X)) \big] \cup \big[Conf_B \cap \widetilde{Pre}(K_\downarrow(X)) \big] \Big).
\end{aligned}
\tag{12}
$$

In (12), the subterm $Pre_{\text{perf}}(K_\downarrow(X))$ accounts for states in which A can choose a perfect move that will end in $K_\downarrow(X)$, i.e., that can be followed by any adversarial message losses and still remain in X. The subterm $\widetilde{Pre}(X)$ accounts for states in which B cannot avoid going to X, even with message losses under his control. $\widetilde{Pre}(X)$ can be rewritten into $\widetilde{Pre}(K_\downarrow(X))$ thanks to Lemma 3.2, so that we end up with a guarded term.

Goals to be Satisfied with Positive Probability. In $2\frac{1}{2}$-player games, it may happen that a given goal can only be attained with some non-zero probability [13]. Observe that, since the games we consider are determined [22], the goals $[\Diamond V]_{>0}$ or $[\Box V]_{>0}$ are the opposite of goals asking for probability 1:

$$
\langle\!\langle A \rangle\!\rangle [\Diamond V]_{>0} = \overline{\langle\!\langle B \rangle\!\rangle [\Box \overline{V}]_{=1}}, \qquad\qquad \langle\!\langle A \rangle\!\rangle [\Box V]_{>0} = \overline{\langle\!\langle B \rangle\!\rangle [\Diamond \overline{V}]_{=1}}.
$$

Theorem 5.2 (Decidability of qualitative symmetric probabilistic LCS-games). *For symmetric probabilistic LCS-games $\mathcal{L}$ and regular regions V, the sets $\langle\!\langle A \rangle\!\rangle [\Diamond V]_{=1}$, $\langle\!\langle A \rangle\!\rangle [\Diamond V]_{>0}$, $\langle\!\langle A \rangle\!\rangle [\Box V]_{=1}$, and $\langle\!\langle A \rangle\!\rangle [\Box V]_{>0}$ are (effective) regions. Hence qualitative reachability and invariance games are decidable on GLCS's.*

Proof (Sketch). These sets can be defined by guarded L_μ terms.   □

6 Conclusion

We defined a notion of upward/downward-guarded fixpoint expressions that define subsets of a well-quasi-ordered set. For these guarded fixpoint expressions, a finite convergence theorem is proved, that shows how the fixpoints can be evaluated with a finite number of operations. This has a number of applications, in particular in the symbolic verification of well-structured systems, our original motivation. We illustrate this in the second part of the paper, with lossy channel systems as a target. For these systems, we derive in an easy and uniform way, a number of decidability theorems that extend or generalize the main existing results in the verification of temporal properties or game-theoretical properties.

These techniques can be applied to other well-structured systems, with a region algebra built on, e.g., upward-closed sets. Such regions are not closed by complementation, hence fewer properties can be written in L_μ. Admittedly, many examples of well-structured systems do not enjoy closure properties as nice as our Lemma 3.2 for LCS's, which will make it more difficult to express interesting properties in the guarded fragment of L_μ. But this can still be done, as witnessed by [27,28] where the authors introduced a concept of B-games and BB-games that captures some essential closure assumptions allowing the kind of rewritings and unfoldings we have justified with Lemma 3.2.

References

1. P. A. Abdulla, N. Bertrand, A. Rabinovich, and Ph Schnoebelen. Verification of probabilistic systems with faulty communication. *Information and Computation*, 202(2):141–165, 2005.
2. P. A. Abdulla, A. Bouajjani, and J. d'Orso. Deciding monotonic games. In *Proc. 17th Int. Workshop Computer Science Logic (CSL 2003) and 8th Kurt Gödel Coll. (KGL 2003), Vienna, Austria, Aug. 2003*, volume 2803 of *Lecture Notes in Computer Science*, pages 1–14. Springer, 2003.
3. P. A. Abdulla, K. Čerāns, B. Jonsson, and Yih-Kuen Tsay. Algorithmic analysis of programs with well quasi-ordered domains. *Information and Computation*, 160(1/2):109–127, 2000.
4. P. A. Abdulla and B. Jonsson. Undecidable verification problems for programs with unreliable channels. *Information and Computation*, 130(1):71–90, 1996.
5. P. A. Abdulla and B. Jonsson. Verifying programs with unreliable channels. *Information and Computation*, 127(2):91–101, 1996.
6. P. A. Abdulla and B. Jonsson. Channel representation in protocol verification. In *Proc. 12th Int. Conf. Concurrency Theory (CONCUR 2001), Aalborg, Denmark, Aug. 2001*, volume 2154 of *Lecture Notes in Computer Science*, pages 1–15. Springer, 2001.
7. A. Arnold and D. Niwiński. *Rudiments of μ-Calculus*, volume 146 of *Studies in Logic and the Foundations of Mathematics*. Elsevier Science, 2001.
8. C. Baier, N. Bertrand, and Ph. Schnoebelen. A note on the attractor-property of infinite-state Markov chains. *Information Processing Letters*, 97(2):58–63, 2006.
9. C. Baier, N. Bertrand, and Ph. Schnoebelen. Verifying nondeterministic probabilistic channel systems against ω-regular linear-time properties. *ACM Transactions on Computational Logic*, 2006. To appear, available at http://arxiv.org/abs/cs.LO/0511023.
10. S. Bardin, A. Finkel, J. Leroux, and Ph. Schnoebelen. Flat acceleration in symbolic model checking. In *Proc. 3rd Int. Symp. Automated Technology for Verification and Analysis (ATVA 2005), Taipei, Taiwan, Oct. 2005*, volume 3707 of *Lecture Notes in Computer Science*, pages 474–488. Springer, 2005.
11. A. Bouajjani, B. Jonsson, M. Nilsson, and T. Touili. Regular model checking. In *Proc. 12th Int. Conf. Computer Aided Verification (CAV 2000), Chicago, IL, USA, July 2000*, volume 1855 of *Lecture Notes in Computer Science*, pages 403–418. Springer, 2000.
12. G. Cécé, A. Finkel, and S. Purushothaman Iyer. Unreliable channels are easier to verify than perfect channels. *Information and Computation*, 124(1):20–31, 1996.
13. K. Chatterjee, L. de Alfaro, and T. A. Henzinger. The complexity of stochastic Rabin and Streett games. In *Proc. 32nd Int. Coll. Automata, Languages, and Programming (ICALP 2005), Lisbon, Portugal, July 2005*, volume 3580 of *Lecture Notes in Computer Science*, pages 878–890. Springer, 2005.

14. L. de Alfaro, T. A. Henzinger, and R. Majumdar. Symbolic algorithms for infinite-state games. In *Proc. 12th Int. Conf. Concurrency Theory (CONCUR 2001), Aalborg, Denmark, Aug. 2001*, volume 2154 of *Lecture Notes in Computer Science*, pages 536–550. Springer, 2001.

15. A. Finkel. Decidability of the termination problem for completely specificied protocols. *Distributed Computing*, 7(3):129–135, 1994.

16. A. Finkel and Ph. Schnoebelen. Well-structured transition systems everywhere! *Theoretical Computer Science*, 256(1–2):63–92, 2001.

17. E. Grädel, W. Thomas, and T. Wilke, editors. *Automata, Logics, and Infinite Games: A Guide to Current Research*, volume 2500 of *Lecture Notes in Computer Science*. Springer, 2002.

18. T. A. Henzinger, R. Majumdar, and J.-F. Raskin. A classification of symbolic transition systems. *ACM Trans. Computational Logic*, 6(1):1–32, 2005.

19. Y. Kesten, O. Maler, M. Marcus, A. Pnueli, and E. Shahar. Symbolic model checking with rich assertional languages. *Theoretical Computer Science*, 256(1–2):93–112, 2001.

20. J. B. Kruskal. The theory of well-quasi-ordering: A frequently discovered concept. *Journal of Combinatorial Theory, Series A*, 13(3):297–305, 1972.

21. A. Kučera and Ph. Schnoebelen. A general approach to comparing infinite-state systems with their finite-state specifications. *Theoretical Computer Science*, 358(2-3):315–333, 2006.

22. D. A. Martin. The determinacy of Blackwell games. *The Journal of Symbolic Logic*, 63(4):1565–1581, 1998.

23. R. Mayr. Undecidable problems in unreliable computations. *Theoretical Computer Science*, 297(1–3):337–354, 2003.

24. E. C. Milner. Basic WQO- and BQO-theory. In I. Rival, editor, *Graphs and Order. The Role of Graphs in the Theory of Ordered Sets and Its Applications*, pages 487–502. D. Reidel Publishing, 1985.

25. J. Ouaknine and J. Worrell. On metric temporal logic and faulty Turing machines. In *Proc. 9th Int. Conf. Foundations of Software Science and Computation Structures (FOSSACS 2006), Vienna, Austria, Mar. 2006*, volume 3921 of *Lecture Notes in Computer Science*, pages 217–230. Springer, 2006.

26. D. Perrin. Finite automata. In J. van Leeuwen, editor, *Handbook of Theoretical Computer Science*, volume B, chapter 1, pages 1–57. Elsevier Science, 1990.

27. J.-F. Raskin, M. Samuelides, and L. Van Begin. Petri games are monotonic but difficult to decide. Tech. Report 2003.21, Centre Fédéré en Vérification, 2003. Available at http://www.ulb.ac.be/di/ssd/cfv/TechReps.

28. J.-F. Raskin, M. Samuelides, and L. Van Begin. Games for counting abstractions. In *Proc. 4th Int. Workshop on Automated Verification of Critical Systems (AVoCS 2004), London, UK, Sep. 2004*, volume 128(6) of *Electronic Notes in Theor. Comp. Sci.*, pages 69–85. Elsevier Science, 2005.

29. Ph. Schnoebelen. The verification of probabilistic lossy channel systems. In *Validation of Stochastic Systems – A Guide to Current Research*, volume 2925 of *Lecture Notes in Computer Science*, pages 445–465. Springer, 2004.

30. J. Sifakis. A unified approach for studying the properties of transitions systems. *Theoretical Computer Science*, 18:227–258, 1982.

Verification Condition Generation
Via Theorem Proving

John Matthews[1], J. Strother Moore[2], Sandip Ray[2], and Daron Vroon[3]

[1] Galois Connections Inc., Beaverton, OR 97005
[2] Dept. of Computer Sciences, University of Texas at Austin, Austin, TX 78712
[3] College of Computing, Georgia Institute of Technology, Atlanta, GA 30332

Abstract. We present a method to convert (i) an operational semantics for a given machine language, and (ii) an off-the-shelf theorem prover, into a high assurance verification condition generator (VCG). Given a program annotated with assertions at cutpoints, we show how to use the theorem prover directly on the operational semantics to generate verification conditions analogous to those produced by a custom-built VCG. Thus no separate VCG is necessary, and the theorem prover can be employed both to generate and to discharge the verification conditions. The method handles both partial and total correctness. It is also compositional in that the correctness of a subroutine needs to be proved once, rather than at each call site. The method has been used to verify several machine-level programs using the ACL2 theorem prover.

1 Introduction

Operational semantics has emerged as a popular approach for formal modeling of complex computing systems. In this approach, a program is modeled by defining an interpreter that specifies the effect of executing its instructions on the states of the underlying machine. Unfortunately, traditional code proofs based on operational models have been tedious and complex, requiring the user to define global invariants which are preserved on each transition or a *clock function* that precisely characterizes the number of machine steps to termination [1,2].

Research in program verification has principally focused on assertional reasoning [3,4]. Here a program is annotated with assertions at cutpoints. From these annotations, one derives a set of formulas or *verification conditions*, which guarantee that whenever program control reaches a cutpoint the associated assertions hold. Assertional methods generally rely on (i) a *verification condition generator* (VCG) to generate verification conditions from an annotated program, and (ii) a theorem prover to discharge these conditions.

In this paper, we present a method for verifying deterministic sequential programs, using operational semantics, that inherits the benefits of the assertional methods. Given an annotated program and an operational semantics, we show how to configure a theorem prover to emulate a VCG for generating (and discharging) the verification conditions.

M. Hermann and A. Voronkov (Eds.): LPAR 2006, LNAI 4246, pp. 362–376, 2006.

In this section, we first provide a brief overview of operational models and assertional proof approaches to establish the relevant background. We then discuss our contributions in greater detail.

1.1   Background

In *operational semantics*, a program is modeled by its effects on the underlying machine state. A state is viewed as a tuple of values of all machine variables like the program counter (pc), registers, memory, etc. One defines a transition function $next : S \rightarrow S$ where S is the set of states: for a state s, $next(s)$ returns the state after executing one instruction from s. Executions are modeled by a function $run : S \times \mathbb{N} \rightarrow S$ which returns the state after n transitions from s.

$$run(s, n) \triangleq \begin{cases} s & \text{if } n = 0 \\ run(next(s), n - 1) & \text{otherwise} \end{cases}$$

Correctness is formalized with three predicates *pre*, *post*, and *exit*, on set S. Predicates *pre* and *post* are the preconditions and postconditions, and *exit* specifies the "final states"; when verifying a program component, *exit* is defined to recognize the return of control from that component. There are two notions of correctness, *partial* and *total*. Partial correctness involves showing that for any state s satisfying *pre*, the predicate *post* holds at the first *exit* state reachable from s (if some such state exists). Total correctness involves showing both partial correctness and *termination*, that is, the machine starting from a state s satisfying *pre* eventually reaches an *exit* state. Partial correctness and termination are formalized as follows:

Partial Correctness: $\forall s, n : pre(s) \wedge exit(run(s, n)) \Rightarrow$
$$(\exists m : (m \leq n) \wedge exit(run(s, m)) \wedge post(run(s, m)))$$
Termination: $\forall s : pre(s) \Rightarrow (\exists n : exit(run(s, n)))$

Several deductive techniques have been devised to facilitate proofs of the above statements. One method is to define a global invariant *inv* satisfying **I1-I3** below:

I1: $\forall s : pre(s) \Rightarrow inv(s)$
I2: $\forall s : inv(s) \wedge \neg exit(s) \Rightarrow inv(next(s))$
I3: $\forall s : inv(s) \wedge exit(s) \Rightarrow post(s)$

Partial correctness follows from **I1-I3**. By **I1** and **I2**, any state reachable from a *pre* state s up to (and including) the first *exit* state p satisfies *inv*; **I3** then guarantees *post(p)*. For total correctness, one also defines a function $rank : S \rightarrow W$ where W is well-founded under some ordering $\prec$, and shows **I4** below. Well-foundedness guarantees termination.

I4: $\forall s : inv(s) \wedge \neg exit(s) \Rightarrow rank(next(s)) \prec rank(s)$.

Another approach is to use *clock functions*. A clock function $clock : S \rightarrow \mathbb{N}$ satisfies conditions **C1-C3** below:

C1: $\forall s : pre(s) \Rightarrow exit(run(s, clock(s)))$
C2: $\forall s : pre(s) \Rightarrow post(run(s, clock(s)))$
C3: $\forall s, n : pre(s) \wedge exit(run(s, n)) \Rightarrow (clock(s) \leq n)$

C1-C3 imply total correctness: for every *pre* state s, there exists an n, namely $clock(s)$, such that $run(s, n)$ is an *exit* state, guaranteeing termination. To express only partial correctness, one weakens **C1** and **C2** by adding the predicate ($\exists n : exit(run(s, n))$) as a conjunct in the antecedents. It is known [5] that global invariants and clock functions have the same logical strength in that a correctness proof in one method can be mechanically transformed into the other.

Assertional methods are based on annotating a program with assertions at certain control points called *cutpoints* that typically include loop tests and program entry and exit [3,6]. To formalize this, assume that we have two predicates *cut* and *assert*, where *cut* recognizes the cutpoints and *assert* specifies the assertions at each cutpoint. Commonly *cut* is a predicate on the pc values but might occasionally involve other state components. A VCG generates a set of *verification conditions* from the annotated program, which are verified using a theorem prover. The guarantee provided by the process is informally stated as: "Let p be a non-exit *cut* state satisfying *assert*. Let q be the next *cut* state in an execution from p. Then *assert*(q) must hold." Thus, if (i) initial (*i.e.*, *pre*) and *exit* states are cutpoints, (ii) *pre* implies *assert*, and (iii) *assert* implies *post* at *exit*, then the first *exit* state reachable from a *pre* state satisfies *post*. Finally, for termination, one also defines a ranking function *rank* : $S \rightarrow W$, where W is a well-founded set, and shows that for any non-exit cutpoint p satisfying *assert*, if q is the next cutpoint, then $rank(q) \prec rank(p)$. Notice that both assertions and ranking functions are attached to cutpoints rather than to every state.

1.2   Contributions of This Paper

Operational semantics and assertional methods have complementary strengths. Operational models have been lauded for clarity and concreteness [1,7], and facilitate the validation of formal models by simulation [7,8]. However, performing code proofs with such models is cumbersome: defining an appropriate global invariant or clock function requires understanding of the effect of *each* transition on the machine state [1,9,2]. Assertional methods factor out verification complexity by restricting user focus to cutpoints, but require a VCG which must be trusted. A VCG encodes the language semantics as formula transformations. Most VCGs also perform on-the-fly simplifications to keep the generated formulas manageable. Implementing a practical VCG, let alone ensuring its correctness by verifying it against an operational semantics, is non-trivial [10].

In this paper, we present a technique to integrate assertional methods with operational semantics that is suitable for use with general-purpose theorem proving and does not depend on a trusted VCG. As in assertional reasoning, the user annotates the program at cutpoints. However, instead of implementing a VCG we show how to configure the theorem prover to generate verification conditions by symbolic simulation on the operational model. The result is a high assurance program verifier with an off-the-shelf theorem prover as the only trusted component. The method handles both partial and total correctness, and recursive procedures. It is also compositional; subroutines can be verified separately rather than at every call site. The method has been mechanized in the ACL2 theorem prover [11], and used to reason about several machine-level programs. The basic approach (*i.e.*, without composition) has also been formalized in the Isabelle theorem prover [12].

The rest of the paper is organized as follows. We present the basic approach in Section 2. In Section 3, we discuss compositionality and means for handling recursive procedures. In Section 4, we present illustrative applications of the method. We discuss related work in Section 5 and conclude in Section 6.

2   Basic Methodology

Assume that we have defined *next, pre, post, exit, cut*, and *assert*, as described in Section 1.1. Consider the following function *csteps*:

$$csteps(s, i) \triangleq \begin{cases} i & \text{if } cut(s) \\ csteps(next(s), i + 1) & \text{otherwise} \end{cases}$$

If j is the minimum number of transitions to a cutpoint from state s, then *csteps*(s, i) returns $i + j$; the recursion does not terminate if no cutpoint is reachable. Generally, defining a recursive function requires showing that the recursion terminates. However, if the definition is tail-recursive as above, then it is admissible in theorem provers whose logics support Hilbert's choice operator; the defining axiom can be witnessed by a total function that returns an arbitrary constant when the recursion does not terminate [13][12, §9.2.3].

We now formalize the notion of "next cutpoint". Fix a state **d** such that $cut(\mathbf{d}) \Leftrightarrow (\forall s : cut(s))$. State **d** can be defined with a choice operator. Then *nextc*(s) returns the first reachable cutpoint from s if any, else **d**:

$$nextc(s) \triangleq \begin{cases} run(s, csteps(s, 0)) & \text{if } cut(run(s, csteps(s, 0))) \\ \mathbf{d} & \text{otherwise} \end{cases}$$

With these definitions, we formalize verification conditions as formulas **V1-V5**. Notice that the formulas involve obligations only about assertions at cutpoints.

V1: $\forall s : pre(s) \Rightarrow assert(s)$
V2: $\forall s : assert(s) \Rightarrow cut(s)$
V3: $\forall s : exit(s) \Rightarrow cut(s)$
V4: $\forall s : assert(s) \wedge exit(s) \Rightarrow post(s)$
V5: $\forall s : assert(s) \wedge \neg exit(s) \Rightarrow assert(nextc(next(s)))$

The formulas imply partial correctness. To prove this, we define function *esteps* to count the number of transitions up to the first *exit* state, and *nexte* that returns the first reachable exit point. Note that *esteps* is tail-recursive.

$$esteps(s, i) \triangleq \begin{cases} i & \text{if } exit(s) \\ esteps(next(s), i + 1) & \text{otherwise} \end{cases}$$

$$nexte(s) \triangleq run(s, esteps(s, 0))$$

We can take $esteps(s, 0)$ as the definition of a generic clock function. Partial correctness now follows from Theorem 1.

Theorem 1. *Suppose conditions* **V1**, **V3-V5** *hold. Let state s and natural number n be such that* $pre(s)$ *and* $exit(run(s, n))$. *Then* $esteps(s, 0) \leq n$, $exit(nexte(s))$, *and* $post(nexte(s)))$.

Proof sketch: $esteps(s, 0) \leq n$ and $exit(nexte(s))$ hold since $esteps(s, 0)$ returns the number of steps to the first reachable *exit* state, if one exists. If *assert* holds for a cutpoint p, then by **V5** *assert* holds for every cutpoint reachable from p until (and, by **V3**, including) the first *exit* state. Since a *pre* state satisfies *assert* (by **V1**), the first *exit* state reachable from a *pre* state satisfies *assert*. Now $post(nexte(s)))$ follows from **V4**.   □

For termination, we also need a well-founded *rank* over cutpoints. **V6** below formalizes the corresponding proof obligation. By Theorem 2, total correctness follows from **V1-V6**.

V6: $\forall s : assert(s) \wedge \neg exit(s) \Rightarrow rank(nextc(next(s))) \prec rank(s)$

Theorem 2. *Suppose* **V1-V6** *hold, and let s satisfy* **pre**. *Then* $exit(nexte(s))$ *and* $post(nexte(s))$ *hold.*

Proof sketch: To prove $exit(nexte(s))$, it suffices to show that some *exit* state is reachable from each *pre* state s. By **V1**, **V2**, and **V5**, for every non-exit cutpoint p reachable from s, there exists a subsequently reachable cutpoint p'. But, by **V6** and well-foundedness of $\prec$, eventually one of these cutpoints must be an *exit* state. Then $post(nexte(s))$ follows from $exit(nexte(s))$ and Theorem 1.   □

We now discuss how the verification conditions are discharged for a concrete program. The non-trivial conditions are **V5** and **V6**, which involve relation between two consecutive cutpoints. To automate their verification, we use theorems **SSR1** and **SSR2** below, which are trivial consequences of the definition of *nextc*.

SSR1: $\forall s : \neg cut(s) \Rightarrow nextc(s) = nextc(next(s))$
SSR2: $\forall s : cut(s) \Rightarrow nextc(s) = s$

We use **SSR1** and **SSR2** as conditional rewrite rules oriented left to right. For any symbolic state s, the rules rewrite the term $nextc(s)$ to either s or $nextc(next(s))$ depending on whether s is a cutpoint, in the latter case causing a symbolic expansion of the definition of *next* possibly with auxiliary simplifications, and applying the rules again on the resulting term. Proofs of **V5** and **V6** thus cause the theorem prover to symbolically simulate the program from each cutpoint satisfying *assert* until the next cutpoint is reached, at which point we check if the new state satisfies assertions. The process mimics a "forward" VCG, but generates and discharges the verification conditions on a case-by-case basis.

3   Composing Correctness Statements

The basic method above did not treat subroutines compositionally. Consider verifying a procedure P that invokes a subroutine Q. Symbolic simulation from a cutpoint of P might encounter an invocation of Q, resulting in symbolic execution of Q. Thus subroutines have been treated as if they were in-lined. We often prefer to separately verify Q, and use its correctness theorem for verifying P. We now extend the method to afford such composition.

We will uniformly use the symbols P and Q to refer to invocations of the caller and callee respectively. We also use a subscript to distinguish between predicates about P and Q when necessary, for example referring to the postcondition for P as $post_P$.

For composition, it is convenient to extend the notion of *exit* states as follows. We define a predicate in_P to characterize states which are poised to execute an instruction in P or one of its callees. Then define $exit_P(s) \triangleq \neg in_P(s)$. Thus, $exit_P$ recognizes *any* state that does not involve execution of P (or any subroutine), not just those that return control from P. Note that this does not change the notion of the *first exit* state from P. With this view, we add the new verification condition **CC** below, stating that no cutpoint of P is encountered during the execution of Q. The condition will be used in the proofs of additional rules **SSR3** and **SSR3$'$** that we define later, which are necessary for composition.

CC: $\forall s : cut_P(s) \Rightarrow exit_Q(s)$

Another key ingredient for composition is the formalization of *frame conditions* necessary to prove that P can continue execution after Q returns. A postcondition specifying that Q correctly performs its desired computation is not sufficient to guarantee this. For instance, Q, while correctly computing its return value, might corrupt the call stack preventing P from executing on return. To account for this, $post_Q$ needs to characterize the global effect of executing Q, that is, specify how *each* state component is affected by the execution of Q. However, such global characterization of the effect of Q might be difficult. In practice, we require that $post_Q$ is strong enough such that for any state s satisfying $exit_Q$ and $post_Q$ we can infer the control flow for continuing execution of P. For instance, if Q updates some "scratch space" which is irrelevant to the execution of P, then $post_Q$ need not characterize such update. Then we prove the additional symbolic simulation rule **SSR3** (resp., **SSR3$'$**) below, which (together with **SSR1** and **SSR2**) affords compositional reasoning about total (resp., partial) correctness of P assuming that Q has been proven totally (resp., partially) correct. Here $excut_P(s) \triangleq cut_P(nextc_P(s))$.

SSR3: $\forall s : pre_Q(s) \Rightarrow nextc_P(s) = nextc_P(nexte_Q(s))$
SSR3$'$: $\forall s : pre_Q(s) \wedge excut_P(s) \Rightarrow nextc_P(s) = nextc_P(nexte_Q(s))$

Proof sketch: We only discuss **SSR3** since the proof of **SSR3$'$** is similar. By **CC** and the definition of $esteps_Q$, if s satisfies pre_Q and $n < esteps_Q(s, 0)$, then $run(s, n)$ does not satisfy cut_P. Hence the next cut_P state after s is the same as the next cut_P state after the first $exit_Q$ state reachable from s. The rule now follows from the definitions of *nextc* and *nexte*.   □

We prioritize rule applications so that **SSR1** and **SSR2** are tried only when **SSR3** (resp., **SSR3$'$**) cannot be applied during symbolic simulation. Therefore, if Q has been proven totally correct and if a non-cutpoint state s encountered during symbolic simulation of P satisfies pre_Q, then **SSR3** "skips past" the execution of Q; otherwise we expand the transition function via **SSR2** as desired.

We need one further observation to apply **SSR3'** for composing partial correctness proofs. Note that **SSR3'** has the hypothesis $excut_P(s)$. To apply the rule, we must therefore know for a symbolic state s satisfying pre_Q whether some subsequent cutpoint of P is reachable from s. However, such a cutpoint, if one exists, can only be encountered *after s*. The solution is to observe that for partial correctness we can weaken the verification condition **V5** to **V5'** below. For a cutpoint s satisfying assertions, **V5'** requires the next subsequent cutpoint to satisfy the assertion only if some such cutpoint is reachable.

V5': $\forall s : assert(s) \land \neg exit(s) \land excut(next(s)) \Rightarrow assert(nextc(next(s)))$

V5' allows us to assume $excut_P(next(s))$ for any non-exit cutpoint s of P. Now let b be some pre_Q state encountered during symbolic simulation. We must have previously encountered a non-exit cutpoint a of P such that there is no cutpoint between $next_P(a)$ and b. Assuming $excut_P(next(a))$ we can infer $excut_P(b)$ by the definitions of $excut$ and $nextc$, enabling application of **SSR3'**.

Note that while we used the word "subroutine" for presentation, our treatment does not require P or Q to be subroutines. One can mark *any* program block by defining an appropriate predicate *in*, verify it separately, and use it to compositionally reason about programs that invoke it. In practice, we separately verify callees that (i) contain one or more loops, and (ii) are invoked several times, possibly by several callers. If Q is a straight-line procedure with complicated semantics, for instance some complex initialization code, we skip composition and allow symbolic simulation of P to emulate in-lining of Q.

We now turn to recursive procedures. So far we have considered the scenario where Q has been verified *before* P. This is not valid for recursive programs where P and Q are invocations of the same procedure. Nevertheless, we can still *assume* the correctness of Q while reasoning about P. The soundness of the assumption is justified by well-founded induction on the number of machine steps needed to reach the first *exit* state for P, and the fact that recursive invocations of P execute in fewer steps than P itself.

We end the description of the method with a note on its mechanization in ACL2. Observe that the proofs of Theorems 1 and 2, the symbolic simulation rules, and the justification for applying induction for recursive procedures above, do not depend on the actual definitions of *next*, *pre*, *post*, etc., but merely on conditions **V1-V5**, **V5'**, and **CC**. Thus we can verify concrete programs by instantiating the correctness theorems with the corresponding functions for the concrete machine model. In ACL2, we make use of a derived rule of inference called *functional instantiation* [14], which enables instantiation of theorems about constrained functions with concrete functions satisfying the constraints. In particular, we have used constrained functions *pre*, *post*, *next*, etc., axiomatized to satisfy the verification conditions, and mechanically derived the remaining theorems and rules. This allows us to automate assertional reasoning on operational models by implementing a macro which performs steps 1-4 below.

1. Mechanically generate concrete versions of the functions *csteps, nextc, esteps*, etc., for the given operational semantics.
2. Functionally instantiate the generic symbolic simulation rules **SSR1, SSR2**, and **SSR3** (resp., **SSR3'**), and the justification for recursive procedures.
3. Use symbolic simulation to prove the verification conditions.
4. Derive correctness by functionally instantiating Theorems 1 and 2.

4   Applications

In this section, we discuss applications of the method in verification of concrete programs. All the examples presented have been verified in ACL2 using the macro mentioned above. We start with an assembly language Fibonacci program on a simple machine model called TINY [8]. The subsequent examples are JVM bytecodes compiled from Java for an operational model of the JVM in ACL2 called M5 [2]. The details of TINY or M5 are irrelevant to this paper; we chose them since they are representative of operational machine models in ACL2, and their formalizations were accessible to us.

4.1   Fibonacci Implementation on TINY

TINY is a stack-based 32-bit processor developed at Rockwell Collins Inc [8]. The Fibonacci program shown in Fig. 1 is the result of compiling the standard iterative implementation for this machine. TINY represents memory as a linear address space. The two most recently computed values of the Fibonacci sequence are stored in addresses 20 and 21, and the loop counter n is maintained on the stack. TINY performs 32-bit integer arithmetic. Given a number k the program computes $fix(fib(k))$, where $fix(n)$ returns the low-order 32 bits of n, and fib is the mathematical Fibonacci function defined below:

$$fib(k) \triangleq \begin{cases} 1 & \text{if } k \leq 1 \\ fib(k-1) + fib(k-2) & \text{otherwise} \end{cases}$$

The *pre, post*, and *exit* predicates for the verification of the Fibonacci program[1] are shown in Fig. 2, and the assertions at the different cutpoints in Fig. 3. They are fairly traditional. The key assertion is the loop invariant which specifies that the numbers at addresses 20 and 21 are $fix(fib(k-n))$ and $fix(fib(k-n-1))$ respectively, where n is the loop count stored at the top of the stack when the control reaches the loop test. For partial correctness, no further user input is necessary. Symbolic simulation proves the standard verification conditions.

For total correctness, we additionally use the function *rank* below that maps the cutpoints to the well-founded set of ordinals below ϵ_0.

$$rank(s) \triangleq \begin{cases} 0 & \text{if } exit(s) \\ (\omega \cdot_o tos(s)) +_o |*\texttt{halt}* - pc(s)| & \text{otherwise} \end{cases}$$

---

[1] Functions *pre* and *post* here take an extra argument k while our generic proofs used unary functions. This is admissible since one can functionally instantiate constraints with concrete functions having extra arguments, as long as such arguments do not affect the parameters (in this case s) involved in the constraints [14].

```
100   pushsi 1      *start*
102   dup
103   dup
104   pop 20                    fib0 := 1;
106   pop 21                    fib1 := 1;
108   sub                       n := max(n-1,0);
109   dup           *loop*
110   jumpz 127                 if n == 0, goto *done*;
112   pushs 20
113   dup
115   pushs 21
117   add
118   pop 20                    fib0 := fib0 + fib1;
120   pop 21                    fib1 := fib0 (old value);
122   pushsi 1
124   sub                       n := max(n-1,0);
125   jump 109                  goto *loop*;
127   pushs 20      *done*
129   add                       return fib0 + n;
130   halt          *halt*
```

Fig. 1. TINY Assembly Code for computing the nth Fibonacci sequence. The numbers to the left of each instruction is the pc value for the loaded program. High-level pseudo-code is shown at the extreme right. The add instruction at pc value 129 removes 0 from the top of stack; this trick is necessary since TINY has no DROP instruction.

- $pre(k, s) \triangleq pc(s) = *\text{start}* \wedge tos(s) = k \wedge k \geq 0 \wedge \textit{fib-loaded}(s)$
- $post(k, s) \triangleq tos(s) = \textit{fix}(\textit{fib}(k))$
- $exit(s) \triangleq pc(s) = *\text{halt}*$

Fig. 2. Predicates *pre*, *post*, and *exit* for the Fibonacci program. Here $pc(s)$ and $tos(s)$ return the program counter and top of stack at state s, and *fib-loaded* holds at state s if the program in Fig. 1 is loaded in the memory starting at location *start*.

Here ω is the first infinite ordinal, and $\cdot_o$ and $+_o$ represent ordinal multiplication and addition. Informally, *rank* is a lexicographic ordering of the loop count and the difference between the location *halt* and $pc(s)$.

4.2   Recursive Factorial Implementation on the JVM

Our next example involves JVM bytecodes for a recursive implementation of the factorial program (Fig. 4). We use an operational model of the JVM called M5, developed at the University of Texas [2]. M5 defines the semantics for 138 JVM instructions, and supports invocation of static, special, and virtual methods, inheritance rules for method resolution, multi-threading, and synchronization via monitors. The bytecodes in Fig. 4 are produced from the Java implementation by disassembling the output of javac and can be executed with M5.

Program Counter	Assertions
start	$tos(s) = k \wedge 0 \leq k \wedge \textit{fib-loaded}(s)$
loop	$mem(20, s) = \textit{fix}(\textit{fib}(k - tos(s))) \wedge 0 \leq tos(s) \leq k \wedge$ $mem(21, s) = \textit{fix}(\textit{fib}(k - tos(s) - 1)) \wedge \textit{fib-loaded}(s)$
done	$mem(20, s) = \textit{fix}(\textit{fib}(k)) \wedge tos(s) = 0 \wedge \textit{fib-loaded}(s)$
halt	$tos(s) = \textit{fix}(\textit{fib}(k))$

Fig. 3. Assertions for the Fibonacci program

```
Method int fact (int)
0   ILOAD_0                                      *start*
1   IFLE 12                                              if (n<=0) goto *done*
4   ILOAD_0
5   ILOAD_0
6   ICONST_1
7   ISUB
8   INVOKESTATIC #4 <Method int fact (int)>      x:= fact(n-1)
11  IMUL                                         x:= n*x
12  IRETURN                                      *ret*    return x
13  ICONST_1                                     *done*
14  IRETURN                                      *base*   return 1
```

Fig. 4. M5 Bytecodes for the Factorial Method

The example is an entertaining illustration of our treatment of recursion. With the exception of the recursive call, the procedure involves a straight line code. Thus we only need to specify the precondition and the postcondition. The precondition posits that the state s is poised to start executing the bytecodes for fact on argument k; the postcondition specifies that the return state pops the top frame from the call stack and stores $\textit{fix}(\textit{fact}(k))$ on the frame of the caller where *fact* is the mathematical factorial function. No further annotation is necessary. When symbolic simulation reaches the state in which the recursive call is invoked, it skips past the call (inferring the postcondition for the recursive call) and continues until the procedure exits. This stands in stark contrast to all the previously published ACL2 proofs of the method [2,15], which require complex assertions to characterize each recursive frame in the call stack.

4.3   CBC-Mode Encryption and Decryption

Our third example is a more elaborate proof of functional correctness of a Java program implementing encryption and decryption of an unbounded array of bits. By *functional correctness*, we mean that the composition of encryption and decryption yields the original plaintext. Functional correctness of cryptographic protocols has received considerable attention recently in formal verification [16,17]. We refer the reader to Schneier [18] for an overview of cryptosystems.

Cryptographic protocols use a *block cipher* that encrypts and decrypts a fixed-size *block* of bits. We use blocks of 128 bits. Encryption and decryption of large data streams additionally require the following operations.

- A *mode of operation* extends the cipher from a single block to arbitrary block sequences. We use *Cipher Block Chaining* (CBC), which 'xor's a plaintext block with the previous ciphertext in the sequence before encryption.
- *Padding* expands a bit sequence to one which is a multiple of a block length, so as to apply a block cipher; *unpadding* drops the padding during decryption.
- *Blocking* involves transforming an array of bits to an array of blocks for use by CBC encryption; *unblocking* is the obvious inverse.

Our Java implementation performs the following sequence of operations on an unbounded bit-array: (i) padding, (ii) blocking, (iii) CBC encoding, (iv) CBC decoding, (v) unblocking, and (vi) unpadding. It follows Slind and Hurd's HOL model of the operations [16], adapted for bit arrays. However, we do *not* implement a practical block cipher; our cipher 'xor's a 128-bit block with a key based on a fixed key schedule. The program constitutes about 300 lines of Java (with 18 subroutines), which compiles to 600 bytecodes.

We verify both partial and total functional correctness. The precondition specifies that the class table containing the routines is loaded and the current call frame contains a reference to an array a of bits in the heap; the postcondition requires that the array on termination is the same as a. Using ACL2 libraries on arithmetic and arrays, the only non-trivial user inputs necessary for the proofs are the loop invariants for the associated procedures. Furthermore, the only property of the block cipher used in reasoning about the CBC methods is that the encryption and decryption of 128-bit blocks are inverses. Thus, it is now possible to independently prove this invertibility property for a practical block cipher, and "plug in" the cipher to obtain a proof of the corresponding unbounded bit-array encryption.

5   Related Work

Operational semantics was introduced by McCarthy [19], and has since been used extensively for mechanical verification of complex programs. In particular, ACL2 and its predecessor Nqthm have used such models extensively [1,2,8,20]. Operational models have also been used in Isabelle/HOL to formalize Java and the JVM [21], and in PVS to model state chart languages [22].

The notion of assertions was used by Goldstein and von Neumann [23], and Turing [24], and made explicit in the classic works of Floyd [3], Manna [6], Hoare [4], and Dijkstra [25]. King [26] wrote the first mechanized VCG. VCGs have been used extensively in practice, for example in the Extended Static Checker for Java (ESC/Java) [27], the Java certifying compiler [10], and the Praxis verification of Spark programs [28]. Several researchers have commented on the complexity of a practical VCG [29,30]. There has also been significant research verifying VCGs via theorem proving [31,32,33]. In the context of theorem proving, assertions have also been used to verify C programs in HOL [34], and reason about pointers and BDD normalization algorithms in Isabelle [35,36].

This work is influenced by two earlier efforts in ACL2 by the individual authors, namely Moore [15] and Matthews and Vroon [37], to emulate VCG reasoning with a theorem prover. Moore defines a tail-recursive predicate *inv* such that the proof of invariance of *inv* reduces to showing that each cutpoint satisfies assertions. However, since the definition of *inv* is tied to assertions, the method cannot be used to reason about ranking functions (and hence termination). Matthews and Vroon prove termination by directly characterizing cutpoints, but conflate assertions and cutpoints in a single predicate. Thus symbolic simulation can skip past cutpoints not satisfying assertions, and partial correctness cannot be inferred. Neither method handles composition or recursive procedures. Our work can be viewed as a unification and substantial extension of these efforts.

There are parallels between our work and research on proof-carrying code (PCC) [38]. VCGs are the key trusted components in PCCs. Similar to our work, foundational PCC research [39] ensures reliability of verification condition generation by relying only on a general-purpose theorem prover and the operational semantics of a machine language. However, while PCCs focus on automatic proofs of fixed safety properties (such as type and memory safety), our approach is geared towards verifying functional program correctness which requires more general-purpose assertions. We achieve this by using the simplification mechanisms of a theorem prover to automate verification condition generation.

An early implementation of our ACL2 macro is currently distributed with ACL2. Several researchers have personally communicated to the authors independent endeavors applying and extending the method. At Galois Connections Inc., Pike has applied the macro to verify programs on the Rockwell Collins AAMP7[TM] processor [40]. At the National Security Agency, Legato has used it to verify an assembly language multiplier for the Mostek 6502 microprocessor. At Rockwell Collins Inc., Hardin *et al.* are independently extending the method and using it for AAMP7 and JVM code verification [41]. Fox has formalized the method in HOL4 and is applying it on ARM assembly language programs.

6   Summary and Conclusion

We have presented a method to apply assertional reasoning for verifying sequential programs based on operational semantics, that is suitable for use in mechanical theorem proving. Symbolic simulation is used for generating and discharging verification conditions, which are then traded for the correctness theorem by automatically generating a tail-recursive clock. Partial and total correctness are handled uniformly. The method is compositional in that individual procedures can be verified component-wise to prove the correctness of their composition. It also provides a natural treatment of recursive procedures.

The method unifies the clarity and concreteness of operational semantics with the abstraction provided by assertional methods without requiring the implementation (or verification) of a VCG for the target language. To understand why implementing a VCG for a realistic programming language is difficult, consider the method invocation instruction of the JVM. This instruction involves method resolution with respect to the object on which the method is invoked, and side effects on many parts of the states such as the call frames, heap (for synchronized methods), and the class table (for dynamic methods). Encoding such operations as predicate transformation instead of state transformation is non-trivial. Furthermore, most VCGs perform on-the-fly formula simplifications to generate manageable verification conditions. As a measure of the complexity, the VCG for the Java certifying compiler ran to about 23000 lines of C in 2001 [10]. In our approach, only one trusted tool, namely an off-the-shelf theorem prover, is necessary, while still inheriting the benefits of a VCG; the requisite simplifications are performed with the full power of the theorem prover.

Note however, that practical VCGs may implement substantial static analysis on the control flow of the program. For instance, the VCG for ESC/Java performs static analysis to elide assertions from join points of conditionals without incurring exponential case blow-up [29]. To emulate them with a theorem prover, the simplification engine and lemma libraries must be powerful enough to encode such transformations. ACL2 provides a *meta reasoning* facility [42], allowing the user to augment its native simplification heuristics. We are investigating its use to encode the analysis performed by a practical VCG.

We are working on making our ACL2 macro more efficient and applying it to verify high-assurance programs on realistic machine models. A target application is the *verifying compiler* being developed at Galois Connections and Rockwell Collins, Inc. to compile programs in the Cryptol^{TM} language into code for the AAMP7^{TM} processor [43]. The goal is to generate, in addition to object code, a proof to certify that the code implements the source program semantics, and our macro can be used with the existing ACL2 model of the AAMP7 [40] to generate the requisite verification conditions.

Acknowledgements. This work has been supported in part by DARPA and the NSF under Grant no. CNS-0429591. Eric Smith and Matt Kaufmann provided many insightful suggestions, and Joe Hurd found an error in an earlier draft of this paper. We thank our colleagues at the National Security Agency, Galois Connections Inc., Rockwell Collins Inc., and the University of Texas, for using our ACL2 macro and providing feedback. The anonymous referees also provided substantial comments that have improved the presentation of the paper.

References

1. Boyer, R.S., Moore, J.S.: Mechanized Formal Reasoning about Programs and Computing Machines. In Veroff, R., ed.: Automated Reasoning and Its Applications: Essays in Honor of Larry Wos, MIT Press (1996) 141–176
2. Moore, J.S.: Proving Theorems about Java and the JVM with ACL2. In Broy, M., Pizka, M., eds.: Models, Algebras, and Logic of Engineering Software, Amsterdam, IOS Press (2003) 227–290

3. Floyd, R.: Assigning Meanings to Programs. In: Mathematical Aspects of Computer Science, Proceedings of Symposia in Applied Mathematcs. Volume XIX., Providence, Rhode Island, American Mathematical Society (1967) 19–32
4. Hoare, C.A.R.: An Axiomatic Basis for Computer Programming. Communications of the ACM **12** (1969) 576–583
5. Ray, S., Moore, J.S.: Proof Styles in Operational Semantics. In: FMCAD 2004. LNCS 3312, Springer-Verlag (2004) 67–81
6. Manna, Z.: The Correctness of Programs. JCSS **3** (1969) 119–127
7. Oheimb, D.v., Nipkow, T.: Machine-checking the Java Specification: Proving Type-Safety. In Alves-Foss, J., ed.: Formal Syntax and Semantics of Java. Volume 1523 of LNCS. Springer (1999) 119–156
8. Greve, D., Wilding, M., Hardin, D.: High-Speed, Analyzable Simulators. In Kaufmann, M., Manolios, P., Moore, J.S., eds.: Computer-Aided Reasoning: ACL2 Case Studies, Kluwer Academic Publishers (2000) 89–106
9. Shankar, N.: Machine-Assisted Verification Using Theorem Proving and Model Checking. In Broy, M., Schieder, B., eds.: Mathematical Methods in Program Development. Volume 158 of NATO ASI Series F: Computer and Systems Science. Springer (1997) 499–528
10. Colby, C., Lee, P., Necula, G.C., Blau, F., Plesko, M., Cline, K.: A Certifying Compiler for Java. In: ACM SIGPLAN 2000 conference on Programming language design and implementation. (2000) 95–107
11. Kaufmann, M., Manolios, P., Moore, J.S.: Computer-Aided Reasoning: An Approach. Kluwer Academic Publishers (2000)
12. Nipkow, T., Paulson, L., Wenzel, M.: Isabelle/HOL: A Proof Assistant for Higher Order Logics. Volume 2283 of LNCS. Springer-Verlag (2002)
13. Manolios, P., Moore, J.S.: Partial Functions in ACL2. Journal of Automated Reasoning **31** (2003) 107–127
14. Boyer, R.S., Goldshlag, D., Kaufmann, M., Moore, J.S.: Functional Instantiation in First Order Logic. In Lifschitz, V., ed.: Artificial Intelligence and Mathematical Theory of Computation: Papers in Honor of John McCarthy, Academic Press (1991) 7–26
15. Moore, J.S.: Inductive Assertions and Operational Semantics. In Geist, D., ed.: CHARME 2003. Volume 2860 of LNCS., Springer-Verlag (2003) 289–303
16. Slind, K., Hurd, J.: Applications of polytypism in theorem proving. In Basin, D., Wolff, B., eds.: 16th International Conference on Theorem Proving in Higher Order Logics. LNCS 2978 (2003) 103–119
17. Toma, D., Borrione, D.: Formal verification of a SHA-1 circuit core using ACL2. In Hurd, J., Melham, T., eds.: TPHOLS 2005. Springer LNCS 3603 (2005) 326–341
18. Schneier, B.: Applied Cryptography (2nd ed.): Protocols, Algorithms, and Source Code in C. John Wiley & Sons, Inc. (1995)
19. McCarthy, J.: Towards a Mathematical Science of Computation. In: Proceedings of the Information Processing Congress. Volume 62., North-Holland (1962) 21–28
20. Yu, Y.: Automated Proofs of Object Code for a Widely Used Microprocessor. PhD thesis, University of Texas at Austin (1992)
21. Strecker, M.: Formal Verification of a Java Compiler in Isabelle. In Voronkov, A., ed.: CADE 2004. LNCS 2392, Springer-Verlag (2002) 63–77
22. Hamon, G., Rushby, J.: An Operational Semantics for Stateflow. In: FASE 2004. LNCS 2984, Springer-Verlag (2004) 229–243
23. Goldstein, H.H., J. von Neumann: Planning and Coding Problems for an Electronic Computing Instrument. In: John von Neumann, Collected Works, Volume V, Pergamon Press, Oxford (1961)

24. Turing, A.M.: Checking a Large Routine. In: Report of a Conference on High Speed Automatic Calculating Machine, University Mathematical Laboratory, Cambridge, England (1949) 67–69
25. Dijkstra, E.W.: Guarded Commands, Non-determinacy and a Calculus for Derivation of Programs. Communications of the ACM **18** (1975) 453–457
26. King, J.C.: A Program Verifier. PhD thesis, Carnegie-Melon University (1969)
27. Detlefs, D.L., Leino, K.R.M., Nelson, G., Saxe, J.B.: Extended Static Checking for Java. Technical Report 159, Compaq Systems Research Center (1998)
28. King, S., Hammond, J., Chapman, R., Pryor, A.: Is Proof More Cost-Effective Than Testing? IEEE Transactions on Software Engineering **26** (2000) 675–686
29. Flanagan, C., Saxe, J.B.: Avoiding Exponential Explosion: Generating Compact Verification Conditions. In: Proceedings of the 28th ACM SIGPLAN-SIGACT symposium on Principles of Programming Languages . (2001) 193–205
30. Leino, K.R.M.: Efficient weakest preconditions. Inf. Process. Lett. **93** (2005) 281–288
31. Homeier, P., Martin, D.: A Mechanically Verified Verification Condition Generator. The Computer Journal **38** (1995) 131–141
32. Gloess, P.Y.: Imperative Program Verification in PVS. Technical report, École Nationale Supérieure Électronique, Informatique et Radiocommunications de bordeaux (1999)
33. Schirmer, N.: A verification environment for sequential imperative programs in Isabelle/HOL. In Baader, F., Voronkov, A., eds.: LPAR 2004. Volume 3452 of LNAI., Springer (2005) 398–414
34. Norrish, M.: C Formalised in HOL. PhD thesis, University of Cambridge (1998)
35. Mehta, F., Nipkow, T.: Proving Pointer Programs in Higher Order Logic. In Baader, F., ed.: CADE 2003. LNAI 2741, Springer-Verlag (2003) 121–135
36. Ortner, V., Schirmer, N.: Verification of bdd normalization. In Hurd, J., Melham, T., eds.: TPHOLS 2005. Springer LNCS 3603 (2005) 261–277
37. Matthews, J., Vroon, D.: Partial Clock Functions in ACL2. In Kaufmann, M., Moore, J.S., eds.: 5th ACL2 Workshop. (2004)
38. Necula, G.C.: Proof-Carrying Code. (In: POPL 1997) 106–119
39. Appel, A.W.: Foundational Proof-Carrying Code. In: LICS 2001. (2001) 247–258
40. Greve, D., Richards, R., Wilding, M.: A Summary of Intrinsic Partitioning Verification. In Kaufmann, M., Moore, J.S., eds.: 5th ACL2 Workshop. (2004)
41. Hardin, D., Smith, E.W., Young, W.D.: A Robust Machine Code Proof Framework for Highly Secure Applications. In Manolios, P., Wilding, M., eds.: 6th ACL2 Workshop. (2006)
42. Hunt Jr., W.A., Kaufmann, M., Krug, R.B., Moore, J.S., Smith, E.W.: Meta Reasoning in ACL2. In Hurd, J., Melham, T., eds.: TPHOLS 2005. Springer LNCS 3603 (2005) 373–384
43. Pike, L., Shields, M., Matthews, J.: A Verifying Core for a Cryptographic Language Compiler. In Manolios, P., Wilding, M., eds.: 6th ACL2 Workshop. (2006)

An Incremental Approach to
Abstraction-Carrying Code*

Elvira Albert[1], Puri Arenas[1], and Germán Puebla[2]

[1] Complutense University of Madrid
{elvira,puri}@sip.ucm.es
[2] Technical University of Madrid
german@fi.upm.es

Abstract. *Abstraction-Carrying Code* (ACC) has recently been proposed as a framework for Proof-Carrying Code (PCC) in which the code supplier provides a program together with an *abstraction* (or abstract model of the program) whose validity entails compliance with a predefined safety policy. Existing approaches for PCC are developed under the assumption that the consumer reads and validates the entire program w.r.t. the *full* certificate at once, in a non incremental way. In the context of ACC, we propose an *incremental* approach to PCC for the generation of certificates and the checking of untrusted *updates* of a (trusted) program, i.e., when a producer provides a modified version of a previously validated program. Our proposal is that, if the consumer keeps the original (fixed-point) abstraction, it is possible to provide only the program updates and the incremental certificate (i.e., the *difference* of abstractions). Furthermore, it is now possible to define an *incremental checking* algorithm which, given the new updates and its incremental certificate, only re-checks the fixpoint for each procedure affected by the updates and the propagation of the effect of these fixpoint changes. As a consequence, both certificate transmission time and checking time can be reduced significantly.

1 Introduction

Proof-Carrying Code (PCC) [13] is a general technique for mobile code safety which proposes to associate safety information in the form of a *certificate* to programs. The certificate (or proof) is created at compile time by the *certifier* on the code supplier side, and it is packaged along with the code. The consumer who receives or downloads the (untrusted) code+certificate package can then run a *checker* which by an efficient inspection of the code and the certificate can verify the validity of the certificate and thus compliance with the safety policy. The key benefit of this "certificate-based" approach to mobile code safety is that

---

* This work was funded in part by the Information Society Technologies program of the European Commission, Future and Emerging Technologies under the IST-15905 *MOBIUS* project, by the Spanish MEC under the TIN-2005-09207 *MERIT* project, and the Regional CAM under the S-0505/TIC/0407 *PROMESAS* project.

M. Hermann and A. Voronkov (Eds.): LPAR 2006, LNAI 4246, pp. 377–391, 2006.

the consumer's task is reduced from proving to checking, a task which should be much simpler, efficient, and automatic than generating the original certificate.

Abstraction-Carrying Code (ACC) [4] has been recently proposed as an enabling technology for PCC in which an *abstraction* (i.e., an abstract model of the program) plays the role of certificate. An important feature of ACC is that not only the checking, but also the generation of the abstraction (or fixpoint) is *automatically* carried out by a fixed-point analyzer. In this paper, we will consider analyzers which construct a program *analysis graph* which is interpreted as an abstraction of the (possibly infinite) set of states explored by the concrete execution. Essentially, the certification/analysis carried out by the supplier is an iterative process which repeatedly traverses the analysis graph until a fixpoint is reached. A key idea in ACC is that, since the certificate is a fixpoint, a single pass over the analysis graph is sufficient to validate the certificate in the consumer side. The ACC framework and our work here are applied at the source-level while in existing PCC frameworks the code supplier typically packages the certificate with the *object* code rather than with the *source* code (both are untrusted). This is without loss of generality because both the ideas in ACC and in our current incremental proposal could also be applied to bytecode.

Non incremental models for PCC (ACC among them) are based on checkers which receive a "certificate+program" package and read and validate the entire program w.r.t. its certificate at once . However, there are situations which are not well suited to this simple model. In particular, we consider possible untrusted *updates* of a validated (trusted) code, i.e., a code producer can (periodically) send to its consumers new updates of a previously submitted package. By updates, we mean any modification over a program including: 1) the *addition* of new data/procedures and the extension of already existing procedures with new functionalities, 2) the *deletion* of procedures or parts of them and 3) the *replacement* of certain (parts of) procedures by new versions for them. In such a context of frequent software updates, it appears inefficient to submit a full certificate (superseding the original one) and to perform the checking of the entire updated program from scratch, as needs to be done with current systems. In the context of ACC, we investigate an *incremental* approach to PCC by considering any arbitrary program update over the original program.

When a program is updated, a new fixpoint has to be computed for the updated program. Such fixpoint differs from the original fixpoint stored in the certificate in a) the new fixpoint for each procedure affected by the changes and b) the update of certain (existing) fixpoints affected by the propagation of the effect of a). However, certain parts of the original certificate may not be affected by the changes. Thus, if the consumer still keeps the original abstraction, it is possible to provide, along with the program updates, only the *difference* of both abstractions, i.e., the *incremental certificate*. The first obvious advantage of an incremental approach is that the size of the certificate may be substantially reduced by submitting only the increment.

Moreover, the task performed by the checker can also be further reduced in incremental PCC. In principle, a non-incremental checker (like the one in [4]) requires a whole traversal of the analysis graph where the entire program + updates is checked against the (full) certificate. However, it is now possible to define an *incremental checking* algorithm which, given the updates and its incremental certificate, only rechecks the part of the analysis graph for the procedures which have been affected by the updates and, also, propagates and rechecks the effect of these changes. In order to perform such propagation of changes, the *dependencies* between the nodes of the original analysis graph have to be computed and stored by the consumers, together with the original certificate. With this, the checking process is carried out in a single pass over the part of the abstraction affected by the updates. Thus, the second advantage of our incremental approach is that checking time is further reduced.

2   Abstraction-Carrying Code

We assume some familiarity with abstract interpretation (see [6]), (Constraint) Logic Programming (C)LP (see, e.g., [11,10]) and PCC [13].

An abstract interpretation-based certifier is a function CERTIFIER: *Prog* × *ADom* × *Approx* ↦ *Approx* which for a given program $P \in Prog$, an abstract domain $D_\alpha \in ADom$ and an abstract safety policy $I_\alpha \in Approx$ generates an abstract certificate $Cert_\alpha \in Approx$, by using an abstract interpreter for D_α, such that the certificate entails that P satisfies I_α. An abstract safety policy I_α is a specification of the safety requirements given in terms of the abstract domain D_α. We denote that I_α and $Cert_\alpha$ are specifications given as abstract semantic values of D_α by using the same subscript α. The basics for defining such certifiers (and their corresponding checkers) in ACC are summarized in the following five points:

Approximation. We consider a *description (or abstract) domain* $\langle D_\alpha, \sqsubseteq \rangle \in ADom$ and its corresponding *concrete domain* $\langle 2^D, \subseteq \rangle$, both with a complete lattice structure. Description (or abstract) values and sets of concrete values are related by an *abstraction* function $\alpha : 2^D \to D_\alpha$, and a *concretization* function $\gamma : D_\alpha \to 2^D$. The pair $\langle \alpha, \gamma \rangle$ forms a Galois connection. The concrete and abstract domains must be related in such a way that the following condition holds [6] $\forall x \in 2^D : \gamma(\alpha(x)) \supseteq x$ and $\forall y \in D_\alpha : \alpha(\gamma(y)) = y$. In general $\sqsubseteq$ is induced by $\subseteq$ and α. Similarly, the operations of *least upper bound* ($\sqcup$) and *greatest lower bound* ($\sqcap$) mimic those of 2^D in a precise sense.

Analysis. We consider the class of *fixed-point semantics* in which a (monotonic) semantic operator, S_P, is associated to each program P. The meaning of the program, $[\![P]\!]$, is defined as the least fixed point of the S_P operator, i.e., $[\![P]\!] = \mathrm{lfp}(S_P)$. If S_P is continuous, the least fixed point is the limit of an iterative process involving at most ω applications of S_P starting from the bottom element of the lattice. Using abstract interpretation, we can usually only compute $[\![P]\!]_\alpha$, as $[\![P]\!]_\alpha = \mathrm{lfp}(S_P^\alpha)$. The operator S_P^α is the abstract counterpart of S_P.

$$\text{analyzer}(P, D_\alpha) = \mathrm{lfp}(S_P^\alpha) = [\![P]\!]_\alpha \qquad (1)$$

Correctness of analysis ensures that $[\![P]\!]_\alpha$ safely approximates $[\![P]\!]$, i.e., $[\![P]\!] \in \gamma([\![P]\!]_\alpha)$. Thus, such *abstraction* can be used as certificate.

Certificate. Let $Cert_\alpha$ be a safe approximation of $[\![P]\!]_\alpha$. If an abstract safety specification I_α can be proved w.r.t. $Cert_\alpha$, then P satisfies the safety policy and $Cert_\alpha$ is a valid certificate:

$$Cert_\alpha \text{ is } a \text{ valid certificate for } P \text{ w.r.t. } I_\alpha \text{ iff } Cert_\alpha \sqsubseteq I_\alpha \qquad (2)$$

Together, Equations (1) and (2) define a certifier which provides program fixpoints, $[\![P]\!]_\alpha$, as certificates which entail a given safety policy, i.e., by taking $Cert_\alpha = [\![P]\!]_\alpha$.

Checking. A checker is a function CHECKER: $Prog \times ADom \times Approx \mapsto bool$ which for a program $P \in Prog$, an abstract domain $D_\alpha \in ADom$ and certificate $Cert_\alpha \in Approx$ checks whether $Cert_\alpha$ is a fixpoint of S_P^α or not:

$$\text{CHECKER}(P, D_\alpha, Cert_\alpha) \text{ returns } true \text{ iff } (S_P^\alpha(Cert_\alpha) \equiv Cert_\alpha) \qquad (3)$$

Verification Condition Regeneration. To retain the safety guarantees, the consumer must regenerate a trustworthy verification condition –Equation (2)– and use the incoming certificate to test for adherence of the safety policy.

$$P \text{ is trusted iff } Cert_\alpha \sqsubseteq I_\alpha \qquad (4)$$

A fundamental idea in ACC is that, while analysis –Equation (1)– is an iterative process, checking –Equation (3)– is guaranteed to be done in a *single pass* over the abstraction.

3   Notions on Certificates

Although ACC and Incremental ACC are general proposals not tied to any particular programming paradigm, our developments for incremental ACC (as well as for the original ACC framework [4]) are formalized in the context of (C)LP. Very briefly, a *constraint* is essentially a conjunction of expressions built from predefined predicates (such as term equations or inequalities over the reals) whose arguments are constructed using predefined functions (such as real addition). An *atom* has the form $p(t_1, ..., t_n)$ where p is a predicate symbol and t_i are terms. A *literal* is either an atom or a constraint. A *goal* is a finite sequence of literals. A *rule* is of the form H :-D where H, the *head*, is an atom and D, the *body*, is a possibly empty finite sequence of literals. A *constraint logic program $P \in Prog$*, or *program*, is a finite set of rules. Program rules are assumed to be normalized: only distinct variables are allowed to occur as arguments to atoms. Furthermore, we require that each rule defining a predicate p has identical sequence of variables $x_{p_1}, ... x_{p_n}$ in the head atom, i.e., $p(x_{p_1}, ... x_{p_n})$. We call this the *base form* of p. This is not restrictive since programs can always be normalized, and it will facilitate the presentation of the checking algorithms.

3.1   The Notion of Full Certificate

For concreteness, we rely on an abstract interpretation-based analysis algorithm in the style of the generic analyzer of [7]. This goal-dependent analysis algorithm, which we refer to as analyzer, given a program P and abstract domain D_α, receives a set $Q_\alpha \in AAtom$ of Abstract Atoms (or *call patterns*) and constructs an *analysis graph* [5] for Q_α. The elements of Q_α are pairs of the form $A : CP$ where A is a procedure descriptor and CP is an abstract substitution (i.e., a condition of the run-time bindings) of A expressed as $CP \in D_\alpha$.[1] Then, the analysis graph is an abstraction of the (possibly infinite) set of (possibly infinite) trees explored by the concrete execution of initial calls described by Q_α in P. The program analysis graph computed by analyzer(Q_α) for P in D_α can be implicitly represented by means of two data structures, the *answer table* and the *dependency arc table* (which are in fact the result of the analysis algorithm).

  Answer Table (AT). Its entries correspond to the *nodes* in the analysis graph. They are of the form $A : CP \mapsto AP$, where A is always an atom in base form. They should be interpreted as "the answer pattern for calls to A satisfying precondition (or call pattern), CP, accomplishes postcondition (or answer pattern), AP." AP and CP are abstract substitutions in D_α.

  Dependency Arc Table (DAT). Dependencies correspond to the *arcs* in the analysis graph. The intended meaning of a dependency $A_k : CP \Rightarrow B_{k,i} : CP_1$ associated to a program rule A_k:-$B_{k,1}, \ldots, B_{k,n}$ with $i \in \{1, ..n\}$, is that the answer for $A_k : CP$ depends on the answer for $B_{k,i} : CP_1$, say AP_1. Thus, if AP_1 changes with the update of some rule for $B_{k,i}$ then, the *arc* $A_k : CP \Rightarrow B_{k,i} : CP_1$ must be reprocessed in order to compute the new answer for $A_k : CP$. This is to say that the rule for A_k has to be processed again starting from atom $B_{k,i}$.

All the details and the formalization of the analysis algorithm analyzer can be found in [7]. Certification in ACC [4] consists in using the *complete* set of entries stored in the answer table as certificate. Dependencies are not needed for certificate generation neither for non-incremental checking though they will be fundamental later for incremental certificate checking.

Definition 1 (certificate [4]). *Let $P \in Prog$, $D_\alpha \in ADom$ and $Q_\alpha \in AAtom$. We define* Cert $\in Approx$, *the certificate for P and Q_α, as the set of entries stored in the answer table computed by* analyzer(Q_α) *[7] for P in D_α.*

Example 1. The next example shows a piece of a module which contains the following (normalized) program for the naive reversal of a list and uses an implementation of app with several base cases (e.g., added automatically by a partial evaluator [8] for efficiency purposes).

  (rev_1) rev(X, Y) : $-$ X = [ ], Y = [ ].
  (rev_2) rev(X, Y) : $-$ X = [U|V], rev(V, W), T = [U], app(W, T, Y).
  (app_1) app(X, Y, Z) : $-$ X = [ ], Y = Z.
  (app_2) app(X, Y, Z) : $-$ X = [U], Z = [U|Y].
  (app_3) app(X, Y, Z) : $-$ X = [U, V], Z = [U, V|Y].
  (app_4) app(X, Y, Z) : $-$ X = [U|V], Z = [U|W], app(V, Y, W).

The description domain that we use in our examples is the domain *Pos* of Positive Boolean functions [12]. The key idea in this description is to use implication to capture groundness dependencies. The reading of the function $x \to y$ is

---

[1] We sometimes omit the subscript α from Q_α when it is clear from the context.

"if the program variable x is (becomes) ground, so is (does) program variable y." For example, the best description of the constraint $\mathtt{f}(\mathtt{X},\mathtt{Y}) = \mathtt{f}(\mathtt{a},\mathtt{g}(\mathtt{U},\mathtt{V}))$ is $\mathtt{X} \wedge (\mathtt{Y} \leftrightarrow (\mathtt{U} \wedge \mathtt{V}))$. Groundness information is of great importance as a safety property in order to verify that (C)LP programs are "well moded" (i.e., arguments are correctly instantiated). The most general description $\top$ does not provide information about any variable. The least general substitution $\bot$ assigns the empty set of values to each variable.

For the analysis of our running example, we consider the calling pattern $\mathtt{rev}(\mathtt{X}, \mathtt{Y}) : \top$, i.e., no entry information is provided on $\mathtt{X}$ nor $\mathtt{Y}$. $\mathtt{analyzer}(\mathtt{rev}(\mathtt{X},\mathtt{Y}) : \top)$ produces **State 0** composed of the following answers and dependencies:

$(A_1)\ \mathtt{rev}(\mathtt{X},\mathtt{Y}) : \top \mapsto \mathtt{X} \leftrightarrow \mathtt{Y}$ $\qquad (D_1)\ \mathtt{rev}(\mathtt{X},\mathtt{Y}) : \top \Rightarrow \mathtt{rev}(\mathtt{V},\mathtt{W}) : \top$

$(A_2)\ \mathtt{app}(\mathtt{X},\mathtt{Y},\mathtt{Z}) : \top \mapsto (\mathtt{X} \wedge \mathtt{Y}) \leftrightarrow \mathtt{Z}$ $\qquad (D_2)\ \mathtt{rev}(\mathtt{X},\mathtt{Y}) : \top \Rightarrow \mathtt{app}(\mathtt{W},\mathtt{T},\mathtt{Y}) : \top$

$\qquad\qquad\qquad\qquad\qquad\qquad\qquad\qquad (D_3)\ \mathtt{app}(\mathtt{X},\mathtt{Y},\mathtt{Z}) : \top \Rightarrow \mathtt{app}(\mathtt{V},\mathtt{Y},\mathtt{W}) : \top$

Intuitively, D_2 denotes that the answer for $\mathtt{rev}(\mathtt{X},\mathtt{Y}) : \top$ may change if the answer for $\mathtt{app}(\mathtt{W},\mathtt{T},\mathtt{Y}) : \top$ changes. In such a case, the second rule for $\mathtt{rev}$ must be processed again starting from atom $\mathtt{app}(\mathtt{W},\mathtt{T},\mathtt{Y})$ in order to recompute the fixpoint for $\mathtt{rev}(\mathtt{X},\mathtt{Y}) : \top$. D_1 and D_3 reflect the recursivity of $\mathtt{rev}(\mathtt{X},\mathtt{Y}) : \top$ and $\mathtt{app}(\mathtt{W},\mathtt{T},\mathtt{Y}) : \top$, respectively, since they depend on themselves. The detailed steps performed by the algorithm can be found in [7] for the same program without the rules $\mathtt{app}_2$ and $\mathtt{app}_3$. However these rules do not add any further information to the fixpoint computation and the steps performed there still apply to our example. According to Definition 1, the certificate Cert for this example is composed of all entries in the answer table, i.e., A_1 and A_2. $\qquad\qquad\square$

3.2   The Notion of Incremental Certificate

Given a program P, we define an *update* of P, written as $Upd(P) \in UProg$, as a set of tuples of the form $\langle A, Add(A), Del(A)\rangle$, where $A = p(x_1, \ldots, x_n)$ is an atom in base form, $Add(A)$ is the set of rules which are to be added to P for predicate p^2 and $Del(A)$ is the set of rules which are to be removed from P for predicate p.

When a program is updated, depending on the kind of update, the new certificate for the modified program can be either equal, more or less precise than the original one, or even not comparable. In any case, it appears inefficient to generate, transmit, and check the full certificate Ext_Cert for the updated program U_P defined as $U_P = P \oplus Upd(P)$.[3] Our proposal is that it is possible to submit only the new program update $Upd(P)$ together with the *incremental certificate* Inc_Cert, i.e., the *difference* of Ext_Cert w.r.t. the original Cert.

Definition 2 (incremental certificate). *In the conditions of Def. 1, we consider $Upd(P) \in UProg$. Let Cert be the certificate for P and Q_α. Let Ext_Cert be*

---

[2] This includes both the case of addition of new procedures, when p did not exist in P, as well as the extension of additional rules (or functionality) for p, if it existed.

[3] The operator "$\oplus$" applies the update to P and generates $U_P = P \oplus Upd(P)$. This can be implemented by using a program in the spirit of the traditional Unix *patch* command as $\oplus$ operator.

the certificate for $P \oplus Upd(P)$ and Q_α. We define Inc_Cert, *the incremental certificate for $Upd(P)$ w.r.t.* Cert, *as* Ext_Cert − Cert, *where* Ext_Cert − Cert *is defined as the set of entries $B : CP_B \mapsto AP_B \in$* Ext_Cert *such that:*

1. $B : CP_B \mapsto \_ \notin$ Cert *or,*
2. $A : CP_A \mapsto AP_A \in$ Cert, $A : CP_A = B : CP_B$ *and* $AP_A \neq AP_B$ *(modulo renaming).*

The definition of incremental certificate for the particular case of program extensions can be found in [2]. The following example illustrates that updating a program can require the change in the analysis information previously computed for other procedures whose fixpoint is indirectly affected by the updates, although their definitions have not been directly changed.

Example 2. Consider the following new definition for app, which is a specialization of the previous app to concatenate lists of a's of the same length :

(Napp₁) $app(X, Y, Z) : - X = [\ ], Y = [\ ], Z = [\ ].$
(Napp₂) $app(X, Y, Z) : - X = [a|V], Y = [a|U], Z = [a, a|W], app(V, U, W).$

The update consists in deleting all rules for app in Ex. 1, and replacing them by Napp₁ and Napp₂. After running the (incremental) analysis algorithm in [7], the following answer table and dependencies are computed **(State 1)**:

(NA_1) $rev(X, Y) : \top \mapsto X \wedge Y$	(ND_1) $rev(X, Y) : \top \Rightarrow rev(V, W) : \top$
(NA_2) $app(X, Y, Z) : \top \mapsto X \wedge Y \wedge Z$	(ND_2) $rev(X, Y) : \top \Rightarrow app(W, T, Y) : W$
(NA_3) $app(X, Y, Z) : X \mapsto X \wedge Y \wedge Z$	(ND_3) $app(X, Y, Z) : X \Rightarrow app(V, U, W) : V$

Note that the analysis information has changed because the new definition of app allows inferring that all its arguments are ground upon success (NA_2 and NA_3). This change propagates to the answer of rev and allows inferring that, regardless of the calling pattern, both arguments of rev will be ground on the exit (NA_1). According to Def. 2, the incremental certificate Inc_Cert contains NA_3, as it corresponds a new calling pattern (point 1), and also NA_1 and NA_2 since their answers have changed w.r.t. the ones in **State 0** (point 2).   □

Note that in a non incremental framework, the size of certificates can be reduced by using compression techniques as in [3]. This approach is not compatible with the incremental setting we discuss in this paper, because information essential for the incremental checker can have been removed by the fixpoint reduction.

4   A Checking Algorithm with Support for Incrementality

In this section, we present a checking algorithm for full certificates which is instrumented with a *Dependency Arc Table* (*DAT* in the following). The DAT stores the dependencies between the atoms in the analysis graph (see Section 3). This structure is not required by non incremental checkers [4] but it is fundamental to support an incremental design.

1: **procedure** checking($P, Q, \text{Cert}, AT_{mem}, DAT_{mem}$)
2:     $AT_{mem} := \emptyset$; $DAT_{mem} := \emptyset$; $CP_{checked} := \emptyset$;
3:     **for all** $A : CP \in Q$ **do**
4:         process_node($P, A : CP, \text{Cert}, AT_{mem}, DAT_{mem}, CP_{checked}$);
5:     **return** Valid;
6: **procedure** process_node($P, A : CP, \text{Cert}, AT_{mem}, DAT_{mem}, CP_{checked}$)
7:     **if** ($\exists$ a renaming σ s.t. $\sigma(A : CP \mapsto AP)$ in Cert) **then**
8:         add $A : CP \mapsto \sigma^{-1}(AP)$ to AT_{mem} ;
9:         $CP_{checked} := CP_{checked} \cup \{A : CP\}$;
10:     **else return** Error;
11:     process_set_of_rules($P, P|_A, A : CP \mapsto \sigma^{-1}(AP), \text{Cert},$
                        $AT_{mem}, DAT_{mem}, CP_{checked}$);
12: **procedure** process_set_of_rules($P, R, A : CP \mapsto AP, \text{Cert},$
                        $AT_{mem}, DAT_{mem}, CP_{checked}$)
13:     **for all** rule $A_k \leftarrow B_{k,1}, \ldots, B_{k,n_k}$ in R **do**
14:         $W := vars(A_k, B_{k,1}, \ldots, B_{k,n_k})$;
15:         $CP_b := \text{Aextend}(CP, vars(B_{k,1}, \ldots, B_{k,n_k}))$;
16:         $CPR_b := \text{Arestrict}(CP_b, B_{k,1})$;
17:         $CP_a := \text{process\_rule}(P, A : CP, A_k \leftarrow B_{k,1}, \ldots, B_{k,n_k}, W, CP_b, CPR_b, \text{Cert},$
                        $AT_{mem}, DAT_{mem}, CP_{checked}$);
18:         $AP_1 := \text{Arestrict}(CP_a, vars(A_k))$; $AP_2 := \text{Alub}(AP_1, AP)$;
19:         **if** ($AP <> AP_2$) **then return** Error;
20: **procedure** process_rule($P, A : CP, A_k \leftarrow B_{k,j}, \ldots, B_{k,n_k}, W, CP_b, CPR_b, \text{Cert},$
                        $AT_{mem}, DAT_{mem}, CP_{checked}$)
21:     **for all** $B_{k,i}$ in the rule body $i = j, ..., n_k$ **do**
22:         $CP_a := \text{process\_arc}(P, A : CP, B_{k,i} : CPR_b, CP_b, W, \text{Cert},$
                        $AT_{mem}, DAT_{mem}, CP_{checked}$);
23:         **if** ($i <> n_k$) **then** $CPR_a := \text{Arestrict}(CP_a, var(B_{k,i+1}))$;
24:         $CP_b := CP_a$; $CPR_b := CPR_a$;
25:     **return** CP_a;
26: **procedure** process_arc($P, A : CP, B_{k,i} : CPR_b, CP_b, W, \text{Cert},$
                        $AT_{mem}, DAT_{mem}, CP_{checked}$)
27:     **if** ($B_{k,i}$ is a constraint) **then** $CP_a := \text{Aadd}(B_{k,i}, CP_b)$;
28:     **else**
29:         **if** ($\not\exists$ a renaming σ s.t. $\sigma(B_{k,i} : CPR_b \mapsto AP')$ in AT_{mem}) **then**
30:             process_node ($P, B_{k,i} : CPR_b, \text{Cert}, AT_{mem}, DAT_{mem}, CP_{checked}$);
31:         $AP_1 := \text{Aextend}(\rho^{-1}(AP), W)$; where ρ is a renaming s.t.
                        $\rho(B_{k,i} : CPR_b \mapsto AP)$ in AT_{mem}
32:         $CP_a := \text{Aconj}(CP_b, AP_1)$;
33:         add $A : CP \Rightarrow B_{k,i}$ to DAT_{mem};
34:     **return** CP_a;

Fig. 1. Checking with Support for Incrementality (Algorithm 1)

Algorithm 1 presents our checker, which receives as parameters a program P, a set Q of call patterns, the certificate Cert returned by analyzer, and two input/output variables AT_{mem} and DAT_{mem} (initially empty) and constructs a program analysis graph in a single iteration by assuming the fixpoint information in Cert. While the graph is being constructed, the obtained answers are stored in AT_{mem} and compared with the corresponding fixpoints stored in Cert. If any of the computed answers is not consistent with the certificate (i.e., it is greater than the fixpoint), the certificate is considered invalid and the program is rejected. Otherwise, Cert gets checked. The checker returns the reconstructed answer table AT_{mem} and the set of dependencies DAT_{mem} which have been traversed. A detailed explanation of this algorithm can be found in [2] (where only program extensions are considered and the parameter $CP_{checked}$ is not needed). Algorithm 1 is parametric w.r.t. the abstract domain of interest D_α and it is hence defined in terms of five abstract operations on D_α:

- Arestrict(CP, V) performs the abstract restriction of a description CP to the set of variables in the set V, denoted $vars(V)$;
- Aextend(CP, V) extends the description CP to the variables in the set V;
- Aadd(C, CP) performs the abstract operation of conjoining the constraint C with the description CP;
- Aconj(CP_1, CP_2) performs the abstract conjunction of two descriptions;
- Alub(CP_1, CP_2) performs the abstract disjunction of two descriptions.

Example 3. The abstract operations for the domain *Pos* (Ex. 1) are:

$$\text{Arestrict}(CP, V) = \exists_{-V} CP \qquad \text{Aconj}(CP_1, CP_2) = CP_1 \wedge CP_2$$
$$\text{Alub}(CP_1, CP_2) = CP_1 \sqcup CP_2 \qquad \text{Aextend}(CP, V) = CP$$
$$\text{Aadd}(C, CP) = \alpha_{Def}(C) \wedge CP \qquad \alpha_{Def}(X = t) = (X \leftrightarrow \bigwedge\{Y \in vars(t)\})$$

where $\exists_{-V} F$ represents $\exists v_1, \ldots, v_n F$, $\{v_1, \ldots, v_n\} = vars(F) - V$, and $\sqcup$ is the least upper bound (lub) operation over the *Pos* lattice. For instance, $\text{Aconj}(X, Y \leftrightarrow (X \wedge Z)) = X \wedge (Y \leftrightarrow Z)$. $\text{Aadd}(X = [U|V], Y) = (X \leftrightarrow (U \wedge V)) \wedge Y$. $\text{Alub}(X, Y) = X \vee Y$. As an example of checking, we illustrate the steps carried out by the checker to validate the rules app_1 and app_4 of Ex. 1 w.r.t. a certificate Cert composed of the entry A_2. We take as call pattern $\text{app}(X, Y, Z) : \top$. Consider the call to procedure process_node for $\text{app}(X, Y, Z) : \top$. The entry A_2 is added (L8) to AT_{mem} (initially empty), and $\text{app}(X, Y, Z) : \top$ is marked as checked by inserting it in $CP_{checked}$. A call to process_set_of_rules is generated for the call at hand w.r.t. app_1 and app_4 (L11). Consider the processing of the two rules.

1. The call to process_rule for app_1 (L17) executes process_arc (L22) for each of the two constraints in the body. The final answer $CP_a \equiv X \wedge (Y \leftrightarrow Z)$ (L17) for app_1 is built up from the abstract conjunction (L32) between X (partial answer from first constraint) and $Y \leftrightarrow Z$ (from second constraint). Since the least upper bound (L18) between CP_a and the answer A_2 is A_2, then no Error is issued (L19) and the first rule app_1 gets successfully checked.
2. As before, the call to process_rule for app_4 executes process_arc for the first two constraints and computes as (partial) solution $CP_a \equiv (X \leftrightarrow (U \wedge V)) \wedge (Z \leftrightarrow (U \wedge W))$ (L22). Since we are not in the last atom of the rule (L23), CP_a is restricted to the variables in $\text{app}(V, Y, W)$, giving as result $CPR_a \equiv \top$. Now, the next call to process_arc for the rightmost body atom $\text{app}(V, Y, W) : \top$ computes as final solution $(X \leftrightarrow (U \wedge V)) \wedge (Z \leftrightarrow (U \wedge W)) \wedge (V \wedge (Y \leftrightarrow W))$, which

is simplified to A_2. The corresponding dependency is stored in DAT_{mem}. Thus, the call to process_rule for app_4 computes as solution A_2 (L17), the same answer stored in Cert, and no Error is issued (L19).

In order to support an incremental extension, the final values of the data structures AT_{mem}, DAT_{mem} and P must be available after the end of the execution of the checker. We denote by $AT_{persist}$, $DAT_{persist}$ and $P_{persist}$ the copy in persistent memory (i.e., in disk) of such structures.

Definition 3 (checker). *We define function* CHECKER:$Prog \times Approx \times AAtom \times ADom \mapsto boolean$ *which takes a program* $P \in Prog$ *and its certificate* Cert $\in Approx$ *for* $Q_\alpha \in AAtom$ *in* $D_\alpha \in ADom$ *and it returns the result of* checking(P, Q_α, Cert, AT_{mem}, DAT_{mem}). *If it does not issue an* Error, *then it stores in memory* $AT_{persist} := AT_{mem}$, $DAT_{persist} := DAT_{mem}$ *and* $P_{persist} := P$.

5   Incremental Checking

In this section, we propose an incremental checking algorithm which deals with all possible updates over a program in a unified form. The basic idea is that the task performed by an incremental checker has to be optimized such that it only: a) rechecks the part of the abstraction for the procedures which have been directly affected by an update and, b) propagates and rechecks the indirect effect of these changes. In order to do this, we will take as starting point the checker in Algorithm 1. Its DAT will allow the incremental algorithm to propagate the changes and carry out the process in a single pass over the subgraph affected by the updates. Algorithm 2 presents our implementation of this intuition. We start by removing all (possibly incorrect or inaccurate) information *directly* affected by the updates from the answer table and DAT (i.e., the information for the updated procedures) and, then, we check it from scratch against the answers provided in the incremental certificate. If the "direct" checking succeeds, we proceed to check the information *indirectly* affected by such changes in a similar way (i.e., delete the information for them from answer and DAT and recheck it from scratch). This iterative process successfully finishes when all directly and indirectly affected information gets checked. Otherwise, an Error is issued.

The incremental checker is defined as follows: replace the procedure checking by the new procedure incremental_checking in Algorithm 2 and use the remaining procedures defined in Algorithm 1. Below we enumerate the points which should be done in a way or another in any incremental checking algorithm beyond the analysis of logic programs.

1. *Retrieve stored data.* After checking the original package, the structures $AT_{persist}$, $DAT_{persist}$ and the program $P_{persist}$ have been stored in persistent memory (see Definition 3). Our checker retrieves such stored data and initializes, respectively, the parameters AT_{mem}, DAT_{mem} and P with them.

2. *Update program and answer table.* Prior to proceeding with the proper checking, the incoming updates $Upd(P)$ are applied (by means of the operator $\oplus$)

```
 1: procedure incremental_checking(P, Upd(P), Inc_Cert, AT_mem, DAT_mem)
 2:     P_mem := P ⊕ Upd(P);  update_answer_table(AT_mem, Inc_Cert);
 3:     call_patterns_to_check(Upd(P), AT_mem, CP_tocheck);
 4:     CP_checked := ∅;        % call patterns already checked
 5:     check_affected_entries(P_mem, Inc_Cert, AT_mem, DAT_mem, CP_tocheck, CP_checked);
 6:     return Valid;
 7: procedure update_answer_table(AT_mem, Inc_Cert)
 8:     for all entry A : CP ↦ AP in AT_mem do
 9:         if (∃ A : CP ↦ AP_A in Inc_Cert and AP ≠ AP_A (modulo renaming))
                then replace entry for A : CP ↦ AP in AT_mem by A : CP ↦ AP_A;
10: procedure call_patterns_to_check(Upd(P), AT_mem, CP_tocheck)
11:     CP_tocheck := ∅;        % call patterns required to be checked
12:     for all entry A : CP ↦ _ ∈ AT_mem do
13:         if A is updated in Upd(P) then   CP_tocheck := CP_tocheck ∪ {A : CP};
14: procedure check_affected_entries(P_mem, Inc_Cert, AT_mem, DAT_mem,
                                        CP_tocheck, CP_checked)
15:     while CP_tocheck ! = ∅ do
16:         select A : CP from CP_tocheck;
17:         remove_previous_info(A : CP, AT_mem, DAT_mem);
18:         if A : CP ∉ Inc_Cert then
19:             let A : CP ↦ AP the entry for A : CP in AT_mem;
20:             Inc_Cert = Inc_Cert ∪ {A : CP ↦ AP}; propagate := false;
21:         else propagate := true;
22:         process_node(P_mem, A : CP, Inc_Cert, AT_mem, DAT_mem, CP_checked);
23:         CP_tocheck := CP_tocheck − CP_checked;
24:         if propagate then  propagate_effects(A : CP, DAT_mem,
                                        CP_tocheck, CP_checked);
25: procedure remove_previous_info(A : CP, AT_mem, DAT_mem)
26:     remove entry for A : CP from AT_mem;
27:     remove from DAT_mem all dependencies of the form A : CP ⇒ _ ;
28: procedure propagate_effects(A : CP, DAT_mem, CP_tocheck, CP_checked)
29:     for all B : CP_B ⇒ A : CP ∈ DAT_mem do
30:         if B : CP_B ∉ CP_checked ∪ CP_tocheck then
31:             CP_tocheck := CP_tocheck ∪ {B : CP_B};
```

Fig. 2. Incremental Checking (Algorithm 2)

to P in order to generate P_{mem} (L2). Also, the procedure update_answer_table updates the answers for those call patterns in AT_{mem} which have a different answer in Inc_Cert (L8-9). The new entries not yet present in AT_{mem} will be asserted upon request, as in the usual checking process (L8 of Algorithm 1).

3. *Initialize call patterns to check.* The procedure call_patterns_to_check initializes the set $CP_{tocheck}$ with those call patterns with an entry in AT_{mem} which correspond to a rule directly affected by an update (L12-13). During the execution of the checker, the set $CP_{tocheck}$ will be dynamically extended to include the additional call patterns whose checking is indirectly affected by the propagation of changes (L31).

4. *Check affected procedures.* Procedure check_affected_entries launches the checking of all procedures affected by the updates, i.e., the call patterns in $CP_{tocheck} - CP_{checked}$. The set $CP_{checked}$ is used to avoid rechecking the same call pattern more than once, if it appears several times in the analysis subgraph to be checked. Three actions are taken in order to check a call pattern:[4] remove its analysis information (L17), proceed to check it by calling process_node of Algorithm 1 (L22) and, propagate the effects of type b) if needed (L24). We only propagate effects if the answer provided in Inc_Cert for the call pattern at hand is different from that originally stored in $AT_{persist}$ (L21). As a technical detail, in L20, we add to Inc_Cert the information which, although has not changed w.r.t. AT_{mem}, needs to be checked and, therefore, it must be available in Inc_Cert (or process_node would issue an error in L10 of Algorithm 1).

5. *Remove previous analysis information.* Before proceeding with the checking, we need to get rid of previous (possibly incorrect or inaccurate) analysis information. Procedure remove_previous_info eliminates the entry to be checked from AT_{mem} (L26) and all its dependencies from DAT_{mem} (L27).

6. *Propagate effects.* After processing the updated rules, the procedure propagate_effects introduces in the set $CP_{tocheck}$ (L31) the calling patterns whose answer depends on the updated one, i.e., those which are indirectly affected by the updates. Their checking will be later required in L15.

7. *Store data.* Upon return, the checker has to store the computed AT_{mem}, DAT_{mem} and P_{mem}, respectively, in $AT_{persist}$, $DAT_{persist}$, and $P_{persist}$ for achieving a compositional design of our incremental approach.

Definition 4 (incremental checker). *We define function* INCR_CHECKER: *UProg* $\times$ *Approx* $\times$ $\mapsto$ *boolean which takes* $Upd(P) \in$ *UProg and its incremental certificate* Inc_Cert $\in$ *Approx and 1) it retrieves from memory* $AT_{mem} :=$ $AT_{persist}$, $DAT_{mem} := DAT_{persist}$ *and* $P := P_{persist}$ *and 2) it returns the result of* incremental_checking(P, $Upd(P)$, Inc_Cert, AT_{mem}, DAT_{mem}) *for* P. *If it does not issue an* Error, *then it stores* $AT_{persist} := AT_{mem}$, $DAT_{persist} := DAT_{mem}$ *and* $P_{persist} := P_{mem}$.

Note that the safety policy has to be tested w.r.t. the answer table for the extended program. Therefore, the checker has reconstructed, from Inc_Cert, the answer table returned by analyzer for the extended program, Ext_Cert, in order to test for adherence to the safety policy –Equation (4), i.e., $AT_{persist} \equiv$ Ext_Cert.

The following example illustrates a situation in which the task performed by the incremental checker is optimized to only check a part of the abstraction.

Example 4. Consider the deletion of rules app$_2$ and app$_3$ of Example 1. The analysis algorithm of [7] returns the same state **(State 0)** since the eliminated rules do not affect the fixpoint result, i.e., they do not add any further information.

---

[4] Note that an updated rule which does not match any entry in AT_{mem} does not need to be processed by now. Its processing may be required by some other new rule or they can simply not be affected by the checking process.

Thus, the incremental certificate Inc_Cert associated to such an update is empty. The checking algorithm proceeds as follows. Initially, AT_{mem} and DAT_{mem} are initialized with the values in **State 0**. P_{mem} is composed of the rules rev_1, rev_2, app_1 and app_4. Procedure update_answer_table (L2) does not modify AT_{mem}. The execution of procedure call_patterns_to_check (L3) adds $E_1 \equiv app(X, Y, Z) : \top$ to $CP_{tocheck}$. Procedure check_affected_entries selects E_1 from $CP_{tocheck}$. The next call to remove_previous_info (L17) removes A_2 from AT_{mem} and D_3 from DAT_{mem}. It then inserts A_2 in Inc_Cert. The variable *"propagate"* takes the value *false*. We now jump to the non incremental checking with a call to procedure process_node (L22). This process corresponds exactly to the checking illustrated in Example 3. Upon return from process_node (since variable *"propagate"* is *false*), no effects have to be propagated.

The important point to note is that the incremental checker has not had to recheck the rules for rev since its answer is not affected by the deletion. Once Inc_Cert has been validated, the consumer memoizes AT_{mem}, DAT_{mem} (which are those of **State 0**) and P_{mem} in disk.   □

Our second example is intended to show how to propagate effects.

Example 5. Let us illustrate the checking process carried out to validate the update proposed in Example 2 with an incremental certificate, Inc_Cert, which contains the entries NA_1, NA_2 and NA_3. The incremental checker retrieves **State 0** from disk. Next, procedure update_answer_table returns as new AT_{mem} the entries NA_1 and NA_2 which replace the old entries A_1 and A_2, respectively. Then, the set $CP_{tocheck}$ is initialized with $E_1 \equiv app(X, Y, Z) : \top$. Procedure check_affected_entries first executes remove_previous_info, which eliminates E_1 from AT_{mem} and dependency D_3 from DAT_{mem}. Moreover, the variable *"propagate"* is initialized to *true*. This annotates that effects have to be propagated later. The execution of process_node for E_1 succeeds and adds the dependency D_3 to DAT_{mem} and the set $CP_{checked}$ is returned with E_1 marked as checked. Upon return, since the variable *"propagate"* is *true*, a call to propagate_effects is generated which forces the checking of rev. After inspecting D_2 and D_3 (the two dependencies for E_1), only the entry $E_2 \equiv rev(X, Y) : \top$ is added to $CP_{tocheck}$. The dependency for D_3 will not be checked because E_1 has been already processed (hence, it belongs to $CP_{checked}$). Now, procedure check_affected_entries takes E_2 from $CP_{tocheck}$, and similarly to the previous case, successfully executes process_node, and replaces D_2 by ND_2. During the checking of rule rev_2, a new call to process_node is generated for $E_3 \equiv app(X, Y, Z) : X$ which introduces E_3 in $CP_{checked}$, and replaces the dependency D_3 in DAT_{mem} by the new one ND_3 of Example 2. Upon return, since the variable *"propagate"* is *true*, a call to propagate_effects is generated from it. But the affected dependency D_1 is not processed because E_1 was processed already and belongs to $CP_{checked}$. The conclusion is that a single pass has been performed on the three provided entries in order to validate the certificate.   □

The following theorem establishes the correctness of incremental checking. The proof can be found in [1].

Theorem 1 (correctness). *Let* $P \in Prog$, $Upd(P) \in UProg$, $D_\alpha \in ADom$ *and* $Q_\alpha \in AAtom$. *Let* Cert *be the certificate for* P *and* Q_α, Ext_Cert *the certificate for* $P \oplus Upd(P)$ *and* Q_α *and* Inc_Cert *the incremental certificate for* $Upd(P)$ *w.r.t.* Cert. *If* INCR_CHECKER$(Upd(P)$, Inc_Cert$)$ *does not issue an Error, then the validation of* Inc_Cert *is done in a single pass over* Inc_Cert *and* $AT_{persist} \equiv AT_{mem}$, $DAT_{persist} \equiv DAT_{mem}$, *where* AT_{mem} *and* DAT_{mem} *are, respectively, the answer table and DAT returned by* checking$(P \oplus Upd(p), Q_\alpha$, Ext_Cert, $AT_{mem}, DAT_{mem})$.

Efforts for coming up with incremental approaches are known in the context of program analysis (see [17,7,14,15]) and program verification (see [18,9,16]). Our work is more closely related to incremental program analysis, although the design of our incremental checking algorithm is notably different from the design of an incremental analyzer (like the ones in [7,14]). In particular, the treatment of deletions and arbitrary changes is completely different. In our case, we can take advantage of the information provided in the certificate in order to avoid the need to compute the strongly connected components (see [7]). This was necessary in the analyzer in order to ensure the correctness of the incremental algorithm. Unlike [7,14], we have integrated in a single algorithm all incremental updates over a program in a seamless way. In [2], we have identified the particular optimization for the addition of rules to a program.

6   Conclusions

Our approach to incremental ACC aims at reducing the size of certificates and the checking time when a supplier provides an untrusted update of a (previously) validated package. Essentially, when a program is subject to an update, the incremental certificate we propose contains only the *difference* between the original certificate for the initial program and the new certificate for the updated one. Checking time is reduced by traversing only those parts of the abstraction which are affected by the changes rather than the whole abstraction. An important point to note is that our incremental approach requires the original certificate and the dependency arc table to be stored on the consumer side for upcoming updates. The appropriateness of using the incremental approach will therefore depend on the particular features of the consumer system and the frequency of software updates. In general, our approach seems to be more suitable when the consumer prefers to minimize as much as possible the waiting time for receiving and validating the certificate while storage requirements are not scarce. We believe that, in everyday practice, time-consuming safety tests would be avoided by many users, while they would probably accept to store the safety certificate and dependencies associated to the package. We are now in the process of extending the ACC implementation already available in the CiaoPP system to support incrementality. Our preliminary results in certificate reduction are very promising. We expect optimizations in the checking time similar to those achieved in the case of incremental analysis (see, e.g., [7]).

References

1. E. Albert, P. Arenas, and G. Puebla. An Incremental Approach to Abstraction-Carrying Code. Technical Report CLIP3/2006, Technical University of Madrid (UPM), School of Computer Science, UPM, March 2006.
2. E. Albert, P. Arenas, and G. Puebla. Incremental Certificates and Checkers for Abstraction-Carrying Code. In *Proc. of WITS 2006*, March 2006.
3. E. Albert, P. Arenas, G. Puebla, and M. Hermenegildo. Reduced Certificates for Abstraction-Carrying Code. In *Proc. of ICLP 2006*, Springer LNCS. To appear.
4. E. Albert, G. Puebla, and M. Hermenegildo. Abstraction-Carrying Code. In *Proc. of LPAR'04*, Springer LNAI 3452, pp. 380–397, 2005.
5. M. Bruynooghe. A Practical Framework for the Abstract Interpretation of Logic Programs. *Journal of Logic Programming*, 10:91–124, 1991.
6. P. Cousot and R. Cousot. Abstract Interpretation: a Unified Lattice Model for Static Analysis of Programs by Construction or Approximation of Fixpoints. In *Proc. POPL 1977*, ACM, pp.238–252, 1977.
7. M. Hermenegildo, G. Puebla, K. Marriott, and P. Stuckey. Incremental Analysis of Constraint Logic Programs. *ACM Transactions on Programming Languages and Systems*, 22(2):187–223, March 2000.
8. N.D. Jones, C.K. Gomard, and P. Sestoft. *Partial Evaluation and Automatic Program Generation*. Prentice Hall, New York, 1993.
9. Y. Lakhnech, S. Bensalem, S. Berezin, and S. Owre. Incremental verification by abstraction. In *Proc. 7th International Conference on Tools and Algorithms for the Construction and Analysis of Systems*, Springer LNCS 2031, pp. 98–112, 2001.
10. J.W. Lloyd. *Foundations of Logic Programming*. Springer, second, extended edition, 1987.
11. Kim Marriot and Peter Stuckey. *Programming with Constraints: An Introduction*. The MIT Press, 1998.
12. K. Marriott and H. Søndergaard. Precise and efficient groundness analysis for logic programs. *ACM Letters on Programming Languages and Systems*, 2(4):181–196, 1993.
13. G. Necula. Proof-Carrying Code. In *Proc. of POPL 1997*, pp. 106–119. ACM Press, 1997.
14. G. Puebla and M. Hermenegildo. Optimized Algorithms for the Incremental Analysis of Logic Programs. In *Proc. SAS'96*, Springer LNCS 1145, pp. 270–284, 1996.
15. B. Ryder. Incremental data-flow analysis algorithms. *ACM Transactions on Programming Languages and Systems*, 10(1):1–50, 1988.
16. O.V. Sokolsky and S.A. Smolka. Incremental model checking in the modal μ-calculus. In *Computer Aided Verification, Proc. 6th International Conference*, Springer LNCS 818, pp. 351–363, 1994.
17. Tim A. Wagner and Susan L. Graham. Incremental analysis of real programming languages. In *Proc. PLDI'97*, pp. 31–43, 1997.
18. M. Wildmoser, A. Chaieb, and T. Nipkow. Bytecode Analysis for Proof Carrying Code. In *Proc. Bytecode'05*, ENTCS 141, pp. 19–34. Elsevier, 2005.

Context-Sensitive Multivariant Assertion Checking in Modular Programs

Paweł Pietrzak[1], Jesús Correas[2],
Germán Puebla[1], and Manuel V. Hermenegildo[1,3]

[1] School of Computer Science, Technical University of Madrid (UPM)
[2] School of Computer Science, Complutense University of Madrid
[3] CS and ECE Departments, University of New Mexico

Abstract. We propose a *modular*, assertion-based system for verification and debugging of large logic programs, together with several interesting models for checking assertions statically in modular programs, each with different characteristics and representing different trade-offs. Our proposal is a *modular* and *multivariant* extension of our previously proposed abstract assertion checking model and we also report on its implementation in the CiaoPP system. In our approach, the specification of the program, given by a set of assertions, may be partial, instead of the complete specification required by traditional verification systems. Also, the system can deal with properties which cannot always be determined at compile-time. As a result, the proposed system needs to work with *safe* approximations: all assertions proved correct are guaranteed to be valid and all errors actual errors. The use of modular, context-sensitive static analyzers also allows us to introduce a new distinction between assertions checked in a particular context or checked in general.

1 Introduction

Splitting program code into modules is widely recognized as a useful technique in the process of software development. In this paper we propose a framework for static (i.e., compile-time) checking of assertions in modular logic programs, based on information from global analysis. We assume a *strict* module system, i.e., a system in which modules can only communicate via their *interface*. The interface of a module contains the names of the *exported* predicates and the names of the *imported* modules.

Within our framework, the programmer is expected to write a (partial) specification for a module (or a set of modules) being subject to the verification process. The specification is written in terms of (Ciao) assertions [13]. From the programmer's viewpoint, these assertions resemble the type (and mode) declarations used in strongly typed logic languages such as Mercury [16] and in functional languages. However, when compared to the latter, note that in logic programming arguments of procedures behave differently in the sense that arguments might be either input or output, depending on the specific *usage* (i.e., the context) of the procedure. For instance, the classical predicate append/3 can be

M. Hermann and A. Voronkov (Eds.): LPAR 2006, LNAI 4246, pp. 392–406, 2006.

used for concatenating lists, for decomposing lists, for checking or finding a prefix of a given list, etc. Therefore, our assertion language and the checking procedure are designed to *allow various usages of a predicate*. Moreover, comparing to the former, herein we are interested in supporting a general setting in which, on one hand assertions can be of a quite general nature, including properties which are *undecidable*, and, on the other hand, only a small number of assertions may be present in the program, i.e., the assertions are *optional*.

Our approach is strongly motivated by the availability of powerful and mature static analyzers for (constraint) logic programs (see, e.g., [8] and its references), generally based on abstract interpretation [6]. Also, since we deal with modular programs, context-sensitive static analyses that handle modules (see, e.g., [7] and its references) provide us with suitable background. Especially relevant is our recent work on context sensitive, multivariant modular analysis (see [15,5] among others). These analysis systems can statically infer a wide range of properties (from types to determinacy or termination) accurately and efficiently, for realistic modular programs. We would like to take advantage of such program analysis tools, rather than developing new abstract procedures, such as concrete [10] or abstract [3,14] diagnosers and debuggers, or using traditional proof-based methods, e.g., [1,9].

The work presented builds on [13] where the assertion language that we use was introduced, and on [14] where a proposal for the formal treatment of assertion checking, both at compile-time and at run-time, was presented. We extend the above-mentioned work in four main directions. Most importantly, the solution of [14] is not modular. We show herein how to check assertions in modular programs in a way that ensures the soundness of the approach. Also, the formalization is different to that of [14], the present one being based on generalized AND trees. In addition, in this work we exploit *multivariant* information generated by the analysis. This essentially means that multiple usages of a procedure can result in multiple descriptions in the analysis output. In consequence, this enables us to verify the code in a more accurate way.

Modular verification has also been studied within OO programming (e.g., [11]) where the importance of contextual correctness, as in our paper, has been recognized. Nevertheless this work differ from ours in several respects, the most important one being that they are based on traditional Hoare-like based verification techniques and the full specification is required, whereas our framework is based on abstract interpretation and allows for partial specifications.

In the context of Logic Programming [4] shows how to perform abstract diagnosis of incomplete logic programs. Our approach is similar to theirs, since the correctness of a modular program is established in terms of the correctness of its modules. However, in [4] the complete specification is needed and, more importantly, context-sensitive analysis information is not used, and therefore there is no concept of correctness in context. We claim that this is an important advantage of our approach, because it allows the validation of a module in a given program even when it is not possible to validate it in a context-independent way.

2   Preliminaries

An *atom* has the form $p(t_1, ..., t_n)$ where p is a predicate symbol and the t_i are terms. A *predicate descriptor* is an atom $p(X_1, ..., X_n)$ where $X_1, ..., X_n$ are distinct variables. We shall use predicate descriptors to refer to a certain form of atoms, as well as to predicate symbols. A *clause* is of the form H :-$B_1, ..., B_n$ where H, the *head*, is an atom and $B_1, ..., B_n$, the *body*, is a possibly empty finite conjunction of atoms. In the following we assume that all clause heads are normalized, i.e., H is of the form of a predicate descriptor. Furthermore, we require that each clause defining a predicate p has an identical sequence of variables $X_{p_1}, ..., X_{p_n}$ in the head. We call this the *base form* of p. This is not restrictive since programs can always be normalized, and it will facilitate the presentation of the algorithms later. However, both in the examples and in the implementation we handle non-normalized programs. A *definite logic program*, or *program*, is a finite sequence of clauses. *ren* denotes a set of renaming substitutions over variables in the program at hand.

The concrete semantics used for reasoning about programs will use the notion of generalized AND trees, as they are described in [2]. Every node of a generalized AND tree, denoted $\langle \theta_c, P, \theta_s \rangle$, contains a call to a predicate P, with a call substitution θ_c and corresponding success subtitution θ_s. The concrete semantics of a program R for a given set of queries Q, $[\![R]\!]_Q$, is the set of generalized AND trees that represent the execution of the queries in Q for the program R.[1]

Definition 1. *calling_context(P, R, Q) of a predicate given by the predicate descriptor P defined in R for a set of queries Q is the set $\{\theta_c | \exists T \in [\![R]\!]_Q$ s.t. $\exists \langle \theta'_c, P', \theta'_s \rangle$ in $T \wedge \exists \sigma \in ren$ s.t. $P = P'\sigma \wedge \theta_c = \theta'_c\sigma\}$*

success_context(P, R, Q) of a predicate given by the predicate descriptor P defined in R for a set of queries Q is the set of pairs $\{(\theta_c, \theta_s) | \exists T \in [\![R]\!]_Q$ s.t. $\exists \langle \theta'_c, P', \theta'_s \rangle$ in $T \wedge \exists \sigma \in ren$ s.t. $P = P'\sigma \wedge \theta_c = \theta'_c\sigma \wedge \theta_s = \theta'_s\sigma\}$.

Our basic tool for checking assertions is *abstract interpretation* [6]. Abstract interpretation is a technique for static program analysis in which semantics of the program is conservatively approximated using an *abstract domain* D_α (equipped with a partial order $\sqsubseteq$) which is simpler than the actual, *concrete domain* D. Abstract values and sets of concrete values are related via a pair of monotonic mappings $\langle \alpha, \gamma \rangle$: *abstraction* $\alpha : D \rightarrow D_\alpha$, and *concretization* $\gamma : D_\alpha \rightarrow D$.

Goal-dependent abstract interpretation takes as input a program R and a call pattern[2] $P{:}\lambda$, where P is an atom, and λ is a restriction of the run-time bindings of P expressed as an abstract substitution in D_α. Such an abstract interpretation (denoted *analysis$(R, P{:}\lambda)$*) computes an *answer table* (AT) whose entries are of the form $P_i{:}\lambda_i^c \mapsto \lambda_i^s$, where P_i is an atom and λ_i^c and λ_i^s are, respectively, the abstract call and success substitutions. An analysis is said to be *multivariant*

---

[1] We find this formalization more suitable than the derivation-based one used in our previous work [14] because it simplifies the presentation of the subsequent material.

[2] Note that we shall use sets of call patterns instead in the subsequent sections –the extension is trivial.

(on calls) if more than one entry $P:\lambda_1^c \mapsto \lambda_1^s, \ldots, P:\lambda_n^c \mapsto \lambda_n^s$ $n \geq 0$ with $\lambda_i^c \neq \lambda_j^c$ for some i, j may be computed for the same predicate. As it is shown in this paper, multivariant analyzers may provide valuable information for assertion checking not obtainable otherwise. An abstract interpretation process is monotonic, in the sense that the more specific the initial call pattern is, the more precise the results of the analysis are.

The abstract semantics of a program (or module) R for a set of queries Q, $[\![R]\!]_{Q_\alpha}^\alpha$, can be represented as a set of abstract AND-OR trees [2]. A context-sensitive, multivariant static analyzer such as that in CiaoPP [12] actually computes this set of trees, and returns the set of nodes in such trees, kept in the answer table AT.

3   Modular Programs and Modular Analysis

We start by introducing some notation. We will use m and n to denote *modules*. Given a module m, by *imports(m)* we denote the set of modules which m imports. By *depends(m)* we refer to the set generated by the transitive closure of *imports*. Note that there may be circular dependencies among modules. The *program unit* of a given module m is the finite set of modules containing m and the modules on which m depends: $program\_unit(m) = \{m\} \cup depends(m)$.[3] m is called the *top-level* module of its program unit. Finally, *exported(m)* is the set of predicate names exported by module m, and *imported(m)* is the set of predicate names imported by m. Given a program unit $program\_unit(m)$, we can always obtain a single-module program that behaves like $program\_unit(m)$. We will denote such program as $flatten(m)$.

In summary, the framework for modular analysis works as follows: given the top-level module m, analysis computes an intermodular fixed point by iterating through the modules in $program\_unit(m)$, and analyzing them one by one. When the intermodular fixed point has been reached, the analysis results for exported predicates are stored in a *Global Answer Table* (*GAT* for short), in the form of $P : CP \mapsto AP$ entries, where CP and AP are the call and the answer patterns of an exported predicate, respectively. In the rest of the paper we will use CP and AP to refer to abstract substituions stored in the GAT, and λ for other abstract substitutions.

We will use the function $GAT = modular\_analysis(m)$ to refer to the analysis of the program unit m, that returns as result the global answer table, and $LAT = analysis(m, E, AT)$ to indicate the analysis of module m, with call patterns for exported predicates E and success patterns of imported predicates contained in AT, and returning the *Local Answer Table* (*LAT*), which contains the results of analyzing m. When computing the intermodular fixed point, $analysis(n, E, AT)$ is invoked for each module n in the program unit, where E is the set of calling patterns in GAT for predicates defined in n which need to be (re)analyzed, AT is the current state of the GAT, and the GAT is updated after analysis with

---

[3] Library modules and *builtins* require special treatment in order to avoid reanalysis of all used library predicates every time a user program is analyzed.

information from the resulting LAT. See [15] for details. We can define a partial ordering on answer tables over a given module in the following sense: $AT_1 \preceq AT_2$ iff $\forall(P : CP_1 \mapsto AP_1) \in AT_1, (\exists(P : CP_2 \mapsto AP_2) \in AT_2$ s.t. $CP_1 \sqsubseteq CP_2$ and $\forall(P : CP_2' \mapsto AP_2') \in AT_2,$ if $CP_1 \sqsubseteq CP_2'$ then $AP_1 \sqsubseteq AP_2')$.

The computation performed by $analysis(m, E, AT)$ has the difficulty that, from the point of view of analysis of a given module m, the code to be analyzed is *incomplete* in the sense that the code for procedures imported from other modules is not available to analysis. During the analysis of a module m there may be calls $P : CP$ such that the procedure P is not defined in m but instead it is imported from another module n. There are several alternatives for computing a temporary answer pattern for $P : CP$, which are selected by means of the *success policy* (*SP* for short). *SP* is needed because given a call pattern $P : CP$ it will often be the case that no entry of exactly the form $P : CP \mapsto AP$ exists in the analysis results stored in the GAT for n (or there may be no entry at all). In such case, the information already present may be of value in order to obtain a (temporary) answer pattern AP, and continue the analysis of module m.

Several success policies can be defined which provide over- or under-approximations of the "exact" answer pattern $AP^=$ with different degrees of accuracy. By this exact value $AP^=$ we refer to the one which would be computed for the flattened program. As shown in [15], using over-approximating success policies (named SP^+) has the advantage that after analyzing any number of modules, even when a fixed point has not been reached yet, the information obtained for each module is always a correct over-approximation. The drawback is that when the fixed point is reached it may not be the least fixed point, i.e., information is not as precise as it could be. In contrast, under-approximating (SP^-) policies obtain the least fixed point (most precise information) but only produce correct results when the fixed point is reached. Therefore, SP^- policies are as accurate as performing the analysis of the flattened program. We will denote with $analysis_{SP}(m, E, AT)$ the analysis of a module m with respect to the set of call patterns E and using a success policy SP applied to the answer table AT.

4   Assertions

We consider two fundamental kinds of (basic) assertions [13].[4] The first one is **success** assertions, which are used to express properties which should hold on termination of a successful computation of a given predicate (*postconditions*). At the time of calling the predicate, the computation should satisfy a certain *precondition*. **success** assertions can be expressed in our assertion language using an expression of the form: **success** $P : Pre \Rightarrow Post$, where P is a predicate descriptor, and Pre and $Post$ are pre- and post-conditions respectively. Without loss of generality, we will consider that Pre and $Post$ correspond to abstract substitutions (λ_{Pre} and λ_{Post} resp.) over $vars(P)$. This kind of assertion should be interpreted as "in any invocation of P if Pre holds in the calling state and

---

[4] [13] presents other types of assertions, but they are outside the scope of this paper.

the computation succeeds, then *Post* should also hold in the success state."
The postcondition stated in a success assertion refers to *all* the success states
(possibly none). Note that success P : *true* $\Rightarrow$ *Post* can be abbreviated as
success $P \Rightarrow Post$.

A second kind of assertions expresses properties which should hold in any
call to a given predicate. These properties are similar in nature to the classical *preconditions* used in program verification. These assertions have the form:
calls P : *Pre*, and should be interpreted as "in all activations of P *Pre* should
hold in the calling state." More than one assertion may be written for each predicate. That means that, in any invocation of P, at least one calls assertion for
P should hold.

Finally, we write pred P : *Pre* $\Rightarrow$ *Post*, as a shortcut for the two assertions:
calls P : *Pre* and success P : *Pre* $\Rightarrow$ *Post*. We claim that the pred form is
a natural way to describe a usage of the predicate. In what follows, we will use
calls (resp. success) assertions when we want to refer to the calls part (resp.
success part) of a pred assertion. We will assume, for simplicity and with no
loss of generality, that all assertions referring to a predicate P defined in module
m are also provided in that module. We will denote with *assertions*(m) the set
of assertions appearing in module m, and *assertions*(P) refers to the assertions
for predicate P.

Example 1. A possible set of calls assertions for the traditional length/2 predicate that relates a list to its length, might be:

```
:- calls length(L,N) : (var(L), int(N)).      %(1)
:- calls length(L,N) : (list(L), var(N)).     %(2)
```

These assertions describe different modes for calling that predicate: either for
(1) generating a list of length N, or (2) to obtain the length of a list L.

Possible success assertions for that predicate are:

```
:- success length(L,N) : (var(L), int(N))  => list(L).
:- success length(L,N) : (var(N), list(L)) => int(N).
```

The following two assertions are equivalent to all the previous assertions for
length/2:

```
:- pred length(L,N) : (var(L), int(N))  => list(L).
:- pred length(L,N) : (var(N), list(L)) => int(N).
```

We assign a *status* to each assertion. The status indicates whether the assertion
refers to intended or actual properties, and the relation between the property
and the program semantics. This section builds on [14], but it has been adapted
to our use of generalized AND trees.

We say that a calls assertion A with predicate descriptor P is *applicable*
to a node $N = \langle \theta_c, P', \theta_s \rangle$ of the generalized AND tree if there is $\sigma \in ren$ (a
renaming substitution) s.t. $P' = P\sigma$ and N is adorned on the left, i.e., the call
substitution θ_c of N has been already computed. A success assertion A with
predicate descriptor P is applicable to a node N if $P' = P\sigma$ (where $\sigma \in ren$)
and N is adorned on the right, i.e., the success substitution θ_s of the call at N

has been computed (the procedure exit has been completed). In what follows, we will denote with ρ a suitable renaming substitution.

If an assertion holds within a fixed set of queries Q then the assertion is said to be *checked* with respect to Q. If this is proved, the assertion receives the corresponding status checked. Formally:

Definition 2 (Checked assertions). *Let R be a program.*

- *An assertion $A = \mathtt{calls}\ P : Pre\ in\ R$ is* checked *w.r.t. the set of queries Q iff $\forall \theta_c \in calling\_context(P, R, Q), \theta_c\rho \in \gamma(\lambda_{Pre})$.*
- *An assertion $A = \mathtt{success}\ P : Pre \Rightarrow Post\ in\ R$ is* checked *w.r.t. a set of queries Q iff $\forall(\theta_c, \theta_s) \in success\_context(P, R, Q), \theta_c\rho \in \gamma(\lambda_{Pre}) \rightarrow \theta_s\rho \in \gamma(\lambda_{Post})$.*

A calls or success assertion can also be *false*, whenever it is known that there is at least one call (or success) pattern in the concrete semantics that violates the property in the assertion. If we can prove this, the assertion is given the status false. In addition, an error message will be issued by the preprocessor.

Definition 3 (False assertions). *Let R be a program.*

- *An assertion $A = \mathtt{calls}\ P : Pre\ in\ R$ is* false *w.r.t. the set of queries Q iff $\exists \theta_c \in calling\_context(P, R, Q)\ s.t.\ \theta_c\rho \notin \gamma(\lambda_{Pre})$.*
- *An assertion $A = \mathtt{success}\ P : Pre \Rightarrow Post\ in\ R$ is* false *w.r.t. the calling context Q iff $\exists(\theta_c, \theta_s) \in success\_context(P, R, Q)\ s.t.\ \theta_c\rho \in \gamma(\lambda_{Pre}) \wedge \theta_s\rho \notin \gamma(\lambda_{Post})$.*

Finally, an assertion which expresses a property which holds for any initial query is a *true* assertion. If it can be proven, independently on the calling context, during compile-time checking, the assertion is rewritten with the status true. Formally:

Definition 4 (True success assertion). *An assertion $A = \mathtt{success}\ P : Pre \Rightarrow Post\ in\ R$ is* true *if and only if for every set of queries Q, $\forall(\theta_c, \theta_s) \in success\_context(P, R, Q), \theta_c\rho \in \gamma(\lambda_{Pre}) \rightarrow \theta_s\rho \in \gamma(\lambda_{Post})$.*

Note that the difference between checked assertions and true ones, is that the latter hold for any context. Thus, the fact that an assertion is true implies that it is also checked.

Assertions are subject to compile-time checking. An assertion which is not determined by compile-time checking to be given any of the above statuses is a *check* assertion. This assertion expresses an intended property. It may hold or not in the current version of the program. This is the default status, i.e., if an assertion has no explicitly written status, it is assumed that the status is check. Before performing a compile-time checking procedure all assertions written by the user have check status.

In our setting, checking assertions must be preceded by analysis, and basically it boils down to comparing assertions (whenever applicable) with the abstract information obtained by analysis. Below we present sufficient conditions for compile-time assertion checking in a program not structured in modules. The following sections will deal with assertion checking of modules and modular programs. In the case of proving a calls assertion, we would like to ensure that all concrete calls are included in the description λ_{Pre}. For disproving calls assertions, i.e., turning them to false, we want to show that there is some concrete call which is not covered by λ_{Pre}.

Definition 5 (Abstract assertion checking). *Let R be a program, and Q_α an abstract description of queries to R.*

- *An assertion $A =$ success $P : Pre \Rightarrow Post$ in R is abstractly true iff $\exists P' : \lambda^c \mapsto \lambda^s \in analysis(R, \{P : \lambda_{Pre}\})$ s.t. $\exists \sigma \in ren,\ P' = P\sigma, \lambda^c = \lambda_{Pre} \wedge \lambda^s \sqsubseteq \lambda_{Post}$.*
- *An assertion $A =$ success $P : Pre \Rightarrow Post$ in R is abstractly checked w.r.t. Q_α iff $\forall P' : \lambda^c \mapsto \lambda^s \in analysis(R, Q_\alpha)$ s.t. $\exists \sigma \in ren,\ P' = P\sigma, \lambda^c \sqsubseteq \lambda_{Pre} \rightarrow \lambda^s \sqsubseteq \lambda_{Post}$.*
- *An assertion $A =$ calls $P : Pre$ in R is abstractly checked w.r.t. Q_α iff $\forall P' : \lambda^c \mapsto \lambda^s \in analysis(R, Q_\alpha)$ s.t. $\exists \sigma \in ren,\ P' = P\sigma, \lambda^c \sqsubseteq \lambda_{Pre}$.*
- *An assertion $A =$ success $P : Pre \Rightarrow Post$ in R is abstractly false w.r.t. Q_α iff $\forall P' : \lambda^c \mapsto \lambda^s \in analysis(R, Q_\alpha)$ s.t. $\exists \sigma \in ren,\ P' = P\sigma, \lambda^c \sqsubseteq \lambda_{Pre} \wedge (\lambda^s \sqcap \lambda_{Post} = \bot)$.*
- *An assertion $A =$ calls $P : Pre$ in R is abstractly false w.r.t. Q_α iff $\forall P' : \lambda^c \mapsto \lambda^s \in analysis(R, Q_\alpha)$ s.t. $\exists \sigma \in ren,\ P' = P\sigma, \lambda^c \sqcap \lambda_{Pre} = \bot$.*

In this definition $analysis(R, Q_\alpha)$ is a generic analysis computation, and therefore the definition is parametric with respect to the analysis actually performed for checking the assertions, as will be shown below. The sufficient conditions are the following:

Proposition 1 (Checking a calls assertion). *Let $A =$ check calls $P : Pre$ be an assertion.*

- *If A is abstractly checked w.r.t. Q_α, then A is checked w.r.t. $\gamma(Q_\alpha)$.*
- *If A is abstractly false w.r.t. Q_α, then A is false w.r.t. $\gamma(Q_\alpha)$.*
- *otherwise, nothing can be deduced about A considered atomically (and it is left in check status).*

Soundness of the above statements can be derived directly from the correctness of abstract interpretation. In the case of checked assertions, we make sure that all call patterns that can appear at run-time belong to $\gamma(\lambda_{Pre})$. The "false" cases are a bit more involved. Due to the approximating nature of abstract interpretation, there is no guarantee that a given abstract call description λ^c corresponds to any call pattern that can appear at run-time. Thus, it is possible that the assertion is never applicable, but if it is, it will be invalid. What is known is that every run-time call pattern is described by one or more entries for P in AT. Thus, in order to ensure that no call pattern will satisfy λ_{Pre}, all λ^c's for P must be taken into account.

Finally, if a calls assertion is not abstractly checked nor abstractly false, we cannot deduce anything about A when it is considered atomically. However, we could still split it, and apply the same process to the parts.

Proposition 2 (Checking a success assertion). *Let $A = $ check success $P :$ Pre $\Rightarrow$ Post be an assertion.*

- *If A is abstractly true, then A is true.*
- *If A is abstractly checked w.r.t. Q_α, then A is checked w.r.t. $\gamma(Q_\alpha)$.*
- *If A is abstractly false w.r.t. Q_α, then A is false w.r.t. $\gamma(Q_\alpha)$.*
- *otherwise, nothing can be deduced about A considered atomically (and it is left in check status).*

In the same way as before, a success assertion remains atomically check when it is not abstractly checked nor abstractly false. We can however simplify the assertion when part of the assertion can be proved to hold, like in a calls assertion. Note that the more precise analysis results are, the more assertions get status true, checked and false.

5   Checking Assertions in a Single Module

The modular analysis framework described in Section 3 is independent from the assertion language. Nevertheless, assertions may contain relevant information for the analyzer. To this end when $analysis(m, E, AT)$ is computed for a module m, the parameters E and AT can also refer to information gathered directly from assertions, rather than from other analysis steps. This yields additional entry and success policies:

- E can be extracted from the call parts of **pred** assertions for exported predicates in m. Such set will be denoted as $\mathcal{CP}_m^{Asst} = \{P : \lambda_{Pre} \mid P \in exported(m) \wedge$ **pred** $P : Pre \Rightarrow Post \in assertions(m)\} \cup \{P : \top \mid P \in exported(m) \wedge assertions(P) = \emptyset\}$.
- AT can also be extracted from **pred** (or **success**) assertions found in the imported modules. Given a module m, the answer table generated from the assertions for imported modules is denoted as $\mathcal{AT}_m^{Asst} = \bigcup_{n \in imports(m)}(\{P : \lambda_{Pre} \mapsto \lambda_{Post} \mid P \in exported(n) \wedge$ **pred** $P : Pre \Rightarrow Post \in assertions(n)\} \cup \{P : \top \mapsto \top \mid P \in exported(n) \wedge assertions(P) = \emptyset\})$.

Note that we assume the topmost patterns if no assertions are present.

When checking assertions of modular programs, a given module can be considered either in the context of a program unit or separately, taking into account only the imported predicates. When treated in the context of a program unit, the calling context of a module m is called the *set of initial queries Q_m*. We say that the set of initial queries Q_m to a module m is *valid* iff for every imported predicate p all the calls assertions related to p are checked w.r.t. Q_m.

Definition 6 (Partially correct in context module). *A module m is partially correct in context with respect to a set of initial queries Q_m iff (1) every calls assertion in m is checked w.r.t. Q_m, and (2) every success assertion in m is true, or checked w.r.t. Q_m, and (3) every calls assertion for a predicate imported by m is checked with respect to Q_m.*

Definition 7 (Partially correct module). *A module* m *is* partially correct *iff* m *is partially correct in context w.r.t. any valid set of initial queries.*

Assertions are checked, as explained above, w.r.t. all analysis information available for a given (call or success of a) predicate after executing the analysis of the code. Such analysis information is multivariant, and covers all the program points in the analyzed code where a given predicate is called and how it succeeds. If available, a GAT table can be used to improve the analysis results with information from previous analyses of imported modules.

In our system, when checking a module, `calls` assertions for imported predicates are visible, and can therefore also be checked. This enables verifying whether a particular call pattern to an imported predicate satisfies its assertions. Of course, a `calls` assertion cannot be given status `true` or `checked`, as in general not all call patterns for the imported predicate occur in the calling module. Nevertheless, a warning or error is issued whenever the assertion is violated and/or cannot be shown to hold.

Proposition 3. *Let* $LAT = analysis_{SP+}(m, \mathcal{CP}_m^{Asst}, AT)$, *where* m *is a module and* AT *is an over-approximating answer table for (some modules in)* imports(m). *The module* m *is partially correct if all success assertions are abstractly true w.r.t.* LAT *and all calls assertions for predicates in* m *and* imported(m) *are abstractly checked w.r.t.* LAT.

This proposition considers correctness of a single module regardless of the calling context of the module, since the starting point of the analysis is the set of preconditions in **pred** assertions. Note that LAT must be computed using an over-approximating success policy, in order to obtain correct results (provided that AT is correct). The answer table AT used for the analysis may be incomplete, or even an empty set: this approach allows us to check the assertions of a given module even when there is no information available from the imported modules. However, the more accurate AT is, the more assertions get status `true` or `checked`. This proposition is especially useful during the development of a modular program (i.e., the "edit-check cycle"), when different programmers develop different modules of the program. A programmer can check the assertions of his/her module as soon as it is syntactically correct. If other programmers in the team have analyzed their modules already, a shared GAT can be used to generate the answer table AT for checking the module more accurately.

Unfortunately, if the modules imported by m are not implemented yet, there is no possibility to analyze them in order to provide more accurate information to the analyzer. In order to overcome that, we can use the assertion information for the exported predicates in imported modules to obtain a more precise LAT. In this case, correctness of the module cannot be guaranteed, but a weaker notion of correctness, conditional partial correctness, may be proved. Note that in this case the analysis relies on possibly unverified assertions written by the user.

Proposition 4. *Let* $LAT = analysis_{SP+}(m, \mathcal{CP}_m^{Asst}, AT_m^{Asst})$, *where* m *is a module. The module* m *is conditionally partially correct if all success assertions* *are abstractly true, and all calls assertions for predicates in m and imported(m) are abstractly checked w.r.t. LAT.*

This conditional partial correctness turns into partial correctness when the program unit is taken as a whole, as we will see in Section 6.

Example 2. Consider the standard `functor/3` predicate. The ISO standard for Prolog states that `functor/3` can only be invoked using two possible calling modes, and any other mode will raise a run-time error. The first mode allows obtaining the functor name and arity of a structure, while the second calling mode builds up a structure given its functor name and arity.

Our assertion checking system is able to statically detect such calling patterns because several assertions are allowed for a given predicate, and the underlying analyzer captures context-sensitive, multivariant abstract information. They can be expressed by means of the following assertions:

```
:- pred functor(+T,Name,Arity) => (atomic(Name), nat(Arity)).
:- pred functor(T,+Name,+Arity) : (atomic(Name), nat(Arity)) => nonvar(T).
```

In these assertions, the plus sign before an argument has the usual meaning of a Prolog mode, i.e., that the argument cannot be a free variable on calls. The calls parts of these assertions will be used when analyzing and checking any module that uses this library predicate, in order to check the calling modes to it.

6   Checking Assertions in a Program Unit

Checking assertions in a program unit consisting of several modules differs from checking assertions in a single module in some ways. First of all, the most accurate initial queries to a given module m are provided by the calls to m made by other modules in the program unit (except the top-level one). Secondly, the success patterns of imported predicates may also be more accurate if we consider a given program unit. This leads us to the notion of correctness for program units. Note that the following definition concerns the concrete semantics.

Definition 8 (Partially correct program unit). *Let m_{top} be a module defining a program unit $U = program\_unit(m_{top})$. U is partially correct iff m_{top} is partially correct and $\forall m \in depends(m_{top})$, m is partially correct in context w.r.t. the sets of initial queries induced by the initial queries to m_{top}.*

Verifying a Program Unit with No Intermodular Analysis Information

As explained in the previous section, every assertion A of the form

$$\text{check calls } P : \lambda_{Pre} \in assertions(m)$$

where $P \in exported(m)$ is verified in every module that imports P from m. If such calls assertions are abstractly true in all importing modules (i.e., for every call pattern CP found in a module importing P we have that $CP \sqsubseteq \lambda_{Pre}$),

Algorithm 1. Checking assertions without modular analysis

Input: top-level module m_{top}
Output: Warning/Error messages, new status in the assertions in $program\_unit\,(m_{top})$

 for all $m \in program\_unit(m_{top})$ **do**
  $LAT_m := analysis_{SP+}(m, \mathcal{CP}_m^{Asst}, \mathcal{AT}_m^{Asst})$
  $check\_assertions(m, LAT_m)$
 end for

then that means that λ_{Pre} approximates all possible calling patterns to P from outside m. Therefore, the `calls` assertions can be used as starting points for analyzing every module in the program unit for checking the assertions. This leads us to a scenario for checking assertions, shown in Algorithm 1, where no prior intermodular analysis is required, and which aims at proving every module to be conditionally correct rather than correct in context.

Observe that Algorithm 1 does not use the modular analysis results as input. Instead, `pred` assertions of exported predicates are taken as input to the single-module analysis phase, $\mathcal{CP}_m^{Asst}$. A similar policy is applied when collecting success patterns of imported predicates.

This scenario can be viewed as proving conditional correctness of each module $m \in program\_unit(m_{top})$, where the conditions are the corresponding `pred` assertions from imported modules, as stated in Proposition 4. On the other hand, since we check all the modules in the program unit, and the program unit is self-contained, the `pred` assertions from imported modules are also the subject of checking. Assume that after checking all the modules in $program\_unit(m_{top})$ all the `pred` assertions get status `checked` or `true`.[5] This means that for every exported/imported predicate P, the analysis information $P : CP \mapsto AP$ generated when analyzing individual modules satisfies the checking conditions of Propositions 1 and 2. Thus, the following result holds:

Proposition 5. *Let m_{top} be a module defining a program unit $U = program\_unit(m_{top})$. If each module $m \in U$ is conditionally partially correct, and m_{top} is partially correct, then U is partially correct.*

If the assertions get true or checked using Algorithm 1, it is easy to see that they would also get true or checked if the (full) modular analysis were used, as modular analysis computes the least fixed point, i.e., it returns the most accurate analysis information. Consequently, if the `calls` assertions receive status `checked` and the `success` assertions receive status `true` when checking with Algorithm 1, there is no need to run a costly modular analysis.

Interleaving Analysis and Checking

Algorithm 1 may not be able to determine that a program unit is partially correct if the user has provided either too few assertions for exported predicates or they

---

[5] In this case the `calls` part originated from the `pred` assertion receives status `checked`, and the `success` part status `true`.

Algorithm 2. Interleaving analysis and checking

Input: top module m_{top}
Output: GAT, Warning/Error messages, new status in the assertions in $program\_unit$ (m_{top})

    Set initial GAT with marked entries for call patterns from $CP_{m_{top}}^{Asst}$
    while there are modules with marked entries in GAT **do**
1   select module m
        $LAT_m := analysis_{SP}(m, CP_m^{GAT}, GAT)$
        $check\_assertions(m, LAT_m)$
        if an error is detected in m **then**
          STOP
        end if
2   update GAT with LAT_m
    end while

---

are not accurate enough. In this case we have to replace information from the missing assertions and to incorporate a certain degree of automatic propagation of call/success patterns among modules during the checking process. The basic idea is to interleave analysis and compile-time checking during modular analysis. The main advantage of this approach is that errors will be detected as soon as possible, without computing an expensive intermodular fixpoint, yet having call and success patterns being propagated among modules. The whole process terminates as soon as an error is detected or when the modular analysis fixed point has been reached, as shown in Algorithm 2. Concrete procedures in steps 1 and 2 depend on a specific intermodular analysis algorithm, success and entry policies, etc. Note that in Algorithm 2 every module is analyzed for CP_m^{GAT}, the set of all call patterns for a module m in the GAT.[6]

If an SP^+ success policy is used in Algorithm 2, then $LAT_m^1 \succeq LAT_m^2 \succeq \cdots \succeq LAT_m^n$, where LAT_m^n coincides with the analysis results of module m when the intermodular fixed point has been reached, and each of the LAT_m^i corresponds to the status of the analysis answer table for m at every iteration of the algorithm that schedules m for analysis.

Proposition 6. *Let LAT_m be an answer table for module m. If an assertion is abstractly checked (resp. abstractly true or abstractly false) w.r.t. LAT_m it will also be abstractly checked (resp. abstractly true or abstractly false) w.r.t. any answer table LAT_m' s.t. $LAT_m' \preceq LAT_m$.*

Thus, the conclusions drawn about the assertions are sound in the following sense: if an assertion is detected to be checked or false in an intermediate step, it will surely remain checked or false at the end of the process. If the assertion is not yet proved not disproved, its status might change in the subsequent steps as the analysis information might be more accurate in future iterations.

---

[6] CP_m^{GAT} is used for simplicity of the presentation. In the actual implementation the modules are analyzed just for the *marked* entries, and only the assertions related to those entries are checked.

Algorithm 2 can be adapted to apply the SP^- success policy. The sequence of answer tables generated during the analysis using that policy is now $LAT_m^1 \preceq LAT_m^2 \preceq \cdots \preceq LAT_m^n$, where only LAT_m^n, i.e. the one corresponding with the global fixpoint, is guaranteed to safely approximate the module's semantics.

Proposition 7. *Let LAT_m be an answer table for module m. If an assertion A is not abstractly checked w.r.t. LAT_m, then $\forall LAT_m'$ s.t. $LAT_m \preceq LAT_m'$, A will not be abstractly checked w.r.t. LAT_m'.*

Therefore, in this case the following conclusions can be made about the final status of assertions: if at any intermediate step the status of an assertion remains as check or becomes false, it will at most be check at the end of the whole process. Therefore, Algorithm 2 must stop and issue an error as soon as false or check assertions are detected (instead of stopping only when there are false assertions, as above).

Sufficient condition for partial correctness follows:

Proposition 8. *Let m_{top} be a module defining a program unit $U = program\_unit(m_{top})$. If Algorithm 2 terminates without issuing error messages, then (1) if SP^+ is used and Algorithm 2 decides that an assertion A is abstractly true (resp. checked), then A is true (resp. checked); and (2) if SP^- is used then all assertions in U are checked.*

7 Conclusions

Algorithms 1 and 2 have different levels of accuracy, computing cost, and verification power. The advantages of Algorithm 2 are that it is potentially more accurate and it does not impose any burden on the user, since no assertions are compulsory. On the other hand, Algorithm 1 has low computing cost, since modules only need to be analyzed once and it can be applied to incomplete programs. All this at the price of a development policy where module interfaces are accurately described using assertions.

Comparing this paper with related work, the scenario described in Section 6 can be seen as an instance of the analysis with user-provided interface of [7]. Our goal is however different than theirs: instead of computing the most precise analysis information we try to prove or disprove assertions, which makes this method more related in fact to the one of [4], focused on program verification. Nevertheless, unlike [4] we do not require the user to provide a complete specification, specially in Algorithm 2 –the missing parts are either described by topmost values or infered by the interleaved analysis algorithm.

Acknowledgements. This work was funded in part by the IST programme of the European Commission, FET project FP6 IST-15905 *MOBIUS*, by Ministry of Education and Science (MEC) projects TIN2005-09207-C03 *MERIT-COMVERS* and *MERIT-FORMS*, and CAM project S-0505/TIC/0407 PROMESAS. M. Hermenegildo is also supported in part by the Prince of Asturias Chair in Information Science and Technology at UNM. P. Pietrzak is supported by a 'Juan de la Cierva' grant provided by the Spanish MEC.

References

1. K. R. Apt and E. Marchiori. Reasoning about Prolog programs: from modes through types to assertions. *Formal Aspects of Computing*, 6(6):743–765, 1994.
2. M. Bruynooghe. A Practical Framework for the Abstract Interpretation of Logic Programs. *JLP*, 10:91–124, 1991.
3. M. Comini, G. Levi, M. C. Meo, and G. Vitiello. Abstract diagnosis. *JLP*, 39(1–3):43–93, 1999.
4. M. Comini, G. Levi, and G. Vitiello. Modular abstract diagnosis. In *APPIA-GULP-PRODE'98*, pages 409–420, 1998.
5. J. Correas, G. Puebla, M. Hermenegildo, and F. Bueno. Experiments in Context-Sensitive Analysis of Modular Programs. In *LOPSTR'05*, LNCS. Springer-Verlag, September 2006.
6. P. Cousot and R. Cousot. Abstract Interpretation: a Unified Lattice Model for Static Analysis of Programs by Construction or Approximation of Fixpoints. In *Proc. of POPL'77*, pages 238–252, 1977.
7. P. Cousot and R. Cousot. Modular Static Program Analysis, invited paper. In *CC 2002*, number 2304 in LNCS, pages 159–178. Springer-Verlag, 2002.
8. M. García de la Banda, M. Hermenegildo, M. Bruynooghe, V. Dumortier, G. Janssens, and W. Simoens. Global Analysis of Constraint Logic Programs. *ACM Trans. on Programming Languages and Systems*, 18(5):564–615, 1996.
9. P. Deransart. Proof methods of declarative properties of definite programs. *Theoretical Computer Science*, 118:99–166, 1993.
10. W. Drabent, S. Nadjm-Tehrani, and J. Maluszynski. Algorithmic debugging with assertions. In H. Abramson and M.H.Rogers, editors, *Meta-programming in Logic Programming*, pages 501–522. MIT Press, 1989.
11. K. R. M. Leino and P. Müller. Modular verification of static class invariants. In J. Fitzgerald, I. Hayes, and A. Tarlecki, editors, *Formal Methods (FM)*, volume 3582 of *LNCS*, pages 26–42. Springer-Verlag, 2005.
12. K. Muthukumar and M. Hermenegildo. Compile-time Derivation of Variable Dependency Using Abstract Interpretation. *JLP*, 13(2/3):315–347, July 1992.
13. G. Puebla, F. Bueno, and M. Hermenegildo. An Assertion Language for Constraint Logic Programs. In *Analysis and Visualization Tools for Constraint Programming*, volume 1870 of *LNCS*, pages 23–61. Springer-Verlag, 2000.
14. G. Puebla, F. Bueno, and M. Hermenegildo. Combined Static and Dynamic Assertion-Based Debugging of Constraint Logic Programs. In *LOPSTR'99*, number 1817 in LNCS, pages 273–292. Springer-Verlag, 2000.
15. G. Puebla, J. Correas, M. Hermenegildo, F. Bueno, M. García de la Banda, K. Marriott, and P. J. Stuckey. A Generic Framework for Context-Sensitive Analysis of Modular Programs. In M. Bruynooghe and K. Lau, editors, *Program Development in Computational Logic, A Decade of Research Advances in Logic-Based Program Development*, number 3049 in LNCS, pages 234–261. Springer-Verlag, 2004.
16. Z. Somogyi, F. Henderson, and T. Conway. The execution algorithm of Mercury: an efficient purely declarative logic programming language. *JLP*, 29(1–3), October 1996.

Representation of Partial Knowledge and Query Answering in Locally Complete Databases

Álvaro Cortés-Calabuig[1], Marc Denecker[1], Ofer Arieli[2], and Maurice Bruynooghe[1]

[1] Department of Computer Science, Katholieke Universiteit Leuven, Belgium
{alvaro, marc.denecker, maurice.bruynooghe}@cs.kuleuven.be
[2] Department of Computer Science, The Academic College of Tel-Aviv, Israel
oarieli@mta.ac.il

Abstract. The *Local Closed-World Assumption* (LCWA) is a generalization of Reiter's Closed-World Assumption (CWA) for relational databases that may be incomplete. Two basic questions that are related to this assumption are: (1) how to *represent* the fact that only part of the information is known to be complete, and (2) how to properly *reason* with this information, that is: how to determine whether an answer to a database query is complete even though the database information is incomplete. In this paper we concentrate on the second issue based on a treatment of the first issue developed in earlier work of the authors. For this we consider a fixpoint semantics for declarative theories that represent locally complete databases. This semantics is based on 3-valued interpretations that allow to distinguish between the certain and possible consequences of the database's theory.

1 Introduction

In database theory it is common to falsify any atomic fact that does not appear in the database instance. This approach follows Reiter's Closed-World Assumption (CWA) [13], that presupposes a complete knowledge about the database's domain of discourse.

Databases, however, are not always complete[1]. There are many reasons for this fact, including ignorance about the domain, lack of proper maintenance, incomplete migration, accidental deletion of tuples, the intrinsic nature of database mediator-based systems (see [10]), and so forth. Unless properly handled, partial information in database systems might lead to erroneous conclusions, as illustrated in the following example:

Example 1. Consider a database of a computer science (CS) department which stores information about the telephone numbers of the department's members and collaborators. A fragment of the database is represented in Figure 1. A reasonable assumption in this case is that this database is complete with respect to all CS department members, but possibly incomplete regarding its external collaborators. Thus, appropriate answers for the queries Telephone(Bart Delvaux,3962836) and Telephone(Leen Desmet,3212445) are "no" and "unknown," respectively.

---

[1] Nor they are always correct, but we do not address this problem here.

M. Hermann and A. Voronkov (Eds.): LPAR 2006, LNAI 4246, pp. 407–421, 2006.

Telephone		Deparment	
Name	Telephone	Name	Department
Leen Desmet	6531421	Bart Delvaux	Computer Science
Bart Delvaux	5985625	Leen Desmet	Philosophy
Tom Demans	5845213	Tom Demans	Computer Science

Fig. 1. A database of contact phone numbers for a CS department

Example 1 illustrates a situation in which database information is *locally* complete, and so applying the CWA is not realistic, and might even lead to wrong conclusions. The other extreme approach, known as *Open-World Assumption* (OWA) [1,9], is often used for maintaining distributed knowledge, e.g. for mediator-based systems. In this approach a relational database is considered as a correct but possibly incomplete representation of the domain of discourse. The main weakness of the OWA is that it does not allow to express locally complete information, and so in the example above, for instance, one cannot state a full knowledge regarding the phone numbers of the CS department members.

In order to overcome the drawbacks of the CWA and the OWA in representing partial knowledge in reality, Etzioni [6] and Motro [12] introduced the notion of *Local Closed-World Assumption* (LCWA) that, intuitively, is *"a specification of the areas in the real world in which a database contains all true tuples"* [3]. In Example 1, for instance, such an assumption would state a meta-knowledge that the information in the Telephone relation is complete for the members of the CS department.

At the practical level, the LCWA poses some important challenges. First, a proper way of *representing* the fact that only part of the information is known to be complete is required. In the literature there are several proposals for this, using e.g. theories in a logic programming style [7] or second-order circumscriptive formulae [5]. Here we follow the first-order representation considered in [3].[2] Another challenge, which is addressed in this paper, is the problem of query answering in the presence of LCWA. This involves not only the query computation itself, but also a determination whether the query answer is complete even though the database information is incomplete. Our approach is based on a 3-valued fixpoint semantics and corresponding algorithms for constructing a 3-valued interpretation that evaluates queries under certain and possible semantics. More specifically, the following issues are addressed:

– **Fixpoint theory for the LCWA.** A sound fixpoint operator for the LCWA is introduced, and conditions for assuring its completeness are defined. This yields a mechanism for computing a 3-valued interpretation that approximates all the 2-valued interpretations of the database's theory and so allows informative query answering.

---

[2] It is shown there that this representation and its second-order derivative capture and generalize both Reiter's CWA and the OWA.

- **Query answering algorithm.** A simple yet general algorithm for query answering under the LCWA is presented. It distinguishes between certain and possible answers and can be easily implemented by standard relational databases engines.

- **Reconciliation of paradigms.** Alternative approaches to the LCWA are considered. In particular, LCWA handling in the context of database systems [3,12,11] is related to LCWA formalizations for modelling logic-based agents [5,6].

The rest of this paper is organized as follows. In Section 2 we recall some preliminary definitions and facts about the LCWA. In Section 3 we introduce a fixpoint semantics for locally complete databases, and in Section 4 we define corresponding query answering formalisms. Some related works are discussed in Section 5 and future research is sketched in Section 6. Full proofs of all the propositions in this paper appear in [2].

2 Preliminaries

In what follows we denote by Σ a first-order vocabulary consisting of predicate symbols $\mathcal{R}(\Sigma)$ (a relational schema in database terminology) and a finite set $\mathcal{C}(\Sigma)$ of constants representing the elements of the domain of discourse. For a formula Ψ in Σ we denote by $\Psi[\overline{x}]$ that the free variables of Ψ are a subset of $\overline{x}$. The Herbrand base of Σ is the set $HB(\Sigma)$ of atomic formulas formed using $\mathcal{C}(\Sigma)$ and the predicate symbols in $\mathcal{R}(\Sigma)$. A *database* is a finite set of ground atoms in Σ.

Definition 1. [3] A *local closed-world assumption* (LCWA), is an expression of the form

$$\mathcal{LCWA}\,(P(\overline{x}), \Psi[\overline{x}]),$$

where $P \in \Sigma$ is a predicate symbol, called the LCWA's *object*; and $\Psi[\overline{x}]$, called a *window of expertise* for P, is a first-order formula over Σ.

Example 2. The expression $\mathcal{LCWA}\,(\mathsf{Tel}(x, y), \mathsf{Dept}(x, \mathsf{CS}))$ is a local closed-world assumption stating that the telephone numbers of all the members of the computer science department are known. That is, for every x_0 in $\{x \mid \mathsf{Dept}(x, \mathsf{CS})\}$ (the window of expertise for Tel), all atoms of the form $\mathsf{Tel}(x_0, y)$ are in the database.

Definition 2. *[3] Let $\theta = \mathcal{LCWA}(P(\overline{x}), \Psi[\overline{x}])$ be a local closed-world assumption and D a database under vocabulary Σ. Denote by P^D the set of tuples corresponding to the set of atoms of P in D. We abbreviate the formula $\bigvee_{\overline{a} \in P^D} (\overline{t} = \overline{a})$ by $P(\overline{t}) \in P^D$, where $\overline{t}$ is a tuple of terms. The meaning of θ under D is the formula*

$$\mathcal{M}_D(\theta) = \forall \overline{x}\Big(\Psi[\overline{x}] \supset \big(P(\overline{x}) \supset (P(\overline{x}) \in P^D)\big)\Big).$$

The intuition behind this formula is simple: for all tuples $\overline{x}$ of domain elements such that $\Psi(\overline{x})$ holds in the *real world*, if $P(\overline{x})$ is true (again, in *reality*), then $\overline{x}$ must be a tuple in the table of P in D.

Example 3. The meaning of $\theta = \mathcal{LCWA}\,(\mathsf{Tel}(x,y),\mathsf{Dept}(x,\mathsf{CS}))$ in the database D of Example 1 is given by

$$\mathcal{M}_D(\theta) = \forall x \forall y \big(\mathsf{Dept}(x,\mathsf{CS}) \supset \mathsf{Tel}(x,y) \supset$$
$$((x = \text{Leen Desmet} \wedge y = 6531421) \vee (x = \text{Bart Delvaux} \wedge y = 5985625)$$
$$\vee\,(x = \text{Tom Demans} \wedge y = 5845213)))$$

In some cases, we may want to express within the same expression local closed-world assumption on different predicates. In doing so, we need to extend the basic notion of an LCWA expression to allow for set of objects:

$$\theta = \mathcal{LCWA}\,(\{P_1(\overline{x}_1),\dots,P_n(\overline{x}_n)\},\Psi[\overline{x}]),$$

where the $P_i \in \Sigma$ are predicate symbols (the LCWA's objects) and $\Psi[\overline{x}]$ is a first-order formula over Σ with free variables $\overline{y}$ s.t. $\overline{y} \subseteq \bigcup_{i=1}^n \overline{x}_i = \overline{x}$. When an LCWA expression takes this form, the meaning of θ under a database D is extended as follows:

$$\mathcal{M}_D(\theta) = \forall \overline{x}\Big(\Psi[\overline{x}] \supset \big(\bigwedge_{i=1}^n \big(P_i(\overline{x}_i) \supset (P_i(\overline{x}_i) \in P_i^D)\big)\big)\Big).$$

In this paper we assume only one predicate object for each LCWA expression. As the following proposition shows, this assumption does not harm generality:

Proposition 1. *[3] Given a formula Ψ, denote by $\exists|_{\overline{x}}\Psi$ the existential quantification of all free variables in Ψ, except those in $\overline{x}$. Let $\theta = \mathcal{LCWA}(\{P_1(\overline{x}_1),\dots,P_n(\overline{x}_n)\},\Psi)$ and $\theta_i = \mathcal{LCWA}(P_i(\overline{x}_i),\exists|_{\overline{x}_i}\Psi)$, $i = 1,\dots n$. Then $\mathcal{M}_D(\theta) \equiv \bigwedge_{i=1}^n \mathcal{M}_D(\theta_i)$.*

Similarly, one may split a disjunctive window of expertise to its disjuncts and still preserve the original LCWA, and any collection of LCWAs on the same predicate may be combined to one (disjunctive) LCWA.

Proposition 2. *Let $\theta = \mathcal{LCWA}\,(P(\overline{x}),\bigvee_{i=1}^n \Psi_i[\overline{x}_i])$ and $\theta_i = \mathcal{LCWA}(P(\overline{x}),\Psi_i[\overline{x}_i])$, $i=1,\dots,n$. Then $\mathcal{M}_D(\theta) \equiv \bigwedge_{i=1}^n \mathcal{M}_D(\theta_i)$.*

In the sequel we assume, without loss of generality, one LCWA expression per predicate of $\mathcal{R}(\Sigma)$. The predicates in $\mathcal{R}(\Sigma)$ that do not appear as objects in any LCWA expression are considered as objects of LCWAs in which the windows of expertise is false. In other words, there is no context in which those predicates are complete.

The meaning of a database is now defined by the conjunction of its atoms augmented with the meaning of the given local closed-word assumptions, and the following two general assumptions:

- *Domain Closure Axiom*: $\mathsf{DCA}(\Sigma) = \forall x(\bigvee_{i=1}^n x = C_i)$,
- *Unique Name Axiom*: $\mathsf{UNA}(\Sigma) = \bigwedge_{1 \leqslant i < j \leqslant n} C_i \neq C_j$,

where $C_1,\dots,C_n$ are the constant symbols of Σ (i.e., in $\mathcal{C}(\Sigma)$).

Definition 3. *Let D be a database and let $\mathcal{L}$ be a set of LCWA expressions $\theta_j = \mathcal{LCWA}(P_j, \Psi_j)$, $j = 1, \ldots, n$ applied on D. The meaning of D and $\mathcal{L}$ is given by:*

$$\mathcal{M}(D, \mathcal{L}) = \bigwedge_{A \in D} A \wedge \bigwedge_{j=1}^{n} \mathcal{M}_D(\theta_j) \wedge \mathsf{UNA}(\Sigma) \wedge \mathsf{DCA}(\Sigma).$$

The theory consisting of the meaning of D and $\mathcal{L}$ is consistent and decidable[3]. Consistency is shown in [3] and decidability follows from the fact that the language does not contain function symbols and that UNA and DCA are imposed, ensuring a fixed and finite domain. Note also that each model of this theory is isomorphic to a Herbrand model.

Our goal is to evaluate queries with respect to the meaning $\mathcal{M}(D, \mathcal{L})$ of a database D and a set $\mathcal{L}$ of LCWA expressions. In this context, particularly interesting queries are those formulas that are either entailed by $\mathcal{M}(D, \mathcal{L})$ or are necessarily falsified by it. Such queries induce definitive answers. This idea is formalized in different ways in [3,6,11]. In what follows we adopt the definition of [6].

Definition 4. *A first-order theory Γ determines* complete world information *(CWI) on a query $\mathcal{Q}[\overline{x}]$ iff for every ground tuple $\overline{d}$, either $\Gamma \models \mathcal{Q}[\overline{d}]$ or $\Gamma \models \neg\mathcal{Q}[\overline{d}]$ holds.*

Observe that the LCWA and CWI are related concepts that capture different phenomena. The LCWA expresses completeness of a set of atoms in a relational database while the CWI identifies completeness of queries posed to the databases. Frequently, one or more LCWAs determine CWI on a query with respect to a given database. In Section 3 we consider sufficient conditions for assuring this.

As the meaning $\mathcal{M}(D, \mathcal{L})$ of a database is a first-order formula, one way of evaluating queries is by using off-the-shelf theorem provers. This requires a new derivation for every ground instance of the query, which makes the whole process time consuming. An alternative approach is to generate a 3-valued Herbrand interpretation approximating all models of $\mathcal{M}(D, \mathcal{L})$ and then evaluate different queries with respect to this interpretation. The advantage of this approach is twofold. From a theoretical point of view, it is a good tool to distinguish the complete consequences of the theory from the incomplete ones, and in particular CWI can be easily determined. From a more practical perspective, the 3-valued Herbrand interpretation can be used to compute approximating answers to queries. In the next sections we consider this approach.

3   3-Valued Fixpoint Theory for LCWA

3.1   3-Valued Semantics

The truth values $\mathcal{THREE} = \{t, u, f\}$, standing for true, unknown and false, of 3-valued semantics are usually arranged in two orders: the truth order, $\leqslant$, which is a linear order given by $f \leqslant u \leqslant t$, and the precision order $\leqslant_p$, which is a partial order on $\mathcal{THREE}$ in which u is the least element, and t and f are incomparable maximal elements. The structure of $\mathcal{THREE}$ is drawn in the following diagram.

---

[3] There is an effective way of deciding whether any given sentence is a theorem of the theory.

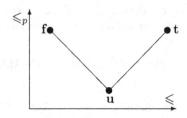

The conjunction $\wedge$ in $\mathcal{THREE}$ is defined by the $\leqslant$-glb of this structure, the disjunction $\vee$ is defined by the $\leqslant$-lub, and the negation operator $\neg$ is associated with the $\leqslant$-involution, that is: $\neg\mathbf{t} = \mathbf{f}$, $\neg\mathbf{f} = \mathbf{t}$, and $\neg\mathbf{u} = \mathbf{u}$.

In this paper we focus on Herbrand interpretations. Two-valued (respectively, 3-valued) (Herbrand) interpretations of Σ are total functions from the set $HB(\Sigma)$ of all ground atoms of Σ to the set of truth values $\{\mathbf{t}, \mathbf{f}\}$ (respectively, to the elements in $\mathcal{THREE}$). Equivalently, two-valued interpretations are sometimes represented as sets of (true) atoms. Extensions to complex formulas are as usual. An interpretation I *satisfies* a formula ψ if $\psi^I = \mathbf{t}$; I satisfies a set Γ of formulas if it satisfies every formula in Γ. In this case I is called a *model* of Γ. The orders $\leqslant$ and $\leqslant_p$ between truth values are extended to 3-valued Herbrand interpretations by pointwise comparisons. For a fixed Σ, the set $\mathfrak{L}$ of 2-valued Herbrand Σ-interpretations forms a complete lattice under $\leqslant$. The set $\mathfrak{L}^c$ of 3-valued Herbrand Σ-interpretations is a chain complete poset[4] under $\leqslant_p$.

There is an interesting lattice theoretic way to construct the 3-valued interpretations from $\mathfrak{L}$. Given a lattice $\mathfrak{L}$, we can define $\mathfrak{L}_c$ as the set of *consistent* pairs $(x, y) \in \mathfrak{L}$, i.e., pairs such that $x \leqslant y$. On $\mathfrak{L}_c$, we can define two orders:

1. $(x, y) \leqslant (x', y')$ if $x \leqslant x'$ and $y \leqslant y'$
2. $(x, y) \leqslant_p (x', y')$ if $x \leqslant x'$ and $y' \leqslant y$

In general, $\leqslant$ is a lattice order and $\leqslant_p$ is a chain-complete order. The following mapping from 3-valued interpretations $\mathcal{K}$ to consistent pairs (I, J) of two-valued interpretations is a one-to-one correspondence from $\mathfrak{L}^c$ to $\mathfrak{L}_c$, preserving both $\leqslant$ and $\leqslant_p$:

$$I = \{P(\bar{a}) \in HB(\Sigma) \mid P(\bar{a})^{\mathcal{K}} = \mathbf{t}\}$$
$$J = \{P(\bar{a}) \in HB(\Sigma) \mid P(\bar{a})^{\mathcal{K}} = \mathbf{t} \text{ or } P(\bar{a})^{\mathcal{K}} = \mathbf{u}\}$$

Conversely, $\mathcal{K}$ can be constructed from (I, J) by defining for every atom $P(\bar{a})$:

$$P(\bar{a})^{\mathcal{K}} = \begin{cases} \mathbf{t} & \text{if } P(\bar{a})^I = \mathbf{t} \\ \mathbf{f} & \text{if } P(\bar{a})^J = \mathbf{f} \\ \mathbf{u} & \text{otherwise} \end{cases}$$

3.2   Fixpoint Operators for LCWAs

Below, we focus on theories Γ that include UNA and DCA, i.e., every model is isomorphic with a Herbrand model.

---

[4] A poset P is chain-complete if every totally ordered subset $C \subseteq P$ has a least upper bound.

Definition 5. *Let Γ be a consistent theory based on Σ. We say that a 3-valued Herbrand Σ-interpretation $\mathcal{K}$ approximates Γ (from below) iff for every 2-valued Herbrand model M of Γ, $\mathcal{K} \leqslant_p M$. The optimal approximation for Γ is a 3-valued Σ-interpretation, defined by $\mathcal{K}_{opt}(\Gamma) = glb_{\leqslant_p}(\{M \mid M \models \Gamma\})$, where M ranges over 2-valued Herbrand models of Γ.*

$\mathcal{K}_{opt}(\Gamma)$ is the most precise of all 3-valued Herbrand Σ-interpretations approximating Γ and is well-defined since every nonempty set $S \subseteq \mathfrak{L}^c$ has a greatest lower bound and Γ is consistent. Back in the LCWA context, note that $\mathcal{M}(D, \mathcal{L})$ satisfies the consistency condition, hence $\mathcal{K}_{opt}(\mathcal{M}(D, \mathcal{L}))$ is well-defined.

In order to construct a 3-valued approximation for $\mathcal{M}(D, \mathcal{L})$, we first introduce a fixpoint operator on the chain complete poset of 3-valued Herbrand Σ-interpretations.

Definition 6. Define an operator $\mathcal{O}_{\mathcal{LCWA}} : \mathfrak{L}^c \to \mathfrak{L}^c$ as follows: for every $\mathcal{K} \in \mathfrak{L}^c$, the interpretation $\mathcal{K}' = \mathcal{O}_{\mathcal{LCWA}}(\mathcal{K})$ is defined for each ground atom $P(\bar{a})$ by:

$$
P(\bar{a})^{\mathcal{K}'} = \begin{cases} \mathbf{t} & \text{if } P(\bar{a}) \in D \\ \mathbf{f} & \text{if there is } \mathcal{LCWA}\,(P(\bar{x}), \Psi[\bar{x}]) \in \mathcal{L} \text{ such that} \\ & \Psi[\bar{a}]^{\mathcal{K}} = \mathbf{t} \text{ and } P(\bar{a}) \notin D \\ \mathbf{u} & \text{otherwise} \end{cases}
$$

The idea is to iterate $\mathcal{O}_{\mathcal{LCWA}}$ starting with total ignorance (a valuation that assigns $\mathbf{u}$ to every ground atom), and gradually extend the definite knowledge according to the database and its LCWAs.

Proposition 3. *$\mathcal{O}_{\mathcal{LCWA}}$ is a $\leqslant_p$-monotone operator on the chain complete poset of 3-valued Σ-interpretations, thus it has a least fixpoint. Moreover, the least fixpoint can be computed in polynomial time in the size of the database.*

Proof. Monotonicity follows from $\leqslant_p$-monotonicity of the truth assignment. By an extension of the well-known Knaster-Tarski theorem, every monotone operator in a chain complete poset has a fixpoint. Polynomial complexity follows from the fact that per application of the operator, the number of queries to be solved is polynomial in the size of the database and each query can be solved in polynomial time, while the number of iterations is at most polynomial in the size of the database. $\qquad\Box$

Definition 7. Denote by $\mathcal{O}_{\mathcal{LCWA}}^{\uparrow}$ the $\leqslant_p$-least fixpoint of $\mathcal{O}_{\mathcal{LCWA}}$.

Example 4.

1. If $D = \emptyset$ and $\theta_1 = \mathcal{LCWA}\,(P, R)$ then $R^{\mathcal{O}_{\mathcal{LCWA}}^{\uparrow}} = \mathbf{u}$ and $P^{\mathcal{O}_{\mathcal{LCWA}}^{\uparrow}} = \mathbf{u}$.
2. Suppose that $D = \emptyset$, $\theta_1 = \mathcal{LCWA}\,(Q, \mathbf{t})$, and $\theta_2 = \mathcal{LCWA}\,(P, \neg Q)$. In this case $Q^{\mathcal{O}_{\mathcal{LCWA}}^{\uparrow}} = \mathbf{f}$ and $P^{\mathcal{O}_{\mathcal{LCWA}}^{\uparrow}} = \mathbf{f}$.
3. Consider the database D of Example 1 and $\mathcal{LCWA}\,(\mathsf{Tel}(x, y), \mathsf{Dept}(x, \mathsf{CS}))$, that is discussed in Example 2. Here $\mathsf{Tel}(\mathsf{Bart\ Delvaux}, 1234567)^{\mathcal{O}_{\mathcal{LCWA}}^{\uparrow}} = \mathbf{f}$, while $\mathsf{Tel}(\mathsf{Leen\ Desmet}, 1234567)^{\mathcal{O}_{\mathcal{LCWA}}^{\uparrow}} = \mathbf{u}$.

The following theorem shows that $\mathcal{O}_{\mathcal{LCWA}}^{\uparrow}$ is a sound approximation of $\mathcal{M}(D, \mathcal{L})$.

Theorem 1. *(Soundness)* $\mathcal{O}^{\uparrow}_{\mathcal{LCWA}}$ *approximates* $\mathcal{M}(D, \mathcal{L})$.

Proof (Outline). Denote by $\bot$ the interpretation that assigns $\mathbf{u}$ to every ground atom, and by $\mathcal{O}_{\mathcal{LCWA}}(\bot)^i$ the i-th iteration of $\mathcal{O}_{\mathcal{LCWA}}$ starting from $\bot$. Let M be a model of $\mathcal{M}(D, \mathcal{L})$. By induction on i, one shows that $\mathcal{O}_{\mathcal{LCWA}}(\bot)^i \leqslant_p M$.   □

Example 5. In the following two cases $\mathcal{O}^{\uparrow}_{\mathcal{LCWA}}$ is strictly less than $\mathcal{K}_{opt}(\mathcal{M}(D, \mathcal{L}))$:

1. $D = \emptyset$, $\theta = \mathcal{LCWA}(Q, P \vee \neg P)$.
   All the models of $\mathcal{M}(D, \mathcal{L})$ assign $\mathbf{f}$ to Q, thus $Q^{\mathcal{K}_{opt}(\mathcal{M}(D,\mathcal{L}))} = \mathbf{f}$. However, as in the standard 3-valued Kripke-Kleene semantics $P \vee \neg P$ is unknown whenever P is unknown, we have that $Q^{\mathcal{O}^{\uparrow}_{\mathcal{LCWA}}} = \mathbf{u}$.
2. $D = \emptyset$, $\theta_1 = \mathcal{LCWA}(P, R)$, $\theta_2 = \mathcal{LCWA}(Q, R \supset \neg P)$.
   Here again $Q^{\mathcal{O}^{\uparrow}_{\mathcal{LCWA}}} = \mathbf{u}$, while $Q^{\mathcal{K}_{opt}(\mathcal{M}(D,\mathcal{L}))} = \mathbf{f}$.   ·

One way to address the phenomenon in item (1) is to extend the Kripke-Kleene semantics to supervaluations [4]. Under this semantics, two-valued and 3-valued tautologies/contradictions coincide. In what follows we avoid this problem by representing tautologies and contradictions only with the standard $\mathbf{t}$ and $\mathbf{f}$ symbols (respectively).

The difference between $\mathcal{K}_{opt}(\mathcal{M}(D, \mathcal{L}))$ and $\mathcal{O}^{\uparrow}_{\mathcal{LCWA}}$ in item 2 is more subtle. In this case $\mathcal{M}(D, \mathcal{L})$ is the formula $(R \supset \neg P) \wedge ((R \supset \neg P) \supset \neg Q)$, which obviously entails $\neg Q$. The intuitive reason for the difference is that the window of expertise in θ_2 is exactly the meaning of θ_1, and this link is not captured by $\mathcal{O}_{\mathcal{LCWA}}$. To gain completeness, some restrictions need to be imposed to the windows of expertise. In the following section we study such conditions.

3.3 A Hierarchy of LCWAs

Definition 8. *An LCWA dependency graph that is determined by a set of LCWAs $\mathcal{L}$, is a directed graph whose nodes correspond to $R(\Sigma)$, such that there is a directed edge from Q to P iff there exists $\mathcal{LCWA}(P(\overline{x}), \Psi[\overline{x}]) \in \mathcal{L}$ such that Q occurs in Ψ.*

Example 6. Consider the following set of local-closed world assumptions:

$$\mathcal{L} = \left\{ \begin{array}{lll} \mathcal{LCWA}(P_1(x), \mathbf{t}), & \mathcal{LCWA}(P_2(x), \mathbf{t}), & \mathcal{LCWA}(Q(x), P_1(x) \wedge P_2(x)) \\ \mathcal{LCWA}(Q(x), S(x)), & \mathcal{LCWA}(S(x), Q(x)), & \mathcal{LCWA}(R(x), Q(x)) \end{array} \right\}$$

The corresponding (cyclic) dependency graph is shown below:

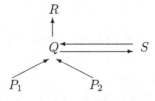

Definition 9. *A local closed-world assumption expression $\mathcal{LCWA}(P(\overline{x}), \Psi[\overline{x}])$ is primitive iff $\Psi[\overline{x}]$ is either $\mathbf{t}, \mathbf{f}$, contains only the equality predicate or any Boolean combination of those. Likewise, a predicate P is primitive iff P appears as object of a primitive LCWA expression.*

Primitive LCWAs induce CWI on appropriate subsets of their object predicates. Consider for instance $\mathcal{LCWA}\,(P(x), x = a)$. This is a primitive LCWA and it specifies that CWI on P is obtained for the domain constant a. Thus $\mathcal{M}(D, \mathcal{L}) \models P(a)$ or $\mathcal{M}(D, \mathcal{L}) \models \neg P(a)$, for any database D. The following proposition formalizes this property and establishes the relationship between primitive LCWA and CWI.

Proposition 4. *Let D be a database and let $\theta = \mathcal{LCWA}(P(\overline{x}), \Psi) \in \mathcal{L}$ be a primitive LCWA on D. Then for any $\overline{c}$ s.t. $\Psi[\overline{c}]$ is true, $\mathcal{M}(D, \mathcal{L}) \models P(\overline{c})$ iff $P(\overline{c}) \in D$ and $\mathcal{M}(D, \mathcal{L}) \models \neg P(\overline{c})$ iff $P(\overline{c}) \notin D$. In this case, then, every model of $\mathcal{M}(D, \mathcal{L})$ satisfies $\neg P(\overline{c})$.*

Proof. Let HU be the Herbrand universe of Σ. As θ is a primitive LCWA, for every $\overline{c} \in HU^n$ either $\Psi[\overline{c}]$ holds in every Herbrand interpretation of $\mathcal{M}(D, \mathcal{L})$ or else $\Psi[\overline{c}]$ is falsified by every Herbrand interpretation. Assume that $\Psi[\overline{c}]$ is true. If $P(\overline{c}) \in D$, then $\mathcal{M}(D, \mathcal{L})$ contains the conjunct $P(\overline{c})$, hence every model of $\mathcal{M}(D, \mathcal{L})$ satisfies $P(\overline{c})$. If $P(\overline{c}) \notin D$, then every model M of $\mathcal{M}(D, \mathcal{L})$ satisfies:

$$\Psi[\overline{c}] \supset (P(\overline{c}) \supset P(\overline{c}) \in D)$$

It follows that $P(\overline{c})$ is false in M. □

Corollary 1. *Let D be a database and let $\theta = \mathcal{LCWA}(P(\overline{x}), \Psi) \in \mathcal{L}$ be a primitive LCWA on D. For any $\overline{c}$ such that $\Psi[\overline{c}]$ holds, $\mathcal{M}(D, \mathcal{L})$ determines CWI on $P(\overline{c})$.*

Another interesting relation between LCWA and CWI is the following:

Proposition 5. *Let $\theta = \mathcal{LCWA}(P(\overline{x}), \Psi[\overline{x}]) \in \mathcal{L}$. If $\mathcal{M}(D, \mathcal{L})$ determines CWI on $\Psi[\overline{x}]$, then it also determines CWI on $P(\overline{x}) \wedge \Psi[\overline{x}]$ and on $\neg P(\overline{x}) \wedge \Psi[\overline{x}]$.*

Proof. Again, denote by HU the Herbrand universe of Σ. By assumption, for every $\overline{c} \in HU^n$ either $\mathcal{M}(D, \mathcal{L}) \models \Psi[\overline{c}]$ or $\mathcal{M}(D, \mathcal{L}) \models \neg \Psi[\overline{c}]$. In the second case, $\mathcal{M}(D, \mathcal{L}) \models \neg(P(\overline{c}) \wedge \Psi[\overline{c}])$ and $\mathcal{M}(D, \mathcal{L}) \models \neg(\neg P(\overline{c}) \wedge \Psi[\overline{c}])$. In the first case, the values of $P(\overline{c}) \wedge \Psi[\overline{c}]$ and $\neg P(\overline{c}) \wedge \Psi[\overline{c}]$ are determined by the question whether $P(\overline{c})$ and $\neg P(\overline{c})$ are true. As in the proof of Proposition 4, this reduces to the validity of $P(\overline{c}) \in P^D$, which is determined by the content of D. □

Example 7. Consider again Example 6. By the last proposition, some of the formulas to which $\mathcal{M}(D, \mathcal{L})$ determines CWI can be inductively defined by the following stages:
1. $P_1(x)$, $\neg P_1(x)$, $P_2(x)$, $\neg P_2(x)$.
2. $P_1(x) \wedge P_2(x)$, $\neg P_1(x) \wedge P_2(x)$, $P_1(x) \wedge \neg P_2(x)$, $\neg P_1(x) \wedge \neg P_2(x)$.
3. $Q(x) \wedge P_1(x) \wedge P_2(x)$, $\neg Q(x) \wedge P_1(x) \wedge P_2(x)$, and so forth.

Definition 10. A *hierarchically closed* database $\mathfrak{D}$ based on vocabulary Σ is a pair $(D, \mathcal{L})$, where D is a database and $\mathcal{L}$ is a set of LCWAs inducing a cycle-free dependency graph.

The transitive closure of a cycle-free LCWA dependency graph is a well-founded strict order on $\mathcal{R}(\Sigma)$, denoted by $<_{\mathcal{L}}$. The minimal predicates in this order are those that are the object of a primitive LCWA (recall that every predicate is the object of exactly one LCWA in $\mathcal{L}$). This property together with the definition of $\mathcal{O}_{\mathcal{LCWA}}$ are the corner stones for the following constructive definition of an approximation of $\mathcal{M}(D, \mathcal{L})$.

Definition 11. Let $\mathfrak{D} = (D, \mathcal{L})$ be a hierarchically closed database. The interpretation $\mathcal{K}_{\mathcal{L}}$ that is *induced* by $\mathfrak{D}$ is defined by induction on $<_{\mathcal{L}}$ as follows: for each predicate P of Σ and every tuple $\bar{a}$,

$$P(\bar{a})^{\mathcal{K}_{\mathcal{L}}} = \begin{cases} \mathbf{t} & \text{if } P(\bar{a}) \in D \\ \mathbf{f} & \text{if there exists } \mathcal{LCWA}\,(P(\bar{x}), \Psi[\bar{x}]) \in \mathcal{L} \text{ s.t.} \\ & \Psi[\bar{a}]^{\mathcal{K}_{\mathcal{L}}} = \mathbf{t} \text{ and } P(\bar{a}) \notin D \\ \mathbf{u} & \text{otherwise} \end{cases}$$

Note 1. In spite of their similar forms, Definitions 6 and 11 define 3-valued interpretations in different ways. In Definition 6 a given operator is iterated so that several 3-valued interpretations are constructed until a fixpoint is reached. Definition 11, on the other hand, induces a gradual construction of a *single* interpretation, starting from bottom elements of the underlying LCWA dependency graph. This construction only works for cycle-free graphs.

It is easy to see how an algorithm to compute $\mathcal{K}_{\mathcal{L}}$ could look like: first, a primitive predicate P from Σ is (non-deterministically) selected. For every tuple $\bar{a}$ of the domain, if $P(\bar{a})$ is in the database, then $P(\bar{a})^{\mathcal{K}_{\mathcal{L}}} = \mathbf{t}$. Otherwise, if the corresponding window of expertise $\Psi_P(\bar{a})$ holds in $\mathcal{K}_{\mathcal{L}}$, then $P(\bar{a})^{\mathcal{K}_{\mathcal{L}}} = \mathbf{f}$. Otherwise, $P(\bar{a})^{\mathcal{K}_{\mathcal{L}}}$ is $\mathbf{u}$. The same steps can be repeated for any predicate Q once all the predicates on which Q depends have been evaluated.

Proposition 6. $\mathcal{K}_{\mathcal{L}}$ *can be computed in polynomial time in the size of the database D.*

Proposition 7. $\mathcal{K}_{\mathcal{L}} \equiv \mathcal{O}^{\uparrow}_{\mathcal{LCWA}}$ *for every hierarchically closed database $\mathfrak{D} = (D, \mathcal{L})$.*

Proof. Let $rank(P) = \max(\{1 + rank(Q) \mid Q <_{\mathcal{L}} P\})$ and $rank(Q) = 1$ iff Q is primitive. The proof is by induction on these ranks: If $rank(P) = 1$ then as P is a primitive predicate, by the definitions of $\mathcal{O}^{\uparrow}_{\mathcal{LCWA}}$ and $\mathcal{K}_{\mathcal{L}}$, $P^{\mathcal{O}^{\uparrow}_{\mathcal{LCWA}}} = P^{\mathcal{K}_{\mathcal{L}}}$. If $rank(P) = n$ for some $n > 1$, then $P^{\mathcal{O}^{\uparrow}_{\mathcal{LCWA}}}$ is computed using the elements in $\{Q \mid Q <_{\mathcal{L}} P\}$. As the rank of each element Q in this set is strictly smaller than n, by induction hypothesis $Q^{\mathcal{O}^{\uparrow}_{\mathcal{LCWA}}} = Q^{\mathcal{K}_{\mathcal{L}}}$. It follows then that $\mathcal{O}_{\mathcal{LCWA}}$ and $\mathcal{K}_{\mathcal{L}}$ must assign the same truth value for P, so again $P^{\mathcal{O}^{\uparrow}_{\mathcal{LCWA}}} = P^{\mathcal{K}_{\mathcal{L}}}$. $\qquad\square$

Given Proposition 7, the soundness of $\mathcal{K}_{\mathcal{L}}$ is obtained as a corollary of Theorem 1.

Corollary 2. *(Soundness) Let $\mathfrak{D} = (D, \mathcal{L})$ be a hierarchically closed database. Then $\mathcal{K}_{\mathcal{L}}$ approximates $\mathcal{M}(D, \mathcal{L})$.*

The next theorem states sufficient conditions under which *optimal* approximation for $\mathcal{M}(D, \mathcal{L})$ can be effectively constructed. Below, $\leq_{\mathcal{L}}$ denotes the reflexive closure of $<_{\mathcal{L}}$.

Theorem 2. *(Completeness) Let $\mathfrak{D} = (D, \mathcal{L})$ be a hierarchically closed database. If Ψ_θ (the windows of expertise of an LCWA expression θ) is a conjunction of literals for every LCWA θ in $\mathcal{L}$, then $\mathcal{K}_{\mathcal{L}} = \mathcal{K}_{opt}(\mathcal{M}(D, \mathcal{L}))$.*

Proof (Sketch). The proof is based on the fact that for every predicate P, $\mathcal{K}_\mathcal{L}|_{\{Q|Q\leqslant_\mathcal{L}P\}}$ $= glb(\{I|_{\{Q|Q\leqslant_\mathcal{L}P\}}|I \models \mathcal{M}(D,\mathcal{L})\})$. This is proven by induction on the dependency order on predicates. The crucial step is when $P(\overline{a})^{\mathcal{K}_\mathcal{L}} = \mathbf{u}$, which is when $P(\overline{a}) \notin D$ and $\Psi_P(\overline{a})^{\mathcal{K}_\mathcal{L}} \neq \mathbf{t}$. In that case, we show the existence of models I and I' of $\mathcal{M}(D,\mathcal{L})$ making $P(\overline{a})$ $\mathbf{t}$, resp. $\mathbf{f}$. The database D itself represents a model of $\mathcal{M}(D,\mathcal{L})$ in which $P(\overline{a})$ is false. In constructing a model in which $P(\overline{a})$ is true, we exploit the fact that $\Psi_P(\overline{a})^{\mathcal{K}_\mathcal{L}} \neq \mathbf{t}$. Since Ψ_P is a conjunction of literals, there is a literal l s.t. $l^{\mathcal{K}_\mathcal{L}} \neq \mathbf{t}$ and l is less than P in the dependency order. Using the induction hypothesis we construct a model I' of $\mathcal{M}(D,\mathcal{L})$ s.t. $P(\overline{a})^{I'} = \mathbf{t}$ but $l^{I'} = \mathbf{f}$ and hence $\Psi_P(\overline{a})^{I'} = \mathbf{f}$. □

Note 2. As Example 5 shows, the requirement in Theorem 2 that Ψ_θ should be a conjunction of literals is indeed necessary.

Example 8. Consider a database in which $D = \{P_1(a), P_1(b), P_2(a), Q(c)\}$ and $\mathcal{L}$ is the set of LCWA of Example 6 without $\mathcal{LCWA}$ $(Q(x), S(x))$. That is,

$$\mathcal{L} = \begin{Bmatrix} \mathcal{LCWA}\,(P_1(x), \mathbf{t}), & \mathcal{LCWA}\,(P_2(x), \mathbf{t}), & \mathcal{LCWA}\,(Q(x), P_1(x) \wedge P_2(x)) \\ \mathcal{LCWA}\,(S(x), Q(x)), & \mathcal{LCWA}\,(R(x), Q(x)) \end{Bmatrix}$$

This database is hierarchically closed as the dependency graph induced by $\mathcal{L}$ is acyclic. Also, as each window of expertise is a conjunction of literals, the conditions of Theorem 2 are satisfied in this case. Clearly, $Q(a)^{\mathcal{K}_\mathcal{L}} = \mathbf{f}$, $Q(b)^{\mathcal{K}_\mathcal{L}} = \mathbf{u}$ and $Q(c)^{\mathcal{K}_\mathcal{L}} = \mathbf{t}$. By Corollary 2, then, $\mathcal{M}(D,\mathcal{L}) \models \neg Q(a)$ and $\mathcal{M}(D,\mathcal{L}) \models Q(c)$. Moreover, by Theorem 2, $\mathcal{K}_\mathcal{L}$ is an optimal approximation of $\mathcal{M}(D,\mathcal{L})$.

4 Query Answering

In the previous section we presented techniques to compute an (optimal) 3-valued interpretation for the meaning of a database and its set of LCWAs. In this section we show how these interpretations can be used for query answering in incomplete databases.

Definition 12. *Given a 3-valued Σ-interpretation $\mathcal{K}$ and a query $\mathcal{Q}[\overline{x}]$ in Σ, define:*

- *Certain answers:* $Cert(\mathcal{Q}[\overline{x}]) = \{\overline{x} \mid \mathcal{Q}[\overline{x}]^\mathcal{K} = \mathbf{t}\}$.
- *Possible answers:* $Poss(\mathcal{Q}[\overline{x}]) = \{\overline{x} \mid \mathcal{Q}[\overline{x}]^\mathcal{K} \geqslant \mathbf{u}\}$.

Note 3. The notions of certain and possible answers proposed here differ from definitions considered in some domains of incomplete databases (see for instance [1]), where the certain and possible answers depend on whether an open or closed-world is assumed. Our definition is based on 3-valued semantics and it does not rely on the assumption that is adopted for the database.

Proposition 8. *Let $\mathfrak{D} = (D, \mathcal{L})$ be a hierarchically closed database. If a ground tuple $\overline{d}$ is a certain answer for $\mathcal{Q}$ in $\mathcal{K}_\mathcal{L}$, then $\mathcal{M}(D,\mathcal{L}) \models \mathcal{Q}[\overline{d}]$.*

We can not prove in general that for any possible answer $\overline{d}$ for a query $\mathcal{Q}$ in $\mathcal{K}_\mathcal{L}$, that $\mathcal{M}(D,\mathcal{L}) \cup \{Q[\overline{d}]\}$ is consistent. All we can assure is that the set of possible answers for $\mathcal{Q}$ constitutes a safe (and usually quite precise) over-approximation of this set.

Proposition 9. *Let* $\mathfrak{D} = (D, \mathcal{L})$ *be a hierarchically closed database and* $\mathcal{Q}$ *a disjunction of literals. If a ground tuple* $\bar{d}$ *is a possible answer for* $\mathcal{Q}$ *in* $\mathcal{K}_{\mathcal{L}}$ *and* $\mathcal{K}_{\mathcal{L}} = \mathcal{K}_{opt}(\mathcal{M}(D, \mathcal{L}))$, *then* $\mathcal{M}(D, \mathcal{L}) \cup \{\mathcal{Q}[\bar{d}]\}$ *is satisfiable.*

Given a 3-valued Herbrand Σ-interpretation $\mathcal{K}$ and a query $\mathcal{Q}[\bar{x}]$ in Σ, we compute certain/possible answers by Algorithm 1 below. In this algorithm, steps 1 and 2 are computed once (unless $\mathcal{K}$ is changed), while step 3 is executed for each new query. Observe that in step 3.a we under-approximate positive occurrences and over-approximate negative occurrences of predicates, while in 3.b we do the converse.

Algorithm 1. Computing Certain/Possible Answers

1: For each predicate P, define $\Sigma' = \{R \in \Sigma : R^{\mathcal{K}} \text{is 2-valued}\} \cup \{P_u, P_t : P^{\mathcal{K}}\text{is 3-valued}\}$.
2: Define $I^{\mathcal{K}}$ as the 2-valued Herbrand Σ'-interpretation, such that:

  - $R^{I^{\mathcal{K}}} = R^{\mathcal{K}}$ if $R^{\mathcal{K}}$ is 2-valued in $\mathcal{K}$.
  - $P_t^{I^{\mathcal{K}}} = \{\bar{d} \mid P(\bar{d})^{\mathcal{K}} = \mathbf{t}\}$.
  - $P_u^{I^{\mathcal{K}}} = \{\bar{d} \mid P(\bar{d})^{\mathcal{K}} \geqslant \mathbf{u}\}$.

3: Consider the query $\mathcal{Q}[\bar{x}]$.

    3.a To obtain **certain** answers for $\mathcal{Q}[\bar{x}]$ compute $\mathcal{Q}^c[\bar{x}]$ as follows:

  - Replace positive occurrences of 3-valued predicates P by P_t.
  - Replace negative occurrences of 3-values predicates P by P_u.

    3.b To obtain **possible** answers for $\mathcal{Q}[\bar{x}]$ compute $\mathcal{Q}^p[\bar{x}]$ as follows:

  - Replace positive occurrences of 3-valued predicates P by P_u.
  - Replace negative occurrences of 3-valued predicates P by P_t.

Theorem 3. *A ground tuple* $\bar{d}$ *is a certain (alternatively possible) answer for* $\mathcal{Q}[\bar{x}]$ *in* $\mathcal{K}$ *iff* $\bar{d}$ *is an answer to* $\mathcal{Q}^c$ *(alternatively* $\mathcal{Q}^p$*) in* $I^{\mathcal{K}}$.

Proof. Consider the (non-standard representation of) truth assignment interpreting a formula φ in a pair of structures (I, J) with the same domain, such that positively occurring atoms of φ are interpreted by I, and negatively occurring ones by J. A satisfaction relation $\models$ between these valuations and formulas in Σ is inductively defined as follows:

  - $(I, J) \models P(\bar{d})$ iff $I \models P(\bar{d})$, i.e., $\bar{d}^I \in P^I$;
  - $(I, J) \models \neg\varphi$ iff $(J, I) \not\models \varphi$;
  - $(I, J) \models \varphi \vee \psi$ iff $(I, J) \models \varphi$ or $(I, J) \models \psi$;
  - $(I, J) \models \exists\bar{x}\, \varphi(\bar{x})$ iff there is a $\bar{d} \in dom(I)$, such that $(I[\bar{x}/\bar{d}], J[\bar{x}/\bar{d}]) \models \varphi(\bar{x})$.

There is a strong link with 3-valued logic. Indeed, when (I, J) is the result of splitting a 3-valued interpretation $\mathcal{K}$ in a 2-valued underestimation I and 2-valued overestimation J (see Section 3.1), then it is well-known that :

- $\varphi^{\mathcal{K}} = \mathbf{f}$ iff $(J, I) \not\models \varphi$;
- $\varphi^{\mathcal{K}} = \mathbf{u}$ iff $(J, I) \models \varphi$ and $(I, J) \not\models \varphi$;
- $\varphi^{\mathcal{K}} = \mathbf{t}$ iff $(I, J) \models \varphi$.

A straightforward consequence of these equalities is $\varphi^{\mathcal{K}} \geqslant \mathbf{u}$ iff $(J, I) \models \varphi$. Let (I, J) be the pair of 2-valued Herbrand Σ-interpretations associated with $\mathcal{K}$. By construction of $I^{\mathcal{K}}$ (see step 2 in Algorithm 1), for every 3-valued predicate P, $(P_t)^{I^{\mathcal{K}}} = P^I$ and $(P_u)^{I^{\mathcal{K}}} = P^J$. It is easy to see that for any tuple of domain elements $\overline{d}$, $(I, J) \models \mathcal{Q}[\overline{d}]$ iff $I^{\mathcal{K}} \models \mathcal{Q}^c[\overline{d}]$ and $(J, I) \models \mathcal{Q}[\overline{d}]$ iff $I^{\mathcal{K}} \models \mathcal{Q}^p[\overline{d}]$. It follows that if $I^{\mathcal{K}} \models \mathcal{Q}^c[\overline{d}]$, then $\mathcal{Q}[\overline{d}]^{\mathcal{K}} = \mathbf{t}$, i.e., $\overline{d}$ is a certain answer for $\mathcal{Q}$, and if $I^{\mathcal{K}} \models \mathcal{Q}^p[\overline{d}]$ then $\mathcal{Q}[\overline{d}]^{\mathcal{K}} \geqslant \mathbf{u}$, i.e., $\overline{d}$ is a possible answer for $\mathcal{Q}$. $\square$

Example 9. Consider the database $\mathfrak{D}$ of Example 8. Let us check the query $\mathcal{Q}[x] = P_1(x) \wedge R(x)$ for $x = b$. Let $\mathcal{K}_{\mathcal{L}}$ be the 3-valued interpretation that is induced by $\mathfrak{D}$ (obtained by the inductive construction of Definition 11), and let I be the 2-valued interpretation derived from $\mathcal{K}_{\mathcal{L}}$ by step 2 of Algorithm 1. Since P_1 is 2-valued in $\mathcal{K}_{\mathcal{L}}$, for every constant a, $P_1(a)^{\mathcal{K}_{\mathcal{L}}} = P_1(a)^I$. The predicate R is 3-valued in $\mathcal{K}_{\mathcal{L}}$, and following step 2 we replace it by R_t and R_u in I. It follows that $R_t(b)^I = \mathbf{f}$ and $R_u(b)^I = \mathbf{t}$. Rewriting $\mathcal{Q}[x]$ using now step 3, we obtain $\mathcal{Q}^c[x] = P_1(x) \wedge R_t(x)$ and $\mathcal{Q}^p[x] = P_1(x) \wedge R_u(x)$. It follows that $x = b$ is a possible but not a certain answer for $\mathcal{Q}[x]$ (that is, $b \in Poss(\mathcal{Q}) - Cert(\mathcal{Q})$).

The last example demonstrates query answering in hierarchically closed databases. The whole process can be summarized as follows:

1) Given a database $\mathfrak{D} = (D, \mathcal{L})$, check whether it is hierarchically closed (this is simple, as both the construction of the dependency graph and cycle checking for it are polynomial in the size of $\mathcal{L}$).
2) Apply the procedure that is sketched in the paragraph above the proof of Proposition 6 for constructing the 3-valued interpretation $\mathcal{K}_{\mathcal{L}}$ that is induced by $\mathfrak{D}$.
3) Given a query $\mathcal{Q}$, apply Algorithm 1 with $\mathcal{K}_{\mathcal{L}}$ and $\mathcal{Q}$.

5   Related Works

In [6], the authors introduced the concept of closed-world information on a formula $\mathcal{Q}$ in the context of logical agents. The idea amounts to the specification of which parts of a logical theory are complete. More formally, an agent has CWI relative to a formula $\mathcal{Q}(\overline{x})$ if every ground instance $\mathcal{Q}(\overline{a})$ is either entailed by the first-order knowledge base or necessarily false. As argued in this paper (see the discussion after Definition 4), the notions of CWI and LCWA (as presented here) are closely related, but they capture different properties of different entities.

Doherty et al. [5] propose a semantics for the CWI of Etzioni et al. in terms of (second-order) circumscription. This approach generalizes the one in [6] by allowing limited use of negation and disjunction in the representation of CWI, while retaining tractability of reasoning. The query processing in [5] is based on fixpoint semantics. One of the robust characteristics of this approach is the possibility to express inductive definitions by means of CWI formulas. The correspondence between this approach and our notion of LCWA is considered in detail in [3].

The database community has made important contributions to the study of locally complete databases. In [12], Motro formalizes the concept of partial completeness in relational databases by means of *completeness constraints*, which are concerned with "true information that must be part of a complete database". Such constraints are represented in the conjunctive relational calculus. The role of Motro's completeness constraints is taken here by the windows of expertise, which are represented by a more expressive language (function-free first-order). In [11], Levy investigates how to determine whether the answer to a given query is complete even if the database is incomplete. The notion of completeness is semantically characterised in terms of *virtual* relations (those that are true in the real world) and *available relations* (the actual database). Neither Motro nor Levy address the problem of obtaining possible answers to queries, as we do in this paper.

In answer-set programming, Gelfond and Lifschitz [7] introduce the possibility to *partially* define a predicate by combining in one rule classical negation and negation as failure. Consider, for instance, the following program[5]: $\{\neg p \leftarrow \text{ not } p, \varphi\}$. Under stable-models semantics [8], the truth of $\neg p$ can be established if no evidence is found about p and φ is provable. The relationship with the LCWA in this context is clear: φ is a window of expertise of p.

6   Conclusions and Future Work

We have presented a general algebraic fixpoint theory for the local closed-world assumption of relational databases. The framework proposed here re-conciliates the notions of CWI and LCWA used in the contexts of knowledge-base agents and relational databases. More specifically, (i) important cases in which LCWA induces CWI are identified, and (ii) a simple query answering mechanism that allows to distinguish between possible and certain answers is introduced. Future lines of research include the following topics:

- **Extension from relational to deductive databases.** In deductive databases (sometimes referred as Datalog), so called intensional predicates are defined in terms of extensional relations. Given a relational database and set of LCWAs, it would be informative to identify where locally complete extensional relations induce complete knowledge on intensional ones. The immaterial nature of intensional predicates presumably requires some extension of the notion of LCWA considered in this paper.

- **Integration with mediator-based systems [10].** In [3] it was shown how to represent LCWA information over a number of different data-sources. Informally, the idea amounts to represent that a set of data-sources, taken together, may store complete knowledge about certain predicates. An open question is how to explore this

---

[5] Following standard conventions, the symbols $\neg$ and not represent classical negation and negation as failure, respectively.

additional knowledge to retrieve more informative answers from queries to the mediator. An approach based on the semantic considerations presented in this paper could provide a well-founded solution to the elusive problem of answering negative queries from mediator systems.

– **Efficient query answering techniques for the LCWA.** The methods we presented here for query answering require the computation of a 3-valued interpretation. This approach allows a straightforward identification of the exact knowledge endorsed by a database, but, if the database or the set of the LCWA expressions is updated, the 3-valued interpretation must be re-computed. Incremental methods for updating 3-valued interpretations may be incorporated for reducing the computational complexity of the revision process.

References

1. S. Abiteboul and O.M. Duschka. Complexity of answering queries using materialized views. In *Proc. 17th PODS*, pages 254–263, 1998.
2. A. Cortés-Calabuig, M. Denecker, O. Arieli, and M. Bruynooghe. Representation of partial knowledge and query answering in locally complete databases. *Technical Report 457, Department of Computer Science, K.U. Leuven, August 2006*, 2006.
3. A. Cortés-Calabuig, M. Denecker, O. Arieli, B. Van Nuffelen, and M. Bruynooghe. On the local closed-world assumption of data-sources. In *Proc. 8th LPNMR, LNCS 3662*, pages 145–157, 2005.
4. M. Denecker, V.W. Marek, and M. Truszczynski. Uniform semantic treatment of default and autoepistemic logics. *Artificial Intelligence*, 143(1):79–122, 2003.
5. P. Doherty, W. Łukaszewicz, and A. Szalas. Efficient reasoning using the local closed-world assumption. In *Proc. 9th AIMSA*, LNCS 2407, pages 49–58, 2000.
6. O. Etzioni, K. Golden, and D. Weld. Sound and efficient closed-world reasoning for planning. *Artificial Intelligence*, 89(1-2):113–148, 1997.
7. M. Gelfond and V. Lifschitz. Logic programs with classical negation. In *Proc. 7th ICLP*, pages 579–597, 1990.
8. M. Gelfond and V. Lifschitz. Classical negation in logic programs and disjunctive databases. *New Generation Comput.*, 9(3/4):365–386, 1991.
9. G. Grahne. Information integration and incomplete information. *IEEE Data Engineering Bulletin*, 25(3):46–52, 2002.
10. M. Lenzerini. Data integration: A theoretical perspective. In *Proc. 21st PODS*, pages 233–246, 2002.
11. A.Y. Levy. Obtaining complete answers from incomplete databases. In *Proc. 22nd VLDB*, pages 402–412, 1996.
12. A. Motro. Integrity = validity + completeness. *ACM Trans. Database Syst.*, 14(4):480–502, 1989.
13. R. Reiter. Towards a logical reconstruction of relational database theory. In *Conceptual Modelling*, pages 191–233, 1982.

Sequential, Parallel, and Quantified Updates of First-Order Structures

Philipp Rümmer

Department of Computer Science and Engineering, Chalmers University of
Technology and Göteborg University, SE-412 96 Göteborg, Sweden
philipp@cs.chalmers.se

Abstract. We present a datastructure for storing memory contents of
imperative programs during symbolic execution—a technique frequently
used for program verification and testing. The concept, called updates,
can be integrated in dynamic logic as runtime infrastructure and models both stack and heap. Here, updates are systematically developed as
an imperative programming language that provides the following constructs: assignments, guards, sequential composition and bounded as
well as unbounded parallel composition. The language is equipped both
with a denotational semantics and a correct rewriting system for execution, whereby the latter is a generalisation of the syntactic application of
substitutions. The normalisation of updates is discussed. The complete
theory of updates has been formalised using Isabelle/HOL.

1 Introduction

First-Order Dynamic Logic [1] is a program logic that enables to reason about the
relation between the initial and final states of imperative programs. One way to
build calculi for dynamic logic is to follow the symbolic execution paradigm and
to execute programs (symbolically) in forward direction. This requires infrastructure for storing the memory contents of the program, for updating the contents
when assignments occur and for accessing information whenever the program
reads from memory. Sequent calculi for dynamic logic often represent memory
using formulas and handle state changes by renaming variables and by relating
pre- and post-states with equations. All information about the considered pro-
gram states is stored in the side-formulas Γ, Δ of a sequent $\Gamma \vdash \langle \alpha \rangle \phi, \Delta$, like
in inequations $0 \doteq x$ and equations $x' \doteq x + 1$.

As an alternative, this paper presents a datastructure called *Updates*, which
are a generalisation of substitutions designed for storing symbolic memory contents. When using updates, typical sequents during symbolic execution have the
shape $\Gamma \vdash \{u\} \langle \alpha \rangle \phi, \Delta$. The program α is preceded by an update u that determines parts of the program state, for instance the update $x := x + 1$. Compared
with side-formulas, updates (i) attach information about the program state directly to the program, (ii) avoid the introduction of new symbols, (iii) can be
simplified and avoid the storage of obsolete information, like of assignments that
have been overridden by other assignments, (iv) represent accesses to variables,

M. Hermann and A. Voronkov (Eds.): LPAR 2006, LNAI 4246, pp. 422–436, 2006.

array cells or instance attributes (in object-oriented languages) in a uniform way, (v) delay case-distinctions that can become necessary due to aliasing, (vi) can be eliminated mechanically once a program has been worked off completely.

Historically, updates have evolved over years as a central component of the KeY system [2], a system for deductive verification of Java programs. They are used both for interactive and automated verification. In the present paper, we define updates as a formal language (independently of particular program logics) and give them a denotational semantics based on model-theoretic semantics of first-order predicate logic. The language is proposed as an intermediate language to which sequential parts of more complicated languages (like Java) can stepwise be translated. The thesis [3] related to this paper gives a rewriting system that allows to execute or eliminate updates mechanically. The main contributions of the paper are new update constructs (in particular quantification), the development of a complete metatheory of updates and its formalisation[1] using the Isabelle/HOL proof assistant [4], including proofs of all lemmas about updates that are given in the present paper or in [3].

The paper is organised as follows: Sect. 2 motivates updates through an example. Sect. 3 and 4 introduce syntax and semantics of a basic version of updates in the context of a minimalist first-order logic. Sect. 5 describes the rewriting system for executing updates. Sect. 6 adds an operator for sequential composition to the update language. Sect. 7 shows how heap structures can be modelled and modified using updates, which is applied in Sect. 8 about symbolic execution. Sect. 9 discusses laws for simplification of updates.

2   Updates for Symbolic Execution in Dynamic Logic

We give an example for symbolic execution using updates in dynamic logic. Notation and constructs used here are later introduced in detail. The program fragment *max* is written in a Java-like language and is executed in the context of a class/record *List* representing doubly-linked lists with attributes *next*, *prev* and *val* for the successor, predecessor and value of list nodes:

$$max = \text{if } (a.val \overset{.}{<} a.next.val) \ g = a.next.val; \text{else } g = a.val;$$

where a and g are program variables pointing to list nodes. The initial state of program execution is specified in an imperative way using an update:

$$init = a.prev := nil \mid b.next := nil \mid a.next := b \mid b.prev := a \mid$$
$$a.val := c \mid b.val := d$$

init can be read as a program that is executing a number of assignments in parallel and that is setting up a list with nodes a and b. In case $a \overset{.}{=} b$—which is possible because we do not specify the opposite—the two nodes will collapse to the single node of a cyclic list and will carry value d: assignments that literally

---

[1] www.cs.chalmers.se/~philipp/updates.thy, ≈ 3500 lines Isabelle/Isar code.

occur later ($b.val := d$) can override earlier assignments ($a.val := c$). This means that parallel composition in updates also has a sequential component: while the left- and right-hand sides of the assignments are all evaluated in parallel, the actual writing to locations is carried out sequentially from left to right.

When adding updates to a dynamic logic, they can be placed in front of modal operators for programs, like in $\{init\} \langle max \rangle \phi$. The diamond formula $\langle max \rangle \phi$ alone expresses that a given formula ϕ holds in at least one final state of max. Putting the update $init$ in front means that first $init$ and then the program max is supposed to be executed—$init$ sets up the pre-state of max.

We execute max symbolically by working off the statements in forward direction. Effects of the program are either appended to the update $init$ or are translated to first-order connectives. We denote execution steps of max by $\rightsquigarrow$ and write $\equiv$ for an update simplification step. $init$ is used as an abbreviation.

$$\{init\} \langle \texttt{if } (a.val \stackrel{<}{.} a.next.val) \ g = a.next.val; \texttt{else } g = a.val; \rangle \ \phi$$

A conditional statement can be translated to propositional connectives. The branch condition is $co = (a.val \stackrel{<}{.} a.next.val)$.

$$\rightsquigarrow \quad \{init\} ((co \wedge \langle g = a.next.val; \rangle \ \phi) \vee (\neg co \wedge \langle g = a.val; \rangle \ \phi))$$

The application of $init$ distributes through propositional connectives. Applying $init$ to co yields the condition $co' = (\{init\} \ co) \equiv ((\texttt{if } a \stackrel{.}{=} b \texttt{ then } d \texttt{ else } c) \stackrel{<}{.} d)$.

$$\equiv \quad (co' \wedge \{init\} \langle g = a.next.val; \rangle \ \phi \vee (\neg co' \wedge \{init\} \langle g = a.val; \rangle \ \phi)$$

The program assignments are turned into update assignments that are sequentially (;) connected with $init$.

$$\rightsquigarrow \quad (co' \wedge \{init \,; \ g := a.next.val\} \ \phi) \vee (\neg co' \wedge \{init \,; \ g := a.val\} \ \phi)$$

The updates are simplified by turning sequential composition ; into parallel composition | . The update $init$ has to be applied to the right-hand sides, which become $(\{init\} \ a.next.val) \equiv d$ and $(\{init\} \ a.val) \equiv (\texttt{if } a \stackrel{.}{=} b \texttt{ then } d \texttt{ else } c)$.

$$\equiv \quad (co' \wedge \{init \mid g := d\} \ \phi) \vee (\neg co' \wedge \{init \mid g := (\texttt{if } a \stackrel{.}{=} b \texttt{ then } d \texttt{ else } c)\} \ \phi)$$

The last formula is logically equivalent to the original formula $\{init\} \langle max \rangle \phi$ and can further be simplified by applying the updates to ϕ. An implementation like in KeY can, of course, easily carry out all shown steps automatically.

3   Syntax of Terms, Formulas, and Updates

The present paper is a self-contained account on updates. To this end, we abstract from concrete program logics and define syntax and semantics of a (minimalist)[2] first-order logic that is equipped with updates. Updates can, however, be integrated in virtually any predicate logic, e.g., in dynamic logic.

We first define a basic version of our logic that contains the most common constructors for terms and formulas (see e.g. [5]), the equality predicate $\stackrel{.}{=}$ and

---

[2] We do not include many common features like arbitrary predicate symbols, in order to keep the presentation concise. Adding such concepts is straightforward.

a strict order relation $\dot{<}$, as well as operators for minimum and conditional terms. The two latter are not strictly necessary, but enable a simpler definition of laws and rewriting rules. In this section, updates are only equipped with the connectives for parallelism, guards and quantification, sequential composition is added later in Sect. 6.

In order to define the syntax of the logic, we need (i) a vocabulary (Σ, α) of function symbols, where $\alpha : \Sigma \rightarrow \mathbb{N}$ defines the arity of each symbol, and (ii) an infinite set *Var* of variables.

Definition 1. *The sets Ter, For and Upd of terms, formulas and updates are defined by the following grammar, in which $x \in Var$ ranges over variables and $f \in \Sigma$ over functions:*

$$Ter ::= x \mid f(Ter, \ldots, Ter) \mid \text{if } For \text{ then } Ter \text{ else } Ter \mid \min x. \, For \mid \{Upd\} \, Ter$$

$$For ::= true \mid false \mid For \wedge For \mid For \vee For \mid \neg For \mid \forall x. \, For \mid \exists x. \, For \mid$$
$$Ter \doteq Ter \mid Ter \dot{<} Ter \mid \{Upd\} \, For$$

$$Upd ::= \texttt{skip} \mid f(Ter, \ldots, Ter) := Ter \mid Upd \mid Upd \mid \texttt{if } For \, \{Upd\} \mid \texttt{for } x \, \{Upd\}$$

The update constructors represent the empty update $\texttt{skip}$, assignments to function terms $f(s_1, \ldots, s_n) := t$, parallel updates $u_1 \mid u_2$, guarded updates $\texttt{if } \phi \, \{u\}$, and quantified updates $\texttt{for } x \, \{u\}$. The possibility of having function terms as left-hand sides of assignments is crucial for modelling heaps. In Sect. 2, expressions like *a.prev* are really function terms *prev(a)*, but we use the more common notation from programming languages. More details are given in Sect. 7. There are also constructors for applying updates to terms and to formulas (like $\{u\} \, \phi$).

We mostly use vector notation for the arguments $\bar{t}$ of functions. Operations on terms are extended canonically or in an obvious way to vectors, for instance $f(\{u\} \, \bar{t}) = f(\{u\} \, t_1, \ldots, \{u\} \, t_n)$, $\text{val}_{S,\beta}(\bar{t}) = (\text{val}_{S,\beta}(t_1), \ldots, \text{val}_{S,\beta}(t_n))$.

4   Semantics of Terms, Formulas, and Updates

The meaning of terms and formulas is defined using classical model-theoretic semantics. We consider interpretations as mappings from *locations* to *individuals* of a universe U (the predicates $\doteq$ and $\dot{<}$ are handled separately):

Definition 2. *Given a vocabulary (Σ, α) of function symbols and an arbitrary set U, we define the set $Loc_{(\Sigma, \alpha), U}$ of locations over (Σ, α) and U by*

$$Loc_{(\Sigma, \alpha), U} := \{ \langle f, (a_1, \ldots, a_n) \rangle \mid f \in \Sigma, \; \alpha(f) = n, \; a_1, \ldots, a_n \in U \} \, .$$

If the indexes are clear from the context, we just write Loc instead of $Loc_{(\Sigma, \alpha), U}$.

The following definition of structures/algebras deviates from common definitions in the addition of a strict well-ordering on the universe.[3] The well-ordering is used for resolving clashes that can occur in quantified updates (see Example 1 and Sect. 8).

---

[3] As every set can be well-ordered (based on Zermelo-Fraenkel set theory [6]) this does not restrict the range of considered universes. Because the well-ordering is also

Definition 3. *Suppose that a vocabulary (Σ, α) of function symbols is given. A well-ordered algebra over (Σ, α) is a tuple $S = (U, <, I)$, where*

- *U is an arbitrary non-empty set (the universe),*
- *$<$ is a strict well-ordering on U, i.e., a binary relation with the properties[4]*
  - *Irreflexivity: $a \not< a$ for all $a \in U$,*
  - *Transitivity: $a_1 < a_2$, $a_2 < a_3$ entails $a_1 < a_3$ $(a_1, a_2, a_3 \in U)$,*
  - *Well-orderedness: Every non-empty set $A \subseteq U$ contains a least element $\min_< A \in A$ such that $\min_< A < a$ for all $a \in A \setminus \{\min_< A\}$,*
- *I is a (total) mapping $Loc_{(\Sigma, \alpha), U} \to U$ (the interpretation).*

A partial interpretation is a partial function $Loc_{(\Sigma, \alpha), U} \twoheadrightarrow U$.

A (partial) function $f : M \twoheadrightarrow N$ is here considered as a subset of the cartesian product $M \times N$. For combining and modifying interpretations, we frequently make use of the *overriding* operator $\oplus$, which can be found in Z [7] and many other specification languages. For two (partial or total) functions $f, g : M \twoheadrightarrow N$ we define

$$f \oplus g := \{(a \mapsto b) \in f \mid \text{for all } c\colon (a \mapsto c) \notin g\} \cup g,$$

i.e., g overrides f but leaves f unchanged at points where g is not defined. For $S = (U, <, I)$, we also write $S \oplus A := (U, <, I \oplus A)$ as a shorthand notation.

Definition 4. *A variable assignment over a set Var of variables and a well-ordered algebra $(U, <, I)$ is a mapping $\beta : Var \to U$.*

Given a variable assignment β, we denote the assignment that is altered in exactly one point as is common:

$$\beta_x^a(y) := \begin{cases} a & \text{for } x = y \\ \beta(y) & \text{otherwise} \end{cases}$$

From now on, we consider the vocabulary (Σ, α) and *Var* as fixed.

Definition 5. *Given a well-ordered algebra $S = (U, <, I)$ and a variable assignment β, we define the evaluation of terms, formulas and updates through the equations of Table 1 as the (overloaded) mapping*

$$\mathrm{val}_{S,\beta} : Ter \to U, \quad \mathrm{val}_{S,\beta} : For \to \{tt, ff\}, \quad \mathrm{val}_{S,\beta} : Upd \to (Loc \twoheadrightarrow U),$$

i.e., in particular updates are evaluated to partial interpretations.

---

accessible through the predicate $\dot{<}$, however, the expressiveness of the logic goes beyond pure first-order predicate logic. One can, for instance, axiomatise natural numbers up to isomorphism with a finite set of formulas. In our experience, this is not a problem for the application of updates, because quantification in updates will in practice only be used for variables representing integers, objects or similar types. On such domains, appropriate well-orderings are readily available and have to be handled anyway.

[4] Note, that well-orderings are linear, i.e., $a < b$, $a = b$, or $b < a$ for arbitrary $a, b \in U$. Further, well-orderings are well-founded—there are no infinite descending chains—which enables us to use well-founded recursion when defining update evaluation.

Table 1. Evaluation of Terms, Formulas, and Updates

For terms:

$$\mathrm{val}_{S,\beta}(x) = \beta(x) \qquad\qquad (x \in Var)$$

$$\mathrm{val}_{S,\beta}(f(\bar{t})) = I\langle f, \mathrm{val}_{S,\beta}(\bar{t})\rangle \qquad (S = (U, <, I))$$

$$\mathrm{val}_{S,\beta}(\text{if } \phi \text{ then } t_1 \text{ else } t_2) = \begin{cases} \mathrm{val}_{S,\beta}(t_1) & \text{for } \mathrm{val}_{S,\beta}(\phi) = tt \\ \mathrm{val}_{S,\beta}(t_2) & \text{otherwise} \end{cases}$$

$$\mathrm{val}_{S,\beta}(\min x.\, \phi) = \begin{cases} \min_< A & \text{for } A \neq \emptyset \\ \min_< U & \text{otherwise} \end{cases}$$

where $S = (U, <, I)$ and $A = \{a \in U \mid \mathrm{val}_{S,\beta_x^a}(\phi) = tt\}$

For formulas:

$$\mathrm{val}_{S,\beta}(\mathit{true}) = tt, \qquad \mathrm{val}_{S,\beta}(\mathit{false}) = ff$$

$$\mathrm{val}_{S,\beta}(\phi_1 \wedge \phi_2) = tt \quad \text{iff} \quad ff \notin \{\mathrm{val}_{S,\beta}(\phi_1), \mathrm{val}_{S,\beta}(\phi_2)\}$$

$$\mathrm{val}_{S,\beta}(\phi_1 \vee \phi_2) = tt \quad \text{iff} \quad tt \in \{\mathrm{val}_{S,\beta}(\phi_1), \mathrm{val}_{S,\beta}(\phi_2)\}$$

$$\mathrm{val}_{S,\beta}(\neg\phi) = tt \quad \text{iff} \quad \mathrm{val}_{S,\beta}(\phi) = ff$$

$$\mathrm{val}_{S,\beta}(\forall x.\, \phi) = tt \quad \text{iff} \quad ff \notin \{\mathrm{val}_{S,\beta_x^a}(\phi) \mid a \in U\}$$

$$\mathrm{val}_{S,\beta}(\exists x.\, \phi) = tt \quad \text{iff} \quad tt \in \{\mathrm{val}_{S,\beta_x^a}(\phi) \mid a \in U\}$$

$$\mathrm{val}_{S,\beta}(t_1 \doteq t_2) = tt \quad \text{iff} \quad \mathrm{val}_{S,\beta}(t_1) = \mathrm{val}_{S,\beta}(t_2)$$

$$\mathrm{val}_{S,\beta}(t_1 \dot{<} t_2) = tt \quad \text{iff} \quad \mathrm{val}_{S,\beta}(t_1) < \mathrm{val}_{S,\beta}(t_2) \qquad (S = (U, <, I))$$

For updates:

$$\mathrm{val}_{S,\beta}(\mathbf{skip}) = \emptyset$$

$$\mathrm{val}_{S,\beta}(f(\bar{s}) := t) = \{\langle f, \mathrm{val}_{S,\beta}(\bar{s})\rangle \mapsto \mathrm{val}_{S,\beta}(t)\}$$

$$\mathrm{val}_{S,\beta}(u_1 \mid u_2) = \mathrm{val}_{S,\beta}(u_1) \oplus \mathrm{val}_{S,\beta}(u_2)$$

$$\mathrm{val}_{S,\beta}(\mathbf{if}\ \phi\ \{u\}) = \begin{cases} \mathrm{val}_{S,\beta}(u) & \text{for } \mathrm{val}_{S,\beta}(\phi) = tt \\ \emptyset & \text{otherwise} \end{cases}$$

$$\mathrm{val}_{S,\beta}(\mathbf{for}\ x\ \{u\}) = \bigcup\{A(a) \mid a \in U\}$$

where $A : U \rightarrow (Loc \nrightarrow U)$ is defined by well-founded recursion on $(U, <)$ and the equation $A(a) = \mathrm{val}_{S,\beta_x^a}(u) \oplus \bigcup\{A(b) \mid b \in U,\, b < a\}$

Application of updates: $(S' = S \oplus \mathrm{val}_{S,\beta}(u)$ and $\alpha \in Ter \cup For)$

$$\mathrm{val}_{S,\beta}(\{u\}\, \alpha) = \mathrm{val}_{S',\beta}(\alpha)$$

The most involved part of the update evaluation concerns quantified expressions for x $\{u\}$, whose value is defined by well-founded recursion on $(U, <)$. The definition shows that quantification is a generalisation of parallel composition: informally, for a well-ordered universe $U = \{a < b < c < \cdots\}$ we have

$$\text{val}_{S,\beta}(\text{for } x \ \{u\}) \ = \ \cdots \oplus \text{val}_{S,\beta_x^c}(u) \oplus \text{val}_{S,\beta_x^b}(u) \oplus \text{val}_{S,\beta_x^a}(u) \ .$$

For a general definition (see Table 1) of the partial interpretation on the right-hand side, we need a union operator on partial functions:[5]

$$\left(\bigcup M\right)(x) = \begin{cases} f(x) & \text{if there is } f \in M \text{ with } f(x) \neq \bot \\ \bot & \text{otherwise} \end{cases},$$

where we write $f(x) = \bot$ if a partial function f is not defined at point x.

Example 1. The following examples refer to the well-ordered algebra $(\mathbb{N}, <, I)$, where $<$ is the standard order on $\mathbb{N}$. We assume that the vocabulary contains literals and operations $+$, $\cdot$, and that these symbols are interpreted as usual for $\mathbb{N}$.

$$\text{val}_{S,\beta}(a := 2) \ = \ \{\langle a \rangle \mapsto 2\}$$

In parallel composition, the effect of the left update is invisible to the right one:

$$\text{val}_{S,\beta}(a := 2 \mid f(a) := 3) \ = \ \{\langle a \rangle \mapsto 2, \ \langle f, (\text{val}_{S,\beta}(a)) \rangle \mapsto 3\}$$

The right update in parallel composition overrides the left update when clashes occur. Here, this happens for $\text{val}_{S,\beta}(a) = 1$:

$$\text{val}_{S,\beta}(f(a) := 1 \mid f(1) := 2) \ = \ \{\langle f, (1) \rangle \mapsto 2\}$$

In contrast, for $\text{val}_{S,\beta}(a) \neq 1$ both assignments have an effect:

$$\text{val}_{S,\beta}(f(a) := 1 \mid f(1) := 2) \ = \ \{\langle f, (\text{val}_{S,\beta}(a)) \rangle \mapsto 1, \ \langle f, (1) \rangle \mapsto 2\}$$

Quantified updates make it possible to define whole functions:

$$\text{val}_{S,\beta}(\{\text{for } x \ \{f(x) := 2 \cdot x + 1\}\} \ f(5)) \ = \ 11$$

When clashes occur in quantified updates, smaller valuations of the quantified variable will dominate. The smallest individual of $(\mathbb{N}, <)$ is 0:

$$\text{val}_{S,\beta}(\text{for } x \ \{a := x\}) \ = \ \{\langle a \rangle \mapsto 0\}$$

Update constructors can be nested arbitrarily, like in quantified parallel updates:

$$\text{val}_{S,\beta}(\text{for } x \ \{(f(x+3) := x \mid f(2 \cdot x) := x + 1)\}) \ =$$

$$\{\langle f, (3) \rangle \mapsto 0, \langle f, (4) \rangle \mapsto 1, \langle f, (5) \rangle \mapsto 2, \cancel{\langle f, (6) \rangle \mapsto 3}, \langle f, (7) \rangle \mapsto 4, \ldots,$$
$$\langle f, (0) \rangle \mapsto 1, \langle f, (2) \rangle \mapsto 2, \cancel{\langle f, (4) \rangle \mapsto 3}, \langle f, (6) \rangle \mapsto 4, \langle f, (8) \rangle \mapsto 5, \ldots \ \}$$

In the last example, both kinds of clashes occur: (i) the pair $\langle f, (6) \rangle \mapsto 3$ stems from $f(x+3) := x$ and is overridden by $\langle f, (6) \rangle \mapsto 4$ (from $f(2 \cdot x) := x + 1$), because updates on the right side of parallel composition dominate updates on the left side ("last-win semantics"). (ii) the pair $\langle f, (4) \rangle \mapsto 3$ stems from the valuation $x \mapsto 2$ and is overridden by $\langle f, (4) \rangle \mapsto 1$ (from $x \mapsto 1$), because small valuations of variables dominate larger valuations ("well-ordered semantics").

---

[5] The operator $\bigcup$ is obviously not uniquely defined by the given equation, but because of $A(a) \subseteq A(b)$ for $a < b$ its result is unique when defining the evaluation function.

We formalise the behaviour of updates for the latter kind of clashes:

Lemma 1. *Small valuations of variables in updates override larger ones:*

$$\mathrm{val}_{S,\beta}(\text{for } x \; \{u\})(loc) \;=\; \mathrm{val}_{S,\beta_x^m}(u)(loc)$$

$$where \quad m = \begin{cases} \min_< A & for \; A \neq \emptyset \\ arbitrary & otherwise \end{cases} \quad and \quad A = \{a \mid \mathrm{val}_{S,\beta_x^a}(u)(loc) \neq \perp\}$$

We can now also introduce the equivalence symbol $\equiv$ used in Sect. 2:

Definition 6. *We call two terms, formulas or updates $\alpha_1, \alpha_2 \in Ter \cup For \cup Upd$ equivalent and write $\alpha_1 \equiv \alpha_2$ if they are necessarily evaluated to the same value: for all well-ordered algebras S and all variable assignments β over S,*

$$\mathrm{val}_{S,\beta}(\alpha_1) = \mathrm{val}_{S,\beta}(\alpha_2) \; .$$

$\equiv$ is a congruence relation for all constructors given in Def. 1 (see Lem. 2).

5 Application of Updates by Rewriting

Updates do in principle not increase the expressiveness of terms or formulas: given an arbitrary term, formula or update α, there will always be an equivalent expression $\alpha' \equiv \alpha$ that does not contain the update application operator.[6] We obtain this result by giving a rewriting system that eliminates updates using altogether 44 rules like $\{u\} (t_1 * t_2) \rightarrow \{u\} t_1 * \{u\} t_2$ (with $* \in \{\doteq, \dot<\}$). For the complete rewriting system, we have to refer to [3].

Syntactic application of updates to terms or formulas, i.e., simplification of expressions $\{u\} \alpha$, is carried out in two phases: first, the update is propagated to subterms or subformulas. In the second phase, when the update has reached a function application, it is analysed whether the update assigns the represented location. For achieving this separation, we need to introduce further operators and extend the syntax given Def. 1 as well as the semantics of Def. 5:

Definition 7. *We define the sets Ter_A, For_A and Upd_A of terms, formulas and updates as in Def. 1, but with further constructors ($x \in Var$ ranges over variables and $f \in \Sigma$ over functions):*

$$Ter_A ::= \cdots \mid \{x/ Ter_A\} \; Ter_A \mid \text{NON-REC}(Upd_A, f, (Ter_A, \ldots, Ter_A))$$
$$For_A ::= \cdots \mid \{x/ Ter_A\} \; For_A \mid \text{IN-DOM}(f, (Ter_A, \ldots, Ter_A), Upd_A)$$
$$Upd_A ::= \cdots \mid \{x/ Ter_A\} \; Upd_A \mid \text{REJECT}(Upd_A, \overline{Upd_A})$$

The constructors represent the explicit application of substitutions to terms, formulas, and to updates (like $\{x/s\} \; t$), the non-recursive application of an update u

---

[6] As we have not formally proven that our rewriting system that turns α into α' is terminating (but consider it as obvious), we do not state this as a theorem.

to function terms $f(\bar{t})$ (like NON-REC$(u, f, \bar{t})$), the test whether an update u assigns to the location denoted by $f(\bar{t})$ (like IN-DOM$(f, \bar{t}, u)$), and filtered updates REJECT$(u_1, \overline{u_2})$ (which are described in Sect. 9). We also extend the evaluation function val$_{S,\beta}$ on Ter_A, For_A and Upd_A by adding the following clauses:

$$\text{val}_{S,\beta}(\{x/s\}\,\alpha) = \text{val}_{S,\beta'}(\alpha)\,,$$

where $\beta' = \beta_x^{\text{val}_{S,\beta}(s)}$ and $\alpha \in Ter_A \cup For_A \cup Upd_A$,

$$\text{val}_{S,\beta}(\text{NON-REC}(u, f, \bar{t})) = I'\langle f, \text{val}_{S,\beta}(\bar{t})\rangle\,,$$

where $S = (U, <, I)$ and $I' = I \oplus \text{val}_{S,\beta}(u)$,

$$\text{val}_{S,\beta}(\text{IN-DOM}(f, \bar{t}, u)) = tt \quad \text{iff} \quad \text{val}_{S,\beta}(u)\langle f, \text{val}_{S,\beta}(\bar{t})\rangle \neq \bot$$

$$\text{val}_{S,\beta}(\text{REJECT}(u_1, \overline{u_2})) = \{(loc \mapsto a) \in \text{val}_{S,\beta}(u_1) \mid \text{val}_{S,\beta}(u_2)(loc) = \bot\}$$

The difference between non-recursive application NON-REC$(u, f, \bar{t})$ and ordinary application $\{u\}\, f(\bar{t})$ is that the subterms $\bar{t}$ are in the first case evaluated in the unmodified algebra, whereas in the latter case the algebra is first updated by u. Formally, we have $\{u\}\, f(\bar{t}) \equiv \text{NON-REC}(u, f, \{u\}\,\bar{t})$. The non-recursive operator enables us to separate the syntactic propagation of updates to subterms and subformulas from the syntactic evaluation of updates.

6   Sequentiality and Application of Updates to Updates

We extend the basic version of updates from Sect. 3 a second time and introduce sequential composition. Sequentiality already occurs when applications of updates are nested, for instance in an expression $\{u_1\}\,\{u_2\}\,\alpha$. It seems natural to make an operator for sequential composition compatible with the nesting of updates: $\{u_1\}\,\{u_2\}\,\alpha \equiv \{u_1\,;\,u_2\}\,\alpha$. Sequential composition of this kind can be reduced to parallel composition by extending the update application operator to updates themselves, i.e., by considering updates $\{u_1\}\,u_2$.

Definition 8. *We define the sets Ter_{AS}, For_{AS} and Upd_{AS} of terms, formulas and updates as in Def. 7, but with two further constructors:*

$$Upd_{AS} ::= \cdots \mid Upd_{AS}\,;\, Upd_{AS} \mid \{Upd_{AS}\}\, Upd_{AS}$$

Again, the evaluation function is extended to Ter_{AS}, For_{AS} and Upd_{AS} by adding two clauses (in both cases $S' = S \oplus \text{val}_{S,\beta}(u_1)$):

$$\text{val}_{S,\beta}(u_1\,;\,u_2) = \text{val}_{S,\beta}(u_1) \oplus \text{val}_{S',\beta}(u_2), \qquad \text{val}_{S,\beta}(\{u_1\}\,u_2) = \text{val}_{S',\beta}(u_2)$$

The second clause resembles the semantics of update application to terms and formulas. The first clause is very similar to the evaluation of parallel updates, with the only difference that the right update u_2 is evaluated in the structure S' updated by u_1. Intuitively, with parallel composition the effect of u_1 is invisible to u_2 (and vice versa), whereas sequential composition carries out u_1 before u_2. This directly leads to the equivalence $u_1\,;\,u_2 \equiv u_1 \mid \{u_1\}\,u_2$ that makes it possible to eliminate sequentiality (see [3]).

The relation $\equiv$ from Def. 6 can be extended to Ter_{AS}, For_{AS} and Upd_{AS}:

Lemma 2. *Equivalence $\equiv$ of terms, formulas and updates is a congruence relation for all constructors given in Def. 1, 7 and 8.*

Example 2. We continue Example 1 and assume the same vocabulary/algebra.

$$a := 1;\; f(a) := 2 \quad\equiv\quad a := 1 \mid f(1) := 2$$
$$\mathrm{val}_{S,\beta}(a := 1;\; f(a) := 2) \;=\; \{\langle a\rangle \mapsto 1,\; \langle f,(1)\rangle \mapsto 2\}$$
$$\mathrm{val}_{S,\beta}(a := 1;\; (a := 3 \mid f(a) := 2)) \;=\; \{\langle a\rangle \mapsto 3,\; \langle f,(1)\rangle \mapsto 2\}$$

7 Modelling Heap Structures

The memory of imperative and object-oriented programs can be modelled as a well-ordered algebra by choosing appropriate vocabularies Σ. By updating the values of function symbols, the memory contents can be modified symbolically. Compared to a more explicit encoding of program states as individuals (for instance, elements of a datatype), directly representing memory using a first-order vocabulary leads to very readable formulas that are in particular suited for interactive proof systems (see [3] for a more detailed discussion).

In the whole section, we assume that the universe for evaluating updates are the natural numbers $\mathbb{N}$, and that the standard well-ordering $<$ is used (as in Example 1). A more realistic application would, of course, require a typed logic and to model the datatypes of programming languages properly. For this section, it shall suffice to treat both data and addresses/pointers as natural numbers.

Variables: The simplest way to store data in programs is the usage of global variables, which can be seen as constants $g, h, i, \ldots \in \Sigma$ when representing program memory using well-ordered algebras $(\alpha(g) = \alpha(h) = \cdots = 0)$. Assignments are naturally performed through updates $g := t$. Expanding a sequential update into a parallel update yields a representation of the post-state by describing the post-values of all modified variables in terms of the pre-values:[7]

$$gswap \;=\; i := g;\; g := h;\; h := i \quad\equiv\quad g := h \mid h := g \mid i := g$$

Classes and Attributes: The individual objects of a class can be distinguished using addresses (natural numbers). Instance attributes of a class C are then unary functions $a_C, b_C \ldots \in \Sigma$ (with $\alpha(a_C) = \alpha(b_C) = \cdots = 1$) that take an address as argument. As an example, we consider again the class *List* representing doubly-linked lists from Sect. 2 (with attributes *next, prev, val* $\in \Sigma$). The following two updates describe the setup of singleton lists (that hold a value v) and the concatenation of two lists (where one list ends with the object e and the second one begins with the object b):

$$setup(o, v) \;=\; o.prev := nil \mid o.val := v \mid o.next := nil$$
$$cat(e, b) \;=\; e.next := b \mid b.prev := e$$

---

[7] We leave out parentheses because both parallel and sequential composition are associative, see (R52) and (R53) in Table 2.

(we assume that $nil \in \Sigma$ denotes invalid addresses and the beginning and end of lists). The update $init$ from Sect. 2 and a list containing the numbers $0, \ldots, n$ can then be set up as follows:

$$init \equiv setup(a, c)\,; \; setup(b, 2)\,; \; cat(a, b)\,; \; a.next.val := d$$

$$seq = \mathbf{for}\; x \;\{\mathbf{if}\; x \stackrel{.}{<} n + 1 \;\{setup(x, x)\}\}\,; \mathbf{for}\; x \;\{\mathbf{if}\; x \stackrel{.}{<} n \;\{cat(x, x + 1)\}\}$$

$$\equiv_{\mathbb{N}} \; 0.prev := nil \mid n.next := nil \mid \mathbf{for}\; x \;\{\mathbf{if}\; x \stackrel{.}{<} n + 1 \;\{x.val := x\}\} \mid$$

$$\mathbf{for}\; x \;\{\mathbf{if}\; x \stackrel{.}{<} n \;\{x.next := x + 1\}\} \mid$$

$$\mathbf{for}\; x \;\{\mathbf{if}\; x \stackrel{.}{<} n \;\{(x + 1).prev := x\}\}$$

Properties about the lists can be proven by applying the updates and performing first-order reasoning:

$$\forall x.\, (\neg x \stackrel{.}{<} n \vee \{seq\}\, x.next.prev \stackrel{.}{=} x) \quad \equiv_{\mathbb{N}} \quad \forall x.\, (\neg x \stackrel{.}{<} n \vee x \stackrel{.}{=} x) \quad \equiv \quad true$$

Object Allocation: Updates cannot add or remove individuals from a universe (*constant-domain semantics*). In modal logic, the usual way to simulate changing universes is to introduce a predicate that distinguishes between existing and non-existing individuals. Likewise, for our heap model "implicit" attributes $created_C$ can be defined that, for instance, have value 1 for existing and 0 for non-existing objects of a class C. An initial state in which no objects are allocated can be reached through the update $\mathbf{for}\; x \;\{x.created_C := 0\}$. We write an allocator for list nodes as follows:[8]

$$alloc(o, v) = o := \min i.\, (i.created_{List} \stackrel{.}{=} 0)\,; \; \big(o.created_{List} := 1 \mid setup(o, v)\big)$$

Note, that allocating objects in parallel using this method will produce clashes, because parallel updates cannot observe each other's effects. When running in parallel, $alloc(a, 1)$ and $alloc(b, 2)$ will deterministically allocate the same object:

$$alloc(a, 1) \mid alloc(b, 2) \quad \equiv \quad alloc(b, 2)\,; \; a := b \quad \not\equiv \quad alloc(a, 1)\,; \; alloc(b, 2)$$

Arrays: Arrays in a Java-like language behave much like objects of classes, with the difference that arrays provide numbered cells instead of attributes. We can model arrays be introducing a binary access function $ar \in \Sigma$ and a unary function $len \in \Sigma$ telling the length of arrays ($\alpha(ar) = 2$ and $\alpha(len) = 1$). Array allocation can be treated just like allocation of objects through an implicit attribute $created_{ar}$. Given this vocabulary, we can allocate an array of length n and fill it with numbers $0, \ldots, n - 1$: (we write $o[x]$ instead of $ar(o, x)$)

$$alloc_{ar}(o, n) = o := \min i.\, (i.created_{ar} \stackrel{.}{=} 0)\,; \; (o.created_{ar} := 1 \mid o.len := n)$$

$$seq_{ar} = alloc_{ar}(o, n)\,; \; \mathbf{for}\; x \;\{\mathbf{if}\; x \stackrel{.}{<} o.len \;\{o[x] := x\}\}.$$

---

[8] For practical purposes, it is reasonable to have more book-keeping about allocated objects than shown here. The approach that is followed in KeY is to introduce variables $nextToCreate_C$ and to allocate objects sequentially.

8   Symbolic Execution in Dynamic Logic Revisited

As shown in Sect. 2, during symbolic execution, updates can represent a certain prefix (or path) of a program, whereas the suffix that remains to be executed is given in the original language. In order to use updates for symbolic execution, first of all a suitable representation of the program states using a first-order vocabulary and algebras (along the lines of Sect. 7) has to be chosen. Rewriting rules then define the semantics of program features in terms of updates and of connectives of first-order logic. This approach has been used to implement symbolic execution for the "real-world" language JavaCard [8]. Examples for the rewriting rules are:[9]

$$\langle \, \rangle \, \phi \; \rightsquigarrow \; \phi, \qquad\qquad \langle \, s = t; \, \alpha \, \rangle \, \phi \; \rightsquigarrow \; \{ s := t \} \, \langle \, \alpha \, \rangle \, \phi$$
$$\langle \, \texttt{if} \, (b) \, \beta_1; \; \texttt{else} \, \beta_2; \, \alpha \, \rangle \, \phi \; \rightsquigarrow \; (b \wedge \langle \, \beta_1; \, \alpha \, \rangle \, \phi) \vee (\neg b \wedge \langle \, \beta_2; \, \alpha \, \rangle \, \phi)$$

It is important to note that updates are *not* intended as an intermediate representation for complete programs: the focus is on handling the sequential parts. For reasoning about general loops or recursion, techniques like induction or invariants are still necessary. It is, nevertheless, possible to translate certain loops directly to an update [9]. An example are many array operations in Java:[10]

$$\langle \, \texttt{System.arrayCopy}(ar_1, o_1, ar_2, o_2, n) \, \rangle \, \phi$$
$$\rightsquigarrow \; \{ \texttt{for} \; x \; \{ \texttt{if} \; \neg x \stackrel{<}{\scriptstyle\cdot} o_2 \wedge x \stackrel{<}{\scriptstyle\cdot} o_2 + n \; \{ ar_2[x] := ar_1[x - o_2 + o_1] \} \} \} \, \phi$$

Compared to a declarative specification of `arrayCopy` using a post-condition that contains a universally quantified formula, the imperative update can be applied to formulas or terms like a substitution. We consider updates as advantageous both for interactive and automated reasoning: the program structure is preserved, and unnecessary non-determinism in a derivation is avoided.

A characteristic of imperative programs is that memory locations can be assigned to/overwritten multiple times. After elimination of sequential composition, overwritten locations occur as clashes in updates. An example is the update *init* from Sect. 2 and 7, which contains potential clashes because of aliasing: for $a \stackrel{.}{=} b$, the expressions $a.val$ and $b.val$ denote the same location. Due to last-win semantics, it is not necessary to distinguish the possible cases when turning sequential composition into parallel composition. Only when applying the update, as in the expression co' in Sect. 2, the case $a \stackrel{.}{=} b$ has to be handled explicitly.

Well-ordered semantics enables an implicit handling of output dependencies in loops (different iterations assign to the same locations) in a similar way [9]. A simple example is: ($e(i)$ is a side-effect free, possibly non-injective expression)

$$\langle \, \texttt{while} \; (\neg i \stackrel{.}{=} 0) \; \{ i = i - 1; \; a[e(i)] = i; \} \, \rangle \, \phi$$
$$\rightsquigarrow \; \{ i := 0 \mid \texttt{for} \; x \; \{ \texttt{if} \; x \stackrel{<}{\scriptstyle\cdot} i \; \{ a[e(x)] := x \} \} \} \, \phi.$$

---

[9] s, t, b have to be free of side-effects. It general, it will also be necessary to define a translation of side-effect free program expressions into terms.

[10]   For sake of clarity, the example ignores the diverse errors that can occur when calling `arrayCopy`, for instance for $ar_1 \stackrel{.}{=} ar_2$.

Table 2. Laws for Commuting and Distributing Update Connectives

---

For $\alpha \in Ter_{AS} \cup For_{AS} \cup Upd_{AS}$:

$$\{u_1\} \{u_2\} \, \alpha \;\equiv\; \{u_1 \,;\, u_2\} \, \alpha \tag{R51}$$

$$u_1 \mid (u_2 \mid u_3) \;\equiv\; (u_1 \mid u_2) \mid u_3 \tag{R52}$$

$$u_1 \,;\, (u_2 \,;\, u_3) \;\equiv\; (u_1 \,;\, u_2) \,;\, u_3 \tag{R53}$$

$$u_1 \mid u_2 \;\equiv\; \text{REJECT}(u_1, \overline{u_2}) \mid u_2 \tag{R54}$$

$$u_1 \mid u_2 \;\equiv\; u_2 \mid \text{REJECT}(u_1, \overline{u_2}) \tag{R55}$$

$$u \;\equiv\; u \mid \text{if } \phi \, \{u\} \qquad (\phi \text{ arbitrary}) \tag{R56}$$

$$u_1 \;\equiv\; u_1 \mid \text{REJECT}(u_1, \overline{u_2}) \qquad (u_2 \text{ arbitrary}) \tag{R57}$$

$$\text{if } \phi \, \{u_1 \mid u_2\} \;\equiv\; \text{if } \phi \, \{u_1\} \mid \text{if } \phi \, \{u_2\} \tag{R58}$$

$$\text{if } \phi_1 \, \{\text{if } \phi_2 \, \{u\}\} \;\equiv\; \text{if } \phi_1 \wedge \phi_2 \, \{u\} \tag{R59}$$

$$\text{for } x \, \{\text{if } \phi \, \{u\}\} \;\equiv\; \text{if } \phi \, \{\text{for } x \, \{u\}\} \qquad (x \notin \text{fv}(\phi)) \tag{R60}$$

$$\text{for } x \, \{\text{if } \phi \, \{u\}\} \;\equiv\; \text{if } \exists x.\, \phi \, \{u\} \qquad (x \notin \text{fv}(u)) \tag{R61}$$

$$\text{for } x \, \{u_1 \mid u_2\} \;\equiv\; \text{for } x \, \{u_1\} \mid u_2 \qquad (x \notin \text{fv}(u_2)) \tag{R62}$$

For $u = \text{for } z \, \{\text{if } z \stackrel{\cdot}{<} x \, \{\{x/z\} \, u_1\}\}$ and $z \neq x$, $z \notin \text{fv}(u_1)$:

$$\text{for } x \, \{u_1\} \;\equiv\; \text{for } x \, \{\text{REJECT}(u_1, \overline{u})\} \tag{R63}$$

$$\text{for } x \, \{u_1 \mid u_2\} \;\equiv\; \text{for } x \, \{u_1\} \mid \text{for } x \, \{\text{REJECT}(u_2, \overline{u})\} \tag{R64}$$

For $u = \text{for } z \, \{\text{if } z \stackrel{\cdot}{<} x \, \{\{x/z\} \, \text{for } y \, \{u_1\}\}\}$ and $|\{x, y, z\}| = 3$, $z \notin \text{fv}(u_1)$:

$$\text{for } x \, \{\text{for } y \, \{u_1\}\} \;\equiv\; \text{for } y \, \{\text{for } x \, \{\text{REJECT}(u_1, \overline{u})\}\} \tag{R65}$$

---

9   Laws for Update Simplification

Sect. 7 demonstrates how updates can be simplified and written as parallel composition of assignments. More formally, we can extend Sect. 5 and state that, given an arbitrary update u, there will always be an equivalent update $u' \equiv u$ of the following shape: (in which ϕ_i, s_i, t_i do not contain further updates)

$$\begin{aligned}
&\text{for } x_{1,1} \, \{\text{for } x_{1,2} \, \{\text{for } \cdots \, \{\text{if } \phi_1 \, \{s_1 := t_1\}\}\}\} \\
&\mid \cdots \\
&\mid \text{for } x_{k,1} \, \{\text{for } x_{k,2} \, \{\text{for } \cdots \, \{\text{if } \phi_k \, \{s_k := t_k\}\}\}\}
\end{aligned} \tag{1}$$

It is usually advantageous to establish this shape: (i) Obvious clashes, like in the update $g := 1 \mid g := 2$, can easily be eliminated. (ii) The update can easily be read and directly tells about the values of variables or heap contents. (iii) When applying updates syntactically using the rewriting system of Sect. 5, this form is more efficient than most other shapes, because it supports the search for matching assignments. (iv) It is possible to define more specialised and efficient rewriting rules for update application (than the ones given in [3]). This has been done for the implementation of updates in KeY.

Table 2 gives, besides others, identities that enable to establish form (1) by turning sequential composition into parallel composition, distributing if and for through parallel composition and commuting if and for. In this table, we denote the set of free variables of an expression α with $\text{fv}(\alpha)$ (see, e.g., [5]). The soundness of all rules and identities, based on the semantics of Sect. 4, has been proven using the Isabelle/HOL proof assistant.

For formulating the transformation rules, we need a further operator from Def. 7: the expression $\text{REJECT}(u_1, \overline{u_2})$ denotes an update that carries out exactly those assignments of u_1 that do *not* define locations that are also assigned to by u_2. This enables us to make updates disjoint, i.e., to prevent updates from assigning to the same locations, which is often a premise for permuting updates. Disjointness is relevant for parallel composition (R55) and for quantification (R64), (R65), where permutation can change the order of assignments.

10 Related Work

A theory that is very similar to updates are abstract state machines (ASMs) [10]. While there are different versions of ASMs, all update constructors of this paper can in similar form also be found in [11]. The main difference is the notion of "consistent updates" that exists for ASMs and that demands clash-freeness. In contrast, the present paper describes a semantics in which clashes are resolved by a last-win strategy or a well-ordering strategy, which we consider as better suited for representing imperative programs.

Substitutions in B [12] have character similar to updates. Like ASMs, they are used for modelling systems and are a complete programming language that also provides loops and non-determinism. Updates are deliberately kept less expressive, focussing on automated simplification and application.

The guarded command language [13] is used as intermediate language in the verification systems ESC/Java2 and Boogie. In contrast to updates, guarded commands are used to represent *complete* object-oriented programs—which requires concepts like loops or non-determinism—and are eliminated using wp-calculus.

In the context of the KeY system, updates turn up in [8] for the first time, where the only update constructor are assignments. Parallel updates are described in [14,15] for the first time, and have the same last-win semantics as in this paper.

11 Conclusions and Future Work

The update language described in this paper has been implemented in the KeY prover. Quantified updates, added most recently, have mostly improved the ability of the prover to handle arrays, as operations like arrayCopy (Sect. 8) can now be specified and symbolically executed very efficiently. Compared to the rules in Sect. 5 and 9 (which are more general), KeY also contains further optimisations for applying updates that have been found to be important in practice.

In the future, an interesting step would be the combination of ordinary substitutions and updates. This would require developing a concept of bound renaming for updates. Another appealing improvement would be the possibility of non-deterministic updates, which would allow to handle object creation (or, generally, under-specification of language features) more naturally.

Acknowledgements

I want to thank Reiner Hähnle for bringing up the idea of extending the update language by adding quantification, as well as for discussions. I am also grateful for discussions and comments from Wolfgang Ahrendt, Richard Bubel, and Steffen Schlager, and for comments from the anonymous referees.

References

1. Harel, D., Kozen, D., Tiuryn, J.: Dynamic Logic. MIT Press (2000)
2. Ahrendt, W., Baar, T., Beckert, B., Bubel, R., Giese, M., Hähnle, R., Menzel, W., Mostowski, W., Roth, A., Schlager, S., Schmitt, P.H.: The KeY Tool. Software and System Modeling **4** (2005) 32–54
3. Rümmer, P.: Proving and disproving in dynamic logic for Java. Licentiate Thesis 2006–26L, Department of Computer Science and Engineering, Chalmers University of Technology, Göteborg, Sweden (2006)
4. Nipkow, T., Paulson, L.C., Wenzel, M.: Isabelle/HOL—A Proof Assistant for Higher-Order Logic. Volume 2283 of LNCS. Springer (2002)
5. Fitting, M.C.: First-Order Logic and Automated Theorem Proving. 2nd edn. Springer-Verlag, New York (1996)
6. Zermelo, E.: Beweis dass jede Menge wohlgeordnet werden kann. Mathematische Annalen **59** (1904) 514–516
7. Spivey, J.M.: The Z Notation: A Reference Manual. 2nd edn. Prentice Hall (1992)
8. Beckert, B.: A dynamic logic for the formal verification of JavaCard programs. In Attali, I., Jensen, T., eds.: Java on Smart Cards: Programming and Security. Revised Papers, Java Card 2000, International Workshop, Cannes, France. Volume 2041 of LNCS., Springer (2001) 6–24
9. Gedell, T., Hähnle, R.: Automating verification of loops by parallelization. In: Proceedings, 13th International Conference on Logic for Programming, Artificial Intelligence and Reasoning. LNAI, Springer (2006) To appear.
10. Gurevich, Y.: Evolving Algebras 1993: Lipari Guide. In Börger, E., ed.: Specification and Validation Methods. Oxford University Press (1995) 9–36
11. Stärk, R.F., Nanchen, S.: A logic for abstract state machines. Journal of Universal Computer Science **7** (2001) 981–1006
12. Abrial, J.R.: The B Book: Assigning Programs to Meanings. Cambridge University Press (1996)
13. Dijkstra, E.W.: A Discipline of Programming. Prentice-Hall (1976)
14. Platzer, A.: An object-oriented dynamic logic with updates. Master's thesis, University of Karlsruhe, Department of Computer Science. Institute for Logic, Complexity and Deduction Systems (2004)
15. Beckert, B., Platzer, A.: Dynamic logic with non-rigid functions: A basis for object-oriented program verification. In Furbach, U., Shankar, N., eds.: Proceedings, IJCAR, Seattle, USA. LNCS, Springer (2006) To appear.

Representing Defaults and Negative Information Without Negation-as-Failure

Pablo R. Fillottrani and Guillermo R. Simari

Department of Computer Science and Engineering
Universidad Nacional del Sur
Av. Alem 1253, 8000 Bahía Blanca, Argentina
{prf, grs}@cs.uns.edu.ar

Abstract. In logic programs, negation-as-failure has been used both for representing negative information and for providing default nonmonotonic inference. In this paper we argue that this twofold role is not only unnecessary for the expressiveness of the language, but it also plays against declarative programming, especially if further negation symbols such as strong negation are also available. We therefore propose a new logic programming approach in which negation and default inference are independent, orthogonal concepts. Semantical characterization of this approach is given in the style of answer sets, but other approaches are also possible. Finally, we compare them with the semantics for logic programs with two kinds of negation.

1 Introduction

The utility of a language as a tool for practical development of knowledge representation systems is grounded on a simple syntax with intuitive semantics, and efficient proof procedures. So, in order to keep a broad scope of users and applications, the language should be both powerful and simple at the same time. The absence of any of these conditions produces languages with theoretical interest, but difficult to use in real applications. We think the original success of Logic Programming was due to the fulfillment of these requirements, so any extension must also preserve them.

Despite its lack of declarative meaning in all programs, negation-as-failure partially satisfied these properties at the beginning. The semantics supported for stratified programs is intuitive and general enough for extended use. Semantics for nonmonotonic reasoning, such as the stable models or the well founded semantics, filled the gap and provided an elegant characterization valid for all programs. They also helped in understanding the close relationship between *"not"* and nonmonotonic reasoning formalisms, such as default logic, circumscription or autoepistemic logics. As soon as this relationship became clear, it was evident that negation-as-failure plays a dual rôle in the language of logic programs: it is both a negative connective, and a default, nonmonotonic rule of inference. As a negative connective, it represents negative information, and as a default rule of inference it allows to draw conclusions from the absence of

M. Hermann and A. Voronkov (Eds.): LPAR 2006, LNAI 4246, pp. 437–451, 2006.

facts. But the Negation-as-failure mechanism was shown to be inadequate for representing explicitly negative information [1,2,3,4]. Extended logic programs were introduced with the possibility of referring to another negation symbol "¬", called strong, explicit, or classical negation. Therefore, syntax and semantics of logic programs have been extended to reflect the distinction between asserting something false, and denying something true.

However, the presence of two negative symbols goes against the necessary simplicity for logic programming languages. When using negative information to infer new facts, it is necessary to evaluate if negation-as-failure or strong negation is the right choice. Moreover, most proposed semantics for extended programs do not relate both meanings, yielding two completely independent semantics for negative connectives.

In this paper we argue that in the presence of strong negation, negation-as-failure is no longer necessary for representing negative information. Consequently, negation-as-failure remains in logic programs only as a nonmonotonic inference rule, which is better referred to independently of the way negative and positive information is represented. Formalisms like default logic, circumscription, or autoepistemic logic can be taken as models in this sense. We propose a syntax of logic programs without negation-as-failure, but with strong negation and non-monotonic inference rules. The semantics associated with this approach is given in the style of answer set semantics, but other approaches such as well founded models are also possible.

The structure of the paper is as follows: in Section 2, we perform a more detailed analysis of the above mentioned problems, mostly attributable to the lack of distinction between negation and nonmonotonic inference in logic programs. In Section 3 we propose to extend the influence of nonmonotonic reasoning into logic programming, not only to provide a semantics for negation-as-failure, but also to induce a framework of logic programs where negation and default reasoning are independent concepts. In Section 4 we apply this approach to some examples and show some semantic properties. Finally, in Section 5 we compare it with known semantics for extended logic programs with two kinds of negation.

2   "*not*" Considered Harmful

We consider in this section the language of extended logic programs from the viewpoint of the requirements for useful knowledge representation tools, identifying some problems and analyzing their causes. In this sense, we will shortly review the concept of declarative language and show that negation-as-failure can be considered harmful for the declarativeness of logic programs, in a similar way Dijkstra [5] analyzed the GOTO statement in the context of structured programming.

Informally, a declarative programming language is one that specifies *what* is computed, instead of *how* it is done. Baral and Gelfond [6] consider McCarthy to be the first advocate for representing knowledge in a declarative way:

"... expressing information in declarative sentences is far more modular than expressing it in segments of computer programs or in tables. Sentences can be true in a much wider context than specific programs can be used. The supplier of a fact does not have to understand much about how the receiver functions or how or whether the receiver will use it. The same fact can be used for many purposes, because the logical consequences of collections of facts can be available."

In our view, the key point is to establish a clear distinction between the supplier of a fact, and its receiver or user. The receiver does not know how the fact is produced, nor does the supplier know how it is used.

In a logical system, this problem is translated into drawing the boundary between logic and control in Kowalski's [7] equation *algorithm = logic+control*. In this sense, John Lloyd [8] proposed that a program is declarative if it may be considered as a formal theory and its results may be obtained as deductions from the theory. This is a broad criterion that all formal systems satisfy as long as they specify a language and a proof theory. But the main advantage of declarativeness is being modular, *i.e.* allowing the theory to be composed with theories, possibly written by other programmers.

One way to achieve this goal in a programming language with a general scope is to define a syntax similar to natural discourse with semantics that coincides with common sense reasoning. Originally, logic programming fell short of this point because its syntax is simpler than that of full first order logic, and the meaning of definite rules is even clearer; furthermore, the efficiency of its proof methods provides an additional benefit. However, negation is necessary in a logic programming language. The question is whether logic programs with several kinds of negation still satisfy the requirements of declarativeness.

Let us then define the components of a formal theory from such logic programs. A *rule* is a clause of the form

$$L_0 \leftarrow L_1, \ldots, L_m, not\, L_{m+1}, \ldots, not\, L_n \tag{1}$$

where all $L_i, 0 \leq i \leq n$ are literals (ground atoms A, or strong negated atoms $\neg A$). A *logic program* is then a set of rules, and a *query* is a finite set of literals. It is clear that literals belong to the language of the formal theory, since they bear truth values and are deduced by the inference rules. Rules are generally not considered as members of the language. Thus, we consider rules of the form (1) as inference rules of the formal theory determined by a specific logic program.

Traditionally, these rules have been split into two parts: head and body. The head, literal L_0 in (1), is where the truth value of the literal is defined. The program containing a rule with a literal in its head may be regarded as the *supplier* of the fact, according to McCarthy's use of the word. On the other hand, in the body of the rule is where facts are *used*. We have not yet established which are the facts in this part since they depend on the interpretation of "*not*". However, since we want the language to be declarative, these facts must not express the way in which they are inferred. Note that a query is the other possible place where facts can be used.

The status of *"not"* is still to be determined. In principle, there are two possible alternatives. It is possible to consider rules where *"not"* appears as nonmonotonic inference rules, similar to the ones in default logic. By doing so, rules of the form (1) are read as "if $L_1, \ldots, L_m$ are true, and there is not enough evidence for $L_{m+1}, \ldots, L_n$, then L_0 is true". If this is the case, then the language only contains literals with explicit negation and *"not"* has nothing to do with negation. Moreover, *"not A"* and *"not ¬A"* do not have truth value; instead, they express conditions in the meta-language, and so should not be part of queries. Otherwise, *"not"* can be treated as a connective. Here, the language is formed by extended literals (literals, and applications of *"not"* to literals), queries may contain *"not"*, and rules of the form (1) are monotonic inference rules with the usual meaning "if $L_1, \ldots, not\, L_n$ are true then L_0 is true". Marc Denecker [9] made a similar critique of the semantics for negation-as-failure, based on the different epistemological interpretations that can be given to models, or in this case, answer sets.

Both alternatives are feasible. In fact, one of the first proposals for the semantics of logic programs with two kinds of negation has been proposed as a translation of the logic program into a default logic theory [10]. However, it is not possible to easily extend this translation to other semantics, and in order to be coherent with its use, a change in the syntax of *"not"* is necessary. General use suggests *"not A"* as being a negative fact, assigning the values true or false just as in any other formula in the language.

Even though "¬" and *"not"* are two connectives in the alphabet of the language, they are very special ones. The primitive function of a connective is to build a new formula from smaller ones. This syntactical view does not require a functional truth definition of the meaning of the new formula from the truth values of its components. Nevertheless, traditional connectives in propositional logics such as "∨", "∧", *etc.* do have clear truth tables. If a formal theory satisfies this property, then it is possible to replace one of the components in a formula by any other formula with the same truth value. However, this is not the case for the two negative connectives in logic programming; truth for negated literals are not a direct consequence of the truth of its components. Furthermore, in the case of "¬", most semantic characterizations only specify a sort of consistency condition when both "A" and "$¬A$" are provable.

Another problem is that these negative connectives cannot be nested, which is not actually a problem for "¬" since it is easy to change syntax and semantics of logic programs to allow nested explicit negation. However, *"not not A"* does not have a clear negative semantics, particularly a declarative one. An approach to assign semantic to these expressions is given in [11]. If we read *"not A"* as "A is not known" or "A is not believed", the problem does not appear. In fact, general usage of this connective suggests this interpretation as it follows from the example below [1].

Example 1. A college is awarding scholarships to its students. Examination scores are represented by predicates highGPA(·) and fairGPA(·), and selected(·) represents those who where chosen.

$$\text{selected}(X) \quad \leftarrow \text{highGPA}(X)$$
$$\text{selected}(X) \quad \leftarrow \text{minority}(X), \text{fairGPA}(X)$$
$$\neg\text{selected}(X) \leftarrow \neg\text{fairGPA}(X), \neg\text{highGPA}(X)$$
$$\text{interview}(X) \leftarrow not\ \text{selected}(X), not\ \neg\text{selected}(X)$$

The last rule in the program shows a body where an atom appears both negatively and positively. Indeed, if "*not*" represents negation, then the rule is meaningless.

The real semantics of these occurrences of "*not*" is "not known", as in Moore's autoepistemic modal operator [12]. The representation of negative information by "*not*" should avoid this confusion, even if it cannot be nested.

From the semantical point of view, another serious problem arises. Even when both are negative connectives, there is no connection between "$\neg$" and "*not*" in most semantics. The following examples show this fact. Example 2 presents an atom A such that in the well-founded semantics $\neg A$ is **true** and *not* A is **false**. Example 3 shows the opposite situation.

Example 2. The following program has no answer set, and its well-founded model is $\langle\{\neg p\}, \emptyset\rangle$.

$$p \leftarrow not\, p$$
$$\neg p \leftarrow$$

The well-founded semantics accepts $\neg p$ and sets *not* p as undefined. Technically, the set of consequences under the answer set semantics is the whole language.

Example 3. In this example, we will follow the definitions and notations in [13]. Suppose the language contains the constant 0 and the unary function symbol $s(\cdot)$ to represent all natural numbers. The logic program

$$\text{even}(0) \quad \leftarrow$$
$$\text{even}(s(X)) \leftarrow not\ \text{even}(X)$$

has a unique answer set $S = \{\text{even}(s^n(0)), \text{for all even } n\}$. Therefore, its well founded model is $\langle S, \mathcal{L}\backslash S\rangle$ implying that for example $\neg\text{even}(s(0))$ is false, as well as $\text{even}(s(0))$. This problem can be solved adding the rule

$$\neg\text{even}(X) \leftarrow not\ \text{even}(X)$$

but this is the programmer's choice. We consider that the semantics should solve this kind of problems for *all* programs, instead of trusting the programmer to include one additional rule for each predicate symbol in such conditions. Thus, the formalization of the semantics avoids the problem from the beginning.

In answer set semantics, the difference between "*not*" and "$\neg$" diminishes since it is a two-valued semantics. However, the different connectives are still there, and when applied to programs with "$\neg$" the semantics lack the necessary connection between them.

Even though there exists a close relationship between logic programming semantics and formalizations of nonmonotonic reasoning, in these systems the problem does not arise. Moreover, negation is represented by only one connective and is completely separated from the nonmonotonic rule of inference.

Example 4. We represent Example 3 in nonmonotonic formalisms. In default logic we need the following default rule D, along with theory $W = \{\text{even}(0)\}$,

$$\frac{: \neg\ \text{even}(x)}{\neg\text{even}(x) \wedge \text{even}(\text{s}(x))}$$

Then we can prove all intuitive positive and negative facts, like $\neg\text{even}(\text{s}(0))$ and $\text{even}(\text{s}(\text{s}(0)))$. Note that atoms, literals, and composed formulas can be obtained by default rules. In circumscription we can represent this problem by means of the theory $\{\text{even}(0), \forall x(\neg\text{even}(x) \supset \text{even}(\text{s}(x)))\}$ where predicate $\text{even}(\cdot)$ is minimized. Apart from the formal theory, circumscription needs to specify which circumscriptive policy is applied. However, the consequences are also formulas in the traditional logic language; there is no connective distinguishing between nonmonotonically and monotonically inferred formulas. Autoepistemic logic, as well as all nonmonotonic modal logics, has a belief modal connective "L". The formula "*not A*" in logic programming is associated with "$\neg LA$". In these systems, the problem of distinguishing between "$\neg A$" and "$\neg LA$" is also present. But here "LA" has an intended semantics of "A is known" or "A is believed" which makes the distinction between "A" and "LA".

These examples show that negative and positive information can be inferred monotonically or not, and a clear distinction is made between the nonmonotonic semantics and the contingently chosen syntactic representation of a piece of information.

Consider for instance an atom A in a logic program under the well-founded semantics. The syntax allows the four alternatives A, $\neg A$, $not\ A$, $not\ \neg A$, and since the semantics is three valued, nine truth value assignments are possible, which are indeed too many cases for easy understanding. Notice the paradox that an inconsistent program, represented by both A and $\neg A$ being true, has $not\ A$ and $not\ \neg A$ as false formulas. In particular, if a programmer is trying to use a positive occurrence of the atom, he/she will need to decide which of A, $not\ \neg A$ or $A \wedge not\ \neg A$ is adequate.

Alferes and Pereira [14] suggested that all semantic formalization should satisfy the following *coherence principle*: " if $\neg A$ belongs to the semantics of a program then $not\ A$ must also belong to the same semantics". Obviously, the well-founded semantics does not observe this principle, and they proposed a variant that complies with it. Even though this principle improves the situation, both connectives are still present in this class of programs. We think this dual representation of negation is the original problem. The *not* is a syntactical device used to refer to the inference rule used to prove the literal. This procedural meaning was the reason for the difficulty in finding its declarative counterpart.

3   Logic Programs with Default Policies

Circumscription is a general term that designates a whole family of nonmonotonic reasoning formalisms which have the minimization of a semantic concept as a distinctive feature (see Lifschitz [15] for a review). Nonmonotonicity in these logics originates from the fact that minimization is always done when it is consistent to do so. Therefore, new facts may block the assumption of previously accepted conclusions. Each theory in these logics is specified by a collection of first order formulas together with a particular *circumscriptive policy*, a set of rules defining the way in which minimization must be applied. A second order logic formula is constructed from these two elements, which determines the semantics of the theory.

In the logic programming language that is defined in this section we introduce, within logic programs, features of two special circumscriptive logics: pointwise circumscription [16] and circumscriptive theories [17]. In pointwise circumscription, minimization is taken to be at the level of ground atoms, rather than at the level of predicates or formulas as it is in the general case. Circumscriptive theories are characterized by the insertion of a circumscriptive policy within the same language of the theory. These two features are incorporated into the definition of *logic programs with default policies*.

Due to the fact that the syntax of these programs should include the circumscriptive policy, one or more second order predicates must be present in the alphabet.

Definition 1. *Let $\sigma = \langle \mathcal{V}, Func, Pred, Pred2 \rangle$ be a signature (set of variable, function, first order predicate, and second order predicate symbols respectively). The set $\mathbf{Lit}(\sigma)$ of all its literals is called a* circumscriptive language *if $Pred2 = \{\mathtt{def}\}$. A circumscriptive language will be noted by $\mathbf{Lit}_{CIRC}(\sigma)$.*

Then a circumscriptive language is just an ordinary language for logic programs, except for the fact that it includes a special "second order" predicate $\mathtt{def}(\cdot)$. This predicate will be used in the definition of minimization policies among atoms, which in turn will be interpreted by the semantics to implement default reasoning. The circumscriptive policy, *i.e.* the set of all atoms containing predicate $\mathtt{def}(\cdot)$, may be considered the extension of a classic second order predicate. However, since there is no quantifier and the semantics will interpret variables as shorthand for subsumed rules, then the language is not as expressive as (and does not have the computational problems of) second order logic.

Logic programs with circumscriptive policies are then basic programs (monotonic programs with strong negation [13]) using a circumscriptive language.

Definition 2. *Let $\mathbf{Lit}_{CIRC}(\sigma)$ be a circumscriptive language. A logic program with default policy (**lpdp**) is a set of basic rules in $\mathbf{Lit}_{CIRC}(\sigma)$.*

Note that the only requirement for these programs is that some of the literals might refer to predicate $\mathtt{def}(\cdot)$. In the same way, the syntax of circumscriptive theories [17] is the same as that of first order logic. Every basic program Π can be considered as an **lpdp** taking its signature σ without second order predicates, and extending it by including $\texttt{def}(\cdot)$ in a signature σ'. Therefore, when referring to a **lpdp** we assume the language and signature are those implicitly determined by the program.

The semantics of an **lpdp** will minimize those ground literals $\bar{L}$ such that $\texttt{def}(L)$ is a consequence in the program. Truth minimization implies that literal L will be assumed by default whenever it is consistent to do so. It will be the only nonmonotonic rule of inference in the program, and it can be applied to positive or negative literals.

For the formal characterization, we need to introduce the concept of the set of default literals for a program with respect to a given answer set. Recall that $\mathbf{Cn}(\Pi)$ is the set of (monotonic) consequences of Π, $i.e.$ the minimal set closed both logically and under the rules of the program.

Definition 3. *Let Π be an **lpdp**, and C a set of literals in its language. The set of default literals of Π with respect to C is the set*

$$\text{Def}_{\Pi}(C) := \{L : \texttt{def}(L) \in \mathbf{Cn}(\Pi) \wedge \bar{L} \notin C\} \tag{2}$$

C is called the consistency basis *of $\text{Def}_{\Pi}(C)$. The* minimization policy *of Π is the set of atoms in $\mathbf{Cn}(\Pi)$ with predicate $\texttt{def}(\cdot)$.*

This means that L is a default literal if $\texttt{def}(L)$ belongs to $\mathbf{Cn}(\Pi)$, and $\bar{L}$ does not belong to C. Then, the set of default literals depends on the minimization policy of the program, and a given consistency basis. From the semantic point of view, this set is important because it contains all literals that are assumed to be true by default. Traditional rules determine monotonic inferences; circumscriptive policies and the consistency basis determine nonmonotonic ones.

We will now introduce the answer set semantics for a **lpdp**. The answer sets definition for extended logic programs [13] constitutes an extension of the stable model semantics [18] definition only for negation as failure. The idea is that, for a set of literals (or only atoms in the original case) to be the consequences of a program, it is necessary to satisfy all negation as failure occurrences in it. However, every literal in the set must have some justification for being in it. In other words, the set should satisfy at the same time a *completeness* property, $i.e.$ it should contain all the rules' consequences, and a *soundness* property, $i.e.$ no other literal should be contained. The negation-as-failure characteristics make these conditions mutually dependent. Technically, this is solved by means of an equation: the sets that satisfy the equation are answer sets of the **lpdp**, or stable models of the extended logic program.

Definition 4. *Let Π an **lpdp**, and S a set of literals in its language. S is called an* answer set *of Π if it satisfies*

$$S = \mathbf{Cn}(\Pi \cup \text{Def}_{\Pi \cup S}(S)) \tag{3}$$

Equation 3 assures that if S is an answer set then the default literals generated by S, with consistency basis S, have as consequence in Π the same set S. The answer set thus provides a certain "stability" to the program since it generates each of its members, and contains all of the generated elements. The difference with the equation for extended programs is that the extended literals are interpreted through the reduct of a program. On the other hand, in equation (3) default literals are generated outside the traditional rules in program Π, and then incorporated as facts in order to obtain the consequences of the program. The program reduct disappears as default literals are introduced.

Example 5. Let Π be the following **lpdp**

1. $\mathtt{def}(\neg\mathtt{p}) \leftarrow$
2. $\mathtt{def}(\mathtt{q}) \quad\leftarrow$
3. $\mathtt{p} \qquad\quad \leftarrow \mathtt{q}$

We can see $\mathrm{Def}_\Pi(\{\}) = \{\neg\mathtt{p}, \mathtt{q}\}$, and $\mathrm{Def}_{\Pi\cup\{\neg\mathtt{p},\mathtt{q}\}}(\{\neg\mathtt{p}, \mathtt{q}\}) = \{\neg\mathtt{p}, \mathtt{q}\}$, but this is not an answer set for Π because $\mathbf{Cn}(\Pi \cup \{\neg\mathtt{p}, \mathtt{q}\})$ is the whole set of literals in the language. If we consider $\{\mathtt{p}, \mathtt{q}\}$, then $\mathrm{Def}_{\Pi\cup\{\mathtt{p},\mathtt{q}\}}(\{\mathtt{p}, \mathtt{q}\}) = \{\mathtt{q}\}$, and $\mathbf{Cn}(\Pi \cup \{\mathtt{p}, \mathtt{q}\}) = \{\mathtt{p}, \mathtt{q}\}$ so this set is an answer set for Π. Considering $\{\neg\mathtt{p}\}$ we have that $\mathrm{Def}_{\Pi\cup\{\neg\mathtt{p}\}}(\{\neg\mathtt{p}\}) = \{\neg\mathtt{p}, \mathtt{q}\}$ and $\mathbf{Cn}(\Pi \cup \{\neg\mathtt{p}, \mathtt{q}\})$ is again the whole set of literals, so $\{\neg\mathtt{p}\}$ is not an answer set for Π.

In a similar manner, it is possible to introduce the well founded model semantics for **lpdp**'s or to include rules in the style of Default Logic instead of the circumscriptive logic [19]. In the next section we present several examples for **lpdp**'s, and we discuss some properties of this semantics.

4   Properties and Examples

We will show an example in which positive and negative default conclusions are possible. This emphasizes the symmetry of our approach with respect to positive and negative data, in contrast to the standard attachment of a "negative" context to negation-as-failure.

Example 6. Suppose we know that every train T is passing through some stations, but we do not know in advance in which of these stations it stops. When the train is announced, information about the stops is given in the shortest possible way. If the train stops in many stations, only information for non-stopping stations is given. If the train stops in a small number of stations, only information for stopping stations is given. The following program formalizes the complete reasoning about stopping and non-stopping stations for a train in this line, beginning with the information given in an announcement.

1. $\mathtt{line\_station}(T, \mathtt{lavis}) \qquad\quad \leftarrow \mathtt{train}(T)$
2. $\mathtt{line\_station}(T, \mathtt{mezzocorona}) \leftarrow \mathtt{train}(T)$
3. $\mathtt{line\_station}(T, \mathtt{salorno}) \qquad \leftarrow \mathtt{train}(T)$
4. $\mathtt{line\_station}(T, \mathtt{egna}) \qquad\quad \leftarrow \mathtt{train}(T)$
5. $\mathtt{def}(\neg\mathtt{stops}(T, X)) \qquad\qquad \leftarrow \mathtt{line\_station}(T, X), \mathtt{stops}(T, Y)$
6. $\mathtt{def}(\mathtt{stops}(T, X)) \qquad\qquad\quad \leftarrow \mathtt{line\_station}(T, X), \neg\mathtt{stops}(T, Y)$

The first four rules define the stations in the line, and the last two formalize the default reasoning. For instance, rule 5 says that if we know that the train stops in some station, then it will be assumed by default that the train does not stop in others. Note that this default is not applied if the conclusion is contradictory with some already known fact; therefore, it is not necessary to include conditions such as $X \neq Y$ in the body of these rules. If the announcement is

$$\texttt{train(r123)}, \texttt{stops(r123, mezzocorona)}$$

then there is only one answer set of the above program together with these facts which contains the following extension of the $\texttt{stop}(\cdot, \cdot)$ predicate

$$\{\texttt{stop(r123, mezzocorona)}, \neg\texttt{stop(r123, lavis)},$$
$$\neg\texttt{stop(r123, salorno)}, \neg\texttt{stops(r123, egna)}\}$$

For a new announcement

$$\texttt{train(r124)}, \neg\texttt{stops(r123, lavis)}$$

then the answer set contains

$$\{\texttt{stop(r124, mezzocorona)}, \neg\texttt{stop(r124, lavis)},$$
$$\texttt{stop(r124, salorno)}, \texttt{stops(r124, egna)}\}$$

In case we only know that $\texttt{train(r125)}$, then no positive nor negative information about stops is inferred from the program.

The same kind of problems represented in extended logic programs need several combinations of "not" and "$\neg$" in the bodies of the rules. This fact affects the objectives mentioned in Section 2, and obviously make the understanding of such programs more difficult.

In order to formalize this reasoning, let S be an answer set for an **lpdp** P. Let us call a literal L *supported* in S for Π iff there is some rule in Π with L in the head, and a body included in S; a literal L is a *default* literal in S for Π if $\texttt{def}(L)$ is supported, and $\bar{L} \notin S$. Intuitively, a supported literal can exhibit some justification to be included in the semantics. Then the following result can be proved.

Proposition 1. *Let Π be an* **lpdp** *with a consistent answer set S. Then, for every literal $L \in S$ either L or $\texttt{def}(L)$ is supported in S for Π*

It is not possible for a similar property to hold for extended logic programs. There is no rule in an extended program for justifying extended literals of the form $not\,L$. Therefore, not only are these literals unsupported, but the rules that use these literals in their body cannot justify their conclusions. In fact, these definitions can be used to characterize answer sets for **lpdp**'s.

Proposition 2. *Let Π be an* **lpdp** *with a consistent answer set S. Then, $S = \{L : L$ is supported or L is default in S for $\Pi\}$*

Naturally enough, several other properties of the answer set semantics for extended logic programs also hold for answer sets in **lpdp**'s. For example, there are **lpdp**'s with no, one, and several answer sets.

In view of the diversity of semantics for negation-as-failure in logic programs, Dix [20,21] proposed a method for classifying and characterizing them. Inspired in similar work in nonmonotonic reasoning [22], he introduced a nonmonotonic entailment relation for normal logic programs and studied its properties under each of the semantics. These principles are classified into two types: *strong properties* are adaptations of those from nonmonotonic reasoning and belief dynamics, such as cumulativity, rationality, cut, and cautious monotony; *weak properties* reflect the specific idea of negation-as-failure in logic programming. The answer set semantics for extended programs does not satisfy most strong properties like cumulativity or rationality, and the same holds for the given semantics for **lpdp**'s. In fact, this allows us to give the name of "answer set" to this semantics. However, there are some weak properties like *reduction* that do not hold for **lpdp**'s even if they are satisfied in extended programs. Reduction removes those literals that are facts in the program from the bodies of all other rules. The idea is to interpret those literals as `true`, and simplifying the rules that refer to them. In the original version [21] for normal logic programs, reduction has two effects: one for positive literals, and the other for negative literals. Positive literals are considered as true with the explained meaning, but negative literals in these programs are interpreted with negation-as-failure semantics. So the effect of reducing a program by a negative literal is to consider the complementary literal as false, and eliminating from the program all rules that have the complement in the head. This is no longer adequate for **lpdp**'s, because negative literals can also be in the head of basic rules, and non-monotonic inference can also be applied to positive literals. In short, we can say **lpdp**'s do not satisfy reduction because negation is no longer the result of only nonmonotonic inferences.

5   Comparison with Related Work

As it was mentioned in the introduction, negation-as-failure preceded explicit negation in its incorporation into a logic programming framework. The first proposals that included the possibility to express both types of negation [10,1,3] did so under the semantics of the stable models. As it was shown in several examples, this semantics has the property of preferring those models that are "as much two-valued as possible". In other words, it maximizes the truth value of literals, according to the ordering $\leq_k$. Therefore, the non orthogonal problems are reduced, since it is often the case that when $\neg L$ belongs to the semantics so does $not\,L$.

On the other hand, the well founded model semantics only assigns a truth value of true or false to a literal if it is safe to do so in every situation. The fact that a default literal is consistent with the set of consequences is not enough justification to include it. When explicit negation was added to this framework [23,24], the lack of semantic connection between $\neg L$ and $not\,L$ was worsened. Literals can be negated in one way or the other, but both negations are completely independent, as it is shown in the following example.

Example 7. Consider the following extended program

1. a ← *not* b
2. b ← *not* a
3. ¬a ←

The well founded model of this program is the set $\{\neg a, not \neg b\}$, where a and b have undefined truth value. In spite of the fact that ¬a is true, *not* a is undefined and this does not allow the application of rule 2. In this case strong negation is not "strong" enough to generate weak negation as failure. Note that the program has only one stable model, $S_1 = \{\neg a, b\}$, so both credulous and sceptic semantics coincide. In this case the relation between ¬a and *not* a is forced by the inconsistent assumption. In this way, however, the semantics assigns a preference of rule 2 over rule 1.

In view of these facts, Alferes and Pereira [25,14] presented a new version of the well founded model semantics, called WFSX, such that the coherence principle (see section 2) is enforced. In order to simplify the presentation, we will not discuss here the precise definitions for the construction of the model according to WFSX. It is based on the traditional well founded model ($\gamma_\Pi(\cdot)$ operator); then, those literals that are necessary for the satisfaction of the coherence principle are added, a new closure is calculate, and a fixpoint of the resulting operator is obtained. The following program shows the result of this semantics.

Example 8. Let Π be the extended program from example 7. Then the set $\{\neg a, b, not\, a, not \neg b\}$ is the set of consequences in the WFSX semantics.

The WFSX semantics, as it is shown in the previous example, considers *"not"* as a connective in the language. Therefore it has an extensional meaning, at the same level as "¬". Besides, WFSX has two fundamental characteristics that distinguish it from most of the other semantics for programs with two types of negation.

- Symmetry in the treatment of positive and negative literals. The fact that a literal is positive or negative doesn't have an impact on the set of consequences of a semantics, and therefore on the truth value assigned. Many times the sign of a literal depends on the election of the name for the predicate, such as for example $guilty(X)$ or $\neg innocent(X)$. In consequence, the programmers will to use one or another version makes a difference in most semantics [3]. The WFSX semantics amends these characteristics if we do not distinguish both types of negations.
- Existence of a semantic connection between the two negative connectives. It solves the problems of Section 2 concerning the negative relationship. Thus it allows to combine both connectives, and the use of negative connectives can be simplified.

The WFSX semantics provides a solution to the problem of semantic connection between negative connectives. However, this formalism doesn't solve other problems, like the non-homogeneous syntax and the poor adaptability to changes in the program. We consider all these problems related by the same cause: the bond of non-monotonic inference and a negative connective. The WFSX semantics does not break this bond. Instead, it attacks one of its effects. The relationship between the WFSX semantics and **lpdp**'s is that both have a similar motivation. The proposal of Alferes and Pereira redefines the well founded process to include those consequences that were intuitively missing. On the other hand, **lpdp** tries to maintain the well known inferences of answer sets and well founded models, but makes a complete revision of the representation of the information and the inference rules in a program. The idea behind this proposal is that both the answer set and the well founded model semantics are sufficiently expressive mechanisms to represent most of the practical problems in which you expect to apply a logic programming system. Therefore, instead of changing the inference methods, it was preferred to change the programming style to separate negation from nonmonotonic inference. This decision not only permits to solve the problem of the semantic connection, but it also establishes a more elegant syntax and allows the resulting logic programs to have more extendibility and composition properties, as it was shown in the previous section.

In **lpdp**'s the use of non-monotonic inference is protected by the language: once it is applied, no clues are left to indicate its application. The representation of information is transparent to the inference procedure. Since the underlying programs in the WFSX semantics are still extended programs, every reference to "*not*" has the modal flavor that makes it incompatible with negation. Further references to explicit negation might not be in concordance with this style. When negation is independent of the inference rules, combinations, extensions, and restrictions of the original program can be more declaratively specified.

Now we briefly compare with other related works. Wagner's proposal for two negations [4,26] is in the same line as the WFSX semantics. It presents a semantics of logical programs with two negative connectives, "$\sim$" and "$-$" which are semantically related. However, both semantic characterizations differ from negation-as-failure. Besides, the connection is carried out at the level of predicates, *e.g.*, all the atoms that contain a predicate father are such that the negation $\sim$ father(X, Y) implies $-$father(X, Y), a kind of selective coherence principle in the sense of WFSX. For **lpdp**'s, the only negation connective can be inferred by monotonic or non-monotonic inference rules, and this fact is not carried out in the representation. In these programs, it is also possible to make nonmonotonic inference only for certain ground atoms (def(father(charles, susan))), instead of applying it to the whole extension of the predicate. On the other hand, Poole proposes in [27] Theorist, a practical implementation of a diagnosis system based on the PROLOG language. It uses a syntax of logic programming such that it incorporates a kind of default rule as an additional type of inference rule. The syntax of these rules is similar that of default rules, but the semantics is different. The nonmonotonic inference is carried out by means of abduction, that is, trying to generate explanations for a given atom. There is no connection in the system among the abducible literals and the possible references to explicit negation. Yann Loyer and Umberto

Straccia presented in [28] the Any-World Assumption, which allows to assign default interpretations for atoms over any truth space that is a bilattice. A default truth value is defined, and then when an atom cannot be assigned a truth value following the rules of the programs, the default truth value is applied. The main difference with our approach is that this default policy if fixed for all atoms.

6   Conclusions

In this paper we presented some problems in the integration of negation-as-failure and strong negation into logic programs. Their origin is the fact that negation-as-failure is both a negative symbol and a nonmonotonic inference rule. We proposed an approach where negation-as-failure is not present in the language, and nonmonotonicity is introduced in the form of default policies. Then, we showed that it is possible to recast the answer set semantics and recover similar properties that hold for extended programs. We conclude that negation-as-failure is not necessary for the semantics of logic programming, or answer set programming. Furthermore, since it also makes the understanding of extended programs more difficult because of the presence of two negation symbols without semantic connection, it is preferable to remove it. In this way, we are encouraging simplicity while maintaining the expressiveness of the language.

References

1. Gelfond, M., Lifschitz, V.: Logic programs with classical negation. In Warren, D.H.D., Szeredi, P., eds.: Proceedings of the 7th. International Logic Programming Conference, Jerusalem, Israel, MIT Press (1990) 579–597
2. Pearce, D.: Reasoning with negative information II: hard negation, strong negation and logic programs. In Pearce, D., Wansing, H., eds.: Nonclassical logics and information processing. Number 619 in Lecture Notes in Computer Science. Springer Verlag (1992) 63–79
3. Kowalski, R.A., Sadri, F.: Logic programs with exceptions. In Warren, D.H.D., Szeredi, P., eds.: Proceedings of the 7th. International Logic Programming Conference, Jerusalem, Israel, MIT Press (1990) 398–613
4. Wagner, G.: Vivid logic: knowledge based reasoning with two kinds of negation. Number 764 in Lecture Notes in Computer Science. Springer Verlag (1994)
5. Dijkstra, E.W.: GOTO statement considered harmful. Communications of the ACM 11 (1968) 147–148
6. Baral, C., Gelfond, M.: Logic programming and knowledge representation. Journal of Logic Programming 19 (1994) 73–148
7. Kowalski, R.A.: Predicate logic as a programming language. In Rosenfeld, J.L., ed.: Proceedings of the IFIP Congress 74, Stockholm, Sweden, North Holland (1974) 569–574
8. Lloyd, J.W.: Practical advantages of declarative programming. In: Proceedings of the 1994 Joint Conference on Declarative Programming, GULP-PRODE'94, Springer Verlag (1994)
9. Denecker, M.: What's in a model? epistemological analysis of logic programming. In Dubois, D., Welty, C.A., Williams, M.A., eds.: KR, AAAI Press (2004) 106–113

10. Gelfond, M., Lifschitz, V.: Classical negation in logic programming and disjunctive databases. New Generation Computing **9** (1991) 365–385
11. Lifschitz, V., Tang, L.R., Turner, H.: Nested expressions in logic programs. Annals of Mathematics and Artificial Intelligence **25** (1999) 369–389
12. Moore, R.C.: Semantical considerations on nonmonotonic logic. Artificial Intelligence **25** (1985) 75–94
13. Lifschitz, V.: Foundations of logic programs. In Brewka, G., ed.: Principles of knowledge representation. Studies in Logic, Language and Information. Cambridge University Press (1996) 69–127
14. Alferes, J.J., Pereira, L.M.: Reasoning with logic programming. Volume 1111 of Lecture Notes in Computer Science. Springer Verlag (1996)
15. Lifschitz, V.: Circumscription. In Gabbay, D.M., Hogger, C.J., Robinson, J.A., eds.: Handbook of logic in artificial intelligence and logic programming. Volume 3. Oxford University Press (1994) 297–352
16. Lifschitz, V.: Pointwise circumscription. In Ginsberg, M.L., ed.: Readings in nonmonotonic reasoning. Morgan Kaufmann Publishers (1987) 179–193
17. Lifschitz, V.: Circumscriptive theories: a logic-based framework for knowledge representation. In Thomason, R.H., ed.: Philosophical logic and artificial intelligence. Kluwer Academic Publishers (1989) 109–159
18. Gelfond, M., Lifschitz, V.: The stable model semantics for logic programming. In Kowalski, R.A., Bowen, K.A., eds.: Proceedings of the 5th. International Logic Programming Conference, Seattle, Washington, MIT Press (1988)
19. Fillottrani, P.R.: Sobre la negación y la inferencia no monótona en la programación en lógica. In: Proceedings CACIC'00, Sexto Congreso Argentino de Ciencias de la Computación. (2000) 489–500
20. Dix, J.: Semantics of logic programs: their intuitions and formal properties. In Fuhrmann, A., Rott, H., eds.: Logic, action and information. de Gruyter, Berlín–New York (1994) 227–313
21. Brewka, G., Dix, J., Konolige, K.: Nonmonotonic reasoning: an overview. Number 73 in Lecture Notes. CSLI Publications (1997)
22. Kraus, S., Lehmann, D., Magidor, M.: Nonmonotonic reasoning, preferential models and cumulative logics. Artificial Intelligence **44** (1990) 167–207
23. Dung, P.M., Ruamviboonsuk, P.: Well-founded reasoning with classical negation. In Nerode, A., Marek, V.W., Subrahmanian, V.S., eds.: Proceedings of the 1st. International Workshop on Logic Programming and Nonmonotonic Reasoning, Washington, DC, MIT Press (1991) 120–132
24. Przymusinski, T.C.: Extended stable semantics for normal and disjunctive logic programs. In Warren, D.H.D., Szeredi, P., eds.: Proc. of the 7th. International Logic Programming Conference, Jerusalem, Israel, MIT Press (1990) 459–477
25. Alferes, J.J., Pereira, L.M.: On logic program semantics with two kinds of negation. In Apt, K.R., ed.: Proceedings of the 1992 Joint International Conference and Symposium on Logic Programming, Washington, DC, MIT Press (1992) 574–588
26. Wagner, G.: Vivid reasoning with negative information. In van der Hoek, W., Meyer, J.J.C., Tan, Y.H., Witteveen, C., eds.: Nonmonotonic reasoning and partial semantics. Ellis Horwood (1992) 181–205
27. Poole, D., Goebel, R., Aleliunas, R.: Theorist: a logical reasoning system for defaults and diagnosis. In Cercone, N., McCalla, G., eds.: The knowledge frontier: essays in the representation of knowledge. Springer Verlag (1987) 331–352
28. Loyer, Y., Straccia, U.: Any-world assumptions in logic programming. Theor. Comput. Sci. **342** (2005) 351–381

Constructing Camin-Sokal Phylogenies Via Answer Set Programming

Jonathan Kavanagh, David Mitchell, Eugenia Ternovska, Ján Maňuch,
Xiaohong Zhao, and Arvind Gupta

Simon Fraser University, Burnaby, B.C. V5A 1S6, Canada
{jkavanag, mitchell, ter, jmanuch, xzhao2, arvind}@cs.sfu.ca

Abstract. Constructing parsimonious phylogenetic trees from species data is a
central problem in phylogenetics, and has diverse applications, even outside biology. Many variations of the problem, including the cladistic Camin-Sokal (CCS)
version, are NP-complete. We present Answer Set Programming (ASP) models
for the binary CCS problem, as well as a simpler perfect phylogeny version, along
with experimental results of applying the models to biological data. Our contribution is three-fold. First, we solve phylogeny problems which have not previously
been tackled by ASP. Second, we report on variants of our CCS model which significantly affect run time, including the interesting case of making the program
"slightly tighter". This version exhibits some of the best performance, in contrast
with a tight version of the model which exhibited poor performance. Third, we
are able to find proven-optimal solutions for larger instances of the CCS problem
than the widely used branch-and-bound-based PHYLIP package.

Keywords: phylogeny, maximum parsimony, Camin-Sokal, answer set
programming.

1 Introduction

Phylogenetics is the taxonomical classification of organisms based on their evolutionary
distance. The central problem is that of constructing phylogenies (evolutionary trees)
which postulate the most likely evolution of a set of extant species. This problem, and
its variations, are widely applicable. For example, they play an important role in ho-
mology determination [1] and haplotyping [2], and can even be applied to the evolution
of natural languages [3]. These variations are, for the most part, NP-complete, however
their wide applicability requires the development of tools that help to overcome this
intractability.

One of the most general and widely used forms of the problem is the maximum
parsimony problem, where the goal is to find the smallest evolutionary tree (called
the most parsimonious tree) that accounts for the diversity of the given species. The
problem is specified as follows: A set of characters, each of which can take on a number
of possible states, characterizes a group of species. The input is a set of species, given as
character vectors. The goal is to construct a tree, with nodes labeled as character vectors,
such that the node labels include all species, and the total number of character changes
along edges is minimized. Variations of the problem arise from different restrictions on
character changes and different metrics on the minimization.

M. Hermann and A. Voronkov (Eds.): LPAR 2006, LNAI 4246, pp. 452–466, 2006.

One traditional approach to solving maximum parsimony phylogeny problems, proposed by Hendy and Penny [4], is branch-and-bound (BNB). The BNB method involves constructing candidate trees in a depth-first manner, keeping track of the best trees found so far. The method benefits from heuristics which direct the search toward promising trees, and often finds optimal or near-optimal trees quickly. However, in the worst case, finding optimal phylogenies requires enumerating all trees. For data sets with many species, this is a daunting task since the number of trees grows exponentially in the number of species.

Due to the success of BNB, most present day software packages for phylogeny construction use this approach. The two most common packages, PHYLIP [5] and PAUP [6], use BNB to solve several variations of the phylogeny construction problem. Many of these packages sacrifice optimality in an effort to improve running times and it can be difficult to know if and when optimality has been reached. Other methods are needed, especially when optimality is required. In particular, we would like to develop a tool which can quickly compute optimal phylogenies for the maximum parsimony problem.

One strategy for dealing with NP-complete problems is to specify a solution's properties declaratively, and solve the declarative model with a general-purpose solver. This contrasts with the procedural approach used in BNB packages such as PHYLIP. In recent years, Answer Set Programming (ASP), a declarative approach, has gained increasing attention in tackling combinatorial search problems. Based on the stable model semantics of logic programming [7], it was identified as a new programming paradigm in 1999 [8,9]. Problems are modeled in extended logic programming notation so that models of the logic program correspond to problem solutions. An answer set solver, such as smodels [10] or Cmodels [11] is used to compute answer sets, which represent models of the program and hence solutions. Phylogeny problems, with their combinatorially large search spaces, seem ideal candidates for ASP formulation.

In attempting to solve the maximum parsimony problem using ASP, we must choose a metric space in which to work. The ultimate goal is to use the Wagner metric [12], the most general metric, in which arbitrary mutations are allowed. In general, this metric yields extremely large search spaces and it seems difficult to find ASP models which perform satisfactorily on substantial data sets. Another well-established metric for the maximum parsimony problem is the cladistic Camin-Sokal (CCS) metric [13]. Though other models are more common, the CCS version is in use for specific applications (see [14,15,16]). In this version, the states of each character are ordered and all changes are to the next state in the order. These changes are irreversible. In the binary version, each character has two states. The CCS problem, even in the binary case, is NP-complete [17].

In this paper, we define an ASP model for the binary CCS problem. As a first step towards modeling this problem, we construct a model for the so-called *perfect phylogeny* problem. So long as the number of character states is constant, perfect phylogenies can be constructed in polynomial-time [18]. Our model to construct perfect binary CCS phylogenies performs well and we base our general CCS model on it. A straightforward implementation gives a model with unsatisfactory running time, which is not uncommon in modeling NP-hard problems. To achieve a speed-up, we experimented with a considerable number of variations of the basic model, of which the seven most interesting are presented here. We present empirical evidence of the performance of the variations tried. Indeed, one of our contributions is a deeper understanding of how ASP models can be modified to potentially reduce running times. In particular, we propose the notion of *slightly tighter* models and show that a slightly tighter model can obtain better performance where a completely tight program fails to do so. We compare the performance of our ASP-based approach with PENNY, the BNB-based program from the PHYLIP package which constructs CCS phylogenies, on two biological data sets, including haplotype data for *Poecilia reticulata* (guppies) which was recently determined experimentally [19]. Our method finds, and proves optimality of, trees for subsets of this data with up to 27 species and 24 characters, or 36 species and 18 characters. PENNY cannot establish optimality of trees for subsets with more than 18 species within a two hour cutoff period. As the number of species grows, our methods seem to yield a more viable technique than PENNY to obtain optimal solutions. This work shows that by refining an original, basic declarative model, one can achieve performance comparable to, or faster than, procedural approaches.

2   Related Work

There are two main approaches (both yielding NP-complete problems) in character-based phylogeny construction: the "maximum parsimony" approach and the "maximum compatibility" approach. The goal of the former approach is to find a phylogeny for the input species with the minimum number of evolutionary changes, and is the approach we use in this paper. The goal of the latter approach is to construct a phylogeny using the maximum number of compatible characters. Brooks *et al.* present an ASP-based method for the "maximum compatibility" approach [20]. ASP solvers have also been used to construct "perfect phylogenetic networks", from phylogenetic trees, to explain the evolution of Indo-European languages [3]. These networks extend given phylogenies with extra edges to create perfect phylogenetic networks which explain how languages are related, both through evolutionary changes and contact amongst different cultures.

This work focuses on the binary CCS version of the "maximum parsimony" approach. Recent biological uses of binary CCS include finding phylogenetic trees of *Saccharomyces sensu stricto* complex of yeast [14]. The model was also applied to DNA fragment data for individuals from *Pellia genus*, where state 1 represents the presence of the particular DNA fragment and state 0 represents its absence [16]. Nozaki *et al.* utilized the irreversibility in the CCS model because they observed that regaining of plastid genes is generally impossible during evolution [15].

As mentioned earlier, BNB is the most common method used in the "maximum parsimony" approach. In recent years, advances have been made to the basic BNB procedure, such as developing tighter lower bounds and better branching heuristics, e.g. [21,22,23]. These advances have helped improve the speed of BNB algorithms for finding the most parsimonious evolutionary trees. We are not aware of any recent developments in BNB techniques which are tailored directly to the CCS version.

3   Cladistic Camin-Sokal Problem

The general large parsimony problem is to construct a tree with the minimum number of mutations, or state changes. In binary CCS, a given character may mutate only once on any directed path from the root. Since this mutation is irreversible, we may assume that all mutations are from state 0 to state 1, and the root of the tree is the zero vector.

The usual convention for phylogenetic tree construction is to construct binary trees, to place all species at the leaves of the tree, and allow any number of characters to change along each edge. For our purposes, it is easier to model phylogenetic trees by dropping the assumptions that the tree is binary and that species appear only in leaves of the tree and enforcing exactly one character state change along each edge. Every leaf will be labeled by a species, but not necessarily vice versa. Since we limit ourselves to one change per edge rather than grouping changes on a single edge, there are more phylogenies possible with our convention. However, each of our phylogenies maps to a unique phylogeny in the standard convention, and each phylogeny in the standard convention can be mapped to a group of isomorphic phylogenies in our convention.

Consider the small 6 species, 5 character example in Figure 1. Notice that exactly one character changes on each edge (labeled by c_i to denote the i-th character has changed) and that species may occur at internal nodes. Both of these properties differ from the phylogenies produced by PENNY, but it is easy to convert trees from either format to the other.

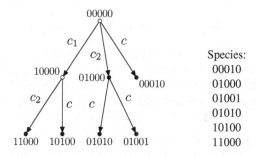

Fig. 1. Example of a binary CCS phylogenetic tree with minimum number of extra vertices. Vertices for species are marked with black dots.

Definition 1. *The binary cladistic Camin-Sokal problem (binary CCS) is:*

> **Instance:** *A set S of n distinct species vectors from $\{0,1\}^m$, and natural number B.*
>
> **Question:** *Is there a directed tree $T = (V, E)$, such that: T is rooted at 0^m; $S \subseteq V \subseteq \{0,1\}^m$; every leaf in T is in S; if $(v_1, v_2) \in E$, v_1 and v_2 differ in exactly one character; $\forall (v_1, v_2) \in E$, if v_1 has character state 1 for character c, then v_2 has state 1 for c (irreversibility); and $|V| \leq B$.*

In a perfect phylogeny, each character mutation occurs only once in the tree. For binary CCS, this is equivalent to setting $B = m$.

4   Models

Before giving our ASP model for binary CCS, we describe a simpler model for the
perfect phylogeny version. This model will help us illustrate our general model, given in
Section 4.2, since we constructed the general model by extending the perfect phylogeny
model to allow for individual characters to mutate multiple times.

4.1   Perfect Phylogeny Model

Our ASP model (program) takes as input a set of facts:

$$a(P, C, S).$$

where P is the species number ranging from 1 to n, C is the character number ranging
from 1 to m, and S is the state, either 0 or 1, of that character.

Let predicate c(C) be true if C is a character. We name each vertex, other than the
root, by the character that has just changed from 0 to 1 (with the rule "v(C) :- c(C).").
This naming scheme identifies each vertex, other than the root, with a character. Since
the root has only character states of 0, and no character/vertex associated with it, we
ignore it in our model. Thus we generate a forest. Connecting the root of each tree
in the forest to our real root in post-processing produces the solution. To enforce this
forest structure, we define relation edge on vertices so that each vertex has at most one
incoming edge:

$$\{ \text{ edge(V1,V): c(V1): V1 != V } \} \text{ 1 :- c(V).}$$

It remains to ensure that each species is represented by a vertex in the tree. We do not
have an explicit mapping between species and vertices, but rather ensure that exactly
those characters with state 1 in a species appear as vertices along the path to it from the
root. For this, we introduce two new relations: above and comparable. Relation above
is the transitive closure of edge:

above(V,V1) :- v(V), v(V1), V != V1, edge(V,V1).
above(V,V2) :- v(V:V1:V2), V != V1, V != V2, V1 != V2, above(V,V1), edge(V1,V2).

Two vertices (characters) are comparable if one is above the other:

comparable(C,C1) :- v(C), v(C1), C != C1, above(C,C1).
comparable(C,C1) :- v(C), v(C1), C != C1, above(C1,C).

We say two characters are shared if, for some species, they both take the value 1. We
require that each pair of shared characters is comparable:

:- a(P,C,1), a(P,C1,1), C != C1, not comparable(C,C1).

The constraint ensures that, for each species, all characters with state value 1 must
appear along a single path in the forest. However, this path should not contain characters
which take value 0 for this species. For any species, we must prevent a character with
state 0 occurring above a character with state 1:

:- a(P,C,0), a(P,C1,1), above(C,C1).

To complete the model, we must ensure a graph is a forest. To eliminate cycles, we add a constraint to prevent any two different characters from being above each other:

:- c(C), c(C1), above(C,C1), above(C1,C).

4.2   General Model

To handle the general problem, we modify our simple model for the perfect version. Predicates c(C) and sp(P) indicate that C is a character and P is a species. In this model, c(C) no longer represents vertices. Since characters can change states multiple times, there is no longer a one-to-one correspondence between vertices and characters. We let v(V) denote that V is a vertex. For m characters, we have $m + k$ vertices, where k is a number of extra vertices:

$$v(C) :- c(C).$$
$$v(m + i). \text{ (for } 1 \leq i \leq k)$$

We create a mapping m(V,C) from vertices to characters. Since each character must change to state 1 at least once, the first m vertices are mapped identically to the characters. The k extra vertices are free to be mapped to any character:

m(C,C) :- c(C).
1 { m(V,C) : c(C) } 1 :- v(V), V > m.

As before, we create a forest by allowing each vertex to have at most one incoming edge and by forbidding cycles. We again use relation above to define paths amongst directed edges, but we modify it to be reflexive (i.e., the reflexive transitive closure of edge):

above(V,V) :- v(V).

This will simplify the remaining specification that each species is properly mapped to a vertex in the tree. In the general case, it is not enough to insist that each pair of characters which take the value 1 for a particular species are comparable, as multiple vertices can be mapped to the same character. For each species, we need a path from a root to a particular vertex such that the vertices in the path map exclusively to all of the characters which take value 1 for that species. To do this, we first introduce a mapping p(P,V) from species to vertices:

1 { p(P,V) : v(V) } 1 :- sp(P).

Suppose that species s is mapped to vertex v (i.e., p(s,v) holds). If character c has state 1 for species s, we require some vertex above v to map to c (above is now reflexive, so v itself could map to c). Similarly, if character c has state 0 for species s, we require that no vertex above v maps to c. To model these requirements, we introduce relation g(P,C), which is true of all characters C which have changed along the path to species P. For example, suppose that species s maps to vertex v which maps to character c. Then g(s,c) holds if there is a vertex v_1, above v, which maps to c:

g(P,C) :- sp(P), c(C), v(V1), v(V), p(P,V), m(V1,C), above(V1,V).

For each species P, we require that all characters with state 1 to be exactly those satisfying g(P,C):

$$:- a(P,C,1), not\ g(P,C).$$
$$:- a(P,C,0), g(P,C).$$

This completes the model.

To solve an instance of this problem, we consider a sequence of instances of the model. In the first instance, we have no extra vertices (i.e., require a perfect phylogeny). In each successive instance, we increase the number of extra vertices by one. We continue until a solution, which must be optimal, is found.

4.3   Model Variations

We were unable to solve the CCS problem for either of the full data sets we obtained. In attempting to improve performance, we tried a number of variations of the basic model just described. We report the most interesting, based on these four strategies: adding redundant constraints; rephrasing constraints; tightening the program; and adding pre-processing steps to reduce the size of the search space.

Model A - Redundant constraints. A common strategy to improve performance of declarative models is to add redundant constraints. Adding redundant constraints to a logic program does not change the resulting answer sets, but can reduce the running time of the solver to find these solutions as candidate solutions can possibly be discarded more quickly.

A species can only be mapped to a vertex which takes state 1 for this species, so we added a constraint which explicitly prevents a species from being mapped to a vertex which maps to a character that has state 0 for this species:

$$:- sp(P), v(V), c(C), p(P,V), m(V,C), a(P,C,0).$$

Note that this constraint does not change the requirements for a candidate tree to be a solution. Without this constraint, it is still impossible for a species to be mapped to a vertex which represents a character for which the species takes a zero.

Model B - Rephrase constraints. Our basic model from Section 4.2 makes use of the fact that above is reflexive. This allows for a more concise definition of predicate g. We tested the idea of making above irreflexive and altering the program to account for this.

We remove the reflexive constraint from our basic model, and replace the rule to remove cycles with our new irreflexive constraint (this will also serve to prevent cycles):

$$:- v(V), above(V,V).$$

To modify relation g(P,C) so that reflexivity is not needed, we introduce a new predicate, ch_above(C,V):

```
ch_above(C,V) :- c(C), v(V), m(V,C).
ch_above(C,V) :- c(C), v(V), v(V1), V != V1, m(V1,C), above(V1,V).
```

ch_above(c,v) is true if vertex v maps to character c or there is a vertex v_1 above v which maps to c. Predicate g can now be simply defined as:

g(P,C) :- sp(P), c(C), v(V), p(P,V), ch_above(C,V).

Model C - Make program tight. If a logic program satisfies a syntactic condition called "tightness" or being "positive-order-consistent", then its stable models can be characterized as the models of its completion (for a discussion of tight logic programs, see [24]). In general, Cmodels may make exponentially many calls to a SAT solver during one execution, but on tight programs it will only make one such call [11]. This may improve the overall run time.

To make our program tight, we create an ordering on the vertices, by replacing our identity mapping rule with a general mapping rule so each vertex can map to any character:

$$1 \{ m(V,C) : c(C) \} 1 :- v(V).$$

We modify the edge selection rule so that only edges from smaller vertices to greater vertices are allowed:

$$\{ edge(V1,V): v(V1): V1 < V \} 1 :- v(V).$$

Model D - Use preprocessing to reduce search space. In an attempt to reduce the size of the search space, we determined which characters are in conflict by constructing a conflict graph, in a preprocessing stage. A conflict graph has a vertex for each character, and edges between characters which are in conflict. Two binary characters are in *conflict* if there are three distinct species in which they take the state pairs '0-1', '1-0', and '1-1'. If two characters are in conflict, at least one of them will require an extra vertex in any resulting phylogenies. This is due to the fact that, from some parent node which has value 0 for both characters, both characters must change state along different paths to produce the '0-1' and '1-0' state pairs. However, one of these two characters must change again to obtain the '1-1' state pair. In this variation, we restrict the possible characters to which the extra vertices can be mapped to those which are in conflict.

We define a predicate con(C) to mean character C is in conflict. When adding extra vertices, we only choose among the characters in conflict:

$$1 \{ m(V,C) : con(C) \} 1 :- v(V), V > m.$$

Surprisingly, only Model A showed improved running time. We take Model A as our base model for these further improvements:

Model E. Our attempt to make the program completely tight resulted in horrendous performance. Using a similar idea we made a 'tighter' program by creating an ordering on the extra vertices only. In this model, there can be edges from the first m vertices to any other vertices, but for each extra vertex numbered $k > m$, there can only be edges to vertices numbered greater than k.

To accomplish this, we create a predicate I which defines which pairs of vertices are allowed to have an edge between them. So $I(v_1,v)$ is true if $v_1 \leq m$ or $m < v_1 < v$:

$$I(V1,V) :\text{-} v(V1), v(V), V1 <= m.$$
$$I(V1,V) :\text{-} v(V1), v(V), V1 > m, V1 < V.$$

With I defined, we can define our new edge relation as:

$$\{ edge(V1,V): v(V1): V1 = V \} 1 :\text{-} v(V), V <= m.$$
$$\{ edge(V1,V): v(V1): I(V1,V) \} 1 :\text{-} v(V), V > m.$$

Model A+. A character cannot change to state 1 more than once along any given path, so we add another redundant constraint which prevents vertices which map to the same character from being comparable. Since the first m vertices map to unique characters, we only need to check a pair of vertices for this condition if at least one of the two vertices is an extra vertex. We add these rules in the preprocessing phase:

$$:\text{-} v(V), v(V1), V > m, V1 <= m, c(C), m(V,C), m(V1,C), above(V,V1).$$
$$:\text{-} v(V), v(V1), V <= m, V1 > m, c(C), m(V,C), m(V1,C), above(V,V1).$$
$$:\text{-} v(V), v(V1), V > m, V1 > m, V = V1, c(C), m(V,C), m(V1,C), above(V,V1).$$

We again note that these constraints do not alter the resulting answer sets.

Model MC. For each pair of conflicting characters, at least one needs an extra vertex (i.e., the extra vertices must form a vertex cover of the conflict graph). Every vertex cover contains a minimal one. We make use of this fact and add mappings, in preprocessing, from the first extra vertices to characters so that a particular minimal vertex cover is a part of the extra vertices. Our iteration procedure begins with minimal covers with the smallest number of vertices, then continuing with these minimal covers and one additional extra vertex, and with minimal vertex covers with one more vertices than the minimum number, etc., until an optimal solution is found. Since we have explicitly chosen the characters some extra vertices map to, we have significantly reduced the number of possible mappings. However, we must (currently) manually find all minimal vertex covers in the conflict graph. For the reported data sets, this is not hard.

As mentioned, Models B, C, and D did not improve the performance of our basic model. The results of tests with the remaining variations are given in the next section.

5   Experimental Results

We present experimental results based on two sets of species data. One set, 'fb65', is haplotype information for *P. reticulata* containing 37 species and 468 characters with 5 states. Since the binary characters (SNPs) of this data are the most important, and our models are restricted to the binary case, we remove non-binary characters, leaving 449. The other set, 'pin', is from a taxonomic study of the *saccharomyces sensu stricto* complex [14], consisting of 20 species and 274 binary characters.

Identical characters form non-branching paths in phylogenies and all but one copy can be removed in preprocessing. Removed characters can easily be added to resulting trees in post processing. After this, the 'fb65' data set is left with 65 characters and 'pin' is left with 75.

Our ASP solver, in all reported results, was Cmodels-2 with zchaff. Cmodels regularly performed much better than smodels on our data. Our model, along with the input, was grounded using lparse [25]. This is always fast and is not included in the timing. Times shown are durations output by Cmodels. In the case of the general CCS problem, the time given is the sum of durations for the sequence of models as the number of extra vertices is increased. All runs were on a Sun Fire V20z, with Opteron 250 (2.4 GHz) CPU, and 4GB DDR1 RAM, running 64-bit Suse Linux Enterprise Server 9.

5.1   Perfect Phylogeny Model Results

To test the performance of our model, we derived subsets of 'fb65' which must have perfect phylogenies. We compared each pair of characters to find conflicting character pairs. For 'fbpp1', the first character in each conflicting pair was removed before continuing, leaving 38 characters. In 'fbppr', a random character from each conflicting pair was removed. This data set has 39 characters. For each, we solved subsets with 12, 24, 36, and 37 species (see Table 1). These results verified the correctness of the model. We found solutions to our full test data sets quickly, as hoped.

Table 1. Running times (in seconds) to construct phylogenies using our perfect phylogeny model on two different data sets, as the number of species (Sp) is varied

Sp	12	24	36	37
fbpp1	0.01	0.09	0.25	0.27
fbppr	0.01	0.07	0.28	0.29

5.2   General Model Results

We also used the 'fb65' data to test the performance of our CCS model and its variations. The 37-species 65-character data set is too large for any solver we tested, so we considered a number of subsets, varying both the number of characters and the number of species. Our notation for these subsets is of the form '15s,39c', for example, which represents the data set comprised of the first 39 characters from each of the first 15 species in our data.

To obtain the minimum number of extra vertices needed to produce a solution, we proceed incrementally from zero, adding a vertex whenever the solver returns false. We do not use binary search since the most time consuming computation often occurs when the number of extra vertices is one less than optimal (see Table 2). To prove a solution is optimal, we must show that no trees can be constructed with one less than the optimal number of vertices. Adding more vertices to the optimal number increases the running time of the solver. For this particular example, where the optimal solutions have four extra vertices, our algorithm requires just 28 seconds to reach three extra vertices when proceeding linearly. Solving even one instance with more than four vertices would be less efficient.

Table 2. Running times (in seconds) as the number of extra vertices (#EV) is increased, for '24s,24c'. Optimal solution has 4 extra vertices.

#EV	0	1	2	3	**4**	5	6
Time	0	1	27	11931	**4845**	8930	9011

Table 3 lists the largest data sets for which we could find solutions, together with run times for our various models. These represent a frontier for the size of problems we are able to solve. We can construct a phylogeny for '36s,18c' in seconds, but are unable to construct one for '36s,21c' in two hours.

Table 3. Model comparsion on 'fb65' data. Column 'Data' shows the largest data sets for which we could find solutions. Column '#EV' shows the optimal number of extra vertices needed. The remaining columns give the running times, in seconds, for each model on each data set.

Data	#EV	Basic	A	E	A+	MC
3s,63c	0	0	0	0	0	0
6s,51c	0	3159	2503	1701	2398	2503
9s,39c	3	3191	4099	4850	1996	1500
12s,39c	3	670	579	496	863	131
15s,39c	3	1107	755	797	4093	73
18s,39c	3	1077	947	1050	3787	191
21s,21c	3	23	5	5	4	10
24s,24c	4	16803	10784	8634	1916	440
27s,24c	4	1990	1180	913	239	6
30s,18c	3	4	3	3	3	2
33s,18c	3	5	4	4	3	2
36s,18c	3	6	5	5	4	4

Since Model A+ generally has the best performance (Model MC performs best, but we exclude it as it requires manual steps), we used it to compare the performance of our ASP-based approach to that of PENNY. Table 4 gives run times for the two methods on our two data sets. For each data set, we construct several subsets, as before. The tables list the largest data sets for which a solution was found with our method (Data), the optimal number of extra vertices (#EV), the total length of time, rounded to the nearest second, to find a solution with Model A+, and the time for PENNY, in seconds (PENNY). Times for PENNY are wall-clock times, as this package does not provide a timing function. An 'X' in the table denotes that PENNY did not halt within the two hour cutoff period.

The best performance we have obtained, to date, is with our Model MC, which, in pre-processing, modifies the ASP program to reduce the search space based on properties of the data. This approach drastically reduced running times, enabling us to solve larger problems within reasonable amounts of time. Figure 2 shows the frontier of largest subsets of our 'fb65' data solvable within two hours, for Models A+ and MC, as well as PENNY.

Table 4. Comparison of performance of Model A+ and PENNY on two data sets: (a) fb65 - 37 species, 65 characters; (b) pin - 20 species, 75 characters. Running times are given in seconds. An 'X' in the table represents failure to return a solution within the two hour cutoff period.

Data	#EV	A+	PENNY
3s,63c	0	0	0
6s,51c	0	2398	0
9s,39c	3	1996	0
12s,39c	3	863	1
15s,39c	3	4093	8
18s,39c	3	3787	5700
21s,21c	3	4	X
24s,24c	4	1916	X
27s,24c	4	239	X
30s,18c	3	3	X
33s,18c	3	3	X
36s,18c	3	4	X

(a)

Data	#EV	A+	PENNY
3s,75c	0	0	0
6s,57c	1	3	0
9s,30c	4	317	0
12s,21c	4	10	46
15s,10c	2	0	1350
18s,9c	3	8	X
20s,9c	3	7	X

(b)

Fig. 2. Frontier for PENNY and Models A+, MC

6 Discussion and Future Work

We presented ASP models for the binary CCS phylogeny problem, and for the restriction to the perfect phylogeny case. We examined the performance of a method using these models and the Cmodels solver on experimentally obtained biological data.

As we would hope, solutions for the polytime perfect phylogeny case were found very quickly. The general problem is much harder, and we know of no method, including ours, that can determine optimal phylogenies for the full data sets we use. We tried several ideas for improving the performance of our model. The best of our model variants can determine optimal phylogenies for larger fragments of the data (measured by number of species included) than can PENNY, the standard branch-and-bound program for the problem.

For data with n species, PENNY essentially enumerates all phylogenetic trees on n nodes, keeping track of the most parsimonious ones found so far (measured by total number of character changes on the tree). PENNY relies on good heuristics which direct the search toward the most promising trees, and trims subspaces which cannot contain optimal solutions. This approach has three main effects: it is very effective at finding good trees quickly, at least on small data sets; its performance is largely unaffected by the number of characters in the data; and it can establish optimality only for data sets with few species, since a large number of species implies too many trees to search.

Our ASP models fix a limit on the number of mutations in the tree to be found. Our method solves a series of models, beginning with the one which requires a perfect phylogeny, and then adding extra vertices until a phylogeny is found. This phylogeny must be optimal. In contrast with PENNY: Our general method relies on no domain-specific heuristics, and searches for a "perfect" tree, rather than enumerating trees; Our model involves mappings between both species and vertices, and vertices and characters, so performance is significantly affected by number of characters as well as number of species; The first phylogeny we find is optimal, and because we do not have to enumerate all trees, we can prove optimality for cases involving larger numbers of species.

Based on our experimental results and our understanding of the performance of the two methods, we conclude that declarative methods, and ASP in particular, are promising for solving hard phylogeny problems, especially when optimality is relevant. We understand that advances have been made in BNB algorithms since PENNY was developed, and that commercial software such as PAUP* 4.0 make use of these more advanced approaches. However, we also feel that time will permit advances in the declarative approach, both through the development of better models (perhaps with non-declarative components) and the development of faster ASP solvers.

Among our model variations, a few deserve attention. Model C was obtained by looking for a straightforward way to make the ASP program tight. Models for a tight program coincide with models for its completion, so some solvers could perform better on an equivalent tight program. Our change involved ordering the vertices. However, off-setting any benefit of tightness is the fact that the solver must also guess the ordering. This significantly enlarges the search space. The resulting performance was very poor. However, Model E, a model which involved ordering the extra vertices only, exhibited good performance in general, and the best performance for some particular data sets. We have simultaneously increased the search space slightly and made the program slightly tighter. In doing so, we have exhibited better performance than a purely tight model or a model with a smaller search space.

The second best model, A+, was the result of adding two sets of redundant constraints to the model. This is a standard technique in constraint satisfaction (CSP) practice, for example, but less used in ASP.

The best performance was with Model MC. This model was based on pre-processing the data to obtain information which was used to revise the model, on an instance-by-instance basis, to reduce the search space. The fact that the performance of this version was significantly better than the others highlights a general problem for declarative approaches, namely, can we always solve problems with a purely declarative approach, or will we always need to consider such non-declarative components when tackling hard problems? Put another way, can we find a way to capture ideas such as the one used in version MC declaratively, or not; if so, how, and if not, under what conditions should we look beyond declarative methods?

Future work includes exploring more ways to improve the performance of our binary CCS models. Possible directions include further attempts at reformulations, incorporating more recent, faster SAT solvers into Cmodels, and exploring hybrid techniques which combine BNB and declarative approaches. The generation of minimal vertex covers for Model MC could be automated, perhaps by using another ASP program. Our CCS model could be extended to the non-binary case. We have made some initial explorations in this direction, but the straightforward model we constructed yields unsatisfactory performance and considerable work remains. Continuing to remove restrictions from our CCS model, until we reach the more general Wagner version of the problem, would make this technique applicable to a wider range of applications.

Acknowledgements. We would like to thank Dr. Nikolay Pelov for his preliminary work in this project. We also wish to thank the three groups who supplied us with their data: Hellman *et al.*, Pacak *et al.*, and Edwards-Ingram *et al.*

References

1. Roderic, D., Page, M., Holmes, E.: Molecular Evolution: A Phylogenetic Approach. Blackwell Science, Oxford, UK (1998)
2. Gusfield, D.: Haplotyping as perfect phylogeny: conceptual framework and efficient solutions. In: RECOMB '02: Proc. of the sixth annual int'l conf. on Comp. biology. (2002) 166–175
3. Erdem, E., Lifschitz, V., Nakhleh, L., Ringe, D.: Reconstructing the evolutionary history of indo-european languages using answer set programming. Proc., Practical Aspects of Declarative Languages: 5th Int'l Symposium (2003) 160–176
4. Hendy, M., Penny, D.: Branch and bound algorithms to determine minimal evolutionary trees. Mathematical Biosciences **59** (1982) 277–290
5. Felsenstein, J.: Phylip home page (1980) http://evolution.genetics.washington.edu/ phylip.
6. Swofford, D.: Paup* 4.0 (2001) Phylogenetic Analysis Using Parsimony (*and Other Methods).
7. Gelfond, M., Lifschitz, V.: The stable model semantics for logic programming. Proc., Int'l Logic Programming Conference and Symposium (1988) 1070–1080
8. Niemelä, I.: Logic programs with stable model semantics as a constraint programming paradigm. Annals of Mathematics and Artificial Intelligence **25** (1999) 241–273
9. Marek, V., Truszczynski, M. In: Stable logic programming - an alternative logic programming paradigm. Springer-Verlag (1999) In: The Logic Programming Paradigm: A 25-Year Perspective, K.R. Apt, V.W. Marek, M. Truszczynski, D.S. Warren, Eds.
10. Niemelä, I., Simons, P., Syrjänen, T.: Smodels: A system for answer set programming. In: Proc. 8th Int'l Workshop on Non-Monotonic Reasoning, April 9-11, 2000, Breckenridge, Colorado. (2000)
11. Lierler, Y., Maratea, M.: Cmodels-2: SAT-based answer set solver enhanced to non-tight programs. In: Logic Programming and Nonmonotonic Reasoning, 7th International Conference. Volume 2923 of LNCS. (2004) 346–350
12. Eck, R., Dayhoff, M.: Atlas of protein sequence and structure. National Biomedical Research Foundation (1966)

13. Camin, J., Sokal, R.: A method for deducing branching sequences in phylogeny. Evolution **19** (1965) 311–326
14. Edwards-Ingram, L., Gent, M., Hoyle, D., Hayes, A., Stateva, L., Oliver, S.: Comparative genomic hybridization provides new insights into the molecular taxonomy of the saccharomyces sensu stricto complex. Genome Research **14** (2004) 1043–1051
15. Nozaki, H., Ohta, N., Matsuzaki, M., Misumi, O., Kuroiwa, T.: Phylogeny of plastids based on cladistic analysis of gene loss inferred from complete plastid genome sequences. J. Molecular Evolution **57** (2003) 377–382
16. Pacak, A., Fiedorow, P., Dabert, J., Szweykowska-Kulińska, Z.: RAPD technique for taxonomic studies of pellia epiphylla-complex (hepaticae, metzgeriales). Genetica **104** (1998) 179–187
17. Day, W., Johnson, D., Sankoff, D.: The computational complexity of inferring rooted phylogenies by parsimony. Mathematical Biosciences **81** (1986) 33–42
18. Agarwala, R., Fernandez-Baca, D.: A polynomial-time algorithm for the perfect phylogeny problem when the number of character states is fixed. SIAM Journal on Computing (1994) 1216–1224
19. Hellman, M., Tripathi, N., Henz, S., Lindholm, A., Weigel, D., Breden, F., Dreyer, C.: Unpublished data. (2006)
20. Brooks, D., Erdem, E., Minett, J., Rings, D.: Character-based cladistics and answer set programming. PADL (2005) 37–51
21. Purdom, Jr., W., Bradford, P., Tamura, K., Kumar, S.: Single column discrepancy and dynamic max-mini optimization for quickly finding the most parsimonious evolutionary trees. Bioinformatics **2** (2000) 140–151
22. Yan, M., Bader, D.A.: Fast character optimization in parsimony phylogeny reconstruction. Technical report (2003)
23. Moret, B., Tang, J., Wang, L., Warnow, T.: Steps toward accurate reconstruction of phylogenies from gene-order data. J. Comput. Syst. Sci. **65** (2002) 508–525
24. Erdem, E., Lifschitz, V.: Tight logic programs. Theory and Practice of Logic Programming **3** (2003) 499–518
25. Syrjänen, T.: Lparse user's manual (1998) http://www.tcs.hut.fi/Software/smodels/.

Automata for Positive Core XPath Queries on Compressed Documents

Barbara Fila and Siva Anantharaman

LIFO - Université d'Orléans (France)
{fila, siva}@univ-orleans.fr

Abstract. Given any dag t representing a fully or partially compressed XML document, we present a method for evaluating any positive unary query expressed in terms of Core XPath axes, on t, without unfolding t into a tree. To each Core XPath query of a certain basic type, we associate a word automaton; these automata run on the graph of dependency between the non-terminals of the straightline regular tree grammar associated to the given dag, or along complete sibling chains in this grammar. Any given Core XPath query can be decomposed into queries of the basic type, and the answer to the query, on the dag t, can then be expressed as a sub-dag of t suitably labeled under the runs of such automata.

Keywords: Automata, Tree grammars, Dags, XML, Core XPath.

1   Introduction

Several algorithms have been optimized in the past, by using structures over dags instead of over trees. Tree automata are widely used for querying XML documents (e.g., [6,11,12]); on the other hand, the notion of a compressed XML document has been introduced in [1,5,9], and a possible advantage of using dag structures for the manipulation of such documents has been brought out in [9]. It is legitimate then to investigate the possibility of using automata over dags instead of over trees, for querying compressed XML documents.

Our aim in this paper is to propose an approach based on word automata, for evaluating queries on any XML document possibly given in a compressed format. With such an objective, we first define the notion of a compressed document as a *tree/dag* (*trdag*, for short), designating a directed acyclic graph that may be partially or fully compressed; the terms 'trdag' and 'document' will therefore be considered synonymous in the sequel. We adopt then the view that a trdag t is equivalent to a minimal straightline regular tree grammar $\mathcal{L}_t$ that one can naturally associate with t, cf. e.g., [2,3]. From the grammar $\mathcal{L}_t$, we construct the graph of dependency $\mathcal{D}_t$ between its non-terminals, and also the *chiblings* (linear graphs formed of complete chains of sibling non-terminals) of $\mathcal{L}_t$. The word automata that we construct below will run on $\mathcal{D}_t$, or on the chiblings of $\mathcal{L}_t$, rather than on the document t itself.

We shall only consider *positive* unary queries expressed in terms of Core XPath axes. (The view we adopt allows us to define the various axes of Core XPath

M. Hermann and A. Voronkov (Eds.): LPAR 2006, LNAI 4246, pp. 467–481, 2006.
© Springer-Verlag Berlin Heidelberg 2006

on compressed documents, in a manner which does not modify their semantics on trees.) For evaluating any such query on any document (trdag) t, we proceed as follows. We first break up the given query into basic sub-queries of the form $Q= //*\mathtt{[axis::}\sigma\mathtt{]}$ where $\mathtt{axis}$ is a Core XPath axis of a certain type. To each such basic query Q, we associate a word automaton $\mathbf{A}_Q$. The automaton $\mathbf{A}_Q$ runs on the graph $\mathcal{D}_t$ when $\mathtt{axis}$ is non-sibling, and on the chiblings of $\mathcal{L}_t$ when $\mathtt{axis}$ is a sibling axis. An essential point in our method is that the runs of $\mathbf{A}_Q$ are guided by some well-defined semantics for the nodes traversed, indicating whether the current node answers Q, or is on a path leading to some other node answering Q. The automaton is not deterministic, but its runs are made effectively unambiguous by defining a priority relation between its transitions, based on the semantics. A basic query Q can then be evaluated in one single top-down pass of $\mathbf{A}_Q$, under such an unambiguous run. An arbitrary positive unary Core XPath query Q can be evaluated on t by combining the answers to its various basic sub-queries, and the answer set for Q is expressed as a sub-trdag of t, whose nodes get labeled in conformity with the semantics. It is important to note that the evaluation is performed on the *given* trdag t; as such, on two different trdags corresponding to two different compressions of the same XML tree, the answers obtained may *not* be the same, in general.

The paper is structured as follows: Section 2 presents the notion of trdags. In Section 3, we construct from any trdag t its normalized straightline regular tree grammar $\mathcal{L}_t$, as well as the dependency graph $\mathcal{D}_t$ and the chiblings of $\mathcal{L}_t$; these will be seen as rooted labeled acyclic graphs (*rlags*, for short); the basic notions of Core XPath are also recalled. Section 4 is devoted to the construction of the word automata for any basic Core XPath query, based on the semantics, and an illustrative example. In Section 5, we prove that the runs of these automata, uniquely and effectively determined under a maximal priority condition, generate the answers to the queries. Section 6 shows how a non basic (composite, or imbricated) Core XPath query can be evaluated in a stepwise fashion.

2   Tree/Dags

Definition 1. *A tree/dag, or trdag for short, over an unranked alphabet Σ is a rooted dag (directed acyclic graph) $t = (Nodes(t), Edges(t))$, where:*

- *every node $u \in Nodes(t)$ has a name $\in \Sigma$, denoted $name_t(u)$ or $name(u)$;*
- *the edges going out of any node are ordered.*

Given any node u on a trdag t, the notion of the sub-trdag of t rooted at u is defined as usual, and denoted as $t|_u$. If v is any node, $\gamma(v) = u_1 \ldots u_n$ will denote the *string* of all its not necessarily distinct *children* nodes. For any node u on t, we set: $Parents(u) = \{v \in Nodes(t) \mid u$ is a child of $v\}$.

A trdag t is said to be a *tree* iff for every node u on t other than the root, $Parents(u)$ is a singleton. For any trdag t, we define the set $Pos(t)$ as the set of all the positions $pos_t(u)$ of all its nodes u, these being defined recursively, as follows: if u is the root node on t, then $pos_t(u) = \epsilon$, otherwise, $pos_t(u) = \{a.i \mid$

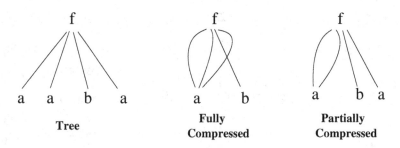

Fig. 1. Tree, tdag, and trdag

$\alpha \in pos_t(v), v$ is a parent of u, u is the i-th child of v}. The elements of $Pos(t)$ are words over natural integers.

The function $name_t$ is extended naturally to the positions in $Pos(t)$ as follows: for every $u \in Nodes(t)$ and $\alpha \in pos_t(u)$, we set $name_t(\alpha) = name_t(u)$. Given a trdag t, we define its tree-equivalent as a tree $\hat{t}$ such that: $Pos(\hat{t}) = Pos(t)$, and for every $\alpha \in Pos(t)$ we have $name_{\hat{t}}(\alpha) = name_t(\alpha)$. A *trdag* is said to be a *tdag*, or *fully compressed*, iff for any two distinct nodes u, u' on t, the two sub-dags $t|_u$ and $t|_{u'}$ have non-isomorphic tree-equivalents; otherwise, the trdag is said to be *partially compressed*, if it is not a tree. For example, the tree to the left of Figure 1 is the tree-equivalent of the partially compressed trdag to the right, and also of the fully compressed tdag to the middle.

3   Querying Compressed Documents: Preliminaries

Given a trdag t, one can naturally construct a regular tree grammar associated with t, which is *straightline* (cf. [3]), in the sense that there are no cycles on the dependency relations between its non-terminals, and each non-terminal produces exactly one sub-trdag of t. Such a grammar will be denoted as $\mathcal{L}_t$, if it is *normalized* in the following sense:

  (i) for every non-terminal A_i of $\mathcal{L}_t$, there is exactly one production of the form $A_i \to f(A_{j_1}, \ldots, A_{j_k})$, where $i < j_r$ for every $1 \le r \le k$; we shall then set $Sons(A_i) = \{A_{j_1}, \ldots, A_{j_k}\}$, and $symb_{\mathcal{L}_t}(A_i) = f$;

  (ii) the number of non-terminals of $\mathcal{L}_t$ is the number of nodes on t.

Such a normalized grammar $\mathcal{L}_t$ is uniquely defined up to a renaming of the non-terminals. For instance, for the trdag t to the left of Figure 2, we get the following normalized grammar:

$$A_1 \to f(A_2, A_3, A_4, A_5, A_2), \quad A_2 \to c, \quad A_3 \to a(A_5), \quad A_4 \to b, \quad A_5 \to b$$

Such a grammar is easily constructed from t, for instance by using a standard algorithm which computes the 'depth' of any node (as the maximal distance from the root), to number the non-terminals so as to satisfy condition (i) above.

The *dependency graph* of the normalized grammar $\mathcal{L}_t$ associated with t, and denoted as $\mathcal{D}_t$, consists of nodes named with the non-terminals $A_i, 1 \le i \le n$,

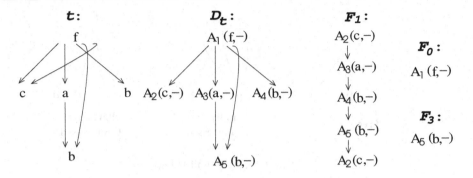

Fig. 2. trdag t, associated rlag $\mathcal{D}_t$, and chiblings of $\mathcal{L}_t$

and *one single* directed arc from any node A_i to a node A_j whenever A_j is a son of A_i. The root of $\mathcal{D}_t$ is by definition the node named A_1. The notion of *Sons* of the nodes on $\mathcal{D}_t$ is derived in the obvious way from that defined above on $\mathcal{L}_t$.

Furthermore, to any production $A_i \rightarrow f(A_{j_1}, \ldots, A_{j_k})$ of $\mathcal{L}_t$, we associate a rooted linear graph composed of k nodes respectively named $A_{j_1}, \ldots, A_{j_k}$, with root at A_{j_1}, and such that for all $l \in \{2, \ldots, k\}$ the node named A_{j_l} is the son of the node named $A_{j_{l-1}}$. This graph is referred to as the *chibling* of $\mathcal{L}_t$ associated with the (unique) A_i-production; it is denoted as $\mathcal{F}_i$. We also define a further chibling denoted $\mathcal{F}_0$, as the linear graph with a single node named A_1, where A_1 is the axiom of $\mathcal{L}_t$.

In the sequel, we designate by $\mathcal{G}$ either $\mathcal{D}_t$ or any of the chiblings $\mathcal{F}$ of $\mathcal{L}_t$. We complete any of these acyclic graphs $\mathcal{G}$ into a rooted labeled acyclic graph (*rlag*, for short), by attaching to each node u on $\mathcal{G}$, with $name(u) = A_i$, a label denoted $label(u)$, and defined as $label(u) = (symb_{\mathcal{L}_t}(A_i), -)$; cf. Figure 2.

3.1   Positive Core XPath Queries on Trdags

In this paper, our study is restricted to positive Core XPath queries on trdags. Recall that Core XPath (cf. [7]) is the navigational segment of XPath, based on the following axes of XPath: `self`, `child`, `parent`, `ancestor`, `descendant`, `following-sibling`, `preceding-sibling`. A location expression is defined as a predicate of the form `[axis::b]`, where `axis` is one of the above axes, and b is a symbol of Σ. Given any trdag t over Σ, a context node u on t and $b \in \Sigma$, the semantics for `axis` is defined by evaluating this predicate at u. The semantics for the axes `self`, `child`, `descendant` are easily defined, exactly as on trees (cf. [14]). For defining the semantics of the remaining axes, we first recall that $Parents(u) = \{v \in Nodes(t) \mid u \text{ is a child of } v\}$.

Definition 2. *Given a context node u on a trdag t, and $b \in \Sigma$:*
i) [`parent::b`] *evaluates to* true *at u, if and only if there exists a b-named node in $Parents(u)$;*

ii) [ancestor::*b*] *evaluates to* true *at u, iff either* [parent::*b*] *evaluates to* true *at u, or there exists a node v* ∈ *Parents(u) such that* [ancestor::*b*] *evaluates to* true *at v;*

iii) [following-sibling::*b*] *evaluates to* true *at u, iff there exists a b-named node u′, and a node v on t such that γ(v) is of the form* ...*u*...*u′*...;

iv) [preceding-sibling::*b*] *evaluates to* true *at u, iff there exists a b-named node u′, and a node v on t such that γ(v) is of the form* ...*u′*...*u*...

For the 'composite' axes descendant-or-self and ancestor-or-self, the semantics are then deduced in an obvious manner. We shall also need position predicates of the form [*position*() = *i*]; their semantics is that the expression [child::*b* [*position*() = *i*]] evaluates to *true* at a context node *u*, iff: [child::*b*] evaluates to *true* at *u*, and *u* is an *i*-th child of some parent.

Positive Core XPath query expressions are usually defined in the literature (cf. e.g., [5]), as those generated by the following grammar:

$$A \quad ::= \texttt{self} \mid \texttt{child} \mid \texttt{descendant} \mid \texttt{parent} \mid \texttt{ancestor} \mid$$
$$\texttt{preceding-sibling} \mid \texttt{following-sibling}$$
$$S_{can} ::= \texttt{A::}\sigma \mid position() = i \mid S_{can} \textit{ and } S_{can} \mid S_{can} \textit{ or } S_{can}$$
$$E_{can} ::= \texttt{A::}*[S_{can}] \mid E_{can}[E_{can}]$$
$$Q_{can} ::= /S_{can} \mid /E_{can} \mid Q_{can}/Q_{can}$$

We shall refer to the query expressions generated by this grammar as *canonical*; they can be shown to be of the type $/C_1/C_2/\dots/C_n$, where each C_i is of the form A::$\sigma[X_{can}]$, or of the form A::$\sigma[X_{can}]$ *conn* A'::$\sigma'[X'_{can}]$, with *conn* ∈ {*and, or*}, and X_{can}, X'_{can} ∈ {$S_{can}, E_{can}, true$}; we agree here to identify A::$\sigma[true]$ with A::σ.

Any such positive Core XPath query expression can be translated into one that is in "standard form", i.e., where the format of the sub-queries is of the type 'axis::*b*'; we formalize this idea now. The axes self, child, descendant, parent, ancestor, preceding-sibling, following-sibling will be referred to as *basic*. A basic Core XPath query is a query of the form //*[axis::σ], where axis is basic. More generally, the queries we propose to evaluate on trdags are defined formally as the expressions Q_{std} generated by the following grammar, where σ stands for any node name on the documents, or for * (meaning 'any'):

$$A \quad ::= \texttt{self} \mid \texttt{child} \mid \texttt{descendant} \mid \texttt{parent} \mid \texttt{ancestor} \mid$$
$$\texttt{preceding-sibling} \mid \texttt{following-sibling}$$
$$S \quad ::= \texttt{A::}\sigma \mid position() = i \mid S \textit{ and } S \mid S \textit{ or } S \mid \texttt{Root}$$
$$E \quad ::= \texttt{A::}*[S] \mid E[E]$$
$$Q_{std} ::= //* \mid //*[S] \mid //*[E]$$

Core XPath queries Q_{std} of the format generated by this grammar are said to be in *standard form*; to be able to handle any positive Core XPath query with such a grammar, we have introduced a special predicate called Root, deemed true only at the root node of the trdag considered.

By the *evaluation* of a given query expression *Q* on any trdag *t*, we mean the assignment: *t* ↦ the set of all context nodes on *t* where the expression *Q* evaluates to true (following the conventions of Definition 2); this latter set is also called the *answer* for Q on t. Two given queries Q_1, Q_2 are said to be *equivalent* iff, on any trdag t, the answer sets for Q_1 and Q_2 are the same. Any positive Core XPath query Q_{can} can be translated into an equivalent one in standard form; e.g., /c[following-sibling::g]/d *is equivalent to* //*[self::d *and* parent::*[Root *and* self::c [following-sibling::g]]] in standard form. An inductive procedure performing such a translation in the general case (of linear complexity w.r.t. the number of location steps in Q_{can}) is given in [4]. The following proposition results from Definition 2.

Proposition 1

(1) For any set of nodes X on a trdag t, and any axis A, *we have*   A$(X) =$

$$\bigcup_{\substack{x \in X, \\ \alpha \in pos_t(x) \\ \alpha = i_1 \ldots i_k}} \{ \text{/child::*}[position() = i_1]/\ldots/\text{child::*}[position() = i_k]/\text{A::*}\}$$

(2) For any trdag t, and any node with name b on t, we have:

i) //*[preceding::b] $= \bigcup_u \{$descendant-or-self(following-sibling(

   //*[self::u *and* (descendant::b *or* self::b)]))}

ii) //*[following::b] $= \bigcup_u \{$descendant-or-self(preceding-sibling(

   //*[self::u *and* (descendant::b *or* self::b)]))}

For any set S of nodes on t, the sets following(S) and preceding(S) can then be defined formally, following [1], as below:

a) following$(S) =$
   descendant-or-self(following-sibling(ancestor-or-self(S))),
b) preceding$(S) =$
   descendant-or-self(preceding-sibling(ancestor-or-self(S))).

Note 1 Unlike on a tree, the ancestor, descendant, following, self and preceding axes do *not* partition the set of nodes on a trdag t, in general.

4   Automata for Basic Core XPath Queries

4.1   The Semantics of the Approach

We first consider basic Core XPath queries. Composite or imbricated queries will subsequently be evaluated in a stepwise fashion; see Section 6.

To any basic query $Q = $ //*[axis::σ], we shall associate a word automaton (actually a transducer), referred to as $\mathbf{A}_Q$. It will run top-down, on the rlag $\mathcal{D}_t$ if axis is non-sibling, and on each of the chiblings $\mathcal{F}$ of $\mathcal{L}_t$ otherwise. In either case, a run will attach, to any node traversed, a pair of the form (l, x), where the first component l will have the intended semantics of selection or not by Q, of the corresponding node on t, and the component x will be a 1 or 0, with the intended semantics that $x = 1$ iff the corresponding node on t has a descendant answering

Q. At the end of the run, $label(u)$, at any node u of $\mathcal{D}_t$, will be replaced by a new label derived from the ll-pairs attached to u by the run.

To formalize these ideas, we introduce a set of new symbols $L = \{s, \eta, \top, \top'\}$ referred to as *llabels* (the term 'llabel' is used so as to avoid confusion with the term label). We define *ll-pairs* as elements of the set $L \times \{0, 1\}$, and the states of $\mathbf{A}_Q$ as elements of the set $\{init\} \cup (L \times \{0, 1\})$. For any Q, the automaton $\mathbf{A}_Q$ is over the alphabet $\Sigma \cup \{s, \eta\}$, has $init$ as its initial state, and has no final state. The set Δ_Q of transitions of $\mathbf{A}_Q$ will consist of rules of the form $(q, \tau) \rightarrow q'$ where $q \in \{init\} \cup (L \times \{0, 1\})$, $q' \in (L \times \{0, 1\})$, and $\tau \in \Sigma \cup \{s, \eta\}$.

For any rlag $\mathcal{G}$, we define a function $llab \colon Nodes(\mathcal{G}) \rightarrow \Sigma \cup \{s, \eta\}$, by setting $llab(u) = \pi_1(label(u))$, the first component of $label(u)$. A *run* of $\mathbf{A}_Q$ on $\mathcal{G}$ is a map $r \colon Nodes(\mathcal{G}) \rightarrow L \times \{0, 1\}$, such that, for every $u \in Nodes(\mathcal{G})$, the following holds:

- if u is $root_{\mathcal{G}}$, then the rule $(init, llab(u)) \rightarrow r(u)$ is in Δ_Q;
- otherwise, for every $v \in \gamma(u)$ the rules $(r(u), llab(v)) \rightarrow r(v)$ are all in Δ_Q.

Note 2 When `axis` is non-sibling, this amounts to requiring that, for any node v, the state $r(v)$ must be in conformity with the states $r(u)$ for *every* parent node u of v, with respect to the rules in Δ_Q.

From the run of the automaton $\mathbf{A}_Q$ and from the states it attaches to the nodes of $\mathcal{D}_t$, we will deduce, at every node u of t, a well-determined ll-pair as (a new) label at u, via the natural bijection between $Nodes(t)$ and $Nodes(\mathcal{D}_t)$. The ll-pairs thus attached to the nodes of t will have the following semantics (where x stands for the name of the node u on t, corresponding to the 'current' node on $\mathcal{D}_t$):

$(s, 1)$: $x \neq \sigma$, current node is selected;

$(\eta, 1)$: $x \neq \sigma$, current node is *not* selected, but has a selected descendant;

$(\eta, 0)$: $x \neq \sigma$, current node is *not* selected, and has *no* selected descendant;

$(\top', 1)$: $x = \sigma$, current node on t is selected by (i.e., is an answer for) Q;

$(\top, 1)$: $x = \sigma$, current node is *not* selected, but has a selected descendant;

$(\top, 0)$: $x = \sigma$, current node is *not* selected, and has *no* selected descendant.

Only the nodes on $\mathcal{D}_t$, to which the run of A_Q associates the labels $(s, 1)$ or $(\top', 1)$, correspond to the nodes of t that will get selected by the query Q. The ll-pairs with boolean component 1 will label the nodes of $\mathcal{D}_t$ corresponding to the nodes of t which are on a path to an answer for the query Q; thus the automaton $\mathbf{A}_Q$ will have *no* transitions from any state with boolean component 0 to a state with boolean component 1. Moreover, with a view to define runs which are unique (or unambiguous in a sense that will be presently made clear), we define the following *priority* relations between the ll-pairs:

$$(\eta, 0) > (\eta, 1) > (s, 1), \quad \text{and} \quad (\top, 0) > (\top, 1) > (\top', 1).$$

A run of the automaton $\mathbf{A}_Q$ will label any node u on $\mathcal{G}$ with an ll-pair coming either from the group $\{(\eta, 0), (\eta, 1), (s, 1)\}$, or from $\{(\top, 0), (\top, 1), (\top', 1)\}$; this group will be determined by $llab(u)$.

For ease of presentation, we agree to set $\eta' := s$, and often denote either of the above two groups of ll-pairs under the uniform notation $\{(l,0),(l,1),(l',1)\}$, where $l \in \{\eta, \top\}$, with the ordering $(l,0) > (l,1) > (l',1)$.

We shall construct a run r of $\mathbf{A}_Q$ on $\mathcal{G}$ that will be uniquely determined by the following *maximal priority* condition:

(**MP**): at any node v on $\mathcal{G}$, $r(v)$ is the maximal ll-pair $(\mathfrak{t}, x)$ for the ordering $>$ in the group $\{(l,0),(l,1),(l',1)\}$ determined by $llab(v)$, such that $\mathbf{A}_Q$ contains a transition rule of the form $(r(u), llab(v)) \rightarrow (\mathfrak{t}, x)$, for *every* parent u of v.

Such a run will assign a label with boolean component 1 only to the nodes corresponding to those of the minimal sub-trdag t containing the root of t and all the answers to Q on t.

4.2   Re-labeling of $\mathcal{D}_t$ by the Runs of $\mathbf{A}_Q$

We first consider a non-sibling basic query Q on a given document t, and a given run r of the automaton $\mathbf{A}_Q$ on $\mathcal{D}_t$; at the end of the run, the nodes on $\mathcal{D}_t$ will get re-labeled with new ll-pairs, computed as below for every $u \in Nodes(\mathcal{D}_t)$:

$$lab_r(u) = (s,1) \quad \text{iff} \quad r(u) \in \{(s,1),(\top',1)\},$$
$$lab_r(u) = (\eta,1) \quad \text{iff} \quad r(u) \in \{(\eta,1),(\top,1)\},$$
$$lab_r(u) = (\eta,0) \quad \text{iff} \quad r(u) \in \{(\eta,0),(\top,0)\}.$$

The rlag obtained in this manner from $\mathcal{D}_t$, following the run r and the associated re-labeling function lab_r, will be denoted as $r(\mathcal{D}_t)$.

For a basic query Q over a sibling axis, the situation is a little more complex, because several different nodes on one chibling of $\mathcal{L}_t$ can have the same name (non-terminal), or several different chiblings can have nodes named by the same non-terminal, or both. Thus, to any node of $\mathcal{D}_t$, named with a non-terminal A, will correspond in general a *set* of ll-pairs, assigned by the various runs of $\mathbf{A}_Q$ to the A-named nodes on the various chiblings of $\mathcal{L}_t$. We therefore proceed as follows: for every complete set $\hat{r}$ of runs of $\mathbf{A}_Q$, formed of one run $r_{\mathcal{F}}$ on each chibling $\mathcal{F}$, we will define $\hat{r}(\mathcal{D}_t)$ as the re-labeled rlag derived from $\mathcal{D}_t$, under $\hat{r}$. With that purpose we associate to $\hat{r}$ and any $u \in Nodes(\mathcal{D}_t)$, a set of ll-pairs:

$$ll_{\hat{r}}(u) = \bigcup_{r_{\mathcal{F}} \in \hat{r}} \{r_{\mathcal{F}}(v) \mid v \in Nodes(\mathcal{F}), \text{ and } name(v) = name(u)\}.$$

We then derive, at each node of $\mathcal{D}_t$ a unique ll-pair in conformity with the semantics of our approach, by using the following function:

$$\lambda_{\hat{r}}(u) = s \iff ll_{\hat{r}}(u) \cap \{(s,1),(\top',1)\} \neq \emptyset,,$$
$$\lambda_{\hat{r}}(u) = \eta < \iff ll_{\hat{r}}(u) \cap \{(s,1),(\top',1)\} = \emptyset.$$

From $\mathcal{D}_t$ and this function $\lambda_{\hat{r}}$, we next derive an rlag $\lambda_{\hat{r}}(\mathcal{D}_t)$ by re-labeling each node u on $\mathcal{D}_t$ with the pair $(\lambda_{\hat{r}}(u), -)$. And finally we define $\hat{r}(\mathcal{D}_t)$ as the rlag obtained from $\lambda_{\hat{r}}(\mathcal{D}_t)$, by running on it the automaton for the basic non-sibling query $//*[\mathtt{self}::s]$, as indicated at the beginning of this subsection.

In practical terms, such a run amounts in essence to setting, as the second component of $label(u)$ at any node u, the boolean 1 iff u is on a path to some node with llab s, and 0 otherwise. All these details are illustrated with an example in the following subsection.

4.3   The Automata

We present the automata for all the basic queries in Figure 3. A few words on some of the automata by way of explanation. First, the reason why the automaton for self does *not* have the states $(\top, 0), (\top, 1), (s, 1)$: for $(\top, 0), (\top, 1)$, by the semantics of Section 4.1 we must have $x = \sigma$, where x is the name of the current node on t, but then the query //*[self::σ] should select the current node, so one cannot be at such a state; as for $(s, 1)$, the reasoning is just the opposite. Next, the reason why the automaton for descendant does *not* have the states $(\eta, 1), (\top, 1)$: if the semantics attribute one of these pairs to any node u, that would mean the node u has a selected descendant u'; which means that u' has some σ-descendant node, which would then be a σ-descendant for u too, so Q should select u.

Figure 4 illustrates the evaluation of $Q = $ //*[following-sibling::b], on the trdag t of Figure 2. We first use the automaton for the basic query //*[following-sibling::σ] with $\sigma = b$, and then the automaton for the query //*[self::σ] with $\sigma = s$. The sub-trdag of t, formed of nodes corresponding to those of $\widehat{r}(\mathcal{D}_t)$ with labels having boolean component 1, contains all the answers to Q on t.

5   Maximal Priority Runs of Basic Query Automata

Note that the following properties, required by our semantics of Section 4.1, hold on the automaton $\mathbf{A}_Q$ for any basic Core XPath query $Q = $ //*[axis::σ]:

i) There are no transitions from any state with boolean component 0 to a state with boolean component 1;

ii) The σ-transitions have all their target states in $\{(\top, 0), (\top, 1), (\top', 1)\}$; for any $\gamma \neq \sigma$, the target states of γ-transitions are all in $\{(\eta, 0), (\eta, 1), (s, 1)\}$.

Theorem 1. *Let Q be any basic Core XPath query, t any given trdag, and let $\mathcal{G}$ denote either the rlag $\mathcal{D}_t$, or any given chibling $\mathcal{F}$ of $\mathcal{L}_t$. Assume given a labeling function $\mathbb{L}$ from $Nodes(\mathcal{G})$ into the set of ll-pairs, which is correct with respect to Q, i.e., in conformity with the semantics of Section 4.1. Then there is a run r of the automaton $\mathbf{A}_Q$ on $\mathcal{G}$, such that:*

i) r is compatible with $\mathbb{L}$; i.e., $r(u) = \mathbb{L}(u)$ for every node u on $\mathcal{G}$;
ii) r satisfies the maximal priority condition (MP) of Section 4.1.

Proof. We first construct, by induction, a 'complete' run (i.e., defined at all the nodes of $\mathcal{G}$) satisfying property i). For that, we shall employ reasonings that will be specific to the axis of the basic query Q. We give here the details only for the axis parent; they are similar for the other axes.

$Q = //*[\texttt{parent}::\sigma]$: (The axis considered is non-sibling so $\mathcal{G} = \mathcal{D}_t$ here.) At the root u node of $\mathcal{D}_t$, we set $r(u) = \mathbb{L}(u)$; we have to show that there is a transition rule in $\mathbf{A}_Q$ of the form $(init, llab(u)) \to \mathbb{L}(u)$. Obviously, for the axis parent, the root node u cannot correspond to a node on t selected by Q, so the only ll-pairs possible for $\mathbb{L}(u)$ are $(l, 0), (l, 1)$, with $l \in \{\eta, \top\}$; for each of these choices, we do have a transition rule of the needed form, on $\mathbf{A}_Q$.

Consider then a node v on $\mathcal{D}_t$ such that, at each of its ancestor nodes u on $\mathcal{D}_t$, the part of the run r of A_Q has been constructed such that $r(u) = \mathbb{L}(u)$; assume that the run cannot be extended at the node by setting $r(v) = \mathbb{L}(v)$. This means that there exists a parent node w of v, such that $(\mathbb{L}(w), llab(v)) \to \mathbb{L}(v)$ is not a transition rule of $\mathbf{A}_Q$; we shall then derive a contradiction. We only have to consider the cases where the boolean component of $\mathbb{L}(w)$ is greater than or equal to that of $\mathbb{L}(v)$. The possible couples $\mathbb{L}(w), \mathbb{L}(v)$ are then respectively:

$$\mathbb{L}(w) : (\top, 0) \mid (\top, 1) \mid (\top, 1) \mid (\top', 1) \mid (\top', 1)$$
$$\mathbb{L}(v) : (\eta, 0) \mid (\top, 1) \mid (\eta, 1) \mid (\top, 1) \mid (\eta, 1)$$

In all cases, we have $llab(w) = \sigma$ because of the semantics, so the node (on t corresponding to the node) v has a σ-parent, so must be selected; thus the above choices for $\mathbb{L}(v)$ are not in conformity with the semantics; contradiction.

We now prove that the complete run r thus constructed, satisfies property ii). For this part of the proof, the reasoning does not need to be specific for each Q; so, write Q more generally, as $//*[\texttt{axis}::\sigma]$ for some given σ. Suppose the run r does not satisfy the maximal priority condition at some node v on $\mathcal{G}$; assume, for instance, that the run r made the choice, say of the ll-pair $(l, 1)$, although the maximal labeling of the node v, in a manner compatible with the ll-pairs of all its parents, was the ll-pair $(l, 0)$. Since $\mathbb{L}$ is assumed correct, and r is compatible with $\mathbb{L}$, the maximal possible labeling $(l, 0)$ would mean that the node (on t corresponding to the node) v has no descendant selected by Q; whereas, the choice that r is assumed to have made at v, namely the ll-pair $(l, 1)$, has the opposite semantics whether or not $llab(v) = \sigma$; in other words, the labeling $\mathbb{L}$ would not be correct with respect to Q; contradiction. The other possibilities for the 'bad' labelings under r also get eliminated in a similar manner.   □

Theorem 2. *Let $Q, t, \mathcal{D}_t, \mathcal{F}, \mathcal{G}$ be as above. Let r be a (complete) run of the automaton $\mathbf{A}_Q$ on $\mathcal{G}$, which satisfies the maximal priority condition (**MP**) of Section 4.1. Then the labeling function $\mathbb{L}$ on $Nodes(\mathcal{G})$, defined as $\mathbb{L}(u) = r(u)$ for any node u, is correct with respect to the semantics of Section 4.1.*

Proof. Let us suppose that the labeling $\mathbb{L}$ deduced from r is *not* correct with respect to Q; we shall then derive a contradiction. The reasoning will be by case analysis, which will be specific to the axis of the basic query Q considered. We give the details here for $Q = //*[\texttt{descendant}::\sigma]$. The axis is non-sibling, so we have $\mathcal{G} = \mathcal{D}_t$. The sets $Nodes(t), Nodes(\mathcal{D}_t)$ are in a natural bijection, so for any node u on $\mathcal{D}_t$ we shall also denote by u the corresponding node on t, in our reasonings below.

We saw that the automaton $\mathbf{A}_Q$ for the `descendant` axis does not have the states $(\eta, 1), (\top, 1)$. Consider then a node u on $\mathcal{D}_t$ such that: for all ancestor nodes w of u, the llabel $r(w)$ is in conformity with the semantics, but the ll-pair $r(u)$ is not in conformity. Now, $\mathbf{A}_Q$ has only 5 states: $(init), (\top', 1), (s, 1), (\top, 0), (\eta, 0)$, of which only the last four can llabel the nodes. So the possible 'bad' choices that r is assumed to have made at our node u, are as follows:

(a) $r(u) = (\top', 1)$, but the node u is *not* an answer to the query Q. Here $name(u)$ must be σ, so the choice of r ought to have been $(\top, 0)$;

(b) $r(u) = (s, 1)$, but the node u is *not* an answer to the query Q. But $name(u) \neq \sigma$, so the choice of r ought to have been $(\eta, 0)$;

(c) $r(u) = (\eta, 0)$, but the node u *is* an answer to the query Q. But $name(u) \neq \sigma$, so the choice of r ought to have been $(s, 1)$;

(d) $r(u) = (\top, 0)$, but the node u *is* an answer to the query Q. Here $name(u)$ must be σ, so the choice of r ought to have been $(\top', 1)$.

In all the four cases, we have to show:

i) that the "ought-to-have-been" choice ll-pair is reachable from *all* the parent nodes of u;

ii) *and* that, with such a new and 'correct' choice made at u, r can be completed from u, into a run on the entire dag $\mathcal{D}_t$.

The reasoning will be similar for cases (a), (b) and for the cases (c), (d). Here are the details for case (a): That u is *not* an answer to Q means that u has no σ-descendant node, so for all nodes v below u on $\mathcal{D}_t$, we have $llab(v) \neq \sigma$. Therefore, assertions i) and ii) above follow from the following observations on the automaton for $Q = //*[\texttt{descendant::}\sigma]$:

i) *if* r could reach the state $(\top', 1)$ at node u (via a σ-transition) from any parent node of u, then $(\top, 0)$ is also reachable thus at u, from any of them;

ii) *if*, from the state $(\top', 1)$, r could reach all the nodes on $\mathcal{D}_t$ below u (with state $(\eta, 0)$), via transitions over $\gamma \neq \sigma$, then it can do exactly the same now, with the 'correct' choice ll-pair $(\top, 0)$ at u.

As for case (c): Node u *is* an answer to Q here, so u has a σ-descendant; let v be a σ-node below u on $\mathcal{D}_t$; the ll-pair $r(v)$ that r assigns to v must then be either $(\top', 1)$ or $(\top, 0)$; this implies that r passed from the state $(\eta, 0)$ – supposedly assigned by r to u – to $(\top', 1)$ or $(\top, 0)$ somewhere between u and v; which is impossible, as is easily seen on the automaton $\mathbf{A}_Q$ for the axis `descendant` considered. The reasoning for case (d) is even easier: from state $(\top, 0)$, no state with an outgoing σ-transition is reachable. □

6   Evaluating Composite Queries

A composite query is a query in standard form, but not basic; it is evaluated incrementally. We first consider queries of the form $//*[\texttt{A::}x \; conn \; \texttt{A'::}x']$, where $conn \in \{and, or\}$, where the axes are all basic. Observe that the answer for $Q = //*[\texttt{A::}x \; conn \; \texttt{A'::}x']$ can be obtained as union (resp. intersection) of the answers for the two 'component' queries $//*[\texttt{A::}x]$, and $//*[\texttt{A'::}x']$, when

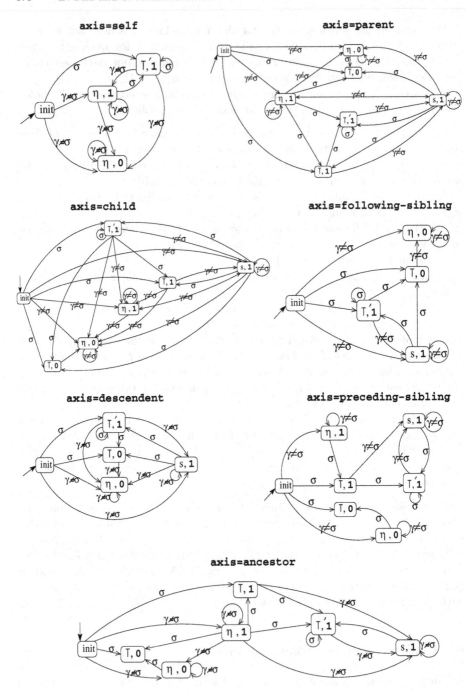

Fig. 3. Automata for //*[axis::σ]

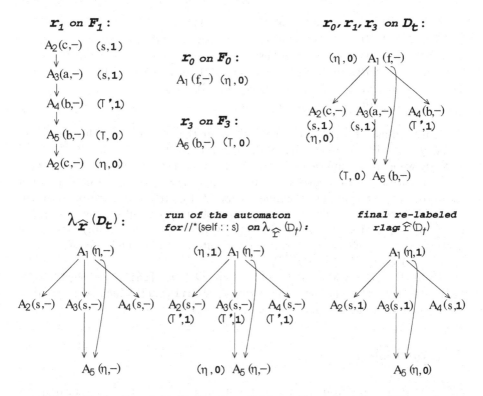

Fig. 4. Evaluation of //*[following-sibling::b] on the trdag of Figure 2

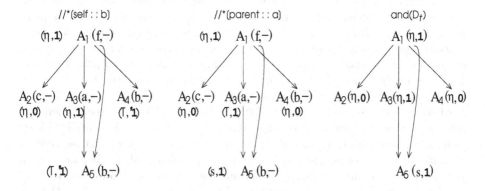

Fig. 5. Evaluation of //*[self::b and parent::a] on the trdag of Figure 2

conn is an *or* (resp. *and*). So, we apply the method described earlier, separately for $Q_1 = //*[A::x]$ and for $Q_2 = //*[A'::x']$, thus getting two respective evaluating runs r_1, r_2. Any node u of the dag $\mathcal{D}_t$ will then be re-labeled, by the composite query Q, with ll-pairs computed by a function AND when *conn* = *and* (resp. OR when *conn* = *or*), in conformity with the semantics of Section 4.1:

$$AND(u) = (s,1) \quad \text{iff} \quad r_1(u) = (l',1) = r_2(u);$$
$$AND(u) = (\eta,0) \quad \text{iff} \quad r_1(u) = (l,0) \text{ or } r_2(u) = (l,0);$$
$$AND(u) = (\eta,1) \quad \text{otherwise.}$$
$$OR(u) = (s,1) \quad \text{iff} \quad r_1(u) = (l',1) \text{ or } r_2(u) = (l',1);$$
$$OR(u) = (\eta,0) \quad \text{iff} \quad r_1(u) = (l,0) = r_2(u);$$
$$OR(u) = (\eta,1) \quad \text{otherwise} \qquad \qquad .$$

Figure 5 illustrates the above reasoning, for the evaluation of the composite query $Q = //*[\texttt{self}::b \text{ } and \text{ } \texttt{parent}::a]$, on the trdag t of Figure 2:

Next, we consider imbricated queries of the form $Q = //*[\texttt{A}_1::*[\texttt{A}_2::\sigma]]$. We first consider a maximal priority run evaluating r_2 (resp. a set of runs $\widehat{r}_2$) of the automaton associated to the inner query $//*[\texttt{A}_2::\sigma]$, on $\mathcal{D}_t$ (resp. on the set of all chiblings of $\mathcal{L}_t$). This run (resp. the set of runs) will output the rlag $r_2(\mathcal{D}_t)$ (resp. $\widehat{r}_2(\mathcal{D}_t)$), as described in Section 4.2. Evaluating the given imbricated query Q on the dag t is then done by running the automaton for the basic outer query $//*[\texttt{A}_1::s]$ on $r_2(\mathcal{D}_t)$ (resp. $\widehat{r}_2(\mathcal{D}_t)$).

Finally, the answer for a query of the type $Q = //*[\texttt{child}::x[position() = k]]$, is the subset of the nodes answering $//*[\texttt{child}::x]$, which correspond to a k-th node on some sibling.

7   Conclusion

Information retrieval from compressed structures, without having to uncompress them, is a field of active research; cf. e.g., [13,8]. Our concern has been the evaluation of queries on XML documents that may be in a compressed form. Limiting our concern to positive Core XPath queries, we have presented a method for evaluating them on any trdag t *without* having to uncompress t; the given query is first translated (in linear time w.r.t. the number of location steps, cf. [4]) into a standard form, where the sub-queries are of a basic type. With each basic query, an automaton is associated such that an unambiguous maximal priority run of this automaton can evaluate the query. An algorithm constructing the maximal priority runs is given in [4]; the complexity bound is $\mathcal{O}(n^3)$ on any trdag t, where n is the number of nodes of t; it reduces to $\mathcal{O}(n^2)$ on trees, where the relation *Parents* is trivial. This algorithm has just been implemented. (*Please note:* given a query Q, the answer for Q on a trdag t can be a strict superset of the answer for the same query Q on the tree-equivalent $\widehat{t}$ of t; it is shown in [4] how to derive the answer for Q on $\widehat{t}$, from the answer for Q on t; the method consists in completing the label associated to any given node u on t by the run of $\mathbf{A}_Q$, by an appropriate subset of $pos_t(u)$.)

An advantage of the approach presented in this paper seems to be that the basic sub-queries "composing" a given query can be evaluated in parallel, in several cases; a detailed analysis of this issue could be a direction for future work. We also expect to be able to extend our approach to the evaluation of more general XPath queries, such as those involving the data values, by adapting its underlying mechanism based on labeling.

References

1. P. Buneman, M. Grohe, C. Koch, *Path queries on compressed XML.* In Proc. of the 29*th* Conf. on VLDB, 2003, pp. 141–152, Ed. Morgan Kaufmann.
2. G. Busatto, M. Lohrey, S. Maneth, *Grammar-Based Tree Compression.* EPFL Technical Report IC/2004/80, http://icwww.epfl.ch/publications.
3. G. Busatto, M. Lohrey, S. Maneth, *Efficient Memory Representation of XML Documents.* In Proc. DBPL'05, LNCS 3774, pp. 199–216, Springer-Verlag, 2005.
4. B. Fila, S. Anantharaman, *Automata for Analyzing and Querying Compressed Documents*, Research Report, RR-2006-03, LIFO, 2006, http://www.univ-orleans.fr/lifo/prodsci/rapports/RR/RR2006/
5. M. Frick, M. Grohe, C. Koch, *Query Evaluation of Compressed Trees*, In Proc. of LICS'03, pp. 188–197, IEEE, 2003.
6. G. Gottlob, C. Koch, *Monadic Queries over Tree-Structured Data*, In Proc. of LICS'02, pp. 189–202, IEEE, 2002.
7. G. Gottlob, C. Koch, R. Pichler, L. Segoufin, *The complexity of XPath query evaluation and XML typing* In Journal of the ACM 52(2):284-335, 2005.
8. M. Lohrey, *Word problems and membership problems on compressed words* In SIAM Journal of Computing, 35(5):1210-1240, 2006.
9. M. Marx, *XPath and Modal Logics for Finite DAGs.* In Proc. of TABLEAUX'03, pp. 150–164, LNAI 2796, 2003.
10. W. Martens, F. Neven, *On the complexity of typechecking top-down XML transformations*, In Theoretical Computer Science, 336(1): 153–180, 2005.
11. F. Neven, *Automata Theory for XML Researchers*, In SIGMOD Record 31(3), September 2002.
12. F. Neven, T. Schwentick, *Query automata over finite trees*, In Theoretical Computer Science, 275(1–2):633–674, 2002.
13. W. Rytter, *Compressed and fully compressed pattern matching in one and two dimensions*, In Proceedings of the IEEE, 88(11):1769–1778, 2000.
14. World Wide Web Consortium, *XML Path Language (XPath Recommendation)*, http://www.w3c.org/TR/xpath/

Boolean Rings for
Intersection-Based Satisfiability

Nachum Dershowitz[1,*], Jieh Hsiang[2,**],
Guan-Shieng Huang[3,***], and Daher Kaiss[4]

[1] School of Computer Science, Tel Aviv University, Ramat Aviv, Israel
nachumd@tau.ac.il
[2] Department of Computer Science and Information Engineering,
National Taiwan University, Taipei, Taiwan
hsiang@csie.ntu.edu.tw
[3] Department of Computer Science and Information Engineering,
National Chi Nan University, Nantou, Taiwan
shieng@ncnu.edu.tw
[4] Design Technology Solutions Group, Intel Corporation, Haifa, Israel
daher.kaiss@intel.com

> There is not a person in this courtroom
> who has never told a lie,
> who has never done an immoral thing,
> and there is no man living
> who has never looked upon a woman
> without desire.[1]
>
> —Harper Lee: *To Kill a Mockingbird*

Abstract. A potential advantage of using a Boolean-ring formalism for propositional formulæ is the large measure of simplification it facilitates. We propose a combined linear and binomial representation for Boolean-ring polynomials with which one can easily apply Gaussian elimination and Horn-clause methods to advantage. We demonstrate that this framework, with its enhanced simplification, is especially amenable to intersection-based learning, as in recursive learning and the method of Stålmarck. Experiments support the idea that problem variables can be eliminated and search trees can be shrunk by incorporating learning in the form of Boolean-ring saturation.

1 Introduction

Simplification has been used successfully in recent years in the context of theorem proving. This process requires a well-founded notion of "simplicity", under

* Research supported in part by the Israel Science Foundation (grant no. 250/05).
** Research supported in part by the National Science Council of the Republic of China, Taiwan (grant no. NSC94-2213-E-002-011).
*** Research supported by the National Science Council of the Republic of China, Taiwan (grant no. NSC94-2213-E-260-016).

[1] Atticus presumably did not mean $\neg\exists m.\neg\exists t,w.\neg Desired(t,m,w)$. Bill Clinton was reported to have used a similar triple negation.

M. Hermann and A. Voronkov (Eds.): LPAR 2006, LNAI 4246, pp. 482–496, 2006.
© Springer-Verlag Berlin Heidelberg 2006

which one can delete intermediate results that follow from known (or yet to be derived) simpler facts, without jeopardizing completeness of the inference mechanism. Simplifying as much as possible at each stage can greatly reduce storage requirements. Simplification-based theorem-proving strategies, as in the popular term-rewriting approach, have been used to solve some difficult problems in mathematics, including the long-open Robbins Algebra Conjecture [19]. Term rewriting means using equations asymmetrically to replace "equals by equals" in the direction that decreases the complexity of the term (according to some well-founded measure). For term rewriting as a tool in automated deduction, see [1,12]. For an abstract theory of inference with simplification, see [11,5].

A natural way of incorporating simplification in propositional reasoning is to use the *Boolean-ring* (BR) formalism. Boolean rings obey the following identities:

$$
\begin{array}{lll}
xx = x & x0 = 0 & x1 = x \\
x + x = 0 & x + 0 = x & -x = x \\
xy = yx & (xy)z = x(yz) & \\
x + y = y + x & (x + y) + z = x + (y + z) & x(y + z) = xy + xz
\end{array}
$$

where (nilpotent) $+$ is *exclusive-or* and (idempotent) juxtaposition is *logical-and*, $\wedge$. (The additive inverse $-x$ is useless.) It is straightforward to express inclusive-or and negation: $x \vee y$ is $xy + x + y$ and $\bar{x}$ is $x + 1$.

The Boolean-ring formalism differs from Boolean algebra in that it defines a unique normal form (up to associativity and commutativity of the two operators) for every Boolean formula, called a *Boolean polynomial* (also known as a *Zhegalkin polynomial* or *Reed-Muller normal form*). It is known [22,21] that circuits based on exclusive-or are smaller, on the average, than those using inclusive-or. A similar advantage should accrue symbolic representations. Like any other normal form, applying the distributive law (the bottom-right equation) can cause the length of a Boolean polynomial to grow exponentially in the worst case.

This paper focuses on satisfiability testing using Boolean rings (which is, of course, NP-hard [4]). Several possibilities are outlined in the next two sections. Section 4 proposes a Davis-Putnam-like method for satisfiability. We use a novel representation, called Bin-Lin, separating the set of formulæ into two parts (linear, binomial), each of which, on its own, can be dealt with efficiently. This is followed (in Sect. 5) by some suggestions for practical improvements. Converting to the Bin-Lin representation is the subject of Sect. 6. Section 7 provides several relevant complexity results, including NP-completeness (via reduction from SAT, which implies completeness of the proposed method). We also give polynomial-time results for restricted classes of Boolean-ring formulæ corresponding to the two parts mentioned above. The latter results provide some justification as to why the proposed method may be efficient.

The main advantage of the proposed Bin-Lin representation is that it allows for a large measure of polynomial-time inference of new facts, using Gaussian elimination on the linear part and Horn methods for the binomial. This suggests incorporating more forward reasoning in a search-based satisfiability procedure than just Boolean constraint propagation. In Sect. 8, we apply the Boolean-ring representation in a framework—akin to Stålmarck's method [23] (see also [3]) and recursive learning [18]—that includes computing the intersection of sets of formulæ. Preliminary experimental results may be found in Sect. 9. This is followed by some brief comments.

2   Satisfiability

To decide satisfiability, one can transform a formula into a normal form that clearly distinguishes between satisfiable and unsatisfiable cases. Such canonical representations include disjunctive normal form (DNF) and conditional normal form (as in OBDDs). The Boolean-ring normal form (BNF), described above, can be obtained directly by using pattern matching and repeatedly applying the emboldened ring axioms (on the previous page) from left to right to any subformula [14]. Tautologies reduce to 1; contradictions, to 0; contingent formulæ, to neither. But a normal form can of necessity be exponentially larger than the original. For example, the BNF of $(p + p')(q + q')(r + r')$ is $pqr + pqr' + pq'r + pq'r' + p'qr + p'qr' + p'q'r + p'q'r'$. Despite the fact that, in the process of normalization, terms that appear twice in a sum cancel each other out (since $x + x = 0$), this method is still, in reality, impractical.

An alternative [7,15] to BNF is to construct a Gröbner basis (confluent and terminating rewrite system) from the initial set of equations, plus idempotence $(xx = x)$ for each propositional variable (x). To begin with, rather than present the whole given formula as one big equation, conjunctions $AB = 1$ are divided into two, $A = 1$ and $B = 1$, and inclusive disjunctions $A \lor B = 0$ into $A = 0$, $B = 0$. The BR axioms are applied at each step, and equations are *inter-reduced* by using each as a simplifier of others (permuting arguments, as necessary to match rule patterns), until no longer possible. The resultant reduced set of Boolean polynomials is unique up to associativity and commutativity of sums and products. By imposing an ordering on (variables and extending it to) monomials, a unique normal form for Boolean functions is obtained. Efficient techniques (congruence closure, Gröbner bases) can be applied to the generation task. A structure-sharing ("decision diagram") exclusive-or normal from is presented in [16].

The Davis-Putnam-Logemann-Loveland (DPLL) procedure [8] was the first attempt to solve the satisfiability problem efficiently, employing a backtracking search strategy, plus heuristics to minimize formulæ. A truth value is assigned to a variable and the formula is recursively solved, trying another value when no solution is found. There are many fast implementations today based on this old procedure.

In the same vein, one can easily represent formulæ as sets of Boolean polynomials (without any exponential blowup in size), and use a similar backtracking method. See [15]. Splitting is done on variables, as usual, but formulæ are kept as simplified BR equations. Section 4 below improves on this by employing a new BR representation.

The traditional mechanical approach to satisfiability of a propositional formula is to assert its negation and try to infer a contradiction. The total number of consequences one needs to derive is, of course, in general, exponential. Most nontrivial proofs require some form of case splitting. In Sect. 8, we show how to combine limited saturation with search, within a BR framework.

3 Simplification

To counter the certain exponential cost of naïve realizations of satisfiability methods, simplification at intermediate stages is of paramount importance. Equations being processed are replaced with simpler ones (in some well-founded sense) by making *polynomial-time* inferences and deleting now-redundant formulæ. Such steps reduce the likelihood of suffering from the potentially exponential aspect of the approach (be it case analysis, splitting, merging, or distributivity).

Regardless of the method, it is helpful to make cheap and valuable deductions—which may enable additional simplifications—as early as possible. In particular, virtually all approaches employ some mechanism for detecting "necessary" assignments. Simplification rules used in DPLL and OBDD provers [6] include tautology, unit (Boolean constraint propagation), pure literal, subsumption, and failed literal. (In practice, tautology and pure-literal are often omitted.) In the search approach, after assigning 0 or 1 to a variable, simplifiers like $x0 = 0$, $x1 = x$, $x \vee 0 = x$, and $x \vee 1 = 1$ should be applied, regardless of the specific manner in which formulæ are represented, since these rules may result in the deletion of all occurrences of some other variables.

Performing simplification during preprocessing can also be useful. In [20], preprocessing CNF formulæ derived from circuit testing, bounded model checking, combinatorial equivalence checking, and superscalar processor verification, was found to reduce the number of variables to $1/3$ in many cases. In a normalization approach, the same simplifiers can dramatically reduce the size of formulæ. The first five Boolean-ring axioms are simplifiers. They can be easily implemented by keeping terms sorted.

4 Representation

We argue that Boolean rings are an especially convenient framework for simplification. As already mentioned, distributivity is the potentially expensive step (even when directed acyclic graphs are used for shared subterms). We propose a new representation, called Bin-Lin, that circumvents this problem.

A *linear equation* (over $\mathbb{Z}_2$) is a Boolean equation of the form $x_1 + \cdots + x_n = 1$ or $x_1 + \cdots + x_n = 0$, where the x_i are distinct propositional variables. A *binomial equation* is a Boolean equation with at most two monomials, that is, an equation of one of the three forms: $P = Q$, $P = 0$, or $Q = 1$, where P and Q are products of distinct propositional variables (distinct on account of idempotence). Simple equations, $x = 0$, $y = 1$, or $x = y$, for propositional variables x, y, as well as degenerate equations, $0 = 0$, $1 = 1$, or $1 = 0$, will be considered both linear and binomial.

Let $\mathcal{B}$ be a set of binomial equations and $\mathcal{L}$ be a set of linear equations over the propositional variables. Instead of solving a general set of Boolean-ring equations (e.g. $xy + x + y = 0$ implies $x = 0$ and $y = 0$), we will decide the satisfiability of $\mathcal{B} \cup \mathcal{L}$. Simplification by $\mathcal{B}$ of $\mathcal{L}$, and vice-versa, will be severely limited.

Given a system $\mathcal{R} = \mathcal{B} \cup \mathcal{L}$ and an ordering $>$ on monomials, inference proceeds as follows:

1. *Termination Test.* If $1 = 0$ has been inferred, the system is unsatisfiable.
2. *Tautology Deletion.* Remove all trivial equations $A = A$.
3. *Decomposition.* Decompose any equation $x_1 x_2 \cdots x_k = 1$ in $\mathcal{B}$ into $x_1 = 1, \ldots, x_k = 1$.
4. *Unit Rule.* Use all unit equations of the form $x = 0$ or $x = 1$ in $\mathcal{R}$ to simplify equations in $\mathcal{R}$.
5. *Equivalence Rule.* If two variables are equated, as in $x = y$ or $x + y = 0$, replace one by the other throughout $\mathcal{R}$.
6. *Simplification.* Inter-reduce one equation by another within $\mathcal{B}$ and within $\mathcal{L}$, by replacing occurrences in $\mathcal{B} \cup \mathcal{L}$ of the larger side (larger, in the given ordering $>$) of any equation $M = N$, say M, with the smaller side, N.
7. *Splitting.* Split the system of equations by considering $\mathcal{R} \cup \{x = 1\}$ and $\mathcal{R} \cup \{x = 0\}$, individually and recursively, for some propositional variable x appearing in $\mathcal{R}$. Heuristics (e.g. [10]) can be applied to decide which variable x to split on.

Equations in $\mathcal{B}$ and $\mathcal{L}$ are processed independently, except for the *Unit Rule* and *Equivalence Rule*. Splitting on x and applying the rule for units eliminates x from both $\mathcal{B} \cup \{x = 1\} \cup \mathcal{L}$ and $\mathcal{B} \cup \{x = 0\} \cup \mathcal{L}$.

This inference procedure is complete for propositional reasoning, because any Boolean formula can be converted into a Bin-Lin form preserving satisfiability, as will be explained in Sect. 6, and splitting with the *Unit Rule* suffices to test satisfiability of BR formulæ.

The *Simplification* step is not needed for completeness, but rather to improve search efficiency. All the steps, save *Splitting*, are encompassed by the replacement rules of Table 1. The choice of ordering $>$ is flexible: It may prefer long monomials, to keep equations short, or short ones, to maximize the likelihood of a simplifier applying.

One advantage of this mixed representation is that relatively fast methods exist for processing each of the two components; see Sect. 7. Software is readily available to handle the computations within each of the two sets, $\mathcal{B}$ and $\mathcal{L}$. Distributivity is not needed when simplifying Boolean terms, because (non-unit) equations in $\mathcal{L}$ are not used to simplify $\mathcal{B}$. So formulæ do not grow very large, as in more conventional Boolean-ring based methods.

Example 1. Suppose we want to prove the validity of the formula

$$(p \vee q) \wedge (\overline{q} \vee s) \wedge (\overline{s} \vee p) \wedge (\overline{p} \vee r) \wedge (\overline{r} \vee \overline{p} \vee t) \Rightarrow (t \wedge r) .$$

Table 1. Inference rules for *replacing* antecendents with consequents (A, B are any formulæ; M, N are monomials, including variables and values; x is any propositional variable; c, d are either Boolean value; $A[N]$ is formula $A[M]$ with subformula N instead of M; $\perp$ signifies unsatisfiability)

$$\frac{1 = 0}{\perp} \qquad \frac{\perp, \; A = B}{\perp} \qquad \frac{A = A}{}$$

$$\frac{MN = 1}{M = 1, \; N = 1} \qquad \frac{M0 = N}{N = 0} \qquad \frac{M1 = N}{M = N} \qquad \frac{Mxx = N}{Mx = N}$$

$$\frac{A + 0 = c}{A = c} \quad \frac{A + 1 = 1}{A = 0} \quad \frac{A + 1 = 0}{A = 1} \quad \frac{A + x + x = c}{A = c} \quad \frac{M + N = 0}{M = N}$$

$$\frac{M = N, \; A[M] = B}{M = N, \; A[N] = B} \; M{>}N \qquad \frac{x + A = c, \; x + B = d}{x + A = c, \; A + B = c + d} \; x{>}B{>}A$$

To represent the clause $p \vee q$, a new variable $\widehat{p}$ for $\overline{p}$ is required. The clausal form of its negation, written as Boolean equations, is as follows:

(1) $qs = q$ (2) $sp = s$ (3) $prt = pr$ (4) $rt = 0$
(5) $p + \widehat{p} = 1$ (6) $q\widehat{p} = \widehat{p}$ (7) $pr = p$.

Equation (4) simplifies (3) to $pr = 0$, which, in turn, simplifies (7) to $p = 0$. This invokes the *Unit Rule*, and (2,5) become $s = 0$ and $\widehat{p} = 1$. The new (2) simplifies (1) to $q = 0$. Finally, $\widehat{p} = 1$ and $q = 0$ simplify (6) into the contradiction $1 = 0$, concluding the proof (*sans* splits). □

Example 2. The Pigeon-Hole Principle for 3 pigeons and 2 holes can be expressed as linear equations $\{a_1 + a_2 + 1 = 0, b_1 + b_2 + 1 = 0, c_1 + c_2 + 1 = 0\}$ and binomial equations $\{x_i y_j = 0 \mid x_i, y_j \in A, x \neq y \vee i \neq j\}$, where $A = \{a_1, a_2, b_1, b_2, c_1, c_2\}$ and x_i means that pigeon x is in the ith hole. One split on a_1, with simplification, proves the principle. If $a_1 = 0$, then $a_2 = 1$ from the linear part, $b_2 = c_2 = 0$ from the binomial part, $b_1 = c_1 = 1$ from the linear part, leading to a contradiction $1 = 0$ from the binomial $b_1 c_1 = 0$. A similar contradiction obtains from $a_1 = 1$. □

5   Cross-Fertilization

It is advantageous to allow some "cross-fertilization" between $\mathcal{B}$ and $\mathcal{L}$, so that useful equations can migrate from one set to the other. A trivial case is when equations can belong to both sets. In fact, the Unit and Equivalence Rules of Sect. 4 belong to this case.

Since $\mathcal{B}$ is Horn, it can express cases where variables propagate values, such as those that can be obtained from equations in $\mathcal{L}$. For example, consider a linear equation $x + y + z = 1$. By assigning 1 to variables x and y, the equation reduces to $z = 1$, since an even number of 1's cancel each other. Thus, we may conclude that the binomial equation $xyz = xy$ (that is, x and y imply z) is a logical

Table 2. Transformation rules

Gate	Bin-Lin
Wide-or: $\quad F := \bigvee_i F_i$	$\mu(F) = \prod_i \mu(F_i)$
Wide-and: $\quad F := \bigwedge_i F_i$	$\nu(F) = \prod_i \nu(F_i)$
Exclusive-or: $F := \bigoplus_i F_i$	$\nu(F) = \sum_i \nu(F_i)$
Negation: $\quad F := \overline{G}$	$\nu(F) = \mu(G)$
Implication: $F := F_1 \Rightarrow F_2$	$\mu(F) = \nu(F_1) \cdot \mu(F_2)$
Equivalence: $F := F_1 \Leftrightarrow F_2 \Leftrightarrow \cdots \Leftrightarrow F_k$	$\nu(F) = \sum_i \nu(F_i) + (k-1) \bmod 2$

consequence of the linear equation. Furthermore, if we are lucky enough to have $xyz = 0$ (equivalent to $\overline{x} \vee \overline{y} \vee \overline{z}$) as a constraint, we can deduce $xy = 0$. In general, a linear equation $y_1 + y_2 + \cdots + y_k = 1$ implies the binomial $y_1 y_2 \cdots y_k = 0$, whenever k is even, while $y_1 + y_2 + \cdots + y_k = 0$ implies $y_1 y_2 \cdots y_k = 0$ when k is odd. The equation $y_1 + y_2 + \cdots + y_k = c$ breeds k binomials of the form $y_1 y_2 \cdots y_k = y_1 \cdots y_{i-1} y_{i+1} \cdots y_k$ in the remaining two cases ($c = 1$ and k odd, or $c = 0$ and k even).

Additional simplifications within $\mathcal{B}$ are also possible. Suppose we have $MP = QR$ and $MQ = 0$, where M, P, Q, R are monomials. Since either M or Q equals 0, it is evident that either MP or QR equals 0. However, $MP = QR$; hence, both must be 0. Therefore, we can use $MQ = 0$ to reduce $MP = QR$ to two equations, $MP = 0$ and $QR = 0$. This is an example of a critical pair computation [12], which results—after simplification—in smaller equations. In general, entailment of equations in either $\mathcal{B}$ or $\mathcal{L}$ alone is cheap (cf. Theorems 1 and 2 below).

Simplification within $\mathcal{B}$ tends to produce equations like $M = 0$, where M is a monomial. However, substituting a variable x in M by its counterpart $1 + \widehat{x}$ can further expand it into a non-degenerate binomial equation.

6   Compilation

Any SAT formula encoded by a Boolean circuit can be recursively compiled into the Bin-Lin representation, as described in Table 2. Each logical gate F is associated with two new variables, $\nu(F)$ and $\mu(F)$, together with the linear equation $\nu(F) + \mu(F) = 1$. Intuitively speaking, $\nu(F)$ is the structure variable for F, $\mu(F)$ is its negation, $\nu(x)$ is x, for input variable x, and $\mu(x)$ is a new variable $\widehat{x}$.

A SAT problem encoded in conjunctive normal form can also be compiled into the Bin-Lin representation in this way. A clause $l_1 \vee l_2 \vee \cdots \vee l_t$ can be easily converted into an equation by expanding $(l_1 + 1)(l_2 + 1) \cdots (l_t + 1) = 0$. If there are more than two positive literals amongst the l_i's, the final equation will contain at least four monomials. To avoid this, we introduce new Boolean variables that serve as *complements* of the positive ones. When l_i is a positive literal, a new variable $\widehat{l_i}$ and new equation $l_1 + \widehat{l_i} = 1$ are introduced, and $l_i + 1$ is replaced by $\widehat{l_i}$. Therefore, at most $2n$ variables remain after compilation.

Additional inference rules can help handle the positive variable $\nu(F)$ and the negative variable $\mu(F)$. Two variables x and y are called *complementary* if the linear equation $x + y = 1$ exists. We proceed as follows:

1. Replace any product of variables by 0 if it contains complementary variables.
2. Replace a negative variable $\widehat{x}$ by $x + 1$ in every linear equation other than $x + \widehat{x} = 1$ (and simplify).
3. Suppose we have $MM'x = N$ and $M'y = 0$, where M, N, M' are monomials. Replace $MM'x = N$ by $MM' = N$ if x and y are complementary.
4. Replace $MN = 1$ by $M = 1$ and $N = 1$.
5. Suppose we have $MP = QR$ and $MQ = 0$. Replace $MP = QR$ by $MP = 0$ and $QR = 0$.
6. Remove an equation $x = M$ if x is a variable that appears only in this equation.

Example 3. Consider, again, the instance in Example 1:

$$(p \vee q) \wedge (\overline{q} \vee s) \wedge (\overline{s} \vee p) \wedge (\overline{p} \vee r) \wedge (\overline{r} \vee \overline{p} \vee t) \Rightarrow (t \wedge r) \ .$$

To prove this formula valid, we set it equal to false and try to find a counterexample. We compile it into the following:

(1) $\widehat{t_1} = \widehat{p}\widehat{q}$ (2) $\widehat{t_2} = q\widehat{s}$ (3) $\widehat{t_3} = s\widehat{p}$

(4) $\widehat{t_4} = p\widehat{r}$ (5) $\widehat{t_5} = rp\widehat{t}$ (6) $t_6 = tr$

(7) $t_7 = t_1 t_2 t_3 t_4 t_5$ (8) $\widehat{t_8} = t_7\widehat{t_6}$ (9) $t_8 = 0 \ .$

Note that the t_i and the variables wearing hats are new. (We've omitted all the duality constraints.) It follows that (9) forces $t_7 = 1$ and $t_6 = 0$ in (8), which further forces $t_1 = t_2 = t_3 = t_4 = t_5 = 1$ in (7). Then repeatedly applying Rule 3 and the *Unit Rule*, we get $rp = 0$ in (5), $p = 0$ in (4), $s = 0$ in (3), $q = 1$ in (1), and finally $0 = 1$ for (2). □

In [23], all formulæ are represented as definitional "triplets", of the form $x \Leftrightarrow y \wedge z$, where x, y, z are propositional variables, which is just the binomial $x = yz$ in BR.

7 Complexity

We next present several simple complexity results, including two polynomial-time subclasses (for $\mathcal{B}$ and $\mathcal{L}$). These results give some indication as to why our Bin-Lin method may be relatively effective.

Let Linear-BRSAT be the problem of solving a system of linear equations over the Boolean ring.

Theorem 1. Linear-BRSAT *is solvable in polynomial time.*

Proof. By Gaussian elimination (modulo 2).   □

Note that, although Tseitin formulæ have an exponential lower bound for resolution [24,2], they can be solved easily within $\mathcal{L}$ alone.

Let Binomial-BRSAT be the problem of solving a system of binomial equations.

Theorem 2. Binomial-BRSAT *is linear-time solvable.*

The well-known Horn-SAT case falls within this class, since any Horn clause $x_1 \wedge \cdots \wedge x_m \to y$ is equivalent to $x_1 \cdots x_m y = x_1 \cdots x_m$ in the Boolean ring. In fact, Binomial-BRSAT defines the same Boolean functions as does Horn-SAT, which has linear complexity [13].

Proof. If $1 = 0$ is in $\mathcal{B}$, then it is unsatisfiable. Variables appearing in an equation $M = 1$ can each be assigned 1. These variables can then be used to simplify the other equations, and this process continues until all equations are of the form $M = 0$ or $M = N$. Observe that these remaining equations can be easily satisfied just by assigning 0 to all variables appearing in them. Implemented appropriately, the process terminates in linear time.   □

Full-fledged computation of the Gröbner basis of $\mathcal{B}$ is not feasible, since its size can be exponential in the number of variables.[2]

Despite the fact that Linear-BRSAT and Binomial-BRSAT are easy, their combination, BRSAT (satisfiability over $\mathcal{B} \cup \mathcal{L}$) is NP-complete, as one would expect. We have already shown how to compile a set of clauses into the Bin-Lin representation (cf. Sect. 6). Thus:

Theorem 3. BRSAT *is NP-complete.*

It is easy to design a polynomial simplification algorithm that uses every binomial to rewrite every other binomial (Step 6), until nothing more can be reduced.[3]

8   Intersection Method

The core idea of recursive learning [18] is to learn as much as possible from shallow case splits, and to use the learned facts to prune the search space. Stålmarck's Prover [23] has used this innovative approach successfully for testing satisfiability of many large-scale industrial problems. Such saturate-by-intersection methods proceed via iterative deepening. Informally, the steps in this learning approach are as follows:

1. Perform cheap (i.e. polynomial) inferences to reduce formulæ. Check if done.
2. Choose a variable to split on; recur on each case.

---

[2] We have not determined the precise complexity of computing an efficient representation of the basis.

[3] We have not, however, found a linear-time algorithm for this purpose.

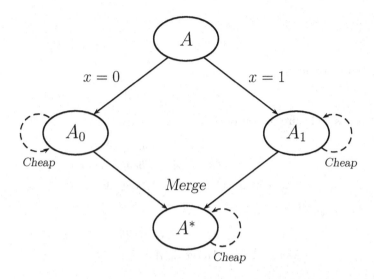

Fig. 1. Intersection-based learning method

3. If either case succeeds, then done; otherwise, merge results.
4. If something learned, add it to formulæ and reset the list of variables.
5. If no unsplit variables remain, increase depth up to current bound; otherwise, continue at same depth.
6. Repeat with incremented bound until maximum depth.

By "merging", we mean looking for consequences that hold in both cases. This, too, should be a polytime step. See Fig. 1.

Suppose, then, that we are provided with the following four polynomial procedures:

1. *Sat A*, which detects "obvious" cases of satisfiability of the formulæ in a set of formulæ A.
2. *Unsat A*, which detects "obvious" cases of unsatisfiability of A.
3. *Cheap A*, which performs simple, but incomplete, "reduction" inferences on A.
4. *Merge A, B*, which returns a set of formulæ that can be inferred from both A and B.

Let *Th A* be the theory (deductive closure) of A, $\perp$ denote unsatisfiability (falsehood, failure), and *Var A* be the (unassigned) variables appearing in A. We need for the above procedures to satisfy the following requirements:

– *Sat* and *Unsat* are sound:

$$Sat\ A = T \Rightarrow (Th\ A)' \neq \emptyset$$
$$Unsat\ A = T \Rightarrow (Th\ A)' = \emptyset$$

where $(Th\ A)'$ are the formulæ that are not theorems.

- *Sat* and *Unsat* do something:

$$Var\ A = \emptyset \Rightarrow (Sat\ A = T) \vee (Unsat\ A = T)$$

- *Cheap* is sound:

$$Cheap\ A \subseteq Th\ A$$

- *Cheap* is a closure operation:

$$A \subseteq Cheap\ A$$
$$Cheap\ A \subseteq Cheap\ (A \cup B)$$
$$Cheap\ (Cheap\ A) = Cheap\ A$$

- *Merge* is sound:

$$Merge\ A, B \subseteq (Th\ A) \cap (Th\ B)$$
$$Merge\ A, T = Merge\ T, A = T$$

- *Merge* does something:

$$Merge\ A, B \supseteq A \cap B$$

- Failure propagates:

$$Sat\ \bot = F$$
$$Unsat\ \bot = T$$
$$Cheap\ \bot = \bot$$
$$Merge\ \bot, A = Merge\ A, \bot \supseteq A$$

With this framework, intersection-based learning (IBL) works as shown in the algorithm of Fig. 2. Assuming the above requirements, we have the following:

$$IBL(A) = T \Leftrightarrow (Th\ A)' \neq \emptyset$$
$$IBL(A) = \bot \Leftrightarrow (Th\ A)' = \emptyset$$
$$IBL(A) \notin \{T, \bot\} \Rightarrow IBL(A) \quad \subseteq \quad Th\ A$$

The original Davis-Putnam satisfiability procedure [9] uses unit propagation and elimination for *Cheap*; it looks for the absence of complementary literals to declare *Sat*; it detects unsatisfiability in the form of an empty set; and merges by generating one round of resolvents.

For the Bin-Lin method, *Cheap* applies the simplifications described above; *Sat* includes checking that there is no 0 occurring in Bin and that all formulæ in Lin are of even parity; *Unsat* looks for $1 = 0$; *Merge* can be simple syntactic intersection. We have implemented such a scheme for the full Bin-Lin representation, as described in the next section.

Better yet, *Merge* could comprise limited generate-and-test. The low complexity of inference for either binomials or linear equations means that one can tractably test for small shared simplifiers, even if they do not appear explicitly in $\mathcal{B}$ or $\mathcal{L}$.

$IBL(P) := I(P, \text{Var } P, N)$
where $I(B, V, n)$ is
    if $n = 0$ then return *Cheap B*
    $A := I(B, V, n - 1)$
    if *Unsat A* then return $\bot$ $\|$ if *Sat A* then return $\top$
    $V' := V \cap \text{Var } A$
    if $V' = \emptyset$ then return A
    choose $p :\in V$
    $V'' := V' \setminus p$
    $A_0 := I(A \cup \{\overline{p}\}, V'', n - 1)$ $\|$ $A_1 := I(A \cup \{p\}, V'', n - 1)$
    $A^* := \text{Merge } A_0, A_1$
    if $A^* \in \{\top, \bot\}$ then return A^*
    if $A = A^*$ then return $I(A, V'', n)$
          else return $I(A^*, \text{Var } A^*, n)$

Fig. 2. Generic intersection-based learning algorithm ($S\|S'$ means that execution of S and S' can be performed in parallel; N is the maximum depth of splits for learning)

9 Results

The degree to which simplification and learning can sometimes reduce the number of splits needed in a backtrack search is the main practical question. In earlier, initial experiments with an implementation of a naïve Boolean-ring-based search method (of Sect. 2), the number of splits was reduced by 30% [17]. This saving, however, came at the price of time-consuming simplification, mainly because—in that implementation—distributivity was needed, which is not the case with the method proposed here.

We conducted several sets of experiments to measure the usefulness of reduction techniques under the Bin-Lin framework:

P: This is a basic DPLL procedure, with learning of conflict clauses. Variables are split according to their given order. This set is intended as a baseline reference.

I: The intersection method described in Sect. 8, with syntactic intersection, is incorporated in this case. The maximum depth for intersection-based learning was set to 3.

GI: Gaussian elimination on linear equations is added to the implementation of Set **I**.

HI: Equivalence of variables are learned from binomial equations, together with Set **I**.

GHI: The features of Sets **GI** and **HI** are combined.

Over 700 satisfiable examples, taken from actual Intel Corp. hardware verification problems, were tested for each set of features. Not surprisingly, using combined simplification (**GHI**) performed best in terms of eliminating splits. Indeed, nearly 14% of these 700 examples have over 50% savings on splits with **GHI**. Some examples can be solved completely—without any splits—just with **I**; this phenomenon occurs more frequently for **GHI**.

Table 3. Representative runs

| Input | | P | I | | GI | | HI | | GHI | | Over- |
Vars	Gates	Splits	Splits	Savings	Splits	Savings	Splits	Savings	Splits	Savings	head
5	18	15	14	6.7%	14	6.7%	14	6.7%	10	33.3%	13
5	38	31	31	0.0%	31	0.0%	13	58.1%	13	58.1%	15
6	10	20	19	5.0%	19	5.0%	17	15.0%	17	15.0%	16
6	37	63	63	0.0%	56	11.1%	63	0.0%	56	11.1%	18
7	33	38	37	2.6%	37	2.6%	37	2.6%	19	50.0%	19
7	36	95	95	0.0%	95	0.0%	95	0.0%	45	52.6%	21
8	30	116	115	0.9%	115	0.9%	115	0.9%	0	100%	22
8	34	191	191	0.0%	191	0.0%	191	0.0%	6	96.9%	24
9	39	507	507	0.0%	507	0.0%	504	0.6%	127	75.0%	27
9	45	17	0	100%	0	100%	0	100%	0	100%	9
10	54	258	257	0.4%	257	0.4%	257	0.4%	65	74.8%	28
10	63	511	511	0.0%	432	15.5%	511	0.0%	214	58.1%	30
11	41	1794	1794	0.0%	1794	0.0%	896	50.1%	896	50.1%	33
11	46	1983	1983	0.0%	1983	0.0%	1983	0.0%	991	50.0%	33
11	52	1187	1187	0.0%	593	50.0%	1187	0.0%	593	50.0%	33

Despite the heavy cost of merging, there was an overall average reduction of 3% in run time, compared to the baseline, since merging often produces simplifiers that greatly reduce the need for splitting.[4]

Table 3 shows some sample results. The savings for **GHI** are usually more than the sum of those obtained by **GI** and **HI**. This is due to the cross-fertilization between $\mathcal{B}$ and $\mathcal{L}$. The last column indicates the additional splits (on average) needed for applying the learning technique. In only two of the smallest cases does this overhead outweigh the benefit in terms of total splits.

10   Discussion

We have endeavored to show that using powerful simplification, such as provided by the Boolean-ring format, combined with the forward reasoning of intersection-based learning, can lead to a significant reduction in the number of variables on which splitting will need to be performed.

Simplification is more time-consuming than splitting on a variable or evaluating a truth-assignment. Splitting a variable can usually be carried out in linear time, but simplification, though polynomial, is not linear. On the other hand, eliminating a split saves space, and may in the long run save time.

Besides the ease of incorporating simplification, Boolean rings are a suitable representation for preprocessing for the following reason: Let $\mathcal{C}$ be the set of

---

[4] The code wasn't designed to be competitive in terms of overall performance, but only as proof of concept. In particular, constant propagation over the Bin-Lin system was noticeably time consuming. Accordingly, there is no point in providing time comparisons with alternative approaches.

Boolean formulæ over all binary and unary operations, $\mathcal{D}$ be over $\{\vee, \wedge, -\}$, and $\mathcal{G}$ over $\{1, +, \wedge\}$. As shown in [16], any formula in $\mathcal{C}$ is linearly reducible to one in $\mathcal{G}$, but may not be linearly reducible to one in $\mathcal{D}$. Hence, Boolean-ring formulæ can preserve the structure of *any* Boolean formula, while Boolean algebra requires additional variables. This ability to preserve structure is also important for Stålmarck's method (cf. Sect. 8), which is sensitive to the structure of the input formula.

Nilpotence of $+$ makes it possible to express parity succinctly as a linear equation in the Boolean ring. This feature allows for very simple BR proofs of the pigeon-hole principle (see Example 2) and the mutilated checkerboard. In contrast, in Boolean algebra, the shortest corresponding formula is of quadratic length, if no new variables are introduced. Introducing new variables normally increases computational effort.

It should also be interesting to identify additional subclasses of Boolean rings (like Binomial-BRSAT) for which satisfiability testing can be accomplished by simplification alone, without splitting.

Acknowledgement

We are grateful to the referees for their comments.

References

1. Baader, F., and Nipkow, T.: *Term Rewriting and All That*. Cambridge University Press (1998)
2. Ben-Sasson, E., and Wigderson, A.: Short proofs are narrow — resolution made simple. Journal of the ACM **48** (2001) 149–169
3. Björk, M.: A First Order Extension of Stålmarck's Method, Ph.D. thesis, Department of Computer Science and Engineering, Göteborg University, Sweden, 2006
4. Bloniarz, P. A., Hunt, H. B., III, and Rosenkrantz, D. J.: Algebraic structures with hard equivalence and minimization problems. Journal of the ACM **31** (1984) 879–904
5. Bonacina, M. P. , and Dershowitz, N.: Abstract canonical inference. ACM Transactions on Computational Logic, to appear
6. Bryant, R. E.: Symbolic Boolean manipulation with ordered binary-decision diagrams. ACM Computing Surveys **24** (1992) 293–318
7. Clegg, M., Edmonds, J., and Impagliazzo, R.: Using the Groebner basis algorithm to find proofs of unsatisfiability. Proc. 28th ACM Symposium on Theory of Computing (1996) 174–183
8. Davis, M., Logemann, G., and Loveland, D.: A machine program for theorem proving. Communications of the ACM **5** (1962) 394–397
9. Davis, M., and Putnam, H.: A computing procedure for quantification theory. Journal of the ACM **7** (1960) 201–215
10. Dershowitz, N., Hanna, Z., and Nadel, A.: A clause-based heuristic for SAT solvers. Proc. Eighth International Conference on Theory and Applications of Satisfiability Testing (SAT 2005; St. Andrews, Scotland), Bacchus, F., and Walsch, T., eds., Lecture Notes in Computer Science **3569**, Springer-Verlag, Berlin (June 2005) 46–60

11. Dershowitz, N., and Kirchner, C.: Abstract canonical presentations. Theoretical Computer Science **357** (2006) 53–69
12. Dershowitz, N., and Plaisted, D. A.: Rewriting. Handbook of Automated Reasoning, Robinson, A., and Voronkov, A., eds., vol. 1, chap. 9, Elsevier (2001) 535–610
13. Dowling, W. F., and Gallier, J. H.: Linear-time algorithms for testing the satisfiability of propositional Horn formulae. Journal of Logic Programming **3** (1984) 267–284
14. Hsiang, J., and Dershowitz, N.: Rewrite methods for clausal and non-clausal theorem proving. Proc. 10th Intl. Colloquium on Automata, Languages and Programming (Barcelona, Spain), Lecture Notes in Computer Science **154**, Springer-Verlag (1983) 331–346
15. Hsiang, J., and Huang, G. S.: Some fundamental properties of Boolean ring normal forms. DIMACS Series in Discrete Mathematics and Theoretical Computer Science **35** (1997) 587–602
16. Hsiang, J., and Huang, G. S.: Compact representation of Boolean formulas. Chinese Journal of Advanced Software Research **6**(2) 178–187 (1999)
17. Jan, R. L.: Experimental results on propositional theorem proving with Boolean ring. Master's thesis, Department of Computer Science and Information Engineering, National Taiwan University (1997)
18. Kunz, W., and Pradhan, D. K.: Recursive learning: A new implication technique for efficient solutions to CAD problems — test, verification, and optimization. IEEE Trans. on Computer-Aided Design of Integrated Circuits and Systems **13** (1994) 1143–1158
19. McCune, W.: Solution of the Robbins problem. Journal of Automated Reasoning **19** (1997) 263-276
20. Marques-Silva, J. P.: Algebraic simplification techniques for propositional satisfiability. Technical Report RT/01/2000, INESC (2000)
21. Sasao, T.: And-exor expressions and their optimization. Logic Synthesis and Optimization, T. Sasao, ed., pp. 287–312, Kluwer, 1993
22. Sasao, T., and Besslich, P.: On the complexity of mod-2 sum PLA's. IEEE Transactions on Computers **C-39**(2) (Feb. 1990) 263–265
23. Sheeran, M., and Stålmarck, G.: A tutorial on Stålmarck's proof procedure for propositional logic. Proc. 2nd Intl. Conference on Formal Methods in Computer-Aided Design, Lecture Notes in Computer Science **1522**, Springer Verlag (1998) 82–99
24. Urquhart, A.: Hard examples for resolution. Journal of the ACM **34** (1987) 209–219

Theory Instantiation

Harald Ganzinger[1] and Konstantin Korovin[2,*]

[1] MPI für Informatik
[2] University of Manchester

Abstract. In this paper we present a method of integrating theory reasoning into the instantiation framework. This integration is done in the black-box style, which allows us to integrate different theories in a uniform way. We prove completeness of the resulting calculus, provided that the theory reasoner is answer-complete and complete for reasoning with ground clauses. One of the distinctive features of our approach is that it allows us to employ off-the-shelf satisfiability solvers for ground clauses modulo theories, as a part of general first-order reasoning. As an application of this approach, we show how it is possible to combine the instantiation calculus with other calculi, such as ordered resolution and paramodulation.

1 Introduction

Instantiation-based theorem proving has been studied intensively in recent years, see, e.g., [6,7,16,18,19,24] among others. It has attractive features of combining efficient reasoning on ground formulas with first-order reasoning.

In this paper we develop a method for integrating theory reasoning into the instantiation-based framework, introduced in [13]. Approaches for integrating theory reasoning into a logical calculus usually fall into two major categories: black-box and glass-box approaches.

In the glass-box approach, theory reasoning is integrated via specialised inference rules, e.g., for the theory of equality, ordered paramodulation can be used. Usually, the resulting calculus is very efficient for a particular theory. However, for each theory one needs to devise specific rules which can make completeness arguments for the resulting calculus highly non-trivial. There is extensive literature on the integration of various theories into the resolution based framework. Much less is known about such integration into the instantiation framework beyond the integration of equality reasoning [8,14,19,24].

In this paper we introduce theory instantiation which is closely related to theory resolution [25], and can be viewed as a black-box approach. Thus we assume only limited knowledge of the theory itself and the theory reasoner. This allows us to integrate theory reasoning in a uniform manner for different theories.

We follow the instantiation framework developed in our earlier papers [13,14]. In our theorem proving process we interleave efficient satisfiability checking for

---

* Supported by the EPSRC grant GR/T08760/01.

M. Hermann and A. Voronkov (Eds.): LPAR 2006, LNAI 4246, pp. 497–511, 2006.

ground clauses with appropriate instantiations witnessing unsatisfiability at the ground level. One of the distinctive features of our approach is that it allows us to employ off-the-shelf satisfiability solvers for ground clauses modulo theories, as a part of general first-order reasoning. Let us note that for many important theories such reasoners have received considerable attention and very efficient implementations are available (see, e.g., [5] and work on DPLL(T) [11,22,26]).

We prove completeness of the resulting calculus provided that the theory reasoner satisfies some general requirements. In particular, we require the theory reasoner to be answer-complete for reasoning with unit clauses, and to be complete for reasoning with ground clauses (formal definitions are given later in the paper). Our completeness proof is based on the model generation technique (see [3,23]), which allows us to justify redundancy elimination based on a semantic notion of redundant clauses and redundant inferences. We also show that the instantiation process can be guided by (partial) information on models for ground clauses.

One of the applications of the presented approach is a method for combining various calculi with instantiation. It is reasonable to assume that some classes of formulas can be efficiently treated by instantiation, e.g., near propositional formulas, whereas other classes by resolution/paramodulation calculi. Therefore, combinations of various calculi is an important issue. In our approach we can divide the set of input clauses into two classes: the first class can be taken as theory clauses and we apply a specialised procedure to them; the second class are clauses treated with the instantiation calculus. In this case, the theory reasoner itself can be a logical calculus which satisfies the abstract requirements on the theory reasoner. We show that the requirements on the theory reasoner can be naturally satisfied by the ordered paramodulation calculus. Let us note that in this setting it is natural to use the black-box approach since the theory axiomatized by the theory part is generally not known in advance.

Our approach for integrating theory reasoning is closely related to theory resolution [9,17,25], (see also work on DPLL(T) [11,26]). Here we consider full first-order reasoning in the instantiation-based framework. We are also concerned with issues of how to restrict instantiation and issues related to permutative theories.

2   Preliminaries

Let $\Sigma = \langle \mathcal{P}, \mathcal{F} \rangle$ be a first-order signature, where $\mathcal{P}$ is the set of predicate symbols and $\mathcal{F}$ is the set of function symbols. We assume that $\mathcal{P}$ contains the equality predicate $\simeq$ and $\mathcal{F}$ contains the constant $\bot$. The term algebra $\mathcal{T}(\mathcal{F})$, with the universe of all ground terms in $\mathcal{F}$ is defined as usual by assigning an interpretation of a function $f^{\mathcal{T}(\mathcal{F})}(t_1, \ldots, t_n)$ to $f(t_1^{\mathcal{T}(\mathcal{F})}, \ldots, t_n^{\mathcal{T}(\mathcal{F})})$.

A clause is a possibly empty multiset of literals denoting their disjunction and is usually written as $L_1 \vee \ldots \vee L_n$; a literal being either an atomic formula or the negation thereof. The logical constant false is denoted as $\Box$. Variables are usually denoted by x, y, and z, whereas, unless indicated otherwise, letters a, b and c

denote constants. If L is a literal, $\overline{L}$ denotes the complement of L. Substitutions are defined as usual and will be denoted by letters ρ, σ, τ, and θ. We will also use $\perp$ to denote the substitution mapping all variables to the constant $\perp$. If S is a set of clauses, by $S\perp$ we denote all ground clauses obtained by applying $\perp$ to each clause in S. *Renamings* are injective substitutions which map variables to variables. Two clauses are *variants* of each other if one can be obtained from the other by applying a renaming.

As in our previous work on instantiation ([13,14]), we consider a refined notion of instances of clauses called closures. A *closure* is a pair consisting of a clause C and a substitution σ written $C \cdot \sigma$. We work modulo renaming, that is, do not distinguish between closures $C \cdot \sigma$ and $D \cdot \tau$ for which C is a variant of D and $C\sigma$ is a variant of $D\tau$. A closure is called *ground* if it represents a ground clause. Let S be a set of clauses and C be a clause in S, then a ground closure $C \cdot \sigma$ is called a *ground instance* of S; we also say that the closure $C \cdot \sigma$ is a *representation (of the clause $C\sigma$) in S*. Truth values for closures are defined from the truth values of the clauses they represent.

We consider a universally axiomatized background theory T in the signature Σ [1] and assume that T implies the usual congruence axioms for equality. We are interested in proving unsatisfiability of sets of clauses modulo T, i.e., in proving that there is no model of T in which the considered clauses are true. Since the theory T is universal, from the Herbrand theorem it follows that a set of clauses is satisfiable in a model of T if and only if it is satisfiable in a Herbrand model of T. Therefore, we can restrict ourselves to Herbrand models. A Herbrand model of T, called *T-model*, is a model of T on the set of all ground terms where all functions are interpreted as in the term algebra $\mathcal{T}(\mathcal{F})$.

We say that a clause C follows from clauses $C_1, \ldots, C_n$ modulo T (or *T-follows*), denoted $C_1, \ldots, C_n \models_T C$, if for all T-models where $C_1, \ldots, C_n$ are true, C is also true. We say that a clause C is *T-satisfiable* if C is true in a T-model, likewise we say C is *T-unsatisfiable* if C is false in all T-models, also denoted as $C \models_T \square$. For two ground clauses C, C' we write $C \leftrightarrow_T C'$ if $\models_T C \leftrightarrow C'$. For two ground terms t and s, we write $t \simeq_T s$ if $\models_T t \simeq s$, and $t \not\simeq_T s$ if $\not\models_T t \simeq s$. Likewise, we write for a pair of n-tuples of ground terms $\bar{t} \simeq_T \bar{s}$ if $t_i \simeq_T s_i$ for all $1 \leq i \leq n$ and write $\bar{t} \not\simeq_T \bar{s}$ if for some $1 \leq i \leq n$, $t_i \not\simeq_T s_i$. Let us note that $\simeq_T$ is the least congruence on the term algebra $\mathcal{T}(\mathcal{F})$, which satisfies all unit equational theorems of T, i.e., theorems of the form $\forall \bar{x}\, t(\bar{x}) \simeq s(\bar{x})$.

The Herbrand *interpretations* we deal with are sometimes partial, given by sets I of ground literals consistent with T. A clause C is called *T-true* in a partial interpretation I, written $I \models_T C$, if C is true in each T-model of I. Otherwise C is called *T-false* in I. This is the case when there is a T-model of I in which C is false. A ground literal L is called *T-undefined* in I if neither L nor $\overline{L}$ is T-true in I. An interpretation I is called *total* if for each ground literal, I either contains the literal or its complement.

Our restrictions on the instantiation calculus and completeness proofs are based on an ordering on closures defined as follows. First we need to adapt the

---

[1] If T is not a universal theory one can consider its Skolemization.

notion of a proper instantiator from [13]. We call a substitution θ a T-*proper instantiator* for a clause C if for some variable x in C, $x\theta\bot \not\approx_T x\bot$. We will show that in our instantiation process it is sufficient to consider only T-proper instantiators. Let $\succ$ be a total simplification ordering on ground terms such that $\bot$ is a minimal term wrt. $\succ$. We assume that $\succ$ is defined on ground clauses by a total, well-founded and monotone extension of the ordering on terms as defined, e.g., in [23]. Now we lift the ordering $\succ$ from ground clauses to ground closures. Let $C \cdot \sigma$ and $D \cdot \tau$ be ground closures. We say that $C \cdot \sigma \succ' D \cdot \tau$ if either (i) $C\sigma \succ D\tau$, or (ii) $C\sigma = D\tau$ and there exists a T-proper instantiator θ for C such that $C\theta = D$. It is obvious that $\succ'$ is well-founded. We define ordering $\succ$ on closures as any total well-founded extension of $\succ'$.

3   An Informal Description of the Instantiation Procedure

Let us first informally describe our instantiation-based inference process for reasoning modulo a universal theory T.

Let S be a given set of first-order clauses. We start by mapping all variables in all clauses in S, into the distinguished constant $\bot$, obtaining a set of ground clauses $S\bot$. If $S\bot$ is T-unsatisfiable, then S is also T-unsatisfiable and we are done. Otherwise, we non-deterministically select a literal in each clause, obtaining a set of literals $\mathcal{L}$ (below we will show how this selection can be guided by information on a T-model of $S\bot$). If $\mathcal{L}$ is T-satisfiable, then S is T-satisfiable and we are done. Otherwise, we generate relevant instances of clauses from S witnessing T-unsatisfiability of $\mathcal{L}$ at the ground level. This is done based on the Unit Calculus (UC). For the refutational completeness of the overall process we need to ensure that sufficiently many instances of clauses are generated. For this we require UC to be answer-complete. Finally, we add obtained instances of clauses to S.

We prove the completeness of this instantiation process, following the steps below. First, in Section 4, we formulate an abstract calculus UC for reasoning with unit clauses, and introduce the notion of answer-completeness. Then, in Section 5, we introduce our main instantiation calculus TInst-Gen, based on an answer-complete UC, together with redundancy notions. Next, we introduce the notion of a saturated set of clauses and show that every saturated set can either be shown to be unsatisfiable by reasoning on ground clauses, or it is satisfiable (modulo the background theory). In Section 6, we show how such saturated sets can be achieved via effective fair saturation processes. We conclude with the theorem which states that every fair saturation process either stops after a finite number of steps detecting satisfiability/unsatisfiability of the initial set of clauses, or in the limit we obtain a saturated set and hence the initial set of clauses is satisfiable (modulo the background theory). In Section 7 we apply our main theorem for combining the ordered paramodulation calculus with instantiation.

4   The Unit Calculus

In this section we formulate requirements on the theory reasoner, wrt. reasoning with literals. This will be done in terms of an abstract calculus UC for proving T-unsatisfiability of sets of (selected) literals, which also provides substitutions for generating relevant instances witnessing T-unsatisfiability.

The Unit Calculus (UC)

$$\frac{L_1, \ldots, L_n}{L_1\theta, \ldots, L_n\theta}$$

where θ is such that $L_1\theta\bot \wedge \ldots \wedge L_n\theta\bot \models_T \Box$.

We assume that literals in the premise do not share variables. Let us note that the premise of UC may contain variants of the same literal.

The unit calculus will be used to generate instantiations based on T-unsatisfiable sets of literals, ensuring that the inconsistency can be detected by a theory reasoner for ground clauses.

Next we introduce the notion of answer-completeness, which is needed for overall completeness of the instantiation process. We say that UC is *answer-complete wrt.* $(T, \succ)$, if the following holds. Let $\mathcal{L} = \{L_1, \ldots, L_n\}$ be a set of literals and τ be a grounding substitution such that (i) $\mathcal{L}\tau$ is T-unsatisfiable and (ii) every proper subset of $\mathcal{L}\tau$ is T-satisfiable. Then, there is an inference in UC with $L_1, \ldots, L_n$ as a premise and $L_1\theta, \ldots, L_n\theta$ as a conclusion and a grounding substitution ρ such that $\bar{x}\tau \simeq_T \bar{x}\theta\rho$ and $\bar{x}\tau \succeq \bar{x}\theta\rho$. Let us note that an answer-complete UC calculus can produce any other instantiations, so in practice we do not need to check condition (ii) that every proper subset of $\mathcal{L}\tau$ is T-satisfiable.

Intuitively, answer-completeness requires UC to instantiate T-unsatisfiable sets of literals, with the restriction that we only need to consider instantiators generalizing minimal (wrt. $\succ$) representatives of the congruence classes defined by T. In Section 8, we show that it is possible to weaken the latter restriction further, to possibly non-minimal representatives, which is more natural in the presence of permutative subtheories.

5   The Instantiation Calculus (TInst-Gen)

In this section we introduce the instantiation calculus TInst-Gen and prove that if a set of clauses S is saturated wrt. TInst-Gen, then either $S\bot$ is already T-unsatisfiable and therefore a theory reasoner for ground clauses can detect the unsatisfiability, or S is T-satisfiable. In Section 6 we show how to achieve saturated sets.

Selection function. Our inference system will be guided by a selection function on clauses which will be based on a model for the ground clauses $S\bot$. A *selection function* sel for a set of clauses S is a mapping from clauses in S to literals such that $\mathsf{sel}(C) \in C$ for each clause $C \in S$. We say that sel is based on a model $I_\bot$ of $S\bot$, if $I_\bot \models \mathsf{sel}(C)\bot$ for all $C \in S$.

Let UC be an answer-complete wrt. $(T, \succ)$ calculus for literals and let sel be a selection function. We define TInst-Gen based on UC and sel as follows.

TInst-Gen
$$\frac{L_1 \vee C_1 \ldots L_n \vee C_n}{(L_1 \vee C_1)\theta \ldots (L_n \vee C_n)\theta}$$

where (i) the literal L_k is selected by sel in the clause $L_k \vee C_k$, for $1 \leq k \leq n$, (ii) there is an inference in UC with $L_1, \ldots, L_n$ as a premise and $L_1\theta, \ldots, L_n\theta$ as a conclusion, (iii) θ is a T-proper instantiator for at least one of $L_1, \ldots, L_n$.

Redundancy. Now we adapt the semantic notion of redundancy from [13]. Let S be a set of clauses. A ground closure C is called T-*redundant* in S if there exist closures $C_1, \ldots, C_k$ that are ground instances of S such that, (i) for each i, $C \succ C_i$, and (ii) $C_1, \ldots, C_k \models_T C$. A clause C (possibly non-ground) is called T-redundant in S if each ground closure $C \cdot \sigma$ is T-redundant in S. An inference with premises $C_1, \ldots, C_n$ and a unifier θ (thus deriving conclusions $C_1\theta, \ldots, C_n\theta$) is T-*redundant* in S if for any substitution ρ grounding all the $C_i\theta$ there exists an index i_0 such that $C_{i_0} \cdot \theta\rho$ is T-redundant in S.

A set of clauses S is called *TInst-saturated up to redundancy* wrt. a selection function sel if all inferences in TInst-Gen with premises from S are T-redundant in S.

Theorem 1. *Let S be a set of clauses such that $S\bot$ is T-satisfiable and* sel *be a selection based on a T-model $I_\bot$ of $S\bot$. If S is TInst-saturated up to redundancy wrt.* sel *then S is T-satisfiable.*

Proof. Suppose that S is a set of clauses such that $S\bot$ is satisfied in a T-model $I_\bot$, and sel is a selection function based on $I_\bot$. By induction over $\succ$ we construct a candidate T-model I_S for all ground instances of S. Let $C = C' \cdot \sigma$ be a ground instance of S. Suppose, as an induction hypothesis, we have defined sets of literals ϵ_D, for all ground instances D of S smaller than C wrt. $\succ$. Let I_C denote the set $\bigcup_{C \succ D} \epsilon_D$. Then, define $\epsilon_C = \{L\sigma\}$, if

1. C is T-false in I_C (i.e., there is a T-model of I_C in which C is false); and
2. L is a literal in C' such that $L\sigma$ is T-undefined in I_C (i.e., neither $I_C \models_T L\sigma$ nor $I_C \models_T \overline{L}\sigma$ holds) and $\text{sel}(C') = L$.

Otherwise define $\epsilon_C = \emptyset$. In the case when $\epsilon_C = \{L\sigma\}$ we say that $L\sigma$ is *produced* by C. Finally, define I_S to be the union of all ϵ_C where C is an instance of S.

Let us first show that I_S is consistent with T. Otherwise, by compactness, there would be a finite set of literals $L_1\sigma_1, \ldots, L_n\sigma_n$ in I_S which is contradictory with T. Let $L_i\sigma$ be produced by a closure C_i for $1 \leq i \leq n$, and C_j be the maximal wrt. $\succ$ closure among them. Then, we have $I_{C_j} \models_T \overline{L}_j\sigma_j$, which contradicts the productiveness of C_j.

Let S be a set of clauses saturated under TInst-Gen and I be a total extension of I_S, consistent with T. We will show that I is a model for all ground instances of S.

First we note that our model construction is monotone: if a ground closure D is T-true in some I_C then it is T-true in all $I_{C' \succ C}$ and also true in I.

Now, by induction on $\succ$ we show that every ground instance D of S, is T-true in $I_D \cup \epsilon_D$. From this the theorem follows. Assume otherwise. Let $D = D' \cdot \sigma$ be the minimal ground instance of S that is not T-true in $I_D \cup \epsilon_D$. Let $L = \mathsf{sel}(D')$. As D is not productive and T-false in I_D we have $I_D \models_T \overline{L}\sigma$. By compactness, there is a finite set $C_1 \cdot \tau_1, \ldots, C_n \cdot \tau_n$ of closures, producing $L_1\tau_1, \ldots, L_n\tau_n$ such that $L_1\tau_1 \wedge \ldots \wedge L_n\tau_n \models_T \overline{L}\sigma$. We can assume that no proper subset of $\{L_1\tau_1, \ldots, L_n\tau_n\}$ T-implies $\overline{L}\sigma$. First we show that neither D nor any of $C_i \cdot \tau_i$ is T-redundant in S. Indeed, if $C_i \cdot \tau_i$ would T-follow from smaller closures in S, then by the induction hypothesis these closures would be T-true in $I_{C_i \cdot \tau_i}$ and hence $C_i \cdot \tau_i$ would not be productive. Similarly, if $D' \cdot \sigma$ would T-follow from smaller closures in S, it would be T-true in I_D contradicting the assumption.

It will be convenient to introduce a substitution τ which is the composition of all substitutions $\sigma, \tau_1, \ldots, \tau_n$, we assume that all clauses $D', C_1, \ldots, C_n$ are renamed apart.

Since the inference system for unit clauses UC is answer-complete wrt. $(T, \succ)$, we have that there is a UC inference with the premise $L, L_1, \ldots, L_n$ and the conclusion $L\theta, L_1\theta, \ldots, L_n\theta$ such that for a grounding substitution ρ, $\bar{x}\tau \simeq_T \bar{x}\theta\rho$ and $\bar{x}\tau \succeq \bar{x}\theta\rho$. Let us show that θ is a T-proper instantiator for at least one of $L, L_1, \ldots, L_n$. Otherwise, we would have $\bar{x}\bot \simeq_T \bar{x}\theta\bot$, where $\bar{x}$ are all variables in $L, L_1, \ldots, L_n$. This implies that $L\bot \leftrightarrow_T L\theta\bot$, $L_i\bot \leftrightarrow_T L_i\theta\bot$ for $1 \leq i \leq n$. Since $L\theta, L_1\theta, \ldots, L_n\theta$ is a conclusion of a UC inference, we have that $L\theta\bot \wedge L_1\theta\bot \wedge \ldots \wedge L_n\theta\bot \models_T \square$ and therefore $L\bot \wedge L_1\bot \wedge \ldots \wedge L_n\bot \models_T \square$, which contradicts that $L\bot$ and each $L_i\bot$ are true in a T-model $I_\bot$.

Since θ is a T-proper instantiator we have that TInst-Gen is applicable to $D', C_1, \ldots, C_n$, with the conclusion $D'\theta, C_1\theta, \ldots, C_n\theta$. To derive a contradiction, let us show that this inference is not redundant. For this it is sufficient to show that all closures $D' \cdot \theta\rho, C_1 \cdot \theta\rho, \ldots, C_n \cdot \theta\rho$ are not redundant. Consider $D' \cdot \theta\rho$. From $\bar{x}\tau \succeq \bar{x}\theta\rho$ and monotonicity of $\succeq$ it follows that $D' \cdot \sigma = D' \cdot \tau \succeq D' \cdot \theta\rho$. Moreover $D'\sigma \leftrightarrow_T D'\theta\rho$. Hence if $D' \cdot \theta\rho$ T-follows from smaller closures then $D' \cdot \sigma$ also T-follows from these closures, this contradicts that $D' \cdot \sigma$ is not redundant which was shown above. In the same way one can show that $C_1 \cdot \theta\rho, \ldots, C_n \cdot \theta\rho$ are not redundant.

Theorem 1 implies that if a set of clauses S is TInst-saturated up to redundancy then we can check T-satisfiability of S by checking T-satisfiability of the ground set of clauses $S\bot$. This can be done by a theory reasoner for ground clauses. In order be able to use the TInst-Gen calculus for TInst-saturation we need to show that adding the conclusion of an TInst-Gen inference to S makes the inference redundant.

Lemma 1. *Let S be a set of clauses. Consider a TInst-Gen inference, applying substitution θ and a clause $C\theta$ in the conclusion, for which θ is a T-proper instantiator (note that such a clause always exists). Then, the inference is redundant if either $C\theta$ is in S or is redundant in S. In particular, adding $C\theta$ to S makes the inference redundant.*

Proof. Let $C\theta$ be in S. Since θ is T-proper for C we have that for every ρ, $C \cdot \theta\rho \succ C\theta \cdot \rho$, and therefore $C \cdot \theta\rho$ is redundant in S. This shows that the inference is redundant. The case when $C\theta$ is redundant in S is similar.

6   Effective Saturation

In this section we show how TInst-Gen saturation of a set of clauses can be achieved as a limit of a fair saturation process.

A *TInst-saturation process* is a sequence $\{\langle S^i, \mathsf{sat}^i_\perp, \mathsf{sel}^i \rangle\}_{i=1}^\infty$, where (i) S^i is a set of clauses, (ii) $\mathsf{sat}^i_\perp$ is a procedure for checking T-satisfiability of finite sets of ground clauses, (iii) sel^i is a selection function. In addition, we require $\{\mathsf{sat}^i_\perp\}_{i=1}^\infty$ and $\{\mathsf{sel}^i\}_{i=1}^\infty$ to satisfy some natural requirements below.

Given $\{\langle S^i, \mathsf{sat}^i_\perp, \mathsf{sel}^i \rangle\}$, a *successor state* $\{\langle S^{i+1}, \mathsf{sat}^{i+1}_\perp, \mathsf{sel}^{i+1} \rangle\}$ is obtained by one of these steps: (i) $S^{i+1} = S^i \cup N$, where N is a set of clauses such that $S^i \models_T N$; or (ii) $S^{i+1} = S^i \setminus \{C\}$, where C is TInst-redundant in S^i. If $\mathsf{sat}^{i+1}_\perp(S^{i+1}\perp)$ returns "unsatisfiable", then the process terminates with the result "unsatisfiable". Define $S^\cup = \cup_{i=1}^\infty S^i$. Let S^∞ denote the set of persisting clauses, that is, the lower limit of $\{S^i\}_{i=1}^\infty$, (i.e., $S^\infty = \cup_{i\geq 1} \cap_{j\geq i} S^j$).

In certain applications, e.g., when the theory is given as a part of the input clause set, it is natural to assume that the theory reasoner can only semi-decide T-unsatisfiability of sets of ground clauses. This is reflected in the requirements on $\{\mathsf{sat}^i_\perp\}_{i=1}^\infty$ and the selection functions $\{\mathsf{sel}^i\}_{i=1}^\infty$ below.

Requirements on $\mathsf{sat}_\perp$

Soundness. For every finite set of clauses $S_{fin} \subseteq S^\cup$, we have: (i) If $\mathsf{sat}^i_\perp(S_{fin}\perp)$ returns "unsatisfiable" then $S_{fin}\perp$ is T-unsatisfiable. (ii) If $\mathsf{sat}^i_\perp(S_{fin}\perp)$ returns "satisfiable" then $S_{fin}\perp$ is T-satisfiable.

Completeness. For every finite set of clauses $S_{fin} \subseteq S^\infty$, we have: If $S_{fin}\perp$ is T-unsatisfiable then there exists i such that for all $j \geq i$, $\mathsf{sat}^j_\perp(S_{fin}\perp)$ returns "unsatisfiable".

Termination. For every finite subset $S_{fin} \subseteq S^\cup$ and every i, $\mathsf{sat}^i_\perp(S_{fin}\perp)$ is terminating, possibly returning "unknown".

The Requirement on sel. For a *TInst-saturation process* $\{\langle S^i, \mathsf{sat}^i_\perp, \mathsf{sel}^i \rangle\}_{i=1}^\infty$, it is desirable that at each step i the selection functions sel^i is based on a T-model of $S^i\perp$. Since we assume that at a step i we do not know all information about T-models of $S^i\perp$, we need a weaker requirement on the selection functions. We require that selection functions only eventually respect the models. More formally, the following should hold: either (i) some finite subset of $S^\infty\perp$ is T-unsatisfiable (hence unsatisfiability will be detected by $\mathsf{sat}^i_\perp$ for some i), or (ii) for each finite subset $S_{fin} \subseteq S^\infty$ there is an index i' such that for all $i \geq i'$ we have that for each $C \in S_{fin}$, $\mathsf{sel}^i(C)\perp$ is true in some T-model $I^i_\perp$ of $S_{fin}\perp$.

Next, in order to ensure that in the limit of a TInst-saturation process we always obtain a TInst-saturated set, we require the saturation process to be TInst-fair. Consider a TInst-saturation process $\{\langle S^i, \mathsf{sat}^i_\perp, \mathsf{sel}^i \rangle\}_{i=1}^\infty$. A TInst-Gen inference from clauses $\{L_1 \vee C_1, \ldots, L_n \vee C_n\}$ (on literals $L_1, \ldots, L_n$) in S^∞ is called *persisting* if there are infinitely many indexes i such that $\mathsf{sel}_i(L_k \vee C_k) = L_k$ for all $1 \leq k \leq n$ and conditions (i-iii) on applicability of TInst-Gen to these clauses are satisfied. A TInst-saturation process is called *TInst-fair* if every persisting TInst-Gen inference in S^∞ is redundant in S^k for some k. Let us note we can make a TInst-Gen inference redundant by simply adding the conclusion of the inference to the current clause set (see Lemma 1).

If we compare our notion of saturation to saturation in the resolution framework (e.g., [3]), one of the key differences is that the literal selection can change at each step of the saturation. In particular, we need to consider an additional problem of showing that in the limit of a TInst-fair saturation process, we obtain a TInst-saturated set wrt. some selection function based on a T-model of the limit set of ground clauses. This is done in the next lemma.

Lemma 2. *Let S^∞ be a set of persistent clauses of a TInst-fair saturation process $\{\langle S^i, \mathsf{sat}^i_\perp, \mathsf{sel}^i \rangle\}_{i=1}^\infty$, and $S^\infty \perp$ is T-satisfiable. Then, there exists a T-model $I\perp$ of $S^\infty \perp$ and a selection function sel based on $I\perp$ such that S^∞ is TInst-saturated wrt. sel.*

Proof. The proof can be found in the full version of this paper [15].

We summarize the obtained results in the following theorem.

Theorem 2. *Let $\{\langle S^i, \mathsf{sat}^i_\perp, \mathsf{sel}^i \rangle\}_{i=1}^\infty$, be a TInst-fair saturation process. Then, either (1) for some i the procedure $\mathsf{sat}^i_\perp(S^i \perp)$ returns "unsatisfiable" and therefore our initial set S^1 is T-unsatisfiable, or (2) for all i, $\mathsf{sat}^i_\perp(S^i \perp)$ returns either "unknown" or "satisfiable" and therefore, (by Lemma 2 and Theorem 1) S^1 is T-satisfiable. Moreover if for some i, S^i is TInst-saturated and $\mathsf{sat}^i_\perp(S^i \perp)$ returns "satisfiable" then at this step we can conclude that S^1 is T-satisfiable.*

Theorem 2 can be applied as follows. Assume that we have an answer-complete theory reasoner for unit clauses and a theory reasoner for ground clauses satisfying the requirements above. Then, based on the TInst-Gen calculus, we can form a TInst-fair saturation process for any set of clauses. Theorem 2 implies that this will be a complete procedure for reasoning modulo this theory. In the next section we will give an example of an application of this approach for combining the ordered paramodulation calculus with instantiation.

7   Combining Instantiation with Other Calculi

In this section we show that the presented approach to theory reasoning is also suitable for combining the instantiation calculus with other calculi. The idea is to divide the set of input clauses into two classes: the first class can be taken as theory clauses and we apply a specialized procedure to them, the second class are the clauses treated with the instantiation calculus. In this case the theory reasoner itself can be a logical calculus which satisfies the abstract requirements introduced above.

As an example, we consider the case when theory clauses are Horn, possibly containing equality and clauses treated by instantiation contain equality only negatively, other predicates can occur positively and negatively. In order to satisfy conditions on the theory reasoner we first need an answer-complete procedure for reasoning with literals. This can be obtained based on ordered paramodulation combined with answer computations on selected literals. Such procedures, complete for answer computations, are well-studied (see [21]). Secondly, we need a procedure for theory reasoning with ground clauses. For this we can interleave ordered paramodulation with propositional reasoning, which can be done in the DPLL(T) framework [26,22]. Let us remark that for the theory of lists and some other data structures we can use paramodulation based decision procedures for ground reasoning, studied in [1].

It is not difficult to define a TInst-fair saturation process interleaving ordered paramodulation between theory clauses, ground satisfiability checking and answer computation on selected literals with corresponding instantiation. Now we can apply Theorem 2 to show that the obtained combination of paramodulation type calculus and instantiation is complete for this class of clauses.

Remarks. Let us first note that based on our notion of redundancy we can easily justify redundancy elimination and in particular simplifications of instantiation clauses by theory clauses, such as demodulation, subsumption and T-tautology deletion. Next, we note that for answer computation we can employ other answer-complete calculi, for example calculi designed for E-unification (see [10,2,20]).

Now we consider the issue of a modular integration of existing reasoners for ground clauses. One of the main issues here is that usually off-the-shelf reasoners for ground clauses can reason only modulo some subtheory T' of the background theory T. (For example T' can be the theory of equality and T extends T' with some theory clauses.) Next we show how to design a reasoner for ground clauses modulo T based on a reasoner for ground clauses modulo a weaker theory T' and additional ground lemmas that can be generated by a T-reasoner for unit clauses. Such a reasoner will be sufficient for the completeness of the instantiation process modulo T.

Let S be a given set of clauses and $T' \subseteq T$. Let $\mathcal{L} = \{L_1, \ldots, L_n\}$ be a set of literals. A T'-*witness* (of T-unsatisfiability) for $\mathcal{L}\bot$ is a set of ground clauses $W = \{C_1, \ldots C_m\}$ such that (i) $S \models_T C_k$ for $1 \leq k \leq m$ and (ii) if $\mathcal{L}\bot \models_T \square$ then $\mathcal{L}\bot \cup W \models_{T'} \square$. In particular, if $\mathcal{L}\bot$ is T-unsatisfiable and W is a T'-witness for $\mathcal{L}\bot$, then a T' reasoner can be used to show that $\mathcal{L}\bot \cup W$ is T'-unsatisfiable. Now we formalise a saturation process based on a T' reasoner for ground clauses, assuming that we are provided with necessary T'-witnesses of T-unsatisfiability. A *TWInst-saturation process with T'-witnesses* is a sequence $\{\langle S^i, \mathsf{sat}^i_\bot, \mathsf{sel}^i, W^i \rangle\}_{i=1}^\infty$ such that the following holds. At each saturation step the clause set is modified as in a usual TInst-saturation. The witness set is modified as follows: $W^1 = \emptyset$ and either $W^{i+1} = W^i$ or $W^{i+1} = W^i \cup \{C_1, \ldots, C_n\}$, where $\{C_1, \ldots, C_n\}$ is a finite set of ground clauses such that $S^1 \models_T C_k$ for $1 \leq k \leq n$. If for some i, $\mathsf{sat}^i_{\perp}(S^i\perp \cup W^i)$ returns "unsatisfiable", then the saturation process terminates with the result "unsatisfiable". We assume that $\mathsf{sat}_{\perp}$, sel and W satisfy the following requirements, where we use $'$ to distinguish new requirements from the requirements on $\mathsf{sat}_{\perp}$ and sel in Section 6.

Requirements$'$ on $\mathsf{sat}_{\perp}$

Soundness$'$. For every finite set of clauses $S_{fin} \subseteq S^{\cup}$, and every i we have: (i) If $\mathsf{sat}^i_{\perp}(S_{fin}\perp \cup W^i)$ returns "unsatisfiable" then $S_{fin}\perp \cup W^i$ is T'-unsatisfiable (and therefore T-unsatisfiable). (ii) If $\mathsf{sat}^i_{\perp}(S_{fin}\perp\cup W^i)$ returns "satisfiable" then $S_{fin}\perp \cup W^i$ is T'-satisfiable and W^i is a T'-witness for $\{L\perp | L = \mathsf{sel}^i(C), C \in S_{fin}\}$ (and therefore $S_{fin}\perp$ is T-satisfiable).

Completeness$'$. For every finite set of clauses $S_{fin} \subseteq S^\infty$, we have: If $S_{fin}\perp \cup W^i$ is T'-unsatisfiable then there exists i such that for all $j \geq i$, $\mathsf{sat}^j_{\perp}(S_{fin}\perp \cup W^j)$ returns "unsatisfiable".

Termination$'$. For every finite subset $S_{fin} \subseteq S^{\cup}$ and every i, $\mathsf{sat}^i_{\perp}(S_{fin}\perp \cup W^i)$ is terminating, possibly returning "unknown".

The Requirement$'$ on W. Let $\{L_1 \vee C_1, \ldots, L_n \vee C_n\} \subseteq S^\infty$, and for infinitely many i we have $L_k = \mathsf{sel}^i(L_k \vee C_k)$ for $1 \leq k \leq n$. Then, for some j, W^j is a T'-witness for $\{L_1\perp, \ldots, L_n\perp\}$.

The Requirement$'$ on sel. The following should hold: either (i) for some j and some finite subset $S_{fin} \subseteq S^\infty$ we have $S_{fin}\perp \cup W^j$ is T'-unsatisfiable (hence unsatisfiability will be detected by $\mathsf{sat}^i_{\perp}$ for some i), or (ii) for each finite subset $S_{fin} \subseteq S^\infty$ there is an index i' such that for all $i \geq i'$ we have that for each $C \in S_{fin}$, $\mathsf{sel}^i(C)\perp$ is true in some T'-model $I^i_{\perp}$ of $S_{fin}\perp \cup W^i$.

Let us remark that based on a sound and complete T'-reasoner for ground clauses we can easily define $\{\mathsf{sat}^i_{\perp}\}^{\infty}_{i=1}$ and $\{\mathsf{sel}^i\}^{\infty}_{i=1}$ satisfying the above requirements.

In order to apply our main Theorem 2 we need to show that for a TWInst-saturation process $\{\langle S^i, \mathsf{sat}^i_{\perp}, \mathsf{sel}^i, W^i\rangle\}^{\infty}_{i=1}$, we have $\{\langle S^i, \mathsf{sat}^i_{\perp}, \mathsf{sel}^i\rangle\}^{\infty}_{i=1}$ is also a TInst-saturation process. The only nontrivial cases to check are the Completeness requirement on $\mathsf{sat}_{\perp}$ and the Requirement on sel. Let $S_{fin} \subseteq S^\infty$ such that $S_{fin}\perp$ is T-unsatisfiable. Let us show that in this case the TWInst-saturation process is finite. Otherwise $S_{fin} = \{L_1 \vee C_1, \ldots, L_n \vee C_n\}$, where for infinitely many i we have $L_k = \mathsf{sel}^i(L_k \vee C_k)$ for $1 \leq k \leq n$. From the Requirement$'$ on W it follows that for some j, W^j is a T'-witness for $\mathcal{L} = \{L_1\perp, \ldots, L_n\perp\}$. Therefore, $\mathcal{L}\perp \cup W^j$ is also T'-unsatisfiable which contradicts the Requirement$'$ on sel. From this it follows that the TWInst-saturation process terminates with "unsatisfiable" and therefore the Completeness requirement is satisfied. Using similar considerations we can show that the Requirement on sel is also satisfied.

We define the notion of the TWInst-fair saturation process in the same way as TInst-fair saturation. From Theorem 2 we obtain.

Corollary 1. *Let* $\{\langle S^i, \mathsf{sat}^i_\perp, \mathsf{sel}^i, W^i \rangle\}_{i=1}^\infty$, *be a TWInst-fair saturation process. Then, either (1) for some i the procedure* $\mathsf{sat}^i_\perp(S^i \perp \cup W^i)$ *returns "unsatisfiable" and therefore our initial set* S^1 *is T-unsatisfiable, or (2) for all i,* $\mathsf{sat}^i_\perp(S^i \perp \cup W^i)$ *returns either "unknown" or "satisfiable" and therefore,* S^1 *is T-satisfiable. Moreover if for some i,* S^i *is TInst-saturated and* $\mathsf{sat}^i_\perp(S^i \perp \cup W^i)$ *returns "satisfiable" then at this step we can conclude that* S^1 *is T-satisfiable.*

The only issue left to consider is how to generate witness sets. Let us consider the case when T' is the theory of equality and the theory reasoner for unit clauses is based on the ordered paramodulation calculus. In order to satisfy the Requirement' on W, we need to ensure that if a set of literals $\mathcal{L} = \{L_1, \ldots, L_n\}$ is persistently selected and $\mathcal{L}\perp$ is T-unsatisfiable then for some i, $\mathcal{L}\perp \cup W^i$ is T'-unsatisfiable. Since the T-reasoner for unit clauses is answer-complete a proof of the empty clause will be generated from theory clauses and $\mathcal{L}$. If we propagate substitutions in such a proof from the root to the leaves (as it is done in [14] in a different context), we obtain a proof of the empty clause from the instances of the theory clauses, denoted as T_{inst}, and $\mathcal{L}$ where all substitutions map variables to variables. Therefore we have that $T_{inst}\perp \cup \mathcal{L}\perp$ is T'-unsatisfiable. Adding instantiations of the theory clauses T_{inst} to the witness set will produce the desired effect. Let us remark that clauses in the witness sets do not participate in the instantiation inferences and are only used as lemmas for the T'-reasoner on ground clauses.

Example 1. Let T' be the theory of equality. Let T extend T' with the axiom:

$$A_1 : \neg P(g(x), y) \vee f(h(x), y) \simeq g(x).$$

Let S^1 be the set of clauses:

$$C_1 : \underline{\neg P(f(x,y), c)} \vee \neg P(x, c) \quad C_2 : \underline{P(g(x), c)} \vee \neg P(h(x), c) \quad C_3 : \underline{P(h(x), c)}.$$

We assume that theory reasoning for unit clauses is based on the ordered paramodulation/resolution calculus wrt. the lexicographic path ordering with the precedence $P \gg f \gg h \gg g$. We assume that the ground reasoner is based on T' and the witness set $W^1 = \emptyset$. Let us describe a possible TWInst-fair saturation process. First, we apply a ground reasoner modulo T' on $S^1\perp$ which selects $\neg P(f(x,y), c)$ in C_1, $P(g(x), c)$ in C_2, and $P(h(x), c)$ in C_3, note that $\{\neg P(f(\perp, \perp), c), P(g(\perp), c), P(h(\perp), c)\}$ is T'-satisfiable. Then we apply the reasoner for unit clauses on the set of selected literals $\{\neg P(f(x,y), c), P(g(x), c), P(h(x), c)\}$. We derive the empty clause by resolving A_1 with $P(g(x), c)$ obtaining $f(h(x), c) \simeq g(x)$, then paramodulating $f(h(x), c) \simeq g(x)$ into $\neg P(f(x,y), c)$ obtaining $\neg P(g(x), c)$ and finally resolving $\neg P(g(x), c)$ with $P(g(x), c)$. Propagating substitutions in this proof (we need to be careful to rename variables) from the root to the leaves, we obtain an instance of C_1, $C'_1 : \neg P(f(h(x), c), c) \vee \neg P(h(x), c)$ and an instance of A_1, $A'_1 : \neg P(g(x), c) \vee f(h(x), c) \simeq g(x)$. We add C'_1 to S and $A'_1\perp$ to the witness set W. At the next step the T' reasoner for ground clauses is able to detect unsatisfiability of $S^2\perp \cup W^2$ and therefore the initial set S^1 is T-unsatisfiable.

8   Permutative Theories

In this section we show that it is possible to relax conditions on answer-completeness to appropriately accommodate reasoning modulo theories containing permutative axioms such as associativity and commutativity (AC). Let T_P be a subtheory of the theory T. Intuitively we want the unit calculus to avoid producing all permutations of witnesses equivalent wrt. T_P. For this we first need to define an appropriate T_P-compatible closure ordering. In order to ensure that such an ordering exists we impose the following restrictions on the theory T_P. Later we show that these restrictions are satisfied by permutative theories such as AC.

Condition on T_P (1). There exists a T_P-compatible simplification ordering $\succ_{T_P}$ on ground terms which is total on T_P congruence classes. An ordering $\succ_{T_P}$ is called T_P-compatible if the following holds: if $t \succ_{T_P} s$, $t \simeq_{T_P} t'$ and $s \simeq_{T_P} s'$ then $t' \succ_{T_P} s'$. We assume that $\succ_{T_P}$ is also defined on all ground clauses by an extension from ground terms, which is also a T_P-compatible T_P-total simplification ordering on ground clauses.

Now we lift the ordering $\succ_{T_P}$ from ground clauses to ground closures. For this we need an auxiliary relation $\succ'_{T_P}$ on closures. Let $C \cdot \sigma$ and $D \cdot \tau$ be ground closures. We say that $C \cdot \sigma \succ'_{T_P} D \cdot \tau$ if either (i) $C\sigma \succ_{T_P} D\tau$ or (ii) there exists a T-proper instantiator θ for C such that $C\theta = D$ and $\bar{x}\sigma \simeq_{T_P} \bar{x}\theta\tau$. Next, we would like to extend $\succ'_{T_P}$ to a well-founded order on closures. Let us show that it is not always possible for certain theories T_P. Indeed, let $\simeq_{T_P}$ be the theory of equality together with the axiom $f(f(x)) \simeq x$. Then, we would have that

$$A(f(x)) \cdot [c/x] \succ'_{T_P} A(f(f(x))) \cdot [f(c)/x] \succ'_{T_P} A(f(f(f(x)))) \cdot [c/x] \succ'_{T_P} \cdots.$$

Therefore we impose the following condition on T_P.

Condition on T_P (2): $\succ'_{T_P}$ is well-founded. Now we can define $\succ_{T_P}$ on ground closures as a T_P-total, well-founded ordering extending $\succ'_{T_P}$. Note that such an extension always exists, since any well-founded relation can be extended to a total well-founded ordering. We call $\succ_{T_P}$ a *closure ordering wrt. T_P*.

Now we show that for some important subtheories T_P, the ordering requirements on T_P can be satisfied.

Lemma 3. *Let T_P be a theory such that Condition (1) is satisfied and each T_P congruence class of ground terms is finite. Then T_P satisfies Condition (2).*

Proof. Let us show that $\succ'_{T_P}$ is well-founded. Indeed, consider an infinite chain of closures $C_1 \succ'_{T_P} C_2 \succ'_{T_P} \cdots$. Since $\succ_{T_P}$ is well-founded on ground clauses, we have that starting from some i, C_{i+k} and C_{i+k+1} satisfy the condition (ii) from the definition of $\succ'_{T_P}$, (for all $k \geq 0$). Therefore we have an infinite chain:

$$C \cdot \sigma \succ'_{T_P} C\theta_1 \cdot \sigma_1 \succ'_{T_P} C\theta_1\theta_2 \cdot \sigma_2 \succ'_{T_P} \cdots \succ'_{T_P} C\theta_1 \cdots \theta_i \cdot \sigma_i \succ'_{T_P} \cdots$$

where $\bar{x}\sigma \simeq_{T_P} \bar{x}\theta_1\sigma_1 \simeq_{T_P} \cdots \simeq_{T_P} \bar{x}\theta_1 \cdots \theta_i\sigma_i \simeq_{T_P} \cdots$. But this is impossible since each θ_i is a T-proper instantiator and therefore has a depth of at least 1 but each T_P congruence class contains only a finite number of terms.

Corollary 2. *For the theory associativity and commutativity Conditions (1-2) can be satisfied.*

Now, assume that a subtheory T_P of our background theory T satisfies Conditions (1-2). Let $\succ_{T_P}$ be a closure ordering wrt. T_P. Now we can relax restrictions on answer-completeness by considering $\succeq_{T_P}$ in place of $\succeq$. It is straightforward to check that all our previous considerations and theorems will hold in this case.

9   Conclusion

In this paper we have presented a framework for integrating theory reasoning into instantiation-based theorem proving. This integration is done in the black-box style, which allows us to integrate different theories in a uniform way. Moreover in this way we can combine different calculi with the instantiation process by treating part of the input clauses as theory clauses. We also show how in this framework it is possible to employ efficient off-the-shelf satisfiability solvers for ground clauses modulo theories. For completeness of the resulting process we impose some general requirements on the theory reasoner and show that these requirements can be naturally satisfied by calculi based on ordered paramodulation. One of our main results is the theorem which implies that if the theory reasoner satisfies the requirements then any fair instantiation process will be complete for reasoning modulo this theory. Moreover, we show how this process can be guided by (partial) information on models for ground clauses. In addition, our framework allows to justify redundancy elimination based on a semantic notion of redundant clause and redundant inference.

For future work let us mention extending our approach to theories with particular properties, like Shostak theories [12]. This would help to integrate reasoning with fragments of Arithmetic. It would also be interesting to study the relationship between our approach and hierarchical reasoning [4]. Currently the implementation of the instantiation calculus is in progress [2] which will be used to evaluate practical applicability of the proposed methods.

Acknowledgements. Many thanks to Robert Nieuwenhuis, Andrei Voronkov and anonymous reviewers for providing useful comments.

In Memoriam. It is to our deep sorrow that Professor Harald Ganzinger passed away on 3th of June 2004. His work was revolutionary in the field of automated deduction and will continue to inspire future researchers.

References

1. A. Armando, S. Ranise, and M. Rusinowitch. A Rewriting Approach to Satisfiability Procedures. *Info. and Comp.*, 183(2):140–164, June 2003.
2. F. Baader and W. Snyder. Unification theory. In A. Robinson and A. Voronkov, editors, *Handbook of Automated Reasoning*, volume I, pages 445–532. Elsevier, 2001.
3. L. Bachmair and H. Ganzinger. Resolution theorem proving. In A. Robinson and A. Voronkov, editors, *Handbook of Automated Reasoning*, volume I, pages 19–100. Elsevier, 2001.

[2] See http://www.cs.man.ac.uk/~korovink/iprover/

4. L. Bachmair, H. Ganzinger, and U. Waldmann. Refutational Theorem Proving for Hierarchic First-Order Theories. *Applicable Algebra in Engineering, Communication and Computing*, 5(3/4):193–212, 1994.
5. C. Barrett, L. de Moura, and A. Stump. Design and results for the 1st satisfiability modulo theories competition. *Journal of Automated Reasoning*, 2006. to appear.
6. P. Baumgartner. FDPLL – a first-order Davis-Putnam-Logeman-Loveland Procedure. In *Proc. CADE*, volume 1831 of *LNAI*, pages 200–219, 2000.
7. P. Baumgartner and C. Tinelli. The model evolution calculus. In *Proc. CADE-19*, number 2741 in LNAI, pages 350–364. Springer, 2003.
8. P. Baumgartner and C. Tinelli. The model evolution calculus with equality. In *Proc. CADE-21*, number 3632 in LNAI, pages 392–408. Springer, 2005.
9. Peter Baumgartner. An order theory resolution calculus. In *LPAR*, volume 624 of *LNAI*, pages 119–130, 1992.
10. J. Gallier and W. Snyder. Complete sets of transformations for general E-unification. *Theoretical Computer Science*, 67(2,3):203–260, 1989.
11. H. Ganzinger, G. Hagen, R. Nieuwenhuis, A. Oliveras, and C. Tinelli. DPLL(T): Fast decision procedures. In *Poc. of CAV'04*, volume 3114 of *LNCS*, pages 175–188. Springer, 2004.
12. H. Ganzinger, T. Hillenbrand, and U. Waldmann. Superposition modulo a Shostak theory. In *CADE-19*, volume 2741 of *LNAI*, pages 182–196. Springer, 2003.
13. H. Ganzinger and K. Korovin. New directions in instantiation-based theorem proving. In *Proc. 18th IEEE Symposium on LICS*, pages 55–64. IEEE, 2003.
14. H. Ganzinger and K. Korovin. Integrating equational reasoning into instantiation-based theorem proving. In *CSL'04*, volume 3210 of *LNCS*, pages 71–84, 2004.
15. H. Ganzinger and K. Korovin. Theory Instantiation, 2006. Full version, available at http://www.cs.man.ac.uk/~korovink/ .
16. J. Hooker, G. Rago, V. Chandru, and A. Shrivastava. Partial instantiation methods for inference in first order logic. *J. of Automated Reasoning*, 28:371–396, 2002.
17. U. Hustadt, B. Motik, and U. Sattler. Reasoning in description logics with a concrete domain in the framework of resolution. In *ECAI*, pages 353–357, 2004.
18. R. Letz and G. Stenz. Proof and model generation with disconnection tableaux. In *Proc. LPAR 2001*, volume 2250 of *LNAI*, pages 142–156, 2001.
19. R. Letz and G. Stenz. Integration of equality reasoning into the disconnection calculus. In *Tableaux 2002*, volume 2381 of *LNAI*, pages 176–190, 2002.
20. C. Lynch and B. Morawska. Goal-directed E-unification. In *Proc. of RTA'2001*, volume 2051 of *LNCS*, pages 231–245. Springer, 2001.
21. R. Nieuwenhuis. On narrowing, refutation proofs and constraints. In *Proc. of RTA'1995*, volume 914 of *LNCS*, pages 56–70. Springer, 1995.
22. R. Nieuwenhuis and A. Oliveras. Decision procedures for SAT, SAT Modulo Theories and Beyond. In *12th Int. Conf. Logic for Prog., Artif. Intell. and Reasoning (LPAR)*, volume 3835 of *LNCS*, pages 23–46, 2005.
23. R. Nieuwenhuis and A. Rubio. Paramodulation-based theorem proving. In A. Robinson and A. Voronkov, editors, *Handbook of Automated Reasoning*, volume I, pages 371–443. Elsevier, 2001.
24. D. Plaisted and Y. Zhu. Ordered semantic hyper-linking. *J. of Automated Reasoning*, 25(3):167–217, 2000.
25. M. Stickel. Automated deduction by theory resolution. *J. Autom. Reasoning*, 1(4):333–355, 1985.
26. C. Tinelli. A DPLL-based calculus for ground satisfiability modulo theories. In *Proceedings of the 8th European Conference on Logics in Artificial Intelligence*, volume 2424 of *LNAI*, pages 308–319. Springer, 2002.

Splitting on Demand in SAT Modulo Theories*

Clark Barrett[1], Robert Nieuwenhuis[2], Albert Oliveras[2], and Cesare Tinelli[3]

[1] New York University
www.cs.nyu.edu/~barrett
[2] Technical Univ. of Catalonia, Barcelona
www.lsi.upc.edu/~roberto|~oliveras
[3] University of Iowa
www.cs.uiowa.edu/~tinelli

Abstract. Lazy algorithms for *Satisfiability Modulo Theories* (SMT) combine a generic DPLL-based SAT *engine* with a *theory solver* for the given theory T that can decide the T-consistency of conjunctions of ground literals. For many theories of interest, theory solvers need to reason by performing internal case splits. Here we argue that it is more convenient to delegate these case splits to the DPLL engine instead. The delegation can be done on demand for solvers that can encode their internal case splits into one or more clauses, possibly including new constants and literals. This results in drastically simpler theory solvers. We present this idea in an improved version of DPLL(T), a general SMT architecture for the lazy approach, and formalize and prove it correct in an extension of *Abstract DPLL Modulo Theories*, a framework for modeling and reasoning about lazy algorithms for SMT. A remarkable additional feature of the architecture, also discussed in the paper, is that it naturally includes an efficient Nelson-Oppen-like combination of multiple theories and their solvers.

1 Introduction

The performance of propositional SAT solvers based on the Davis-Putnam-Logemann-Loveland (DPLL) procedure [9,8] has importantly improved during the last years, and DPLL-based solvers are becoming the tool of choice for attacking more and more practical problems. The DPLL procedure has also been adapted for handling problems in more expressive logics, and, in particular, for the *Satisfiability Modulo Theories (SMT)* problem: deciding the satisfiability of ground first-order formulas with respect to background theories such as the integer or real numbers, or arrays. SMT problems frequently arise in formal hardware and software verification applications, where typical formulas consist of very large sets of clauses like:

$$p \quad \vee \quad \neg q \quad \vee \quad a{=}f(b-c) \quad \vee \quad read(s,\, f(b-c)){=}d \quad \vee \quad a - g(c) \le 7$$

* Partially supported by Spanish Ministry of Education and Science through the Logic-Tools project TIN2004-03382 (Nieuwenhuis and Oliveras), FPU grant AP2002-3533 (Oliveras), and by NSF grant 0237422 (Tinelli).

M. Hermann and A. Voronkov (Eds.): LPAR 2006, LNAI 4246, pp. 512–526, 2006.
© Springer-Verlag Berlin Heidelberg 2006

with propositional atoms as well as atoms over (combined) theories like the integers, arrays, or Equality with Uninterpreted Functions (EUF). SMT has become a very active area of research, and efficient SMT solvers exist that can handle (combinations of) many such theories T. Currently most SMT solvers follow the so-called *lazy* approach to SMT, combining (i) *theory solvers* that can handle *conjunctions* of literals over the given theory T, with (ii) DPLL *engines* for dealing with the Boolean structure of the formulas.

DPLL(T) is a general SMT architecture for the lazy approach [10]. It consists of a DPLL(X) engine, whose parameter X can be instantiated with a T-solver $Solver_T$, thus producing a DPLL(T) system. The DPLL(X) engine always considers the problem as a purely propositional one. For example, if the theory T is EUF, at some point DPLL(X) might consider a partial assignment containing, among many others, the four literals $a{=}b$, $f(a){=}c$, $f(b){=}d$, and $c{\neq}d$ without noticing its T-inconsistency, because it just considers such literals as propositional (syntactic) objects. But $Solver_T$ continuously analyzes the partial model that DPLL(X) is building (a conjunction of literals). It can warn DPLL(X) about this T-inconsistency, and generate a clause, called a *theory lemma*, like $a{\neq}b \lor f(a){\neq}c \lor f(b){\neq}d \lor c{=}d$, which can be used by DPLL(X) for backjumping. $Solver_T$ sometimes also does *theory propagation*: as soon as, e.g., $a{=}b$, $f(a){=}c$, and $f(b){=}d$ become true, it can notify DPLL(X) about T-consequences like $c{=}d$ that occur in the input formula. The modular DPLL(T) architecture is flexible, and can be implemented efficiently: the BarcelogicTools implementation of DPLL(T) won all the four divisions it entered at the 2005 SMT Competition [1].

Here we propose an improved version of the DPLL(T) architecture, to rationalize and simplify the construction of lazy SMT systems where $Solver_T$ does reasoning by cases. We present it formally by means of a corresponding extension of *Abstract DPLL Modulo Theories*, a uniform, declarative framework introduced in [12] for modeling and reasoning about lazy SMT procedures.

Example 1. In the array theory, the equation $read(write(A, i, v), j) = read(A, j)$ holds in two situations: when the indices i and j are distinct, or when they are equal but the $write(A, i, v)$ changes nothing, i.e., the value of array A at position i is already v. Deciding the T-consistency of a large conjunction of equations and disequations over arrays essentially requires $Solver_T$ to do an analysis of many Boolean combinations of such cases. In the extension of DPLL(T) we propose here, $Solver_T$ can delegate all such case splittings to the DPLL(X) engine, e.g., it can *demand* DPLL(X) to split on atoms like $i{=}j$, by sending it a *theory lemma* (i.e., a ground clause valid in the theory) that encodes the split—for instance, a clause like $read(write(A, i, v), j){\neq}read(A, j) \lor i{\neq}j \lor read(A, i) = v$.   □

The main novelty, and complication, versus the previous version of DPLL(T) is that the lemma may contain atoms that *do not occur in the input formula*. Sometimes even new constant symbols may be introduced. For example, in (fragments of) set theory [7], a set disequality $s \neq s'$ may be handled by the theory solver by reducing it to the disjunction $(a \in s \land a \notin s') \lor (a \notin s \land a \in s')$, where a is a fresh Skolem constant.

Centralizing all case splitting in the engine allows one to avoid the duplication of search functionality in the theory solver and drastically simplify its implementation, since a case splitting infrastructure is no longer necessary. Roughly, the solver's only requirement reduces to being able to detect T-inconsistencies once all case splits it has requested have been done.

The main contribution of this paper is a general and formal specification of this sort of architecture, together with a rigorous proof of its correctness. The relevance of this architecture is that it unquestionably leads to simpler solvers for theories that require case splits—in practice, all theories T where checking the T-inconsistency of ground literals is NP-hard.

In many SMT applications the background theory T is defined as a combination of several component theories $T_1, \ldots, T_n$, each with its own local solver. An important aspect of our approach is that it can be naturally refined to accommodate such combined theories, giving rise to a DPLL$(T_1, \ldots, T_n)$ architecture.

Example 2. Let T be the union of two disjoint theories T_1 and T_2 where T_1 is EUF and T_2 is (some fragment of) arithmetic, two of the most common theories in SMT. Let F be the conjunction $a=b \ \wedge \ f(a) - c \leq 3 \ \wedge \ f(b) - c \geq 4$ over the combined signature of T_1 and T_2. Introducing new constants c_1 and c_2, F can be *purified*, into an equisatisfiable conjunction of the T_1-pure formula F_1 and the T_2-pure formula F_2 below:

$$a=b \ \wedge \ c_1=f(a) \ \wedge \ c_2=f(b) \qquad\qquad c_1 - c \leq 3 \ \wedge \ c_2 - c \geq 4 \ .$$

In general, an *arrangement* A for such pure conjunctions $F_1 \ldots F_n$ is a conjunction saying, for every two constants *shared* between at least two different F_i's, whether the constants are equal or distinct. A general combination result underpinning the Nelson-Oppen method [11] states that for *stably infinite* and *signature disjoint* T_i's, F is T-consistent if, and only if, for some arrangement A each $F_i \wedge A$ is T_i-consistent (see, e.g., [14] for precise definitions and details). This can be decided by the respective T_i-solvers. In this example, F is T-inconsistent since $F_1 \wedge c_1 \neq c_2$ is T_1-inconsistent and $F_2 \wedge c_1 = c_2$ is T_2-inconsistent.

In practice, it is useful if each T_i-solver is able to *generate* all clauses $c_1 = c'_1 \vee \cdots \vee c_k = c'_k$ over the shared constants that are T_i-entailed by the conjunction F_i. For *convex* T_i, these entailed clauses are in fact always unit. It is not difficult to see that, if these two properties hold for all T_i, we only have to consider one arrangement: the one where every two constants not equated in a propagated equality are distinct. But usually the situation is less ideal. If some T_i is non-convex, it is necessary to do case splitting over the T_i-entailed non-unit clauses, and if some T_i-solver has limited or too expensive generation capabilities, the possible arrangements need to be (partially) guessed and tried.

By centralizing case splitting into the DPLL(X) engine and extending it to equalities over shared constants we can use the engine, in effect, to efficiently enumerate the arrangements on demand, that is, as requested by the individual theory solvers. Note that in the resulting DPLL$(T_1, \ldots, T_n)$ architecture, the engine will again handle literals possibly not in the input clauses, namely, (dis)equalities between shared variables.   □

Section 2 of this paper introduces and discusses the correctness of an Extended Abstract DPLL Modulo Theories framework that formalizes our approach.[1] Section 3 illustrates how to use the framework to avoid internal case splits in a very general class of theory solvers. Section 4 discusses the application of the framework to $DPLL(T_1, \ldots, T_n)$. Finally, Section 5 concludes.

Related work. Some of the ideas formalized in this paper on centralizing case splits in the Boolean engine are implemented in the system CVC [5] and CVC-Lite [4]. But apart from a brief note in Clark Barrett's PhD thesis (in Section 3.5.1 of [3]), we are not aware of any other description of them in the literature.

Bozzano *et al.* propose in [6] to use the Boolean engine in multi-theory SMT systems to do case splitting over the space of all possible arrangements. In contrast to this work, there the centralization of case-splitting concerns only equalities between shared constants, as needed by the Nelson-Oppen method. As far as theory solver combination is concerned, our approach and that in [6] are in a sense dual, possibly as a consequence of their different motivations. Simplifying a bit, in [6] the theory solvers are (or can be) completely unaware of each other. The DPLL engine is in charge of identifying shared constants and feeding (dis)equalities between them as appropriate to the solvers. This way, off-the-shelf decision procedures can be used as theory solvers. In our case, the roles are reversed. As we will see, the solvers are aware of their shared constants, and are in charge of producing lemmas containing (dis)equalities between them, for the engine to split on. The advantage in this case is that the same mechanism already in place for splitting on demand can be used for combination as well, with no changes to the engine.

2   Extended Abstract DPLL Modulo Theories

In this section, we briefly describe the Abstract DPLL Modulo Theories framework (see [12] for more details) and then extend it so that it can be used to formalize our new version of $DPLL(T)$ and, more generally, SMT approaches where new atoms and new symbols are introduced.

2.1   Abstract DPLL Modulo Theories

As usual in SMT, given a theory T (a set of closed first-order formulas), we will only consider the SMT problem for *ground* (and hence quantifier-free) CNF formulas F. Such formulas may contain *free* constants, i.e., constant symbols not in the signature of T, which, as far as satisfiability is concerned, can be equivalently seen as existential variables. Other than free constants, all other predicate and function symbols in the formulas will instead come from the signature of T. From now on, we will assume that all formulas satisfy these restrictions.

The formalism we describe is based on a set of *states* together with a binary relation $\Longrightarrow$ (called the *transition relation*) over these states, defined by means

---

[1] Because of space constraints we cannot provide the correctness proof here. The complete proof can be found in [2].

of *transition rules*. Starting with a state containing an input formula F, one can use the rules to generate a finite sequence of states, where the final state indicates whether or not F is T-consistent.

A *state* is either the distinguished state *FailState* (denoting T-unsatisfiability) or a pair of the form $M \parallel F$, where M is a sequence of literals, with $\emptyset$ denoting the empty sequence, and F is a formula in conjunctive normal form (CNF), i.e., a finite set of disjunctions of literals. We additionally require that M never contains both a literal and its negation and that each literal in M is annotated as either a *decision* literal (indicated by l^d) or not. Frequently, we will refer to M as a *partial assignment* or consider M just as a set or conjunction of literals, ignoring both the annotations and the order of its elements.

In what follows, a possibly subscripted or primed lowercase l *always* denotes a literal. Similarly C and D always denote clauses (disjunctions of literals), F and G denote conjunctions of clauses, and M and N denote partial assignments.

We write $M \models F$ to indicate that M propositionally satisfies F. If C is a clause $l_1 \vee \cdots \vee l_n$, we sometimes write $\neg C$ to denote the formula $\neg l_1 \wedge \cdots \wedge \neg l_n$. We say that C is *conflicting* in a state $M \parallel F, C$ if $M \models \neg C$.

A formula F is called T-*(in)consistent* if $F \wedge T$ is (un)satisfiable in the first-order sense. We say that M *is a T-model of* F if $M \models F$ and M, seen as a conjunction of literals, is T-consistent. It is not difficult to see that F is T-consistent if, and only if, it has a T-model. If F and G are formulas, then F *entails G in T*, written $F \models_T G$, if $F \wedge \neg G$ is T-inconsistent. If $F \models_T G$ and $G \models_T F$, we say that F and G are T-*equivalent*. A *theory lemma* is a clause C such that $\emptyset \models_T C$.

We start with the transition system first presented in [12].[2]

Definition 1. *Abstract DPLL Modulo Theories consists of the rules in Figure 1.*

The Basic DPLL Modulo Theories system *consists of the rules* Decide, Fail, UnitPropagate, T-Propagate *and* T-Backjump. *We denote the transition relation defined by these rules by* $\Longrightarrow_B$. *We denote the transition relation defined by all the rules by* $\Longrightarrow_{FT}$.

For a transition relation $\Longrightarrow$, we denote by $\Longrightarrow^*$ the reflexive-transitive closure of $\Longrightarrow$. We call any sequence of the form $S_0 \Longrightarrow S_1$, $S_1 \Longrightarrow S_2$, ... a *derivation*, and denote it by $S_0 \Longrightarrow S_1 \Longrightarrow S_2 \Longrightarrow \ldots$. We call any subsequence of a derivation a *subderivation*. If $S \Longrightarrow S'$ we say that there is a *transition* from S to S'. A state S is *final* with respect to $\Longrightarrow$ if there are no transitions from S.

The relevant derivations in the Abstract DPLL Modulo Theories system are those that start with a state of the form $\emptyset \parallel F$, where F is a formula to be checked for T-consistency, and end in a state that is final with respect to $\Longrightarrow_B$.

2.2   The Extended Abstract DPLL Modulo Theories System

Any realization of the Abstract DPLL Modulo Theories framework, in addition to implementing the rules and an execution strategy, must be able to determine

---

[2] For simplicity, we omit the Restart and T-Forget rules. A complete treatment of these rules is included in the full report [2].

UnitPropagate :

$$M \parallel F, C \vee l \implies M\, l \parallel F, C \vee l \quad \text{if} \quad \begin{cases} M \models \neg C \\ l \text{ is undefined in } M \end{cases}$$

Decide :

$$M \parallel F \qquad\qquad \implies M\, l^{\mathsf{d}} \parallel F \quad \text{if} \quad \begin{cases} l \text{ or } \neg l \text{ occurs in a clause of } F \\ l \text{ is undefined in } M \end{cases}$$

Fail :

$$M \parallel F, C \qquad \implies \textit{FailState} \quad \text{if} \quad \begin{cases} M \models \neg C \\ M \text{ contains no decision literals} \end{cases}$$

T-Learn :

$$M \parallel F \qquad\qquad \implies M \parallel F, C \quad \text{if} \quad \begin{cases} \text{each atom of } C \text{ occurs in } F \text{ or in } M \\ F \models_T C \end{cases}$$

T-Backjump :

$$M\, l^{\mathsf{d}}\, N \parallel F, C \implies M\, l' \parallel F, C \quad \text{if} \quad \begin{cases} M\, l^{\mathsf{d}}\, N \models \neg C, \text{ and there is} \\ \text{some clause } C' \vee l' \text{ such that:} \\ \quad F, C \models_T C' \vee l' \text{ and } M \models \neg C', \\ \quad l' \text{ is undefined in } M, \text{ and} \\ \quad l' \text{ or } \neg l' \text{ occurs in } F \text{ or in } M\, l^{\mathsf{d}}\, N \end{cases}$$

T-Propagate :

$$M \parallel F \quad \implies M\, l \parallel F \quad \text{if} \quad \begin{cases} M \models_T l \\ l \text{ or } \neg l \text{ occurs in } F \\ l \text{ is undefined in } M \end{cases}$$

Fig. 1. Rules for Abstract DPLL Modulo Theories

the T-consistency of M when a final state $M \parallel F$ is reached. For this purpose, one typically assumes the existence of $Solver_T$ which can do precisely that.

However, for some important theories, determining the T-consistency of a conjunction of literals requires additional *internal* case splitting. In order to simplify $Solver_T$ and centralize the case splitting in the DPLL engine, it is desirable to relax the requirement on $Solver_T$ by allowing it to demand that the DPLL engine do additional case splits before determining the T-consistency of the partial assignment. For flexibility—and because it is needed by actual theories of interest—the theory solver should be able to demand case splits on literals that do not appear in M or F and possibly even contain fresh constant symbols.

It is not hard to see, however, that allowing this kind of flexibility poses a potential termination problem. We can overcome this difficulty if, for any input formula F, the set of all literals needed to check the T-consistency of F is finite. More precisely, as a purely theoretical construction, we assume that for every input formula F there is a finite set $\mathcal{L}(F)$ of literals containing all literals on which a given theory solver may demand case splits when starting with a conjunction of literals from F. For example, for a solver for the theory of arrays $\mathcal{L}(F)$ could contain atoms of the form $i = j$, where i and j are array indices occurring in F. This technical requirement poses no limitations on any of the practically useful theory solver procedures we are aware of (see Section 3). Also, for the proofs here there is no need to construct the set $\mathcal{L}(F)$. It is enough to know that it exists. Formally, we require the following.

Definition 2. $\mathcal{L}$ *is a* suitable literal-generating function *if for every finite set of literals L:*

1. $\mathcal{L}$ *maps L to a new finite set of literals L' such that $L \subseteq L'$.*
2. *For each atomic formula α, $\alpha \in \mathcal{L}(L)$ iff $\neg\alpha \in \mathcal{L}(L)$.*
3. *If L' is a set of literals and $L \subseteq L'$, then, $\mathcal{L}(L) \subseteq \mathcal{L}(L')$ (monotonicity).*
4. *$\mathcal{L}(\mathcal{L}(L)) = \mathcal{L}(L)$ (idempotence).*

For convenience, given a formula F, we denote by $\mathcal{L}(F)$ the result of applying $\mathcal{L}$ to the set of all literals appearing in F.

The introduction of new constant symbols poses potential problems not only for termination, but also for soundness. One property of the transition relation $\Longrightarrow_{FT}$ is that whenever $\emptyset \parallel F \Longrightarrow^*_{FT} M \parallel F'$, the formulas F and F' are T-equivalent. This will no longer be true if we allow the introduction of new constant symbols. However, it is sufficient to simply ensure T-equisatisfiability of F and F'. To this end, we introduce the following definition.

Definition 3. *Given a formula F and a formula G, we define $\gamma_F(G)$ as follows:*

1. *Let G' be the formula obtained by replacing each free constant symbol in G that does not appear in F with a fresh variable.*
2. *Let $\overline{v}$ be the set of all fresh variables introduced in the previous step.*
3. *Then, $\gamma_F(G) = \exists\, \overline{v}.\, G'$.*

Now we can give a new transition rule called Extended T-Learn which replaces T-Learn and allows for the desired additional flexibility.

Definition 4. *The* Extended DPLL Modulo Theories system, *denoted as* $\Longrightarrow_{XT}$, *consists of the rules of Basic DPLL Modulo Theories, together with the rule:*

Extended T-Learn

$$M \parallel F \implies M \parallel F, C \quad \text{if} \quad \begin{cases} \text{each atom of } C \text{ occurs in } F \text{ or in } \mathcal{L}(M) \\ F \models_T \gamma_F(C) \end{cases}$$

The key observation is that an implementation using Extended T-Learn has more flexibility when a state $M \parallel F$ is reached which is final with respect to $\Longrightarrow_B$. Whereas before it would have been necessary for the theory solver to determine the T-consistency of M when such a state was reached, the Extended T-Learn rule allows the possibility of *delaying* a response by demanding that additional case splits (on possibly new literals appearing in the clause C) be done first. As we will show below, the properties of $\mathcal{L}$ ensure that the solver's response cannot be delayed indefinitely.

2.3   Correctness of Extended Abstract DPLL Modulo Theories

A decision procedure for SMT can be obtained by generating a derivation using $\Longrightarrow_{\text{XT}}$ with a particular strategy. As with $\Longrightarrow_{\text{FT}}$, the aim of a derivation is to compute a state S such that: (i) S is final with respect to the rules of Basic DPLL Modulo Theories and (ii) if S is of the form $M \parallel F$ then M is T-consistent.

Lemma 1. *If* $\emptyset \parallel F \Longrightarrow^{*}_{\text{XT}} M \parallel G$ *then the following hold.*

1. *All the literals in M and all the literals in G are in $\mathcal{L}(F)$.*
2. *M contains no literal more than once and is indeed an assignment, i.e., it contains no pair of literals of the form p and $\neg p$.*
3. *$G \models_T F$ and for some H, $F \models_T \gamma_H(G)$.*
4. *If M is of the form $M_0 \, l_1 \, M_1 \, \ldots \, l_n \, M_n$, where $l_1, \ldots, l_n$ are all the decision literals of M, then $G, l_1, \ldots, l_i \models_T M_i$ for all i in $0 \ldots n$.*

Theorem 1 (Termination of $\Longrightarrow_{\text{XT}}$). *There is no infinite derivation of the form $\emptyset \parallel F \Longrightarrow_{\text{XT}} S_1 \Longrightarrow_{\text{XT}} \ldots$*

The main difference in the termination argument with respect to $\Longrightarrow_{\text{FT}}$ is that, while Extended T-Learn can produce lemmas with new literals, it can only produce a finite number of them thanks to the properties of $\mathcal{L}$.

Lemma 2. *If* $\emptyset \parallel F \Longrightarrow^{*}_{\text{XT}} M \parallel F'$ *and there is some conflicting clause in $M \parallel F'$, i.e., $M \models \neg C$ for some clause C in F', then either* Fail *or* T-Backjump *applies to $M \parallel F'$.*

Property 1. If $\emptyset \parallel F \Longrightarrow^{*}_{\text{XT}} M \parallel F'$ and M is T-inconsistent, then either there is a conflicting clause in $M \parallel F'$, or else Extended T-Learn applies to $M \parallel F'$, generating a clause enabling some Basic DPLL Modulo Theories step.

Lemma 2 and Property 1 show that, for a state of the form $M \parallel F$, if there is some literal of F undefined in M, or there is some conflicting clause, or M is T-inconsistent, then a rule of Basic DPLL Modulo Theories is always applicable, possibly after a single Extended T-Learn step. Together with Theorem 1 (Termination), this shows how to compute a state to which the following main theorem is applicable.

Theorem 2. *Let Der be a derivation* $\emptyset \parallel F \Longrightarrow^{*}_{\text{XT}} S$, *where S is (i) final with respect to Basic DPLL Modulo Theories, and (ii) if S is of the form $M \parallel F'$ then M is T-consistent. Then*

1. *S is FailState if, and only if, F is T-inconsistent.*
2. *If S is of the form $M \parallel F'$ then M is a T-model of F.*

For a given theory T, Theorems 1 and 2 show how to obtain a decision procedure for the T-consistency of formulas as long as we have a theory solver and can prove for it the existence of a suitable literal-generating function $\mathcal{L}$ such that the following holds: for every state of the form $M \parallel F$ that is final with respect to $\Longrightarrow_{\text{B}}$, the theory solver is able to (i) determine that M is T-inconsistent, (ii) determine that M is T-consistent, or (iii) generate a new clause via Extended T-Learn that enables some Basic DPLL Modulo Theories step.

3   Avoiding Case Splitting Within Theory Solvers

In this section, we show how rule-based theory solvers can be used in the context of Extended DPLL Modulo Theories.

Recall that theory solvers only need to deal with conjunctions (equivalently, sets) of literals. Then observe that any solver deciding the T-consistency of such conjunctions in a theory where this problem is NP-hard is bound to resort to some form of case splitting.[3] We show how the Extended T-Learn rule allows such solvers to avoid any internal case splitting, and we explain why, for rule-based solvers, the existence of $\mathcal{L}$ is reasonable.

3.1   Rule-Based Theory Solvers

A large class of theory solvers can be defined using inference rules that describe how to take a set of literals and transform it in some way to get new sets of literals (or $\perp$, indicating T-inconsistency). Consider a theory T. For our purposes, let us assume that an inference rule has one of the following two formats:

$$\frac{\Gamma, \Delta}{\perp} \qquad\qquad \frac{\Gamma, \Delta}{\Gamma, \Delta_1 \quad \Gamma, \Delta_2 \quad \cdots \quad \Gamma, \Delta_n}$$

where the meta-variables Γ, Δ and Δ_i represent sets of literals. We call rules of the first kind *refuting* rules and rules of the second kind *progress* rules. Typically, Δ has side-conditions or is a schema, while Γ can represent any set of literals. Progress rules describe a local change based on a small number of literals (the ones in Δ), while all of the other literals (the ones in Γ) are unchanged.

A refuting rule is *sound* if and only if any legal instance δ of Δ is T-inconsistent. A progress rule is *sound* if whenever $\Delta, \Delta_1, \ldots, \Delta_n$ are instantiated with $\delta, \delta_1, \ldots, \delta_n$ respectively, δ is T-consistent iff $\bigvee_{i=1}^{n} \delta_i$ is T-consistent. We say that a set Φ of literals is *(ir)reducible* with respect to a set of derivation rules R if (n)one of the rules in R applies to it, i.e., if (no) some subset of Φ is a legal instance of Δ in a rule of R. A *strategy* is a function that, given a reducible set of literals Φ, chooses a rule from R to apply.

Given a set R of rules and a strategy S, a *derivation tree* for a set of literals Φ is a finite tree with root Φ such that for each internal node E of the tree, E is reducible and its children are the conclusions of the rule selected by S for E. A *refutation tree* (for Φ) is a derivation tree all of whose leaves are $\perp$. A *derivation* is a sequence of derivation trees starting with the single-node tree containing Φ, where each tree is derived from the previous one by the application of a rule from R to one of its leaves. A *refutation* is a finite derivation ending with a refutation tree. A strategy S is *terminating* if every derivation using S is finite. A strategy S is *complete* if whenever Φ is T-inconsistent, S produces a refutation for Φ.

It is not hard to see that a set R of sound inference rules together with a terminating and complete strategy S provide a decision procedure for the

---

[3] In fact, conceivably a solver may be based on case splitting even if the above T-consistency problem is polynomial, for simplicity or convenience.

T-consistency of sets of ground literals. In fact, all decision procedures typically associated with applications of Satisfiability Modulo Theories can be described in this way. We will now describe how such decision procedures can be incorporated into the Extended Abstract DPLL Modulo Theories formalism.

3.2 Integration with Rule-Based Theory Solvers

Recall that the original DPLL Modulo Theories framework requires that for every state $M \parallel F$ that is final with respect to Basic DPLL Modulo Theories, the theory solver can determine the T-consistency of M. Given a set of sound inference rules and a terminating and complete strategy, M can be checked for T-consistency simply by generating the derivation starting with M and determining whether it results in a refutation tree or not.

Note that this process may require a large derivation tree with many branches. The purpose of the Extended T-Learn rule is to allow the theory solver to avoid having to do any splitting itself. This can be accomplished as follows. Given a state $M \parallel F$ which is final with respect to Basic DPLL Modulo Theories, the theory solver begins applying rules starting with M. However, this time, as soon as a splitting rule is encountered (a progress rule with $n > 1$), the theory solver halts and uses Extended T-Learn to return one or more clauses representing the case split. The theory solver is then suspended until another final state $M' \parallel F'$ is reached.

The obvious remaining question is how to capture the case split with a learned clause. As we show in [2], one way to do this that will work for any rule-based theory solver is to encode the number of possible case splits using Boolean constants. In practice, however, it is usually possible and desirable to encode splitting rules more directly. For example, a progress rule of the form seen in the previous subsection (where $n > 1$) corresponds to the following formula schema: $\neg(\Delta) \vee \bigvee_{i=1}^{n} \Delta_i$. Any instance of this schema can be converted into CNF and the resulting clauses sent to the DPLL engine via Extended T-Learn. For this to work, one additional requirement is that the rules be *refining*. We say that an inference rule is *refining* if it is a refuting rule or if whenever $\Delta, \Delta_1, \ldots, \Delta_n$ are instantiated with $\delta, \delta_1, \ldots, \delta_n$ respectively, $\delta \models_T \gamma_\delta(\bigvee_{i=1}^{n} \delta_i)$. This is essentially a stronger version of soundness. It requires that any model of the premise can be refined into a model of some of the consequents. It is necessary in order to satisfy the side conditions of Extended T-Learn.

We must also check that an appropriate literal-generating function $\mathcal{L}$ exists. Assume we are given a set R of rules and a terminating strategy S. First, define $\mathcal{D}$ to be a function which, given a set Φ of literals returns all literals that may appear along any branch of the derivation tree with any subset of Φ at its root. And let $\mathcal{N}$ be a function which, given a set Φ of literals, returns all literals that can be formed from the atomic formulas in Φ. Now, we define a series of functions $\mathcal{L}_i$ as follows. Let $\mathcal{L}_0$ be the identity function and for $i > 0$, let $\mathcal{L}_i(\Phi) = \mathcal{N}(\mathcal{D}(\mathcal{L}_{i-1}(\Phi)))$. If for some $k > 0$, $\mathcal{L}_k = \mathcal{L}_{k+1}$, then we say that R is *literal-bounded under S*, and define $\mathcal{L} = \mathcal{L}_k$.

Property 2. If R is a set of sound refining rules for a theory T, S is a strategy for R that is terminating and complete, and R is literal-bounded under S, then R can be integrated with the Extended DPLL Modulo Theories framework.

Proof. We first show that $\mathcal{L}$ satisfies Definition 2. It is easy to see that Properties 1 and 2 in the definition are satisfied. Because $\mathcal{D}(\Phi)$ considers derivations starting with any subset of Φ, Property 3 must also be satisfied. Finally, because $\mathcal{L}$ is a fixed point of $\mathcal{L}_i$, it must be idempotent.

Now, we must show that whenever a state $M \parallel F$ is reached that is final with respect to Basic DPLL Modulo Theories, the theory solver can do one of the following: determine that M is T-consistent; determine that M is T-inconsistent; or introduce a new clause via Extended T-Learn that enables some Basic DPLL Modulo Theories step.

Given a state $M \parallel F$, we simply apply rules from R to M according to strategy S. If $\bot$ is derived, then by soundness, M is T-inconsistent. If an irreducible set of literals is derived, then by completeness, M must be T-consistent. If a splitting rule is reached, and $\Gamma, \Delta, \Delta_1, \ldots, \Delta_n$ are instantiated with $\phi, \delta, \delta_1, \ldots, \delta_n$ respectively, there are three possibilities:

1. For all i, $M \models \neg\delta_i$. In this case, we apply Extended T-Learn to learn $\neg(\delta) \lor \bigvee_{i=1}^n \delta_i$, which will result in one or more clauses that are conflicting in M, thus enabling either Fail or T-Backjump by Lemma 2.
2. For some i, $M \models \delta_i$, or else δ_i is undefined in M and $M \models \neg\delta_j$ for every $j \neq i$. In either case, no split is necessary and we simply proceed by applying rules of R to ϕ, δ_i.
3. The final case is when at least two of the δ_i are undefined in M. Then we apply Extended T-Learn to learn $\neg(\delta) \lor \bigvee_{i=1}^n \delta_i$ which is guaranteed to contain at least one clause that is not satisfied by M, thus enabling Decide.   □

Example 3. As we saw in a previous example the theory of arrays requires case splitting. One (sound and refining) rule-based decision procedure for this theory is given in [13]. A careful examination of the decision procedure reveals the following: (i) each term can be categorized as an *array* term, an *index* term, a *value* term, or a *set* term; (ii) no new array terms are ever introduced by the inference rules; (iii) at most one new index term for every pair of array terms is introduced; (iv) set terms are made up of some finite number of index terms; (v) the only new value terms introduced are of the form $read(a, i)$ where a is an array term and i is an index term. It follows that the total number of possible terms that can be generated by the procedure starting with any finite set of literals is finite. Because there are only a finite number of predicates, it then follows that this set of rules is literal-bounded.   □

4   Application to Satisfiability Modulo Multiple Theories

In this section, we focus on background theories T that are actually the union of two or more component theories $T_1, \ldots, T_n$, each equipped with its own solver.

We first show how to obtain an Abstract DPLL Modulo Theories transition system for the combined theory T as a *refinement* of the system XT described in Section 2 using only the solvers of the theories T_i. Then we show how to refine the new DPLL(T) architecture into a DPLL($T_1, \ldots, T_n$) architecture in which each T_i-solver is directly integrated into the DPLL($X_1, \ldots, X_n$) engine.

We will work here in the context of first-order logic with equality. For the rest of the section we fix $n > 1$ *stably infinite* theories[4] $T_1, \ldots, T_n$ with respective, mutually disjoint signatures $\Sigma_1, \ldots, \Sigma_n$. We will consider the theory $T = T_1 \cup \cdots \cup T_n$ with signature $\Sigma = \Sigma_1 \cup \cdots \cup \Sigma_n$. We are interested in the T-satisfiability of ground formulas over the signature Σ extended with an infinite set K of *free constants*. For any signature Ω we will denote by $\Omega(K)$ the signature $\Omega \cup K$. We say that a ground clause or literal is *(i-)pure* if it has signature $\Sigma_i(K)$ where $i \in \{1, \ldots, n\}$. Given a CNF formula F of signature $\Sigma(K)$, by abstracting subterms with fresh constants from K, it is possible to convert F in linear time into an equisatisfiable CNF formula, all of whose atoms are pure. See [14], for instance, for details on this purification procedure. From now on, we will limit ourselves with no loss of generality to pure formulas.

Following the Nelson-Oppen combination method, the various solvers will cooperate by exchanging entailed equalities over *shared* constants. Let L be a set of pure literals over the signature $\Sigma(K)$. We say that a constant $k \in K$ is an *(ij-)shared constant* of L if it occurs in an i-pure and a j-pure literal of L for some distinct i and j. For $i = 1, \ldots, n$, we denote by L^i the set of all the $\Sigma_i(K)$-literals of L and by $\mathcal{S}_i(L)$ the set of all equalities between distinct ij-shared constants of L for every $j \neq i$. Note that for every $j \neq i$, $L^j \cap L^i$ contains at most equalities or the negation of equalities from $\mathcal{S}_i(L)$. An *arrangement for* L is a set containing for each equality $e \in \bigcup_i \mathcal{S}_i(L)$ either e or $\neg e$ (but not both), and nothing else.

The extended Abstract DPLL Modulo theories framework can be refined to take into account that T is a combined theory by imposing the following additional requirements on the XT system.

Refinement 1. We consider only derivations starting with states of the form $\emptyset \parallel F$, where each atom of F is a pure $\Sigma(K)$-atom.

Refinement 2. We consider only applications $M \parallel F \implies M\, l \parallel F$ of the rule T-Propagate and applications $M \parallel F \implies M \parallel F, C$ of Extended T-Learn where l and each literal of C are pure.

Refinement 1 and 2 maintain the invariant that all the literals occurring in a state are pure, and so can be fed to the corresponding local solvers. Given these minimal requirements, it will be sufficient for T-Propagate to propagate only literals l that are i-pure for some $i = 1, \ldots, n$ and such that and $M^i \models_{T_i} l$, where the entailment $M^i \models_{T_i} l$ is determined by the T_i-solver. Similarly, Extended T-Learn will rely on the local solvers only to learn T_i-lemmas, i.e., i-pure clauses C such that $\emptyset \models_{T_i} \gamma_F(C)$. Note that we do allow lemmas C consisting

---

[4] A theory T is stably infinite if every T-consistent quantifier-free formula F over T's signature is satisfiable in an infinite model of T.

of pure literals from different theories and such that $F \models_T \gamma_F(C)$, as lemmas of this sort can be computed even if one only has local solvers (consider for example the backjump clauses generated by standard conflict analysis mechanisms).

Refinement 3. The suitable literal-generating function $\mathcal{L}$ maps every finite set L of pure $\Sigma(K)$-literals to a finite set of pure $\Sigma(K)$-literals including $\bigcup_i \mathcal{S}_i(L)$.

To use the various solvers together in a refutationally complete way for T-consistency, it is necessary to make them agree on an arrangement. To do this efficiently, they should be able to share the entailed (disjunctions) of equalities of shared constants. Refinement 3 then essentially states that theory lemmas can include shared equalities.

4.1   From DPLL(T) to DPLL($T_1, \ldots, T_n$)

Assuming the previous refinements at the abstract level, we now show in concrete how the DPLL(T) architecture can be specialized to use the various local solvers directly and to facilitate cooperation among them. Here we define a local requirement on each T_i-solver that does not even need refutational completeness for T_i-consistency. If M is an assignment consisting of pure literals and $i \in \{1, \ldots, n\}$, we call the *(default) completion* of M^i and denote by $\widehat{M^i}$ the smallest extension of M^i falsifying every shared equation for M^i that is undefined in M, that is, $\widehat{M^i} = M^i \cup \{\neg e \mid e \in \mathcal{S}_i(M), e \text{ undefined in } M\}$.

Requirement 1. For each $i = 1, \ldots, n$, the solver for T_i, given a state $M \parallel F$, must be able to do one of the following:

1. determine that $\widehat{M^i}$ is T_i-consistent, or
2. identify a T_i-inconsistent subset of M^i, or
3. produce an i-pure clause C containing at least one literal of $\mathcal{L}(M)$ undefined in M and such that $\emptyset \models_{T_i} \gamma_F(C)$.

The computational cost of the test in Point 1 of this requirement depends on the deduction capabilities of the theory solver.[5] Note, however, that the test can be deferred thanks to Point 3. The solver may choose not to generate the completion of M^i explicitly and test it for T_i-inconsistency, and instead generate a lemma for the engine containing one of the undefined equalities.

If a solver meeting Requirement 1 cannot determine the T_i-consistency of the completion $\widehat{M^i}$, it must be either because it has determined that a subset of M^i (possibly of M^i alone) is in fact inconsistent, or that it needs more information about some of the undefined literals of $\mathcal{L}(M)$ first. However, once every literal of $\mathcal{L}(M)$ is defined in M, including the equalities in $\mathcal{S}_i(M)$, the solver *must* be able to tell whether M^i is T_i-consistent or not. This is a minimal requirement for any solver to be used in a Nelson-Oppen style combination procedure.

Usually though it is desirable for Nelson-Oppen solvers to also be able to compute (disjunctions of) shared equalities entailed by a given set of literals, so

---

[5] For some solvers, such as the common ones for EUF or linear rational arithmetic, this additional cost is actually zero as these solvers already explicitly maintain complete information on all the entailed equalities between the known terms.

that only these equalities can be propagated to the other solvers, and guessing is minimized. For instance, if one solver communicates that a is equal to either b or c, then the other solvers do not have to consider cases where a is equal to some fourth constant. Requirement 1 allows that possibility, as illustrated by the following example.

Example 4. Assume, just for simplicity, that for every M, $\mathcal{L}(M)$ is no more than $M \cup \bigcup_i \mathcal{S}_i(M)$, which entails that each T_i-solver is refutationally complete for T_i-consistency. Then consider an assignment M where M_i is T_i-consistent, for some i, and let $e_1, \ldots, e_n$ be equalities in $\mathcal{S}_i(M)$ undefined in M such that $l_1, \ldots, l_m \models \bigvee_k e_k$ for some $\{l_1, \ldots, l_m\} \subseteq M^i$. In this case, $\widehat{M^i}$ is clearly T_i-inconsistent. However, since M^i alone is consistent, by Requirement 1 the T_i-solver must return a lemma containing one or more undefined literals of $\mathcal{L}(M)$.

Now, if the solver can in fact compute (deterministically, with no internal case splits!) the clause $\bigwedge_j l_j \Rightarrow \bigvee_k e_k$, that clause will be the ideal lemma to return. Otherwise, it is enough for the solver to return *any* lemma that contains at least one shared equality e (in the worst case, even a tautology of the form $e \vee \neg e$ will do). Intuitively, this marks a progress in the computation because eventually one of the shared equalities will be added to M (for instance, by an application of Decide), reducing the number of undefined literals in $\mathcal{L}(M)$. □

Requirement 1 and the earlier refinements are enough to guarantee that we can use the local T_i-solvers directly—as opposed to building a solver for the combined theory T—to generate derivations satisfying Theorem 2. The first thing we need for Theorem 2 is easy to see: it is always possible to derive from a state $\emptyset \parallel F$ a final state S with respect to Basic DPLL Modulo Theories ($\Longrightarrow_B$). The second thing we need is that whenever the final state S has the form $M \parallel F'$, the assignment M is T-consistent. Although none of the local solvers is able to determine that by itself, it can do it in cooperation with the other solvers thanks to Requirement 1. It is then not difficult to show (see [2]) that, under the assumptions in this section, the following property holds.

Property 3. Each derivation of the form $\emptyset \parallel F \Longrightarrow_{\mathrm{XT}}^* M \parallel G$ where $M \parallel G$ is final wrt. Basic DPLL Modulo Theories can be extended in finitely many steps using the solvers for $T_1, \ldots, T_n$ to a derivation of the form $\emptyset \parallel F \Longrightarrow_{\mathrm{XT}}^* M \parallel G \Longrightarrow_{\mathrm{XT}}^* S$ where S is either *FailState* or a state $M' \parallel G'$ with a T-consistent M'.

5 Conclusions and Further Work

We have proposed a new version of DPLL(T) in which theory solvers can delegate all case splits to the DPLL engine. This can be done *on demand* for solvers that can encode their internal case splits into one or more clauses, possibly including new constants and literals. We have formalized this in an extension of Abstract DPLL and proved it correct. We think that the new insights gained by this formalization will help us and others when incorporating these ideas into our respective SMT solvers. We have also introduced a DPLL($T_1, \ldots, T_n$) architecture for combined theories, which also fits naturally into the extended Abstract DPLL framework. This refinement is crucial in practice because most SMT applications are based on combinations of theories. Our splitting on demand approach leads to significantly simpler theory solvers. The price to pay is an increase in the complexity of the DPLL(X) engine, which must be able to deal with a dynamically expanding set of literals. However, we believe that doing this once and for all is better than paying the price of building a far more complex theory solver for each theory that requires case splits. Moreover, the requirement of being able to deal dynamically with new literals and clauses is needed in general for flexibility in applications, not just for our approach.

As future work, we plan to evaluate the approach experimentally. We also plan to investigate theory-dependent splitting heuristics, and effective ways for a theory solver to share such heuristic information with the DPLL(X) engine.

References

1. C. Barrett, L. de Moura, and A. Stump. SMT-COMP: Satisfiability Modulo Theories Competition. In *CAV'05*, LNCS 3576, pages 20–23. Springer, 2005.
2. C. Barrett, R. Nieuwenhuis, A. Oliveras, and C. Tinelli. Splitting on demand in satisfiability modulo theories. Technical report. University of Iowa, 2006. Available at ftp://ftp.cs.uiowa.edu/pub/tinelli/papers/BarNOT-RR-06.pdf.
3. C. W. Barrett. *Checking Validity of Quantifier-Free Formulas in Combinations of First-Order Theories*. PhD thesis, Stanford University, 2003.
4. C. W. Barrett and S. Berezin. CVC lite: A new implementation of the cooperating validity checker. In *CAV'04*, LNCS 3114, pages 515–518. Springer, 2004.
5. C. Barrett, D. Dill, and A. Stump. Checking satisfiability of first-order formulas by incremental translation into SAT. In *CAV'02*, LNCS 2404, pages 236–249, 2002.
6. M. Bozzano, R. Bruttomesso, A. Cimatti, T. A. Junttila, S. Ranise, P. van Rossum, and R. Sebastiani. Efficient theory combination via boolean search. *Information and Computation*. To appear. Cf. conference paper at CAV'05.
7. D. Cantone and C. G. Zarba. A new fast tableau-based decision procedure for an unquantified fragment of set theory. In *Automated Deduction in Classical and Non-Classical Logics*, LNCS 1761, pages 127–137. Springer, 2000.
8. M. Davis, G. Logemann, and D. Loveland. A machine program for theorem-proving. *Comm. of the ACM*, 5(7):394–397, 1962.
9. M. Davis and H. Putnam. A computing procedure for quantification theory. *Journal of the ACM*, 7:201–215, 1960.
10. H. Ganzinger, G. Hagen, R. Nieuwenhuis, A. Oliveras, and C. Tinelli. DPLL(T): Fast Decision Procedures. In *CAV'04*, LNCS 3114, pages 175–188. Springer, 2004.
11. G. Nelson and D. C. Oppen. Simplification by cooperating decision procedures. *ACM Trans. Program. Lang. Syst.*, 1(2):245–257, 1979.
12. R. Nieuwenhuis, A. Oliveras, and C. Tinelli. Abstract DPLL and Abstract DPLL Modulo Theories. In *LPAR'04*, LNAI 3452, pages 36–50. Springer, 2005.
13. A. Stump, C. W. Barrett, D. L. Dill, and J. R. Levitt. A decision procedure for an extensional theory of arrays. In *LICS'01*, pages 29–37. IEEE Computer Society.
14. C. Tinelli and M. T. Harandi. A new correctness proof of the Nelson–Oppen combination procedure. In *FroCoS'96*, pages 103–120. Kluwer Academic Publishers.

Delayed Theory Combination vs. Nelson-Oppen for Satisfiability Modulo Theories: A Comparative Analysis[*]

Roberto Bruttomesso[1], Alessandro Cimatti[1], Anders Franzén[1,2],
Alberto Griggio[2], and Roberto Sebastiani[2]

[1] ITC-IRST, Povo, Trento, Italy
{bruttomesso, cimatti, franzen}@itc.it
[2] DIT, Università di Trento, Italy
{griggio, rseba}@dit.unitn.it

Abstract. Many approaches for Satisfiability Modulo Theory ($SMT(\mathcal{T})$) rely on the integration between a SAT solver and a decision procedure for sets of literals in the background theory $\mathcal{T}$ ($\mathcal{T}$-solver). When $\mathcal{T}$ is the combination $\mathcal{T}_1 \cup \mathcal{T}_2$ of two simpler theories, the approach is typically handled by means of Nelson-Oppen's (NO) theory combination schema in which two specific $\mathcal{T}$-solvers deduce and exchange (disjunctions of) interface equalities.

In recent papers we have proposed a new approach to $SMT(\mathcal{T}_1 \cup \mathcal{T}_2)$, called *Delayed Theory Combination* (DTC). Here part or all the (possibly very expensive) task of deducing interface equalities is played by the SAT solver itself, at the potential cost of an enlargement of the boolean search space. In principle this enlargement could be up to exponential in the number of interface equalities generated.

In this paper we show that this estimate was too pessimistic. We present a comparative analysis of DTC vs. NO for $SMT(\mathcal{T}_1 \cup \mathcal{T}_2)$, which shows that, using state-of-the-art SAT-solving techniques, the amount of boolean branches performed by DTC can be upper bounded by the number of deductions and boolean branches performed by NO on the same problem. We prove the result for different deduction capabilities of the $\mathcal{T}$-solvers and for both convex and non-convex theories.

1 Introduction

Satisfiability Modulo a Theory $\mathcal{T}$ ($SMT(\mathcal{T})$) is the problem of checking the satisfiability of a quantifier-free (or ground) first-order formula with respect to a given first-order theory $\mathcal{T}$. Theories of interest for many applications are, e.g., the theory of difference logic $\mathcal{DL}$, the theory $\mathcal{EUF}$ of equality and uninterpreted functions, the quantifier-free fragment of Linear Arithmetic over the rationals $\mathcal{LA}(\mathbb{Q})$ and that over the integers $\mathcal{LA}(\mathbb{Z})$. Particularly relevant is the case of $SMT(\mathcal{T}_1 \cup \mathcal{T}_2)$, where the background theory $\mathcal{T}$ is the combination of two (or more) simpler theories $\mathcal{T}_1$ and $\mathcal{T}_2$. [1]

---

[*] This work has been partly supported by ISAAC, an European sponsored project, contract no. AST3-CT-2003-501848, by ORCHID, a project sponsored by Provincia Autonoma di Trento, and by a grant from Intel Corporation.

[1] For better readability, and as it is common practice in papers dealing with combination of theories, in this paper we always deal with only two theories $\mathcal{T}_1$ and $\mathcal{T}_2$. The discourse generalizes to more than two theories.

M. Hermann and A. Voronkov (Eds.): LPAR 2006, LNAI 4246, pp. 527–541, 2006.
© Springer-Verlag Berlin Heidelberg 2006

A prominent approach to $SMT(\mathcal{T})$ which underlies several systems (e.g., CVCLITE [2], DLSAT [8], DPLL(T)/BarceLogic [10], MATHSAT [4], TSAT++ [1], ICS/YICES [9]), is based on extensions of SAT technology: a SAT engine is modified to enumerate boolean assignments, and integrated with a decision procedure for sets of literals in the theory $\mathcal{T}$ ($\mathcal{T}$-solver). The above schema is also followed to tackle the $SMT(\mathcal{T}_1 \cup \mathcal{T}_2)$ problem. The approach relies on a decision procedure able to decide the satisfiability of sets of literals in $\mathcal{T}_1 \cup \mathcal{T}_2$, that is typically based on an integration schema like Nelson-Oppen (NO) [11] (or its variant due to Shostak [13]): the $\mathcal{T}_i$-solvers are combined by means of a structured exchange of (disjunctions of) interface equalities (e_{ij}'s).

Unfortunately from a practical point of view this schema poses some challenges. First, the integration between the two $\mathcal{T}_i$-solvers is not trivial to implement. Second, the ability of $\mathcal{T}_i$-solvers of inferring (disjunctions of) interface equalities (hereafter e_{ij}-*deduction completeness*) required by NO is neither always easy to achieve nor always cheap to perform. (E.g., e_{ij}-deduction is cheap for $\mathcal{EUF}$ but can be very expensive for $\mathcal{LA}(\mathbb{Z})$.) Third, in case of non-convex theories (e.g., $\mathcal{LA}(\mathbb{Z})$), a backtrack search must be used to take care of the disjunctions that need to be managed.

In recent papers [3,6] we have proposed a novel approach to $SMT(\mathcal{T}_1 \cup \mathcal{T}_2)$, called *Delayed Theory Combination* (DTC). The main idea is to avoid the integration schema between $\mathcal{T}_1$ and $\mathcal{T}_2$, and tighten the connection between each $\mathcal{T}_i$ and the SAT engine. While the truth assignment is being constructed, it is checked for consistency with respect to each theory in isolation. This can be seen as constructing two (possibly inconsistent) partial models for the original formula; the "merging" of the two partial models is enforced, on demand, since the solver is requested to find a complete assignment to the e_{ij}'s.

Compared to the NO schema, this approach has several advantages [3,6]. First, it is easier to implement and analyze. Second, the approach does not rely on the $\mathcal{T}_i$-*solvers* being e_{ij}-deduction complete, although it can fully benefit from this property. Third, the DTC nicely encompasses the case of non-convex theories. On the negative side, in [3,6] we noticed that these benefits are traded with a potential enlargement of the boolean search space which, in principle, could be up to exponential in the number of interface equalities generated. Thus, despite the positive empirical results presented in [3,6], the latter fact represented, at least in theory, one possible drawback of DTC.

In this paper we show that this latter point was way too pessimistic. We present a comparative analysis of DTC vs. NO for $SMT(\mathcal{T}_1 \cup \mathcal{T}_2)$, and we introduce some novel theoretical results, for both convex and non-convex theories and for different deduction capabilities of the $\mathcal{T}$-solvers. These results show that, by exploiting the full power of advanced SAT techniques like backjumping and learning, DTC can be implemented in such a way as to mimic the behavior of NO, so that the amount of boolean branches required by DTC can be upper-bounded by the sum of the number of deductions and branches required by NO in order to perform the same tasks.

From these results we have that DTC generalizes NO, in the sense that:

- under the same hypotheses of e_{ij}-deduction-completeness of the $\mathcal{T}_i$-*solvers* required by NO, DTC emulates NO with no extra cost in terms of boolean search;
- in the more general case ($\mathcal{T}_i$-*solvers* with partial or no e_{ij}-deduction capabilities) DTC can mimic the behavior of NO, in such a way that all or part of the (possibly very expensive) e_{ij}-deductions are substituted with only few extra boolean branches.

We also notice that the capability of learning conflict clauses containing interface equalities, which is typical of DTC, allows for cutting branches corresponding to repeated deductions in an equivalent NO schema.

The paper is structured as follows. In Section 2 we present some background and introduce the Nelson-Oppen combination schema for $SMT(\mathcal{T}_1 \cup \mathcal{T}_2)$. DTC is then discussed in Section 3. We present our analysis in Sections 4 (where the case of e_{ij}-deduction completeness in the $\mathcal{T}_i$-solvers of DTC is examined) and 5 (where the $\mathcal{T}_i$-solvers employed by DTC are assumed to have limited or no deduction capabilities). Finally, in Section 6 we draw some conclusions.

For lack of space, the proofs of the theorems and a more detailed description of the algorithms are omitted here, and they are reported in an extended technical report [7].

2 SMT for Combined Theories Via Nelson-Oppen's Integration

2.1 Basic Definitions and Properties

Consider a theory $\mathcal{T}$ with equality. $\mathcal{T}$ is *stably-infinite* iff every quantifier-free $\mathcal{T}$-satisfiable formula is satisfiable in an infinite model of $\mathcal{T}$. Notice that $\mathcal{EUF}$, $\mathcal{DL}(\mathbb{Q})$, $\mathcal{DL}(\mathbb{Z})$, $\mathcal{LA}(\mathbb{Q})$, $\mathcal{LA}(\mathbb{Z})$ are stably-infinite, whereas e.g. theories of bit-vectors $\mathcal{BV}$ are typically not. In what follows, we shall assume to deal only with stably-infinite theories with equality and with disjoint signatures.

$\mathcal{T}$ is *convex* iff, for every collection $l_1, \ldots, l_k, e_1, \ldots, e_n$ of literals in $\mathcal{T}$ s.t. $e_1, \ldots, e_n$ are in the form $(x = y)$, x, y being variables, we have that

$$\{l_1, ..., l_k\} \models_{\mathcal{T}} \bigvee_{i=1}^{n} e_i \Longleftrightarrow \{l_1, ..., l_k\} \models_{\mathcal{T}} e_i \text{ for some } 1 \le i \le n.$$

Notice that $\mathcal{EUF}$, $\mathcal{DL}(\mathbb{Q})$, $\mathcal{LA}(\mathbb{Q})$ are convex, whereas $\mathcal{DL}(\mathbb{Z})$ and $\mathcal{LA}(\mathbb{Z})$ are not.

Consider two theories $\mathcal{T}_1, \mathcal{T}_2$ with equality and disjoint signatures Σ_1, Σ_2. An atom ψ is *i-pure* if only $=$, variables and symbols from Σ_i occur in ψ. A formula φ is *pure* iff every atom in φ is *i-pure* for some $i \in \{1, 2\}$. Every non-pure $\mathcal{T}_1 \cup \mathcal{T}_2$ formula φ can be converted into an equivalently satisfiable pure formula φ' by recursively labeling terms t with fresh variables v_t, and by adding the atom $(v_t = t)$. E.g.:

$$(f(x+3y) = g(2x-y)) \Rightarrow (f(v_{x+3y}) = g(v_{2x-y})) \wedge (v_{x+3y} = x+3y) \wedge (v_{2x-y} = 2x-y).$$

This process is called *purification*, and is linear in the size of the input formula. Thus, henceforth we assume w.l.o.g. that all input formulas $\varphi \in \mathcal{T}_1 \cup \mathcal{T}_2$ are pure.

If φ is a pure $\mathcal{T}_1 \cup \mathcal{T}_2$ formula, then v is an *interface variable* for φ iff it occurs in both 1-pure and 2-pure atoms of φ. An equality $(v_i = v_j)$ is an *interface equality* for φ iff v_i, v_j are interface variables for φ. We assume an unique representation for $(v_i = v_j)$ and $(v_j = v_i)$. Henceforth we denote the interface equality $(v_i = v_j)$ by "e_{ij}".

Given a $\mathcal{T}$-inconsistent set of literals $L = \{l_1, \ldots, l_n\}$ in a theory $\mathcal{T}$, a *conflict set* η is an $(\mathcal{T}$-)inconsistent subset of L. η is *minimal* if none of its strict subsets is $\mathcal{T}$-inconsistent. We say that η is $\neg e_{ij}$-*minimal* iff $\eta \setminus \{\neg e_{ij}\}$ is no more $\mathcal{T}$-inconsistent, for every $\neg e_{ij} \in \eta$.

```
function Bool+T (φ: quantifier-free formula)
1       A^p ⟵ T2B(Atoms(φ))
2       φ^p ⟵ T2B(φ)
3       while Bool-satisfiable(φ^p) do
4           μ^p ⟵ pick_total_assign(A^p, φ^p)
5           (ρ, π) ⟵ T − satisfiable(B2T(μ^p))
6           if ρ = sat then return sat
7           φ^p ⟵ φ^p ∧ T2B(¬π)
8       end while
9       return unsat
end function
```

Fig. 1. A simplified view of enumeration-based T-satisfiability procedure: Bool+T

A T-*solver* is a procedure that decides the consistency of an assignment μ in T. An (propositional) assignment μ for a formula φ is a function $\mu : Atoms(\varphi) \mapsto \{true, false\}$. μ can be equivalently represented as a set of literals μ_S, where $\neg A \in \mu_S$ if $\mu(A) = false$, and $A \in \mu_S$ otherwise. μ can also equivalently be seen as a formula μ_φ, built as the conjunction of the literals in the set μ_S. (In the following, we will denote all such equivalent representations with μ. Moreover, we will denote with μ_{T_i} the subassignment of μ containing only i-pure literals.) When a T-*solver* detects the inconsistency of μ, it also returns a conflict set η of μ. Finally, we also require every T-*solver* involved in either the NO schema or DTC to be *incremental* (it does not need to restart the computation from scratch to decide the satisfiability of μ' if it had already proved that of $\mu \subset \mu'$) and *backtrackable* (it can return to a previous state in an efficient manner) [11].

We say that a T-*solver* is $\neg e_{ij}$-*minimal* (resp. *minimal*) if the conflict sets it returns are always $\neg e_{ij}$-minimal (resp. *minimal*). Notice that $\neg e_{ij}$-minimality is a much weaker requirement than minimality.

2.2 Satisfiability Modulo Theory

Fig. 1 presents Bool+T, a (much simplified) decision procedure for $SMT(T)$. The function $Atoms(\varphi)$ takes a ground formula φ and returns the set of atoms which occur in φ. We use the notation φ^p to denote the *propositional abstraction* of φ, which is formed by the function $T2B$ that maps propositional variables to themselves, ground atoms into fresh propositional variables, and is homomorphic w.r.t. boolean operators and set inclusion. The function $B2T$ is the inverse of $T2B$. We use μ^p to denote a propositional assignment. (If $T2B(\mu) \models T2B(\varphi)$, then we say that μ *propositionally satisfies* φ.) The idea underlying the algorithm is that the truth assignments for the propositional abstraction of φ are enumerated and checked for satisfiability in T. The procedure either returns sat if one such model is found, or returns unsat otherwise. The function $pick\_total\_assign$ returns a total assignment to the propositional variables in φ^p, that is, it assigns a truth value to all variables in A^p. The function T-satisfiable(μ) detects if the set of conjuncts μ is T-satisfiable: if so, it returns (sat, $\emptyset$); otherwise, it returns (unsat, π), where $\pi \subseteq \mu$ is a T-unsatisfiable set, called a *theory conflict set*. We call the negation of a conflict set, a *conflict clause*.

The algorithm is a coarse abstraction of the ones underlying TSAT++, MATHSAT, DLSAT, DPLL(T) /BarceLogic, CVCLITE, and ICS /YICES. The test for satisfiability and the extraction of the corresponding truth assignment are kept separate in this description only for the sake of simplicity.

In practice, the enumeration of truth assignments is carried out by means of efficient implementations of the DPLL algorithm [15], where a *partial assignment* μ^p is built incrementally, each time selecting an unassigned literal l (*literal selection*), called *decision literal*, according to some heuristic criterion, adding it to μ^p and performing all the other assignments which derive deterministically from this choice (*unit propagation*). When some assignment μ^p falsifies the formula returning a (boolean) conflict set π^p, or when $\mathcal{T}$-satisfiable($\mathcal{B}2\mathcal{T}(\mu^p)$) fails returning a theory conflict set π, the negation $\neg\pi^p$ of (the boolean abstraction of) the conflict set is passed as a conflict clause to the boolean solver. Then $\neg\pi^p$ is added in conjunction to φ^p either temporarily or permanently (*learning*), and the algorithm backtracks up to the highest point in the search where a literal can be unit-propagated on $\neg\pi^p$ (*backjumping*). Learning also avoids generating the same conflicts in future branches.

An important variant [10] is that of building from $\neg\pi^p$ a "mixed boolean+theory conflict clause", by recursively removing non-decision literals l from the conflict clause by resolving the latter with the clause C_l which caused the unit-propagation of l; this is done until the conflict clause contains only decision literals (*last-UIP strategy*) or at most one non-decision literal assigned after the last decision (*first-UIP strategy*).[2]

Another important improvement is *early pruning (EP)*: before every literal selection, intermediate assignments are checked for $\mathcal{T}$-satisfiability and, if not $\mathcal{T}$-satisfiable, they are pruned (since no refinement can be $\mathcal{T}$-satisfiable). Finally, *theory deduction* can be used to reduce the search space by allowing the $\mathcal{T}$-solvers to explicitly return truth values for unassigned literals, which can be unit-propagated by the SAT solver. The interested reader is pointed to, e.g., [1,4,10,5] for details and further references.

2.3 Nelson-Oppen's Schema

Given two signature-disjoint stably infinite theories $\mathcal{T}_1$ and $\mathcal{T}_2$, the Nelson-Oppen combination schema [11], in the following referred to as NO, allows for solving the satisfiability problem for $\mathcal{T}_1 \cup \mathcal{T}_2$ (i.e. the problem of checking the $\mathcal{T}_1 \cup \mathcal{T}_2$-satisfiability of sets of $\Sigma_1 \cup \Sigma_2$-literals) by using the satisfiability procedures for $\mathcal{T}_1$ and $\mathcal{T}_2$. The procedure is basically a structured interchange of information inferred from either theory and propagated to the other, until convergence is reached. The schema requires the exchange of information, the kind of which depends on the *convexity* of the involved theories. In the case of convex theories, the two solvers communicate to each other single interface equalities. In the case of non-convex theories, the NO schema becomes more complicated, because the two solvers need to exchange *arbitrary disjunctions of interface equalities*, which have to be managed within the decision procedure by means of case splitting and of *backtrack* search. In the latter case, the NO schema performs a number of *branches* to check the consistency of a set of literals which depends on how many

---

[2] These are standard techniques implemented in most SAT solvers in order to build the boolean conflict clauses [14].

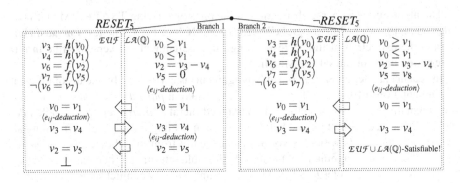

Fig. 2. Representation of the search tree for the formula of Example 1

disjunctions of equalities are exchanged at each step: if the current set of literals is μ, and one of the $\mathcal{T}_i$-solver sends the disjunction $\bigvee_{k=1}^{n}(e_{ij})_k$ to the other, the latter must further investigate up to n branches to check the consistency of each of the $\mu \cup \{(e_{ij})_k\}$ sets separately.

Example 1 (convex case). Consider the following $\mathcal{EUF} \cup \mathcal{LA}(\mathbb{Q})$ formula φ (cf Fig. 2)

$$\mathcal{EUF}: \quad (v_3 = h(v_0)) \wedge (v_4 = h(v_1)) \wedge (v_6 = f(v_2)) \wedge (v_7 = f(v_5)) \wedge$$
$$\mathcal{LA}(\mathbb{Q}): (v_0 \geq v_1) \wedge (v_0 \leq v_1) \wedge (v_2 = v_3 - v_4) \wedge (RESET_5 \rightarrow (v_5 = 0)) \wedge \quad (1)$$
$$Both: \quad (\neg RESET_5 \rightarrow (v_5 = v_8)) \wedge \neg(v_6 = v_7).$$

$v_0, v_1, v_2, v_3, v_4, v_5$ are interface variables, v_6, v_7, v_8 are not. (Thus, e.g., $(v_0 = v_1)$ is an interface equality, whilst $(v_0 = v_6)$ is not.) $RESET_5$ is a boolean variable.

After the first run of unit propagations, assume DPLL selects the literal $RESET_5$, resulting in the assignment

$$\mu = \{ (v_3 = h(v_0)), (v_4 = h(v_1)), (v_6 = f(v_2)), (v_7 = f(v_5)), (v_0 \geq v_1),$$
$$(v_0 \leq v_1), (v_2 = v_3 - v_4), \neg(v_6 = v_7), RESET_5, (v_5 = 0) \}, \quad (2)$$

which propositionally satisfies φ. Now, the set of literals $\mu_{\mathcal{EUF}} \subseteq \mu$ is given to the $\mathcal{EUF}$ solver, which reports its consistency and deduces no new interface equality. Then the set $\mu_{\mathcal{LA}(\mathbb{Q})} \subseteq \mu$ is given to the $\mathcal{LA}(\mathbb{Q})$ solver, which reports consistency and deduces the interface equality $(v_0 = v_1)$, which is passed to the $\mathcal{EUF}$ solver. The new set $\mu_{\mathcal{EUF}} \cup \{(v_0 = v_1)\}$ is still $\mathcal{EUF}$-consistent, but this time the $\mathcal{EUF}$ solver deduces the equality $(v_3 = v_4)$, which is in turn passed to the $\mathcal{LA}(\mathbb{Q})$ solver, that now as a consequence of this and the assignment $\mu_{\mathcal{LA}(\mathbb{Q})}$ deduces $(v_2 = v_5)$. The $\mathcal{EUF}$ solver is then invoked again to check the $\mathcal{EUF}$-consistency of the assignment $\mu_{\mathcal{EUF}} \cup \{(v_0 = v_1), (v_2 = v_5)\}$: since this check fails, the Nelson-Oppen method reports the $\mathcal{EUF} \cup \mathcal{LA}(\mathbb{Q})$-unsatisfiability of φ under the whole assignment μ. At this point, then, DPLL backtracks and tries assigning false to $RESET_5$, resulting in the new assignment

$$\mu = \{ (v_3 = h(v_0)), (v_4 = h(v_1)), (v_6 = f(v_2)), (v_7 = f(v_5)), (v_0 \geq v_1), (v_0 \leq v_1),$$
$$(v_2 = v_3 - v_4), \neg(v_6 = v_7), \neg RESET_5, (v_5 = v_8)) \},$$

which is found $\mathcal{EUF} \cup \mathcal{LA}(\mathbb{Q})$-satisfiable (see Fig. 2).   □

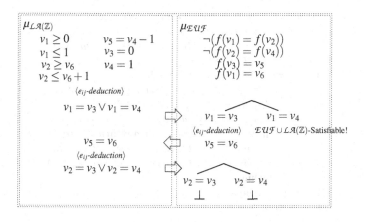

Fig. 3. Representation of the search tree for the formula of Example 2

Example 2 (non-convex case). Consider the following $\mathcal{EUF} \cup \mathcal{LA}(\mathbb{Z})$ formula φ

$$\mathcal{EUF} : \ \neg(f(v_1) = f(v_2)) \wedge \neg(f(v_2) = f(v_4)) \wedge (f(v_3) = v_5) \wedge (f(v_1) = v_6) \wedge$$
$$\mathcal{LA}(\mathbb{Z}) : (v_1 \geq 0) \wedge (v_1 \leq 1) \wedge (v_5 = v_4 - 1) \wedge (v_3 = 0) \wedge (v_4 = 1) \wedge \qquad (3)$$
$$(v_2 \geq v_6) \wedge (v_2 \leq v_6 + 1).$$

Here (see Fig. 3) all the variables $(v_1, \ldots, v_6)$ are interface ones. φ contains only unit clauses, so after the first run of unit propagations, DPLL generates the assignment μ which is simply the set of literals in φ. The Nelson-Oppen combination schema then runs as follows. First, the sub-assignment $\mu_{\mathcal{EUF}}$ is given to the $\mathcal{EUF}$ solver, which reports its consistency and deduces no interface equality. Then, the sub-assignment $\mu_{\mathcal{LA}(\mathbb{Z})}$ is given to the $\mathcal{LA}(\mathbb{Z})$ solver, which reports its consistency and deduces the disjunction $(v_1 = v_3) \vee (v_1 = v_4)$. Next, there is a case-splitting and the two equalities $(v_1 = v_3)$ and $(v_1 = v_4)$ are passed to the $\mathcal{EUF}$ solver. The first branch, corresponding to selecting $(v_1 = v_3)$, is opened: then the set $\mu_{\mathcal{EUF}} \cup \{(v_1 = v_3)\}$ is $\mathcal{EUF}$-consistent, and the equality $(v_5 = v_6)$ is deduced. After that, the assignment $\mu_{\mathcal{LA}(\mathbb{Z})} \cup \{(v_5 = v_6)\}$ is passed to the $\mathcal{LA}(\mathbb{Z})$ solver, that reports its consistency and deduces another disjunction, $(v_2 = v_3) \vee (v_2 = v_4)$. At this point, another case-splitting is needed in the $\mathcal{EUF}$ solver, resulting in the two branches $\mu_{\mathcal{EUF}} \cup \{(v_1 = v_3), (v_2 = v_3)\}$ and $\mu_{\mathcal{EUF}} \cup \{(v_1 = v_3), (v_2 = v_4)\}$. Both of them are found inconsistent, so the whole branch previously opened by the selection of $(v_1 = v_3)$ is found inconsistent; at this point, the other case of the branch (i.e. the equality $(v_1 = v_4)$) is selected, and since the assignment $\mu_{\mathcal{EUF}} \cup \{(v_1 = v_4)\}$ is $\mathcal{EUF}$-consistent and no new interface equality is deduced, the Nelson-Oppen method reports the $\mathcal{EUF} \cup \mathcal{LA}(\mathbb{Z})$-satisfiability of φ under the whole assignment μ. □

3 SMT for Combined Theories Via Delayed Theory Combination

In the Delayed Theory Combination (DTC) schema [3,6], the $SMT(\mathcal{T}_1 \cup \mathcal{T}_2)$ problem is tackled in a different way: each of the two $\mathcal{T}_i$ solvers works in isolation, without

function Bool+$\mathcal{T}_1$+$\mathcal{T}_2$ (φ_i: *quantifier-free formula*)
1       $\varphi \longleftarrow$ *purify*(φ_i)
2       $\mathcal{A}^p \longleftarrow \mathcal{T}2\mathcal{B}(Atoms(\varphi) \cup interface\_equalities(\varphi))$
3       $\varphi^p \longleftarrow \mathcal{T}2\mathcal{B}(\varphi)$
4   **while** Bool-*satisfiable* (φ^p) **do**
5           $\mu_1^p \wedge \mu_2^p \wedge \mu_e^p = \mu^p \longleftarrow$ *pick_total_assign*($\mathcal{A}^p, \varphi^p$)
6           $(\rho_1, \pi_1) \longleftarrow \mathcal{T}_1$-*satisfiable* ($\mathcal{B}2\mathcal{T}(\mu_1^p \wedge \mu_e^p)$)
7           $(\rho_2, \pi_2) \longleftarrow \mathcal{T}_2$-*satisfiable* ($\mathcal{B}2\mathcal{T}(\mu_2^p \wedge \mu_e^p)$)
8   **if** ($\rho_1 = $ sat $\wedge \rho_2 = $ sat) **then return** sat **else**
9   **if** $\rho_1 = $ unsat **then** $\varphi^p \longleftarrow \varphi^p \wedge \mathcal{T}2\mathcal{B}(\neg\pi_1)$
10   **if** $\rho_2 = $ unsat **then** $\varphi^p \longleftarrow \varphi^p \wedge \mathcal{T}2\mathcal{B}(\neg\pi_2)$
11   **end while**
12   **return** unsat
end function

Fig. 4. A simplified view of the Delayed Theory Combination procedure for $SMT(\mathcal{T}_1 \cup \mathcal{T}_2)$

direct exchange of information. Their mutual consistency is ensured by augmenting the input problem with all interface equalities e_{ij}, even if these do not occur in the original problem. The enumeration of assignments includes not only the atoms in the formula, but also the interface equalities e_{ij}. Both theory solvers receive, from the boolean level, the same truth assignment μ_e for e_{ij}: under such conditions, the two "partial" models found by each decision procedure can be merged into a model for the input formula.

A simplified view of the algorithm is presented in Fig. 4. Initially (lines 1–3), the formula is purified, the *new* e_{ij}'s are created and added to the set of propositional symbols $\mathcal{A}^p$, and the propositional abstraction φ^p of φ is created. Then, the main loop is entered (lines 4–11): while φ^p is propositionally satisfiable (line 4), a satisfying truth assignment μ^p is selected (line 5). It is important to stress that truth values are associated not only to atoms in φ, but also to the e_{ij} atoms, even though they do not occur in φ. μ^p is then (implicitly) separated into $\mu_1^p \wedge \mu_e^p \wedge \mu_2^p$, where $\mathcal{B}2\mathcal{T}(\mu_i^p)$ is a set of i-pure literals and $\mathcal{B}2\mathcal{T}(\mu_e^p)$ is a set of e_{ij}-literals. The relevant parts of μ^p are checked for consistency against each theory (lines 6–7); $\mathcal{T}_i$-satisfiable(μ) returns a pair (ρ_i, π_i), where ρ_i is unsat iff μ is unsatisfiable in $\mathcal{T}_i$, and sat otherwise. If both calls to $\mathcal{T}_i$-satisfiable return sat, then the formula is satisfiable. Otherwise, when ρ_i is unsat, then π_i is a theory conflict set, i.e. $\pi_i \subseteq \mu$ and π_i is $\mathcal{T}_i$-unsatisfiable. Then, φ^p is strengthened to exclude truth assignments which may fail in the same way (line 9–10), and the loop is resumed. Unsatisfiability is returned (line 12) when the loop is exited without having found a model.

In practical implementations of DTC, the search for a satisfactory assignment is based on a modern DPLL engine, performing literal selection, unit-propagation, backjumping and learning, early pruning, and theory deduction, as explained in §2.2. In particular, DTC can be enhanced by e_{ij}-deduction, in which e_{ij}'s can by deduced by the $\mathcal{T}_i$-*solvers* and hence unit-propagated. We refer the reader to [3,6] for a more detailed discussion.

Notation-wise, we call "*new*" e_{ij}'s all the interface equalities e_{ij}'s which do not occur in any clause of the input formula φ (including all the clauses learned). Moreover, we often write sets of literals $\{l_1, ..., l_n\}$ as conjunctions $l_1 \wedge ... \wedge l_n$, and we often write clauses $(\bigvee_i l_i) \vee (\bigvee_j l_j)$ as implications: $(\bigwedge_i \neg l_i) \rightarrow (\bigvee_j l_j)$ or $(\bigwedge_i \neg l_i \wedge \bigwedge_j \neg l_j) \rightarrow \bot$.

Hereafter, for the sake of proving the theoretical results in §4 and §5, we assume that DTC implements the following strategy.

Strategy 1 (NO emulation)

1. *All the conflict clauses derived by theory conflicts are learned.* [3]
2. *Each conflict clause in 1. is a mixed boolean+theory conflict clause which is built from the theory conflict set by means of the last-UIP strategy described in §2.2.* [4]
3. *The literal selection heuristic and the $\mathcal{T}_i$-solvers calls are such that:*
   - (i) *new e_{ij}'s are selected only after all the other literals have been assigned,*
   - (ii) *Early pruning (EP) is applied before every selection of a new e_{ij},* [5]
   - (iii) *the new e_{ij}'s selected are always assigned false,*
   - (iv) *each $\mathcal{T}_i$-solver is invoked only if at least one literal (which has not been deduced singularly by $\mathcal{T}_i$-solver itself) has been added to its input since the last call.* [6]
4. *At every early-pruning call on a branch (namely μ) which is found both $\mathcal{T}_1$- and $\mathcal{T}_2$-consistent, if one $\mathcal{T}_i$-solver performs the e_{ij}-deduction $\mu^* \models_{\mathcal{T}_i} \bigvee_{j=1}^k e_j$, s.t. $\mu^* \subseteq \mu_{\mathcal{T}_i}$, each e_j being an unassigned interface equality on variables in μ, then:*
   - (i) *the clause $T2\mathcal{B}(\mu^* \rightarrow \bigvee_{j=1}^k e_j)$ is learned immediately;*
   - (ii) *if $k = 1$, then e_k is added to the current assignment and unit-propagated immediately;*
   - (iii) *if $k > 1$, then $\neg e_1, ..., \neg e_k$ are put on the top of the literal selection list, so that to be the next $\neg e_{ij}$'s selected by the literal selection heuristic.*
5. **[If and only if both $\mathcal{T}_i$-solvers are e_{ij}-deduction complete]**
   If a total assignment μ which propositionally satisfies φ is found $\mathcal{T}_i$-satisfiable for both $\mathcal{T}_i$'s, and neither $\mathcal{T}_i$-solver performs any e_{ij}-deduction from μ, then DTC stops returning "Sat". [7]

4 DTC with e_{ij}-Deduction-Complete $\mathcal{T}_i$-solvers vs. NO

In this section, we assume that both the $\mathcal{T}_i$-solvers employed by DTC are e_{ij}-deduction complete. Under these assumptions, we have the following result.

---

[3] That is, if one $\mathcal{T}_i$-solver returns a conflict set π, then the conflict clauses $T2\mathcal{B}(\neg\pi)$ is always added to φ^p, either temporarily or permanently.

[4] That is, each conflict clause contains all and only (the negation of) the decision literals which forced the unit-propagation or the e_{ij}-deduction of those in the theory conflict.

[5] That is, before adding a new (negated) e_{ij} to μ, the $\mathcal{T}_i$-satisfiability of μ is checked for both $\mathcal{T}_i$'s by calling the $\mathcal{T}_i$-solver's. If μ is found $\mathcal{T}_i$-inconsistent for some $\mathcal{T}_i$, then the procedure backtracks.

[6] This avoids invoking a $\mathcal{T}_i$-solver twice in sequence on the same input. The restriction "which ... by $\mathcal{T}_i$-solver itself" means that, if $\mathcal{T}_i$-solver (μ) returns "Sat" and deduces e_{ij}, then $\mathcal{T}_i$-solver is not invoked on $\mu \cup \{e_{ij}\}$.

[7] Step 5. is identical to the $\mathcal{T}_1 \cup \mathcal{T}_2$-satisfiability termination condition of NO.

$$\mu_{\mathcal{EUF}} : \{\, (v_3 = h(v_0)), (v_4 = h(v_1)), \neg(v_6 = v_7),$$
$$(v_6 = f(v_2)), (v_7 = f(v_5)))\}$$

$$\mu_{\mathcal{LA}(\mathbb{Q})} :$$
$$\{(v_0 \geq v_1), (v_0 \leq v_1),$$
$$(v_2 = v_3 - v_4)\}$$

	$RESET_5$		$\neg RESET_5$	
		$(v_5 = 0)$	$(v_5 = v_8)$	
$\mathcal{LA}(\mathbb{Q})$-deduce $(v_0 = v_1)$ learn C_{01}	$(v_0 = v_1)$		$(v_0 = v_1)$	$\mathcal{LA}(\mathbb{Q})$-deduce $(v_0 = v_1)$ learn C'_{01}
$\mathcal{EUF}$-deduce $(v_3 = v_4)$ learn C_{34}	$(v_3 = v_4)$		$(v_3 = v_4)$	
$\mathcal{LA}(\mathbb{Q})$-deduce $(v_2 = v_5)$ learn C_{25}	$(v_2 = v_5)$		SAT	
$\mathcal{EUF}$-unsat C_{67}				

$$C_{01} : (\mu'_{\mathcal{LA}(\mathbb{Q})}) \rightarrow (v_0 = v_1)$$
$$C_{34} : (\mu'_{\mathcal{EUF}} \wedge (v_0 = v_1)) \rightarrow (v_3 = v_4)$$
$$C_{25} : (\mu''_{\mathcal{LA}(\mathbb{Q})} \wedge (v_5 = 0) \wedge (v_3 = v_4)) \rightarrow (v_2 = v_5)$$
$$C_{67} : (\mu''_{\mathcal{EUF}} \wedge (v_2 = v_5)) \rightarrow (v_6 = v_7)$$

Fig. 5. DTC execution of Example 3 on $\mathcal{LA}(\mathbb{Q}) \cup \mathcal{EUF}$, with e_{ij}-deduction-complete $\mathcal{T}_i$-solvers

Theorem 1. *Let $\mathcal{T}_1$ and $\mathcal{T}_2$ be two stably-infinite (possibly non-convex) theories and let both $\mathcal{T}_i$-solvers be e_{ij}-deduction complete; let φ be a pure $\mathcal{T}_1 \cup \mathcal{T}_2$ formula and let μ be a total assignment propositionally satisfying φ. Let DTC with Strategy 1 prove the $\mathcal{T}_1 \cup \mathcal{T}_2$-consistency (resp. $\mathcal{T}_1 \cup \mathcal{T}_2$-inconsistency) of μ, returning a conflict set η in the case of inconsistency. Let dtc_br be the number of boolean branches required in the DTC proof. Then we have:*

$$dtc\_br \leq no\_br \qquad\qquad (4)$$

no_br being the number of branches performed by a corresponding NO proof of the $\mathcal{T}_1 \cup \mathcal{T}_2$-consistency (resp. $\mathcal{T}_1 \cup \mathcal{T}_2$-inconsistency) of μ.

Theorem 1 states that, under the same hypotheses of e_{ij}-deduction as NO, DTC emulates NO with no extra cost in terms of boolean search.

Example 3 (convex case). Consider again the $\mathcal{EUF} \cup \mathcal{LA}(\mathbb{Q})$ formula φ of Example 1. Figure 5 illustrates a DTC execution when both $\mathcal{T}_i$-solvers are e_{ij}-deduction complete.

On the left branch (when $RESET_5$ is selected), after the unit-propagation of $(v_5 = 0)$, the $\mathcal{LA}(\mathbb{Q})$ solver deduces $(v_0 = v_1)$, and thus by Step 4. (i) of Strategy 1, the clause C_{01} is learned and $(v_0 = v_1)$ is unit-propagated. As a consequence of this, the $\mathcal{EUF}$ solver can deduce $(v_3 = v_4)$, resulting in the learning of C_{34} and the unit-propagation of $(v_3 = v_4)$, which in turn causes the $\mathcal{LA}(\mathbb{Q})$-deduction of $(v_2 = v_5)$, with the resulting learning of C_{25} and unit-propagation of the deduced equality.

At this point, $\mu''_{\mathcal{EUF}} \cup \{(v_2 = v_5)\}$ [8] is found $\mathcal{EUF}$-inconsistent, so that the $\mathcal{EUF}$-solver returns (the negation of) the clause C_{67}, which is resolved backward with the clauses C_{25}, C_{34}, C_{01}, $\neg(v_6 = v_7)$, and $(RESET_5 \rightarrow (v_5 = 0))$ as explained in Step 2. of Strategy 1, obtaining a mixed theory+boolean conflict clause C'_{67} in the form $(\mu^* \wedge RESET_5) \rightarrow \perp$ s.t. μ^* contains no interface equality. C'_{67} forces DTC to backjump up to the last branching point. Then the execution of the right branch begins with the

---

[8] Hereafter, $\mu'_T, \mu''_T, \mu'''_T$ will denote generic subsets of μ_T, $T \in \{\mathcal{EUF}, \mathcal{LA}(\mathbb{Q}), \mathcal{LA}(\mathbb{Z})\}$.

$$\mu_{\mathcal{EUF}}: \qquad \mu_{\mathcal{LA(Z)}}:$$

$$\begin{array}{l} \neg(f(v_1) = f(v_2)) \\ \neg(f(v_2) = f(v_4)) \\ f(v_3) = v_5 \\ f(v_1) = v_6 \end{array} \quad \begin{array}{l} v_1 \geq 0 \\ v_1 \leq 1 \\ v_2 \geq v_6 \\ v_2 \leq v_6 + 1 \end{array} \quad \begin{array}{l} v_5 = v_4 - 1 \\ v_3 = 0 \\ v_4 = 1 \end{array}$$

$$\begin{array}{ll} C_{13}: & (\mu'_{\mathcal{LA(Z)}}) \rightarrow ((v_1 = v_3) \vee (v_1 = v_4)) \\ C_{56}: & (\mu^m_{\mathcal{EUF}} \wedge (v_1 = v_3)) \rightarrow (v_5 = v_6) \\ C_{23}: & (\mu^n_{\mathcal{LA(Z)}} \wedge (v_5 = v_6)) \rightarrow ((v_2 = v_3) \vee (v_2 = v_4)) \\ C_{24}: & (\mu^p_{\mathcal{EUF}} \wedge (v_1 = v_3) \wedge (v_2 = v_3)) \rightarrow \bot \\ C_{14}: & (\mu^h_{\mathcal{EUF}} \wedge (v_1 = v_3) \wedge (v_2 = v_4)) \rightarrow \bot \end{array}$$

$$\mathcal{LA(Z)}\text{-deduce } (v_1 = v_4) \vee (v_1 = v_3), \text{ learn } C_{13}$$

$$\begin{array}{l} \neg(v_1 = v_4) \Big/ \;\; v_1 = v_4 \\ \qquad\qquad\;\; \diagup \; \text{SAT} \\ v_1 = v_3 \,\Big|\, \mathcal{EUF}\text{-deduce } (v_5 = v_6), \text{ learn } C_{56} \\ v_5 = v_6 \,\Big|\, \mathcal{LA(Z)}\text{-deduce } (v_2 = v_4) \vee (v_2 = v_3), \text{ learn } C_{23} \\ \neg(v_2 = v_4) \Big/ \;\; v_2 = v_4 \\ v_2 = v_3 \,\Big|\, \mathcal{EUF}\text{-unsat}, C_{14} \\ \mathcal{EUF}\text{-unsat}, C_{24} \end{array}$$

Fig. 6. DTC execution of Ex 4 on $\mathcal{LA(Z)} \cup \mathcal{EUF}$, with e_{ij}-deduction-complete $\mathcal{T}_i$-solvers

unit-propagation of $\neg RESET_5$ on C'_{67} and hence of $(v_5 = v_8)$ on $\neg RESET_5 \rightarrow (v_5 = v_8)$, which produces an assignment propositionally satisfying φ. The theory solvers are invoked, and the $\mathcal{LA(Q)}$ solver deduces again $(v_0 = v_1)$, learning a clause C'_{01} which is similar to C_{01} except for the fact that it may contain the redundant literal $(v_5 = v_8)$ instead of $(v_5 = 0)$. [9] Then $(v_3 = v_4)$ is unit-propagated on C_{34}. At this point, since both theory solvers cannot deduce any new e_{ij}, by Step 5. of Strategy 1 DTC concludes that φ is $\mathcal{EUF} \cup \mathcal{LA(Q)}$-satisfiable. □

Notice that the left branch of the DTC search tree of Figure 5 mimics directly that of the NO execution of Figure 2. The main difference relies on the fact that, unlike with NO, the deduced e_{ij}'s are not exchanged directly by the $\mathcal{T}_i$-solvers, but rather they are added to the current assignment μ and unit-propagated.

In the right branch, instead, all values are assigned directly by unit-propagation. This fact illustrates one further potential advantage of DTC with respect to NO: the fact that new e_{ij}'s are known a priori to the DPLL engine allows their inclusion in the learned clauses derived by theory conflicts. Thanks to unit-propagation, this makes it possible to assign truth values to them *directly at the boolean level*, without performing the (potentially costly) invocation of the $\mathcal{T}_i$-solvers. In the traditional NO schema, this fact does not come naturally, because the boolean solver knows nothing about the e_{ij}'s.

We consider now the case where some $\mathcal{T}_i$'s are non-convex.

Example 4 (non-convex case). Consider the $\mathcal{EUF} \cup \mathcal{LA(Z)}$ formula φ and assignment μ of Example 2. Figure 6 illustrates a DTC execution when both $\mathcal{T}_i$-solvers are e_{ij}-deduction complete.

The first invocation of the $\mathcal{LA(Z)}$ solver results in deducing of the disjunction $(v_1 = v_4) \vee (v_1 = v_3)$ and learning of the corresponding clause C_{13}. By Step 4.(iii) of Strategy 1, then, $(v_1 = v_4)$ and $(v_1 = v_3)$ are put on the top of the literal selection list.

---

[9] Here we assume the "worst" case in which $\mu'_{\mathcal{LA(Q)}}$ in C_{01} contains the (redundant) literal $(v_5 = 0)$. If this is not the case, then $(v_0 = v_1)$ is directly unit-propagated on C_{01}, without calling the theory solvers.

As a consequence, DTC selects $\neg(v_1 = v_4)$, and thanks to C_{13} it immediately unit-propagates $(v_1 = v_3)$. At this point the $\mathcal{EUF}$ solver can deduce $(v_5 = v_6)$, so that the clause C_{56} is learned and the deduced equality is unit-propagated immediately. When $\mu_{\mathcal{LA}(\mathbb{Z})} \cup \{(v_5 = v_6)\}$ is passed to the $\mathcal{LA}(\mathbb{Z})$ solver, this deduces the disjunction $(v_2 = v_4) \vee (v_2 = v_3)$, learning C_{23}. Selecting $\neg(v_2 = v_4)$ results in the unit-propagation of $(v_2 = v_3)$, which in turn causes a $\mathcal{EUF}$ conflict. After the $\mathcal{EUF}$-solver returns (the negation of) C_{24}, DTC backjumps up to a point where $(v_2 = v_4)$ can be unit-propagated. This results again in an $\mathcal{EUF}$-conflict, so that the $\mathcal{EUF}$-solver returns (the negation of) C_{14}, which causes another backjumping up to where $(v_1 = v_4)$ can be unit-propagated. Then, after another invocation to the theory solvers, DTC stops, declaring φ to be $\mathcal{EUF} \cup \mathcal{LA}(\mathbb{Z})$-satisfiable.   □

As with the convex example, notice that the DTC search tree of Figure 6 mimics directly that of the NO execution of Figure 3 (both *dtc_br* and *no_br* are equal to 3.)

5   DTC with Non e_{ij}-Deduction-Complete $\mathcal{T}_i$-solvers vs. NO

In this section, we assume that both the $\mathcal{T}_i$-solvers employed by DTC are $\neg e_{ij}$-minimal and have limited or no e_{ij}-deduction capabilities. Under these assumptions, we have the following result.

Theorem 2. *Let $\mathcal{T}_1$ and $\mathcal{T}_2$ be two stably-infinite (possibly non-convex) theories. Let both $\mathcal{T}_i$-solvers be $\neg e_{ij}$-minimal, and possibly have some e_{ij}-deduction capabilities; let φ be a pure $\mathcal{T}_1 \cup \mathcal{T}_2$ formula and let μ be a total assignment propositionally satisfying φ. Let DTC with Strategy 1 prove the $\mathcal{T}_1 \cup \mathcal{T}_2$-consistency (resp. $\mathcal{T}_1 \cup \mathcal{T}_2$-inconsistency) of μ, returning a conflict set η in the case of inconsistency. Let dtc_br and dtc_ded be the number of boolean branches and of e_{ij}-deductions performed in the DTC proof. Then we have:*

$$dtc\_br + dtc\_ded \leq no\_br + no\_ded, \tag{5}$$

no_ded and no_br being respectively the number of deductions and of branches performed by a corresponding NO proof of the $\mathcal{T}_1 \cup \mathcal{T}_2$-consistency (resp. $\mathcal{T}_1 \cup \mathcal{T}_2$-inconsistency) of μ.

Theorem 2 states that, if the $\mathcal{T}_i$-solvers are both $\neg e_{ij}$-minimal, then there is a strategy for DTC which emulates some NO proof (even though the $\mathcal{T}_i$-solvers have limited or no e_{ij}-deduction capabilities!) at the cost of (at most) one extra boolean branch for every e_{ij}-deduction performed by NO. Therefore the (possibly very expensive) e_{ij}-deduction steps of the NO schema can be avoided at the cost of one extra boolean branch each.

More generally, we notice that one key idea in the proof of Theorem 2 is that, when the DPLL engine fails and generates a conflict set π, it backjumps up to the second-most-recently-assigned $\neg e_{ij}$ in π, if any [7]. (See, e.g., the case of C_{23} in Figure 7.) Therefore, in a more general case than that of Theorem 2 (no $\neg e_{ij}$-minimality), *the more redundant $\neg e_{ij}$'s the $\mathcal{T}_i$-solvers are able to remove from the conflict set returned, the more boolean branches are skipped by backjumping.*

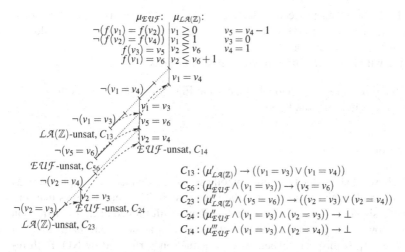

$$C_{13} : (\mu'_{\mathcal{LA}(\mathbb{Z})}) \rightarrow ((v_1 = v_3) \vee (v_1 = v_4))$$
$$C_{56} : (\mu'_{\mathcal{EUF}} \wedge (v_1 = v_3)) \rightarrow (v_5 = v_6)$$
$$C_{23} : (\mu''_{\mathcal{LA}(\mathbb{Z})} \wedge (v_5 = v_6)) \rightarrow ((v_2 = v_3) \vee (v_2 = v_4))$$
$$C_{24} : (\mu''_{\mathcal{EUF}} \wedge (v_1 = v_3) \wedge (v_2 = v_3)) \rightarrow \bot$$
$$C_{14} : (\mu'''_{\mathcal{EUF}} \wedge (v_1 = v_3) \wedge (v_2 = v_4)) \rightarrow \bot$$

Fig. 7. DTC execution of Example 5 on $\mathcal{LA}(\mathbb{Z}) \cup \mathcal{EUF}$, with no e_{ij}-deduction. The clauses C_{ij}'s are the same as those of Fig. 6.

Example 5 (no e_{ij}-deduction, non-convex case). Consider the $\mathcal{EUF} \cup \mathcal{LA}(\mathbb{Z})$ formula φ (3) and the assignment μ of Example 2. Look at Fig. 7. Both $\mu_{\mathcal{LA}(\mathbb{Z})}$ and $\mu_{\mathcal{EUF}}$ are found consistent in the respective theories by the respective solvers.

Then DTC starts selecting new $\neg e_{ij}$'s, and proceeds without causing conflicts, until it selects $\neg(v_1 = v_4)$ and $\neg(v_1 = v_3)$, which cause a $\mathcal{LA}(\mathbb{Z})$ conflict. The branch is in the form $\mu \cup \bigcup_j \neg e_j$, so that, the $\neg e_{ij}$-minimal conflict set η_{13} returned is in the form $\mu'_{\mathcal{LA}(\mathbb{Z})} \cup \{\neg(v_1 = v_3), \neg(v_1 = v_4)\}$. Thus DTC learns the corresponding clause C_{13} (see Fig 7) and backjumps up to the highest point which allows for unit-propagating $(v_1 = v_3)$ on C_{13}, and performs such unit propagation. Then DTC starts and proceeds selecting new $\neg e_{ij}$'s without causing conflicts, until it selects $\neg(v_5 = v_6)$, which causes a $\mathcal{EUF}$ conflict represented by the clause C_{56}. As $\mathcal{EUF}$ is convex, $\neg(v_5 = v_6)$ is the only $\neg e_{ij}$ occurring in the conflict set, so that DTC backtracks over the last chain of $\neg e_{ij}$'s and unit-propagates $(v_5 = v_6)$.

Again, DTC selects a chain of new $\neg e_{ij}$'s without causing conflicts, until it selects $\neg(v_2 = v_4)$ and $\neg(v_2 = v_3)$, which cause a $\mathcal{LA}(\mathbb{Z})$ conflict represented by clause C_{23}. As before, it backjumps to the highest point where it can unit-propagate $(v_2 = v_3)$. Performing the latter unit propagation causes a $\mathcal{EUF}$ conflict, learning the clause C_{24}. By applying Step 2. of Strategy 1, resolving on literal $(v_2 = v_3)$ the conflicting clause C_{24} with the clause C_{23} (which caused the unit-propagation of $(v_2 = v_3)$), DTC obtains a clause $C'_{24} : (\mu''_{\mathcal{LA}(\mathbb{Z})} \wedge \mu''_{\mathcal{EUF}} \wedge (v_5 = v_6) \wedge (v_1 = v_3)) \rightarrow (v_2 = v_4)$, which allows it for backjumping over all the remaining $\neg e_{ij}$'s of the current chain and unit-propagating $(v_2 = v_4)$.

The latter causes a new $\mathcal{EUF}$ conflict represented by the clause C_{14}. By Step 2. of Strategy 1, C_{14} is resolved with the clauses C'_{24}, C_{56}, C_{13} (which caused the propagation of $(v_2 = v_4)$, $(v_5 = v_6)$, $(v_1 = v_3)$ respectively), obtaining the clause $C'_{14} : (\mu'_{\mathcal{LA}(\mathbb{Z})} \wedge \mu''_{\mathcal{LA}(\mathbb{Z})} \wedge \mu''_{\mathcal{EUF}} \wedge \mu'''_{\mathcal{EUF}} \wedge \mu'''_{\mathcal{EUF}}) \rightarrow (v_1 = v_4)$, which allows for backjumping up to μ and unit-propagating $(v_1 = v_4)$.

Finally, DTC starts and proceeds selecting $\neg e_{ij}$'s (possibly unit-propagating some value due to the clauses learned) without generating conflicts, so that to conclude that the formula is $\mathcal{T}_1 \cup \mathcal{T}_2$-satisfiable.

Comparing with Fig. 3, $dtc\_br = 6$, $dtc\_ded = 0$, $no\_ded = 3$ and $no\_br = 3$.   □

Notice that the three leftmost diagonal branches in Fig. 7 obtain the same effect as the e_{ij}-deduction steps in Fig. 6 (and in Fig. 3).

6   Conclusions

Theorem 1 shows that, under the same hypotheses of e_{ij}-deduction-completeness as NO, DTC can emulate NO, with no extra boolean search. Theorem 2 shows that, under the hypothesis of $\neg e_{ij}$-minimality, even $\mathcal{T}_i$-solvers with limited or no e_{ij}-deduction capabilities allow DTC to emulate NO, at the cost of (at most) one extra boolean branch for every (possibly very expensive) e_{ij}-deduction performed by NO. Both results also highlight the fact that DTC naturally allows for learning clauses containing e_{ij}'s, which can be used in subsequent branches to prune search and avoid redoing the same search/deductions from scratch.

We remark that Strategy 1 has been conceived only for mimicking NO, and by no means it is assumed to be the most efficient strategy for DTC. (E.g., Step 3.(ii) can be substituted with a weakened version of EP [4], and more efficient literal selection strategies might be preferable to Step 3.(i) and (iii).) Some alternatives are currently under investigation, and their theoretical properties and practical performance are subjects for future work.

As far as the $\neg e_{ij}$-minimality hypothesis is concerned, we notice that, at least for theories like $\mathcal{EUF}$ and $\mathcal{LA}(\mathbb{Q})$, there are known decision procedures that fulfill this requirement (see [12] and [4] respectively.) For other theories, the problem of $\neg e_{ij}$-minimization opens a novel research branch. [10] However, we remark that DTC works also when the $\mathcal{T}_i$-solvers are not $\neg e_{ij}$-minimal, at the cost of (at most) one extra branch to explore for each redundant $\neg e_{ij}$ returned in a conflict set.

It is also important to notice that, in general, only a fraction of the assignments μ enumerated turn out to be $\mathcal{T}_i$-satisfiable for both $\mathcal{T}_i$'s, so that to require the boolean search on the e_{ij}'s. Thus, for all the other branches, DTC may save the effort of many failed attempts of deducing implied e_{ij}'s.

On the whole, the results presented in this paper show that DTC allows for trading boolean search for e_{ij}-deduction. Thus everyone can choose and implement the most suitable $\mathcal{T}_i$-solvers without being forced by the e_{ij}-deduction-completeness straitjacket: for theories for which efficient e_{ij}-deduction complete procedures are available (e.g., $\mathcal{EUF}$ [12]), DTC allows for exploiting the full power of e_{ij}-deduction; for harder theories (e.g., $\mathcal{LA}(\mathbb{Z})$), the research task changes from that of finding e_{ij}-deduction complete $\mathcal{T}$-solvers to that of finding $\neg e_{ij}$-minimal or nearly-$\neg e_{ij}$-minimal ones.

---

[10] Bottom line, one can always make μ $\neg e_{ij}$-minimal by dropping the remaining $\neg e_{ij}$'s one by one, each time checking $\mu \setminus \{\neg e_{ij}\}$. Notice that, in general, with $\neg e_{ij}$-minimization the search for the candidate $\neg e_{ij}$'s to drop is restricted to only those occurring in μ, whilst with e_{ij}-deduction the search for the candidate e_{ij}'s to deduce extends to all the unassigned e_{ij}'s.

References

1. A. Armando, C. Castellini, E. Giunchiglia, and M. Maratea. A SAT-based Decision Procedure for the Boolean Combination of Difference Constraints. In *Proc. SAT'04*, 2004.
2. C.L. Barrett and S. Berezin. CVC Lite: A New Implementation of the Cooperating Validity Checker. In *Proc. CAV'04*, volume 3114 of *LNCS*. Springer, 2004.
3. M. Bozzano, R. Bruttomesso, A. Cimatti, T. Junttila, P.van Rossum, S. Ranise, and R. Sebastiani. Efficient Satisfiability Modulo Theories via Delayed Theory Combination. In *Proc. Int. Conf. on Computer-Aided Verification, CAV 2005.*, volume 3576 of *LNCS*. Springer, 2005.
4. M. Bozzano, R. Bruttomesso, A. Cimatti, T. Junttila, P.van Rossum, S. Schulz, and R. Sebastiani. An incremental and Layered Procedure for the Satisfiability of Linear Arithmetic Logic. In *Proc. TACAS'05*, volume 3440 of *LNCS*. Springer, 2005.
5. M. Bozzano, R. Bruttomesso, A. Cimatti, T. Junttila, P.van Rossum, S. Schulz, and R. Sebastiani. MathSAT: A Tight Integration of SAT and Mathematical Decision Procedure. *Journal of Automated Reasoning*, 2005. to appear.
6. M. Bozzano, R. Bruttomesso, A. Cimatti, T. Junttila, P. van Rossum, S. Ranise, and R. Sebastiani. Efficient Theory Combination via Boolean Search. *Information and Computation*, 2005. To appear.
7. R. Bruttomesso, A. Cimatti, A. Franzén, A. Griggio, and R. Sebastiani. Delayed Theory Combination vs. Nelson-Oppen for Satisfiability Modulo Theories: a Comparative Analysis. Technical Report DIT-06-032, DIT, University of Trento, 2006. Available at http://dit.unitn.it/~rseba/papers/lpar06_dtc_extended.pdf.
8. S. Cotton, E. Asarin, O. Maler, and P. Niebert. Some Progress in Satisfiability Checking for Difference Logic. In *Proc. FORMATS-FTRTFT 2004*, 2004.
9. J.-C. Filliâtre, S. Owre, H. Rueß, and N. Shankar. ICS: Integrated Canonizer and Solver. In *Proc. CAV'01*, volume 2102 of *LNCS*, pages 246–249, 2001.
10. H. Ganzinger, G. Hagen, R. Nieuwenhuis, A. Oliveras, and C. Tinelli. DPLL(T): Fast decision procedures. In *Proc. CAV'04*, volume 3114 of *LNCS*, pages 175–188. Springer, 2004.
11. G. Nelson and D.C. Oppen. Simplification by Cooperating Decision Procedures. *ACM Trans. on Programming Languages and Systems*, 1(2):245–257, 1979.
12. R. Nieuwenhuis and A. Oliveras. Congruence Closure with Integer Offsets. In *Proc. 10th LPAR*, number 2850 in LNAI, pages 77–89. Springer, 2003.
13. R.E. Shostak. Deciding Combinations of Theories. *Journal of the ACM*, 31:1–12, 1984.
14. L. Zhang, C. F. Madigan, M. H. Moskewicz, and S. Malik. Efficient conflict driven learning in a boolean satisfiability solver. In *Proc. ICCAD '01*. IEEE Press, 2001.
15. L. Zhang and S. Malik. The quest for efficient boolean satisfiability solvers. In *Proc. CAV'02*, number 2404 in LNCS, pages 17–36. Springer, 2002.

Automatic Combinability of Rewriting-Based Satisfiability Procedures

Hélène Kirchner[1], Silvio Ranise[1,2],
Christophe Ringeissen[1], and Duc-Khanh Tran[1]

[1] LORIA & INRIA-Lorraine
[2] Università di Milano

Abstract. We address the problems of combining satisfiability procedures and consider two combination scenarios: (i) the combination within the class of rewriting-based satisfiability procedures and (ii) the Nelson-Oppen combination of rewriting-based satisfiability procedures and arbitrary satisfiability procedures. In each scenario, we use meta-saturation, which schematizes saturation of the set containing the axioms of a given theory and an arbitrary set of ground literals, to syntactically decide sufficient conditions for the combinability of rewriting-based satisfiability procedures. For (i), we give a sufficient condition for the modular termination of meta-saturation. When meta-saturation for the union of theories halts, it yields a rewriting-based satisfiability procedure for the union. For (ii), we use meta-saturation to prove the stable infiniteness of the component theories and deduction completeness of their rewriting-based satisfiability procedures. These properties are important to establish the correctness of the Nelson-Oppen combination method and to obtain an efficient implementation.

1 Introduction

Satisfiability procedures for theories of data types such as arrays, lists, or integers are at the core of many state-of-the-art verification tools. The task of designing, proving correct, and implementing such procedures is far from simple. One of the main problems is proving their correctness. To overcome this difficulty, an approach to flexibly build satisfiability procedures based on saturation has been proposed in [3]. The key idea is that proving correctness of the procedure for a theory T reduces to showing the termination of the fair and exhaustive application of the rules of the superposition calculus [10] on an axiomatization of T plus an arbitrary set S of (ground) literals. The approach has been shown competitive with *ad hoc* satisfiability procedures in [1]. An automated method to check the termination of superposition for a theory T is given in [8] by using a *meta-saturation* calculus schematizing the inferences of the standard superposition calculus relevant to solve the satisfiability problem of T.

Most verification problems require reasoning in a combination of theories. As a consequence, there is a need to modularly build procedures for the composed theory by re-using available procedures for the component theories. In this respect, there are two possible approaches:

M. Hermann and A. Voronkov (Eds.): LPAR 2006, LNAI 4246, pp. 542–556, 2006.

(i) use superposition on the union of the axioms of the theories being combined or

(ii) use the Nelson-Oppen combination schema [9] to modularly combine procedures for the component theories.

For (i), [2] provides a sufficient condition on component theories to guarantee the termination of the superposition calculus on their union. Here, the problem is the possibility to have "across-theories inferences," which are likely to prevent termination when theories are not considered in isolation. To avoid this problem, in this paper, we give a condition (along the lines of [2]) on the component theories to guarantee that superposition may derive only finitely many new clauses when considering the composed theory. Also, we go a step further by describing an automatic test to check that a component theory satisfies the sufficient condition for modular termination by using meta-saturation.

For (ii), it is particularly interesting to study how to efficiently incorporate rewriting-based procedures in the Nelson-Oppen schema. One of the key problems to obtain an efficient integration is the capability to derive equalities between shared constants. Theoretically, it is not a problem: to check that a (ground) formula ϕ is entailed by a theory T, it is sufficient to check that the negation of ϕ is unsatisfiable in T. Practically, this solution requires guessing which may decrease performance unacceptably (see [6] for an in-depth discussion of this issue). To overcome this problem, [7] shows that—under certain assumptions—the exhaustive application of the rules of the superposition calculus derives enough equalities between shared constants to guarantee the completeness of the Nelson-Oppen schema. This result is not obvious since superposition is not complete for consequence finding. Here, we give a sufficient condition for a rewriting-based satisfiability procedure to be deduction complete, thereby generalizing the results in [7] which were developed for some theories in an *ad hoc* way. More importantly, we give an automatic test to check the condition for deduction completeness, again, by using meta-saturation.

The final contribution of this paper is an automatic test for establishing whether a theory admitting a rewriting-based satisfiability procedure is stably infinite[1] by using meta-saturation. To our knowledge, this is the first time that an automatic check for stable infiniteness is described.

Plan of the paper. Section 2 introduces some background notions. Section 3 overviews the main ideas of the rewriting-based [3] and the meta-saturation [8] approaches. Section 4 presents the modularity result on the termination of superposition and its automatic check. Section 5 describes the conditions for stable infiniteness and deduction completeness, and their automatic tests. Section 6 illustrates the results of Sections 4 and 5 on some interesting theories. Section 7 discusses the relevance of the results and compares them with related work.

---

[1] Roughly, a theory T is stably infinite iff for every satisfiable quantifier-free formula φ, we have that φ is satisfiable in an infinite model of T.

2 Preliminaries

We assume the usual first-order syntactic notions of signature, term, position, and substitution, as defined, e.g., in [5]. If l and r are two terms, then $l = r$ is an *equality* and $\neg(l = r)$ (also written as $l \neq r$) is a *disequality*. A *literal* is either an equality or a disequality. A first-order *formula* is built in the usual way over the universal and existential quantifiers, Boolean connectives, and symbols in a given first-order signature. We call a formula *ground* if it has no variables. A *clause* is a disjunction of literals. A *unit* clause is a clause with only one disjunct, equivalently a literal. A *Horn* clause is a clause with at most one equality. The *empty* clause is the clause with no disjunct, equivalently an unsatisfiable formula. We denote with $Vars(t)$, $Vars(l)$, $Vars(\phi)$ the sets of variables appearing respectively in a term t, a literal l and a formula ϕ. For a term t, $depth(t) = 0$, if t is a constant or a variable, and $depth(f(t_1, \ldots, t_n)) = 1 + max\{depth(t_i) \mid 1 \leq i \leq n\}$. A term is *flat* if its depth is 0 or 1. For a literal, $depth(l \bowtie r) = depth(l) + depth(r)$, where $\bowtie \in \{=, \neq\}$. A positive literal is *flat* if its depth is 0 or 1. A negative literal is *flat* if its depth is 0. A positive literal of the form $f(k_1, \ldots, k_m) = k_0$, where k_i is a constant or a variable for $i \in \{0, \ldots, m\}$, is called a flat f-equality.

We also assume the usual first-order notions of model, satisfiability, validity, logical consequence. A *first-order theory* (with finite signature) is a set of first-order formulae with no free variables. When T is a finitely axiomatized theory, $Ax(T)$ denotes the set of axioms of T. All the theories in this paper are first-order theories *with equality*, which means that the equality symbol $=$ is always interpreted as the equality relation. A formula is *satisfiable in a theory* T if it is satisfiable in a model of T. The *satisfiability problem* for a theory T amounts to establishing whether any given finite conjunction of literals (or equivalently, any given finite set of literals) is T-satisfiable or not. A *satisfiability procedure* for T is any algorithm that solves the satisfiability problem for T (the satisfiability of any quantifier-free formula can be reduced to the satisfiability of sets of literals by converting to disjunctive normal form and then splitting on disjunctions).

3 Rewriting-Based Satisfiability Procedure

3.1 The Superposition Calculus ($\mathcal{SP}$)

In the sequel, $=$ is (unordered) equality, $\equiv$ is identity, l, r, u, t are terms, v, w, x, y, z are variables, all other lower case letters are constant or function symbols. A fundamental feature of $\mathcal{SP}$ is the usage of a *reduction ordering* $\succ$ which is total on ground terms, for example the lexicographic path ordering [5]. We also assume that if a term t is not a variable or constant, then for any constant c we have that $t \succ c$. The ordering $\succ$ is extended to positive literals by considering them as multisets of terms, and then to the clauses by considering them as multisets of positive literals. Also, we define $\succ$ in such a way that negative literals are always bigger than the positive ones.

$$\text{Superposition} \quad \frac{\Gamma \Rightarrow \Delta, l[u'] = r \quad \Pi \Rightarrow \Sigma, u = t}{\sigma(\Gamma, \Pi \Rightarrow \Delta, \Sigma, l[t] = r)} (i), (ii), (iii), (iv)$$

$$\text{Paramodulation} \quad \frac{\Gamma, l[u'] = r \Rightarrow \Delta \quad \Pi \Rightarrow \Sigma, u = t}{\sigma(l[t] = r, \Gamma, \Pi \Rightarrow \Delta, \Sigma)} (i), (ii), (iii), (iv)$$

$$\text{Reflection} \quad \frac{\Gamma, u' = u \Rightarrow \Delta}{\sigma(\Gamma \Rightarrow \Delta)} (v)$$

$$\text{Eq. Factoring} \quad \frac{\Gamma \Rightarrow \Delta, u = t, u' = t'}{\sigma(\Gamma, t = t' \Rightarrow \Delta, u = t')} (i), (vi)$$

where a clause $\neg A_1 \vee \cdots \vee \neg A_n \vee B_1 \vee \cdots \vee B_n$ is written in sequent style as $\{A_1, \ldots, A_n\} \Rightarrow \{B_1, \ldots, B_m\}$ (where the A_i's and B_j's are equalities), equality is the only predicate symbol, σ is the most general unifier of u and u', u' is not a variable in *Superposition* and *Paramodulation*, L is a literal, and the following hold:

(i) $\sigma(u) \not\preceq \sigma(t)$, *(ii)* $\forall L \in \Pi \cup \Sigma : \sigma(u = t) \not\preceq \sigma(L)$, *(iii)* $\sigma(l[u']) \not\preceq \sigma(r)$, *(iv)* $\forall L \in \Gamma \cup \Delta : \sigma(l[u'] = r) \not\preceq \sigma(L)$, and *(v)* for all $L \in \Gamma \cup \Delta : \sigma(u' = u) \not\prec \sigma(L)$, and *(vi)* for all $L \in \Gamma : \sigma(u) \not\preceq \sigma(L)$, and for all $L \in \{u' = t'\} \cup \Delta : \sigma(u = t) \not\prec \sigma(L)$.

Fig. 1. Expansion Inference Rules of $\mathcal{SP}$

$$\text{Subsumption} \quad \frac{S \cup \{C, C'\}}{S \cup \{C\}} \quad \text{if for some substitution } \theta, \ \theta(C) \subseteq C'$$

$$\text{Simplification} \quad \frac{S \cup \{C[l'], l = r\}}{S \cup \{C[\theta(r)], l = r\}} \quad \begin{array}{l} \text{if } l' \equiv \theta(l), \theta(l) \succ \theta(r), \text{ and} \\ \forall L \in C[\theta(l)] : L \succ (\theta(l) = \theta(r)) \end{array}$$

$$\text{Deletion} \quad \frac{S \cup \{\Gamma \Rightarrow \Delta, t = t\}}{S}$$

where C and C' are clauses and S is a set of clauses.

Fig. 2. Contraction Inference Rules of $\mathcal{SP}$

A clause C is *redundant* with respect to a set S of clauses if either $C \in S$ or S can be obtained from $S \cup \{C\}$ by a sequence of application of the contraction rules of Figure 2. An inference is *redundant* with respect to a set S of clauses if its conclusion is redundant with respect to S. A set S of clauses is *saturated* with respect to $\mathcal{SP}$ if every inference of $\mathcal{SP}$ with a premise in S is redundant with respect to S. A *derivation* is a sequence $S_0, S_1, \ldots, S_i, \ldots$ of sets of clauses where at each step an inference of $\mathcal{SP}$ is applied to generate and add a clause (cf. expansion rules in Figure 1) or to delete or reduce a clause (cf. contraction rules in Figure 2). A derivation is characterized by its *limit*, defined as the set of persistent clauses $S_\infty = \bigcup_{j \geq 0} \bigcap_{i > j} S_i$.

A derivation $S_0, S_1, \ldots, S_i, \ldots$ with limit S_∞ is *fair* with respect to $\mathcal{SP}$ if for every inference in $\mathcal{SP}$ with premises in S_∞, there is some $j \geq 0$ such that the inference is redundant in S_j.

Theorem 1 ([10]). *If $S_0, S_1, \ldots$ is a fair derivation of $\mathcal{SP}$, then* (i) *its limit S_∞ is saturated with respect to $\mathcal{SP}$,* (ii) *S_0 is unsatisfiable iff the empty clause is in S_j for some j, and* (iii) *if such a fair derivation is finite, i.e. it is of the form $S_0, \ldots, S_n$, then S_n is saturated and logically equivalent to S_0.*

We say that $\mathcal{SP}$ is *refutation complete* since it is possible to derive the empty clause with a finite derivation from an unsatisfiable set of clauses (cf. (*ii*) of Theorem 1).

3.2   Rewriting-Based Methodology

The rewriting-based methodology for T-satisfiability consists of two phases:

1. *Flattening:* all ground literals are flattened by introducing new constants, yielding an equisatisfiable *flat* problem.
2. *Ordering selection and termination:* any fair derivation of $\mathcal{SP}$ is shown to be finite when applied to a flat problem together with the axioms of T, provided that $\succ$ satisfies a few properties depending on T.

If T is a theory for which the rewriting-based methodology applies, a T-satisfiability procedure can be built by implementing the flattening (this can be done once and for all), and by using a prover mechanizing $\mathcal{SP}$ with a suitable ordering $\succ$. If the final set of clauses returned by the prover contains the empty clause, then the T-satisfiability procedure returns unsatisfiable; otherwise, it returns satisfiable.

3.3   Meta-saturation

Meta-saturation [8] has been designed to simulate the saturation process of the axioms of a given theory T together with an arbitrary set S of ground flat literals. It works by saturating the axioms $Ax(T)$ together with the set G_0^T schematizing any finite set of ground flat literals built out of symbols in the signature of T, with respect to the inference system $m\mathcal{SP}$ (see Figures 3 and 4). Intuitively, the saturation of $Ax(T) \cup G_0^T$ schematizes the saturation of $Ax(T)$ together with any finite set of ground flat literals. Therefore if the meta-saturation halts for the theory T, then any saturation of $Ax(T) \cup S$ will be finite and consequently the T-satisfiability problem is decidable. Below, we quickly overview the formal concepts underlying the meta-saturation approach of [8].

An *atomic constant constraint* is of the form $const(t)$ and it is true if t is a constant. A *constant constraint* is of the form $const(t_1) \wedge \ldots \wedge const(t_n), n \geq 0$. A substitution λ satisfies a constant constraint ϕ if $\lambda(\phi)$ is true. A constrained clause is of the form $C \parallel \phi$, where C is a (unconstrained) clause and ϕ is a constant constraint. We say that $\lambda(C)$ is a *constraint instance* of $C \parallel \phi$ if $dom(\lambda) = Vars(\phi)$ and $ran(\lambda)$ only contains constants. There are standard techniques to define the ordering on constrained clauses by comparing all ground instances of constrained clauses (see [10] for details).

Define G_0^T as follows:

$$G_0^T = \{x = y \parallel const(x) \wedge const(y)\} \cup \{x \neq y \parallel const(x) \wedge const(y)\} \cup$$

$$\bigcup_{f \in \Sigma_T} \{f(x_1, \ldots, x_n) = x_0 \parallel \bigwedge_{i=0}^{n} const(x_i)\},$$

where Σ_T is the signature of T.

The inference system $m\mathcal{SP}$ (see Figures 3 and 4) is almost identical to $\mathcal{SP}$, except that all clauses now have constraints (unconstrained clauses have empty constraints), which are inherited by the conclusions of an inference; also Constrained Contraction Rules have different applicability conditions. This is because we cannot simulate every subsumption, deletion or simplification since we cannot assume that ground literals are always present in a saturation of $Ax(T) \cup S$, on which such contraction inferences depend.

Superposition	$\dfrac{\Gamma \Rightarrow \Delta, l[u'] = r \parallel \phi \quad \Pi \Rightarrow \Sigma, u = t \parallel \varphi}{\sigma(\Gamma, \Pi \Rightarrow \Delta, \Sigma, l[t] = r \parallel \phi \wedge \varphi)}$	$(i), (ii), (iii), (iv)$
Paramodulation	$\dfrac{\Gamma, l[u'] = r \Rightarrow \Delta \parallel \phi \quad \Pi \Rightarrow \Sigma, u = t \parallel \varphi}{\sigma(l[t] = r, \Gamma, \Pi \Rightarrow \Delta, \Sigma \parallel \phi \wedge \varphi)}$	$(i), (ii), (iii), (iv)$
Reflection	$\dfrac{\Gamma, u' = u \Rightarrow \Delta \parallel \phi}{\sigma(\Gamma \Rightarrow \Delta \parallel \phi)}$ (v)	
Eq. Factoring	$\dfrac{\Gamma \Rightarrow \Delta, u = t, u' = t' \parallel \phi}{\sigma(\Gamma, t = t' \Rightarrow \Delta, u = t' \parallel \phi)}$ $(i), (vi)$	

where a clause $\neg A_1 \vee \cdots \vee \neg A_n \vee B_1 \vee \cdots \vee B_n$ is written in sequent style as $\{A_1, \ldots, A_n\} \Rightarrow \{B_1, \ldots, B_m\}$ (where the A_i's and B_j's are equalities), equality is the only predicate symbol, σ is the most general unifier of u and u', u' is not a variable in Superposition and Paramodulation, L is a literal, and the following hold:

(i) $\sigma(u) \not\preceq \sigma(t)$, **(ii)** $\forall L \in \Pi \cup \Sigma : \sigma(u = t) \not\preceq \sigma(L)$, **(iii)** $\sigma(l[u']) \not\preceq \sigma(r)$, **(iv)** $\forall L \in \Gamma \cup \Delta : \sigma(l[u'] = r) \not\preceq \sigma(L)$, and **(v)** for all $L \in \Gamma \cup \Delta : \sigma(u' = u) \not\prec \sigma(L)$, and **(vi)** for all $L \in \Gamma : \sigma(u) \not\preceq \sigma(L)$, and for all $L \in \{u' = t'\} \cup \Delta : \sigma(u = t) \not\prec \sigma(L)$.

Fig. 3. Constrained Expansion Inference Rules of $m\mathcal{SP}$

Subsumption	$\dfrac{S \cup \{C, C' \parallel \phi\}}{S \cup \{C\}}$	if $C \in Ax(T)$ and for some substitution θ, $\theta(C) \subseteq C'$, or if C and $C' \parallel \phi$ are renamings of each other.
Simplification	$\dfrac{S \cup \{C[l'] \parallel \phi, l = r\}}{S \cup \{C[\theta(r) \parallel \phi], l = r\}}$	if $l = r \in Ax(T)$, $l' \equiv \theta(l)$, $\theta(l) \succ \theta(r)$, and $\forall L \in C[\theta(l)] : L \succ (\theta(l) = \theta(r))$
Deletion	$\dfrac{S \cup \{\Gamma \Rightarrow \Delta, t = t \parallel \phi\}}{S}$	
	$\dfrac{S \cup \{\Gamma \Rightarrow \Delta \parallel \phi\}}{S}$	if ϕ is unsatisfiable

where C and C' are clauses and S is a set of clauses.

Fig. 4. Constrained Contraction Inference Rules of $m\mathcal{SP}$

Lemma 1 (Theorem 5 of [8]). *Let T be a theory axiomatized by a finite set $Ax(T)$ of clauses, which is saturated with respect to $\mathcal{SP}$. Let G_∞^T be the set of all clauses generated in a finite saturation of $Ax(T) \cup G_0^T$ by $m\mathcal{SP}$. Let S be a set of ground flat literals. Then, we can saturate $Ax(T) \cup S$ by $\mathcal{SP}$ such that every clause generated in the saturation is*

(A) a disjunction of equalities between constants $c_1 = c'_1 \vee \ldots \vee c_n = c'_n$, where $n \geq 1$, or

(B) a clause of the form $C \vee c_1 = c'_1 \vee \ldots \vee c_n = c'_n$, where $n \geq 0$ and C is a constraint instance of a clause C' in G^T_∞, or

(C) a clause of the form $C \vee c_1 = c'_1 \vee \ldots \vee c_n = c'_n$ such that $n \geq 0$ and C is a ground flat f-equality and $f \notin \Sigma_T$.

In [8], an extension of the Superposition Calculus $\mathcal{SP}$ by a special rule — called, the Orient rule — is used, which is crucial to obtain better complexity results than those in [3]. However, Lemma 1 continues to hold for the Superposition Calculus $\mathcal{SP}$ used in this paper. In fact, a proof of Lemma 1 can be obtained from that of Theorem 2 in [8] by simply omitting the case for the Orient rule. For the sake of simplicity, we have chosen to disregard complexity issues in this paper and hence we have omitted the Orient rule. It would be straightforward to include such a rule to give similar complexity results as those in [8] to complement the results obtained in this paper.

4   Modular Termination of Rewriting-Based Procedures

We study conditions under which the theory $T_1 \cup T_2$ admits a rewriting-based satisfiability procedure, provided that T_1 and T_2 are disjoint theories admitting rewriting-based satisfiability procedures. To this end, we have to consider termination of the $\mathcal{SP}$-saturation process of $Ax(T_1) \cup Ax(T_2) \cup S$ for an arbitrary set of ground flat literals S. Since the signatures of the component theories are disjoint, across-theories $\mathcal{SP}$-inferences can only take place on variables, constants, or flat uninterpreted terms. It is easy to see that $\mathcal{SP}$-inferences on constants or flat uninterpreted terms generate finitely many clauses. It simply remains to exclude across-theories $\mathcal{SP}$-inferences on variables to ensure the modular termination. Before stating formally the results, we need to introduce the following definition.

Definition 1 (Variable-active Clause). *A clause C is variable-active with respect to an ordering $\succ$ if*

- *C contains a literal of the form $X = t$, where $X \notin Vars(t)$, and*
- *there exists some substitution λ such that $\lambda(X = t)$ is maximal in $\lambda(C)$ and $\lambda(X)$ is maximal in $\lambda(X = t)$ with respect to $\succ$.*

A constrained clause is variable-active with respect to $\succ$ if one of its constraint instances is variable-active with respect to $\succ$.

From now on, when we say that a clause C is variable-active we mean that C is variable-active with respect to $\succ$ used by $\mathcal{SP}$. The following proposition provides us with a syntactic criterion to check whether a clause is variable-active or not.

Proposition 1. *A clause C is variable-active if and only if C contains a maximal literal of the form $X = t$ and $X \notin Vars(t)$.*

Proof. ($\Rightarrow$). If C contains no literals of the form $X = t$ then C is not variable-active. If C contains literals of the form $X = t$ but they are not maximal in C then C is still not variable-active. Assume that a maximal literal $X = t$ is in C but $X \in Vars(t)$. Then by subterm property, $\lambda(t) \succ \lambda(X)$ for every substitution λ and hence $\lambda(X)$ is not maximal in $\lambda(X = t)$. Consequently C is not variable-active.

($\Leftarrow$). Assume that C contains a maximal literal of the form $X = t$, where $X \notin Vars(t)$, then we can choose a substitution λ such that $\lambda(X)$ is maximal in $\lambda(X = t)$ and $\lambda(X = t)$ is maximal in $\lambda(C)$ and thereby C is variable-active. $\square$

Lemma 2. *Let T be a theory axiomatized by a finite set $Ax(T)$ of clauses, which is saturated with respect to SP. Assume that any saturation of $Ax(T) \cup G_0^T$ by mSP is finite and does not contain any variable-active clauses. Then for every set S of ground flat literals, any saturation of $Ax(T) \cup S$ by SP does not contain any variable-active clauses.*

Proof. Assume that a saturation of $Ax(T) \cup S$ by SP contains a clause variable-active D, then D must have the form (B) in Lemma 1, i.e. a clause of the form $C \vee c_1 = c_1' \vee \ldots \vee c_n = c_n'$, where $n \geq 0$ and C is a constraint instance of a clause C' in G_∞^T. That would imply that C is variable-active and C' also is, and this contradicts the hypothesis of the lemma. $\square$

Lemma 3. *Let T_i be a theory axiomatized by a finite set $Ax(T_i)$ of clauses, which is saturated with respect to SP for $i = 1, 2$. Assume that*

- *the signatures of T_1 and T_2 are disjoint, and*
- *for every set S of ground flat literals, any saturation of $Ax(T_i) \cup S$ by SP is finite and does not contain any variable-active clauses, for $i = 1, 2$.*

Then for every set S of ground flat literals, any saturation of $Ax(T_1) \cup Ax(T_2) \cup S$ by SP is finite.

Proof. We consider all possible across-theories inferences between clauses of the forms listed in Lemma 1. Inferences between clauses of the form (A) generate finitely many clauses of this form. Inferences between clauses of the form (C) also generate finitely many clauses of the form (A). Inferences between a clause of the form (A) and a clause of the form (C) also generate finitely many clauses of the form (C). Now, let us consider inferences between clauses of the form (B), i.e. $C \vee c_1 = c_1' \vee \ldots \vee c_n = c_n'$, where C is a constraint instance of a clause C' in $G_\infty^{T_i}$, for $i = 1, 2$ and other clauses. This kind of inferences is possible if and only if C is variable-active because the signatures of the theories are disjoint; that would contradict the hypothesis of the theorem. Consequently, the number of clauses generated in any saturation of $Ax(T_1) \cup Ax(T_2) \cup S$ by mSP is finite. $\square$

Lemma 2 and Lemma 3 allow us to state the first important result of the paper regarding the modular termination of rewriting-based satisfiability procedures.

Theorem 2. *Let T_i be a theory axiomatized by a finite set $Ax(T_i)$ of clauses, which is already saturated with respect to SP for $i = 1, 2$. Assume that*

- *the signatures of T_1 and T_2 are disjoint, and*
- *any saturation of $Ax(T_i) \cup G_0^{T_i}$ by $m\mathcal{SP}$ is finite and does not contain any variable-active clauses, for $i = 1, 2$.*

Then, $\mathcal{SP}$ is a satisfiability procedure for $T_1 \cup T_2$.

5   Stable Infiniteness and Deduction Completeness

The Nelson-Oppen combination method allows us to combine satisfiability procedures for the class of stably infinite theories (cf. Definition 2 below) in a modular way.

Definition 2 (Stably Infinite Theory). *Let T be a consistent theory. T is stably infinite iff for every T-satisfiable conjunction φ of ground literals, we have that φ is T-satisfiable in an infinite model.*

Since the requirement of being stably infinite is important for the Nelson-Oppen combination method, it is interesting to develop automated techniques to prove stable infiniteness. Here, we develop such a technique for theories admitting rewriting-based satisfiability procedures by using meta-saturation.

5.1   Deciding Stable Infiniteness

Let $\exists^{\geq n}$ be $\exists x_1 \ldots x_n. \bigwedge_{j \neq k}(x_j \neq x_k)$, $\exists^{\leq n}$ be $\forall x_0 \ldots x_n. \bigvee_{j \neq k}(x_j = x_k)$, and $\exists^{\infty}$ stand for the infinite set $\{\exists^{\geq n}|n \geq 2\}$. It is easy to see that $\exists^{\geq n}$, $\exists^{\leq n}$, and $\exists^{\infty}$ constrain the cardinality of each one of their models to be at least n, at most n, and infinite, respectively.

Lemma 4. *Let T be a first-order theory. If T has no infinite models, then there exists a positive integer n such that, for each model $\mathcal{M}$ of T, the cardinality of $\mathcal{M}$ is bounded by n.*

The proof of this lemma can be found in any introductory textbook about model theory (see, e.g., [12]). The key idea is to apply compactness to $T \cup \exists^{\infty}$.

Definition 3 (Finite Cardinality Clause). *A clause is a finite cardinality clause if it has the form $\exists^{\leq n}$, for some positive integer n.*

Lemma 5. *Let T be a consistent theory. If T has no infinite models then T entails a finite cardinality clause.*

Proof. Assume that T has no infinite models. Let $\mathcal{M}$ be a model of T. Then, we have $\mathcal{M} \models \exists^{\leq \kappa}$ (i.e. M contains at most κ elements) for $|M| = \kappa$. By Lemma 4, we know that there exists some positive integer n such that the cardinality of every model of T is bounded by n, which implies that there are finitely many models $\mathcal{M}_1, \ldots, \mathcal{M}_r$ (for some $r \geq 1$) of T, up to isomorphism. Let C be the clause $\bigvee_{i=1}^r \exists^{\leq \kappa_i}$, where $\mathcal{M}_i$ is a model of T, $|M_i| = \kappa_i$ (for $i = 1, \ldots, r$), and we have left implicit the universal quantifiers of $\exists^{\leq \kappa_i}$. Clearly, we have $T \models C$ and C entails necessarily a finite cardinality clause. $\square$

Lemma 6. *Let T be a consistent theory axiomatized by a finite set $Ax(T)$ of clauses and S be a finite T-satisfiable set of ground literals. If $T \cup S$ entails a finite cardinality clause, then any saturation of $Ax(T) \cup S$ by $\mathcal{SP}$ contains a variable-active clause.*

Proof. Assume that there is some finite cardinality clause C such that $T \cup S \models C$. Reasoning by refutation, $T \cup S \models C$ iff $S \wedge \neg C$ is not T-satisfiable. Hence, it must be possible to derive the empty clause by applying $\mathcal{SP}$ to the set $Ax(T) \cup S \cup Sk(\neg C)$, where $C \equiv \exists^{\leq n}$ and $Sk(\neg C)$ being the set $\{c_i^{sk} \neq c_j^{sk} \mid 0 \leq i \neq j \leq n\}$ such that c_i^{sk}, c_j^{sk} are Skolem constants (recall that each implicitly universally quantified variable in C becomes existentially quantified in $\neg C$). To obtain a saturation of $Ax(T) \cup S \cup Sk(\neg C)$, it is possible to obtain the saturation S' of $Ax(T) \cup S$ first (which is saturated by $\mathcal{SP}$ with respect to the extension of the signature of the clauses in $Ax(T) \cup S$ by the Skolem constants introduced by Sk because $\mathcal{SP}$ is stable under signature extensions [10]) and then consider all possible inferences between a clause in S' and one in $Sk(\neg C)$.[2] Let us analyze such inferences, i.e. inferences between a clause $c_i^{sk} \neq c_j^{sk}$ and some clause $s = t \vee D$ in S'. This kind of inference is possible only if s, t are variables or constants and $s = t$ is maximal in $s = t \vee D$. If both s and t are constants, then an inference between $c_i^{sk} \neq c_j^{sk}$ and $s = t \vee D$ is not possible. Let t be a variable. Now if s is a term containing a function symbol of arity greater than zero then an inference is not possible since $\sigma(s) \succ c_j^{sk}$, where σ is the most general unifier of t and c_j^{sk}. Therefore s is a variable or a constant, which implies $t \notin Vars(s)$, otherwise we have a tautology clause which is immediately deleted. But then by Proposition 1, we have that $s = t \vee D$ is a variable-active clause, and this completes the proof. □

We are now ready to state and to prove the second important result of this paper for automatically recognizing stably infinite theories.

Theorem 3. *Let T be a consistent theory axiomatized by a finite set $Ax(T)$ of clauses, which is saturated with respect to $\mathcal{SP}$. Let G_∞^T be the set of all clauses generated in a finite saturation of $Ax(T) \cup G_0^T$ by $m\mathcal{SP}$. If G_∞^T contains no variable-active clauses, then T is stably infinite.*

Proof. By contradiction, assume that T is not stably infinite. Then, there must exist a T-satisfiable set S of ground literals such that $T \cup S$ has no infinite models. By Lemma 5, $T \cup S$ entails some finite cardinality clause. It follows from Lemma 6 that any saturation of $Ax(T) \cup S$ contains some variable-active clause. Then, by Lemma 2, G_∞^T contains a variable-active clause, which contradicts the hypothesis of the theorem. □

---

[2] No other inferences are possible between two clauses in $S' \cup Sk(\neg C)$ since S' has already been saturated by $\mathcal{SP}$ and $Sk(\neg C)$ contains only negative unit clauses to which only Reflection (cf. Figure 1) can be applied obtaining the empty clause, thereby concluding the proof.

5.2   Deciding Deduction Completeness

The crux of the Nelson-Oppen combination method is to exchange entailed equalities between satisfiability procedures. There does not seem to be any problem in using a satisfiability procedure to check whether a set S of literals entails a formula ϕ in a theory since we can check whether S and the negation of ϕ is unsatisfiable. However, to implement the Nelson-Oppen combination method efficiently, the satisfiability procedure for the component theories must be capable to derive the equalities to exchange with other procedures.

Definition 4 (Elementary Equality). *An elementary equality is an equality between constants.*

Satisfiability procedures capable of deriving sufficiently many elementary equalities to ensure the completeness of the Nelson-Oppen method will be called *deduction complete*.

Definition 5 (Deduction Complete Satisfiability Procedure). *A T-satisfiability procedure is* deduction complete *with respect to elementary equalities iff for any T-satisfiable conjunction ϕ of ground literals it returns, in addition to satisfiable, a set S_e of elementary equalities such that for every elementary equality $c = c'$, the following holds: $T \models \phi \Rightarrow c = c'$ iff $S_e \models c = c'$.*

Lemma 7. *Assume*

- *T to be a theory axiomatized by a finite set $Ax(T)$ of Horn clauses, which is saturated with respect to $\mathcal{SP}$;*
- *G_∞^T to be the set of all clauses generated in a finite saturation of $Ax(T) \cup G_0^T$ by $m\mathcal{SP}$ such that G_∞^T contains no variable-active clauses;*
- *S to be a finite T-satisfiable set of ground flat literals;*
- *S' to be a saturation of $Ax(T) \cup S$ by $\mathcal{SP}$.*

Then, for every elementary equality $c = c'$ such that $Ax(T) \cup S \models c = c'$, we have that the subset containing all elementary equalities in S' entails $c = c'$.

Proof. Assume that there is some elementary equality $c = c'$ such that $T \cup S \models c = c'$. Reasoning by refutation, $T \cup S \models c = c'$ iff $S \wedge c \neq c'$ is not T-satisfiable. Hence, it must be possible to derive the empty clause by applying $\mathcal{SP}$ to the set $S' \cup \{c \neq c'\}$. Since S' is T-satisfiable and saturated, only inferences involving both clauses from (or inferred from) S' and $c \neq c'$ can infer the empty clause. Let us analyze such inferences, i.e. inferences between $c \neq c'$ and some clause C' in S'. If there is an inference between $c \neq c'$ and C', then C' must be an equality between constants or variables. This is because the ordering $\succ$ is defined such that a disequality is always bigger than an equality and as consequence an equality is maximal in a clause only if the latter contains no disequalities. If C' contains a variable, then C' is variable-active. This implies that G_∞^T contains a variable-active clause because C' must have the form (B) listed in Lemma 1; that would contradict the assumption of the lemma. If C' only contains constants, then C' is an elementary equality and the clause inferred from $c \neq c'$

and C' must be a disequality between constants. This means that an inference between $c \neq c'$ and a clause in S' is possible only if the latter is an elementary equality and only derives a disequality between constants. Therefore, the subset containing all elementary equalities in S' together with $c \neq c'$ suffice to infer the empty clause. Or equivalently the subset containing all elementary equalities in S' entails $c = c'$.   □

The next theorem, which directly follows from Lemma 7, offers an automated check for deduction completeness by meta-saturation.

Theorem 4. *Let T be a theory axiomatized by a finite set $Ax(T)$ of Horn clauses, which is saturated with respect to $\mathcal{SP}$. Let G_∞^T be the set of all clauses generated in a finite saturation of $Ax(T) \cup G_0^T$ by $m\mathcal{SP}$. If G_∞^T contains no variable-active clauses, then $\mathcal{SP}$ is a deduction complete T-satisfiability procedure with respect to elementary equalities.*

6 Application

We apply the main results of this paper (Theorem 2, 3, and 4) to some of the theories considered in [3]. For the sake of conciseness, let $const(x_1, ..., x_n)$ abbreviate $const(x_1) \wedge \cdots \wedge const(x_n)$, where $x_1, ..., x_n$ are variables.

Theory of Equality. The theory $\mathcal{E}$ of equality is considered primitive in our framework and so it is axiomatized by the empty set of sentences. Then, $G_0^{\mathcal{E}}$ consists of the following constrained clauses

$$x = y \parallel const(x, y) \quad \text{and} \quad x \neq y \parallel const(x, y).$$

Now, $G_\infty^{\mathcal{E}}$ contains all clauses in $G_0^{\mathcal{E}}$. Indeed, $G_\infty^{\mathcal{E}}$ is finite and contains no variable-active clauses. It follows from Theorem 3 that $\mathcal{E}$ is stably infinite. And $\mathcal{SP}$ is a deduction complete procedure for $\mathcal{E}$ by Theorem 4.

Theory of Lists. Let $\Sigma_{\mathcal{L}} = \{cons, car, cdr\}$. The theory $\mathcal{L}$ of lists is axiomatized by the following set $Ax(\mathcal{L})$ of axioms:

$$\{car(cons(X, Y)) = X, \quad cdr(cons(X, Y)) = Y, \quad cons(car(X), cdr(X)) = X\}$$

where X and Y are implicitly universally quantified variables. Then, $G_0^{\mathcal{L}}$ consists of the clauses in $G_0^{\mathcal{E}} \cup Ax(\mathcal{L})$ and the following clauses:

$$car(x) = y \parallel const(x, y),$$
$$cdr(x) = y \parallel const(x, y),$$
$$cons(x, y) = z \parallel const(x, y, z).$$

Now, $G_\infty^{\mathcal{L}}$ consists of all clauses in $G_\infty^{\mathcal{E}} \cup Ax(\mathcal{L}) \cup G_0^{\mathcal{L}}$ and the following clauses:

$$cons(car(x), y) = z \parallel const(x, y, z)$$
$$cons(x, cdr(y)) = z \parallel const(x, y, z)$$

Again, we have that $G_\infty^\mathcal{L}$ is finite and no variable-active clause is in $G_\infty^\mathcal{L}$. It follows from Theorem 3 that $\mathcal{L}$ is stably infinite. Since $\mathcal{L}$ is equational, $\mathcal{SP}$ is a deduction complete satisfiability procedure for $\mathcal{L}$ by Theorem 4.

Theory of Arrays. Let $\Sigma_\mathcal{A} = \{select, store\}$. The theory $\mathcal{A}$ of arrays is axiomatized by the following finite set $Ax(\mathcal{A})$ of axioms:

$$\{select(store(A, I, E), I) = E, \ I = J \lor select(store(A, I, E), J) = select(A, J)\}$$

where A, I, J, E are implicitly universally quantified variables. Then, $G_0^\mathcal{A}$ consists of the clauses in $G_0^\mathcal{E}$ and the following clauses:

$$select(x, y) = z \parallel const(x, y, z)$$
$$store(x, y, z) = t \parallel const(x, y, z, t)$$

And $G_\infty^\mathcal{A}$ consists of all clauses in $G_\infty^\mathcal{E} \cup Ax(\mathcal{A}) \cup G_0^\mathcal{A}$ and the following clauses:

$$select(x, t) = select(z, t) \lor y = t \parallel const(x, y, z)$$
$$select(x, t) = z \lor y = t \parallel const(x, y, z, t)$$
$$x = y \lor z = t \parallel const(x, y, z, t)$$
$$x = y \lor z = t \lor u = v \parallel const(x, y, z, t, u, v)$$

$G_\infty^\mathcal{A}$ is finite and does not contain any variable-active clauses; and consequently $\mathcal{A}$ is stably infinite and $\mathcal{SP}$ is a satisfiability procedure for $\mathcal{A}$.

Union of the theories of Lists and Arrays. Since $G_\infty^\mathcal{L}$ and $G_\infty^\mathcal{A}$ are both finite and contain no variable-active clauses, it follows from Theorem 2 that $\mathcal{SP}$ is a satisfiability procedure for $\mathcal{L} \cup \mathcal{A}$. Unsurprisingly, $\mathcal{L}$, $\mathcal{A}$, and $\mathcal{L} \cup \mathcal{A}$ are all stably infinite theories (respectively) by Theorem 3.

7   Discussion

In this paper, we have shown that the meta-saturation approach to rewriting-based satisfiability procedures can be used not only to derive complexity bounds on the obtained procedures as in [8], but also to provide automatic checks for (1) the modular termination of superposition, (2) stable infiniteness, and (3) deduction completeness. For the sake of simplicity, we use for all these problems the same assumptions on the ordering and the same criterion for the meta-saturation, based on variable-active clauses.

Regarding (1), the work described here extends the results in [2], where the authors define a class of variable-inactive theories. Any saturation of the axioms of two variable-inactive theories together with an arbitrary set of ground flat literals do not allow for across-theories inferences. Modular termination is guaranteed as soon as it is possible to show the termination of the saturation for each component theory. In this paper, we have introduced variable-active clauses which allow for across-theories inferences. We have shown that if meta-saturation for each component theory halts and derives no variable-active clauses, then we obtain modular termination of meta-saturation and hence a rewriting-based satisfiability procedure for the union of the theories. We have also given a syntactical criterion to decide whether a clause is variable-active or not, provided that the ordering used by the superposition calculus is defined in such a way that a negative literal is larger than a positive literal whenever they contain the same maximal term. This requirement is easily implemented using standard orderings and it is commonly used by superposition provers because of efficiency. This is so because such a prover is trying to refute the set of input clauses, i.e. to derive the empty clause, which can only be inferred by an inference involving a negative literal. For this reason, we believe that such a requirement on the ordering used by the superposition calculus is both natural and does not restrict the scope of (practical) applicability of the results in this paper.

For (2), by using again the concept of variable-active clauses, we have developed an automatic check for stable infiniteness for theories admitting a rewriting-based procedure: if, for given a theory T, meta-saturation halts, and does not infer any variable-active clauses, then T is stably infinite. To our knowledge, this is the first time that an automatic check for stable infiniteness is given. This result complements that in [4] about the relationship between the variable-inactivity condition of [2] and stable infiniteness. In fact, [4] shows that, under certain assumptions, if a theory is not stably infinite, then superposition is guaranteed to generate clauses (which are a particular case of the variable-active clauses introduced here) that constrain the cardinality of its models, so that the theory is not variable-inactive. It is important to note that our automatic check relies on a condition which is sufficient but not necessary. Indeed, meta-saturation may infer a variable-active clause whilst the theory is stably infinite. A possible extension of this work would be to find a better criterion for the particular problem of stably infiniteness using meta-saturation.

Regarding (3), the work in this paper complements the results in [7] where it is shown that superposition yields a deduction complete procedure for the theories of equality, and lists. In this paper, the concept of variable-active clauses allows us to develop an automatic method to check whether a rewriting-based satisfiability procedure is deduction complete: if, for an equational theory or a Horn theory T, meta-saturation halts, and does not infer any variable-active clauses, then superposition is a deduction complete satisfiability procedure for T. In order to obtain deduction completeness for non-Horn theories, we could use a clause splitting rule, along the lines of [11], to activate every possible inference and therefore derive sufficiently many disjunctions of elementary equalities.

References

1. A. Armando, M. P. Bonacina, S. Ranise, and S. Schulz. On a Rewriting Approach to Satisfiability Procedures: Extension, Combination of Theories and an Experimental Appraisal. In *Proc. of the 5th Int. Workshop on Frontiers of Combining Systems (FroCoS'05)*, volume 3717 of *LNCS*, pages 65–80. Springer, 2005.

2. A. Armando, M. P. Bonacina, S. Ranise, and S. Schulz. New results on rewrite-based satisfiability procedures, 2006. Extended version of [1], available at http://arxiv.org/abs/cs.AI/0604054.

3. A. Armando, S. Ranise, and M. Rusinowitch. A Rewriting Approach to Satisfiability Procedures. *Info. and Comp.*, 183(2):140–164, June 2003.

4. M. P. Bonacina, S. Ghilardi, E. Nicolini, S. Ranise, and D. Zucchelli. Decidability and Undecidability Results for Nelson-Oppen and Rewrite-Based Decision Procedures. In *Proc. of the 3rd International Joint Conference on Automated Reasoning (IJCAR'06)*, volume 4130 of *LNAI*, pages 513–527. Springer, 2006.

5. N. Dershowitz and J.-P. Jouannaud. *Handbook of Theoretical Computer Science*, volume B, chapter 6: Rewrite Systems, pages 244–320. Elsevier Science Publishers B. V. (North-Holland), 1990.

6. D. Detlefs, G. Nelson, and J. B. Saxe. Simplify: A Theorem Prover for Program Checking. Technical Report HPL-2003-148, HP Laboratories, 2003.

7. H. Kirchner, S. Ranise, C. Ringeissen, and D.-K. Tran. On superposition-based satisfiability procedures and their combination. In *Second International Colloquium on Theoretical Aspects of Computing — ICTAC 2005, Hanoi, Vietnam*, volume 3722 of *LNCS*, pages 594–608. Springer, Oct 2005.

8. C. Lynch and B. Morawska. Automatic decidability. In *Proc. of the IEEE Symposium on Logic in Computer Science*, July 2002.

9. G. Nelson and D. C. Oppen. Simplification by cooperating decision procedures. *ACM Trans. on Programming Languages and Systems*, 1(2):245–257, Oct. 1979.

10. R. Nieuwenhuis and A. Rubio. Paramodulation-based theorem proving. In A. Robinson and A. Voronkov, editors, *Handbook of Automated Reasoning*, volume I, chapter 7, pages 371–443. Elsevier Science, 2001.

11. A. Riazanov and A. Voronkov. Splitting without backtracking. In *Seventeenth International Joint Conference on Artificial Intelligence*, pages 611–617, 2001.

12. D. van Dalen. *Logic and Structure*. Springer-Verlag, 1989. Second edition.

To Ackermann-ize or Not to Ackermann-ize?
On Efficiently Handling Uninterpreted Function
Symbols in $SMT(\mathcal{EUF} \cup \mathcal{T})^\star$

Roberto Bruttomesso[1], Alessandro Cimatti[1], Anders Franzén[1,2],
Alberto Griggio[2], Alessandro Santuari[2], and Roberto Sebastiani[2]

[1] ITC-IRST, Povo, Trento, Italy
{bruttomesso, cimatti, franzen}@itc.it
[2] DIT, Università di Trento, Italy
{griggio, santuari, rseba}@dit.unitn.it

Abstract. Satisfiability Modulo Theories $(SMT(\mathcal{T}))$ is the problem of deciding the satisfiability of a formula with respect to a given background theory $\mathcal{T}$. When $\mathcal{T}$ is the combination of two simpler theories $\mathcal{T}_1$ and $\mathcal{T}_2$ $(SMT(\mathcal{T}_1 \cup \mathcal{T}_2))$, a standard and general approach is to handle the integration of $\mathcal{T}_1$ and $\mathcal{T}_2$ by performing some form of search on the equalities between the shared variables.

A frequent and very relevant sub-case of $SMT(\mathcal{T}_1 \cup \mathcal{T}_2)$ is when $\mathcal{T}_1$ is the theory of Equality and Uninterpreted Functions $(\mathcal{EUF})$. For this case, an alternative approach is to eliminate first all uninterpreted function symbols by means of Ackermann's expansion, and then to solve the resulting $SMT(\mathcal{T}_2)$ problem.

In this paper we build on the empirical observation that there is no absolute winner between these two alternative approaches, and that the performance gaps between them are often dramatic, in either direction.

We propose a simple technique for estimating a priori the costs and benefits, in terms of the size of the search space of an SMT tool, of applying Ackermann's expansion to all or part of the function symbols.

A thorough experimental analysis, including the benchmarks of the SMT'05 competition, shows that the proposed technique is extremely effective in improving the overall performance of the SMT tool.

1 Introduction

Satisfiability Modulo a Theory $\mathcal{T}$ $(SMT(\mathcal{T}))$ is the problem of checking the satisfiability of a quantifier-free (or ground) first-order formula with respect to a given first-order theory $\mathcal{T}$ (we are considering theories with equality). Theories of interest for many applications are, e.g., the theory of difference logic $\mathcal{DL}$, the theory $\mathcal{EUF}$ of equality and uninterpreted functions, the quantifier-free fragment of Linear Arithmetic over the rationals $\mathcal{LA}(\mathbb{Q})$ and that over the integers $\mathcal{LA}(\mathbb{Z})$, the theory of bit-vectors $\mathcal{BV}$. The prominent *lazy* approach to $SMT(\mathcal{T})$, which underlies several systems (e.g., CV-CLite [3], DLSAT [10], DPLL(T) /BarceLogic [12], MATHSAT [5], TSAT++ [2],

---

* This work has been partly supported by ISAAC, an European sponsored project, contract no. AST3-CT-2003-501848, by ORCHID, a project sponsored by Provincia Autonoma di Trento, and by a grant from Intel Corporation.

M. Hermann and A. Voronkov (Eds.): LPAR 2006, LNAI 4246, pp. 557–571, 2006.

ICS /YICES [11]), is based on extensions of propositional SAT technology: a SAT solver is modified to enumerate boolean assignments, and integrated with a decision procedure for sets of literals in the theory $\mathcal{T}$ ($\mathcal{T}$-solver).

When $\mathcal{T}$ is the combination of two simpler theories $\mathcal{T}_1$ and $\mathcal{T}_2$ ($SMT(\mathcal{T}_1 \cup \mathcal{T}_2)$), a standard and general approach is to handle the integration of $\mathcal{T}_1$ and $\mathcal{T}_2$ by performing some form of search on the equalities between the variables which are shared between the theories (*interface equalities*): in the Nelson-Oppen [13] and Shostak [15] schemata (NO hereafter), the interface equalities are deduced by the $\mathcal{T}$-*solvers*; in the Delayed Theory Combination schema (DTC hereafter) [6,7] all or part of them are assigned to truth values also by the underlying SAT solver.

A frequent and very relevant sub-case is when one of the two theories is that of equality and uninterpreted functions $\mathcal{EUF}$. (Hereafter we refer to this problem as *SMT* ($\mathcal{EUF} \cup \mathcal{T}$).) For this case, an alternative approach is to eliminate first all uninterpreted function symbols by means of Ackermann's expansion [1], and then to solve the resulting single-theory $SMT(\mathcal{T})$ problem. (Hereafter we refer to this approach as ACK.)

In this paper we focus on *SMT* ($\mathcal{EUF} \cup \mathcal{T}$). Comparing the performances of DTC and ACK approaches, we notice that not only there is no absolute winner, but also the performance gaps are often dramatic, in either direction. We investigate the causes of this fact, and we introduce a technique for estimating off-line the costs and benefits, in terms of the size of the search space of an *SMT* tool, of applying Ackermann's expansion to all or part of the function symbols.

We have implemented a preprocessor which analyzes the input formula, decides autonomously which functions to expand, performs such expansions and gives the resulting formula as input to an *SMT* tool.

A thorough experimental analysis, including the benchmarks of the SMT'05 competition, shows that our preprocessor performs the best choice(s) nearly always, and that the proposed technique is extremely effective in improving the overall performance of the *SMT* tool.

The paper is organized as follows. In §2 we introduce the necessary background information on *SMT*, $SMT(\mathcal{T}_1 \cup \mathcal{T}_2)$, DTC and Ackermann's expansion. In §3 we present the main intuitions and ideas underlying our work. In §4 we present our new preprocessor. In §5 we present the experimental evaluation of our work. In §6 we conclude and briefly present potential future developments.

2   Background

2.1   Satisfiability Modulo Theory

Fig. 1 presents Bool+$\mathcal{T}$, (a much simplified version of) a standard schema of a decision procedure for $SMT(\mathcal{T})$. The function $Atoms(\varphi)$ takes a ground formula φ and returns the set of atoms which occur in φ. We use the notation φ^p to denote the *propositional abstraction* of φ, which is formed by the function $\mathcal{T}2\mathcal{B}$ that maps propositional variables to themselves, ground atoms into fresh propositional variables, and is homomorphic w.r.t. boolean operators and set inclusion. The function $\mathcal{B}2\mathcal{T}$ is the inverse of $\mathcal{T}2\mathcal{B}$. We use μ^p to denote a propositional assignment, i.e. a conjunction (a set) of propositional literals. (If $\mathcal{T}2\mathcal{B}(\mu) \models \mathcal{T}2\mathcal{B}(\varphi)$, then we say that μ *propositionally satisfies* φ.)

```
function Bool+T (φ: quantifier-free formula)
1       A^p ⟵ T2B(Atoms(φ))
2       φ^p ⟵ T2B(φ)
3       while Bool-satisfiable(φ^p) do
4           μ^p ⟵ pick_total_assign(A^p, φ^p)
5           (ρ, π) ⟵ T − satisfiable(B2T(μ^p))
6           if ρ = sat then return sat
7           φ^p ⟵ φ^p ∧ ¬T2B(π)
8       end while
9       return unsat
end function
```

Fig. 1. A simplified view of enumeration-based T-satisfiability procedure: Bool+T

The idea underlying the algorithm is that the truth assignments for the propositional abstraction of φ are enumerated and checked for satisfiability in T. The procedure either returns sat if one such model is found, or returns unsat otherwise. The function *pick_total_assign* returns a total assignment to the propositional variables in $φ^p$, that is, it assigns a truth value to all variables in A^p. The function T-satisfiable($μ$) detects if the set of conjuncts $μ$ is T-satisfiable: if so, it returns (sat, $\emptyset$); otherwise, it returns (unsat, $π$), where $π ⊆ μ$ is a T-unsatisfiable set, called a *theory conflict set*. We call the negation of a conflict set, a *conflict clause*.

The algorithm is a coarse abstraction of the ones underlying most *SMT* tools (including, e.g., TSAT++, MATHSAT, DLSAT, DPLL(T) /BarceLogic, CVCLITE, and ICS /YICES).

In practice, the enumeration is carried out by means of efficient implementations of the DPLL algorithm [16], where a *partial assignment* $μ^p$ is built incrementally, and *unit propagation* is used extensively to perform all the assignments which derive deterministically from the current $μ^p$. Conflict sets, generated because either the current $μ^p$ falsifies the formula or because T-satisfiable($B2T(μ^p)$) fails, are used to prune the search tree and to backtrack as high as possible (*backjumping*), and *learned* as conflict clauses to avoid generating the same conflicts in future branches. Another important improvement is *early pruning*: intermediate assignments are checked for T-satisfiability and, if not T-satisfiable, then are pruned (since no refinement can be T-satisfiable); finally, *theory deduction* can be used to reduce the search space by explicitly returning truth values for unassigned literals, as well as constructing/learning implications. The interested reader is pointed to [5,8,3,12,11] for details and further references.

2.2 *SMT*($T_1 ∪ T_2$) **Via Theory Combination**

In many practical applications of *SMT*(T), the background theory is a combination of two (or more) theories T_1 and T_2. Most approaches to *SMT*($T_1 ∪ T_2$) rely on the adaptation of the Bool+T schema, by instantiating T-satisfiable with some decision procedure for the satisfiability of $T_1 ∪ T_2$, typically based on an integration schema like Nelson-Oppen (NO) [13] (or its variant due to Shostak [15]), or on the more recent Delayed Theory Combination (DTC) schema [6,7].

function DTC (φ_i: *quantifier-free formula*)

1      $\varphi \longleftarrow purify(\varphi_i)$

2      $\mathcal{A}^p \longleftarrow \mathcal{T}2\mathcal{B}(Atoms(\varphi) \cup interface\_equalities(\varphi))$

3      $\varphi^p \longleftarrow \mathcal{T}2\mathcal{B}(\varphi)$

4   **while** Bool-*satisfiable* (φ^p) **do**

5          $\mu_1^p \wedge \mu_2^p \wedge \mu_e^p = \mu^p \longleftarrow pick\_total\_assign(\mathcal{A}^p, \varphi^p)$

6          $(\rho_1, \pi_1) \longleftarrow \mathcal{T}_1\text{-}satisfiable\ (\mathcal{B}2\mathcal{T}(\mu_1^p \wedge \mu_e^p))$

7          $(\rho_2, \pi_2) \longleftarrow \mathcal{T}_2\text{-}satisfiable\ (\mathcal{B}2\mathcal{T}(\mu_2^p \wedge \mu_e^p))$

8   **if** ($\rho_1 = $ sat $\wedge \rho_2 = $ sat) **then return** sat **else**

9   **if** $\rho_1 = $ unsat **then** $\varphi^p \longleftarrow \varphi^p \wedge \neg \mathcal{T}2\mathcal{B}(\pi_1)$

10   **if** $\rho_2 = $ unsat **then** $\varphi^p \longleftarrow \varphi^p \wedge \neg \mathcal{T}2\mathcal{B}(\pi_2)$

11   **end while**

12   **return** unsat

end function

Fig. 2. A simplified view of the DTC procedure for $SMT(\mathcal{T}_1 \cup \mathcal{T}_2)$

Both the NO and DTC schemata work only for combinations of *stably-infinite* and *signature-disjoint* theories $\mathcal{T}_i$ with equality (we recall that $\mathcal{T}_i$ is stably-infinite iff every quantifier-free $\mathcal{T}_i$-satisfiable formula is satisfiable in an infinite model of $\mathcal{T}_i$). Moreover, they require the input formula to be *pure*: a formula φ is pure iff every atom ψ in φ is *i-pure* for some $i \in \{1,2\}$, that is ψ contains only $=$, variables and symbols from the signature of $\mathcal{T}_i$. Every non-pure $\mathcal{T}_1 \cup \mathcal{T}_2$ formula φ can be converted into an equivalently satisfiable pure formula φ' by recursively labeling terms t with fresh variables v_t, and by conjoining the definition atom $(v_t = t)$ to the formula. E.g.:

$$(f(x+3y) = g(2x-y)) \Rightarrow (f(v_{x+3y}) = g(v_{2x-y})) \wedge (v_{x+3y} = x+3y) \wedge (v_{2x-y} = 2x-y).$$

This process is called *purification*, and is linear in the size of the input formula.

In a pure formula φ, an *interface variable* is a variable appearing in both 1-pure and 2-pure atoms. An *interface equality* is an equality between two interface variables.

In the NO schema, the two decision procedures for $\mathcal{T}_1$ and $\mathcal{T}_2$ ($\mathcal{T}_i$-solvers) cooperate by exchanging (disjunctions of) interface equalities (e_{ij}'s). In the DTC schema, each of the two $\mathcal{T}_i$-solvers works in isolation, without direct exchange of information. Their mutual consistency is ensured by augmenting the input problem with all interface equalities e_{ij}, even if these do not occur in the original problem. The enumeration of assignments includes not only the atoms in the formula, but also the interface equalities e_{ij}. Both theory solvers receive, from the boolean level, the same truth assignment μ_e for e_{ij}: under such conditions, the two "partial" models found by each decision procedure can be merged into a model for the input formula.

A simplified view of the DTC algorithm is presented in Fig. 2. Initially (lines 1–3), the formula is purified, the e_{ij}'s which do not occur in the purified formula are created and added to the set of propositional symbols $\mathcal{A}^p$, and the propositional abstraction φ^p of φ is created. Then, the main loop is entered (lines 4–11): while φ^p is propositionally satisfiable (line 4), a satisfying truth assignment μ^p is selected (line 5). Truth values are associated not only to atoms in φ, but also to the e_{ij} atoms, even though they do not occur in φ. μ^p is then (implicitly) separated into $\mu_1^p \wedge \mu_e^p \wedge \mu_2^p$, where $\mathcal{B}2\mathcal{T}(\mu_i^p)$ is a set of i-pure literals and $\mathcal{B}2\mathcal{T}(\mu_e^p)$ is a set of e_{ij}-literals. The relevant part of μ^p are checked for consistency against each theory (lines 6–7); $\mathcal{T}_i$-satisfiable(μ) returns a pair (ρ_i, π_i), where ρ_i is unsat iff μ is unsatisfiable in $\mathcal{T}_i$, and sat otherwise. If both calls to $\mathcal{T}_i$-satisfiable return sat, then the formula is satisfiable. Otherwise, when ρ_i is unsat, then π_i is a theory conflict set, i.e. $\pi_i \subseteq \mu$ and π_i is $\mathcal{T}_i$-unsatisfiable. Then, φ^p is strengthened to exclude truth assignments which may fail in the same way (line 9–10), and the loop is resumed. Unsatisfiability is returned (line 12) when the loop is exited without having found a model.

In practical implementations of DTC, as before, the enumeration is carried out by means of efficient implementations of the DPLL engine, where a *partial assignment* μ^p is built incrementally, exploiting unit-propagation, backjumping and learning, early pruning and theory deduction. Moreover, if one or both $\mathcal{T}_i$-*satisfiable* have the capability of deducing (disjunctions of) interface equalities which derive from $\mathcal{T}_i$ from a partial assignment μ, [1] then such a deduction is exploited to prune the boolean search on the interface equalities (e_{ij}-*deduction*). To this extent, DTC extends the NO schema, in the sense that it allows for using $\mathcal{T}_i$-*satisfiable* procedures with every deduction capability, trading e_{ij}-deduction power with boolean search, and allows for emulating the NO schema [9]. For the sake of simplicity, in this paper we do not consider e_{ij}-deduction for DTC. We refer the reader to [7,9] for a more detailed discussion.

Example 1. Let φ be the following $\mathcal{EUF} \cup \mathcal{LA}(\mathbb{Z})$-pure formula

$$
\begin{aligned}
\varphi \;\equiv\; & w = h(x) \wedge a = h(y) \wedge c = f(z) \wedge d = f(b) \wedge f(c) = f(b) \wedge \\
& w = f(d) \wedge \neg(c = d) \wedge x \geq y \wedge x \leq y \wedge z = w - a \wedge b = 0.
\end{aligned}
\tag{1}
$$

x, y, z, w, a, b are the interface variables, so that there are 15 interface equalities: $z = b, w = b, a = b, x = b, y = b, z = w, z = a, x = z, y = z, w = a, x = w, y = w, x = a, y = a, x = y$.

The DPLL solver generates first the assignment $\mu := \mu_{\mathcal{EUF}} \cup \mu_{\mathcal{LA}(\mathbb{Z})}$ satisfying φ, s.t.
$\mu_{\mathcal{EUF}} := \{w = h(x), a = h(y), c = f(z), d = f(b), f(c) = f(b), w = f(d), \neg(c = d)\}$,
$\mu_{\mathcal{LA}(\mathbb{Z})} := \{x \geq y, x \leq y, z = w - a, b = 0\}$.

Then it tries to extend it with a total truth assignment μ_e to the interface equalities such that $\mu_{\mathcal{EUF}} \cup \mu_e$ and $\mu_{\mathcal{LA}(\mathbb{Z})} \cup \mu_e$ are consistent in $\mathcal{EUF}$ and $\mathcal{LA}(\mathbb{Z})$ respectively. This requires some search on the 15 interface equalities.

E.g, if the DPLL engine is smart or lucky enough to select first $x = y$, $w = a$, $z = b$, then we have
$\mu_{\mathcal{LA}(\mathbb{Z})} \cup \{\neg(x = y)\} \models_{\mathcal{LA}(\mathbb{Z})} \bot$, so that $x = y$ is added to μ,
$\mu_{\mathcal{EUF}} \cup \{x = y, \neg(w = a)\} \models_{\mathcal{EUF}} \bot$, so that $w = a$ is added to μ,
$\mu_{\mathcal{LA}(\mathbb{Z})} \cup \{x = y, w = a, \neg(z = b)\} \models_{\mathcal{LA}(\mathbb{Z})} \bot$, so that $z = b$ is added to μ,
$\mu_{\mathcal{EUF}} \cup \{x = y, w = a, z = b\} \models_{\mathcal{EUF}} \bot$, hence φ is $\mathcal{EUF} \cup \mathcal{LA}(\mathbb{Z})$-inconsistent. $\qquad\square$

Notice that on a single-theory $SMT(\mathcal{T})$ problem, DTC behaves as a standard SMT tool, because there are no interface equalities.

---

[1] In the NO schema this capability is strictly required for both $\mathcal{T}_i$-*satisfiable*'s [13].

2.3 $SMT(\mathcal{EUF} \cup \mathcal{T})$ **Via Ackermann's Expansion**

When one of the theories $\mathcal{T}_i$ is $\mathcal{EUF}$, another possible approach to the $SMT(\mathcal{T}_1 \cup \mathcal{T}_2)$ problem is to eliminate uninterpreted function symbols by means of Ackermann's expansion [1] so to obtain an $SMT(\mathcal{T})$ problem with only one theory. The method works by replacing every function application occurring in the input formula φ with a fresh variable and then adding to φ all the needed functional consistency constraints. The new formula φ' obtained is equisatisfiable with φ, and contains no uninterpreted function symbols. First, each distinct function application $f(x_1, \ldots, x_n)$ is replaced by a fresh variable $v_{f(x_1, \ldots, x_n)}$. Then, for every pair of distinct applications of the same function, $f(x_1, \ldots, x_n)$ and $f(y_1, \ldots, y_n)$, a constraint

$$(\bigwedge_{i=1}^{arity(f)} ack(x_i) = ack(y_i)) \rightarrow v_{f(x_1, \ldots, x_n)} = v_{f(y_1, \ldots, y_n)}, \tag{2}$$

is added, where ack is a function that maps each function application $g(z_1, \ldots, z_n)$ into the corresponding variable $v_{g(z_1, \ldots, z_n)}$, each variable into itself and is homomorphic wrt. the interpreted symbols. The atom $ack(x_i) = ack(y_i)$ is not added if the two sides of the equality are syntactically identical.

Example 2. Let φ be the pure formula (1) of Example 1. Then, replacing every function application with a fresh variable, and adding all the functional consistency constraints, we obtain the formula

$$
\begin{aligned}
\varphi_{ACK} \equiv \ & w = v_{h(x)} \wedge a = v_{h(y)} \wedge c = v_{f(z)} \wedge d = v_{f(b)} \wedge v_{f(c)} = v_{f(b)} \wedge \\
& w = v_{f(d)} \wedge \neg(c = d) \wedge x \geq y \wedge x \leq y \wedge z = w - a \wedge b = 0 \wedge \\
& (x = y \rightarrow v_{h(x)} = v_{h(y)}) \wedge (z = b \rightarrow v_{f(z)} = v_{f(b)}) \wedge \\
& (z = c \rightarrow v_{f(z)} = v_{f(c)}) \wedge (z = d \rightarrow v_{f(z)} = v_{f(d)}) \wedge \\
& (c = b \rightarrow v_{f(c)} = v_{f(b)}) \wedge (c = d \rightarrow v_{f(c)} = v_{f(d)}) \wedge \\
& (b = d \rightarrow v_{f(b)} = v_{f(d)}).
\end{aligned}
\tag{3}
$$

The DPLL solver first deterministically selects the truth assignment
$$\mu_{LA(\mathbb{Z})} := \{ \ w = v_{h(x)}, a = v_{h(y)}, c = v_{f(z)}, d = v_{f(b)}, v_{f(c)} = v_{f(b)}, w = v_{f(d)}, \\ \neg(c = d), x \geq y, x \leq y, z = w - a, b = 0 \},$$
which is consistent in $LA(\mathbb{Z})$. Then, it performs some search on the remaining 12 equalities. [2]

E.g., if it is smart or lucky enough to select first $x = y, z = b$, then we have:
$\mu_{LA(\mathbb{Z})} \cup \{\neg(x = y)\} \models_{LA(\mathbb{Z})} \bot$, so that $x = y$ is added to μ,
$\mu_{LA(\mathbb{Z})} \cup \{x = y, v_{h(x)} = v_{h(y)}, \neg(z = b)\} \models_{LA(\mathbb{Z})} \bot$, so that $z = b$ is added to μ,
$\mu_{LA(\mathbb{Z})} \cup \{x = y, v_{h(x)} = v_{h(y)}, z = b, v_{f(z)} = v_{f(b)}\} \models_{LA(\mathbb{Z})} \bot$, hence φ is $\mathcal{EUF} \cup LA(\mathbb{Z})$-inconsistent. □

---

[2] The remaining equalities are only 12 because $v_{f(c)} = v_{f(b)}$ causes the removal of the 5th implication.

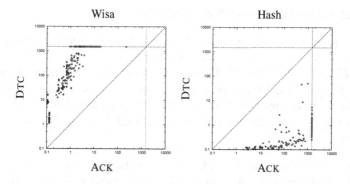

Fig. 3. Execution time ratio (in logarithmic scale) for DTC and ACK on the benchmarks Wisa and Hash, using MATHSAT. A dot above the diagonal line means better performance of ACK and vice versa. The horizontal and vertical dashed lines represent time-out.

Notice that, for simplicity, in Example 1 we have considered a pure formula φ, which might be the result of purifying some non-pure formula φ'. If so, applying Ackermann expansion directly to φ' might result into a more compact formula than (3).

Henceforth, we call respectively *Ackermann constraints* or *Ackermann implications* the functional consistency constraints added by Ackermann expansion, *Ackermann equalities* the equalities occurring in the Ackermann constraints, and *Ackermann variables* the variables occurring in the Ackermann equalities.

3 To Ackermann-ize or Not to Ackermann-ize?

We start from a simple empirical observation: neither DTC or ACK always prevails in the task of solving $SMT(\mathcal{EUF} \cup \mathcal{T})$ problems, and the performance gaps between the two approaches may be dramatic, in either direction. As an example, Figure 3 shows the execution times of the two approaches on two different groups of benchmarks, for the MATHSAT [8] solver (both tests will be described in §5). For the Wisa benchmarks (left), ACK is up to 1000 times faster than DTC (or even more, considering also the timed-out examples), whilst for the Hash benchmarks (right) the converse is true.

By tracing the behavior of MATHSAT on these tests, we notice that the performance gaps mirror the different amount of boolean search performed by the two techniques. From which we argue that one of the main reasons of such big performance gaps is the different size of the boolean search space that each technique has to explore in order to decide the satisfiability of its input.

Thus, we look to both techniques from the perspective of the boolean search only. Both DTC and ACK require the SAT solver to perform an extra boolean search on equalities which did not occur in the original formula (i.e., on the interface equalities and on the Ackermann equalities respectively). Thus the enlargement of the boolean search space with the two techniques depends directly on the number of these new equalities introduced.

3.1   Enlargement of the Search Space with DTC

In the DTC approach it may be necessary to assign a truth value to up to all the interface equalities. If φ is a pure $\mathcal{E}\mathcal{U}\mathcal{F} \cup \mathcal{T}$ formula, then the number of interface equalities is given by $|\mathcal{V}| \cdot (|\mathcal{V}| - 1)/2$, where $|\mathcal{V}|$ is the number of interface variables in φ. (Notice that this is an upper bound for the number of the *new* equalities introduced, since some of them might already appear in φ.) Thus, with DTC, the number of boolean atoms the SAT solver may have to explore is enlarged by a factor that is quadratic in the number of the interface variables.

Example 3. The formula φ of Example 1 has 6 interface variables, so that the number of atoms the SAT solver may have to explore is increased by $(6 \cdot 5)/2 = 15$ interface equalities, all of which are new.   □

Notice that, in general, the input problem φ must be purified to be handled by DTC. The purification process adds a number of new variables and atoms that is linear in the size of φ. However, this does not cause an enlargement of the boolean search space, because all the atoms added are definitions of terms like $(v_t = t)$ and occur as unit clauses in the resulting formula, so that they are assigned a priori and deterministically to true by the SAT solver.

3.2   Enlargement of the Search Space with ACK

In the ACK approach, the increase in the boolean search space depends on the number of (new) equalities in the Ackermann constraints introduced.

Let $\mathcal{F}$ be the set of (distinct) function symbols occurring in φ, and let O_f be the set of all (distinct) applications of the function f in the input formula φ. Then the number of new Ackermann equalities introduced is less than or equal to

$$\sum_{f \in \mathcal{F}} \frac{|O_f| \cdot (|O_f| - 1)}{2} \cdot (arity(f) + 1). \tag{4}$$

In fact, for each $f \in \mathcal{F}$ and for each of the $(|O_f| \cdot (|O_f| - 1))/2$ pairs of distinct occurrences of f, Equation (2) causes the introduction of up to $(arity(f) + 1)$ new Ackermann equalities. (As with DTC, this is an upper bound, both because some of the equalities in one constraint could already occur in the formula or in other constraints, and because identities like $x = x$ are dropped by construction.)

Thus, with ACK, the number of boolean atoms the SAT solver may have to explore is enlarged by a factor that is quadratic in the number of occurrences of each function symbol, and linear in the number of distinct function symbols and in their arity.

Example 4. In the formula φ (1) of Example 1, $O_h = 1$ and $O_f = 4$. Thus the Ackermann constraints introduced in the formula φ_{ACK} (3) of Example 2 contain $(2 \cdot 1)/2 \cdot (1+1) + (4 \cdot 3)/2 \cdot (1+1) = 14$ equalities. Since $v_{f(c)} = v_{f(b)}$ is not new, the new equalities are 13. Notice that also $c = b$ does not really increase the boolean search space, because the 5th implication is immediately removed by the DPLL solver (Footnote 2).   □

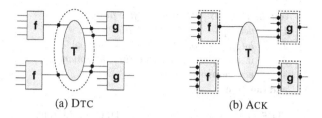

(a) DTC   (b) ACK

Fig. 4. Schemas of the frontier between $\mathcal{EUF}$ and $\mathcal{T}$ in the DTC and ACK approaches

3.3   Intuition: the "frontier" Between $\mathcal{EUF}$ and $\mathcal{T}$ in DTC and ACK

Both DTC and ACK introduce an enlargement of the search space of the input problem φ. Intuitively, we can think of this extra boolean search as the *cost* associated to each of the two approaches for handling the interaction between the two theories. We notice that the set of new equivalences introduced by either approach corresponds to a distinct notion of "frontier" between $\mathcal{EUF}$ and $\mathcal{T}$ in the two approaches.

In DTC, the frontier is given by the interface variables (see Figure 4.a). As the cost of DTC depends quadratically on the size of the frontier, DTC is expected to perform better for those examples where the two theories are loosely coupled, and worse when there is a strong connection between them.

With ACK, the frontier between the two theories is potentially much larger, because it consists of the inputs and outputs of all (distinct) function applications (i.e, the Ackermann variables), including those which do not interact with terms of the theory $\mathcal{T}$ (see Figure 4.b). However, in this case the cost is not quadratic in the number of variables in the frontier; rather, it depends on the number of different functions and of distinct occurrences of each function invocation (4). Thus ACK is expected to perform better when the number of the distinct function invocations for the same function is low.

4   Cost-Driven Ackermann-ization

When we want to check the satisfiability of an $SMT(\mathcal{EUF} \cup \mathcal{T})$ formula φ, no matter which of the two approaches (DTC or ACK) we use, we must pay a price in terms of enlargement of the boolean search space. We believe that this cost is one of the main factors which influence the performance of the two methods. Thus, being able to estimate this cost a priori can drive the choice of which technique to apply.

4.1   A Global-Decision Approach: DECIDE

Our first, basic idea is that of trying to estimate a priori the difference of costs of applying ACK or DTC, and to simply select the technique that costs less. We call this first idea "a global-decision approach" because here the decision involves all function symbols altogether.

The resulting algorithm DECIDE is outlined in Figure 5. Let φ be a (possibly non-pure) $SMT(\mathcal{EUF} \cup \mathcal{T})$ formula. The function *countAckEqualities* returns the number of new Ackermann equalities added by the Ackermann's expansion of φ. The function

function DECIDE (φ: *quantifier-free formula*)
1   *ack_eq* ⟵ *countAckEqualities*(φ)
2   *int_eq* ⟵ *countInterfaceEqualities*(φ)
3   **if** *ack_eq* < *int_eq* **then return** *ackermanize*(φ)
4   **else return** φ
end function

Fig. 5. High-level description of the DECIDE algorithm

countInterfaceEqualities returns the number of new interface equalities in (the formula resulting from purifying) φ. Notice that both functions return the *exact* number of equalities introduced, avoiding counting repeated equalities, identities, etc. Both functions are straightforward to implement, and their complexity is linear in the size of φ.

DECIDE works as a preprocessor for an *SMT* solver for $SMT(\mathcal{EUF} \cup \mathcal{T})$ which uses DTC: the algorithm either returns an Ackermann-ized version of the input φ (if ACK costs less), or leaves the input untouched. As noticed in §2, in the first case DTC behaves as a standard single-theory *SMT* tool, so that the two options correspond to ACK and DTC respectively.

Example 5. Consider again the formulas (1) and (3) of Examples 1 and 2 respectively. DTC would introduce 15 new interface equalities, whilst ACK would introduce 13 new Ackermann equalities. Therefore DECIDE in this case would choose ACK.   □

4.2 A Local-Decision Approach: PARTIAL

The idea just described can be generalized in the following way. From §3 we know that the cost of DTC depends quadratically on the global number of interface variables, whilst the cost of ACK, *for each function symbol f*, depends quadratically on the number of the distinct occurrences of f and linearly on its arity. Thus, we can decide to apply Ackermann's expansions only to *subsets* of the function symbols, according to their relative costs. We call this second idea "a local-decision approach" because here the decision involves subsets of function symbols.

Let f be a function in φ with very few occurrences but many arguments shared between $\mathcal{EUF}$ and $\mathcal{T}$. Then f causes a low increase of the ACK costs and a big increase of the DTC costs, because Ackermann's expansion will introduce few constraints, whilst the high number of interface variables would make DTC generate many new equalities. On the other hand, a function g with many occurrences but few or no arguments shared among the theories is going to cost much less for DTC than for ACK for the very same reason. Thus, if we consider a formula which contains both f and g, then applying Ackermann's expansion only *partially*, so that to remove only f, and solving the resulting problem with DTC, is going to cost less than pure ACK or pure DTC.

Example 6. Consider again the formula (1) of Example 1. If we expand only h, we get the following formula:

$$\varphi' \equiv w = v_{h(x)} \wedge c = f(z) \wedge d = f(b) \wedge f(c) = f(b) \wedge w = f(d) \wedge \neg(c = d) \wedge$$
$$x \geq y \wedge x \leq y \wedge z = w - v_{h(y)} \wedge b = 0 \wedge x = y \rightarrow v_{h(x)} = v_{h(y)}, \tag{5}$$

function PARTIAL (φ: *quantifier-free formula*)
1 $\mathcal{A} \longleftarrow \emptyset$
2 $\psi \longleftarrow purify(\varphi)$
3 **do**
4    $\mathcal{B} \longleftarrow selectFunctionsToAckermanize(\psi)$
5    $\psi \longleftarrow ackermanizeFunctions(\psi, \mathcal{B})$
6    $\mathcal{A} \longleftarrow \mathcal{A} \cup \mathcal{B}$
7 **while** $\mathcal{B} \neq \emptyset$
8 $\varphi' \longleftarrow ackermanizeFunctions(\varphi, \mathcal{A})$
9 **return** φ'
end function

Fig. 6. High-level description of the PARTIAL algorithm

which has only 3 interface variables (z, b and w). Using DTC on φ' would then enlarge the search space by 3 interface equalities. Therefore, the mixed approach would cost in total 5 new equalities (2 for the Ackermann constraints and 3 for the interface equalities), which is less than with ACK (13) and DTC (15).   ☐

The ideal solution would be to develop an algorithm that applies Ackermann's expansion to the subset of the function symbols corresponding to a global minimum in the number of new equalities to add. Unfortunately, finding such a global optimal solution seems to be very expensive. Intuitively, this is because both the cost and the benefit of applying Ackermann's expansion to each function symbol —in terms of more Ackermann equalities and less interface equalities to add respectively— depend on the previous eliminations of some other functions. (For example, as a consequence of the elimination of a function f, it may become convenient to eliminate also g because they had many pairs of corresponding arguments in common.) Thus, finding the global optimum may require exploring up to all the $2^{|\mathcal{F}|}$ possible subsets of function symbols.

For this reason, we have conceived instead the algorithm PARTIAL (outlined in Figure 6) which finds a local optimum. PARTIAL is a greedy algorithm that starts from the purified formula and that finds at each step a set of function symbols $\mathcal{B}$ whose removal causes a reduction in the number of equivalences to add. When this set is empty, a local minimum has been reached, and the algorithm terminates. Then the Ackermann's expansion on the set of selected functions $\mathcal{A}$ is performed on the original input formula φ, and the result is returned.

The core of PARTIAL is the function *selectFunctionsToAckermanize*, which returns the set of functions to remove in order to reduce the number of new equalities to add, according to the following heuristic. The function symbols occurring in φ are divided into (possibly overlapping) subgroups G_v's, one for every interface variable v in φ, G_v consisting of the set of all the function symbols that cause v to be an interface variable. Then the group G_v is returned which causes the maximum reduction gain$_{G_v}$ in terms of equivalences to add. (That is, gain$_{G_v}$ is defined as the difference between the number of interface equalities to remove and the number of equalities in the functional consistency constraints to add, if all the functions in the group were removed with

Ackermann's expansion.) If for no group G_v the value gain_{G_v} is positive, then the empty set is returned. [3]

Example 7. Consider the pure formula (1) used in all the previous examples. When invoked for the first time, *selectFunctionsToAckermanize* constructs for the set of functions $\{f, h\}$ in (1) six groups, one for each interface variable:

$$G_x = G_y = G_a = \{h\} \qquad\qquad G_w = G_z = G_b = \{f\}.$$

Then, for each of them, the associated gain (i.e. the difference between the number of interface equalities to remove and the number of equalities to add for the functional consistency constraints) is computed:

$$\text{gain}_{G_x} = \text{gain}_{G_y} = \text{gain}_{G_a} = 12 - 2 = 10, \ \text{gain}_{G_w} = \text{gain}_{G_z} = \text{gain}_{G_b} = 12 - 11 = 1$$

because removing h makes x, y and a loose the status of interface variables, whilst removing f the same happens for w, z and b. Thus *selectFunctionsToAckermanize* selects $\{h\}$ only, causing the generation of the formula (5) of Example 6. At the next iteration of the main loop of PARTIAL, the only function symbol is f, which is not removed since all gain_{G_v}'s are negative.   □

5 Empirical Evaluation

We implemented both DECIDE and PARTIAL in a preprocessor program, written in C++. It handles $SMT(\mathcal{EUF} \cup \mathcal{LA})$ problems, and has four different operational modes:

transparent (DTC), which simply reads a problem from its standard input and outputs it to its standard output without doing anything;
ackermanize, which removes every uninterpreted function symbol;
decide, which applies the DECIDE algorithm; and
partial, which applies the PARTIAL algorithm to remove a subset of the uninterpreted function symbols.

We tested our preprocessor with the MATHSAT [8] solver, which handles $SMT(\mathcal{EUF} \cup \mathcal{LA})$ problems with DTC. We used different benchmarks, coming from different domains:

QF_UFIDL comes from the SMT-LIB [14], and is made of formulas with $\mathcal{EUF}$ and integer difference logic. It is a superset of the QF_UFIDL set used in the SMT-COMP'05 competition [4];
Wisa are software verification benchmarks from the Wisconsin Safety Analyzer, created with a slightly modified version of the generator available at http://www.cs.wisc.edu/wisa/papers/icse05/wisa-benchmarks.html;

---

[3] As a direct consequence of how the groups are built, removing the functions in a group removes at least one interface variable from $\mathcal{V}$, so that at least $|\mathcal{V}| - 1$ interface equalities are removed. It may be the case that more than one interface variable is removed: e.g., if $G_x \subseteq G_y$, then removing all the function symbols in G_y causes the removal of both x and y from $\mathcal{V}$.

EufLaArithmetic are simulations of arithmetic operations (succ, pred, sum) modulo N, using $\mathcal{EUF}$ and $\mathcal{LA}(\mathbb{Z})$. This and the following groups of benchmarks were introduced in [7];

Hash are problems over hash tables, modeled with a combination of $\mathcal{EUF}$ and $\mathcal{LA}(\mathbb{Z})$;

RandomCoupled are randomly generated $SMT(\mathcal{EUF} \cup \mathcal{LA}(\mathbb{Q}))$ problems, with a propositional 3-CNF structure. In this group, there is a high coupling between the two theories, that is there is a high probability that for instance an argument of a function is a $\mathcal{LA}(\mathbb{Q})$ term;

RandomDecoupled are tests generated in the same way as the previous group, but where the coupling between $\mathcal{EUF}$ and $\mathcal{LA}(\mathbb{Q})$ is low.

The tests were run on a machine with an Intel Xeon 3GHz processor running Linux. The memory limit was set to 1GB, and the time limit to 1000 sec.

Figure 7 shows the results, both for the individual suites singularly and for the union of all the suites. A point in $\langle X, Y \rangle$ states that X problems have been solved each in less than or equal to Y seconds. (Notice the logarithmic scale of the Y axis.) A higher number of tests solved means better performance. When this number is the same, the lowest line is the best. All the plots include the cost of preprocessing, which however is negligible.

The following table summarizes the total results. The rows are sorted from the worst to the best, while the columns show details of the performances in terms of total number of tests solved, total running time, and total time to solve a fixed amount N of tests, for various values of N.

	Number of tests solved	Total time (for all tests)	Total time for solving N tests					
			300	600	1200	1384	1479	1513
transparent (DTC)	1384	34500	25.9	100.8	1804	34500	-	-
ackermanize	1479	41431	33.0	149.3	1402	5436	41431	-
decide	1513	12891	22.1	82.4	629	1646	3577	12891
partial	1516	13393	21.1	75.9	602	1495	3450	11335

We can see from both Figure 7 and the above table that different suites show very different performance gaps between **transparent** (DTC) and **ackermanize** (ACK), as observed in §2, and that both **decide** (DECIDE) and **partial** (PARTIAL) always behave quite similarly to the best of the two. (E.g., looking at the data, we noticed that **decide** chooses the most efficient option nearly always, and that the few samples for which it does not are such that the performance gaps between ACK and DTC are minor.)

The overall result shows that both DECIDE and PARTIAL are globally much more efficient than both ACK and DTC, with PARTIAL being the best technique. The reason why the performances of two techniques are so similar is that, on these benchmarks, it turns out that PARTIAL either removes all or most of the functions or it removes none, thus behaving very similarly to DECIDE.

6   Conclusions

In this paper we have focused on the $SMT(\mathcal{EUF} \cup \mathcal{T})$ problem. We have proposed a simple technique for estimating a priori the costs and benefits, in terms of the size of

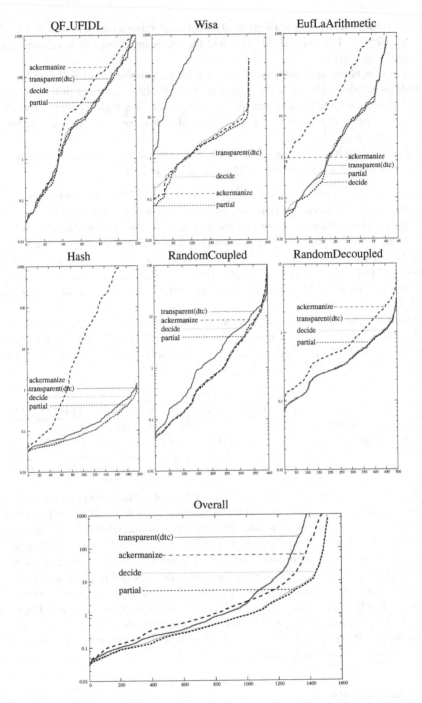

Fig. 7. Results of the benchmarks for the MATHSAT solver. For each technique, the X axis represents the number of tests solved and the Y axis the time required (in log scale). The labels in the plots are sorted according to performance: from the worst to the best.

the search space of an *SMT* tool, of applying Ackermann's expansion to all or part of the function symbols; we have implemented a preprocessor which analyzes the input formula, decides autonomously which functions to expand, performs such expansions and gives the resulting formula as input to an *SMT* tool; we have performed a thorough experimental analysis with MATHSAT on $SMT(\mathcal{EUF} \cup \mathcal{DL})$, $SMT(\mathcal{EUF} \cup \mathcal{LA}(\mathbb{Q}))$ and $SMT(\mathcal{EUF} \cup \mathcal{LA}(\mathbb{Z}))$, showing that the proposed technique is extremely effective in improving the overall performance of the *SMT* tool.

As future developments, we plan to experiment the effectiveness of our techniques also with other *SMT* tools (e.g., CVCLITE [3], ICS /YICES [11]), and with other theories (e.g., $\mathcal{EUF}$ with the theory of bit-vectors $\mathcal{BV}$).

References

1. W. Ackermann. Solvable Cases of the Decision Problem. North Holland Pub. Co., 1954.
2. A. Armando, C. Castellini, E. Giunchiglia, and M. Maratea. A SAT-based Decision Procedure for the Boolean Combination of Difference Constraints. In *Proc. SAT'04*, 2004.
3. C.L. Barrett and S. Berezin. CVC Lite: A New Implementation of the Cooperating Validity Checker. In *Proc. CAV'04*, volume 3114 of *LNCS*. Springer, 2004.
4. C. Barrett, L. de Moura, and A. Stump. SMT-COMP: Satisfiability Modulo Theories Competition. In *Proc. CAV'05*, volume 3576 of *LNCS*. Springer, 2005.
5. M. Bozzano, R. Bruttomesso, A. Cimatti, T. Junttila, P. van Rossum, S. Schulz, and R. Sebastiani. An incremental and Layered Procedure for the Satisfiability of Linear Arithmetic Logic. In *Proc. TACAS'05*, volume 3440 of *LNCS*. Springer, 2005.
6. M. Bozzano, R. Bruttomesso, A. Cimatti, T. Junttila, P. van Rossum, S. Ranise, and R. Sebastiani. Efficient Satisfiability Modulo Theories via Delayed Theory Combination. In *Proc. Int. Conf. on Computer-Aided Verification, CAV 2005.*, volume 3576 of *LNCS*. Springer, 2005.
7. M. Bozzano, R. Bruttomesso, A. Cimatti, T. Junttila, P. van Rossum, S. Ranise, and R. Sebastiani. Efficient Theory Combination via Boolean Search. *Information and Computation*, 2005. To appear.
8. M. Bozzano, R. Bruttomesso, A. Cimatti, T. Junttila, P. van Rossum, S. Schulz, and R. Sebastiani. MathSAT: A Tight Integration of SAT and Mathematical Decision Procedure. *Journal of Automated Reasoning*, 2005. to appear.
9. R. Bruttomesso, A. Cimatti, A. Franzén, A. Griggio, and R. Sebastiani. Delayed Theory Combination vs. Nelson-Oppen for Satisfiability Modulo Theories: a Comparative Analysis. In *Proc. LPAR'06*, 2006.
10. S. Cotton, E. Asarin, O. Maler, and P. Niebert. Some Progress in Satisfiability Checking for Difference Logic. In *Proc. FORMATS-FTRTFT 2004*, 2004.
11. J.-C. Filliâtre, S. Owre, H. Rueß, and N. Shankar. ICS: Integrated Canonizer and Solver. In *Proc. CAV'01*, volume 2102 of *LNCS*, pages 246–249, 2001.
12. H. Ganzinger, G. Hagen, R. Nieuwenhuis, A. Oliveras, and C. Tinelli. DPLL(T): Fast decision procedures. In *Proc. CAV'04*, volume 3114 of *LNCS*, pages 175–188. Springer, 2004.
13. G. Nelson and D.C. Oppen. Simplification by Cooperating Decision Procedures. *ACM Trans. on Programming Languages and Systems*, 1(2):245–257, 1979.
14. S. Ranise and C. Tinelli. The SMT-LIB Standard: Version 1.1. Technical Report, 2005.
15. R.E. Shostak. Deciding Combinations of Theories. *Journal of the ACM*, 31:1–12, 1984.
16. L. Zhang and S. Malik. The quest for efficient boolean satisfiability solvers. In *Proc. CAV'02*, number 2404 in LNCS, pages 17–36. Springer, 2002.

Lemma Learning in the Model Evolution Calculus

Peter Baumgartner[1], Alexander Fuchs[2], and Cesare Tinelli[2]

[1] National ICT Australia (NICTA)
Peter.Baumgartner@nicta.com.au
[2] The University of Iowa, USA
{fuchs, tinelli}@cs.uiowa.edu

Abstract. The Model Evolution ($\mathcal{ME}$) Calculus is a proper lifting to first-order logic of the DPLL procedure, a backtracking search procedure for propositional satisfiability. Like DPLL, the ME calculus is based on the idea of incrementally building a model of the input formula by alternating constraint propagation steps with non-deterministic decision steps. One of the major conceptual improvements over basic DPLL is *lemma learning*, a mechanism for generating new formulae that prevent later in the search combinations of decision steps guaranteed to lead to failure. We introduce two lemma generation methods for $\mathcal{ME}$ proof procedures, with various degrees of power, effectiveness in reducing search, and computational overhead. Even if formally correct, each of these methods presents complications that do not exist at the propositional level but need to be addressed for learning to be effective in practice for $\mathcal{ME}$. We discuss some of these issues and present initial experimental results on the performance of an implementation of the two learning procedures within our $\mathcal{ME}$ prover *Darwin*.

1 Introduction

The Model Evolution ($\mathcal{ME}$) Calculus [5] is a proper lifting to first-order logic of the DPLL procedure, a backtracking search procedure for propositional satisfiability. Like DPLL, the calculus is based on the idea of incrementally building a model of the input formula by alternating constraint propagation steps with non-deterministic decision steps. Two of the major conceptual improvements over basic DPLL developed over the years are *backjumping*, a form of intelligent backtracking of wrong decision steps, and *lemma learning*, a mechanism for generating new formulae that prevent later in the search combinations of decision steps guaranteed to lead to failure.

Adapting backjumping techniques from the DPLL world to $\mathcal{ME}$ implementations is relatively straightforward and does lead to performance improvements, as our past experience with *Darwin*, our $\mathcal{ME}$-based theorem prover, has shown [2]. In contrast, adding learning capabilities is not immediate, first because one needs to lift properly to the first-order level both the notion of lemma and the lemma generation process itself, and second because any first-order lemma generation process adds a significant computation overhead that can offset the potential advantages of learning.

In this paper, we introduce two lemma learning procedures for $\mathcal{ME}$ with different degrees of power, effectiveness in reducing search, and computational overhead. Even if formally correct, each of these procedures presents issues and complications that do not arise at the propositional level and need to be addressed for learning to be effective

M. Hermann and A. Voronkov (Eds.): LPAR 2006, LNAI 4246, pp. 572–586, 2006.

for $\mathcal{ME}$. We mention some of these issues and then present initial experimental results on the performance of an implementation of the learning procedures within *Darwin*.

The $\mathcal{ME}$ calculus is a sequent-style calculus consisting of three basic derivation rules: Split, Assert and Close, and three more optional rules. To simplify the exposition we will consider here a restriction of the calculus to only the non-optional rules. The learning methods presented in this paper extend with minor modifications to $\mathcal{ME}$ derivations that use the optional rules as well. The derivation rules are presented in [5] and in more detail in [6]. We do not present them directly here because in this paper we focus on *proof procedures* for $\mathcal{ME}$, which are better described in terms of abstract transition systems (see Section 2). It suffices to say that Split, with two possible conclusions instead of one, is the only non-deterministic rule of the calculus, and that the calculus is proof-confluent, i.e., the rules may be applied in any order, subject to fairness conditions, without endangering completeness. Derivations in $\mathcal{ME}$ are defined as sequences of *derivation trees*, trees whose nodes are pairs of the form $\Lambda \vdash \Phi$ where Λ is a literal set and Φ a clause set. A derivation for a clause set Φ_0 starts with a single-node derivation tree containing the clause set Φ_0 and grows the tree by applying one of the rules to one of the leaves, adding to that leaf the rule's conclusions as children.

A proof procedure for $\mathcal{ME}$ in effect grows the initial derivation tree in a depth-first manner, backtracking on *closed branches*, i.e., failed branches whose leaf results from an application of Close.[1] The procedure determines that the initial clause set Φ_0 is unsatisfiable after it has determined that all possible branches are closed. Conversely, it finds a model of Φ_0 if it reaches a node that does not contain the empty clause and to which no derivation rule applies.

Like in all backtracking procedures, performance of a proof procedure for $\mathcal{ME}$ can be improved in principle by analyzing the sequence of non-deterministic choices (i.e, Split decisions) that have led to a *conflict*, a closed branch. The analysis determines which of the choices were really relevant to the conflict and saves this information so that the same choices, or *similar* choices that can also lead to a conflict, are avoided later in the search. In the next section, we present two methods for implementing this sort of *learning* process. The methods follow the footprints of popular learning methods from the DPLL literature: conflict analysis is performed by means of a guided resolution derivation that synthesizes a new clause, a *lemma*, containing the reasons for the conflict; then learning is achieved simply by adding the lemma to the clause set and using it like any other clause in constraint propagation steps during the rest of the derivation. These methods can be given a logical justification by seeing them just as another derivation rule that adds to the clause set selected logical consequences of the set. In our experiments we also tried, as a sanity check, a third and much simpler learning method based on purely propositional techniques. While this method has low overhead it is also a lot less general than the other two and did not fare well experimentally. Because of this we do not discuss it here and instead refer the reader to [3] for more details.

Related work. To our knowledge there is little work in the literature on conflict-driven lemma learning in first-order theorem proving. One of them is described in [1] and consists of the "caching" and "lemmaizing" techniques for the model elimination calculus.

---

[1] More precisely, the proof procedure performs a sort of iterative-deepening search, to avoid getting stuck in infinite branches.

Caching means to store solutions to subgoals (which are single literals) in the proof search. The idea is to look up a solution (a substitution) that solves the current subgoal, based on the solution of a previously computed solution of a compatible subgoal. This idea of replacing search by lookup is thus conceptually related to lemma learning as we consider it here. However, as far as we can tell from [1] (and other publications), the use of lemmas there seems having been restricted to *unit* lemmas, perhaps for pragmatic reasons, although the mechanism has been defined more generally (already in [12]). A more general caching mechanism for unit clauses has been described in [11].

A recent paper [8] describes the Geometric Resolution calculus, which includes a lemma learning mechanism that is closely related to our lifted method (cf. Section 2.2). A major difference is that lemmas learned there are used only to close branches, but not to derive new information such as implied unit clauses. Unfortunately, [8] does not contain an experimental analysis describing the impact of their learning technique.

Further related work comes from Explanation-Based Learning (EBL), which allows the learning of logical descriptions of a concept from the description of a single concept instance and a preexisting knowledge base. A comprehensive and powerful EBL framework based on the language of definite logic programs and SLD-resolution is presented in [15]. As depicted there, EBL is essentially the process of deriving from a given SLD proof a (definite) clause representing parts of the proof or even generalizations thereof. The goal is to derive clauses that are of high *utility*, that is, that help find shorter proofs of similar theorems without broadening the search space too much. The learning procedures we present here follows a similar process. Structurally, they are SLD-derivations producing lemma clauses, and have a role comparable to the derivations of [15].

2   An Abstract Proof Procedure $\mathcal{ME}$

Being a *calculus*, $\mathcal{ME}$ abstracts away many control aspects of a proof search. As a consequence, one cannot formalize in it stateful operational improvements such as learning. Following an approach first introduced in [14] for the DPLL procedure, one can however formalize general classes of proof procedures for $\mathcal{ME}$ in a way that makes it easy to model and analyze operational features like backtracking and learning.

An $\mathcal{ME}$ proof procedure can be described abstractly as a transition system over *states* of the form $\perp$, a distinguished fail state, or the form $\Lambda \vdash \Phi$ where Φ is a clause set and Λ is an *(ordered) context*, that is, a sequence of *annotated literals*, literals with an annotation that marks each of them as a *decision* or a *propagated* literal. We model generic $\mathcal{ME}$ proof procedures by means of a set of states of the kind above together with a binary *transition relation* over these states defined by means of conditional *transition rules*. For a given state S, a transition rule precisely defines whether there is a transition from S by this rule and, if so, to which state S'. A proof procedure is then a *transition system*, a set of transition rules defined over some given set of states. In the following, we first introduce a basic transition system for $\mathcal{ME}$ and then extend it with learning capabilities.

Formal Preliminaries. If $\Longrightarrow$ is a transition relation between states we write, as usual, $S \Longrightarrow S'$ instead of $(S, S') \in \Longrightarrow$. We denote by $\Longrightarrow^*$ the reflexive-transitiveclosure of $\Longrightarrow$. Given a transition system R, we denote by $\Longrightarrow_R$ the transition relation defined by R. We call any sequence of transitions of the form $S_0 \Longrightarrow_R S_1$, $S_1 \Longrightarrow_R S_2$, ... a *derivation in R*, and denote it by $S_0 \Longrightarrow_R S_1 \Longrightarrow_R S_2 \Longrightarrow \cdots$

The concatenation of two ordered contexts will be denoted by simple juxtaposition. When we want to stress that a context literal L is annotated as a decision literal we will write it as L^d. With an ordered context of the form $\Lambda_0 L_1 \Lambda_1 \cdots L_n \Lambda_n$ where $L_1, \ldots L_n$ are all the decision literals of the context, we say that the literals in Λ_0 are at *decision level* 0, and those in $L_i \Lambda_i$ are at decision level i, for all $i = 1, \ldots, n$.

The $\mathcal{ME}$ calculus uses two disjoint, infinite sets of variables: a set X of *universal variables*, which we will refer to just as variables, and another set V, which we will always refer to as *parameters*. We will use u and v to denote elements of V and x, y and z to denote elements of X. If t is a term we denote by $\mathcal{V}ar(t)$ the set of t's variables and by $\mathcal{P}ar(t)$ the set of t's parameters. A term t is *ground* iff $\mathcal{V}ar(t) = \mathcal{P}ar(t) = \emptyset$. A substitution ρ is a *renaming on* $W \subseteq (V \cup X)$ iff its restriction to W is a bijection of W onto itself. A substitution σ is *p-preserving* (short for parameter preserving) if it is a renaming on V. If s and t are two terms, we say that s is a *p-variant of* t iff there is a p-preserving renaming ρ such that $s\rho = t$. We write $s \geq t$ iff there is a p-preserving substitution σ such that $s\sigma = t$. We write t^{sko} to denote the term obtained from t by replacing each variable in t by a fresh Skolem constant. All of the above is extended from terms to literals in the obvious way.

Every (ordered) context the proof procedure works with starts with a *pseudo-literal* of the form $\neg v$ (which, intuitively, stands for all negative ground literals). Where L is a literal and Λ a context, we will write $L \in_{\approx} \Lambda$ if L is a p-variant of a literal in Λ. A literal L is *contradictory with* a context Λ iff $L\sigma = \overline{K}\sigma$ for some $K \in_{\approx} \Lambda$ and some p-preserving substitution σ. (We write $\overline{K}$ to denote the complement of the literal K.) A context Λ is contradictory if one of its literals is contradictory with Λ.

Each non-contradictory context containing $\neg v$ determines a Herbrand interpretation I^Λ over the input signature extended by a countable set of Skolem constants. We refer the reader to [5,6] for the formal definition of I^Λ. Here it should suffice to say that the difference between (universal) variables and parameters in $\mathcal{ME}$ lies mainly in the definition of this Herbrand interpretation. Roughly, a literal with a parameter, like $A(u)$, in a context assigns true to all of its ground instances that are not also an instance of a more specific literal, like $\neg A(f(u))$, with opposite sign. In contrast, a literal with a variable, like $A(x)$, assigns true to all of its ground instances, with no exceptions.

In a state of the form $\Lambda \vdash \Phi$, the interpretation I^Λ is a *candidate* model for Φ. The purpose of the proof procedure is to recognize whether the candidate model is in fact a model of Φ or whether it possibly falsifies a clause of Φ. The latter situation is detectable syntactically through the computation of *context unifiers*.

Definition 1 (Context Unifier). *Let Λ be a context and $C = L_1 \vee \cdots \vee L_m \vee L_{m+1} \vee \cdots \vee L_n$ a parameter-free clause, where $0 \leq m \leq n$. A substitution σ is a context unifier of C against Λ with remainder $L_{m+1}\sigma \vee \cdots \vee L_n\sigma$ iff there are fresh p-variants $K_1, \ldots, K_n \in_{\approx} \Lambda$ such that (i) σ is a most general simultaneous unifier of $\{K_1, \overline{L_1}\}, \ldots, \{K_n, \overline{L_n}\}$, (ii) for all $i = 1, \ldots, m$, $(\mathcal{P}ar(K_i))\sigma \subseteq V$, (iii) for all $i = m+1, \ldots, n$, $(\mathcal{P}ar(K_i))\sigma \not\subseteq V$. A context unifier σ of C against Λ with remainder $L_{m+1}\sigma \vee \cdots \vee L_n\sigma$ is admissible (for* Split*) iff for all distinct $i, j = m+1, \ldots, n$, $\mathcal{V}ar(L_i\sigma) \cap \mathcal{V}ar(L_j\sigma) = \emptyset$.*

If σ is a context unifier with remainder D of a clause C against a context Λ, we call each literal of D *a remainder literal* of σ. We say that C is *conflicting (in Λ because of σ)* if σ has an empty remainder.

For space constraints we must refer the reader again to [5,6] for the rationale behind context unifiers and how parameters arise in $\mathcal{ME}$ derivations. Intuitively, the existence of a context unifier σ for a clause C indicates that $C\sigma$ is possibly falsified by the current I^Λ. If σ has a remainder literal $L\sigma$, adding $L\sigma$ to the context makes progress towards making I^Λ eventually satisfy $C\sigma$. If σ has no remainder literals, the problem is not repairable and backtracking is instead needed.

2.1 A Basic Proof Procedure for $\mathcal{ME}$

A basic proof procedure for $\mathcal{ME}$ is the transition system B defined by the rules Decide, Propagate, Backjump and Fail below. Since the transition system B is at a lower level of abstraction, its rules do not correspond one-to-one to the derivation rules of $\mathcal{ME}$. Roughly speaking, Decide implements Split, Propagate implements Assert, while Backjump and Fail implement Close. The relevant derivations in this system are those that start with a state of the form $\{\neg v\} \vdash \Phi$, where Φ is the clause set whose unsatisfiability one is interested in.

Decide: $\Lambda \vdash \Phi, C \vee L \implies \Lambda (L\sigma)^{\mathrm{d}} \vdash \Phi, C \vee L$ if $(*)$

$$\text{where } (*) = \begin{cases} \sigma \text{ is an admissible context unifier of } C \vee L \text{ against } \Lambda \text{ (cf. Def. 1)} \\ \text{with at least two remainder literals,} \\ L\sigma \text{ is a remainder literal, and} \\ \text{neither } L\sigma \text{ nor } (\overline{L\sigma})^{\mathrm{sko}} \text{ is contradictory with } \Lambda \end{cases}$$

We call the literal $L\sigma$ above a *decision literal* of the context unifier σ and the clause $C \vee L$. Decide makes the non-deterministic decision of adding the literal $L\sigma$ to the context. It is the only rule that adds a literal as a decision literal.

Propagate: $\Lambda \vdash \Phi, C \vee L \implies \Lambda, L\sigma \vdash \Phi, C \vee L$ if $(*)$

$$\text{where } (*) = \begin{cases} \sigma \text{ is an admissible context unifier of } C \vee L \text{ against } \Lambda \\ \text{with a single remainder literal } L\sigma, \\ L\sigma \text{ is not contradictory with } \Lambda, \text{ and} \\ \text{there is no } K \in \Lambda \text{ such that } K \geq L\sigma \end{cases}$$

We call the literal $L\sigma$ in the rule above the *propagated literal* of the context unifier σ and the clause $C \vee L$.

Backjump: $\Lambda L^{\mathrm{d}} \Lambda' \vdash \Phi, C \implies \Lambda \overline{L}^{\mathrm{sko}} \vdash \Phi, C$ if $\begin{cases} C \text{ is conflicting in} \\ \Lambda L^{\mathrm{d}} \text{ but not in } \Lambda \end{cases}$

Backjump models both chronological and non-chronological backtracking by allowing, but not requiring, that the undone decision literal L be the most recent one. Note that L's complement is added as a propagated literal, after all (and only) the variables of L have been Skolemized, which is needed for soundness. More general versions of

Backjump are conceivable, for instance along the lines of the backjump rule of Abstract DPLL [14]. Again, we present this one here mostly for simplicity.

Fail: $\Lambda \vdash \Phi, C \implies \bot$ if $\begin{cases} C \text{ is conflicting in } \Lambda, \\ \Lambda \text{ contains no decision literals} \end{cases}$

Fail ends a derivation once all possible decisions have generated a conflict.

Restart: $\Lambda \vdash \Phi \implies \{\neg v\} \vdash \Phi$

Restart is used to generate fair derivations that explore the search space in an iterative-deepening fashion.

Although it is beyond the scope of this paper, one can show that there are (deterministic) rule application strategies for this transition system that are refutationally sound and complete, that is, that reduce a state of the form $\{\neg v\} \vdash \Phi$ to the state $\bot$ if and only if Φ is unsatisfiable.

2.2 Adding Learning to $\mathcal{ME}$ Proof Procedures

To illustrate the potential usefulness of learning techniques for a transition system like the system B defined in the previous subsection, it is useful to look first at an example of a derivation in B.

Example 1. Let Φ be a clause set containing, among others, the clauses:

(1) $\neg B(x) \lor C(x,y)$ (2) $\neg A(x) \lor \neg C(y,x) \lor D(y)$ (3) $\neg C(x,y) \lor E(x)$ (4) $\neg D(x) \lor \neg E(x)$.

The table below provides a trace of a possible derivation of Φ. The first column shows the literal added to the context by the current derivation step, the second column specifies the rule used in that step, and the third indicates which instance of a clause in Φ was used by the rule. A row with ellipses stands for zero or more intermediate steps. Note that Backjump *replaces* the whole subsequence $B(u)^d C(u,y) D(u) E(u)$ of the current context with $\neg B(u)$.

Context Literal	Derivation Rule	Clause Instance
$\ldots$	$\ldots$	$\ldots$
$A(t(x))$	Propagate	instance $A(t(x)) \lor \cdots$ of some clause in Φ where $t(x)$ is a term with a single variable x.
$\ldots$	$\ldots$	$\ldots$
$B(u)^d$	Decide	instance $B(u) \lor \cdots$ of some clause in Φ
$C(u,y)$	Propagate	instance $\neg B(u) \lor C(u,y)$ of (1)
$D(u)$	Propagate	instance $\neg A(t(x)) \lor \neg C(u,t(x)) \lor D(u)$ of (2)
$E(u)$	Propagate	instance $\neg C(u,y) \lor E(u)$ of (3)
$\neg B(u)$	Backjump	instance $\neg D(u) \lor \neg E(u)$ of (4)

It is clear by inspection of the trace that any intermediate decisions made between the additions of $A(t(x))$ and $B(u)$ are irrelevant in making clause (4) conflicting at the point of the Backjump application. The fact that (4) is conflicting depends only on the decisions that lead to the propagation of $A(t(x))$—say, some decision literals $S_1, \ldots, S_n$ with $n \geq 0$—and the decision to add $B(u)$. This means that the decision literals $S_1, \ldots, S_n, B(u)$ will eventually produce a conflict (i.e., make some clause conflicting) in any context that contains them. The basic goal of this work is to define efficient conflict analysis procedures that can come to this conclusion automatically and store it into the system in such a way that Backjump is applicable, possibly with few propagation steps, whenever the current context happens to contain again the literals $S_1, \ldots, S_n, B(u)$. Even better would be the possibility to avoid altogether the addition of $B(u)$ as a decision literal in any context containing $S_1, \ldots, S_n$, and instead add the literal $\neg B(u)$ as a propagated literal. We discuss how to do these in the rest of the paper.   □

Within the abstract framework of Section 2.1, and in perfect analogy to the Abstract DPPL framework of Nieuwenhuis *et al.* [14], learning can be modeled very simply and generally by the addition of the following two rules to the transition system B:

Learn: $\Lambda \vdash \Phi \implies \Lambda \vdash \Phi, C$ if $\Phi \models C$

Forget: $\Lambda \vdash \Phi, C \implies \Lambda \vdash \Phi$ if $\Phi \models C$

Note that adding entailed clauses to the clause set is superfluous for completeness. The Learn rule then is meant to be used only to add clauses that are more likely to cause further propagations and correspondingly reduce the number of needed decisions. The intended use of the Forget rule is to control the growth of the clause set, by removing entailed clauses that cause little propagation.

Because of the potentially high overhead involved in generating lemmas and propagating them in practice, we focus in this work on only the kind of *conflict-driven* learning that has proven to be very effective in DPLL-based solvers. In the following we discuss two methods for doing that. Both of them are directly based on a lemma generation technique common in DPLL implementations. This technique can be described proof-theoretically as a linear resolution derivation whose initial central clause is a conflicting clause in the DPLL computation, and whose side clauses are clauses used in unit propagation steps. In terms of the abstract framework above, the linear resolution derivation proceeds as follows. The central clause $C \vee \overline{L}$ is resolved with a clause $L \vee D$ in the clause set only if L was added to the current context by a Propagate step with clause $L \vee D$. Since the net effect of each resolution step is to replace $\overline{L}$ in $C \vee \overline{L}$ by L's "causes" D, we can also see this resolution derivation as a *regression* process.

Both of the methods we present below lift this regression to the first-order case, although with different degrees of generality. The first method produces lemmas that are strictly subsumed by the lemmas produced by the second method. We present it here because it is practically interesting in its own right, and because it can be used to greatly simplify the presentation of the second method.

The Grounded Method. Let $\mathbf{D} = (\{\neg v\} \vdash \Phi_0 \implies_L \ldots \implies_L \Lambda \vdash \Phi)$ be a derivation in the transition system L where Λ contains at least one decision literal and Φ contains a clause C_0 conflicting in Λ. We describe a process for generating from $\mathbf{D}$ a *lemma*, a clause logically entailed by Φ, which can be *learned* in the derivation by an application of Learn to the state $\Lambda \vdash \Phi$.

We describe the lemma generation process itself as a transition system, this time applied to *annotated clauses*, pairs of the form $C \mid S$ where C is a clause and S is finite mapping $\{L \mapsto M, \ldots\}$ from literals in C to context literals of $\mathbf{D}$. A transition invariant for $C \mid S$ will be that C consists of negated ground instances of context literals, while S specifies for each literal L of C the context literal M of which $\overline{L}$ is an instance, provided that M is a propagated literal. The mapping $L \mapsto M$ will be used to *regress* L, that is, to resolve it with M in the clause used in $\mathbf{D}$ to add M to the context.

The initial annotated clause A_0 will be built from the conflicting clause of $\mathbf{D}$ and will be regressed by applying to it the GRegress rule, defined below, one or more times. In the definition of A_0 and of GRegress we use the following notational conventions: if σ is a substitution and C a clause or a literal, $C\underline{\sigma}$ denotes the expression obtained by replacing each variable or parameter of $C\sigma$ by a fresh Skolem constant (one per variable or parameter); if σ is a context unifier of a clause $L_1 \vee \cdots \vee L_n$ against some context, we denote by L_i^σ the context literal paired with L_i by σ.

Assume that C_0 is conflicting in Λ because of some context unifier σ_0. Then A_0 is defined as the annotated lemma

$$A_0 = C_0\underline{\sigma_0} \mid \{L\underline{\sigma_0} \mapsto L^{\sigma_0} \mid L \in C_0 \text{ and } L^{\sigma_0} \text{ is a propagated literal}\}$$

consisting of a fresh grounding of $C_0\sigma_0$ by Skolem constants (hence the name "grounded method") and a mapping of each literal of $C_0\underline{\sigma_0}$ to its pairable literal in Λ if that literal is a propagated literal. The regression rule is

GRegress: $D \vee M \mid S, M \mapsto L\sigma \implies_{gr} D \vee C\sigma\underline{\mu} \mid S, T$ if $(*)$

where $(*) = \begin{cases} L\sigma \text{ is the propagated literal of some context unifier } \sigma \text{ and clause } L \vee C, \\ \mu \text{ is a most general unifier of } M \text{ and } \overline{L\sigma}, \\ T = \{N\sigma\underline{\mu} \mapsto N^\sigma \mid N \in C \text{ and } N^\sigma \text{ is a propagated literal}\} \end{cases}$

Note that the mapping is used by GRegress to guide the regression so that no search is needed. The regression process simply repeatedly applies the rule GRegress an arbitrary number of times starting from A_0 and returns the last clause. While this clause is ground by construction, it can be generalized to a non-ground clause C by replacing each of its Skolem constants by a distinct variable. As stated in the next result, this generalized clause is a logical consequence of the current clause set Φ in the derivation, and so can be learned with an application of the Learn rule.[2]

Proposition 1. *If $A_0 \implies_{gr}^* C' \mid S$, the clause C obtained from C' by replacing each constant of C' not in Φ by a fresh variable is a consequence of Φ_0.*

An important invariant in practice is that one can continue regressing the initial clause until it contains only decision literals. This result, expressed in the next proposition, gives one great latitude in terms of how far to push the regression. In our implementation, to reduce the regression overhead, and following a common practice in DPLL solvers, we regress only propagated literals belonging to the last decision level of Λ.

Proposition 2. *If $A_0 \implies_{gr}^* A$ and A has the form $D \vee M \mid S, M \mapsto N$, then the GRegress rule applies to A.*

Example 2. Figure 1 shows a possible regression of the conflicting clause $\neg D(x) \vee \neg E(x)$ in the derivation of Example 1. This clause is conflicting because of the con-

---

[2] We refer the reader to a longer version of this paper [3] for all the proofs of the results below.

$$\frac{\neg D(a) \vee \neg \mathbf{E(a)} \quad \neg C(u,y) \vee E(u)}{\underbrace{\neg \mathbf{D(a)} \vee \neg C(a,b)}_{} \qquad \neg A(t(x)) \vee \neg C(u,t(x)) \vee D(u)}$$

Grounded regression tree:

$$\cfrac{\cfrac{\cfrac{\neg D(a) \vee \neg \mathbf{E(a)} \quad \neg C(u,y) \vee E(u)}{\neg \mathbf{D(a)} \vee \neg C(a,b) \qquad \neg A(t(x)) \vee \neg C(u,t(x)) \vee D(u)}}{\neg \mathbf{C(a,b)} \vee \neg A(t(c)) \vee \neg C(a,t(c)) \qquad \neg B(u) \vee C(u,y)}}{\cfrac{\neg A(t(c)) \vee \neg \mathbf{C(a,t(c))} \vee \neg B(a) \qquad \neg B(u) \vee C(u,y)}{\neg A(t(c)) \vee \neg B(a)}}$$

Fig. 1. Grounded regression of $\neg D(u) \vee \neg E(u)$

text unifier $\sigma_0 = \{x \mapsto u\}$, pairing the clause literals $\neg D(x)$ and $\neg E(x)$ respectively with the context literals $D(u)$ and $E(u)$. So we start with the initial annotated clause: $A_0 = (\neg D(x) \vee \neg E(x))\sigma_0 \mid \{(\neg D(x))\sigma_0 \mapsto (\neg D(x))^{\sigma_0}, (\neg E(x))\sigma_0 \mapsto (\neg E(x))^{\sigma_0}\} = \neg D(a) \vee \neg E(a) \mid \{\neg D(\overline{a}) \mapsto D(u), \neg \overline{E(a)} \mapsto E(u)\}$. To ease the notation burden, we represent the regression in the more readable form of a linear resolution tree, where at each step the central clause is the regressed clause, the literal in bold font is the regressed literal, and the side clause is the clause $(L \vee C)\sigma$ identified in the precondition of GRegress. The introduced Skolem constants are a, b and c. Stopping the regression with the resolvent $\neg A(t(c)) \vee \neg B(a)$ gives, after replacing the Skolem constants by fresh variables, the lemma $\neg A(t(z_c)) \vee \neg B(z_a)$. (Similarly for the previous resolvents.) □

To judge the effectiveness of lemmas learned with this process in reducing the explored search space we also need to argue that they let the system later recognize more quickly, or possibly avoid altogether, the set of decisions responsible for the conflict in $\mathbf{D}$. This is not obvious within the $\mathcal{ME}$ calculus because of the role played by parameters in the definition of a conflicting clause. (Recall that a clause is conflicting because of some context unifier σ iff it moves parameters only to parameters in the context literals associated with the clause.) To show that lemmas can have the intended consequences, we start by observing that, by construction, every literal L_i in a lemma $C = L_1 \vee \cdots \vee L_m$ generated with the process above is a negated instance of some context literal K_i in Λ. Let us write C^Λ to denote the set $\{K_1, \ldots, K_m\}$.

Proposition 3. *Any lemma C produced from $\mathbf{D}$ by the regression method in this section is conflicting in any context that contains C^Λ.*

Proposition 3 implies, as we wanted, that having had the lemma C in the clause set from the beginning could have led to the discovery of a conflict sooner, that is, with less propagation work and possibly also less decisions than in $\mathbf{D}$. Moreover, the more regressed the lemma, the sooner the conflict would have been discovered. For instance, looking back at the lemmas generated in Example 2, it is easy to see that the lemma $\neg C(z_a, z_b) \vee \neg A(t(z_c)) \vee \neg C(z_a, t(z_c))$ becomes conflicting in the derivation of Example 1 as soon as $C(u, y)$ is added to the context. In contrast, the more regressed lemma $\neg A(t(z_c)) \vee \neg B(z_a)$ becomes conflicting as soon as the decision $B(u)$ is made. Since a lemma generated from $\mathbf{D}$ is typically conflicting once a *subset* of the decisions in Λ are taken, learning it in the state $\Lambda \vdash \Phi, C_0$ will help recognize more quickly these wrong decisions later in extensions of $\mathbf{D}$ that undo parts of Λ by backjumping. In fact, if the lemma is regressed enough, one can do even better and completely avoid the conflict later on if one uses a derivation strategy that prefers applications of Propagate to applications of Decide.

$$\dfrac{\dfrac{\neg D(x) \vee \neg \mathbf{E(x)} \quad \neg C(x_1,y_1) \vee E(x_1)}{\neg \mathbf{D(x)} \vee \neg C(x,y_1)} \quad \neg A(x_2) \vee \neg C(y_2,x_2) \vee D(y_2)}{\dfrac{\dfrac{\neg \mathbf{C(x,y_1)} \vee \neg A(x_2) \vee \neg C(x,x_2)}{\neg A(x_2) \vee \neg C(\mathbf{x},\mathbf{x_2}) \vee \neg B(x)} \quad \neg B(x_3) \vee C(x_3,y_3)}{\neg A(x_2) \vee \neg B(x)} \quad \neg B(x_4) \vee C(x_4,y_4)}$$

Fig. 2. Lifted regression of $\neg D(x) \vee \neg E(x)$

Example 3. Consider an extension of the derivation in Example 1 where the context has been undone enough that now its last literal is $A(t(x))$. By applying Propagate to the lemma $\neg A(t(z_c)) \vee \neg B(z_a)$ it is possible to add $\neg B(z_a)$ to the context, thus preventing the addition of $B(u)$ as a decision literal (because $B(u)$ is contradictory with $\neg B(z_a)$) and avoiding the conflict with clause (4). With the less regressed lemma $\neg C(z_a,z_b) \vee \neg A(t(z_c)) \vee \neg C(z_a,t(z_c))$ it is still possible to add $\neg B(z_a)$, but with two applications of Propagate—to the lemma and then to clause (1). □

So far, what we have described mirrors what happens with propositional clause sets in DPLL SAT solvers. What is remarkable about learning at the $\mathcal{ME}$ level, besides producing the same nice effects obtained in DPLL, is that its lemmas are not just caching compactly the reasons for a specific conflict. For being a *first-order* formula, a lemma in $\mathcal{ME}$ represents an *infinite* class of conflicts of the same form. For instance, the lemma $\neg A(t(z_c)) \vee \neg B(z_a)$ in our running example will become conflicting once the context contains *any* instance of $A(t(z_c))$ and $B(z_a)$, not just the original $A(t(x))$ and $B(u)$.

Our lemma generation process then does learning in a more proper sense of the word, as it can generalize over a single instance of a conflict, and later recognize *unseen* instances in the same class, and so lead to additional pruning of the search space.

A slightly more careful look at the derivation in Example 1 shows that the lemma $\neg A(t(z_c)) \vee \neg B(z_a)$ is actually not as general as it could be. The reason is that a conflict arises also in contexts that contain, in addition to any instance of $B(z_a)$, also any *generalization* of $A(t(z_c))$. So a better possible lemma is $\neg A(z) \vee \neg B(z_a)$. We can produce generalized lemmas like the above by lifting the regression process similarly as in Explanation-Based Learning (cf. Section 1). We describe this lifted process next.

The Lifted Method. Consider again the derivation **D** from the previous subsection, whose last state $\Lambda \vdash \Phi$ contains a clause C_0 that is conflicting in Λ because of some context unifier σ_0. Using basic results about resolution and unification, this derivation can be lifted to the first-order level. The lifted derivation can be built simply by following the steps of the grounded derivation, but this time using the original clauses in Φ for the initial central clause and the side clauses. In practice of course, the lifted derivation can be built directly, without building the grounded derivation first. As in the grounded case, we can use any regressed clause C as a lemma but with the difference that we do not need to abstract away Skolem constants because the regression process resolves only input clauses of C. Again, the resulting clause is a logical consequence of Φ.

More details, including a soundness proof can be found in the long version [3]. Here we will only present the main idea by means of an example.

Example 4. Figure 2 shows the lifting of the grounded regression in Figure 1 for the conflicting clause $\neg D(x) \vee \neg E(x)$ in the derivation of Example 1. This time, we start with the initial annotated clause: $(\neg D(x) \vee \neg E(x)) \mid \{\neg D(x) \mapsto D(u), \neg E(x) \mapsto E(u)\}$. As before, we represent the regression as a linear resolution tree, where this time at each step the central clause is the regressed clause, the literal in bold font is the regressed literal, and the side clause corresponds to the clause $L \vee C$ in the precondition of the lifted version of GRegress. The lemma learned in this case is $\neg A(x_2) \vee \neg B(x)$.   □

3   Experimental Evaluation

A detailed discussion on implementing the various methods can be found in [3], where we describe the regression processes more concretely. We also discuss some memoization techniques used to reduce the regression cost, condensing techniques to limit the size of lemmas, and a simple lemma forgetting policy. Here we focus on our initial experimental results.

First problem set. We first evaluated the effectiveness of lemma learning with version 1.2 of *Darwin* over version 3.1.1 of the TPTP problem library. Since *Darwin* can handle only clause logic, and has no dedicated inference rules for equality, we considered only clausal problems without equality, both satisfiable and unsatisfiable ones. Furthermore, as *Darwin* never applies the Decide rule in Horn problems [10], and thus also never backtracks, we further restricted the selection to non-Horn problems only. All tests were run on Xeon 2.4Ghz machines with 1GB of RAM. The imposed limit on the prover were 300s of CPU time and 512MB of RAM.

The first 4 rows of Table 1 summarize the results for various configurations of *Darwin*, namely, not using lemmas and using lemmas with the grounded and lifted regression methods. The first significant observation is that all configurations solve almost exactly the same number of problems, which is somewhat disappointing. The situation is similar even with an increased timeout of one hour per problem. A sampling of the derivation traces of the unsolved problems, however, reveals that they contain only a handful of Backjump steps, suggesting that the system spends most of the time in propagation steps and supporting operations such as the computation of context unifiers.

The second observation is that for the solved problems the search space, measured in the number of Decide applications, is significantly pruned by all learning methods (with 18% to 58% less decisions), although this improvement is only marginally reflected in the run times. This too seems to be due to the fact that most derivations involve only a few applications of Backjump in the configuration without lemmas. Indeed, 652 of the 898 problems solved with the lifted technique require at most 2 backjumps. This implies that only a few lemmas can be learned, and thus their effect is limited and the run time of most problems remains unchanged. Based on these tests alone, it is not clear if the small number of backjumps is an artifact of the specific proof procedure implemented by *Darwin* or a characteristic of the problems in the TPTP library.

The rest of Table 1 shows the same statistics, but restricted to the problems solved by the no lemmas configuration using, respectively, at least 3, 20, and 100 applications of Backjump within the 300s time limit. There, the effect of the search space pruning is more pronounced and does translate into reduced run times. In particular, the speed

Table 1. Problems that respectively take at least 0, 3, 20, and 100 applications of Backjump without lemmas within 300s, where **Solved Problems** gives the number of problems solved by a configuration, while the remaining values are for the subsets of 894, 241, 106, 65 problems solved by *all* configurations. **Avg Time** (**Total Time**) gives the average (total) time needed for the problems solved by all configurations, **Speed up** shows the run time speed up factor of each configuration versus the one with no lemmas. **Failure**, **Propagate**, and **Decide** give the number of rule applications, with **Failure** including both Backjump and Fail applications.

Method	Solved Probls	Avg Time	Total Time	Speed up	Failure Steps	Propag. Steps	Decide Steps
no lemmas	896	2.7	2397.0	1.00	24991	597286	45074
grounded	895	2.4	2135.6	1.12	9476	391189	18935
lifted	898	2.4	2173.4	1.10	9796	399525	19367
no lemmas	244	3.0	713.9	1.00	24481	480046	40766
grounded	243	1.8	445.1	1.60	8966	273849	14627
lifted	246	2.0	493.7	1.45	9286	282600	15059
no lemmas	108	5.2	555.7	1.00	23553	435219	38079
grounded	108	2.2	228.5	2.43	8231	228437	12279
lifted	111	2.6	274.4	2.02	8535	238103	12688
no lemmas	66	5.0	323.9	1.00	21555	371145	34288
grounded	67	1.7	111.4	2.91	6973	183292	9879
lifted	70	2.3	151.4	2.14	7275	193097	10294

up of each lemma configuration with respect to the no lemmas one steadily increases with the difficulty of the problems, reaching a factor of almost 3 for the most difficult problems in the grounded case. Moreover, the lifted lemmas configuration always solves a few more problems than the no lemmas one.

Because of the way *Darwin*'s proof procedure is designed [3], in addition to pruning search space, lemmas may also cause changes to the order in which the search space is explored. Since experimental results for unsatisfiable problems are usually more stable with respect to different space exploration orders, it is instructive to separate the data in Table 1 between satisfiable and unsatisfiable problems. For lack of space, we must refer the reader to [3] for detailed tables with this breakdown. Here it suffices to say that the results for unsatisfiable problems show the same pattern as the aggregate results in Table 1. Those solved by all configurations and solved by the no lemmas one with at least 0, 3, 20, and 100 backjumps are respectively 561, 191, 89, and 61. For these unsatisfiable problems, the speed up factors for grounded lemmas in particular are respectively 1.07, 1.55, 3.74, and 4.19, which actually compares more favorably overall to the corresponding speed up factors in Table 1: resp., 1.12, 1.60, 2.43, and 2.91.

In Figure 3 we plot the individual run times of the no lemmas configuration against the lemma configurations for all problems solved by at least one configuration and generating at least 3 backjumps in the no lemma one. The scatter plots clearly show the positive effect of learning. For nearly all of the problems, the performance of the

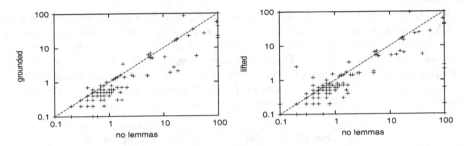

Fig. 3. Comparative performance, on a log-log scale, for different configurations for problems with at least 3 applications of Backjump. For readability, the cutoff is set at 100s instead of 300s, because in all cases less than a handful of problems are solved in the 100-300s range.

grounded lemmas configuration is better, often by a large margin, than the one with no lemmas. A similar situation occurs with lifted lemmas, although there are more problems for which the no lemmas configuration is faster.

Overall, our results indicate that lifted lemmas generate more Decide applications and have higher overhead than grounded lemmas. The larger number of decision steps of the lifted method versus the grounded one seems paradoxical at first sight, but can be explained by observing that lifted lemmas—in addition to avoiding or detecting early a larger number of conflicts—also cause the addition of more general propagated literals to a context, leading to a higher number of (possibly useless) context unifiers. Furthermore, due to the increased generality of lifted lemmas and the way they are condensed when they are too long, sometimes Propagate applies to a grounded lemma but not the corresponding lifted lemma, making the latter *less* effective at avoiding conflicts (see [3] for more details).

The higher overhead of the lifted method can be attributed to two main reasons. The first is of course the increased number of context unifiers to be considered for rule applications. The second is the intrinsically higher cost of the lifted method versus the grounded one, because of its use of unification—as opposed to matching—operations during regression, and its considerable post-processing work in removing multiple variants of the same literals from a lemma—something that occurs quite often.

Second problem set. Given that only a minority of the TPTP problems we could use in the first experiment cause a considerable amount of search and backtracking, and that, on the other hand, many decidable fragments of first-order logic are NP-hard, we considered a second problem set, stemming from an application of *Darwin* for finite model finding [4]. This application follows an approach similar to that of systems like Paradox [7]. To find a finite model of a given cardinality n, a clause set, with or without equality, is converted into an equisatisfiable Bernays-Schönfinkel problem (instead of a propositional problem as in Paradox) that includes the cardinality restriction. If *Darwin* proves the latter clause set unsatisfiable, it increases the value of n by 1 and restarts, repeating the process until it finds a model—and diverging if the original problem has no finite models. Since *Darwin* is a decision procedure for the Bernays-Schönfinkel class, starting with n above at 1, it is guaranteed to find a finite model of minimum size if one exists. In the configurations with learning, *Darwin* uses lemmas during each

Table 2. Satisfiable problems that transformed to a finite model representation respectively take at least 0, 100, and 1000 applications of Backjump without lemmas within 300s, where **Solved Problems** gives the number of problems solved by a configuration, while the remaining values are for the subsets of 647, 152, 47 problems solved by *all* configurations.

Method	Solved Probls	Average Time	Total Time	Speed up	Failure Steps	Propagate Steps	Decide Steps
no lemmas	657	5.6	3601.3	1.00	404237	16122392	628731
grounded	669	3.3	2106.3	1.71	74559	4014058	99865
lifted	657	4.7	3043.9	1.18	41579	1175468	68235
no lemmas	162	17.8	2708.6	1.00	398865	15911006	614572
grounded	174	7.9	1203.1	2.25	70525	3833986	87834
lifted	162	14.0	2126.2	1.27	38157	1023589	57070
no lemmas	52	36.2	1702.9	1.00	357663	14580056	555015
grounded	64	10.5	495.3	3.44	53486	3100339	64845
lifted	57	11.5	538.7	3.16	26154	678319	39873

iteration of the process and carries over to the next iteration those lemmas not depending on the cardinality restriction. Since a run over a problem with a model of minimum size n includes $n - 1$ iterations over unsatisfiable clause sets, it is reasonable to consider together all the n iterations in the run when measuring the effect of learning.

Table 2 shows our results for (the BS translation of) all the 815 satisfiable problems of the TPTP library.[3] In general, solving a problem in *Darwin* with the process above requires significantly more applications of Backjump than for the set of experiments presented earlier. As a consequence, the grounded lemmas configuration performs significantly better than the no lemmas configuration, solving the same problems in about half the time, and also solving 12 new problems. The lifted configuration on the other hand performs only moderately better. Although the search space is drastically reduced (the number of decisions is reduced by an order of magnitude in all cases), the overhead of lemma simplification almost outweighs the positive effects of pruning. Restricting the analysis to harder problems shows that the speed up factor of grounded lemmas increases gradually to about 3.5.

This second set of results then confirms that learning has a significant positive effect in solving problems that require a lot of search and produce comparatively few unit propagations.

4   Conclusion and Further Work

We have presented two methods for implementing conflict-based learning in proof procedures for the Model Evolution calculus. The methods have different degrees of

---

[3] For an idea how we compare with other systems, Mace 4 [13] and Paradox 1.3, currently the fastest finite model finders available, respectively solve 553 and 714 of those problems, making *Darwin* second only to Paradox.

generality, implementation difficulty, and effectiveness in practice. Our initial experimental results indicate that for problems that are not trivially solvable by the *Darwin* implementation and do not cause too much constraint propagation all methods have a dramatic pruning effect on the search space. The grounded method, however, is the most effective at reducing the run time as well.

We plan to investigate the grounded and the lifted methods further, possibly adapting to our setting some of the heuristics developed in [15], in order to make learning more effective and reduce its computational overhead. We also plan to evaluate experimentally our learning methods with sets of problems not (yet) in the TPTP library.

References

1. O. L. Astrachan and M. E. Stickel. Caching and Lemmaizing in Model Elimination Theorem Provers. In D. Kapur, ed., *Proc. CADE-11*, LNAI 607. Springer, 1992.

2. P. Baumgartner, A. Fuchs, and C. Tinelli. Implementing the Model Evolution Calculus. *International Journal of Artificial Intelligence Tools*, 15(1):21–52, 2006.

3. P. Baumgartner, A. Fuchs, and C. Tinelli. Lemma Learning in the Model Evolution Calculus. Technical Report no. 06-04, Department of Computer Science, The University of Iowa, 2006. (Available at http://www.cs.uiowa.edu/~tinelli/papers.html.)

4. P. Baumgartner, A. Fuchs, C. Tinelli and H. de Nivelle, and Cesare Tinelli. Computing Finite Models by Reduction to Function-Free Clause Logic. In W. Ahrendt, P. Baumgartner and H. de Nivelle, eds., *IJCAR'06 Workshop on Disproving*, 2006.

5. P. Baumgartner and C. Tinelli. The Model Evolution Calculus. In Franz Baader, ed., *Proc. CADE-19*, LNAI 2741. Springer, 2003.

6. P. Baumgartner and C. Tinelli. The Model Evolution Calculus. Fachberichte Informatik 1–2003, Universität Koblenz-Landau, Germany, 2003.

7. K. Claessen and N. Sörensson. New Techniques that Improve MACE-Style Finite Model Building. In P. Baumgartner and C. G. Fermüller, eds., *CADE-19 Workshop on Model Computation*, 2003.

8. H. de Nivelle and J. Meng. Geometric resolution: A Proof Procedure Based on Finite Model Search. In U. Furbach and N. Shankar, eds., *Proc. IJCAR, LNAI 4130*. Springer, 2006.

9. G. DeJong and R. J. Mooney. Explanation-Based Learning: An Alternative View. *Machine Learning*, 1(2):145–176, 1986.

10. A. Fuchs. Darwin: A Theorem Prover for the Model Evolution Calculus. Master's thesis, University of Koblenz-Landau, 2004.

11. R. Letz and G. Stenz. Model Elimination and Connection Tableau Procedures. In A. Robinson and A. Voronkov, eds., *Handbook of Automated Reasoning*, Elsevier, 2001.

12. D. Loveland. *Automated Theorem Proving - A Logical Basis*. North Holland, 1978.

13. William McCune. Mace4 Reference Manual and Guide. Technical Report ANL/MCS-TM-264, Argonne National Laboratory, 2003.

14. R. Nieuwenhuis, A. Oliveras, and C. Tinelli. Abstract DPLL and Abstract DPLL Modulo Theories. In F. Baader and A. Voronkov, eds., *Proc. LPAR'04*, LNCS 3452, Springer, 2005.

15. A. Segre and C. Elkan. A High-Performance Explanation-Based Learning Algorithm. *Artificial Intelligence*, 69:1–50, 1994.

Author Index

Lecture Notes in Artificial Intelligence (LNAI)

Vol. 4088: Z.-Z. Shi, R. Sadananda (Eds.), Agent Computing and Multi-Agent Systems. XVII, 827 pages. 2006.

Vol. 4087: F. Schwenker, S. Marinai (Eds.), Artificial Neural Networks in Pattern Recognition. IX, 299 pages. 2006.

Vol. 4068: H. Schärfe, P. Hitzler, P. Øhrstrøm (Eds.), Conceptual Structures: Inspiration and Application. XI, 455 pages. 2006.

Vol. 4065: P. Perner (Ed.), Advances in Data Mining. XI, 592 pages. 2006.

Vol. 4062: G. Wang, J.F. Peters, A. Skowron, Y. Yao (Eds.), Rough Sets and Knowledge Technology. XX, 810 pages. 2006.

Vol. 4049: S. Parsons, N. Maudet, P. Moraitis, I. Rahwan (Eds.), Argumentation in Multi-Agent Systems. XIV, 313 pages. 2006.

Vol. 4048: L. Goble, J.-J.C.. Meyer (Eds.), Deontic Logic and Artificial Normative Systems. X, 273 pages. 2006.

Vol. 4045: D. Barker-Plummer, R. Cox, N. Swoboda (Eds.), Diagrammatic Representation and Inference. XII, 301 pages. 2006.

Vol. 4031: M. Ali, R. Dapoigny (Eds.), Advances in Applied Artificial Intelligence. XXIII, 1353 pages. 2006.

Vol. 4029: L. Rutkowski, R. Tadeusiewicz, L.A. Zadeh, J.M. Zurada (Eds.), Artificial Intelligence and Soft Computing – ICAISC 2006. XXI, 1235 pages. 2006.

Vol. 4027: H.L. Larsen, G. Pasi, D. Ortiz-Arroyo, T. Andreasen, H. Christiansen (Eds.), Flexible Query Answering Systems. XVIII, 714 pages. 2006.

Vol. 4021: E. André, L. Dybkjær, W. Minker, H. Neumann, M. Weber (Eds.), Perception and Interactive Technologies. XI, 217 pages. 2006.

Vol. 4020: A. Bredenfeld, A. Jacoff, I. Noda, Y. Takahashi (Eds.), RoboCup 2005: Robot Soccer World Cup IX. XVII, 727 pages. 2006.

Vol. 4013: L. Lamontagne, M. Marchand (Eds.), Advances in Artificial Intelligence. XIII, 564 pages. 2006.

Vol. 4012: T. Washio, A. Sakurai, K. Nakajima, H. Takeda, S. Tojo, M. Yokoo (Eds.), New Frontiers in Artificial Intelligence. XIII, 484 pages. 2006.

Vol. 4008: J.C. Augusto, C.D. Nugent (Eds.), Designing Smart Homes. XI, 183 pages. 2006.

Vol. 4005: G. Lugosi, H.U. Simon (Eds.), Learning Theory. XI, 656 pages. 2006.

Vol. 3978: B. Hnich, M. Carlsson, F. Fages, F. Rossi (Eds.), Recent Advances in Constraints. VIII, 179 pages. 2006.

Vol. 3963: O. Dikenelli, M.-P. Gleizes, A. Ricci (Eds.), Engineering Societies in the Agents World VI. XII, 303 pages. 2006.

Vol. 3960: R. Vieira, P. Quaresma, M.d.G.V. Nunes, N.J. Mamede, C. Oliveira, M.C. Dias (Eds.), Computational Processing of the Portuguese Language. XII, 274 pages. 2006.

Vol. 3955: G. Antoniou, G. Potamias, C. Spyropoulos, D. Plexousakis (Eds.), Advances in Artificial Intelligence. XVII, 611 pages. 2006.

Vol. 3949: F.A. Savacı (Ed.), Artificial Intelligence and Neural Networks. IX, 227 pages. 2006.

Vol. 3946: T.R. Roth-Berghofer, S. Schulz, D.B. Leake (Eds.), Modeling and Retrieval of Context. XI, 149 pages. 2006.

Vol. 3944: J. Quiñonero-Candela, I. Dagan, B. Magnini, F. d'Alché-Buc (Eds.), Machine Learning Challenges. XIII, 462 pages. 2006.

Vol. 3937: H. La Poutré, N.M. Sadeh, S. Janson (Eds.), Agent-Mediated Electronic Commerce. X, 227 pages. 2006.

Vol. 3932: B. Mobasher, O. Nasraoui, B. Liu, B. Masand (Eds.), Advances in Web Mining and Web Usage Analysis. X, 189 pages. 2006.

Vol. 3930: D.S. Yeung, Z.-Q. Liu, X.-Z. Wang, H. Yan (Eds.), Advances in Machine Learning and Cybernetics. XXI, 1110 pages. 2006.

Vol. 3918: W.-K. Ng, M. Kitsuregawa, J. Li, K. Chang (Eds.), Advances in Knowledge Discovery and Data Mining. XXIV, 879 pages. 2006.

Vol. 3913: O. Boissier, J. Padget, V. Dignum, G. Lindemann, E. Matson, S. Ossowski, J.S. Sichman, J. Vázquez-Salceda (Eds.), Coordination, Organizations, Institutions, and Norms in Multi-Agent Systems. XII, 259 pages. 2006.

Vol. 3910: S.A. Brueckner, G.D.M. Serugendo, D. Hales, F. Zambonelli (Eds.), Engineering Self-Organising Systems. XII, 245 pages. 2006.

Vol. 3904: M. Baldoni, U. Endriss, A. Omicini, P. Torroni (Eds.), Declarative Agent Languages and Technologies III. XII, 245 pages. 2006.

Vol. 3900: F. Toni, P. Torroni (Eds.), Computational Logic in Multi-Agent Systems. XVII, 427 pages. 2006.

Vol. 3899: S. Frintrop, VOCUS: A Visual Attention System for Object Detection and Goal-Directed Search. XIV, 216 pages. 2006.

Vol. 3898: K. Tuyls, P.J. 't Hoen, K. Verbeeck, S. Sen (Eds.), Learning and Adaption in Multi-Agent Systems. X, 217 pages. 2006.

Vol. 3891: J.S. Sichman, L. Antunes (Eds.), Multi-Agent-Based Simulation VI. X, 191 pages. 2006.

Vol. 3890: S.G. Thompson, R. Ghanea-Hercock (Eds.), Defence Applications of Multi-Agent Systems. XII, 141 pages. 2006.

Vol. 3885: V. Torra, Y. Narukawa, A. Valls, J. Domingo-Ferrer (Eds.), Modeling Decisions for Artificial Intelligence. XII, 374 pages. 2006.

Vol. 3881: S. Gibet, N. Courty, J.-F. Kamp (Eds.), Gesture in Human-Computer Interaction and Simulation. XIII, 344 pages. 2006.

Vol. 3874: R. Missaoui, J. Schmidt (Eds.), Formal Concept Analysis. X, 309 pages. 2006.

Vol. 3873: L. Maicher, J. Park (Eds.), Charting the Topic Maps Research and Applications Landscape. VIII, 281 pages. 2006.

Vol. 3864: Y. Cai, J. Abascal (Eds.), Ambient Intelligence in Everyday Life. XII, 323 pages. 2006.

Vol. 3863: M. Kohlhase (Ed.), Mathematical Knowledge Management. XI, 405 pages. 2006.